1991-92 Accredited Institutions of Postsecondary Education

1991-92
Accredited Institutions of Postsecondary Education
Programs
Candidates

A directory of accredited institutions, professionally accredited programs, and candidates for accreditation

Edited by William A. Wade
Published for the Council on Postsecondary Accreditation

American Council on Education
Washington, DC

Copyright © 1992 American Council on Education

All rights reserved. No part of this book may be reproduced or transmitted in any form or by any means, electronic or mechanical, including photocopying, recording, or by any information storage and retrieval system, without permission in writing from the Publisher.

American Council on Education
One Dupont Circle, N.W.
Washington, DC 20036

Printed in the United States of America

printing number
1 2 3 4 5 6 7 8 9 10

This publication was prepared on an Apple Macintosh SE computer, using QuarkXPress desktop publishing software, and was printed on an Apple LaserWriter IINT laser printer.

Library of Congress Cataloging in Publication Data

The Library of Congress has catalogued this serial as follows:

Accredited institutions of postsecondary education, programs,
   candidates / published for the Council on Postsecondary
   Accreditation.— —Washington, DC: American
   Council on Education.

   v.; 24 cm.

   Annual
   Began with issue for 1976-77.
   A directory of accredited institutions, professionally accredited programs, and candidates for accreditation.
   Description based on: 1980-81.
   Spine title: Accredited Institutions of Postsecondary Education

   ISSN 0270-1715 = Accredited institutions of postsecondary education, programs, candidates.

I. Education, Higher—United States—Directories   I. Council on Postsecondary Accreditation.   II. American Council on Education.   III. Title: Accredited Institutions of Postsecondary Education.
   [DNLM: L901 A172]

L901.A48   378.73   81-641495
                                                                                           AACR2   MARC-S

Table of Contents

About This Directory vii
How To Use This Directory ix
Abbreviations x
Key to Institutional Accrediting Bodies xi
Key to Specialized Accrediting Bodies xii
Accredited Institutions (United States) 1
    Accredited Institutions Outside the United States 555
Major Changes 562
Candidates for Accreditation 563
Public Systems of Higher Education 573

Appendices 691
    A. The Accrediting Process 692
    B. Accrediting Groups Recognized by COPA 694
    C. Joint Statement on Transfer and Award of Academic
        Credits 702

Institutional Index 705

About This Directory

Accredited Institutions of Postsecondary Education is an annual publication of the American Council on Education (ACE) for the Council on Postsecondary Accreditation (COPA). Neither COPA nor ACE is an accrediting body; the listings in the directory are supplied by the numerous national and regional accrediting groups that have been evaluated by COPA and recognized as meeting acceptable levels of quality and performance.

The institutions and programs listed, in turn, have been evaluated by the recognized accreditors and determined by their peers to meet acceptable levels of educational quality.

Those institutions designated as "candidates for accreditation" have achieved initial recognition from the appropriate accrediting commission or association. The designation "candidate" means that an institution is progressing toward accreditation, but that does not assure the achievement of accredited status.

Most of the data contained in each entry have been provided by the individual accrediting bodies. They, in turn, have had an opportunity to verify the listings as late in the publication process as possible.

The user of the directory is cautioned that the entries show only accredited institutions and indicate professional programs within those institutions that have sought and attained specialized accreditation. *The listings do not include all curricula offered by an institution.* For example, curricula in anthropology, English, physics, and many other disciplines are not listed because no recognized specialized accreditation exists in those fields. The absence of a particular discipline or course of study in these listings does not necessarily mean that it is not offered at that institution, nor that it is not a quality program if offered.

Also, the user is reminded that the process of accreditation is an ongoing one and that institutions and programs are accredited (or dropped from accredited status) throughout the year. Information about the accreditation status of a specific institution or program beyond what is given should be sought directly from the appropriate accrediting body. (Addresses, names, and telephone numbers of persons to contact begin on page 694.)

Please take time to review the section on how to use this directory and interpret the listings (page ix). For further clarification regarding entries in the directory, please contact the Council on Postsecondary Accreditation, One Dupont Circle, N.W., Suite 305, Washington, DC 20036, (202) 452-1433.

To order this directory, contact American Council on Education, Publications Division, One Dupont Circle, N.W., Washington, DC 20036, (202) 939-9380.

How To Use This Directory

Initial entry into the directory should be through the index, which lists over 5,500 accredited institutions alphabetically by institutional name.

The main body of the directory lists institutions alphabetically by state.

Information for the individual listings is arranged as follows (not all categories are listed for each institution):

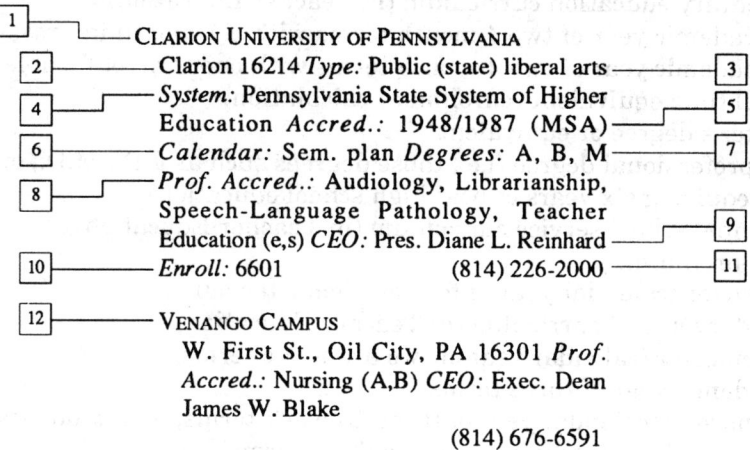

1. Name of the institution.

2. Address.

3. Brief description of *(a)* control (e.g., Public); *(b)* type of institution; and *(c)* type of student body (no indication means coeducational).

4. Indication of membership in a public system of higher education.

5. Dates of first accreditation (or of admission as candidate) and of latest renewal or reaffirmation of this status, followed by accrediting body. (Consult accrediting body for dates of interruption in or limitations on accreditation status.)

6. Type of academic calendar.

7. Level of degrees offered.

8. Specialized accreditation by 45 professional accrediting agencies, including one umbrella organization representing 20 joint review committees.

9. Name and title of chief executive officer.

10. Latest enrollment figure. Figures are included to provide indication of relative size of student body and indicate either total number enrolled or full time equivalent (FTE) calculated figures.

11. Telephone number.

12. Branch campus(es).

Abbreviations

A—associate degree or equivalent
ABA—American Bar Association
AMA—American Medical Association
B—bachelor's degree or equivalent
D—doctoral degree
e—elementary education curriculum (in Teacher Education)
4-1-4—academic year of two 4-month terms with a 1-month intersession
4-4-x—academic year of two 4-month terms with one term of flexible length
FTE—full time equivalent (enrollment calculation)
M—master's degree or equivalent
P—first professional degree (i.e., those degrees such as J.D., M.D., or M.Div. requiring six years of post-high school education)
p—personnel school service curriculum (in Teacher Education)
prelim.—preliminary
Qtr.—quarter (calendar year of four academic terms)
s—secondary school curriculim (in Teacher Education)
Sem.—semester (calendar year of two academic terms)
3-3—academic year of three terms
Tri.—trimester (calendar year of three 15-week terms, with students generally attending two of the three terms)

Key to Institutional Accrediting Bodies

AABC	American Association of Bible Colleges
AARTS	Association of Advanced Rabbinical and Talmudic Schools
ATS	The Association of Theological Schools in the United States and Canada
CCA-ACICS	Career College Association/Accrediting Commission for Independent Colleges and Schools
CCA-ACTTS	Career College Association/Accrediting Commission for Trade and Technical Schools
MSA	Middle States Association of Colleges and Schools
NASC	The Northwest Association of Schools and Colleges
NCA	North Central Association of Colleges and Schools
NEASC-CIHE	New England Association of Schools and Colleges, Inc./Commission on Institutions of Higher Education
NEASC-CVTCI	New England Association of Schools and Colleges, Inc./Commission on Vocational, Technical, Career Institutions
NHSC	National Home Study Council
SACS-CC	Southern Association of Colleges and Schools/Commission on Colleges
SACS-COEI	Southern Association of Colleges and Schools/Commission on Occupational Educational Institutions
WASC-Jr.	Western Association of Schools and Colleges/Accrediting Commission for Community and Junior Colleges
WASC-Sr.	Western Association of Schools and Colleges/Accrediting Commission for Senior Colleges and Universities

Key to Specialized Accrediting Bodies

Accounting	American Assembly of Collegiate Schools of Business
Acupuncture	National Accreditation Commission for Schools and Colleges of Acupuncture and Oriental Medicine
Administration Health Care Management	National Association of Schools of Public Affairs and Administration
Anesthesiologist Assisting	American Medical Association
Animal Health Technology	American Veterinary Medical Association
Animal Medical Technology	American Veterinary Medical Association
Animal Science Technology	American Veterinary Medical Association
Animal Technology	American Veterinary Medical Association
Architecture	National Architectural Accrediting Board
Art	National Association of Schools of Art and Design
Audiology	American Speech-Language-Hearing Association
Blood Bank Technology	American Medical Association
Business	American Assembly of Collegiate Schools of Business
Cardiovascular Technology	American Medical Association
Chiropractic Education	The Council on Chiropractic Education
Clinical Psychology	American Psychological Association
Combined Maxillofacial Prosthodontics	American Dental Association
Combined Professional-Scientific Psychology	American Psychological Association
Combined Prosthodontics	American Dental Association
Community Health	The Council on Education for Public Health
Community Health/Preventive Medicine	The Council on Education for Public Health
Computer Science	Computing Sciences Accreditation Board, Inc.
Construction Education	American Council for Construction Education
Construction Management	American Council for Construction Education
Counseling	American Association for Counseling and Development
Counseling Psychology	American Psychological Association
Cytotechnology	American Medical Association
Dance	National Association of Schools of Dance
Dental Assisting	American Dental Association
Dental Hygiene	American Dental Association
Dental Laboratory Technology	American Dental Association
Dental Public Health	American Dental Association
Dentistry	American Dental Association
Diagnostic Medical Sonography	American Medical Association
Dietetics	The American Dietetic Association
Electroneurodiagnostic Technology	American Medical Association
EMT-Paramedic	American Medical Association
Endodontics	American Dental Association
Engineering	Accreditation Board for Engineering and Technology, Inc.
Engineering Technology	Accreditation Board for Engineering and Technology, Inc.
Forestry	Society of American Foresters

Key to Specialized Accrediting Bodies (continued)

Funeral Service Education	American Board of Funeral Service Education, Inc.
General Dentistry	American Dental Association
General Practice Residency	American Dental Association
Health Education	Accrediting Bureau of Health Education Schools
Health Services Administration	Accrediting Commission on Education for Health Services Administration
Histologic Technology	American Medical Association
Home Economics	American Home Economics Association
Interior Design	Foundation for Interior Design Education Research
Journalism	Accrediting Council on Education in Journalism and Mass Communications
Landscape Architecture	American Society of Landscape Architects
Law	American Bar Association/Association of American Law Schools
Leisure Management and Tourism	National Recreation and Park Association
Leisure Services and Studies	National Recreation and Park Association
Leisure Studies	National Recreation and Park Association
Leisure Studies and Resources	National Recreation and Park Association
Leisure Systems Studies	National Recreation and Park Association
Librarianship	American Library Association
Management	National Association of Schools of Public Affairs and Administration
Maxillofacial Prosthodontics	American Dental Association
Medical Assisting	Accrediting Bureau of Health Education Schools/ American Medical Association
Medical Illustration	American Medical Association
Medical Laboratory Technology	Accrediting Bureau of Health Education Schools/ American Medical Association
Medical Record Administration	American Medical Association
Medical Record Technology	American Medical Association
Medical Technology	American Medical Association
Medicine	American Medical Association
Mortuary Science	American Board of Funeral Service Education, Inc.
Music	National Association of Schools of Music
Nuclear Medicine Technology	American Medical Association
Nurse Anesthesia Education	Council on Accreditation of Nurse Anesthesia Educational Programs
Nursing	National League for Nursing
Occupational Therapy	American Medical Association
Occupational Therapy Assisting	American Medical Association
Ophthalmic Medical Technology	American Medical Association
Optometric Technology	American Optometric Association
Optometric/Opthalmic Technology	American Optometric Association
Optometry	American Optometric Association
Oral and Maxillofacial Surgery	American Dental Association
Oral Pathology	American Dental Association
Orthodontics	American Dental Association
Osteopathy	American Osteopathic Association

Key to Specialized Accrediting Bodies (continued)

Park Administration	National Recreation and Park Association
Parks and Recreation	National Recreation and Park Association
Parks, Recreation and Tourism	National Recreation and Park Association
Pediatric Dentistry	American Dental Association
Perfusion	American Medical Association
Periodontics	American Dental Association
Pharmacy	The American Council on Pharmaceutical Education
Physical Therapy	American Physical Therapy Association
Physical Therapy Assisting	American Physical Therapy Association
Physician Assisting	American Medical Association
Planning	Association of Collegiate Schools of Planning
Podiatry	American Podiatric Medical Association
Policy Science	National Association of Schools of Public Affairs and Administration
Practical Nursing	National League for Nursing
Psychology Internship	American Psychological Association
Public Administration	National Association of Schools of Public Affairs and Administration
Public Affairs	National Association of Schools of Public Affairs and Administration
Public Health	The Council on Education for Public Health
Public Management	National Association of Schools of Public Affairs and Administration
Public Management and Policy	National Association of Schools of Public Affairs and Administration
Public Policy	National Association of Schools of Public Affairs and Administration
Public Policy Administration	National Association of Schools of Public Affairs and Administration
Public Policy and Administration	National Association of Schools of Public Affairs and Administration
Radiation Therapy Technology	American Medical Association
Radiography	American Medical Association
Recreation	National Recreation and Park Association
Recreation Administration	National Recreation and Park Association
Recreation and Leisure Services	National Recreation and Park Association
Recreation and Leisure Studies	National Recreation and Park Association
Recreation and Park Administration	National Recreation and Park Association
Recreation and Park Management	National Recreation and Park Association
Recreation Management	National Recreation and Park Association
Recreation, Park and Leisure Studies	National Recreation and Park Association
Recreation, Park and Tourism Administration	National Recreation and Park Association
Recreation, Parks and Leisure Services	National Recreation and Park Association
Recreation, Parks and Tourism	National Recreation and Park Association
Recreation Resources	National Recreation and Park Association
Recreation Resources Administration	National Recreation and Park Association

Key to Specialized Accrediting Bodies (continued)

Rehabilitation Counseling	Council on Rehabilitation Education
Resource Recreation and Tourism	National Recreation and Park Association
Respiratory Therapy	American Medical Association
Respiratory Therapy Technology	American Medical Association
School Psychology	American Psychological Association
Social Work	Council on Social Work Education
Speech-Language Pathology	American Speech-Language-Hearing Association
Surgeon Assisting	American Medical Association
Surgical Technology	American Medical Association
Teacher Education	National Council for Accreditation of Teacher Education
Theatre	National Association of Schools of Theatre
Urban Affairs and Policy Analysis	National Association of Schools of Public Affairs and Administration
Urban Studies and Public Administration	National Association of Schools of Public Affairs and Administration
Veterinary and Animal Science	American Veterinary Medical Association
Veterinary Assisting	American Veterinary Medical Association
Veterinary Medical Technology	American Veterinary Medical Association
Veterinary Medicine	American Veterinary Medical Association
Veterinary Science Technology	American Veterinary Medical Association
Veterinary Technology	American Veterinary Medical Association

Accredited Institutions

ALABAMA

ALABAMA AGRICULTURAL AND MECHANICAL UNIVERSITY
P.O. Box 285, 4107 Meridian St., Normal 35762 *Type:* Public (state) liberal arts *System:* Alabama Commission on Higher Education *Accred.:* 1963/1984 (SACS-CC) *Calendar:* Sem. plan *Degrees:* A, B, M, D (candidate) *Prof. Accred.:* Engineering Technology (civil/construction, electrical, mechanical, mechanical drafting/design), Home Economics, Planning (community/urban), Social Work (B), Teacher Education (e,s,p) *CEO:* Interim Pres. Alan L. Keyes
Enroll: 4283   (205) 851-5000

ALABAMA AVIATION AND TECHNICAL COLLEGE
U.S. Hwy. 231 S., Ozark 36361-1209 *Type:* Public (state) *Accred.:* 1991 (SACS-CC) *Calendar:* Qtr. plan *Degrees:* A *CEO:* Pres. Shirley Woodie
Enroll: 475   (205) 774-5113

ALABAMA CHRISTIAN SCHOOL OF RELIGION
1200 Taylor Rd., Montgomery 36117-3553 *Type:* Private professional *Accred.:* 1989 (SACS-CC) *Calendar:* Qtr. plan *Degrees:* B, M *CEO:* Pres. Rex A. Turner, Jr.
Enroll: 64   (205) 277-2277

ALABAMA STATE COLLEGE OF BARBER STYLING
9480 Pkwy. E., Birmingham 35215-8308 *Type:* Private *Accred.:* 1991 (CCA-ACTTS) *Calendar:* Courses of varying lengths *Degrees:* certificates *CEO:* Dir. Donald S. Mathews
                      (205) 836-2404

ALABAMA STATE UNIVERSITY
915 S. Jackson St., Montgomery 36101-0271 *Type:* Public liberal arts *System:* Alabama Commission on Higher Education *Accred.:* 1966/1990 (SACS-CC) *Calendar:* Sem. plan *Degrees:* A, B, M *Prof. Accred.:* Music, Social Work (B), Teacher Education (e,s,p) *CEO:* Interim Pres. C.C. Baker
Enroll: 4590   (205) 293-4100

ATHENS STATE COLLEGE
Beaty St., Athens 35611 *Type:* Public (state) liberal arts *System:* Alabama Commission on Higher Education *Accred.:* 1955/1991 (SACS-CC) *Calendar:* Qtr. plan *Degrees:* B *CEO:* Pres. Jerry Bartlett
Enroll: 2770   (205) 233-1800

ATMORE STATE TECHNICAL COLLEGE
P.O. Box 1119, Atmore 36504 *Type:* Public (state) *Accred.:* 1978/1988 (SACS-COEI) *Calendar:* Courses of varying lengths *Degrees:* certificates *CEO:* Pres. Malcolm A. Jones
Enroll: 547   (205) 368-8118

AUBURN UNIVERSITY
Auburn University 36849-5113 *Type:* Public (state) *System:* Auburn University Central Office *Accred.:* 1922/1984 (SACS-CC) *Calendar:* Qtr. plan *Degrees:* B, P, M, D *Prof. Accred.:* Architecture (B), Art, Audiology, Business (B,M), Clinical Psychology, Computer Science, Construction Education, Counseling, Counseling Psychology, Dietetics (coordinated), Engineering (aerospace, agricultural, chemical, civil, computer, electrical, industrial, materials, mechanical), Engineering Technology (textile), Forestry, Home Economics, Interior Design, Landscape Architecture (B), Music, Nursing (B), Pharmacy, Rehabilitation Counseling, Social Work (B), Speech-Language Pathology, Teacher Education (e,s,p), Theatre *CEO:* Pres. James E. Martin
Enroll: 19862   (205) 844-4000

AUBURN UNIVERSITY AT MONTGOMERY
7300 University Dr., Montgomery 36117-3596 *Type:* Public (state) *System:* Auburn University Central Office *Accred.:* 1968/1988 (SACS-CC) *Calendar:* Qtr. plan *Degrees:* B, M *Prof. Accred.:* Business (B,M), Medical Technology, Nursing (B), Public Administration, Teacher Education (e,s,p) *CEO:* Chanc. James O. Williams
Enroll: 6383   (205) 244-3000

Alabama

BESSEMER STATE TECHNICAL COLLEGE
Hwy. 11 S., P.O. Box 308, Bessemer 35021 *Type:* Public (state) *Accred.:* 1972/1987 (SACS-COEI) *Calendar:* Qtr. plan *Degrees:* A *Prof. Accred.:* Dental Assisting *CEO:* Pres. W. Michael Bailey
Enroll: 790   (205) 428-6391

BIRMINGHAM-SOUTHERN COLLEGE
900 Arkadelphia Rd., Birmingham 35254 *Type:* Private (United Methodist) liberal arts *Accred.:* 1922/1984 (SACS-CC) *Calendar:* 4-1-4 plan *Degrees:* B, M *Prof. Accred.:* Music, Teacher Education (e,s) *CEO:* Pres. Neal R. Berte
Enroll: 1902   (205) 226-4600

BISHOP STATE COMMUNITY COLLEGE
351 N. Broad St., Mobile 36690 *Type:* Public *System:* Alabama College System (Two-Year Institutions) *Accred.:* 1970/1984 (SACS-CC) *Calendar:* Qtr. plan *Degrees:* A *Prof. Accred.:* Mortuary Science, Nursing (A) *CEO:* Pres. Yvonne Kennedy
Enroll: 2060   (205) 690-6416

SOUTHWEST CAMPUS
925 Dauphin Island Pkwy., Mobile, AL 36605-3299 *CEO:* Provost Earl Roberson
          (205) 479-7476

BREWER STATE JUNIOR COLLEGE
2631 Temple Ave., N., Fayette 35555 *Type:* Public *System:* Alabama College System (Two-Year Institutions) *Accred.:* 1973/1988 (SACS-CC) *Calendar:* Qtr. plan *Degrees:* A *CEO:* Pres. Wayland K. DeWitt
Enroll: 774   (205) 932-3221

CAPPS COLLEGE
2970 Cottage Hill Rd., Bldg. #5, Mobile 36606 *Type:* Private *Calendar:* Courses of varying lengths *Degrees:* diplomas *Prof. Accred.:* Health Education, Medical Assisting *CEO:* Admin. Bruce G. Capps
Enroll: 28   (205) 473-1393

CAREER DEVELOPMENT CENTER
518 14th St., Tuscaloosa 35401 *Type:* Private technical *Accred.:* 1989/1990 (SACS-COEI) *Calendar:* Qtr. plan *Degrees:* diplomas *CEO:* Dir. Art Lovett
Enroll: 113   (205) 752-6025

CAREER DEVELOPMENT INSTITUTE
2233 Fourth Ave., N., Birmingham 35203 *Type:* Private *Accred.:* 1988 (SACS-COEI) *Calendar:* Qtr. plan *Degrees:* diplomas *CEO:* Dir. Darlene Mosley
Enroll: 316   (205) 252-6396

BRANCH CAMPUS
2314 9th Ave., N., Bessemer, AL 35020 *CEO:* Dir. Darrell Glaze
          (205) 425-6757

CAREER DEVELOPMENT INSTITUTE
Old American Ctr., 301 N. 12th St., Gadsden 35901 *Type:* Private business *Accred.:* 1991 (SACS-COEI) *Calendar:* Qtr. plan *Degrees:* diplomas *CEO:* Dir. Catherine Vogel
Enroll: 56   (205) 543-8844

CAREER DEVELOPMENT INSTITUTE
1060 Springhill Ave., Mobile 36604 *Type:* Private *Accred.:* 1988 (SACS-COEI) *Calendar:* Qtr. plan *Degrees:* diplomas *CEO:* Dir. Bertha George
Enroll: 92   (205) 433-5042

BRANCH CAMPUS
22 Cloverleaf Plaza, Tillman's Corner, Mobile, AL 36619 *CEO:* Dir. Jean Brown
          (205) 666-8822

CAREER DEVELOPMENT INSTITUTE
505-507 Montgomery St., Montgomery 36104 *Type:* Private *Accred.:* 1988 (SACS-COEI) *Calendar:* Qtr. plan *Degrees:* diplomas *CEO:* Dir. Amie Garrett
Enroll: 237   (205) 262-3131

BRANCH CAMPUS
418 E. Battle St., No. 11 Talladega Plaza, Talladega, AL 35160 *CEO:* Dir. Steve Hanks
          (205) 761-9228

CARVER STATE TECHNICAL COLLEGE
414 Stanton St., Mobile 36617 *Type:* Public (state) *Accred.:* 1975/1990 (SACS-COEI)

Calendar: Qtr. plan *Degrees:* A, certificates *CEO:* Pres. Earl Roberson, Sr.
Enroll: 278 (205) 473-8692

CENTRAL ALABAMA COMMUNITY COLLEGE
P.O. Box 699, 908 Cherokee Rd., Alexander City 35010 *Type:* Public *System:* Alabama College System (Two-Year Institutions) *Accred.:* 1969/1984 (SACS-CC) *Calendar:* Qtr. plan *Degrees:* A *CEO:* Pres. James H. Cornell
Enroll: 1951 (205) 234-6346

CENTRAL ALABAMA SKILLS CENTER
Two East Bldg., No. 20400, Montgomery 36103-4839 *Type:* Public (state) *Accred.:* 1988 (SACS-COEI) *Calendar:* Courses of varying lengths *Degrees:* certificates *CEO:* Dir. Claude McCartney
Enroll: 296 (205) 242-5121

CHATTAHOOCHEE VALLEY STATE COMMUNITY COLLEGE
2602 College Dr., Phenix City 36867 *Type:* Public *System:* Alabama College System (Two-Year Institutions) *Accred.:* 1976/1982 (SACS-CC) *Calendar:* Qtr. plan *Degrees:* A *Prof. Accred.:* Nursing (A) *CEO:* Pres. James E. Owen
Enroll: 1315 (205) 291-4900

CHOCTAW TRAINING INSTITUTE
218 W. Church St., Butler 36904 *Type:* Private *Accred.:* 1988/1991 (SACS-COEI) *Calendar:* Courses of varying lengths *Degrees:* certificates *CEO:* Dir. Ruth Corley
Enroll: 38 (205) 459-4331

COMMUNITY COLLEGE OF THE AIR FORCE
Bldg. 836, Maxwell Air Force Base 36112-6655 *Type:* Public (federal) technical *Accred.:* 1980/1986 (SACS-CC) *Calendar:* Courses of varying lengths *Degrees:* A *Prof. Accred.:* Physical Therapy Assisting *CEO:* Pres. Russell A. Gregory
Enroll: 59011 (205) 593-7847

CONCORDIA COLLEGE
1804 Green St., Selma 36701 *Type:* Private (Lutheran) junior *Accred.:* 1983/1989 (SACS-CC) *Calendar:* Sem. plan *Degrees:* A, B (candidate) *CEO:* Pres. Julius Jenkins
Enroll: 370 (205) 874-5700

DEBBIE'S SCHOOL OF BEAUTY CULTURE
1911 Third Ave., N., Birmingham 35203 *Type:* Private *Accred.:* 1984/1989 (SACS-COEI) *Calendar:* Courses of varying lengths *Degrees:* certificates *CEO:* Pres. Deborah Howell
Enroll: 227 (205) 252-2552

BRANCH CAMPUS
3521 Memorial Dr., Decatur, GA 30032 *CEO:* Dir. Jan Stenson
 (404) 286-0208

BRANCH CAMPUS
10340 Eastex Fwy., Houston, TX 77093 *CEO:* Pres. Deborah Howell
 (713) 699-2561

DOUGLAS MACARTHUR STATE TECHNICAL COLLEGE
1708 N. Main St., P.O. Box 649, Opp 36467 *Type:* Public (state) *Accred.:* 1972/1987 (SACS-COEI) *Calendar:* Qtr. plan *Degrees:* A *CEO:* Pres. Raymond V. Chisum
Enroll: 395 (205) 493-3573

DRAUGHONS JUNIOR COLLEGE
122 Commerce St., Montgomery 36104 *Type:* Private business *Accred.:* 1954/1991 (CCA-ACICS) *Calendar:* Qtr. plan *Degrees:* A *CEO:* Dean Conley D. Siler
Enroll: 415 (205) 263-1013

EAST ALABAMA SKILLS CENTER
1001 E. Broad St., Gadsden 35999 *Type:* Public (state) *Accred.:* 1987 (SACS-COEI) *Calendar:* Courses of varying lengths *Degrees:* certificates *CEO:* Dir. William B. Tumlin
Enroll: 253 (205) 543-3623

ENTERPRISE STATE JUNIOR COLLEGE
600 Plaza Dr., Enterprise 36330-1300 *Type:* Public *System:* Alabama College System (Two-Year Institutions) *Accred.:* 1969/1984

Alabama

(SACS-CC) *Calendar:* Qtr. plan *Degrees:* A *CEO:* Pres. Joseph D. Talmadge
Enroll: 3559   (205) 347-2623

THE EXTENSION COURSE INSTITUTE OF THE UNITED STATES AIR FORCE
Gunter Air Force Sta., Montgomery 36118-5643 *Type:* Public (federal) home study *Accred.:* 1981/1991 (NHSC) *Calendar:* Courses of varying lengths *Degrees:* certificates, diplomas *CEO:* Commandant Jerry Sailors
            (205) 279-4252

FAULKNER AREA VOCATIONAL CENTER
32 W. Elm St., Prichard 36610 *Type:* Public (state) *Accred.:* 1986 (SACS-CC); 1986 (SACS-COEI) *Calendar:* Courses of varying length *Degrees:* certificates *CEO:* Dir. Hershel Wilson
Enroll: 200   (205) 452-3445

FAULKNER UNIVERSITY
5345 Atlanta Hwy., Montgomery 36109-3378 *Type:* Private (Church of Christ) liberal arts *Accred.:* 1971/1990 (SACS-CC) *Calendar:* Sem. plan *Degrees:* A, B, P, D *CEO:* Pres. Billy D. Hilyer
Enroll: 1820   (205) 272-5820

FREDD STATE TECHNICAL COLLEGE
3401 Martin Luther King Blvd., Tuscaloosa 35401 *Type:* Public (state) *Accred.:* 1973/1988 (SACS-COEI) *Calendar:* Courses of varying lengths *Degrees:* certificates *CEO:* Dir. Norman C. Cephus
Enroll: 836   (205) 758-3361

GADSDEN BUSINESS COLLEGE
750 Forrest Ave., P.O. Box 1544, Gadsden 35901 *Type:* Private business *Accred.:* 1962/1991 (CCA-ACICS) *Calendar:* Qtr. plan *Degrees:* certificates *CEO:* Pres. Michael Beecham
Enroll: 355   (205) 546-2863

BRANCH CAMPUS
P.O. Box 1575, 630 S. Wilmer Ave., Anniston, AL 36202-1575 *CEO:* Dir. Deborah Hawkins
            (205) 237-7517

GADSDEN STATE COMMUNITY COLLEGE
P.O. Box 227, Gadsden 35902-0227 *Type:* Public *System:* Alabama College System (Two-Year Institutions) *Accred.:* 1968/1982 (SACS-CC) *Calendar:* Qtr. plan *Degrees:* A *Prof. Accred.:* EMT-Paramedic, Medical Laboratory Technology (AMA), Nursing (A), Radiography *CEO:* Pres. Victor B. Ficker
Enroll: 4595   (205) 549-8200

GEORGE C. WALLACE STATE COMMUNITY COLLEGE
Napier Field, Dothan 36303 *Type:* Public *System:* Alabama College System (Two-Year Institutions) *Accred.:* 1969/1984 (SACS-CC) *Calendar:* Qtr. plan *Degrees:* A *Prof. Accred.:* EMT-Paramedic, Medical Assisting (AMA), Medical Laboratory Technology (AMA), Nursing (A), Respiratory Therapy *CEO:* Interim Pres. Imogene Mixson
Enroll: 3215   (205) 983-3521

GEORGE CORLEY WALLACE STATE COMMUNITY COLLEGE
3000 Range Line Rd., P.O. Box 1049, Selma 36702-1049 *Type:* Public *System:* Alabama College System (Two-Year Institutions) *Accred.:* 1974/1989 (SACS-CC) *Calendar:* Qtr. plan *Degrees:* A *Prof. Accred.:* Nursing (A), Practical Nursing *CEO:* Pres. Julius R. Brown
Enroll: 1586   (205) 875-2634

HARRY M. AYERS STATE TECHNICAL COLLEGE
1801 Coleman Rd., P.O. Box 1647, Anniston 36201 *Type:* Public (state) *Accred.:* 1972/1987 (SACS-COEI) *Calendar:* Courses of varying lengths *Degrees:* A *CEO:* Pres. Pierce C. Cain
Enroll: 367   (205) 831-4540

HERZING INSTITUTE
1218 S. 20th St., Birmingham 35205 *Type:* Private *Accred.:* 1971/1983 (CCA-ACTTS) *Calendar:* Courses of varying length *Degrees:* certificates, diplomas *CEO:* Dir. Donald Lewis
Enroll: 854   (205) 933-8536

Accredited Institutions **Alabama**

HOBSON STATE TECHNICAL COLLEGE
Hwy. 43, P.O. Box 489, Thomasville 36784 *Type:* Public (state) *Accred.:* 1972/1987 (SACS-COEI) *Calendar:* Qtr. plan *Degrees:* A *CEO:* Pres. Hoyt Jones
Enroll: 413   (205) 636-9642

HUNTINGDON COLLEGE
1500 E. Fairview Ave., Montgomery 36106-2148 *Type:* Private (United Methodist) liberal arts *Accred.:* 1928/1990 (SACS-CC) *Calendar:* Sem. plan *Degrees:* A, B *Prof. Accred.:* Music *CEO:* Pres. Allen K. Jackson
Enroll: 698   (205) 265-0511

HUNTSVILLE BUSINESS INSTITUTE SCHOOL OF COURT REPORTING
3315 S. Memorial Pkwy., Huntsville 35801 *Type:* Private *Accred.:* 1990 (SACS-COEI) *Calendar:* Courses of varying lengths *Degrees:* certificates, diplomas *CEO:* Dir. Bonnie Gray
Enroll: 10   (205) 880-7530

INTERNATIONAL BIBLE COLLEGE
P.O. Box IBC, Florence 35630 *Type:* Private (Churches of Christ) professional *Accred.:* 1988 (AABC) *Calendar:* Sem. plan *Degrees:* A, B *CEO:* Pres. Dennis Jones
Enroll: 61   (205) 766-6610

INTERNATIONAL CAREER INSTITUTE
Phenix Plaza, Phenix City 36867 *Type:* Private business *Accred.:* 1984/1989 (SACS-COEI) *Calendar:* Courses of varying lengths *Degrees:* certificates *CEO:* Dir. Sandy Cox
Enroll: 231   (205) 297-6355

BRANCH CAMPUS
2101 Seminole Dr., Huntsville, AL 35805 *CEO:* Dir. Kathy Cheatum
                      (205) 533-2727

BRANCH CAMPUS
Cherry Valley Shopping Center, Lanett, AL 36863 *CEO:* Dir. Scott Waldrop
                      (205) 644-7511

BRANCH CAMPUS
1600 Whitesville St., LaGrange, GA 30240 *CEO:* Dir. Connie Manning
                      (404) 882-8287

J.F. DRAKE STATE TECHNICAL COLLEGE
34321 Meridian St., Huntsville 35811 *Type:* Public (state) *Accred.:* 1971/1991 (SACS-COEI) *Calendar:* Qtr. plan *Degrees:* A *CEO:* Pres. Johnny L. Harris, Ph.D.
Enroll: 497   (205) 539-8161

J.F. INGRAM STATE TECHNICAL COLLEGE
Country Rd. No. 3, P.O. Box 209, Deatsville 36022 *Type:* Public (state) *Accred.:* 1977/1987 (SACS-COEI) *Calendar:* Courses of varying lengths *Degrees:* A *CEO:* Pres. Murry C. Gregg
Enroll: 1015   (205) 285-5177

J.R. PITTARD AREA VOCATIONAL SCHOOL
22401 Hwy. 21, Alpine 35014 *Type:* Public (state) *Accred.:* 1990 (SACS-COEI) *Calendar:* Courses of varying lengths *Degrees:* certificates *CEO:* Dir. L. C. McMurphy
Enroll: 136   (205) 539-8161

JACKSONVILLE STATE UNIVERSITY
N. Pelham Rd., Jacksonville 36265 *Type:* Public *System:* Alabama Commission on Higher Education *Accred.:* 1935/1983 (SACS-CC) *Calendar:* Sem. plan *Degrees:* B, M *Prof. Accred.:* Music, Nursing (B), Social Work (B-candidate), Teacher Education (e,s,p) *CEO:* Pres. Harold J. McGee
Enroll: 7453   (205) 782-5781

JAMES H. FAULKNER STATE JUNIOR COLLEGE
Hwy. 31 S., Bay Minette 36507 *Type:* Public *System:* Alabama College System (Two-Year Institutions) *Accred.:* 1970/1985 (SACS-CC) *Calendar:* Qtr. plan *Degrees:* A *Prof. Accred.:* Dental Assisting *CEO:* Pres. Gary L. Branch
Enroll: 2666   (205) 937-9581

JEFFERSON DAVIS STATE JUNIOR COLLEGE
220 Aleo Dr., Brewton 36426 *Type:* Public *System:* Alabama College System (Two-Year Institutions) *Accred.:* 1968/1985 (SACS-CC) *Calendar:* Qtr. plan *Degrees:* A *Prof. Accred.:* Nursing (A) *CEO:* Pres. Sandra K. McCleod
Enroll: 916   (205) 867-4832

Alabama

JEFFERSON STATE COMMUNITY COLLEGE
2601 Carson Rd., Birmingham 35215-3098 *Type:* Public *System:* Alabama College System (Two-Year Institutions) *Accred.:* 1968/1983 (SACS-CC) *Calendar:* Qtr. plan *Degrees:* A *Prof. Accred.:* Engineering Technology (electrical), Funeral Service Education, Medical Laboratory Technology (AMA), Nursing (A), Radiography *CEO:* Pres. Judy M. Merritt
Enroll: 5590   (205) 853-1200

JOHN C. CALHOUN STATE COMMUNITY COLLEGE
P.O. Box 2216, Decatur 35609-2216 *Type:* Public *System:* Alabama College System (Two-Year Institutions) *Accred.:* 1968/1982 (SACS-CC) *Calendar:* Qtr. plan *Degrees:* A, certificates *Prof. Accred.:* Dental Assisting, Nursing (A), Practical Nursing *CEO:* Interim Pres. Jack Sasser
Enroll: 7833   (205) 353-3102

JOHN M. PATTERSON STATE TECHNICAL COLLEGE
3920 Troy Hwy., Montgomery 36116-2699 *Type:* Public (state) *Accred.:* 1972/1987 (SACS-COEI) *Calendar:* Qtr. plan *Degrees:* A *CEO:* Pres. J. L. Taunton
Enroll: 448   (205) 288-1080

JOHN POPE EDEN AREA VOCATIONAL EDUCATION CENTER
Route 2, Box 166-C, Ashville 35953 *Type:* Public (state) *Accred.:* 1984/1989 (SACS-CC); 1984/1989 (SACS-COEI) *Calendar:* Courses of varying lengths *Degrees:* certificates *CEO:* Dir. John Hazelwood
Enroll: 188   (205) 594-7055

JUDSON COLLEGE
P.O. Box 120, Marion 36756 *Type:* Private (Southern Baptist) liberal arts for women *Accred.:* 1925/1984 (SACS-CC) *Calendar:* Sem. plan *Degrees:* B *Prof. Accred.:* Music *CEO:* Pres. David E. Potts
Enroll: 351   (205) 683-6161

LAWSON STATE COMMUNITY COLLEGE
3060 Wilson Rd., S.W., Birmingham 35221 *Type:* Public *System:* Alabama College System (Two-Year Institutions) *Accred.:* 1968/1982 (SACS-CC) *Calendar:* Qtr. plan *Degrees:* A *Prof. Accred.:* Nursing (A) *CEO:* Pres. Perry W. Ward
Enroll: 2011   (205) 925-2515

LIVINGSTON UNIVERSITY
Hwy. 11, Livingston 35470 *Type:* Public (state) liberal arts *System:* Alabama Commission on Higher Education *Accred.:* 1938/1984 (SACS-CC) *Calendar:* Qtr. plan *Degrees:* A, B, M *Prof. Accred.:* Nursing (A), Teacher Education (e,s,p) *CEO:* Pres. Asa N. Green
Enroll: 1774   (205) 652-9661

LURLEEN B. WALLACE STATE JUNIOR COLLEGE
Hwy. 84 E., P.O. Box 1418, Andalusia 36420 *Type:* Public *System:* Alabama College System (Two-Year Institutions) *Accred.:* 1972/1987 (SACS-CC) *Calendar:* Qtr. plan *Degrees:* A *CEO:* Pres. Seth Hammett
Enroll: 1012   (205) 222-6591

MANLEY L. CUMMINS SCHOOL OF ANESTHESIA
P.O. Drawer 6987, Dothan 36302 *Type:* Private *Calendar:* 2-year program *Degrees:* certificates *Prof. Accred.:* Nurse Anesthesia Education *CEO:* Dir. Linda L. Callahan
                              (205) 793-8104

MARION MILITARY INSTITUTE
Washington St., Marion 36756 *Type:* Private junior for men *Accred.:* 1926/1984 (SACS-CC) *Calendar:* Sem. plan *Degrees:* A *CEO:* Pres. Joseph L. Fant, III
                              (205) 683-2301

MILES COLLEGE
P.O. Box 3800, Birmingham 35208 *Type:* Private (Christian Methodist Episcopal) liberal arts *Accred.:* 1969/1983 (SACS-CC) *Calendar:* Sem. plan *Degrees:* A, B *CEO:* Pres. Albert J.H. Sloan
Enroll: 542   (205) 923-2771

MOBILE COLLEGE
P.O. Box 13220, Mobile 36613 *Type:* Private (Southern Baptist) liberal arts *Accred.:* 1968/1983 (SACS-CC) *Calendar:* Sem. plan *Degrees:* A, B, M *Prof. Accred.:*

Music, Nursing (A,B) *CEO:* Pres. Michael A. Magnoli, Jr.
Enroll: 1183 (205) 675-5990

NATIONAL CAREER COLLEGE
224 Second Ave., S.E., Decatur 35601 *Type:* Private business *Accred.:* 1978/1990 (CCA-ACICS) *Calendar:* Qtr. plan *Degrees:* diplomas *CEO:* Dir. Dianne Phipps
Enroll: 409 (205) 353-6243

NATIONAL CAREER COLLEGE
1351 McFarland Blvd., E., East Tuscaloosa 35405 *Type:* Private business *Accred.:* 1984/1990 (CCA-ACICS) *Calendar:* Qtr. plan *Degrees:* diplomas *CEO:* Pres. Dave Tracy
Enroll: 371 (205) 758-9091

NATIONAL CAREER COLLEGE
1626 Florence Blvd., Florence 35630 *Type:* Private business *Accred.:* 1990 (CCA-ACICS) *Calendar:* Qtr. plan *Degrees:* certificates, diplomas *CEO:* Dir. Teresa Wright
(205) 764-4417

NATIONAL CAREER COLLEGE
1309 N. Memorial Pkwy., Huntsville 35801 *Type:* Private business *Accred.:* 1984/1990 (CCA-ACICS) *Calendar:* Qtr. plan *Degrees:* diplomas *CEO:* Dir. Bob Guthrie
Enroll: 371 (205) 539-4100

NATIONAL EDUCATION CENTER—NATIONAL INSTITUTE OF TECHNOLOGY CAMPUS
1900 28th Ave., S., Homewood 35209-2667 *Type:* Private *Accred.:* 1972/1991 (CCA-ACTTS) *Calendar:* Qtr. plan *Degrees:* A *CEO:* Dir. Robert L. Lott
Enroll: 200 (205) 871-2131

NEW WORLD COLLEGE OF BUSINESS
1031 Noble St., Anniston 36201 *Type:* Private business *Accred.:* 1979/1991 (CCA-ACICS) *Calendar:* Qtr. plan *Degrees:* certificates, diplomas *CEO:* Dir. Barbara Turner
Enroll: 229 (205) 236-7578

NEW WORLD COLLEGE OF BUSINESS
434-400 Broad St., Gadsden 35901 *Type:* Private business *Accred.:* 1983/1988 (CCA-ACICS) *Calendar:* Qtr. plan *Degrees:* certificates, diplomas *CEO:* Dir. Alta Pittman
(205) 543-1060

NORTH ALABAMA COLLEGE OF COMMERCE
2820 Holmes Ave., Huntsville 35816-3900 *Type:* Private *Accred.:* 1979/1989 (SACS-COEI) *Calendar:* Qtr. plan *Degrees:* certificates, diplomas *CEO:* Pres. JoAnn Butler
Enroll: 300 (205) 539-0428

NORTH ALABAMA SKILLS CENTER
3400 Blue Spring Road, P.O. Box 3269, Huntsville 35810 *Type:* Public (state) *Accred.:* 1987 (SACS-COEI) *Calendar:* Courses of varying lengths *Degrees:* certificates *CEO:* Dir. Betty L. Smith
Enroll: 219 (205) 852-5051

NORTHEAST ALABAMA STATE JUNIOR COLLEGE
Hwy. 35, P.O. Box 159, Rainsville 35986 *Type:* Public *System:* Alabama College System (Two-Year Institutions) *Accred.:* 1969/1984 (SACS-CC) *Calendar:* Qtr. plan *Degrees:* A *Prof. Accred.:* Nursing (A) *CEO:* Pres. Charles M. Pendley
Enroll: 1365 (205) 638-4418

NORTHWEST ALABAMA COMMUNITY COLLEGE
Rte. 3, P.O. Box 77, Phil Campbell 35581 *Type:* Public (state) *System:* Alabama College System (Two-Year Institutions) *Accred.:* 1967/1982 (SACS-CC) *Calendar:* Qtr. plan *Degrees:* A *Prof. Accred.:* Nursing (A), Practical Nursing *CEO:* Pres. Charles W. Britnell
Enroll: 1940 (205) 993-5331

OAKWOOD COLLEGE
Oakwood Rd., N.W., Huntsville 35896 *Type:* Private (Seventh-Day Adventist) liberal arts *Accred.:* 1958/1991 (SACS-CC) *Calendar:* Qtr. plan *Degrees:* A, B *Prof. Accred.:* Social Work (B), Teacher Education (e,s) *CEO:* Pres. Benjamin F. Reaves
Enroll: 1266 (205) 726-7000

OPELIKA STATE TECHNICAL COLLEGE
1701 Lafayette Pkwy., P.O. Box 2268, Opelika 36803-2268 *Type:* Public (state) *Accred.:* 1971/1991 (SACS-COEI) *Calen-*

Alabama

dar: Courses of varying lengths *Degrees:* A *CEO:* Interim Pres. Bob Boothe
Enroll: 372 (205) 745-6437

PATRICK HENRY STATE JUNIOR COLLEGE
P.O. Box 2000, Monroeville 36461 *Type:* Public *System:* Alabama College System (Two-Year Institutions) *Accred.:* 1970/1985 (SACS-CC) *Calendar:* Qtr. plan *Degrees:* A *CEO:* Pres. John A. Johnson
Enroll: 1160 (205) 575-3158

PHOENIX COLLEGE
336 S. Wilson Ave., Prichard 36610 *Type:* Private *Accred.:* 1985/1990 (SACS-COEI) *Calendar:* Courses of varying lengths *Degrees:* certificates *CEO:* Dir. Sally Conlee
Enroll: 241 (205) 497-3000

PRINCE INSTITUTE OF PROFESSIONAL STUDIES
6001 E. Shirley La., Montgomery 36117 *Type:* Private business *Accred.:* 1984/1991 (CCA-ACICS) *Calendar:* 2-year program *Degrees:* diplomas *CEO:* Dir. Sara Prince
Enroll: 141 (205) 271-1670

BRANCH CAMPUS
242 A&B Club Manor Dr., Mobile, AL 36615 *CEO:* Dir. Ann C. Schmidt
(205) 432-4232

R.E.T.S. ELECTRONIC INSTITUTE
2812 12th Ave., N., Birmingham 35234 *Type:* Private *Accred.:* 1980/1986 (CCA-ACTTS) *Calendar:* Sem. plan *Degrees:* A *CEO:* Dir. Victor L. Reiley
Enroll: 550 (205) 251-7962

BRANCH CAMPUS
2800A Bob Wallace Dr., Huntsville, AL 35805 *CEO:* Dir. Ira Vatandoost
(205) 533-7387

REID STATE TECHNICAL COLLEGE
P.O. Box 588, I-65Y Hwy. 83, Evergreen 36401 *Type:* Public (state) *Accred.:* 1972/1988 (SACS-COEI) *Calendar:* Qtr. plan *Degrees:* A *CEO:* Pres. Wiley Salter
Enroll: 272 (205) 578-1313

RICE COLLEGE
2116 Bessemer Rd., Birmingham 35208 *Type:* Private *Accred.:* 1983/1988 (SACS-COEI) *Calendar:* Courses of varying lengths *Degrees:* certificates, diplomas *CEO:* Dir. Ronald P. Beals
Enroll: 80 (205) 781-8600

RILEY COLLEGE
4129 Ross Clark Cir., N.W., P.O. Box 7001, Dothan 36303 *Type:* Private business *Accred.:* 1983/1988 (SACS-COEI) *Calendar:* Qtr. plan *Degrees:* certificates, diplomas *CEO:* Pres. Peggy Rice
Enroll: 1009 (205) 794-4296

BRANCH CAMPUS
901-A Jeff Davis St., Selma, AL 36701 *CEO:* Dir. Michael Rawls
(205) 872-2904

BRANCH CAMPUS
610 W. Oglethorpe Blvd., Albany, GA 31701 *CEO:* Dir. Carlton Vurrell
(912) 883-8048

BRANCH CAMPUS
2514 Abercorn St., Savannah, GA 31402 *CEO:* Dir. Sheila Phelts
(912) 234-9911

BRANCH CAMPUS
1410 E. Park Ave., Valdosta, GA 31601-1410 *CEO:* Dir. Margaret Price
(912) 242-0092

BRANCH CAMPUS
201-S Alabama St., Columbus, MS 39702 *CEO:* Dir. David Smart
(601) 328-9484

BRANCH CAMPUS
108 N. Harvey St., Greenville, MS 38701 *CEO:* Dir. Nancy Spears
(601) 378-8011

SAMFORD UNIVERSITY
800 Lakeshore Dr., Birmingham 35229 *Type:* Private (Southern Baptist) *Accred.:* 1920/1986 (SACS-CC) *Calendar:* 4-1-4 plan *Degrees:* A, B, P, M, D *Prof. Accred.:* Law,

Music, Nursing (A,B), Pharmacy, Teacher Education (e,s,p) *CEO:* Pres. Thomas E. Corts
Enroll: 4151 (205) 870-2011

SELMA UNIVERSITY
1501 Lapsley St., Selma 36701 *Type:* Private (Baptist) liberal arts and teachers *Accred.:* 1991 (SACS-CC) *Calendar:* Sem. plan *Degrees:* A, B *CEO:* Pres. Burnest W. Dawson
Enroll: 179 (205) 872-2533

SHELTON STATE COMMUNITY COLLEGE
202 Skyland Blvd., Tuscaloosa 35405 *Type:* Public (state) technical *System:* Alabama College System (Two-Year Institutions) *Accred.:* 1979/1984 (SACS-CC) *Calendar:* Qtr. plan *Degrees:* A *Prof. Accred.:* Nursing (A) *CEO:* Pres. Thomas E. Umphrey
Enroll: 3327 (205) 759-1541

SHOALS COMMUNITY COLLEGE
George Wallace Blvd., P.O. Box 2545, Muscle Shoals 35662 *Type:* Public (state) *System:* Alabama College System (Two-Year Institutions) *Accred.:* 1991 (SACS-CC) *Calendar:* Qtr. plan *Degrees:* A *CEO:* Pres. Larry McCoy
Enroll: 2127 (205) 381-2813

SNEAD STATE JUNIOR COLLEGE
200 Walnut St., P.O. Drawer D, Boaz 35957 *Type:* Public *System:* Alabama College System (Two-Year Institutions) *Accred.:* 1941/1983 (SACS-CC) *Calendar:* Qtr. plan *Degrees:* A *Prof. Accred.:* Veterinary Technology *CEO:* Pres. William H. Osborn
Enroll: 1462 (205) 593-5120

SOUTH ALABAMA SKILLS CENTER
846 Butler Dr., Ste. A, Mobile 36693 *Type:* Public (state) *Accred.:* 1988 (SACS-COEI) *Calendar:* Courses of varying lengths *Degrees:* certificates *CEO:* Dir. Charles Lang
Enroll: 254 (205) 661-0215

SOUTHEAST ALABAMA SKILLS CENTER
1416 Lena St., P.O. Box 6268, Dothan 36302 *Type:* Public (state) *Accred.:* 1988 (SACS-COEI) *Calendar:* Courses of varying lengths *Degrees:* certificates *CEO:* Dir. Wendell Payne
Enroll: 295 (205) 793-2896

SOUTHEAST COLLEGE OF TECHNOLOGY
828 Downtowner Loop Long W., Mobile 36609 *Type:* Private *Accred.:* 1986 (CCA-ACTTS) *Calendar:* Courses of varying lengths *Degrees:* certificates *CEO:* Pres. Jerry Barnett
Enroll: 454 (205) 343-8200

BRANCH CAMPUS
2731 Nonconnah Blvd., Memphis, TN 38132-2799 *CEO:* Dir. J. Matthews Bonnell
(901) 345-1000

SOUTHEASTERN BIBLE COLLEGE
3001 Hwy. 280 E., Birmingham 35243 *Type:* Private *Accred.:* 1962/1983 (AABC) *Calendar:* Sem. plan *Degrees:* A, B, M, certificates *CEO:* Pres. John Talley, Jr.
Enroll: 123 (205) 969-0880

SOUTHERN JUNIOR COLLEGE
1710 First Ave., N., Birmingham 35203 *Type:* Private junior *Accred.:* 1969/1987 (CCA-ACICS); 1980/1986 (SACS-CC) *Calendar:* Qtr. plan *Degrees:* A *CEO:* Pres. Diane Clower
Enroll: 1462 (205) 251-2821

BRANCH CAMPUS
2015-2019 Highland Ave., S., Birmingham, AL 35205 *Accred.:* 1969/1987 (CCA-ACICS) *CEO:* Dir. Bibbie McLaughlin
(205) 933-8242

BRANCH CAMPUS
4900 Corporate Dr., Ste. E, Huntsville, AL 35805-9601 *CEO:* Dir. Carol Titolo

SOUTHERN TECHNICAL COLLEGE
4116 Narrow Lane Rd., Montgomery 36111-2699 *Type:* Private *Accred.:* 1991 (CCA-ACTTS) *Calendar:* Qtr. plan *Degrees:* A *CEO:* Dir. Chris White
(205) 281-2100

Alabama

SOUTHERN UNION STATE JUNIOR COLLEGE
Roberts St., Wadley 36276 *Type:* Public *System:* Alabama College System (Two-Year Institutions) *Accred.:* 1970/1986 (SACS-CC) *Calendar:* Qtr. plan *Degrees:* A *Prof. Accred.:* Nursing (A) *CEO:* Pres. Richard J. Federinko
Enroll: 2693   (205) 395-2211

SOUTHERN VOCATIONAL COLLEGE
225 S. Main St., P.O. Box 688, Tuskegee 36083 *Type:* Private *Accred.:* 1983/1989 (SACS-COEI) *Calendar:* Courses of varying lengths *Degrees:* certificates, diplomas *CEO:* Pres. Lawrence F. Haygood, Jr.
Enroll: 80   (205) 727-5220

SPARKS STATE TECHNICAL COLLEGE
Hwy. 431, S., P.O. Drawer 580, Eufaula 36072-0580 *Type:* Public (state) *Accred.:* 1973/1988 (SACS-COEI) *Calendar:* Qtr. plan *Degrees:* A *CEO:* Pres. Linda C. Wilson
Enroll: 302   (205) 687-5288

SPRING HILL COLLEGE
4000 Dauphin St., Mobile 36608 *Type:* Private (Roman Catholic) liberal arts *Accred.:* 1922/1985 (SACS-CC) *Calendar:* Sem. plan *Degrees:* B, M *CEO:* Pres. William J. Rewak, S.J.
Enroll: 1055   (205) 460-2121

STILLMAN COLLEGE
P.O. Drawer 1430, Tuscaloosa 35403 *Type:* Private (Presbyterian) liberal arts *Accred.:* 1953/1990 (SACS-CC) *Calendar:* Sem. plan *Degrees:* B *CEO:* Pres. Cordell Wynn
Enroll: 772   (205) 349-4240

TALLADEGA COLLEGE
627 W. Battle St., Talladega 35160 *Type:* Private liberal arts *Accred.:* 1931/1989 (SACS-CC) *Calendar:* Sem. plan *Degrees:* B *Prof. Accred.:* Social Work (B) *CEO:* Pres. Joseph B. Johnson
Enroll: 642   (205) 362-0206

TALLAPOOSA-ALEXANDER CITY AREA VOCATIONAL CENTER
100 E. Junior College Dr., Alexander City 35010 *Type:* Public (state) *Accred.:* 1984/1989 (SACS-CC); 1984/1989 (SACS-COEI) *Calendar:* Courses of varying lengths *Degrees:* certificates *CEO:* Dir. Joe Martin
Enroll: 165   (205) 329-8448

TRENHOLM STATE TECHNICAL COLLEGE
1225 Air Base Blvd., P.O. Box 9000, Montgomery 36108 *Type:* Public (state) *Accred.:* 1972/1987 (SACS-COEI) *Calendar:* Qtr.plan *Degrees:* A *Prof. Accred.:* Dental Assisting, Dental Laboratory Technology (conditional), EMT-Paramedic, Medical Assisting (AMA), Practical Nursing *CEO:* Pres. Thad McClammy
Enroll: 607   (205) 832-9000

TROY STATE UNIVERSITY
University Ave., Troy 36082 *Type:* Public liberal arts and teachers *System:* Troy State University System *Accred.:* 1934/1983 (SACS-CC) *Calendar:* Qtr. plan *Degrees:* A, B, M *Prof. Accred.:* Nursing (A,B,M), Social Work (B), Teacher Education (e,s,p) *CEO:* Chanc. Jack Hawkins, Jr., Ph.D.
Enroll: 8134   (205) 566-8112

TROY STATE UNIVERSITY AT DOTHAN
3601 U.S. Hwy. 231 N., P.O. Box 8368, Dothan 36304-0368 *Type:* Public liberal arts and teachers *System:* Troy State University System *Accred.:* 1985/1990 (SACS-CC) *Calendar:* Qtr. plan *Degrees:* A, B, M *CEO:* Pres. Thomas E. Harrison
Enroll: 1483   (205) 983-6556

TROY STATE UNIVERSITY IN MONTGOMERY
231 Montgomery St., P.O. Drawer 4419, Montgomery 36103-4419 *Type:* Public liberal arts and teachers *System:* Troy State University System *Accred.:* 1983/1989 (SACS-CC) *Calendar:* Qtr. plan *Degrees:* A, B, M *CEO:* Pres. Millard E. Elrod
Enroll: 1894   (205) 834-1400

TUSKEGEE UNIVERSITY
Tuskegee 36088 *Type:* Private *Accred.:* 1933/1988 (SACS-CC) *Calendar:* Sem. plan *Degrees:* B, P, M, D *Prof. Accred.:* Architecture (B), Engineering (chemical, electrical, mechanical), Medical Technology, Nurs-

Accredited Institutions   **Alabama**

ing (B), Occupational Therapy, Social Work (B) *CEO:* Pres. Benjamin F. Payton
Enroll: 3510   (205) 727-8011

TWENTIETH CENTURY COLLEGE
352 Government St., Mobile 36602 *Type:* Private business *Accred.:* 1966/1991 (CCA-ACICS) *Calendar:* Courses of varying lengths *Degrees:* certificates, diplomas *CEO:* Pres. John P. Hornung
Enroll: 439   (205) 438-9837

UNITED STATES ARMY ORDNANCE MISSILE AND MUNITIONS CENTER AND SCHOOL
Redstone Arsenal, Huntsville 35897-6000 *Type:* Public (federal) technical *Accred.:* 1975/1990 (SACS-COEI)*Calendar:* Courses of varying lengths *Degrees:* certificates *CEO:* Commandant James Boddie
Enroll: 2060   (205) 876-3349

UNITED STATES SPORTS ACADEMY
One Academy Dr., Daphne 36526 *Type:* Private professional *Accred.:* 1983/1988 (SACS-CC) *Calendar:* Qtr. plan *Degrees:* M, D (candidate) *CEO:* Pres. Thomas P. Rosandich
Enroll: 148   (205) 626-3303

THE UNIVERSITY OF ALABAMA
Tuscaloosa 35487 *Type:* Public (state) *System:* University of Alabama System *Accred.:* 1897/1984 (SACS-CC) *Calendar:* Sem. plan *Degrees:* B, P, M, D *Prof. Accred.:* Accounting (Type A,C), Art, Audiology, Business (B,M), Clinical Psychology, Computer Science, Counseling, Dietetics (coordinated), EMT-Paramedic, Engineering (aerospace, chemical, civil, electrical, industrial, mechanical, metallurgical, mineral), Engineering Technology (civil/construction, electrical), Home Economics, Interior Design, Journalism, Law, Librarianship, Music, Nursing (B), Rehabilitation Counseling, Social Work (B,M), Speech-Language Pathology, Teacher Education (e,s,p), Theatre *CEO:* Pres. Roger Sayers
Enroll: 18037   (205) 348-6010

THE UNIVERSITY OF ALABAMA AT BIRMINGHAM
UAB Sta., Birmingham 35294 *Type:* Public (state) *System:* University of Alabama System *Accred.:* 1970/1984 (SACS-CC) *Calendar:* Qtr. plan *Degrees:* B, P, M, D *Prof. Accred.:* Accounting (Type A,C), Business (B,M), Clinical Psychology, Combined Prosthodontics, Combined Maxillofacial Prosthodontics, Cytotechnology, Dental Assisting, Dental Hygiene, Dental Public Health, Dentistry, Dietetics (internship), EMT-Paramedic, Endodontics, Engineering (civil, electrical, materials, mechanical), General Dentistry (provisional), General Practice Residency (provisional), Health Services Administration, Histologic Technology, Medical Assisting (AMA), Medical Laboratory Technology (AMA), Medical Record Administration, Medical Record Technology, Medical Technology, Medicine, Nuclear Medicine Technology, Nurse Anesthesia Education, Nursing (B,M), Occupational Therapy, Occupational Therapy Assisting, Optometry, Oral and Maxillofacial Surgery, Oral Pathology, Orthodontics, Pediatric Dentistry, Periodontics, Physical Therapy, Physical Therapy Assisting, Psychology Internship, Public Administration, Public Health, Radiation Therapy Technology, Radiography, Rehabilitation Counseling, Respiratory Therapy, Social Work (B), Surgeon Assisting, Teacher Education (e,s,p) *CEO:* Pres. Charles A. McCallum, Jr.
Enroll: 13700   (205) 934-4011

THE UNIVERSITY OF ALABAMA IN HUNTSVILLE
Huntsville 35899 *Type:* Public (state) *Accred.:* 1970/1985 (SACS-CC) *Calendar:* Sem. plan *Degrees:* B, M, D *Prof. Accred.:* Computer Science, EMT-Paramedic, Engineering (chemical, civil, electrical, industrial, mechanical), Music, Nursing (B,M) *CEO:* Pres. Frank A. Franz
Enroll: 4160   (205) 895-6120

UNIVERSITY OF MONTEVALLO
Sta. 6001, Montevallo 35115-6001 *Type:* Public (state) liberal arts and professional *System:* Alabama Commission on Higher

Alabama

Education *Accred.:* 1925/1990 (SACS-CC) *Calendar:* Sem. plan *Degrees:* B, M *Prof. Accred.:* Art, Audiology, Business (B), Home Economics, Music, Social Work (B), Speech-Language Pathology, Teacher Education (e,s) *CEO:* Pres. John W. Stewart
Enroll: 2869 (205) 665-6001

UNIVERSITY OF NORTH ALABAMA
Florence 35632-0001 *Type:* Public liberal arts and teachers *System:* Alabama Commission on Higher Education *Accred.:* 1934/1982 (SACS-CC) *Calendar:* Sem. plan *Degrees:* B, M *Prof. Accred.:* Art, Music, Nursing (B), Social Work (B), Teacher Education (e,s) *CEO:* Pres. Robert L. Potts
Enroll: 5685 (205) 760-4100

UNIVERSITY OF SOUTH ALABAMA
307 University Blvd., Mobile 36688 *Type:* Public (state) liberal arts *System:* Alabama Commission on Higher Education *Accred.:* 1968/1983 (SACS-CC) *Calendar:* Qtr. plan *Degrees:* B, P, M, D *Prof. Accred.:* Audiology, Business (B,M), Computer Science, EMT-Paramedic, Engineering (chemical, electrical, mechanical), Medical Technology, Medicine, Music, Nursing (B,M), Physical Therapy, Radiography, Respiratory Therapy, Speech-Language Pathology, Teacher Education (e,s,p) *CEO:* Pres. Frederick P. Whiddon
Enroll: 10307 (205) 460-6101

WALKER COLLEGE
1411 Indiana Ave., Jasper 35501 *Type:* Private junior *Accred.:* 1959/1990 (SACS-CC) *Calendar:* Sem. plan *Degrees:* A *Prof. Accred.:* Nursing (A) *CEO:* Pres. Jack L. Mott
Enroll: 1071 (205) 387-0511

WALKER STATE TECHNICAL COLLEGE
P.O. Drawer K, Sumiton 35148 *Type:* Public (state) *Accred.:* 1991 (SACS-CC candidate); 1973/1988 (SACS-COEI) *Calendar:* Qtr. plan *Degrees:* A *CEO:* Pres. Harold Wade
Enroll: 791 (205) 648-3271

WALLACE STATE COMMUNITY COLLEGE
801 Main St., Hanceville 35077 *Type:* Public (state) technical *System:* Alabama College System (Two-Year Institutions) *Accred.:* 1978/1984 (SACS-CC) *Calendar:* Qtr. plan *Degrees:* A *Prof. Accred.:* Dental Assisting, EMT-Paramedic, Medical Laboratory Technology (AMA), Medical Record Technology, Nursing (A), Radiography, Respiratory Therapy *CEO:* Pres. James C. Bailey
Enroll: 3510 (205) 352-6403

WEST CENTRAL ALABAMA SKILLS CENTER
2112 11th Ave., S., No. 201, Birmingham 35205 *Type:* Public (state) *Accred.:* 1987 (SACS-COEI) *Calendar:* Courses of varying lengths *Degrees:* certificates *CEO:* Dir. Henry L. Rookis
Enroll: 695 (205) 322-0504

WINSTON COUNTY AREA VOCATIONAL CENTER
Holly Grove Rd., P.O. Box 146, Double Springs 35553 *Type:* Public (state) *Accred.:* 1985/1990 (SACS-CC); 1985/1990 (SACS-COEI) *Calendar:* Courses of varying lengths *Degrees:* certificates *CEO:* Dir. Betty Porter
Enroll: 111 (205) 489-2121

ALASKA

ALASKA BIBLE COLLEGE
P.O. Box 289, Glennallen 99588 *Type:* Private *Accred.:* 1982/1987 (AABC) *Calendar:* Sem. plan *Degrees:* A, B, certificates *CEO:* Pres. Gary J. Ridley, Sr.
Enroll: 46 (907) 822-3201

ALASKA JUNIOR COLLEGE
800 E. Dimond Blvd., Ste. 3-350, Anchorage 99515 *Type:* Private *Accred.:* 1970/1988 (CCA-ACICS) *Calendar:* Qtr. plan *Degrees:* A *CEO:* Pres. Kathryn Smith
Enroll: 655 (907) 349-1905

ALASKA PACIFIC UNIVERSITY
4101 University Dr., Anchorage 99508 *Type:* Private (United Methodist) *Accred.:* 1981/1986 (NASC) *Calendar:* Tri. plan *Degrees:* A, B, M *CEO:* Pres. F. Thomas Trotter
Enroll: 1591 (907) 564-8248

CHARTER COLLEGE
2221 E. Northern Lights Blvd., Ste. 120, Anchorage 99508-4140 *Type:* Private business *Accred.:* 1984/1989 (CCA-ACICS) *Calendar:* Courses of varying lengths *Degrees:* certificates *CEO:* Pres. Milton Byrd
Enroll: 917 (907) 227-1000

PRINCE WILLIAM SOUND COMMUNITY COLLEGE
P.O. Box 97, Valdez 99686 *Type:* Public junior *System:* University of Alaska System *Accred.:* 1989 (NASC) *Calendar:* Sem. plan *Degrees:* A *CEO:* Pres. John M. Devens
Enroll: 493 (907) 835-2421

SHELDON JACKSON COLLEGE
Sitka 99835 *Type:* Private (United Presbyterian) liberal arts *Accred.:* 1966/1988 (NASC) *Calendar:* 4-1-4 plan *Degrees:* A, B *CEO:* Pres. Michael E. Kaelke
Enroll: 268 (907) 747-5231

THE TRAVEL ACADEMY
540 W.International Airport Rd, Anchorage 99518 *Type:* Private *Accred.:* 1987 (CCA-ACTTS) *Calendar:* Courses of varying lengths *Degrees:* certificates *CEO:* Pres. Jennifer A. Deitz
(907) 563-7575

UNIVERSITY OF ALASKA ANCHORAGE
3211 Providence Dr., Anchorage 99508 *Type:* Public (state) *System:* University of Alaska System *Accred.:* 1974/1990 (NASC) *Calendar:* Sem. plan *Degrees:* A, B, M *Prof. Accred.:* Dental Assisting, Dental Hygiene, Engineering (civil), Journalism, Medical Assisting (AMA), Medical Laboratory Technology (AMA), Nursing (A,B,M), Social Work (B) *CEO:* Chanc. Donald Behrend
Enroll: 17551 (907) 786-1437

UNIVERSITY OF ALASKA ANCHORAGE—KENAI PENINSULA COLLEGE
34820 College Drive, Soldotna 99669 *Type:* Public junior *System:* University of Alaska System *Accred.:* 1974/1990 (NASC) *Calendar:* Sem. plan *Degrees:* A *CEO:* Dir. Ginger Steffy
Enroll: 1764 (907) 262-5801

UNIVERSITY OF ALASKA ANCHORAGE—KODIAK COLLEGE
Kodiak 99615 *Type:* Public junior *System:* University of Alaska System *Accred.:* 1974/1990 (NASC) *Calendar:* Sem. plan *Degrees:* A *CEO:* Dir. Carol Hagel
Enroll: 803 (907) 486-4161

UNIVERSITY OF ALASKA ANCHORAGE—MATANUSKA-SUSITNA COLLEGE
Palmer 99645 *Type:* Public junior *System:* University of Alaska System *Accred.:* 1974/1990 (NASC) *Calendar:* Sem. plan *Degrees:* A *CEO:* Dir. Glenn Massay, Ph.D.
Enroll: 1543 (907) 745-9774

UNIVERSITY OF ALASKA FAIRBANKS
320 Signers' Hall, Fairbanks 99775 *Type:* Public (state) *System:* University of Alaska System *Accred.:* 1934/1990 (NASC) *Calendar:* Sem. plan *Degrees:* A, B, M, D *Prof. Accred.:* Accounting (Type A), Business (B,M), Engineering (civil, electrical, geolog-

ical/geophysical, mechanical, mining), Journalism, Music, Social Work (B), Teacher Education (e,s,p) *CEO:* Chanc. Joan Wadlow
Enroll: 7569   (907) 474-7112

UNIVERSITY OF ALASKA FAIRBANKS—CHUKCHI
P.O. Box 297, Kotzebue 99752 *Type:* Public junior *System:* University of Alaska System *Accred.:* 1934/1990 (NASC) *Calendar:* Sem. plan *Degrees:* A *CEO:* Dir. Lynn Johnson
Enroll: 221   (907) 442-3400

UNIVERSITY OF ALASKA FAIRBANKS—KUSKOKWIM
Bethel 99559 *Type:* Public junior *System:* University of Alaska System *Accred.:* 1934/1990 (NASC) *Calendar:* Sem. plan *Degrees:* A *CEO:* Pres. Linwood Laughy
Enroll: 449   (907) 543-4502

UNIVERSITY OF ALASKA FAIRBANKS—NORTHWEST
P.O. Box 1023, Nome 99762 *Type:* Public junior *System:* University of Alaska System *Accred.:* 1934/1990 (NASC) *Calendar:* Sem. plan *Degrees:* A *CEO:* Dir. Nancy Mendenhall
Enroll: 293   (907) 443-2201

UNIVERSITY OF ALASKA SOUTHEAST
11120 Glacier Hwy., Juneau 99801 *Type:* Public (state) *System:* University of Alaska System *Accred.:* 1983/1989 (NASC) *Calendar:* Sem. plan *Degrees:* A, B, M *CEO:* Chanc. Marshall L. Lind
Enroll: 4674   (907) 789-4509

UNIVERSITY OF ALASKA SOUTHEAST—KETCHIKAN
Ketchikan 99901 *Type:* Public junior *System:* University of Alaska System *Accred.:* 1983/1989 (NASC) *Calendar:* Sem. plan *Degrees:* A *CEO:* Dir. Francis Feinerman
Enroll: 632   (907) 225-6177

UNIVERSITY OF ALASKA SOUTHEAST—SITKA
1332 Seward Ave., Sitka 99835 *Type:* Public junior *System:* University of Alaska System *Accred.:* 1983/1989 (NASC) *Calendar:* Sem. plan *Degrees:* A *CEO:* Dir. Richard Griffin
Enroll: 1254   (907) 747-6653

AMERICAN SAMOA

AMERICAN SAMOA COMMUNITY COLLEGE
P.O. Box 2609, Pago Pago 96799 *Type:* Public (state) junior *Accred.:* 1976/1991 (WASC-Jr.) *Calendar:* Sem. plan *Degrees:* A *CEO:* Pres. Saeu L. Scanlan *Enroll:* 1235   (684) 699-9155

ARIZONA

ABC TECHNICAL AND TRADE SCHOOL
3761 E. Technical Dr., Tucson 85713 *Type:* Private *Accred.:* 1977/1988 (CCA-ACTTS) *Calendar:* Courses of varying lengths *Degrees:* certificates *CEO:* Dir. Ron Kessler
Enroll: 650 (602) 748-1762

ABC WELDING SCHOOL
2345 W. Thomas Rd., Phoenix 85015-5904 *Type:* Private *Accred.:* 1978/1984 (CCA-ACTTS) *Calendar:* Courses of varying lengths *Degrees:* certificates, diplomas *CEO:* Dir. Torch Hall
Enroll: 454 (602) 258-1808

ACADEMY OF BUSINESS COLLEGE
3320 W. Cheryl Dr., Ste. 115, Phoenix 85051 *Type:* Private business *Accred.:* 1984/1990 (CCA-ACICS) *Calendar:* Courses of varying lengths *Degrees:* certificates *CEO:* Dir. Toby D. Jalowsky
Enroll: 363 (602) 942-4141

AL COLLINS GRAPHIC DESIGN SCHOOL
1140 S. Priest Dr., P.O. Box 3178, Tempe 85281 *Type:* Private *Accred.:* 1981/1987 (CCA-ACTTS) *Calendar:* Qtr. plan *Degrees:* certificates *CEO:* Dir. Chuck Collins
Enroll: 490 (602) 966-3000

AMERICAN COLLEGE
1002 E. Tuckey La., Phoenix 85014-1248 *Type:* Private *Accred.:* 1985 (CCA-ACTTS) *Calendar:* Courses of varying lengths *Degrees:* certificates *CEO:* Dir. Charles R. Wirth
Enroll: 57 (602) 890-8900

AMERICAN GRADUATE SCHOOL OF INTERNATIONAL MANAGEMENT
Thunderbird Campus, Glendale 85306 *Type:* Private professional; graduate only *Accred.:* 1969/1985 (NCA) *Calendar:* Sem. plan *Degrees:* M *CEO:* Pres. Roy A. Herberger, Jr.
Enroll: 1236 (602) 978-7200

AMERICAN INDIAN BIBLE COLLEGE
10020 N. Fifteenth Ave., Phoenix 85021 *Type:* Private (Assemblies of God) *Accred.:* 1988 (NCA) *Calendar:* Sem. plan *Degrees:* A, B, certificates *CEO:* Pres. David J. Moore
Enroll: 125 (602) 944-3335

AMERICAN INSTITUTE
3443 North Central Avenue, Phoenix 85012 *Type:* Private business *Accred.:* 1981 (CCA-ACICS) *Calendar:* Sem. plan *Degrees:* certificates, diplomas *CEO:* Exec. Dir. Mary Park
Enroll: 600 (602) 252-4986

AMERICAN INSTITUTE OF TECHNOLOGY
1917 W. Glendale Ave., Phoenix 85021 *Type:* Private *Accred.:* 1985 (CCA-ACTTS) *Calendar:* Courses of varying lengths *Degrees:* certificates *CEO:* Pres. R. Wade Murphree
Enroll: 129 (602) 433-1076

AMERICAN TECHNICAL CENTER
4201 N. 47th Ave., Phoenix 85031 *Type:* Private *Accred.:* 1983/1987 (CCA-ACTTS) *Calendar:* Courses of varying lengths *Degrees:* certificates *CEO:* Pres. George Milhoan
Enroll: 463 (602) 245-0090

AMERICAN TELLER SCHOOLS
635 W. Indian School Rd., Ste. 201, Phoenix 85013 *Type:* Private *Accred.:* 1988 (CCA-ACTTS) *Calendar:* Courses of varying lengths *Degrees:* certificates *CEO:* Pres. Randy Utley
(602) 248-0885

BRANCH CAMPUS
1819 S. Dobson Rd., Mesa, AZ 85202 *CEO:* Dir. Shelly Navarro
(602) 730-8191

BRANCH CAMPUS
4023 E. Grant Rd., Tucson, AZ 85712 *CEO:* Dir. Betty Moseman
(602) 881-1541

Accredited Institutions   **Arizona**

APOLLO COLLEGE OF MEDICAL AND DENTAL CAREERS
8503 N. 27th Ave., Phoenix 85051 *Type:* Private *Accred.:* 1979/1986 (CCA-ACTTS) *Calendar:* Courses of varying lengths *Degrees:* diplomas *Prof. Accred.:* Medical Assisting, Respiratory Therapy, Respiratory Therapy Technology *CEO:* Pres. Margaret M. Carlson
Enroll: 914   (602) 864-1571

BRANCH CAMPUS
630 W. Southern Ave., Mesa, AZ 85202 *CEO:* Dir. Craig Milgrim
                       (602) 864-1571

BRANCH CAMPUS
7502 W. Thomas Rd., Phoenix, AZ 85033 *Prof. Accred.:* Medical Assisting *CEO:* Dir. Frederick D. Lockhart
                       (602) 849-9000

BRANCH CAMPUS
114 Camelback Rd., Phoenix, AZ 85013 *CEO:* Dir. Vicki Lynn Lusk
                       (602) 230-1168

BRANCH CAMPUS
3870 N. Oracle Rd., Tucson, AZ 85705 *CEO:* Dir. Luba Chiliwnenk
                       (602) 888-5885

BRANCH CAMPUS
310 Third Ave., Ste. B22, Chula Vista, CA 92010 *Prof. Accred.:* Medical Assisting *CEO:* Dir. Mark R. Bowlds
                       (619) 585-3320

BRANCH CAMPUS
1333 Camino Del Rio S., Ste. 313, San Diego, CA 92108 *Prof. Accred.:* Medical Assisting *CEO:* Dir. Roy Papenhaus
                       (619) 291-4181

ARIZONA ACADEMY OF MEDICAL AND DENTAL ASSISTANTS
2725 E. Seventh Ave., Flagstaff 86004 *Type:* Private *Calendar:* Courses of varying lengths *Degrees:* certificates *Prof. Accred.:* Health Education, Medical Assisting *CEO:* Pres./Dir. David M. Schrader
Enroll: 63   (602) 526-6359

ARIZONA COLLEGE OF THE BIBLE
2045 W. Northern Ave., Phoenix 85021 *Type:* Private *Accred.:* 1981/1986 (AABC); 1991 (NCA candidate) *Calendar:* Sem. plan *Degrees:* A, B, D, certificates *CEO:* Pres. Robert W. Benton
Enroll: 88   (602) 995-2670

ARIZONA INSTITUTE OF BUSINESS AND TECHNOLOGY
6049 N. 43rd Ave., Phoenix 85019 *Type:* Private business *Accred.:* 1982/1988 (CCA-ACICS) *Calendar:* Courses of varying lengths *Degrees:* certificates, diplomas *CEO:* Dir. Lynda Angel
Enroll: 875   (602) 242-6265

BRANCH CAMPUS
925 S. Gilbert Rd., Ste. 201, Mesa, AZ 85204 *CEO:* Dir. Sue Boyer
                       (602) 545-8755

BRANCH CAMPUS
2330 N. 75th Ave., Ste. 110, Phoenix, AZ 85035 *CEO:* Pres. Logan P. Bauer
                       (602) 849-8208

ARIZONA STATE UNIVERSITY
Tempe 85287-2203 *Type:* Public *System:* Arizona Board of Regents *Accred.:* 1931/1983 (NCA) *Calendar:* Sem. plan *Degrees:* B, P, M, D *Prof. Accred.:* Accounting (Type A,C), Architecture (M), Audiology, Business (B,M), Clinical Psychology, Construction Education, Counseling Psychology, Dance, Engineering (aerospace, bioengineering, chemical, civil, computer, electrical, general, industrial, mechanical), Engineering Technology (aerospace, electrical, manufacturing), Health Services Administration, Interior Design, Journalism, Law, Medical Technology, Music, Nursing (B,M), Public Administration, School Psychology, Social Work (B,M), Speech-Language Pathology,

Arizona

Teacher Education (e,s,p), Theatre *CEO:* Pres. Lattie F. Coor
Enroll: 36094   (602) 965-5606

ARIZONA WESTERN COLLEGE
P.O. Box 929, Yuma 85366 *Type:* Public (county) junior *System:* Arizona State Board of Directors for Community Colleges *Accred.:* 1968/1989 (NCA) *Calendar:* Sem. plan *Degrees:* A *Prof. Accred.:* Nursing (A) *CEO:* Pres. James Carruthers
Enroll: 2217   (602) 726-1000

AZTECH COLLEGE
1131 W. Broadway, Tempe 85282-1225 *Type:* Private *Accred.:* 1991 (CCA-ACTTS) *Calendar:* Courses of varying lengths *Degrees:* diplomas *CEO:* Pres. Mark Luebke
    (602) 967-7813

CAREER TRAINING INTERNATIONAL
4002 E. Main St., Mesa 85205 *Type:* Private home study *Accred.:* 1991 (NHSC) *Calendar:* Courses of varying lengths *Degrees:* certificates *CEO:* Pres. Nancy S. Ledins
    (800) 545-4466

CENTRAL ARIZONA COLLEGE
8470 N. Overfield Rd., Coolidge 85228 *Type:* Public (district) junior *System:* Arizona State Board of Directors for Community Colleges *Accred.:* 1973/1986 (NCA) *Calendar:* Sem. plan *Degrees:* A, certificates *Prof. Accred.:* Nursing (A) *CEO:* Pres. John J. Klein
Enroll: 2081   (602) 723-4141

CHAPARRAL CAREER COLLEGE
4585 E. Speedway Blvd., Ste. 204, Tucson 85712 *Type:* Private business *Accred.:* 1969/1987 (CCA-ACICS) *Calendar:* Qtr. plan *Degrees:* A *CEO:* Pres. A. Lauren Rhude
Enroll: 900   (602) 327-6866

CLINTON TECHNICAL INSTITUTE/MOTORCYCLE MECHANICS INSTITUTE
2844 W. Deer Valley Rd., Phoenix 85027 *Type:* Private *Accred.:* 1979/1986 (CCA-ACTTS) *Calendar:* Courses of varying lengths *Degrees:* certificates *CEO:* Dir. David Miller
Enroll: 739   (602) 869-2871

BRANCH CAMPUS
4065 L.B. McCleod Rd., Orlando, FL 32811 *CEO:* Dir. Dennis Hendrix
    (305) 423-1514

BRANCH CAMPUS
9751 Delegates Dr., Orlando, FL 32821-9835 *CEO:* Dir. Dennis Hendrix
    (407) 240-2422

COCHISE COLLEGE
Douglas 85607 *Type:* Public (district) junior *System:* Arizona State Board of Directors for Community Colleges *Accred.:* 1969/1989 (NCA) *Calendar:* Sem. plan *Degrees:* A, certificates *Prof. Accred.:* Nursing (A) *CEO:* Pres. Dan Rehurek
Enroll: 2458   (602) 364-7943

CONSERVATORY OF RECORDING ARTS AND SCIENCES
1110 E. Missouri Ave., No. 400, Phoenix 85014-2704 *Type:* Private *Accred.:* 1991 (CCA-ACTTS) *Calendar:* Courses of varying lengths *Degrees:* diplomas *CEO:* Chf. Admin. Jacqueline F. Vican
    (602) 493-9898

DEVRY INSTITUTE OF TECHNOLOGY, PHOENIX
4702 N. 24th St., Phoenix 85016 *Type:* Private *Accred.:* 1981/1987 (NCA) *Calendar:* Tri. plan *Degrees:* A, B, certificates *Prof. Accred.:* Engineering Technology (electrical) *CEO:* Pres. James A. Dugan
Enroll: 5404   (602) 870-9222

DESERT INSTITUTE OF THE HEALING ARTS
639 N. Sixth Ave., Tucson 85705 *Type:* Private *Accred.:* 1987 (CCA-ACTTS) *Calendar:* Courses of varying lengths *Degrees:* certificates *CEO:* Dir. Janice Hollender
    (602) 882-0899

THE DOGGIE MAT
10628 N. 51st Ave., Glendale 85301 *Type:* Private *Accred.:* 1988 (CCA-ACTTS) *Cal-

endar: Courses of varying lengths *Degrees:* certificates *CEO:* Dir. Elizabeth Berger
(602) 342-9630

EASTERN ARIZONA COLLEGE
600 Church St., Thatcher 85552-0769 *Type:* Public (district) junior *System:* Arizona State Board of Directors for Community Colleges *Accred.:* 1966/1986 (NCA) *Calendar:* Sem. plan *Degrees:* A, certificates *CEO:* Pres. Gherald L. Hoopes, Jr.
Enroll: 2107 (602) 428-8233

FRANK LLOYD WRIGHT SCHOOL OF ARCHITECTURE
Taliesin West, Scottsdale 85261 *Type:* Private professional; graduate only *Accred.:* 1987 (NCA) *Calendar:* yearly plan *Degrees:* M *CEO:* Managing Trustee Richard Carney
Enroll: 36 (602) 860-2700

GATEWAY COMMUNITY COLLEGE
108 N. 40th St., Phoenix 85034 *Type:* Public junior *System:* Maricopa County Community College District *Accred.:* 1971/1990 (NCA) *Calendar:* Sem. plan *Degrees:* A, certificates *Prof. Accred.:* Nuclear Medicine Technology, Nursing, Radiography, Respiratory Therapy, Respiratory Therapy Technology *CEO:* Pres. Phil D. Randolph
Enroll: 1930 (602) 275-8500

GLENDALE COMMUNITY COLLEGE
6000 W. Olive Ave., Glendale 85302-3090 *Type:* Public junior *System:* Maricopa County Community College District *Accred.:* 1967/1984 (NCA) *Calendar:* Sem. plan *Degrees:* A, certificates *Prof. Accred.:* Engineering Technology (electrical), Nursing (A) *CEO:* Pres. John R. Waltrip
Enroll: 7818 (602) 435-3000

GRAND CANYON UNIVERSITY
3300 W. Camelback Rd., Phoenix 85017 *Type:* Private (Southern Baptist) liberal arts and teachers *Accred.:* 1968/1987 (NCA) *Calendar:* 4-1-4 plan *Degrees:* B, M *Prof. Accred.:* Nursing (B) *CEO:* Pres. Bill Williams
Enroll: 1825 (602) 249-3300

HIGH-TECH INSTITUTE
1515 E. Indian School Rd., Phoenix 85016 *Type:* Private *Accred.:* 1984 (CCA-ACTTS) *Calendar:* Courses of varying lengths *Degrees:* certificates *CEO:* Dir. Marilyn Pobiak
Enroll: 270 (602) 279-9700

THE BRYMAN SCHOOL
4343 N. 16th St., Phoenix, AZ 85016 *Prof. Accred.:* Medical Assisting, Medical Assisting (AMA) *CEO:* Dir. Carol Miller
(602) 274-4300

ITT TECHNICAL INSTITUTE
4837 E. McDowell Rd., Phoenix 85008 *Type:* Private *Accred.:* 1977 (CCA-ACTTS) *Calendar:* Courses of varying lengths *Degrees:* diplomas *CEO:* Dir. Michael Henry
Enroll: 300 (602) 252-2331

ITT TECHNICAL INSTITUTE
1840 E. Benson Hwy., Tucson 85714 *Type:* Private *Accred.:* 1986 (CCA-ACTTS) *Calendar:* Courses of varying lengths *Degrees:* diplomas *CEO:* Dir. Richard Freund
(602) 294-2944

INSTITUTE OF MEDICAL-DENTAL TECHNOLOGY AT MESA
240 W. First St., Mesa 85201 *Type:* Private *Accred.:* 1980/1987 (CCA-ACTTS) *Calendar:* Courses of varying lengths *Degrees:* diplomas *CEO:* Dir. Jule J. Goldberg
Enroll: 77 (602) 969-5505

LAMSON BUSINESS COLLEGE
6367 E. Tanque Verde Rd., Ste. 100, Tucson 85715 *Type:* Private business *Accred.:* 1977/1989 (CCA-ACICS) *Calendar:* Qtr. plan *Degrees:* A, certificates, diplomas *CEO:* Dir. Jim Mullen
Enroll: 387 (602) 327-6851

LAMSON JUNIOR COLLEGE
1980 W. Main St., Mesa 85201 *Type:* Private *Accred.:* 1981/1990 (CCA-ACICS) *Calendar:* Qtr. plan *Degrees:* A, certificates, diplomas *CEO:* Dir. Jerome L. Thompson
Enroll: 1158 (602) 898-7000

Arizona

LAMSON JUNIOR COLLEGE
2701 W. Bethany Home Rd., Phoenix 85017 *Type:* Private *Accred.:* 1966/1990 (CCA-ACICS) *Calendar:* Qtr. plan *Degrees:* A, certificates, diplomas *CEO:* Pres. James W. Cox
Enroll: 1101 (602) 433-2000

THE LAURAL SCHOOL
2538 N. Eighth St., P.O. Box 5338, Phoenix 85006 *Type:* Private home study *Accred.:* 1980/1991 (NHSC) *Calendar:* Courses of varying lengths *Degrees:* certificates, diplomas *CEO:* Admin. Laura Orman Fabricant
(602) 994-3460

LONG MEDICAL INSTITUTE
4126 N. Black Canyon Hwy., Phoenix 85017 *Type:* Private *Accred.:* 1981/1987 (CCA-ACTTS) *Calendar:* Courses of varying lengths *Degrees:* diplomas *Prof. Accred.:* Respiratory Therapy Technology *CEO:* Dir. Galyn Smock
Enroll: 405 (602) 279-9333

MESA COMMUNITY COLLEGE
1833 W. Southern Ave., Mesa 85202 *Type:* Public junior *System:* Maricopa County Community College District *Accred.:* 1967/1985 (NCA) *Calendar:* Sem. plan *Degrees:* A, certificates *Prof. Accred.:* Nursing (A) *CEO:* Pres. Larry K. Christiansen
Enroll: 9159 (602) 461-7000

CHANDLER EXTENSION
Chandler, AZ 85227 *CEO:* Provost Arnette Ward
(602) 461-7407

MODERN SCHOOLS OF AMERICA, INC.
2538 N. 8th St., P.O. Box 5338, Phoenix 85010-5338 *Type:* Private home study *Accred.:* 1980/1991 (NHSC) *Calendar:* Courses of varying lengths *Degrees:* certificates *CEO:* Dir. Paul Fabricant
(602) 990-8346

MOHAVE COMMUNITY COLLEGE
1971 Jagerson Ave., Kingman 86401 *Type:* Public junior *System:* Arizona State Board of Directors for Community Colleges *Accred.:* 1981/1986 (NCA) *Calendar:* Sem. plan *Degrees:* A, certificates *CEO:* Pres. Charles W. Hall
Enroll: 1533 (602) 757-4331

MOUNTAIN STATES TECHNICAL INSTITUTE
3120 N. 34th Dr., Phoenix 85017 *Type:* Private *Accred.:* 1977/1987 (CCA-ACTTS) *Calendar:* Courses of varying lengths *Degrees:* diplomas *CEO:* Dir. Ernest L. Gaddie
Enroll: 1351 (602) 269-7555

MUNDUS INSTITUTE
4745 N. Seventh St., Ste. 425, Phoenix 85014 *Type:* Private *Accred.:* 1990 (CCA-ACTTS) *Calendar:* Courses of varying lengths *Degrees:* certificates *CEO:* Vice Pres. Irene J. Hickman
(602) 248-8548

NATIONAL EDUCATION CENTER—ARIZONA AUTOMOTIVE INSTITUTE CAMPUS
6829 N. 46th Ave., Glendale 85301 *Type:* Private *Accred.:* 1972/1988 (CCA-ACTTS) *Calendar:* Qtr. plan *Degrees:* diplomas *CEO:* Dir. Allan J. Reed
Enroll: 999 (602) 934-7273

NAVAJO COMMUNITY COLLEGE
Tsaile 86556 *Type:* Public junior *Accred.:* 1976/1990 (NCA) *Calendar:* Sem. plan *Degrees:* A, certificates *CEO:* Pres. Laurence Gischi
Enroll: 1011 (602) 724-3311

NORTH AMERICAN COLLEGE
5035 N. 35th Ave., Phoenix 85017 *Type:* Private business *Accred.:* 1982/1988 (CCA-ACICS) *Calendar:* Courses of varying lengths *Degrees:* certificates, diplomas *CEO:* Pres. Stacy Vagts
Enroll: 788 (602) 248-0648

BRANCH CAMPUS
2108 E. Thomas Rd., Phoenix, AZ 85016 *CEO:* Dir. Charles Schrader

NORTHERN ARIZONA INSTITUTE OF TECHNOLOGY
1120 Kaibab La., Flagstaff 86001 *Type:* Private business *Accred.:* 1989 (CCA-ACICS) *Calendar:* Qtr. plan *Degrees:* cer-

tificates, diplomas *CEO:* Pres. John H. Biggar
Enroll: 169 (602) 779-4532

NORTHERN ARIZONA UNIVERSITY
Box 4092, Flagstaff 86011 *Type:* Public (state) *System:* Arizona Board of Regents *Accred.:* 1930/1988 (NCA) *Calendar:* Sem. plan *Degrees:* B, M, D *Prof. Accred.:* Business (B,M), Dental Hygiene, Engineering (civil, computer, electrical, mechanical), Engineering Technology (civil/construction, electrical, mechanical), Forestry, Music, Nursing (B), Physical Therapy, Social Work (B), Speech-Language Pathology, Teacher Education (e,s,p) *CEO:* Pres. Eugene M. Hughes
Enroll: 15006 (602) 523-3232

NORTHLAND PIONEER COLLEGE
1200 E. Hermosa Dr., P.O. Box 610, Holbrook 86025-1993 *Type:* Public junior *System:* Arizona State Board of Directors for Community Colleges *Accred.:* 1980/1990 (NCA) *Calendar:* Sem. plan *Degrees:* A, certificates *CEO:* Pres. John H. Anderson
Enroll: 1796 (602) 524-6111

PARADISE VALLEY COMMUNITY COLLEGE
18401 N. 32nd St., Phoenix 85032 *Type:* Public junior *System:* Maricopa County Community College District *Accred.:* 1990 (NCA) *Calendar:* Sem. plan *Degrees:* A, certificates *CEO:* Pres. John A. Cordova
Enroll: 2082 (602) 493-2600

PARALEGAL INSTITUTE, INC.
2922 N. 35th Ave., Suite 4, P.O. Drawer 11408, Phoenix 85061-1408 *Type:* Private home study *Accred.:* 1979/1988 (NHSC) *Calendar:* Courses of varying lengths *Degrees:* certificates *CEO:* Pres. John W. Morrison
(602) 272-1855

PEDIGREE CAREER INSTITUTE
3037 W. Clarendon Ave., Phoenix 85017 *Type:* Private *Accred.:* 1987 (CCA-ACTTS) *Calendar:* Courses of varying lengths *Degrees:* certificates *CEO:* Dir. Michael Kessler
(602) 264-3647

PEDIGREE CAREER INSTITUTE
3781 E. Technical Dr., No. 1, Tucson 85713 *Type:* Private *Accred.:* 1986 (CCA-ACTTS) *Calendar:* Courses of varying lengths *Degrees:* certificates *CEO:* Dir. Ron B. Kessler
Enroll: 113 (602) 745-3647

PHOENIX COLLEGE
1202 W. Thomas Rd., Phoenix 85013 *Type:* Public junior *System:* Maricopa County Community College District *Accred.:* 1928/1986 (NCA) *Calendar:* Sem. plan *Degrees:* A, certificates *Prof. Accred.:* Dental Assisting, Dental Hygiene, Medical Assisting (AMA), Medical Laboratory Technology (AMA), Medical Record Technology, Nursing (A) *CEO:* Pres. Myrna Harrison
Enroll: 5830 (602) 285-7433

PHOENIX INSTITUTE OF TECHNOLOGY
2555 E. University Dr., Phoenix 85034 *Type:* Private *Accred.:* 1973/1985 (CCA-ACTTS) *Calendar:* Qtr. plan *Degrees:* diplomas *CEO:* Pres. W. Ray Sevy
Enroll: 2391 (602) 244-8111

PIMA COUNTY COMMUNITY COLLEGE DISTRICT
200 N. Stone Ave., P.O. Box 3010, Tucson 85702 *Type:* Public *System:* Arizona State Board of Directors for Community Colleges *Accred.:* 1975/1991 (NCA) *Calendar:* Sem. plan *Degrees:* A, certificates *Prof. Accred.:* Dental Assisting, Dental Laboratory Technology, Nursing (A), Radiography, Respiratory Therapy *CEO:* Pres. Johnas F. Hockaday
Enroll: 13471 (602) 884-6047

PIMA MEDICAL INSTITUTE
3350 E. Grant Rd., Tucson 85716 *Type:* Private *Calendar:* Courses of varying lengths *Degrees:* A *Prof. Accred.:* Health Education, Radiography, Respiratory Therapy, Respiratory Therapy Technology *CEO:* Pres. Richard L. Luebke, Sr.
Enroll: 68 (602) 326-1600

Arizona

BRANCH CAMPUS
2300 E. Broadway Rd., Tempe, AZ 85282 *Prof. Accred.:* Health Education, Radiography *CEO:* Pres. Richard L. Luebke, Sr.
(602) 345-7777

BRANCH CAMPUS
7290 Samuel Dr., Ste. 200, Denver, CO 80221 *Prof. Accred.:* Health Education, Radiography *CEO:* Pres. Richard L. Luebke
(303) 426-1800

BRANCH CAMPUS
2201 San Pedro Dr., N.E., Bldg. 3, Ste. 100, Albuquerque, NM 87110 *Prof. Accred.:* Health Education, Radiography *CEO:* Pres. Richard L. Luebke
(505) 881-1234

BRANCH CAMPUS
1627 Eastlake Ave. E., Seattle, WA 98102 *Prof. Accred.:* Health Education *CEO:* Dir. Walter Greenly
(206) 322-6100

PRESCOTT COLLEGE
220 Grove Ave., Prescott 86301 *Type:* Private liberal arts *Accred.:* 1984/1990 (NCA) *Calendar:* 4-1-4 plan *Degrees:* B *CEO:* Pres. Douglas M. North
Enroll: 574 (602) 778-2090

THE REFRIGERATION SCHOOL
4210 E. Washington St., Phoenix 85034 *Type:* Private *Accred.:* 1973/1985 (CCA-ACTTS) *Calendar:* Courses of varying lengths *Degrees:* diplomas *CEO:* Dir. Ola L. Loney
Enroll: 794 (602) 275-7133

RIO SALADO COMMUNITY COLLEGE
640 N. First Ave., Phoenix 85003 *Type:* Public junior *System:* Maricopa County Community College District *Accred.:* 1981/1986 (NCA) *Calendar:* Sem. plan *Degrees:* A, certificates *CEO:* Pres. Linda M. Thor
Enroll: 4110 (602) 243-4000

ROBERTO-VENN SCHOOL OF LUTHIERY
4011 S. 16th St., Phoenix 85040 *Type:* Private *Accred.:* 1979 (CCA-ACTTS) *Calendar:* Courses of varying lengths *Degrees:* certificates *CEO:* Dir. John H. Roberto
Enroll: 43 (602) 243-1179

SCOTTSDALE COMMUNITY COLLEGE
9000 E. Chaparral Rd., Scottsdale 85256 *Type:* Public junior *System:* Maricopa County Community College District *Accred.:* 1975/1987 (NCA) *Calendar:* Sem. plan *Degrees:* A, certificates *Prof. Accred.:* Nursing (A) *CEO:* Pres. Arthur W. DeCabooter
Enroll: 4249 (602) 423-6000

SCOTTSDALE CULINARY INSTITUTE
8100 E. Camelback Rd., Scottsdale 85251 *Type:* Private *Accred:* 1989 (CCA-ACTTS) *Calendar:* Courses of varying lengths *Degrees:* certificates *CEO:* Pres. Elizabeth Leite
(602) 990-3773

SOUTH MOUNTAIN COMMUNITY COLLEGE
7050 S. 24th St., Phoenix 85040 *Type:* Public junior *System:* Maricopa County Community College District *Accred.:* 1984/1989 (NCA) *Calendar:* Sem. plan *Degrees:* A, certificates *CEO:* Pres. Raul Cardenas
Enroll: 1232 (602) 243-8000

SOUTH WEST ACADEMY OF TECHNOLOGY
1333 W. Camelback Rd., Phoenix 85013 *Type:* Private *Accred.:* 1983/1988 (CCA-ACTTS) *Calendar:* Qtr. plan *Degrees:* certificates *CEO:* Pres. Alan Hatch
Enroll: 358 (602) 277-0237

BRANCH CAMPUS
1660 S. Alma School Rd., Ste. 227, Mesa, AZ 85210 *Prof. Accred.:* Respiratory Therapy, Respiratory Therapy Technology *CEO:* Dir. Tom Mathews
(602) 820-3003

BRANCH CAMPUS
1020 Sandretto Dr., Prescott, AZ 86301 *Accred.:* 1987 (CCA-ACTTS) *CEO:* Dir. Joanne Hobbs
(602) 776-0700

Accredited Institutions   **Arizona**

SOUTHWESTERN COLLEGE
2625 E. Cactus Rd., Phoenix 85032 *Type:* Private (Conservative Baptist) *Accred.:* 1977/1987 (AABC); 1990 (NCA candidate) *Calendar:* Sem. plan *Degrees:* A, B, certificates *CEO:* Pres. Wesley A. Olsen
Enroll: 126   (602) 992-6101

STERLING SCHOOL
801 E. Indian School Rd., Phoenix 85014 *Type:* Private business *Accred.:* 1981/1990 (CCA-ACICS) *Calendar:* Courses of varying lengths *Degrees:* certificates, diplomas *CEO:* Dir. Ruby Sterling
Enroll: 96   (602) 277-5276

TUCSON COLLEGE OF BUSINESS
7830 E. Broadway, Tucson 85710 *Type:* Private *Accred.:* 1966/1990 (CCA-ACICS) *Calendar:* Courses of varying lengths *Degrees:* certificates, diplomas *Prof. Accred.:* Medical Assisting *CEO:* Pres. M.A. Mikhail
Enroll: 802   (602) 296-3261

UNITED STATES ARMY INTELLIGENCE CENTER AND SCHOOL
Fort Huachuca 85613 *Type:* Public (federal) *Accred.:* 1980/1990 (NCA) *Calendar:* Courses of varying lengths *Degrees:* certificates *CEO:* Commander Julius Parker
Enroll: 5733   (602) 538-2830

UNIVERSAL TECHNICAL INSTITUTE
3121 W. Waldon Ave., Phoenix 85017 *Type:* Private *Accred.:* 1968/1983 (CCA-ACTTS) *Calendar:* Courses of varying lengths *Degrees:* certificates *CEO:* Dir. Randy Smith
Enroll: 294   (602) 264-4164

BRANCH CAMPUS
601 Regency Dr., Glendale Heights, IL 60139 *CEO:* Dir. Gerald Murphy
                                      (312) 529-2662

UNIVERSITY OF ARIZONA
Tucson 85721 *Type:* Public (state) *System:* Arizona Board of Regents *Accred.:* 1917/1990 (NCA) *Calendar:* Sem plan. *Degrees:* B, M, D *Prof. Accred.:* Architecture (B), Audiology, Business (B,M), Clinical Psychology, Dance, Dietetics (internship), Engineering (aerospace, agricultural, chemical, civil, computer, electrical, geological/geophysical, industrial, materials, mechanical, mining, nuclear, systems), Journalism, Landscape Architecture (B), Law, Librarianship, Medical Technology, Medicine, Music, Nursing (B,M), Perfusion, Pharmacy, Psychology Internship, Public Administration, Rehabilitation Counseling, School Psychology, Speech-Language Pathology, Teacher Education, Theatre *CEO:* Pres. Manuel T. Pacheco
Enroll: 31879   (602) 621-2211

UNIVERSITY OF PHOENIX
4615 E. Elwood Ave., Phoenix 85040 *Type:* Private professional *Accred.:* 1978/1987 (NCA) *Calendar:* Sem. plan *Degrees:* A, B, M *Prof. Accred.:* Nursing (B) *CEO:* Pres. William H. Gibbs
Enroll: 8070   (602) 966-9577

WESTERN INTERNATIONAL UNIVERSITY
10202 N. 19th Ave., Phoenix 85021 *Type:* Private *Accred.:* 1984/1987 (NCA) *Calendar:* Tri. plan *Degrees:* A, B, M, certificates *CEO:* Chanc./C.E.O. Robert S. Webber
Enroll: 2150   (602) 943-2311

YAVAPAI COLLEGE
1100 E. Sheldon St., Prescott 86301 *Type:* Public (district) junior *System:* Arizona State Board of Directors for Community Colleges *Accred.:* 1975/1987 (NCA) *Calendar:* Sem. plan *Degrees:* A, certificates *Prof. Accred.:* Nursing (A) *CEO:* Pres. Paul D. Walker
Enroll: 2582   (602) 445-7300

ARKANSAS

ARKANSAS BAPTIST COLLEGE
1600 High St., Little Rock 72202 *Type:* Private (Baptist) liberal arts *Accred.:* 1987/1990 (NCA) *Calendar:* Sem. plan *Degrees:* B, certificates *CEO:* Pres. W. Thomas Keaton
Enroll: 249 (501) 372-6883

ARKANSAS COLLEGE
P.O. Box 2317, Batesville 72503 *Type:* Private (Presbyterian) *Accred.:* 1959/1982 (NCA) *Calendar:* 4-1-4 plan *Degrees:* B, certificates *Prof. Accred.:* Social Work (B), Teacher Education (e,s,p) *CEO:* Pres. John V. Griffith
Enroll: 664 (501) 793-9813

ARKANSAS COLLEGE OF BARBERING AND HAIR DESIGN
200 Washington Ave., North Little Rock 72114-5615 *Type:* Private *Accred.:* 1991 (CCA-ACTTS) *Calendar:* Courses of varying lengths *Degrees:* certificates *CEO:* Pres. Larry Little
(501) 376-9696

ARKANSAS STATE UNIVERSITY
P.O. Box 76, State University 72467 *Type:* Public *System:* Arkansas State University System Office *Accred.:* 1928/1983 (NCA) *Calendar:* Sem. plan *Degrees:* A, B, M, certificates *Prof. Accred.:* Business (B,M), Engineering (agricultural, general), Journalism, Medical Laboratory Technology (AMA), Medical Technology, Music, Nursing (A,B), Radiography, Rehabilitation Counseling, Social Work (B), Speech-Language Pathology, Teacher Education (e,s,p) *CEO:* Pres. Eugene W. Smith
Enroll: 7838 (501) 972-3030

ARKANSAS STATE UNIVERSITY—BEEBE
Drawer H, Beebe 72012 *Type:* Public junior *System:* Arkansas State University System Office *Accred.:* 1971/1982 (NCA) *Calendar:* Sem. plan *Degrees:* A, certificates *CEO:* Chanc. William H. Owen, Jr.
Enroll: 1142 (501) 882-6452

ARKANSAS TECH UNIVERSITY
Russellville 72801 *Type:* Public (state) liberal arts *System:* Arkansas Department of Higher Education *Accred:* 1930/1991 (NCA) *Calendar:* Sem. plan *Degrees:* A, B, M *Prof. Accred.:* Engineering (general), Medical Assisting (AMA), Medical Record Administration, Music, Nursing (B), Teacher Education (e,s,p) *CEO:* Pres. Kenneth G. Kersh
Enroll: 3417 (501) 968-0237

ARKANSAS VALLEY VOCATIONAL-TECHNICAL SCHOOL
P.O. Box 506, Ozark 72949 *Type:* Private *Calendar:* Courses of varying lengths *Degrees:* diplomas *Prof. Accred.:* Respiratory Therapy Technology *CEO:* Pres. Carl Jones
Enroll: 45 (501) 667-2117

BLACK RIVER VOCATIONAL-TECHNICAL SCHOOL
P.O. Box 468, Pocahontas 72455 *Type:* Private *Calendar:* Courses of varying lengths *Degrees:* certificates *Prof. Accred.:* Respiratory Therapy Technology *CEO:* Dir. Richard Gaines
Enroll: 26 (501) 892-4565

CARTI SCHOOL OF RADIATION THERAPY TECHNOLOGY
P.O. Box 5210, Little Rock 72215 *Type:* Private *Calendar:* Courses of varying lengths *Degrees:* certificates *Prof. Accred.:* Radiation Therapy Technology *CEO:* Dir. Edward Rensch, Jr.
Enroll: 12 (501) 664-8573

CAPITAL CITY BUSINESS COLLEGE
K-Mart Ctr., Hwy. 64 E., P.O. Box 790, Russellville 72801 *Type:* Private business *Accred.:* 1973/1985 (CCA-ACICS) *Calendar:* Qtr. plan *Degrees:* certificates, diplomas *CEO:* Dir. Barbara G. Dunn
Enroll: 153 (501) 968-1825

CAPITAL CITY JUNIOR COLLEGE
7723 Asher Ave., P.O. Box 4818, Little Rock 72214 *Type:* Private *Accred.:* 1966/1986 (CCA-ACICS); 1987/1991 (NCA pro-

bational) *Calendar:* Qtr. plan *Degrees:* A, certificates, diplomas *Prof. Accred.:* Medical Assisting (AMA) *CEO:* Pres. Carolyn Butler
Enroll: 244 (501) 562-0700

CENTRAL BAPTIST COLLEGE
CBC Sta., 1501 College Ave., Conway 72032 *Type:* Private (Baptist Missionary Association) *Accred.:* 1977/1987 (AABC); 1990 (NCA candidate) *Calendar:* Sem. plan *Degrees:* A, B, M, certificates *CEO:* Pres. Charles Atteberry
Enroll: 239 (501) 329-6872

COTTON BOLL VOCATIONAL-TECHNICAL SCHOOL
Box 36, Burdette 72321 *Type:* Private *Calendar:* Courses of varying lengths *Prof. Accred.:* Dental Assisting *CEO:* Pres. William Nelson
(501) 763-1486

DELTA CAREER COLLEGE
6909 Geyer Springs Rd., Little Rock 72204 *Type:* Private business *Accred.:* 1988 (CCA-ACICS) *Calendar:* Qtr. plan *Degrees:* diplomas *CEO:* Dir. Steve McCray
Enroll: 672 (501) 666-8509

DRAUGHON BUSINESS COLLEGE
4821 S. University Ave., Little Rock 72209 *Type:* Private business *Accred.:* 1953/1990 (CCA-ACICS) *Calendar:* Courses of varying lengths *Degrees:* certificates, diplomas *CEO:* Dir. Marty Berry
Enroll: 635 (501) 562-6626

EAST ARKANSAS COMMUNITY COLLEGE
Forrest City 72335 *Type:* Public junior *Accred.:* 1979/1989 (NCA) *Calendar:* Sem. plan *Degrees:* certificates *CEO:* Pres. Tom Spencer
Enroll: 949 (501) 633-4480

EASTERN COLLEGE OF HEALTH VOCATIONS
6423 Forbing Rd., Little Rock 72209 *Type:* Private *Calendar:* Courses of varying lengths *Degrees:* diplomas *Prof. Accred.:* Health Education *CEO:* Dir. Susan M. Dalto
Enroll: 402 (501) 568-0211

GARLAND COUNTY COMMUNITY COLLEGE
One College Dr., Mid-America Park, Hot Springs 71913 *Type:* Public junior *Accred.:* 1981/1986 (NCA) *Calendar:* Sem. plan *Degrees:* A, certificates *Prof. Accred.:* Medical Laboratory Technology (AMA), Medical Record Technology, Nursing (A), Radiography *CEO:* Pres. Gerald H. Fisher
Enroll: 1136 (501) 767-9371

HARDING UNIVERSITY
Box 761, Sta. A, Searcy 72143 *Type:* Private (Churches of Christ) liberal arts *Accred.:* 1954/1985 (NCA) *Calendar:* Sem plan. *Degrees:* A, B, M *Prof. Accred.:* Music, Nursing (B), Social Work (B), Teacher Education (e,s) *CEO:* Pres. David B. Burks, Jr.
Enroll: 3100 (501) 279-4274

HENDERSON STATE UNIVERSITY
1100 Henderson St., Arkadelphia 71923 *Type:* Public liberal arts and teachers *System:* Arkansas Department of Higher Education *Accred:* 1934/1982 (NCA) *Calendar:* Sem. plan *Degrees:* A, B, M *Prof. Accred.:* Music, Nursing (B), Teacher Education (e,s,p) *CEO:* Pres. Charles D. Dunn
Enroll: 3081 (501) 246-5511

HENDRIX COLLEGE
Conway 72032 *Type:* Private (United Methodist) liberal arts *Accred.:* 1924/1989 (NCA) *Calendar:* Sem. plan *Degrees:* B *Prof. Accred.:* Music, Teacher Education (e,s) *CEO:* Interim Pres. John Curchill
Enroll: 1001 (501) 329-6811

JOHN BROWN UNIVERSITY
Siloam Springs 72761 *Type:* Private liberal arts *Accred.:* 1962/1982 (NCA) *Calendar:* Sem. plan *Degrees:* A, B *Prof. Accred.:* Teacher Education (e,s) *CEO:* Pres. John E. Brown, III
Enroll: 878 (501) 524-3131

MISSISSIPPI COUNTY COMMUNITY COLLEGE
P.O Drawer 1109, Blytheville 72316-1109 *Type:* Public junior *Accred.:* 1980/1985 (NCA) *Calendar:* Sem. plan *Degrees:* A,

Arkansas

certificates *Prof. Accred.:* Nursing (A) *CEO:* Pres. John P. Sullins
Enroll: 1016 (501) 762-1020

NATIONAL EDUCATION CENTER—ARKANSAS COLLEGE OF TECHNOLOGY
9720 Rodney Parham Rd., Little Rock 72207 *Type:* Private *Accred.:* 1972/1988 (CCA-ACTTS) *Calendar:* Qtr. plan *Degrees:* diplomas *CEO:* Pres. Allen J. Reed
Enroll: 635 (501) 224-8200

NEW TYLER BARBER COLLEGE
1221 Seventh St., North Little Rock 72114 *Type:* Private *Accred.:* 1984 (CCA-ACTTS) *Calendar:* Courses of varying lengths *Degrees:* certificates *CEO:* Pres. Daniel Bryant
Enroll: 58 (501) 375-0377

NORTH ARKANSAS COMMUNITY COLLEGE
Pioneer Ridge, Harrison 72601 *Type:* Public junior *Accred.:* 1979/1991 (NCA) *Calendar:* Sem. plan *Degrees:* A, certificates *Prof. Accred.:* Nursing (A) *CEO:* Pres. William Bert Baker
Enroll: 800 (501) 743-3000

OUACHITA BAPTIST UNIVERSITY
Arkadelphia 71923 *Type:* Private (Southern Baptist) *Accred.:* 1927/1990 (NCA) *Calendar:* Sem. plan *Degrees:* B, M, certificates *Prof. Accred.:* Music, Teacher Education (e,s,p) *CEO:* Pres. Ben Elrod
Enroll: 1280 (501) 246-4531

PHILANDER SMITH COLLEGE
812 W. 13th St., Little Rock 72202 *Type:* Private (United Methodist) liberal arts *Accred.:* 1949/1990 (NCA) *Calendar:* Sem. plan *Degrees:* B *CEO:* Pres. Myer L. Titus
Enroll: 664 (501) 375-9845

PHILLIPS COUNTY COMMUNITY COLLEGE
Box 785, Helena 72342 *Type:* Public junior *Accred.:* 1972/1985 (NCA) *Calendar:* Sem. plan *Degrees:* A, certificates *Prof. Accred.:* Medical Laboratory Technology (AMA), Nursing (A) *CEO:* Pres. Steven M. Jones
Enroll: 1012 (501) 338-6474

PULASKI VOCATIONAL-TECHNICAL SCHOOL
3000 West Scenic Dr., North Little Rock 72118 *Type:* Private *Calendar:* Courses of varying lengths *Degrees:* certificates, diplomas *Prof. Accred.:* Dental Assisting, Respiratory Therapy Technology *CEO:* Admin. Ben Wyatt
(501) 771-1000

RED RIVER VOCATIONAL-TECHNICAL SCHOOL
P.O. Box 140, Hope 71801 *Type:* Private *Calendar:* Courses of varying lengths *Prof. Accred.:* Respiratory Therapy Technology *CEO:* Dir. Johnny Rapert
(501) 777-5722

RICH MOUNTAIN COMMUNITY COLLEGE
601 Bush St., Mena 71953 *Type:* Public junior *Accred.:* 1990 (NCA) *Calendar:* Sem. plan *Degrees:* A, certificates *CEO:* Pres. Bill Abernathy
Enroll: 309 (501) 394-5012

SHORTER COLLEGE
604 Locust St., North Little Rock 72114 *Type:* Private junior *Accred.:* 1981/1986 (NCA) *Calendar:* Sem. plan *Degrees:* A, certificates *CEO:* Pres. Katherine P. Mitchell
Enroll: 140 (501) 374-6305

SOUTH CENTRAL CAREER COLLEGE
4500 W. Commercial Dr., North Little Rock 72116 *Type:* Private business *Accred.:* 1979/1988 (CCA-ACICS) *Calendar:* Qtr. plan *Degrees:* certificates, diplomas *CEO:* Dir. Sandy Locke
Enroll: 424 (501) 758-6800

BRANCH CAMPUS
2311 E. Nettleton, Ste. G, Jonesboro, AR 72401 *CEO:* Dir. Richard Pierce
(501) 972-6999

SOUTH CENTRAL CAREER COLLEGE
1614 Brentwood Dr., Pine Bluff 71601 *Type:* Private business *Accred.:* 1986/1989 (CCA-ACICS) *Calendar:* Qtr. plan *Degrees:* certificates, diplomas *CEO:* Dir. Gene Owens
Enroll: 242 (501) 535-6800

Accredited Institutions   **Arkansas**

SOUTHERN ARKANSAS UNIVERSITY
Magnolia 71753 *Type:* Public (state) liberal arts and teachers *Accred.:* 1929/1983 (NCA) *Calendar:* Sem. plan *Degrees:* A, B, M *Prof. Accred.:* Music, Nursing (A), Teacher Education (e,s,p) *CEO:* Pres. Steven G. Gamble
Enroll: 2230   (501) 235-4001

SOUTHERN ARKANSAS UNIVERSITY TECH
SAU Tech Sta., Camden 71701 *Type:* Public (state) 2-year *Accred.:* 1980/1990 (NCA) *Calendar:* Sem. plan *Degrees:* A, certificates *CEO:* Chanc. George J. Brown
Enroll: 534   (501) 574-4500

SOUTHERN ARKANSAS UNIVERSITY—EL DORADO
300 S. West Ave., El Dorado 71730 *Type:* Public (state) 2-year *Accred.:* 1983/1988 (NCA) *Calendar:* Sem. plan *Degrees:* A, certificates *Prof. Accred.:* Medical Laboratory Technology (AMA), Radiogra-phy *CEO:* Chanc. Ben T. Whitfield
Enroll: 481   (501) 862-8131

SOUTHERN TECHNICAL COLLEGE
100 Greenwood St., Hot Springs 71913 *Type:* Private business *Accred.:* 1988 (CCA-ACICS) *Calendar:* Courses of varying lengths *Degrees:* certificates, diplomas *CEO:* Dir. Steven B. Jarratt
     (501) 623-4300

SOUTHERN TECHNICAL COLLEGE
7601 Scott Hamilton Dr., Little Rock 72209 *Type:* Private business *Accred.:* 1989 (CCA-ACICS) *Calendar:* Qtr. plan *Degrees:* certificates, diplomas *CEO:* Dir. Charles E. Carlisle
Enroll: 1207   (501) 565-7000

UNIVERSITY OF ARKANSAS AT LITTLE ROCK
2801 S. University Ave., Little Rock 72204 *Type:* Public (state) *System:* University of Arkansas System *Accred.:* 1929/1980 (NCA) *Calendar:* Sem. plan *Degrees:* A, B, P, M *Prof. Accred.:* Art, Audiology, Business (B,M), Dental Hygiene, Engineering Technology (civil/construction, computer, electrical, manufacturing, mechanical), Health Services Administration, Journalism, Law (ABA only), Music, Nursing (A), Social Work (M), Speech-Language Pathology, Surgical Technology, Teacher Education (e,s), Theatre *CEO:* Chanc. James H. Young
Enroll: 7842   (501) 569-3200

UNIVERSITY OF ARKANSAS AT MONTICELLO
Monticello 71655 *Type:* Public (state) *System:* University of Arkansas System *Accred.:* 1928/1985 (NCA) *Calendar:* Sem. plan *Degrees:* A, B, M, certificates *Prof. Accred.:* Forestry, Music, Nursing (A), Teacher Education (e,s) *CEO:* Chanc. Fred J. Taylor
Enroll: 1929   (501) 460-1020

UNIVERSITY OF ARKANSAS AT PINE BLUFF
Pine Bluff 71601 *Type:* Public (state) *System:* University of Arkansas System *Accred.:* 1950/1987 (NCA) *Calendar:* Sem. plan *Degrees:* A, B, M *Prof. Accred.:* Home Economics, Music, Nursing (B), Social Work (B), Teacher Education (e,s) *CEO:* Interim Chanc. Carolyn Blakely
Enroll: 3195   (501) 541-6512

UNIVERSITY OF ARKANSAS FOR MEDICAL SCIENCES
4301 W. Markham St., Little Rock 72205 *Type:* Public *System:* University of Arkansas System *Accred.:* 1987 (NCA) *Calendar:* Sem. plan *Degrees:* A, B, M, D, certificates *Prof. Accred.:* Cytotechnology, Dietetics (internship), Medical Technology, Medicine, Nuclear Medicine Technology, Nursing (B,M), Pharmacy, Psychology Internship, Radiography, Respiratory Therapy, Respiratory Therapy Technology *CEO:* Chanc. Harry P. Ward
Enroll: 1274   (501) 686-5680

UNIVERSITY OF ARKANSAS, FAYETTEVILLE
Fayetteville 72701 *Type:* Public (state) *System:* University of Arkansas System *Accred.:* 1924/1987 (NCA) *Calendar:* Sem. plan *Degrees:* A, B, M, D *Prof. Accred.:* Accounting (Type A,C), Architecture (B), Business (B,M), Clinical Psychology, Engineering (agricultural, chemical, civil, electri-

Arkansas

cal, industrial, mechanical), Home Economics, Journalism, Landscape Architecture (B), Law, Music, Nursing (A), Rehabilitation Counseling, Social Work (B), Speech-Language Pathology, Teacher Education (e,s,p) *CEO:* Chanc. Daniel E. Ferritor
Enroll: 12611 (501) 575-4148

UNIVERSITY OF CENTRAL ARKANSAS
Conway 72032 *Type:* Public liberal arts and teachers *System:* Arkansas Department of Higher Education *Accred.:* 1931/1990 (NCA) *Calendar:* Sem. plan *Degrees:* A, B, M *Prof. Accred.:* Business (B,M), Music, Nursing (B,M), Occupational Therapy, Physical Therapy, Physical Therapy Assisting, Teacher Education (e,s,p) *CEO:* Pres. Winfred Thompson
Enroll: 9108 (501) 329-2931

UNIVERSITY OF THE OZARKS
415 College Ave., Clarksville 72830 *Type:* Private (United Presbyterian) liberal arts *Accred.:* 1931/1983 (NCA) *Calendar:* 4-1-4 plan *Degrees:* A, B, M *Prof. Accred.:* Teacher Education (e,s) *CEO:* Pres. Gene Stephenson
Enroll: 674 (501) 754-3839

WESTARK COMMUNITY COLLEGE
P.O. Box 3649, Fort Smith 72913 *Type:* Public junior *Accred.:* 1973/1985 (NCA) *Calendar:* Sem. plan *Degrees:* A, certificates *Prof. Accred.:* Nursing (A), Surgical Technology *CEO:* Pres. Joel Stubblefield
Enroll: 3006 (501) 785-7004

WILLIAMS BAPTIST COLLEGE
Box 3667, Walnut Ridge 72476 *Type:* Private (Southern Baptist) *Accred.:* 1963/1987 (NCA) *Calendar:* Sem. plan *Degrees:* A, B, certificates *CEO:* Pres. D. Jack Nicholas
Enroll: 485 (501) 886-6741

CALIFORNIA

A B INSTITUTE
2855 Market Street, P.O. Box 8069, San Diego 92102 *Type:* Private *Accred.:* 1988 (CCA-ACTTS) *Calendar:* Courses of varying lengths *Degrees:* certificates *CEO:* Dir. Larry Doria
(619) 231-0052

ABS TRAINING CENTER
5140 Vineland Ave., North Hollywood 91601 *Type:* Private *Accred.:* 1986 (CCA-ACTTS) *Calendar:* Courses of varying lengths *Degrees:* certificates *CEO:* Dir. Steven P. Mahoney
Enroll: 421   (818) 761-6188

BRANCH CAMPUS
22505 Montgomery St., Hayward, CA 94541-5035 *CEO:* Dir. Sandra Pella
(510) 538-6151

BRANCH CAMPUS
7132 Garden Grove Blvd., Westminster, CA 92683 *CEO:* Dir. Joanne T. Riordan
(714) 895-6990

ACADEMY PACIFIC BUSINESS AND TRAVEL COLLEGE
1777 N. Vine St., Hollywood 90028-5384 *Type:* Private *Accred.:* 1973/1985 (CCA-ACTTS) *Calendar:* Courses of varying lengths *Degrees:* diplomas *CEO:* Pres. Marsha Toy
Enroll: 942   (213) 462-3211

ACADEMY OF ART COLLEGE
540 Powell St., San Francisco 94108-3895 *Type:* Private professional *Accred.:* 1973/1985 (CCA-ACTTS) *Calendar:* Qtr. plan *Degrees:* B, M, certificates *Prof. Accred.:* Art, Interior Design *CEO:* Pres. Richard A. Stephens
Enroll: 272   (415) 765-4200

ADVANCE SCHOOL OF DRIVING
20825 Currier Rd., Box 443, Walnut 91789 *Type:* Private *Accred.:* 1988 (CCA-ACTTS) *Calendar:* Courses of varying lengths *Degrees:* certificates *CEO:* Pres. Barry Bither
(714) 595-2292

ALLAN HANCOCK COLLEGE
800 S. College Dr., Santa Maria 93454 *Type:* Public (district) junior *System:* Allan Hancock Joint Community College District *Accred.:* 1952/1986 (WASC-Jr.) *Calendar:* Sem. plan *Degrees:* A *CEO:* Interim Pres. Frances Conn
Enroll: 8105   (805) 922-6966

AMERICAN ACADEMY FOR CAREER EDUCATION
520 N. Euclid Ave., Ontario 91762 *Type:* Private *Accred.:* 1986/1988 (CCA-ACTTS) *Calendar:* Courses of varying lengths *Degrees:* certificates *CEO:* Dir. Mary Herling
Enroll: 88   (714) 984-5027

AMERICAN ACADEMY OF DRAMATIC ARTS WEST
2550 Paloma St., Pasadena 91107 *Type:* Private 2-year professional *Accred.:* 1981/1991 (WASC-Jr.) *Calendar:* Sem. plan *Degrees:* A *Prof. Accred.:* Theatre *CEO:* Dir. George C. Cuttingham
Enroll: 300   (818) 798-0777

AMERICAN ACADEMY OF NUTRITION
3408 Sausalito, Corona del Mar 92625 *Type:* Private home study *Accred.:* 1989 (NHSC) *De-grees:* certificates *CEO:* Admin. Peter Berwick
(714) 760-5081

AMERICAN BAPTIST SEMINARY OF THE WEST
2606 Dwight Way, Berkeley 94704-3029 *Type:* Private (Baptist) professional; graduate only *Accred.:* 1938/1989 (ATS) *Calendar:* Sem. plan *Degrees:* P, M, D *CEO:* Pres. Theodore Keaton
Enroll: 31   (510) 841-1905

AMERICAN BUSINESS COLLEGE
2011 Fresno St., Fresno 93721 *Type:* Private business *Accred.:* 1976/1991 (CCA-ACICS) *Calendar:* Courses of varying lengths *Degrees:* A, certificates *CEO:* Dir. Nina M. Stamoulis
Enroll: 219   (209) 268-4481

California

AMERICAN BUSINESS COLLEGE
5952 El Cajon Blvd., San Diego 92115
Type: Private *Accred.:* 1970/1981 (CCA-ACTTS) *Calendar:* Courses of varying lengths *Degrees:* certificates, diplomas *CEO:* Pres. Michael L. Dawson
Enroll: 360   (619) 582-1319

ABC TECH
4560 Alvarado Canyon Rd., San Diego, CA 92120-4309 *CEO:* Dir. Linda Hawk
(619) 280-9922

AMERICAN COLLEGE OF ELECTROLOGY
2285 Willow Pass Rd., Concord 94520
Type: Private *Accred.:* 1986 (CCA-ACTTS) *Calendar:* Courses of varying lengths *Degrees:* certificates *CEO:* Dir. Misao Makino
(415) 682-1776

AMERICAN COLLEGE OF OPTICS
4021 Rosewood Ave., Los Angeles 90004
Type: Private *Accred.:* 1989 (CCA-ACTTS) *Calendar:* Courses of varying lengths *Degrees:* certificates *Prof. Accred.:* Health Education *CEO:* Pres. David A. Pyle
Enroll: 174   (213) 383-2862

AMERICAN CONSERVATORY THEATRE
450 Geary St., San Francisco 94102 *Type:* Independent professional *Accred.:* 1984 (WASC-Sr.) *Calendar:* Sem. plan *Degrees:* M *CEO:* Dir. Susan Stauter
Enroll: 99   (415) 749-2200

THE AMERICAN FILM INSTITUTE CENTER FOR ADVANCED FILM AND TELEVISION STUDIES
2021 N. Western Ave., Los Angeles 90027 *Type:* Private professional; graduate only *Calendar:* 2-year program *Degrees:* M *Prof. Accred.:* Art *CEO:* Dir. Jean Firstenberg
Enroll: 160   (213) 856-7627

AMERICAN RIVER COLLEGE
4700 College Oak Dr., Sacramento 95841 *Type:* Public (district) junior *System:* Los Rios Community College District *Accred.:* 1959/1989 (WASC-Jr.) *Calendar:* Sem. plan *Degrees:* A *Prof. Accred.:* Respiratory Therapy *CEO:* Pres. Queen F. Randall
Enroll: 21514   (916) 484-8011

Accredited Institutions

AMERICAN TECHNICAL COLLEGE FOR CAREER TRAINING
191 South E St., San Bernardino 92401
Type: Private *Accred.:* 1989 (CCA-ACTTS) *Calendar:* Courses of varying lengths *Degrees:* certificates, diplomas *CEO:* Dir. Steve S. Hu
Enroll: 75   (714) 885-3857

AMERITECH COLLEGE
6843 Lennox Ave., Van Nuys 91405-7311
Type: Private *Accred.:* 1991 (CCA-ACTTS) *Calendar:* Courses of varying lengths *Degrees:* certificates *CEO:* Dir. Tauni Murphy
(818) 901-7311

AMERITECH COLLEGE
15374 Beach Blvd., Westminster 92683
Type: Private *Accred.:* 1991 (CCA-ACTTS) *Calendar:* Courses of varying lengths *Degrees:* certificates *CEO:* Dir. Tami Freedman
(714) 981-9211

AMERITECH COLLEGE OF BAKERSFIELD
4600 Ashe Rd., Ste. 313, Bakersfield 93313-2041 *Type:* Private *Accred.:* 1991 (CCA-ACTTS) *Calendar:* Courses of varying lengths *Degrees:* certificates *CEO:* Dir. Tami Freedman
805-83-9225

ANDON COLLEGE AT MODESTO
1314 H St., Modesto 95354 *Type:* Private *Calendar:* Courses of varying lengths *Degrees:* certificates *Prof. Accred.:* Health Education *CEO:* Pres. Gary D. Kerber
(209) 571-8777

ANDON COLLEGE AT STOCKTON
1201 N. El Dorado St., Stockton 95202
Type: Private *Calendar:* Courses of varying lengths *Degrees:* certificates *Prof. Accred.:* Health Education *CEO:* Pres. Gary D. Kerber
(209) 462-8777

ANJONS SCHOOL OF COSMETOLOGY
3031 W. Florida Ave., Hemet 92343-3607
Type: Private *Accred.:* 1991 (CCA-ACTTS) *Calendar:* Courses of varying lengths *De-

grees: certificates *CEO:* Pres. Keith A. Wood
(714) 652-7856

ANTELOPE VALLEY COLLEGE
3041 W. Ave. K, Lancaster 93536 *Type:* Public (district) junior *System:* Antelope Valley Community College District *Accred.:* 1952/1987 (WASC-Jr.) *Calendar:* Sem. plan *Degrees:* A *CEO:* Pres. Allan W. Kurki
Enroll: 9833 (805) 943-3241

ARMSTRONG COLLEGE
2222 Harold Way, Berkeley 94704 *Type:* Public *Accred.:* 1990 (CCA-ACICS) *Calendar:* Courses of varying lengths *Degrees:* A, B, M *CEO:* Pres. Franklin T. Burroughs
(510) 848-2500

ART CENTER COLLEGE OF DESIGN
1700 Lida St., P.O. Box 7197, Pasadena 91109 *Type:* Independent professional *Accred.:* 1955/1988 (WASC-Sr.) *Calendar:* Tri. plan *Degrees:* B, M *Prof. Accred.:* Art *CEO:* Pres. David R. Brown
Enroll: 1433 (818) 584-5000

ART INSTITUTE OF SOUTHERN CALIFORNIA
2222 Laguna Canyon Rd., Laguna Beach 92651 *Type:* Independent *Accred.:* 1990 (WASC-Sr. candidate) *Calendar:* Sem. plan *Degrees:* B *Prof. Accred.:* Art *CEO:* Pres. Russell E. Lewis
Enroll: 129 (714) 497-3309

ASSOCIATED TECHNICAL COLLEGE
1177 N. Magnolia Ave., Anaheim 92801-2606 *Type:* Private *Accred.:* 1987 (CCA-ACTTS) *Calendar:* Courses of varying lengths *Degrees:* certificates *CEO:* Dir. Christine A. Szymanski
Enroll: 773 (714) 229-8785

ASSOCIATED TECHNICAL COLLEGE
1670 W. Wilshire Blvd., Los Angeles 90017 *Type:* Private *Accred.:* 1969/1987 (CCA-ACTTS) *Calendar:* Courses of varying lengths *Degrees:* certificates *CEO:* Dir. Jeanette Muhlstein
Enroll: 3368 (213) 484-2444

ASSOCIATED TECHNICAL COLLEGE
4295 Brockton Ave., Riverside 92501 *Type:* Private *Accred.:* 1991 (CCA-ACTTS) *Calendar:* Courses of varying lengths *Degrees:* certificates *CEO:* Dir. Ali Khalaj
(714) 369-0303

ASSOCIATED TECHNICAL COLLEGE
395 N. E St., San Bernardino 92418 *Type:* Private *Accred.:* 1991 (CCA-ACTTS) *Calendar:* Courses of varying lengths *Degrees:* certificates *CEO:* Dir. William Basham
(714) 885-1888

ASSOCIATED TECHNICAL COLLEGE
1475 Sixth Ave., San Diego 92101 *Type:* Private *Accred.:* 1984 (CCA-ACTTS) *Calendar:* Courses of varying lengths *Degrees:* certificates *CEO:* Dir. Ali Pourhosseini
Enroll: 693 (619) 234-2181

AZUSA PACIFIC UNIVERSITY
Citrus and Alosta, P.O. Box APU, Azusa 91702 *Type:* Independent liberal arts *Accred.:* 1964/1982 (WASC-Sr.) *Calendar:* 4-4-1 plan *Degrees:* A, B, M *Prof. Accred.:* Nursing (B,M), Social Work (B) *CEO:* Pres. Richard E. Felix
Enroll: 2455 (818) 969-3434

BAKERSFIELD COLLEGE
1801 Panorama Dr., Bakersfield 93305 *Type:* Public (district) junior *System:* Kern Community College District *Accred.:* 1952/1988 (WASC-Jr.) *Calendar:* Sem. plan *Degrees:* A *Prof. Accred.:* Radiography *CEO:* Pres. Richard L. Wright
Enroll: 12473 (805) 395-4011

BARCLAY COLLEGE
1752 E. Bullard Ave., Fresno 93710 *Type:* Private business *Accred.:* 1979/1991 (CCA-ACICS) *Calendar:* Courses of varying lengths *Degrees:* certificates *CEO:* Dir. Marjorie Mrasek
Enroll: 1202 (209) 436-1138

BRANCH CAMPUS
777 Twelfth St., Ste. 300, Sacramento, CA 95814 *CEO:* Exec. Dir. Zoe Smith
(916) 448-8118

California

BRANCH CAMPUS
10403 International Plaza Dr., St. Ann, MO 63074 *CEO:* Dir. Kathryn Klee
(314) 426-4200

BARSTOW COLLEGE
2700 Barstow Rd., Barstow 92311 *Type:* Public (district) junior *System:* Barstow Community College District *Accred.:* 1962/1989 (WASC-Jr.) *Calendar:* Sem. plan *Degrees:* A *CEO:* Pres. John C. Menzie
Enroll: 2365   (619) 252-2411

BELLFLOWER BUSINESS COLLEGE
16620 Bellflower Blvd., Bellflower 90706 *Type:* Private business *Accred.:* 1985/1990 (CCA-ACICS) *Calendar:* Courses of varying lengths *Degrees:* certificates *CEO:* Dir. Ann Keiner
Enroll: 592   (213) 804-4523

BETHANY COLLEGE OF THE ASSEMBLIES OF GOD
800 Bethany Dr., Scotts Valley 95066 *Type:* Independent (Assemblies of God) *Accred.:* 1959/1985 (AABC); 1966/1985 (WASC-Sr.) *Calendar:* 4-1-4 plan *Degrees:* A, B *CEO:* Pres. Richard B. Foth
Enroll: 445   (408) 438-3800

BIOLA UNIVERSITY
13800 Biola Ave., La Mirada 90639 *Type:* Independent liberal arts and professional *Accred.:* 1977/1988 (ATS); 1961/1988 (WASC-Sr.) *Calendar:* 4-1-4 plan *Degrees:* B, P, M, D *Prof. Accred.:* Clinical Psychology, Music, Nursing (B) *CEO:* Pres. Clyde Cook
Enroll: 2566   (213) 903-6000

BROOKLINE TECHNICAL INSTITUTE
1814 W. Lincoln Ave., Anaheim 92801 *Type:* Private *Accred.:* 1988 (CCA-ACTTS) *Calendar:* Courses of varying lengths *Degrees:* certificates *CEO:* Pres. Elton Pamplin
(714) 635-5030

BROOKS COLLEGE
4825 E. Pacific Coast Hwy., Long Beach 90804 *Type:* Private 2-year *Accred.:* 1976/1988 (CCA-ACTTS); 1977/1987 (WASC-Jr.) *Calendar:* Qtr. plan *Degrees:* A, diplomas *CEO:* Admin. Dir. Steven B. Sotraidis
Enroll: 641   (310) 597-6611

BROOKS INSTITUTE OF PHOTOGRAPHY
801 Alston Rd., Santa Barbara 93108 *Type:* Private senior business *Accred.:* 1984/1991 (CCA-ACICS) *Calendar:* Tri. plan *Degrees:* B, M *CEO:* Pres. Ernest H. Brooks, II
Enroll: 918   (805) 966-3888

BRYAN COLLEGE OF COURT REPORTING
2511 Beverly Blvd., Los Angeles 90057 *Type:* Private business *Accred.:* 1971/1989 (CCA-ACICS) *Calendar:* Courses of varying lengths *Degrees:* certificates *CEO:* Pres. James T. Patterson
Enroll: 876   (213) 484-8850

BUSINESS INDUSTRY SCHOOL
3721 W. Washington Blvd., Los Angeles 90018 *Type:* Private professional *Calendar:* Courses of varying lengths *Degrees:* certificates *Prof. Accred.:* Dental Assisting *CEO:* Prin. Barbara Arney
(213) 742-7390

BUTTE COLLEGE
3536 Butte Campus Dr., Oroville 95965 *Type:* Public (district) junior *System:* Butte Community College District *Accred.:* 1972/1991 (WASC-Jr.) *Calendar:* Sem. plan *Degrees:* A *Prof. Accred.:* Respiratory Therapy *CEO:* Pres. Betty M. Dean
Enroll: 12400   (916) 895-2511

CDI CAREER DEVELOPMENT INSTITUTE
100 N. Sepulveda Blvd., Ste. 110, El Segunda 90245 *Type:* Private *Accred.:* 1968/1990 (CCA-ACTTS) *Calendar:* Courses of varying lengths *Degrees:* certificates *CEO:* Dir. William Naj
Enroll: 694   (213) 322-1440

CDI CAREER DEVELOPMENT INSTITUTE
814 Mission St., San Francisco 94103 *Type:* Private *Accred.:* 1969/1986 (CCA-ACTTS) *Calendar:* Courses of varying lengths *Degrees:* certificates *CEO:* Dir. F.X. Syster
Enroll: 270   (415) 882-4545

CDI CAREER DEVELOPMENT INSTITUTE
1950 E. 17th St., Santa Ana 92701 *Type:* Private *Accred.:* 1969/1987 (CCA-ACTTS) *Calendar:* Courses of varying lengths *Degrees:* certificates *CEO:* Dir. Robert A. Dickinson
Enroll: 660 (714) 643-0214

BRANCH CAMPUS
3800 Main St., Riverside, CA 92501 *CEO:* Dir. K. Kilgore
(714) 781-8911

CABRILLO COLLEGE
6500 Soquel Dr., Aptos 95003 *Type:* Public (district) junior *System:* Cabrillo Community College District *Accred.:* 1961/1989 (WASC-Jr.) *Calendar:* Sem. plan *Degrees:* A *Prof. Accred.:* Dental Hygiene, Radiography *CEO:* Pres. John D. Hurd
Enroll: 13027 (408) 479-6100

CALIFORNIA BAPTIST COLLEGE
8432 Magnolia Ave., Riverside 92504 *Type:* Independent (Southern Baptist) liberal arts *Accred.:* 1961/1987 (WASC-Sr.) *Calendar:* Early sem. and Jan. term *Degrees:* B, M *Prof. Accred.:* Music *CEO:* Pres. Russell R. Tuck
Enroll: 617 (714) 689-5771

CALIFORNIA CAREER SCHOOL
392 W. Cerritos Ave., Anaheim 92805 *Type:* Private *Accred.:* 1987 (CCA-ACTTS) *Calendar:* Courses of varying lengths *Degrees:* certificates *CEO:* Pres. Victor Ziebelman
Enroll: 54 (714) 635-6585

CALIFORNIA COLLEGE FOR HEALTH SCIENCES
222 W. 24th St., National City 92050 *Type:* Private *Accred.:* 1980/1987 (CCA-ACTTS); 1981/1987 (NHSC) *Calendar:* Courses of varying lengths *Degrees:* A, certificates *Prof. Accred.:* Respiratory Therapy, Respiratory Therapy Technology *CEO:* Dir. Dale Dean
Enroll: 22 (619) 477-4800

CALIFORNIA COLLEGE OF ARTS AND CRAFTS
5212 Broadway, Oakland 94618 *Type:* Independent professional *Accred.:* 1954/1984 (WASC-Sr.) *Calendar:* Tri. plan *Degrees:* B, M *Prof. Accred.:* Architecture (B-candidate), Art, Interior Design *CEO:* Pres. Neil J. Hoffman
Enroll: 933 (510) 653-8118

CALIFORNIA COLLEGE OF PODIATRIC MEDICINE
1210 Scott St., San Francisco 94115 *Type:* Private professional *Accred.:* 1961/1983 (WASC-Sr.) *Calendar:* Sem. plan *Degrees:* B, P, M, D *Prof. Accred.:* Podiatry *CEO:* Pres. Richard H. Lanham, Jr.
Enroll: 349 (415) 563-8070

CALIFORNIA CULINARY ACADEMY
625 Polk St., San Francisco 94102 *Type:* Private *Accred.:* 1982/1988 (CCA-ACTTS) *Calendar:* Courses of varying lengths *Degrees:* certificates *CEO:* Pres. Thomas A. Bloom, Ph.D.
Enroll: 496 (415) 771-3536

CALIFORNIA FAMILY STUDY CENTER
5433 Laurel Canyon Blvd., North Hollywood 91607-2193 *Type:* Independent *Accred.:* 1983/1988 (WASC-Sr.) *Calendar:* Sem. plan *Degrees:* M *CEO:* Pres. Edwin S. Cox, Ph.D.
Enroll: 263 (818) 509-5959

CALIFORNIA INSTITUTE OF INTEGRAL STUDIES
765 Ashbury St., San Francisco 94117 *Type:* Independent graduate only *Accred.:* 1981/1984 (WASC-Sr.) *Calendar:* Qtr. plan *Degrees:* M, D *CEO:* Pres. Robert McDermott
Enroll: 445 (415) 753-6100

CALIFORNIA INSTITUTE OF TECHNOLOGY
1201 E. California Blvd., Pasadena 91125 *Type:* Independent *Accred.:* 1949/1990 (WASC-Sr.) *Calendar:* Qtr. plan *Degrees:* B, M, D *Prof. Accred.:* Engineering (chemical, engineering physics/science) *CEO:* Pres. Thomas E. Everhart
Enroll: 1822 (818) 356-6811

CALIFORNIA INSTITUTE OF THE ARTS
24700 McBean Pkwy., Valencia 91355 *Type:* Independent *Accred.:* 1955/1986 (WASC-Sr.) *Calendar:* Sem. plan *Degrees:*

B, M *Prof. Accred.:* Art, Dance, Music *CEO:* Pres. Steven D. Lavine
Enroll: 950   (805) 255-1050

CALIFORNIA LUTHERAN UNIVERSITY
60 Olsen Rd., Thousand Oaks 91360 *Type:* Independent (Evangelical Lutheran) liberal arts *Accred.:* 1962/1989 (WASC-Sr.) *Calendar:* 4-1-4 plan *Degrees:* B, M *CEO:* Pres. Jerry H. Miller
Enroll: 2081   (805) 493-3145

CALIFORNIA MARITIME ACADEMY
P.O. Box 1392, Vallejo 94590 *Type:* Public (state) *Accred.:* 1977/1987 (WASC-Sr.) *Calendar:* Tri. plan *Degrees:* B *Prof. Accred.:* Engineering Technology (naval architecture/marine) *CEO:* Pres. Mary E. Lyons
Enroll: 359   (707) 648-4200

CALIFORNIA NANNIE COLLEGE
910 Howe Ave., Sacramento 95815 *Type:* Private *Accred.:* 1988 (CCA-ACTTS) *Calendar:* Courses of varying lengths *Degrees:* certificates *CEO:* Dir. Larry Leonetti
    (916) 484-0163

CALIFORNIA PARAMEDICAL AND TECHNICAL COLLEGE
3745 Long Beach Blvd., Long Beach 90807 *Type:* Private *Accred.:* 1980/1987 (CCA-ACTTS) *Calendar:* Courses of varying lengths *Degrees:* diplomas *Prof. Accred.:* Medical Assisting, Respiratory Therapy Technology, Surgical Technology *CEO:* Dir. Julia Morally
Enroll: 416   (213) 426-9359

CALIFORNIA PARAMEDICAL AND TECHNICAL SCHOOL
4550 LaSierra Ave., Riverside 92505 *Type:* Private *Accred.:* 1982/1987 (CCA-ACTTS) *Calendar:* Courses of varying lengths *Degrees:* diplomas *Prof. Accred.:* Medical Assisting, Respiratory Therapy *CEO:* Dir. Julia Morally
    (714) 687-9006

CALIFORNIA POLYTECHNIC STATE UNIVERSITY, SAN LUIS OBISPO
San Luis Obispo 93407 *Type:* Public (state) *System:* California State University System *Accred.:* 1951/1990 (WASC-Sr.) *Calendar:* Qtr. plan *Degrees:* B, M *Prof. Accred.:* Architecture (B), Business (B,M), Computer Science, Construction Management, Engineering (aerospace, agricultural, architectural, civil, electrical, environmental/sanitary, industrial, mechanical, metallurgical), Engineering Technology (air conditioning, electrical, manufacturing, mechanical, welding), Forestry (candidate), Interior Design, Landscape Architecture (B), Planning (city/regional), Recreation Administration *CEO:* Pres. Warren J. Baker
Enroll: 15658   (805) 756-1111

CALIFORNIA SCHOOL OF COURT REPORTING
1201 N. Main St., Santa Ana 92701 *Type:* Private business *Accred.:* 1979/1985 (CCA-ACICS) *Calendar:* Courses of varying lengths *Degrees:* certificates *CEO:* Pres. Virginia Wilcke
Enroll: 710   (714) 541-6892

BRANCH CAMPUS
3510 Adams St., Riverside, CA 92504 *CEO:* Admin. Marianne Evans
    (714) 359-0293

CALIFORNIA SCHOOL OF PROFESSIONAL PSYCHOLOGY, BERKELEY/ALAMEDA
1005 Atlantic Ave., Alameda 94501 *Type:* Independent professional *Accred.:* 1977/1989 (WASC-Sr.) *Calendar:* Sem. plan *Degrees:* M, D *Prof. Accred.:* Clinical Psychology *CEO:* Dir. Katsuyuki Sakamoto
Enroll: 294   (510) 523-2300

CALIFORNIA SCHOOL OF PROFESSIONAL PSYCHOLOGY, FRESNO
1350 M St., Fresno 93721 *Type:* Independent professional *Accred.:* 1977/1989 (WASC-Sr.) *Calendar:* Sem. plan *Degrees:* M, D *Prof. Accred.:* Clinical Psychology *CEO:* Provost W. Gary Cannon
Enroll: 265   (209) 486-8420

California School of Professional Psychology, Los Angeles
1000 S. Fremont Ave., Alhambra 91803-1360 *Type:* Independent professional *Accred.:* 1977/1989 (WASC-Sr.) *Calendar:* Sem. plan *Degrees:* M, D *Prof. Accred.:* Clinical Psychology *CEO:* Provost Connell F. Persico
Enroll: 438 (818) 284-2777

California School of Professional Psychology, San Diego
6212 Ferris Sq., San Diego 92121 *Type:* Independent professional *Accred.:* 1977/1989 (WASC-Sr.) *Calendar:* Sem. plan *Degrees:* M, D *Prof. Accred.:* Clinical Psychology *CEO:* Provost Raymond J. Trybus
Enroll: 350 (619) 452-1664

California State Polytechnic University, Pomona
3801 W. Temple Ave., Pomona 91768 *Type:* Public (state) *System:* California State University System *Accred.:* 1970/1990 (WASC-Sr.) *Calendar:* Qtr. plan *Degrees:* B, M *Prof. Accred.:* Architecture (B,M), Engineering (aerospace, agricultural, chemical, civil, electrical, industrial, manufacturing, mechanical), Engineering Technology (general), Landscape Architecture (B,M), Park Administration, Planning (regional/urban), Recreation Administration, Social Work (B) *CEO:* Pres. Bob H. Suzuki
Enroll: 15445 (714) 869-7659

California State University, Bakersfield
9001 Stockdale Hwy., Bakersfield 93311-1099 *Type:* Public (state) *System:* California State University System *Accred.:* 1970/1990 (WASC-Sr.) *Calendar:* Qtr. plan *Degrees:* B, M *Prof. Accred.:* Administration Health Care Management, Business (B,M), Medical Technology, Nursing (B,M), Public Administration, Teacher Education (e,s,p) *CEO:* Pres. Tomas A. Arciniega
Enroll: 3971 (805) 664-2011

California State University, Chico
First and Normal Sts., Chico 95929-0110 *Type:* Public (state) *System:* California State University System *Accred.:* 1949/1989 (WASC-Sr.) *Calendar:* Sem. plan *Degrees:* B, M *Prof. Accred.:* Art, Business (B,M), Computer Science, Construction Management, Engineering (civil, computer, electrical, mechanical), Home Economics, Music, Nursing (B), Recreation and Park Management, Social Work (B), Speech-Language Pathology, Teacher Education (e,s,p) *CEO:* Pres. Robin S. Wilson
Enroll: 14321 (916) 898-4636

California State University, Dominguez Hills
1000 E. Victoria St., Carson 90747 *Type:* Public (state) *System:* California State University System *Accred.:* 1965/1990 (WASC-Sr.) *Calendar:* Qtr. plan *Degrees:* B, M *Prof. Accred.:* Art, Medical Technology, Music, Nuclear Medicine Technology, Nursing (B,M), Public Administration, Teacher Education (e,s), Theatre *CEO:* Pres. Robert C. Detweiler
Enroll: 6886 (213) 516-3300

California State University, Fresno
5241 N. Maple Ave., Fresno 93740 *Type:* Public (state) *System:* California State University System *Accred.:* 1949/1989 (WASC-Sr.) *Calendar:* Sem. plan *Degrees:* B, M *Prof. Accred.:* Audiology, Business (B,M), Engineering (civil, electrical, industrial, mechanical, surveying), Interior Design, Journalism, Music, Nursing (B,M), Physical Therapy, Recreation Administration, Rehabilitation Counseling, Social Work (B,M), Speech-Language Pathology, Teacher Education (e,s,p), Theatre *CEO:* Pres. John D. Welty
Enroll: 15675 (209) 278-4240

California State University, Fullerton
800 N. State College Blvd., Fullerton 92634 *Type:* Public (state) *System:* California State University System *Accred.:* 1961/1991 (WASC-Sr.) *Calendar:* Sem. plan *Degrees:* B, M *Prof. Accred.:* Art, Business (B,M), Computer Science, Dance, Engineering (civil, electrical, mechanical), Journalism, Music, Nursing (B), Public Administration,

California

Speech-Language Pathology, Teacher Education (e,s,p), Theatre *CEO:* Pres. Milton A. Gordon
Enroll: 17518 (714) 773-2011

CALIFORNIA STATE UNIVERSITY, HAYWARD
Hayward 94542 *Type:* Public (state) *System:* California State University System *Accred.:* 1961/1989 (WASC-Sr.) *Calendar:* Qtr. plan *Degrees:* B, M *Prof. Accred.:* Art, Business (B,M), Music, Nursing (B), Public Administration, Teacher Education (e,s,p) *CEO:* Pres. Norma Rees
Enroll: 9572 (510) 881-3000

CALIFORNIA STATE UNIVERSITY, LONG BEACH
1250 Bellflower Blvd., Long Beach 90840 *Type:* Public (state) *System:* California State University System *Accred.:* 1957/1987 (WASC-Sr.) *Calendar:* Sem. plan *Degrees:* B, M *Prof. Accred.:* Art, Audiology, Business (B,M), Community Health, Construction Education, Dance, Engineering (chemical, civil, computer, electrical, mechanical), Home Economics, Interior Design, Journalism, Music, Nurse Anesthesia Education, Nursing (B,M), Physical Therapy, Psychology Internship, Public Administration, Recreation and Leisure Studies, Social Work (B,M), Speech-Language Pathology, Theatre *CEO:* Pres. Curtis McCray
Enroll: 23266 (213) 985-4111

CALIFORNIA STATE UNIVERSITY, LOS ANGELES
5151 State University Dr., Los Angeles 90032-8508 *Type:* Public (state) *System:* California State University System *Accred.:* 1954/1990 (WASC-Sr.) *Calendar:* Qtr. plan *Degrees:* B, M *Prof. Accred.:* Art, Audiology, Business (B,M), Counseling, Dietetics (coordinated), Engineering (civil, electrical, mechanical), Home Economics, Music, Nursing (B,M), Public Administration, Rehabilitation Counseling, Social Work (B), Speech-Language Pathology, Teacher Education (e,s,p) *CEO:* Pres. James M. Rosser
Enroll: 14044 (213) 343-3000

CALIFORNIA STATE UNIVERSITY, NORTHRIDGE
18111 Nordhoff St., Northridge 91330 *Type:* Public (state) *System:* California State University System *Accred.:* 1958/1991 (WASC-Sr.) *Calendar:* Sem. plan *Degrees:* B, M *Prof. Accred.:* Audiology, Business (B,M), Community Health, Computer Science, Counseling, Engineering (general), Home Economics, Journalism, Music, Physical Therapy, Radiography, Recreation and Leisure Studies, Speech-Language Pathology, Teacher Education (e,s,p), Theatre *CEO:* Pres. James W. Cleary
Enroll: 21675 (818) 885-1200

CALIFORNIA STATE UNIVERSITY, SACRAMENTO
6000 J St., Sacramento 95819-2694 *Type:* Public (state) *System:* California State University System *Accred.:* 1951/1990 (WASC-Sr.) *Calendar:* Sem. plan *Degrees:* B, M *Prof. Accred.:* Art, Audiology, Business (B,M), Computer Science, Construction Education, Counseling, Engineering (civil, computer, electrical, mechanical), Engineering Technology (civil/construction, mechanical), Music, Nursing (B,M), Recreation and Park Administration, Rehabilitation Counseling, Social Work (B,M), Speech-Language Pathology, Theatre *CEO:* Pres. Donald R. Gerth
Enroll: 19303 (916) 278-6011

CALIFORNIA STATE UNIVERSITY, SAN BERNARDINO
5500 State University Pkwy., San Bernardino 92407 *Type:* Public (state) *System:* California State University System *Accred.:* 1965/1989 (WASC-Sr.) *Calendar:* Qtr. plan *Degrees:* B, M *Prof. Accred.:* Art, Computer Science, Nursing (B), Public Administration, Rehabilitation Counseling (prelim.), Social Work (M-candidate) *CEO:* Pres. Anthony H. Evans
Enroll: 7612 (714) 880-5000

CALIFORNIA STATE UNIVERSITY, STANISLAUS
801 W. Monte Vista Ave., Turlock 95380 *Type:* Public (state) *System:* California State University System *Accred.:* 1963/1991 (WASC-Sr.) *Calendar:* 4-1-4 plan *Degrees:* B, M *Prof. Accred.:* Art, Computer Science,

Music, Nursing (B), Public Administration, Theatre *CEO:* Pres. John W. Moore
Enroll: 3670 (209) 667-3122

CALIFORNIA WESTERN SCHOOL OF LAW
350 Cedar St., San Diego 92101 *Type:* Private professional *Calendar:* Sem. plan *Degrees:* P *Prof. Accred.:* Law *CEO:* Dean Michael H. Dessent
Enroll: 631 (619) 239-0391

CAÑADA COLLEGE
4200 Farm Hill Blvd., Redwood City 94061 *Type:* Public (district) junior *System:* San Mateo County Community College District *Accred.:* 1970/1986 (WASC-Jr.) *Calendar:* Sem. plan *Degrees:* A *CEO:* Pres. Miles D. Ketcher
Enroll: 7600 (415) 364-1212

CAREER INSTITUTE
717 Pine Ave., Long Beach 90813 *Type:* Private *Accred.:* 1976/1988 (CCA-ACTTS) *Calendar:* Courses of varying lengths *Degrees:* certificates *CEO:* Dir. Lee Schnuchow
Enroll: 49 (213) 436-2510

CAREERCOM COLLEGE OF BUSINESS
5337 Truxton Ave., Bakersfield 93309 *Type:* Private business *Accred.:* 1988 (CCA-ACICS) *Calendar:* Courses of varying lengths *Degrees:* certificates *CEO:* Dir. Phyllis Smith
Enroll: 893 (805) 323-1747

BRANCH CAMPUS
10 Eastmont Mall, Ste. 200, Oakland, CA 94605 *CEO:* Dir. Sidney Carey
(510) 569-2632

BRANCH CAMPUS
7667 Folsom Blvd., Ste. 200, Sacramento, CA 95826 *CEO:* Dir. George Evans
(916) 456-5100

CASA LOMA COLLEGE
11620 Eldridge Ave., Lakeview Terrace 91342 *Type:* Private *Calendar:* Courses of varying lengths *Degrees:* certificates *CEO:* Dir. Norma Jones
(818) 899-1175

BRANCH CAMPUS
3761 Stocker St., Los Angeles, CA 90008 *Prof. Accred.:* Practical Nursing *CEO:* Dir. Geraldine Gores
(213) 290-6440

CATHERINE COLLEGE
8155 Van Nuys Blvd., Ste. 200, Panorama City 91402 *Type:* Private business *Accred.:* 1984/1990 (CCA-ACICS) *Calendar:* Courses of varying lengths *Degrees:* certificates *CEO:* Dir. Ione Gamrat
Enroll: 566 (818) 989-9000

CENTURY SCHOOLS
2665 Fifth Ave., San Diego 92104 *Type:* Private *Accred.:* 1985 (CCA-ACTTS) *Calendar:* Courses of varying lengths *Degrees:* certificates *CEO:* Vice Pres. Wayne O. Miletta
Enroll: 391 (619) 233-0184

BRANCH CAMPUS
3325 Wilshire Blvd., Ste. 200, Los Angeles, CA 90010 *CEO:* Dir. Howard Heller
(213) 383-1585

BRANCH CAMPUS
3075 E. Flamingo Rd., Las Vegas, NV 89121 *CEO:* Vice Pres. Scotty Wetxel

CERRITOS COLLEGE
11110 E. Alondra Blvd., Norwalk 90650 *Type:* Public (district) junior *System:* Cerritos Community College District *Accred.:* 1959/1990 (WASC-Jr.) *Calendar:* Sem. plan *Degrees:* A *Prof. Accred.:* Dental Assisting, Dental Hygiene, Nursing (A), Physical Therapy Assisting *CEO:* Pres. Ernest A. Martinez
Enroll: 19030 (310) 860-2451

CERRO COSO COMMUNITY COLLEGE
3000 College Heights Blvd., Ridgecrest 93555 *Type:* Public (district) junior *System:* Kern Community College District *Accred.:*

1975/1990 (WASC-Jr.) *Calendar:* Sem. plan *Degrees:* A *CEO:* Pres. Raymond A. McCue
Enroll: 4085   (619) 375-5001

CHABOT COLLEGE
25555 Hesperian Blvd., Hayward 94545 *Type:* Public (district) junior *System:* Chabot-Las Positas Community College District *Accred.:* 1963/1991 (WASC-Jr.) *Calendar:* Qtr. plan *Degrees:* A *Prof. Accred.:* Dental Assisting, Dental Hygiene, Medical Assisting (AMA), Medical Record Technology *CEO:* Pres. Raul Cardoza
Enroll: 19686   (510) 786-6600

CHAFFEY COLLEGE
5885 Haven Ave., Rancho Cucamonga 91701 *Type:* Public (district) junior *System:* Chaffey Community College District *Accred.:* 1952/1987 (WASC-Jr.) *Calendar:* Qtr. plan *Degrees:* A *Prof. Accred.:* Dental Assisting, Nursing (A), Radiography *CEO:* Pres. Jerry W. Young
Enroll: 14563   (714) 987-1737

CHAPMAN UNIVERSITY
333 N. Glassell St., Orange 92666 *Type:* Independent (Disciples of Christ) liberal arts *Accred.:* 1956/1988 (WASC-Sr.) *Calendar:* 4-1-4 plan *Degrees:* A, B, M *Prof. Accred.:* Physical Therapy *CEO:* Pres. James Doti
Enroll: 6662   (714) 997-6611

CHARLES R. DREW UNIVERSITY
1621 E. 120th St., Los Angeles 90059 *Type:* Private *Accred.:* 1988 (WASC-Sr. candidate) *Calendar:* Sem. plan *Degrees:* A, B, M, D *Prof. Accred.:* Dietetics (coordinated), Medical Record Technology, Medical Technology, Nuclear Medicine Technology, Physician Assisting, Radiography *CEO:* Pres. Reed V. Tuckson
Enroll: 430   (213) 563-4800

CHARTERWAY COLLEGE
1975 Long Beach Blvd., Long Beach 90806 *Type:* Private business *Accred.:* 1985 (CCA-ACICS); 1991 (CCA-ACTTS) *Calendar:* Qtr. plan *Degrees:* certificates *CEO:* Pres. Edmund G. Lau
Enroll: 878   (213) 599-2122

CHRIST COLLEGE, IRVINE
1530 Concordia, Irvine 92715 *Type:* Independent (Lutheran-Missouri Synod) liberal arts *Accred.:* 1981/1985 (WASC-Sr.) *Calendar:* Qtr. plan *Degrees:* A, B, M *CEO:* Pres. D. Ray Halm
Enroll: 536   (714) 854-8002

CHRISTIAN HERITAGE COLLEGE
2100 Greenfield Dr., El Cajon 92019 *Type:* Independent (Scott Memorial Baptist Church) liberal arts *Accred.:* 1984 (WASC-Sr. probational) *Calendar:* Sem. plan *Degrees:* B *CEO:* Pres. David P. Jeremiah
Enroll: 316   (619) 440-3043

CHURCH DIVINITY SCHOOL OF THE PACIFIC
2451 Ridge Rd., Berkeley 94709-1211 *Type:* Independent (Episcopal) professional; graduate only *Accred.:* 1954/1984 (ATS); 1978/1989 (WASC-Sr.) *Calendar:* Qtr. plan *Degrees:* P, M, D *CEO:* Dean/Pres. Charles A. Perry
Enroll: 93   (510) 848-3282

CITRUS COLLEGE
1000 W. Foothill Blvd., Glendora 91740 *Type:* Public (district) junior *System:* Citrus Community College District *Accred.:* 1952/1987 (WASC-Jr.) *Calendar:* Sem. plan *Degrees:* A *Prof. Accred.:* Dental Assisting *CEO:* Pres. Louis E. Zellers
Enroll: 9766   (818) 963-0323

CITY COLLEGE OF SAN FRANCISCO
50 Phelan Ave., San Francisco 94112 *Type:* Public (district) junior *System:* San Francisco Community College District *Accred.:* 1952/1988 (WASC-Jr.) *Calendar:* Sem. plan *Degrees:* A *Prof. Accred.:* Dental Assisting, Dental Laboratory Technology, Engineering Technology (electrical, electromechanical, mechanical), Medical Assisting (AMA), Radiation Therapy Technology, Radiography *CEO:* Chanc. Evan S. Dobelle
Enroll: 64085   (415) 239-3000

California

THE CLAREMONT GRADUATE SCHOOL
160 E. 10th St., Claremont 91711 *Type:* Independent graduate only *Accred.:* 1949/1987 (WASC-Sr.) *Calendar:* Sem. plan *Degrees:* M, D *CEO:* Pres. John D. Maguire
Enroll: 775   (714) 621-8000

CLAREMONT MCKENNA COLLEGE
850 Columbia Ave., Pitzer Hall, Claremont 91711 *Type:* Independent liberal arts *Accred.:* 1949/1991 (WASC-Sr.) *Calendar:* Sem. plan *Degrees:* B *CEO:* Pres. Jack L. Stark
Enroll: 906   (714) 621-8111

CLEVELAND CHIROPRACTIC COLLEGE OF CLEVELAND UNIVERSITY LOS ANGELES
590 N. Vermont Ave., Los Angeles 90004 *Type:* Private professional *Accred.:* 1987 (WASC-Sr. candidate) *Calendar:* Tri. plan *Degrees:* B, P *Prof. Accred.:* Chiropractic Education *CEO:* Pres. Carl S. Cleveland, Jr.
Enroll: 367   (213) 660-6166

COASTLINE COMMUNITY COLLEGE
11460 Warner Ave., Fountain Valley 92708 *Type:* Public (district) junior *System:* Coast Community College District *Accred.:* 1978/1988 (WASC-Jr.) *Calendar:* Sem. plan *Degrees:* A *CEO:* Pres. William M. Vega
Enroll: 16000   (714) 546-7600

COGSWELL POLYTECHNICAL COLLEGE
10420 Bubb Rd., Cupertino 95014 *Type:* Independent technical *Accred.:* 1977/1982 (WASC-Sr. probational) *Calendar:* Tri. plan *Degrees:* A, B *Prof. Accred.:* Engineering Technology (electrical, mechanical) *CEO:* Pres. Ted Kastelic, Ph.D.
Enroll: 254   (408) 252-5550

BRANCH CAMPUS
10626 N.E. 37th Cir., Kirkland, WA 98033 *Prof. Accred.:* Engineering Technology (electrical, mechanical) *CEO:* Dir. Bill Sutton
                              (206) 822-3137

COLEMAN COLLEGE
7380 Parkway Dr., La Mesa 91942 *Type:* Private *Accred.:* 1967/1988 (CCA-ACICS) *Calendar:* Qtr. plan *Degrees:* A, B, M, certificates *CEO:* Pres. Michael Flood
Enroll: 1844   (619) 465-3990

COLLEGE OF ALAMEDA
555 Atlantic Ave., Alameda 94501 *Type:* Public (district) junior *System:* Peralta Community College District *Accred.:* 1973/1988 (WASC-Jr.) *Calendar:* Qtr. plan *Degrees:* A *Prof. Accred.:* Dental Assisting *CEO:* Pres. Marie Smith
Enroll: 6156   (510) 522-7221

COLLEGE OF MARIN
College Ave., Kentfield 94904 *Type:* Public (district) junior *System:* Marin Community College District *Accred.:* 1952/1988 (WASC-Jr.) *Calendar:* Sem. plan *Degrees:* A *Prof. Accred.:* Dental Assisting, Nursing (A) *CEO:* Pres. Myrna R. Miller
Enroll: 9640   (415) 457-8811

COLLEGE OF NOTRE DAME
1500 Ralston Ave., Belmont 94002 *Type:* Independent (Roman Catholic) liberal arts *Accred.:* 1955/1991 (WASC-Sr.) *Calendar:* Sem. plan *Degrees:* B, M *Prof. Accred.:* Music *CEO:* Pres. Veronica Skillin
Enroll: 806   (415) 593-1601

COLLEGE OF OCEANEERING
272 S. Fries Ave., Wilmington 90744 *Type:* Private *Accred.:* 1982/1987 (WASC-Jr.) *Calendar:* Courses of varying lengths *Degrees:* A *CEO:* Pres. James T. Joiner
Enroll: 481   (310) 834-2501

COLLEGE OF OSTEOPATHIC MEDICINE OF THE PACIFIC
College Plaza, Pomona 91766-1889 *Type:* Private *Accred.:* 1990 (WASC-Sr. candidate) *Calendar:* Sem. plan *Degrees:* B, M *Prof. Accred.:* Osteopathy, Physician Assisting *CEO:* Pres. Philip Pumerantz
Enroll: 428   (714) 623-6116

COLLEGE OF RECORDING ARTS
665 Harrison St., San Francisco 94107 *Type:* Private *Accred.:* 1977/1990 (CCA-ACTTS)

Calendar: Sem. plan *Degrees:* diplomas
CEO: Pres. Leo de Gar Kulka
Enroll: 120 (415) 781-6306

COLLEGE OF SAN MATEO
1700 W. Hillsdale Blvd., San Mateo 94402 *Type:* Public (district) junior *System:* San Mateo County Community College District *Accred.:* 1952/1989 (WASC-Jr.) *Calendar:* Sem. plan *Degrees:* A *Prof. Accred.:* Dental Assisting *CEO:* Interim Pres. Richard A. Jones
Enroll: 15148 (415) 574-6161

COLLEGE OF THE CANYONS
26455 N. Rockwell Canyon Rd., Santa Clarita 91355 *Type:* Public (district) junior *System:* Santa Clarita Community College District *Accred.:* 1972/1990 (WASC-Jr.) *Calendar:* Sem. plan *Degrees:* A *CEO:* Pres. Dianne G. Van Hook
Enroll: 5200 (805) 259-7800

COLLEGE OF THE DESERT
43-500 Monterey Ave., Palm Desert 92260 *Type:* Public (district) junior *System:* Desert Community College District *Accred.:* 1963/1989 (WASC-Jr.) *Calendar:* Sem. plan *Degrees:* A *Prof. Accred.:* Nursing (A), Respiratory Therapy *CEO:* Pres. David A. George
Enroll: 11029 (619) 346-8041

COLLEGE OF THE REDWOODS
7351 Tompkins Hill Rd., Eureka 95501 *Type:* Public (district) junior *System:* Redwoods Community College District *Accred.:* 1967/1989 (WASC-Jr.) *Calendar:* Sem. plan *Degrees:* A *Prof. Accred.:* Dental Assisting *CEO:* Pres. Cedric A. Sampson
Enroll: 7369 (707) 445-6700

COLLEGE OF THE SEQUOIAS
915 S. Mooney Blvd., Visalia 93277 *Type:* Public (district) junior *System:* Sequoias Community College District *Accred.:* 1952/1989 (WASC-Jr.) *Calendar:* Sem. plan *Degrees:* A *CEO:* Pres. Robert A. Lombardi
Enroll: 9086 (209) 730-3700

COLLEGE OF THE SISKIYOUS
800 College Ave., Weed 96094 *Type:* Public (district) junior *System:* Siskiyous Joint Community College District *Accred.:* 1961/1987 (WASC-Jr.) *Calendar:* Sem. plan *Degrees:* A *CEO:* Pres. Eugene Schumacher
Enroll: 2923 (916) 938-4461

COLUMBIA COLLEGE
P.O. Box 1849, Columbia 95310 *Type:* Public (district) junior *System:* Yosemite Community College District *Accred.:* 1972/1989 (WASC-Jr.) *Calendar:* Sem. plan *Degrees:* A *CEO:* Pres. W. Dean Cunningham
Enroll: 2912 (209) 533-5100

COLUMBIA COLLEGE HOLLYWOOD
925 N. La Brea Ave., Hollywood 90038 *Type:* Private technical *Accred.:* 1979/1986 (CCA-ACTTS) *Calendar:* Qtr. plan *Degrees:* A, B, diplomas *CEO:* Pres. Ernest M. Baumeister
Enroll: 270 (213) 851-0550

COMPTON COMMUNITY COLLEGE
1111 E. Artesia Blvd., Compton 90221 *Type:* Public (district) junior *System:* Compton Community College District *Accred.:* 1952/1988 (WASC-Jr.) *Calendar:* Sem. plan *Degrees:* A *CEO:* Pres. Warren A. Washington
Enroll: 5200 (310) 637-2660

COMPUTER LEARNING CENTER
1240 S. State College Blvd., Anaheim 92806 *Type:* Private business *Accred.:* 1990 (CCA-ACICS) *Calendar:* Courses of varying lengths *Degrees:* diplomas *CEO:* Educ. Dir. Selwin Brent
(714) 239-8060

COMPUTER LEARNING CENTER
3130 Wilshire Blvd., Los Angeles 90010 *Type:* Private *Accred.:* 1970/1986 (CCA-ACTTS) *Calendar:* Courses of varying lengths *Degrees:* diplomas *CEO:* Dir. Stephen J. Woody
Enroll: 1456 (213) 386-6311

Accredited Institutions California

COMPUTER LEARNING CENTER
661 Howard St., San Francisco 94105 *Type:* Private business *Accred.:* 1985/1991 (CCA-ACICS) *Calendar:* Courses of varying lengths *Degrees:* diplomas *CEO:* Dir. Alec Winters
(415) 498-0800

BRANCH CAMPUS
45 Cabot St., Santa Clara, CA 95051 *CEO:* Dir. Al Nederhood
(408) 983-5950

CONCORDE CAREER INSTITUTE
1717 S. Brookhurst St., Anaheim 92804-6461 *Type:* Private *Accred.:* 1991 (CCA-ACTTS) *Calendar:* Courses of varying lengths *Degrees:* certificates *Prof. Accred.:* Medical Assisting (AMA) *CEO:* Dir. Sue McGuire
(714) 635-3450

CONCORDE CAREER INSTITUTE
4150 Lankershim Blvd., North Hollywood 91602 *Type:* Private *Accred.:* 1991 (CCA-ACTTS) *Calendar:* Courses of varying lengths *Degrees:* certificates *Prof. Accred.:* Respiratory Therapy Technology *CEO:* Dir. Jeri Weinstein
(818) 766-8151

CONCORDE CAREER INSTITUTE
600 N. Sierra Way, San Bernardino 92410-4414 *Type:* Private *Accred.:* 1991 (CCA-ACTTS) *Calendar:* Courses of varying lengths *Degrees:* certificates *CEO:* Dir. Jeanne Thompson
(714) 884-8891

CONCORDE CAREER INSTITUTE
7510 Clairemont Mesa Blvd., Ste. 101, San Diego 92111-9702 *Type:* Private *Accred.:* 1991 (CCA-ACTTS) *Calendar:* Courses of varying lengths *Degrees:* certificates *CEO:* Dir. Tony Galang
(619) 569-7306

CONCORDE CAREER INSTITUTE
4411 30th St., San Diego 92116-4295 *Type:* Private *Accred.:* 1991 (CCA-ACTTS) *Calendar:* Courses of varying lengths *Degrees:* certificates *CEO:* Dir. Nelson Melchior
(619) 280-5005

CONCORDE CAREER INSTITUTE
1290 N. First St., San Jose 95112 *Type:* Private *Accred.:* 1989 (CCA-ACTTS) *Calendar:* Courses of varying lengths *Degrees:* certificates *Prof. Accred.:* Health Education *CEO:* Dir. Maurice Crowley
Enroll: 96   (408) 244-8777

CONCORDE CAREER INSTITUTE
6850 Van Nuys Blvd., Ste. 210, Van Nuys 91405 *Type:* Private *Calendar:* Courses of varying lengths *Degrees:* certificates *Prof. Accred.:* Health Education, Medical Assisting *CEO:* Dir. Robert Serin
(818) 780-5252

CONSOLIDATED WELDING SCHOOLS
4343 Imperial Hwy. E., Lynwood 90262 *Type:* Private *Accred.:* 1985/1990 (CCA-ACTTS) *Calendar:* Courses of varying lengths *Degrees:* certificates *CEO:* Dir. Robert Swanson
Enroll: 18   (213) 638-0418

CONTRA COSTA COLLEGE
2600 Mission Bell Dr., San Pablo 94806 *Type:* Public (district) junior *System:* Contra Costa Community College District *Accred.:* 1952/1989 (WASC-Jr.) *Calendar:* Sem. plan *Degrees:* A *Prof. Accred.:* Dental Assisting *CEO:* Pres. D. Candy Rose
Enroll: 9700   (510) 235-7800

COSUMNES RIVER COLLEGE
8401 Center Pkwy., Sacramento 95823 *Type:* Public (district) junior *System:* Los Rios Community College District *Accred.:* 1972/1991 (WASC-Jr.) *Calendar:* Sem. plan *Degrees:* A *Prof. Accred.:* Animal Health Technology, Medical Assisting (AMA), Medical Record Technology *CEO:* Pres. Marc E. Hall
Enroll: 10962   (916) 686-7300

CRAFTON HILLS COLLEGE
11711 Sand Canyon Rd., Yucaipa 92399 *Type:* Public (district) junior *System:* San

Bernardino Community College District *Accred.*: 1975/1990 (WASC-Jr.) *Calendar*: Sem. plan *Degrees*: A *Prof. Accred.*: EMT-Paramedic, Respiratory Therapy, Respiratory Therapy Technology *CEO*: Acting Pres. Luis S. Gomez
Enroll: 5111   (714) 794-2161

CRENSHAW TECHNICAL INSTITUTE
4625 Crenshaw Blvd., Los Angeles 90043-0099 *Type*: Private *Accred.*: 1991 (CCA-ACTTS) *Calendar*: Courses of varying lengths *Degrees*: certificates *CEO*: Dir. Arthur R. Dansby
     (213) 294-2271

CUESTA COLLEGE
P.O. Box 8106, San Luis Obispo 93403 *Type*: Public (district) junior *System*: San Luis Obispo Community College District *Accred.*: 1968/1991 (WASC-Jr.) *Calendar*: Sem. plan *Degrees*: A *CEO*: Pres. Grace N. Mitchell
Enroll: 7508   (805) 546-3101

CUYAMACA COLLEGE
2950 Jamacha Rd., El Cajon 92019 *Type*: Public (district) junior *System*: Grossmont-Cuyamaca Community College District *Accred.*: 1980/1990 (WASC-Jr.) *Calendar*: Sem. plan *Degrees*: A *CEO*: Pres. Samuel M. Ciccati
Enroll: 3700   (619) 670-1980

CYPRESS COLLEGE
9200 Valley View St., Cypress 90630 *Type*: Public (district) junior *System*: North Orange County Community College District *Accred.*: 1968/1986 (WASC-Jr.) *Calendar*: Sem. plan *Degrees*: A *Prof. Accred.*: Dental Assisting, Dental Hygiene, Medical Record Technology, Mortuary Science, Radiography *CEO*: Pres. Kirk Avery
Enroll: 15274   (714) 826-2220

D-Q UNIVERSITY
P.O. Box 409, Davis 95617 *Type*: Public junior *Accred.*: 1977/1989 (WASC-Jr.) *Calendar*: Sem. plan *Degrees*: A *CEO*: Pres. Carlos Cordero
Enroll: 192   (916) 758-0470

DEANZA COLLEGE
21250 Stevens Creek Blvd., Cupertino 95014 *Type*: Public (district) junior *System*: Foothill-DeAnza Community College District *Accred.*: 1969/1987 (WASC-Jr.) *Calendar*: Qtr. plan *Degrees*: A *Prof. Accred.*: Medical Assisting (AMA), Physical Therapy Assisting *CEO*: Pres. A. Robert DeHart
Enroll: 27208   (408) 996-4760

DEVRY INSTITUTE OF TECHNOLOGY, LOS ANGELES
12801 Crossroads Pkwy., S., City of Industry 91746 *Type*: Private *Accred.*: 1985 (CCA-ACTTS); 1981/1987 (NCA) *Calendar*: Tri. plan *Degrees*: A, B, certificates *Prof. Accred.*: Engineering Technology (electrical) *CEO*: Pres. Paul R. McGuirk
Enroll: 2200   (213) 699-9927

DEEP SPRINGS COLLEGE
via Dyer, Nevada, Deep Springs 89010 *Type*: Private junior for men *Accred.*: 1952/1987 (WASC-Jr.) *Calendar*: Sem. plan *Degrees*: A *CEO*: Dir. Edward Hoenicke
Enroll: 24   (619) 872-2000

DEFENSE LANGUAGE INSTITUTE
Presidio of Monterey 93944 *Type*: Public (federal) technical *Accred.*: 1979/1989 (WASC-Jr.) *Calendar*: Courses of varying lengths *Degrees*: certificates *CEO*: Commandant Donald C. Fischer, Jr.
Enroll: 3501   (408) 647-5324

DELL'ARTE SCHOOL OF PHYSICAL THEATRE
P.O. Box 816, Blue Lake 95525 *Type*: Private *Calendar*: Courses of varying lengths *Degrees*: certificates *Prof. Accred.*: Theatre *CEO*: Dir. Jane Hill
     (707) 668-5663

DENTAL TECHNOLOGY INSTITUTE
1937 W. Chapman Ave., Ste. 100, Orange 92668 *Type*: Private *Accred.*: 1976/1989 (CCA-ACTTS) *Calendar*: Courses of vary-

ing lengths *Degrees:* diplomas *CEO:* Dir. Phillip J. Hassan
Enroll: 97 (714) 937-3989

DESIGN INSTITUTE OF SAN DIEGO
8555 Commerce Ave., San Diego 92121 *Type:* Private professional *Calendar:* Courses of varying lengths *Degrees:* P *Prof. Accred.:* Interior Design *CEO:* Pres. Arthur Rosenstein
(619) 566-1200

DIABLO VALLEY COLLEGE
321 Golf Club Rd., Pleasant Hill 94523 *Type:* Public (district) junior *System:* Contra Costa Community College District *Accred.:* 1952/1991 (WASC-Jr.) *Calendar:* Sem. plan *Degrees:* A *Prof. Accred.:* Dental Assisting, Dental Hygiene, Dental Laboratory Technology *CEO:* Pres. Phyllis L. Peterson
Enroll: 23000 (510) 685-1230

DICKINSON-WARREN BUSINESS COLLEGE
1001 S. 57th St., Richmond 94804 *Type:* Private business *Accred.:* 1979/1988 (CCA-ACICS) *Calendar:* Courses of varying lengths *Degrees:* certificates *CEO:* Pres. Ramon Flores
Enroll: 505 (415) 236-5627

DOMINICAN COLLEGE OF SAN RAFAEL
50 Acacia St., San Rafael 94901 *Type:* Independent (Roman Catholic) liberal arts *Accred.:* 1949/1987 (WASC-Sr.) *Calendar:* Sem. plan *Degrees:* B, M *Prof. Accred.:* Nursing (B) *CEO:* Pres. Joseph R. Fink
Enroll: 619 (415) 457-4440

DOMINICAN SCHOOL OF PHILOSOPHY AND THEOLOGY
2401 Ridge Rd., Berkeley 94709 *Type:* Independent (Roman Catholic) professional *Accred.:* 1978/1983 (ATS); 1964/1988 (WASC-Sr.) *Calendar:* Sem. plan *Degrees:* B, P, M *CEO:* Pres. Allen Duston, O.P.
Enroll: 75 (510) 849-2030

DON BOSCO TECHNICAL INSTITUTE
1151 San Gabriel Blvd., Rosemead 91770 *Type:* Private (Roman Catholic) 2-year *Accred.:* 1972/1989 (WASC-Jr.) *Calendar:* Sem. plan *Degrees:* A *CEO:* Pres. Nicholos Reina, S.D.B.
Enroll: 260 (818) 280-0451

DOOTSON SCHOOL OF TRUCKING
11625 Clark St., Arcadia 91006-5804 *Type:* Private *Accred.:* 1986 (CCA-ACTTS) *Calendar:* Courses of varying lengths *Degrees:* certificates *CEO:* Vice Pres. John Dootson
(818) 303-1900

EAST LOS ANGELES COLLEGE
1301 Brooklyn Ave., Monterey Park 91754 *Type:* Public (district) junior *System:* Los Angeles Community College District *Accred.:* 1952/1987 (WASC-Jr.) *Calendar:* Sem. plan *Degrees:* A *Prof. Accred.:* Medical Record Technology, Respiratory Therapy *CEO:* Pres. Omero Suarez
Enroll: 12973 (213) 265-8650

EAST LOS ANGELES OCCUPATIONAL CENTER
2100 Marengo St., Los Angeles 90033 *Type:* Private professional *Calendar:* Courses of varying lengths *Degrees:* certificates *Prof. Accred.:* Dental Assisting *CEO:* Prin. Joe Tijerina
(213) 223-1283

EDUCORP CAREER COLLEGE/ROSSTON SCHOOL
230 E. Third St., Long Beach 90802 *Type:* Private *Accred.:* 1975/1987 (CCA-ACTTS) *Calendar:* Courses of varying lengths *Degrees:* certificates, diplomas *CEO:* Dir. Kenneth Boyle
(213) 437-0501

EDUPLEX CAREER CENTER
1028 E. Compton Blvd., Compton 90221 *Type:* Private *Accred.:* 1989 (CCA-ACTTS) *Calendar:* Courses of varying lengths *Degrees:* certificates, diplomas *CEO:* Dir. Mary A. Jenkins
(213) 537-3824

EL CAMINO COLLEGE
16007 S. Crenshaw Blvd., Torrance 90506 *Type:* Public (district) junior *System:* El Camino Community College District *Accred.:* 1952/1990 (WASC-Jr.) *Calendar:* Sem. plan *Degrees:* A *Prof. Accred.:* Nurs-

ing (A), Radiography, Respiratory Therapy *CEO:* Pres. Sam Schauerman
Enroll: 27330 (310) 715-3111

ELDORADO COLLEGE
2204 El Camino Real, Ste. 104, Oceanside 92054 *Type:* Private business *Accred.:* 1980/1986 (CCA-ACICS) *Calendar:* Qtr. plan *Degrees:* certificates, diplomas *CEO:* Dir. Marti Cockell
Enroll: 610 (619) 433-3660

BRANCH CAMPUS
385 N. Escondido Blvd., Escondido, CA 92025 *CEO:* Dir. Deborah Kelley
(619) 743-2100

ELDORADO COLLEGE
1901 Pacific Ave., West Covina 91790 *Type:* Private business *Accred.:* 1986 (CCA-ACICS) *Calendar:* Qtr. plan *Degrees:* certificates, diplomas *CEO:* Dir. Joan E. Muse
Enroll: 528 (818) 960-5173

ELECTRONIC TECHNICAL INSTITUTE
1201 W. Foothill Blvd., Azusa 91702 *Type:* Private *Accred.:* 1988 (CCA-ACTTS) *Calendar:* Courses of varying lengths *Degrees:* certificates *CEO:* Admin. Tony Zarza
(818) 334-0236

ELEGANCE INTERNATIONAL
3912 Wilshire Blvd., Los Angeles 90010 *Type:* Private *Accred.:* 1978/1989 (CCA-ACTTS) *Calendar:* Sem. plan *Degrees:* diplomas *CEO:* Pres. Wynna Miller
Enroll: 207 (213) 385-4026

EMPEROR'S COLLEGE OF TRADITIONAL ORIENTAL MEDICINE
2515 Wilshire Blvd., Santa Monica 90403 *Type:* Private professional *Calendar:* 3-year plan *Degrees:* M *Prof. Accred.:* Acupuncture *CEO:* Pres. Bong D. Kim
(213) 453-8833

EMPIRE COLLEGE
3033 Cleveland Ave., Ste. 107, Santa Rosa 95401 *Type:* Private business *Accred.:* 1969/1987 (CCA-ACICS) *Calendar:* Sem. plan *Degrees:* A, certificates, diplomas *CEO:* Pres. Roy O. Hurd
Enroll: 1253 (707) 546-4000

ESTELLE HARMAN ACTORS' WORKSHOP
522 N. La Brea Ave., Los Angeles 90036 *Type:* Private *Accred.:* 1976/1988 (CCA-ACTTS) *Calendar:* Qtr. plan *Degrees:* certificates *CEO:* Dir. Estelle Harman
Enroll: 176 (213) 931-8137

EVERGREEN VALLEY COLLEGE
3095 Yerba Buena Rd., San Jose 95135 *Type:* Public (district) junior *System:* San Jose-Evergreen Community College District *Accred.:* 1977/1987 (WASC-Jr.) *Calendar:* Sem. plan *Degrees:* A *Prof. Accred.:* Nursing (A) *CEO:* Pres. Richard G. Carpenter
Enroll: 13024 (408) 274-7900

FASHION CAREERS OF CALIFORNIA
1923 Morena Blvd., San Diego 92110 *Type:* Private business *Accred.:* 1983/1989 (CCA-ACICS) *Calendar:* Courses of varying lengths *Degrees:* certificates *CEO:* Dir. Patricia G. O'Connor
Enroll: 127 (619) 275-4700

THE FASHION INSTITUTE OF DESIGN AND MERCHANDISING
919 S. Grand Ave., Los Angeles 90015 *Type:* Private 2-year *Accred.:* 1978/1988 (WASC-Jr.) *Calendar:* Qtr. plan *Degrees:* A *Prof. Accred.:* Interior Design *CEO:* Pres. Tonian Hohberg
Enroll: 2694 (213) 624-1200

BRANCH CAMPUS
3420 S. Bristol St., Ste. 400, Costa Mesa, CA 92626 *CEO:* Dir. Dorothy Metcalfe
(714) 546-0930

BRANCH CAMPUS
1010 Second Ave., Ste. 200, San Diego, CA 92101 *CEO:* Dir. Ann Poloko
(619) 235-4515

BRANCH CAMPUS
55 Stockton St., San Francisco, CA 94108 *CEO:* Dir. Kathryn Caulfield
(415) 433-6691

BRANCH CAMPUS
13701 Riverside Dr., 2nd Fl., Sherman Oaks, CA 91423 *CEO:* Dir. Sheryl Stern
(818) 990-2133

FEATHER RIVER COLLEGE
570 Golden Eagle Ave., Quincy 95971 *Type:* Public (district) junior *System:* Feather River Community College District *Accred.:* 1973/1988 (WASC-Jr.) *Calendar:* Sem. plan *Degrees:* A *CEO:* Pres. Donald J. Donato
Enroll: 2650 (916) 283-0202

FIELDING INSTITUTE
2112 Santa Barbara St., Santa Barbara 93105 *Type:* Independent professional; graduate only *Accred.:* 1982 (WASC-Sr.) *Calendar:* Tri. plan *Degrees:* M, D *CEO:* Pres. William H. Maehl
Enroll: 652 (805) 687-1099

FOOTHILL COLLEGE
12345 El Monte Rd., Los Altos Hills 94022 *Type:* Public (district) junior *System:* Foothill-DeAnza Community College District *Accred.:* 1959/1988 (WASC-Jr.) *Calendar:* Qtr. plan *Degrees:* A *Prof. Accred.:* Animal Health Technology, Dental Assisting, Dental Hygiene, Radiation Therapy Technology, Radiography, Respiratory Therapy *CEO:* Pres. Thomas H. Clements
Enroll: 20029 (415) 960-4600

FRANCISCAN SCHOOL OF THEOLOGY
1712 Euclid Ave., Berkeley 94709 *Type:* Independent (Roman Catholic) professional; graduate only *Accred.:* 1975/1988 (ATS); 1975/1988 (WASC-Sr.) *Calendar:* Qtr. plan *Degrees:* P, M *CEO:* Pres. William J. Short, O.F.M.
Enroll: 61 (510) 848-5232

FRESNO CITY COLLEGE
1101 E. University Ave., Fresno 93741 *Type:* Public (district) junior *System:* State Center Community College District *Accred.:* 1952/1988 (WASC-Jr.) *Calendar:* Sem. plan *Degrees:* A *Prof. Accred.:* Dental Hygiene, Radiography, Respiratory Therapy *CEO:* Pres. Brice W. Harris
Enroll: 18500 (209) 442-4600

FRESNO PACIFIC COLLEGE
1717 S. Chestnut Ave., Fresno 93702 *Type:* Independent (Mennonite) liberal arts *Accred.:* 1961/1986 (WASC-Sr.) *Calendar:* Sem. plan *Degrees:* A, B, M *CEO:* Pres. Richard Kriegbaum
Enroll: 876 (209) 453-2000

FULLER THEOLOGICAL SEMINARY
135 N. Oakland Ave., Pasadena 91182 *Type:* Independent (interdenominational) professional; graduate only *Accred.:* 1957/1990 (ATS); 1969/1990 (WASC-Sr.) *Calendar:* Qtr. plan *Degrees:* P, M, D *Prof. Accred.:* Clinical Psychology, Psychology Internship (provisional) *CEO:* Pres. David A. Hubbard
Enroll: 1399 (818) 584-5200

FULLERTON COLLEGE
321 E. Chapman Ave., Fullerton 92634 *Type:* Public (district) junior *System:* North Orange County Community College District *Accred.:* 1952/1987 (WASC-Jr.) *Calendar:* Sem. plan *Degrees:* A *CEO:* Pres. Philip W. Borst
Enroll: 19236 (714) 992-7000

FUTURES IN EDUCATION, INC.
1249 F St., San Diego 92101 *Type:* Private home study *Accred.:* 1989 (NHSC) *Calendar:* Courses of varying lengths *Degrees:* diplomas *CEO:* Pres. Karen Bishop
(619) 235-4100

GALEN COLLEGE OF MEDICAL AND DENTAL ASSISTANTS
1325 N. Wishon Ave., Fresno 93728 *Type:* Private *Accred.:* 1974/1988 (CCA-ACTTS) *Calendar:* Courses of varying lengths *Degrees:* diplomas *CEO:* Pres. Stelia Mesple
Enroll: 240 (209) 264-9726

BRANCH CAMPUS
1604 Ford Ave., Ste. 10, Modesto, CA 95350 *CEO:* Dir. Marylin Heath
(209) 527-5084

California

BRANCH CAMPUS
3746 W. Mineral King Ave., Ste. C, Visalia, CA 93277 *CEO:* Dir. Joyce Thompson
(209) 732-2217

GAVILAN COLLEGE
5055 Santa Teresa Blvd., Gilroy 95020 *Type:* Public (district) junior *System:* Gavilan Community College District *Accred.:* 1952/1989 (WASC-Jr.) *Calendar:* Sem. plan *Degrees:* A *CEO:* Pres. John J. Holleman
Enroll: 4586 (408) 848-4712

GEMOLOGICAL INSTITUTE OF AMERICA
1660 Stewart St., Santa Monica 90404-4088 *Type:* Private technical and home study *Accred.:* 1973/1986 (CCA-ACTTS); 1965/1982 (NHSC) *Calendar:* Courses of varying lengths *Degrees:* certificates, diplomas *CEO:* Pres. William E. Boyajian
Enroll: 1106 (213) 829-2991

BRANCH CAMPUS
580 Fifth Ave., New York, NY 10036 *CEO:* Dir. Seung H. Moon
(212) 944-5900

GLENDALE CAREER COLLEGE
1021 Grandview Ave., Glendale 91201 *Type:* Private *Calendar:* 28-wk. program *Degrees:* diplomas *Prof. Accred.:* Medical Assisting *CEO:* Exec. Dir. Gloria Green
Enroll: 28 (818) 243-1131

GLENDALE COMMUNITY COLLEGE
1500 N. Verdugo Rd., Glendale 91208 *Type:* Public (district) junior *System:* Glendale Community College District *Accred.:* 1952/1987 (WASC-Jr.) *Calendar:* Sem. plan *Degrees:* A *CEO:* Pres. John A. Davitt
Enroll: 14516 (818) 240-1000

GOLDEN GATE BAPTIST THEOLOGICAL SEMINARY
Strawberry Pt., Mill Valley 94941 *Type:* Independent (Southern Baptist) professional; graduate only *Accred.:* 1962/1990 (ATS); 1971/1990 (WASC-Sr.) *Calendar:* Sem. plan *Degrees:* P, M, D *Prof. Accred.:* Music *CEO:* Pres. William O. Crews, Jr.
Enroll: 441 (415) 388-8080

GOLDEN GATE UNIVERSITY
536 Mission St., San Francisco 94105-2968 *Type:* Independent business *Accred.:* 1959/1986 (WASC-Sr. probational) *Calendar:* Tri. plan *Degrees:* A, B, P, M, D *Prof. Accred.:* Law *CEO:* Pres. Otto Butz
Enroll: 4769 (415) 442-7000

GOLDEN STATE SCHOOL
1661 N. Raymond St., Anaheim 92801-1121 *Type:* Private *Accred.:* 1991 (CCA-ACTTS) *Calendar:* Courses of varying lengths *Degrees:* certificates *CEO:* Dir. James Swigart
(714) 680-0102

GOLDEN STATE SCHOOL
195 W. Benedict St., San Bernardino 92408-5807 *Type:* Private *Accred.:* 1991 (CCA-ACTTS) *Calendar:* Courses of varying lengths *Degrees:* certificates *CEO:* Dir. Bill Jackson
(805) 833-0123

GOLDEN STATE SCHOOL
P.O. Box 6869, Santa Maria 93456-6869 *Type:* Private *Accred.:* 1991 (CCA-ACTTS) *Calendar:* Courses of varying lengths *Degrees:* certificates *CEO:* Dir. Marc Marchwardt
(805) 922-0454

GOLDEN WEST COLLEGE
15744 Golden West St., Huntington Beach 92647 *Type:* Public (district) junior *System:* Coast Community College District *Accred.:* 1969/1987 (WASC-Jr.) *Calendar:* Sem. plan *Degrees:* A *Prof. Accred.:* Nursing (A) *CEO:* Pres. Judith Valles
Enroll: 15079 (714) 892-7711

GOLF ACADEMY OF SAN DIEGO
P.O. Box 3050, Rancho Santa Fe 92067 *Type:* Private *Accred.:* 1982/1988 (CCA-ACICS) *Calendar:* Courses of varying lengths *Degrees:* certificates *CEO:* Pres. Frederick L. Schwartz
Enroll: 220 (619) 756-2486

GOLF ACADEMY OF THE SOUTH
P.O. Box 3609, Winter Springs, FL 32708
CEO: Dir. Richard B. Rogers
(407) 699-1990

GRADUATE THEOLOGICAL UNION
2400 Ridge Rd., Berkeley 94709 *Type:* Independent professional; graduate only *Accred.:* 1969/1988 (ATS); 1966/1988 (WASC-Sr.) *Calendar:* Sem. plan *Degrees:* M, D *CEO:* Pres. Robert M. Barr
Enroll: 383   (510) 649-2400

GROSSMONT COLLEGE
8800 Grossmont College Dr., El Cajon 92020 *Type:* Public (district) junior *System:* Grossmont-Cuyamaca Community College District *Accred.:* 1963/1990 (WASC-Jr.) *Calendar:* Sem. plan *Degrees:* A *Prof. Accred.:* Cardiovascular Technology, Nursing (A), Perfusion, Respiratory Therapy *CEO:* Pres. Richard Sanchez
Enroll: 17441   (619) 465-1700

THE GROVE SCHOOL OF MUSIC
14539 Sylvan St., Van Nuys 91411 *Type:* Private *Calendar:* Courses of varying lengths *Degrees:* certificates, diplomas *Prof. Accred.:* Music *CEO:* Pres. Dick Grove
Enroll: 800   (818) 904-9400

HARTNELL COLLEGE
156 Homestead Ave., Salinas 93901 *Type:* Public (district) junior *System:* Hartnell Community College District *Accred.:* 1952/1989 (WASC-Jr.) *Calendar:* Sem. plan *Degrees:* A *Prof. Accred.:* Animal Health Technology *CEO:* Pres. James R. Hardt
Enroll: 7587   (408) 755-6700

HARVEY MUDD COLLEGE
260 E. Foothill Blvd., Claremont 91711 *Type:* Independent professional *Accred.:* 1959/1987 (WASC-Sr.) *Calendar:* Sem. plan *Degrees:* B, M *Prof. Accred.:* Engineering (general) *CEO:* Pres. Henry E. Riggs
Enroll: 563   (714) 621-8000

HEALD 4C'S COLLEGE
255 W. Bullard Ave., Fresno 93704 *Type:* Private business *Accred.:* 1983/1989 (WASC-Jr.) *Calendar:* Qtr. plan *Degrees:* A *CEO:* Dir. John Swiger
(209) 438-4222

HEALD BUSINESS COLLEGE—HAYWARD
22730 Mission Blvd., Hayward 94541 *Type:* Private business *Accred.:* 1983/1989 (WASC-Jr.) *Calendar:* Qtr. plan *Degrees:* A *CEO:* Dir. Barbara Gordon
(510) 886-3101

HEALD BUSINESS COLLEGE—OAKLAND
1000 Broadway, Oakland 94612 *Type:* Private business *Accred.:* 1983/1989 (WASC-Jr.) *Calendar:* Qtr. plan *Degrees:* A *CEO:* Vice Pres./Dir. Marie-Louise Coppinger
(510) 444-0201

HEALD BUSINESS COLLEGE—ROHNERT PARK
100 Professional Center Dr., Rohnert Park 94928 *Type:* Private business *Accred.:* 1983/1989 (WASC-Jr.) *Calendar:* Qtr. plan *Degrees:* A *CEO:* Dir. Janet A. Englebert
(707) 584-5900

HEALD BUSINESS COLLEGE—SACRAMENTO
2910 Prospect Park Dr., Rancho Cordova 95670 *Type:* Private business *Accred.:* 1983/1989 (WASC-Jr.) *Calendar:* Qtr. plan *Degrees:* A *CEO:* Dir. David B. Raulston
(916) 638-1616

HEALD BUSINESS COLLEGE—SALINAS
P.O. Box 3167, Salinas 93912 *Type:* Private business *Accred.:* 1983/1988 (WASC-Jr.) *Calendar:* Qtr. plan *Degrees:* A *CEO:* Dir. Tim Knapp
(408) 757-1700

HEALD BUSINESS COLLEGE—SAN FRANCISCO
1453 Mission St., San Francisco 94103 *Type:* Private business *Accred.:* 1983/1989 (WASC-Jr.) *Calendar:* Qtr. plan *Degrees:* A *CEO:* Dir. Edward B. Boscacci
(415) 673-5500

HEALD BUSINESS COLLEGE—SAN JOSE
684 El Paseo de Saratoga, Ste. B, San Jose 95130 *Type:* Private business *Accred.:* 1983/

California

1989 (WASC-Jr.) *Calendar:* Qtr. plan *Degrees:* A *CEO:* Dir. Richard Launey
(408) 370-2400

HEALD BUSINESS COLLEGE—STOCKTON
1776 W. March La., Stockton 95207 *Type:* Private business *Accred.:* 1983/1989 (WASC-Jr.) *Calendar:* Qtr. plan *Degrees:* A *CEO:* Dir. Patricia Fechner
(209) 477-1114

HEALD BUSINESS COLLEGE—WALNUT CREEK
2085 N. Broadway, Walnut Creek 94596 *Type:* Private business *Accred.:* 1983/1989 (WASC-Jr.) *Calendar:* Qtr. plan *Degrees:* A *CEO:* Dir. William B. Collins
Enroll: 300   (510) 933-2436

HEALD INSTITUTE OF TECHNOLOGY—HAYWARD
24301 Southland Dr., Hayward 94545 *Type:* Private *Accred.:* 1983/1989 (WASC-Jr.) *Calendar:* Qtr. plan *Degrees:* A *CEO:* Dir. Chester J. Schaufel
(510) 783-2100

HEALD INSTITUTE OF TECHNOLOGY—MARTINEZ
2860 Howe Rd., Martinez 94553 *Type:* Private *Accred.:* 1983/1989 (WASC-Jr.) *Calendar:* Qtr. plan *Degrees:* A *CEO:* Dir. Marykay Michaels
(510) 228-9000

HEALD INSTITUTE OF TECHNOLOGY—SACRAMENTO
2920 Prospect Park Dr., Rancho Cordova 95670 *Type:* Private *Accred.:* 1983/1989 (WASC-Jr.) *Calendar:* Qtr. plan *Degrees:* A *CEO:* Dir. Ralph Roe
(916) 638-0999

HEALD INSTITUTE OF TECHNOLOGY—SAN FRANCISCO
150 Fourth St., San Francisco 94103 *Type:* Private *Accred.:* 1983/1989 (WASC-Jr.) *Calendar:* Qtr. plan *Degrees:* A *CEO:* Dir. Dale Walls
(415) 441-5555

HEALD INSTITUTE OF TECHNOLOGY—SAN JOSE
684 El Paseo de Saratoga, Ste. A, San Jose 95130 *Accred.:* 1983/1989 (WASC-Jr.) *Degrees:* A *CEO:* Dir. Nagar L. Ramesh
(408) 295-8000

HEALTH STAFF TRAINING INSTITUTE
1505 E. 17th St., Ste. 122, Santa Ana 92701 *Type:* Private *Calendar:* Courses of varying lengths *Degrees:* certificates, diplomas *Prof. Accred.:* Health Education *CEO:* Pres. Beverly Carpenter
(714) 543-9828

HEBREW UNION COLLEGE—JEWISH INSTITUTE OF RELIGION
3077 University Ave., Los Angeles 90007 *Type:* Independent (Reform Judaism) *Accred.:* 1960/1985 (WASC-Sr.) *Calendar:* Sem. plan *Degrees:* B, M, D *CEO:* Exec. Vice Pres. Uri D. Herscher
Enroll: 56   (213) 749-3424

HEMPHILL SCHOOLS
510 S. Alvarado St., Los Angeles 90057-2998 *Type:* Private home study *Accred.:* 1966/1987 (NHSC) *Calendar:* Courses of varying lengths *Degrees:* diplomas *CEO:* Pres. Arturo Delgado
(213) 413-6323

HOLLYWOOD SCRIPTWRITING INSTITUTE
1605 N. Cahuenga Blvd., Ste. 216, Hollywood 90028 *Type:* Private home study *Accred.:* 1985/1991 (NHSC) *Calendar:* Courses of varying lengths *Degrees:* certificates *CEO:* Dir. Donna Lee
(213) 461-8333

HOLY NAMES COLLEGE
3500 Mountain Blvd., Oakland 94619-9989 *Type:* Independent (Roman Catholic) liberal arts *Accred.:* 1949/1986 (WASC-Sr.) *Calendar:* Sem., Tri., and weekend plans *Degrees:* B, M *Prof. Accred.:* Music, Nursing (B) *CEO:* Pres. Lois A. MacGillivray, S.N.J.M.
Enroll: 800   (510) 436-1000

HUMBOLDT STATE UNIVERSITY
Arcata 95521 *Type:* Public (state) *System:* California State University System *Accred.:*

1949/1990 (WASC-Sr.) *Calendar:* Sem. plan *Degrees:* B, M *Prof. Accred.:* Art, Engineering (environmental/sanitary), Forestry, Journalism, Music, Nursing (B), Social Work (B-candidate), Theatre *CEO:* Pres. Alistair W. McCrone
Enroll: 6742 (707) 826-3011

HUMPHREYS COLLEGE
6650 Inglewood St., Stockton 95207 *Type:* Private *Accred.:* 1972/1990 (WASC-Jr.); 1985 (WASC-Sr. candidate) *Calendar:* Qtr. plan *Degrees:* A, B (candidate), P (candidate) *CEO:* Pres. Robert G. Humphreys
Enroll: 374 (209) 478-0800

HUNTINGTON COLLEGE OF DENTAL TECHNOLOGY
7466 Edinger Ave., Huntington Beach 92647 *Type:* Private *Accred.:* 1987 (CCA-ACTTS) *Calendar:* Courses of varying lengths *Degrees:* certificates *CEO:* Pres. Edward M. Beram
Enroll: 54 (714) 841-9500

HYPNOSIS MOTIVATION INSTITUTE
18607 Ventura Blvd., Ste. 310, Tarzana 91356 *Type:* Private home study *Accred.:* 1989 (NHSC) *Calendar:* Courses of varying lengths *Degrees:* certificates *CEO:* Pres. John J. Kappas
(818) 344-4464

ITT TECHNICAL INSTITUTE
7100 Knott Ave., Buena Park 90620 *Type:* Private *Accred.:* 1983/1988 (CCA-ACTTS) *Calendar:* Qtr. plan *Degrees:* A *CEO:* Dir. Cynthia J. Norman
Enroll: 580 (714) 523-9080

ITT TECHNICAL INSTITUTE
9680 Granite Ridge Dr., San Diego 92123-2662 *Type:* Private *Accred.:* 1983/1988 (CCA-ACTTS) *Calendar:* Qtr. plan *Degrees:* A *CEO:* Dir. Mark Bowilds
Enroll: 999 (714) 462-0682

ITT TECHNICAL INSTITUTE
6723 Van Nuys Blvd., Van Nuys 91405 *Type:* Private *Accred.:* 1984/1989 (CCA-ACTTS) *Calendar:* Qtr. plan *Degrees:* A *CEO:* Pres. William M. Allan
Enroll: 419 (818) 989-1177

ITT TECHNICAL INSTITUTE
1530 W. Cameron Ave., West Covina 91790 *Type:* Private *Accred.:* 1983/1989 (CCA-ACTTS) *Calendar:* Qtr. plan *Degrees:* A *CEO:* Dir. Michael Arterburn
Enroll: 1303 (213) 960-8681

IMPERIAL VALLEY COLLEGE
380 E. Ira Aten Rd., P.O. Box 158, Imperial 92251 *Type:* Public (district) junior *System:* Imperial Community College District *Accred.:* 1952/1989 (WASC-Jr.) *Calendar:* Sem. plan *Degrees:* A *CEO:* Pres. John A. DePaoli, Jr.
Enroll: 3839 (619) 352-8320

INSTITUTE FOR BUSINESS AND TECHNOLOGY
2550 Scott Blvd., Santa Clara 95050 *Type:* Private *Accred.:* 1979/1986 (CCA-ACTTS) *Calendar:* Courses of varying lengths *Degrees:* certificates *CEO:* Dir. M.A. Mikhail
Enroll: 446 (408) 727-1060

BRANCH CAMPUS
6060 Sunrise Vista Dr., Citrus Heights, CA 95610 *CEO:* Dir. Lynn Kretzinger
(916) 969-4900

INSTITUTE OF AUDIOVISUAL ENGINEERING
1831 Hyperion Ave., Hollywood 90027 *Type:* Private *Accred.:* 1987 (CCA-ACTTS) *Calendar:* Courses of varying lengths *Degrees:* certificates *CEO:* Dir. Lominic A. Lacasse
(213) 666-2380

INSTITUTE OF COMPUTER TECHNOLOGY
3200 Wilshire Blvd., Los Angeles 90010 *Type:* Private *Accred.:* 1985 (CCA-ACTTS) *Calendar:* Courses of varying lengths *Degrees:* diplomas *CEO:* Pres. K.C. You
Enroll: 780 (213) 381-3333

INSTITUTE OF DEVELOPMENT TECH
2315 E. Anaheim St., Long Beach 90804 *Type:* Private *Accred.:* 1988 (CCA-ACTTS)

California

Calendar: Courses of varying lengths *Degrees:* certificates *CEO:* Pres. Richard Wong
(213) 434-6758

INTERIOR DESIGNERS INSTITUTE
1061 Camelback Rd., Newport Beach 92660 *Type:* Private *Accred.:* 1987 (CCA-ACTTS) *Calendar:* Courses of varying lengths *Degrees:* A, certificates *CEO:* Dir. Judy Deaton
Enroll: 248   (714) 675-4451

INTERNATIONAL AIR ACADEMY
2980 Inland Empire Blvd., Ontario 91764-4804 *Type:* Private *Accred.:* 1991 (CCA-ACTTS) *Calendar:* Courses of varying lengths *Degrees:* certificates *CEO:* Vice Pres. Daniel C. Day
(714) 989-5222

INTERNATIONAL DEALER'S SCHOOL
7230 S. Eastern Ave., Ste. B, Bell Gardens 90201 *Type:* Private *Accred.:* 1985 (CCA-ACTTS) *Calendar:* Courses of varying lengths *Degrees:* certificates, diplomas *CEO:* Pres. Gary Mahoney
Enroll: 88   (213) 927-6733

IRVINE COLLEGE OF BUSINESS
16591 Noyes Ave., Irvine 92714 *Type:* Private business *Accred.:* 1977/1983 (CCA-ACICS) *Calendar:* Courses of varying lengths *Degrees:* certificates *CEO:* Pres. W. D. Polick
Enroll: 162   (714) 863-1145

IRVINE VALLEY COLLEGE
5500 Irvine Center Dr., Irvine 92720 *Type:* Public (district) junior *System:* Saddleback Community College District *Accred.:* 1988 (WASC-Jr.) *Calendar:* Sem. plan *Degrees:* A *CEO:* Pres. Anna L. McFarlin
Enroll: 7114   (714) 559-9300

JESUIT SCHOOL OF THEOLOGY AT BERKELEY
1735 LeRoy Ave., Berkeley 94709-8804 *Type:* Independent (Roman Catholic) professional; graduate only *Accred.:* 1971/1989 (ATS); 1971/1989 (WASC-Sr.) *Calendar:* Qtr. plan *Degrees:* P, M *CEO:* Pres. Thomas F. Gleeson, S.J.
Enroll: 164   (510) 841-8804

JOHN F. KENNEDY UNIVERSITY
12 Altarinda Rd., Orinda 94563 *Type:* Independent liberal arts and professional *Accred.:* 1977/1985 (WASC-Sr.) *Calendar:* Qtr. plan *Degrees:* B, P, M *CEO:* Pres. Charles E. Glasser
Enroll: 1245   (510) 254-0200

JOHN TRACY CLINIC
806 West Adams Blvd., Los Angeles 90007 *Type:* Private home study *Accred.:* 1965/1987 (NHSC) *Calendar:* Courses of varying lengths *Degrees:* certificates *CEO:* Dir. Sandra Meyer
(213) 748-5481

KELSEY-JENNY BUSINESS COLLEGE
201 A St., San Diego 92101 *Type:* Private *Accred.:* 1983/1989 (WASC-Jr.) *Calendar:* Qtr. plan *Degrees:* A *CEO:* Dir. J. Robert Evans
Enroll: 630   (619) 233-7418

KINGS RIVER COMMUNITY COLLEGE
995 N. Reed Ave., Reedley 93654 *Type:* Public (district) junior *System:* State Center Community College District *Accred.:* 1952/1988 (WASC-Jr.) *Calendar:* Sem. plan *Degrees:* A *Prof. Accred.:* Dental Assisting *CEO:* Pres. Richard J. Giese
Enroll: 5400   (209) 638-3641

L.I.F.E. BIBLE COLLEGE
1100 Covina Blvd., San Dimas 91773 *Type:* Private (International Four Square Gospel) *Accred.:* 1980/1990 (AABC) *Calendar:* Sem. plan *Degrees:* A, B, diplomas *CEO:* Pres. Jack E. Hamilton
Enroll: 297   (714) 599-5433

LA JOLLA ACADEMY OF ADVERTISING ARTS
10025 Mesa Rim Rd., San Diego 92121-2913 *Type:* Private *Accred.:* 1986 (CCA-ACTTS) *Calendar:* Courses of varying lengths *Degrees:* certificates, diplomas *CEO:* Dir. Gary Cantor
Enroll: 216   (619) 546-8400

LA SIERRA UNIVERSITY
4700 Pierce St., Riverside 92515 *Type:* Independent (Seventh-Day Adventist) liberal

arts and professional *Accred.:* 1960 (WASC-Sr. probational) *Calendar:* Qtr. plan *Degrees:* A, B, P, M, D *Prof. Accred.:* Social Work (B) *CEO:* Pres. Fritz Guy
Enroll: 1219 (714) 785-2022

LAKE TAHOE COMMUNITY COLLEGE
One College Dr., P.O. Box 14445, South Lake Tahoe 95702 *Type:* Public (district) junior *System:* Lake Tahoe Community College District *Accred.:* 1979/1989 (WASC-Jr.) *Calendar:* Qtr. plan *Degrees:* A *CEO:* Pres. Guy F. Lease
Enroll: 2500 (916) 541-4660

LANEY COLLEGE
900 Fallon St., Oakland 94607 *Type:* Public (district) junior *System:* Peralta Community College District *Accred.:* 1956/1991 (WASC-Jr.) *Calendar:* Sem. plan *Degrees:* A *CEO:* Pres. Odell Johnson
Enroll: 11909 (510) 834-5740

LAS POSITAS COLLEGE
3033 Collier Canyon Rd., Livermore 94550 *Type:* Public (district) junior *System:* Chabot-Las Positas Community College District *Accred.:* 1991 (WASC-Jr.) *Calendar:* Qtr. plan *Degrees:* A *CEO:* Pres. Barbara A. Adams
Enroll: 5723 (415) 373-5800

LASSEN COLLEGE
Hwy. 139, P.O. Box 3000, Susanville 96130 *Type:* Public (district) junior *System:* Lassen Community College District *Accred.:* 1952/1990 (WASC-Jr.) *Calendar:* Sem. plan *Degrees:* A *CEO:* Supt./Pres. Larry J. Blake
Enroll: 1836 (916) 257-6181

LAWTON SCHOOL
950 S. Bascom Ave., Ste. 2011, San Jose 95128 *Type:* Private *Accred.:* 1990 (CCA-ACTTS) *Calendar:* Courses of varying lengths *Degrees:* certificates *CEO:* Exec. Dir. Ronald Gerhardt
Enroll: 41 (408) 288-8400

BRANCH CAMPUS
1077 Lexington Ave., Columbus, OH 43201 *CEO:* Dir. Al Haro
(614) 299-0444

LEDERWOLFF CULINARY ACADEMY
3300 Stockton Blvd., Sacramento 95820-1450 *Type:* Private *Accred.:* 1991 (CCA-ACTTS) *Calendar:* Courses of varying lengths *Degrees:* certificates *CEO:* Owner Ronald Lederman
(916) 456-7002

LIFE CHIROPRACTIC COLLEGE—WEST
2005 Via Barrett, P.O. Box 367, San Lorenzo 94580 *Type:* Private professional *Calendar:* Sem. plan *Degrees:* P *Prof. Accred.:* Chiropractic Education *CEO:* Pres. Gerard Clum
(415) 276-9013

LINCOLN UNIVERSITY
281 Masonic Ave., San Francisco 94118 *Type:* Independent professional *Accred.:* 1990 (CCA-ACICS); 1987 (WASC-Sr. candidate) *Calendar:* Sem. plan *Degrees:* B, P, M *CEO:* Pres. Luke T. Chang
Enroll: 417 (415) 221-1212

LOMA LINDA UNIVERSITY
Loma Linda 92350 *Type:* Independent (Seventh-Day Adventist) liberal arts and professional *Accred.:* 1960/1980 (WASC-Sr. probational) *Calendar:* Qtr. plan *Degrees:* A, B, P, M, D *Prof. Accred.:* Cytotechnology, Dental Hygiene, Dentistry, Diagnostic Medical Sonography, Dietetics (coordinated), Endodontics, Medical Record Administration, Medical Technology, Medicine, Nuclear Medicine Technology, Nursing (B,M), Occupational Therapy, Occupational Therapy Assisting, Oral and Maxillofacial Surgery, Orthodontics, Periodontics, Physical Therapy, Physical Therapy Assisting, Public Health, Radiation Therapy Technology, Radiography, Respiratory Therapy *CEO:* Pres. B. Lyn Behrens
Enroll: 2134 (714) 824-4300

LONG BEACH CITY COLLEGE
4901 E. Carson St., Long Beach 90808 *Type:* Public (district) junior *System:* Long Beach Community College District *Accred.:* 1952/1990 (WASC-Jr.) *Calendar:* Sem. plan *Degrees:* A *Prof. Accred.:* Nursing (A), Radiography *CEO:* Pres. Beverly L. O'Neill
Enroll: 29456   (310) 420-4111

LONG BEACH COLLEGE OF BUSINESS
455 E. Artesia Blvd., Long Beach 90805 *Type:* Private business *Accred.:* 1972/1990 (CCA-ACICS) *Calendar:* Courses of varying lengths *Degrees:* diplomas *CEO:* Pres. Marcus Hawkins
Enroll: 324   (213) 423-6610

LOS ANGELES CITY COLLEGE
855 N. Vermont Ave., Los Angeles 90029 *Type:* Public (district) junior *System:* Los Angeles Community College District *Accred.:* 1952/1985 (WASC-Jr.) *Calendar:* Sem. plan *Degrees:* A *Prof. Accred.:* Dental Laboratory Technology, Radiography *CEO:* Acting Pres. Jose Robledo
Enroll: 17087   (213) 669-4000

LOS ANGELES COLLEGE OF CHIROPRACTIC
16200 E. Amber Valley Dr., P.O. Box 1166, Whittier 90609-1166 *Type:* Private professional *Accred.:* 1986 (WASC-Sr. candidate) *Calendar:* Sem. plan *Degrees:* B, P *Prof. Accred.:* Chiropractic Education *CEO:* Pres. Reed B. Phillips
Enroll: 1003   (213) 947-8755

LOS ANGELES HARBOR COLLEGE
1111 Figueroa Pl., Wilmington 90744 *Type:* Public (district) junior *System:* Los Angeles Community College District *Accred.:* 1952/1990 (WASC-Jr.) *Calendar:* Sem. plan *Degrees:* A *CEO:* Pres. James Heinselman
Enroll: 8908   (310) 518-1000

LOS ANGELES MISSION COLLEGE
13356 Eldridge Ave., Sylmar 91342 *Type:* Public (district) junior *System:* Los Angeles Community College District *Accred.:* 1978/1991 (WASC-Jr.) *Calendar:* Sem. plan *Degrees:* A *CEO:* Pres. Jack Fujimoto
Enroll: 5769   (818) 364-7600

LOS ANGELES ORT TECHNICAL INSTITUTE
635 S. Harvard Blvd., Ste. 116, Los Angeles 90015 *Type:* Private *Accred.:* 1988 (CCA-ACTTS) *Calendar:* Courses of varying lengths *Degrees:* certificates *CEO:* Dir. Arthur Cherdack
          (213) 788-7222

BRANCH CAMPUS
15130 Ventura Blvd., Sherman Oaks, CA 91403 *CEO:* Dir. Chris Mahdesian
          (818) 288-7222

LOS ANGELES PIERCE COLLEGE
6201 Winnetka Ave., Woodland Hills 91371 *Type:* Public (district) junior *System:* Los Angeles Community College District *Accred.:* 1952/1989 (WASC-Jr.) *Calendar:* Sem. plan *Degrees:* A *Prof. Accred.:* Animal Health Technology (probational), Nursing (A) *CEO:* Pres. Daniel G. Means
Enroll: 17957   (818) 347-0551

LOS ANGELES SOUTHWEST COLLEGE
1600 W. Imperial Hwy., Los Angeles 90047 *Type:* Public (district) junior *System:* Los Angeles Community College District *Accred.:* 1980/1989 (WASC-Jr.) *Calendar:* Sem. plan *Degrees:* A *CEO:* Interim Pres. Patricia Wainwright
Enroll: 4642   (310) 777-2225

LOS ANGELES TRADE-TECHNICAL COLLEGE
400 W. Washington Blvd., Los Angeles 90015 *Type:* Public (district) junior *System:* Los Angeles Community College District *Accred.:* 1952/1987 (WASC-Jr.) *Calendar:* Sem. plan *Degrees:* A *CEO:* Pres. Thomas L. Stevens, Jr.
Enroll: 13925   (213) 744-9500

LOS ANGELES VALLEY COLLEGE
5800 Fulton Ave., Van Nuys 91401 *Type:* Public (district) junior *System:* Los Angeles Community College District *Accred.:* 1952/1989 (WASC-Jr.) *Calendar:* Sem. plan *De-

grees: A *Prof. Accred.:* Nursing (A), Respiratory Therapy *CEO:* Pres. Mary E. Lee
Enroll: 17701 (818) 781-1200

LOS MEDANOS COLLEGE
2700 E. Leland Rd., Pittsburg 94565 *Type:* Public (district) junior *System:* Contra Costa Community College District *Accred.:* 1977/1987 (WASC-Jr.) *Calendar:* Sem. plan *Degrees:* A *CEO:* Pres. Stanley Chin
Enroll: 6016 (510) 798-3500

LOUISE SALINGER ACADEMY OF FASHION
101 Jessie St., San Francisco 94105 *Type:* Private *Accred.:* 1971/1989 (CCA-ACTTS) *Calendar:* Qtr. plan *Degrees:* A, B, diplomas *CEO:* Pres. Esther Herschelle
Enroll: 100 (415) 974-6666

LOYOLA MARYMOUNT UNIVERSITY
Loyola Blvd. at W. 80th St., Los Angeles 90045 *Type:* Independent (Roman Catholic) liberal arts and professional *Accred.:* 1949/1988 (WASC-Sr.) *Calendar:* Sem. plan *Degrees:* B, P, M *Prof. Accred.:* Art, Business (B,M), Dance, Engineering (civil, electrical, mechanical), Law, Music, Theatre *CEO:* Pres. Thomas P. O'Malley, S.J.
Enroll: 6587 (213) 338-2700

MTI BUSINESS COLLEGE OF STOCKTON
6006 N. El Dorado St., Stockton 95207-4349 *Type:* Private *Accred.:* 1987 (CCA-ACTTS) *Calendar:* Courses of varying lengths *Degrees:* certificates *CEO:* Dir. Felix G. Brenner
Enroll: 91 (209) 957-3030

MTI COLLEGE
2011 W. Chapman Ave., No. 100, Orange 92668 *Type:* Private *Accred.:* 1988 (CCA-ACTTS) *Calendar:* Qtr. plan *Degrees:* certificates, diplomas *CEO:* Pres. Ton Bui
Enroll: 300 (714) 385-1132

MTI-WESTERN BUSINESS COLLEGE
2731 Capitol Ave., Sacramento 95816 *Type:* Private *Accred.:* 1975/1987 (CCA-ACICS) *Calendar:* Courses of varying lengths *Degrees:* diplomas *CEO:* Pres. John A. Zimmerman
Enroll: 822 (916) 442-8933

MANOR FASHION INSTITUTE
1111 Howe Ave., Ste. 150, Sacramento 95825 *Type:* Private *Accred.:* 1986 (CCA-ACICS) *Calendar:* Courses of varying lengths *Degrees:* diplomas *CEO:* Admin. Linda Weldon
Enroll: 46 (916) 927-7769

MARIC COLLEGE OF MEDICAL CAREERS
7202 Princess View Dr., San Diego 92120 *Type:* Private *Accred.:* 1982/1988 (CCA-ACTTS) *Calendar:* 28-wk. courses *Degrees:* certificates *Prof. Accred.:* Health Education, Medical Assisting *CEO:* Exec. Dir. Gerry Taylor
Enroll: 515 (619) 583-8232

BRANCH CAMPUS
1593-C E. Vista Way, Vista, CA 92084 *CEO:* Dir. Peter Hansen
(619) 758-8640

MARIC COLLEGE OF MEDICAL CAREERS
1300 Rancheros Dr., San Marcos 92069 *Type:* Private *Accred.:* 1984/1990 (CCA-ACTTS) *Calendar:* 28-wk. courses *Degrees:* certificates *Prof. Accred.:* Health Education, Medical Assisting *CEO:* Pres. Richard I. Lyles
Enroll: 163 (619) 747-1555

MARIN BALLET SCHOOL
100 Elm St., San Rafael 94901 *Type:* Private *Calendar:* Courses of varying lengths *Degrees:* certificates *Prof. Accred.:* Dance *CEO:* Dir. Margaret Swarthout
(415) 453-6705

MARYMOUNT COLLEGE
30800 Palos Verdes Dr., E., Rancho Palos Verdes 90274 *Type:* Private (Roman Catholic) junior *Accred.:* 1971/1989 (WASC-Jr.) *Calendar:* 4-1-4 plan *Degrees:* A *CEO:* Pres. Thomas D. Wood
Enroll: 1077 (310) 377-5501

California

THE MASTER'S COLLEGE
21726 W. Placerita Canyon Rd., P.O. Box 878, Newhall 91322 *Type:* Independent (Baptist) liberal arts *Accred.:* 1975/1985 (WASC-Sr.) *Calendar:* Sem plan. *Degrees:* B *CEO:* Pres. John MacArthur, Jr.
Enroll: 957 (805) 259-3540

MASTERS INSTITUTE
50 Airport Pkwy., Ste. 8, San Jose 95110 *Type:* Private *Accred.:* 1984/1989 (CCA-ACTTS) *Calendar:* Courses of varying lengths *Degrees:* certificates *CEO:* Pres. Les Nicholaeff
Enroll: 88 (408) 249-6861

MED-HELP TRAINING SCHOOL
2702 Clayton Rd., Ste. 201, Concord 95519 *Type:* Private *Accred.:* 1981/1987 (CCA-ACTTS) *Calendar:* Courses of varying lengths *Degrees:* certificates *CEO:* Dir. Ronald Hare
Enroll: 243 (415) 934-1947

MENDOCINO COLLEGE
P.O. Box 3000, Ukiah 95482 *Type:* Public (district) junior *System:* Mendocino Lake Community College District *Accred.:* 1980/1990 (WASC-Jr.) *Calendar:* Sem. plan *Degrees:* A *CEO:* Pres. Carl J. Ehmann
Enroll: 4570 (707) 468-3100

MENLO COLLEGE
1000 El Camino Real, Atherton 94027-4185 *Type:* Independent *Accred.:* 1952/1987 (WASC-Sr.) *Calendar:* 4-1-4 plan *Degrees:* A, B *CEO:* Pres. David W. Butler
Enroll: 530 (415) 323-6141

MENNONITE BRETHREN BIBLICAL SEMINARY
4824 E. Butler and Chestnut Aves., Fresno 93727 *Type:* Independent (Mennonite) professional; graduate only *Accred.:* 1977/1981 (ATS); 1972/1987 (WASC-Sr.) *Calendar:* 4-1-4 plan *Degrees:* P, M *CEO:* Pres. Larry D. Martens
Enroll: 93 (209) 251-8628

MERCED COLLEGE
3600 M St., Merced 95348 *Type:* Public (district) junior *System:* Merced Community College District *Accred.:* 1965/1988 (WASC-Jr.) *Calendar:* Sem. plan *Degrees:* A *Prof. Accred.:* Dental Assisting, Dental Laboratory Technology, Radiography *CEO:* Pres. E. Jan Moser
Enroll: 7929 (209) 384-6000

MERIT COLLEGE
7101 Sepulveda Blvd., Van Nuys 91405 *Type:* Private business *Accred.:* 1972/1991 (CCA-ACICS) *Calendar:* Courses of varying lengths *Degrees:* diplomas *CEO:* Pres. Mel Baron
Enroll: 1007 (818) 988-6640

MERRITT COLLEGE
12500 Campus Dr., Oakland 94619 *Type:* Public (district) junior *System:* Peralta Community College District *Accred.:* 1956/1991 (WASC-Jr.) *Calendar:* Sem. plan *Degrees:* A *Prof. Accred.:* Radiography *CEO:* Pres. Donald R. Hongisto
Enroll: 6023 (510) 531-4911

MILLS COLLEGE
Oakland 94613 *Type:* Independent liberal arts for women *Accred.:* 1949/1986 (WASC-Sr.) *Calendar:* Sem. plan *Degrees:* B, M *CEO:* Pres. Janet Holmgren McKay
Enroll: 998 (510) 430-2255

MIRACOSTA COLLEGE
One Barnard Dr., Oceanside 92056 *Type:* Public (district) junior *System:* MiraCosta Community College District *Accred.:* 1952/1987 (WASC-Jr.) *Calendar:* Sem. plan *Degrees:* A *CEO:* Pres. H. Deon Holt
Enroll: 8934 (619) 757-2121

MISSION COLLEGE
3000 Mission College Blvd., Santa Clara 95054 *Type:* Public (district) junior *System:* West Valley-Mission Community College District *Accred.:* 1979/1989 (WASC-Jr.) *Calendar:* Sem. plan *Degrees:* A *CEO:* Pres. Floyd M. Hogue
Enroll: 11576 (408) 988-2200

MODERN TECHNOLOGY SCHOOL X-RAY
1232 E. Katella Ave., Anaheim 92805 *Type:* Private *Accred.:* 1987 (CCA-ACTTS) *Cal-*

endar: Courses of varying lengths *Degrees:* certificates *CEO:* Dir. Linda Ermshar
(714) 978-7702

MODERN TECHNOLOGY SCHOOL X-RAY
6180 Laurel Canyon Blvd., North Hollywood 91601 *Type:* Private *Accred.:* 1987 (CCA-ACTTS) *Calendar:* Courses of varying lengths *Degrees:* certificates *CEO:* Dir. Donna Juds-Caplan
(818) 763-2563

MODESTO JUNIOR COLLEGE
435 College Ave., Modesto 95350 *Type:* Public (district) junior *System:* Yosemite Community College District *Accred.:* 1952/1989 (WASC-Jr.) *Calendar:* Sem. plan *Degrees:* A *Prof. Accred.:* Dental Assisting, Medical Assisting (AMA), Respiratory Therapy, Respiratory Therapy Technology *CEO:* Pres. Stanley Hodges
Enroll: 15817   (209) 575-6067

MOLER BARBER COLLEGE
3500 Broadway, Oakland 94611 *Type:* Private *Accred.:* 1980/1988 (CCA-ACTTS) *Calendar:* Courses of varying lengths *Degrees:* certificates, diplomas *CEO:* Owner Willie C. McHenry
Enroll: 126   (510) 652-4177

MOLER BARBER COLLEGE
727 J St., Sacramento 95814 *Type:* Private *Accred.:* 1980/1987 (CCA-ACTTS) *Calendar:* Courses of varying lengths *Degrees:* diplomas *CEO:* Dir. James A. Murray, Jr.
Enroll: 89   (916) 441-0072

MOLER BARBER COLLEGE
50 Mason St., San Francisco 94102 *Type:* Private *Accred.:* 1980/1987 (CCA-ACTTS) *Calendar:* Courses of varying lengths *Degrees:* diplomas *CEO:* Pres. Donald A. Forfang, II
Enroll: 48   (415) 362-5885

MONTEREY INSTITUTE OF INTERNATIONAL STUDIES
425 Van Buren, Monterey 93940 *Type:* Independent liberal arts; graduate only *Accred.:* 1961/1985 (WASC-Sr.) *Calendar:* Sem. plan *Degrees:* B, M *CEO:* Pres. Robert G. Gard, Jr.
Enroll: 587   (408) 647-4100

MONTEREY PENINSULA COLLEGE
980 Fremont St., Monterey 93940 *Type:* Public (district) junior *System:* Monterey Peninsula Community College District *Accred.:* 1952/1987 (WASC-Jr.) *Calendar:* Sem. plan *Degrees:* A *Prof. Accred.:* Dental Assisting *CEO:* Pres. David W. Hopkins, Jr.
Enroll: 10500   (408) 646-4010

MOORPARK COLLEGE
7075 Campus Rd., Moorpark 93021 *Type:* Public (district) junior *System:* Ventura County Community College District *Accred.:* 1969/1987 (WASC-Jr.) *Calendar:* Sem. plan *Degrees:* A *Prof. Accred.:* Nursing (A) *CEO:* Acting Pres. Roger Boedecker
Enroll: 10562   (805) 378-1400

MOUNT ST. MARY'S COLLEGE
12001 Chalon Rd., Los Angeles 90049 *Type:* Independent (Roman Catholic) liberal arts primarily for women *Accred.:* 1949/1986 (WASC-Sr.) *Calendar:* 4-1-4 plan *Degrees:* A, B, M *Prof. Accred.:* Music, Nursing (B), Occupational Therapy Assisting, Physical Therapy, Physical Therapy Assisting *CEO:* Pres. Karen Kennelly, C.S.J.
Enroll: 1043   (213) 476-2237

DOHENY CAMPUS
10 Chester Pl., Los Angeles, CA 90007 *CEO:* Dean Kathleen Kelly
(213) 746-0450

MOUNT SAN ANTONIO COLLEGE
1100 N. Grand Ave., Walnut 91789 *Type:* Public (district) junior *System:* Mount San Antonio Community College District *Accred.:* 1952/1987 (WASC-Jr.) *Calendar:* Sem. plan *Degrees:* A *Prof. Accred.:* Animal Health Technology, Radiography, Respiratory Therapy *CEO:* Pres. William H. Feddersen
Enroll: 41413   (714) 594-5611

California

MOUNT SAN JACINTO COLLEGE
1499 N. State St., San Jacinto 92383 *Type:* Public (district) junior *System:* Mount San Jacinto Community College District *Accred.:* 1965/1988 (WASC-Jr.) *Calendar:* Sem. plan *Degrees:* A *CEO:* Pres. Richard H. Lowe
Enroll: 3581 (714) 654-8011

MUSICIANS INSTITUTE
1655 N. McCadden Pl., Hollywood 90028 *Type:* Private professional *Calendar:* 1-year program *Degrees:* certificates *Prof. Accred.:* Music *CEO:* Pres. Patrick Hicks
(213) 462-1384

NAPA VALLEY COLLEGE
2277 Napa-Vallejo Hwy., Napa 94558 *Type:* Public (district) junior *System:* Napa Valley Community College District *Accred.:* 1952/1986 (WASC-Jr.) *Calendar:* Sem. plan *Degrees:* A *Prof. Accred.:* Respiratory Therapy *CEO:* Pres. William H. Feddersen
Enroll: 6991 (707) 253-3095

NATIONAL BROADCASTING SCHOOL
2033 Howe Ave., Ste. 110, Sacramento 95825 *Type:* Private *Accred.:* 1985 (CCA-ACTTS) *Calendar:* Courses of varying lengths *Degrees:* certificates, diplomas *CEO:* Dir. Michael Davling
Enroll: 42 (916) 922-2366

NATIONAL EDUCATION CENTER—BRYMAN CAMPUS
5350 Atlantic Ave., Long Beach 90805 *Type:* Private *Accred.:* 1968/1989 (CCA-ACTTS) *Calendar:* Courses of varying lengths *Degrees:* diplomas *Prof. Accred.:* Medical Assisting (AMA) *CEO:* Dir. Jane Parker
Enroll: 511 (213) 422-6007

NATIONAL EDUCATION CENTER—BRYMAN CAMPUS
1017 Wilshire Blvd., Los Angeles 90017 *Type:* Private *Accred.:* 1973/1985 (CCA-ACTTS) *Calendar:* Courses of varying lengths *Degrees:* diplomas *CEO:* Dir. David Corson
Enroll: 589 (213) 481-1640

Accredited Institutions

NATIONAL EDUCATION CENTER—BRYMAN CAMPUS
3505 N. Hart Ave., Rosemead 91770 *Type:* Private *Accred.:* 1968/1985 (CCA-ACTTS) *Calendar:* Courses of varying lengths *Degrees:* diplomas *Prof. Accred.:* Medical Assisting (AMA) *CEO:* Dir. George Ballew
Enroll: 596 (818) 573-5470

BRANCH CAMPUS
1600 Broadway, Oakland, CA 94612 *CEO:* Dir. Carol Carter
(510) 763-0800

NATIONAL EDUCATION CENTER—BRYMAN CAMPUS
731 Market St., San Francisco 94103 *Type:* Private *Accred.:* 1972/1985 (CCA-ACTTS) *Calendar:* Courses of varying lengths *Degrees:* diplomas *Prof. Accred.:* Medical Assisting (AMA) *CEO:* Dir. Vicki Wallace
Enroll: 697 (415) 777-2500

NATIONAL EDUCATION CENTER—BRYMAN CAMPUS
2015 Naglee Ave., San Jose 95128 *Type:* Private *Accred.:* 1973/1986 (CCA-ACTTS) *Calendar:* Courses of varying lengths *Degrees:* diplomas *Prof. Accred.:* Medical Assisting (AMA) *CEO:* Dir. Sherry De Los Santos
Enroll: 541 (408) 275-8800

NATIONAL EDUCATION CENTER—BRYMAN CAMPUS
1302 N. Fourth St., San Jose 95112 *Type:* Private *Accred.:* 1991 (CCA-ACTTS) *Calendar:* Courses of varying lengths *Degrees:* diplomas *CEO:* Dir. Gary Finch
(408) 452-8800

NATIONAL EDUCATION CENTER—BRYMAN CAMPUS
4212 W. Artesia Blvd., Torrance 90504 *Type:* Private *Accred.:* 1973/1985 (CCA-ACTTS) *Calendar:* Courses of varying lengths *Degrees:* diplomas *Prof. Accred.:* Medical Assisting (AMA) *CEO:* Dir. Michele Huggard
Enroll: 408 (213) 542-6951

Accredited Institutions **California**

NATIONAL EDUCATION CENTER—BRYMAN CAMPUS
20835 Sherman Way, Winnetka 91306 *Type:* Private *Accred.:* 1974/1987 (CCA-ACTTS) *Calendar:* Courses of varying lengths *Degrees:* diplomas *Prof. Accred.:* Medical Assisting *CEO:* Dir. Don Hyde
Enroll: 292 (818) 887-7911

NATIONAL EDUCATION CENTER—NATIONAL INSTITUTE OF TECHNOLOGY
1120 N. Brookhurst St., Anaheim 92801 *Type:* Private *Accred.:* 1983/1985 (CCA-ACTTS) *Calendar:* Courses of varying lengths *Degrees:* diplomas *CEO:* Dir. Cheryl Smith
Enroll: 716 (714) 778-6500

NATIONAL EDUCATION CENTER—SAWYER CAMPUS
5500 S. Eastern Ave., Commerce 90040 *Type:* Private business *Accred.:* 1972/1990 (CCA-ACICS) *Calendar:* Courses of varying lengths *Degrees:* A *CEO:* Dir. Delores Morann
Enroll: 1764 (213) 724-1800

NATIONAL EDUCATION CENTER—SAWYER CAMPUS
8475 Jackson Rd., Sacramento 95826 *Type:* Private business *Accred.:* 1973/1991 (CCA-ACICS) *Calendar:* Courses of varying lengths *Degrees:* certificates *CEO:* Dir. Albert H. Plante
Enroll: 1041 (916) 383-1909

NATIONAL EDUCATION CENTER—SKADRON CAMPUS
825 E. Hospitality La., San Bernardino 92408 *Type:* Private business *Accred.:* 1962/1985 (CCA-ACICS) *Calendar:* Qtr. plan *Degrees:* A, certificates *CEO:* Pres. Pamela Burns
Enroll: 1587 (714) 885-3896

NATIONAL UNIVERSITY
4025 Camino del Rio S., San Diego 92108 *Type:* Independent business *Accred.:* 1977/1982 (WASC-Sr.) *Calendar:* 12-term plan *Degrees:* A,B,P,M *CEO:* Pres. Jerry C. Lee
Enroll: 10157 (619) 563-7100

NEW COLLEGE OF CALIFORNIA
50 Fell St., San Francisco 94102 *Type:* Independent liberal arts *Accred.:* 1976/1985 (WASC-Sr.) *Calendar:* Sem. plan *Degrees:* B, P, M *CEO:* Pres. Peter Gabel
Enroll: 639 (415) 623-1694

NEW SCHOOL OF ARCHITECTURE
1249 F St., San Diego 92101-6634 *Type:* Private *Accred.:* 1991 (CCA-ACTTS) *Calendar:* Courses of varying lengths *Degrees:* certificates *CEO:* Pres. Gordon Bishop
(619) 235-4100

NEWBRIDGE COLLEGE
700 El Camino Real, Tustin 92680 *Type:* Private *Accred.:* 1991 (CCA-ACTTS) *Calendar:* Courses of varying lengths *Degrees:* certificates *CEO:* Admin. Ricci Siegel
(213) 941-7071

NORTH PARK COLLEGE
3956 30th St., San Diego 92104-3005 *Type:* Private *Accred.:* 1991 (CCA-ACTTS) *Calendar:* Courses of varying lengths *Degrees:* certificates *CEO:* Pres. Gerald Farkas
(619) 297-3333

NORTH VALLEY OCCUPATIONAL CENTER
11450 Sharp Ave., Mission Hills 91345 *Type:* Private professional *Calendar:* Courses of varying lengths *Prof. Accred.:* Dental Assisting (conditional) *CEO:* Prin. Gloria Martinez
(818) 365-9645

NORTHROP UNIVERSITY[*]
5800 W. Arbor Vitae St., Inglewood 90306 *Type:* Independent technological *Accred.:* 1960/1985 (WASC-Sr.) *Calendar:* Qtr. plan *Degrees:* A, B, P *Prof. Accred.:* Engineering (aerospace, electrical), Engineering Technology (aerospace) *CEO:* Pres. John R. Beljun
Enroll: 425 (213) 337-4400

[*]Northrop University will be closing in June 1992

California

NORTHWEST COLLEGE OF MEDICAL AND DENTAL ASSISTANTS
124 S. Glendale Ave., Glendale 91205 *Type:* Private *Accred.:* 1986 (CCA-ACTTS) *Calendar:* Courses of varying lengths *Degrees:* diplomas *CEO:* Exec. Dir. Bonnie Granger
Enroll: 425 (818) 242-0205

NORTHWEST COLLEGE OF MEDICAL AND DENTAL ASSISTANTS
530 E. Union St., Pasadena 91101 *Type:* Private *Accred.:* 1983/1988 (CCA-ACTTS) *Calendar:* Courses of varying lengths *Degrees:* diplomas *CEO:* Exec. Dir. Marsha Fuerst
Enroll: 60 (213) 796-5815

NORTHWEST COLLEGE OF MEDICAL AND DENTAL ASSISTANTS
134 W. Holt Ave., Pomona 91768 *Type:* Private *Accred.:* 1976/1988 (CCA-ACTTS) *Calendar:* Courses of varying lengths *Degrees:* diplomas *CEO:* Exec. Dir. Marsha Fuerst
Enroll: 517 (714) 623-1552

NORTHWEST COLLEGE OF MEDICAL AND DENTAL ASSISTANTS
2121 W. Garvey Ave., West Covina 91790 *Type:* Private *Accred.:* 1973/1980 (CCA-ACTTS) *Calendar:* Courses of varying lengths *Degrees:* diplomas *Prof. Accred.:* Medical Assisting *CEO:* Exec. Dir. Marsha Fuerst
Enroll: 100 (818) 960-5046

NOVA INSTITUTE OF HEALTH TECHNOLOGY
2400 S. Western Ave., Los Angeles 90018 *Type:* Private *Accred.:* 1991 (CCA-ACTTS) *Calendar:* Courses of varying lengths *Degrees:* certificates, diplomas *CEO:* Dir. Elyas Rashed
(213) 735-2222

OAKLAND COLLEGE OF COURT REPORTING
343 19th St., Oakland 94612 *Type:* Private business *Accred.:* 1982/1988 (CCA-ACICS) *Calendar:* Courses of varying lengths *Degrees:* certificates, diplomas *CEO:* Dir. Frank Hutchinson
Enroll: 220 (510) 287-5290

OCCIDENTAL COLLEGE
1600 Campus Rd., Los Angeles 90041 *Type:* Independent liberal arts *Accred.:* 1949/1990 (WASC-Sr.) *Calendar:* 3-term plan *Degrees:* B, M *CEO:* Pres. John B. Slaughter
Enroll: 1677 (213) 259-2500

OHLONE COLLEGE
43600 Mission Blvd., Fremont 94539 *Type:* Public (district) junior *System:* Fremont-Newark Community College District *Accred.:* 1970/1990 (WASC-Jr.) *Calendar:* Sem. plan *Degrees:* A *Prof. Accred.:* Nursing (A), Respiratory Therapy *CEO:* Pres. Peter Blomerley
Enroll: 8867 (510) 659-6000

ORANGE COAST COLLEGE
2701 Fairview Rd., P.O. Box 5005, Costa Mesa 92628 *Type:* Public (district) junior *System:* Coast Community College District *Accred.:* 1952/1990 (WASC-Jr.) *Calendar:* Sem. plan *Degrees:* A *Prof. Accred.:* Dental Assisting, Dental Laboratory Technology, Electroneurodiagnostic Technology, Medical Assisting (AMA), Radiography, Respiratory Therapy *CEO:* Pres. David A. Grant
Enroll: 23314 (714) 432-0202

ORANGE COUNTY BUSINESS COLLEGE
1401 S. Anaheim Blvd., Anaheim 92805 *Type:* Private business *Accred.:* 1973/1985 (CCA-ACICS) *Calendar:* Courses of varying lengths *Degrees:* certificates, diplomas *CEO:* Dir. Pamela Fechtman
Enroll: 583 (714) 772-6941

OTIS ART INSTITUTE OF PARSONS SCHOOL OF DESIGN
2401 Wilshire Blvd., Los Angeles 90057 *Type:* Independent professional; graduate only *Accred.:* 1956/1990 (WASC-Sr.) *Calendar:* Sem. plan *Degrees:* B, M *Prof. Accred.:* Art *CEO:* Dean Roger Workman
Enroll: 711 (213) 251-0500

Accredited Institutions   **California**

OXNARD COLLEGE
4000 S. Rose Ave., Oxnard 93033 *Type:* Public (district) junior *System:* Ventura County Community College District *Accred.:* 1978/1988 (WASC-Jr.) *Calendar:* Sem. plan *Degrees:* A *CEO:* Pres. Elise D. Schneider
Enroll: 6207   (805) 488-0911

PACIFIC CHRISTIAN COLLEGE
2500 E. Nutwood Ave., Fullerton 92631 *Type:* Independent (Christian Churches /Churches of Christ) liberal arts *Accred.:* 1963/1983 (AABC); 1969/1988 (WASC-Sr.) *Calendar:* 4-1-4 plan *Degrees:* A, B, M *CEO:* Pres. E. LeRoy Lawson
Enroll: 474   (714) 879-3901

PACIFIC COAST COLLEGE
118 W. Fifth St., Santa Ana 92701 *Type:* Private *Accred.:* 1972/1987 (CCA-ACTTS) *Calendar:* Courses of varying lengths *Degrees:* diplomas *CEO:* Exec. Dir. Charles Murray, Jr.
Enroll: 536   (714) 558-8700

PACIFIC COAST TECHNICAL INSTITUTE
14620 Keswick St., Van Nuys 91405 *Type:* Private *Accred.:* 1985 (CCA-ACTTS) *Calendar:* Courses of varying lengths *Degrees:* diplomas *CEO:* Dir. Kathleen Cooperstein
Enroll: 924   (818) 781-9500

PACIFIC COLLEGE OF ORIENTAL MEDICINE
702 W. Washington St., San Diego 92103 *Type:* Private professional *Calendar:* 3-year plan *Degrees:* M *Prof. Accred.:* Acupuncture *CEO:* Exec. Dir. Jack Miller
     (619) 574-6909

PACIFIC GRADUATE SCHOOL OF PSYCHOLOGY
935 E. Meadow Dr., Palo Alto 94303 *Type:* Independent professional *Accred.:* 1986 (WASC-Sr.) *Calendar:* Qtr. plan *Degrees:* D *Prof. Accred.:* Clinical Psychology (provisional) *CEO:* Pres. Allen Calvin
Enroll: 213   (415) 494-7477

PACIFIC LUTHERAN THEOLOGICAL SEMINARY
2770 Marin Ave., Berkeley 94708 *Type:* Private (Evangelical Lutheran) professional; graduate only *Accred.:* 1964/1986 (ATS) *Calendar:* Sem. plan *Degrees:* P, M *CEO:* Pres. Jerry L. Schmalenberger
Enroll: 124   (510) 524-5264

PACIFIC OAKS COLLEGE
5 Westmoreland Pl., Pasadena 91103 *Type:* Independent professional; graduate only *Accred.:* 1959/1985 (WASC-Sr.) *Calendar:* Sem. plan *Degrees:* B, M *CEO:* Pres. Katherine Gabel
Enroll: 296   (818) 397-1300

PACIFIC SCHOOL OF RELIGION
1798 Scenic Ave., Berkeley 94709 *Type:* Independent (interdenominational) professional; graduate only *Accred.:* 1938/1988 (ATS); 1971/1988 (WASC-Sr.) *Calendar:* Sem. plan *Degrees:* P, M, D *CEO:* Pres. Eleanor Scott Meyers
Enroll: 156   (510) 848-0528

PACIFIC TRAVEL SCHOOL
2515 N. Main St., Santa Ana 92701 *Type:* Private *Accred.:* 1968/1985 (CCA-ACTTS) *Calendar:* Courses of varying lengths *Degrees:* diplomas *CEO:* Dir. Celia Sifry
Enroll: 839   (714) 543-9495

PACIFIC UNION COLLEGE
One Angwin Ave., Angwin 94508 *Type:* Independent (Seventh-Day Adventist) liberal arts *Accred.:* 1951/1991 (WASC-Sr.) *Calendar:* Qtr. plan *Degrees:* A, B, M *Prof. Accred.:* Music, Nursing (A,B), Social Work (B) *CEO:* Pres. D. Malcolm Maxwell
Enroll: 1556   (707) 965-6234

PALMER COLLEGE OF CHIROPRACTIC—WEST
1095 Dunford Way, Sunnyvale 94087 *Type:* Private professional *Calendar:* Qtr. plan *Degrees:* P *Prof. Accred.:* Chiropractic Education *CEO:* Pres. John L. Miller
Enroll: 591   (408) 244-8907

PALO VERDE COLLEGE
811 W. Chanslor Way, Blythe 92225 *Type:* Public (district) junior *System:* Palo Verde Community College District *Accred.:* 1951/1990 (WASC-Jr.) *Calendar:* Sem. plan *De-*

California

grees: A *Prof. Accred.:* Nursing (A) *CEO:* Pres. Wilford J. Beumel
Enroll: 700 (619) 922-6168

PALOMAR COLLEGE
1140 W. Mission Rd., San Marcos 92069 *Type:* Public (district) junior *System:* Palomar Community College District *Accred.:* 1951/1991 (WASC-Jr.) *Calendar:* Sem. plan *Degrees:* A *Prof. Accred.:* Dental Assisting, Nursing (A) *CEO:* Pres. George R. Boggs
Enroll: 22600 (619) 744-1150

PASADENA CITY COLLEGE
1570 E. Colorado Blvd., Pasadena 91106 *Type:* Public (district) junior *System:* Pasadena Area Community College District *Accred.:* 1952/1991 (WASC-Jr.) *Calendar:* Sem. plan *Degrees:* A *Prof. Accred.:* Dental Assisting, Dental Hygiene, Dental Laboratory Technology, Medical Assisting (AMA), Nursing (A), Radiography *CEO:* Pres. Jack A. Scott
Enroll: 28000 (818) 585-7123

PATTEN COLLEGE
2433 Coolidge Ave., Oakland 94601 *Type:* Independent (Christian Evangelical Church) liberal arts *Accred.:* 1980/1983 (WASC-Sr.) *Calendar:* Sem. plan *Degrees:* A, B *CEO:* Pres. Priscilla C. Patten
Enroll: 105 (510) 533-8300

PEPPERDINE UNIVERSITY
24255 Pacific Coast Hwy., Malibu 90263 *Type:* Independent (Church of Christ) liberal arts and professional *Accred.:* 1949/1988 (WASC-Sr.) *Calendar:* Tri-plan *Degrees:* B, P, M, D *Prof. Accred.:* Clinical Psychology, Law, Music *CEO:* Pres. David Davenport
Enroll: 5783 (213) 456-4000

PHILLIPS COLLEGE
4300 Central Ave., Riverside 92506 *Type:* Private business *Accred.:* 1982/1988 (CCA-ACICS) *Calendar:* Courses of varying lengths *Degrees:* A, certificates *CEO:* Dir. Tom Beckerle
Enroll: 526 (714) 787-9300

Accredited Institutions

PHILLIPS JUNIOR COLLEGE
One W. Campbell Ave., Campbell 95008 *Type:* Private junior *Accred.:* 1974/1990 (CCA-ACICS); 1991 (WASC-Jr.) *Calendar:* Courses of varying lengths *Degrees:* A, diplomas *CEO:* Pres. Leslie E. Pritchard
Enroll: 1417 (408) 866-6666

FRESNO CAMPUS
390 W. Fir Ave., Clovis, CA 93612 *CEO:* Dir. Diane Donally
 (209) 297-9000

PHILLIPS JUNIOR COLLEGE
One Civic Plaza, Ste. 110, Carson 90745-2264 *Type:* Private junior *Accred.:* 1991 (CCA-ACTTS) *Calendar:* Courses of varying lengths *Degrees:* A, diplomas *CEO:* Dir. Rosie Crown
 (213) 518-2600

PHILLIPS JUNIOR COLLEGE
8520 Balboa Blvd., Northridge 91325-3561 *Type:* Private junior *Accred.:* 1991 (CCA-ACTTS) *Calendar:* Courses of varying lengths *Degrees:* A, diplomas *CEO:* Dir. John Kolacinski
 (818) 875-2220

PITZER COLLEGE
1050 N. Mills Ave., Claremont 91711-6110 *Type:* Independent liberal arts *Accred.:* 1965/1990 (WASC-Sr.) *Calendar:* Sem. plan *Degrees:* B *CEO:* Interim Pres. Paul Ranslow
Enroll: 789 (714) 621-8000

PLATT COLLEGE
10900 E. 183rd St., Ste. 290, Cerritos 90701-5342 *Type:* Private *Accred.:* 1991 (CCA-ACTTS) *Calendar:* Courses of varying lengths *Degrees:* certificates *CEO:* Dir. Margaret Potter Simons
 (213) 809-5100

PLATT COLLEGE
2361 McGaw Ave., Irvine 92714-5831 *Type:* Private *Accred.:* 1991 (CCA-ACTTS) *Calendar:* Courses of varying lengths *Degrees:*

Accredited Institutions   **California**

certificates *CEO:* Pres. William W. Lockwood
(714) 833-2300

PLATT COLLEGE
7470 N. Figueroa St., Los Angeles 90041 *Type:* Private *Accred.:* 1987 (CCA-ACTTS) *Calendar:* Courses of varying lengths *Degrees:* certificates *CEO:* Dir. William W. Lockwood
(213) 258-8050

PLATT COLLEGE
2920 Inland Empire Blvd., Ste. 102, Ontario 91764-4801 *Type:* Private *Accred.:* 1989 (CCA-ACTTS) *Calendar:* Courses of varying lengths *Degrees:* certificates *CEO:* Dir. Jan E. Hartz
(714) 989-1187

PLATT COLLEGE
6250 El Cajon Blvd., San Diego 92115 *Type:* Private *Accred.:* 1985 (CCA-ACTTS) *Calendar:* Courses of varying lengths *Degrees:* certificates *CEO:* Dir. Marshall D. Payn
Enroll: 630   (619) 265-0107

PLATT COLLEGE
301 Mission St., No. 450, San Francisco 94105-2243 *Type:* Private *Accred.:* 1991 (CCA-ACTTS) *Calendar:* Courses of varying lengths *Degrees:* certificates *CEO:* Dir. Carel Owens
(415) 495-4000

POINT LOMA NAZARENE COLLEGE
3900 Lomaland Dr., San Diego 92106 *Type:* Independent (Nazarene) liberal arts *Accred.:* 1949/1990 (WASC-Sr.) *Calendar:* Qtr. plan *Degrees:* A, B, M *Prof. Accred.:* Nursing (B) *CEO:* Pres. Jim L. Bond
Enroll: 1787   (619) 221-2200

POMONA COLLEGE
333 N. College Way, Claremont 91711 *Type:* Independent liberal arts *Accred.:* 1949/1987 (WASC-Sr.) *Calendar:* Early sem. plan *Degrees:* B *CEO:* Pres. Peter W. Stanley
Enroll: 1485   (714) 621-8000

PORTERVILLE COLLEGE
900 S. Main St., Porterville 93257 *Type:* Public (district) junior *System:* Kern Community College District *Accred.:* 1952/1989 (WASC-Jr.) *Calendar:* Sem. plan *Degrees:* A *CEO:* Pres. Paul D. Alcantra
Enroll: 2374   (209) 781-3130

PRACTICAL SCHOOLS
900 E. Ball St., Anaheim 92805 *Type:* Private *Accred.:* 1973/1985 (CCA-ACTTS) *Calendar:* Courses of varying lengths *Degrees:* diplomas *CEO:* Pres. Marilyn B. Sheehan
Enroll: 156   (714) 630-9614

PROFESSIONAL CAREER COLLEGE
75-110 St. Charles Pl., Palm Desert 92260 *Type:* Private *Accred.:* 1988 (CCA-ACTTS) *Calendar:* Courses of varying lengths *Degrees:* certificates *CEO:* Dir. Bette Kieffe
Enroll: 593   (619) 341-0151

QUEEN OF THE HOLY ROSARY COLLEGE
43326 Mission Blvd., Mission San Jose 94539 *Type:* Private (Roman Catholic) junior *Accred.:* 1979/1989 (WASC-Jr.) *Calendar:* Sem. plan *Degrees:* A *CEO:* Dean Mary P. Mehegan
Enroll: 269   (510) 657-2468

RANCHO SANTIAGO COMMUNITY COLLEGE
17th and Bristol Sts., Santa Ana 92706 *Type:* Public (district) junior *System:* Rancho Santiago Community College District *Accred.:* 1952/1990 (WASC-Jr.) *Calendar:* Sem. plan *Degrees:* A *CEO:* Chanc. Vivian B. Blevins
Enroll: 34095   (714) 667-3000

RAND GRADUATE SCHOOL OF POLICY STUDIES
1700 Main St., Santa Monica 90407-2138 *Type:* Independent graduate only *Accred.:* 1975/1990 (WASC-Sr.) *Calendar:* Qtr. plan *Degrees:* D *CEO:* Dean Charles Wolf, Jr.
Enroll: 66   (213) 393-0411

RIO HONDO COLLEGE
3600 Workman Mill Rd., Whittier 90608 *Type:* Public (district) junior *System:* Rio Hondo Community College District *Accred.:*

1967/1990 (WASC-Jr.) *Calendar:* Sem. plan *Degrees:* A *Prof. Accred.:* Respiratory Therapy *CEO:* Pres. Alex A. Sanchez
Enroll: 18400 (310) 692-0921

RIVERSIDE COMMUNITY COLLEGE
4800 Magnolia Ave., Riverside 92506 *Type:* Public (district) junior *System:* Riverside Community College District *Accred.:* 1952/1989 (WASC-Jr.) *Calendar:* Sem. plan *Degrees:* A *Prof. Accred.:* Nursing (A) *CEO:* Pres. Charles A. Kane
Enroll: 16227 (714) 684-3240

ROSSTON SCHOOL OF MEN'S HAIR DESIGN
673 W. Fifth St., San Bernardino 92410 *Type:* Private *Accred.:* 1976/1988 (CCA-ACTTS) *Calendar:* Courses of varying lengths *Degrees:* certificates, diplomas *CEO:* Pres. John Olivas
Enroll: 90 (800) 821-4934

ROUSE SCHOOL OF SPECIAL DETECTIVE TRAINING
3410-G W. MacArthur Blvd., P.O. Box 25750, Santa Ana 92799-5750 *Type:* Private home study *Accred.:* 1988 (NHSC) *Calendar:* Courses of varying lengths *Degrees:* certificates *CEO:* Pres. Art Kassel
(714) 540-9391

ROYAL HAIR INSTITUTE
5924 Whittier Blvd., Los Angeles 90022 *Type:* Private *Accred.:* 1979/1986 (CCA-ACTTS) *Calendar:* Courses of varying lengths *Degrees:* certificates *CEO:* Pres. Loran Keller
Enroll: 113 (213) 724-1087

SACRAMENTO CITY COLLEGE
3835 Freeport Blvd., Sacramento 95822 *Type:* Public (district) junior *System:* Los Rios Community College District *Accred.:* 1952/1986 (WASC-Jr.) *Calendar:* Sem. plan *Degrees:* A *Prof. Accred.:* Dental Assisting, Dental Hygiene *CEO:* Pres. Robert M. Harris
Enroll: 16131 (916) 449-7111

SADDLEBACK COLLEGE
28000 Marguerite Pkwy., Mission Viejo 92692 *Type:* Public (district) junior *System:* Saddleback Community College District *Accred.:* 1971/1988 (WASC-Jr.) *Calendar:* Sem. plan *Degrees:* A *Prof. Accred.:* Nursing (A) *CEO:* Pres. Constance M. Carroll
Enroll: 22908 (714) 582-4500

ST. JOHN'S SEMINARY
5012 Seminary Rd., Camarillo 93012-2598 *Type:* Independent (Roman Catholic) *Accred.:* 1976/1981 (ATS); 1951/1986 (WASC-Sr.) *Calendar:* Sem. plan *Degrees:* B, P, M *CEO:* Pres./Rector George H. Niederauer
Enroll: 116 (805) 482-2755

ST. JOHN'S SEMINARY COLLEGE
5118 E. Seminary Rd., Camarillo 93012 *Type:* Independent (Roman Catholic) liberal arts *Accred.:* 1951/1981 (WASC-Sr.) *Calendar:* Sem. plan *Degrees:* B *CEO:* Pres./Rector Rafael Luevano
Enroll: 88 (805) 482-2755

ST. JOSEPH'S COLLEGE
P.O. Box 7009, Mountain View 94039 *Type:* Independent (Roman Catholic) professional *Accred.:* 1954/1986 (WASC-Sr.) *Calendar:* Sem. plan *Degrees:* B *CEO:* Pres. Cale J. Crowley, S.S.
Enroll: 57 (408) 345-4600

ST. MARY'S COLLEGE OF CALIFORNIA
P.O. Box 4267, Moraga 94575 *Type:* Independent (Roman Catholic) liberal arts *Accred.:* 1949/1986 (WASC-Sr.) *Calendar:* 4-1-4 plan *Degrees:* A, B, M *Prof. Accred.:* Nursing (B) *CEO:* Pres. Mel Anderson, F.S.C.
Enroll: 3321 (510) 631-4000

ST. PATRICK'S SEMINARY
320 Middlefield Rd., Menlo Park 94025 *Type:* Independent (Roman Catholic) professional; graduate only *Accred.:* 1971/1984 (ATS); 1971/1989 (WASC-Sr.) *Calendar:*

Sem. plan *Degrees:* P, M *CEO:* Rector/Pres. Gerald D. Coleman, S.S.
Enroll: 97 (415) 325-5621

SALVATION ARMY SCHOOL FOR OFFICERS' TRAINING
30840 Hawthorne Blvd., Rancho Palos Verdes 90274 *Type:* Private *Accred.:* 1990 (WASC-Jr.) *Calendar:* Courses of varying lengths *Degrees:* certificates *CEO:* Training Princ. Bill Luttrell
Enroll: 100 (310) 377-0481

SAMRA UNIVERSITY OF ORIENTAL MEDICINE
2828 Beverly Blvd., Los Angeles 90057 *Type:* Private professional *Calendar:* 3-year plan *Degrees:* M *Prof. Accred.:* Acupuncture *CEO:* Pres. Norman Bleicher
(213) 487-2672

SAMUEL MERRITT COLLEGE
370 Hawthorne Ave., Oakland 94609 *Type:* Private professional *Accred.:* 1984/1990 (WASC-Sr.) *Calendar:* 4-1-4 plan *Degrees:* A, B *Prof. Accred.:* Nursing (B) *CEO:* Pres. Sharon Diaz
Enroll: 142 (510) 420-6011

SAN BERNARDINO VALLEY COLLEGE
701 S. Mt. Vernon Ave., San Bernardino 92410 *Type:* Public (district) junior *System:* San Bernardino Community College District *Accred.:* 1952/1991 (WASC-Jr.) *Calendar:* Sem. plan *Degrees:* A *Prof. Accred.:* Nursing (A) *CEO:* Pres. Donald L. Singer
Enroll: 11271 (714) 888-6511

SAN DIEGO CITY COLLEGE
1313 12th Ave., San Diego 92101 *Type:* Public (district) junior *System:* San Diego Community College District *Accred.:* 1952/1987 (WASC-Jr.) *Calendar:* Sem. plan *Degrees:* A *CEO:* Pres. Jeanne L. Atherton
Enroll: 13280 (619) 230-2400

SAN DIEGO COLLEGE FOR MEDICAL AND DENTAL CAREERS
5952 El Cajon Blvd., San Diego 92115 *Type:* Private *Accred.:* 1969/1987 (CCA-ACTTS) *Calendar:* Courses of varying lengths *Degrees:* certificates, diplomas *CEO:* Pres. Frank E. Hollar
Enroll: 542 (619) 582-1319

SAN DIEGO MESA COLLEGE
7250 Mesa College Dr., San Diego 92111 *Type:* Public (district) junior *System:* San Diego Community College District *Accred.:* 1966/1987 (WASC-Jr.) *Calendar:* Sem. plan *Degrees:* A *Prof. Accred.:* Animal Health Technology (probational), Medical Assisting (AMA), Medical Record Technology, Physical Therapy Assisting, Radiography *CEO:* Pres. Allen Brooks
Enroll: 27825 (619) 560-2600

SAN DIEGO MIRAMAR COLLEGE
10440 Black Mountain Rd., San Diego 92126 *Type:* Public (district) junior *System:* San Diego Community College District *Accred.:* 1982/1987 (WASC-Jr.) *Calendar:* Sem. plan *Degrees:* A *CEO:* Pres. Jerome Hunter, Ed.D.
Enroll: 8513 (619) 693-6800

SAN DIEGO STATE UNIVERSITY
5300 Campanile Dr., San Diego 92182 *Type:* Public (state) *System:* California State University System *Accred.:* 1949/1989 (WASC-Sr.) *Calendar:* Sem. plan *Degrees:* B, M, D *Prof. Accred.:* Accounting (Type A,C), Art, Audiology, Business (B,M), Clinical Psychology, Engineering (aerospace, civil, electrical, mechanical), Health Services Administration, Interior Design, Journalism, Music, Nursing (B,M), Public Administration, Public Health, Recreation, Rehabilitation Counseling, Social Work (B,M), Speech-Language Pathology, Teacher Education (e,s,p), Theatre *CEO:* Pres. Thomas B. Day
Enroll: 26670 (619) 594-5200

SAN FRANCISCO ART INSTITUTE
800 Chestnut St., San Francisco 94133 *Type:* Independent professional *Accred.:* 1954/1984 (WASC-Sr.) *Calendar:* Sem. plan *Degrees:* B, M *Prof. Accred.:* Art *CEO:* Pres. William O. Barrett
Enroll: 580 (415) 771-7020

California

SAN FRANCISCO BALLET SCHOOL
455 Franklin St., San Francisco 94102 *Type:* Private *Calendar:* Courses of varying lengths *Degrees:* certificates *Prof. Accred.:* Dance *CEO:* Dir. Nancy Johnson
(415) 861-5600

SAN FRANCISCO BARBER COLLEGE
64 Sixth St., San Francisco 94103 *Type:* Private *Accred.:* 1984 (CCA-ACTTS) *Calendar:* Courses of varying lengths *Degrees:* certificates *CEO:* Pres. Frank Yorkis
Enroll: 14 (415) 621-6802

SAN FRANCISCO COLLEGE OF MORTUARY SCIENCE
1363 Divisadero St., San Francisco 94115 *Type:* Private professional *Accred.:* 1962/1987 (WASC-Jr.) *Calendar:* Sem. plan *Degrees:* A *Prof. Accred.:* Mortuary Science *CEO:* Pres. Jacquelyn S. Taylor
Enroll: 65 (415) 567-0674

SAN FRANCISCO CONSERVATORY OF MUSIC
1201 Ortega St., San Francisco 94122 *Type:* Independent professional *Accred.:* 1960/1988 (WASC-Sr.) *Calendar:* Sem. plan *Degrees:* B, M *Prof. Accred.:* Music *CEO:* Interim Pres. Milton Salkind
Enroll: 222 (415) 564-8086

SAN FRANCISCO STATE UNIVERSITY
1600 Holloway Ave., San Francisco 94132 *Type:* Public (state) *System:* California State University System *Accred.:* 1949/1987 (WASC-Sr.) *Calendar:* Sem. plan *Degrees:* B, M *Prof. Accred.:* Art, Audiology, Business (B,M), Counseling, Engineering (civil, electrical, mechanical), Home Economics, Journalism, Medical Technology, Music, Nursing (B,M), Recreation and Leisure Studies, Rehabilitation Counseling, Social Work (B,M), Speech-Language Pathology, Teacher Education (e,s,p), Theatre *CEO:* Pres. Robert A. Corrigan
Enroll: 20981 (415) 338-1111

SAN FRANCISCO THEOLOGICAL SEMINARY
2 Kensington Rd., San Anselmo 94960 *Type:* Independent (United Presbyterian) professional; graduate only *Accred.:* 1938/1988 (ATS); 1973/1988 (WASC-Sr.) *Calendar:* Sem. plan *Degrees:* P, M, D *CEO:* Pres. J. Randolph Taylor
Enroll: 307 (415) 258-6500

SAN JOAQUIN DELTA COLLEGE
5151 Pacific Ave., Stockton 95207 *Type:* Public (district) junior *System:* San Joaquin Delta Community College District *Accred.:* 1952/1990 (WASC-Jr.) *Calendar:* Sem. plan *Degrees:* A *Prof. Accred.:* Nursing (A) *CEO:* Pres. L.H. Horton, Jr.
Enroll: 13633 (209) 474-5625

SAN JOAQUIN VALLEY COLLEGE
201 New Stine Rd., Bakersfield 93309 *Type:* Private *Accred.:* 1982/1988 (CCA-ACTTS) *Calendar:* Courses of varying lengths *Degrees:* diplomas *Prof. Accred.:* Medical Assisting *CEO:* Dir. Raelene Vanek
Enroll: 94 (805) 834-0126

SAN JOAQUIN VALLEY COLLEGE
3333 N. Bond St., Fresno 93726 *Type:* Private *Accred.:* 1981/1987 (CCA-ACTTS) *Calendar:* Courses of varying lengths *Degrees:* diplomas *Prof. Accred.:* Medical Assisting *CEO:* Dir. Michael Perry
(209) 229-7800

SAN JOAQUIN VALLEY COLLEGE
8400 W. Mineral King Ave., Visalia 93291 *Type:* Private *Accred.:* 1981/1987 (CCA-ACTTS) *Calendar:* Courses of varying lengths *Degrees:* diplomas *Prof. Accred.:* Medical Assisting, Respiratory Therapy Technology *CEO:* Pres. Robert F. Perry
Enroll: 946 (209) 651-2500

SAN JOSE CHRISTIAN COLLEGE
P.O. Box 1090, San Jose 95108 *Type:* Private (Christian Churches/Church of Christ) *Accred.:* 1969/1989 (AABC) *Calendar:* Qtr. plan *Degrees:* A, B, certificates *CEO:* Pres. Bryce L. Jessup
Enroll: 179 (408) 293-9058

SAN JOSE CITY COLLEGE
2100 Moorpark Ave., San Jose 95128 *Type:* Public (district) junior *System:* San Jose-

Evergreen Community College District *Accred.:* 1953/1986 (WASC-Jr.) *Calendar:* Sem. plan *Degrees:* A *Prof. Accred.:* Dental Assisting *CEO:* Pres. Del Anderson
Enroll: 11423 (408) 298-2181

SAN JOSE STATE UNIVERSITY
One Washington Sq., San Jose 95192 *Type:* Public (state) *System:* California State University System *Accred.:* 1949/1989 (WASC-Sr.) *Calendar:* Sem. plan *Degrees:* B, M *Prof. Accred.:* Art, Audiology, Business (B,M), Community Health, Dance, Engineering (chemical, civil, electrical, industrial, materials, mechanical), Journalism, Librarianship, Music, Nursing (B,M), Occupational Therapy, Planning (regional/urban), Public Administration, Public Health, Recreation and Leisure Studies, Social Work (B,M), Speech-Language Pathology, Teacher Education (e,s,p), Theatre *CEO:* Interim Pres. J. Handel Evans
Enroll: 21402 (408) 924-1000

SANTA BARBARA BUSINESS COLLEGE
211 S. Real Rd., Bakersfield 93301 *Type:* Private business *Accred.:* 1983 (CCA-ACICS) *Calendar:* Qtr. plan *Degrees:* diplomas *CEO:* Dir. Lynda Jones
Enroll: 281 (805) 322-3006

SANTA BARBARA BUSINESS COLLEGE
740 State St., Santa Barbara 93101 *Type:* Private business *Accred.:* 1976/1990 (CCA-ACICS) *Calendar:* Qtr. plan *Degrees:* diplomas *CEO:* Pres. Karen Selby
Enroll: 302 (805) 963-8681

BRANCH CAMPUS
4333 Hansen Ave., Fremont, CA 94536 *CEO:* Dir. Susan Corvino
Enroll: 266 (510) 793-4342

SANTA BARBARA BUSINESS COLLEGE
303 E. Plaza Dr., Santa Maria 93454 *Type:* Private business *Accred.:* 1983/1985 (CCA-ACICS) *Calendar:* Qtr. plan *Degrees:* diplomas *CEO:* Dir. Carol Gastiger
Enroll: 435 (805) 922-8256

SANTA BARBARA CITY COLLEGE
721 Cliff Dr., Santa Barbara 93109 *Type:* Public (district) junior *System:* Santa Barbara Community College District *Accred.:* 1952/1991 (WASC-Jr.) *Calendar:* Sem. plan *Degrees:* A *Prof. Accred.:* Dental Assisting, Nursing (A), Radiography *CEO:* Pres. Peter R. MacDougall
Enroll: 11602 (805) 965-0581

SANTA CLARA UNIVERSITY
Santa Clara 95053 *Type:* Independent (Roman Catholic) liberal arts and professional *Accred.:* 1949/1988 (WASC-Sr.) *Calendar:* Qtr. plan *Degrees:* B, P, M, D *Prof. Accred.:* Business (B,M), Engineering (civil, computer, electrical, mechanical), Law, Music, Theatre *CEO:* Pres. Paul L. Locatelli, S.J.
Enroll: 6528 (408) 554-4764

SANTA MONICA COLLEGE
1900 Pico Blvd., Santa Monica 90405 *Type:* Public (district) junior *System:* Santa Monica Community College District *Accred.:* 1952/1986 (WASC-Jr.) *Calendar:* Sem. plan *Degrees:* A *Prof. Accred.:* Nursing (A), Respiratory Therapy *CEO:* Pres. Richard L. Moore
Enroll: 22091 (310) 450-5150

SANTA ROSA JUNIOR COLLEGE
1501 Mendocino Ave., Santa Rosa 95401 *Type:* Public (district) junior *System:* Sonoma County Junior College District *Accred.:* 1952/1991 (WASC-Jr.) *Calendar:* Sem. plan *Degrees:* A *Prof. Accred.:* Dental Assisting, Radiography *CEO:* Pres. Robert F. Agrella
Enroll: 25038 (707) 527-4443

SAWYER COLLEGE
441 W. Trimble Rd., San Jose 95181 *Type:* Private business *Accred.:* 1973/1990 (CCA-ACICS) *Calendar:* Courses of varying lengths *Degrees:* certificates *CEO:* Pres. Sharon Turnoy
Enroll: 1164 (408) 954-8200

SAWYER COLLEGE AT POMONA
1021 E. Holt Ave., Pomona 91767 *Type:* Private business *Accred.:* 1967/1985 (CCA-

California

ACICS) *Calendar:* Courses of varying lengths *Degrees:* certificates *CEO:* Chf. Exec. Ofcr. Denise Berson
Enroll: 273 (714) 629-2534

SAWYER COLLEGE AT VENTURA
470 E. Thompson Blvd., Ventura 93001-2729 *Type:* Private business *Accred.:* 1969/1987 (CCA-ACICS) *Calendar:* Courses of varying lengths *Degrees:* certificates, diplomas *CEO:* Pres. Doreen E. Adamache
Enroll: 537 (805) 648-6877

SAWYER COLLEGE OF BUSINESS
5507 El Cajon Blvd., San Diego 92115 *Type:* Private business *Accred.:* 1973/1991 (CCA-ACICS) *Calendar:* Courses of varying lengths *Degrees:* certificates, diplomas *CEO:* Exec. Dir. Berta Cuaron
Enroll: 370 (619) 286-4770

SAYBROOK INSTITUTE
1550 Sutter St., San Francisco 94109 *Type:* Independent professional *Accred.:* 1984/1988 (WASC-Sr.) *Calendar:* Sem. plan *Degrees:* M, D *CEO:* Pres. J. Bruce Francis
Enroll: 200 (415) 441-5034

SCHOOL OF COMMUNICATION ELECTRONICS
184 Second St., San Francisco 94105 *Type:* Private *Accred.:* 1986 (CCA-ACTTS) *Calendar:* Courses of varying lengths *Degrees:* certificates *CEO:* Owner Robert W. Lew
(415) 392-0194

SCHOOL OF THEOLOGY AT CLAREMONT
1325 N. College Ave., Claremont 91711 *Type:* Independent (Disciples of Christ/United Methodist) graduate only *Accred.:* 1944/1989 (ATS); 1971/1984 (WASC-Sr.) *Calendar:* Sem. plan *Degrees:* P, M, D *CEO:* Pres. Robert W. Edgar
Enroll: 255 (714) 626-3521

SCRIPPS COLLEGE
1030 Columbia Ave., Claremont 91711 *Type:* Independent liberal arts for women *Accred.:* 1949/1988 (WASC-Sr.) *Calendar:* Sem. plan *Degrees:* B *CEO:* Pres. Nancy Y. Bekavac
Enroll: 612 (714) 621-8178

SEQUOIA AUTOMOTIVE INSTITUTE
420 Whitney Pl., Fremont 94539 *Type:* Private *Accred.:* 1977/1989 (CCA-ACTTS) *Calendar:* Courses of varying lengths *Degrees:* certificates *CEO:* Dir. Kenneth E. Years
Enroll: 2212 (510) 490-6900

SHASTA COLLEGE
P.O. Box 496006, Redding 96049 *Type:* Public (district) junior *System:* Shasta-Tehama Trinity Joint Community College District *Accred.:* 1952/1989 (WASC-Jr.) *Calendar:* Sem. plan *Degrees:* A *CEO:* Pres. Kenneth B. Cerreta
Enroll: 10200 (916) 225-4600

SIERRA ACADEMY OF AERONAUTICS TECHNOLOGY INSTITUTE
Oakland International Airport, Oakland 94614 *Type:* Private *Accred.:* 1987 (CCA-ACTTS) *Calendar:* Courses of varying lengths *Degrees:* certificates, diplomas *CEO:* Pres. Norris N. Everett
(510) 568-6100

SIERRA COLLEGE
5000 Rocklin Rd., Rocklin 95677 *Type:* Public (district) junior *System:* Sierra Joint Community College District *Accred.:* 1952/1990 (WASC-Jr.) *Calendar:* Sem. plan *Degrees:* A *CEO:* Pres. Gerald C. Angove
Enroll: 11194 (916) 624-3333

SIERRA VALLEY BUSINESS COLLEGE
4747 N. First St., Bldg. D, Fresno 93701 *Type:* Private business *Accred.:* 1981/1987 (CCA-ACICS) *Calendar:* Courses of varying lengths *Degrees:* certificates *CEO:* Pres. Donald D. Goodpaster
Enroll: 381 (209) 222-0947

SIMI VALLEY ADULT SCHOOL
3192 Los Angeles Ave., Simi Valley 93065 *Type:* Private *Calendar:* 12-mo. plan *Degrees:* certificates, diplomas *Prof. Accred.:* Dental Assisting (conditional), Respiratory Therapy Technology, Surgical Technology *CEO:* Dir. Wilfred M. Hopp
(805) 527-4840

SIMPSON COLLEGE
2211 College View Dr., Redding 96003
Type: Independent (Christian and Missionary Alliance) liberal arts *Accred.:* 1969/1981 (WASC-Sr.) *Calendar:* 4-1-4 plan *Degrees:* B, M *CEO:* Pres. Francis W. Grubbs
Enroll: 233   (916) 222-6360

SKYLINE COLLEGE
3300 College Dr., San Bruno 94066 *Type:* Public (district) junior *System:* San Mateo County Community College District *Accred.:* 1971/1989 (WASC-Jr.) *Calendar:* Sem. plan *Degrees:* A *Prof. Accred.:* Respiratory Therapy *CEO:* Pres. Linda Graef Salter
Enroll: 9451   (415) 355-7000

SOLANO COMMUNITY COLLEGE
4000 Suisun Valley Rd., Suisun 94585 *Type:* Public (district) junior *System:* Solano County Community College District *Accred.:* 1952/1989 (WASC-Jr.) *Calendar:* Sem. plan *Degrees:* A *CEO:* Pres. Virginia L. Holten
Enroll: 11192   (707) 864-7000

SONOMA STATE UNIVERSITY
Rohnert Park 94928 *Type:* Public (state) *System:* California State University System *Accred.:* 1963/1989 (WASC-Sr.) *Calendar:* Sem. plan *Degrees:* B, M *Prof. Accred.:* Art, Counseling, Music, Nursing (B,M) *CEO:* Pres. David W. Benson
Enroll: 5418   (707) 664-2880

SOUTH COAST COLLEGE OF COURT REPORTING
7122 Maple St., Westminster 92683 *Type:* Private business *Accred.:* 1984/1990 (CCA-ACICS) *Calendar:* Courses of varying lengths *Degrees:* diplomas *CEO:* Dir. Jean Gonzalez
Enroll: 1033   (714) 897-6464

SOUTHERN CALIFORNIA COLLEGE
55 Fair Dr., Costa Mesa 92626 *Type:* Independent (Assemblies of God) liberal arts *Accred.:* 1964/1991 (WASC-Sr.) *Calendar:* 4-1-4 plan *Degrees:* B, M *CEO:* Pres. Wayne E. Kraiss
Enroll: 720   (714) 556-3610

SOUTHERN CALIFORNIA COLLEGE OF OPTOMETRY
2575 Yorba Linda Blvd., Fullerton 92631 *Type:* Independent professional *Accred.:* 1961/1991 (WASC-Sr.) *Calendar:* Qtr. plan *Degrees:* A, B, P *Prof. Accred.:* Optometry *CEO:* Pres. Richard L. Hopping
Enroll: 390   (714) 870-7226

SOUTHERN CALIFORNIA INSTITUTE OF ARCHITECTURE
1800 Berkeley St., Santa Monica 90404 *Type:* Private professional *Accred.:* 1991 (WASC-Sr. candidate) *Calendar:* Sem. plan *Degrees:* B, M, P *Prof. Accred.:* Architecture (B,M) *CEO:* Dir. Michael Rotondi
Enroll: 364   (213) 829-3482

SOUTHWEST COLLEGE
22505 Montgomery St., Hayward 94541 *Type:* Private *Accred.:* 1988 (CCA-ACTTS) *Calendar:* Courses of varying lengths *Degrees:* certificates *CEO:* Gen. Mgr. Karen James
Enroll: 601   (510) 538-6151

SOUTHWEST COLLEGE
2901 N. Park Way, San Diego 92104 *Type:* Private *Accred.:* 1984 (CCA-ACTTS) *Calendar:* Courses of varying lengths *Degrees:* certificates *CEO:* Dir. Ruth French
(619) 574-6268

SOUTHWEST COLLEGE
667 Mission St., San Francisco 94105 *Type:* Private *Accred.:* 1988 (CCA-ACTTS) *Calendar:* Courses of varying lengths *Degrees:* certificates *CEO:* Dir. Kathy Ghisell
Enroll: 857   (415) 777-5327

SOUTHWESTERN COLLEGE
900 Otay Lakes Rd., Chula Vista 91910 *Type:* Public (district) junior *System:* Southwestern Community College District *Accred.:* 1964/1991 (WASC-Jr.) *Calendar:*

California

Sem. plan *Degrees:* A *CEO:* Pres. Joseph M. Conte
Enroll: 20897 (619) 421-6700

SOUTHWESTERN UNIVERSITY SCHOOL OF LAW
675 S. Westmoreland Ave., Los Angeles 90005 *Type:* Private professional *Calendar:* Sem. plan *Degrees:* P *Prof. Accred.:* Law *CEO:* Dean Leigh H. Taylor
Enroll: 1063 (213) 738-6710

STANFORD UNIVERSITY
Stanford 94305 *Type:* Independent liberal arts and professional *Accred.:* 1949/1991 (WASC-Sr.) *Calendar:* Qtr. plan *Degrees:* B, P, M, D *Prof. Accred.:* Business (M), Counseling Psychology, Engineering (aerospace, chemical, civil, electrical, industrial, mechanical, petroleum), Law, Medicine, Physician Assisting *CEO:* Pres. Donald Kennedy
Enroll: 12447 (415) 723-2300

STARR KING SCHOOL FOR THE MINISTRY
2441 LeConte Ave., Berkeley 94709 *Type:* Private (Unitarian Universalist) professional; graduate only *Accred.:* 1978/1988 (ATS) *Calendar:* Sem. plan *Degrees:* P, M *CEO:* Pres. Rebecca Parker
Enroll: 54 (510) 845-6232

STUDIO SEVEN FASHION CAREER COLLEGE
304 E. San Bernadino Rd., Covina 91723 *Type:* Private *Accred.:* 1977/1989 (CCA-ACTTS) *Calendar:* Qtr. plan *Degrees:* diplomas *CEO:* Dir. Leslie Stevenson
Enroll: 284 (818) 915-1711

SYSTEMS PROGRAMMING DEVELOPMENT INSTITUTE
4900 Triggs St., City of Commerce 90022 *Type:* Private *Accred.:* 1984/1989 (CCA-ACTTS) *Calendar:* Courses of varying lengths *Degrees:* certificates *CEO:* Pres. Jose Segura
Enroll: 687 (213) 261-8181

TAFT COLLEGE
29 Emmons Park Dr., Taft 93268 *Type:* Public (district) junior *System:* West Kern Community College District *Accred.:* 1952/1991 (WASC-Jr.) *Calendar:* Sem. plan *Degrees:* A *CEO:* Pres. David Cothrun
Enroll: 1125 (805) 763-4282

TECHNICAL HEALTH CAREERS SCHOOL
11603 S. Western Ave., Los Angeles 90047 *Type:* Private *Calendar:* Courses of varying lengths *Degrees:* certificates *Prof. Accred.:* Health Education, Medical Assisting *CEO:* Pres. Sharon L. Hughes
(213) 757-0273

TECHNICAL TRAINING CENTER
3550 Stevens Creek Blvd., San Jose 95117 *Type:* Private *Accred.:* 1985 (CCA-ACTTS) *Calendar:* Courses of varying lengths *Degrees:* certificates *CEO:* Dir. Jim Harris
Enroll: 197 (408) 554-0300

THOMAS AQUINAS COLLEGE
10000 N. Ojai Rd., Santa Paula 93060 *Type:* Independent liberal arts *Accred.:* 1980/1988 (WASC-Sr.) *Calendar:* Sem. plan *Degrees:* B *CEO:* Pres. Thomas E. Dillon
Enroll: 176 (805) 525-4417

TRAVEL UNIVERSITY INTERNATIONAL
3655 Ruffin Rd., N., Ste. 225, San Diego 92123 *Type:* Private *Accred.:* 1988 (CCA-ACTTS) *Calendar:* Courses of varying lengths *Degrees:* certificates *CEO:* Dir. Nancy Chappie
Enroll: 117 (619) 292-9755

TRAVEL AND TRADE CAREER INSTITUTE
1541 Brookhurst St., Ste. 1, Garden Grove 92641 *Type:* Private *Accred.:* 1972/1989 (CCA-ACTTS) *Calendar:* Courses of varying lengths *Degrees:* diplomas *CEO:* Exec. Vice Pres. Karen R. Erickson
(714) 636-2611

TRAVEL AND TRADE CAREER INSTITUTE
3635 Atlantic Ave., Long Beach 90807 *Type:* Private *Accred.:* 1972/1989 (CCA-ACTTS) *Calendar:* Courses of varying lengths *Degrees:* diplomas *CEO:* Pres. Roger Erickson
Enroll: 783 (800) 777-8824

Accredited Institutions California

TRUCK DRIVING ACADEMY
5711 Florin-Perkins Rd., Sacramento 95828 *Type:* Private *Accred.:* 1988 (CCA-ACTTS) *Calendar:* Courses of varying lengths *Degrees:* certificates *CEO:* Dir. Charles J. Grant
(916) 381-2285

BRANCH CAMPUS
5168 N. Blythe Ave., Ste. 102, Fresno, CA 93722 *CEO:* Dir. Shirley Ross
(209) 276-5708

TRUCK MARKETING INSTITUTE
1090 Eugenia Pl., P.O. Box 5000, Carpinteria 93014-5000 *Type:* Private home study *Accred.:* 1968/1989 (NHSC) *Calendar:* Courses of varying lengths *Degrees:* diplomas *CEO:* Dir. Robert Godfrey
(805) 684-4558

UNIFIED SCHOOLS OF AMERICA
461 Arrow Hwy., Azusa 91702 *Type:* Private *Accred.:* 1988 (CCA-ACTTS) *Calendar:* Courses of varying lengths *Degrees:* certificates *CEO:* Dir. Arthur Hillard
(818) 915-7659

ARIZONA INSTITUTE OF ELECTROLYSIS
4000 E. Main St., Ste. A, Mesa, AZ 85205 *CEO:* Dir. Demnise Horvath
(602) 832-8999

UNIFIED SCHOOLS OF AMERICA
302 N. Long Beach Blvd., Compton 90221-2869 *Type:* Private *Accred.:* 1988 (CCA-ACTTS) *Calendar:* Courses of varying lengths *Degrees:* certificates *CEO:* Dir. Robert Hysong
(213) 608-2355

UNIFIED SCHOOLS OF AMERICA
15111 Hawthorne Blvd., Lawndale 90260-2137 *Type:* Private *Accred.:* 1988 (CCA-ACTTS) *Calendar:* Courses of varying lengths *Degrees:* certificates *CEO:* Dir. Murray Cohen
(213) 676-0110

UNIFIED SCHOOLS OF AMERICA
4545 W. Washington Blvd., Los Angeles 90019-1717 *Type:* Private *Accred.:* 1988 (CCA-ACTTS) *Calendar:* Courses of varying lengths *Degrees:* certificates *CEO:* Dir. Alejandra Corrales
(213) 965-1410

UNIFIED SCHOOLS OF AMERICA
130 S. Harbor Blvd., Santa Ana 92704 *Type:* Private *Accred.:* 1988 (CCA-ACTTS) *Calendar:* Courses of varying lengths *Degrees:* certificates *CEO:* Dir. Barbara West
(714) 775-0785

UNIFIED SCHOOLS OF AMERICA
14550 Lanark St., Van Nuys 91402-4915 *Type:* Private *Accred.:* 1988 (CCA-ACTTS) *Calendar:* Courses of varying lengths *Degrees:* certificates *CEO:* Pres. Murray Cohen
(818) 782-0700

UNIFIED SCHOOLS OF AMERICA
12519 E. Washington Blvd., Whittier 90602 *Type:* Private *Accred.:* 1988 (CCA-ACTTS) *Calendar:* Courses of varying lengths *Degrees:* certificates *CEO:* Dir. Barbara West
(213) 907-4300

UNITED HEALTH CAREERS INSTITUTE
600 N. Sierra Way, San Bernardino 92401 *Type:* Private *Calendar:* Sem. plan *Degrees:* certificates, diplomas *Prof. Accred.:* Practical Nursing *CEO:* Dir. Jeanne Thompson
(714) 884-8891

UNITED STATES INTERNATIONAL UNIVERSITY
10455 Pomerado Rd., San Diego 92131 *Type:* Independent liberal arts and professional *Accred.:* 1956/1984 (WASC-Sr. probational) *Calendar:* Qtr. plan *Degrees:* A, B, P, M, D *Prof. Accred.:* Engineering (civil) *CEO:* Acting Pres. Kenneth McLennan *Enroll:* 3086
(619) 271-4300

UNITED STATES NAVAL AMPHIBIOUS SCHOOL
U.S. Dept. of the Navy, Coronado 92155 *Type:* Public (federal) technical *Accred.:* 1979/1989 (SACS-COEI) *Calendar:* Courses

of varying lengths *Degrees:* certificates *CEO:* Commanding Ofcr. Stephen G. Young
Enroll: 10930 (619) 437-2236

UNITED STATES NAVAL CONSTRUCTION TRAINING CENTER
Construction Battalion Ctr., Port Hueneme 93043-5005 *Type:* Public (federal) technical *Accred.:* 1979/1988 (SACS-COEI) *Calendar:* Courses of varying lengths *Degrees:* certificates *CEO:* Commanding Ofcr. J.R. Dunbar
Enroll: 510 (805) 982-5556

UNITED STATES NAVAL POSTGRADUATE SCHOOL
Monterey 93943-5000 *Type:* Public (federal) science and technology; graduate only *Accred.:* 1955/1990 (WASC-Sr.) *Calendar:* Qtr. plan *Degrees:* B, M, D *Prof. Accred.:* Engineering (aerospace, electrical, mechanical), Public Management *CEO:* Supt. Ralph W. West, Jr.
Enroll: 1829 (408) 646-2411

UNITED STATES NAVAL SERVICE SCHOOL COMMAND
Naval Training Ctr., San Diego 92133-3000 *Type:* Public (federal) technical *Accred.:* 1985/1989 (SACS-COEI) *Calendar:* Courses of varying lengths *Degrees:* certificates *CEO:* Commanding Ofcr. J.R. Beinbrink
Enroll: 23344 (619) 524-4857

UNITED STATES NAVAL TECHNICAL TRAINING CENTER
Treasure Island, San Francisco 94130 *Type:* Public (federal) technical *Accred.:* 1987 (SACS-COEI) *Calendar:* Courses of varying lengths *Degrees:* certificates *CEO:* Commanding Ofcr. Patricia M. Spishock
Enroll: 18000 (415) 395-3073

UNITED STATES NAVAL TRANSPORTATION MANAGEMENT SCHOOL
Oakland Army Base, Bldg. 790, Oakland 94625 *Type:* Public (federal) technical *Accred.:* 1986/1991 (SACS-COEI) *Calendar:* Courses of varying lengths *Degrees:* certificates *CEO:* Commanding Ofcr. Samuel J. Major, Jr.
Enroll: 1456 (510) 466-2155

UNITED STATES NAVY COMBAT SYSTEMS TECHNICAL SCHOOLS COMMAND
Mare Island, Vallejo 94592-5050 *Type:* Public (federal) technical *Accred.:* 1986/1990 (SACS-COEI) *Calendar:* Courses of varying lengths *Degrees:* certificates *CEO:* Commanding Ofcr. Harvey Holden, U.S.N.
Enroll: 1200 (707) 554-8550

UNITED STATES TRUCK DRIVER SCHOOL
924 Rialto Ave., Rialto 92376 *Type:* Private *Accred.:* 1988 (CCA-ACTTS) *Calendar:* Courses of varying lengths *Degrees:* certificates *CEO:* Dir. Ray Jarman
(714) 875-8000

UNITED TRAINING INSTITUTE, INC.
9966 Dolores St., Ste. 203, Spring Valley 91977 *Type:* Private home study *Accred.:* 1989 (NHSC) *Calendar:* Course in private *Degrees:* certificates *CEO:* Pres. Lee Schwuchow
(619) 698-9600

UNIVERSITY OF CALIFORNIA, BERKELEY
Berkeley 94720 *Type:* Public (state) *System:* University of California Office of the President *Accred.:* 1949/1990 (WASC-Sr.) *Calendar:* Sem. plan *Degrees:* B, P, M, D *Prof. Accred.:* Architecture (M), Business (B,M), Clinical Psychology, Dietetics (coordinated), Engineering (chemical, civil, computer, electrical, industrial, mechanical, mineral, naval architecture/marine, nuclear), Forestry, Health Services Administration, Journalism, Landscape Architecture (M), Law, Librarianship, Optometry, Planning (city/regional), Psychology Internship, Public Health, School Psychology, Social Work (M) *CEO:* Chanc. Chang-Lin Tien
Enroll: 31123 (510) 642-6000

UNIVERSITY OF CALIFORNIA, DAVIS
Davis 95616 *Type:* Public (state) *System:* University of California Office of the President *Accred.:* 1954/1987 (WASC-Sr.)

Calendar: Qtr. plan *Degrees:* B, P, M, D *Prof. Accred.:* Engineering (aerospace, agricultural, chemical, civil, computer, electrical, mechanical), Landscape Architecture (B), Law, Medical Technology, Medicine, Physician Assisting, Psychology Internship (provisional) *CEO:* Chanc. Theodore L. Hullar
Enroll: 21115   (916) 752-1011

UNIVERSITY OF CALIFORNIA, HASTINGS COLLEGE OF THE LAW
200 McAllister St., San Francisco 94102 *Type:* Public (state) *System:* University of California Office of the President *Calendar:* Sem. plan *Degrees:* P *Prof. Accred.:* Law *CEO:* Dean Frank T. Read
Enroll: 1347   (415) 565-4600

UNIVERSITY OF CALIFORNIA, IRVINE
Irvine 92717 *Type:* Public (state) *System:* University of California Office of the President *Accred.:* 1965/1986 (WASC-Sr.) *Calendar:* Qtr. plan *Degrees:* B, P, M, D *Prof. Accred.:* Business (M), Engineering (civil, electrical, mechanical), Medical Technology, Medicine, Psychology Internship, Theatre *CEO:* Chanc. Jack W. Peltason
Enroll: 16149   (714) 856-6345

UNIVERSITY OF CALIFORNIA, LOS ANGELES
405 Hilgard Ave., Los Angeles 90024 *Type:* Public (state) *System:* University of California Office of the President *Accred.:* 1949/1989 (WASC-Sr.) *Calendar:* Qtr. plan *Degrees:* B, P, M, D *Prof. Accred.:* Architecture (M), Business (M), Clinical Psychology, Combined Prosthodontics, Dance, Dentistry, Engineering (aerospace, chemical, civil, computer, electrical, materials, mechanical), General Dentistry (provisional), General Practice Residency, Health Services Administration, Interior Design, Law, Librarianship, Maxillofacial Prosthodontics, Medicine, Nurse Anesthesia Education, Nursing (B,M), Oral and Maxillofacial Surgery, Orthodontics, Pediatric Dentistry, Periodontics, Planning (urban), Psychology Internship, Radiography, Public Health, Social Work (M) *CEO:* Chanc. Charles E. Young
Enroll: 32092   (213) 825-4321

UNIVERSITY OF CALIFORNIA, RIVERSIDE
Riverside 92502-9879 *Type:* Public (state) *System:* University of California Office of the President *Accred.:* 1956/1988 (WASC-Sr.) *Calendar:* Qtr. plan *Degrees:* B, M, D *CEO:* Chanc. Rosemary Schraer, SJ
Enroll: 7886   (714) 787-1012

UNIVERSITY OF CALIFORNIA, SAN DIEGO
La Jolla 92092 *Type:* Public (state) *System:* University of California Office of the President *Accred.:* 1964/1986 (WASC-Sr.) *Calendar:* Qtr. plan *Degrees:* B, P, M, D *Prof. Accred.:* Clinical Psychology, Computer Science, Engineering (bioengineering, chemical, civil, electrical, mechanical, systems), Medicine, Psychology Internship *CEO:* Chanc. Richard C. Atkinson
Enroll: 16614   (619) 534-2230

UNIVERSITY OF CALIFORNIA, SAN FRANCISCO
Third and Parnassus Aves., San Francisco 94143 *Type:* Public (state) *System:* University of California Office of the President *Accred.:* 1976/1986 (WASC-Sr.) *Calendar:* Qtr. plan *Degrees:* B, P, M, D *Prof. Accred.:* Combined Prosthodontics, Dental Hygiene, Dentistry, Dental Public Health, Dietetics (internship), General Dentistry, Medicine, Nuclear Medicine Technology, Nursing (B,M), Oral and Maxillofacial Surgery, Orthodontics, Pediatric Dentistry (conditional), Periodontics, Pharmacy, Physical Therapy, Psychology Internship *CEO:* Chanc. Julius R. Krevans, M.D.
Enroll: 3657   (415) 476-9000

UNIVERSITY OF CALIFORNIA, SANTA BARBARA
Santa Barbara 93106 *Type:* Public (state) *System:* University of California Office of the President *Accred.:* 1949/1991 (WASC-Sr.) *Calendar:* Qtr. plan *Degrees:* B, M, D *Prof. Accred.:* Audiology, Computer Science, Counseling Psychology, Dance, Engineering (chemical, electrical, mechanical, nuclear), Psychology Internship, Speech-

Language Pathology *CEO:* Chanc. Barbara S. Uehling
Enroll: 17879 (805) 893-2231

UNIVERSITY OF CALIFORNIA, SANTA CRUZ
Santa Cruz 95064 *System:* University of California Office of the President *Accred.:* 1965/1986 (WASC-Sr.) *Calendar:* Qtr. plan *Degrees:* B, M, D *Prof. Accred.:* Engineering (computer) *CEO:* Interim Chanc. Karl S. Piester
Enroll: 9152 (408) 459-0111

UNIVERSITY OF JUDAISM
15600 Mulholland Dr., Los Angeles 90077 *Type:* Independent *Accred.:* 1961/1988 (WASC-Sr.) *Calendar:* Sem. plan *Degrees:* B, M *CEO:* Pres. David L. Lieber
Enroll: 116 (213) 476-9777

UNIVERSITY OF LA VERNE
1950 Third St., La Verne 91750 *Type:* Independent liberal arts and professional *Accred.:* 1955/1991 (WASC-Sr.) *Calendar:* 4-1-4 plan *Degrees:* B, P, M, D *CEO:* Pres. Stephen C. Morgan
Enroll: 4653 (714) 593-3511

UNIVERSITY OF REDLANDS
1200 E. Colton Ave., Redlands 92373-0999 *Type:* Independent liberal arts and professional *Accred.:* 1949/1987 (WASC-Sr.) *Calendar:* 4-1-4 plan *Degrees:* B, M *Prof. Accred.:* Music *CEO:* Pres. James R. Appleton
Enroll: 2947 (714) 793-2121

UNIVERSITY OF SAN DIEGO
Alcala Pike, San Diego 92110 *Type:* Independent (Roman Catholic) liberal arts and professional *Accred.:* 1956/1988 (WASC-Sr.) *Calendar:* 4-1-4 plan *Degrees:* B, P, M, D *Prof. Accred.:* Business (B,M), Law, Nursing (B,M) *CEO:* Pres. Author E. Hughes
Enroll: 5143 (619) 260-4600

UNIVERSITY OF SAN FRANCISCO
2130 Fulton St., Ignatian Hgts., San Francisco 94117-1080 *Type:* Independent (Roman Catholic) liberal arts and professional *Accred.:* 1949/1981 (WASC-Sr.) *Calendar:* Sem. plan *Degrees:* B, P, M, D *Prof. Accred.:* Business (B,M), Computer Science, Law, Nursing (B) *CEO:* Pres. John P. Schlegel, S.J.
Enroll: 6593 (415) 666-6163

UNIVERSITY OF SOUTHERN CALIFORNIA
University Park, Los Angeles 90089-0012 *Type:* Independent liberal arts and professional *Accred.:* 1949/1987 (WASC-Sr.) *Calendar:* Sem. plan *Degrees:* B, P, M, D *Prof. Accred.:* Architecture (B), Business (B,M), Clinical Psychology, Combined Prosthodontics, Computer Science, Dental Hygiene, Dentistry, Endodontics, Engineering (aerospace, chemical, civil, electrical, industrial, mechanical, petroleum), Health Services Administration, Journalism, Law, Medicine, Music, Nursing (B), Occupational Therapy, Oral and Maxillofacial Surgery, Orthodontics, Pediatric Dentistry, Periodontics, Pharmacy, Physical Therapy, Physician Assisting, Planning (regional/urban), Psychology Internship, Public Administration, Social Work (M) *CEO:* Pres. Steven B. Sample
Enroll: 23859 (213) 740-2311

UNIVERSITY OF WEST LOS ANGELES
12201 Washington Pl., Los Angeles 90066 *Type:* Independent professional *Accred.:* 1983/1988 (WASC-Sr.) *Calendar:* Tri. plan *Degrees:* B, P *CEO:* Pres. Bernard S. Jefferson
Enroll: 523 (213) 313-1011

UNIVERSITY OF THE PACIFIC
3601 Pacific Ave., Stockton 95211 *Type:* Independent liberal arts and professional *Accred.:* 1949/1987 (WASC-Sr.) *Calendar:* Sem. plan *Degrees:* B, P, M, D *Prof. Accred.:* Art, Business (B), Computer Science, Dentistry, Engineering (civil, computer, electrical, engineering physics/science, mechanical), General Dentistry (provisional), Law, Music, Orthodontics, Pharmacy, Physical Therapy, Speech-Language Pathology, Teacher Education (e,s,p) *CEO:* Pres. William L. Atchley
Enroll: 5110 (209) 946-2011

Accredited Institutions   **California**

VALLEY COMMERCIAL COLLEGE
910 12th St., Modesto 95354 *Type:* Private business *Accred.:* 1970/1989 (CCA-ACICS) *Calendar:* Courses of varying lengths *Degrees:* certificates, diplomas *CEO:* Pres./C.E.O. Gregory L. Martin
Enroll: 709   (209) 578-0616

VAN NUYS COLLEGE OF BUSINESS
8041 Van Nuys Blvd., Van Nuys 91402 *Type:* Private business *Accred.:* 1972/1984 (CCA-ACICS) *Calendar:* Courses of varying lengths *Degrees:* diplomas *CEO:* Educ. Dir. Linda Wollaston
Enroll: 688   (818) 782-0550

VENTURA COLLEGE
4667 Telegraph Rd., Ventura 93003 *Type:* Public (district) junior *System:* Ventura County Community College District *Accred.:* 1952/1990 (WASC-Jr.) *Calendar:* Sem. plan *Degrees:* A *CEO:* Pres. Robert W. Long
Enroll: 12350   (805) 642-3211

VICTOR VALLEY COLLEGE
18422 Bear Valley Rd., Victorville 92392 *Type:* Public (district) junior *System:* Victor Valley Community College District *Accred.:* 1963/1987 (WASC-Jr.) *Calendar:* Sem. plan *Degrees:* A *Prof. Accred.:* Nursing (A), Respiratory Therapy *CEO:* Pres. Ed Gould
Enroll: 5859   (619) 245-4271

VISTA COLLEGE
2020 Milvia St., Berkeley 94704 *Type:* Public (district) junior *System:* Peralta Community College District *Accred.:* 1981/1991 (WASC-Jr.) *Calendar:* Sem. plan *Degrees:* A *CEO:* Pres. Barbara A. Beno
Enroll: 4680   (510) 841-8431

WATTERSON COLLEGE
1165 E. Colorado Blvd., Pasadena 91106 *Type:* Private business *Accred.:* 1953/1990 (CCA-ACICS) *Calendar:* Qtr. plan *Degrees:* certificates *CEO:* Dir. Robert M. Toren
Enroll: 1141   (818) 449-3990

WATTERSON COLLEGE
5121 Van Nuys Blvd., Sherman Oaks 91403 *Type:* Private business *Accred.:* 1966/1991 (CCA-ACICS) *Calendar:* Qtr. plan *Degrees:* certificates *CEO:* Dir. Kevin Kurth
Enroll: 1097   (818) 990-4070

BRANCH CAMPUS
1835 S. La Cienaga Blvd., Los Angeles, CA 90035 *CEO:* Dir. Joyce Saul
                             (213) 299-2966

WATTERSON COLLEGE
1422 S. Azusa Ave., West Covina 91791 *Type:* Private business *Accred.:* 1988 (CCA-ACICS) *Calendar:* Qtr. plan *Degrees:* certificates *CEO:* Dir. John Walker
Enroll: 1579   (818) 919-8701

WATTERSON COLLEGE PACIFIC
41 E. 12th St., National City 92050 *Type:* Private business *Accred.:* 1988 (CCA-ACICS) *Calendar:* Qtr. plan *Degrees:* certificates *CEO:* Pres. Marga Dussman
Enroll: 426   (619) 474-8017

WATTERSON COLLEGE PACIFIC
815 N. Oxnard Blvd., Oxnard 93030 *Type:* Private business *Accred.:* 1979/1990 (CCA-ACICS) *Calendar:* Courses of varying lengths *Degrees:* certificates *CEO:* Dir. Julie Martin
Enroll: 810   (805) 656-5566

BRANCH CAMPUS
336 Rancheros Dr., San Marcos, CA 92069 *CEO:* Dir. Kevin Michie
                             (619) 471-9100

WEBSTER CAREER COLLEGE
222 S. Hill St., Ste. 400, Los Angeles 90012 *Type:* Private business *Accred.:* 1969/1983 (CCA-ACICS) *Calendar:* Qtr. plan *Degrees:* diplomas *CEO:* Pres. Glenn Blackwell
Enroll: 519   (213) 625-1201

WEST COAST CHRISTIAN JUNIOR COLLEGE
6901 N. Maple Ave., Fresno 93710 *Type:* Private (Church of God) junior and professional *Accred.:* 1976/1986 (AABC); 1976/1991 (WASC-Jr. probational) *Calendar:*

Sem. plan *Degrees:* B *CEO:* Pres. H.B. Thompson, Jr.
Enroll: 144 (209) 299-7204

WEST COAST UNIVERSITY
440 S. Shatto Pl., Los Angeles 90020 *Type:* Independent *Accred.:* 1963/1982 (WASC-Sr.) *Calendar:* Tri. plan *Degrees:* B, M *CEO:* Pres. Robert M.L. Baker, Jr.
Enroll: 1225 (213) 487-4433

WEST HILLS COMMUNITY COLLEGE
300 Cherry La., Coalinga 93210 *Type:* Public (district) junior *System:* West Hills Community College District *Accred.:* 1952/1988 (WASC-Jr.) *Calendar:* Sem. plan *Degrees:* A *CEO:* Pres. Stan Arterberry
Enroll: 1283 (209) 935-0801

WEST LOS ANGELES COLLEGE
4800 Freshman Dr., Culver City 90230 *Type:* Public (district) junior *System:* Los Angeles Community College District *Accred.:* 1971/1989 (WASC-Jr.) *Calendar:* Sem. plan *Degrees:* A *Prof. Accred.:* Dental Hygiene *CEO:* Pres. Evelyn C. Wong
Enroll: 9500 (310) 836-7110

WEST VALLEY COLLEGE
14000 Fruitvale Ave., Saratoga 95070 *Type:* Public (district) junior *System:* West Valley-Mission Community College District *Accred.:* 1966/1990 (WASC-Jr.) *Calendar:* Sem. plan *Degrees:* A *Prof. Accred.:* Interior Design, Medical Assisting (AMA) *CEO:* Pres. Leo Chavez
Enroll: 14407 (408) 867-2200

WESTECH COLLEGE
500 W. Mission Blvd., Pomona 91766 *Type:* Private *Accred.:* 1991 (CCA-ACTTS) *Calendar:* Courses of varying lengths *Degrees:* certificates *CEO:* Exec. Dir. Barry Maleki
(714) 622-6486

WESTERN CAREER COLLEGE
4000 El Camino Ave., Sacramento 95821 *Type:* Private *Accred.:* 1970/1987 (CCA-ACTTS) *Calendar:* Courses of varying lengths *Degrees:* diplomas *Prof. Accred.:* Medical Assisting *CEO:* Dir. Richard G. Nathanson
Enroll: 644 (916) 486-0533

WESTERN CAREER COLLEGE
170 Bay Fair Mall, San Leandro 94578-3711 *Type:* Private *Accred.:* 1986 (CCA-ACTTS) *Calendar:* Courses of varying lengths *Degrees:* diplomas *Prof. Accred.:* Medical Assisting *CEO:* Dir. Ann Tye
Enroll: 459 (415) 278-3888

WESTERN CAREER INSTITUTE
2029 N. Keith St., Los Angeles 90031 *Type:* Private *Accred.:* 1988 (CCA-ACTTS) *Calendar:* Courses of varying lengths *Degrees:* certificates *CEO:* Dir. John R. Phalen
(213) 227-9001

WESTERN STATE UNIVERSITY COLLEGE OF LAW OF ORANGE COUNTY
1111 N. State College Blvd., Fullerton 92631 *Type:* Private *Accred.:* 1976/1990 (WASC-Sr.) *Calendar:* Sem. plan *Degrees:* B, P *CEO:* Pres. John C. Monks
Enroll: 996 (714) 738-1000

WESTERN STATE UNIVERSITY COLLEGE OF LAW OF SAN DIEGO
2121 San Diego Ave., San Diego 92110 *Type:* Private *Accred.:* 1976/1990 (WASC-Sr.) *Calendar:* Sem. plan *Degrees:* B, P *CEO:* Pres. John C. Monks
Enroll: 368 (619) 297-9700

WESTERN TECHNICAL COLLEGE
5400 Van Nuys Blvd., Van Nuys 91401 *Type:* Private *Accred.:* 1968/1985 (CCA-ACTTS) *Calendar:* Courses of varying lengths *Degrees:* certificates, diplomas *CEO:* Dir. Yekta Badie
Enroll: 1058 (818) 783-6520

WESTERN TRUCK SCHOOL
4565 N. Golden State Blvd., Fresno 93711 *Type:* Private *Accred.:* 1988 (CCA-ACTTS) *Calendar:* Courses of varying lengths *Degrees:* certificates *CEO:* Mgr. Garland Alcorn
(209) 276-1220

Accredited Institutions   California

WESTERN TRUCK SCHOOL
2101 Carden St., San Leandro 94577 *Type:* Private *Accred.:* 1987 (CCA-ACTTS) *Calendar:* Courses of varying lengths *Degrees:* certificates *CEO:* Pres. Everett G. Nord
(415) 430-1120

WESTERN TRUCK SCHOOL
4521 W. Capitol Ave., West Sacramento 95691 *Type:* Private *Accred.:* 1980/1987 (CCA-ACTTS) *Calendar:* Courses of varying lengths *Degrees:* certificates *CEO:* Pres. Everett G. Nord
Enroll: 268 (916) 372-6500

BRANCH CAMPUS
3405 S. 40th St., Phoenix, AZ 85040 *CEO:* Dir. Bill Williams
(602) 437-5303

BRANCH CAMPUS
1100 E. Fifth St., Oxnard, CA 93030 *CEO:* Dir. Dale Shubert
(805) 486-0960

BRANCH CAMPUS
4612 E. Nunes Rd., Turlock, CA 95380 *CEO:* Dir. Mike Montgomery
(209) 667-7002

WESTLAND COLLEGE
300 S. Hobart Blvd., Los Angeles 90020 *Type:* Private *Accred.:* 1988 (CCA-ACTTS) *Calendar:* Courses of varying lengths *Degrees:* certificates *CEO:* Dir. Eric Hyde
(213) 385-2600

WESTMINSTER THEOLOGICAL SEMINARY IN CALIFORNIA
1725 Bear Valley Pkwy., Escondido 92027 *Type:* Independent (Presbyterian) professional *Accred.:* 1984 (WASC-Sr. probational) *Calendar:* 1-4-1-4 plan *Degrees:* P, M *CEO:* Pres. Robert G. den Dulk
Enroll: 104 (619) 480-8474

WESTMONT COLLEGE
955 La Paz Rd., Santa Barbara 93108 *Type:* Independent liberal arts *Accred.:* 1957/1989 (WASC-Sr.) *Calendar:* Sem. plan *Degrees:* B *CEO:* Pres. David K. Winter
Enroll: 1254 (805) 565-6000

WHITTIER COLLEGE
P.O. Box 634, Whittier 90608 *Type:* Independent liberal arts *Accred.:* 1949/1990 (WASC-Sr.) *Calendar:* 4-1-4 modular curriculum *Degrees:* B, P, M *Prof. Accred.:* Law, Social Work (B) *CEO:* Pres. James L. Ash, Jr.
Enroll: 1126 (213) 693-0771

WILSHIRE COMPUTER COLLEGE
12912 Brookhurst St., Garden Grove 92640 *Type:* Private business *Accred.:* 1989 (CCA-ACICS) *Calendar:* Courses of varying lengths *Degrees:* certificates *CEO:* Dir. Alan Sleiman
Enroll: 490 (714) 536-2800

BRANCH CAMPUS
12901 Ramona Blvd., Stes. A-D, Irwindale, CA 91706 *CEO:* Dir. Al Carpenter
(818) 338-0111

BRANCH CAMPUS
7012 Greenleaf Ave., Whittier, CA 90601 *CEO:* Dir. Wambi Cook
(213) 945-9535

WILSHIRE COMPUTER COLLEGE
3000 Wilshire Blvd., Ste. B, Los Angeles 90010 *Type:* Private business *Accred.:* 1988 (CCA-ACICS) *Calendar:* Courses of varying lengths *Degrees:* certificates *CEO:* Pres. Lena Krill
Enroll: 1160 (213) 480-4806

WOODBURY UNIVERSITY
7500 Glenoaks Blvd., P.O. Box 7846, Burbank 91510-7846 *Type:* Independent professional *Accred.:* 1961/1991 (WASC-Sr.) *Calendar:* Qtr. plan *Degrees:* B, M *Prof. Accred.:* Architecture (B-candidate) *CEO:* Pres. Paul E. Sago
Enroll: 838 (818) 767-0888

WORLD COLLEGE WEST
101 S. San Antonio Rd., Petaluma 94952 *Type:* Independent liberal arts *Accred.:* 1981/1984 (WASC-Sr.) *Calendar:* Qtr. plan *Degrees:* B *CEO:* Pres. Douglas G. Trout
Enroll: 108 (707) 765-4500

California

WRIGHT INSTITUTE
2728 Durant Ave., Berkeley 94704 *Type:* Independent professional *Accred.:* 1977/1987 (WASC-Sr.) *Calendar:* Qtr. plan *Degrees:* D *Prof. Accred.:* Clinical Psychology (provisional) *CEO:* Pres. Peter Dybwad
Enroll: 178 (510) 841-9230

YESHIVA OHR ELCHONON-CHABAD/WEST COAST TALMUDIC SEMINARY
7215 Waring Ave., Los Angeles 90046 *Type:* Private professional *Accred.:* 1983/1989 (AARTS) *Calendar:* Sem. plan *Degrees:* B *CEO:* Pres. D. Weiss
Enroll: 50 (213) 937-3763

YUBA COLLEGE
2088 N. Beale Rd., Marysville 95901 *Type:* Public (district) junior *System:* Yuba Community College District *Accred.:* 1952/1989 (WASC-Jr.) *Calendar:* Sem. plan *Degrees:* A *Prof. Accred.:* Animal Health Technology, Radiography *CEO:* Pres. Patricia L. Wirth
Enroll: 12262 (916) 741-6700

COLORADO

ACADEMY OF FLORAL DESIGN
837 Acoma St., Denver 80204 *Type:* Private business *Accred.:* 1989 (CCA-ACICS) *Calendar:* Courses of varying lengths *Degrees:* certificates *CEO:* Pres. Noel S. Valnes
Enroll: 62   (303) 623-8855

ADAMS STATE COLLEGE
Alamosa 81102 *Type:* Public liberal arts and teachers *System:* State Colleges in Colorado *Accred.:* 1950/1987 (NCA) *Calendar:* Sem. plan *Degrees:* A, B, M *Prof. Accred.:* Music, Teacher Education (e,s,p) *CEO:* Pres. William Fulkerson, Jr.
Enroll: 2215   (719) 589-7341

AIMS COMMUNITY COLLEGE
5401 W. 20th St., P.O. Box 69, Greeley 80632 *Type:* Public (district) junior *System:* Colorado Community College and Occupational Education System *Accred.:* 1977/1989 (NCA) *Calendar:* Qtr. plan *Degrees:* A, certificates *Prof. Accred.:* Radiography *CEO:* Pres. George R. Conger
Enroll: 3082   (303) 330-8008

AMERICAN DIESEL AND AUTOMOTIVE COLLEGE
1002 S. Jason St., Denver 80223-2868 *Type:* Private *Accred.:* 1981/1987 (CCA-ACTTS) *Calendar:* Qtr. plan *Degrees:* diplomas *CEO:* Pres. Mel Jones
Enroll: 113   (303) 778-6772

ARAPAHOE COMMUNITY COLLEGE
2500 W. College Dr., P.O. Box 9002, Littleton 80160-9002 *Type:* Public (state) junior *System:* Colorado Community College and Occupational Education System *Accred.:* 1970/1987 (NCA) *Calendar:* Sem. plan *Degrees:* A, certificates *Prof. Accred.:* Medical Laboratory Technology (AMA), Medical Record Technology, Physical Therapy Assisting *CEO:* Pres. James F. Weber
Enroll: 3677   (303) 794-1550

BARNES BUSINESS COLLEGE
150 N. Sheridan Blvd., Denver 80226 *Type:* Private *Accred.:* 1953/1987 (CCA-ACICS) *Calendar:* Qtr. plan *Degrees:* certificates, diplomas *CEO:* Dir. Shirley C. Lowery
Enroll: 2747   (303) 922-8454

BEL-REA INSTITUTE OF ANIMAL TECHNOLOGY
1681 S. Dayton St., Denver 80231 *Type:* Private *Accred.:* 1975/1987 (CCA-ACTTS) *Calendar:* Qtr. plan *Degrees:* A *Prof. Accred.:* Animal Technology *CEO:* Dir. Marc Schapiro
Enroll: 234   (303) 751-8700

BETH-EL COLLEGE OF NURSING
10 N. Farragut Ave., Colorado Springs 80909 *Type:* Private professional *Accred.:* 1988 (NCA) *Calendar:* Sem. plan. *Degrees:* B *Prof. Accred.:* Nursing (B) *CEO:* Dean Carole Schaffstall, Ph.D.
Enroll: 117   (719) 475-5170

BLAIR JUNIOR COLLEGE
828 Wooten Rd., Colorado Springs 80915 *Type:* Private junior *Accred.:* 1953/1988 (CCA-ACICS) *Calendar:* Qtr. plan *Degrees:* A *CEO:* Dir. Tara B. Phillips
Enroll: 1704   (719) 574-1082

BOULDER SCHOOL OF MASSAGE THERAPY
3285 30th St., Boulder 80301-1451 *Type:* Private *Accred.:* 1991 (CCA-ACTTS) *Calendar:* Courses of varying lengths *Degrees:* certificates *CEO:* Dir. Lorraine M. Zinn
    (303) 443-5131

BOULDER VALLEY AREA VOCATIONAL-TECHNICAL CENTER
6600 E. Arapahoe Ave., Boulder 80303 *Type:* Private *Calendar:* Courses of varying lengths *Degrees:* certificates *Prof. Accred.:* Medical Assisting (AMA) *CEO:* Exec. Dir. Lonnie M. Hart, Ph.D.
Enroll: 36   (303) 447-5247

CDI CAREER DEVELOPMENT INSTITUTE
720 S. Colorado Blvd., Denver 80222 *Type:* Private *Accred.:* 1984 (CCA-ACTTS) *Cal-

Colorado

endar: Courses of varying lengths *Degrees:* certificates *CEO:* Dir. Kathy Metcalf
Enroll: 115   (303) 691-9756

CAPITOL CITY BARBER COLLEGE
1523 S. Nevada Ave., Colorado Springs 80906 *Type:* Private *Accred.:* 1985 (CCA-ACTTS) *Calendar:* Courses of varying lengths *Degrees:* certificates *CEO:* Dir. Allen Hossfeld
Enroll: 34   (719) 633-2400

CAPITOL CITY BARBER COLLEGE
1631 S. Prairie Ave., Pueblo 81005 *Type:* Private *Accred.:* 1985 (CCA-ACTTS) *Calendar:* Courses of varying lengths *Degrees:* certificates *CEO:* Dir. Julie Herrem
Enroll: 48   (719) 564-3004

COLORADO AERO TECH
10851 W. 120th Ave., Broomfield 80020 *Type:* Private *Accred.:* 1972/1987 (CCA-ACTTS) *Calendar:* Courses of varying lengths *Degrees:* certificates *CEO:* Dir. William C. Bottoms
Enroll: 1623   (303) 466-1714

COLORADO CHRISTIAN UNIVERSITY
180 S. Garrison St., Lakewood 80226 *Type:* Private *Accred.:* 1974/1984 (AABC); 1981/1985 (NCA) *Calendar:* Sem. plan *Degrees:* A, B, M, certificates, diplomas *CEO:* Pres. Joe L. Wall
Enroll: 908   (303) 238-5386

COLORADO COLLEGE
Colorado Springs 80903 *Type:* Private liberal arts *Accred.:* 1915/1989 (NCA) *Calendar:* Sem. plan *Degrees:* B, M *CEO:* Acting Pres. Thomas E. Cronin
Enroll: 1956   (719) 389-6000

COLORADO INSTITUTE OF ART
200 E. Ninth Ave., Denver 80203 *Type:* Private *Accred.:* 1977/1988 (CCA-ACTTS) *Calendar:* Qtr. plan *Degrees:* A, diplomas *CEO:* Pres. Cheryl Murphy
Enroll: 1100   (303) 837-0825

COLORADO MOUNTAIN COLLEGE
215 9th St., Glenwood Springs 81602 *Type:* Public (district) *System:* Colorado Community College and Occupational Education System *Accred.:* 1974/1985 (NCA) *Calendar:* Qtr. plan *Degrees:* A, certificates *Prof. Accred.:* Veterinary Technology *CEO:* Pres. Dennis Mayer
Enroll: 1224   (303) 945-8691

EAST CAMPUS
Leadville, CO 80461 *CEO:* Dean Joe D. Forrester
    (719) 486-2015

WEST CAMPUS
Glenwood Springs, CO 81601 *CEO:* Dean David Beyer
    (303) 945-7481

COLORADO NORTHWESTERN COMMUNITY COLLEGE
500 Kennedy Dr., Rangely 81648 *Type:* Public (district) junior *System:* Colorado Community College and Occupational Education System *Accred.:* 1976/1986 (NCA) *Calendar:* Sem. plan *Degrees:* A, certificates *Prof. Accred.:* Dental Hygiene *CEO:* Pres. Aubrey Holderness
Enroll: 322   (303) 675-2261

COLORADO SCHOOL OF DOG GROOMING
95 S. Wadsworth Blvd., Lakewood 80215 *Type:* Private *Accred.:* 1985 (CCA-ACTTS) *Calendar:* Courses of varying lengths *Degrees:* certificates *CEO:* Dir. Madeleine Athanasiou
Enroll: 68   (303) 234-0401

COLORADO SCHOOL OF MINES
1500 Illinois St., Golden 80401 *Type:* Public (state) technological *Accred.:* 1929/1983 (NCA) *Calendar:* Sem. plan *Degrees:* B, M, D *Prof. Accred.:* Engineering (chemical, engineering physics/science, general, geological/geophysical, metallurgical, mining, petroleum) *CEO:* Pres. George S. Ansell
Enroll: 2361   (303) 273-3280

Colorado

COLORADO SCHOOL OF TRADES
1575 Hoyt St., Lakewood 80215 *Type:* Private *Accred.:* 1973/1985 (CCA-ACTTS) *Calendar:* Courses of varying lengths *Degrees:* certificates *CEO:* Dir. Robert Martin
Enroll: 310 (303) 233-4697

COLORADO SCHOOL OF TRAVEL
608 Garrison St., Unit G, Lakewood 80215-5881 *Type:* Private *Accred.:* 1991 (CCA-ACTTS) *Calendar:* Courses of varying lengths *Degrees:* certificates *CEO:* Pres. Paula E. Wagner
(303) 233-8654

COLORADO STATE UNIVERSITY
Fort Collins 80523 *Type:* Public (state) *System:* Colorado State University System *Accred.:* 1925/1984 (NCA) *Calendar:* Sem. plan *Degrees:* B, M, D *Prof. Accred.:* Audiology, Business (B,M), Construction Management, Counseling Psychology, Engineering (agricultural, chemical, civil, electrical, engineering physics/science, mechanical), Forestry, Journalism, Landscape Architecture (B), Medical Illustration, Music, Occupational Therapy, Psychology Internship, Recreation Resources, Social Work (B,M), Speech-Language Pathology, Teacher Education (s,p) *CEO:* Pres. Albert C. Yates
Enroll: 20795 (303) 491-6211

COLORADO TECHNICAL COLLEGE
4435 N. Chestnut St., Colorado Springs 80907 *Type:* Private *Accred.:* 1980/1991 (NCA) *Calendar:* Qtr. plan *Degrees:* A, B, M, certificates *Prof. Accred.:* Engineering Technology (bioengineering, electrical) *CEO:* Pres. David O'Donnell
Enroll: 975 (719) 598-0200

COMMUNITY COLLEGE OF AURORA
16000 E. Centretech Pkwy., Aurora 80011 *Type:* Public (district) junior *System:* Colorado Community College and Occupational Education System *Accred.:* 1988 (NCA) *Calendar:* Sem. plan *Degrees:* A, certificates *CEO:* Pres. Larry D. Carter
Enroll: 1798 (303) 360-4700

COMMUNITY COLLEGE OF DENVER
1111 W. Colfax Ave., Denver 80204 *Type:* Public (district) junior *System:* Colorado Community College and Occupational Education System *Accred.:* 1975/1988 (NCA) *Calendar:* Qtr. plan *Degrees:* A, certificates *Prof. Accred.:* Nuclear Medicine Technology, Radiation Therapy Technology, Radiography, Surgical Technology *CEO:* Pres. Byron N. McClenney
Enroll: 3174 (303) 556-2411

CONCORDE CAREER INSTITUTE
770 Grant St., Denver 80203-3517 *Type:* Private *Accred.:* 1991 (CCA-ACTTS) *Calendar:* Courses of varying lengths *Degrees:* certificates *CEO:* Dir. Richard K. Shepard
(303) 861-1151

DENVER ACADEMY OF COURT REPORTING
1000 Speer Blvd., Denver 80204 *Type:* Private business *Accred.:* 1982/1987 (CCA-ACICS) *Calendar:* Qtr. plan *Degrees:* certificates, diplomas *CEO:* Dir. Charles W. Jarstfer
Enroll: 325 (303) 629-1291

DENVER AUTOMOTIVE AND DIESEL COLLEGE
405 S. Platte River Dr., Denver 80223 *Type:* Private *Accred.:* 1968/1988 (CCA-ACTTS) *Calendar:* Courses of varying lengths *Degrees:* diplomas *CEO:* Dir. Paul G. Hoffman
Enroll: 706 (303) 347-3232

DENVER BUSINESS COLLEGE
7350 N. Broadway, Denver 80221 *Type:* Private business *Accred.:* 1986 (CCA-ACICS) *Calendar:* Qtr. plan *Degrees:* diplomas *CEO:* Pres. William E. Winger
Enroll: 623 (303) 426-1000

BRANCH CAMPUS
1731 W. Baseline Rd., Ste. A-109, Mesa, AZ 85202 *CEO:* Dir. Dayna P. Hughes
(602) 834-1000

BRANCH CAMPUS
1916 Young St., Ste. 101, Honolulu, HI 96826 *CEO:* Dir. John Rybczyk
(808) 942-1000

Colorado

BRANCH CAMPUS
2520 Fifth Ave., S., Billings, MT 59102
CEO: Dir. Ray L. Mace
(406) 256-1000

DENVER CONSERVATIVE BAPTIST SEMINARY
P.O. Box 10000, Denver 80210 *Type:* Private (Conservative Baptist) professional; graduate only *Accred.:* 1970/1981 (ATS); 1972/1982 (NCA) *Calendar:* Qtr. plan *Degrees:* P, M, D *CEO:* Pres. Haddon W. Robinson
Enroll: 285 (303) 761-2482

DENVER INSTITUTE OF TECHNOLOGY
The Educational Plaza, 7350 N. Broadway, Denver 80221 *Type:* Private *Accred.:* 1968/1985 (CCA-ACTTS) *Calendar:* Qtr. plan *Degrees:* A *CEO:* Pres. Kirk Riedinger
Enroll: 1157 (303) 426-1808

DENVER PARALEGAL INSTITUTE
1401 19th St., Denver 80202 *Type:* Private *Accred.:* 1979/1985 (CCA-ACTTS) *Calendar:* Courses of varying lengths *Degrees:* certificates *CEO:* Dir. Betsy O'Neil
Enroll: 388 (800) 848-0550

DENVER TECHNICAL COLLEGE
925 South Niagara St., Denver 80224 *Type:* Private *Accred.:* 1979/1988 (CCA-ACTTS) *Calendar:* Courses of varying lengths *Degrees:* A, certificates *Prof. Accred.:* Medical Assisting *CEO:* Pres. Donald Richardson
Enroll: 1262 (303) 329-3000

BRANCH CAMPUS
225 S. Union Blvd., Colorado Springs, CO 80910 *Prof. Accred.:* Medical Assisting *CEO:* Dean Karen McGrath
(303) 632-3000

EMILY GRIFFITH OPPORTUNITY SCHOOL
1250 Welton St., Denver 80204 *Type:* Private *Calendar:* Courses of varying lengths *Degrees:* certificates *Prof. Accred.:* Dental Assisting, Medical Assisting (AMA) *CEO:* Prin. Mary Ann Parthum, Ph.D.
(303) 572-8218

EMPIRE BUSINESS COLLEGE
1609 Oak Ridge Dr., No. 104, Fort Collins 80525-5563 *Type:* Private *Accred.:* 1991 (CCA-ACTTS) *Calendar:* Courses of varying lengths *Degrees:* certificates *CEO:* Pres. Douglas Dodds
(303) 229-9926

EXECUTIVE SECURITY INTERNATIONAL, LTD.
605 W. Main St., Ste. 103, Aspen 81611 *Type:* Private home study *Accred.:* 1988 (NHSC) *Calendar:* Courses of varying lengths *Degrees:* certificates *CEO:* Pres. Robert Duggan
(303) 920-2323

FORT LEWIS COLLEGE
Durango 81301 *Type:* Public (state) liberal arts *System:* Colorado State University System *Accred.:* 1958/1986 (NCA) *Calendar:* Tri. plan *Degrees:* A, B *Prof. Accred.:* Business (B), Music, Teacher Education (e,s) *CEO:* Pres. Joel M. Jones
Enroll: 4001 (303) 247-7100

FRONT RANGE COMMUNITY COLLEGE
3645 W. 112th Ave., Westminster 80030 *Type:* Public (district) junior *System:* Colorado Community College and Occupational Education System *Accred.:* 1975/1988 (NCA) *Calendar:* Qtr. plan *Degrees:* A, certificates *Prof. Accred.:* Dental Assisting, Respiratory Therapy *CEO:* Pres. Thomas Gonzales
Enroll: 3836 (303) 466-8811

HERITAGE COLLEGE OF HEALTH CAREERS
12 Lakeside La., Denver 80212-7413 *Type:* Private *Accred.:* 1991 (CCA-ACTTS) *Calendar:* Courses of varying lengths *Degrees:* certificates *CEO:* Dir. Richard Herold
(303) 477-7240

ITT TECHNICAL INSTITUTE
2121 S. Blackhawk St., Aurora 80014 *Type:* Private *Accred.:* 1985 (CCA-ACTTS) *Calendar:* Courses of varying lengths *Degrees:* certificates *CEO:* Dir. Coy Ritchie
Enroll: 536 (303) 695-1913

Accredited Institutions   **Colorado**

ILIFF SCHOOL OF THEOLOGY
2201 S. University Blvd., Denver 80210 *Type:* Private (United Methodist) professional; graduate only *Accred.:* 1938/1987 (ATS); 1973/1988 (NCA) *Calendar:* Qtr. plan *Degrees:* P, M, D *CEO:* Pres. Donald E. Messer
Enroll: 320   (303) 744-1287

INTERIOR DESIGN INSTITUTE OF DENVER
1401 Blake St., Denver 80202 *Type:* Private professional *Calendar:* Sem. plan *Degrees:* B *Prof. Accred.:* Interior Design *CEO:* Pres. Edward A. Jensen
                      (303) 893-3002

INTERMOUNTAIN COLLEGE
3754 E. LaSalle St., Colorado Springs 80909 *Type:* Private *Accred.:* 1991 (CCA-ACTTS) *Calendar:* Courses of varying lengths *Degrees:* certificates *CEO:* Dir. Peter Schlosser
                      (719) 574-8777

INTERMOUNTAIN COLLEGE
3100 S. Sheridan Blvd., Denver 80227-5528 *Type:* Private *Accred.:* 1991 (CCA-ACTTS) *Calendar:* Courses of varying lengths *Degrees:* certificates *CEO:* Dir. Peter Schlosser
                      (303) 935-2266

LAMAR COMMUNITY COLLEGE
2401 S. Main St., Lamar 81052 *Type:* Public (district) junior *System:* Colorado Community College and Occupational Education System *Accred.:* 1976/1987 (NCA) *Calendar:* Qtr. plan *Degrees:* A, certificates *CEO:* Pres. Marvin E. Lane
Enroll: 650   (719) 336-2248

MEDICAL CAREERS TRAINING CENTER
4020 S. College Ave., Fort Collins 80524 *Type:* Private *Calendar:* Courses of varying lengths *Degrees:* certificates *Prof. Accred.:* Health Services Administration *CEO:* Pres. Carolyn Norrgard
                      (303) 223-2669

MESA STATE COLLEGE
P.O. Box 2647, Grand Junction 81502 *Type:* Public (state) *System:* State Colleges in Colorado *Accred.:* 1957/1989 (NCA) *Calendar:* Sem. plan *Degrees:* A, B, certificates *Prof. Accred.:* Nursing (A,B), Radiography *CEO:* Pres. Raymond N. Kieft
Enroll: 1742   (303) 248-1498

METROPOLITAN STATE COLLEGE OF DENVER
1006 11th St., P.O. Box 173362, Denver 80217-3362 *Type:* Public liberal arts *System:* State Colleges in Colorado *Accred.:* 1971/1987 (NCA) *Calendar:* Sem. plan *Degrees:* B, certificates *Prof. Accred.:* Engineering Technology (civil/construction, electrical, mechanical), Leisure Studies, Music, Nursing (B), Teacher Education (e,s) *CEO:* Pres. Thomas B. Brewer
Enroll: 11571   (303) 556-3022

MILE HI COLLEGE
6464 W. 14th Ave., Lakewood 80214 *Type:* Private business *Accred.:* 1977/1989 (CCA-ACICS) *Calendar:* Qtr. plan *Degrees:* diplomas *CEO:* Dir. Elizabeth J. Midyett
Enroll: 419   (303) 233-7973

MORGAN COMMUNITY COLLEGE
17800 Rd. 20, Fort Morgan 80701 *Type:* Public (district) junior *System:* Colorado Community College and Occupational Education System *Accred.:* 1980/1989 (NCA) *Calendar:* Qtr. plan *Degrees:* A, certificates *Prof. Accred.:* Physical Therapy Assisting *CEO:* Pres. Richard Bond
Enroll: 424   (303) 867-3081

THE NAROPA INSTITUTE
2130 Arapahoe Ave., Boulder 80302 *Type:* Private *Accred.:* 1986/1990 (NCA) *Calendar:* Sem. plan *Degrees:* B, M, certificates *CEO:* Pres. Barbara Dilley
Enroll: 269   (303) 444-0202

NATIONAL TECHNOLOGICAL UNIVERSITY
700 Centre Ave., Fort Collins 80526 *Type:* Private graduate only *Accred.:* 1987 (NCA) *Calendar:* Sem. plan *Degrees:* M *CEO:* Pres. Lionel Baldwin
Enroll: 1679   (303) 484-1184

NAZARENE BIBLE COLLEGE
P.O. Box 15749, Colorado Springs 80935 *Type:* Private (Nazarene) junior *Accred.:*

Colorado

1976/1986 (AABC) *Calendar:* Qtr. plan *Degrees:* A, certificates, diplomas *CEO:* Pres. Jerry D. Lambert
Enroll: 392 (719) 596-5110

BRANCH CAMPUS
2315 Markham Rd., S.W., Albuquerque, NM 87105 *CEO:* Dir. R.T. Bolerjack
Enroll: 46 (505) 877-0240

NORTHEASTERN JUNIOR COLLEGE
Sterling 80751 *Type:* Public junior *System:* Colorado Community College and Occupational Education System *Accred.:* 1964/1989 (NCA) *Calendar:* Qtr. plan *Degrees:* A, certificates *CEO:* Pres. Henry M. Milander
Enroll: 1454 (303) 522-6600

OTERO JUNIOR COLLEGE
La Junta 81050 *Type:* Public junior *System:* Colorado Community College and Occupational Education System *Accred.:* 1967/1987 (NCA) *Calendar:* Qtr. plan *Degrees:* A, certificates *Prof. Accred.:* Nursing (A) *CEO:* Pres. William L. McDivitt
Enroll: 660 (719) 384-8721

PPI HEALTH CAREERS SCHOOL
2345 N. Academy Blvd., Colorado Springs 80909 *Type:* Private *Calendar:* Courses of varying lengths *Degrees:* diplomas *Prof. Accred.:* Health Education, Medical Assisting, Medical Laboratory Technology *CEO:* Pres. Thomas J. Twardowski
(719) 596-7400

PARKS JUNIOR COLLEGE
9065 Grant St., Denver 80229 *Type:* Private business *Accred.:* 1962/1991 (CCA-ACICS) *Calendar:* Qtr. plan *Degrees:* A, certificates, diplomas *Prof. Accred.:* Medical Assisting (AMA) *CEO:* Pres. Linda S. Bowman
Enroll: 2165 (303) 457-2757

BRANCH CAMPUS
6 Abilene St., Aurora, CO 80011 *CEO:* Dir. Patricia Hardy
(303) 367-2757

PIKES PEAK COMMUNITY COLLEGE
5675 S. Academy Blvd., Colorado Springs 80906 *Type:* Public (district) junior *System:* Colorado Community College and Occupational Education System *Accred.:* 1975/1987 (NCA) *Calendar:* Sem. plan *Degrees:* A, certificates *Prof. Accred.:* Dental Assisting *CEO:* Pres. Marijane A. Paulsen
Enroll: 3876 (719) 540-7551

PLATT COLLEGE
3100 S. Parker Rd., Aurora 80014 *Type:* Private *Accred.:* 1987 (CCA-ACTTS) *Calendar:* Courses of varying lengths *Degrees:* certificates, diplomas *CEO:* Dir. Jerald Sirbur
(303) 369-5152

PRESBYTERIAN-ST. LUKE CENTER FOR HEALTH SCIENCE EDUCATION
1719 E. 19th Ave., Denver 80218 *Type:* Private *Calendar:* Courses of varying lengths *Degrees:* certificates, diplomas *Prof. Accred.:* Medical Technology, Radiography *CEO:* Pres. Thomas Petty, M.D.
(303) 839-6740

PUEBLO COLLEGE OF BUSINESS AND TECHNOLOGY
4035 Fortino Blvd., Pueblo 81008 *Type:* Private business *Accred.:* 1969/1987 (CCA-ACICS) *Calendar:* Qtr. plan *Degrees:* certificates, diplomas *CEO:* Dir. Karen Thompson
Enroll: 257 (719) 545-3100

PUEBLO COMMUNITY COLLEGE
900 W. Orman Ave., Pueblo 81004 *Type:* Public (state) junior *System:* Colorado Community College and Occupational Education System *Accred.:* 1979/1984 (NCA) *Calendar:* Sem. plan *Degrees:* A, certificates *Prof. Accred.:* Dental Hygiene, Occupational Therapy Assisting, Physical Therapy Assisting, Radiography, Respiratory Therapy *CEO:* Pres. P. Anthony Zeiss
Enroll: 973 (719) 549-3213

RED ROCKS COMMUNITY COLLEGE
13300 W. Sixth Ave., Lakewood 80401 *Type:* Public (state) *System:* Colorado Community College and Occupational Education System *Accred.:* 1975/1988 (NCA) *Calendar:* Sem. plan *Degrees:* A, certificates *CEO:* Pres. Dorothy Horrell
Enroll: 1365 (303) 988-6160

REGIS UNIVERSITY
3539 W. 50th Pkwy., Denver 80221 *Type:* Private (Roman Catholic) liberal arts *Accred.:* 1922/1988 (NCA) *Calendar:* Sem. plan *Degrees:* A, B, M, certificates *Prof. Accred.:* Medical Record Administration, Nursing (B) *CEO:* Pres. David M. Clarke, S.J.
Enroll: 4457 (303) 458-4190

ROCKY MOUNTAIN COLLEGE OF ART AND DESIGN
6875 E. Evans Ave., Denver 80224 *Type:* Private *Accred.:* 1977/1984 (CCA-ACTTS) *Calendar:* Qtr. plan *Degrees:* A *CEO:* Pres. Steven M. Steele
Enroll: 327 (800) 888-2787

ST. THOMAS THEOLOGICAL SEMINARY
1300 S. Steele St., Denver 80210 *Type:* Private (Roman Catholic) for men *Accred.:* 1970/1984 (ATS); 1961/1984 (NCA) *Calendar:* Qtr. plan *Degrees:* P, M *CEO:* Pres./Rector John E. Rybolt, C.M.
Enroll: 96 (303) 722-4687

T.H. PICKENS TECHNICAL CENTER
500 Buckley Rd., Aurora 80011 *Type:* Private *Calendar:* Courses of varying lengths *Degrees:* certificates *Prof. Accred.:* Dental Assisting, Medical Assisting (AMA), Medical Laboratory Technology (AMA), Respiratory Therapy Technology *CEO:* Dir. Dale McCall
(303) 344-4910

TECHNICAL TRADES INSTITUTE
2315 E. Pikes Peak Ave., Colorado Springs 80909 *Type:* Private *Accred.:* 1983/1988 (CCA-ACTTS) *Calendar:* Courses of varying lengths *Degrees:* certificates, diplomas *CEO:* Dir. Fred Harring
Enroll: 885 (303) 632-7626

TECHNICAL TRADES INSTITUTE
772 Horizon Dr., Grand Junction 81506 *Type:* Private *Accred.:* 1987 (CCA-ACTTS) *Calendar:* Courses of varying lengths *Degrees:* certificates *CEO:* Dir. Ernest Ashley
Enroll: 185 (303) 245-8101

TECHNICAL TRADES INSTITUTE
661 Buss Ave., Greeley 80631-9779 *Type:* Private *Accred.:* 1991 (CCA-ACTTS) *Calendar:* Courses of varying lengths *Degrees:* certificates *CEO:* Dir. Ed L. Behr
(719) 632-8116

TRINIDAD STATE JUNIOR COLLEGE
600 Prospect St., Trinidad 81082 *Type:* Public (district) junior *System:* Colorado Community College and Occupational Education System *Accred.:* 1962/1988 (NCA) *Calendar:* Qtr. plan *Degrees:* A, certificates *CEO:* Pres. Harold Deselms
Enroll: 1055 (719) 846-5541

UNITED STATES AIR FORCE ACADEMY
USAF Academy 80840 *Type:* Public (federal) military and technological *Accred.:* 1959/1989 (NCA) *Calendar:* Sem. plan *Degrees:* B *Prof. Accred.:* Computer Science, Engineering (aerospace, civil, electrical, engineering mechanics, engineering physics/science) *CEO:* Supt. Charles R. Hamm
Enroll: 4438 (719) 472-4140

UNITED STATES TRUCK DRIVING SCHOOL
19825 Wigwam Rd., Midway 81008 *Type:* Private *Accred.:* 1986 (CCA-ACTTS) *Calendar:* Courses of varying lengths *Degrees:* certificates *CEO:* Pres. Richard Lammers
Enroll: 425 (719) 382-3000

UNITED STATES TRUCK DRIVING SCHOOL
8150 W. 48th St., Wheatridge 80033 *Type:* Private *Accred.:* 1985 (CCA-ACTTS) *Calendar:* Courses of varying lengths *Degrees:* certificates *CEO:* Pres. Richard Lammers
Enroll: 852 (800) 727-7364

Colorado

BRANCH CAMPUS
7500 New Sapulpa Rd., Tulsa, OK 75131
CEO: Dir. Mark Byrns
(918) 227-4100

UNIVERSITY OF COLORADO HEALTH SCIENCES CENTER
4200 E. Ninth Ave., Denver 80262 *Type:* Public (state) *System:* University of Colorado System *Accred.:* 1913/1989 (NCA) *Calendar:* Sem. plan *Degrees:* B, M, D, certificates *Prof. Accred.:* Clinical Psychology, Dental Hygiene, Dentistry, General Dentistry, General Practice Residency, Medical Technology, Medicine, Nursing (B,M), Physical Therapy, Physician Assisting, Psychology Internship *CEO:* Chanc. Bernard W. Nelson
Enroll: 1993 (303) 270-7682

UNIVERSITY OF COLORADO AT BOULDER
Boulder 80309 *Type:* Public (state) *System:* University of Colorado System *Accred.:* 1913/1990 (NCA) *Calendar:* Sem. plan *Degrees:* B, P, M, D *Prof. Accred.:* Audiology, Business (B,M), Engineering (aerospace, architectural, chemical, civil, computer, electrical, mechanical), Journalism, Law, Music, Pharmacy, Speech-Language Pathology, Teacher Education (e,s,p) *CEO:* Chanc. James N. Corbridge, Jr.
Enroll: 22182 (303) 492-8908

UNIVERSITY OF COLORADO AT COLORADO SPRINGS
P.O. Box 7150, Colorado Springs 80933 *Type:* Public (state) *System:* University of Colorado System *Accred.:* 1970/1988 (NCA) *Calendar:* Sem. plan *Degrees:* B, M, D *Prof. Accred.:* Business (B,M), Computer Science, Engineering (electrical), Teacher Education (e,s) *CEO:* Chanc. Dwayne C. Nuzum
Enroll: 3707 (719) 593-3119

UNIVERSITY OF COLORADO AT DENVER
1200 Larimer St., Denver 80204 *Type:* Public (state) *System:* University of Colorado System *Accred.:* 1970/1988 (NCA) *Calendar:* Sem. plan *Degrees:* B, P, M, D *Prof. Accred.:* Architecture (M), Business (B,M), Community Health/Preventive Medicine, Engineering (civil, electrical, mechanical), Health Services Administration, Landscape Architecture (M), Music, Nursing (B,M), Planning (regional/urban), Public Administration, Teacher Education (e,s,p) *CEO:* Chanc. John C. Buechner
Enroll: 5891 (303) 556-3279

UNIVERSITY OF DENVER
2199 S. University Blvd., Denver 80208 *Type:* Private (United Methodist) *Accred.:* 1914/1986 (NCA) *Calendar:* Qtr. plan *Degrees:* B, P, M, D, certificates *Prof. Accred.:* Accounting (Type A,B,C), Business (B,M), Clinical Psychology, Counseling Psychology, Engineering (electrical, mechanical), Law, Music, Social Work (M) *CEO:* Chanc. Daniel L. Ritchie
Enroll: 6515 (303) 871-2111

UNIVERSITY OF NORTHERN COLORADO
Greeley 80639 *Type:* Public (state) *Accred.:* 1916/1985 (NCA) *Calendar:* Sem. plan *Degrees:* B, P, M, D *Prof. Accred.:* Audiology, Community Health, Counseling, Music, Nursing (B,M), Recreation, Rehabilitation Counseling, School Psychology, Speech-Language Pathology, Teacher Education (e,s,p) *CEO:* Pres. Herman D. Lujan
Enroll: 8938 (303) 351-2121

UNIVERSITY OF SOUTHERN COLORADO
2200 Bonforte Blvd., Pueblo 81001 *Type:* Public liberal arts and technological *System:* Colorado State University System *Accred.:* 1951/1987 (NCA) *Calendar:* Qtr. plan *Degrees:* B, M *Prof. Accred.:* Engineering Technology (civil/construction, electrical, mechanical), Music, Nursing (B), Social Work (B), Teacher Education (e,s,p) *CEO:* Pres. Robert C. Shirley
Enroll: 3873 (719) 549-2306

WESTERN STATE COLLEGE OF COLORADO
Gunnison 81231 *Type:* Public liberal arts *System:* State Colleges in Colorado *Accred.:* 1915/1985 (NCA) *Calendar:* Sem. plan *Degrees:* B, M *Prof. Accred.:* Music, Teacher Education (e,s,p) *CEO:* Pres. Kaye Howe
Enroll: 2274 (303) 943-2114

YESHIVA TORAS CHAIM TALMUDIC SEMINARY
  1400 Quitman St., P.O. Box 4067, Denver
  80204 *Type:* Private professional *Accred.:*
1979/1990 (AARTS) *Calendar:* Sem. plan
Degrees: B, M *CEO:* Pres. S. Beren
Enroll: 35   (303) 629-8200

CONNECTICUT

ALBERT I. PRINCE REGIONAL VOCATIONAL-TECHNICAL SCHOOL
500 Brookfield St., Hartford 06106 *Type:* Private *Calendar:* Courses of varying lengths *Degrees:* certificates *Prof. Accred.:* Dental Assisting (prelim. provisional) *CEO:* Dir. Silas Shannon
(203) 246-8594

ALBERTUS MAGNUS COLLEGE
New Haven 06511-1189 *Type:* Private (Roman Catholic) liberal arts *Accred.:* 1932/1986 (NEASC-CIHE) *Calendar:* Sem. plan *Degrees:* A, B *CEO:* Pres. Julia M. McNamara
Enroll: 540 (203) 773-8550

ALLSTATE TRACTOR TRAILER TRAINING SCHOOL
2064 Main St., Bridgeport 06004 *Type:* Private *Accred.:* 1989 (CCA-ACTTS) *Calendar:* Courses of varying lengths *Degrees:* certificates *CEO:* Pres. George Delibro
Enroll: 19 (203) 336-9567

AMERICAN EDUCATIONAL INSTITUTE
3787 Main St., Bridgeport 06606 *Type:* Private home study *Accred.:* 1989 (NHSC) *Calendar:* Courses of varying lengths *Degrees:* certificates *CEO:* Pres. Joseph M. Monaco
(203) 371-0088

ASNUNTUCK COMMUNITY COLLEGE
Enfield 06082 *Type:* Public (state) junior *System:* Connecticut Community-Technical Colleges *Accred.:* 1976/1986 (NEASC-CIHE) *Calendar:* Sem. plan *Degrees:* A *CEO:* Pres. Harvey S. Irlen
Enroll: 682 (203) 253-3000

BERKELEY DIVINITY SCHOOL
363 St. Roman St., New Haven 06511 *Type:* Private (Episcopal) professional; graduate only *Accred.:* 1954/1991 (ATS) *Calendar:* Sem. plan *Degrees:* P, M *CEO:* Dean James E. Annand
(203) 432-6105

BETH BENJAMIN ACADEMY OF CONNECTICUT
132 Prosect St., Stamford 06901 *Type:* Private professional *Accred.:* 1990 (AARTS) *Calendar:* Tri. plan *Degrees:* Rabbinic (1st), Talmudic (1st) *CEO:* Pres. S. Schustal
Enroll: 25 (203) 325-4351

BRANFORD HALL SCHOOL OF BUSINESS
9 Business Park Dr., Branford 06405 *Type:* Private business *Accred.:* 1977/1987 (CCA-ACICS) *Calendar:* Courses of varying lengths *Degrees:* certificates *CEO:* Pres. Nelson Bernabucci
Enroll: 216 (203) 488-2525

BRIARWOOD COLLEGE
2279 Mt. Vernon Rd., Southington 06489 *Type:* Private business *Accred.:* 1982 (NEASC-CVTCI) *Calendar:* Sem. plan *Degrees:* A, diplomas *Prof. Accred.:* Dental Assisting, Medical Record Technology *CEO:* Pres. John J. LeConche
Enroll: 333 (203) 628-4751

BRIDGEPORT ENGINEERING INSTITUTE
Fairfield 06430 *Type:* Private professional *Accred.:* 1977/1990 (NEASC-CIHE) *Calendar:* Tri. plan *Degrees:* A, B *CEO:* Pres. William M. Krummel
Enroll: 264 (203) 259-5717

BUSINESS CAREERS INSTITUTE
95 Scoville St., Waterbury 06706 *Type:* Private business *Accred.:* 1970/1981 (CCA-ACICS) *Calendar:* Sem. plan *Degrees:* certificates *CEO:* Dir. Sally L. Deegan
Enroll: 258 (203) 573-8338

BUTLER BUSINESS SCHOOL
2710 North Ave., Bridgeport 06604 *Type:* Private business *Accred.:* 1979/1985 (CCA-ACICS) *Calendar:* Courses of varying lengths *Degrees:* certificates, diplomas *CEO:* Pres. Robert M. Butler
Enroll: 335 (203) 333-3601

Accredited Institutions — Connecticut

CENTRAL CONNECTICUT STATE UNIVERSITY
New Britain 06050 *Type:* Public liberal arts and teachers *System:* Connecticut State University Central Office *Accred.:* 1947/1988 (NEASC-CIHE) *Calendar:* Sem. plan *Degrees:* A, B, M *Prof. Accred.:* Computer Science, Engineering Technology (civil/construction, manufacturing), Nurse Anesthesia Education, Nursing (B), Social Work (B-candidate), Teacher Education (e,s) *CEO:* Pres. John W. Shumaker
Enroll: 8722 (203) 827-7000

CHARTER OAK COLLEGE
270 Farmington Ave., Ste. 171, Farmington 06032-1909 *Type:* Public (state) liberal arts *Accred.:* 1981/1987 (NEASC-CIHE) *Calendar:* Sem. plan *Degrees:* A, B *CEO:* Pres. Merle W. Harris
Enroll: 884 (203) 566-7230

COMPUTER PROCESSING INSTITUTE
111 Ash St., East Hartford 06108 *Type:* Private business *Accred.:* 1971/1983 (CCA-ACICS) *Calendar:* Courses of varying length *Degrees:* diplomas *CEO:* Pres. David S. Shefrin
Enroll: 2616 (203) 528-9211

BRANCH CAMPUS
305 Boston Ave., Stratford, CT 06497 *CEO:* Dir. Steve Denegre
(203) 378-2800

CONNECTICUT BUSINESS INSTITUTE
605 Broad St., Stratford 06497 *Type:* Private business *Accred.:* 1972/1988 (CCA-ACICS) *Calendar:* Tri. plan *Degrees:* certificates, diplomas *CEO:* Pres. Emanuel Pallant
Enroll: 457 (203) 377-1775

CONNECTICUT CENTER FOR MASSAGE THERAPY, INC.
75 Kitts La., Newington 06111 *Type:* Private *Accred.:* 1985 (CCA-ACTTS) *Calendar:* Courses of varying lengths *Degrees:* certificates *CEO:* Dir. Stephen Kitts
Enroll: 195 (203) 667-1886

CONNECTICUT COLLEGE
New London 06320 *Type:* Private liberal arts *Accred.:* 1932/1987 (NEASC-CIHE) *Calendar:* Sem. plan *Degrees:* B, M *CEO:* Pres. Claire L. Gaudiani
Enroll: 1816 (203) 447-1911

CONNECTICUT INSTITUTE OF ART
581 W. Putnam Ave., Greenwich 06830 *Type:* Private *Accred.:* 1980/1985 (CCA-ACTTS) *Calendar:* Sem. plan *Degrees:* diplomas *CEO:* Dir. August J. Propersi
Enroll: 66 (203) 869-4430

CONNECTICUT INSTITUTE OF HAIR DESIGN
1681 Meriden Rd., Wolcott 06716 *Type:* Private *Accred.:* 1980/1987 (CCA-ACTTS) *Calendar:* Courses of varying lengths *Degrees:* diplomas *CEO:* Dir. John Varanelli
Enroll: 37 (203) 879-4247

CONNECTICUT SCHOOL OF ELECTRONICS
586 Grasso Blvd., P.O. Box 7308, New Haven 06519 *Type:* Private *Accred.:* 1968/1989 (CCA-ACTTS) *Calendar:* Sem. plan *Degrees:* certificates, diplomas *CEO:* Vice Pres. Karen George
Enroll: 778 (203) 624-2121

COUNTY SCHOOLS, INC.
3787 Main St., Bridgeport 06606 *Type:* Private home study *Accred.:* 1976/1987 (NHSC) *Calendar:* Courses of varying lengths *Degrees:* certificates *CEO:* Pres. Joseph M. Monaco
(203) 374-5000

AIRLINE/TRAVEL AND HOTEL-MANAGEMENT TRAINING SITE
3851 Main St., Bridgeport, CT 06606 *CEO:* Dir. Allison Golding
(203) 371-0088

NURSE'S AIDE TRAINING SITE
Barnett Multi-Health Care Facility, 2875 Main St., Bridgeport, CT 06606 *CEO:* Dir. Robin Santiago
(203) 336-0232

Connecticut

DATA INSTITUTE
745 Burnside Ave., East Hartford 06108 *Type:* Private business *Accred.:* 1983 (CCA-ACICS) *Calendar:* Courses of varying lengths *Degrees:* certificates *CEO:* Pres. Mark Scheinberg
Enroll: 2410   (203) 528-4111

DIESEL TECHNOLOGY INSTITUTE
105 Phoenix Ave., Enfield 06082 *Type:* Private *Accred.:* 1983/1988 (CCA-ACTTS) *Calendar:* Courses of varying lengths *Degrees:* certificates *CEO:* Pres. Arthur Bertrand
Enroll: 108   (203) 745-2010

EASTERN CONNECTICUT STATE UNIVERSITY
Willimantic 06226 *Type:* Public liberal arts and teachers *System:* Connecticut State University Central Office *Accred.:* 1958/1990 (NEASC-CIHE) *Calendar:* Sem. plan *Degrees:* A, B, M *CEO:* Pres. David G. Carter
Enroll: 3126   (203) 456-2231

ELI WHITNEY REGIONAL VOCATIONAL-TECHNICAL SCHOOL
71 Jones Rd., Hamden 06514 *Type:* Private *Calendar:* Courses of varying lengths *Degrees:* certificates *Prof. Accred.:* Dental Assisting *CEO:* Dir. Cecil Robinson
                (203) 397-4031

FAIRFIELD UNIVERSITY
Fairfield 06430-7524 *Type:* Private (Roman Catholic) liberal arts *Accred.:* 1953/1988 (NEASC-CIHE) *Calendar:* Sem. plan *Degrees:* B, M *Prof. Accred.:* Counseling, Nursing (B) *CEO:* Pres. Aloysius P. Kelley, S.J.
Enroll: 3677   (203) 254-4000

GREATER HARTFORD COMMUNITY COLLEGE
Hartford 06105 *Type:* Public (state) junior *System:* Connecticut Community-Technical Colleges *Accred.:* 1975/1986 (NEASC-CIHE) *Calendar:* Sem. plan *Degrees:* A *Prof. Accred.:* Nursing (A) *CEO:* Pres. Conrad L. Mallett
Enroll: 1307   (203) 520-7800

GREATER NEW HAVEN STATE TECHNICAL COLLEGE
88 Bassett Rd., North Haven 06473 *Type:* Public 2-year *System:* Connecticut Community-Technical Colleges *Accred.:* 1983 (NEASC-CVTCI) *Calendar:* Sem. plan *Degrees:* A *Prof. Accred.:* Engineering Technology (manufacturing, mechanical) *CEO:* Pres. George D. Harris
Enroll: 531   (203) 234-3300

HARTFORD CAMERATA CONSERVATORY
834 Asylum Ave., Hartford 06105 *Type:* Private professional *Accred.:* 1979/1985 (NEASC-CVTCI) *Calendar:* Sem. plan *Degrees:* diplomas *CEO:* Dir. Claudia Bell
Enroll: 18   (203) 246-2588

HARTFORD COLLEGE FOR WOMEN
Hartford 06105 *Type:* Private junior *Accred.:* 1962/1983 (NEASC-CIHE) *Calendar:* Sem. plan *Degrees:* A *CEO:* Acting Pres. Jane M. Barstow
Enroll: 157   (203) 236-1215

HARTFORD GRADUATE CENTER
275 Windsor St., Hartford 06120 *Type:* Private graduate only *Accred.:* 1966/1983 (NEASC-CIHE) *Calendar:* Sem. plan *Degrees:* M *CEO:* Pres. Worth Loomis
Enroll: 1044   (203) 548-2400

HARTFORD SECRETARIAL SCHOOL
765 Asylum Ave., Hartford 06105 *Type:* Private business *Accred.:* 1979/1985 (CCA-ACICS) *Calendar:* Qtr. plan *Degrees:* certificates, diplomas *CEO:* Pres. Patrick J. Fox
Enroll: 193   (203) 522-2888

HARTFORD SEMINARY
77 Sherman St., Hartford 06105 *Type:* Private (interdenominational) graduate only *Accred.:* 1938/1983 (ATS); 1983/1988 (NEASC-CIHE) *Calendar:* Sem. plan *Degrees:* M, D *CEO:* Pres. Barbara Brown Zikmund
Enroll: 51   (203) 232-4451

HARTFORD STATE TECHNICAL COLLEGE
401 Flatbush Ave., Hartford 06106 *Type:* Public 2-year technical *System:* Connecticut

Community-Technical Colleges *Accred.:* 1970/1991 (NEASC-CVTCI) *Calendar:* Sem. plan *Degrees:* A *Prof. Accred.:* Engineering Technology (civil/construction, electrical, manufacturing, mechanical) *CEO:* Pres. John E. Arnet
Enroll: 549 (203) 527-4111

HARTFORD TECHNICAL INSTITUTE
424 Homestead Ave., Hartford 06112 *Type:* Private *Accred.:* 1981/1987 (CCA-ACTTS) *Calendar:* Courses of varying lengths *Degrees:* certificates, diplomas *CEO:* Pres. Robert M. Meyers
Enroll: 289 (203) 249-8688

HOLY APOSTLES COLLEGE AND SEMINARY
Cromwell 06416 *Type:* Private (Roman Catholic) liberal arts for men *Accred.:* 1979/1986 (NEASC-CIHE) *Calendar:* Sem. plan *Degrees:* A, B, M *CEO:* Pres. Francis J. Lescoe, Ph.D.
Enroll: 154 (203) 635-5311

HOUSATONIC COMMUNITY COLLEGE
510 Barnum Ave., Bridgeport 06608 *Type:* Public (state) junior *System:* Connecticut Community-Technical Colleges *Accred.:* 1972/1985 (NEASC-CIHE) *Calendar:* Sem. plan *Degrees:* A *Prof. Accred.:* Medical Laboratory Technology (AMA), Physical Therapy Assisting *CEO:* Pres. Vincent S. Darnowski
Enroll: 1064 (203) 579-6400

HUNTINGTON INSTITUTE
193 Broadway, Norwich 06360 *Type:* Private business *Accred.:* 1980/1986 (CCA-ACICS) *Calendar:* Courses of varying lengths *Degrees:* certificates *CEO:* Dir. Thomas Haggerty
Enroll: 224 (203) 886-0507

KATHARINE GIBBS SCHOOL
142 East Ave., Norwalk 06851 *Type:* Private business *Accred.:* 1975/1986 (CCA-ACICS) *Calendar:* Sem. plan *Degrees:* A, certificates *CEO:* Dir. Frank Gallo
Enroll: 552 (203) 838-4173

MANCHESTER COMMUNITY COLLEGE
P.O. Box 1046, P.P. Sta., Manchester 06040 *Type:* Public (state) junior *System:* Connecticut Community-Technical Colleges *Accred.:* 1971/1982 (NEASC-CIHE) *Calendar:* Sem. plan *Degrees:* A *Prof. Accred.:* Medical Laboratory Technology (AMA), Occupational Therapy Assisting, Respiratory Therapy, Surgical Technology *CEO:* Pres. Jonathan M. Daube
Enroll: 3376 (203) 647-6000

MATTATUCK COMMUNITY COLLEGE
Waterbury 06708 *Type:* Public (state) junior *System:* Connecticut Community-Technical Colleges *Accred.:* 1973/1983 (NEASC-CIHE) *Calendar:* Sem. plan *Degrees:* A *Prof. Accred.:* Nursing (A), Radiography, Respiratory Therapy Technology *CEO:* Pres. Richard L. Sanders
Enroll: 2369 (203) 575-0328

MIDDLESEX COMMUNITY COLLEGE
Middletown 06457 *Type:* Public (state) junior *System:* Connecticut Community-Technical Colleges *Accred.:* 1973/1983 (NEASC-CIHE) *Calendar:* Sem. plan *Degrees:* A *Prof. Accred.:* Radiography *CEO:* Pres. Leila G. Sullivan
Enroll: 1393 (203) 344-3011

MITCHELL COLLEGE
New London 06320 *Type:* Private junior *Accred.:* 1956/1983 (NEASC-CIHE) *Calendar:* Sem. plan *Degrees:* A *CEO:* Pres. David A. Sandell
Enroll: 673 (203) 443-2811

MOHEGAN COMMUNITY COLLEGE
Norwich 06360 *Type:* Public (state) junior *System:* Connecticut Community-Technical Colleges *Accred.:* 1973/1986 (NEASC-CIHE) *Calendar:* Sem. plan *Degrees:* A *Prof. Accred.:* Nursing (A) *CEO:* Interim Pres. Diann Williams
Enroll: 1447 (203) 886-1931

MORSE SCHOOL OF BUSINESS
275 Asylum St., Hartford 06103 *Type:* Private business *Accred.:* 1953/1990 (CCA-

ACICS) *Calendar:* Courses of varying lengths *Degrees:* diplomas *Prof. Accred.:* Medical Assisting (AMA) *CEO:* Pres. Michael S. Taub
Enroll: 742 (203) 522-2261

NEW ENGLAND TECHNICAL INSTITUTE OF CONNECTICUT
200 John Downey Dr., New Britain 06051 *Type:* Private *Accred.:* 1983 (CCA-ACTTS) *Calendar:* 66-week program *Degrees:* diplomas *CEO:* Dir. Paul Taub
Enroll: 375 (203) 225-8641

NEW ENGLAND TRACTOR TRAILER TRAINING
32 Field Rd., P.O. Box 326, Somers 06071 *Type:* Private combination home study and resident *Accred.:* 1982/1988 (CCA-ACTTS); 1989 (NHSC) *Calendar:* 4-week courses *Degrees:* diplomas *CEO:* Dir. Arian Greenberg
Enroll: 524 (203) 749-0711

NORTHWESTERN CONNECTICUT COMMUNITY COLLEGE
Winsted 06098 *Type:* Public (state) junior *System:* Connecticut Community-Technical Colleges *Accred.:* 1971/1983 (NEASC-CIHE) *Calendar:* Sem. plan *Degrees:* A *CEO:* Pres. Booker T. DeVaughn
Enroll: 919 (203) 738-6300

NORWALK COMMUNITY COLLEGE
Norwalk 06854 *Type:* Public (state) junior *System:* Connecticut Community-Technical Colleges *Accred.:* 1973/1982 (NEASC-CIHE) *Calendar:* Sem. plan *Degrees:* A *Prof. Accred.:* Nursing (A) *CEO:* Pres. William H. Schwab
Enroll: 1610 (203) 853-2040

NORWALK STATE TECHNICAL COLLEGE
181 Richards Ave., Norwalk 06850 *Type:* Public 2-year technical *System:* Connecticut Community-Technical Colleges *Accred.:* 1970/1991 (NEASC-CVTCI) *Calendar:* Sem. plan *Degrees:* A *Prof. Accred.:* Engineering Technology (architectural, civil/construction, computer, electrical, electro-mechanical, mechanical) *CEO:* Pres. John K. Fisher
Enroll: 552 (203) 855-6600

PAIER COLLEGE OF ART, INC.
6 Prospect Ct., Hamden 06517 *Type:* Private *Accred.:* 1991 (CCA-ACTTS) *Calendar:* Courses of varying lengths *Degrees:* B, certificates, diplomas *CEO:* Pres. Edward T. Paier
Enroll: 191 (203) 777-7319

PORTER AND CHESTER INSTITUTE
138 Weymouth St., Enfield 06082 *Type:* Private *Accred.:* 1980/1985 (CCA-ACTTS) *Calendar:* Qtr. plan *Degrees:* diplomas *CEO:* Exec. Dir. Joseph M. Doering
Enroll: 324 (203) 741-2561

PORTER AND CHESTER INSTITUTE
670 Lordship Blvd., P.O. Box 364, Stratford 06497 *Type:* Private *Accred.:* 1972/1985 (CCA-ACTTS) *Calendar:* Qtr. plan *Degrees:* diplomas *CEO:* Exec. Dir. Raymond R. Clark
Enroll: 585 (203) 375-4463

PORTER AND CHESTER INSTITUTE
320 Sylvan Lake Rd., Watertown 06705 *Type:* Private *Accred.:* 1972/1987 (CCA-ACTTS) *Calendar:* Qtr. plan *Degrees:* diplomas *CEO:* Dir. Louis Giannelli
Enroll: 1036 (203) 274-9294

PORTER AND CHESTER INSTITUTE
125 Silas Deane Hwy., Wethersfield 06109 *Type:* Private *Accred.:* 1979/1985 (CCA-ACTTS) *Calendar:* Qtr. plan *Degrees:* diplomas *CEO:* Dir. John Mashia
Enroll: 671 (203) 529-2519

QUINEBAUG VALLEY COMMUNITY COLLEGE
724 Upper Maple St., Danielson 06239 *Type:* Public (state) junior *System:* Connecticut Community-Technical Colleges *Accred.:* 1978/1985 (NEASC-CIHE) *Calendar:* Sem. plan *Degrees:* A *CEO:* Pres. Robert E. Miller
Enroll: 554 (203) 774-1130

Accredited Institutions   **Connecticut**

QUINNIPIAC COLLEGE
Hamden 06518 *Type:* Private liberal arts and professional *Accred.:* 1958/1989 (NEASC-CIHE) *Calendar:* Sem. plan *Degrees:* A, B, M *Prof. Accred.:* Animal Technology, Medical Technology, Nursing (A), Occupational Therapy, Perfusion, Physical Therapy, Radiography, Respiratory Therapy, Respiratory Therapy Technology *CEO:* Pres. John L. Lahey
Enroll: 2762   (203) 288-5251

RIDLEY-LOWELL BUSINESS AND TECHNICAL INSTITUTION
P.O. Box 652, New London 06320 *Type:* Private business *Accred.:* 1979/1985 (CCA-ACICS) *Calendar:* Courses of varying lengths *Degrees:* certificates *CEO:* Dir. Karen Harden
Enroll: 152   (203) 443-7441

ROFFLER ACADEMY FOR HAIRSTYLISTS
454 Park St., Hartford 06106 *Type:* Private *Accred.:* 1974 (CCA-ACTTS) *Calendar:* Courses of varying lengths *Degrees:* diplomas *CEO:* Pres. Stewart Smith
Enroll: 27   (203) 522-2359

   BRANCH CAMPUS
   106 Elm St., Cheshire, CT 06410 *CEO:* Dir. Douglas Hiltz
   (203) 272-4333

SACRED HEART UNIVERSITY
5151 Park Ave., Fairfield 06432-1000 *Type:* Private (Roman Catholic) liberal arts *Accred.:* 1969/1983 (NEASC-CIHE) *Calendar:* Sem. plan *Degrees:* A, B, M *Prof. Accred.:* Nursing (B), Respiratory Therapy, Social Work (B) *CEO:* Pres. Anthony J. Cernera, Ph.D.
Enroll: 2538   (203) 371-7999

ST. JOSEPH COLLEGE
1678 Asylum Ave., West Hartford 06117 *Type:* Private (Roman Catholic) liberal arts *Accred.:* 1938/1986 (NEASC-CIHE) *Calendar:* Sem. plan *Degrees:* B, M *Prof. Accred.:* Dietetics (coordinated), Nursing (B,M), Social Work (B) *CEO:* Pres. Winifred E. Coleman
Enroll: 1026   (203) 232-4571

SCHOOL OF THE HARTFORD BALLET
Hartford Courant Arts Ctr., 224 Farmington Ave., Hartford 06105 *Type:* Private *Calendar:* Courses of varying lengths *Degrees:* certificates *Prof. Accred.:* Dance *CEO:* Dir. Enid Lynn
     (203) 525-9396

SOUTH CENTRAL COMMUNITY COLLEGE
60 Sargent Dr., New Haven 06511 *Type:* Public (state) junior *System:* Connecticut Community-Technical Colleges *Accred.:* 1981/1986 (NEASC-CIHE) *Calendar:* Sem. plan *Degrees:* A *Prof. Accred.:* Nuclear Medicine Technology, Radiation Therapy Technology, Radiography *CEO:* Pres. Antonio Perez
Enroll: 1712   (203) 789-7071

SOUTHERN CONNECTICUT STATE UNIVERSITY
New Haven 06515 *Type:* Public liberal arts and teachers *System:* Connecticut State University Central Office *Accred.:* 1952/1986 (NEASC-CIHE) *Calendar:* Sem. plan *Degrees:* A, B, M *Prof. Accred.:* Librarianship, Nurse Anesthesia Education, Nursing (B,M), Social Work (B,M), Speech-Language Pathology *CEO:* Pres. Michael J. Adanti
Enroll: 9197   (203) 397-4000

STONE ACADEMY
1315 Dixwell Ave., Hamden 06514 *Type:* Private business and technical *Accred.:* 1953/1990 (CCA-ACICS) *Calendar:* 9-1/2 month program *Degrees:* diplomas *Prof. Accred.:* Medical Assisting (AMA) *CEO:* Pres. Janet S. Arena
Enroll: 459   (203) 288-7474

TECHNICAL CAREERS INSTITUTE
11 Kimberly Ave., West Haven 06516 *Type:* Private *Accred.:* 1974/1987 (CCA-ACTTS) *Calendar:* Courses of varying lengths *De-

grees: certificates *CEO:* Dir. Richard Barnikow
Enroll: 2129 (203) 932-2282

BRANCH CAMPUS
605 Day Hill Rd., Windsor, CT 06095 *Accred.:* 1986 (CCA-ACTTS) *CEO:* Pres. Linda Perkins
(203) 688-8351

TEIKYO POST UNIVERSITY
Waterbury 06708 *Type:* Private liberal arts *Accred.:* 1972/1985 (NEASC-CIHE) *Calendar:* Sem. plan *Degrees:* A, B *CEO:* Pres. Phyllis C. DeLeo
Enroll: 996 (203) 755-0121

THAMES VALLEY STATE TECHNICAL COLLEGE
574 New London Tpke., Norwich 06360 *Type:* Public 2-year technical *System:* Connecticut Community-Technical Colleges *Accred.:* 1970/1991 (NEASC-CVTCI) *Calendar:* Sem. plan *Degrees:* A *Prof. Accred.:* Engineering Technology (chemical, electrical, manufacturing, mechanical, nuclear) *CEO:* Pres. R. Eileen Baccus
Enroll: 725 (203) 886-0177

TRINITY COLLEGE
Hartford 06106 *Type:* Private liberal arts *Accred.:* 1929/1986 (NEASC-CIHE) *Calendar:* Sem. plan *Degrees:* B, M *CEO:* Pres. Tom Gerety
Enroll: 1898 (203) 297-2000

TUNXIS COMMUNITY COLLEGE
Farmington 06032 *Type:* Public (state) junior *System:* Connecticut Community-Technical Colleges *Accred.:* 1975/1984 (NEASC-CIHE) *Calendar:* Sem. plan *Degrees:* A *Prof. Accred.:* Dental Assisting, Dental Hygiene *CEO:* Pres. Marilyn Menack
Enroll: 1681 (203) 677-7701

UNITED STATES COAST GUARD ACADEMY
15 Mohegan Ave., New London 06320-4195 *Type:* Public (federal) professional *Accred.:* 1952/1990 (NEASC-CIHE) *Calendar:* Sem. plan *Degrees:* B *Prof. Accred.:* Engineering (civil, electrical, naval architecture/marine) *CEO:* Supt. Thomas T. Matteson
Enroll: 1108 (203) 444-8444

UNIVERSITY OF BRIDGEPORT
Bridgeport 06602 *Type:* Private *Accred.:* 1951/1989 (NEASC-CIHE) *Calendar:* Sem. plan *Degrees:* A, B, M, D *Prof. Accred.:* Art, Business (B,M), Dental Hygiene, Engineering (computer, electrical, mechanical), Law *CEO:* Pres. Edwin G. Eigel, Jr.
Enroll: 3005 (203) 576-4000

THE UNIVERSITY OF CONNECTICUT
Storrs 06269 *Type:* Public (state) *System:* University of Connecticut System *Accred.:* 1931/1987 (NEASC-CIHE) *Calendar:* Sem. plan *Degrees:* B, P, M, D *Prof. Accred.:* Accounting (Type A,B), Art, Audiology, Business (B,M), Clinical Psychology, Community Health/Preventive Medicine, Dietetics (coordinated), Engineering (chemical, civil, computer, electrical, mechanical), Law, Music, Nursing (B,M), Pharmacy, Physical Therapy, Public Affairs, Social Work (M), Speech-Language Pathology, Teacher Education, Theatre *CEO:* Pres. Harry J. Hartley
Enroll: 19479 (203) 486-2000

THE UNIVERSITY OF CONNECTICUT HEALTH CENTER
263 Farmington Ave., Farmington 06032 *Type:* Public *System:* University of Connecticut System *Accred.:* 1931/1987 (NEASC-CIHE) *Calendar:* 4-1-4 plan *Degrees:* B, P *Prof. Accred.:* Cytotechnology, Dentistry, Endodontics, General Dentistry (prelim. provisional), General Practice Residency, Medicine, Oral and Maxillofacial Surgery, Orthodontics, Pediatric Dentistry, Periodontics *CEO:* Interim Pres. Harry J. Hartley
Enroll: 507 (203) 679-2000

UNIVERSITY OF HARTFORD
200 Bloomfield Ave., West Hartford 06117 *Type:* Private *Accred.:* 1961/1982 (NEASC-CIHE) *Calendar:* Sem. plan *Degrees:* A, B, M, D *Prof. Accred.:* Art, Engineering (civil, electrical, mechanical), Engineering Tech-

nology (electrical), Medical Technology, Music, Nursing (B), Radiography, Respiratory Therapy, Teacher Education (e,s,p) *CEO:* Pres. Humphrey Tonkin
Enroll: 6224 (203) 243-4100

UNIVERSITY OF NEW HAVEN
West Haven 06516 *Type:* Private *Accred.:* 1966/1990 (NEASC-CIHE) *Calendar:* Sem. plan *Degrees:* A, B, M, D *Prof. Accred.:* Engineering (civil, electrical, industrial, mechanical) *CEO:* Pres. Lawrence J. DeNardis
Enroll: 3853 (203) 932-7000

WATERBURY STATE TECHNICAL COLLEGE
750 Chase Pkwy., Waterbury 06708 *Type:* Public 2-year technical *System:* Connecticut Community-Technical Colleges *Accred.:* 1970/1991 (NEASC-CVTCI) *Calendar:* Sem. plan *Degrees:* A *Prof. Accred.:* Engineering Technology (chemical, electrical, manufacturing, mechanical, mechanical drafting/design) *CEO:* Pres. Charles A. Ekstrom
Enroll: 838 (203) 575-8082

WESLEYAN UNIVERSITY
Middletown 06457 *Type:* Private liberal arts *Accred.:* 1929/1980 (NEASC-CIHE) *Calendar:* Sem. plan *Degrees:* B, M, D *CEO:* Pres. William M. Chace
Enroll: 3028 (203) 347-9411

WESTERN CONNECTICUT STATE UNIVERSITY
Danbury 06810 *Type:* Public liberal arts and teachers *System:* Connecticut State University Central Office *Accred.:* 1954/1984 (NEASC-CIHE) *Calendar:* Sem. plan *Degrees:* A, B, M *Prof. Accred.:* Nursing (B,M), Social Work (B) *CEO:* Pres. Stephen Feldman
Enroll: 4006 (203) 797-4347

WESTLAWN SCHOOL OF MARINE TECHNOLOGY
733 Summer St., Stamford 06901 *Type:* Private home study *Accred.:* 1971/1987 (NHSC) *Calendar:* Courses of varying lengths *Degrees:* certificates *CEO:* Dir. Norman Nudelman
(203) 359-0500

WINDHAM REGIONAL VOCATIONAL-TECHNICAL SCHOOL
210 Birch St., Willimantic 06226 *Type:* Private *Calendar:* Courses of varying lengths *Degrees:* certificates *Prof. Accred.:* Dental Assisting (conditional) *CEO:* Dir. Charles Wilt
(203) 456-3879

YALE UNIVERSITY
New Haven 06520 *Type:* Private *Accred.:* 1929/1989 (NEASC-CIHE) *Calendar:* Sem. plan *Degrees:* B, P, M, D *Prof. Accred.:* Architecture (M), Business (M), Clinical Psychology, Engineering (chemical, electrical, mechanical), Forestry, Health Services Administration, Law, Medicine, Music, Nursing (M), Physician Assisting, Psychology Internship, Public Health *CEO:* Pres. Benno C. Schmidt, Jr.
Enroll: 10711 (203) 432-4771

DELAWARE

DAWN AERONAUTICS
New Castle County Airport, 120 Old Churchmans Rd., New Castle 19720-3116 *Type:* Private *Accred.:* 1991 (CCA-ACTTS) *Calendar:* Courses of varying lengths *Degrees:* certificates *CEO:* Pres. Hollis Anglin
(302) 328-9695

DELAWARE STATE COLLEGE
1200 N. Dupont Hwy., Dover 19901 *Type:* Public liberal arts and teachers *System:* Delaware Postsecondary Education Commission *Accred.:* 1945/1987 (MSA) *Calendar:* Tri. plan *Degrees:* B, M *Prof. Accred.:* Nursing (B), Social Work (B,M) *CEO:* Pres. William DeLauder
Enroll: 2510   (302) 736-4901

DELAWARE TECHNICAL AND COMMUNITY COLLEGE SOUTHERN
P.O. Box 610, Georgetown 19947 *Type:* Public (state) 2-year technological *System:* Delaware Technical and Community College President's Office *Accred.:* 1972/1988 (MSA) *Calendar:* Qtr. plan *Degrees:* A *Prof. Accred.:* Medical Laboratory Technology (AMA), Radiography *CEO:* Vice Pres./Dir. Jack F. Owens
Enroll: 2520   (302) 856-5422

DELAWARE TECHNICAL AND COMMUNITY COLLEGE STANTON
400 Christiana-Stanton Rd., Newark 19713 *Type:* Public (state) 2-year technological *System:* Delaware Technical and Community College President's Office *Accred.:* 1972/1988 (MSA) *Calendar:* Qtr. plan *Degrees:* A *Prof. Accred.:* Engineering Technology (mechanical) *CEO:* Vice Pres./Dir. Lawrence Miller
(302) 454-3917

DELAWARE TECHNICAL AND COMMUNITY COLLEGE TERRY
1832 N. Dupont Pkwy., Dover 19903 *Type:* Public (state) 2-year technological *System:* Delaware Technical and Community College President's Office *Accred.:* 1972/1988 (MSA) *Calendar:* Qtr. plan *Degrees:* A *Prof. Accred.:* Radiography *CEO:* Vice Pres./Dir. Linda C. Jolly
Enroll: 1535   (302) 736-5321

DELAWARE TECHNICAL AND COMMUNITY COLLEGE WILMINGTON
333 Shipley St., Wilmington 19801 *Type:* Public (state) 2-year technological *System:* Delaware Technical and Community College President's Office *Accred.:* 1972/1988 (MSA) *Calendar:* Qtr. plan *Degrees:* A *Prof. Accred.:* Dental Hygiene, Nuclear Medicine Technology, Nursing (A), Physical Therapy Assisting, Respiratory Therapy *CEO:* Vice Pres./Dir. Orlando J. George
Enroll: 5078   (302) 573-5481

GOLDEY BEACOM COLLEGE
4701 Limestone Rd., Wilmington 19808 *Type:* Private *Accred.:* 1976/1986 (MSA) *Calendar:* Sem. plan *Degrees:* A, B, certificates *CEO:* Pres. William R. Baldt
Enroll: 1827   (302) 998-8814

STAR TECHNICAL INSTITUTE
3301 N. Market St., Wilmington 19802 *Type:* Private *Accred.:* 1988 (CCA-ACTTS) *Calendar:* Courses of varying lengths *Degrees:* certificates *CEO:* Dir. Joseph Commisso
Enroll: 175   (302) 762-8324

USA TRAINING ACADEMY, INC.
955 S. Chapel St., P.O. Box 6032, Newark 19714-6032 *Type:* Private home study *Accred.:* 1974/1984 (NHSC) *Calendar:* Courses of varying lengths *Degrees:* certificates *CEO:* Pres. Paul L. Teeven
(302) 731-1555

UNIVERSITY OF DELAWARE
Newark 19716 *Type:* Public (state-related) *System:* Delaware Postsecondary Education Commission *Accred.:* 1921/1986 (MSA) *Calendar:* 4-1-4 plan *Degrees:* A, B, M, D *Prof. Accred.:* Accounting (Type A,C), Business (B,M), Clinical Psychology, Dietetics

(coordinated), Engineering (chemical, civil, electrical, mechanical), Engineering Technology (agricultural, general), Medical Technology, Music, Nursing (B,M), Physical Therapy, Psychology Internship, Public Administration *CEO:* Pres. David P. Roselle
Enroll: 19818 (302) 831-2000

WESLEY COLLEGE
120 N. State St., Dover 19901 *Type:* Private (United Methodist) liberal arts *Accred.:* 1950/1988 (MSA) *Calendar:* Sem. plan *Degrees:* A, B, certificates *Prof. Accred.:* Nursing (A) *CEO:* Pres. Reed M. Stewart
Enroll: 1187 (302) 736-2300

WIDENER UNIVERSITY SCHOOL OF LAW
4601 Concord Pike, P.O. Box 7474, Wilmington 19803 *Type:* Private professional *Calendar:* Sem. plan *Degrees:* P *Prof. Accred:* Law *CEO:* Dean Anthony J. Santoro
Enroll: 1286 (302) 477-2100

WILMINGTON COLLEGE
320 Dupont Hwy., New Castle 19720 *Type:* Private liberal arts *Accred.:* 1975/1985 (MSA) *Calendar:* Tri. plan *Degrees:* A, B, M *Prof. Accred.:* Nursing (B) *CEO:* Pres. Audrey K. Doberstein
Enroll: 1548 (302) 328-9401

DISTRICT OF COLUMBIA

THE AMERICAN UNIVERSITY
4400 Massachusetts Ave., N.W., Washington 20016 *Type:* Private (United Methodist) *Accred.:* 1928/1989 (MSA) *Calendar:* Sem. plan *Degrees:* A, B, P, M, D *Prof. Accred.:* Business (B,M), Clinical Psychology, Computer Science, Law, Music, Public Administration, Teacher Education (e,s) *CEO:* Pres. Joseph A. Duffey
Enroll: 11659   (202) 885-1000

AUTOMATION ACADEMY
666 11th St., N.W., Ste. 750, Washington 20001 *Type:* Private *Accred.:* 1988 (CCA-ACTTS) *Calendar:* Courses of varying lengths *Degrees:* certificates *CEO:* Dir. Gerald W. Newman
Enroll: 317   (202) 638-6677

BARCLAY CAREER SCHOOL
1511 K St., N.W., Ste. 200, Washington 20005 *Type:* Private *Accred.:* 1991 (CCA-ACTTS) *Calendar:* Courses of varying lengths *Degrees:* certificates *CEO:* Dir. Lynn Johnson
        (202) 347-7200

CATHOLIC UNIVERSITY OF AMERICA
620 Michigan Ave., N.E., Washington 20064 *Type:* Private (Roman Catholic) *Accred.:* 1980/1985 (ATS); 1921/1980 (MSA) *Calendar:* Sem. plan *Degrees:* B, P, M, D *Prof. Accred.:* Architecture (B,M), Clinical Psychology, Engineering (bioengineering, civil, electrical, mechanical), Law, Librarianship, Medical Technology, Music, Nursing (B,M), Social Work (B,M), Teacher Education (e,s,p) *CEO:* Pres. William J. Byron, S.J.
Enroll: 7005   (202) 319-5000

CORCORAN SCHOOL OF ART
17th St. and New York Ave., NW, Washington 20006 *Type:* Private professional *Accred.:* 1985 (MSA) *Calendar:* Sem. plan *Degrees:* B *Prof. Accred.:* Art *CEO:* Pres./Dir. David Levy
Enroll: 280   (202) 628-9484

DE SALES SCHOOL OF THEOLOGY
721 Lawrence St., N.E., Washington 20017 *Type:* Private (Roman Catholic) graduate only *Accred.:* 1976/1986 (MSA) *Calendar:* Sem. plan *Degrees:* P, M *CEO:* Pres. John W. Crossin
Enroll: 34   (202) 269-9412

DEFENSE INTELLIGENCE COLLEGE
Defense Intelligence Analysis Ctr., Washington 20340 *Type:* Public (federal) graduate only *Accred.:* 1983/1988 (MSA) *Calendar:* Qtr. plan *Degrees:* M, certificates *CEO:* Commandant Howard J. Roop, U.S.N. (Ret.)
Enroll: 2302   (202) 373-3344

DISTRICT OF COLUMBIA SCHOOL OF LAW
719 13th St., N.W., Washington 20005 *Type:* Public *Calendar:* Sem. plan *Degrees:* P *Prof. Accred.:* Law (ABA only) *CEO:* Dean William L. Robinson
        (202) 727-5225

DOMINICAN HOUSE OF STUDIES
487 Michigan Ave., N.E., Washington 20017 *Type:* Private (Roman Catholic) graduate for men *Accred.:* 1976/1986 (ATS); 1976/1986 (MSA) *Calendar:* Sem. plan *Degrees:* M *CEO:* Pres. William C. Dettling
Enroll: 41   (202) 529-5300

GALLAUDET UNIVERSITY
800 Florida Ave., N.E., Washington 20002 *Type:* Private liberal arts *Accred.:* 1957/1986 (MSA) *Calendar:* Sem. plan *Degrees:* A, B, P, M, D, certificates *Prof. Accred.:* Audiology, Recreation and Leisure Studies, Rehabilitation Counseling, Social Work (B,M-candidate), Teacher Education (e,s,p) *CEO:* Pres. Irving King Jordan
Enroll: 2060   (202) 651-5000

GEORGE WASHINGTON UNIVERSITY
Washington 20052 *Type:* Private *Accred.:* 1922/1988 (MSA) *Calendar:* Sem. plan *Degrees:* A, B, P, M, D, certificates *Prof. Accred.:* Audiology, Business (B,M), Clinical Psychology, Community Health/ Preven-

tive Medicine, Computer Science, Counseling, Engineering (civil, computer, electrical, mechanical, systems), Health Services Administration, Law, Medical Record Administration, Medical Technology, Medicine, Music, Nuclear Medicine Technology, Nurse Anesthesia Education, Physician Assisting, Planning (regional/urban), Psychology Internship (provisional), Public Administration, Radiation Therapy Technology, Rehabilitation Counseling, Speech-Language Pathology, Teacher Education *CEO:* Pres. Stephen Joel Trachtenberg
Enroll: 19236 (202) 994-1000

GEORGETOWN UNIVERSITY
37th and O Sts., N.W., Washington 20057 *Type:* Private (Roman Catholic) *Accred.:* 1921/1987 (MSA) *Calendar:* Sem. plan *Degrees:* B, P, M, D, certificates *Prof. Accred.:* Business (B,M), Law, Medicine, Nursing (B,M), Ophthalmic Medical Technology *CEO:* Pres. Leo J. O'Donovan, S.J.
Enroll: 11516 (202) 687-0100

HANNAH HARRISON CAREER SCHOOL
4470 MacArthur Blvd., N.W., Washington 20007 *Type:* Private *Calendar:* Courses of varying lengths *Degrees:* diplomas *Prof. Accred.:* Practical Nursing *CEO:* Dir. Jane Town
(202) 333-3500

HOWARD UNIVERSITY
2400 Sixth St., N.W., Washington 20059 *Type:* Private *Accred.:* 1921/1989 (MSA) *Calendar:* Sem. plan *Degrees:* B, P, M, D, certificates *Prof. Accred.:* Accounting (Type A), Architecture (B), Art, Business (B,M), Clinical Psychology, Computer Science, Dental Hygiene, Dentistry, Dietetics (coordinated), Engineering (chemical, civil, electrical, mechanical), General Dentistry, General Practice Residency, Health Services Administration, Home Economics, Journalism, Law, Medical Technology, Medicine, Music, Nursing (B,M), Occupational Therapy, Oral and Maxillofacial Surgery, Orthodontics, Pediatric Dentistry, Pharmacy, Physical Therapy, Physician Assisting, Psychology Internship, Radiation Therapy Technology, Radiography, School Psychology, Social Work (B,M), Speech-Language Pathology, Theatre *CEO:* Pres. Franklyn G. Jenifer
Enroll: 11742 (202) 806-6100

SCHOOL OF DIVINITY
1400 Shepherd St., N.E., Washington, DC 20017 *Accred.:* 1940/1982 (ATS) *CEO:* Acting Dean Clarence G. Newsome
(202) 806-0500

LEVINE SCHOOL OF MUSIC
1690 36th St., N.W., Washington 20007 *Type:* Private *Calendar:* Courses of varying lengths *Degrees:* certificates *Prof. Accred.:* Music *CEO:* Dir. Joanne Hoover
(202) 337-2227

MARGARET MURRAY WASHINGTON VOCATIONAL SCHOOL
27 O St., N.W., Washington 20001 *Type:* Public *Calendar:* Courses of varying lengths *Degrees:* certificates *Prof. Accred.:* Dental Assisting, Practical Nursing *CEO:* Prin. Alethia Spraggins
(202) 673-7224

MCGRAW-HILL CONTINUING EDUCATION CENTER
4401 Connecticut Ave., N.W., Washington 20008 *Type:* Private home study *Accred.:* 1956/1988 (NHSC) *Calendar:* Courses of varying lengths *Degrees:* certificates *CEO:* Pres. Harold B. Reeb
(202) 244-1600

MOUNT VERNON COLLEGE
2100 Foxhall Rd., N.W., Washington 20007 *Type:* Private liberal arts for women *Accred.:* 1958/1987 (MSA) *Calendar:* Modular plan *Degrees:* A, B *Prof. Accred.:* Interior Design *CEO:* Pres. LucyAnn Geiselman
Enroll: 551 (202) 331-0400

NATIONAL CONSERVATORY OF DRAMATIC ARTS
1556 Wisconsin Ave., N.W., Washington 20007 *Type:* Private *Accred.:* 1980/1987 (CCA-ACTTS) *Calendar:* Sem. plan *Degrees:* diplomas *CEO:* Pres. C. Wayne Rudisill
Enroll: 70 (202) 333-2202

District of Columbia

NATIONAL EDUCATION CENTER—CAPITOL HILL CAMPUS
810 First St., N.E., Washington 20002 *Type:* Private business *Accred.:* 1969/1989 (CCA-ACICS) *Calendar:* Qtr. plan *Degrees:* certificates, diplomas *Prof. Accred.:* Medical Assisting *CEO:* Dir. Christopher Hanley
Enroll: 698   (202) 289-7700

OBLATE COLLEGE
391 Michigan Ave., N.E., Washington 20017 *Type:* Private (Roman Catholic) *Accred.:* 1976/1986(ATS); 1966/1986(MSA) *Calendar:* Sem. plan *Degrees:* B, P, M, certificates *CEO:* Pres. Dennis Cooney
Enroll: 36   (202) 529-6544

PTC CAREER INSTITUTE
529 14th St., N.W., Ste. 350, Washington 20004 *Type:* Private *Accred.:* 1991 (CCA-ACTTS) *Calendar:* Courses of varying lengths *Degrees:* certificates *CEO:* Dir. Esther Reid
   (202) 638-5300

SMITH BUSINESS SCHOOL
601 Indiana Ave., N.W., Ste. 800, Washington 20004 *Type:* Private business *Accred.:* 1979/1985 (CCA-ACICS) *Calendar:* Courses of varying lengths *Degrees:* certificates, diplomas *CEO:* Pres. Barbara Herold
Enroll: 374   (202) 638-1700

SOUTHEASTERN UNIVERSITY
501 Eye St., S.W., Washington 20024 *Type:* Private *Accred.:* 1988 (CCA-ACICS); 1977 (MSA) *Calendar:* Qtr. plan *Degrees:* A, B, M *CEO:* Pres. W. Robert Higgins
Enroll: 1309   (202) 488-8162

STRAYER COLLEGE
1111 18th St., N.W., Washington 20036 *Type:* Private business *Accred.:* 1959/1985 (CCA-ACICS); 1981/1985 (MSA) *Calendar:* Qtr. plan *Degrees:* A, B, M, certificates *CEO:* Pres. Ron K. Bailey
Enroll: 1797   (202) 728-0355

Accredited Institutions

TRINITY COLLEGE
125 Michigan Ave., N.E., Washington 20017 *Type:* Private (Roman Catholic) liberal arts for women *Accred.:* 1921/1986 (MSA) *Calendar:* Sem. plan *Degrees:* B, M *CEO:* Pres. Patricia A. McGuire
Enroll: 1125   (202) 939-5000

UNITED STATES MARINE CORPS INSTITUTE
Marine Barracks, Eighth and Eye Sts., S.E., Washington 20390 *Type:* Public (federal) home study *Accred.:* 1977/1988 (NHSC) *Calendar:* Courses of varying lengths *Degrees:* certificates *CEO:* Dir. P. Pace
   (202) 433-2632

UNIVERSITY OF THE DISTRICT OF COLUMBIA
4200 Connecticut Ave., N.W., Washington 20008 *Type:* Public (federal) *Accred.:* 1976/1985 (MSA) *Calendar:* Sem. plan *Degrees:* A, B, M *Prof. Accred.:* Engineering (civil, electrical, mechanical), Engineering Technology (aerospace, architectural, civil/construction, computer, electrical, mechanical), Mortuary Science, Nursing (A,B), Planning (regional/urban), Radiography, Respiratory Therapy, Social Work (B), Speech-Language Pathology *CEO:* Pres. Tilden J. LeMelle
Enroll: 11263   (202) 282-7300

GEORGIA/HARVARD STREET CAMPUS
11th and Harvard Sts., N.W., Washington, DC 20009
   (202) 673-7021

MOUNT VERNON SQUARE CAMPUS
900 F St., N.W., Washington, DC 20004
   (202) 282-7300

WESLEY THEOLOGICAL SEMINARY
4500 Massachusetts Ave., N.W., Washington 20016 *Type:* Private (United Methodist) professional; graduate only *Accred.:* 1940/1990 (ATS); 1975/1981 (MSA) *Calendar:* Sem. plan *Degrees:* P, M, D, certificates *CEO:* Pres. G. Douglass Lewis
Enroll: 262   (202) 885-8600

FLORIDA

ATI CAREER TRAINING CENTER
2880 N.W. 62nd St., Fort Lauderdale 33309
Type: Private *Accred.:* 1989 (CCA-ACTTS)
Calendar: Qtr. plan *Degrees:* A *CEO:* Pres. Joseph Mehlmann
Enroll: 200   (305) 973-4760

ATI CAREER TRAINING CENTER
One N.E. 19th St., Miami 33132 *Type:* Private *Accred.:* 1991 (CCA-ACTTS) *Calendar:* Qtr. plan *Degrees:* certificates *CEO:* Dir. Mark Gutmann
(305) 573-1600

ATI CAREER TRAINING CENTER
3501 N.W. 9th Ave., Oakland Park 33309-5900 *Type:* Private *Accred.:* 1984/1989 (CCA-ACTTS) *Calendar:* Qtr. plan *Degrees:* certificates *CEO:* Dir. Mike Forte
(800) 848-3500

ATI HEALTH EDUCATION CENTER
1395 N.W. 167th St., Ste. 200, Miami 33169-5745 *Type:* Private *Accred.:* 1991 (CCA-ACTTS) *Calendar:* Qtr. plan *Degrees:* certificates *CEO:* Dir. Michael Hoffman
(305) 628-1000

ALL POINTS TRAVEL SCHOOL
3324 Edgewater Dr., Orlando 32804-3742 *Type:* Private *Accred.:* 1988 (CCA-ACTTS) *Calendar:* Courses of varying lengths *Degrees:* certificates *CEO:* Dir. Jean Pangborn
(407) 291-2200

AMERICAN MEDICAL TRAINING INSTITUTE
10700 Caribbean Blvd., Ste. 301, Miami 33189 *Type:* Private technical *Calendar:* Courses of varying lengths *Degrees:* diplomas *Prof. Accred.:* Health Education, Medical Assisting *CEO:* Admin. James K. Brodie
(305) 253-8028

ART INSTITUTE OF FORT LAUDERDALE
1799 S.E. 17th St., Fort Lauderdale 33316-3013 *Type:* Private *Accred.:* 1971/1988 (CCA-ACTTS) *Calendar:* Qtr. plan *Degrees:* A, B *CEO:* Pres. David P. Higley
Enroll: 2266   (305) 463-3000

ATLANTIC VOCATIONAL-TECHNICAL CENTER
4700 Coconut Creek Pkwy., Coconut Creek 33066 *Type:* Public (state) technical *Accred.:* 1978/1989 (SACS-COEI) *Calendar:* Courses of varying lengths *Degrees:* certificates *Prof. Accred.:* Practical Nursing *CEO:* Dir. Robert Crawford
Enroll: 1744   (305) 977-2000

BRANCH CAMPUS
Pompano Multi-Purpose Ctr., 1400 N.E. Sixth St., Pompano Beach, FL 33060 *CEO:* Dir. Bob Crawford
(305) 786-7630

AUTOMOTIVE TRANSMISSION SCHOOL
453 E. Okeechobee Rd., Hialeah 33010 *Type:* Private *Accred.:* 1985 (CCA-ACTTS) *Calendar:* Courses of varying lengths *Degrees:* certificates *CEO:* Dir. Manuel J. Safon, Jr.
Enroll: 20   (305) 888-4898

BARCLAY CAREER SCHOOL
421 W. Church St., No. 501, Jacksonville 32202 *Type:* Private *Accred.:* 1991 (CCA-ACTTS) *Calendar:* Courses of varying lengths *Degrees:* certificates *CEO:* Exec. Dir. Rowland Adams
(904) 632-1903

BARNA INSTITUTE
1050 N.E. Fifth Terr., Fort Lauderdale 33304 *Type:* Private technical *Accred.:* 1984/1989 (SACS-COEI) *Calendar:* Courses of varying lengths *Degrees:* certificates *CEO:* Dir. Patricia Araujo-Wetstein
Enroll: 226   (305) 525-5069

BARRY UNIVERSITY
11300 N.E. Second Ave., Miami Shores 33161 *Type:* Private (Roman Catholic) *Accred.:* 1947/1991 (SACS-CC) *Calendar:* Sem. plan *Degrees:* B, M, D *Prof. Accred.:*

Nursing (B,M), Podiatry, Social Work (M) *CEO:* Pres. Jeanne O'Laughlin, O.P.
Enroll: 3625 (305) 899-3000

BAY AREA LEGAL ACADEMY
3924 Coconut Palm Dr., Tampa 33619 *Type:* Private business *Accred.:* 1979/1988 (CCA-ACICS) *Calendar:* Courses of varying lengths *Degrees:* certificates *CEO:* Dir. Isabelle Gibson
Enroll: 526 (813) 621-8074

BAY AREA VOCATIONAL-TECHNICAL SCHOOL
1976 Lewis Turner Blvd., Fort Walton Beach 32548 *Type:* Public (state) *Accred.:* 1979/1989 (SACS-COEI) *Calendar:* Courses of varying lengths *Degrees:* certificates *CEO:* Dir. Edward V. Baker
Enroll: 402 (904) 833-3500

BAY MEDICAL CENTER SCHOOL OF NURSE ANESTHESIA
615 N. Bonita Ave., P.O. Box 2515, Panama City 32401 *Type:* Private *Calendar:* Courses of varying lengths *Degrees:* certificates *Prof. Accred.:* Nurse Anesthesia Education *CEO:* Dir. William McCall
(904) 872-4918

BEACON CAREER INSTITUTE
2900 N.W. 183rd St., Miami 33056 *Type:* Private technical *Accred.:* 1990 (SACS-COEI candidate) *Calendar:* Courses of varying lengths *Degrees:* diplomas *Prof. Accred.:* Health Education *CEO:* Dir. Patricia Donawa
Enroll: 139 (305) 620-4637

BEAUTY SCHOOLS OF AMERICA
7942 W. Sample Rd., Margate 33063 *Type:* Private *Accred.:* 1989 (SACS-COEI) *Calendar:* Courses of varying lengths *Degrees:* diplomas *CEO:* Dir. John Rebstock
Enroll: 75 (305) 755-2014

BRANCH CAMPUS
1176 S.W. 67th Ave., Miami, FL 33144 *CEO:* Dir. John Rebstock
(305) 267-6604

BETHUNE-COOKMAN COLLEGE
640 Second Ave., Daytona Beach 32115 *Type:* Private liberal arts *Accred.:* 1947/1990 (SACS-CC) *Calendar:* Sem. plan *Degrees:* B, M (candidate) *Prof. Accred.:* Medical Technology, Teacher Education (e,s) *CEO:* Pres. Oswald P. Bronson, Sr.
Enroll: 2290 (904) 255-1401

BREVARD COMMUNITY COLLEGE
1519 Clearlake Rd., Cocoa 32922 *Type:* Public (district) junior *System:* Florida State Board of Community Colleges *Accred.:* 1963/1991 (SACS-CC) *Calendar:* Sem. plan *Degrees:* A *Prof. Accred.:* Dental Assisting, Dental Hygiene (conditional), EMT-Paramedic, Medical Laboratory Technology (AMA), Radiography, Respiratory Therapy *CEO:* Pres. Maxwell C. King
Enroll: 15152 (407) 632-1111

BRIARCLIFF COLLEGE
11401 S.W. 40th St., Miami 33165 *Type:* Private junior *Accred.:* 1987 (CCA-ACICS) *Calendar:* Courses of varying lengths *Degrees:* A *CEO:* Dir. Robert Hayward
(305) 551-9700

BROWARD COMMUNITY COLLEGE
225 E. Las Olas Blvd., Fort Lauderdale 33301 *Type:* Public (district) junior *System:* Florida State Board of Community Colleges *Accred.:* 1963/1983 (SACS-CC) *Calendar:* Sem. plan *Degrees:* A, certificates *Prof. Accred.:* Diagnostic Medical Sonography, Dental Assisting, EMT-Paramedic, Engineering Technology (electrical), Medical Assisting (AMA), Medical Laboratory Technology (AMA), Medical Record Technology, Nursing (A), Physical Therapy Assisting, Radiography, Respiratory Therapy, Respiratory Therapy Technology *CEO:* Pres. Willis N. Holcombe
Enroll: 19715 (305) 761-7400

BUSINESS TRAINING INSTITUTE
301 U.S. 19 N., Ste. 200, Clearwater 34625 *Type:* Private business *Accred.:* 1987 (CCA-ACICS) *Calendar:* Courses of varying

lengths *Degrees:* certificates, diplomas *CEO:* Dir. Nancy O'Donnell-Kenny
Enroll: 93 (813) 791-7833

BUSINESS TRAINING INSTITUTE
1900 Evans Rd., Ste. 131, Melbourne 32901 *Type:* Private business *Accred.:* 1988 (CCA-ACICS) *Calendar:* Courses of varying lengths *Degrees:* certificates, diplomas *CEO:* Dir. Darlene Wohl
Enroll: 165 (407) 724-0707

CAMBRIDGE ACADEMY
P.O Box 1290, Hwy. 319, Fort McCoy 32134 *Type:* Private home study *Accred.:* 1990 (NHSC) *Calendar:* Courses of varying lengths *Degrees:* certificates, diplomas *CEO:* C.E.O. Tanzee Nahas
(904) 595-5810

CAREER CITY COLLEGE
1317 N.E. Fourth Ave., Fort Lauderdale 33304 *Type:* Private junior *Accred.:* 1990 (CCA-ACICS) *Calendar:* Courses of varying lengths *Degrees:* A, certificates, diplomas *CEO:* Pres. C.M. Fike
Enroll: 538 (305) 764-4660

BRANCH CAMPUS
2400 S.W. 13th St., Gainesville, FL 32608 *CEO:* Dir. Karen L. Young
(904) 335-4000

CAREER INSTITUTE OF AMERICA
1205 Washington Ave., Miami Beach 33139-9883 *Type:* Private *Accred.:* 1985/1989 (CCA-ACTTS) *Calendar:* Courses of varying lengths *Degrees:* certificates *CEO:* Pres. Mort Paul
(305) 531-3300

CENTRAL FLORIDA COMMUNITY COLLEGE
3001 S.W. College Rd., Ocala 32678 *Type:* Public (district) junior *System:* Florida State Board of Community Colleges *Accred.:* 1964/1985 (SACS-CC) *Calendar:* Sem. plan *Degrees:* A *Prof. Accred.:* EMT-Paramedic *CEO:* Pres. William J. Campion
Enroll: 4186 (904) 237-2111

CHAPMAN SCHOOL OF SEAMANSHIP
4343 S.E. St. Lucie Blvd., Stuart 43997 *Type:* Private *Accred.:* 1983/1988 (CCA-ACTTS) *Calendar:* Courses of varying lengths *Degrees:* certificates *CEO:* Pres. Jennifer Castle-Field
Enroll: 159 (800) 225-2841

CHARLOTTE VOCATIONAL-TECHNICAL CENTER
18300 Toledo Blade Blvd., Port Charlotte 33948 *Type:* Public (state) *Accred.:* 1983/1988 (SACS-COEI) *Calendar:* Courses of varying lengths *Degrees:* certificates *Prof. Accred.:* Dental Assisting *CEO:* Dir. Roseann Keller Samson
Enroll: 499 (813) 629-6819

CHIPOLA JUNIOR COLLEGE
1200 College St., Marianna 32446 *Type:* Public (district) junior *System:* Florida State Board of Community Colleges *Accred.:* 1957/1988 (SACS-CC) *Calendar:* Sem. plan *Degrees:* A *CEO:* Pres. Jerry W. Kandzer
Enroll: 2818 (904) 526-2761

CLEARWATER CHRISTIAN COLLEGE
3400 Gulf-to-Bay Blvd., Clearwater 34619 *Type:* Private *Accred.:* 1984/1989 (SACS-CC) *Calendar:* Sem. plan *Degrees:* A, B *CEO:* Pres. George D. Youstra
Enroll: 421 (813) 726-1153

COLLEGE OF THE PALM BEACHES
1750 45th St., West Palm Beach 33407 *Type:* Private business *Accred.:* 1985 (CCA-ACICS) *Calendar:* Courses of varying lengths *Degrees:* A *CEO:* Exec. Dir. Don W. Schaefer
Enroll: 958 (407) 881-0220

CONCORDE CAREER INSTITUTE
7960 Arlington Expy., Jacksonville 32211-7429 *Type:* Private *Accred.:* 1991 (CCA-ACTTS) *Calendar:* Courses of varying lengths *Degrees:* certificates *CEO:* Dir. Jeanette Erdel
(904) 725-0525

CONCORDE CAREER INSTITUTE
4000 N. State Rd. 7, Lauderdale Lakes 33319 *Type:* Private *Accred.:* 1991 (CCA-

ACTTS) *Calendar:* Courses of varying lengths *Degrees:* certificates *CEO:* Dir. Patricia Trax
(305) 731-8880

CONCORDE CAREER INSTITUTE
4202 W. Spruce St., Tampa 33607-0094 *Type:* Private *Accred.:* 1991 (CCA-ACTTS) *Calendar:* Courses of varying lengths *Degrees:* certificates *CEO:* Dir. Thomas L. Buck
(813) 874-0094

COOPER ACADEMY OF COURT REPORTING
400 Executive Center Dr., Ste. 203, West Palm Beach 33401 *Type:* Private business *Accred.:* 1990 (CCA-ACICS) *Calendar:* Courses of varying lengths *Degrees:* certificates, diplomas *CEO:* Pres. Brenda J. Cooper
(407) 478-5389

COURT REPORTING CAREERS, INC.
1750 45th St., Ste. 204, West Palm Beach 33406 *Type:* Private *Accred.:* 1989 (CCA-ACTTS) *Calendar:* Courses of varying lengths *Degrees:* certificates *CEO:* Dir. David Schaefer
(305) 683-3388

CREATIVE SCHOOL OF BEAUTY
866 N. Federal Hwy., Pompano Beach 33062 *Type:* Private *Accred.:* 1989 (SACS-COEI) *Calendar:* Courses of varying lengths *Degrees:* diplomas *CEO:* Dir. Fran Stabinsky
Enroll: 90   (305) 943-8140

CROWN BUSINESS INSTITUTE
1223 S.W. Fourth St., Miami 33135 *Type:* Private business *Accred.:* 1981/1990 (CCA-ACICS) *Calendar:* Courses of varying lengths *Degrees:* certificates, diplomas *CEO:* Dir. Zuleica Perdomo-Martell
Enroll: 1229   (305) 643-1600

DAVID G. ERWIN TECHNICAL CENTER
2010 E. Hillsborough Ave., Tampa 33610 *Type:* Public (state) *Accred.:* 1981/1991 (SACS-COEI) *Calendar:* Courses of varying lengths *Degrees:* certificates *Prof. Accred.:* Medical Assisting (AMA), Medical Laboratory Technology (AMA), Respiratory Therapy Technology, Surgical Technology *CEO:* Dir. Janice Velez
Enroll: 1325   (813) 238-8631

DAYTONA BEACH COMMUNITY COLLEGE
1200 Volusia Ave., P.O. Box 2811, Daytona Beach 32114 *Type:* Public (district) junior *System:* Florida State Board of Community Colleges *Accred.:* 1963/1983 (SACS-CC) *Calendar:* Sem. plan *Degrees:* A *Prof. Accred.:* Dental Assisting, EMT-Paramedic, Medical Record Technology, Nursing (A), Respiratory Therapy, Respiratory Therapy Technology, Surgical Technology *CEO:* Pres. Philip R. Day, Jr.
Enroll: 14238   (904) 255-8131

DEFENSE EQUAL OPPORTUNITY MANAGEMENT INSTITUTE
DEOMI Library, Bldg. 560, Patrick Air Force Base 32925-6685 *Type:* Public (federal) *Accred.:* 1983/1988 (SACS-COEI) *Calendar:* Courses of varying lengths *Degrees:* certificates *CEO:* Dir. Patrick Connor
Enroll: 203   (305) 494-6976

DIANA RAMSAY'S SPECIALTY BEAUTY SCHOOL
2245 W. Hillsboro Blvd., Deerfield Beach 33442 *Type:* Private *Accred.:* 1990 (SACS-COEI) *Calendar:* Courses of varying lengths *Degrees:* certificates, diplomas *CEO:* Dir. Diana Ramsay
Enroll: 13   (305) 429-8358

DIESEL INSTITUTE OF AMERICA
4710 E. Broadway Ave., Tampa 33605 *Type:* Private *Accred.:* 1988 (CCA-ACTTS) *Calendar:* Courses of varying lengths *Degrees:* certificates *CEO:* Pres. Jeffrey Monsein
Enroll: 70   (813) 623-9990

ECKERD COLLEGE
P.O. Box 12560, St. Petersburg 33733 *Type:* Private (Presbyterian) liberal arts *Accred.:* 1963/1991 (SACS-CC) *Calendar:* 4-1-4 plan *Degrees:* B *CEO:* Pres. Peter H. Armacost
Enroll: 1983   (813) 867-1166

EDISON COMMUNITY COLLEGE
8099 College Pkwy., P.O. Box 06210, Fort Myers 33906-6210 *Type:* Public (district) junior *System:* Florida State Board of Community Colleges *Accred.:* 1964/1991 (SACS-CC) *Calendar:* Sem. plan *Degrees:* A *Prof. Accred.:* EMT-Paramedic, Respiratory Therapy *CEO:* Pres. Kenneth P. Walker
Enroll: 6001   (813) 489-9300

EDWARD WATERS COLLEGE
1658 Kings Rd., Jacksonville 32209 *Type:* Private (African Methodist Episcopal) liberal arts and teachers *Accred.:* 1979/1984 (SACS-CC) *Calendar:* Sem. plan *Degrees:* B *CEO:* Pres. Robert L. Mitchell
Enroll: 691   (904) 366-3030

ELINOR SMITH SCHOOL
207 Santillane Ave., Coral Gables 33134 *Type:* Private *Accred.:* 1991 (SACS-COEI) *Calendar:* Courses of varying lengths *Degrees:* certificates, diplomas *CEO:* Pres. Pierre Lepoureau
Enroll: 25   (305) 442-4480

ELKINS INSTITUTE OF JACKSONVILLE
3947 Boulevard Center Dr., Ste. 6, Jacksonville 32207 *Type:* Private *Accred.:* 1989 (SACS-COEI) *Calendar:* Courses of varying lengths *Degrees:* certificates *CEO:* Dir. John Heath
Enroll: 29   (904) 398-6211

EMBRY-RIDDLE AERONAUTICAL UNIVERSITY
Daytona Beach 32114-3900 *Type:* Private technological *Accred.:* 1968/1991 (SACS-CC) *Calendar:* Sem. plan *Degrees:* A, B, M *Prof. Accred.:* Engineering (aerospace), Engineering Technology (aerospace) *CEO:* Pres. Steven M. Sliwa
Enroll: 8504   (904) 239-6000

BRANCH CAMPUS
3200 N. Willow Creek Rd., Prescott, AZ 86301 *Prof. Accred.:* Engineering (aerospace) *CEO:* Chanc. Paul S. Daly
Enroll: 1069   (602) 776-3728

ENGINE TECHNICAL INSTITUTE/PRATT AND WHITNEY AIRCRAFT
P.O. Box 109600, Mail Stop 723-01, West Palm Beach 33410-9600 *Type:* Private *Accred.:* 1983/1988 (SACS-COEI) *Calendar:* Courses of varying lengths *Degrees:* certificates *CEO:* Dir. Joseph F. Manning
Enroll: 24   (407) 796-1073

FAA CENTER FOR MANAGEMENT DEVELOPMENT
4500 Palm Coast Pkwy., S.E., Palm Coast 32137 *Type:* Private *Accred.:* 1989 (SACS-COEI) *Calendar:* Courses of varying length *Degrees:* certificates *CEO:* Dir. Raymond Salazar
Enroll: 118   (904) 446-7136

FEDERAL CORRECTIONAL INSTITUTION
Capital Cir., N.E., Tallahassee 32301-3400 *Type:* Public (federal) *Accred.:* 1985/1990 (SACS-CC); 1985/1990 (SACS-COEI) *Calendar:* Courses of varying lengths *Degrees:* certificates *CEO:* Dir. Davey Edwards
Enroll: 463   (904) 878-2173

FLAGLER CAREER INSTITUTE—JACKSONVILLE
3225 University Blvd., S., Jacksonville 32216 *Type:* Private *Accred.:* 1982 (CCA-ACTTS) *Calendar:* Qtr. plan *Degrees:* A *Prof. Accred.:* Respiratory Therapy, Respiratory Therapy Technology *CEO:* Dir. Elaine Sapp
Enroll: 87   (904) 721-1622

FLAGLER CAREER INSTITUTE—MIAMI
1395 N.W. 167th St., 2nd Fl., Miami 33169 *Type:* Private *Calendar:* Courses of varying lengths *Degrees:* A, certificates, diplomas *Prof. Accred.:* Respiratory Therapy, Respiratory Therapy Technology *CEO:* Pres. Michael Hoffman
                                  (305) 628-1000

FLAGLER COLLEGE
P.O. Box 1027, St. Augustine 32085-1027 *Type:* Private liberal arts *Accred.:* 1973/1988 (SACS-CC) *Calendar:* Sem. plan *Degrees:* B *CEO:* Pres. William L. Proctor
Enroll: 1206   (904) 829-6481

Florida

FLIGHT SAFETY INTERNATIONAL
P.O. Box 2708, Vero Beach Airport, Vero Beach 32961 *Type:* Private *Accred.:* 1975/1988 (CCA-ACTTS) *Calendar:* Courses of varying lengths *Degrees:* certificates *CEO:* Dir. Thomas W. Gillespie
Enroll: 376 (305) 567-5178

FLORIDA AGRICULTURAL AND MECHANICAL UNIVERSITY
Tallahassee 32307 *Type:* Public (state) *System:* State University System of Florida *Accred.:* 1935/1988 (SACS-CC) *Calendar:* Sem. plan *Degrees:* B, P, M, D *Prof. Accred.:* Architecture (B,M), Engineering (chemical, civil, electrical, mechanical), Engineering Technology (civil/construction, electrical), Journalism, Medical Record Administration, Nursing (B), Occupational Therapy, Pharmacy, Physical Therapy, Respiratory Therapy, Social Work (B), Teacher Education (e,s,p) *CEO:* Pres. Frederick S. Humphries
Enroll: 8346 (904) 599-3000

FLORIDA ATLANTIC UNIVERSITY
500 N.W. 20th St., Boca Raton 33431-0991 *Type:* Public (state) graduate only *System:* State University System of Florida *Accred.:* 1965/1982 (SACS-CC) *Calendar:* Sem. plan *Degrees:* B, M, D *Prof. Accred.:* Business (B,M), Engineering (electrical, mechanical, ocean), Medical Technology, Music, Nursing (B,M), Public Administration, Social Work (B), Teacher Education (e,s,p) *CEO:* Pres. Anthony J. Catanese
Enroll: 9065 (407) 367-3000

FLORIDA BAPTIST THEOLOGICAL COLLEGE
1306 College Dr., Graceville 32440-1830 *Type:* Private (Southern Baptist) *Accred.:* 1981/1987 (SACS-CC) *Calendar:* Sem. plan *Degrees:* B *CEO:* Pres. Thomas A. Kinchen
Enroll: 416 (904) 263-3261

FLORIDA BIBLE COLLEGE
1701 Poinciana Blvd., Kissimmee 32758 *Type:* Private (Fundamentalist Churches of America) *Accred.:* 1989 (AABC) *Calendar:* Sem. plan *Degrees:* A, B *CEO:* Pres. Ron Vonbehren
Enroll: 89 (407) 933-4500

FLORIDA CAREER INSTITUTE
1685 Medical La., Ste. 200, Fort Myers 33907 *Type:* Private business *Accred.:* 1984/1990 (CCA-ACICS) *Calendar:* Qtr. plan *Degrees:* A *CEO:* Dir. Sandra Duttko
Enroll: 611 (813) 939-4766

FLORIDA CHRISTIAN COLLEGE
1011 Osceola Blvd., Kissimmee 32744 *Type:* Private (Christian Churches/Church of Christ) *Accred.:* 1985/1990 (AABC) *Calendar:* Qtr. plan *Degrees:* B *CEO:* Pres. A. Wayne Lowen
Enroll: 104 (407) 847-8966

FLORIDA COLLEGE
119 N. Glen Arven Ave., Temple Terrace 33617 *Type:* Private junior *Accred.:* 1954/1988 (SACS-CC) *Calendar:* Sem. plan *Degrees:* A *CEO:* Pres. Bob F. Owen
Enroll: 378 (813) 988-5131

FLORIDA COMMUNITY COLLEGE AT JACKSONVILLE
501 W. State St., Jacksonville 32202-4030 *Type:* Public (district) junior *System:* Florida State Board of Community Colleges *Accred.:* 1969/1984 (SACS-CC) *Calendar:* Sem. plan *Degrees:* A *Prof. Accred.:* Dental Hygiene (conditional), EMT-Paramedic, Medical Laboratory Technology (AMA), Nursing (A), Respiratory Therapy *CEO:* Pres. Charles C. Spence
Enroll: 29885 (904) 632-3224

FLORIDA COMPUTER AND BUSINESS COLLEGE
8300 Flagler St., Ste. 200, Miami 33144 *Type:* Private business *Accred.:* 1985 (CCA-ACICS) *Calendar:* Courses of varying lengths *Degrees:* A *CEO:* Pres. Carlos E. Rossie
Enroll: 464 (305) 553-6065

FLORIDA INSTITUTE OF MASSAGE THERAPY
3866 N. University Dr., Sunrise 33351-6303 *Type:* Private *Accred.:* 1991 (CCA-ACTTS)

Calendar: Courses of varying lengths *Degrees:* certificates *CEO:* Dir. Neal R. Heller
(305) 742-8259

FLORIDA INSTITUTE OF TECHNOLOGY
150 W. University Blvd., Melbourne 32901-6988 *Type:* Private technological *Accred.:* 1964/1985 (SACS-CC) *Calendar:* Qtr. plan *Degrees:* A, B, M, D *Prof. Accred.:* Clinical Psychology, Engineering (chemical, civil, computer, electrical, environmental/sanitary, mechanical, ocean) *CEO:* Pres. Lynn E. Weaver
Enroll: 4191 (407) 768-8000

FLORIDA INSTITUTE OF ULTRASOUND, INC.
8800 University Pkwy., P.O. Box 15135, Pensacola 32514 *Type:* Private technical *Calendar:* Courses of varying lengths *Degrees:* certificates *Prof. Accred.:* Diagnostic Medical Sonography, Health Education *CEO:* Dir. J. Jay Crittenden, M.D.
(904) 478-7300

FLORIDA INTERNATIONAL UNIVERSITY
University Park, Miami 33199 *Type:* Public (state) liberal arts; graduate only *System:* State University System of Florida *Accred.:* 1974/1990 (SACS-CC) *Calendar:* Sem. plan *Degrees:* A, B, M, D *Prof. Accred.:* Accounting (Type A,C), Business (B,M), Construction Education, Dietetics (coordinated), Engineering (civil, electrical, industrial, mechanical), Journalism, Medical Record Administration, Medical Technology, Nursing (B), Occupational Therapy, Physical Therapy, Public Administration, Social Work (B,M) *CEO:* Pres. Modesto A. Maidique
Enroll: 16280 (305) 348-2000

FLORIDA KEYS COMMUNITY COLLEGE
5901 W. Junior College Rd., Key West 33040 *Type:* Public (district) junior *System:* Florida State Board of Community Colleges *Accred.:* 1968/1982 (SACS-CC) *Calendar:* Sem. plan *Degrees:* A *CEO:* Pres. William A. Seeker
Enroll: 1966 (305) 296-9081

FLORIDA MEMORIAL COLLEGE
15800 N.W. 42nd Ave., Miami 33054 *Type:* Private (Baptist) liberal arts *Accred.:* 1951/1982 (SACS-CC) *Calendar:* Sem. plan *Degrees:* B *CEO:* Pres. Lee A. Monroe
Enroll: 1715 (305) 625-4141

FLORIDA NATIONAL COLLEGE
4206 W. 12th Ave., Hialeah 33012 *Type:* Private *Accred.:* 1983/1990 (SACS-COEI) *Calendar:* Courses of varying lengths *Degrees:* certificates *CEO:* Dir. Jose Requeiro
Enroll: 382 (305) 821-3333

BRANCH CAMPUS
11373 W. Flagler St., Ste. 208, Miami, FL 33174 *CEO:* Dir. Gorge Alfonso
(305) 226-9999

BRANCH CAMPUS
5761 S.W. Bird Rd., Miami, FL 33155 *CEO:* Dir. Joan Erica
(305) 663-6464

FLORIDA SCHOOL OF BUSINESS
2990 N.W. 81st Terr., Miami 33147 *Type:* Private business *Accred.:* 1986 (CCA-ACICS) *Calendar:* Qtr. plan *Degrees:* certificates, diplomas *CEO:* Dir. Michael D. Beauregard
Enroll: 426 (305) 696-6312

FLORIDA SCHOOL OF BUSINESS
405 E. Polk St., Tampa 33602 *Type:* Private business *Accred.:* 1986 (CCA-ACICS) *Calendar:* Qtr. plan *Degrees:* certificates, diplomas *CEO:* Dir. Lucille Sanders
Enroll: 288 (813) 221-4200

FLORIDA SOUTHERN COLLEGE
111 Lake Hollingsworth Dr., Lakeland 33801-5698 *Type:* Private (United Methodist) liberal arts *Accred.:* 1935/1988 (SACS-CC) *Calendar:* Sem. plan *Degrees:* B, M *CEO:* Pres. Robert A. Davis
Enroll: 1765 (813) 680-4111

FLORIDA STATE UNIVERSITY
Tallahassee 32306-1037 *Type:* Public (state) *System:* State University System of Florida *Accred.:* 1915/1984 (SACS-CC) *Calendar:*

Sem. plan *Degrees:* A, B, P, M, D *Prof. Accred.:* Accounting (Type A,C), Audiology, Business (B,M), Clinical Psychology, Computer Science, Dance, Engineering (chemical, civil, electrical, mechanical), Home Economics, Interior Design, Law, Leisure Services and Studies, Librarianship, Music, Nursing (B,M), Planning (regional/urban), Public Administration, Rehabilitation Counseling, School Psychology, Social Work (B,M), Speech-Language Pathology, Teacher Education, Theatre *CEO:* Pres. Dale W. Lick
Enroll: 28149   (904) 644-2525

FLORIDA TECHNICAL COLLEGE
8711 Lone Star Rd., Jacksonville 32211 *Type:* Private business *Accred.:* 1984 (CCA-ACICS) *Calendar:* Courses of varying lengths *Degrees:* certificates, diplomas *CEO:* Dir. Robert E. Lee
Enroll: 461   (904) 724-2229

FLORIDA TECHNICAL COLLEGE
1819 N. Semoran Blvd., Orlando 32807 *Type:* Private business *Accred.:* 1982/1990 (CCA-ACICS) *Calendar:* Courses of varying lengths *Degrees:* A *CEO:* Dean James J. Roberts
Enroll: 662   (407) 678-5600

FLORIDA TECHNICAL COLLEGE
4750 E. Adamo Dr., Tampa 33605 *Type:* Private business *Accred.:* 1982/1990 (CCA-ACICS) *Calendar:* Courses of varying lengths *Degrees:* certificates, diplomas *CEO:* Dean Kenneth B. Dowling
Enroll: 249   (813) 247-1700

FORT LAUDERDALE COLLEGE
100 E. Broward Blvd., Fort Lauderdale 33301 *Type:* Private senior *Accred.:* 1968/1987 (CCA-ACICS) *Calendar:* Qtr. plan *Degrees:* A, B, certificates, diplomas *CEO:* Dir. Glen Dorman
Enroll: 1656   (305) 462-3761

BRANCH CAMPUS
551 W. 51st Pl., Hialeah 33012, FL *CEO:* Dir. Diego Valero
         (305) 558-1949

BRANCH CAMPUS
1303 Thomasville Rd., Tallahassee, FL 32303-5675 *CEO:* Dir. Maura Freeberg
         (904) 224-8083

FULL SAIL CENTER FOR THE RECORDING ARTS
3300 University Blvd., Winter Park 32792 *Type:* Private *Accred.:* 1986 (CCA-ACTTS) *Calendar:* Courses of varying lengths *Degrees:* diplomas *CEO:* Pres. Jon Phelps
Enroll: 243   (407) 679-6333

GARCES COMMERCIAL COLLEGE
1301 S.W. First St., Miami 33135 *Type:* Private *Accred.:* 1990 (SACS-COEI) *Calendar:* Courses of varying lengths *Degrees:* diplomas *CEO:* Dir. Elena Nespereira
Enroll: 1030   (305) 643-1044

BRANCH CAMPUS
5385 N.W. 36th St., Miami Springs, FL 33166 *CEO:* Dir. Gabriel Torres
         (305) 871-6535

GEORGE STONE VOCATIONAL-TECHNICAL CENTER
2400 Longleaf Dr., Pensacola 32526-8922 *Type:* Public (state) *Accred.:* 1981/1991 (SACS-COEI) *Calendar:* Courses of varying lengths *Degrees:* certificates *CEO:* Dir. Robert Lindner
Enroll: 821   (904) 944-1424

GEORGE T. BAKER AVIATION SCHOOL
3275 N.W. 42nd Ave., Miami 33142 *Type:* Public technical *Accred.:* 1978/1988 (SACS-COEI) *Calendar:* Courses of varying lengths *Degrees:* certificates *CEO:* Dir. Thomas Gilmour
Enroll: 550   (305) 871-3143

GULF COAST COMMUNITY COLLEGE
5230 W. Hwy. 98, Panama City 32401 *Type:* Public (district) junior *System:* Florida State Board of Community Colleges *Accred.:* 1962/1990 (SACS-CC) *Calendar:* Sem. plan *Degrees:* A *Prof. Accred.:* Dental Assisting, EMT-Paramedic, Nursing (A), Radiography, Respiratory Therapy Technology *CEO:* Pres. Robert L. McSpadden
Enroll: 5243   (904) 872-3800

HENRY W. BREWSTER VOCATIONAL-TECHNICAL CENTER
2222 N. Tampa St., Tampa 33602 *Type:* Public (state) *Accred.:* 1989/1990 (SACS-COEI) *Calendar:* Courses of varying lengths *Degrees:* certificates *CEO:* Dir. Peter Labruzzo
Enroll: 264 (813) 273-9240

HILLSBOROUGH COMMUNITY COLLEGE
P.O. Box 31127, Tampa 33631-3127 *Type:* Public (district) junior *System:* Florida State Board of Community Colleges *Accred.:* 1971/1986 (SACS-CC) *Calendar:* Sem. plan *Degrees:* A *Prof. Accred.:* Diagnostic Medical Sonography, EMT-Paramedic, Nuclear Medicine Technology, Nursing (A), Radiation Therapy Technology, Radiography *CEO:* Pres. Andreas A. Paloumpis
Enroll: 12257 (813) 253-7000

HOBE SOUND BIBLE COLLEGE
P.O. Box 1065, Hobe Sound 33475 *Type:* Private (Wesleyan) *Accred.:* 1986 (AABC) *Calendar:* 4-1-4 plan *Degrees:* A, B *CEO:* Pres. Robert Whitaker
Enroll: 147 (407) 546-5534

HUMANITIES CENTER SCHOOL OF THERAPUTIC MASSAGE
4045 Park Blvd., Pinellas Park 34665 *Type:* Private *Accred.:* 1984/1989 (CCA-ACTTS) *Calendar:* Courses of varying lengths *Degrees:* certificates *CEO:* Dir. Sherry I. Fears
Enroll: 92 (813) 522-1697

ITT TECHNICAL INSTITUTE
5225 Memorial Hwy., Tampa 33634 *Type:* Private *Accred.:* 1983/1988 (CCA-ACTTS) *Calendar:* Qtr. plan *Degrees:* A, B, certificates, diplomas *CEO:* Dir. Larry Graphman
Enroll: 184 (813) 885-2244

INDIAN RIVER COMMUNITY COLLEGE
3209 Virginia Ave., Fort Pierce 34981-5599 *Type:* Public (district) junior *System:* Florida State Board of Community Colleges *Accred.:* 1963/1983 (SACS-CC) *Calendar:* Sem. plan *Degrees:* A *Prof. Accred.:* Dental Assisting, Dental Hygiene, Dental Laboratory Technology, EMT-Paramedic, Medical Laboratory Technology (AMA), Nursing (A), Radiography *CEO:* Pres. Edwin R. Massey
Enroll: 5875 (407) 468-4700

INSTITUTE OF SECURITY AND TECHNOLOGY
13850 N.W. 26th Ave., Miami 33054 *Type:* Private *Accred.:* 1986 (CCA-ACTTS) *Calendar:* Courses of varying lengths *Degrees:* certificates *CEO:* Dir. Leonard Capuzzi
Enroll: 232 (305) 953-0500

INTERNATIONAL ACADEMY OF MERCHANDISING AND DESIGN
200 South Hanover Boulevard, 211 Mariner Square Park, Tampa 33609-9960 *Type:* Private *Accred.:* 1985 (CCA-ACICS) *Calendar:* Sem. plan *Degrees:* A, certificates, diplomas *CEO:* Exec. Dir. Michael Santoro
Enroll: 235 (813) 286-8588

INTERNATIONAL CAREER INSTITUTE
900 N.W. Fifth Ave., Fort Lauderdale 33311 *Type:* Private *Accred.:* 1984/1989 (SACS-COEI) *Calendar:* Courses of varying lengths *Degrees:* certificates *CEO:* Pres. Jeannie Allsage
Enroll: 39 (305) 522-6448

INTERNATIONAL CAREER INSTITUTE
888 W. 11th St., Panama City 32401 *Type:* Private *Accred.:* 1989 (SACS-COEI) *Calendar:* Courses of varying lengths *Degrees:* certificates *CEO:* Dir. William Hanks
Enroll: 397 (904) 784-1802

BRANCH CAMPUS
118 E. Moulton St., Ste. A, Decatur, AL 35601 *CEO:* Dir. Dorothy Wilburn
(205) 351-0204

BRANCH CAMPUS
85-B Elgin Pkwy., N.E., Fort Walton, FL 32458 *CEO:* Dir. Monica Fazio
(904) 244-2365

BRANCH CAMPUS
1412 W. Fairfield Dr., Pensacola, FL 32501 *CEO:* Dir. Bill Bailey
(904) 438-3167

Florida   **Accredited Institutions**

BRANCH CAMPUS
Towne Shopping Ctr., 2525 South Monroe St., Tallahassee, FL 32301 *CEO:* Dir. Jim Bailey
(904) 656-8014

INTERNATIONAL COLLEGE
2654 E. Tamiami Tr., Naples 33962-5790 *Type:* Private senior *Accred.:* 1990 (CCA-ACICS) *Calendar:* Sem. plan *Degrees:* A, B, M *CEO:* Dir. Richard Ashley
(813) 774-4700

INTERNATIONAL FINE ARTS COLLEGE
1737 N. Bayshore Dr., Miami 33132 *Type:* Private *Accred.:* 1979/1984 (SACS-CC) *Calendar:* Sem. plan *Degrees:* A *CEO:* Pres. Edward Porter
Enroll: 610   (305) 373-4684

INTERNATIONAL TECHNICAL INSTITUTE
8407 Laurel Fair Cir., Tampa 33610 *Type:* Private *Accred.:* 1973/1986 (CCA-ACTTS) *Calendar:* Qtr. plan *Degrees:* A, diplomas *CEO:* Pres. Larry J. Nero
Enroll: 500   (813) 621-3566

JACKSONVILLE UNIVERSITY
2800 University Blvd. N., Jacksonville 32211 *Type:* Private *Accred.:* 1961/1983 (SACS-CC) *Calendar:* Sem. plan *Degrees:* B, M *Prof. Accred.:* Dance, Music, Nursing (B) *CEO:* Pres. James J. Brady
Enroll: 2197   (904) 744-3950

JAMES L. WALKER VOCATIONAL-TECHNICAL CENTER
3702 Estey Ave., Naples 33942-4498 *Type:* Public (state) *Accred.:* 1980/1990 (SACS-COEI) *Calendar:* Courses of varying lengths *Degrees:* certificates *CEO:* Dir. Leo Mediavilla
Enroll: 1262   (813) 643-0919

BRANCH CAMPUS
Immokalee High Sch., 701 Immokalee Dr., Immokalee, FL 33934 *CEO:* Coord. Gloria Dominguez
(813) 643-0919

BRANCH CAMPUS
Radisson Suite Beach Resort, 600 S. Collier Blvd., Marco Island, FL 33937 *CEO:* Coord. Kevin Donovan
(813) 643-0919

BRANCH CAMPUS
Marco Marriott Hotel, 400 S. Colleir Blvd., Marco Island, FL 33937 *CEO:* Coord. Roberta Horton
(813) 643-0919

BRANCH CAMPUS
Marco Beach Hilton, 560 S. Collier Blvd., Marco Island, FL 33937 *CEO:* Coord. Kevin Donovan
(813) 643-0919

BRANCH CAMPUS
Naples Beach Hotel, 851 Gulf Shore Blvd., N., Naples, FL 33940 *CEO:* Coord. Garciela Somoza
(813) 643-0919

BRANCH CAMPUS
The Registry Resort, 476 Seagate Dr., Naples, FL 33940 *CEO:* Coord. Garciela Somoza
(813) 643-0919

JOHN B. STETSON UNIVERSITY
401 N. Woodland Blvd., DeLand 32720 *Type:* Private (Southern Baptist) *Accred.:* 1932/1991 (SACS-CC) *Calendar:* 4-1-4 plan *Degrees:* B, P, M, D *Prof. Accred.:* Law, Music *CEO:* Pres. H. Douglas Lee
Enroll: 2830   (904) 822-7000

JONES COLLEGE
5353 Arlington Expy., Jacksonville 32211-5588 *Type:* Private senior *Accred.:* 1957/1988 (CCA-ACICS) *Calendar:* Qtr. plan *Degrees:* A, B, certificates, diplomas *CEO:* Pres. James M. Patch
Enroll: 1421   (904) 743-1122

BRANCH CAMPUS
5975 Sunset Dr., Ste. 100, Miami, FL 33143 *CEO:* Dir. Juan Barreto
(305) 669-9606

KEISER COLLEGE OF TECHNOLOGY
1401 W. Cypress Creek Rd., Fort Lauderdale 33309 *Type:* Private technical *Accred.:* 1981/1988 (CCA-ACTTS); 1991 (SACS-CC); 1984/1989 (SACS-COEI) *Calendar:* Sem. plan *Degrees:* A, certificates *Prof. Accred.:* Medical Assisting, Medical Laboratory Technology *CEO:* Pres. Arthur Keiser
Enroll: 622 (305) 776-4456

BRANCH CAMPUS
410 N. Wickham Rd., Melbourne, FL 32935 *Prof. Accred.:* Medical Assisting *CEO:* Dir. Susan J. Siemsglusz
(407) 255-2255

LAKE CITY COMMUNITY COLLEGE
Rte. 3, Box 7, Lake City 32055 *Type:* Public (district) junior *System:* Florida State Board of Community Colleges *Accred.:* 1964/1990 (SACS-CC) *Calendar:* Sem. plan *Degrees:* A *Prof. Accred.:* EMT-Paramedic, Medical Laboratory Technology (AMA) *CEO:* Pres. Muriel K. Heimer
Enroll: 3064 (904) 752-1822

LAKE COUNTY AREA VOCATIONAL-TECHNICAL CENTER
2001 Kurt St., Eustis 32726 *Type:* Public (state) *Accred.:* 1974/1989 (SACS-COEI) *Calendar:* Courses of varying lengths *Degrees:* certificates *Prof. Accred.:* EMT-Paramedic *CEO:* Dir. Jack Partlow
Enroll: 671 (904) 357-8222

LAKE-SUMTER COMMUNITY COLLEGE
9501 U.S. Hwy. 441, Leesburg 34788 *Type:* Public (district) junior *System:* Florida State Board of Community Colleges *Accred.:* 1965/1990 (SACS-CC) *Calendar:* Sem. plan *Degrees:* A *CEO:* Pres. Carl C. Andersen
Enroll: 1525 (904) 787-3747

LEE COUNTY AREA VOCATIONAL-TECHNICAL SCHOOL
3800 Michigan Ave., Fort Myers 33916 *Type:* Public (state) *Accred.:* 1978/1988 (SACS-COEI) *Calendar:* Courses of varying lengths *Degrees:* certificates *CEO:* Dir. Ronald E. Pentiuk
Enroll: 1081 (813) 334-4544

LEGAL CAREER INSTITUTE
5225 W. Broward Blvd., Fort Lauderdale 33317 *Type:* Private business *Accred.:* 1985 (CCA-ACICS) *Calendar:* Courses of varying lengths *Degrees:* A, certificates, diplomas *CEO:* Dir. Martha Metz
Enroll: 567 (305) 581-2223

BRANCH CAMPUS
7289 Garden Rd., Ste. 204, Riviera Beach, FL 33404 *CEO:* Academic Dean Cynthia Dell Cioppia
(305) 848-2223

LINDSEY HOPKINS TECHNICAL EDUCATION CENTER
750 N.W. 20th St., Miami 33127 *Type:* Public (state) *Accred.:* 1972/1987 (SACS-COEI) *Calendar:* Courses of varying lengths *Degrees:* certificates *Prof. Accred.:* Dental Laboratory Technology, Practical Nursing, Surgical Technology *CEO:* Dir. John T. Coursey
Enroll: 2361 (305) 324-6070

LIVELY AREA VOCATIONAL-TECHNICAL CENTER
500 N. Appleyard Dr., Tallahassee 32304-2895 *Type:* Public (state) *Accred.:* 1977/1987 (SACS-COEI) *Calendar:* Courses of varying lengths *Degrees:* certificates *CEO:* Dir. Tom Dunn
Enroll: 1343 (904) 487-7401

LYNN UNIVERSITY
3601 N. Military Tr., Boca Raton 33431 *Type:* Private *Accred.:* 1964/1991 (SACS-CC) *Calendar:* Sem. plan *Degrees:* A, B, M *Prof. Accred.:* Mortuary Science *CEO:* Pres. Donald E. Ross
Enroll: 948 (407) 994-0770

MTA SCHOOL
6000 Cinderiane Pkwy., Orlando 32810 *Type:* Private *Accred.:* 1991 (CCA-ACTTS) *Calendar:* Courses of varying lengths *De-*

grees: certificates *CEO:* Dir. Vernon Edwards
(407) 299-7447

MANATEE AREA VOCATIONAL-TECHNICAL CENTER
5603 34th St., W., Bradenton 34210 *Type:* Public (state) *Accred.:* 1980/1990 (SACS-COEI) *Calendar:* Courses of varying lengths *Degrees:* certificates *Prof. Accred.:* Dental Assisting, EMT-Paramedic *CEO:* Dir. Walter Bucklin
Enroll: 578 (813) 755-2641

MANATEE COMMUNITY COLLEGE
5840 26th St., W., Bradenton 34206 *Type:* Public (district) junior *System:* Florida State Board of Community Colleges *Accred.:* 1963/1984 (SACS-CC) *Calendar:* Sem. plan *Degrees:* A *Prof. Accred.:* Nursing (A), Radiography *CEO:* Pres. Stephen J. Korcheck
Enroll: 5756 (813) 755-1511

MARION COUNTY SCHOOL OF RADIOLOGIC TECHNOLOGY
438 S.W. Third St., Ocala 32674 *Type:* Private *Calendar:* 2-year program *Degrees:* certificates *Prof. Accred.:* Radiography *CEO:* Admin. Sam Lauff, Jr.
Enroll: 28 (904) 629-7545

MARTIN TECHNICAL COLLEGE
1901 N.W. Seventh St., Miami 33125 *Type:* Private *Accred.:* 1978/1986 (CCA-ACTTS) *Calendar:* Courses of varying lengths *Degrees:* certificates, diplomas *CEO:* Dir. Fernando A. Alvarez
Enroll: 237 (305) 541-8140

MASTER SCHOOL OF BARTENDING
824 S.W. 24th St., Fort Lauderdale 33315 *Type:* Private *Accred.:* 1991 (CCA-ACTTS) *Calendar:* Courses of varying lengths *Degrees:* certificates *CEO:* Pres. Judi Snelling
(305) 467-8829

MASTER SCHOOL OF BARTENDING
4315 N.W. 7th St., Ste. 36, Miami 33126 *Type:* Private *Accred.:* 1991 (CCA-ACTTS)

Calendar: Courses of varying lengths *Degrees:* certificates *CEO:* Dir. Mindy Levine
(305) 373-3036

MEDICAL ARTS TRAINING CENTER
441 State Rd. 7, Ste. 4, Margate 33068-1934 *Type:* Private technical *Calendar:* Courses of varying lengths *Degrees:* certificates *Prof. Accred.:* EMT-Paramedic, Health Education, Medical Assisting *CEO:* Chrmn. Lauren Hemedinger
(305) 968-3500

MIAMI CHRISTIAN COLLEGE
2300 N.W. 135th St., Miami 33167 *Type:* Private (Evangelical Free Church) *Accred.:* 1975/1985 (AABC) *Calendar:* Sem. plan *Degrees:* A, B *CEO:* Pres. Larry D. McCullough
Enroll: 189 (305) 953-1100

MIAMI INSTITUTE OF PSYCHOLOGY
8180 N.W. 36th St., 2nd Fl., Miami 33166-6612 *Type:* Private *Accred.:* 1981/1989 (MSA) *Calendar:* Sem. plan *Degrees:* B, M, D, certificates, diplomas *CEO:* Chanc. Evelyn Diaz
Enroll: 204 (305) 593-1223

MIAMI JOB CORPS CENTER
660 S.W. Third St., Miami 33130 *Type:* Private *Accred.:* 1986 (SACS-COEI) *Calendar:* Courses of varying lengths *Degrees:* certificates *CEO:* Dir. Don E. DeJarnett
Enroll: 222 (305) 325-1276

MIAMI LAKES TECHNICAL EDUCATION CENTER
5780 N.W. 158th St., Miami 33014 *Type:* Public (state) *Accred.:* 1983/1988 (SACS-COEI) *Calendar:* Courses of varying lengths *Degrees:* certificates *Prof. Accred.:* Practical Nursing *CEO:* Dir. Noward Dean
Enroll: 1136 (305) 557-1100

MIAMI TECHNICAL COLLEGE
1001 N. Federal Hwy., Hollywood 33009 *Type:* Private *Accred.:* 1991 (CCA-ACTTS) *Calendar:* Courses of varying lengths *Degrees:* certificates *CEO:* Dir. Alex Diaz
(305) 457-5900

MIAMI TECHNICAL COLLEGE
14701 N.W. Seventh St., Miami 33130 *Type:* Private *Accred.:* 1987 (CCA-ACTTS) *Calendar:* Courses of varying lengths *Degrees:* certificates *CEO:* Dir. Robert Piacenti
(305) 688-8811

MIAMI TECHNICAL COLLEGE
19151 S. Dixie Hwy., Miami 33157 *Type:* Private *Accred.:* 1988 (CCA-ACTTS) *Calendar:* Courses of varying lengths *Degrees:* certificates *CEO:* Dir. Joaquin Bassolles
(305) 254-0995

MIAMI TECHNICAL COLLEGE
1001 S.W. First St., Miami 33130 *Type:* Private *Accred.:* 1980/1987 (CCA-ACTTS) *Calendar:* Courses of varying lengths *Degrees:* certificates *CEO:* Dir. Sergio Delgado
(305) 324-6781

BRANCH CAMPUS
1753 Alton Rd., Miami, FL 33126 *CEO:* Dir. Angel Alonso
(305) 538-3835

BRANCH CAMPUS
7061 W. Flagler St., Miami, FL 33126 *CEO:* Dir. Victor Suarez
(305) 263-9618

MIAMI TECHNICAL COLLEGE
8672 S.W. 40th St., Miami 33142 *Type:* Private *Accred.:* 1988 (CCA-ACTTS) *Calendar:* Courses of varying lengths *Degrees:* certificates *CEO:* Dir. Graciela Scotta
(305) 858-1350

MIAMI-DADE COMMUNITY COLLEGE
300 N.E. Second Ave., Miami 33132 *Type:* Public (district) junior *System:* Florida State Board of Community Colleges *Accred.:* 1964/1985 (SACS-CC) *Calendar:* Sem. plan *Degrees:* A *Prof. Accred.:* Dental Hygiene, Electroneurodiagnostic Technology, EMT-Paramedic, Funeral Service Education, Medical Laboratory Technology (AMA), Medical Record Technology, Nursing (A), Physical Therapy Assisting, Radiation Therapy Technology, Radiography, Respiratory Therapy, Respiratory Therapy Technology *CEO:* Pres. Robert H. McCabe
Enroll: 39206   (305) 237-3100

MID-FLORIDA TECHNICAL INSTITUTE
2900 W. Oak Ridge Rd., Orlando 32809 *Type:* Public (state) *Accred.:* 1974/1989 (SACS-COEI) *Calendar:* Courses of varying lengths *Degrees:* certificates *CEO:* Dir. Robert J. Clark
Enroll: 4793   (305) 855-5880

NATIONAL AVIATION ACADEMY
St. Clearwater/Clearwater Apt., Wick Wing No. 236, Clearwater 34622 *Type:* Private *Accred.:* 1991 (SACS-COEI) *Calendar:* Courses of varying lengths *Degrees:* diplomas *CEO:* Pres. Edward Moore
Enroll: 138   (813) 531-2080

NATIONAL CAREER INSTITUTE
3910 U.S. Hwy. 301 N., Tampa 33619 *Type:* Private *Accred.:* 1985 (CCA-ACTTS) *Calendar:* Courses of varying lengths *Degrees:* diplomas *CEO:* Dir. Carroll Gossage
(813) 238-6441

NATIONAL EDUCATION CENTER—BAUDER FASHION COLLEGE
4801 N. Dixie Hwy., Fort Lauderdale 33334 *Type:* Private *Accred.:* 1970/1988 (CCA-ACTTS) *Calendar:* Qtr. plan *Degrees:* A, certificates *CEO:* Dir. Dale Oakley
Enroll: 1200   (305) 491-7171

BRANCH CAMPUS
7955 N.W. 12th St., Ste. 300, Miami, FL 33126-1823 *CEO:* Dir. Allen Rice
(305) 477-0251

NATIONAL SCHOOL OF TECHNOLOGY, INC.
16150 N.E. 17th Ave., North Miami Beach 33162 *Type:* Private *Accred.:* 1983/1988 (CCA-ACTTS) *Calendar:* Courses of 24-wks. plus externship *Degrees:* diplomas *Prof. Accred.:* Medical Assisting *CEO:* Pres. Martin Knobel
Enroll: 550   (305) 949-5500

Florida

BRANCH CAMPUS
4355 W. 16th Ave., Hialeah, FL 33012 *Prof. Accred.:* Medical Assisting *CEO:* Dir. Clare Lodermeier
(305) 558-9500

NATIONAL TRAINING, INC.
188 College Dr., P.O. Box 1899, Orange Park 32067-1899 *Type:* Private combination home study and resident *Accred.:* 1982/1988 (NHSC) *Calendar:* Courses of varying lengths *Degrees:* certificates *CEO:* Pres. Frank Lark
(904) 272-4000

NEW ENGLAND INSTITUTE OF TECHNOLOGY AT PALM BEACH
1126 53rd Ct., West Palm Beach 33407 *Type:* Private *Accred.:* 1984 (CCA-ACTTS) *Calendar:* Qtr. plan *Degrees:* A *CEO:* Pres. Richard I. Gouse
Enroll: 631 (305) 842-8324

NORTH FLORIDA JUNIOR COLLEGE
1000 Turner Davis Dr., Madison 32340 *Type:* Public (district) junior *System:* Florida State Board of Community Colleges *Accred.:* 1963/1984 (SACS-CC) *Calendar:* Sem. plan *Degrees:* A *CEO:* Pres. William H. McCoy
Enroll: 698 (904) 973-2288

NORTH TECHNICAL EDUCATION CENTER
7071 Garden Rd., Riviera Beach 33404 *Type:* Public (state) *Accred.:* 1976/1991 (SACS-COEI) *Calendar:* Courses of varying lengths *Degrees:* certificates *CEO:* Dir. Patricia I. Nugent
Enroll: 1050 (407) 881-4600

NOVA UNIVERSITY
3301 College Ave., Fort Lauderdale 33314 *Type:* Private liberal arts and professional *Accred.:* 1971/1985 (SACS-CC) *Calendar:* Tri. plan *Degrees:* B, P, M, D *Prof. Accred.:* Clinical Psychology, Law, Psychology Internship, Speech-Language Pathology *CEO:* Pres. Abraham S. Fischler
Enroll: 7041 (305) 475-7300

OKALOOSA-WALTON COMMUNITY COLLEGE
100 College Blvd., Niceville 32578 *Type:* Public (district) junior *System:* Florida State Board of Community Colleges *Accred.:* 1965/1991 (SACS-CC) *Calendar:* Sem. plan *Degrees:* A *CEO:* Pres. James R. Richburg
Enroll: 9288 (904) 729-5360

ORLANDO COLLEGE
5500-5800 Diplomat Cir., Orlando 32810 *Type:* Private senior *Accred.:* 1957/1981 (CCA-ACICS) *Calendar:* Qtr. plan *Degrees:* A, B, M *CEO:* Dir. Ouida B. Kirby
Enroll: 1902 (407) 628-5870

BRANCH CAMPUS
925 S. Orange Ave., Orlando, FL 32806 *CEO:* Dir. Barbara Huybers
Enroll: 1037 (407) 841-1410

ORLANDO VOCATIONAL-TECHNICAL CENTER
301 W. Amelia St., Orlando 32801 *Type:* Public (state) *Accred.:* 1983/1988 (SACS-COEI) *Calendar:* Courses of varying lengths *Degrees:* certificates *Prof. Accred.:* Dental Assisting *CEO:* Dir. James Subbs
Enroll: 1032 (305) 425-2756

PRS CAREER ACADEMY
2648 W. Highway 434, Longwood 32779 *Type:* Private business *Accred.:* 1989 (CCA-ACICS) *Calendar:* Courses of varying lengths *Degrees:* certificates, diplomas *CEO:* Pres. Earl Shomber
Enroll: 83 (407) 682-4777

PSI INSTITUTE OF MIAMI
1440 Biscayne Blvd., Miami 33132-1417 *Type:* Private *Accred.:* 1991 (CCA-ACTTS) *Calendar:* Courses of varying lengths *Degrees:* certificates *CEO:* Dir. John Koff
(305) 358-0400

PALM BEACH ATLANTIC COLLEGE
901 S. Flagler Dr., P.O. Box 24708, West Palm Beach 33416-4708 *Type:* Private liberal arts *Accred.:* 1972/1988 (SACS-CC) *Calendar:* Sem. plan *Degrees:* B, M (candidate) *CEO:* Pres. Paul R. Corts
Enroll: 1464 (407) 650-7700

PALM BEACH COMMUNITY COLLEGE
4200 Congress Ave., Lake Worth 33461-4796 *Type:* Public (district) junior *System:* Florida State Board of Community Colleges *Accred.:* 1942/1991 (SACS-CC) *Calendar:* Sem. plan *Degrees:* A *Prof. Accred.:* Dental Hygiene, Dental Laboratory Technology, EMT-Paramedic, Occupational Therapy Assisting *CEO:* Pres. Edward M. Eissey
Enroll: 10177 (407) 439-8000

PANAMA CANAL COLLEGE
Panama Region, APO Miami 34002 *Type:* Private DoDDS-Dependent *Accred.:* 1941/1983 (MSA) *Calendar:* Sem. plan *Degrees:* A *CEO:* Dean Joseph F. Shields
Enroll: 1390 507-52-3107

PARALEGAL CAREERS
1211 N. Westshore Blvd., Ste. 100, Tampa 33607 *Type:* Private *Accred.:* 1988 (SACS-COEI) *Calendar:* Courses of varying lengths *Degrees:* diplomas *CEO:* Dir. Charles Sweet
Enroll: 30 (813) 289-6025

PASCO-HERNANDO COMMUNITY COLLEGE
2401 State Hwy. 41, N., Dade City 33525-7599 *Type:* Public (district) junior *System:* Florida State Board of Community Colleges *Accred.:* 1974/1989 (SACS-CC) *Calendar:* Sem. plan *Degrees:* A *Prof. Accred.:* EMT-Paramedic *CEO:* Pres. Milton O. Jones
Enroll: 3685 (904) 567-6701

PENSACOLA JUNIOR COLLEGE
1000 College Blvd., Pensacola 32504 *Type:* Public (district) junior *System:* Florida State Board of Community Colleges *Accred.:* 1956/1987 (SACS-CC) *Calendar:* Sem. plan *Degrees:* A *Prof. Accred.:* Dental Assisting, Dental Hygiene, Dental Laboratory Technology, EMT-Paramedic, Medical Record Technology, Physical Therapy Assisting, Radiography, Respiratory Therapy, Respiratory Therapy Technology *CEO:* Pres. Horace E. Hartsell
Enroll: 25134 (904) 484-1000

PHILLIPS JUNIOR COLLEGE
2401 N. Harbor City Blvd., Melbourne 32935 *Type:* Private junior *Accred.:* 1966/1987 (CCA-ACICS) *Calendar:* Qtr. plan *Degrees:* A, certificates, diplomas *CEO:* Dir. Sharlee Brittingham
Enroll: 1710 (305) 254-6459

BRANCH CAMPUS
2455 Volusia Ave., Daytona Beach, FL 32114 *CEO:* Dir. Rhonda Olins
(904) 255-1707

PHOENIX EDUCATIONAL SYSTEMS
3300 N. Pace Blvd., Ste. 30, Pensacola 32505 *Type:* Private *Accred.:* 1985 (SACS-COEI) *Calendar:* Courses of varying lengths *Degrees:* certificates *CEO:* Dir. Bonnie Fischer
Enroll: 379 (904) 434-3505

BRANCH CAMPUS
328 Ross Clark Cir., N.E., Dothan, AL 36303 *CEO:* Dir. Marilyn Barnes
(205) 671-0900

BRANCH CAMPUS
405 E. Pass Rd., Gulfport, MS 39507 *CEO:* Dir. Vickie Cheshire
(601) 896-7000

PINELLAS TECHNICAL EDUCATION CENTER—CLEARWATER
6100 154th Ave., N., Clearwater 34620 *Type:* Public (state) *Accred.:* 1970/1990 (SACS-COEI) *Calendar:* Courses of varying lengths *Degrees:* certificates *CEO:* Dir. Clide Cassity
Enroll: 1816 (813) 531-3531

PINELLAS TECHNICAL EDUCATION CENTER—ST. PETERSBURG CAMPUS
910 34th St., St. Petersburg 33711-2298 *Type:* Public (state) *Accred.:* 1975/1990 (SACS-COEI) *Calendar:* Courses of varying lengths *Degrees:* certificates *Prof. Accred.:* Dental Assisting, Medical Assisting (AMA), Respiratory Therapy Technology *CEO:* Dir. Warren Laux
Enroll: 1650 (813) 327-3671

Florida

POLITECHNICAL INSTITUTE
11865 (H3) Coral Way, Miami 33165 *Type:* Private *Accred.:* 1989 (SACS-COEI) *Calendar:* Courses of varying lengths *Degrees:* certificates *CEO:* Dir. Ivan Curiel
Enroll: 731 (305) 226-8099

POLK COMMUNITY COLLEGE
999 Ave. H, N.E., Winter Haven 33881-4299 *Type:* Public (district) junior *System:* Florida State Board of Community Colleges *Accred.:* 1965/1990 (SACS-CC) *Calendar:* Sem. plan *Degrees:* A *Prof. Accred.:* EMT-Paramedic, Nursing (A), Radiography *CEO:* Pres. Maryly V. Peck
Enroll: 5286 (813) 297-1000

THE POYNTER INSTITUTE FOR MEDIA STUDIES
801 Third St., S., St. Petersburg 33701 *Type:* Private *Accred.:* 1983/1988 (SACS-COEI) *Calendar:* Courses of varying lengths *Degrees:* certificates *CEO:* Pres. Robert J. Haiman
Enroll: 1254 (813) 821-9494

PROFESSIONAL HAIR DESIGN ACADEMY
1927 34th St., N., St. Petersburg 333713 *Type:* Private *Accred.:* 1988 (CCA-ACTTS) *Calendar:* Courses of varying lengths *Degrees:* diplomas *CEO:* Dir. Gail E. McCanless
(813) 327-0999

BRANCH CAMPUS
27380 U.S. Hwy. 19 S., Clearwater, FL 34621 *CEO:* Admin. Gail Simon
(813) 791-7438

PROSPECT HALL COLLEGE
1725 Monroe St., Hollywood 33020 *Type:* Private business *Accred.:* 1971/1986 (CCA-ACICS) *Calendar:* Qtr. plan *Degrees:* A, certificates, diplomas *CEO:* Pres. F. Moorghem
Enroll: 572 (305) 923-8100

QUALTEC INSTITUTE FOR COMPETITIVE ADVANTAGE
11300 U.S. Hwy. 1, Ste. 400, Palm Beach Gardens 33408 *Type:* Private *Accred.:* 1990 (SACS-COEI) *Calendar:* Courses of varying lengths *Degrees:* certificates *CEO:* Dir. Elizabeth Hirst
Enroll: 114 (800) 247-9871

RADFORD M. LOCKLIN VOCATIONAL-TECHNICAL CENTER
2216 Berryhill Rd., Milton 32570 *Type:* Public (state) *Accred.:* 1988 (SACS-COEI) *Calendar:* Courses of varying lengths *Degrees:* certificates *CEO:* Dir. Raymond Rogers
Enroll: 266 (904) 626-1918

RECREATIONAL VEHICLE SERVICE ACADEMY
721 Cattleman Rd., Sarasota 34233 *Type:* Private *Accred.:* 1991 (CCA-ACTTS) *Calendar:* Courses of varying lengths *Degrees:* certificates *CEO:* Dir. Thomas J. Santoro
(813) 379-9511

REESE INSTITUTE SCHOOL OF MASSAGE THERAPY
425 Geneva Dr., Oviedo 32765-9115 *Type:* Private *Accred.:* 1991 (CCA-ACTTS) *Calendar:* Courses of varying lengths *Degrees:* certificates *CEO:* Dean Dave Epley, Ph.D.
(407) 365-9283

REGIONAL SEMINARY OF ST. VINCENT DE PAUL
10701 S. Military Tr., Boynton Beach 33436-4811 *Type:* Private (Roman Catholic) graduate only *Accred.:* 1968/1990 (SACS-CC) *Calendar:* Sem. plan *Degrees:* P, M *CEO:* Pres./Rector Joseph L. Cunningham
Enroll: 91 (407) 732-4424

RIDGE VOCATIONAL-TECHNICAL CENTER
7700 State Rd. 544, Winter Haven 33881 *Type:* Public (state) *Accred.:* 1982/1987 (SACS-COEI) *Calendar:* Courses of varying lengths *Degrees:* certificates *CEO:* Dir. Bill Hampton
Enroll: 1031 (813) 422-6402

RINGLING SCHOOL OF ART AND DESIGN
2700 N. Tamiami Tr., Sarasota 34234-5896 *Type:* Private professional *Accred.:* 1979/1985 (SACS-CC) *Calendar:* Sem. plan *Degrees:* B, certificates *Prof. Accred.:* Art, Interior Design *CEO:* Pres. Arland F. Christ-Janer
Enroll: 608 (813) 351-4614

Accredited Institutions **Florida**

ROBERT MORGAN VOCATIONAL-TECHNICAL INSTITUTE
18180 S.W. 122nd Ave., Miami 33177 *Type:* Public (state) *Accred.:* 1983/1988 (SACS-COEI) *Calendar:* Courses of varying lengths *Degrees:* certificates *Prof. Accred.:* Dental Assisting *CEO:* Dir. John Leyva
Enroll: 1014   (305) 253-9920

ROFFLER HAIR DESIGN COLLEGE
2242 W. Broward Blvd., Fort Lauderdale 33312 *Type:* Private *Accred.:* 1979/1986 (CCA-ACTTS) *Calendar:* Courses of varying lengths *Degrees:* diplomas *CEO:* Dir. Stewart A. Smith
Enroll: 57   (305) 584-4730

ROFFLER HAIR DESIGN COLLEGE
5110 University Blvd., Jacksonville 32216 *Type:* Private *Accred.:* 1979/1986 (CCA-ACTTS) *Calendar:* Courses of varying lengths *Degrees:* diplomas *CEO:* Pres. Stewart A. Smith, Jr.
Enroll: 222   (904) 731-5060

ROFFLER HAIR DESIGN COLLEGE
905 E. Memorial Blvd., Lakeland 33801 *Type:* Private *Accred.:* 1987 (CCA-ACTTS) *Calendar:* Courses of varying lengths *Degrees:* diplomas *CEO:* Dir. Joan Ogden
Enroll: 156   (813) 686-2224

ROFFLER HAIR DESIGN COLLEGE
1710 N.W. Seventh St., Miami 33125-3502 *Type:* Private *Accred.:* 1978/1985 (CCA-ACTTS) *Calendar:* Courses of varying lengths *Degrees:* diplomas *CEO:* Dir. Hipolite Ramas
Enroll: 76   (305) 541-6200

BRANCH CAMPUS
5433 Lake Howell Rd., Winter Park, FL 32792 *CEO:* Dir. Kim Pfeifer
Enroll: 55   (305) 657-0700

ROFFLER HAIR DESIGN COLLEGE
4122-4126 Park Blvd., Pinellas Park 33565 *Type:* Private *Accred.:* 1988 (CCA-ACTTS) *Calendar:* Courses of varying lengths *Degrees:* diplomas *CEO:* Pres. Stewart A. Smith
(813) 541-2600

ROFFLER HAIR DESIGN COLLEGE
1964 W. Tennessee St., No. 14, Tallahassee 32304 *Type:* Private *Accred.:* 1983/1988 (CCA-ACTTS) *Calendar:* Courses of varying lengths *Degrees:* diplomas *CEO:* Dir. Stewart A. Smith
Enroll: 45   (904) 576-2174

ROFFLER HAIR DESIGN COLLEGE
8851 N. 56th St., Temple Terrace 33617 *Type:* Private *Accred.:* 1981/1988 (CCA-ACTTS) *Calendar:* Courses of varying lengths *Degrees:* diplomas *CEO:* Dir. Dwayne Adams
Enroll: 227   (813) 985-8785

ROFFLER TECHNICAL INSTITUTE
1412 W. Fairfield Dr., Pensacola 32501 *Type:* Private *Accred.:* 1985 (CCA-ACTTS) *Calendar:* Courses of varying lengths *Degrees:* certificates *CEO:* Dir. Larry Bryant
Enroll: 38   (904) 433-6547

ROLLINS COLLEGE
1000 Holt Ave., Winter Park 32789-4499 *Type:* Private liberal arts *Accred.:* 1927/1984 (SACS-CC) *Calendar:* 4-1-4 plan *Degrees:* A, B, M *Prof. Accred.:* Business (M), Music *CEO:* Pres. Rita Bornstein
Enroll: 3589   (407) 646-2000

ROMAR HAIRSTYLING ACADEMY
1608 S. Federal Hwy., Boynton Beach 33435 *Type:* Private *Accred.:* 1990 (SACS-COEI) *Calendar:* Courses of varying lengths *Degrees:* certificates, diplomas *CEO:* Dir. Peter Ross
Enroll: 85   (407) 737-3430

ROSS TECHNICAL INSTITUTE
839 N.W. 119th St., North Miami 33168-2336 *Type:* Private *Accred.:* 1991 (CCA-ACTTS) *Calendar:* Courses of varying lengths *Degrees:* certificates *CEO:* Dir. Barbara Franklin
(305) 769-3991

Florida

BRANCH CAMPUS
1490 S. Military Tr., Ste. 11, West Palm Beach, FL 33415 *Prof. Accred.:* Health Education *CEO:* Exec. Dir. Teri Sullivan
(407) 433-1288

ROSS TECHNICAL INSTITUTE
1490 S. Military Tr., Ste. 11, West Palm Beach 33415 *Type:* Private *Accred.:* 1991 (CCA-ACTTS) *Calendar:* Courses of varying lengths *Degrees:* certificates *CEO:* Dir. Teri Sullivan
(407) 433-1288

SER-IBM BUSINESS INSTITUTE
42 N.W. 27th Ave., Miami 33125 *Type:* Private *Accred.:* 1985/1991 (SACS-COEI) *Calendar:* Courses of varying lengths *Degrees:* certificates *CEO:* Dir. Melvin Chaves
Enroll: 334 (305) 649-7500

ST. AUGUSTINE TECHNICAL CENTER
2980 Collins Ave., St. Augustine 32095-9970 *Type:* Public (state) *Accred.:* 1980/1990 (SACS-COEI) *Calendar:* Courses of varying lengths *Degrees:* certificates *Prof. Accred.:* EMT-Paramedic *CEO:* Dir. R.E. Upton, Jr.
Enroll: 1770 (904) 824-4401

ST. JOHN VIANNEY COLLEGE SEMINARY
2900 S.W. 87th Ave., Miami 33165 *Type:* Private (Roman Catholic) for men *Accred.:* 1970/1986 (SACS-CC) *Calendar:* Sem. plan *Degrees:* B *CEO:* Pres. Thomas O'Dwyer
Enroll: 37 (305) 223-4561

ST. JOHNS RIVER COMMUNITY COLLEGE
5001 St. Johns Ave., Palatka 32177 *Type:* Public (district) junior *System:* Florida State Board of Community Colleges *Accred.:* 1963/1983 (SACS-CC) *Calendar:* Sem. plan *Degrees:* A *CEO:* Pres. Robert L. McLendon, Jr.
Enroll: 2434 (904) 328-1571

ST. LEO COLLEGE
P.O. Box 2187, St. Leo 33574 *Type:* Private (Roman Catholic) liberal arts and teachers *Accred.:* 1967/1991 (SACS-CC) *Calendar:* Sem. plan *Degrees:* A, B *Prof. Accred.:* Social Work (B) *CEO:* Pres. Frank Mouch
Enroll: 3959 (904) 588-3000

ST. PETERSBURG JUNIOR COLLEGE
P.O. Box 13489, St. Petersburg 33733 *Type:* Public (district) *System:* Florida State Board of Community Colleges *Accred.:* 1931/1990 (SACS-CC) *Calendar:* Sem. plan *Degrees:* A *Prof. Accred.:* Dental Hygiene, EMT-Paramedic, Engineering Technology (electrical), Medical Laboratory Technology (AMA), Medical Record Technology, Physical Therapy Assisting, Radiography, Respiratory Therapy, Veterinary Technology *CEO:* Pres. Carl M. Kuttler, Jr.
Enroll: 13401 (813) 341-3600

ST. THOMAS UNIVERSITY
16400 N.W. 32nd Ave., Miami 33054 *Type:* Private (Roman Catholic) liberal arts *Accred.:* 1968/1983 (SACS-CC) *Calendar:* Sem. plan *Degrees:* B, M, D *Prof. Accred.:* Law (ABA only) *CEO:* Pres. Richard E. Greene
Enroll: 1744 (305) 625-6000

SANTA FE COMMUNITY COLLEGE
3000 N.W. 83rd St., Gainesville 32606 *Type:* Public (district) junior *System:* Florida State Board of Community Colleges *Accred.:* 1968/1982 (SACS-CC) *Calendar:* Sem. plan *Degrees:* A *Prof. Accred.:* Dental Assisting, Dental Hygiene, EMT-Paramedic, Engineering Technology (computer), Nuclear Medicine Technology, Nursing (A), Radiation Therapy Technology, Radiography, Respiratory Therapy *CEO:* Pres. Lawrence W. Tyree
Enroll: 13617 (904) 395-5000

SARASOTA COUNTY VOCATIONAL-TECHNICAL CENTER
4748 Beneva Rd., Sarasota 34233 *Type:* Public (state) *Accred.:* 1971/1991 (SACS-COEI) *Calendar:* Courses of varying lengths *Degrees:* certificates *Prof. Accred.:* EMT-Paramedic, Medical Assisting (AMA), Practical Nursing *CEO:* Dir. Steve Harvey
Enroll: 2339 (813) 924-1365

SEGAL INSTITUTE OF COURT REPORTING
P.O. Box 6822, Clearwater 34618-6822
Type: Private *Accred.:* 1991 (CCA-ACTTS) *Calendar:* Courses of varying lengths *Degrees:* certificates *CEO:* Dir. Susan Segal
(813) 535-0608

SEMINOLE COMMUNITY COLLEGE
100 Weldon Blvd., Sanford 32773-6199
Type: Public (district) junior *System:* Florida State Board of Community Colleges *Accred.:* 1969/1983 (SACS-CC) *Calendar:* Sem. plan *Degrees:* A *Prof. Accred.:* Nursing (A), Respiratory Therapy, Respiratory Therapy Technology *CEO:* Pres. Earl S. Weldon
Enroll: 11485 (407) 323-1450

SHERIDAN VOCATIONAL-TECHNICAL CENTER
5400 Sheridan St., Hollywood 33021 *Type:* Public (state) *Accred.:* 1974/1989 (SACS-COEI) *Calendar:* Courses of varying lengths *Degrees:* certificates *Prof. Accred.:* Medical Laboratory Technology (AMA), Practical Nursing *CEO:* Dir. Robert Boegli
Enroll: 1440 (305) 985-3233

SOUTH FLORIDA COMMUNITY COLLEGE
600 W. College Dr., Avon Park 33825 *Type:* Public (district) junior *System:* Florida State Board of Community Colleges *Accred.:* 1968/1982 (SACS-CC) *Calendar:* Sem. plan *Degrees:* A *CEO:* Pres. Catherine P. Cornelius
Enroll: 2508 (813) 453-6661

SOUTH TECHNICAL EDUCATION CENTER
1300 S. West Ave., Boynton Beach 33426-9099 *Type:* Public (state) *Accred.:* 1980/1991 (SACS-COEI) *Calendar:* Courses of varying lengths *Degrees:* certificates *CEO:* Dir. Leonard Goforth
Enroll: 1951 (407) 369-7000

SOUTHEASTERN ACADEMY
233 Academy Dr., P.O. Drawer 1768, Kissimmee 32742-1768 *Type:* Private combination home study and resident *Accred.:* 1986 (CCA-ACTTS); 1977/1988 (NHSC) *Calendar:* Courses of varying lengths *Degrees:* A, B, diplomas *CEO:* Pres. D. Keith Peoples
Enroll: 681 (305) 847-4444

SOUTHEASTERN COLLEGE OF THE ASSEMBLIES OF GOD
1000 Longfellow Blvd., Lakeland 33801 *Type:* Private (Assemblies of God) *Accred.:* 1954/1983 (AABC); 1986/1991 (SACS-CC) *Calendar:* Sem. plan *Degrees:* B *CEO:* Pres. James L. Hennesy
Enroll: 1146 (813) 665-4404

SOUTHEASTERN UNIVERSITY OF HEALTH SCIENCES
1750 N.E. 168th St., North Miami Beach 33162-3097 *Type:* Private professional *Calendar:* Sem. plan *Degrees:* B, P, M, D *Prof. Accred.:* Optometry, Osteopathy, Pharmacy *CEO:* Pres. Morton Terry, D.O.
Enroll: 85 (305) 949-4000

SOUTHERN CAREER INSTITUTE
164 W. Royal Palm Rd., P.O. Drawer 2158, Boca Raton 33427-2158 *Type:* Private home study *Accred.:* 1979/1989 (NHSC) *Calendar:* Courses of varying lengths *Degrees:* certificates *CEO:* Admin. Richard Capezzali
(407) 368-2522

SOUTHERN COLLEGE
5600 Lake Underhill Rd., Orlando 32807 *Type:* Private junior *Accred.:* 1970/1988 (CCA-ACICS) *Calendar:* Qtr. plan *Degrees:* A, certificates, diplomas *Prof. Accred.:* Dental Assisting, Dental Laboratory Technology *CEO:* Vice Pres. Daniel F. Moore
Enroll: 1074 (407) 273-1000

STENOTYPE INSTITUTE OF JACKSONVILLE
500 Ninth Ave., N., P.O. Box 50009, Jacksonville Beach 32250 *Type:* Private business and home study *Accred.:* 1968/1989 (CCA-ACICS); 1987 (NHSC) *Calendar:* Courses of varying lengths *Degrees:* certificates, diplomas *CEO:* Pres. Thyra D. Ellis
Enroll: 95 (904) 246-7466

SUNCOAST SCHOOL OF MASSAGE THERAPY
4910 W. Cypress St., Tampa 33607 *Type:* Private *Accred.:* 1986 (CCA-ACTTS) *Cal-

endar: Courses of varying lengths *Degrees:* diplomas *CEO:* Dir. Daniel A. Ulrich
Enroll: 54 (813) 287-1099

SUNSTATE COLLEGE OF HAIR DESIGN, INC.
4901 Palm Beach Blvd., Ste. 12, Fort Myers 33905 *Type:* Private *Accred.:* 1983/1986 (CCA-ACTTS) *Calendar:* Courses of varying lengths *Degrees:* diplomas *CEO:* Dir. Kenneth F. Stone
Enroll: 94 (813) 694-6979

SUNSTATE COLLEGE OF HAIR DESIGN, INC.
2418 Colonial Blvd., Fort Myers 33907 *Type:* Private *Accred.:* 1990 (CCA-ACTTS) *Calendar:* Courses of varying lengths *Degrees:* diplomas *CEO:* Dir. Kenneth F. Stone
 (813) 278-1311

SUNSTATE COLLEGE OF HAIR DESIGN, INC.
4424 Bee Ridge Rd., Sarasota 34233 *Type:* Private *Accred.:* 1983/1989 (CCA-ACTTS) *Calendar:* Courses of varying lengths *Degrees:* diplomas *CEO:* Dir. James A. Stone
Enroll: 70 (813) 377-4880

SUPERIOR SCHOOL
3990 W. Flagler St., Miami 33134 *Type:* Private *Accred.:* 1989 (SACS-COEI) *Calendar:* Courses of varying lengths *Degrees:* certificates *CEO:* Dir. Herbert Sosa
Enroll: 550 (305) 441-1121

SUWANEE-HAMILTON AREA VOCATIONAL, TECHNICAL AND ADULT CENTER
415 Pinewood Dr., S.W., Live Oak 32060 *Type:* Public (state) *Accred.:* 1973/1990 (SACS-COEI) *Calendar:* Courses of varying lengths *Degrees:* certificates *CEO:* Dir. Bill McMillian
Enroll: 197 (904) 362-2751

TALLAHASSEE COMMUNITY COLLEGE
444 Appleyard Dr., Tallahassee 32304-2895 *Type:* Public (district) junior *System:* Florida State Board of Community Colleges *Accred.:* 1969/1984 (SACS-CC) *Calendar:* Sem. plan *Degrees:* A *Prof. Accred.:* Dental Hygiene, EMT-Paramedic, Respiratory Therapy *CEO:* Pres. James H. Hinson, Jr.
Enroll: 6906 (904) 488-9200

TALMUDIC COLLEGE OF FLORIDA
4014 Chase Ave., Miami Beach 32304-2895 *Type:* Private professional *Accred.:* 1989 (AARTS) *Calendar:* Sem. plan *Degrees:* B, P, M, D *CEO:* Pres. Jerome Zweig
Enroll: 86 (305) 534-7050

TAMPA COLLEGE
15064 U.S. Hwy. 19 N., Clearwater 33624 *Type:* Private senior *Accred.:* 1989 (CCA-ACICS) *Calendar:* Qtr. plan *Degrees:* A, B, M *CEO:* Dir. Mark Page
Enroll: 1542 (813) 530-9495

TAMPA COLLEGE
3319 W. Hillsborough Ave., Tampa 33614 *Type:* Private senior *Accred.:* 1966/1987 (CCA-ACICS) *Calendar:* Qtr. plan *Degrees:* A, B, M, certificates, diplomas *CEO:* Exec. Dir. David C. Zorn
Enroll: 2184 (813) 879-6000

BRANCH CAMPUS
Sabal Business Ctr., 3924 Coconut Palm Dr., Tampa, FL 33619 *CEO:* Dir. Judy Lima
 (813) 621-0041

TAMPA TECHNICAL INSTITUTE
3920 E. Hillsborough Ave., Tampa 33610-4595 *Type:* Private *Accred.:* 1991 (CCA-ACTTS) *Calendar:* Courses of varying lengths *Degrees:* certificates *CEO:* Dir. Mark W. Johnson
 (813) 238-0455

TOM P. HANEY VOCATIONAL-TECHNICAL CENTER
3026 Hwy. 77, Panama City 32405 *Type:* Public (state) *Accred.:* 1977/1987 (SACS-COEI) *Calendar:* Courses of varying lengths *Degrees:* certificates *CEO:* Dir. Marion Riviere
Enroll: 604 (904) 769-2191

BRANCH CAMPUS
Bay-St. Joseph Care Ctr., Port St. Joe, FL 32456 *CEO:* Dir. Marion Riviere
 (904) 769-2191

Accredited Institutions **Florida**

TRAVISS VOCATIONAL-TECHNICAL CENTER
3225 Winterlake Rd., P.O. Box 720, Eaton Park 33840 *Type:* Public (state) *Accred.:* 1978/1988 (SACS-COEI) *Calendar:* Courses of varying lengths *Degrees:* certificates *CEO:* Dir. Thaliah S. Harris
Enroll: 945   (813) 665-1220

UNITED ELECTRONICS INSTITUTE
3924 Coconut Palm Dr., Tampa 33619 *Type:* Private *Accred.:* 1973/1985 (CCA-ACTTS) *Calendar:* Qtr. plan *Degrees:* A *CEO:* Dir. Paul Alkisson
Enroll: 600   (813) 626-2999

UNITED STATES NAVAL DIVING AND SALVAGE TRAINING CENTER
Panama City 32407 *Type:* Public (federal) *Accred.:* 1983/1988 (SACS-COEI) *Calendar:* Courses of varying lengths *Degrees:* certificates *CEO:* Commandant D.P. McCampbell
Enroll: 161   (904) 235-5207

UNITED STATES NAVAL TECHNICAL TRAINING CENTER—CORRY STATION
Pensacola 32511-5000 *Type:* Public (federal) technical *Accred.:* 1975/1990 (SACS-COEI) *Calendar:* Courses of varying lengths *Degrees:* certificates *CEO:* Commander Ivan Dunn
Enroll: 2642   (904) 452-6558

UNITED STATES NAVY SERVICE SCHOOL COMMAND
Naval Training Ctr., Orlando 32813-5800 *Type:* Public (federal) technical *Accred.:* 1976/1986(SACS-COEI) *Calendar:* Courses of varying lengths *Degrees:* certificates *CEO:* Commandant R. Sloane
Enroll: 1127   (407) 646-4122

UNITED STATES SCHOOLS
100 N. Plaza, Miami 33147 *Type:* Private *Accred.:* 1989 (SACS-COEI) *Calendar:* Courses of varying lengths *Degrees:* certificates *CEO:* Dir. Hugh Alpeter
Enroll: 119   (305) 836-7424

UNIVERSITY OF CENTRAL FLORIDA
4000 Central Florida Blvd., Orlando 32816 *Type:* Public (state) liberal arts and professional *System:* State University System of Florida *Accred.:* 1970/1985 (SACS-CC) *Calendar:* Sem. plan *Degrees:* A, B, M, D *Prof. Accred.:* Accounting (Type A,C), Audiology, Business (B,M), Computer Science, Engineering (aerospace, civil, computer, electrical, environmental/sanitary, industrial, mechanical), Engineering Technology (computer, electrical, information systems, mechanical drafting/design, operations technology), Medical Record Administration, Medical Technology, Music, Nursing (B), Radiography, Respiratory Therapy, Social Work (B), Speech-Language Pathology, Teacher Education (e,s,p) *CEO:* Interim Pres. Robert A. Bryan
Enroll: 17062   (407) 823-2000

UNIVERSITY OF FLORIDA
Gainesville 32611 *Type:* Public (state) *System:* State University System of Florida *Accred.:* 1913/1983 (SACS-CC) *Calendar:* Sem. plan *Degrees:* A, B, P, M, D *Prof. Accred.:* Accounting (Type A,C), Architecture (M), Audiology, Business (B,M), Clinical Psychology, Construction Education, Counseling, Counseling Psychology, Dentistry, Dental Public Health, Dietetics (coordinated), Engineering (aerospace, agricultural, chemical, civil, computer, electrical, engineering physics/science, environmental/sanitary, industrial, materials, mechanical, nuclear, ocean), Forestry, General Dentistry, General Practice Residency, Health Services Administration, Interior Design, Journalism, Landscape Architecture (B), Law, Medical Technology, Medicine, Music, Nursing (B,M), Occupational Therapy, Ophthalmic Medical Technology, Oral and Maxillofacial Surgery, Orthodontics, Pediatric Dentistry, Periodontics, Pharmacy, Physical Therapy, Physician Assisting, Planning (regional/urban), Psychology Internship, Recreation, Parks and Tourism, Rehabilitation Counseling, Speech-Language Pathology, Teacher

Education (e,s,p), Theatre *CEO:* Pres. John V. Lombardi
Enroll: 30451 (904) 392-3261

UNIVERSITY OF MIAMI
P.O. Box 248006, Coral Gables 33124 *Type:* Private *Accred.:* 1940/1987 (SACS-CC) *Calendar:* Sem. plan *Degrees:* B, P, M, D *Prof. Accred.:* Accounting (Type A,C), Architecture (B), Business (B,M), Clinical Psychology, Community Health/Preventive Medicine, Counseling Psychology (provisional), Cytotechnology, Diagnostic Medical Sonography, Engineering (architectural, civil, computer, electrical, industrial, mechanical), Health Services Administration, Histologic Technology, Law, Medicine, Music, Nuclear Medicine Technology, Nursing (B,M), Physical Therapy, Planning (regional/urban), Psychology Internship, Public Health, Radiography, Teacher Education (e,s,p), Theatre *CEO:* Pres. Edward T. Foote, II
Enroll: 11585 (305) 284-2211

UNIVERSITY OF NORTH FLORIDA
4567 St. Johns Bluff Rd., S., Jacksonville 32216 *Type:* Public (state) graduate only *System:* State University System of Florida *Accred.:* 1974/1989 (SACS-CC) *Calendar:* Sem. plan *Degrees:* B, M *Prof. Accred.:* Business (B,M), Computer Science, Nursing (B), Teacher Education (e,s,p) *CEO:* Pres. Adam W. Herbert, Jr.
Enroll: 5436 (904) 646-2666

THE UNIVERSITY OF SARASOTA
950 S. Tamiami Tr., Sarasota 34236-7825 *Type:* Private professional; graduate only *Accred.:* 1990 (SACS-CC probational) *Calendar:* Sem. plan *Degrees:* M, D *CEO:* Pres. Robert H. Zeller
Enroll: 60 (813) 355-2906

UNIVERSITY OF SOUTH FLORIDA
4202 E. Fowler Ave., Tampa 33620-6100 *Type:* Public (state) *System:* State University System of Florida *Accred.:* 1963/1984 (SACS-CC) *Calendar:* Sem. plan *Degrees:* A, B, P, M, D *Prof. Accred.:* Accounting (Type A,C), Architecture (M-candidate), Audiology, Business (B,M), Clinical Psychology, Computer Science, Engineering (chemical, civil, computer, electrical, industrial, mechanical), Journalism, Librarianship, Medicine, Music, Nursing (B,M), Psychology Internship, Public Administration, Public Health, Rehabilitation Counseling, Social Work (B,M), Speech-Language Pathology, Teacher Education (e,s,p), Theatre *CEO:* Pres. Francis T. Borkowski
Enroll: 28998 (813) 974-2011

UNIVERSITY OF TAMPA
401 W. Kennedy Blvd., Tampa 33606-1490 *Type:* Private liberal arts *Accred.:* 1951/1986 (SACS-CC) *Calendar:* Sem. plan *Degrees:* A, B, M *Prof. Accred.:* Music, Nursing (B) *CEO:* Pres. David G. Ruffer
Enroll: 2161 (813) 253-3333

THE UNIVERSITY OF WEST FLORIDA
11000 University Pkwy., Pensacola 32514-5750 *Type:* Public (state) liberal arts and professional *System:* State University System of Florida *Accred.:* 1969/1985 (SACS-CC) *Calendar:* Sem. plan *Degrees:* A, B, M *Prof. Accred.:* Journalism, Medical Technology, Music, Nursing (B), Public Administration, Social Work (B), Teacher Education (e,s,p) *CEO:* Pres. Morris L. Marx
Enroll: 7613 (904) 474-2000

VALENCIA COMMUNITY COLLEGE
P.O. Box 3028, Orlando 32802 *Type:* Public (district) junior *System:* Florida State Board of Community Colleges *Accred.:* 1969/1983 (SACS-CC) *Calendar:* Sem. plan *Degrees:* A *Prof. Accred.:* Dental Hygiene, EMT-Paramedic, Medical Laboratory Technology (AMA), Nursing (A), Radiography, Respiratory Therapy *CEO:* Pres. Paul C. Gianini, Jr.
Enroll: 13370 (407) 299-5000

VOCATIONAL INSTITUTE
3768 W. 12th Ave., Hialeah 33012 *Type:* Private *Calendar:* 35-week courses *Degrees:* diplomas *Prof. Accred.:* Health Education *CEO:* Pres. Juan Del Pozo
  (305) 822-7073

WARD STONE COLLEGE
9200 S. Dadeland Blvd., N. Tower, Ste. 123, Miami 33156 *Type:* Private business *Accred.:* 1989 (CCA-ACICS) *Calendar:* Courses of varying lengths *Degrees:* A, certificates, diplomas *CEO:* Pres. Kathy Arista-Salado
(305) 670-2082

WARNER SOUTHERN COLLEGE
5301 U.S. Hwy. 27 S., Lake Wales 33853-8725 *Type:* Private liberal arts *Accred.:* 1977/1982 (SACS-CC) *Calendar:* Sem. plan *Degrees:* A, B *CEO:* Pres. Gregory V. Hall
Enroll: 401 (813) 638-1426

WASHINGTON HOLMES AREA VOCATIONAL-TECHNICAL CENTER
209 Hoyt St., Chipley 32428 *Type:* Public (state) *Accred.:* 1976/1991 (SACS-COEI) *Calendar:* Courses of varying lengths *Degrees:* certificates *CEO:* Dir. Gene Prough
Enroll: 681 (904) 638-1180

WEBBER COLLEGE
P.O. Box 96, Babson Park 33827 *Type:* Private 4-year business *Accred.:* 1969/1988 (SACS-CC) *Calendar:* Sem. plan *Degrees:* A, B *CEO:* Pres. Rex R. Yentes
Enroll: 219 (813) 638-1431

WEST TECHNICAL EDUCATION CENTER
2625 State Rd. 715, Belle Glade 33430 *Type:* Public (state) *Accred.:* 1984/1989 (SACS-COEI) *Calendar:* Courses of varying lengths *Degrees:* certificates *CEO:* Dir. Shirley W. Maxson
Enroll: 424 (407) 996-4930

WESTSIDE VOCATIONAL-TECHNICAL CENTER
731 E. Story Rd., Winter Garden 34787 *Type:* Public (state) *Accred.:* 1981/1991 (SACS-COEI) *Calendar:* Courses of varying lengths *Degrees:* certificates *CEO:* Dir. Walt Cobb
Enroll: 894 (305) 656-2851

BRANCH CAMPUS
Apopka Sch., 555 Martin St., Apopka, FL 32703 *CEO:* Asst. Dir. Tony Encinias
(407) 889-3448

BRANCH CAMPUS
Wymore Adult Career Ctr., 100 E. Kennedy Ave., Eatonville, FL 32751 *CEO:* Asst. Dir. Tony Encinias
(407) 644-7518

BRANCH CAMPUS
6628 Old Winter Garden Rd., Orlando, FL 32811 *CEO:* Asst. Dir. Tom Winters
(407) 292-8696

BRANCH CAMPUS
1625 Beulah Rd., Winter Garden, FL 34781 *CEO:* Asst. Dir. Tony Encinias
(407) 656-2424

WILLIAM T. MCFATTER VOCATIONAL-TECHNICAL CENTER
6500 Nova Dr., Davie 33317 *Type:* Public (state) *Accred.:* 1989 (SACS-COEI) *Calendar:* Courses of varying lengths *Degrees:* certificates *Prof. Accred.:* Dental Laboratory Technology (prelim. provisional), Practical Nursing *CEO:* Dir. Horace McLeod
Enroll: 970 (305) 370-8324

BRANCH CAMPUS
2600 S.W. 71 Terr., Davie, FL 33314 *CEO:* Asst. Prin. Patricia Gaiefsky
(305) 474-8219

BRANCH CAMPUS
3501 S.W. Davie Rd., Davie, FL 33314 *CEO:* Asst. Prin. Patricia Gaiefsky
(305) 474-8219

WINTER PARK ADULT VOCATIONAL CENTER
901 Webster Ave., Winter Park 32789 *Type:* Public (county) *Accred.:* 1986/1988 (SACS-COEI) *Calendar:* Courses of varying lengths *Degrees:* certificates *Prof. Accred.:* Medical Assisting (AMA) *CEO:* Dir. Kaye Chastain
Enroll: 954 (407) 647-6366

WITHLACOOHEE VOCATIONAL AND ADULT EDUCATIONAL CENTER
1201 W. Main St., Inverness 32650-4696 *Type:* Public (state) *Accred.:* 1984/1989 (SACS-COEI) *Calendar:* Courses of varying lengths *Degrees:* certificates *CEO:* Dir. Steven S. Kinard
Enroll: 717 (904) 726-2430

GEORGIA

ABRAHAM BALDWIN AGRICULTURAL COLLEGE
P.O. Box 1, ABAC Sta., Tifton 31794-2693 *Type:* Public (state) junior *System:* Board of Regents, University System of Georgia *Accred.:* 1953/1986 (SACS-CC) *Calendar:* Qtr. plan *Degrees:* A *Prof. Accred.:* Nursing (A) *CEO:* Pres. Harold J. Loyd
Enroll: 2611 (912) 386-3236

AGNES SCOTT COLLEGE
Decatur 30030 *Type:* Private liberal arts for women *Accred.:* 1907/1984 (SACS-CC) *Calendar:* Sem. plan *Degrees:* B *CEO:* Pres. Ruth A. Schmidt
Enroll: 560 (404) 371-6000

ALBANY STATE COLLEGE
504 College Dr., Albany 31705-2794 *Type:* Public (state) liberal arts and professional *System:* Board of Regents, University System of Georgia *Accred.:* 1951/1988 (SACS-CC) *Calendar:* Qtr. plan *Degrees:* B, M *Prof. Accred.:* Nursing (B), Teacher Education (e,s) *CEO:* Pres. Billy C. Black
Enroll: 2405 (912) 430-4600

ALBANY TECHNICAL INSTITUTE
1021 Lowe Rd., Albany 31708 *Type:* Public (state) *Accred.:* 1974/1989 (SACS-COEI) *Calendar:* Courses of varying lengths *Degrees:* certificates *Prof. Accred.:* Dental Assisting, Respiratory Therapy Technology *CEO:* Dir. Nathaniel Cross
Enroll: 905 (912) 888-1320

ALLIANCE TRACTOR TRAILER TRAINING
333 Industrial Blvd., P.O. Box 1008, McDonough 30253 *Type:* Private *Accred.:* 1988 (CCA-ACTTS) *Calendar:* Courses of varying lengths *Degrees:* certificates *CEO:* Dir. Richard W. Grassette
Enroll: 544 (404) 957-6401

THE AMERICAN COLLEGE FOR THE APPLIED ARTS
3330 Peachtree Rd., N.E., Atlanta 30326 *Type:* Private professional *Accred.:* 1987 (SACS-CC) *Calendar:* Qtr. plan *Degrees:* A, B *CEO:* Pres. Rafael A. Lago
Enroll: 2182 (404) 231-9000

BRANCH CAMPUS
110 Marylebone High St., London, England, United Kingdom W1M 3DB *CEO:* Pres. Jack Clancy
[44] (1) 486-1772

ANDREW COLLEGE
413 College St., Cuthbert 31740 *Type:* Private (United Methodist) junior *Accred.:* 1927/1986 (SACS-CC) *Calendar:* Qtr. plan *Degrees:* A *CEO:* Pres. Kirk Treible
Enroll: 303 (912) 732-2171

ARMSTRONG STATE COLLEGE
11935 Abercorn Ext., Savannah 31419-1997 *Type:* Public (state) liberal arts *System:* Board of Regents, University System of Georgia *Accred.:* 1940/1982 (SACS-CC) *Calendar:* Qtr. plan *Degrees:* A, B *Prof. Accred.:* Dental Hygiene, Medical Technology, Music, Nursing (A,B), Radiography, Respiratory Therapy, Teacher Education (e,s) *CEO:* Pres. Robert A. Burnett
Enroll: 3649 (912) 927-5211

ARMSTRONG UNIVERSITY OF BEAUTY
101 E. Fourth St., Rome 30161 *Type:* Private *Accred.:* 1989 (SACS-COEI) *Calendar:* Courses of varying lengths *Degrees:* diplomas *CEO:* Dir. Bobbie Wilson
Enroll: 37 (404) 232-6565

THE ART INSTITUTE OF ATLANTA
3376 Peachtree Rd., N.E., Atlanta 30326 *Type:* Private *Accred.:* 1985 (SACS-CC) *Calendar:* Qtr. plan *Degrees:* A, diplomas *CEO:* Pres. Hal R. Griffith
Enroll: 1185 (404) 266-1341

ARTISTIC BEAUTY COLLEGE
1820 Hwy. 20, Conyers 30208 *Type:* Private *Accred.:* 1990 (SACS-COEI) *Calendar:*

Georgia

Courses of varying lengths *Degrees:* certificates, diplomas *CEO:* Mgr. Margaret Moody
Enroll: 78 (404) 922-7653

ASHER SCHOOL OF BUSINESS
100 Pinnacle Way, Ste. 110, Norcross 30071 *Type:* Private *Accred.:* 1989/1990 (SACS-COEI) *Calendar:* Courses of varying lengths *Degrees:* certificates *CEO:* Dir. Bonnie Mittelstadt
Enroll: 175 (404) 368-0800

ATHENS AREA TECHNICAL INSTITUTE
U.S. Hwy. 29 N., Athens 30610 *Type:* Public (state) 2-year *Accred.:* 1988 (SACS-CC) *Calendar:* Qtr. plan *Degrees:* A, certificates *Prof. Accred.:* Engineering Technology (electrical), Radiography, Respiratory Therapy Technology *CEO:* Pres. Kenneth C. Easom
Enroll: 920 (404) 542-8050

ATLANTA AREA TECHNICAL SCHOOL
1560 Stewart Ave., S.W., Atlanta 30310 *Type:* Public (state) *Accred.:* 1971/1991 (SACS-COEI) *Calendar:* Courses of varying lengths *Degrees:* certificates *Prof. Accred.:* Dental Assisting, Dental Laboratory Technology, Medical Assisting (AMA), Medical Laboratory Technology (AMA) *CEO:* Dir. Betty T. Campbell
Enroll: 7869 (404) 758-9451

BRANCH CAMPUS
4191 Northside Dr., N.W., Atlanta, GA 30342 *CEO:* Dir. Betty T. Campbell
(404) 842-3117

ATLANTA CHRISTIAN COLLEGE
2605 Ben Hill Rd., East Point 30344 *Type:* Private (Christian Churches/Churches of Christ) professional *Accred.:* 1965/1984 (AABC); 1990 (SACS-CC) *Calendar:* Sem. plan *Degrees:* A, B *CEO:* Pres. James C. Donovan
Enroll: 146 (404) 761-8861

THE ATLANTA COLLEGE OF ART
1280 Peachtree St., N.E., Atlanta 30309 *Type:* Private professional *Accred.:* 1969/1984 (SACS-CC) *Calendar:* Sem. plan *Degrees:* B *Prof. Accred.:* Art *CEO:* Interim Pres. Manning Pattillo, Jr.
Enroll: 360 (404) 898-1164

ATLANTA COLLEGE OF MEDICAL AND DENTAL CAREERS
1400 W. Peachtree St., N.W., Atlanta 30309 *Type:* Private *Accred.:* 1978/1988 (SACS-COEI) *Calendar:* Courses of varying length *Degrees:* diplomas *Prof. Accred.:* Medical Assisting (AMA), Medical Laboratory Technology (AMA) *CEO:* Exec. Dir. Kenneth Humphrey
Enroll: 291 (404) 249-8222

ATLANTA JOB CORPS CENTER
239 W. Lake Ave., N.W., Atlanta 30314 *Type:* Public (federal) *Accred.:* 1985/1990 (SACS-COEI) *Calendar:* Courses of varying lengths *Degrees:* diplomas *CEO:* Dir. Lonnie Hall
Enroll: 483 (404) 794-9512

ATLANTA METROPOLITAN COLLEGE
1630 Stewart Ave., S.W., Atlanta 30310 *Type:* Public (state) junior *System:* Board of Regents, University System of Georgia *Accred.:* 1976/1991 (SACS-CC) *Calendar:* Qtr. plan *Degrees:* A *CEO:* Pres. Edwin A. Thompson
Enroll: 1761 (404) 756-4441

ATLANTA SCHOOL OF MASSAGE
2300 Peachford Rd., Ste. 3200, Atlanta 30338 *Type:* Private *Accred.:* 1988 (CCA-ACTTS) *Calendar:* Courses of varying lengths *Degrees:* certificates *CEO:* Dir. Leticia Allen
(404) 454-7167

AUGUSTA COLLEGE
2500 Walton Way, Augusta 30910 *Type:* Public (state) liberal arts *System:* Board of Regents, University System of Georgia *Accred.:* 1926/1991 (SACS-CC) *Calendar:* Qtr. plan *Degrees:* A, B, M *Prof. Accred.:* Music, Nursing (A) *CEO:* Pres. Richard S. Wallace
Enroll: 4665 (404) 737-1401

Georgia

AUGUSTA TECHNICAL INSTITUTE
3116 Deans Bridge Rd., Augusta 30906 *Type:* Public (state and district) *Accred.:* 1988 (SACS-CC) *Calendar:* Qtr. plan *Degrees:* A, certificates *Prof. Accred.:* Dental Assisting, Dental Laboratory Technology, Medical Assisting (AMA), Medical Laboratory Technology (AMA), Practical Nursing, Respiratory Therapy Technology *CEO:* Pres. Jack B. Patrick
Enroll: 3291 (404) 796-6900

BAINBRIDGE COLLEGE
Highway 84 E., Bainbridge 31717 *Type:* Public (state) junior *System:* Board of Regents, University System of Georgia *Accred.:* 1975/1990 (SACS-CC) *Calendar:* Qtr. plan *Degrees:* A *CEO:* Pres. Edward D. Mobley
Enroll: 769 (912) 248-2500

BALIN INSTITUTE
1285 Peachtree St., N.E., Atlanta 30309 *Type:* Private *Accred.:* 1981/1986 (SACS-COEI) *Calendar:* Courses of varying lengths *Degrees:* diplomas *CEO:* Dir. Joe Brown
Enroll: 278 (404) 874-5278

BAUDER FASHION COLLEGE—ATLANTA
Phipps Plaza, 3500 Peachtree Rd., N.E., Atlanta 30326 *Type:* Private *Accred.:* 1973/1985 (CCA-ACTTS); 1985/1990 (SACS-CC) *Calendar:* Qtr. plan *Degrees:* A *CEO:* Exec. Dir. Shelley T. McDougal
Enroll: 500 (404) 237-7573

BEN HILL-IRWIN AREA VOCATIONAL-TECHNICAL SCHOOL
Perry House Rd., P.O. Box 1069, Fitzgerald 31750 *Type:* Public (state) *Accred.:* 1973/1989 (SACS-COEI) *Calendar:* Courses of varying lengths *Degrees:* certificates *CEO:* Dir. Edgar B. Greene
Enroll: 272 (912) 468-7487

BRANCH CAMPUS
187 Airport Cir., Douglas, GA 31533 *CEO:* Dir. Jim Mills
(912) 384-7520

BERRY COLLEGE
39 Mount Berry Sta., Rome 30149-0039 *Type:* Private liberal arts *Accred.:* 1957/1988 (SACS-CC) *Calendar:* Sem. plan *Degrees:* A, B, M *Prof. Accred.:* Music, Teacher Education (e,s) *CEO:* Pres. Gloria M. Shatto
Enroll: 1775 (404) 232-5374

BRANELL COLLEGE
4876 Riverdale Rd., Ste. A, College Park 30337 *Type:* Private business *Accred.:* 1972/1991 (CCA-ACICS); 1988 (SACS-COEI) *Calendar:* Courses of varying lengths *Degrees:* certificates, diplomas *CEO:* Dir. John B. Riley
Enroll: 611 (404) 997-1300

BRANCH CAMPUS
1000 Circle 75 Pkwy., Ste. 100, Atlanta, GA 30339 *CEO:* Dir. Kim Howell
(404) 951-0051

BRANCH CAMPUS
41 Marietta St., Ste. 900, Atlanta, GA 30303 *CEO:* Dir. Lee Caters
(404) 525-1800

BRANCH CAMPUS
6600 Bldg., 182 Eastgate Ctr., Chattanooga, TN 37411 *CEO:* Dir. T. Darlene Johnston
(615) 899-3060

BRANCH CAMPUS
5110 Park Ave., Memphis, TN 38117 *CEO:* Dir. Mary Pate
(901) 763-3400

BRENAU COLLEGE
204 Blvd., Gainesville 30501 *Type:* Private liberal arts *Accred.:* 1947/1991 (SACS-CC) *Calendar:* Qtr. plan *Degrees:* B, M *Prof. Accred.:* Nursing (B) *CEO:* Pres. John S. Burd
Enroll: 1501 (404) 534-6299

BREWTON-PARKER COLLEGE
P.O. Box 197, Mount Vernon 30445-0197 *Type:* Private (Southern Baptist) liberal arts *Accred.:* 1962/1991 (SACS-CC) *Calendar:*

Qtr. plan *Degrees:* A, B *CEO:* Pres. Y. Lynn Holmes
Enroll: 1636 (912) 583-2241

BROWN COLLEGE OF COURT REPORTING AND BUSINESS
1100 Spring St., N.W., Ste. 220, Atlanta 30309 *Type:* Private *Accred.:* 1984/1989 (SACS-COEI) *Calendar:* Courses of varying lengths *Degrees:* certificates *CEO:* Dir. Forrest Brown
Enroll: 214 (404) 876-1227

BRANCH CAMPUS
501 Spur 63, Ste. B-3, Longview, TX 75601 *CEO:* Dir. Phyllis Lorenzen
(903) 757-4338

BRUNSWICK COLLEGE
Altama at Fourth St., Brunswick 31523 *Type:* Public (state) junior *System:* Board of Regents, University System of Georgia *Accred.:* 1965/1991 (SACS-CC) *Calendar:* Qtr. plan *Degrees:* A *Prof. Accred.:* Medical Laboratory Technology (AMA), Nursing (A), Radiography *CEO:* Pres. Dorothy L. Lord
Enroll: 1281 (912) 264-7235

CDI CAREER DEVELOPMENT INSTITUTE
3379 Peachtree Rd., N.E., Atlanta 30326 *Type:* Private *Accred.:* 1978/1988 (CCA-ACTTS) *Calendar:* Courses of varying lengths *Degrees:* certificates *CEO:* Dir. Michael D. Sykes
Enroll: 175 (404) 261-7700

CARROLL TECHNICAL INSTITUTE
997 S. Hwy. 16, Carrollton 30117 *Type:* Public (state) *Accred.:* 1973/1987 (SACS-COEI) *Calendar:* Courses of varying lengths *Degrees:* certificates *CEO:* Pres. Judy Hulsey
Enroll: 409 (404) 834-6800

CHATTAHOCHEE TECHNICAL INSTITUTE
980 S. Cobb Dr., S.E., Marietta 30060 *Type:* Public (state) *Accred.:* 1988 (SACS-CC) *Calendar:* Qtr. plan *Degrees:* A *Prof. Accred.:* Engineering Technology (electrical, electromechanical) *CEO:* Pres. Harlon D. Crimm
Enroll: 1494 (404) 528-4500

CITIZENS' HIGH SCHOOL
5115 New Peachtree Rd., Ste. 300, Atlanta 30341 *Type:* Private home study *Accred.:* 1984/1989 (NHSC) *Calendar:* Courses of varying lengths *Degrees:* certificates *CEO:* Pres. Teresa L. Bueno
(404) 455-8358

CLARK ATLANTA UNIVERSITY
James Brawley Dr. at Fair St., Atlanta 30314 *Type:* Private (United Methodist) *Accred.:* 1932/1990 (SACS-CC) *Calendar:* Sem. plan *Degrees:* B, M, D *Prof. Accred.:* Business (M), Librarianship, Medical Record Administration, Social Work (B,M), Teacher Education (e,s,p) *CEO:* Pres. Thomas W. Cole, Jr.
(404) 880-8000

CLAYTON STATE COLLEGE
5900 Lee St., Morrow 30260 *Type:* Public (state) *System:* Board of Regents, University System of Georgia *Accred.:* 1971/1986 (SACS-CC) *Calendar:* Qtr. plan *Degrees:* A, B *Prof. Accred.:* Dental Hygiene, Nursing (A,B) *CEO:* Pres. Harry S. Downs
Enroll: 3787 (404) 961-3400

COLUMBIA THEOLOGICAL SEMINARY
701 Columbia Dr., Decatur 30030 *Type:* Private (Presbyterian) professional; graduate only *Accred.:* 1938/1982 (ATS); 1983 (SACS-CC) *Calendar:* 4-1-4 plan *Degrees:* P, M, D *CEO:* Pres. Douglas W. Oldenburg
Enroll: 266 (404) 378-8821

COLUMBUS COLLEGE
Algonquin Dr., Columbus 31993-2399 *Type:* Public (state) liberal arts *System:* Board of Regents, University System of Georgia *Accred.:* 1963/1985 (SACS-CC) *Calendar:* Qtr. plan *Degrees:* A, B, M *Prof. Accred.:* Dental Hygiene, Medical Laboratory Technology (AMA), Medical Technology, Music, Nursing (A,B), Respiratory Therapy, Teach-

er Education (e,s,p) *CEO:* Pres. Frank D. Brown
Enroll: 3835 (404) 568-2001

COLUMBUS TECHNICAL INSTITUTE
928 45th St., Columbus 31995 *Type:* Public (state) *Accred.:* 1990 (SACS-CC) *Calendar:* Qtr.plan *Degrees:* A, certificates *Prof. Accred.:* Medical Assisting (AMA) *CEO:* Pres. W.G. Hartline
Enroll: 1045 (404) 649-1800

COOSA VALLEY TECHNICAL INSTITUTE
112 Hemlock St., Rome 30161 *Type:* Public (state) *Accred.:* 1972/1987 (SACS-COEI) *Calendar:* Courses of varying lengths *Degrees:* certificates *Prof. Accred.:* Respiratory Therapy Technology *CEO:* Dir. J.D. Powell
Enroll: 398 (404) 235-1142

COVENANT COLLEGE
Scenic Hwy., Lookout Mountain 30750 *Type:* Private (Reformed Presbyterian) liberal arts *Accred.:* 1971/1987 (SACS-CC) *Calendar:* Sem. plan *Degrees:* A, B, M (candidate) *CEO:* Pres. Frank A. Brock
Enroll: 604 (404) 820-1560

CRANDALL JUNIOR COLLEGE
2490 Riverside Dr., Macon 31204-9978 *Type:* Private junior *Accred.:* 1969/1986 (CCA-ACICS) *Calendar:* Qtr. plan *Degrees:* A, certificates, diplomas*CEO:* Pres. John Mills
Enroll: 1201 (912) 745-6593

DALTON COLLEGE
213 N. College Dr., Dalton 30720 *Type:* Public (state) junior *System:* Board of Regents, University System of Georgia *Accred.:* 1969/1984 (SACS-CC) *Calendar:* Qtr. plan *Degrees:* A *Prof. Accred.:* Medical Laboratory Technology (AMA), Nursing (A) *CEO:* Pres. Derrell C. Roberts
Enroll: 2378 (404) 272-4436

DALTON VOCATIONAL SCHOOL OF HEALTH OCCUPATIONS
1221 Elkwood Dr., Dalton 30720 *Type:* Public (state) technical *Accred.:* 1975/1990 (SACS-COEI) *Calendar:* Courses of varying lengths *Degrees:* certificates *CEO:* Dir. Rubye P. Sane
Enroll: 49 (404) 278-8922

DARTON COLLEGE
2400 Gillionville Rd., Albany 31707-3098 *Type:* Public (state) junior *System:* Board of Regents, University System of Georgia *Accred.:* 1968/1983 (SACS-CC) *Calendar:* Qtr. plan *Degrees:* A *Prof. Accred.:* Dental Hygiene, Medical Laboratory Technology (AMA), Nursing (A)*CEO:* Pres. Peter Sireno
Enroll: 1773 (912) 888-8888

DEKALB BEAUTY COLLEGE
6254 Memorial Dr., Ste. M, Stone Mountain 30083 *Type:* Private *Accred.:* 1987 (SACS-COEI) *Calendar:* Courses of varying lengths *Degrees:* certificates *CEO:* Dir. Betty Lyon
Enroll: 87 (404) 879-6673

DEKALB COLLEGE
3251 Panthersville Rd., Decatur 30034 *Type:* Public (state) junior *Accred.:* 1965/1982 (SACS-CC) *Calendar:* Qtr. plan *Degrees:* A *Prof. Accred.:* Dental Hygiene, Nursing (A) *CEO:* Pres. Marvin M. Cole
Enroll: 10867 (404) 244-5090

DEKALB COUNTY OCCUPATIONAL EDUCATION CENTER—CENTRAL
3075 Alton Rd., Chamblee 30341 *Type:* Private *Accred.:* 1988 (SACS-CC); 1988 (SACS-COEI) *Calendar:* Courses of varying lengths *Degrees:* certificates *CEO:* Dir. Robert Burns
Enroll: 121 (404) 457-3393

DEKALB COUNTY OCCUPATIONAL EDUCATION CENTER—NORTH
1995 Womack Rd., Dunwoody 30338 *Type:* Private *Accred.:* 1988 (SACS-CC); 1988 (SACS-COEI) *Calendar:* Courses of varying lengths *Degrees:* certificates *CEO:* Dir. Frank Hall
Enroll: 249 (404) 394-0321

DEKALB COUNTY OCCUPATIONAL EDUCATION CENTER—SOUTH
3303 Pantherville Rd., Decatur 30034 *Type:* Private *Accred.:* 1988 (SACS-CC); 1988

Accredited Institutions

Georgia

(SACS-COEI) *Calendar:* Courses of varying lengths *Degrees:* certificates *CEO:* Dir. Larry Ladner
Enroll: 190   (404) 241-9400

DEKALB TECHNICAL INSTITUTE
495 N. Indian Creek Dr., Clarkston 30021 *Type:* Public (state) 2-year *Accred.:* 1965/1982 (SACS-CC) *Calendar:* Qtr. plan *Degrees:* A *Prof. Accred.:* Engineering Technology (electrical, electromechanical), Medical Laboratory Technology (AMA), Surgical Technology *CEO:* Pres. Paul M. Starnes
Enroll: 4011   (404) 297-9522

DEVRY INSTITUTE OF TECHNOLOGY, ATLANTA
250 N. Arcadia Ave., Decatur 30030-2198 *Type:* Private *Accred.:* 1981/1987 (NCA) *Calendar:* Tri. plan *Degrees:* A, B, certificates *Prof. Accred.:* Engineering Technology (electrical) *CEO:* Pres. Ronald Bush
Enroll: 3801   (404) 292-7900

DERMACLINIC ACADEMY OF MAKE-UP AND SKIN CARE FOR ESTHETICIANS
6649 Roswell Rd., Atlanta 30328 *Type:* Private *Accred.:* 1987 (SACS-COEI) *Calendar:* Courses of varying lengths *Degrees:* certificates *CEO:* Dir. Margaret A. Ruffin
Enroll: 32   (404) 250-9600

DRAUGHONS COLLEGE
805 Peachtree St., Ste. 100, Atlanta 30308 *Type:* Private business *Accred.:* 1990 (CCA-ACICS) *Calendar:* Courses of varying lengths *Degrees:* certificates, diplomas *CEO:* Dir. Gary Vance
Enroll: 434   (404) 892-0814

EAST GEORGIA COLLEGE
237 Thigpen Dr., Swainsboro 30401 *Type:* Public (state) junior *System:* Board of Regents, University System of Georgia *Accred.:* 1975/1990 (SACS-CC) *Calendar:* Qtr. plan *Degrees:* A *CEO:* Pres. Willie D. Gunn
Enroll: 461   (919) 237-7831

EMMANUEL COLLEGE
P.O. Box 129, Franklin Springs 30639 *Type:* Private (International Pentecostal Holiness) *Accred.:* 1979/1989 (AABC); 1967/1991 (SACS-CC) *Calendar:* Qtr. plan *Degrees:* A, B *CEO:* Pres. David R. Hopkins
Enroll: 384   (404) 245-7226

EMORY UNIVERSITY
Atlanta 30322 *Type:* Private (United Methodist) *Accred.:* 1938/1983 (ATS); 1917/1983 (SACS-CC) *Calendar:* Sem. plan *Degrees:* A, B, P, M, D *Prof. Accred.:* Anesthesiologist Assisting, Business (B,M), Clinical Psychology, Community Health/Preventive Medicine, Law, Medicine, Music, Nursing (B,M), Oral and Maxillofacial Surgery, Oral Pathology, Physical Therapy, Physician Assisting, Radiography *CEO:* Pres. James T. Laney
Enroll: 8603   (404) 727-6123

FLOYD COLLEGE
P.O. Box 1864, Rome 30162-1864 *Type:* Public (state) *System:* Board of Regents, University System of Georgia *Accred.:* 1972/1987 (SACS-CC) *Calendar:* Qtr. plan *Degrees:* A *Prof. Accred.:* Nursing (A) *CEO:* Acting Pres. Richard W. Trimble
Enroll: 2340   (404) 295-6328

FORT VALLEY STATE COLLEGE
1005 State College Dr., Fort Valley 31030-3298 *Type:* Public (state) liberal arts and teachers *System:* Board of Regents, University System of Georgia *Accred.:* 1951/1990 (SACS-CC) *Calendar:* Qtr. plan *Degrees:* A, B, M *Prof. Accred.:* Engineering Technology (electrical), Home Economics, Rehabilitation Counseling, Teacher Education (e,s,p), Veterinary Technology *CEO:* Pres. Oscar L. Prater
Enroll: 2513   (912) 825-6315

GAINESVILLE COLLEGE
Mundy Mill Rd., P.O. Box 1358, Gainesville 30503 *Type:* Public (state) junior *System:* Board of Regents, University System of Georgia *Accred.:* 1968/1982 (SACS-CC) *Calendar:* Qtr. plan *Degrees:* A *Prof. Accred.:* Nursing (A) *CEO:* Pres. J. Foster Watkins
Enroll: 2031   (404) 535-6239

Georgia

GEORGIA COLLEGE
231 W. Hancock St., Milledgeville 31061 *Type:* Public (state) liberal arts *System:* Board of Regents, University System of Georgia *Accred.:* 1925/1984 (SACS-CC) *Calendar:* Qtr. plan *Degrees:* A, B, M *Prof. Accred.:* Music, Nursing (B), Teacher Education (e,s) *CEO:* Pres. Edwin G. Speir, Jr.
Enroll: 4321   (912) 453-5350

GEORGIA INSTITUTE OF TECHNOLOGY
225 North Ave., N.W., Atlanta 30332-0325 *Type:* Public (state) technological *System:* Board of Regents, University System of Georgia *Accred.:* 1923/1984 (SACS-CC) *Calendar:* Qtr. plan *Degrees:* B, M, D *Prof. Accred.:* Architecture (M), Business (B,M), Computer Science, Engineering (aerospace, ceramic, chemical, civil, electrical, engineering mechanics, environmental/sanitary, industrial, mechanical, nuclear, textile), Planning (city) *CEO:* Pres. John P. Crecine
Enroll: 12525   (404) 894-2000

GEORGIA MEDICAL INSTITUTE
42 Spring St., Ste. 295, Atlanta 30303 *Type:* Private *Calendar:* Courses of varying lengths *Degrees:* diplomas *Prof. Accred.:* Health Education *CEO:* Pres./Dir. Dominic J. Dean
Enroll: 44   (404) 525-3272

GEORGIA MILITARY COLLEGE
201 E. Greene St., Milledgeville 31061-3398 *Type:* Public junior *Accred.:* 1940/1987 (SACS-CC) *Calendar:* Qtr. plan *Degrees:* A *CEO:* Pres. William P. Acker
Enroll: 1918   (912) 453-3481

GEORGIA SOUTHERN UNIVERSITY
Landrum Box 8033, Statesboro 30460-8033 *Type:* Public (state) liberal arts and teachers *System:* Board of Regents, University System of Georgia *Accred.:* 1935/1984 (SACS-CC) *Calendar:* Qtr. plan *Degrees:* A, B, P, M *Prof. Accred.:* Business (B,M), Engineering Technology (civil/construction, electrical, industrial, mechanical), Music, Nursing (A,B), Public Administration, Recreation and Leisure Services, Teacher Education (e,s,p) *CEO:* Pres. Nicholas Henry
Enroll: 11618   (912) 681-5611

GEORGIA SOUTHWESTERN COLLEGE
Americus 31709 *Type:* Public (state) liberal arts *System:* Board of Regents, University System of Georgia *Accred.:* 1932/1983 (SACS-CC) *Calendar:* Qtr. plan *Degrees:* A, B, M *Prof. Accred.:* Nursing (B), Teacher Education (e,s) *CEO:* Pres. William H. Capitan
Enroll: 2670   (912) 928-1278

GEORGIA STATE UNIVERSITY
Univ. Plaza, Atlanta 30303-3083 *Type:* Public (state) *System:* Board of Regents, University System of Georgia *Accred.:* 1952/1988 (SACS-CC) *Calendar:* Qtr. plan *Degrees:* A, B, M, D *Prof. Accred.:* Accounting (Type A,B,C), Art, Business (B,M), Clinical Psychology, Counseling, Counseling Psychology, Dietetics (coordinated), Health Services Administration, Law (ABA only), Medical Technology, Music, Nursing (B,M), Physical Therapy, Psychology Internship, Public Administration, Rehabilitation Counseling, Respiratory Therapy, Respiratory Therapy Technology, School Psychology (B), Social Work (B), Teacher Education (e,s,p) *CEO:* Acting Pres. Sherman R. Day
Enroll: 19935   (404) 651-2000

GORDON COLLEGE
103 College Dr., Barnesville 30204 *Type:* Public (state) junior *System:* Board of Regents, University System of Georgia *Accred.:* 1941/1986 (SACS-CC) *Calendar:* Qtr. plan *Degrees:* A *Prof. Accred.:* Nursing (A) *CEO:* Pres. Jerry M. Williamson
Enroll: 1366   (404) 358-5016

GRIFFIN TECHNICAL INSTITUTE
501 Varsity Rd., Griffin 30223 *Type:* Public (state) *Accred.:* 1971/1991 (SACS-COEI) *Calendar:* Courses of varying lengths *Degrees:* certificates *Prof. Accred.:* Radiography *CEO:* Dir. Coy L. Hodges
Enroll: 526   (404) 228-7365

Accredited Institutions   **Georgia**

GUPTON-JONES COLLEGE OF FUNERAL SERVICE
280 Mt. Zion Rd., Atlanta 30354 *Type:* Private *Calendar:* 1- and 2-year programs *Degrees:* A, diplomas *Prof. Accred.:* Funeral Service Education *CEO:* Pres. Daniel E. Buchanan
(404) 761-3118

GWINNETT COLLEGE
1075-E Old Norcross Rd., Lawrenceville 30245 *Type:* Private business *Accred.:* 1989 (CCA-ACICS) *Calendar:* Qtr. plan *Degrees:* certificates, diplomas *CEO:* Pres. Billy L. Clark
Enroll: 99   (404) 963-5429

GWINNETT TECHNICAL INSTITUTE
1250 Atkinson Rd., P.O. Box 1505, Lawrenceville 30246-1505 *Type:* Public (county) *Accred.:* 1991 (SACS-CC); 1986/1991 (SACS-COEI) *Calendar:* Courses of varying lengths *Degrees:* A, certificates *Prof. Accred.:* Dental Assisting, Dental Laboratory Technology, Physical Therapy Assisting, Radiography, Respiratory Therapy Technology *CEO:* Dir. J. Alvin Wilbanks
Enroll: 1165   (404) 962-7580

HEART OF GEORGIA TECHNICAL INSTITUTE
I-16 at 441 S. Rte. 5, Box 136A-1, Dublin 31021 *Type:* Public (federal) *Accred.:* 1986/1991 (SACS-COEI) *Calendar:* Courses of varying lengths *Degrees:* certificates *CEO:* Pres. W.R. Stewart
Enroll: 323   (912) 275-6589

BRANCH CAMPUS
1124 College St., Eastman, GA 31023 *CEO:* Pres. W.R. Stewart
(912) 374-7122

HOUSTON AERONAUTICAL COLLEGE
Rte. 3, Box 250, Sandersville 31082 *Type:* Private *Accred.:* 1990 (SACS-COEI) *Calendar:* Courses of varying lengths *Degrees:* certificates, diplomas *CEO:* Pres. Ray Houston
Enroll: 218   (912) 552-6100

INSTITUTE OF PAPER SCIENCE AND TECHNOLOGY
575 14th St., N.W., Atlanta 30318 *Type:* Private graduate only *Accred.:* 1989 (SACS-CC) *Calendar:* Qtr. plan *Degrees:* M, D *CEO:* Pres. Richard A. Matula
Enroll: 64   (404) 853-9500

INTERACTIVE LEARNING SYSTEMS
480 N. Thomas St., Athens 30601 *Type:* Private business *Accred.:* 1984/1989 (CCA-ACICS); 1989 (SACS-COEI) *Calendar:* Courses of varying lengths *Degrees:* certificates, diplomas *CEO:* Dir. Fannie Smith
Enroll: 397   (404) 548-9800

INTERACTIVE LEARNING SYSTEMS
5600 Roswell Rd., N.E., Atlanta 30342 *Type:* Private *Accred.:* 1989 (SACS-COEI) *Calendar:* Courses of varying lengths *Degrees:* certificates *CEO:* Pres. Gail Hester
Enroll: 301   (404) 250-9000

BRANCH CAMPUS
4812 Old National Hwy., College Park, GA 30337 *CEO:* Dir. JoAnn Wilson
(404) 765-9777

BRANCH CAMPUS
2759 Delk Rd., Ste. 101, Marietta, GA 30067 *CEO:* Dir. Lynn Haltiwanger
(404) 951-2367

BRANCH CAMPUS
2191 Northlake Pkwy., Bldg. 11, Ste. 33, Tucker, GA 30084 *CEO:* Dir. Doug Cole
(404) 939-6008

BRANCH CAMPUS
6612 Dixie Hwy., Ste. 2, Florence, KY 41042 *CEO:* Dir. Richard Ellison
(606) 282-8989

BRANCH CAMPUS
103 S. Main St., Williamstown, KY 41097 *CEO:* Dir. Janelle McKinney
(606) 824-3573

INTERDENOMINATIONAL THEOLOGICAL CENTER
671 Beckwith St., S.W., Atlanta 30314 *Type:* Private (interdenominational) professional; graduate only *Accred.:* 1960/1991 (ATS);

1984/1991 (SACS-CC) *Calendar:* Sem. plan *Degrees:* P, M, D *CEO:* Pres. James H. Costen
Enroll: 271 (404) 527-7700

INTERNATIONAL SCHOOL OF SKIN AND NAILCARE
5600 Roswell Rd., Atlanta 30342 *Type:* Private *Accred.:* 1987 (SACS-COEI) *Calendar:* Courses of varying lengths *Degrees:* certificates *CEO:* Dir. Liddell McQuinn
Enroll: 232 (404) 843-1005

KENNESAW STATE COLLEGE
P.O. Box 444, Marietta 30061 *Type:* Public (state) liberal arts *System:* Board of Regents, University System of Georgia *Accred.:* 1968/1986 (SACS-CC) *Calendar:* Qtr. plan *Degrees:* A, B, M *Prof. Accred.:* Music, Nursing (A,B), Teacher Education (e,s) *CEO:* Pres. Betty L. Siegel
Enroll: 8339 (404) 423-6000

KERR BUSINESS COLLEGE
3011 Hogansville Rd., P.O. Box 976, LaGrange 30241 *Type:* Private business *Accred.:* 1976/1985 (CCA-ACICS) *Calendar:* Qtr. plan *Degrees:* certificates, diplomas *CEO:* Exec. Vice Pres. Fred R. Kerr
Enroll: 105 (404) 884-1751

BRANCH CAMPUS
2175 Northlake Pkwy., Atlanta, GA 30345 *CEO:* Exec. Vice Pres. Fred Randall Kerr
Enroll: 143 (404) 934-3353

BRANCH CAMPUS
2623 Washington Rd., Bldg. B, P.O. Box 1986, Augusta, GA 30903 *CEO:* Pres. Darryl H. Kerr
(404) 738-5046

LAGRANGE COLLEGE
601 Broad St., LaGrange 30240-2999 *Type:* Private (United Methodist) liberal arts *Accred.:* 1946/1982 (SACS-CC) *Calendar:* Qtr. plan *Degrees:* A, B, M *Prof. Accred.:* Nursing (A) *CEO:* Pres. Walter Y. Murphy
Enroll: 916 (404) 882-2911

LANIER TECHNICAL INSTITUTE
3082 Mundy Mill Rd., P.O. Box 58, Oakwood 30566 *Type:* Public (state) *Accred.:* 1972/1991 (SACS-COEI) *Calendar:* Courses of varying lengths *Degrees:* A, certificates *Prof. Accred.:* Dental Assisting, Dental Hygiene (conditional), Medical Laboratory Technology (AMA) *CEO:* Pres. Joe E. Hill
Enroll: 300 (404) 531-6300

LIFE COLLEGE
1269 Barclay Cir., Marietta 30060 *Type:* Private professional *Accred.:* 1986/1991 (SACS-CC) *Calendar:* Qtr. plan *Degrees:* B, P, D *Prof. Accred.:* Chiropractic Education *CEO:* Pres. Sid Williams
Enroll: 1867 (404) 424-0554

MABLE BAILEY FASHION COLLEGE
1332 13th St., Columbus 31901 *Type:* Private *Accred.:* 1983/1988 (SACS-COEI) *Calendar:* Courses of varying lengths *Degrees:* certificates *CEO:* Dir. Mable Bailey
Enroll: 22 (404) 324-4295

MACON BEAUTY SCHOOL
Baconsfield Shopping Ctr., 630-J North Ave., Macon 31211 *Type:* Private *Accred.:* 1990 (SACS-COEI) *Calendar:* Courses of varying lengths *Degrees:* certificates, diplomas *CEO:* Dir. Roger Sisler
Enroll: 71 (912) 746-3243

MACON COLLEGE
College Station Dr., Macon 31298 *Type:* Public (state) junior *System:* Board of Regents, University System of Georgia *Accred.:* 1970/1985 (SACS-CC) *Calendar:* Qtr. plan *Degrees:* A *Prof. Accred.:* Dental Hygiene, Nursing (A) *CEO:* Pres. S. Aaron Hyatt
Enroll: 3164 (912) 471-2700

MACON TECHNICAL INSTITUTE
3300 Macon Tech Dr., Macon 31206 *Type:* Public (state) *Accred.:* 1973/1988 (SACS-COEI) *Calendar:* Courses of varying lengths *Degrees:* certificates *Prof. Accred.:* Medical

Laboratory Technology (AMA) *CEO:* Pres. Melton Palmer
Enroll: 849　　　　　　　　(912) 781-0551

MARIETTA UNIVERSITY OF COSMETOLOGY
1963 Dorsey Rd., Marietta 30066 *Type:* Private *Accred.:* 1989 (SACS-COEI) *Calendar:* Courses of varying lengths *Degrees:* diplomas *CEO:* Dir. Richard Shepard
Enroll: 43　　　　　　　　(404) 427-6536

MASSEY BUSINESS COLLEGE
120 Ralph McGill Blvd., N.E., Atlanta 30308 *Type:* Private business *Accred.:* 1977/1989 (CCA-ACICS) *Calendar:* Qtr. plan *Degrees:* A *CEO:* Dir. Garrett S. Hall
Enroll: 1055　　　　　　　(404) 872-1900

BRANCH CAMPUS
5299 Roswell Rd., Ste. 320, Atlanta, GA 30342 *CEO:* Dir. Barry Cermack
　　　　　　　　　　　　　(404) 256-3533

MEADOWS COLLEGE OF BUSINESS
832 S. Slappey Blvd., Albany 31701 *Type:* Private business *Accred.:* 1976/1986 (CCA-ACICS) *Calendar:* Qtr. plan *Degrees:* certificates, diplomas *CEO:* Dir. Michael Davis
Enroll: 501　　　　　　　(912) 883-1736

MEADOWS COLLEGE OF BUSINESS
1170 Brown Ave., Columbus 31906 *Type:* Private junior *Accred.:* 1974/1987 (CCA-ACICS) *Calendar:* Qtr. plan *Degrees:* A *CEO:* Pres. William F. Meadows, Jr.
Enroll: 1105　　　　　　　(404) 327-7668

MEDICAL COLLEGE OF GEORGIA
1120 15th St., Augusta 30912 *Type:* Public (state) professional *System:* Board of Regents, University System of Georgia *Accred.:* 1973/1990 (SACS-CC) *Calendar:* Qtr. plan *Degrees:* A, B, P, M, D *Prof. Accred.:* Combined Prosthodontics, Dental Hygiene, Dentistry, Diagnostic Medical Sonography, Endodontics, General Practice Residency, Medical Illustration, Medical Record Administration, Medical Record Technology, Medical Technology, Medicine, Nuclear Medicine Technology, Nursing (B,M), Occupational Therapy, Occupational Therapy Assisting, Oral and Maxillofacial Surgery, Orthodontics, Pediatric Dentistry, Periodontics, Physical Therapy, Physical Therapy Assisting, Physician Assisting, Psychology Internship, Radiation Therapy Technology, Radiography, Respiratory Therapy *CEO:* Pres. Francis J. Tedesco
Enroll: 1877　　　　　　　(407) 721-0211

MEDIX SCHOOL
2480 Windy Hill Rd., Ste. 100, Marietta 30067 *Type:* Private *Calendar:* Courses of varying lengths *Prof. Accred.:* Dental Assisting, Medical Assisting (AMA) *CEO:* Dir. Larry Ritchie
　　　　　　　　　　　　　(404) 980-0002

MERCER UNIVERSITY
1400 Coleman Ave., Macon 31207-0001 *Type:* Private (Southern Baptist) *Accred.:* 1911/1984 (SACS-CC) *Calendar:* Qtr. plan *Degrees:* B, P, M, D *Prof. Accred.:* Engineering (general), Law, Medicine, Music, Pharmacy, Teacher Education (e,s) *CEO:* Pres. R. Kirby Godsey
Enroll: 4144　　　　　　　(912) 752-2700

METROPOLITAN COLLEGE OF BUSINESS
4319 Covington Hwy., No. 303, Decatur 30035 *Type:* Private *Accred.:* 1990 (SACS-COEI) *Calendar:* Courses of varying lengths *Degrees:* certificates, diplomas *CEO:* Pres. Bernard Clay
Enroll: 11　　　　　　　　(404) 288-6241

METROPOLITAN SCHOOL OF HAIR DESIGN
5481 Memorial Dr., Ste. E, Stone Mountain 30083 *Type:* Private *Accred.:* 1989 (SACS-COEI) *Calendar:* Courses of varying lengths *Degrees:* diplomas *CEO:* Dir. Jerry Vaughn
Enroll: 40　　　　　　　　(404) 294-5697

MIDDLE GEORGIA COLLEGE
Sarah St., Cochran 31014 *Type:* Public (state) junior *System:* Board of Regents, University System of Georgia *Accred.:* 1933/1989 (SACS-CC) *Calendar:* Qtr. plan *Degrees:* A *Prof. Accred.:* Nursing (A) *CEO:* Pres. Joe B. Welch
Enroll: 1213　　　　　　　(912) 934-6221

Georgia

MIDDLE GEORGIA TECHNICAL INSTITUTE
1311 Corder Rd., Warner Robins 31088 *Type:* Public (state) *Accred.:* 1978/1988 (SACS-COEI) *Calendar:* Courses of varying lengths *Degrees:* certificates, diplomas *CEO:* Pres. Billy Edenfield
Enroll: 390   (912) 929-6800

MOREHOUSE COLLEGE
830 Westview Dr., S.W., Atlanta 30314 *Type:* Private liberal arts for men *Accred.:* 1932/1988 (SACS-CC) *Calendar:* Sem. plan *Degrees:* B *CEO:* Pres. Leroy Keith, Jr.
Enroll: 2663   (404) 681-2800

MOREHOUSE SCHOOL OF MEDICINE
720 Westview Dr., S.W., Atlanta 30310-1495 *Type:* Private professional *Accred.:* 1986/1991 (SACS-CC) *Calendar:* Sem. plan *Degrees:* P, D *Prof. Accred.:* Medicine *CEO:* Pres. James A. Goodman
Enroll: 146   (404) 752-1500

MORRIS BROWN COLLEGE
643 Martin Luther King, Jr.Dr., Atlanta 30314 *Type:* Private (African Methodist Episcopal) liberal arts *Accred.:* 1941/1989 (SACS-CC) *Calendar:* Sem. plan *Degrees:* B *CEO:* Pres. Calvert H. Smith
Enroll: 1939   (404) 220-0270

MOULTRIE AREA TECHNICAL INSTITUTE
P.O. Box 520, Moultrie 31776 *Type:* Public (state) *Accred.:* 1974/1990 (SACS-COEI) *Calendar:* Courses of varying lengths *Degrees:* certificates *CEO:* Pres. Jack N. Gay
Enroll: 390   (912) 985-2297

BRANCH CAMPUS
314 E. 14th St., Tifton, GA 31794 *CEO:* Dir. Wanda Golden
  (912) 382-2767

THE NATIONAL BUSINESS INSTITUTE
243 W. Ponce de Leon Ave., Decatur 30030-3270 *Type:* Private *Accred.:* 1990 (SACS-COEI) *Calendar:* Courses of varying lengths *Degrees:* certificates *CEO:* Pres. Mark Lavinsky
Enroll: 47   (404) 352-0800

NATIONAL EDUCATION CENTER—BRYMAN CAMPUS
40 Marietta St., Atlanta 30309 *Type:* Private *Accred.:* 1973/1986 (CCA-ACTTS) *Calendar:* Courses of varying lengths *Degrees:* diplomas *Prof. Accred.:* Medical Assisting (AMA) *CEO:* Dir. Alfred Haro
Enroll: 504   (404) 524-8800

NORTH GEORGIA COLLEGE
College Ave., Dahlonega 30597 *Type:* Public (state) liberal arts and teachers *System:* Board of Regents, University System of Georgia *Accred.:* 1948/1987 (SACS-CC) *Calendar:* Qtr. plan *Degrees:* A, B, M *Prof. Accred.:* Nursing (A,B), Teacher Education (e,s) *CEO:* Pres. John H. Owen
Enroll: 2355   (404) 864-1600

NORTH GEORGIA TECHNICAL INSTITUTE
Georgia Hwy. 197 N., P.O. Box 65, Clarksville 30523 *Type:* Public (state) *Accred.:* 1972/1987(SACS-COEI) *Calendar:* Courses of varying lengths *Degrees:* certificates *Prof. Accred.:* Medical Laboratory Technology (AMA) *CEO:* Dir. James H. Marlowe
Enroll: 666   (404) 754-7702

OCCUPATIONAL EDUCATION CENTER—CENTRAL
3075 Alton Rd., Chamblee 30341 *Type:* Public (state) *Accred.:* 1988 (SACS-COEI) *Calendar:* Courses of varying lengths *Degrees:* certificates *CEO:* Dir. Robert Burns
Enroll: 121   (404) 457-3393

OCCUPATIONAL EDUCATION CENTER—NORTH
1995 Womack Rd., Dunwoody 30338 *Type:* Public (state) *Accred.:* 1988 (SACS-COEI) *Calendar:* Courses of varying lengths *Degrees:* certificates *CEO:* Dir. Frank Hall
Enroll: 249   (404) 394-0321

OCCUPATIONAL EDUCATION CENTER—SOUTH
3303 Pantherville Rd., Decatur 30034 *Type:* Public (state) *Accred.:* 1988 (SACS-COEI) *Calendar:* Courses of varying lengths *Degrees:* certificates *CEO:* Dir. Larry Ladner
Enroll: 190   (404) 241-9400

OGLETHORPE UNIVERSITY
4484 Peachtree Rd., N.E., Atlanta 30319-2797 *Type:* Private liberal arts *Accred.:* 1950/1986 (SACS-CC) *Calendar:* Sem. plan *Degrees:* B, M *CEO:* Pres. Donald Stanton
Enroll: 880 (404) 261-1441

OKEFENOKEE TECHNICAL INSTITUTE
1701 Carswell Ave., Waycross 31501 *Type:* Public (state) *Accred.:* 1972/1987 (SACS-COEI) *Calendar:* Courses of varying lengths *Degrees:* certificates *Prof. Accred.:* Medical Laboratory Technology (AMA), Radiography, Surgical Technology *CEO:* Dir. Joseph R. Miller
Enroll: 282 (912) 283-2002

PAINE COLLEGE
1235 15th St., Augusta 30910-2799 *Type:* Private (United Methodist/Christian Methodist Episcopal) liberal arts *Accred.:* 1944/1991 (SACS-CC) *Calendar:* Sem. plan *Degrees:* B *CEO:* Pres. Julius S. Scott, Jr.
Enroll: 525 (404) 722-4471

PHILLIPS COLLEGE OF ATLANTA
1400 W. Peachtree St., N.W., Atlanta 30309 *Type:* Private business *Accred.:* 1973/1985 (CCA-ACICS) *Calendar:* Qtr. plan *Degrees:* A, certificates, diplomas *CEO:* Exec. Dir. Kenneth A. Humphrey
Enroll: 1533 (404) 249-8200

PHILLIPS JUNIOR COLLEGE
745 Greene St., Augusta 30901 *Type:* Private junior *Accred.:* 1973/1985 (CCA-ACICS) *Calendar:* Qtr. plan *Degrees:* A, certificates, diplomas *CEO:* Pres. Linda Rox
Enroll: 1844 (404) 724-7719

PHILLIPS JUNIOR COLLEGE
1622 13th Ave., Columbus 31901 *Type:* Private junior *Accred.:* 1972/1986 (CCA-ACICS) *Calendar:* Qtr. plan *Degrees:* A, certificates, diplomas *CEO:* Pres. Joyce Meadows
Enroll: 1383 (404) 327-4381

PICKENS TECHNICAL INSTITUTE
240 Burnt Mountain Rd., Jasper 30143 *Type:* Public (state) *Accred.:* 1971/1991 (SACS-COEI) *Calendar:* Courses of varying lengths *Degrees:* certificates *CEO:* Dir. Tom Harrison
Enroll: 424 (404) 692-3411

PIEDMONT COLLEGE
P.O. Box 10, Demorest 30535 *Type:* Independent liberal arts *Accred.:* 1965/1987 (SACS-CC) *Calendar:* Sem. plan *Degrees:* B *CEO:* Pres. John F. Elger
Enroll: 452 (404) 778-8009

PORTFOLIO CENTER
125 Bennett St., N.W., Atlanta 30309 *Type:* Private technical *Accred.:* 1982/1987 (SACS-COEI) *Calendar:* Courses of varying lengths *Degrees:* certificates *CEO:* Dir. Gemma Gatt
Enroll: 206 (404) 351-5055

PRO-WAY HAIR SCHOOL
Hwy. 34 W., 8-B Franklin St., Newnan 30263 *Type:* Private *Accred.:* 1983/1990 (SACS-COEI) *Calendar:* 1,500-hour program *Degrees:* certificates *CEO:* Dir. Francis Sullivan
Enroll: 160 (404) 251-4592

BRANCH CAMPUS
3099 S. Perkins Rd., Memphis, TN 38118-3239 *CEO:* Dir. Steve Sullivan
(901) 363-3553

QUALITY PLUS OFFICE SKILLS AND MOTIVATIONAL TRAINING CENTER
1655 Peachtree St., Ste. 450, Atlanta 30309 *Type:* Private business *Accred.:* 1990 (CCA-ACICS) *Calendar:* Courses of varying lengths *Degrees:* certificates, diplomas *CEO:* Pres. Kathleen Bacon
(404) 892-6669

REINHARDT COLLEGE
P.O. Box 128, Waleska 30183 *Type:* Private (United Methodist) junior *Accred.:* 1953/1988 (SACS-CC) *Calendar:* Qtr. plan *Degrees:* A *CEO:* Pres. Floyd A. Falany
Enroll: 706 (404) 479-1454

Georgia

ROFFLER-MOLER HAIRSTYLING
4023 Jonesboro Rd., P.O. Box 518, Forest Park 30050 *Type:* Private *Accred.:* 1985 (CCA-ACTTS) *Calendar:* Courses of varying lengths *Degrees:* certificates *CEO:* Dir. Ruby Sheffield
Enroll: 80 (404) 366-2838

BRANCH CAMPUS
1311 Roswell Rd., Marietta, GA 30062 *Accred.:* 1985 (CCA-ACTTS) *CEO:* Dir. Ruby Sheffield
(404) 565-3285

RUSH INSTITUTE
571 Ashby St., S.W., Atlanta 30310 *Type:* Private *Accred.:* 1988 (SACS-COEI) *Calendar:* Courses of varying lengths *Degrees:* certificates *CEO:* Dir. Margaret Rush
Enroll: 176 (404) 765-9325

BRANCH CAMPUS
1050 Baxter St., Athens, GA 30606 *CEO:* Dir. Margaret Rush
(404) 354-0373

THE SAVANNAH COLLEGE OF ART AND DESIGN
342 Bull St., P.O. Box 4146, Savannah 31402 *Type:* Private *Accred.:* 1983/1989 (SACS-CC) *Calendar:* Qtr. plan *Degrees:* B, M *Prof. Accred.:* Architecture (B-candidate) *CEO:* Pres. Richard G. Rowan
Enroll: 1912 (912) 238-2400

SAVANNAH STATE COLLEGE
State Coll. Branch, Savannah 31404 *Type:* Public (state) liberal arts and professional *System:* Board of Regents, University System of Georgia *Accred.:* 1951/1991 (SACS-CC) *Calendar:* Qtr. plan *Degrees:* B *Prof. Accred.:* Engineering Technology (civil/construction, computer, electrical, mechanical), Social Work (B) *CEO:* Acting Pres. Annette K. Brock
Enroll: 2517 (912) 356-2186

SAVANNAH TECHNICAL INSTITUTE
5717 White Bluff Rd., Savannah 31499 *Type:* Public (state) *Accred.:* 1991 (SACS-CC) *Degrees:* A, certificates, diplomas *Prof. Accred.:* Dental Assisting, Engineering Technology (electrical, electromechanical), Medical Assisting (AMA), Practical Nursing, Surgical Technology *CEO:* Pres. Billy B. Hair
Enroll: 2013 (912) 351-6362

SHORTER COLLEGE
315 Shorter Ave., Rome 30161 *Type:* Private (Southern Baptist) liberal arts *Accred.:* 1923/1982 (SACS-CC) *Calendar:* Sem. plan *Degrees:* B, M (candidate) *Prof. Accred.:* Music *CEO:* Pres. James D. Jordan
Enroll: 780 (404) 291-2121

SOUTH COLLEGE
709 Mall Blvd., Savannah 31406 *Type:* Private junior *Accred.:* 1975/1989 (CCA-ACICS); 1985/1990 (SACS-CC) *Calendar:* Qtr. plan *Degrees:* A, certificates, diplomas *Prof. Accred.:* Medical Assisting (AMA) *CEO:* Pres. John T. South, III
Enroll: 724 (912) 651-8100

BRANCH CAMPUS
1760 N. Congress Ave., West Palm Beach, FL 33409 *Accred.:* 1975/1989 (CCA-ACICS) *Prof. Accred.:* Medical Assisting (AMA) *CEO:* Dir. William G. Faour
Enroll: 425 (407) 697-9200

SOUTH GEORGIA COLLEGE
Douglas 31533-5098 *Type:* Public (state) junior *System:* Board of Regents, University System of Georgia *Accred.:* 1934/1987 (SACS-CC) *Calendar:* Qtr. plan *Degrees:* A *Prof. Accred.:* Nursing (A) *CEO:* Pres. Edward D. Jackson, Jr.
Enroll: 1114 (912) 383-4220

SOUTH GEORGIA TECHNICAL INSTITUTE
Southfield Rd., P.O. Box 1088, Americus 31709 *Type:* Public (state) *Accred.:* 1973/1988 (SACS-COEI) *Calendar:* Courses of varying lengths *Degrees:* certificates *CEO:* Dir. Dea Pounders
Enroll: 427 (912) 928-0283

SOUTHEASTERN CENTER FOR THE ARTS
1935 Cliff Valley Way, Ste. 210, Atlanta 30329 *Type:* Private *Accred.:* 1983/1988

(SACS-COEI) *Calendar:* Courses of varying lengths *Degrees:* certificates *CEO:* Dir. Fred Rick
Enroll: 84 (404) 633-1990

SOUTHERN COLLEGE OF TECHNOLOGY
S. Marietta Pkwy., Marietta 30060-2896 *Type:* Public (state) *System:* Board of Regents, University System of Georgia *Accred.:* 1964/1988 (SACS-CC) *Calendar:* Qtr. plan *Degrees:* A, B, M *Prof. Accred.:* Engineering Technology (apparel, architectural, civil/construction, electrical, industrial, mechanical, textile) *CEO:* Pres. Stephen R. Cheshier
Enroll: 3386 (404) 528-7230

SPELMAN COLLEGE
350 Spelman La., S.W., Atlanta 30314 *Type:* Private liberal arts for women *Accred.:* 1932/1990 (SACS-CC) *Calendar:* Sem. plan *Degrees:* B *Prof. Accred.:* Music, Teacher Education (e,s) *CEO:* Pres. Johnnetta B. Cole
Enroll: 1677 (404) 681-3643

SWAINSBORO TECHNICAL INSTITUTE
201 Kite Rd., Swainsboro 30401 *Type:* Public (state) *Accred.:* 1973/1988 (SACS-COEI) *Calendar:* Courses of varying lengths *Degrees:* certificates *CEO:* Dir. Donald Speir
Enroll: 716 (912) 237-6465

THOMAS COLLEGE
1501 Millpond Rd., Thomasville 31792-7499 *Type:* Private *Accred.:* 1984/1989 (SACS-CC) *Calendar:* Qtr. plan *Degrees:* A, B *CEO:* Pres. H. Douglas Meyers
Enroll: 300 (912) 226-1621

THOMAS TECHNICAL INSTITUTE
Hwy. 19 at Rte. 319, P.O. Box 1578, Thomasville 31792 *Type:* Public (state) *Accred.:* 1973/1988 (SACS-COEI) *Calendar:* Courses of varying lengths *Degrees:* certificates *Prof. Accred.:* Radiography, Respiratory Therapy Technology, Surgical Technology *CEO:* Dir. Charles R. DeMott
Enroll: 566 (912) 225-4094

TOCCOA FALLS COLLEGE
Toccoa Falls 30598 *Type:* Private (Christian and Missionary Alliance) *Accred.:* 1957/1987 (AABC); 1983/1989 (SACS-CC) *Calendar:* Sem. plan *Degrees:* A, B *Prof. Accred.:* Music *CEO:* Pres. Paul L. Alford
Enroll: 741 (404) 886-6831

TRUETT MCCONNELL COLLEGE
Rte. 6, Box 6000, Cleveland 30528 *Type:* Private (Southern Baptist) junior *Accred.:* 1966/1990 (SACS-CC) *Calendar:* Qtr. plan *Degrees:* A *Prof. Accred.:* Music *CEO:* Pres. H.M. Fulbright
Enroll: 1209 (404) 865-2134

TURNER JOB CORPS CENTER
2000 Schilling Ave., Albany 31708 *Type:* Public (district) *Accred.:* 1984/1989 (SACS-COEI) *Calendar:* Courses of varying lengths *Degrees:* certificates *CEO:* Dir. Hal Schmitz
Enroll: 1269 (912) 431-1820

UNITED STATES ARMY SIGNAL CENTER AND SCHOOL
Fort Gordon 30905-5070 *Type:* Public (federal) technical *Accred.:* 1976/1986 (SACS-COEI) *Calendar:* Courses of varying lengths *Degrees:* certificates *CEO:* Commandant Peter Kind, U.S.A.
Enroll: 8365 (404) 791-4588

UNITED STATES NAVY SUPPLY CORPS SCHOOL
Athens 30635-5000 *Type:* Public (federal) technical *Accred.:* 1981/1991 (SACS-COEI) *Calendar:* Courses of varying lengths *Degrees:* certificates *CEO:* Commanding Ofcr. A.J. Waldron
Enroll: 468 (404) 354-7200

THE UNIVERSITY OF GEORGIA
Athens 30602 *Type:* Public (state) *System:* Board of Regents, University System of Georgia *Accred.:* 1909/1991 (SACS-CC) *Calendar:* Qtr. plan *Degrees:* A, B, P, M, D *Prof. Accred.:* Art, Audiology, Business (B,M), Clinical Psychology, Counseling, Counseling Psychology, Engineering (agricultural), Forestry, Home Economics, Interior Design, Journalism, Landscape

Architecture (B,M), Law, Music, Pharmacy, Psychology Internship, Public Administration, Recreation and Leisure Studies, Rehabilitation Counseling, School Psychology, Social Work (B,M), Speech-Language Pathology, Teacher Education (e,s,p), Theatre *CEO:* Pres. Charles B. Knapp
Enroll: 28538 (404) 542-3000

UPSON TECHNICAL INSTITUTE
Hwy. 19 S., P.O. Box 1089, Thomaston 30286 *Type:* Public (state) *Accred.:* 1973/1990 (SACS-COEI) *Calendar:* Courses of varying lengths *Degrees:* certificates *CEO:* Dir. Carlos Schmidt
Enroll: 149 (404) 647-0928

VALDOSTA STATE COLLEGE
Patterson St., Valdosta 31698 *Type:* Public liberal arts and teachers *System:* Board of Regents, University System of Georgia *Accred.:* 1929/1990 (SACS-CC) *Calendar:* Qtr. plan *Degrees:* A, B, M *Prof. Accred.:* Business (B), Music, Nursing (B,M), Teacher Education (e,s,p) *CEO:* Pres. Hugh C. Bailey
Enroll: 6382 (912) 333-5800

VALDOSTA TECHNICAL INSTITUTE
Rte. 1, Box 202, Val-Tech Rd., Valdosta 31602 *Type:* Public (state) *Accred.:* 1974/1990 (SACS-COEI) *Calendar:* Courses of varying lengths *Degrees:* certificates *Prof. Accred.:* Medical Assisting, Medical Assisting (AMA), Radiography *CEO:* Dir. James Bridges
Enroll: 557 (912) 333-2100

WALKER TECHNICAL INSTITUTE
Hwy. 27 N., Rte. 2, Box 185, Rock Spring 30739 *Type:* Public (state) *Accred.:* 1972/1987 (SACS-COEI) *Calendar:* Courses of varying lengths *Degrees:* certificates *CEO:* Dir. Ray Brooks
Enroll: 783 (404) 764-1016

WAYCROSS COLLEGE
2001 Francis St., Waycross 31501 *Type:* Public (state) junior *System:* Board of Regents, University System of Georgia *Accred.:* 1978/1983 (SACS-CC) *Calendar:* Qtr. plan *Degrees:* A *Prof. Accred.:* Nursing *CEO:* Pres. James M. Dye
Enroll: 704 (912) 285-6130

WESLEYAN COLLEGE
4760 Forsyth Rd., Macon 31297-4299 *Type:* Private (United Methodist) liberal arts for women *Accred.:* 1919/1984 (SACS-CC) *Calendar:* Sem. plan *Degrees:* B *Prof. Accred.:* Music *CEO:* Pres. Robert K. Ackerman
Enroll: 463 (912) 477-1110

WEST GEORGIA COLLEGE
Carrollton 30118-0001 *Type:* Public (state) liberal arts and professional *System:* Board of Regents, University System of Georgia *Accred.:* 1963/1983 (SACS-CC) *Calendar:* Qtr. plan *Degrees:* A, B, M *Prof. Accred.:* Business (B,M), Music, Nursing (A,B), Teacher Education (e,s,p) *CEO:* Pres. Maurice K. Townsend
Enroll: 6412 (404) 836-6500

WEST GEORGIA TECHNICAL INSTITUTE
303 Fort Dr., LaGrange 30240 *Type:* Public (state) *Accred.:* 1973/1988 (SACS-COEI) *Calendar:* Courses of varying lengths *Degrees:* certificates *Prof. Accred.:* Radiography *CEO:* Dir. Roger Slater
Enroll: 274 (404) 882-2518

YOUNG HARRIS COLLEGE
P.O. Box 98, Young Harris 30582 *Type:* Private (United Methodist) junior *Accred.:* 1938/1991 (SACS-CC) *Calendar:* Qtr. plan *Degrees:* A *CEO:* Pres. Thomas S. Yow, III
Enroll: 434 (404) 379-3111

GUAM

GUAM COMMUNITY COLLEGE
P.O. Box 23069, Guam Main Facility, M.I. 96921 *Type:* Public (territorial) junior *Accred.:* 1979/1989 (WASC-Jr.) *Calendar:* Sem. plan *Degrees:* A *CEO:* Pres. John T. Cruz
Enroll: 2736 (671) 734-4311

INTERNATIONAL BUSINESS COLLEGE OF GUAM
P.O. Box 3783, Agana 96910 *Type:* Private *Accred.:* 1978/1986 (CCA-ACICS) *Calendar:* Qtr. plan *Degrees:* certificates, diplomas *CEO:* Dir. Dennis M. Wible
Enroll: 586 (671) 646-6901

UNIVERSITY OF GUAM
UOG Sta., Mangilao 96923 *Type:* Public (territorial) liberal arts and professional *Accred.:* 1963/1988 (WASC-Sr.) *Calendar:* Sem. plan *Degrees:* A, B, M *CEO:* Pres. Wilfred P. Leon Guerrero
Enroll: 4644 (671) 734-2177

HAWAII

BRIGHAM YOUNG UNIVERSITY—HAWAII CAMPUS
55-220 Kulanui St., Laie, Oahu 96762 *Type:* Independent (Latter-Day Saints) liberal arts *Accred.:* 1959/1986 (WASC-Sr.) *Calendar:* 4-4-2-2 plan *Degrees:* A, B *Prof. Accred.:* Social Work (B) *CEO:* Pres. Alton L. Wade
Enroll: 2040 (808) 293-3700

CANNON'S INTERNATIONAL BUSINESS COLLEGE OF HONOLULU
1500 Kapiolani Blvd., Honolulu 96814 *Type:* Private junior *Accred.:* 1954/1987 (CCA-ACICS) *Calendar:* Qtr. plan *Degrees:* A *CEO:* Pres. Evelyn A. Schemmel
Enroll: 1277 (808) 955-1500

CHAMINADE UNIVERSITY OF HONOLULU
3140 Waialae Ave., Honolulu 96816 *Type:* Independent (Roman Catholic) liberal arts and professional *Accred.:* 1960/1983 (WASC-Sr.) *Calendar:* Sem. plan *Degrees:* A, B, M *CEO:* Pres. Kent M. Keith
Enroll: 1508 (808) 735-4711

HAWAII BUSINESS COLLEGE
111 N. King St., Penthouse, Honolulu 96817 *Type:* Private business *Accred.:* 1976/1988 (CCA-ACICS) *Calendar:* Courses of varying lengths *Degrees:* certificates, diplomas *CEO:* Vice Pres. Walter Omori
Enroll: 825 (808) 524-4014

HAWAII COMMUNITY COLLEGE
523 W. Lanikaula St., Hilo 96720-4091 *Type:* Public (state) junior *System:* University of Hawaii Community Colleges *Accred.:* 1973/1989 (WASC-Jr.) *Calendar:* Sem. plan *Degrees:* A *CEO:* Provost Sandra Sakaguchi
Enroll: 1526 (808) 933-3311

HAWAII INSTITUTE OF HAIR DESIGN
71 S. Hotel St., Honolulu 96813 *Type:* Private *Accred.:* 1978/1985 (CCA-ACTTS) *Calendar:* Courses of varying lengths *Degrees:* certificates, diplomas *CEO:* Pres. Margaret Williams
Enroll: 200 (808) 533-6496

HAWAII LOA COLLEGE
45-045 Kamehameha Hwy., Kaneohe, Oahu 96744 *Type:* Independent (Episcopal) liberal arts *Accred.:* 1971/1982 (WASC-Sr.) *Calendar:* 4-4-4 plan *Degrees:* B *CEO:* Pres. Dwight M. Smith
Enroll: 501 (808) 235-3641

HAWAII PACIFIC UNIVERSITY
1166 Fort St., Honolulu 96813 *Type:* Independent liberal arts and business *Accred.:* 1973/1988 (WASC-Sr.) *Calendar:* Sem. plan *Degrees:* A, B, M *CEO:* Pres. Chatt G. Wright
Enroll: 3796 (808) 544-0200

HAWAII TRANSPORTATION SYSTEM
419 Waiakami Rd., Ste. 204, Honolulu 96617 *Type:* Private *Accred.:* 1988 (CCA-ACTTS) *Calendar:* Courses of varying lengths *Degrees:* certificates *CEO:* Dir. John C. Dunston
(808) 847-3221

HONOLULU COMMUNITY COLLEGE
874 Dillingham Blvd., Honolulu 96817 *Type:* Public (state) junior *System:* University of Hawaii Community Colleges *Accred.:* 1970/1989 (WASC-Jr.) *Calendar:* Sem. plan *Degrees:* A *CEO:* Provost Peter R. Kessinger
Enroll: 4523 (808) 845-9225

KANSAI GAIDAI-HAWAII COLLEGE
5257 Kalanianaole Hwy., Honolulu 96821 *Type:* Private 2-year *Accred.:* 1985/1990 (WASC-Jr.) *Calendar:* Qtr. plan *Degrees:* A *CEO:* Provost Andrew H. Dykstra
Enroll: 112 (808) 377-5402

KAPIOLANI COMMUNITY COLLEGE
4303 Diamond Head Rd., Honolulu 96816 *Type:* Public (state) junior *System:* University of Hawaii Community Colleges *Accred.:* 1970/1989 (WASC-Jr.) *Calendar:* Sem. plan *Degrees:* A *Prof. Accred.:* Medical Assisting (AMA), Medical Laboratory Technology (AMA), Occupational

Therapy Assisting, Physical Therapy Assisting, Radiography, Respiratory Therapy, Respiratory Therapy Technology *CEO:* Provost John E. Morton
Enroll: 6399 (808) 734-9111

KAUAI COMMUNITY COLLEGE
3-1901 Kaumualii Hwy., Lihue, Kauai 96766 *Type:* Public (state) junior *System:* University of Hawaii Community Colleges *Accred.:* 1971/1989 (WASC-Jr.) *Calendar:* Sem. plan *Degrees:* A *Prof. Accred.:* Nursing (A) *CEO:* Provost David Iha
Enroll: 1231 (808) 245-8311

LEEWARD COMMUNITY COLLEGE
96-045 Ala Ike, Pearl City 96782 *Type:* Public (state) junior *System:* University of Hawaii Community Colleges *Accred.:* 1971/1989 (WASC-Jr.) *Calendar:* Sem. plan *Degrees:* A *CEO:* Provost Barbara Polk
Enroll: 5804 (808) 455-0011

MAUI COMMUNITY COLLEGE
310 Kaahumanu Ave., Kahului 96732 *Type:* Public (state) junior *System:* University of Hawaii Community Colleges *Accred.:* 1980/1989 (WASC-Jr.) *Calendar:* Sem. plan *Degrees:* A *Prof. Accred.:* Nursing (A) *CEO:* Provost Clyde Sakamoto
Enroll: 1915 (808) 244-9181

MED-ASSIST SCHOOL OF HAWAII
1164 Bishop St., Ste. 912, Honolulu 96813 *Type:* Private *Calendar:* Courses of varying lengths *Degrees:* certificates *Prof. Accred.:* Health Education, Medical Assisting *CEO:* Prin. Barbara E. Weinberg
Enroll: 42 (808) 524-3363

NEW YORK TECHNICAL INSTITUTE OF HAWAII
1375 Dillingham Blvd., Honolulu 96817-4415 *Type:* Private *Accred.:* 1991 (CCA-ACTTS) *Calendar:* Courses of varying lengths *Degrees:* certificates *CEO:* Co-Owner Tracy Hamilton
(808) 841-5827

TRAVEL INSTITUTE OF THE PACIFIC
1314 S. King St., Ste. 1164, Honolulu 96814-2004 *Type:* Private *Accred.:* 1991 (CCA-ACTTS) *Calendar:* Courses of varying lengths *Degrees:* certificates *CEO:* Dir. James Hughes
(808) 531-2708

TRAVEL UNIVERSITY INTERNATIONAL
1441 Kapiolani Blvd., Ste. 1414, Honolulu 96814 *Type:* Private *Accred.:* 1988 (CCA-ACTTS) *Calendar:* Courses of varying lengths *Degrees:* certificates *CEO:* Dir. David Emery
(808) 946-3535

UNIVERSITY OF HAWAII AT HILO
Hilo 96720-4091 *Type:* Public (state) liberal arts and professional *System:* University of Hawaii System *Accred.:* 1976/1989 (WASC-Sr.) *Calendar:* Sem. plan *Degrees:* A, B *CEO:* Chanc. Edward J. Kormondy
Enroll: 2794 (808) 933-3311

UNIVERSITY OF HAWAII AT MANOA
2444 Dole St., Honolulu 96822 *Type:* Public (state) liberal arts and professional *System:* University of Hawaii System *Accred.:* 1952/1991 (WASC-Sr.) *Calendar:* Sem. plan *Degrees:* A, B, P, M, D *Prof. Accred.:* Architecture (B,M), Audiology, Business (B,M), Clinical Psychology, Counseling, Dental Hygiene, Engineering (civil, electrical, mechanical, ocean), Journalism, Law, Librarianship, Medical Technology, Medicine, Music, Nursing (A,B,M), Planning (regional/urban), Public Health, Rehabilitation Counseling, Social Work (B,M), Speech-Language Pathology *CEO:* Chanc. Albert J. Simone
Enroll: 14444 (808) 956-8111

UNIVERSITY OF HAWAII AT WEST OAHU
96-043 Ala Ike, Pearl City 96782 *Type:* Public (state) liberal arts; upper division only *System:* University of Hawaii System *Accred.:* 1981 (WASC-Sr.) *Calendar:* Sem. plan *Degrees:* B *CEO:* Chanc. Edward J. Kormondy
Enroll: 346 (808) 456-5921

WINDWARD COMMUNITY COLLEGE
45-720 Keaahala Rd., Kaneohe, Oahu 96744 *Type:* Public (state) junior *System:* University of Hawaii Community Colleges *Accred.:* 1977/1989 (WASC-Jr.) *Calendar:* Sem. plan *Degrees:* A *CEO:* Provost Peter T. Dyer *Enroll:* 1633 (808) 235-0077

IDAHO

ALBERTSON COLLEGE
2112 Cleveland Blvd., Caldwell 83605 *Type:* Private (United Presbyterian) liberal arts *Accred.:* 1922/1982 (NASC) *Calendar:* 4-1-4 plan *Degrees:* B, M *CEO:* Pres. Robert L. Hendren, Jr.
Enroll: 941 (208) 459-5011

BOISE BIBLE COLLEGE
8695 Marigold St., Boise 83714 *Type:* Private (Christian Churches/Churches of Christ) *Accred.:* 1988 (AABC) *Calendar:* Sem. plan *Degrees:* A, B, certificates *CEO:* Pres. Charles A. Crane
Enroll: 66 (208) 376-7731

BOISE STATE UNIVERSITY
Boise 83725 *Type:* Public liberal arts and teachers *System:* State Board of Education and Board of Regents of the University of Idaho *Accred.:* 1941/1984 (NASC) *Calendar:* Sem. plan *Degrees:* A, B, M *Prof. Accred.:* Accounting (Type A), Business (B,M), Construction Management, Dental Assisting, Medical Record Technology, Music, Nursing (A,B), Radiography, Respiratory Therapy, Respiratory Therapy Technology, Social Work (B), Surgical Technology, Teacher Education (e,s) *CEO:* Interim Pres. Larry Selland
Enroll: 13421 (208) 385-1491

COLLEGE OF SOUTHERN IDAHO
315 Falls Ave., P.O. Box 1238, Twin Falls 83303-1238 *Type:* Public (district) junior *System:* State Board of Education and Board of Regents of the University of Idaho *Accred.:* 1968/1984 (NASC) *Calendar:* Sem. plan *Degrees:* A *Prof. Accred.:* Medical Assisting (AMA), Nursing (A) *CEO:* Pres. Gerald R. Meyerhoeffer
Enroll: 3480 (208) 733-9554

EASTERN IDAHO TECHNICAL COLLEGE
1600 S. 2500 E., Idaho Falls 83404 *Type:* Public (district) 2-year *Accred.:* 1982/1987 (NASC) *Calendar:* Modified qtr. plan *Degrees:* certificates *CEO:* Dir. Grace Guemple
Enroll: 355 (208) 524-3000

ITT TECHNICAL INSTITUTE
970 Lusk St., P.O. Box 7567, Boise 83706-1567 *Type:* Private *Accred.:* 1985 (CCA-ACTTS) *Calendar:* Qtr. plan *Degrees:* diplomas *CEO:* Dir. N. Dale Reynolds
Enroll: 966 (208) 344-8376

IDAHO STATE UNIVERSITY
Pocatello 83209-0009 *Type:* Public (state) *System:* State Board of Education and Board of Regents of the University of Idaho *Accred.:* 1923/1984 (NASC) *Calendar:* Sem. plan *Degrees:* A, B, M, D *Prof. Accred.:* Audiology, Business (B,M), Counseling, Dental Hygiene, Dental Laboratory Technology (prelim. provisional), Engineering (general), Music, Nursing (B,M), Pharmacy, Physical Therapy, Radiography, Social Work (B), Speech-Language Pathology, Teacher Education *CEO:* Pres. Richard L. Bowen
Enroll: 9139 (208) 236-3340

LEWIS-CLARK STATE COLLEGE
Lewiston 83501 *Type:* Public (state) 4-year liberal arts and teachers *System:* State Board of Education and Board of Regents of the University of Idaho *Accred.:* 1964/1989 (NASC) *Calendar:* Sem. plan *Degrees:* A, B *Prof. Accred.:* Nursing (A,B), Teacher Education (e,s) *CEO:* Pres. Lee A. Vickers
Enroll: 2667 (208) 799-2216

NORTH IDAHO COLLEGE
Coeur d'Alene 83814 *Type:* Public (district) junior *System:* State Board of Education and Board of Regents of the University of Idaho *Accred.:* 1947/1983 (NASC) *Calendar:* Sem. plan *Degrees:* A *Prof. Accred.:* Nursing (A) *CEO:* Pres. C. Robert Bennett
Enroll: 2960 (208) 769-3300

NORTHWEST NAZARENE COLLEGE
Nampa 83686 *Type:* Private (Nazarene) liberal arts *Accred.:* 1930/1987 (NASC) *Calendar:* Qtr. plan *Degrees:* A, B, M *Prof. Accred.:* Music, Social Work (B), Teacher Education (e,s,p) *CEO:* Pres. A. Gordon Wetmore
Enroll: 1201 (208) 467-8011

Idaho

RICKS COLLEGE
Rexburg 83460 *Type:* Private (Latter-day Saints) junior *Accred.:* 1936/1989 (NASC) *Calendar:* Sem. plan *Degrees:* A *Prof. Accred.:* Engineering Technology (electrical, manufacturing, mechanical drafting/design, welding), Interior Design, Music, Nursing (A) *CEO:* Pres. Steven D. Bennion
Enroll: 7795   (208) 356-2411

STATE BARBER/STYLING COLLEGE
2210 Main St., Boise 83702 *Type:* Private *Accred.:* 1985 (CCA-ACTTS) *Calendar:* Courses of varying lengths *Degrees:* certificates, diplomas *CEO:* Dir./Owner D. Ray Williams
Enroll: 16   (208) 342-4213

UNIVERSITY OF IDAHO
Moscow 83843 *Type:* Public (state) *System:* State Board of Education and Board of Regents of the University of Idaho *Accred.:* 1918/1984 (NASC) *Calendar:* Sem. plan *Degrees:* B, P, M, D *Prof. Accred.:* Architecture (B), Counseling, Dietetics (coordinated), Engineering (agricultural, chemical, civil, electrical, geological/geophysical, mechanical, metallurgical, mining), Forestry, Landscape Architecture (B), Law, Music, Recreation, Teacher Education (e,s,p) *CEO:* Pres. Elisabeth A. Zinser
Enroll: 10544   (208) 885-6365

ILLINOIS

ACADEMY OF ALLIED HEALTH CAREERS
20 N. Michigan Ave., Chicago 60602 *Type:* Private *Accred.:* 1991 (CCA-ACTTS) *Calendar:* Courses of varying lengths *Degrees:* certificates *CEO:* Dir. Robert Clark
(312) 782-7800

ADLER SCHOOL OF PROFESSIONAL PSYCHOLOGY
618 S. Michigan Ave., Chicago 60605 *Type:* Private professional; graduate only *Accred.:* 1978/1990 (NCA) *Calendar:* Tri. plan *Degrees:* M, D, certificates, diplomas *CEO:* Pres. Randall L. Thompson
Enroll: 154   (312) 294-7100

AMERICAN ACADEMY OF ART
122 S. Michigan Ave., 16th Fl., Chicago 60616 *Type:* Private *Accred.:* 1974/1979 (CCA-ACTTS) *Calendar:* Sem. plan *Degrees:* A *CEO:* Educ. Dir. Irene S. McCauley
Enroll: 1079   (312) 939-3883

AMERICAN COLLEGE OF TECHNOLOGY
1300 W. Washington St., Bloomington 61701 *Type:* Private *Accred.:* 1983/1988 (CCA-ACTTS) *Calendar:* 26-wk. courses *Degrees:* diplomas *CEO:* Pres. Freddie H. Clark
Enroll: 87   (309) 828-5151

AMERICAN CONSERVATORY OF MUSIC
16 N. Wabash Ave., Ste. 1850, Chicago 60602-4792 *Type:* Private professional *Calendar:* Courses of varying lengths *Degrees:* A, B, M, D, certificates *Prof. Accred.:* Music *CEO:* Dean Carl L. Waldschmidt
Enroll: 100   (312) 263-4161

AMERICAN MEDICAL RECORD ASSOCIATION
919 N. Michigan Ave., Ste. 1400, Chicago 60611 *Type:* Private home study *Accred.:* 1970/1985 (NHSC) *Calendar:* Courses of varying lengths *Degrees:* certificates *CEO:* Dir. Margaret Amatayakul
(312) 787-2672

AMERICAN SCHOOL
850 E. 58th St., Chicago 60637 *Type:* Private home study *Accred.:* 1956/1991 (NHSC) *Calendar:* Courses of varying lengths *Degrees:* diplomas *CEO:* Pres. William Wright
(312) 947-3300

AMERICAN SCHOOLS OF PROFESSIONAL PSYCHOLOGY
220 S. State St., Chicago 60604 *Type:* Private *Accred.:* 1981/1991 (NCA) *Calendar:* Sem. plan *Degrees:* M, D *CEO:* Pres. James D. McHolland
Enroll: 365   (312) 341-6500

AUGUSTANA COLLEGE
Rock Island 61201 *Type:* Private (Lutheran) liberal arts *Accred.:* 1913/1986 (NCA) *Calendar:* Qtr. plan *Degrees:* B *Prof. Accred.:* Music, Social Work (B), Teacher Education (e,s) *CEO:* Pres. Thomas Tredway
Enroll: 2227   (309) 794-7208

AURORA UNIVERSITY
347 S. Gladstone Ave., Aurora 60506 *Type:* Private (Advent Christian) liberal arts *Accred.:* 1938/1989 (NCA) *Calendar:* Sem. plan *Degrees:* B, M *Prof. Accred.:* Nursing (B), Recreation Resources, Social Work (M) *CEO:* Pres. Thomas H. Zarle
Enroll: 1401   (708) 892-6431

AUTOMOTIVE TECHNICAL INSTITUTE
5567 N. Elston Ave., Chicago 60630 *Type:* Private *Accred.:* 1985 (CCA-ACTTS) *Calendar:* Courses of varying lengths *Degrees:* certificates, diplomas *CEO:* Dir. Robert Snow
(312) 275-8116

BARAT COLLEGE
700 E. Westleigh Rd., Lake Forest 60045 *Type:* Private (Roman Catholic) liberal arts *Accred.:* 1943/1988 (NCA) *Calendar:* Sem. plan *Degrees:* B *Prof. Accred.:* Nursing (B) *CEO:* Pres. Lucy S. Morros
Enroll: 555   (708) 234-3000

Illinois

BELLEVILLE AREA COLLEGE
2500 Carlyle Rd., Belleville 62221 *Type:* Public (district) junior *System:* Illinois Community College Board *Accred.:* 1961/1983 (NCA) *Calendar:* Sem. plan *Degrees:* A, certificates, diplomas *Prof. Accred.:* Medical Assisting (AMA), Medical Laboratory Technology (AMA), Medical Record Technology, Nursing (A), Physical Therapy Assisting, Radiography, Respiratory Therapy Technology *CEO:* Pres. Joseph J. Cipfl
Enroll: 6450   (618) 235-2700

BELLEVILLE BARBER COLLEGE
329 N. Illinois St., Belleville 62220 *Type:* Private *Accred.:* 1985 (CCA-ACTTS) *Calendar:* Courses of varying lengths *Degrees:* certificates *CEO:* Owner/Mgr. Cornelius Boeving
Enroll: 42   (618) 234-4424

BETHANY THEOLOGICAL SEMINARY
Butterfield and Meyers Rds., Oak Brook 60521 *Type:* Private (Brethren) professional; graduate only *Accred.:* 1940/1981 (ATS); 1971/1982 (NCA) *Calendar:* Qtr. plan *Degrees:* P, M, D *CEO:* Pres. Wayne L. Miller
Enroll: 62   (708) 620-2200

BLACK HAWK COLLEGE—EAST
Rtes. 34 and 78, P.O. Box 489, Kewanee 61443-0489 *Type:* Public (district) junior *System:* Illinois Community College Board *Accred.:* 1986 (NCA) *Calendar:* Sem. plan *Degrees:* A, certificates, diplomas *CEO:* Pres. Charles E. Warthen
          (309) 852-5671

BLACK HAWK COLLEGE—QUAD CITITES
6600 34th Ave., Moline 61265-5899 *Type:* Public (district) junior *System:* Illinois Community College Board *Accred.:* 1986 (NCA) *Calendar:* Sem. plan *Degrees:* A, certificates, diplomas *Prof. Accred.:* Dental Assisting, Nursing (A), Respiratory Therapy, Respiratory Therapy Technology *CEO:* Pres. Herbert C. Lyon
Enroll: 3813   (309) 796-1311

BLACKBURN COLLEGE
700 College Ave., Carlinville 62626 *Type:* Private (United Presbyterian) liberal arts *Accred.:* 1918/1986 (NCA) *Calendar:* Sem. plan *Degrees:* B, M *CEO:* Pres. Miriam R. Pride
Enroll: 471   (217) 854-3231

BLESSING-RIEMAN COLLEGE OF NURSING
Broadway at 11th St., Quincy 62301 *Type:* Private professional *Accred.:* 1989 (NCA) *Calendar:* Sem. plan *Degrees:* B *CEO:* Pres. Lawrence Swearingen
Enroll: 105   (217) 223-5811

BLOOMINGTON-NORMAL SCHOOL OF RADIOGRAPHY
900 Franklin Ave., Normal 61761 *Type:* Private *Calendar:* 24-month course *Degrees:* certificates *Prof. Accred.:* Radiography *CEO:* Pres. Jeffrey B. Schaub
Enroll: 18   (309) 452-2834

BRADLEY UNIVERSITY
1501 W. Bradley Ave., Peoria 61625 *Type:* Private *Accred.:* 1913/1990 (NCA) *Calendar:* Sem. plan *Degrees:* B, M *Prof. Accred.:* Accounting (Type A), Art, Business (B,M), Construction Education, Engineering (civil, electrical, industrial, manufacturing, mechanical), Engineering Technology (electrical, manufacturing), Music, Nurse Anesthesia Education, Nursing (B), Teacher Education (e,s,p) *CEO:* Pres. John R. Brazil
Enroll: 5254   (309) 676-7611

BROWN'S BUSINESS COLLEGE
601 Bruns La., Springfield 62702 *Type:* Private business *Accred.:* 1987 (CCA-ACICS) *Calendar:* Courses of varying lengths *Degrees:* certificates, diplomas *CEO:* Admin. Kendra Hurd
Enroll: 272   (217) 787-8797

CCI TRAVEL CAREERS
1315 Butterfield Rd., Ste. 204, Downers Grove 60515-5602 *Type:* Private *Accred.:* 1991 (CCA-ACTTS) *Calendar:* Courses of

varying lengths *Degrees:* certificates *CEO:* Dir. Donna Will
(708) 960-2710

CDI CAREER DEVELOPMENT INSTITUTE
67 E. Madison St., Chicago 60603 *Type:* Private *Accred.:* 1972/1988 (CCA-ACTTS) *Calendar:* Courses of varying lengths *Degrees:* certificates *CEO:* Dir. Elmer Hass
Enroll: 1034 (312) 630-9494

CARL SANDBURG COLLEGE
2232 S. Lake Storey Rd., Galesburg 61401 *Type:* Public (district) junior *System:* Illinois Community College Board *Accred.:* 1974/1991 (NCA) *Calendar:* Qtr. plan *Degrees:* A, certificates, diplomas *Prof. Accred.:* Radiography *CEO:* Interim Pres. Donald Christ
Enroll: 1542 (309) 344-2518

CATHERINE COLLEGE
Two N. La Salle St., Mezzanine Level, Chicago 60602 *Type:* Private business *Accred.:* 1969/1990 (CCA-ACICS) *Calendar:* Courses of varying lengths *Degrees:* certificates, diplomas *CEO:* Pres. Richard H. Otto
Enroll: 1660 (312) 263-7800

CATHOLIC THEOLOGICAL UNION
5401 S. Cornell Ave., Chicago 60615-5698 *Type:* Private (Roman Catholic) professional; graduate only *Accred.:* 1972/1981 (ATS); 1972/1982 (NCA) *Calendar:* Qtr. plan *Degrees:* P, M *CEO:* Pres. Donald Senior, C.P.
Enroll: 233 (312) 324-8000

CAVE TECHNICAL INSTITUTE
2804 Lock Port Rd., Lock Port 60444 *Type:* Private *Accred.:* 1988 (CCA-ACTTS) *Calendar:* Courses of varying lengths *Degrees:* certificates *CEO:* Dir. Harold L. Jones
(815) 723-7572

CHICAGO CITY-WIDE COLLEGE
226 W. Jackson Blvd., Chicago 60606 *Type:* Public *System:* City Colleges of Chicago *Accred.:* 1980/1985 (NCA) *Calendar:* Sem. plan *Degrees:* A, certificates, diplomas *Prof. Accred.:* Mortuary Science, Physician Assisting *CEO:* Pres. Martha S. Bazik
Enroll: 4722 (312) 641-2595

CHICAGO COLLEGE OF COMMERCE
11 E. Adams St., Chicago 60603 *Type:* Private business *Accred.:* 1968/1986 (CCA-ACICS) *Calendar:* Qtr. plan *Degrees:* A *CEO:* Chrmn. of the Bd. Mae S. Glassbrenner
Enroll: 507 (312) 236-3312

CHICAGO COLLEGE OF OSTEOPATHIC MEDICINE
5200 S. Ellis Ave., Chicago 60615 *Type:* Private professional *Calendar:* Sem. plan *Degrees:* P *Prof. Accred.:* Osteopathy *CEO:* Pres. Jack B. Kinsinger, Ph.D.
Enroll: 416 (312) 947-3000

BRANCH CAMPUS
555 31st St., Downers Grove, IL 60515 *CEO:* Pres. Jack B. Kinsinger, Ph.D.
(708) 515-6060

CHICAGO SCHOOL OF PROFESSIONAL PSYCHOLOGY
806 S. Plymouth Ct., Chicago 60605 *Type:* Private *Accred.:* 1984/1987 (NCA) *Calendar:* Sem. plan *Degrees:* D *CEO:* Pres./Dean Jeffrey C. Grip
Enroll: 127 (312) 786-9443

CHICAGO STATE UNIVERSITY
9501 S. Martin Luther King Dr., Chicago 60628 *Type:* Public liberal arts and teachers *System:* Illinois Board of Governors of State Colleges and Universities *Accred.:* 1941/1983 (NCA) *Calendar:* Tri. plan *Degrees:* B, M *Prof. Accred.:* Clinical Psychology (provisional), Dietetics (coordinated), Medical Record Administration, Nursing (B), Occupational Therapy, Radiation Therapy Technology, Teacher Education (e,s,p) *CEO:* Pres. Dolores E. Cross
Enroll: 4331 (312) 995-2000

CHICAGO THEOLOGICAL SEMINARY
5757 S. University Ave., Chicago 60637 *Type:* Private (United Church of Christ) professional; graduate only *Accred.:* 1938/1986 (ATS); 1982/1987 (NCA) *Calendar:* Qtr.

plan *Degrees:* P, M, D *CEO:* Pres. Kenneth B. Smith
Enroll: 117 (312) 752-5757

CHICAGO TRUCK DRIVING SCHOOL
2235 W. 74th St., Chicago 60636 *Type:* Private *Accred.:* 1988 (CCA-ACTTS) *Calendar:* Courses of varying lengths *Degrees:* certificates *CEO:* Dir. Joseph A. Passananti
Enroll: 146 (312) 434-5005

COLLEGE OF DU PAGE
22nd St. and Lambert Rd., Glen Ellyn 60137 *Type:* Public (district) junior *System:* Illinois Community College Board *Accred.:* 1932/1984 (NCA) *Calendar:* Qtr. plan *Degrees:* A, certificates, diplomas *Prof. Accred.:* Medical Record Technology, Nuclear Medicine Technology, Nursing (A), Occupational Therapy Assisting, Radiography, Respiratory Therapy Technology *CEO:* Pres. Harold D. McAninch
Enroll: 15035 (708) 858-2800

COLLEGE OF LAKE COUNTY
19351 W. Washington St., Grayslake 60030 *Type:* Public (district) junior *System:* Illinois Community College Board *Accred.:* 1974/1986 (NCA) *Calendar:* Sem. plan *Degrees:* A, certificates, diplomas *Prof. Accred.:* Medical Laboratory Technology (AMA), Medical Record Technology, Nursing (A), Radiography *CEO:* Pres. Daniel J. LaVista
Enroll: 5646 (708) 223-6601

THE COLLEGE OF OFFICE TECHNOLOGY
1520 W. Division St., 2nd Fl., Chicago 60622 *Type:* Private business *Accred.:* 1985 (CCA-ACICS) *Calendar:* 20-week program *Degrees:* certificates, diplomas *CEO:* Pres. Pedro A. Galva
Enroll: 239 (312) 278-0042

COLLEGE OF ST. FRANCIS
500 N. Wilcox St., Joliet 60435 *Type:* Private (Roman Catholic) liberal arts *Accred.:* 1938/1989 (NCA) *Calendar:* Sem. plan *Degrees:* B, M *Prof. Accred.:* Leisure Studies, Social Work (B) *CEO:* Pres. John C. Orr
Enroll: 1853 (815) 740-3369

COLUMBIA COLLEGE
600 S. Michigan Ave., Chicago 60605 *Type:* Private liberal arts *Accred.:* 1974/1989 (NCA) *Calendar:* Sem. plan *Degrees:* B, M *CEO:* Pres. Mirron Alexandroff
Enroll: 5894 (312) 663-1600

COMPUTER LEARNING CENTER
200 S. Michigan Ave., 3rd Fl., Chicago 60604-2404 *Type:* Private *Accred.:* 1985 (CCA-ACICS) *Calendar:* Courses of varying lengths *Degrees:* certificates, diplomas *CEO:* Dir. Richard Wechner
Enroll: 839 (312) 427-2700

CONCORDIA UNIVERSITY
7400 Augusta St., River Forest 60305 *Type:* Private (Lutheran-Missouri Synod) teachers *Accred.:* 1950/1982 (NCA) *Calendar:* Qtr. plan *Degrees:* B, M, certificates, diplomas *Prof. Accred.:* Clinical Psychology, Teacher Education (e,s,p) *CEO:* Pres. Eugene L. Krentz
Enroll: 1006 (708) 209-3004

COOKING AND HOSPITALITY INSTITUTE OF CHICAGO
361 W. Chestnut St., Chicago 60610 *Type:* Private *Accred.:* 1988 (CCA-ACTTS) *Calendar:* Courses of varying lengths *Degrees:* certificates *CEO:* Dir. Linda Calafore
Enroll: 283 (312) 944-0882

COYNE-AMERICAN INSTITUTE
1235 W. Fullerton Ave., Chicago 60614 *Type:* Private *Accred.:* 1965/1987 (CCA-ACTTS) *Calendar:* Qtr. plan *Degrees:* diplomas *CEO:* Dir. John J. Freeman
(312) 935-2520

DANVILLE AREA COMMUNITY COLLEGE
2000 E. Main St., Danville 61832 *Type:* Public (district) junior *System:* Illinois Community College Board *Accred.:* 1967/1989 (NCA) *Calendar:* Sem. plan *Degrees:*

A, certificates, diplomas *CEO:* Pres. Harry J. Braun
Enroll: 1958 (217) 443-1811

DEPAUL UNIVERSITY
25 E. Jackson Blvd., Chicago 60604 *Type:* Private (Roman Catholic) liberal arts and professional *Accred.:* 1925/1987 (NCA) *Calendar:* Qtr. plan *Degrees:* B, P, M, D, certificates, diplomas *Prof. Accred.:* Accounting (Type A,B,C), Business (B,M), Clinical Psychology, Law, Music, Nurse Anesthesia Education, Nursing (B,M), Teacher Education (e,s,p) *CEO:* Pres. John T. Richardson, C.M.
Enroll: 10974 (312) 362-8000

DEVRY INSTITUTE OF TECHNOLOGY, LOMBARD
2000 S. Finley Rd., Lombard 60148-4892 *Type:* Private *Accred.:* 1981/1987 (NCA) *Calendar:* Tri. plan *Degrees:* A, B, certificates *Prof. Accred.:* Engineering Technology (electrical) *CEO:* Pres. Jerry R. Dill
Enroll: 4080 (708) 953-1300

DEVRY INSTITUTES
2201 W. Howard St., Evanston 60202 *Type:* Private *Accred.:* 1981/1987 (NCA) *Calendar:* Tri. plan *Degrees:* A, B, certificates *Prof. Accred.:* Engineering Technology (electrical) *CEO:* Pres. Ronald Taylor
Enroll: 20770 (708) 328-8100

DR. WILLIAM M. SCHOLL COLLEGE OF PODIATRIC MEDICINE
1001 N. Dearborn St., Chicago 60610 *Type:* Private professional *Accred.:* 1985/1990 (NCA) *Calendar:* Sem. plan *Degrees:* B, D *Prof. Accred.:* Podiatry *CEO:* Pres. Richard B. Patterson
Enroll: 375 (312) 280-2910

EAST-WEST UNIVERSITY
816 S. Michigan Ave., Chicago 60605 *Type:* Private technical *Accred.:* 1984/1991 (NCA) *Calendar:* Qtr. plan *Degrees:* A, B *CEO:* Chanc. M. Wasi Kahn
Enroll: 195 (312) 939-0111

EASTERN ILLINOIS UNIVERSITY
Charleston 61920 *Type:* Public (state) *System:* Illinois Board of Governors of State Colleges and Universities *Accred.:* 1915/1985 (NCA) *Calendar:* Sem. plan *Degrees:* B, M *Prof. Accred.:* Art, Home Economics, Journalism, Music, Recreation and Leisure Studies, Speech-Language Pathology, Teacher Education (e,s,p) *CEO:* Pres. Stanley G. Rives
Enroll: 10301 (217) 581-2011

ECHOLS INTERNATIONAL HOTEL SCHOOL
676 N. St. Clair St., Ste. 1950, Chicago 60611 *Type:* Private *Accred.:* 1986 (CCA-ACTTS) *Calendar:* Courses of varying lengths *Degrees:* certificates *CEO:* Owner Evelyn Echols
Enroll: 250 (312) 943-5500

ELGIN COMMUNITY COLLEGE
1700 Spartan Dr., Elgin 60123 *Type:* Public (district) junior *System:* Illinois Community College Board *Accred.:* 1968/1986 (NCA) *Calendar:* Sem. plan *Degrees:* A, certificates, diplomas *Prof. Accred.:* Dental Assisting, Nursing (A) *CEO:* Pres. Paul R. Heath
Enroll: 3776 (708) 697-1000

ELMHURST COLLEGE
190 Prospect St., Elmhurst 60126 *Type:* Private (United Church of Christ) liberal arts *Accred.:* 1924/1989 (NCA) *Calendar:* 4-1-4 plan *Degrees:* B *Prof. Accred.:* Nursing (B), Teacher Education (e,s) *CEO:* Pres. Ivan E. Frick
Enroll: 2298 (708) 617-3100

THE ENGLISH LANGUAGE INSTITUTE OF AMERICA
332 S. Michigan Ave., Ste. 1518, Chicago 60604 *Type:* Private home study *Accred.:* 1981/1987 (NHSC) *Calendar:* Courses of varying lengths *Degrees:* certificates *CEO:* Pres. Graham Dunbar
(312) 663-0880

ENVIRONMENTAL TECHNICAL SCHOOL
1054 E. Irving Park, Bensenville 60106 *Type:* Private *Accred.:* 1988 (CCA-ACTTS) *Calendar:* Courses of varying lengths *De-

grees: certificates *CEO:* Pres. James C. Argyilan
(312) 350-9100

BRANCH CAMPUS
13010 S. Division St., Blue Island, IL 60406 *CEO:* Dir. Jim Argyilan
(312) 385-0707

EUREKA COLLEGE
300 E. College Ave., Eureka 61530 *Type:* Private (Disciples of Christ) liberal arts *Accred.:* 1924/1990 (NCA) *Calendar:* Four 8-wk. terms *Degrees:* B *CEO:* Pres. George A. Hearne
Enroll: 453 (309) 467-3721

FOREST INSTITUTE OF PROFESSIONAL PSYCHOLOGY
200 Glendale St., Wheeling 60090 *Type:* Private *Accred.:* 1984/1987 (NCA) *Calendar:* Tri. plan *Degrees:* M, D *CEO:* Pres. Robert V. Moriarty
Enroll: 142 (708) 215-7870

BRANCH CAMPUS
2611 Leeman Ferry Rd., Huntsville, AL 35801 *Type:* Private *CEO:* Dean Edwin Wagner
(205) 536-9088

BRANCH CAMPUS
46-005 Kawa St., Ste. 306, Kaneohe, Oahu, HI 96744 *CEO:* Dean Terri Needels
(808) 247-2117

BRANCH CAMPUS
1322 S. Campbell Ave., Springfield, MO 65807 *CEO:* Dean Richard Cox
(417) 831-7902

FOX SECRETARIAL COLLEGE
4201 W. 93rd St., Oak Lawn 60453 *Type:* Private business *Accred.:* 1987 (CCA-ACICS) *Calendar:* Qtr. plan *Degrees:* certificates, diplomas *CEO:* Pres. Edward L. Kapelinski
Enroll: 105 (708) 636-7700

FRONTIER COMMUNITY COLLEGE
Frontier Dr., Rural Rte. 1, Fairfield 62837-9701 *Type:* Public (district) junior *System:* Illinois Eastern Community College System *Accred.:* 1984/1988 (NCA) *Calendar:* Qtr. plan *Degrees:* A, certificates, diplomas *Prof. Accred.:* Nursing (A) *CEO:* Pres. Richard L. Mason
(618) 842-3711

GARRETT-EVANGELICAL THEOLOGICAL SEMINARY
2121 Sheridan Rd., Evanston 60201 *Type:* Private (United Methodist) professional; graduate only *Accred.:* 1938/1988 (ATS); 1972/1988 (NCA) *Calendar:* Qtr. plan *Degrees:* P, M, D *CEO:* Pres. Neal F. Fisher
Enroll: 358 (708) 866-3900

GEM CITY COLLEGE
700 State St., Quincy 62301 *Type:* Private business and technical *Accred.:* 1954/1988 (CCA-ACICS) *Calendar:* Courses of varying lengths *Degrees:* A, certificates, diplomas *Prof. Accred.:* Medical Assisting *CEO:* Pres. Russell H. Hagenah
Enroll: 219 (217) 222-0391

GOVERNORS STATE UNIVERSITY
University Park 60466 *Type:* Public liberal arts; graduate only *System:* Illinois Board of Governors of State Colleges and Universities *Accred.:* 1975/1990 (NCA) *Calendar:* Tri. plan *Degrees:* B, M *Prof. Accred.:* Medical Technology, Nursing (B,M), Social Work (B-candidate), Speech-Language Pathology *CEO:* Pres. Leo Goodman-Malamuth, II
Enroll: 2428 (708) 534-5000

GREENVILLE COLLEGE
Greenville 62246 *Type:* Private (Free Methodist) liberal arts *Accred.:* 1948/1986 (NCA) *Calendar:* 4-1-4 plan *Degrees:* B *Prof. Accred.:* Teacher Education (e,s) *CEO:* Pres. W. Richard Stephens
Enroll: 809 (618) 664-1840

THE HADLEY SCHOOL FOR THE BLIND
700 Elm St., Winnetka 60093 *Type:* Private home study *Accred.:* 1958/1989 (NHSC)

Calendar: Courses of varying lengths *Degrees:* certificates *CEO:* Pres. Robert J. Winn
(708) 446-8111

HAROLD WASHINGTON COLLEGE
30 E. Lake St., Chicago 60601 *Type:* Public *System:* City Colleges of Chicago *Accred.:* 1967/1986 (NCA) *Calendar:* Sem. plan *Degrees:* A, certificates, diplomas *CEO:* Pres. Bernice J. Miller
Enroll: 3688 (312) 781-9430

HARRINGTON INSTITUTE OF INTERIOR DESIGN
410 S. Michigan Ave., Chicago 60605 *Type:* Private *Calendar:* Sem. plan *Degrees:* P *Prof. Accred.:* Interior Design *CEO:* Dean Robert C. Marks
Enroll: 412 (312) 939-4975

HARRY S TRUMAN COLLEGE
1145 W. Wilson Ave., Chicago 60640 *Type:* Public *System:* City Colleges of Chicago *Accred.:* 1967/1990 (NCA) *Calendar:* Sen. plan *Degrees:* A, certificates, diplomas *Prof. Accred.:* Medical Record Technology *CEO:* Pres. Wallace B. Appelson
Enroll: 3709 (312) 989-6125

HIGHLAND COMMUNITY COLLEGE
2998 W. Pearl City Rd., Freeport 61032 *Type:* Public (district) junior *System:* Illinois Community College Board *Accred.:* 1973/1986 (NCA) *Calendar:* Sem. plan *Degrees:* A, certificates, diplomas *CEO:* Pres. Ruth M. Smith
Enroll: 1687 (815) 235-6121

ILLINOIS BENEDICTINE COLLEGE
5700 College Rd., Lisle 60532 *Type:* Private (Roman Catholic) liberal arts *Accred.:* 1958/1986 (NCA) *Calendar:* Sem. plan *Degrees:* B, M *Prof. Accred.:* Computer Science, Nursing (B) *CEO:* Pres. Richard C. Becker
Enroll: 1644 (708) 960-1500

ILLINOIS CENTRAL COLLEGE
One College Dr., East Peoria 61635 *Type:* Public (district) community *System:* Illinois Community College Board *Accred.:* 1972/1982 (NCA) *Calendar:* Sem. plan *Degrees:* A, certificates, diplomas *Prof. Accred.:* Dental Assisting, Dental Hygiene, Medical Laboratory Technology (AMA), Music, Nursing (A), Occupational Therapy Assisting, Physical Therapy Assisting, Radiography, Respiratory Therapy, Respiratory Therapy Technology, Surgical Technology *CEO:* Pres. Thomas K. Thomas
Enroll: 6378 (309) 694-5431

ILLINOIS COLLEGE
Jacksonville 62650 *Type:* Private (United Presbyterian/United Church of Christ) liberal arts *Accred.:* 1913/1985 (NCA) *Calendar:* Sem. plan *Degrees:* B *CEO:* Pres. Donald C. Mundinger
Enroll: 866 (217) 245-3000

ILLINOIS COLLEGE OF OPTOMETRY
3241 S. Michigan Ave., Chicago 60616 *Type:* Private professional *Accred.:* 1969/1989 (NCA) *Calendar:* Sem. plan *Degrees:* B, P, D *Prof. Accred.:* Optometry *CEO:* Pres. Boyd B. Banwell
Enroll: 936 (312) 225-1700

ILLINOIS INSTITUTE OF TECHNOLOGY
330 S. Federal St., Chicago 60616 *Type:* Private *Accred.:* 1941/1987 (NCA) *Calendar:* Sem. plan *Degrees:* B, M, D *Prof. Accred.:* Architecture (B), Clinical Psychology, Engineering (aerospace, chemical, civil, electrical, mechanical, metallurgical), Law, Rehabilitation Counseling *CEO:* Pres. Lewis Collens
Enroll: 4388 (312) 567-3000

ILLINOIS MEDICAL TRAINING CENTER
162 N. State St., Chicago 60601 *Type:* Private *Calendar:* Courses of varying lengths *Degrees:* diplomas *Prof. Accred.:* Health Education, Medical Assisting, Respiratory Therapy Technology *CEO:* Pres. John R. Gibson, Ph.D.
Enroll: 901 (312) 782-2061

ILLINOIS STATE UNIVERSITY
Normal 61761 *Type:* Public (state) *System:* Regency Universities System *Accred.:* 1913/1985 (NCA) *Calendar:* Sem. plan *Degrees:*

B, M, D, certificates, diplomas *Prof. Accred.:* Art, Audiology, Business (B,M), Home Economics, Medical Record Administration, Music, Psychology Internship, Recreation and Park Administration, Social Work (B), Speech-Language Pathology, Teacher Education (e,s,p), Theatre *CEO:* Pres. Thomas Wallace
Enroll: 19450 (309) 438-5677

ILLINOIS VALLEY COMMUNITY COLLEGE
2578 E. 350th Rd., Oglesby 61348 *Type:* Public (district) community *System:* Illinois Community College Board *Accred.:* 1929/1988 (NCA) *Calendar:* Sem. plan *Degrees:* A, certificates, diplomas *Prof. Accred.:* Dental Assisting, Nursing (A) *CEO:* Pres. Alfred E. Wisgoski
Enroll: 2399 (815) 224-2720

ILLINOIS WESLEYAN UNIVERSITY
P.O. Box 2900, Bloomington 61702 *Type:* Private (United Methodist) *Accred.:* 1916/1983 (NCA) *Calendar:* Sem. plan *Degrees:* B *Prof. Accred.:* Music, Nursing (B) *CEO:* Pres. Minor Myers, Jr.
Enroll: 1751 (309) 556-3131

INTERNATIONAL ACADEMY OF MERCHANDISING AND DESIGN
350 N. Orleans St., Chicago 60654-1596 *Type:* Private *Accred.:* 1981/1990 (CCA-ACICS) *Calendar:* Qtr. plan *Degrees:* A, B, diplomas *CEO:* Pres. Clem Stein, Jr.
Enroll: 1289 (312) 828-0202

JOHN A. LOGAN COLLEGE
Rte. 2, Carterville 62918 *Type:* Public (district) junior *System:* Illinois Community College Board *Accred.:* 1972/1987 (NCA) *Calendar:* Sem. plan *Degrees:* A, certificates, diplomas *Prof. Accred.:* Dental Assisting *CEO:* Pres. J. Ray Hancock
Enroll: 3349 (618) 985-3741

THE JOHN MARSHALL LAW SCHOOOL
315 S. Plymouth Ct., Chicago 60604 *Type:* Private professional *Calendar:* Sem. plan *Degrees:* P, M *Prof. Accred.:* Law *CEO:* Acting Dean Fred R. Herzog
Enroll: 9 (312) 427-2737

JOHN WOOD COMMUNITY COLLEGE
150 S. 48th St., Quincy 62301 *Type:* Public (district) junior *System:* Illinois Community College Board *Accred.:* 1980/1986 (NCA) *Calendar:* Sem. plan *Degrees:* A, certificates, diplomas *CEO:* Pres. Robert C. Keys
Enroll: 1218 (217) 224-6500

JOLIET JUNIOR COLLEGE
1216 Houbolt Ave., Joliet 60436 *Type:* Public (district) junior *System:* Illinois Community College Board *Accred.:* 1917/1984 (NCA) *Calendar:* Sem. plan *Degrees:* A, certificates, diplomas *Prof. Accred.:* Nursing (A) *CEO:* Pres. Raymond A. Pietak
Enroll: 5079 (815) 729-9020

JUDSON COLLEGE
1151 N. State St., Elgin 60123 *Type:* Private (Baptist) liberal arts *Accred.:* 1973/1988 (NCA) *Calendar:* Tri. plan *Degrees:* B *CEO:* Pres. Harm A. Weber
Enroll: 511 (708) 695-2500

KANKAKEE COMMUNITY COLLEGE
P.O. Box 888, Kankakee 60901 *Type:* Public (district) junior *System:* Illinois Community College Board *Accred.:* 1974/1984 (NCA) *Calendar:* 4-1-4 plan *Degrees:* A, certificates, diplomas *Prof. Accred.:* Medical Laboratory Technology (AMA), Radiography, Respiratory Therapy Technology *CEO:* Pres. Lawrence D. Huffman
Enroll: 1851 (815) 933-0211

KASKASKIA COLLEGE
Shattuc Rd., Centralia 62801 *Type:* Public (district) junior *System:* Illinois Community College Board *Accred.:* 1964/1989 (NCA) *Calendar:* Sem. plan *Degrees:* A, certificates, diplomas *Prof. Accred.:* Dental Assisting, Nursing (A), Radiography *CEO:* Pres. Raymond D. Woods
Enroll: 2190 (618) 532-1981

Accredited Institutions   **Illinois**

KELLER GRADUATE SCHOOL OF MANAGEMENT
10 S. Riverside Plaza, Chicago 60606 *Type:* Private professional *Accred.:* 1977/1986 (NCA) *Calendar:* Qtr. plan *Degrees:* M *CEO:* Pres./C.E.O. Ronald L. Taylor
Enroll: 1784   (312) 454-0880

KENDALL COLLEGE
2408 Orrington Ave., Evanston 60201 *Type:* Private (United Methodist) liberal arts *Accred.:* 1962/1988 (NCA) *Calendar:* 4-1-4 plan *Degrees:* A, B, certificates, diplomas *CEO:* Pres. Thomas J. Kerr, IV
Enroll: 350   (708) 866-1300

KENNEDY-KING COLLEGE
6800 S. Wentworth Ave., Chicago 60621 *Type:* Public *System:* City Colleges of Chicago *Accred.:* 1967/1989 (NCA) *Calendar:* Sem. plan *Degrees:* A, certificates, diplomas *CEO:* Pres. Harold Pates
Enroll: 1905   (312) 962-3200

KISHWAUKEE COLLEGE
21193 Malta Rd., Malta 60150 *Type:* Public (district) *System:* Illinois Community College Board *Accred.:* 1974/1989 (NCA) *Calendar:* Sem. plan *Degrees:* A, certificates, diplomas *Prof. Accred.:* Radiography *CEO:* Pres. Norman J. Jenkins
Enroll: 1704   (815) 825-2086

KNOWLEDGE SYSTEMS INSTITUTE
3420 Main St., Skokie 60076 *Type:* Private *Accred.:* 1991 (NCA) *Calendar:* Qtr. plan *Degrees:* M *CEO:* Exec. Dir. Shi-Kuo Chang
Enroll: 15   (708) 679-3135

KNOX COLLEGE
2 E. South St., Galesburg 61401 *Type:* Private liberal arts *Accred.:* 1913/1989 (NCA) *Calendar:* 3-3-3 plan *Degrees:* B *CEO:* Pres. John P. McCall
Enroll: 922   (309) 343-0112

LAKE FOREST COLLEGE
College and Sheridan Rds., Lake Forest 60045 *Type:* Private (United Presbyterian) liberal arts *Accred.:* 1913/1987 (NCA) *Calendar:* Qtr. plan *Degrees:* B, M *CEO:* Pres. Eugene Hotchkiss, III
Enroll: 1071   (708) 234-3100

LAKE FOREST GRADUATE SCHOOL OF MANAGEMENT
Lake Forest 60045 *Type:* Private graduate only *Accred.:* 1978/1983 (NCA) *Calendar:* Qtr. plan *Degrees:* M, certificates, diplomas *CEO:* Pres. Raymond E. Britt
Enroll: 269   (708) 234-5005

LAKE LAND COLLEGE
5001 Lake Land Blvd., Mattoon 61938 *Type:* Public (district) junior *System:* Illinois Community College Board *Accred.:* 1973/1988 (NCA) *Calendar:* Qtr. plan *Degrees:* A, certificates, diplomas *Prof. Accred.:* Dental Assisting, Dental Hygiene, Nursing (A), Practical Nursing *CEO:* Pres. Robert K. Luther
Enroll: 2737   (217) 235-3131

LEWIS UNIVERSITY
Rte. 53, Romeoville 60441 *Type:* Private (Roman Catholic) liberal arts *Accred.:* 1963/1987 (NCA) *Calendar:* 4-1-4 plan *Degrees:* A, B, P, M, certificates, diplomas *Prof. Accred.:* Nursing (B,M), Social Work (B-candidate) *CEO:* Pres. James Gaffney, F.S.C.
Enroll: 2526   (815) 838-0500

LEWIS AND CLARK COMMUNITY COLLEGE
5800 Godfrey Rd., Godfrey 62035 *Type:* Public (district) junior *System:* Illinois Community College Board *Accred.:* 1971/1986 (NCA) *Calendar:* Sem. plan *Degrees:* A, certificates, diplomas *Prof. Accred.:* Dental Assisting, Medical Laboratory Technology (AMA), Nursing (A) *CEO:* Pres. J. Neil Admire
Enroll: 2907   (618) 466-3411

LINCOLN CHRISTIAN COLLEGE
P.O. Box 178, 100 Campus View Dr., Lincoln 62656 *Type:* Private (Christian Churches/Church of Christ) *Accred.:* 1954/1985 (AABC); 1991 (ATS); 1991 (NCA)

Illinois

Calendar: Sem. plan *Degrees:* A, B, P, M, certificates *CEO:* Pres. Charles A. McNeely
Enroll: 385 (217) 732-3168

LINCOLN COLLEGE
300 Keokuk St., Lincoln 62656 *Type:* Private junior *Accred.:* 1929/1986 (NCA) *Calendar:* 4-1-4 plan *Degrees:* A, certificates, diplomas *CEO:* Pres. Jack D. Nutt
Enroll: 937 (217) 732-3155

LINCOLN LAND COMMUNITY COLLEGE
Shepherd Rd., Springfield 62794 *Type:* Public (district) community *System:* Illinois Community College Board *Accred.:* 1973/1983 (NCA) *Calendar:* Sem. plan *Degrees:* A, certificates, diplomas *Prof. Accred.:* Dental Assisting (conditional), Nursing (A), Radiography, Respiratory Therapy *CEO:* Pres. William D. Law, Jr.
Enroll: 4011 (217) 786-2268

LINCOLN TECHNICAL INSTITUTE
7320 W. Agatite Ave., Norridge 60656 *Type:* Private *Accred.:* 1971/1985 (CCA-ACTTS) *Calendar:* Courses of varying lengths *Degrees:* certificates, diplomas *CEO:* Dir. Jack B. Wendt
Enroll: 1987 (312) 625-1535

LINCOLN TECHNICAL INSTITUTE
8920 S. Cicero Ave., Oak Lawn 60453 *Type:* Private *Accred.:* 1986 (CCA-ACTTS) *Calendar:* Courses of varying lengths *Degrees:* certificates *CEO:* Dir. Kenneth R. Ruff
(708) 423-9000

LINCOLN TRAIL COLLEGE
Rte. 3, Box 82A, Robinson 62454-9524 *Type:* Public (district) *System:* Illinois Eastern Community College System *Accred.:* 1984/1988 (NCA) *Calendar:* Qtr. plan *Degrees:* A, certificates, diplomas *Prof. Accred.:* Nursing (A) *CEO:* Pres. Donald E. Donnay
(618) 544-8657

LOYOLA UNIVERSITY OF CHICAGO
820 N. Michigan Ave., Chicago 60611 *Type:* Private (Roman Catholic) *Accred.:* 1921/1985 (NCA) *Calendar:* Sem. plan *Degrees:* B, P, M, D *Prof. Accred.:* Business (B,M), Clinical Psychology, Combined Prosthodontics, Counseling Psychology, Dental Hygiene, Dentistry, Endodontics, Law, Medicine, Nursing (B,M), Oral and Maxillofacial Surgery, Orthodontics, Pediatric Dentistry, Periodontics, Social Work (B,M), Teacher Education (e,s,p) *CEO:* Pres. Raymond C. Baumhart, S.J.
Enroll: 10964 (312) 915-6402

MALLINCKRODT CAMPUS
1041 Ridge Rd., Wilmette, IL 60091-1560 *CEO:* Assoc. Vice Pres. Marjorie Noterman
Enroll: 140 (312) 256-1094

LUTHERAN SCHOOL OF THEOLOGY AT CHICAGO
1100 E. 55th St., Chicago 60615-5199 *Type:* Private (Evangelical Lutheran) graduate only *Accred.:* 1945/1987 (ATS); 1982/1988 (NCA) *Calendar:* Qtr. plan *Degrees:* P, M, D, certificates, diplomas *CEO:* Pres. William E. Lesher
Enroll: 289 (312) 753-0700

MACCORMAC JUNIOR COLLEGE
327 S. La Salle St., Chicago 60604 *Type:* Private junior *Accred.:* 1979/1989 (NCA) *Calendar:* Qtr. plan *Degrees:* A, certificates, diplomas *CEO:* Pres. Gordon C. Borchardt
Enroll: 415 (312) 922-1884

MACMURRAY COLLEGE
447 E. College Ave., Jacksonville 62650 *Type:* Private (United Methodist) liberal arts *Accred.:* 1921/1989 (NCA) *Calendar:* 4-1-4 plan *Degrees:* A, B *Prof. Accred.:* Nursing (B) *CEO:* Pres. Edward J. Mitchell
Enroll: 1044 (217) 479-7000

MALCOLM X COLLEGE
1900 W. Van Buren St., Chicago 60612 *Type:* Private *System:* City Colleges of Chicago *Accred.:* 1967/1983 (NCA) *Calendar:* Sem. plan *Degrees:* A, certificates, diplomas *Prof. Accred.:* Medical Laboratory Technology (AMA), Radiography, Respiratory Therapy *CEO:* Pres. Milton F. Brown
Enroll: 676 (312) 942-3000

Accredited Institutions — Illinois

MARYCREST COLLEGE
280 E. Merchant St., Kankakee 60901 *Type:* Private business *Accred.:* 1979/1982 (CCA-ACICS) *Calendar:* Qtr. plan *Degrees:* certificates, diplomas *CEO:* Dir. Michael Steinbach
Enroll: 44   (815) 932-8724

McCORMICK THEOLOGICAL SEMINARY
5555 S. Woodlawn Ave., Chicago 60637 *Type:* Private (Presbyterian) professional; graduate only *Accred.:* 1938/1987 (ATS); 1982/1987 (NCA) *Calendar:* Qtr. plan *Degrees:* P, M, D, certificates, diplomas *CEO:* Pres. David Ramage, Jr.
Enroll: 303   (312) 241-7800

McHENRY COUNTY COLLEGE
Rte. 14 and Lucas Rd., Crystal Lake 60012 *Type:* Public (district) junior *System:* Illinois Community College Board *Accred.:* 1976/1981 (NCA) *Calendar:* Sem. plan *Degrees:* A, certificates, diplomas *CEO:* Pres. Robert C. Bartlett
Enroll: 1622   (815) 455-3700

McKENDREE COLLEGE
701 College Rd., Lebanon 62254 *Type:* Private (United Methodist) liberal arts *Accred.:* 1970/1989 (NCA) *Calendar:* 4-1-4 plan *Degrees:* A, B *Prof. Accred.:* Nursing (B) *CEO:* Pres. Gerrit J. TenBrink
Enroll: 784   (618) 537-4481

MEADVILLE/LOMBARD THEOLOGICAL SCHOOL
5701 S. Woodlawn Ave., Chicago 60637 *Type:* Private (Unitarian Universalist) graduate only *Accred.:* 1940/1987 (ATS) *Calendar:* Qtr. plan. *Degrees:* P,M,D *CEO:* Dean/C.E.O. Spencer Lavan
Enroll: 29   (312) 753-4065

MEDICAL CAREERS INSTITUTE
116 S. Michigan Ave., 2nd Fl., Chicago 60603 *Type:* Private *Calendar:* Courses of varying lengths *Degrees:* diplomas *Prof. Accred.:* Health Education *CEO:* Dir. William Zane
Enroll: 511   (312) 782-9804

MENNONITE COLLEGE OF NURSING
804 N. East St., Bloomington 61701 *Type:* Private *Accred.:* 1986/1991 (NCA) *Calendar:* Qtr. plan *Degrees:* B *Prof. Accred.:* Nursing (B) *CEO:* Pres. Kathleen Hogan
Enroll: 117   (309) 829-0715

METROPOLITAN BUSINESS COLLEGE
2658 W. 95th St., Evergreen Park 60642 *Type:* Private business *Accred.:* 1961/1990 (CCA-ACICS) *Calendar:* Tri. plan *Degrees:* A, certificates, diplomas *CEO:* Dir. Pamela Sargis
Enroll: 668   (708) 424-3000

MIDSTATE COLLEGE
244 S.W. Jefferson St., Peoria 61602 *Type:* Private junior *Accred.:* 1982/1987 (NCA) *Calendar:* Qtr. plan *Degrees:* A, certificates, diplomas *Prof. Accred.:* Medical Assisting (AMA) *CEO:* Pres. R. Dale Bunch
Enroll: 417   (309) 673-6365

MILLIKIN UNIVERSITY
1184 W. Main St., Decatur 62522 *Type:* Private (United Presbyterian) liberal arts and professional *Accred.:* 1914/1987 (NCA) *Calendar:* 4-1-4 plan *Degrees:* B *Prof. Accred.:* Music, Nursing (B) *CEO:* Pres. John Roger Miltner
Enroll: 1960   (217) 424-6211

MOLER HAIRSTYLING COLLEGE
5840 W. Madison St., Aurora 60644 *Type:* Private *Accred.:* 1982/1988 (CCA-ACTTS) *Calendar:* Courses of varying lengths *Degrees:* certificates *CEO:* Pres./Dir. Kenneth M. Edwards
    (708) 851-7505

MOLER HAIRSTYLING COLLEGE
1152 N. Milwaukee Ave., Chicago 60622-4019 *Type:* Private *Accred.:* 1991 (CCA-ACTTS) *Calendar:* Courses of varying lengths *Degrees:* certificates *CEO:* Pres./Dir. Kenneth M. Edwards
    (312) 235-6575

MOLER HAIRSTYLING COLLEGE
924 W. Jefferson St., Joliet 60435 *Type:* Private *Accred.:* 1982/1988 (CCA-ACTTS)

Illinois

Calendar: Courses of varying lengths *Degrees:* certificates *CEO:* Pres./Dir. Kenneth M. Edwards
(815) 725-2225

MONMOUTH COLLEGE
700 E. Broadway, Monmouth 61462 *Type:* Private (United Presbyterian) liberal arts *Accred.:* 1913/1988 (NCA) *Calendar:* 3-3-3 plan *Degrees:* B *CEO:* Pres. Bruce Haywood
Enroll: 662   (309) 457-2127

MONTAY COLLEGE
3750 W. Peterson Ave., Chicago 60659 *Type:* Private (Roman Catholic) 2-year liberal arts *Accred.:* 1977/1989 (NCA) *Calendar:* 4-1-4 plan *Degrees:* A, certificates, diplomas *CEO:* Pres. Mary Charlene Endecavage
Enroll: 238   (312) 539-1919

MOODY BIBLE INSTITUTE
820 N. La Salle Dr., Chicago 60610 *Type:* Private *Accred.:* 1951/1982 (AABC); 1989 (NCA) *Calendar:* Sem. plan *Degrees:* A, B, M, certificates, diplomas *Prof. Accred.:* Music *CEO:* Pres. Joseph Stowell, III
Enroll: 2292   (312) 329-4000

MORAINE VALLEY COMMUNITY COLLEGE
10900 S. 88th Ave., Palos Hills 60465 *Type:* Public (district) junior *System:* Illinois Community College Board *Accred.:* 1975/1986 (NCA) *Calendar:* Sem. plan *Degrees:* A, certificates, diplomas *Prof. Accred.:* Medical Laboratory Technology (AMA), Medical Record Technology, Nursing (A), Radiography, Respiratory Therapy *CEO:* Pres. Vernon O. Crawley
Enroll: 7244   (708) 974-4300

MORRISON INSTITUTE OF TECHNOLOGY
P.O. Box 410, Morrison 61270 *Type:* Private 2-year *Calendar:* Sem. plan *Degrees:* A *Prof. Accred.:* Engineering Technology (general) *CEO:* C.E.O. Don D. Vandercreek
Enroll: 250   (815) 772-7218

MORTON COLLEGE
3801 S. Central Ave., Cicero 60650 *Type:* Public (district) junior *System:* Illinois Community College Board *Accred.:* 1927/1984 (NCA) *Calendar:* Sem. plan *Degrees:* A, certificates, diplomas *Prof. Accred.:* Dental Assisting, Physical Therapy Assisting *CEO:* Pres. Charles P. Ferro
Enroll: 1842   (708) 656-8000

MUSIC CENTER OF THE NORTH SHORE
300 Green Bay Rd., Winnetka 60093 *Type:* Private professional *Calendar:* Courses of varying lengths *Degrees:* certificates *Prof. Accred.:* Music *CEO:* Exec. Dir. Frank Little
Enroll: 1243   (708) 446-3822

NAES COLLEGE
2838 W. Peterson Ave., Chicago 60659 *Type:* Private *Accred.:* 1984/1989 (NCA) *Calendar:* Sem. plan *Degrees:* B *CEO:* Pres. Faith Smith
Enroll: 80   (312) 761-5000

NAPOLEON HILL FOUNDATION
1440 Paddock Dr., Northbrook 60062 *Type:* Private home study *Accred.:* 1986 (NHSC) *Calendar:* Courses of varying lengths *Degrees:* certificates *CEO:* Exec. Dir. Michael J. Ritt, Jr.
(708) 998-0408

NATIONAL BARBER COLLEGE
1035 W. Jefferson St., Springfield 62702 *Type:* Private *Accred.:* 1989 (CCA-ACTTS) *Calendar:* Courses of varying lengths *Degrees:* certificates *CEO:* Dir. Gerald Higgins
(217) 793-3222

NATIONAL COLLEGE OF CHIROPRACTIC
200 E. Roosevelt Rd., Lombard 60148 *Type:* Private professional *Accred.:* 1981/1986 (NCA) *Calendar:* Tri. plan *Degrees:* B, D *Prof. Accred.:* Chiropractic Education *CEO:* Pres. James F. Winterstein
Enroll: 785   (708) 629-2000

NATIONAL EDUCATION CENTER—BRYMAN CAMPUS
17 N. State St., No. 1800, Chicago 60602 *Type:* Private *Accred.:* 1991 (CCA-ACTTS) *Calendar:* Courses of varying lengths *Degrees:* diplomas *CEO:* Dir. Frank Jordan
Enroll: 690   (312) 368-4911

Accredited Institutions **Illinois**

NATIONAL EDUCATION CENTER—BRYMAN CAMPUS
4101 W. 95th St., Oak Lawn 60453-1000 *Type:* Private *Accred.:* 1991 (CCA-ACTTS) *Calendar:* Courses of varying lengths *Degrees:* diplomas *CEO:* Dir. Doloris Reynolds
(708) 423-0411

NATIONAL-LOUIS UNIVERSITY
2840 Sheridan Rd., Evanston 60201 *Type:* Private liberal arts and business *Accred.:* 1946/1991 (NCA) *Calendar:* Qtr. plan *Degrees:* B, M, D, certificates, diplomas *Prof. Accred.:* Medical Technology, Radiation Therapy Technology, Respiratory Therapy, Teacher Education (e,p) *CEO:* Pres. Orley R. Herron
Enroll: 5370   (708) 475-1100

NATIONAL SAFETY COUNCIL SAFETY TRAINING INSTITUTE
444 N. Michigan Ave., Chicago 60611 *Type:* Private home study *Accred.:* 1962/1987 (NHSC) *Calendar:* Courses of varying lengths *Degrees:* certificates *CEO:* Mgr. Carlton D. Piepho
(312) 527-4800

NORTH CENTRAL COLLEGE
30 N. Brainard St., P.O. Box 3063, Naperville 60566-7063 *Type:* Private (United Methodist) liberal arts *Accred.:* 1914/1990 (NCA) *Calendar:* 3-3 plan *Degrees:* B, M *CEO:* Pres. Harold R. Wilde
Enroll: 1765   (708) 420-3400

NORTH PARK COLLEGE AND THEOLOGICAL SEMINARY
3225 W. Foster Ave., Chicago 60625-4987 *Type:* Private (Evangelical Covenant) liberal arts and theology *Accred.:* 1963/1986 (ATS); 1926/1991 (NCA) *Calendar:* 3-3 plan *Degrees:* B, P, M *Prof. Accred.:* Music, Nursing (B) *CEO:* Pres. David G. Horner
Enroll: 954   (312) 478-2696

NORTHEASTERN ILLINOIS UNIVERSITY
5500 N. St. Louis Ave., Chicago 60625 *Type:* Public liberal arts and teachers *System:* Illinois Board of Governors of State Colleges and Universities *Accred.:* 1961/1987 (NCA) *Calendar:* Tri. plan *Degrees:* B, M *Prof. Accred.:* Music, Social Work (B), Teacher Education (e,s,p) *CEO:* Pres. Gordon H. Lamb
Enroll: 6183   (312) 583-4050

NORTHERN BAPTIST THEOLOGICAL SEMINARY
660 E. Butterfield Rd., Lombard 60148 *Type:* Private (Baptist) graduate only *Accred.:* 1968/1981 (ATS); 1947/1982 (NCA) *Calendar:* Qtr. plan *Degrees:* P, M, D *CEO:* Pres. Ian M. Chapman
Enroll: 172   (708) 620-2100

NORTHERN ILLINOIS UNIVERSITY
De Kalb 60115 *Type:* Public (state) *System:* Regency Universities System *Accred.:* 1915/1984 (NCA) *Calendar:* Sem. plan *Degrees:* B, M, D *Prof. Accred.:* Accounting (Type A,C), Art, Audiology, Business (B,M), Clinical Psychology, Counseling, Counseling Psychology, Engineering (electrical, industrial, mechanical), Journalism, Law, Librarianship, Nursing (B,M), Physical Therapy, Psychology Internship, Public Affairs, Rehabilitation Counseling, Speech-Language Pathology, Teacher Education, Theatre *CEO:* Pres. John E. LaTourette
Enroll: 20051   (815) 753-1271

NORTHWESTERN BUSINESS COLLEGE
4829 N. Lipps Ave., Chicago 60630-2298 *Type:* Private business *Accred.:* 1974/1986 (CCA-ACICS); 1991 (NCA candidate); *Calendar:* Qtr. plan *Degrees:* A, certificates, diplomas *Prof. Accred.:* Medical Assisting (AMA) *CEO:* Pres. Lawrence Schumacher
Enroll: 956   (312) 777-4220

BRANCH CAMPUS
10059 S. Roberts Rd., Palos Hills, IL 60465 *CEO:* Academic Dean Tony Sapata
(708) 430-0990

NORTHWESTERN UNIVERSITY
633 Clark St., Evanston 60208 *Type:* Private *Accred.:* 1913/1985 (NCA) *Calendar:* Sem. plan *Degrees:* B, P, M, D *Prof. Accred.:* Audiology, Business (M), Clinical Psych-

Illinois

ology, Combined Prosthodontics, Counseling Psychology, Dental Hygiene, Dentistry, Endodontics, Engineering (bioengineering, chemical, civil, electrical, environmental/sanitary, industrial, materials, mechanical), General Dentistry, Health Services Administration, Journalism, Law, Medicine, Music, Nursing (B,M), Oral and Maxillofacial Surgery, Oral Pathology, Orthodontics, Pediatric Dentistry, Periodontics, Physical Therapy, Psychology Internship, Speech-Language Pathology, Theatre *CEO:* Pres. Arnold R. Weber
Enroll: 14692 (708) 491-7456

OAKTON COMMUNITY COLLEGE
1600 E. Golf Rd., Des Plaines 60016 *Type:* Public (district) junior *System:* Illinois Community College Board *Accred.:* 1976/1988 (NCA) *Calendar:* Sem. plan *Degrees:* A, certificates, diplomas *Prof. Accred.:* Medical Laboratory Technology (AMA), Medical Record Technology, Nursing (A), Physical Therapy Assisting *CEO:* Pres. Thomas TenHoeve
Enroll: 5269 (708) 635-1600

OLIVE-HARVEY COLLEGE
10001 S. Woodlawn Ave., Chicago 60628 *Type:* Public *System:* City Colleges of Chicago *Accred.:* 1967/1990 (NCA) *Calendar:* Sem. plan *Degrees:* A, certificates, diplomas *CEO:* Pres. Homer D. Franklin
Enroll: 2467 (312) 568-3700

OLIVET NAZARENE UNIVERSITY
Kankakee 60901 *Type:* Private (Nazarene) liberal arts *Accred.:* 1956/1985 (NCA) *Calendar:* Sem. plan *Degrees:* A, B, M *Prof. Accred.:* Music, Nursing (B), Teacher Education (e,s) *CEO:* Pres. A. Leslie Parrott
Enroll: 1560 (815) 939-5011

OLNEY CENTRAL COLLEGE
305 N. West St., Olney 62450-1099 *Type:* Public (district) *System:* Illinois Eastern Community College System *Accred.:* 1984/1988 (NCA) *Calendar:* Qtr. plan *Degrees:* A, certificates, diplomas *Prof. Accred.:* Nursing (A), Radiography *CEO:* Pres. Judith Hansen
(618) 395-4351

OMAR RIVAS ACADEMY OF BARBER ARTS AND SCIENCE
5912 W. Roosevelt Rd., Chicago 60650 *Type:* Private *Accred.:* 1986 (CCA-ACTTS) *Calendar:* Courses of varying lengths *Degrees:* diplomas *CEO:* Dir. Omar Rivas
(312) 287-3400

PBS TRAINING CENTER
1153 Tower Rd., Schaumburg 60173-4305 *Type:* Private *Accred.:* 1991 (CCA-ACTTS) *Calendar:* Courses of varying lengths *Degrees:* certificates *CEO:* Pres. Anthony McElligott
(312) 882-7900

PTC CAREER INSTITUTE
11 E. Adams St., Ste. 400, Chicago 60603-6305 *Type:* Private *Accred.:* 1991 (CCA-ACTTS) *Calendar:* Courses of varying lengths *Degrees:* certificates *CEO:* Dir. Greg Reger
(312) 922-2005

PARKLAND COLLEGE
2400 W. Bradley Ave., Champaign 61821 *Type:* Public (district) junior *System:* Illinois Community College Board *Accred.:* 1972/1982 (NCA) *Calendar:* Sem. plan *Degrees:* A, certificates, diplomas *Prof. Accred.:* Dental Assisting, Dental Hygiene, Engineering Technology (electrical), Nursing (A), Occupational Therapy Assisting, Practical Nursing, Radiography, Respiratory Therapy, Surgical Technology, Veterinary Technology *CEO:* Pres. Zelema M. Harris
Enroll: 4837 (217) 351-2200

PARKS COLLEGE OF ST. LOUIS UNIVERSITY
Falling Springs Rd., Cahokia 62206 *Type:* Private (Roman Catholic) *Accred.:* 1970/1985 (NCA) *Calendar:* Tri. plan *Degrees:* A, B, certificates, diplomas *Prof. Accred.:* Engineering (aerospace) *CEO:* Vice Pres. Paul A. Whelan
Enroll: 1077 (618) 337-7500

Accredited Institutions — Illinois

PHILLIPS COLLEGE OF CHICAGO
205 W. Randolph St., 2nd Fl., Chicago 60606 *Type:* Private business *Accred.:* 1969/1987 (CCA-ACICS) *Calendar:* Sem. plan *Degrees:* A, certificates, diplomas *CEO:* Dir. Ron Friedrich
Enroll: 488 (312) 419-1711

PRAIRIE STATE COLLEGE
202 S. Halsted St., Chicago Heights 60411 *Type:* Public (district) junior *System:* Illinois Community College Board *Accred.:* 1965/1989 (NCA) *Calendar:* Sem. plan *Degrees:* A, certificates, diplomas *Prof. Accred.:* Dental Assisting, Dental Hygiene, Nursing (A) *CEO:* Pres. E. Timothy Lightfield
Enroll: 2442 (708) 756-3110

PRINCIPIA COLLEGE
Elsah 62028 *Type:* Private (Christian Science) liberal arts *Accred.:* 1923/1985(NCA) *Calendar:* Qtr. plan *Degrees:* B, certificates, diplomas *CEO:* Pres. David E. Pfeifer
Enroll: 632 (618) 374-2131

QUINCY COLLEGE
1800 College Ave., Quincy 62301 *Type:* Private (Roman Catholic) liberal arts *Accred.:* 1954/1982 (NCA) *Calendar:* Sem. plan *Degrees:* A, B, M *Prof. Accred.:* Music *CEO:* Pres. James Toal, O.F.M.
Enroll: 1164 (217) 228-5270

QUINCY TECHNICAL SCHOOLS
501 N. 3rd St., Quincy 62301 *Type:* Private *Accred.:* 1977/1988 (CCA-ACTTS) *Calendar:* Qtr. plan *Degrees:* diplomas *CEO:* Pres. W.G. Dubuque
Enroll: 497 (217) 224-0600

RAY COLLEGE OF DESIGN
401 N. Wabash St., Chicago 60611 *Type:* Private *Accred.:* 1975/1988 (CCA-ACTTS) *Calendar:* Sem. plan *Degrees:* A, B *CEO:* Pres. Wade F. Ray
Enroll: 933 (312) 280-3500

BRANCH CAMPUS
1051 Perimeter Dr., Schaumburg, IL 60173 *CEO:* Dir. Jerrold Molepske
(312) 619-3450

REND LAKE COLLEGE
Rural Rte. 1, Ina 62846 *Type:* Public (district) junior *System:* Illinois Community College Board *Accred.:* 1969/1989 (NCA) *Calendar:* Sem. plan *Degrees:* A, certificates, diplomas *Prof. Accred.:* Nursing (A) *CEO:* Pres. Mark Kern
Enroll: 1907 (618) 437-5321

RICHARD J. DALEY COLLEGE
7500 S. Pulaski Rd., Chicago 60652 *Type:* Public *System:* City Colleges of Chicago *Accred.:* 1967/1991 (NCA) *Calendar:* Sem. plan *Degrees:* A, certificates, diplomas *CEO:* Pres. William P. Conway
Enroll: 3223 (312) 735-3000

RICHLAND COMMUNITY COLLEGE
One College Park, Decatur 62521 *Type:* Public (district) junior *System:* Illinois Community College Board *Accred.:* 1978/1986 (NCA) *Calendar:* Qtr. plan *Degrees:* A, certificates, diplomas *CEO:* Pres. Charles R. Novak
Enroll: 1889 (217) 875-7200

ROBERT MORRIS COLLEGE
180 N. La Salle St., Chicago 60601 *Type:* Private *Accred.:* 1986/1991 (NCA) *Calendar:* Qtr. plan *Degrees:* A, certificates, diplomas *Prof. Accred.:* Medical Assisting (AMA) *CEO:* Pres. Richard D. Pickett
Enroll: 1820 (312) 836-4888

ROCK VALLEY COLLEGE
3301 N. Mulford Rd., Rockford 61111 *Type:* Public (district) junior *System:* Illinois Community College Board *Accred.:* 1971/1984 (NCA) *Calendar:* Sem. plan *Degrees:* A, certificates, diplomas *Prof. Accred.:* Respiratory Therapy, Respiratory Therapy Technology *CEO:* Pres. Karl J. Jacobs
Enroll: 3921 (815) 654-4260

ROCKFORD BUSINESS COLLEGE
730 N. Church St., Rockford 61103 *Type:* Private business *Accred.:* 1968/1987 (CCA-ACICS) *Calendar:* Qtr. plan *Degrees:* A,

Illinois

certificates, diplomas *CEO:* Pres. David G. Swank
Enroll: 501   (815) 965-8616

ROCKFORD COLLEGE
5050 E. State St., Rockford 61108 *Type:* Private liberal arts *Accred.:* 1913/1984 (NCA) *Calendar:* 4-1-4 plan *Degrees:* A, B, M *Prof. Accred.:* Nursing (B) *CEO:* Pres. Gretchen von Loewe Kreuter
Enroll: 991   (815) 226-4000

ROOSEVELT UNIVERSITY
430 S. Michigan Ave., Chicago 60605 *Type:* Private *Accred.:* 1946/1986 (NCA) *Calendar:* Sem. plan *Degrees:* B, M, D, certificates, diplomas *Prof. Accred.:* Music, Teacher Education (e,s,p) *CEO:* Pres. Theodore L. Gross
Enroll: 3159   (312) 341-3500

ROSARY COLLEGE
7900 W. Division St., River Forest 60305 *Type:* Private (Roman Catholic) liberal arts *Accred.:* 1919/1985 (NCA) *Calendar:* Sem. plan *Degrees:* B, M *Prof. Accred.:* Librarianship *CEO:* Pres. Jean Murray
Enroll: 1207   (708) 366-2490

RUSH UNIVERSITY
1653 W. Congress Pkwy., Chicago 60612 *Type:* Private professional *Accred.:* 1974/1989 (NCA) *Calendar:* Qtr. plan *Degrees:* B, M, D *Prof. Accred.:* Health Services Administration, Medicine, Nurse Anesthesia Education, Nursing (B,M) *CEO:* Pres. Leo M. Henikoff
Enroll: 1032   (312) 942-5474

ST. AUGUSTINE COLLEGE
1333 W. Argyle St., Chicago 60604 *Type:* Private *Accred.:* 1987 (NCA) *Calendar:* Sem. plan *Degrees:* A, certificates, diplomas *CEO:* Pres. Carlos A. Plazas
Enroll: 1149   (312) 878-8756

ST. FRANCIS MEDICAL CENTER COLLEGE OF NURSING
211 Greenleaf St., Peoria 61603 *Type:* Private professional *Accred.:* 1991 (NCA) *Calendar:* Qtr. plan *Degrees:* B *CEO:* Dean Mary Ludgera, O.S.F.
Enroll: 99   (309) 655-2086

ST. XAVIER COLLEGE
3700 W. 103rd St., Chicago 60655 *Type:* Private (Roman Catholic) liberal arts *Accred.:* 1937/1988 (NCA) *Calendar:* 4-1-4 plan *Degrees:* B, M, certificates, diplomas *Prof. Accred.:* Music, Nursing (B,M) *CEO:* Pres. Ronald O. Champagne
Enroll: 2043   (312) 779-3300

SANGAMON STATE UNIVERSITY
Springfield 62794 *Type:* Public liberal arts; graduate only *System:* Regency Universities System *Accred.:* 1975/1987 (NCA) *Calendar:* Sem. plan *Degrees:* B, M *Prof. Accred.:* Medical Technology, Nursing (B), Public Administration *CEO:* Pres. Naomi D. Lynn
Enroll: 2538   (217) 786-6634

SAUK VALLEY COMMUNITY COLLEGE
173 Illinois Rte. 2, Dixon 61021 *Type:* Public (district) junior *System:* Illinois Community College Board *Accred.:* 1972/1985 (NCA) *Calendar:* Sem. plan *Degrees:* A, certificates, diplomas *Prof. Accred.:* Medical Laboratory Technology (AMA), Radiography *CEO:* Pres. Richard L. Behrendt
Enroll: 1568   (815) 288-5511

THE SCHOOL OF THE ART INSTITUTE OF CHICAGO
37 S. Wabash Ave., Chicago 60603 *Type:* Private professional *Accred.:* 1936/1982 (NCA) *Calendar:* Sem. plan *Degrees:* B, M, certificates, diplomas *Prof. Accred.:* Art *CEO:* Pres. Anthony Jones
Enroll: 1695   (312) 899-5135

SEABURY-WESTERN THEOLOGICAL SEMINARY
2122 Sheridan Rd., Evanston 60201 *Type:* Private (Episcopal) graduate only *Accred.:* 1938/1987 (ATS); 1981/1987 (NCA) *Calendar:* Sem. plan *Degrees:* P, M, D, certificates, diplomas *CEO:* Pres./Dean Mark S. Sisk
Enroll: 78   (708) 328-9300

Shawnee Community College
Shawnee College Rd., Ullin 62992 *Type:* Public (district) junior *System:* Illinois Community College Board *Accred.:* 1974/1990 (NCA) *Calendar:* Sem. plan *Degrees:* A, certificates, diplomas *CEO:* Pres. Jack D. Hill
Enroll: 1051   (618) 634-2242

Shimer College
P.O. Box A500, Waukegan 60079 *Type:* Private liberal arts *Accred.:* 1991 (NCA) *Calendar:* Sem. plan *Degrees:* B, certificates, diplomas *CEO:* Pres. Don P. Moon
Enroll: 61   (708) 623-8400

South Suburban College of Cook County
15800 S. State St., South Holland 60473 *Type:* Public (district) junior *System:* Illinois Community College Board *Accred.:* 1933/1989 (NCA) *Calendar:* Sem. plan *Degrees:* A, certificates, diplomas *Prof. Accred.:* Music, Nursing (A), Occupational Therapy Assisting, Practical Nursing, Radiography *CEO:* Pres. Richard W. Fonte
Enroll: 3824   (708) 596-2000

Southeastern Illinois College
Rural Rte. 4, Box 510, Harrisburg 62946 *Type:* Public (district) junior *System:* Illinois Community College Board *Accred.:* 1976/1988 (NCA) *Calendar:* Sem. plan *Degrees:* A, certificates, diplomas *CEO:* Pres. Harry W. Abell
Enroll: 1866   (618) 252-4411

Southern Illinois University at Carbondale
Carbondale 62901 *Type:* Public (state) *System:* Southern Illinois University System *Accred.:* 1913/1989 (NCA) *Calendar:* Sem. plan *Degrees:* A, B, P, M, D *Prof. Accred.:* Accounting (Type A,C), Art, Business (B,M), Clinical Psychology, Counseling, Counseling Psychology, Dental Hygiene, Dental Laboratory Technology, Engineering (civil, electrical, mechanical, mining), Engineering Technology (civil/construction, electrical, mechanical), Forestry, Interior Design, Journalism, Law, Medicine, Mortuary Science, Music, Physical Therapy Assisting, Psychology Internship, Public Affairs, Radiography, Recreation, Rehabilitation Counseling, Respiratory Therapy, Social Work (B,M), Speech-Language Pathology, Teacher Education (e,s,p) *CEO:* Pres. John C. Guyon
Enroll: 20664   (618) 453-2341

Southern Illinois University at Edwardsville
Edwardsville 62026 *Type:* Public (state) *System:* Southern Illinois University System *Accred.:* 1969/1986 (NCA) *Calendar:* Qtr. plan *Degrees:* A, B, P, M, D *Prof. Accred.:* Accounting (Type A), Business (B,M), Dentistry, Engineering (civil, electrical), General Practice Residency, Music, Nursing (B,M), Social Work (B), Speech-Language Pathology, Teacher Education (e,s,p) *CEO:* Pres. Earl E. Lazerson
Enroll: 9268   (618) 692-2475

Sparks College
131 S. Morgan St., Shelbyville 62565 *Type:* Private business *Accred.:* 1954/1985 (CCA-ACICS) *Calendar:* Courses of varying lengths *Degrees:* certificates, diplomas *CEO:* Dir. Juanita Jesse
Enroll: 93   (217) 774-5112

Spertus College of Judaica
618 S. Michigan Ave., Chicago 60605 *Type:* Private (Jewish) liberal arts and teachers *Accred.:* 1971/1987 (NCA) *Calendar:* Qtr. plan *Degrees:* B, M, certificates, diplomas *CEO:* Pres. Howard A. Sulkin
Enroll: 223   (312) 922-9012

Spoon River College
Rural Rte. 1, Canton 61520 *Type:* Public (district) junior *System:* Illinois Community College Board *Accred.:* 1977/1982 (NCA) *Calendar:* Sem. plan *Degrees:* A, certificates, diplomas *CEO:* Pres. Felix T. Haynes
Enroll: 1261   (309) 647-4645

Springfield College in Illinois
1500 N. Fifth St., Springfield 62702 *Type:* Private (Roman Catholic) junior *Accred.:*

Illinois

1933/1986 (NCA) *Calendar:* 4-1-4 plan *Degrees:* A *CEO:* Pres. H. Brent De Land
Enroll: 238 (217) 525-1420

STATE COMMUNITY COLLEGE OF EAST ST. LOUIS
601 James R. Thompson Blvd., East St. Louis 62201 *Type:* Public (state) junior *System:* Illinois Community College Board *Accred.:* 1978/1988 (NCA probational) *Calendar:* Sem. plan *Degrees:* A, certificates, diplomas *CEO:* Pres. Cunthia O. Pace
Enroll: 755 (618) 583-2500

TAYLOR BUSINESS INSTITUTE
36 S. State St., 8th Fl., Chicago 60603 *Type:* Private business *Accred.:* 1973/1985 (CCA-ACICS) *Calendar:* Courses of varying lengths *Degrees:* certificates, diplomas *CEO:* Pres. Janice C. Parker
Enroll: 557 (312) 236-6400

TELSHE YESHIVA-CHICAGO
3535 W. Foster Ave., Chicago 60625 *Type:* Private professional *Accred.:* 1976/1989 (AARTS) *Calendar:* Sem. plan *Degrees:* Rabbinic (1st and 2nd) *CEO:* Pres. A. Levin
Enroll: 71 (312) 463-7738

TRINITY CHRISTIAN COLLEGE
6601 W. College Dr., Palos Heights 60463 *Type:* Private (Christian Reformed) liberal arts *Accred.:* 1976/1991 (NCA) *Calendar:* Sem. plan *Degrees:* B *Prof. Accred.:* Nursing (B) *CEO:* Pres. Kenneth B. Bootsma
Enroll: 521 (708) 597-3000

TRINITY COLLEGE
2077 Half Day Rd., Deerfield 60015 *Type:* Private (Evangelical Free Church) liberal arts and professional *Accred.:* 1969/1987 (NCA) *Calendar:* Sem. plan *Degrees:* B *CEO:* Pres. Kenneth M. Meyer
Enroll: 826 (708) 948-8980

TRINITY EVANGELICAL DIVINITY SCHOOL
2065 Half Day Rd., Deerfield 60015 *Type:* Private (Evangelical Free Church) graduate only *Accred.:* 1973/1989 (ATS); 1969/1990 (NCA) *Calendar:* Qtr. plan *Degrees:* M, D, certificates, diplomas *CEO:* Pres. Kenneth M. Meyer
Enroll: 999 (708) 945-8800

TRITON COLLEGE
2000 Fifth Ave., River Grove 60171 *Type:* Public (district) junior *System:* Illinois Community College Board *Accred.:* 1972/1982 (NCA) *Calendar:* Sem. plan *Degrees:* A, certificates, diplomas *Prof. Accred.:* Dental Laboratory Technology, Diagnostic Medical Sonography, Engineering Technology (electrical), Medical Laboratory Technology (AMA), Nuclear Medicine Technology, Nursing (A), Ophthalmic Medical Technology, Practical Nursing, Radiography, Respiratory Therapy, Surgical Technology *CEO:* Pres. Michael J. Bakalis
Enroll: 8222 (708) 456-0300

TYLER SCHOOL OF SECRETARIAL SCIENCES
8030 S. Kedzie Ave., Chicago 60652 *Type:* Private business *Accred.:* 1984/1987 (CCA-ACICS) *Calendar:* Courses of varying lengths *Degrees:* certificates, diplomas *CEO:* Pres. Michael Franzak
Enroll: 189 (312) 436-5050

UNIVERSITY OF CHICAGO
5801 S. Ellis Ave., Chicago 60637 *Type:* Private *Accred.:* 1938/1982 (ATS); 1913/1986 (NCA) *Calendar:* Qtr. plan *Degrees:* B, M, D, certificates, diplomas *Prof. Accred.:* Accounting (Type B), Business (M), General Practice Residency, Health Services Administration, Histologic Technology, Law, Maxillofacial Prosthodontics, Medicine, Oral and Maxillofacial Surgery, Psychology Internship (provisional), Social Work (M) *CEO:* Pres. Hanna H. Gray
Enroll: 10034 (312) 702-8001

UNIVERSITY OF HEALTH SCIENCES/THE CHICAGO MEDICAL SCHOOL
3333 S. Green Bay Rd., North Chicago 60064 *Type:* Private professional *Accred.:* 1980/1988 (NCA) *Calendar:* Qtr. plan *Degrees:* B, M, D *Prof. Accred.:* Clinical Psychology, Medical Technology, Medicine,

Nursing (B), Physical Therapy *CEO:* Pres. Myron Winick
Enroll: 883   (708) 578-3000

UNIVERSITY OF ILLINOIS AT CHICAGO
P.O. Box 4348, Chicago 60680 *Type:* Public (state) *System:* University of Illinois System *Accred.:* 1970/1987 (NCA) *Calendar:* Qtr. plan *Degrees:* B, M, D *Prof. Accred.:* Architecture (B,M), Art, Blood Bank Technology, Business (B,M), Clinical Psychology, Dentistry, Dietetics (coordinated), Endodontics, Engineering (bioengineering, chemical, civil, computer, electrical, industrial, mechanical, metallurgical), Medical Illustration, Medical Record Administration, Medical Technology, Medicine, Nursing (B,M), Occupational Therapy, Oral and Maxillofacial Surgery, Orthodontics, Pediatric Dentistry, Periodontics, Pharmacy, Physical Therapy, Planning (urban), Psychology Internship, Public Administration, Public Health, Social Work (B,M) *CEO:* Chanc. James J. Stuckel
Enroll: 23437   (312) 996-3000

UNIVERSITY OF ILLINOIS AT URBANA—CHAMPAIGN
601 E. John St., Champaign 61820 *Type:* Public (state) *System:* University of Illinois System *Accred.:* 1913/1989 (NCA) *Calendar:* Sem. plan *Degrees:* B, M, D *Prof. Accred.:* Accounting (Type A,C), Architecture (M), Art, Audiology, Business (B,M), Clinical Psychology, Community Health, Counseling Psychology, Dance, Engineering (aerospace, agricultural, ceramic, chemical, civil, computer, electrical, engineering mechanics, general, industrial, mechanical, metallurgical, nuclear), Forestry, Home Economics, Journalism, Landscape Architecture (B,M), Law, Leisure Studies, Librarianship, Music, Planning (regional/urban), Psychology Internship, Rehabilitation Counseling (candidate), Social Work (B,M), Speech-Language Pathology, Theatre *CEO:* Chanc. Morton W. Weir
Enroll: 35766   (217) 333-1000

UNIVERSITY OF ST. MARY OF THE LAKE, MUNDELEIN SEMINARY
Rte. 176, Mundelein 60060-1174 *Type:* Private (Roman Catholic) graduate only *Accred.:* 1972/1982 (ATS) *Calendar:* Sem. plan *Degrees:* P, M, D *CEO:* Pres. Gerald F. Kicanas
Enroll: 265   (708) 566-6401

VANDERCOOK COLLEGE OF MUSIC
3209 S. Michigan Ave., Chicago 60616 *Type:* Private professional *Accred.:* 1972/1987 (NCA) *Calendar:* Sem. plan *Degrees:* B, M *Prof. Accred.:* Music *CEO:* Pres. Roseanne K. Rosenthal
Enroll: 84   (312) 225-6288

WABASH VALLEY COLLEGE
2200 College Dr., Mount Carmel 62863-2699 *Type:* Public (district) *System:* Illinois Eastern Community College System *Accred.:* 1984/1988 (NCA) *Calendar:* Qtr. plan *Degrees:* A, certificates, diplomas *Prof. Accred.:* Nursing (A) *CEO:* Pres. Harry K. Benson
   (618) 262-8641

WASHINGTON BUSINESS INSTITUTE
819 S. Wabash Ave., Ste. 300, Chicago 60605 *Type:* Private business *Accred.:* 1984/1990 (CCA-ACICS) *Calendar:* Courses of varying lengths *Degrees:* certificates, diplomas *CEO:* Pres. Robert Triplett
Enroll: 173   (312) 663-1851

BRANCH CAMPUS
142 E. 154th St., Harvey, IL 60426 *CEO:* Dir. Raelyn Lilly-Riley
   (312) 333-8220

WAUBONSEE COMMUNITY COLLEGE
Rte. 47 at Harter Rd., Sugar Grove 60554 *Type:* Public (district) junior *System:* Illinois Community College Board *Accred.:* 1972/1986 (NCA) *Calendar:* Sem. plan *Degrees:* A, certificates, diplomas *CEO:* Pres. John J. Swalec
Enroll: 2558   (708) 466-4811

Illinois

WEST SUBURBAN COLLEGE OF NURSING
Erie St. and N. Austin Blvd., Oak Park 60302 *Type:* Private professional *Accred.:* 1986/1989 (NCA) *Calendar:* Qtr. plan *Degrees:* B *Prof. Accred.:* Nursing (B) *CEO:* Provost Sandra Greniewicki
Enroll: 90   (708) 383-6200

WESTERN ILLINOIS UNIVERSITY
900 W. Adams St., Macomb 61455 *Type:* Public (state) *System:* Illinois Board of Governors of State Colleges and Universities *Accred.:* 1913/1991 (NCA) *Calendar:* Sem. plan *Degrees:* B, P, M *Prof. Accred.:* Audiology, Business (B,M), Counseling, Music, Recreation, Park and Tourism Administration, Speech-Language Pathology, Teacher Education (e,s,p) *CEO:* Pres. Ralph H. Wagoner
Enroll: 11616   (309) 295-1414

WHEATON COLLEGE
501 E. College Ave., Wheaton 60187 *Type:* Private liberal arts *Accred.:* 1913/1984 (NCA) *Calendar:* Sem. plan *Degrees:* B, M, certificates, diplomas *Prof. Accred.:* Music, Teacher Education (e,s) *CEO:* Pres. J. Richard Chase
Enroll: 2449   (708) 260-5000

WILBUR WRIGHT COLLEGE
3400 N. Austin Ave., Chicago 60634 *Type:* Public *System:* City Colleges of Chicago *Accred.:* 1967/1983 (NCA) *Calendar:* Sem. plan *Degrees:* A, certificates, diplomas *Prof. Accred.:* Diagnostic Medical Sonography, Occupational Therapy Assisting, Radiography *CEO:* Pres. Raymond F. Le Fevour
Enroll: 4616   (312) 794-3182

WILLIAM RAINEY HARPER COLLEGE
1200 W. Algonquin Rd., Palatine 60067-7398 *Type:* Public (district) junior *System:* Illinois Community College Board *Accred.:* 1971/1988 (NCA) *Calendar:* Sem. plan *Degrees:* A *Prof. Accred.:* Dental Hygiene, Medical Assisting (AMA), Music, Nursing (A) *CEO:* Pres. Paul N. Thompson
Enroll: 7022   (708) 397-3000

WORSHAM COLLEGE OF MORTUARY SCIENCE
1767 S. Wolf Rd., Des Plaines 60018-1900 *Type:* Private *Calendar:* 1-year program *Degrees:* diplomas *Prof. Accred.:* Mortuary Science *CEO:* Chf. Admin. Frederick C. Cappetta
     (708) 297-4411

INDIANA

ACADEMY OF HAIR DESIGN
2150 Lafayette Rd., Indianapolis 46222 *Type:* Private *Accred.:* 1982/1988 (CCA-ACTTS) *Calendar:* Courses of varying lengths *Degrees:* diplomas *CEO:* Dir. Jack Hale
Enroll: 53   (317) 637-7227

ANCILLA COLLEGE
Donaldson 46513 *Type:* Private (Roman Catholic) junior *Accred.:* 1973/1988 (NCA) *Calendar:* Sem. plan *Degrees:* A, certificates, diplomas *CEO:* Pres. Virginia Kampwerth
Enroll: 515   (219) 936-8898

ANDERSON UNIVERSITY
1100 E. Fifth Ave., Anderson 46012 *Type:* Private (Church of God) liberal arts *Accred.:* 1965/1989 (ATS); 1946/1989 (NCA) *Calendar:* Sem. plan *Degrees:* A, B, P, M *Prof. Accred.:* Music, Social Work (B), Teacher Education (e,s) *CEO:* Pres. James L. Edwards
Enroll: 1858   (317) 649-9071

ARISTOTLE COLLEGE OF MEDICAL AND DENTAL TECHNOLOGY
5425 S. U.S. 31, Indianapolis 46227 *Type:* Private technical *Calendar:* Courses of varying lengths *Degrees:* certificates, diplomas *Prof. Accred.:* Health Education, Medical Assisting *CEO:* Pres. Michael A. Walker
   (317) 784-5400

  BRANCH CAMPUS
  5255 Hohman Ave., Hammond, IN 46320 *Prof. Accred.:* Health Education *CEO:* Dir. Carol G. Walker
     (219) 931-1917

BALL STATE UNIVERSITY
2000 University Ave., Muncie 47306 *Type:* Public *System:* Indiana Commission for Higher Education *Accred.:* 1925/1984 (NCA) *Calendar:* Sem. plan *Degrees:* A, B, P, M, D *Prof. Accred.:* Accounting (Type A), Architecture (B), Audiology, Business (B,M), Computer Science, Counseling, Counseling Psychology, Journalism, Landscape Architecture (B,M), Music, Nuclear Medicine Technology, Nursing (B,M), Psychology Internship, Radiography, Respiratory Therapy, School Psychology, Social Work (B), Speech-Language Pathology, Teacher Education *CEO:* Pres. John E. Worthen
Enroll: 17804   (317) 285-5555

BETHEL COLLEGE
1001 W. McKinley, Mishawaka 46545 *Type:* Private (United Missionary) liberal arts *Accred.:* 1971/1991 (NCA) *Calendar:* Sem. plan *Degrees:* A, B, M *Prof. Accred.:* Nursing (B) *CEO:* Pres. Norman Bridges
Enroll: 597   (219) 259-8511

BUTLER UNIVERSITY
4600 Sunset Ave., Indianapolis 46208 *Type:* Private *Accred.:* 1915/1983 (NCA) *Calendar:* Sem. plan *Degrees:* A, B, P, M, certificates, diplomas *Prof. Accred.:* Dance, Music, Pharmacy *CEO:* Pres. Geoffrey Bannister
Enroll: 3697   (317) 283-9900

CALUMET COLLEGE OF SAINT JOSEPH
2400 New York Ave., Whiting 46394 *Type:* Private (Roman Catholic) liberal arts *Accred.:* 1968/1989 (NCA) *Calendar:* Sem. plan *Degrees:* A, B, certificates, diplomas *CEO:* Pres. Dennis C. Rittenmeyer
Enroll: 696   (219) 473-7770

CHRISTIAN THEOLOGICAL SEMINARY
1000 W. 42nd St., Indianapolis 46208 *Type:* Private (Christian Churches/Disciples of Christ); graduate only *Accred.:* 1944/1988 (ATS); 1973/1988 (NCA) *Calendar:* Sem. plan *Degrees:* P, M, D *CEO:* Pres. Richard N. Dickinson, Jr.
Enroll: 209   (317) 924-1331

CLARK COLLEGE
1840 N. Meridian St., Indianapolis 46204 *Type:* Private junior *Accred.:* 1969/1991

Indiana

(CCA-ACICS) *Calendar:* Qtr. plan *Degrees:* A, certificates, diplomas *Prof. Accred.:* Medical Assisting (AMA) *CEO:* Pres. Linda Harverstick
Enroll: 697 (317) 923-3933

BRANCH CAMPUS
6000 E. 46th St., Indianapolis, IN 46226 *CEO:* Dir. Barri Shirk
(317) 546-1535

COLLEGE OF COURT REPORTING
111 W. 10th St., Hobart 46342 *Type:* Private business *Accred.:* 1989 (CCA-ACICS) *Calendar:* Courses of varying lengths *Degrees:* certificates, diplomas *CEO:* Dir. Kay Moody
Enroll: 86 (219) 942-1459

COMMONWEALTH BUSINESS COLLEGE
4200 W. 81st Ave., Merrillville 46410 *Type:* Private business *Accred.:* 1978/1990 (CCA-ACICS) *Calendar:* Qtr. plan *Degrees:* A, certificates, diplomas *Prof. Accred.:* Medical Assisting *CEO:* Dir. Laura J. Smith
Enroll: 292 (219) 769-3321

BRANCH CAMPUS
1527 47th Ave., Moline, IL 61265 *CEO:* Dir. Janice DeTaeye
(309) 762-2100

BRANCH CAMPUS
8995 N. State Rte. 39, LaPorte, IN 46350 *CEO:* Dir. Darlene J. DeRyke
(219) 362-3338

CONCORDIA THEOLOGICAL SEMINARY
6600 N. Clinton St., Fort Wayne 46825 *Type:* Private (Lutheran-Missouri Synod) professional; graduate only *Accred.:* 1968/1991 (ATS); 1981/1991 (NCA) *Calendar:* Qtr. plan *Degrees:* P, M, D *CEO:* Pres. Robert D. Preus
Enroll: 353 (219) 481-2100

DAVENPORT COLLEGE
7121 Grape Road, Granger 46530 *Type:* Private *Calendar:* Courses of varying lengths *Degrees:* certificates *Prof. Accred.:* Medical Assisting *CEO:* Dir. Edward Bauer
(219) 297-8447

BRANCH CAMPUS
8200 Georgia St., Merrillville, IN 46410 *Prof. Accred.:* Medical Assisting *CEO:* Exec. Dir. Thomas Olech
(219) 769-5556

DEPAUW UNIVERSITY
Greencastle 46135 *Type:* Private (United Methodist) *Accred.:* 1915/1988 (NCA) *Calendar:* 4-1-4 plan *Degrees:* B, M *Prof. Accred.:* Music, Nursing (B), Teacher Education (e,s) *CEO:* Pres. Robert G. Bottoms
Enroll: 2331 (317) 658-4800

DEFENSE INFORMATION SCHOOL
Bldg. 400, Fort Benjamin Harrison 46216 *Type:* Public (federal) *Accred.:* 1979/1990 (NCA) *Calendar:* Courses of varying lengths *Degrees:* certificates, diplomas *CEO:* Commandant Richard Hahn
Enroll: 1522 (317) 542-4046

EARLHAM COLLEGE
Richmond 47374 *Type:* Private (Friends) liberal arts *Accred.:* 1973/1986 (ATS); 1915/1984 (NCA) *Calendar:* 3-3 plan *Degrees:* B, P, M *CEO:* Pres. Richard J. Wood
Enroll: 1148 (317) 983-1200

FORT WAYNE SCHOOL OF RADIOGRAPHY
700 Broadway, Fort Wayne 46802 *Type:* Private *Calendar:* 24-mo. plan *Degrees:* certificates *Prof. Accred.:* Radiography *CEO:* C.E.O. Allen Rupiper
Enroll: 46 (219) 425-3000

FRANKLIN COLLEGE OF INDIANA
501 E. Monroe St., Franklin 46131 *Type:* Private (Baptist) liberal arts *Accred.:* 1915/1982 (NCA) *Calendar:* 4-1-4 plan *Degrees:* A, B *CEO:* Pres. William Bryan Martin
Enroll: 833 (317) 738-8000

GOSHEN BIBLICAL SEMINARY
3003 Benham Ave., Elkhart 46517 *Type:* Private (Mennonite) professional; graduate only *Accred.:* 1958/1989 (ATS); 1974/1989 (NCA) *Calendar:* Sem. plan *Degrees:* P, M, certificates, diplomas *CEO:* Pres. Marlin E. Miller
Enroll: 61 (219) 295-3726

Accredited Institutions   **Indiana**

GOSHEN COLLEGE
Goshen 46526 *Type:* Private (Mennonite) liberal arts *Accred.:* 1941/1985 (NCA) *Calendar:* Tri. plan *Degrees:* B, certificates, diplomas *Prof. Accred.:* Nursing (B), Social Work (B), Teacher Education (e,s) *CEO:* Pres. Victor E. Stoltzfus
Enroll: 1048   (219) 535-7000

GRACE COLLEGE
200 Seminary Dr., Winona Lake 46590 *Type:* Private (National Fellowship of Brethren Churches) liberal arts *Accred.:* 1976/1984 (NCA) *Calendar:* Sem. plan *Degrees:* A, B *CEO:* Pres. John J. Davis
Enroll: 591   (219) 372-5101

GRACE THEOLOGICAL SEMINARY
200 Seminary Dr., Winona Lake 46590 *Type:* Private (National Fellowship of Brethren Churches) graduate only *Accred.:* 1982/1987 (NCA) *Calendar:* Sem. plan *Degrees:* M, D, certificates, diplomas *CEO:* Pres. John J. Davis
Enroll: 90   (219) 372-5100

HANOVER COLLEGE
Hanover 47243 *Type:* Private (United Presbyterian) liberal arts *Accred.:* 1915/1990 (NCA) *Calendar:* 4-4-1 plan *Degrees:* B, certificates, diplomas *CEO:* Pres. Russell L. Nichols
Enroll: 1051   (812) 866-7000

HOLY CROSS COLLEGE
Notre Dame 46556 *Type:* Private *Accred.:* 1987/1990 (NCA) *Calendar:* Sem. plan *Degrees:* A *CEO:* Pres. Raphael Wilson, C.S.C.
Enroll: 376   (219) 233-6813

HUNTINGTON COLLEGE
2303 College Ave., Huntington 46750 *Type:* Private (United Brethren in Christ) liberal arts *Accred.:* 1961/1984 (NCA) *Calendar:* 4-1-4 plan *Degrees:* A, B, M, certificates, diplomas *CEO:* Pres. G. Blair Dowden
Enroll: 563   (219) 356-6000

ITT TECHNICAL INSTITUTE
5115 Oak Grove Rd., Evansville 47715 *Type:* Private *Accred.:* 1967/1989 (CCA-ACTTS) *Calendar:* Qtr. plan *Degrees:* A, diplomas *CEO:* Dir. Harry E. Strong
Enroll: 514   (812) 479-1441

ITT TECHNICAL INSTITUTE
4919 Coldwater Rd., Fort Wayne 46825 *Type:* Private *Accred.:* 1968/1985 (CCA-ACTTS) *Calendar:* Qtr. plan *Degrees:* A, diplomas *CEO:* Dir. Jack Cozad
Enroll: 2111   (219) 484-4107

BRANCH CAMPUS
2600 Memorial Hwy., Maitland, FL 32751 *CEO:* Dir. Gary Cosgrove
                        (407) 660-2900

ITT TECHNICAL INSTITUTE
9511 Angola Ct., Indianapolis 46268 *Type:* Private *Accred.:* 1967/1989 (CCA-ACTTS) *Calendar:* Qtr. plan *Degrees:* A, diplomas *CEO:* Dir. Alan Crews
Enroll: 2622   (317) 875-8640

INDIANA BARBER/STYLIST COLLEGE
5536 E. Washington St., Indianapolis 46219 *Type:* Private *Accred.:* 1973/1988 (CCA-ACTTS) *Calendar:* Courses of varying lengths *Degrees:* diplomas *CEO:* Pres. Kenneth L. Fleener
Enroll: 126   (317) 356-8222

INDIANA BUSINESS COLLEGE
802 N. Meridian St., Indianapolis 46204 *Type:* Private business *Accred.:* 1980/1986 (CCA-ACICS) *Calendar:* Courses of varying lengths *Degrees:* A, certificates, diplomas *CEO:* Pres. William N. Griffin, III
Enroll: 983   (317) 634-8337

BRANCH CAMPUS
1320 E. 53rd St., Ste. 106, Anderson, IN 46103 *CEO:* Dir. Carla L. Burke
                        (317) 644-7414

BRANCH CAMPUS
3550 Two Mile House Rd., Columbus, IN 47201 *CEO:* Dir. Judy J. Jackson
                        (812) 342-1000

Indiana

BRANCH CAMPUS
1170 S. Creasy La., Lafayette, IN 47905
CEO: Dir. James F. Kiefer
(317) 447-9550

BRANCH CAMPUS
417 S. Branson St., Marion, IN 46952
CEO: Dir. Teresa B. Hutcheson
(317) 662-7497

BRANCH CAMPUS
618 Wabash Ave., Terre Haute, IN 47807
CEO: Dir. Margaret A. York
(812) 232-4458

BRANCH CAMPUS
1431 Willow St., Vincennes, IN 47591
CEO: Dir. Carol A. Carroll
(812) 882-2550

INDIANA BUSINESS COLLEGE
1809 N. Walnut St., Muncie 47303 *Type:* Private business *Accred.:* 1989 (CCA-ACICS) *Calendar:* Courses of varying lengths *Degrees:* A, certificates, diplomas *CEO:* Dir. John E. Burton
Enroll: 408   (317) 288-8681

INDIANA INSTITUTE OF TECHNOLOGY
1600 E. Washington Blvd., Fort Wayne 46803 *Type:* Private technological *Accred.:* 1962/1986 (NCA) *Calendar:* Sem. plan *Degrees:* A, B, certificates, diplomas *CEO:* Pres. Donald J. Andorfer
Enroll: 637   (219) 422-5561

INDIANA STATE UNIVERSITY
Terre Haute 47809 *Type:* Public *System:* Indiana Commission for Higher Education *Accred.:* 1915/1990 (NCA) *Calendar:* Sem. plan *Degrees:* A, B, P, M, D *Prof. Accred.:* Art, Business (B,M), Clinical Psychology (provisional), Counseling Psychology, Dietetics (coordinated), Home Economics, Medical Laboratory Technology (AMA), Medical Technology, Music, Nursing (A,B,M), Recreation and Leisure Studies, School Psychology, Speech-Language Pathology, Teacher Education (e,s,p) *CEO:* Pres. Richard G. Landini
Enroll: 9596   (812) 237-6311

INDIANA UNIVERSITY BLOOMINGTON
Bloomington 47405 *Type:* Public (state) *System:* Indiana University System *Accred.:* 1913/1987 (NCA) *Calendar:* Sem. plan *Degrees:* A, B, P, M, D, certificates, diplomas *Prof. Accred.:* Art, Audiology, Business (B,M), Clinical Psychology, Journalism, Law, Librarianship, Music, Optometry, Public Affairs, Recreation and Park Administration, Speech-Language Pathology, Teacher Education (e,s,p), Theatre *CEO:* Chanc. Kenneth R. Gros Louis
Enroll: 30589   (812) 855-4602

INDIANA UNIVERSITY EAST
2325 N. Chester Blvd., Richmond 47374 *Type:* Public (state) *System:* Indiana University System *Accred.:* 1971/1982 (NCA) *Calendar:* Sem. plan *Degrees:* A, B, certificates, diplomas *CEO:* Chanc. Charlie Nelms
Enroll: 1088   (317) 973-8200

INDIANA UNIVERSITY NORTHWEST
3400 Broadway, Gary 46408 *Type:* Public (state) *System:* Indiana University System *Accred.:* 1969/1984 (NCA) *Calendar:* Sem. plan *Degrees:* A, B, M, certificates, diplomas *Prof. Accred.:* Business (B,M), Dental Assisting, Dental Hygiene, Medical Laboratory Technology (AMA), Medical Record Technology, Nursing (A), Radiography, Respiratory Therapy, Teacher Education (e,s) *CEO:* Chanc. Peggy Elliott
Enroll: 3154   (219) 980-6700

INDIANA UNIVERSITY SOUTHEAST
4201 Grant Line Rd., New Albany 47150 *Type:* Public (state) *System:* Indiana University System *Accred.:* 1969/1990 (NCA) *Calendar:* Sem. plan *Degrees:* A, B, M, certificates, diplomas *Prof. Accred.:* Business (B), Engineering Technology (mechanical), Teacher Education (e,s,p) *CEO:* Chanc. Leon Rand
Enroll: 3392   (812) 941-2000

INDIANA UNIVERSITY AT KOKOMO
P.O. Box 9003, Kokomo 46904-9003 *Type:* Public (state) *System:* Indiana University System *Accred.:* 1969/1989 (NCA) *Calen-*

dar: Sem. plan *Degrees:* A, B, certificates, diplomas *Prof. Accred.:* Engineering Technology (electrical), Nursing (A), Teacher Education (e) *CEO:* Chanc. Emita B. Hill
Enroll: 1750 (317) 455-9225

INDIANA UNIVERSITY AT SOUTH BEND
1700 Mishawaka Ave., South Bend 46634 *Type:* Public (state) *System:* Indiana University System *Accred.:* 1969/1990 (NCA) *Calendar:* Sem. plan *Degrees:* A, B, M, certificates, diplomas *Prof. Accred.:* Business (B,M), Dental Assisting, Dental Hygiene, Teacher Education (e,s,p) *CEO:* Chanc. H. Daniel Cohen
Enroll: 3952 (219) 237-4181

INDIANA UNIVERSITY-PURDUE UNIVERSITY AT FORT WAYNE
2101 Coliseum Blvd. E., Fort Wayne 46805 *Type:* Public (state) *System:* Indiana University System *Accred.:* 1969/1990 (NCA) *Calendar:* Sem. plan *Degrees:* A, B, P, M, D, certificates, diplomas *Prof. Accred.:* Business (B,M), Dental Assisting, Dental Hygiene, Dental Laboratory Technology (conditional), Engineering Technology (architectural, civil/construction, electrical, industrial, mechanical, mechanical drafting/design), Music, Nursing (A,B), Teacher Education (e,s,p) *CEO:* Chanc. Joanne B. Lantz
Enroll: 6701 (219) 481-6100

INDIANA UNIVERSITY-PURDUE UNIVERSITY AT INDIANAPOLIS
355 N. Lansing St., Indianapolis 46202 *Type:* Public (state) *System:* Indiana University System *Accred.:* 1969/1983 (NCA) *Calendar:* Sem. plan *Degrees:* A, B, P, M, D, certificates, diplomas *Prof. Accred.:* Art, Combined Prosthodontics, Combined Maxillofacial Prosthodontics, Counseling Psychology (provisional), Cytotechnology, Dental Assisting, Dental Hygiene, Dentistry, Dietetics (internship), Endodontics, Engineering (electrical, mechanical), Engineering Technology (civil/construction, electrical, mechanical, mechanical drafting/design), General Dentistry, Health Services Administration, Law, Medical Record Administration, Medical Technology, Medicine, Nuclear Medicine Technology, Nursing (A,B,M), Occupational Therapy, Occupational Therapy Assisting, Oral and Maxillofacial Surgery, Oral Pathology, Orthodontics, Pediatric Dentistry, Periodontics, Physical Therapy, Psychology Internship, Radiation Therapy Technology, Radiography, Respiratory Therapy, School Psychology, Social Work (B,M) *CEO:* Chanc. Gerald L. Bepko
Enroll: 16532 (317) 264-4417

INDIANA VOCATIONAL-TECHNICAL COLLEGE—CENTRAL INDIANA TECHNICAL INSTITUTE
One W. 26th St., P.O. Box 1763, Indianapolis 46206 *Type:* Public (state) 2-year *System:* Indiana Vocational-Technical College Executive Headquarters *Accred.:* 1977/1988 (NCA) *Calendar:* Qtr. plan *Degrees:* A, certificates, diplomas *Prof. Accred.:* Medical Assisting (AMA), Practical Nursing, Radiography, Respiratory Therapy, Respiratory Therapy Technology, Surgical Technology *CEO:* Vice Pres./Chanc. Meredith L. Carter
Enroll: 2431 (317) 921-4882

INDIANA VOCATIONAL-TECHNICAL COLLEGE—COLUMBUS TECHNICAL INSTITUTE
4475 Central Ave., Columbus 47203 *Type:* Public (state) 2-year *System:* Indiana Vocational-Technical College Executive Headquarters *Accred.:* 1978/1987 (NCA) *Calendar:* Qtr. plan *Degrees:* A, certificates, diplomas *Prof. Accred.:* Medical Assisting (AMA) *CEO:* Vice Pres./Chanc. Homer B. Smith
Enroll: 1103 (812) 372-9925

INDIANA VOCATIONAL-TECHNICAL COLLEGE—EASTCENTRAL TECHNICAL INSTITUTE
4301 S. Cowan Rd., P.O. Box 3100, Muncie 47307 *Type:* Public (state) 2-year *System:* Indiana Vocational-Technical College Executive Headquarters *Accred.:* 1979/1984 (NCA) *Calendar:* Qtr. plan *Degrees:* A, certificates, diplomas *Prof. Accred.:* Medical

Indiana

Assisting (AMA) *CEO:* Vice Pres./Chanc. Judith A. Redwine
Enroll: 990 (317) 289-2291

INDIANA VOCATIONAL-TECHNICAL COLLEGE—
KOKOMO TECHNICAL INSTITUTE
1815 E. Morgan St., Kokomo 46901 *Type:* Public (state) 2-year *System:* Indiana Vocational-Technical College Executive Headquarters *Accred.:* 1978/1987 (NCA) *Calendar:* Qtr. plan *Degrees:* A, certificates, diplomas *Prof. Accred.:* Medical Assisting (AMA) *CEO:* Vice Pres./Chanc. Carl F. Lutz
Enroll: 634 (317) 459-0561

INDIANA VOCATIONAL-TECHNICAL COLLEGE—
LAFAYETTE TECHNICAL INSTITUTE
3208 Ross Rd., P.O. Box 6299, Lafayette 47903 *Type:* Public (state) 2-year *System:* Indiana Vocational-Technical College Executive Headquarters *Accred.:* 1980/1990 (NCA) *Calendar:* Qtr. plan *Degrees:* A, certificates, diplomas *Prof. Accred.:* Dental Assisting, Medical Assisting (AMA), Nursing (A), Respiratory Therapy, Surgical Technology *CEO:* Vice Pres./Chanc. H. Victor Baldi
Enroll: 798 (317) 477-9138

INDIANA VOCATIONAL-TECHNICAL COLLEGE—
NORTHCENTRAL TECHNICAL INSTITUTE
1534 W. Sample St., South Bend 46619 *Type:* Public (state) 2-year *System:* Indiana Vocational-Technical College Executive Headquarters *Accred.:* 1977/1990 (NCA) *Calendar:* Qtr. plan *Degrees:* A, certificates, diplomas *Prof. Accred.:* Medical Assisting (AMA), Medical Laboratory Technology (AMA), Nursing (A) *CEO:* Vice Pres./Chanc. Carl F. Lutz
Enroll: 1118 (219) 289-7001

INDIANA VOCATIONAL-TECHNICAL COLLEGE—
NORTHEAST TECHNICAL INSTITUTE
3800 N. Anthony Blvd., Fort Wayne 46805 *Type:* Public (state) 2-year *System:* Indiana Vocational-Technical College Executive Headquarters *Accred.:* 1977/1990 (NCA) *Calendar:* Qtr. plan *Degrees:* A, certificates, diplomas *Prof. Accred.:* Medical Assisting (AMA), Respiratory Therapy, Respiratory Therapy Technology *CEO:* Vice Pres./Dean Jon L. Rupright
Enroll: 1455 (219) 482-9171

INDIANA VOCATIONAL-TECHNICAL COLLEGE—
NORTHWEST TECHNICAL INSTITUTE
1440 E. 35th Ave., Gary 46409 *Type:* Public (state) 2-year *System:* Indiana Vocational-Technical College Executive Headquarters *Accred.:* 1981/1986 (NCA) *Calendar:* Qtr. plan *Degrees:* A, certificates, diplomas *Prof. Accred.:* Medical Assisting (AMA) *CEO:* Vice Pres./Chanc. Ernest Jones
Enroll: 1287 (219) 981-1111

BRANCH CAMPUS
2401 Valley Dr., Valparaiso, IN 46383 *Prof. Accred.:* Medical Assisting (AMA), Respiratory Therapy Technology, Surgical Technology *CEO:* Vice Pres./Chanc. Ernest Jones
(219) 464-8514

INDIANA VOCATIONAL-TECHNICAL COLLEGE—
SOUTHCENTRAL TECHNICAL INSTITUTE
8204 Hwy. 311, Sellersburg 47171 *Type:* Public (state) 2-year *System:* Indiana Vocational-Technical College Executive Headquarters *Accred.:* 1980/1985 (NCA) *Calendar:* Qtr. plan *Degrees:* A, certificates, diplomas *Prof. Accred.:* Medical Assisting (AMA) *CEO:* Vice Pres./Chanc. Homer B. Smith
Enroll: 863 (812) 246-3301

INDIANA VOCATIONAL-TECHNICAL COLLEGE—
SOUTHEAST TECHNICAL INSTITUTE
Hwy. 62 and Ivy Tech Dr., Madison 47250 *Type:* Public (state) 2-year *System:* Indiana Vocational-Technical College Executive Headquarters *Accred.:* 1981/1986 (NCA) *Calendar:* Qtr. plan *Degrees:* A, certificates, diplomas *Prof. Accred.:* Medical Assisting (AMA) *CEO:* Vice Pres./Chanc. Homer B. Smith
Enroll: 461 (812) 265-2580

Accredited Institutions **Indiana**

INDIANA VOCATIONAL-TECHNICAL COLLEGE—
SOUTHWEST TECHNICAL INSTITUTE
3501 First Ave., Evansville 47710 *Type:* Public (state) 2-year *System:* Indiana Vocational-Technical College Executive Headquarters *Accred.:* 1977/1986 (NCA) *Calendar:* Qtr. plan *Degrees:* A, certificates, diplomas *Prof. Accred.:* Medical Assisting (AMA), Surgical Technology *CEO:* Vice Pres./Chanc. H. Victor Baldi
Enroll: 1051   (812) 426-2865

INDIANA VOCATIONAL-TECHNICAL COLLEGE—
WABASH VALLEY TECHNICAL INSTITUTE
7377 S. Dixie Bee Hwy., Terre Haute 47802 *Type:* Public (state) 2-year *System:* Indiana Vocational-Technical College Executive Headquarters *Accred.:* 1977/1985 (NCA) *Calendar:* Qtr. plan *Degrees:* A, certificates, diplomas *Prof. Accred.:* Radiography *CEO:* Vice Pres./Dean Sam Borden
Enroll: 1241   (812) 299-1121

INDIANA VOCATIONAL-TECHNICAL COLLEGE—
WHITEWATER TECHNICAL INSTITUTE
2325 Chester Blvd., Richmond 47374 *Type:* Public (state) 2-year *System:* Indiana Vocational-Technical College Executive Headquarters *Accred.:* 1981/1986 (NCA) *Calendar:* Qtr. plan *Degrees:* A, certificates, diplomas *Prof. Accred.:* Medical Laboratory Technology, Nursing (A) *CEO:* Vice Pres./Chanc. Judith A. Redwine
Enroll: 580   (317) 966-2656

INDIANA WESLEYAN UNIVERSITY
4201 S. Washington St., Marion 46953 *Type:* Private (Wesleyan Methodist) liberal arts *Accred.:* 1966/1990 (NCA) *Calendar:* Sem. plan *Degrees:* A, B, M *Prof. Accred.:* Medical Laboratory Technology (AMA), Nursing (B,M), Social Work (B) *CEO:* Pres. James Barnes
Enroll: 2499   (317) 677-2100

INSTITUTE OF DATA PROCESSING
9521 Indianapolis Blvd., Highland 46322 *Type:* Private *Accred.:* 1988 (CCA-ACTTS) *Calendar:* Courses of varying lengths *Degrees:* certificates *CEO:* Dir. Nikolaus Goregijewski
    (219) 924-1553

INTERNATIONAL BUSINESS COLLEGE—FORT WAYNE
3811 Old Illinois Rd., Fort Wayne 46804 *Type:* Private junior *Accred.:* 1953/1986 (CCA-ACICS) *Calendar:* Sem. and qtr. plans *Degrees:* A, certificates, diplomas *Prof. Accred.:* Medical Assisting (AMA) *CEO:* Pres. Jim C. Zillman
Enroll: 752   (219) 432-8702

INTERNATIONAL BUSINESS COLLEGE—
INDIANAPOLIS
7205 Shadeland Sta., Indianapolis 46256 *Type:* Private junior *Accred.:* 1986 (CCA-ACICS) *Calendar:* Sem. and qtr. plans *Degrees:* A, certificates, diplomas *Prof. Accred.:* Medical Assisting (AMA) *CEO:* Educ. Dir. Sharon M. Roeder
Enroll: 207   (317) 841-6400

LINCOLN TECHNICAL INSTITUTE
1201 Stadium Dr., Indianapolis 46202 *Type:* Private *Accred.:* 1968/1988 (CCA-ACTTS) *Calendar:* Courses of varying lengths *Degrees:* A, certificates, diplomas *CEO:* Dir. Thomas Wilson
Enroll: 2487   (317) 632-5553

LOCKYEAR COLLEGE
6666 E. 75th St., Ste. 300, Indianapolis 46250 *Type:* Private *Accred.:* 1953 (CCA-ACICS) *Calendar:* Sem. plan *Degrees:* A, B *CEO:* Dir. Howard A. Graves
    (317) 849-6666

MTA SCHOOL
325 N. Taylor Rd., Garrett 46738-9984 *Type:* Private *Accred.:* 1991 (CCA-ACTTS) *Calendar:* Courses of varying lengths *Degrees:* certificates *CEO:* Dir. David Antonelli
    (219) 357-5146

MANCHESTER COLLEGE
604 College Ave., North Manchester 46962 *Type:* Private (Church of Brethren) liberal arts *Accred.:* 1932/1983 (NCA) *Calendar:* 4-

1-4 plan *Degrees:* A, B, M *Prof. Accred.:* Social Work (B), Teacher Education (e,s) *CEO:* Pres. William P. Robinson
Enroll: 1094 (219) 982-5000

MARIAN COLLEGE
3200 Cold Spring Rd., Indianapolis 46222 *Type:* Private (Roman Catholic) liberal arts *Accred.:* 1956/1986 (NCA) *Calendar:* Sem. plan *Degrees:* A, B *Prof. Accred.:* Nursing (A), Radiography, Respiratory Therapy, Teacher Education (e,s) *CEO:* Pres. Daniel A. Felicetti
Enroll: 1094 (317) 929-0237

MARTIN UNIVERSITY
P.O. Box 18567, Indianapolis 46218-3250 *Type:* Private *Accred.:* 1987/1990 (NCA) *Calendar:* Sem. plan *Degrees:* B *CEO:* Pres. Boniface Hardin
Enroll: 360 (317) 543-3235

MENNONITE BIBLICAL SEMINARY
3003 Benham Ave., Elkhart 46517 *Type:* Private (Mennonite) professional; graduate only *Accred.:* 1964/1989 (ATS); 1974/1989 (NCA) *Calendar:* Sem. plan *Degrees:* P, M *CEO:* Pres. Marlin E. Miller
Enroll: 56 (219) 295-3726

MICHIANA COLLEGE
1030 E. Jefferson Blvd., South Bend 46617 *Type:* Private business *Accred.:* 1961/1991 (CCA-ACICS) *Calendar:* Qtr. plan *Degrees:* certificates, diplomas *Prof. Accred.:* Medical Assisting (AMA) *CEO:* Pres. David M. Krueper
Enroll: 542 (219) 237-0774

MID-AMERICA COLLEGE OF FUNERAL SERVICE
3111 Hamburg Pike, Jeffersonville 47130 *Type:* Private *Calendar:* 1- and 2-year programs *Degrees:* A, diplomas *Prof. Accred.:* Funeral Service Education *CEO:* Pres. John Rice
(812) 288-8878

MR. JAY'S HAIR ACADEMY
2045 W. Washington St., Indianapolis 46222-4221 *Type:* Private *Accred.:* 1977/1984 (CCA-ACTTS) *Calendar:* Courses of varying lengths *Degrees:* certificates *CEO:* Dir. John Scott
Enroll: 91 (317) 637-0839

BRANCH CAMPUS
3798 Garfield St., Gary, IN 46408 *CEO:* Dir. Jack Smitherman
(219) 884-2222

OAKLAND CITY COLLEGE
200 Lucretia St., Oakland City 47660 *Type:* Private (Baptist) liberal arts *Accred.:* 1977/1988 (NCA) *Calendar:* Sem. plan *Degrees:* A, B, M, certificates, diplomas *CEO:* Chanc./Pres. James W. Murray
Enroll: 655 (812) 749-1213

PSI INSTITUTE
20 N. Meridan St., Indianapolis 46204 *Type:* Private *Accred.:* 1987 (CCA-ACTTS) *Calendar:* Courses of varying lengths *Degrees:* certificates *CEO:* Dir. Tim Johnson
Enroll: 717 (317) 631-8700

PONTIAC BUSINESS INSTITUTE
47 E. Washington St., Indianapolis 46204 *Type:* Private business *Accred.:* 1984/1986 (CCA-ACICS) *Calendar:* Qtr. plan *Degrees:* certificates, diplomas *CEO:* Dir. Donna Reed
Enroll: 552 (317) 634-2901

PROFESSIONAL CAREERS INSTITUTE, INC.
2611 Waterfront Pkwy. E. Dr., Indianapolis 46214-4198 *Type:* Private *Accred.:* 1970/1985 (CCA-ACTTS) *Calendar:* Courses of varying lengths *Degrees:* certificates *Prof. Accred.:* Dental Assisting, Medical Assisting (AMA) *CEO:* Pres. Richard H. Weiss
Enroll: 962 (317) 299-6001

PURDUE UNIVERSITY
West Lafayette 47907 *Type:* Public (state) *System:* Purdue University System *Accred.:* 1913/1990 (NCA) *Calendar:* Sem. plan *Degrees:* A, B, M, D *Prof. Accred.:* Audiology, Business (B,M), Clinical Psychology, Construction Education, Counseling, Dietetics (coordinated), Engineering (aerospace, agricultural, chemical, civil, computer, construction, electrical, food process, industrial,

mechanical, metallurgical, nuclear, surveying), Engineering Technology (electrical, mechanical), Forestry, Landscape Architecture (B), Nursing (B), Pharmacy, Social Work (B), Speech-Language Pathology, Teacher Education (e,s,p), Veterinary Technology, Theatre *CEO:* Pres. Steven C. Beering
Enroll: 33738 (317) 494-4600

PURDUE UNIVERSITY—CALUMET
Hammond 46323 *Type:* Public (state) *System:* Purdue University System *Accred.:* 1969/1983 (NCA) *Calendar:* Sem. plan *Degrees:* A, B, certificates, diplomas *Prof. Accred.:* Engineering (electrical, mechanical), Engineering Technology (architectural, civil/construction, electrical, industrial, mechanical), Nursing (A,B,M), Teacher Education (e,s) *CEO:* Chanc. James W. Yackel
Enroll: 5195 (219) 989-2203

PURDUE UNIVERSITY—NORTH CENTRAL
1401 S. U.S. Hwy. 421, Westville 46391 *Type:* Public (state) *System:* Purdue University System *Accred.:* 1971/1986 (NCA) *Calendar:* Sem. plan *Degrees:* A, certificates, diplomas *Prof. Accred.:* Engineering Technology (electrical, industrial), Nursing (A), Radiography *CEO:* Chanc. Dale W. Alspaugh
Enroll: 1794 (219) 785-5200

ROSE-HULMAN INSTITUTE OF TECHNOLOGY
5500 Wabash Ave., Terre Haute 47803 *Type:* Private professional for men *Accred.:* 1916/1982 (NCA) *Calendar:* Qtr. plan *Degrees:* B, M *Prof. Accred.:* Engineering (chemical, civil, electrical, mechanical) *CEO:* Pres. Samuel F. Hulbert
Enroll: 1467 (812) 877-1511

ST. FRANCIS COLLEGE
2701 Spring St., Fort Wayne 46808 *Type:* Private (Roman Catholic) liberal arts *Accred.:* 1957/1986 (NCA) *Calendar:* Sem. plan *Degrees:* A, B, M, certificates, diplomas *Prof. Accred.:* Business (B), Social Work (B), Teacher Education (e,s) *CEO:* Pres. M. JoEllen Scheetz
Enroll: 614 (219) 434-3229

ST. JOSEPH'S COLLEGE
Rensselaer 47978 *Type:* Private (Roman Catholic) liberal arts *Accred.:* 1932/1982 (NCA) *Calendar:* Sem. plan *Degrees:* A, B, M *Prof. Accred.:* Teacher Education (e,s) *CEO:* Pres. Charles Banet
Enroll: 1033 (219) 866-6157

ST. MARY'S COLLEGE
Notre Dame 46556 *Type:* Private (Roman Catholic) liberal arts primarily for women *Accred.:* 1922/1986 (NCA) *Calendar:* Sem. plan *Degrees:* B *Prof. Accred.:* Art, Music, Nursing (B), Social Work (B-candidate), Teacher Education (e,s) *CEO:* Pres. William A. Hickey
Enroll: 1782 (219) 284-4603

ST. MARY-OF-THE-WOODS COLLEGE
St. Mary-of-the-Woods 47876 *Type:* Private (Roman Catholic) liberal arts for women *Accred.:* 1919/1989 (NCA) *Calendar:* Sem. plan *Degrees:* A, B, M, certificates, diplomas *Prof. Accred.:* Music *CEO:* Pres. Barbara Doherty
Enroll: 529 (812) 535-5151

ST. MEINRAD COLLEGE
St. Meinrad 47577 *Type:* Private (Roman Catholic) liberal arts *Accred.:* 1961/1991 (NCA) *Calendar:* Sem. plan *Degrees:* B *CEO:* Pres./Rector Eugene Hensell, O.S.B.
Enroll: 116 (812) 357-6611

ST. MEINRAD SCHOOL OF THEOLOGY
St. Meinrad 47577 *Type:* Private (Roman Catholic) professional; graduate only *Accred.:* 1968/1983(ATS); 1979/1984(NCA) *Calendar:* Sem. plan *Degrees:* P, M *CEO:* Pres./Rector Eugene Hensell, O.S.B.
Enroll: 102 (812) 357-6611

SAWYER COLLEGE
6040 Hohman Ave., Hammond 46320 *Type:* Private business *Accred.:* 1982/1988 (CCA-ACICS) *Calendar:* Qtr. plan *Degrees:* cer-

tificates, diplomas *Prof. Accred.:* Medical Assisting *CEO:* Dir. Mary Jo Dixon
Enroll: 601 (219) 931-0436

BRANCH CAMPUS
3803 E. Lincoln Hwy., Merrillville, IN 46410 *Prof. Accred.:* Medical Assisting *CEO:* Educ. Dir. Mary Ann Livovich
(219) 736-0436

SUMMIT CHRISTIAN COLLEGE
1025 W. Rudisill Blvd., Fort Wayne 46807 *Type:* Private (Missionary Church) *Accred.:* 1948/1985 (AABC); 1985/1990 (NCA) *Calendar:* Sem. plan *Degrees:* A, B, certificates, diplomas *CEO:* Pres. Donald D. Gerig
Enroll: 344 (219) 456-2111

TAYLOR UNIVERSITY
Upland 46989 *Type:* Private liberal arts *Accred.:* 1947/1987 (NCA) *Calendar:* Sem. plan *Degrees:* A, B, certificates, diplomas *Prof. Accred.:* Music, Social Work (B), Teacher Education (e,s) *CEO:* Pres. Jay L. Kesler
Enroll: 1758 (317) 998-5201

TRI-STATE UNIVERSITY
Angola 46703 *Type:* Private business *Accred.:* 1966/1990 (NCA) *Calendar:* Qtr. plan *Degrees:* A, B, certificates, diplomas *Prof. Accred.:* Engineering (aerospace, chemical, civil, electrical, mechanical), Engineering Technology (mechanical drafting/design) *CEO:* Pres. Richard A. Kenyon
Enroll: 1046 (219) 665-4100

UNITED STATES ARMY SOLDIER SUPPORT CENTER
Fort Benjamin Harrison 46216-5505 *Type:* Public (federal) *Accred.:* 1980/1985 (NCA) *Calendar:* Courses of varying lengths *Degrees:* certificates, diplomas *CEO:* Commandant Robert J. Bavis, III
Enroll: 1885 (317) 542-4969

UNIVERSITY OF EVANSVILLE
1800 Lincoln Ave., Evansville 47722 *Type:* Private (United Methodist) *Accred.:* 1931/1986 (NCA) *Calendar:* Qtr. plan *Degrees:* A, B, M, certificates, diplomas *Prof. Accred.:* Engineering (electrical, mechanical), Music, Nursing (A,B), Physical Therapy, Physical Therapy Assisting, Teacher Education (e,s,p) *CEO:* Pres. James S. Vinson
Enroll: 2554 (812) 479-2000

UNIVERSITY OF INDIANAPOLIS
1400 E. Hanna Ave., Indianapolis 46227 *Type:* Private (United Methodist) liberal arts *Accred.:* 1947/1988 (NCA) *Calendar:* Qtr. plan *Degrees:* A, B, M *Prof. Accred.:* Music, Nursing (A,B), Occupational Therapy, Physical Therapy, Teacher Education (e,s) *CEO:* Pres. G. Benjamin Lantz
Enroll: 2356 (317) 788-3211

UNIVERSITY OF NOTRE DAME
Notre Dame 46556 *Type:* Private (Roman Catholic) *Accred.:* 1977/1983 (ATS); 1913/1984 (NCA) *Calendar:* Sem. plan *Degrees:* B, P, M, D *Prof. Accred.:* Accounting (Type A), Architecture (B), Art, Business (B,M), Counseling Psychology, Engineering (aerospace, chemical, civil, electrical, mechanical, metallurgical), Law, Music, Psychology Internship *CEO:* Pres. Edward A. Malloy, C.S.C.
Enroll: 10026 (219) 293-5000

UNIVERSITY OF SOUTHERN INDIANA
8600 University Blvd., Evansville 47712 *Type:* Public (state) *System:* Indiana Commission for Higher Education *Accred.:* 1974/1987 (NCA) *Calendar:* Sem. plan *Degrees:* A, B, M, certificates, diplomas *Prof. Accred.:* Dental Assisting, Dental Hygiene, Engineering Technology (civil/construction, electrical, mechanical), Radiography, Respiratory Therapy, Social Work (B), Teacher Education (e,s) *CEO:* Pres. David L. Rice
Enroll: 4367 (812) 464-1756

VALPARAISO UNIVERSITY
Valparaiso 46383 *Type:* Private (Lutheran-Missouri Synod) *Accred.:* 1929/1988 (NCA) *Calendar:* Sem. plan *Degrees:* A, B, M, D *Prof. Accred.:* Engineering (civil, computer, electrical, mechanical), Law, Music, Nursing

(B), Social Work (B), Teacher Education (e,s) *CEO:* Pres. Alan F. Harre
Enroll: 3621 (219) 464-5115

VINCENNES UNIVERSITY
1002 N. First St., Vincennes 47591 *Type:* Public (county and state) junior *System:* Indiana Commission for Higher Education *Accred.:* 1958/1986 (NCA) *Calendar:* Sem. plan *Degrees:* A, certificates, diplomas *Prof. Accred.:* Art, Funeral Service Education, Medical Laboratory Technology (AMA), Medical Record Technology, Nursing (A), Physical Therapy Assisting, Practical Nursing, Respiratory Therapy, Theatre *CEO:* Pres. Phillip M. Summers
Enroll: 7277 (812) 882-3350

WABASH COLLEGE
301 W. Wabash Ave., Crawfordsville 47933 *Type:* Private liberal arts for men *Accred.:* 1913/1983 (NCA) *Calendar:* Sem. plan *Degrees:* B *CEO:* Pres. F. Sheldon Wettack
Enroll: 851 (317) 362-1400

IOWA

AMERICAN INSTITUTE OF BUSINESS
2500 Fleur Dr., Des Moines 50321 *Type:* Private junior *Accred.:* 1986/1989 (NCA) *Calendar:* Qtr. plan *Degrees:* A, certificates, diplomas *CEO:* Pres. Keith Fenton
Enroll: 1060 (515) 244-4221

AMERICAN INSTITUTE OF COMMERCE
1801 E. Kimberly Rd., Davenport 52807 *Type:* Private junior *Accred.:* 1957/1989 (CCA-ACICS); 1991 (NCA candidate) *Calendar:* Courses of varying lengths *Degrees:* A, certificates, diplomas *CEO:* Pres. John Huston
Enroll: 783 (319) 355-3500

BRANCH CAMPUS
2302 W. First St., Cedar Falls, IA 50613 *CEO:* Dir. Donald Elmore
(319) 277-0220

BRIAR CLIFF COLLEGE
3303 Rebecca St., Sioux City 51104 *Type:* Private (Roman Catholic) liberal arts *Accred.:* 1945/1985 (NCA) *Calendar:* 3-3 plan *Degrees:* A, B *Prof. Accred.:* Nursing (B), Social Work (B) *CEO:* Pres. Margaret Wick
Enroll: 949 (712) 279-5400

BUENA VISTA COLLEGE
610 W. Fourth St., Storm Lake 50588 *Type:* Private (United Presbyterian) liberal arts *Accred.:* 1952/1991 (NCA) *Calendar:* Sem. plan *Degrees:* B *Prof. Accred.:* Social Work (B), Teacher Education (e,s) *CEO:* Pres. Keith G. Briscoe
Enroll: 2171 (712) 749-2103

CAPRI COSMETOLOGY COLLEGE
395 Main St., P.O. Box 873, Dubuque 52004-0873 *Type:* Private *Accred.:* 1991 (CCA-ACTTS) *Calendar:* Courses of varying lengths *Degrees:* certificates *CEO:* Owner Chuck Fiegin
(319) 588-4545

CEDAR RAPIDS SCHOOL OF HAIRSTYLING
1531 First Ave., S.E., Cedar Rapids 52402-5123 *Type:* Private *Accred.:* 1991 (CCA-ACTTS) *Calendar:* Courses of varying lengths *Degrees:* certificates *CEO:* Pres. T.L. Millis
(515) 362-1488

CENTRAL COLLEGE
Pella 50219 *Type:* Private (Reformed Church in America) liberal arts *Accred.:* 1942/1984 (NCA) *Calendar:* 3-3 plan *Degrees:* B *Prof. Accred.:* Music, Teacher Education (e,s) *CEO:* Pres. William M. Wiebenga
Enroll: 1674 (515) 628-9000

CLARKE COLLEGE
Dubuque 52001 *Type:* Private (Roman Catholic) liberal arts *Accred.:* 1918/1984 (NCA) *Calendar:* Sem. plan *Degrees:* A, B, M *Prof. Accred.:* Music, Social Work (B) *CEO:* Pres. Catherine Dunn
Enroll: 645 (319) 588-6385

CLINTON COMMUNITY COLLEGE
1000 Lincoln Blvd., Clinton 52732 *Type:* Public (district) junior *System:* Eastern Iowa Community College District *Accred.:* 1983 (NCA) *Calendar:* Qtr. plan *Degrees:* A, certificates, diplomas *CEO:* Pres. Desna I. Wallin
(319) 242-6841

COE COLLEGE
1220 First Ave., N.E., Cedar Rapids 52402 *Type:* Private (United Presbyterian) liberal arts *Accred.:* 1913/1988 (NCA) *Calendar:* 4-1-4 plan *Degrees:* B *Prof. Accred.:* Music, Nursing (B) *CEO:* Pres. John E. Brown
Enroll: 1077 (319) 399-8686

CORNELL COLLEGE
600 First St. W., Mount Vernon 52314 *Type:* Private (United Methodist) liberal arts *Accred.:* 1913/1983 (NCA) *Calendar:* Sem. plan *Degrees:* B *Prof. Accred.:* Music *CEO:* Pres. David G. Marker
Enroll: 1136 (319) 895-4324

Accredited Institutions **Iowa**

DAVENPORT BARBER COLLEGE
730 E. Kimberly Rd., Davenport 52807 *Type:* Private *Accred.:* 1988 (CCA-ACTTS) *Calendar:* Courses of varying lengths *Degrees:* certificates *CEO:* Dir. David Morrissey
Enroll: 34   (319) 391-9950

DES MOINES AREA COMMUNITY COLLEGE
2006 S. Ankeny Blvd., Ankeny 50021 *Type:* Public (district) junior *System:* Iowa Community Colleges and Vocational Schools *Accred.:* 1974/1989 (NCA) *Calendar:* Sem. plan *Degrees:* A, certificates, diplomas *Prof. Accred.:* Dental Assisting, Dental Hygiene, Medical Assisting (AMA), Medical Laboratory Technology (AMA), Nursing (A), Practical Nursing, Respiratory Therapy *CEO:* Pres. Joseph A. Borgen, Ph.D.
Enroll: 6735   (515) 964-6260

DIVINE WORD COLLEGE
Epworth 52045 *Type:* Private (Roman Catholic) liberal arts *Accred.:* 1970/1986 (NCA) *Calendar:* Sem. plan *Degrees:* A, B *CEO:* Pres. Joseph D. Simon
Enroll: 58   (319) 876-3353

DORDT COLLEGE
Sioux Center 51250 *Type:* Private (Christian Reformed) liberal arts *Accred.:* 1969/1981 (NCA) *Calendar:* Sem. plan *Degrees:* A, B *Prof. Accred.:* Social Work (B) *CEO:* Pres. John B. Hulst
Enroll: 1027   (712) 722-6000

DRAKE UNIVERSITY
26th St. and University Ave., Des Moines 50311 *Type:* Private *Accred.:* 1913/1988 (NCA) *Calendar:* Sem. plan *Degrees:* B, P, M, D *Prof. Accred.:* Art, Business (B,M), Journalism, Law, Music, Pharmacy, Teacher Education (e,s,p) *CEO:* Pres. Michael R. Ferrari
Enroll: 5468   (515) 271-2191

ELLSWORTH COMMUNITY COLLEGE
1100 College Ave., Iowa Falls 50126 *Type:* Public (district) junior *System:* Iowa Valley Community College District *Accred.:* 1963/1982 (NCA) *Calendar:* Qtr. plan *Degrees:* A, certificates, diplomas *CEO:* Dean Duane R. Lloyd
Enroll: 865   (515) 648-4611

EMMAUS BIBLE COLLEGE
2570 Asbury Rd., Dubuque 52001 *Type:* Private (Christian Brethren Assemblies) *Accred.:* 1986 (AABC) *Calendar:* Sem. plan *Degrees:* A, B, certificates *CEO:* Pres. Daniel Smith
Enroll: 134   (319) 588-8000

FAITH BAPTIST BIBLE COLLEGE AND THEOLOGICAL SEMINARY
1900 N.W. Fourth St., Ankeny 50021 *Type:* Private *Accred.:* 1969/1989 (AABC); 1991 (NCA candidate) *Calendar:* Sem. plan *Degrees:* A, B, M *CEO:* Pres. Robert L. Domokos
Enroll: 271   (515) 964-0601

GRACELAND COLLEGE
Lamoni 50140 *Type:* Private (Latter-Day Saints) liberal arts *Accred.:* 1920/1987 (NCA) *Calendar:* 4-1-4 plan *Degrees:* B, certificates, diplomas *Prof. Accred.:* Nursing (B), Teacher Education (e,s) *CEO:* Pres. Barbara J. Higdon
Enroll: 1607   (515) 784-5000

GRAND VIEW COLLEGE
1200 Grandview Ave., Des Moines 50316 *Type:* Private (Lutheran) liberal arts *Accred.:* 1959/1985 (NCA) *Calendar:* 4-1-4 plan *Degrees:* A, B *Prof. Accred.:* Nursing (B) *CEO:* Pres. Arthur E. Puotinen
Enroll: 1162   (515) 263-2800

GRINNELL COLLEGE
P.O. Box 805, Grinnell 50112 *Type:* Private liberal arts *Accred.:* 1913/1989 (NCA) *Calendar:* Sem. plan *Degrees:* B, certificates, diplomas *CEO:* Pres. Pamela A. Ferguson
Enroll: 1269   (515) 269-3000

HAMILTON BUSINESS COLLEGE
1924 D St., S.W., Cedar Rapids 52404 *Type:* Private business *Accred.:* 1957/1991 (CCA-ACICS); 1990 (NCA candidate) *Calendar:*

Courses of varying lengths *Degrees:* certificates, diplomas *CEO:* Dir. Robert Mata
Enroll: 689 (319) 363-0481

BRANCH CAMPUS
2300 Euclid Ave., Des Moines, IA 50310
CEO: Dir. John Six
(515) 279-0253

BRANCH CAMPUS
100 First St., N.W., Mason City, IA 50401
CEO: Dir. Laurie Wagner
(515) 423-2530

HAMILTON TECHNICAL COLLEGE
1011 E. 53rd St., Davenport 52807 *Type:* Private *Accred.:* 1974/1985 (CCA-ACTTS) *Calendar:* Sem. plan *Degrees:* A *CEO:* Pres. Charles L. Hamilton, Jr.
Enroll: 721 (319) 386-3570

HAWKEYE INSTITUTE OF TECHNOLOGY
1501 E. Orange Rd., Waterloo 50704 *Type:* Public 2-year technical *System:* Iowa Community Colleges and Vocational Schools *Accred.:* 1975/1987 (NCA) *Calendar:* Qtr. plan *Degrees:* A, certificates, diplomas *Prof. Accred.:* Dental Assisting, Dental Hygiene, Engineering Technology (civil/construction), Medical Laboratory Technology (AMA), Respiratory Therapy Technology *CEO:* Pres. John E. Hawse
Enroll: 1646 (319) 296-2320

INDIAN HILLS COMMUNITY COLLEGE
525 Grandview Ave., Ottumwa 52501 *Type:* Public (district) junior *System:* Iowa Community Colleges and Vocational Schools *Accred.:* 1977/1983 (NCA) *Calendar:* Qtr. plan *Degrees:* A, certificates, diplomas *Prof. Accred.:* Medical Record Technology, Physical Therapy Assisting, Radiography *CEO:* Pres. Lyle Adrian Hellyer
Enroll: 1149 (515) 683-5111

CENTERVILLE CAMPUS
Centerville, IA 52544 *CEO:* Dean Richard Sharp
(515) 856-2143

IOWA CENTRAL COMMUNITY COLLEGE
330 Ave. M, Fort Dodge 50501 *Type:* Public (district) junior *System:* Iowa Community Colleges and Vocational Schools *Accred.:* 1974/1991 (NCA) *Calendar:* Sem. plan *Degrees:* A, certificates, diplomas *Prof. Accred.:* Medical Assisting (AMA) *CEO:* Pres. Jack Bottenfield
Enroll: 988 (515) 576-7201

IOWA LAKES COMMUNITY COLLEGE
19 S. 7th St., Estherville 51334 *Type:* Public (district) junior *System:* Iowa Community Colleges and Vocational Schools *Accred.:* 1976/1988 (NCA) *Calendar:* Sem. plan *Degrees:* A, certificates, diplomas *CEO:* Pres. Richard H. Blacker
Enroll: 3470 (712) 362-2601

IOWA SCHOOL OF BARBERING AND HAIRSTYLING
603 E. Sixth St., Des Moines 50309 *Type:* Private *Accred.:* 1975/1986 (CCA-ACTTS) *Calendar:* Courses of varying lengths *Degrees:* diplomas *CEO:* Pres. T.L. Millis
Enroll: 63 (515) 244-0971

IOWA STATE UNIVERSITY
Ames 50011 *Type:* Public *System:* Iowa State Board of Regents *Accred.:* 1916/1986 (NCA) *Calendar:* Sem. plan *Degrees:* B, P, M, D, certificates, diplomas *Prof. Accred.:* Architecture (B,M), Business (B,M), Computer Science, Counseling Psychology, Dietetics (coordinated), Engineering (aerospace, agricultural, ceramic, chemical, civil, computer, construction, electrical, engineering physics/science, industrial, mechanical, metallurgical, nuclear), Forestry, Home Economics, Interior Design, Journalism, Landscape Architecture (B), Leisure Studies, Music, Planning (community/regional), Psychology Internship, Social Work (B), Teacher Education (e,s,p) *CEO:* Pres. Martin Jischke
Enroll: 23136 (515) 294-2042

IOWA WESLEYAN COLLEGE
601 N. Main St., Mount Pleasant 52641 *Type:* Private (United Methodist) liberal arts *Accred.:* 1916/1988 (NCA) *Calendar:* 4-1-4

plan *Degrees:* A, B, certificates, diplomas *Prof. Accred.:* Nursing (B) *CEO:* Pres. Robert J. Prins
Enroll: 701 (319) 385-8021

IOWA WESTERN COMMUNITY COLLEGE
2700 College Rd., Council Bluffs 51501 *Type:* Public (district) junior *System:* Iowa Community Colleges and Vocational Schools *Accred.:* 1975/1990 (NCA) *Calendar:* Sem. plan *Degrees:* A, certificates, diplomas *Prof. Accred.:* Dental Assisting, Engineering Technology (civil/construction), Medical Assisting (AMA) *CEO:* Pres. Carl L. Heinrich
Enroll: 2213 (712) 325-3201

KIRKWOOD COMMUNITY COLLEGE
6301 Kirkwood Blvd., S.W., Cedar Rapids 52406 *Type:* Public (district) junior *System:* Iowa Community Colleges and Vocational Schools *Accred.:* 1970/1990 (NCA) *Calendar:* Sem. plan *Degrees:* A, certificates, diplomas *Prof. Accred.:* Animal Technology (probational), Dental Assisting, Dental Laboratory Technology, Electroneurodiagnostic Technology, Medical Assisting (AMA), Medical Record Technology, Occupational Therapy Assisting, Respiratory Therapy *CEO:* Pres. Norman R. Nielsen
Enroll: 6007 (319) 398-5411

LINCOLN TECHNICAL INSTITUTE
2501 Vine St., West Des Moines 50265 *Type:* Private *Accred.:* 1971/1988 (CCA-ACTTS) *Calendar:* Sem. plan *Degrees:* diplomas *CEO:* Pres. Terry Johnson
Enroll: 662 (515) 225-8433

LORAS COLLEGE
1450 Alta Vista, Dubuque 52001 *Type:* Private (Roman Catholic) liberal arts *Accred.:* 1917/1990 (NCA) *Calendar:* Sem. plan *Degrees:* A, B, M *Prof. Accred.:* Social Work (B) *CEO:* Pres. James Barta
Enroll: 1737 (319) 588-7103

LUTHER COLLEGE
700 College Dr., Decorah 52101 *Type:* Private (Lutheran) liberal arts *Accred.:* 1915/1989 (NCA) *Calendar:* 4-1-4 plan *Degrees:* B *Prof. Accred.:* Music, Nursing (B), Social Work (B), Teacher Education (e,s) *CEO:* Pres. H. George Anderson
Enroll: 2219 (319) 387-1001

MAHARISHI INTERNATIONAL UNIVERSITY
Rte. 1, Fairfield 52556 *Type:* Private liberal arts *Accred.:* 1980/1991 (NCA) *Calendar:* Sem. plan *Degrees:* A, B, M, D, certificates, diplomas *CEO:* Pres. Bevan Morris
Enroll: 948 (515) 472-5031

MARSHALLTOWN COMMUNITY COLLEGE
3700 S. Center St., P.O. Box 430, Marshalltown 50158 *Type:* Public (district) junior *System:* Iowa Valley Community College District *Accred.:* 1966/1982 (NCA) *Calendar:* Qtr. plan *Degrees:* A, certificates, diplomas *Prof. Accred.:* Dental Assisting, Medical Assisting (AMA), Surgical Technology *CEO:* Dean William M. Simpson
Enroll: 563 (515) 752-7106

MIDWEST TRAVEL INSTITUTE
1301 W. Lombard St., Davenport 52804-2100 *Type:* Private *Accred.:* 1991 (CCA-ACTTS) *Calendar:* Courses of varying lengths *Degrees:* certificates *CEO:* Dir. Cynthia S. DeCook
(319) 322-1690

MORNINGSIDE COLLEGE
1501 Morningside Ave., Sioux City 51106 *Type:* Private (United Methodist) liberal arts *Accred.:* 1913/1984 (NCA) *Calendar:* Sem. plan *Degrees:* A, B, M *Prof. Accred.:* Music, Nursing (B), Teacher Education (e,s) *CEO:* Pres. Miles Tommeraasen
Enroll: 1385 (712) 274-5000

MOUNT MERCY COLLEGE
1330 Elmhurst Dr., N.E., Cedar Rapids 52402 *Type:* Private (Roman Catholic) liberal arts *Accred.:* 1932/1983 (NCA) *Calendar:* 4-1-4 plan *Degrees:* B *Prof. Accred.:* Nursing (B), Social Work (B) *CEO:* Pres. Thomas R. Feld
Enroll: 1177 (319) 363-8213

Iowa

MOUNT ST. CLARE COLLEGE
400 N. Bluff Blvd., Clinton 52732 *Type:* Private (Roman Catholic) liberal arts *Accred.:* 1950/1989 (NCA) *Calendar:* Sem. plan *Degrees:* A, B, certificates, diplomas *CEO:* Pres. Charles E. Lang
Enroll: 264 (319) 242-4023

MUSCATINE COMMUNITY COLLEGE
152 Colorado St., Muscatine 52761 *Type:* Public (district) junior *System:* Eastern Iowa Community College District *Accred.:* 1983 (NCA) *Calendar:* Qtr. plan *Degrees:* A, certificates, diplomas *CEO:* Pres. Victor G. McAvoy
(319) 263-8250

NATIONAL EDUCATION CENTER—NATIONAL INSTITUTE OF TECHNOLOGY
1119 Fifth St., West Des Moines 50265 *Type:* Private *Accred.:* 1968/1986 (CCA-ACTTS) *Calendar:* Qtr. plan *Degrees:* A, diplomas *CEO:* Dir. Richard W. Poyner
Enroll: 540 (515) 223-1486

NORTH IOWA AREA COMMUNITY COLLEGE
500 College Dr., Mason City 50401 *Type:* Public (district) junior *System:* Iowa Community Colleges and Vocational Schools *Accred.:* 1919/1984 (NCA) *Calendar:* Sem. plan *Degrees:* A, certificates, diplomas *Prof. Accred.:* Nursing (A) *CEO:* Pres. David L. Buettner
Enroll: 2257 (515) 423-1264

NORTHEAST IOWA COMMUNITY COLLEGE
Box 400, Calmar 52132 *Type:* Public (district) junior *System:* Iowa Community Colleges and Vocational Schools *Accred.:* 1977/1991 (NCA) *Calendar:* Qtr. plan *Degrees:* A, certificates, diplomas *Prof. Accred.:* Dental Assisting, Medical Record Technology, Radiography, Respiratory Therapy Technology *CEO:* Pres. Don Roby
Enroll: 1527 (319) 562-3263

NORTHWEST IOWA TECHNICAL COLLEGE
Hwy. 18 W., Sheldon 51201 *Type:* Public (district) junior *System:* Iowa Community Colleges and Vocational Schools *Accred.:* 1980/1985 (NCA) *Calendar:* Qtr. plan *Degrees:* A, certificates, diplomas *CEO:* Pres. Carl H. Rolf
Enroll: 483 (712) 324-5061

NORTHWESTERN COLLEGE
Orange City 51041 *Type:* Private (Reformed Church in America) liberal arts and teachers *Accred.:* 1953/1986 (NCA) *Calendar:* Sem. plan *Degrees:* A, B, M *Prof. Accred.:* Social Work (B), Teacher Education (e,s) *CEO:* Pres. James E. Bultman
Enroll: 1024 (712) 737-4821

PALMER COLLEGE OF CHIROPRACTIC
1000 Brady St., Davenport 52803 *Type:* Private professional *Accred.:* 1984/1989 (NCA) *Calendar:* Tri. plan *Degrees:* A, B, M, D, certificates, diplomas *Prof. Accred.:* Chiropractic Education *CEO:* Pres. Donald P. Kern
(319) 326-9600

ST. AMBROSE UNIVERSITY
518 W. Locust St., Davenport 52803 *Type:* Private (Roman Catholic) liberal arts *Accred.:* 1927/1988 (NCA) *Calendar:* Sem. plan *Degrees:* B, M, certificates, diplomas *Prof. Accred.:* Occupational Therapy *CEO:* Pres. Edward J. Rogalski
Enroll: 1789 (319) 383-8800

SCOTT COMMUNITY COLLEGE
500 Belmont Rd., Bettendorf 52722 *Type:* Public (district) junior *System:* Eastern Iowa Community College District *Accred.:* 1983 (NCA) *Calendar:* Qtr. plan *Degrees:* A, certificates, diplomas *Prof. Accred.:* Medical Laboratory Technology (AMA), Radiography *CEO:* Pres. Lenny E. Stone
(319) 359-7531

SIMPSON COLLEGE
701 N. C St., Indianola 50125 *Type:* Private (United Methodist) liberal arts *Accred.:* 1913/1986 (NCA) *Calendar:* 4-1-4 plan *Degrees:* B *Prof. Accred.:* Music, Teacher Education (e,s) *CEO:* Pres. Stephen G. Jennings
Enroll: 1299 (515) 961-1611

Accredited Institutions Iowa

SIOUX CITY BARBER COLLEGE
1014 Fourth St., Sioux City 51101-1807 *Type:* Private *Accred.:* 1991 (CCA-ACTTS) *Calendar:* Courses of varying lengths *Degrees:* certificates *CEO:* Dir. Richard Shaffer
(712) 277-9047

SOUTHEASTERN COMMUNITY COLLEGE
1015 S. Gear Ave., Drawer F, West Burlington 52655 *Type:* Public (district) junior *System:* Iowa Community Colleges and Vocational Schools *Accred.:* 1974/1989 (NCA) *Calendar:* Qtr. plan *Degrees:* A, certificates, diplomas *Prof. Accred.:* Medical Assisting (AMA) *CEO:* Pres. R. Gene Gardner
Enroll: 1186 (319) 752-2731

SOUTHWESTERN COMMUNITY COLLEGE
1501 Townline St., Creston 50801 *Type:* Public (district) junior *System:* Iowa Community Colleges and Vocational Schools *Accred.:* 1975/1989 (NCA) *Calendar:* Sem. plan *Degrees:* A, certificates, diplomas *CEO:* Supt./Pres. Richard L. Byerly
Enroll: 884 (515) 782-7081

SPENCER SCHOOL OF BUSINESS
217 W. Fifth St., Spencer 51301 *Type:* Private *Accred.:* 1972/1990 (CCA-ACICS); 1991 (NCA candidate) *Calendar:* Qtr. plan *Degrees:* certificates, diplomas *Prof. Accred.:* Medical Assisting (AMA) *CEO:* Pres. James R. Grove
Enroll: 209 (712) 262-7290

STOREY'S SCHOOL OF TAXIDERMY
Hwy. 18E, Box 5112, Spencer 51301-0112 *Type:* Private *Accred.:* 1991 (CCA-ACTTS) *Calendar:* Courses of varying lengths *Degrees:* certificates *CEO:* Dir. Diane Storey
(712) 262-6441

TEIKYO MARYCREST UNIVERSITY
1607 W. 12th St., Davenport 52804 *Type:* Private liberal arts *Accred.:* 1955/1986 (NCA) *Calendar:* Sem. plan *Degrees:* A, B, M, certificates, diplomas *Prof. Accred.:* Nursing (B), Social Work (B) *CEO:* Pres. Wanda D. Bigham
Enroll: 760 (319) 326-9221

TEIKYO WESTMAR UNIVERSITY
1002 Third Ave., S.E., Le Mars 51031 *Type:* Private (United Methodist) liberal arts *Accred.:* 1953/1991 (NCA) *Calendar:* 4-1-4 plan *Degrees:* B, certificates, diplomas *CEO:* Pres. Arthur W. Richardson
Enroll: 513 (712) 546-7081

UNIVERSITY OF DUBUQUE
2000 University Ave., Dubuque 52001 *Type:* Private (United Presbyterian) liberal arts *Accred.:* 1921/1989 (NCA) *Calendar:* Sem. plan *Degrees:* A, B, M, D *Prof. Accred.:* Nursing (B), Social Work (B), Teacher Education (e,s) *CEO:* Pres. John J. Agria
Enroll: 946 (319) 589-3223

UNIVERSITY OF DUBUQUE—THEOLOGICAL SEMINARY
2000 University Ave., Dubuque 52001 *Type:* Private (Presbyterian) graduate only *Accred.:* 1944/1989 (ATS); 1976/1990 (NCA) *Calendar:* 4-1-4 plan *Degrees:* P, M, D *CEO:* Pres. Walter F. Peterson
Enroll: 142 (319) 589-3000

UNIVERSITY OF IOWA
Iowa City 52242 *Type:* Public (state) *System:* Iowa State Board of Regents *Accred.:* 1913/1988 (NCA) *Calendar:* Sem. plan *Degrees:* B, P, M, D *Prof. Accred.:* Audiology, Business (B,M), Clinical Psychology, Combined Prosthodontics, Combined Maxillofacial Prosthodontics, Counseling, Counseling Psychology, Dental Hygiene, Dentistry, Dental Public Health, Diagnostic Medical Sonography, Dietetics (internship), Endodontics, Engineering (bioengineering, chemical, civil, electrical, industrial, mechanical), General Dentistry, Health Services Administration, Journalism, Law, Leisure Studies, Librarianship, Medical Technology, Medicine, Music, Nuclear Medicine Technology, Nursing (B,M), Oral and Maxillofacial Surgery, Oral Pathology, Orthodontics, Pediatric Dentistry, Periodontics,

Pharmacy, Physical Therapy, Physician Assisting, Planning (regional/urban), Psychology Internship, Radiation Therapy Technology, Radiography, Rehabilitation Counseling, Social Work (B,M), Speech-Language Pathology, Teacher Education (e,s,p), Theatre *CEO:* Pres. Hunter J. Rawlings, III
Enroll: 23588 (319) 335-3549

UNIVERSITY OF NORTHERN IOWA
Cedar Falls 50614 *Type:* Public (state) *System:* Iowa State Board of Regents *Accred.:* 1913/1991 (NCA) *Calendar:* Sem. plan *Degrees:* B, P, M, D *Prof. Accred.:* Art, Audiology, Counseling, Home Economics, Music, Recreation, Social Work (B), Speech-Language Pathology, Teacher Education (e,s,p) *CEO:* Pres. Constantine W. Curris
Enroll: 10089 (319) 273-2566

UNIVERSITY OF OSTEOPATHIC MEDICINE AND HEALTH SCIENCES
3200 Grand Ave., Des Moines 50312 *Type:* Private professional *Accred.:* 1986/1991 (NCA) *Calendar:* Sem. plan *Degrees:* B, M, D, certificates, diplomas *Prof. Accred.:* Osteopathy, Physical Therapy, Physician Assisting, Podiatry *CEO:* Pres. J. Leonard Azneer
Enroll: 1164 (515) 271-1650

UPPER IOWA UNIVERSITY
College and Washington Sts., P.O. Box 1857, Fayette 52142 *Type:* Private liberal arts *Accred.:* 1913/1991 (NCA) *Calendar:* 4-1-4 plan *Degrees:* B *CEO:* Pres. James R. Rocheleau
Enroll: 1622 (319) 425-5200

VENNARD COLLEGE
P.O. Box 29, University Park 52595-0029 *Type:* Private (Wesleyan) *Accred.:* 1948/1984 (AABC) *Calendar:* Sem. plan *Degrees:* A, B, certificates *CEO:* Pres. Warthen Israel
Enroll: 137 (515) 673-8391

WALDORF COLLEGE
Forest City 50436 *Type:* Private (Lutheran) junior *Accred.:* 1948/1990 (NCA) *Calendar:* Sem. plan *Degrees:* A, certificates, diplomas *CEO:* Pres. William E. Hamm
Enroll: 601 (515) 582-2450

WARTBURG COLLEGE
Waverly 50677-1003 *Type:* Private (Lutheran) liberal arts *Accred.:* 1948/1987 (NCA) *Calendar:* 4-4-1 plan *Degrees:* B, certificates, diplomas *Prof. Accred.:* Music, Social Work (B) *CEO:* Pres. Robert L. Vogel
Enroll: 1386 (319) 352-8450

WARTBURG THEOLOGICAL SEMINARY
333 Wartburg Pl., Dubuque 52001 *Type:* Private (Lutheran) professional; graduate only *Accred.:* 1944/1986 (ATS); 1976/1987 (NCA) *Calendar:* 4-1-4 plan *Degrees:* P, M, D *CEO:* Pres. Roger W. Fjeld
Enroll: 211 (319) 589-0200

WESTERN IOWA TECH COMMUNITY COLLEGE
4647 Stone Ave., P.O. Box 265, Sioux City 51102 *Type:* Public junior *System:* Iowa Community Colleges and Vocational Schools *Accred.:* 1977/1985 (NCA) *Calendar:* Qtr. plan *Degrees:* A, certificates, diplomas *Prof. Accred.:* Dental Assisting, Surgical Technology *CEO:* Pres. Robert Dunker
Enroll: 1477 (712) 274-6400

WILLIAM PENN COLLEGE
Oskaloosa 52577 *Type:* Private (Friends) liberal arts *Accred.:* 1913/1987 (NCA) *Calendar:* Sem. plan *Degrees:* B *Prof. Accred.:* Teacher Education (e,s) *CEO:* Pres. John D. Wagoner
Enroll: 663 (515) 673-1001

KANSAS

ALLEN COUNTY COMMUNITY COLLEGE
1801 N. Central, Iola 66749 *Type:* Public (district) junior *System:* Kansas State Board of Education *Accred.:* 1974/1989 (NCA) *Calendar:* Sem. plan *Degrees:* A, certificates, diplomas *CEO:* Pres. William A. Griffin, Jr.
Enroll: 737 (316) 365-5116

AMERICAN CAREER COLLEGE
2010 California St., Topeka 66607 *Type:* Private business *Accred.:* 1984/1990 (CCA-ACICS) *Calendar:* Qtr. plan *Degrees:* certificates, diplomas *CEO:* Chf. Admin. Ofcr. Carol Urbanski
Enroll: 248 (913) 232-6352

AMTECH INSTITUTE
4011 E. 31st St., Wichita 67210 *Type:* Private *Accred.:* 1986 (CCA-ACTTS) *Calendar:* Courses of varying lengths *Degrees:* certificates *CEO:* Pres. Thomas M. Sullivan
Enroll: 666 (316) 682-6548

BAKER UNIVERSITY
Eighth and Grove St., Baldwin City 66006 *Type:* Private (United Methodist) liberal arts *Accred.:* 1913/1985 (NCA) *Calendar:* 4-1-4 plan *Degrees:* A, B, M *CEO:* Pres. Daniel M. Lambert
Enroll: 1217 (913) 594-6451

BARCLAY COLLEGE
P.O. Box 288, Haviland 67059 *Type:* Private (Evangelical Friends Alliance) *Accred.:* 1975/1985 (AABC) *Calendar:* Sem. plan *Degrees:* B, certificates *CEO:* Pres. Robin W. Johnston
Enroll: 85 (316) 862-5252

BARTON COUNTY COMMUNITY COLLEGE
Rural Rte. 3, Box 136Z, Great Bend 67530 *Type:* Public (district) junior *System:* Kansas State Board of Education *Accred.:* 1974/1985 (NCA) *Calendar:* Sem. plan *Degrees:* A, certificates, diplomas *Prof. Accred.:* Medical Laboratory Technology (AMA), Nursing (A) *CEO:* Pres. Jimmie L. Downing
Enroll: 1967 (316) 792-2701

BENEDICTINE COLLEGE
1020 N. Second St., Atchison 66002 *Type:* Private (Roman Catholic) liberal arts *Accred.:* 1971/1988 (NCA) *Calendar:* 4-1-4 plan *Degrees:* A, B, M *Prof. Accred.:* Music, Teacher Education (e,s) *CEO:* Pres. Thomas O. James
Enroll: 697 (913) 367-5340

BETHANY COLLEGE
Lindsborg 67456 *Type:* Private (Lutheran) liberal arts *Accred.:* 1932/1990 (NCA) *Calendar:* 4-1-4 plan *Degrees:* B *Prof. Accred.:* Music, Social Work (B), Teacher Education (e,s) *CEO:* Pres. Joel M. McKean
Enroll: 633 (913) 227-3311

BETHEL COLLEGE
300 E. 27th St., North Newton 67117 *Type:* Private (Mennonite) liberal arts *Accred.:* 1938/1989 (NCA) *Calendar:* 4-1-4 plan *Degrees:* A, B *Prof. Accred.:* Nursing (B), Social Work (B) *CEO:* Pres. John E. Zehr
Enroll: 552 (316) 283-2500

THE BROWN MACKIE COLLEGE
126 S. Santa Fe Ave., Salina 67401 *Type:* Private business *Accred.:* 1980/1990 (NCA) *Calendar:* Qtr. plan *Degrees:* A, certificates, diplomas *CEO:* Pres. M. Gary Talley
Enroll: 749 (913) 825-5422

BRYAN INSTITUTE
1004 S. Oliver St., Wichita 67218 *Type:* Private *Accred.:* 1971/1983 (CCA-ACTTS) *Calendar:* Courses of varying lengths *Degrees:* diplomas *Prof. Accred.:* Medical Assisting *CEO:* Pres. Brian Dickinson
Enroll: 203 (316) 685-2284

BRYAN TRAVEL COLLEGE
1527 Fairlawn Rd., Topeka 66604 *Type:* Private *Accred.:* 1991 (CCA-ACTTS) *Calendar:* Courses of varying lengths *Degrees:*

Kansas

certificates, diplomas *CEO:* Dir. Melody Rust
(913) 272-7511

BUTLER COUNTY COMMUNITY COLLEGE
901 Haverhill Rd., El Dorado 67042 *Type:* Public (district) junior *System:* Kansas State Board of Education *Accred.:* 1970/1990 (NCA) *Calendar:* Sem. plan *Degrees:* A, certificates, diplomas *Prof. Accred.:* Nursing (A) *CEO:* Pres. Rodney V. Cox
Enroll: 2460 (316) 321-5083

CAPITOL CITY BARBER COLLEGE
812 N. Kansas Ave., Topeka 66608 *Type:* Private *Accred.:* 1982/1987 (CCA-ACTTS) *Calendar:* Courses of varying lengths *Degrees:* diplomas *CEO:* Dir. Larry Ross
Enroll: 64 (913) 234-5401

CENTER FOR TRAINING IN BUSINESS AND INDUSTRY
2211 Silicon Ave., Lawrence 66046 *Type:* Private business *Accred.:* 1989 (CCA-ACICS) *Calendar:* Courses of varying lengths *Degrees:* certificates, diplomas *CEO:* Pres. Patricia M. Anderson
Enroll: 68 (913) 841-9640

CENTRAL BAPTIST THEOLOGICAL SEMINARY
Seminary Heights, 741 N. 31st St., Kansas City 66102-3964 *Type:* Private (Baptist) professional; graduate only *Accred.:* 1962/1984 (ATS); 1979/1990 (NCA) *Calendar:* Sem. plan *Degrees:* M *CEO:* Pres. John R. Landgraf
Enroll: 111 (913) 371-5313

CENTRAL BUSINESS COLLEGE
2502 E. Douglas Ave., Wichita 67214 *Type:* Private business and technical *Accred.:* 1966/1990 (CCA-ACICS) *Calendar:* Qtr. plan *Degrees:* certificates, diplomas *CEO:* Dean Marta A. Wishart
Enroll: 432 (316) 684-5138

CENTRAL COLLEGE
1200 S. Main St., McPherson 67460 *Type:* Private (Free Methodist) *Accred.:* 1975/1987 (NCA) *Calendar:* 4-1-4 plan *Degrees:* A, B, certificates, diplomas *CEO:* Pres. Harvey L. Ludwick
Enroll: 231 (316) 241-0723

CLIMATE CONTROL INSTITUTE
3030 N. Hillside St., Wichita 67219 *Type:* Private *Accred.:* 1976/1985 (CCA-ACTTS) *Calendar:* Courses of varying lengths *Degrees:* certificates *CEO:* Pres. D.J. Hampton
Enroll: 244 (316) 686-7355

CLOUD COUNTY COMMUNITY COLLEGE
2221 Campus Dr., P.O. Box 1002, Concordia 66901-1002 *Type:* Public (county) junior *System:* Kansas State Board of Education *Accred.:* 1977/1986 (NCA) *Calendar:* Sem. plan *Degrees:* A, certificates, diplomas *Prof. Accred.:* Nursing (A), Practical Nursing *CEO:* Pres. James P. Ihrig
Enroll: 1098 (913) 243-1435

COFFEYVILLE COMMUNITY COLLEGE
11th and Willow, Coffeyville 67337 *Type:* Public (district) junior *System:* Kansas State Board of Education *Accred.:* 1972/1988 (NCA) *Calendar:* Sem. plan *Degrees:* A, certificates, diplomas *CEO:* Pres. Dan D. Kinney
Enroll: 1028 (316) 251-7700

COLBY COMMUNITY COLLEGE
1255 S. Range, Colby 67701 *Type:* Public (district) junior *System:* Kansas State Board of Education *Accred.:* 1972/1985 (NCA) *Calendar:* Sem. plan *Degrees:* A, certificates, diplomas *Prof. Accred.:* Physical Therapy Assisting, Practical Nursing, Veterinary Technology *CEO:* Pres. Mikel V. Ary
Enroll: 1020 (913) 462-3984

COWLEY COUNTY COMMUNITY COLLEGE
125 S. Second St., P.O. Box 1147, Arkansas City 67005 *Type:* Public (district) junior *System:* Kansas State Board of Education *Accred.:* 1975/1990 (NCA) *Calendar:* Sem. plan *Degrees:* A, certificates, diplomas *CEO:* Pres. Patrick J. McAtee
Enroll: 1391 (316) 442-0430

Accredited Institutions — Kansas

CRANFORD COLLEGE
1600 N. Lorraine St., Hutchinson 67501 *Type:* Private business *Accred.:* 1966/1984 (CCA-ACICS) *Calendar:* Courses of varying lengths *Degrees:* certificates, diplomas *CEO:* Pres./Dir. Sharon K. Arney
Enroll: 210 (316) 663-4419

CRANFORD COLLEGE TRAVEL CAREER INSTITUTE
7777 E. Osie St., Ste. 301, Wichita, KS 67207 *CEO:* Dir. Francie Dix
(316) 687-4240

DODGE CITY COMMUNITY COLLEGE
2501 N. 14th St., Dodge City 67801 *Type:* Public (county) junior *System:* Kansas State Board of Education *Accred.:* 1966/1986 (NCA) *Calendar:* Sem. plan *Degrees:* A, certificates, diplomas *Prof. Accred.:* Medical Record Technology, Nursing (A), Practical Nursing *CEO:* Pres. Thomas E. Gamble
Enroll: 1161 (316) 225-1321

DONNELLY COLLEGE
608 N. 18th St., Kansas City 66102 *Type:* Private (Roman Catholic) junior *Accred.:* 1958/1989 (NCA) *Calendar:* Sem. plan *Degrees:* A *CEO:* Pres. John P. Murry
Enroll: 324 (913) 621-6070

EMPORIA STATE UNIVERSITY
1200 Commercial St., Emporia 66801 *Type:* Public liberal arts and teachers *System:* Kansas Board of Regents *Accred.:* 1915/1985 (NCA) *Calendar:* Sem. plan *Degrees:* A, B, P, M *Prof. Accred.:* Librarianship, Music, Rehabilitation Counseling, Teacher Education (e,s,p) *CEO:* Pres. Robert E. Glennen, Jr.
Enroll: 5047 (316) 343-1200

FLINT HILLS TECHNICAL SCHOOL
3301 W. 18th Ave., Emporia 66801 *Type:* Private *Calendar:* Courses of varying lengths *Degrees:* certificates *Prof. Accred.:* Dental Assisting *CEO:* Dir. Keith Stover
(316) 342-6404

FORT HAYS STATE UNIVERSITY
600 Park St., Hays 67601 *Type:* Public liberal arts and teachers *System:* Kansas Board of Regents *Accred.:* 1915/1982 (NCA) *Calendar:* Sem. plan *Degrees:* A, B, P, M *Prof. Accred.:* Music, Nursing (B), Radiography, Speech-Language Pathology, Teacher Education (e,s,p) *CEO:* Pres. Edward H. Hammond
Enroll: 4339 (913) 628-5880

FORT SCOTT COMMUNITY COLLEGE
2108 S. Horton St., Fort Scott 66701 *Type:* Public (district) junior *System:* Kansas State Board of Education *Accred.:* 1976/1981 (NCA) *Calendar:* Sem. plan *Degrees:* A, certificates, diplomas *Prof. Accred.:* Nursing (A) *CEO:* Pres. Laura Meeks
Enroll: 1141 (316) 223-2700

FRIENDS UNIVERSITY
2100 W. University St., Wichita 67213 *Type:* Private (Friends) liberal arts *Accred.:* 1915/1991 (NCA) *Calendar:* Sem. plan *Degrees:* A, B, M *Prof. Accred.:* Music, Teacher Education (e,s) *CEO:* Pres. Biff Green
Enroll: 1393 (316) 261-5800

GARDEN CITY COMMUNITY COLLEGE
801 Campus Dr., Garden City 67846 *Type:* Public (district) junior *System:* Kansas State Board of Education *Accred.:* 1975/1985 (NCA) *Calendar:* Sem. plan *Degrees:* A, certificates, diplomas *Prof. Accred.:* Nursing (A) *CEO:* Pres. James H. Tangeman
Enroll: 1155 (316) 276-7611

HASKELL INDIAN JUNIOR COLLEGE
155 Indian Ave., No. 1305, Lawrence 66046-4800 *Type:* Public (state) junior *Accred.:* 1979/1989 (NCA) *Calendar:* Sem. plan *Degrees:* A, certificates, diplomas *CEO:* Pres. Robert G. Martin
Enroll: 805 (913) 749-8450

HESSTON COLLEGE
P.O. Box 3000, Hesston 67062-9989 *Type:* Private (Mennonite) junior *Accred.:* 1964/1991 (NCA) *Calendar:* 4-1-4 plan *Degrees:*

Kansas

A *Prof. Accred.:* Nursing (A) *CEO:* Pres. Kirk Alliman
Enroll: 504   (316) 327-8233

HIGHLAND COMMUNITY COLLEGE
Box 68, Highland 66035 *Type:* Public (district) junior *System:* Kansas State Board of Education *Accred.:* 1977/1989 (NCA) *Calendar:* Sem. plan *Degrees:* A, certificates, diplomas *CEO:* Pres. Eric M. Priest
Enroll: 868   (913) 442-3236

HUTCHINSON COMMUNITY COLLEGE
1300 N. Plum St., Hutchinson 67501 *Type:* Public (county and state) junior *System:* Kansas State Board of Education *Accred.:* 1960/1984 (NCA) *Calendar:* Sem. plan *Degrees:* A, certificates, diplomas *Prof. Accred.:* Medical Record Technology, Nursing (A), Radiography *CEO:* Pres. James H. Stringer
Enroll: 2147   (316) 665-3500

INDEPENDENCE COMMUNITY COLLEGE
College Ave. and Brookside Dr., Independence 67301 *Type:* Public (district) junior *System:* Kansas State Board of Education *Accred.:* 1957/1988 (NCA) *Calendar:* Sem. plan *Degrees:* A, certificates, diplomas *CEO:* Pres. Jo Ann C. McDowell
Enroll: 1011   (316) 331-4100

JOHNSON COUNTY COMMUNITY COLLEGE
12345 College Blvd. at Quivira, Overland Park 66210 *Type:* Public (district) junior *System:* Kansas State Board of Education *Accred.:* 1975/1987 (NCA) *Calendar:* Sem. plan *Degrees:* A, certificates, diplomas *Prof. Accred.:* Dental Hygiene, EMT-Paramedic, Nursing (A), Respiratory Therapy *CEO:* Pres. Charles J. Carlsen
Enroll: 6972   (913) 469-8500

KANSAS CITY KANSAS COMMUNITY COLLEGE
7250 State Ave., Kansas City 66112 *Type:* Public (county and state) junior *System:* Kansas State Board of Education *Accred.:* 1951/1986 (NCA) *Calendar:* Sem. plan *Degrees:* A, certificates, diplomas *Prof. Accred.:* Mortuary Science, Nursing (A) *CEO:* Pres. Bill R. Spencer
Enroll: 2795   (913) 334-1100

KANSAS COLLEGE OF TECHNOLOGY
2409 Scanlan Ave., Salina 67401-8196 *Type:* Public (state) 2-year *Accred.:* 1980/1990 (NCA) *Calendar:* Sem. plan *Degrees:* A, certificates, diplomas *Prof. Accred.:* Engineering Technology (chemical, civil/construction, computer, electrical, mechanical) *CEO:* Dean Jerry Cole
Enroll: 393   (913) 825-0275

KANSAS NEWMAN COLLEGE
3100 McCormick Ave., Wichita 67213 *Type:* Private (Roman Catholic) liberal arts *Accred.:* 1967/1987 (NCA) *Calendar:* Sem. plan *Degrees:* A, B *Prof. Accred.:* Nursing (A,B) *CEO:* Pres. Tarcisia Roths
Enroll: 657   (316) 942-4291

KANSAS SCHOOL OF HAIRSTYLING
1207 E. Douglas Ave., Wichita 67211 *Type:* Private *Accred.:* 1985 (CCA-ACTTS) *Calendar:* Courses of varying lengths *Degrees:* certificates *CEO:* Dir. Joe Hancock
Enroll: 86   (316) 264-4891

KANSAS STATE UNIVERSITY
Manhattan 66506-0113 *Type:* Public *System:* Kansas Board of Regents *Accred.:* 1916/1982 (NCA) *Calendar:* Sem. plan *Degrees:* A, B, M, D, certificates, diplomas *Prof. Accred.:* Accounting (Type A,C), Architecture (B), Audiology, Business (B,M), Construction Management, Dietetics (coordinated), Engineering (agricultural, architectural, chemical, civil, electrical, industrial, mechanical, nuclear), Engineering Technology (electrical, mechanical), Home Economics, Interior Design, Journalism, Landscape Architecture (B,M), Leisure Studies, Music, Planning (community/regional), Psychology Internship, Public Administration, Social Work (B), Speech-Language Pathology, Teacher Education (e,s,p), Theatre, Veterinary Medicine *CEO:* Pres. Jon Wefald
Enroll: 18873   (913) 532-6222

Kansas

KANSAS WESLEYAN UNIVERSITY
100 E. Clafin, Salina 67401 *Type:* Private (United Methodist) liberal arts *Accred.:* 1916/1990 (NCA) *Calendar:* 4-1-4 plan *Degrees:* A, B *CEO:* Pres. Marshall P. Stanton
Enroll: 654 (913) 827-5541

LABETTE COMMUNITY COLLEGE
200 S. 14th St., Parsons 67357 *Type:* Public (district) junior *System:* Kansas State Board of Education *Accred.:* 1976/1988 (NCA) *Calendar:* Sem. plan *Degrees:* A, certificates, diplomas *Prof. Accred.:* Nursing (A), Radiography, Respiratory Therapy, Respiratory Therapy Technology *CEO:* Interim Pres. John Patterson
Enroll: 1591 (316) 421-6700

MANHATTAN CHRISTIAN COLLEGE
1415 Anderson Ave., Manhattan 66502 *Type:* Private (Christian Churches/Churches of Christ) *Accred.:* 1948/1986 (AABC) *Calendar:* Sem. plan *Degrees:* A, B, certificates *CEO:* Pres. Kenneth D. Cable
Enroll: 172 (913) 539-3571

MCPHERSON COLLEGE
1600 E. Euclid, P.O. Box 1402, McPherson 67460 *Type:* Private (Church of Brethren) liberal arts *Accred.:* 1921/1990 (NCA) *Calendar:* 4-1-4 plan *Degrees:* A, B, certificates, diplomas *CEO:* Pres. Paul W. Hoffman
Enroll: 390 (316) 241-0731

MIDAMERICA NAZARENE COLLEGE
P.O. Box 1776, Olathe 66061 *Type:* Private (Nazarene) liberal arts *Accred.:* 1974/1989 (NCA) *Calendar:* Sem. plan *Degrees:* A, B, M *Prof. Accred.:* Nursing (B), Music *CEO:* Pres. Richard L. Spindle
Enroll: 1093 (913) 782-3750

NEOSHO COUNTY COMMUNITY COLLEGE
1000 S. Allen, Chanute 66720 *Type:* Public (district) junior *System:* Kansas State Board of Education *Accred.:* 1976/1986 (NCA) *Calendar:* Sem. plan *Degrees:* A, certificates, diplomas *Prof. Accred.:* Nursing (A) *CEO:* Pres. George H. Van Allen
Enroll: 719 (316) 431-2820

NORTH CENTRAL KANSAS AREA VOCATIONAL-TECHNICAL SCHOOL
P.O. Box 507, Beloit 67420 *Type:* Public *Accred.:* 1981/1986 (NCA) *Calendar:* Qtr. plan *Degrees:* certificates *Prof. Accred.:* Practical Nursing *CEO:* Dir. Robert J. Severance
Enroll: 414 (913) 738-2276

OTTAWA UNIVERSITY
Tenth and Cedar, Ottawa 66067 *Type:* Private (Baptist) liberal arts *Accred.:* 1914/1989 (NCA) *Calendar:* Sem. plan *Degrees:* B, M, certificates, diplomas *CEO:* Pres. Wilbur D. Wheaton
Enroll: 899 (913) 242-5200

PITTSBURG STATE UNIVERSITY
1701 S. Broadway, Pittsburg 66762 *Type:* Public liberal arts and professional *System:* Kansas Board of Regents *Accred.:* 1915/1983 (NCA) *Calendar:* Sem. plan *Degrees:* A, B, P, M, certificates, diplomas *Prof. Accred.:* Counseling, Engineering Technology (civil/construction, electrical, manufacturing, mechanical, plastics), Music, Nursing (B), Social Work (B), Teacher Education (e,s,p) *CEO:* Pres. Donald W. Wilson
Enroll: 4911 (316) 231-7000

PRATT COMMUNITY COLLEGE
Hwy. 61, Pratt 67124 *Type:* Public (district) junior *System:* Kansas State Board of Education *Accred.:* 1976/1988 (NCA) *Calendar:* Sem. plan *Degrees:* A, certificates, diplomas *CEO:* Pres. William A. Wojciechowski
Enroll: 744 (316) 672-5641

ST. MARY COLLEGE
4100 S. 4th St., Leavenworth 66048-5082 *Type:* Private (Roman Catholic) liberal arts primarily for women *Accred.:* 1928/1987 (NCA) *Calendar:* Sem. plan *Degrees:* A, B *Prof. Accred.:* Nursing (B), Teacher Education (e,s) *CEO:* Pres. Peter Clifford
Enroll: 584 (913) 682-5151

Kansas · **Accredited Institutions**

ST. MARY OF THE PLAINS COLLEGE
240 San Jose Dr., Dodge City 67801 *Type:* Private (Roman Catholic) liberal arts *Accred.:* 1963/1984 (NCA) *Calendar:* 4-1-4 plan *Degrees:* A, B, certificates, diplomas *Prof. Accred.:* Music, Nursing (A,B), Social Work (B), Teacher Education (e,s) *CEO:* Pres. Bernard S. Parker
Enroll: 857   (316) 225-4171

SEWARD COUNTY COMMUNITY COLLEGE
1801 N. Kansas St., Liberal 67901 *Type:* Public (district) *System:* Kansas State Board of Education *Accred.:* 1975/1990 (NCA) *Calendar:* Sem. plan *Degrees:* A, certificates, diplomas *Prof. Accred.:* Medical Laboratory Technology (AMA), Nursing (A), Practical Nursing, Respiratory Therapy, Respiratory Therapy Technology *CEO:* Pres. Donald E. Guild
Enroll: 795   (316) 624-1951

SOUTHERN TECHNICAL COLLEGE
2105 S. Meridian St., Wichita 67213 *Type:* Private *Accred.:* 1981/1986 (CCA-ACTTS) *Calendar:* Courses of varying lengths *Degrees:* certificates *CEO:* Pres. Joseph F. Gasper
Enroll: 432   (316) 942-7733

SOUTHWESTERN COLLEGE
100 College St., Winfield 67156 *Type:* Private (United Methodist) liberal arts *Accred.:* 1918/1982 (NCA) *Calendar:* 4-1-4 plan *Degrees:* B, M, certificates, diplomas *Prof. Accred.:* Music, Nursing (B), Social Work (B) *CEO:* Pres. Carl Martin
Enroll: 618   (316) 221-4150

STERLING COLLEGE
Sterling 67579 *Type:* Private (United Presbyterian) liberal arts *Accred.:* 1928/1987 (NCA) *Calendar:* 4-1-4 plan *Degrees:* A, B *CEO:* Pres. Roger Parrott
Enroll: 438   (316) 278-2173

TABOR COLLEGE
400 S. Jefferson St., Hillsboro 67063 *Type:* Private (Mennonite) liberal arts *Accred.:* 1965/1985 (NCA) *Calendar:* Sem. plan *Degrees:* A, B *Prof. Accred.:* Music, Social Work (B) *CEO:* Pres. Le Von Balzer
Enroll: 409   (316) 947-3121

TOPEKA SCHOOL OF MEDICAL TECHNOLOGY
1505 W. Eighth St., Topeka 66604 *Type:* Private *Calendar:* 12-mo. plan *Degrees:* B, certificates *Prof. Accred.:* Medical Technology *CEO:* Pres. Patrick Gilles
Enroll: 16   (913) 295-8933

TOPEKA TECHNICAL COLLEGE
1620 Gage Blvd., N.W., Topeka 66618 *Type:* Private *Accred.:* 1971/1987 (CCA-ACTTS) *Calendar:* Qtr. plan *Degrees:* diplomas *CEO:* Dir. Allen Calmes
Enroll: 237   (913) 232-5858

UNITED STATES ARMY COMMAND AND GENERAL STAFF COLLEGE
Fort Leavenworth 66027 *Type:* Public (federal) *Accred.:* 1976/1985 (NCA) *Calendar:* Sem. plan *Degrees:* M, certificates, diplomas *CEO:* Commandant Leonard Wishart
Enroll: 1280   (913) 684-5621

UNIVERSITY OF KANSAS
Lawrence 66045 *Type:* Public (state) *System:* Kansas Board of Regents *Accred.:* 1913/1985 (NCA) *Calendar:* Sem. plan *Degrees:* B, P, M, D *Prof. Accred.:* Architecture (B), Art, Audiology, Business (B,M), Clinical Psychology, Counseling Psychology, Dietetics (internship), Engineering (aerospace, architectural, chemical, civil, electrical, engineering physics/science, mechanical, petroleum), Health Services Administration, Journalism, Law, Music, Pharmacy, Physical Therapy, Planning (urban), Public Administration, School Psychology, Social Work (B,M), Speech-Language Pathology, Teacher Education (e,s,p) *CEO:* Chanc. Gene A. Budig
Enroll: 26328   (913) 864-2700

UNIVERSITY OF KANSAS MEDICAL CENTER
39th St. and Rainbow Blvd., Kansas City 66103 *Type:* Public *Calendar:* Courses of varying lengths *Degrees:* B, M, certificates, diplomas *Prof. Accred.:* Cytotechnology,

Medical Record Administration, Medical Technology, Medicine, Nurse Anesthesia Education, Nursing (B,M), Occupational Therapy, Radiation Therapy Technology, Respiratory Therapy *CEO:* Exec. Vice Chanc. D. Kay Clawson, M.D.
(913) 588-9207

WASHBURN UNIVERSITY OF TOPEKA
17th and College Sts., Topeka 66621 *Type:* Public (city) *Accred.:* 1913/1988 (NCA) *Calendar:* Sem. plan *Degrees:* A, B, M, D, certificates, diplomas *Prof. Accred.:* Law, Medical Record Technology, Music, Nursing (B), Physical Therapy Assisting, Radiation Therapy Technology, Radiography, Respiratory Therapy, Respiratory Therapy Technology, Social Work (B), Teacher Education (e,s,p) *CEO:* Pres. Hugh L. Thompson
Enroll: 4531 (913) 295-6300

WICHITA AREA VOCATIONAL-TECHNICAL SCHOOL
217 N. Water St., Wichita 67202 *Type:* Private *Calendar:* Courses of varying lengths *Degrees:* certificates *Prof. Accred.:* Medical Laboratory Technology (AMA), Practical Nursing, Surgical Technology *CEO:* Dir. Rosemary A. Kirby, Ph.D.
(316) 833-4455

WICHITA BUSINESS COLLEGE
501 E. Pawnee St., Ste. 515, Wichita 67211 *Type:* Private *Accred.:* 1963/1987 (CCA-ACICS) *Calendar:* Qtr. plan *Degrees:* certificates, diplomas *CEO:* Pres. Faith Kite
Enroll: 186 (316) 263-1261

WICHITA STATE UNIVERSITY
1845 Fairmont St., Wichita 67208 *Type:* Public *System:* Kansas Board of Regents *Accred.:* 1927/1987 (NCA) *Calendar:* Sem. plan *Degrees:* A, B, P, M, D, certificates, diplomas *Prof. Accred.:* Audiology, Business (B,M), Dance, Dental Hygiene, Engineering (aerospace, electrical, industrial, mechanical), Medical Technology, Music, Nursing (B,M), Physical Therapy, Physician Assisting, Respiratory Therapy, Social Work (B), Speech-Language Pathology, Teacher Education (e,s,p) *CEO:* Pres. Warren B. Armstrong
Enroll: 11278 (316) 689-3001

WICHITA TECHNICAL INSTITUTE
942 S. West St., Wichita 67213 *Type:* Private *Accred.:* 1971/1988 (CCA-ACTTS) *Calendar:* Courses of varying lengths *Degrees:* certificates, diplomas *Prof. Accred.:* Dental Assisting *CEO:* Pres. Paul D. Moore
Enroll: 171 (316) 943-2241

WRIGHT BUSINESS SCHOOL
Indian Springs Shopping Mall, 4601 State Ave., Kansas City 66102 *Type:* Private business *Accred.:* 1984 (CCA-ACICS) *Calendar:* Courses of varying lengths *Degrees:* certificates, diplomas *CEO:* Dir./Pres. James Miller, Jr.
Enroll: 407 (913) 287-1600

BRANCH CAMPUS
9500 Marshall Dr., Lenexa, KS 66215 *CEO:* Dir. Anna Selleck
(913) 599-0220

BRANCH CAMPUS
5528 N.E. Antioch Rd., Kansas City, MO 64119 *CEO:* Dir. Jerri Abbott
(816) 452-4411

KENTUCKY

ALICE LLOYD COLLEGE
Purpose Rd., Pippa Passes 41844 *Type:* Private liberal arts *Accred.:* 1952/1987 (SACS-CC) *Calendar:* Sem. plan *Degrees:* B *CEO:* Pres. M. Fred Mullinax
Enroll: 528 (606) 368-2101

ASBURY COLLEGE
201 N. Lexington Ave., Wilmore 40390-1198 *Type:* Private liberal arts and teachers *Accred.:* 1940/1989 (SACS-CC) *Calendar:* Qtr. plan *Degrees:* B *Prof. Accred.:* Music *CEO:* Pres. Edwin G. Blue
Enroll: 1124 (606) 858-3511

ASBURY THEOLOGICAL SEMINARY
204 N. Lexington Ave., Wilmore 40390-1199 *Type:* Private (interdenominational) professional; graduate only *Accred.:* 1946/1984 (ATS); 1984 (SACS-CC) *Calendar:* 4-1-4 plan *Degrees:* P, M, D *CEO:* Pres. David L. McKenna
Enroll: 610 (606) 858-3581

ASHLAND COMMUNITY COLLEGE
1400 College Dr., Ashland 41101-3617 *Type:* Public junior *System:* University of Kentucky Community College System *Accred.:* 1957/1991 (SACS-CC) *Calendar:* Sem. plan *Degrees:* A *CEO:* Pres. Anthony Newberry
Enroll: 3632 (606) 329-2999

BALLARD COUNTY AREA VOCATIONAL EDUCATION CENTER
Rte. 1, Box 214, Barlow 42024 *Type:* Public (state) technical *Accred.:* 1975/1990 (SACS-CC); 1975/1990 (SACS-COEI) *Calendar:* Courses of varying lengths *Degrees:* certificates *CEO:* Dir. Donald G. Wells
Enroll: 85 (502) 665-5112

BARRETT & COMPANY SCHOOL OF HAIR DESIGN
973 Kimberly Sq., Nicholasville 40356 *Type:* Private *Accred.:* 1987 (SACS-COEI) *Calendar:* Courses of varying lengths *Degrees:* certificates *CEO:* Dir. James Barrett
Enroll: 40 (606) 885-9136

BELLARMINE COLLEGE
2001 Newburg Rd., Louisville 40205-0671 *Type:* Private (Roman Catholic) liberal arts *Accred.:* 1949/1988 (SACS-CC) *Calendar:* Sem. plan *Degrees:* A, B, M *Prof. Accred.:* Nursing (B) *CEO:* Pres. Joseph J. McGowan, Jr.
Enroll: 1733 (502) 452-8211

BEREA COLLEGE
Berea 40404 *Type:* Private liberal arts *Accred.:* 1926/1985 (SACS-CC) *Calendar:* 4-1-4 plan *Degrees:* B *Prof. Accred.:* Nursing (B), Teacher Education (e,s) *CEO:* Pres. John B. Stephenson
Enroll: 1588 (606) 986-9341

BRANNON BUSINESS SCHOOL
400 S. 6th St., P.O. Box 1680, Paducah 42002-1680 *Type:* Private *Accred.:* 1985/1990 (SACS-COEI) *Calendar:* Courses of varying lengths *Degrees:* certificates *CEO:* Dir. Carroll Walker
Enroll: 109 (502) 442-8222

BRESCIA COLLEGE
717 Frederica St., Owensboro 42301 *Type:* Private (Roman Catholic) liberal arts *Accred.:* 1957/1989 (SACS-CC) *Calendar:* Sem. plan *Degrees:* A, B *CEO:* Pres. Ruth Gehres
Enroll: 625 (502) 685-3131

CAMPBELLSVILLE COLLEGE
200 W. College St., Campbellsville 42718-2799 *Type:* Private (Southern Baptist) liberal arts *Accred.:* 1963/1984 (SACS-CC) *Calendar:* Sem. plan *Degrees:* B *Prof. Accred.:* Music *CEO:* Pres. Kenneth W. Winters
Enroll: 732 (502) 465-8158

CAREERCOM JUNIOR COLLEGE OF BUSINESS
1102 S. Virginia St., Hopkinsville 42240 *Type:* Private junior *Accred.:* 1988 (CCA-ACICS) *Calendar:* Qtr. plan *Degrees:* A, certificates, diplomas *CEO:* Dir. Kim Hall
Enroll: 512 (502) 886-1302

BRANCH CAMPUS
5564 Norwood Ave., Jacksonville, FL 32208 *CEO:* Dir. Willard R. Lively
(904) 766-6010

BRANCH CAMPUS
1314 Burch Dr., Evansville, IN 47701 *CEO:* Dir. Sherri Sherrod
(812) 867-0074

BRANCH CAMPUS
7166 Crowder Blvd., New Orleans, LA 70127 *CEO:* Dir. Ken Evans
(504) 242-2109

CARL D. PERKINS JOB CORPS CENTER
Goble Roberts Rd., Box G-11, Prestonsburg 41653 *Type:* Private *Accred.:* 1985/1990 (SACS-COEI) *Calendar:* Courses of varying lengths *Degrees:* certificates *CEO:* Dir. Edna Higginbotham
Enroll: 206 (606) 886-1037

CENTRE COLLEGE
W. Walnut St., Danville 40422 *Type:* Private liberal arts *Accred.:* 1904/1985 (SACS-CC) *Calendar:* 4-1-4 plan *Degrees:* B *CEO:* Pres. Michael F. Adams
Enroll: 877 (606) 236-5211

CLEAR CREEK BAPTIST BIBLE COLLEGE
300 Clear Creek Rd., Pineville 40977 *Type:* Private (Southern Baptist) *Accred.:* 1986 (AABC) *Calendar:* Sem. plan *Degrees:* A, B, certificates, diplomas *CEO:* Pres. Bill Whittaker
Enroll: 138 (606) 337-3196

CUMBERLAND COLLEGE
Box 6191, College Sta., Williamsburg 40769 *Type:* Private (Southern Baptist) liberal arts and teachers *Accred.:* 1964/1985 (SACS-CC) *Calendar:* Sem. plan *Degrees:* A, B, M *Prof. Accred.:* Music *CEO:* Pres. James H. Taylor
Enroll: 1699 (606) 549-2200

EARLE C. CLEMENTS JOB CORPS CENTER
Morganfield 42437 *Type:* Private *Accred.:* 1983/1988 (SACS-COEI)*Calendar:* Courses of varying lengths *Degrees:* certificates *CEO:* Dir. Gerald A. Oettle
Enroll: 959 (502) 389-2419

EASTERN KENTUCKY UNIVERSITY
Richmond 40475-3101 *Type:* Public (state) *System:* Kentucky Council on Higher Education *Accred.:* 1928/1986 (SACS-CC) *Calendar:* Sem. plan *Degrees:* A, B, M *Prof. Accred.:* EMT-Paramedic, Interior Design, Medical Assisting (AMA), Medical Laboratory Technology (AMA), Medical Record Administration, Medical Record Technology, Medical Technology, Music, Nursing (A,B), Occupational Therapy, Public Administration, Recreation and Park Administration, Social Work (B), Speech-Language Pathology, Teacher Education (e,s,p) *CEO:* Pres. Hanly Funderburk
Enroll: 13989 (606) 622-1000

ELIZABETHTOWN COMMUNITY COLLEGE
600 College Street Rd., Elizabethtown 42701 *Type:* Public junior *System:* University of Kentucky Community College System *Accred.:* 1964/1991 (SACS-CC) *Calendar:* Sem. plan *Degrees:* A *Prof. Accred.:* Nursing (A) *CEO:* Pres. Charles E. Stebbins
Enroll: 2302 (502) 769-2371

FRANKLIN COLLEGE
218 N. Fifth St., Paducah 42001 *Type:* Private junior *Accred.:* 1966/1985 (CCA-ACICS) *Calendar:* Qtr. plan *Degrees:* A, certificates, diplomas *CEO:* Pres. Wayne F. Mullis
Enroll: 234 (502) 443-8478

BRANCH CAMPUS
222 W. Water St., Mayfield, KY 42066 *CEO:* Dir. Ralph Garrett
(502) 247-1366

FUGAZZI COLLEGE
406 Lafayette Ave., Lexington 40502 *Type:* Private business *Accred.:* 1957/1986 (CCA-ACICS) *Calendar:* Qtr. plan *Degrees:* A, certificates, diplomas *Prof. Accred.:* Medical Assisting (AMA) *CEO:* Dir. Bernard Bever
Enroll: 404 (606) 266-0401

Kentucky

GEORGETOWN COLLEGE
400 E. College St., Georgetown 40324-1696 *Type:* Private (Southern Baptist) liberal arts *Accred.:* 1919/1982 (SACS-CC) *Calendar:* Sem. plan *Degrees:* B, M *CEO:* Pres. William H. Crouch, Jr.
Enroll: 1307 (502) 863-8011

HAZARD COMMUNITY COLLEGE
One Community College Dr., Hazard 41701-2402 *Type:* Public junior *System:* University of Kentucky Community College System *Accred.:* 1968/1991 (SACS-CC) *Calendar:* Sem. plan *Degrees:* A *CEO:* Pres. G. Edward Hughes
Enroll: 1126 (606) 436-5721

HEALTH CAREERS OCCUPATIONS SCHOOL
701 N. Laffoon St., Madisonville 42431 *Type:* Private *Calendar:* Courses of varying lengths *Degrees:* certificates *Prof. Accred.:* Medical Laboratory Technology, Radiography, Respiratory Therapy Technology, Surgical Technology *CEO:* Dir. Bill M. Hatley
(502) 825-6546

HENDERSON COMMUNITY COLLEGE
2660 S. Green St., Henderson 42420 *Type:* Public junior *System:* University of Kentucky Community College System *Accred.:* 1960/1991 (SACS-CC) *Degrees:* A *Prof. Accred.:* Medical Laboratory Technology (AMA), Nursing (A) *CEO:* Pres. Patrick R. Lake
Enroll: 113 (502) 827-1867

HOPKINSVILLE COMMUNITY COLLEGE
P.O. Box 2100, Hopkinsville 42241-2100 *Type:* Public junior *System:* University of Kentucky Community College System *Accred.:* 1965/1991 (SACS-CC) *Calendar:* Sem. plan *Degrees:* A *Prof. Accred.:* Dental Hygiene *CEO:* Pres. A. James Kerley
Enroll: 1200 (502) 886-3921

HUMANA HEALTH INSTITUTE
612 S. Fourth St., No. 400, Louisville 40202 *Type:* Private *Accred.:* 1983/1991 (SACS-COEI) *Calendar:* Courses of varying lengths *Degrees:* certificates *CEO:* Dir. Linda Blair
Enroll: 42 (502) 580-3660

BRANCH CAMPUS
11500 Ninth St., N., St. Petersburg, FL 33716 *Accred.:* 1983/1991 (SACS-COEI) *CEO:* Dir. Sharon Roberts
(813) 577-1497

BRANCH CAMPUS
6800 Park Ten Blvd., Ste. 160 S., San Antonio, TX 78213 *CEO:* Dir. Adrienne Lyons
(512) 580-3660

INSTITUTE OF ELECTRONIC TECHNOLOGY
509 S. 30th St., Paducah 42001 *Type:* Private *Accred.:* 1968/1989 (CCA-ACTTS) *Calendar:* Sem. plan *Degrees:* A *CEO:* Dir. Lee Hicklin
Enroll: 275 (502) 444-9676

JEFFERSON COMMUNITY COLLEGE
109 E. Broadway, Louisville 40202-2005 *Type:* Public junior *System:* University of Kentucky Community College System *Accred.:* 1968/1991 (SACS-CC) *Calendar:* Sem. plan *Degrees:* A *Prof. Accred.:* Medical Laboratory Technology (AMA), Nursing (A), Physical Therapy Assisting, Respiratory Therapy *CEO:* Pres. Ronald J. Horvath
Enroll: 6020 (502) 584-0181

KENTUCKY CHRISTIAN COLLEGE
617 N. Carole Malone Blvd., Grayson 41143 *Type:* Private (Christian Churches/Churches of Christ) *Accred.:* 1962/1981 (AABC); 1984/1989 (SACS-CC) *Calendar:* Sem. plan *Degrees:* A, B, M *CEO:* Pres. Keith P. Keeran
Enroll: 554 (606) 474-6613

KENTUCKY COLLEGE OF BARBERING AND HAIRSTYLING
1230 S. Third St., Louisville 40203 *Type:* Private *Accred.:* 1983/1988 (CCA-ACTTS) *Calendar:* Courses of varying lengths *Degrees:* diplomas *CEO:* Dir. David Durbin
Enroll: 71 (502) 634-0521

Kentucky

KENTUCKY COLLEGE OF BUSINESS
628 E. Main St., Lexington 40508 *Type:* Private junior *Accred.:* 1970/1989 (CCA-ACICS) *Calendar:* Qtr. plan *Degrees:* A, certificates, diplomas *CEO:* Dir. Ed Stafford
Enroll: 390   (606) 253-0621

BRANCH CAMPUS
115 E. Lexington Ave., Danville, KY 40422 *CEO:* Dir. Brent Brenard
(606) 236-6991

BRANCH CAMPUS
7627 Tanners La., Florence, KY 41042 *CEO:* Dir. Scott Carlton
(606) 525-6510

BRANCH CAMPUS
3950 Dixie Hwy., Louisville, KY 40216 *CEO:* Dir. Daisy Terrell
(502) 447-7665

BRANCH CAMPUS
198 S. Mayo Tr., Pikeville, KY 41501 *CEO:* Dir. Billie J. Coggins
(606) 432-5477

BRANCH CAMPUS
218 S. Porter St., Richmond, KY 40475 *CEO:* Dir. Keeley Gadd
(606) 623-8956

KENTUCKY POLYTECHNIC INSTITUTE
7410 LaGrange Rd., Ste. 100, Louisville 40222 *Type:* Private *Accred.:* 1990 (CCA-ACTTS) *Calendar:* Courses of varying lengths *Degrees:* certificates *CEO:* Dir. Jim Vernon
Enroll: 155   (502) 426-7744

KENTUCKY SCHOOL OF FINANCIAL EDUCATION
1930 Bishop La., Ste. 720, Louisville 40218-1925 *Type:* Private *Accred.:* 1991 (SACS-COEI) *Calendar:* Courses of varying lengths *Degrees:* certificates *CEO:* Pres. J. Martin Gossman
Enroll: 6   (502) 451-7615

KENTUCKY STATE UNIVERSITY
Frankfort 40601-2355 *Type:* Public liberal arts and teachers *System:* Kentucky Council on Higher Education *Accred.:* 1939/1989 (SACS-CC) *Calendar:* Sem. plan *Degrees:* A, B, M *Prof. Accred.:* Music, Nursing (A), Social Work (B), Teacher Education (e,s) *CEO:* Pres. Mary L. Smith
Enroll: 1914   (502) 227-6000

KENTUCKY TECH—ASHLAND STATE VOCATIONAL-TECHNICAL SCHOOL
4818 Roberts Dr., Ashland 41102-9046 *Type:* Public (state) technical *System:* Vocational Education Region 10 (Fivco) *Accred.:* 1971/1989 (SACS-COEI)*Calendar:* Courses of varying lengths *Degrees:* certificates *CEO:* Prin. Howard Moore
(606) 928-6427

KENTUCKY TECH—BARREN COUNTY AREA VOCATIONAL EDUCATION CENTER
491 Trojan Tr., Glasgow 42141 *Type:* Public (state) technical *System:* Vocational Education Region 4 (Barren River) *Accred.:* 1972/1987 (SACS-COEI) *Calendar:* Courses of varying lengths *Degrees:* certificates *CEO:* Coord. Max Doty
(502) 651-2196

KENTUCKY TECH—BELFRY AREA VOCATIONAL EDUCATION CENTER
P.O. Box 280, Belfry 41514 *Type:* Public (state) technical *System:* Vocational Education Region 11 (Big Sandy) *Accred.:* 1974/1989 (SACS-COEI) *Calendar:* Courses of varying lengths *Degrees:* certificates *CEO:* Prin. Brad W. May
(606) 353-4951

KENTUCKY TECH—BELL COUNTY AREA VOCATIONAL EDUCATION CENTER
Box 199-A, Rte. 7, Pineville 40977 *Type:* Public (state) technical *System:* Vocational Education Region 13 (Cumberland Valley) *Accred.:* 1975/1990 (SACS-COEI) *Calendar:* Courses of varying lengths *Degrees:* certificates *CEO:* Coord. Ron Mason
(606) 337-3094

KENTUCKY TECH—BLACKBURN CORRECTIONAL COMPLEX
3111 Spurr Rd., Lexington 40511 *Type:* Public (state) technical *System:* Vocational

Kentucky

Education Region 15 (Bluegrass) *Accred.:* 1972/1987 (SACS-COEI)*Calendar:* Courses of varying lengths *Degrees:* certificates *CEO:* Coord. Clyde Carroll
(606) 254-2791

KENTUCKY TECH—BOONE COUNTY AREA VOCATIONAL EDUCATION CENTER
3320 Cougar Path, Hebron 41048 *Type:* Public (state) technical *System:* Vocational Education Region 7 (Northern Kentucky) *Accred.:* 1973/1988 (SACS-COEI) *Calendar:* Courses of varying lengths *Degrees:* certificates *CEO:* Coord. Stephanie Rottman
(606) 689-7855

KENTUCKY TECH—BOWLING GREEN STATE TRANSPORTATION CENTER
6198 Nashville Rd., Bowling Green 42101 *Type:* Public (state) technical *System:* Vocational Education Region 4 (Barren River) *Accred.:* 1972/1987 (SACS-COEI) *Calendar:* Courses of varying lengths *Degrees:* certificates *CEO:* Coord. Robert Bierman
(502) 781-0711

KENTUCKY TECH—BOWLING GREEN STATE VOCATIONAL-TECHNICAL SCHOOL
1845 Loop Dr., Bowling Green 42101 *Type:* Public (state) technical *System:* Vocational Education Region 4 (Barren River) *Accred.:* 1972/1987 (SACS-COEI)*Calendar:* Courses of varying lengths *Degrees:* certificates *Prof. Accred.:* Dental Assisting (conditional), Radiography, Respiratory Therapy Technology, Surgical Technology *CEO:* Prin. Donald R. Williams
(502) 843-5461

KENTUCKY TECH—BREATHITT COUNTY AREA VOCATIONAL EDUCATION CENTER
P.O. Box 786, Jackson 41339 *Type:* Public (state) technical *System:* Vocational Education Region 12 (Kentucky River) *Accred.:* 1973/1988 (SACS-COEI)*Calendar:* Courses of varying lengths *Degrees:* certificates *CEO:* Coord. Fred Deaton
(606) 666-5153

KENTUCKY TECH—BRECKINRIDGE COUNTY AREA VOCATIONAL EDUCATION CENTER
P.O. Box 68, Harnet 40144 *Type:* Public (state) technical *System:* Vocational Education Region 5 (Elizabethtown) *Accred.:* 1974/1987 (SACS-COEI)*Calendar:* Courses of varying lengths *Degrees:* certificates *CEO:* Coord. Wayne A. Spencer
(502) 756-2138

KENTUCKY TECH—BULLITT COUNTY AREA VOCATIONAL EDUCATION CENTER
395 High School Dr., Sheperdsville 40165 *Type:* Public (state) technical *System:* Vocational Education Regions 6 and 8 (Jefferson) *Accred.:* 1973/1988 (SACS-COEI) *Calendar:* Courses of varying lengths *Degrees:* certificates *CEO:* Coord. Robert Hazelrigg
(502) 543-7018

KENTUCKY TECH—CALDWELL COUNTY AREA VOCATIONAL EDUCATION CENTER
P.O. Box 350, Princeton 42445 *Type:* Public (state) technical *System:* Vocational Education Region 2 (Pennyrile) *Accred.:* 1971/1991 (SACS-COEI) *Calendar:* Courses of varying lengths *Degrees:* certificates *CEO:* Coord. Arthur Dunn
(502) 365-5563

KENTUCKY TECH—CAMPBELL COUNTY AREA VOCATIONAL EDUCATION CENTER
50 Orchard La., Alexandria 41001 *Type:* Public (state) technical *System:* Vocational Education Region 7 (Northern Kentucky) *Accred.:* 1973/1988 (SACS-COEI) *Calendar:* Courses of varying lengths *Degrees:* certificates *CEO:* Coord. Kenneth McCormick
(606) 635-4101

KENTUCKY TECH—CARROLL COUNTY AREA VOCATIONAL EDUCATION CENTER
1704 Highland Ave., Carrollton 41008 *Type:* Public (state) technical *System:* Vocational Education Region 7 (Northern Kentucky) *Accred.:* 1973/1988 (SACS-COEI) *Calendar:* Courses of varying lengths *Degrees:* certificates *CEO:* Coord. Donald W. Garner
(502) 732-4479

Accredited Institutions **Kentucky**

KENTUCKY TECH—CASEY COUNTY AREA VOCATIONAL EDUCATION CENTER
Rte. 4, Box 49, Liberty 42539 *Type:* Public (state) technical *System:* Vocational Education Region 14 (Lake Cumberland) *Accred.:* 1974/1989 (SACS-COEI)*Calendar:* Courses of varying lengths *Degrees:* certificates *CEO:* Coord. J.D. Shugars
(606) 787-6241

KENTUCKY TECH—CENTRAL KENTUCKY STATE VOCATIONAL-TECHNICAL SCHOOL
104 Vo-Tech Rd., Lexington 40510 *Type:* Public (state) technical *System:* Vocational Education Region 15 (Bluegrass) *Accred.:* 1972/1987 (SACS-COEI)*Calendar:* Courses of varying lengths *Degrees:* certificates *Prof. Accred.:* Dental Assisting, Respiratory Therapy, Surgical Technology *CEO:* Prin. Patrick White
(606) 255-8500

KENTUCKY TECH—CHRISTIAN COUNTY AREA VOCATIONAL EDUCATION CENTER
109 Hamond Plaza, Ste. 2, Fort Campbell Blvd., Hopkinsville 42240 *Type:* Public (state) technical *System:* Vocational Education Region 2 (Pennyrile) *Accred.:* 1971/1991 (SACS-COEI) *Calendar:* Courses of varying lengths *Degrees:* certificates *CEO:* Coord. Ann Claxton
(502) 887-2524

KENTUCKY TECH—CLARK COUNTY AREA VOCATIONAL EDUCATION CENTER
650 Boone Ave., Winchester 40391 *Type:* Public (state) technical *System:* Vocational Education Region 15 (Bluegrass) *Accred.:* 1972/1987 (SACS-COEI)*Calendar:* Courses of varying lengths *Degrees:* certificates *CEO:* Coord. William Lockhart
(606) 744-1250

KENTUCKY TECH—CLAY COUNTY AREA VOCATIONAL EDUCATION CENTER
Rte. 2, Box 256, Manchester 40962 *Type:* Public (state) technical *System:* Vocational Education Region 13 (Cumberland Valley) *Accred.:* 1975/1990 (SACS-COEI) *Calendar:* Courses of varying lengths *Degrees:* certificates *CEO:* Coord. Charles McWhorter
(606) 598-2194

KENTUCKY TECH—CLINTON COUNTY AREA VOCATIONAL EDUCATION CENTER
Rte. 3, Box 8, Albany 42602 *Type:* Public (state) technical *System:* Vocational Education Region 14 (Lake Cumberland) *Accred.:* 1974/1989 (SACS-COEI)*Calendar:* Courses of varying lengths *Degrees:* certificates *CEO:* Coord. Preston Sparks
(606) 387-6448

KENTUCKY TECH—CORBIN AREA VOCATIONAL EDUCATION CENTER
1909 S. Snyder Ave., Corbin 40701 *Type:* Public (state) technical *System:* Vocational Education Region 13 (Cumberland Valley) *Accred.:* 1975/1990 (SACS-COEI) *Calendar:* Courses of varying lengths *Degrees:* certificates *CEO:* Coord. Ronnie Partin
(606) 528-5338

KENTUCKY TECH—CUMBERLAND VALLEY HEALTH OCCUPATIONS CENTER
U.S. 25E S., P.O. Box 187, Pineville 40977 *Type:* Public (state) technical *System:* Vocational Education Region 13 (Cumberland Valley) *Accred.:* 1975/1990 (SACS-COEI) *Calendar:* Courses of varying lengths *Degrees:* certificates *Prof. Accred.:* Radiography, Surgical Technology *CEO:* Coord. Mildred Winkler
(606) 337-3106

KENTUCKY TECH—DANVILLE SCHOOL OF HEALTH OCCUPATIONS
448 S. Third St., Danville 40422 *Type:* Public (state) technical *System:* Vocational Education Region 15 (Bluegrass) *Accred.:* 1972/1987 (SACS-COEI) *Calendar:* Courses of varying lengths *Degrees:* certificates *CEO:* Coord. Sandra Houston
(606) 236-2053

KENTUCKY TECH—DAVIESS COUNTY STATE VOCATIONAL-TECHNICAL SCHOOL
P.O. Box 1677, Owensboro 42303-1677 *Type:* Public (state) technical *System:* Voca-

tional Education Region 3 (Green River) *Accred.:* 1973/1988 (SACS-COEI) *Calendar:* Courses of varying lengths *Degrees:* certificates *CEO:* Prin. Ray Gillaspie
(502) 686-3321

KENTUCKY TECH—EDDYVILLE VOCATIONAL EDUCATION CENTER
P.O. Box 128, Eddyville 42038-0128 *Type:* Public (state) technical *System:* Vocational Education Region 2 (Pennyrile) *Accred.:* 1971/1991 (SACS-COEI)*Calendar:* Courses of varying lengths *Degrees:* certificates *CEO:* Coord. Jim Creekmur
(502) 388-2211

KENTUCKY TECH—ELIZABETHTOWN STATE VOCATIONAL-TECHNICAL SCHOOL
505 University Dr., Elizabethtown 42701 *Type:* Public (state) technical *System:* Vocational Education Region 5 (Elizabethtown) *Accred.:* 1974/1987 (SACS-COEI) *Calendar:* Courses of varying lengths *Degrees:* certificates *CEO:* Prin. Neil Ramer
(502) 765-2104

KENTUCKY TECH—FAIRDALE VOCATIONAL EDUCATION CENTER
907 Fairdale Rd., Fairdale 40118 *Type:* Public (state) technical *System:* Vocational Education Regions 6 and 8 (Jefferson) *Accred.:* 1973/1988 (SACS-COEI) *Calendar:* Courses of varying lengths *Degrees:* certificates *CEO:* Coord. David Schalk
(502) 473-8249

KENTUCKY TECH—FULTON COUNTY AREA VOCATIONAL EDUCATION CENTER
Rte. 4, Hickman 42050 *Type:* Public (state) technical *System:* Vocational Education Region 1 (Purchase) *Accred.:* 1975/1990 (SACS-COEI) *Calendar:* Courses of varying lengths *Degrees:* certificates *CEO:* Coord. Larry Lynch
(502) 236-2517

KENTUCKY TECH—GARRAD COUNTY AREA VOCATIONAL EDUCATION CENTER
306 W. Maple Ave., Lancaster 40444 *Type:* Public (state) technical *System:* Vocational

Education Region 15 (Bluegrass) *Accred.:* 1972/1987 (SACS-COEI)*Calendar:* Courses of varying lengths *Degrees:* certificates *CEO:* Coord. James Spurlin
(606) 792-2144

KENTUCKY TECH—GARTH AREA VOCATIONAL EDUCATION CENTER
HC 79, Box 205, Martin 41649 *Type:* Public (state) technical *System:* Vocational Education Region 11 (Big Sandy) *Accred.:* 1974/1989 (SACS-COEI) *Calendar:* Courses of varying lengths *CEO:* Prin. Ronald Turner
(606) 285-3088

KENTUCKY TECH—GLASGOW SCHOOL FOR HEALTH OCCUPATIONS
1215 N. Race St., Glasgow 42141 *Type:* Public (state) technical *System:* Vocational Education Region 4 (Barren River) *Accred.:* 1972/1987 (SACS-COEI)*Calendar:* Courses of varying lengths *Degrees:* certificates *CEO:* Coord. Rebecca Forrest
(502) 651-5673

KENTUCKY TECH—GREEN COUNTY AREA VOCATIONAL EDUCATION CENTER
P.O. Box H, Greensburg 42743 *Type:* Public (state) technical *System:* Vocational Education Region 14 (Lake Cumberland) *Accred.:* 1974/1989 (SACS-COEI)*Calendar:* Courses of varying lengths *Degrees:* certificates *CEO:* Coord. Jerry O. Rogers
(502) 932-4263

KENTUCKY TECH—GREENUP COUNTY AREA VOCATIONAL EDUCATION CENTER
P.O. Box 7, South Shore 41175 *Type:* Public (state) technical *System:* Vocational Education Region 10 (Fivco) *Accred.:* 1971/1985 (SACS-COEI) *Calendar:* Courses of varying lengths *Degrees:* certificates *CEO:* Coord. Helen Spears
(606) 932-3107

KENTUCKY TECH—HARLAN STATE VOCATIONAL-TECHNICAL SCHOOL
21 Ballpark Rd., Harlan 40831 *Type:* Public (state) technical *System:* Vocational Education Region 13 (Cumberland Valley)

Accred.: 1975/1990 (SACS-COEI) *Calendar:* Courses of varying lengths *Degrees:* certificates *CEO:* Prin. Harve J. Couch
(606) 573-1506

KENTUCKY TECH—HARRISON COUNTY AREA VOCATIONAL EDUCATION CENTER
551 Webster Ave., Cynthiana 41031 *Type:* Public (state) technical *System:* Vocational Education Region 15 (Bluegrass) *Accred.:* 1972/1987 (SACS-COEI)*Calendar:* Courses of varying lengths *Degrees:* certificates *CEO:* Coord. James Plummer
(606) 234-5286

KENTUCKY TECH—HARRODSBURG AREA VOCATIONAL EDUCATION CENTER
661 Tapt Rd., P.O. Box 628, Harrodsburg 40330 *Type:* Public (state) technical *System:* Vocational Education Region 15 (Bluegrass) *Accred.:* 1972/1987 (SACS-COEI) *Calendar:* Courses of varying lengths *Degrees:* certificates *CEO:* Coord. L. Hughes Jones
(606) 734-9329

KENTUCKY TECH—HAZARD STATE VOCATIONAL-TECHNICAL SCHOOL
101 Vo-Tech Dr., Hazard 41701 *Type:* Public (state) technical *System:* Vocational Education Region 12 (Kentucky River) *Accred.:* 1973/1988 (SACS-COEI) *Calendar:* Courses of varying lengths *Degrees:* certificates *CEO:* Prin. Connie W. Johnson
(606) 436-3101

KENTUCKY TECH—HENDERSON COUNTY AREA VOCATIONAL EDUCATION CENTER
2440 Zion Rd., Henderson 42420 *Type:* Public (state) technical *System:* Vocational Education Region 3 (Green River) *Accred.:* 1973/1988 (SACS-COEI)*Calendar:* Courses of varying lengths *Degrees:* certificates *CEO:* Prin. Dennis Harrell
(502) 827-3810

KENTUCKY TECH—JEFFERSON STATE VOCATIONAL-TECHNICAL SCHOOL
727 W. Chestnut St., Louisville 40203 *Type:* Public (state) technical *System:* Vocational Education Regions 6 and 8 (Jefferson)

Accred.: 1973/1988 (SACS-COEI) *Calendar:* Courses of varying lengths *Degrees:* certificates *CEO:* Prin. James Woodrow
(502) 588-4223

KENTUCKY TECH—JEFFERSONTOWN VOCATIONAL EDUCATION CENTER
9127-E Galene Dr., Louisville 40299 *Type:* Public (state) technical *System:* Vocational Education Regions 6 and 8 (Jefferson) *Accred.:* 1973/1988 (SACS-COEI) *Calendar:* Courses of varying lengths *Degrees:* certificates *CEO:* Coord. Jim Floyd
(502) 267-9187

KENTUCKY TECH—KENTUCKY ADVANCED TECHNOLOGY CENTER
1845 Loop Dr., Bowling Green 42101 *Type:* Public (state) technical *System:* Vocational Education Region 4 (Barren River) *Accred.:* 1972/1987 (SACS-COEI)*Calendar:* Courses of varying lengths *Degrees:* certificates *CEO:* Coord. Jack Thomas
(502) 843-5807

KENTUCKY TECH—KNOTT COUNTY AREA VOCATIONAL EDUCATION CENTER
HCR 60, Box 1100, Hindman 41822 *Type:* Public (state) technical *System:* Vocational Education Region 12 (Kentucky River) *Accred.:* 1973/1988 (SACS-COEI) *Calendar:* Courses of varying lengths *Degrees:* certificates *CEO:* Coord. Sonny Smith
(606) 785-5350

KENTUCKY TECH—KNOX COUNTY AREA VOCATIONAL EDUCATION CENTER
210 Wall St., Barbourville 40906 *Type:* Public (state) technical *System:* Vocational Education Region 13 (Cumberland Valley) *Accred.:* 1975/1990 (SACS-COEI) *Calendar:* Courses of varying lengths *Degrees:* certificates *CEO:* Coord. Charles Frasier
(606) 546-5320

KENTUCKY TECH—LAGRANGE VOCATIONAL EDUCATION CENTER
3001 W. Hwy. 146, LaGrange 40031 *Type:* Public (state) technical *System:* Vocational Education Regions 6 and 8 (Jefferson)

Accred.: 1973/1988 (SACS-COEI) *Calendar:* Courses of varying lengths *Degrees:* certificates *CEO:* Coord. Margaret Moore
(502) 222-9441

KENTUCKY TECH—LAUREL COUNTY STATE VOCATIONAL-TECHNICAL SCHOOL
235 S. Laurel Rd., London 40741 *Type:* Public (state) technical *System:* Vocational Education Region 13 (Cumberland Valley) *Accred.:* 1975/1990 (SACS-COEI) *Calendar:* Courses of varying lengths *Degrees:* certificates *CEO:* Prin. Donnie Robinson
(606) 864-7311

KENTUCKY TECH—LEE COUNTY AREA VOCATIONAL EDUCATION CENTER
P.O. Box B, Beattyville 41311 *Type:* Public (state) technical *System:* Vocational Education Region 12 (Kentucky River) *Accred.:* 1973/1988 (SACS-COEI)*Calendar:* Courses of varying lengths *Degrees:* certificates *CEO:* Coord. Fred Kincaid
(606) 464-2475

KENTUCKY TECH—LESLIE COUNTY AREA VOCATIONAL EDUCATION CENTER
P.O. Box 902, Hyden 41749 *Type:* Public (state) technical *System:* Vocational Education Region 12 (Kentucky River) *Accred.:* 1973/1988 (SACS-COEI)*Calendar:* Courses of varying lengths *Degrees:* certificates *CEO:* Coord. Betty Huff
(606) 672-2859

KENTUCKY TECH—LETCHER COUNTY AREA VOCATIONAL EDUCATION CENTER
610 Circle Dr., Whitesburg 41858 *System:* Vocational Education Region 12 (Kentucky River) *Accred.:* 1973/1988 (SACS-COEI) *Degrees:* certificates *CEO:* Coord. James G. Estep
(606) 633-5053

KENTUCKY TECH—LUCKETT VOCATIONAL EDUCATION CENTER
1612 Dawkins Rd., Box 6, LaGrange 40031 *Type:* Public (state) technical *System:* Vocational Education Regions 6 and 8 (Jefferson) *Accred.:* 1973/1988 (SACS-COEI) *Calendar:* Courses of varying lengths *Degrees:* certificates *CEO:* Coord. David Visel
(502) 222-0363

KENTUCKY TECH—MADISON COUNTY AREA VOCATIONAL EDUCATION CENTER
P.O. Box 809, 703 N. Second St., Richmond 40476-0809 *Type:* Public (state) technical *System:* Vocational Education Region 15 (Bluegrass) *Accred.:* 1972/1987 (SACS-COEI) *Calendar:* Courses of varying lengths *Degrees:* certificates *CEO:* Coord. Evelyn Watson
(606) 623-4061

KENTUCKY TECH—MADISONVILLE HEALTH OCCUPATIONS CENTER
701 N. Laffoon, Madisonville 42431 *Type:* Public (state) technical *System:* Vocational Education Region 2 (Pennyrile) *Accred.:* 1971/1991 (SACS-COEI)*Calendar:* Courses of varying lengths *Degrees:* certificates *CEO:* Coord. Mary Stanley
(502) 825-6552

KENTUCKY TECH—MADISONVILLE STATE VOCATIONAL-TECHNICAL SCHOOL
150 School Ave., Madisonville 42431 *Type:* Public (state) technical *System:* Vocational Education Region 2 (Pennyrile) *Accred.:* 1971/1991 (SACS-COEI)*Calendar:* Courses of varying lengths *Degrees:* certificates *CEO:* Prin. James Pfeffer
(502) 825-6544

KENTUCKY TECH—MARION COUNTY AREA VOCATIONAL EDUCATION CENTER
Rte. 3, Box 100, Lebanon 40033 *Type:* Public (state) technical *System:* Vocational Education Region 5 (Elizabethtown) *Accred.:* 1974/1987 (SACS-COEI)*Calendar:* Courses of varying lengths *Degrees:* certificates *CEO:* Coord. John Coyle
(502) 692-3155

KENTUCKY TECH—MARTIN COUNTY AREA VOCATIONAL EDUCATION CENTER
HC 68, Box 2177, Inez 41224 *Type:* Public (state) technical *System:* Vocational Education Region 11 (Big Sandy) *Accred.:* 1974/

1989 (SACS-COEI) *Calendar:* Courses of varying lengths *Degrees:* certificates *CEO:* Coord. Robert L. Allen
(606) 298-3879

KENTUCKY TECH—MAYFIELD AREA VOCATIONAL EDUCATION CENTER
710 Doughtit Rd., Mayfield 42066 *Type:* Public (state) technical *System:* Vocational Education Region 1 (Purchase) *Accred.:* 1975/1990 (SACS-COEI)*Calendar:* Courses of varying lengths *Degrees:* certificates *CEO:* Coord. Jim Lawson
(502) 247-4710

KENTUCKY TECH—MAYO STATE VOCATIONAL-TECHNICAL SCHOOL
Third St., Paintsville 41240 *Type:* Public (state) technical *System:* Vocational Education Region 11 (Big Sandy) *Accred.:* 1974/1989 (SACS-COEI) *Calendar:* Courses of varying lengths *Degrees:* certificates *CEO:* Prin. Gary Coleman
(606) 789-5321

KENTUCKY TECH—MAYSVILLE AREA VOCATIONAL EDUCATION CENTER
646 Kent Station Rd., Maysville 41056 *Type:* Public (state) technical *System:* Vocational Education Region 9 (Buffalo Trace) *Accred.:* 1975/1988 (SACS-COEI) *Calendar:* Courses of varying lengths *Degrees:* certificates *CEO:* Coord. Glenn Collins
(606) 759-7101

KENTUCKY TECH—MEADE COUNTY AREA VOCATIONAL EDUCATION CENTER
Old State Rd., Brandenburg 40108 *Type:* Public (state) technical *System:* Vocational Education Region 5 (Elizabethtown) *Accred.:* 1974/1987 (SACS-COEI) *Calendar:* Courses of varying lengths *Degrees:* certificates *CEO:* Coord. William Whalen
(502) 422-3955

KENTUCKY TECH—MILLARD AREA VOCATIONAL EDUCATION CENTER
430 Millard Hwy., Pikeville 41501 *Type:* Public (state) technical *System:* Vocational Education Region 11 (Big Sandy) *Accred.:* 1974/1989 (SACS-COEI)*Calendar:* Courses of varying lengths *Degrees:* certificates *CEO:* Prin. William Justice
(606) 437-6059

KENTUCKY TECH—MONROE COUNTY AREA VOCATIONAL EDUCATION CENTER
4th and Emmerton Sts., Tompkinsville 42167 *Type:* Public (state) technical *System:* Vocational Education Region 4 (Barren River) *Accred.:* 1972/1987 (SACS-COEI) *Calendar:* Courses of varying lengths *Degrees:* certificates *CEO:* Coord. Bill Polland
(502) 487-8261

KENTUCKY TECH—MONTGOMERY COUNTY AREA VOCATIONAL EDUCATION CENTER
682 Woodford Dr., Mount Sterling 40353 *Type:* Public (state) technical *System:* Vocational Education Region 9 (Buffalo Trace) *Accred.:* 1975/1988 (SACS-COEI) *Calendar:* Courses of varying lengths *Degrees:* certificates *CEO:* Coord. Norma Willoughby
(606) 498-1103

KENTUCKY TECH—MOREHEAD TREATMENT CENTER
100 Pine Crest Rd., Morehead 40351 *Type:* Public (state) technical *System:* Vocational Education Region 9 (Buffalo Trace) *Accred.:* 1975/1988 (SACS-COEI)*Calendar:* Courses of varying lengths *Degrees:* certificates *CEO:* Acting Supt. Jamie Brown
(606) 784-6421

KENTUCKY TECH—MORGAN COUNTY AREA VOCATIONAL EDUCATION CENTER
P.O. Box 249, West Liberty 41472 *Type:* Public (state) technical *System:* Vocational Education Region 9 (Buffalo Trace) *Accred.:* 1975/1988 (SACS-COEI)*Calendar:* Courses of varying lengths *Degrees:* certificates *CEO:* Coord. Willis Lyon
(606) 743-4321

KENTUCKY TECH—MUHLENBERG COUNTY AREA VOCATIONAL EDUCATION CENTER
R.R. Box 67, Greenville 42345 *Type:* Public (state) technical *System:* Vocational Education Region 2 (Pennyrile) *Accred.:* 1971/

Kentucky

1991 (SACS-COEI) *Calendar:* Courses of varying lengths *Degrees:* certificates *CEO:* Coord. Andrew Swansey
(502) 338-1271

KENTUCKY TECH—MURRAY AREA VOCATIONAL EDUCATION CENTER
18th and Sycamore Sts., Murray 42071 *Type:* Public (state) technical *System:* Vocational Education Region 1 (Purchase) *Accred.:* 1975/1990 (SACS-COEI) *Calendar:* Courses of varying lengths *Degrees:* certificates *CEO:* Prin. Lynn Tackett
(502) 753-1870

KENTUCKY TECH—NELSON COUNTY AREA VOCATIONAL EDUCATION CENTER
1060 Bloomfield Rd., Bardstown 40004 *Type:* Public (state) technical *System:* Vocational Education Region 5 (Elizabethtown) *Accred.:* 1974/1987 (SACS-COEI) *Calendar:* Courses of varying lengths *Degrees:* certificates *CEO:* Coord. John T. Kromer
(502) 348-9096

KENTUCKY TECH—NORTHERN CAMPBELL COUNTY VOCATIONAL-TECHNICAL SCHOOL
Campbell Dr., Highland Heights 41076 *Type:* Public (state) technical *System:* Vocational Education Region 7 (Northern Kentucky) *Accred.:* 1973/1988 (SACS-COEI) *Calendar:* Courses of varying lengths *Degrees:* certificates *CEO:* Coord. Earl Wittenrock
(606) 441-2010

KENTUCKY TECH—NORTHERN KENTUCKY HEALTH OCCUPATIONS CENTER
790 Thomas More Pkwy., Edgewood 41017 *Type:* Public (state) technical *System:* Vocational Education Region 7 (Northern Kentucky) *Accred.:* 1973/1988 (SACS-COEI) *Calendar:* Courses of varying lengths *Degrees:* certificates *CEO:* Coord. Wade Halsey
(606) 341-5200

KENTUCKY TECH—NORTHERN KENTUCKY STATE VOCATIONAL-TECHNICAL SCHOOL
1025 Amsterdam Rd., Covington 41011 *Type:* Public (state) technical *System:* Vocational Education Region 7 (Northern Kentucky) *Accred.:* 1973/1988 (SACS-COEI) *Calendar:* Courses of varying lengths *Degrees:* certificates *CEO:* Prin. Edward Burton
(606) 431-2700

KENTUCKY TECH—NORTHPOINT EDUCATION CENTER
P.O. Box 479, Burgin 40310 *Type:* Public (state) technical *System:* Vocational Education Region 15 (Bluegrass) *Accred.:* 1972/1987 (SACS-COEI) *Calendar:* Courses of varying lengths *Degrees:* certificates *CEO:* Coord. Luther Spotts
(606) 236-9012

KENTUCKY TECH—OHIO COUNTY AREA VOCATIONAL EDUCATION CENTER
P.O. Box 1406, U.S. 231 S., Hartford 42347 *Type:* Public (state) technical *System:* Vocational Education Region 3 (Green River) *Accred.:* 1973/1988 (SACS-COEI) *Calendar:* Courses of varying lengths *CEO:* Coord. Ray Price
(502) 274-9612

KENTUCKY TECH—OLDHAM COUNTY VOCATIONAL EDUCATION CENTER
P.O. Box 127, Hwy. 393, Buckner 40065 *Type:* Public (state) technical *System:* Vocational Education Regions 6 and 8 (Jefferson) *Accred.:* 1973/1988 (SACS-COEI) *Calendar:* Courses of varying lengths *Degrees:* certificates *CEO:* Prin. Jeanette Stratton
(502) 222-0131

KENTUCKY TECH—OWENSBORO VOCATIONAL-TECHNICAL SCHOOL
1501 Frederica St., Owensboro 42301 *Type:* Public (state) technical *System:* Vocational Education Region 3 (Green River) *Accred.:* 1973/1988 (SACS-COEI)*Calendar:* Courses of varying lengths *Degrees:* certificates *CEO:* Prin. Tara Parker
(502) 686-3255

KENTUCKY TECH—PADUCAH AREA VOCATIONAL EDUCATION CENTER
2400 Adams St., Paducah 42001 *Type:* Public (state) technical *System:* Vocational

Education Region 1 (Purchase) *Accred.:* 1975/1990 (SACS-COEI)*Calendar:* Courses of varying lengths *Degrees:* certificates *CEO:* Prin. Robert Rouff
(502) 443-6592

KENTUCKY TECH—PATTON VOCATIONAL EDUCATION CENTER
3234 Turkeyfoot Rd., Fort Mitchell 41017 *Type:* Public (state) technical *System:* Vocational Education Region 7 (Northern Kentucky) *Accred.:* 1973/1988 (SACS-COEI) *Calendar:* Courses of varying lengths *Degrees:* certificates *CEO:* Coord. Eugene Penn
(606) 341-2266

KENTUCKY TECH—PEEWEE VALLEY EDUCATION CENTER
P.O. Box 337, Peewee Valley 40056 *Type:* Public (state) technical *System:* Vocational Education Regions 6 and 8 (Jefferson) *Accred.:* 1973/1988 (SACS-COEI) *Calendar:* Courses of varying lengths *Degrees:* certificates *CEO:* Prin. Vivian Whitehouse
(502) 241-8454

KENTUCKY TECH—PHELPS AREA VOCATIONAL EDUCATION CENTER
HC 67, No. 1002, Phelps 41553 *Type:* Public (state) technical *System:* Vocational Education Region 11 (Big Sandy) *Accred.:* 1974/1989 (SACS-COEI) *Calendar:* Courses of varying lengths *Degrees:* certificates *CEO:* Prin. Curtis Akers
(606) 456-8136

KENTUCKY TECH—ROCKCASTLE COUNTY AREA VOCATIONAL EDUCATION CENTER
P.O. Box 275, Mount Vernon 40456 *Type:* Public (state) technical *System:* Vocational Education Region 13 (Cumberland Valley) *Accred.:* 1975/1990 (SACS-COEI) *Calendar:* Courses of varying lengths *Degrees:* certificates *Prof. Accred.:* Respiratory Therapy Technology *CEO:* Coord. Donna Hopkins
(606) 256-4346

KENTUCKY TECH—ROWAN STATE VOCATIONAL-TECHNICAL SCHOOL
100 Vo-Tech Dr., Morehead 40351 *Type:* Public (state) technical *System:* Vocational Education Region 9 (Buffalo Trace) *Accred.:* 1975/1988 (SACS-COEI)*Calendar:* Courses of varying lengths *Degrees:* certificates *CEO:* Prin. Jamie Brown
(606) 783-1538

KENTUCKY TECH—RUSSELL AREA VOCATIONAL EDUCATION CENTER
705 Red Devil La., Russell 41169 *Type:* Public (state) technical *System:* Vocational Education Region 10 (Fivco) *Accred.:* 1971/1989 (SACS-COEI) *Calendar:* Courses of varying lengths *Degrees:* certificates *CEO:* Coord. Michael Chapman
(606) 836-1256

KENTUCKY TECH—RUSSELL COUNTY AREA VOCATIONAL EDUCATION CENTER
P.O. Box 599, Russell Springs 42642 *Type:* Public (state) technical *System:* Vocational Education Region 14 (Lake Cumberland) *Accred.:* 1974/1989 (SACS-COEI) *Calendar:* Courses of varying lengths *Degrees:* certificates *CEO:* Prin. Chester Taylor
(502) 866-6175

KENTUCKY TECH—RUSSELLVILLE AREA VOCATIONAL EDUCATION CENTER
1103 W. 9th St., Russellville 42276 *Type:* Public (state) technical *System:* Vocational Education Region 4 (Barren River) *Accred.:* 1972/1987 (SACS-COEI)*Calendar:* Courses of varying lengths *Degrees:* certificates *CEO:* Coord. Maurice Grayson
(502) 726-8433

KENTUCKY TECH—SHELBY COUNTY AREA VOCATIONAL EDUCATION CENTER
Rte. 7, Box 331, Shelbyville 40065 *Type:* Public (state) technical *System:* Vocational Education Regions 6 and 8 (Jefferson) *Accred.:* 1973/1988 (SACS-COEI) *Calendar:* Courses of varying lengths *Degrees:* certificates *CEO:* Coord. Ruth Bunch
(502) 633-6554

Kentucky

KENTUCKY TECH—SOMERSET STATE VOCATIONAL-TECHNICAL SCHOOL
714 Airport Rd., Somerset 42501 *Type:* Public (state) technical *System:* Vocational Education Region 14 (Lake Cumberland) *Accred.:* 1974/1989 (SACS-COEI) *Calendar:* Courses of varying lengths *Degrees:* certificates *CEO:* Prin. J.P. McCarty
(606) 679-4303

KENTUCKY TECH—UNION COUNTY AREA VOCATIONAL EDUCATION CENTER
Rte. 4, Morganfield 42437 *Type:* Public (state) technical *System:* Vocational Education Region 3 (Green River) *Accred.:* 1973/1988 (SACS-COEI) *Calendar:* Courses of varying lengths *Degrees:* certificates *CEO:* Coord. Michael Helm
(502) 389-3120

KENTUCKY TECH—WAYNE COUNTY AREA VOCATIONAL EDUCATION CENTER
Rte. 4, Box 1B, Monticello 42633 *Type:* Public (state) technical *System:* Vocational Education Region 14 (Lake Cumberland) *Accred.:* 1974/1989 (SACS-COEI) *Calendar:* Courses of varying lengths *Degrees:* certificates *CEO:* Coord. Sharon Tiller
(606) 348-8424

KENTUCKY TECH—WEBSTER COUNTY AREA VOCATIONAL EDUCATION CENTER
P.O. Box 188, Dixon 42409 *Type:* Public (state) technical *System:* Vocational Education Region 2 (Pennyrile) *Accred.:* 1971/1991 (SACS-COEI) *Calendar:* Courses of varying lengths *Degrees:* certificates *CEO:* Coord. Claude Hicks
(502) 639-5035

KENTUCKY TECH—WEST KENTUCKY STATE VOCATIONAL-TECHNICAL SCHOOL
Blandville Rd., P.O. Box 7408, Paducah 42002-7408 *Type:* Public (state) technical *System:* Vocational Education Region 1 (Purchase) *Accred.:* 1975/1990 (SACS-COEI) *Calendar:* Courses of varying lengths *Degrees:* certificates *Prof. Accred.:* Dental Assisting, Diagnostic Medical Sonography, Medical Assisting, Physical Therapy Assisting, Radiography, Respiratory Therapy, Surgical Technology *CEO:* Prin. William D. Houston
(502) 554-4991

PURCHASE TRAINING CENTER
Rte. 2, Lee Powell Rd., Mayfield, KY 42006 *CEO:* Acting Dir. Bob Town
(502) 247-9633

KENTUCKY TECH—WOODSBEND BOYS' CAMP
Rte. 1, Box 765, West Liberty 41472 *Type:* Public (state) technical *System:* Vocational Education Region 9 (Buffalo Trace) *Accred.:* 1975/1988 (SACS-COEI)*Calendar:* Courses of varying lengths *Degrees:* certificates *CEO:* Prin. Willis Lyon
(606) 743-3177

KENTUCKY WESLEYAN COLLEGE
3000 Frederica St., P.O. Box 1039, Owensboro 42302-1039 *Type:* Private (United Methodist) liberal arts *Accred.:* 1948/1988 (SACS-CC) *Calendar:* Sem. plan *Degrees:* A, B *CEO:* Pres. Paul W. Hartman
Enroll: 665   (502) 926-3111

LEES COLLEGE
601 Jefferson Ave., Jackson 41339 *Type:* Private (Presbyterian) *Accred.:* 1951/1989 (SACS-CC) *Calendar:* Sem. plan *Degrees:* A *CEO:* Pres. William B. Bradshaw
Enroll: 352   (606) 666-7521

LEXINGTON COMMUNITY COLLEGE
Oswald Bldg., Cooper Dr., Lexington 40506-0235 *Type:* Public junior *System:* University of Kentucky Community College System *Accred.:* 1965/1991 (SACS-CC) *Calendar:* Sem. plan *Degrees:* A *Prof. Accred.:* Dental Hygiene, Dental Laboratory Technology, Nuclear Medicine Technology, Nursing (A), Radiography, Respiratory Therapy *CEO:* Pres. Allen G. Edwards
Enroll: 3425   (606) 257-4831

LEXINGTON THEOLOGICAL SEMINARY
631 S. Limestone St., Lexington 40508 *Type:* Private (Disciples of Christ) professional; graduate only *Accred.:* 1938/1983 (ATS); 1984 (SACS-CC) *Calendar:* Sem.

plan *Degrees:* P, M, D *CEO:* Pres. William O. Paulsell
Enroll: 107 (606) 252-0361

LINDSEY WILSON COLLEGE
210 Lindsey Wilson St., Columbia 42728 *Type:* Private (United Methodist) junior *Accred.:* 1951/1985 (SACS-CC) *Calendar:* Sem. plan *Degrees:* A, B *CEO:* Pres. John B. Begley
Enroll: 1451 (502) 384-2126

LOUISVILLE PRESBYTERIAN THEOLOGICAL SEMINARY
1044 Alta Vista Rd., Louisville 40205-1798 *Type:* Private (Presbyterian) professional; graduate only *Accred.:* 1938/1989 (ATS); 1973/1989 (SACS-CC) *Calendar:* 4-1-4 plan *Degrees:* P, M, D *CEO:* Pres. John M. Mulder
Enroll: 177 (502) 895-3411

LOUISVILLE TECHNICAL INSTITUTE
Atkinson Sq., 3901 Atkinson Dr., Louisville 40218 *Type:* Private *Accred.:* 1974/1983 (CCA-ACTTS) *Calendar:* Qtr. plan *Degrees:* A, certificates, diplomas *CEO:* Dir. David B. Keene
Enroll: 625 (502) 456-6509

MADISONVILLE COMMUNITY COLLEGE
2000 College Dr., Madisonville 42431 *Type:* Public junior *System:* University of Kentucky Community College System *Accred.:* 1968/1991 (SACS-CC) *Calendar:* Sem. plan *Degrees:* A *Prof. Accred.:* Respiratory Therapy *CEO:* Pres. Arthur D. Stumpf
Enroll: 1483 (502) 821-2250

MARSHALL COUNTY AREA VOCATIONAL EDUCATION CENTER
Rte. 7, Box 100-A, Benton 42025 *Type:* Public (state) technical *Accred.:* 1975 (SACS-CC); 1975/1990 (SACS-COEI) *Calendar:* Courses of varying lengths *Degrees:* certificates *CEO:* Dir. James Cothran
Enroll: 94 (502) 527-8648

MAYSVILLE COMMUNITY COLLEGE
Rte. 2, Maysville 41056 *Type:* Public junior *System:* University of Kentucky Community College System *Accred.:* 1968/1991 (SACS-CC) *Calendar:* Sem. plan *Degrees:* A *CEO:* Pres. James C. Shires
Enroll: 720 (606) 759-7141

MID-CONTINENT BAPTIST BIBLE COLLEGE
P.O. Box 7010, Mayfield 42066 *Type:* Private (Baptist) professional *Accred.:* 1987 (SACS-CC) *Calendar:* Sem. plan *Degrees:* B *CEO:* Pres. LaVerne Butler
Enroll: 74 (502) 247-8521

MIDWAY COLLEGE
512 E. Stephens St., Midway 40347-1120 *Type:* Private junior for women *Accred.:* 1949/1984 (SACS-CC) *Calendar:* Sem. plan *Degrees:* A, B *Prof. Accred.:* Nursing (A) *CEO:* Pres. Robert Botkin
Enroll: 492 (606) 846-4421

MOREHEAD STATE UNIVERSITY
Morehead 40351-1663 *Type:* Public *System:* Kentucky Council on Higher Education *Accred.:* 1930/1990 (SACS-CC) *Calendar:* Sem. plan *Degrees:* A, B, M *Prof. Accred.:* Music, Nursing (B), Radiography, Social Work (B), Teacher Education (e,s,p), Veterinary Technology *CEO:* Pres. C. Nelson Grote
Enroll: 7427 (606) 783-2221

MURRAY STATE UNIVERSITY
Murray 42071-3305 *Type:* Public *System:* Kentucky Council on Higher Education *Accred.:* 1928/1984 (SACS-CC) *Calendar:* Sem. plan *Degrees:* A, B, M *Prof. Accred.:* Animal Health Technology (probational), Art, Business (B,M), Counseling, Engineering Technology (civil/construction, electrical, manufacturing), Journalism, Music, Nursing (B), Social Work (B), Speech-Language Pathology, Teacher Education (e,s,p) *CEO:* Pres. Ronald J. Kurth
Enroll: 7242 (502) 762-3011

NATIONAL EDUCATION CENTER—KENTUCKY COLLEGE OF TECHNOLOGY
300 Highrise Dr., Louisville 40213 *Type:* Private *Accred.:* 1968/1986 (CCA-ACTTS)

Kentucky

Calendar: Qtr. plan *Degrees:* A *CEO:* Dir. Jim Vernon
Enroll: 1164 (502) 966-5555

NEW IMAGE COLLEGE OF COSMETOLOGY
109 E. Sixth St., Corbin 40701 *Type:* Private *Accred.:* 1984/1989 (SACS-COEI) *Calendar:* Courses of varying lengths *Degrees:* certificates *CEO:* Dir. Wanda Powers
Enroll: 92 (606) 528-1490

NORTHERN KENTUCKY UNIVERSITY
Highland Heights 41076-1448 *Type:* Public *System:* Kentucky Council on Higher Education *Accred.:* 1973/1988 (SACS-CC) *Calendar:* Sem. plan *Degrees:* A, B, P, M, D *Prof. Accred.:* Dental Hygiene, Law, Music, Nursing (A,B), Radiography, Social Work (B), Teacher Education (e,s) *CEO:* Pres. Leon E. Boothe
Enroll: 8269 (606) 572-5100

NU-TEK ACADEMY OF BEAUTY
Mount Sterling Plaza, Ste. 6, Mount Sterling 40353 *Type:* Private *Accred.:* 1990 (SACS-COEI) *Calendar:* Courses of varying lengths *Degrees:* certificates, diplomas *CEO:* Dir. Thelma C. Horton
Enroll: 25 (606) 498-4460

OWENSBORO COMMUNITY COLLEGE
4800 New Hartford Rd., Owensboro 42303 *Type:* Public junior *System:* University of Kentucky Community College System *Accred.:* 1990 (SACS-CC) *Calendar:* Sem. plan *Degrees:* A *CEO:* Pres. John M. McGuire
Enroll: 1662 (502) 686-4400

OWENSBORO JUNIOR COLLEGE OF BUSINESS
1515 E. 18th St., Owensboro 42303 *Type:* Private junior *Accred.:* 1969/1990 (CCA-ACICS) *Calendar:* Tri. plan *Degrees:* A, certificates, diplomas *CEO:* Dir. Lenda Anderson
Enroll: 625 (502) 926-4040

PJ'S COLLEGE OF COSMETOLOGY
Russellville Rd., Bowling Green 42101 *Type:* Private *Accred.:* 1986/1991 (SACS-COEI) *Calendar:* Courses of varying lengths

Accredited Institutions

Degrees: certificates *CEO:* Dir. Judith Stewart
Enroll: 218 (502) 842-8149

BRANCH CAMPUS
113 N. Washington St., Crawfordsville, IN 47933 *CEO:* Dir. Judith Stewart
(800) 627-2566

BRANCH CAMPUS
1400 W. Main St., Greenfield, IN 46140 *CEO:* Dir. Judith Stewart
(800) 627-2566

BRANCH CAMPUS
5539 S. Madison Ave., Indianapolis, IN 46227 *CEO:* Dir. Judith Stewart
(800) 627-2566

BRANCH CAMPUS
3023 S. Lafountain St., Kokomo, IN 46902 *CEO:* Dir. Judith Stewart
(800) 627-2566

BRANCH CAMPUS
2006 N. Walnut St., Muncie, IN 47303 *CEO:* Dir. Judith Stewart
(800) 627-2566

BRANCH CAMPUS
2026 Stafford Rd., Plainfield, IN 46168 *CEO:* Dir. Judith Stewart
(800) 627-2566

BRANCH CAMPUS
207 E. Main St., Washington, IN 47501 *CEO:* Dir. Judith Stewart
(800) 627-2566

PJ'S COLLEGE OF COSMETOLOGY
124 W. Washington St., Glasgow 42141 *Type:* Private *Accred.:* 1987 (SACS-COEI) *Calendar:* Courses of varying lengths *Degrees:* certificates *CEO:* Dir. Rita Aikins
Enroll: 27 (502) 651-6553

PADUCAH COMMUNITY COLLEGE
Alben Barkley Dr., P.O. Box 7380, Paducah 42002-7380 *Type:* Public junior *System:* University of Kentucky Community College System *Accred.:* 1932/1991 (SACS-CC)

Calendar: Sem. plan *Degrees:* A *Prof. Accred.:* Nursing (A), Physical Therapy Assisting *CEO:* Pres. Leonard O'Hara
Enroll: 2034   (502) 554-9200

PHILLIPS COLLEGE
1512 Crums La., Louisville 40216 *Type:* Private *Accred.:* 1978/1988 (CCA-ACTTS) *Calendar:* Courses of varying lengths *Degrees:* A, diplomas *Prof. Accred.:* Dental Laboratory Technology, Medical Assisting, Medical Laboratory Technology (AMA) *CEO:* Dir. David Nance
Enroll: 1022   (502) 448-1800

PIKEVILLE COLLEGE
214 Sycamore St., Pikeville 41501-1194 *Type:* Private (United Presbyterian) liberal arts *Accred.:* 1961/1982 (SACS-CC) *Calendar:* Sem. plan *Degrees:* A, B *CEO:* Pres. William H. Owens
Enroll: 996   (606) 432-9200

PRESTONSBURG COMMUNITY COLLEGE
One Bert T. Combs Dr., Prestonsburg 41653 *Type:* Public junior *System:* University of Kentucky Community College System *Accred.:* 1964/1991 (SACS-CC) *Calendar:* Sem. plan *Degrees:* A *CEO:* Pres. Deborah Lee Floyd
Enroll: 2091   (606) 886-3863

R.E.T.S. ELECTRONIC INSTITUTE
4146 Outer Loop, Louisville 40219 *Type:* Private *Accred.:* 1978 (CCA-ACTTS) *Calendar:* Sem. plan *Degrees:* A *CEO:* Pres. Robert Woolridge
Enroll: 1310   (502) 968-7191

ROY'S OF LOUISVILLE BEAUTY ACADEMY
151 Chenowith La., Louisville 40207 *Type:* Private *Accred.:* 1989 (SACS-COEI) *Calendar:* Courses of varying lengths *Degrees:* certificates *CEO:* Dir. Thomas Esrey
Enroll: 212   (502) 897-9401

BRANCH CAMPUS
5200 Dixie Hwy., Louisville, KY 40216 *CEO:* Dir. Thomas Esrey
   (502) 448-1016

ST. CATHARINE COLLEGE
Hwy. 150, St. Catharine 40061 *Type:* Private (Roman Catholic) junior *Accred.:* 1957/1988 (SACS-CC) *Calendar:* Sem. plan *Degrees:* A *CEO:* Pres. Martha L. Collins
Enroll: 207   (606) 336-9303

SOMERSET COMMUNITY COLLEGE
808 Monticello Rd., Somerset 42501-2999 *Type:* Public junior *System:* University of Kentucky Community College System *Accred.:* 1965/1991 (SACS-CC) *Calendar:* Sem. plan *Degrees:* A *Prof. Accred.:* Medical Laboratory Technology (AMA), Physical Therapy Assisting *CEO:* Pres. Rollin J. Watson
Enroll: 1766   (606) 679-8501

SOUTHEAST COMMUNITY COLLEGE
300 College Rd., Cumberland 40823-1099 *Type:* Public junior *System:* University of Kentucky Community College System *Accred.:* 1960/1991 (SACS-CC) *Calendar:* Sem. plan *Degrees:* A *CEO:* Pres. W. Bruce Ayers
Enroll: 1571   (606) 589-2145

THE SOUTHERN BAPTIST THEOLOGICAL SEMINARY
2825 Lexington Rd., Louisville 40280 *Type:* Private (Southern Baptist) professional; graduate only *Accred.:* 1938/1983 (ATS); 1968/1983 (SACS-CC) *Calendar:* Sem. plan *Degrees:* P, M, D *Prof. Accred.:* Music, Social Work (M) *CEO:* Pres. Roy L. Honeycutt
   (502) 897-4011

SPALDING UNIVERSITY
851 S. Fourth St., Louisville 40203-2115 *Type:* Private (Roman Catholic) liberal arts *Accred.:* 1938/1986 (SACS-CC) *Calendar:* Sem. plan *Degrees:* A, B, M, D *Prof. Accred.:* Clinical Psychology (provisional), Dietetics (coordinated), Nursing (B,M), Social Work (B), Teacher Education (e,s,p) *CEO:* Pres. Eileen M. Egan
Enroll: 732   (502) 585-9911

Kentucky

SPENCERIAN COLLEGE
914 E. Broadway, Louisville 40204 *Type:* Private business *Accred.:* 1954/1987 (CCA-ACICS); 1977/1987 (SACS-COEI) *Calendar:* Qtr. plan *Degrees:* certificates, diplomas *Prof.Accred.:* Medical Assisting (AMA) *CEO:* Exec. Dir. David E. Gray
Enroll: 245 (502) 584-7105

SUE BENNETT COLLEGE
151 College Street, London 40741 *Type:* Private (United Methodist) junior *Accred.:* 1932/ 1985 (SACS-CC) *Calendar:* Sem. plan *Degrees:* A *CEO:* Pres. Paul G. Bunnell
Enroll: 455 (606) 864-2238

SULLIVAN COLLEGE
3101 Bardstown Rd., Louisville 40232 *Type:* Private junior *Accred.:* 1965/1988 (CCA-ACICS); 1979/1991 (SACS-CC) *Calendar:* Qtr. plan *Degrees:* A, B (candidate), certificates, diplomas *CEO:* Pres. A.R. Sullivan
Enroll: 1909 (502) 456-6504

BRANCH CAMPUS
2659 Regency Rd., Lexington, KY 40503 *CEO:* Vice Pres./Dir. Bill Noel
(606) 276-4357

THOMAS MORE COLLEGE
333 Thomas More Pkwy., Crestview Hills 41017-3428 *Type:* Private (Roman Catholic) liberal arts *Accred.:* 1959/1990 (SACS-CC) *Calendar:* Sem. plan *Degrees:* A, B *Prof. Accred.:* Nursing (B), Social Work (B) *CEO:* Pres. Charles J. Bensman
Enroll: 1084 (606) 341-5800

TRANSYLVANIA UNIVERSITY
300 N. Broadway, Lexington 40508 *Type:* Private liberal arts *Accred.:* 1915/1983 (SACS-CC) *Calendar:* 4-4-1 plan *Degrees:* B *CEO:* Pres. Charles L. Shearer
Enroll: 1058 (606) 233-8300

TRI-STATE BEAUTY ACADEMY
219 W. Main St., Morehead 40351 *Type:* Private *Accred.:* 1983/1988 (SACS-COEI) *Calendar:* Courses of varying lengths *Degrees:* certificates *CEO:* Dir. Betty Stucky
Enroll: 53 (606) 784-6725

UNION COLLEGE
310 College St., Barbourville 40906 *Type:* Private (United Methodist) liberal arts *Accred.:* 1932/1984 (SACS-CC) *Calendar:* Sem. plan *Degrees:* A, B, M *CEO:* Pres. Jack C. Phillips
Enroll: 800 (606) 546-4151

UNIVERSITY OF KENTUCKY
Lexington 40506-0032 *Type:* Public (state) *System:* Kentucky Council on Higher Education *Accred.:* 1915/1982 (SACS-CC) *Calendar:* Sem. plan *Degrees:* A, B, P, M, D *Prof. Accred.:* Accounting (Type A,C), Architecture (B), Business (B,M), Clinical Psychology, Counseling Psychology, Dentistry, Dietetics (coordinated), Engineering (agricultural, chemical, civil, electrical, mechanical, metallurgical, mining), Forestry, General Practice Residency, Home Economics, Interior Design, Journalism, Landscape Architecture (B-provisional), Law, Librarianship, Medical Technology, Medicine, Music, Nursing (B,M), Oral and Maxillofacial Surgery, Orthodontics, Pediatric Dentistry, Periodontics, Pharmacy, Physical Therapy, Physician Assisting, Public Administration, Radiation Therapy Technology, Recreation and Leisure Studies, Rehabilitation Counseling, School Psychology, Social Work (B,M), Speech-Language Pathology, Teacher Education (e,s,p) *CEO:* Pres. Charles T. Wethington, Jr.
Enroll: 18336 (606) 257-9000

UNIVERSITY OF LOUISVILLE
Louisville 40292-0001 *Type:* Public (state) *System:* Kentucky Council on Higher Education *Accred.:* 1915/1987 (SACS-CC) *Calendar:* Sem. plan *Degrees:* A, B, P, M, D, certificates *Prof. Accred.:* Accounting (Type A), Audiology, Business (B,M), Clinical Psychology, Combined Prosthodontics, Cytotechnology, Dental Hygiene, Dentistry, Endodontics, Engineering (chemical, civil, computer, electrical, industrial, mechanical), General Dentistry, General Practice Residency, Law, Medical Technology, Medicine, Music, Nuclear Medicine Technology, Nursing (B,M), Oral and Maxillofacial Surgery,

Orthodontics, Physical Therapy, Psychology Internship, Radiography, Respiratory Therapy, Social Work (M), Speech-Language Pathology, Teacher Education (e,s,p) *CEO:* Pres. Donald C. Swain
Enroll: 18297 (502) 588-5555

VOGUE COLLEGE OF HAIR DESIGN
2331 Alexandria Pike, Highland Heights 41076-1313 *Type:* Private *Accred.:* 1983/1988 (SACS-COEI) *Calendar:* Courses of varying lengths *Degrees:* certificates *CEO:* Dir. Diane Hight
Enroll: 298 (606) 781-1554

WATTERSON CAREER CENTER
915 S. Third St., Louisville 40203 *Type:* Private business *Accred.:* 1989 (CCA-ACTTS) *Calendar:* Courses of varying lengths *Degrees:* certificates, diplomas *CEO:* Dir. Fred Curtis
Enroll: 404 (502) 585-1670

WATTERSON COLLEGE
4400 Breckinridge La., Louisville 40218 *Type:* Private junior *Accred.:* 1965/1989 (CCA-ACICS); 1982 (SACS-CC) *Calendar:* Qtr. plan *Degrees:* A, certificates, diplomas *CEO:* Pres. John Mathias
Enroll: 817 (502) 491-5000

BRANCH CAMPUS
Fairfield Park, 1064 Gardner Rd., Ste. 105, Charleston, SC 29407 *CEO:* Dir. Carol L. Feldman
(803) 571-4000

WESTERN KENTUCKY UNIVERSITY
Bowling Green 42101-3576 *Type:* Public (state) *System:* Kentucky Council on Higher Education *Accred.:* 1926/1984 (SACS-CC) *Calendar:* Sem. plan *Degrees:* A, B, M *Prof. Accred.:* Art, Business (B), Dental Hygiene, Engineering Technology (civil/construction, electrical, mechanical), Journalism, Medical Record Technology, Music, Nursing (A,B), Recreation and Park Administration, Social Work (B), Teacher Education (e,s,p) *CEO:* Pres. Thomas C. Meredith
Enroll: 14449 (502) 745-0111

LOUISIANA

ACADIANA TECHNICAL COLLEGE
500 Ambassador Caffery Pkwy., P.O. Box 633, Scott 70583 *Type:* Private business *Accred.:* 1985 (CCA-ACICS) *Calendar:* Courses of varying lengths *Degrees:* A, certificates, diplomas *CEO:* Pres. Lester J. Mitchell
Enroll: 804 (318) 235-7327

ALEXANDRIA REGIONAL TECHNICAL INSTITUTE
P.O. Box 5698, 4311 S. MacArthur Dr., Alexandria 71307-5698 *Type:* Public (state) *Accred.:* 1976/1991 (SACS-COEI) *Calendar:* Courses of varying lengths *Degrees:* certificates *CEO:* Dir. Patricia F. Juneau
Enroll: 328 (318) 487-5698

AMERICAN COLLEGE
2559 Plank Rd., Baton Rouge 70805 *Type:* Private *Accred.:* 1986/1990 (SACS-COEI) *Calendar:* Courses of varying lengths *Degrees:* certificates *CEO:* Dir. Glenda Grice
Enroll: 81 (504) 355-7500

AMERICAN COLLEGE
2025 Canal St., Ste. 210, New Orleans 70112 *Type:* Private *Accred.:* 1986/1990 (SACS-COEI) *Calendar:* Courses of varying lengths *Degrees:* certificates *CEO:* Dir. Robert Bradley
Enroll: 149 (504) 522-8824

AMERICAN COLLEGE
820 Cotton St., Shreveport 71101 *Type:* Private *Accred.:* 1990 (SACS-COEI) *Calendar:* Courses of varying lengths *Degrees:* certificates *CEO:* Dir. Arthur Lovett
Enroll: 81 (318) 424-1000

AMERICAN SCHOOL OF BUSINESS
701 Professional Dr. N., Shreveport 71105 *Type:* Private business *Accred.:* 1988 (CCA-ACICS) *Calendar:* Courses of varying lengths *Degrees:* certificates, diplomas *CEO:* Dir. Jerry W. Wood
Enroll: 233 (318) 798-3333

AMERICO TECHNICAL CAREER INSTITUTE
4900 Chef Menteur Hwy., New Orleans 70126 *Type:* Private *Accred.:* 1985/1990 (SACS-COEI) *Calendar:* Courses of varying lengths *Degrees:* certificates *CEO:* Dir. Joseph Lieman
Enroll: 120 (504) 943-7373

ASCENSION COLLEGE
320 E. Ascension St., Gonzales 70737 *Type:* Private technical *Accred.:* 1991 (SACS-COEI) *Calendar:* Courses of varying lengths *Degrees:* certificates, diplomas *CEO:* Dir. Midge Jacobsen
Enroll: 10 (504) 647-6609

ASCENSION TECHNICAL INSTITUTE
9697 Airline Hwy., P.O. Box 38, Sorrento 70778 *Type:* Public (state) *Accred.:* 1982/1987 (SACS-COEI) *Calendar:* Courses of varying lengths *Degrees:* certificates *CEO:* Dir. Charles A. Tassin
Enroll: 175 (504) 675-5397

AVOYELLES TECHNICAL INSTITUTE
P.O. Box 307, Choupique St., Cottonport 71327 *Type:* Public (state) *Accred.:* 1979/1991 (SACS-COEI) *Calendar:* Courses of varying lengths *Degrees:* certificates *CEO:* Dir. Ward Nash
Enroll: 230 (318) 876-2701

AYERS INSTITUTE
3003 Knight St., Ste. 244, Shreveport 71105 *Type:* Private business *Accred.:* 1963/1986 (CCA-ACICS) *Calendar:* Courses of varying lengths *Degrees:* certificates, diplomas *CEO:* Pres. Pat J. Furlong
Enroll: 527 (318) 868-3000

BASTROP TECHNICAL INSTITUTE
P.O. Box 1120, Kammell St., Bastrop 71221-1120 *Type:* Public (state) *Accred.:* 1981/1989 (SACS-COEI) *Calendar:* Courses of varying lengths *Degrees:* certificates *CEO:* Dir. Norene Smith
Enroll: 136 (318) 283-0836

Accredited Institutions — Louisiana

BATON ROUGE SCHOOL OF COMPUTERS
9255 Interline Ave., Baton Rouge 70809 *Type:* Private *Accred.:* 1982/1988 (CCA-ACTTS) *Calendar:* Courses of varying lengths *Degrees:* diplomas *CEO:* Pres. Betty Truxillo
Enroll: 878 (504) 923-2525

BATON ROUGE TECHNICAL INSTITUTE
3250 N. Acadian Thruway, Baton Rouge 70805 *Type:* Public (state) *Accred.:* 1973/1987 (SACS-COEI) *Calendar:* Courses of varying lengths *Degrees:* certificates *CEO:* Dir. Robert R. Buck
Enroll: 570 (504) 359-9201

FRAZIER CAMPUS
555 Julia St., Baton Rouge, LA 70802 *CEO:* Dir. Robert R. Buck
(504) 359-9201

BAYOU TECHNICAL INSTITUTE
P.O. Box 13128, 7818 Earhart Blvd., New Orleans 70185 *Type:* Private *Accred.:* 1980/1987 (CCA-ACTTS) *Calendar:* Courses of varying lengths *Degrees:* certificates *CEO:* Pres. Albert B. Murphy, Jr.
Enroll: 120 (504) 866-7703

BAYTOWN TECHNICAL SCHOOL
2013 Oak Park Blvd., Lake Charles 70601 *Type:* Private *Accred.:* 1990/1991 (SACS-COEI) *Calendar:* Courses of varying lengths *Degrees:* certificates *CEO:* Dir. Margaret Walker
Enroll: 303 (318) 478-6390

BOLTON AVENUE BEAUTY SCHOOL
5623 Jackson St., Alexandria 71301 *Type:* Private *Accred.:* 1988 (SACS-COEI) *Calendar:* Courses of varying lengths *Degrees:* certificates *CEO:* Dir. Winn Johnson
Enroll: 36 (318) 422-6143

BOSSIER PARISH COMMUNITY COLLEGE
2719 Airline Dr., Bossier City 71111 *Type:* Public *Accred.:* 1983/1989 (SACS-CC) *Calendar:* Sem. plan *Degrees:* A *Prof. Accred.:* Respiratory Therapy Technology *CEO:* Chanc. James M. Conerly
Enroll: 2470 (318) 746-9851

CAMELOT CAREER COLLEGE
P.O. Box 53326, 2618 Wooddale Blvd., Baton Rouge 70805 *Type:* Private business *Accred.:* 1990 (CCA-ACICS) *Calendar:* Courses of varying lengths *Degrees:* certificates, diplomas *CEO:* Pres. Ronnie Williams
(504) 928-3005

CAMERON COLLEGE
2740 Canal St., New Orleans 70119 *Type:* Private technical *Accred.:* 1982/1987 (SACS-COEI) *Calendar:* Courses of varying lengths *Degrees:* certificates *CEO:* Dir. Eleanor Cameron
Enroll: 256 (504) 821-5881

CAREER INSTITUTE
2026 E. Texas St., Bossier City 71111 *Type:* Private *Accred.:* 1983/1988 (SACS-COEI) *Calendar:* Courses of varying lengths *Degrees:* certificates *CEO:* Dir. David Broussard
Enroll: 95 (318) 742-4011

CAREER TRAINING SPECIALISTS
Mid City Plaza, 1611 Louisville Ave., Monroe 71201 *Type:* Private *Accred.:* 1989 (SACS-COEI) *Calendar:* Courses of varying lengths *Degrees:* certificates, diplomas *CEO:* Dir. Lloydelle Hopkins
Enroll: 125 (318) 323-2889

CENTENARY COLLEGE OF LOUISIANA
P.O. Box 41188, Shreveport 71134-1188 *Type:* Private (United Methodist) liberal arts *Accred.:* 1925/1987 (SACS-CC) *Calendar:* Sem. plan *Degrees:* B, M *Prof. Accred.:* Music *CEO:* Pres. Kenneth Schwab
Enroll: 848 (318) 869-5011

CLAIBORNE TECHNICAL INSTITUTE
3001 Minden Rd., Homer 71040 *Type:* Public (state) *Accred.:* 1989 (SACS-COEI) *Calendar:* Courses of varying lengths *Degrees:* certificates *CEO:* Dir. Thomas Ragland
Enroll: 129 (318) 927-2034

CLARK COLLEGE
4420 E. Prien Lake Dr., Lake Charles 70605 *Type:* Private *Accred.:* 1988/1991 (SACS-COEI) *Calendar:* Courses of varying lengths

Degrees: certificates *CEO:* Dir. Linda Langford
Enroll: 808 (318) 478-9326

BRANCH CAMPUS
1229 Peters Rd., Harvey, LA 70058 *CEO:* Dir. Jerry Jones
(504) 366-0107

BRANCH CAMPUS
3505 Fifth Ave., Lake Charles, LA 70605 *CEO:* Dir. Rene Lewis
(318) 478-8095

COASTAL COLLEGE
2001 Canal St., Ste. 101, New Orleans 70112 *Type:* Private *Accred.:* 1985/1990 (SACS-COEI) *Calendar:* Courses of varying lengths *Degrees:* certificates *CEO:* Dir. Randi Reboul
Enroll: 3230 (504) 522-2400

BRANCH CAMPUS
5520 Industrial Dr. Ext., Bossier City, LA 71112 *CEO:* Dir. L.C. Farrier
(318) 746-8800

BRANCH CAMPUS
110 Yokum Rd., Hammond, LA 70403 *CEO:* Dir. Randy Reboul
(504) 345-3200

BRANCH CAMPUS
2318 W. Park Ave., Houma, LA 70364 *CEO:* Dir. Mac Le Blanc
(504) 872-2800

BRANCH CAMPUS
320 Howze Beach Rd., Slidell, LA 70461 *CEO:* Dir. Kay Cook
(504) 641-2121

COMMERCIAL COLLEGE OF BATON ROUGE
5677 Florida Blvd., Baton Rouge 70806 *Type:* Private business *Accred.:* 1972/1984 (CCA-ACICS) *Calendar:* Courses of varying lengths *Degrees:* certificates, diplomas *CEO:* Dir. Todd Gordon
Enroll: 617 (504) 927-3470

COMMERCIAL COLLEGE OF SHREVEPORT
2640 Youree Dr., Shreveport 71104 *Type:* Private business *Accred.:* 1971/1989 (CCA-ACICS) *Calendar:* Courses of varying lengths *Degrees:* certificates, diplomas *CEO:* Dir. Teri L. Kelsall
Enroll: 606 (318) 865-6571

CONCORDIA TECHNICAL INSTITUTE
E.E. Wallace Blvd., P.O. Box 152, Ferriday 71334 *Type:* Public (state) *Accred.:* 1980/1990 (SACS-COEI) *Calendar:* Courses of varying lengths *Degrees:* certificates *CEO:* Dir. Ray King
Enroll: 113 (318) 757-6501

CRESCENT CITY TECH
4441 Utica St., Metairie 70006 *Type:* Private *Accred.:* 1981/1986 (SACS-COEI) *Calendar:* Courses of varying lengths *Degrees:* certificates *CEO:* Dir. Manolo Arevalo, Jr.
Enroll: 98 (504) 885-1496

DELGADO COMMUNITY COLLEGE
501 City Park Ave., New Orleans 70119-4399 *Type:* Public (city) junior *Accred.:* 1971/1986 (SACS-CC) *Calendar:* Sem. plan *Degrees:* A, certificates *Prof. Accred.:* Funeral Service Education, Nuclear Medicine Technology, Radiography, Respiratory Therapy, Respiratory Therapy Technology *CEO:* Pres. James A. Caillier
Enroll: 9791 (504) 483-4114

DELTA CAREER COLLEGE
Detroit St. Ext., Alexandria 71302 *Type:* Private business *Accred.:* 1970/1988 (CCA-ACICS) *Calendar:* Qtr. plan *Degrees:* A *CEO:* Pres. John F. McCray
Enroll: 533 (318) 442-9586

BRANCH CAMPUS
600 Ash St., Pine Bluff, AR 71603 *CEO:* Dir. Kyle Treat
(501) 534-0494

BRANCH CAMPUS
110 Bolton Ave., Alexandria, LA 71301 *CEO:* Dir. Phil Mayeaux
(318) 442-4818

Accredited Institutions **Louisiana**

BRANCH CAMPUS
64 Homochitto St., Natchez, MS 39120 *CEO:* Dir. Rhonda Yeates
(601) 446-8894

DELTA CAREER COLLEGE
1900 Cameron St., Lafayette 70506 *Type:* Private business *Accred.:* 1988 (CCA-ACICS); 1990 (SACS-COEI) *Calendar:* Qtr. plan *Degrees:* certificates, diplomas *CEO:* Dir. Tina Soignier
Enroll: 611 (318) 235-1147

DELTA CAREER COLLEGE
1702 Hudson La., Monroe 71201 *Type:* Private business *Accred.:* 1988 (CCA-ACICS); 1990 (SACS-COEI) *Calendar:* Qtr. plan *Degrees:* certificates, diplomas *CEO:* Dir. Bill Rachal
Enroll: 323 (318) 322-8870

DELTA JUNIOR COLLEGE
7290 Exchange Pl., Baton Rouge 70806 *Type:* Private junior *Accred.:* 1973/1989 (CCA-ACICS) *Calendar:* Qtr. plan *Degrees:* A, certificates, diplomas *CEO:* Pres. Billy B. Clark
Enroll: 1092 (504) 927-7780

BRANCH CAMPUS
511 Westbank Expy., Gretna, LA 70053 *CEO:* Dir. Randall Wagley
(504) 362-5445

BRANCH CAMPUS
3827 W. Main St., Houma, LA 70360 *CEO:* Dir. Park Haussler
(504) 868-3074

BRANCH CAMPUS
3321 Hessmer Ave., Metairie, LA 70002 *CEO:* Dir. Danny R. Bedford
(504) 889-6612

DELTA SCHOOL OF BUSINESS AND TECHNOLOGY
517 Broad St., Lake Charles 70601 *Type:* Private business *Accred.:* 1976/1988 (CCA-ACICS) *Calendar:* Courses of varying lengths *Degrees:* A, certificates, diplomas *CEO:* Pres. Gary J. Holt
Enroll: 924 (318) 439-5765

DELTA SCHOOLS
4549 Johnston St., Lafayette 70503 *Type:* Private business *Accred.:* 1971/1989 (CCA-ACICS) *Calendar:* Courses of varying lengths *Degrees:* certificates, diplomas *CEO:* Pres. Peggy Fassio
Enroll: 351 (318) 988-2211

BRANCH CAMPUS
413 W. Admiral Doyle St., New Iberia, LA 70560 *CEO:* Dir. Shirlene Stewart
(318) 365-7348

DELTA-OUACHITA TECHNICAL INSTITUTE
609 Vocaitonal Pkwy., West Monroe 71292 *Type:* Public (state) *Accred.:* 1976/1991 (SACS-COEI) *Calendar:* Courses of varying lengths *Degrees:* certificates *CEO:* Dir. Irving D. Adkins
Enroll: 399 (318) 396-7431

DENHAM SPRINGS BEAUTY COLLEGE
923 Florida Ave., S.E., Denham Springs 70726 *Type:* Private *Accred.:* 1989 (SACS-COEI) *Calendar:* Courses of varying lengths *Degrees:* certificates *CEO:* Dir. Frances Hand
Enroll: 60 (504) 665-6188

DIESEL DRIVING ACADEMY
8136 Airline Hwy., Baton Rouge 70815 *Type:* Private *Accred.:* 1990 (SACS-COEI) *Calendar:* Courses of varying lengths *Degrees:* certificates *CEO:* Dir. Willie Price
Enroll: 56 (504) 929-9990

DIESEL DRIVING ACADEMY
4709 Greenwood Rd., Shreveport 71133 *Type:* Private *Accred.:* 1982/1988 (SACS-COEI) *Calendar:* Courses of varying lengths *Degrees:* certificates *CEO:* Dir. Bruce Busada
Enroll: 358 (318) 636-6300

BRANCH CAMPUS
3295 Wetumpka Hwy., Montgomery, AL 36110 *CEO:* Dir. Jerry Coley
(205) 270-0510

Louisiana

BRANCH CAMPUS
9725 Interstate 30, Little Rock, AR 72209
CEO: Dir. Ron Nahlen
(501) 565-1166

DILLARD UNIVERSITY
2601 Gentilly Blvd., New Orleans 70122 *Type:* Private (United Church of Christ/United Methodist) liberal arts *Accred.:* 1937/1989 (SACS-CC) *Calendar:* Sem. plan *Degrees:* B *Prof. Accred.:* Nursing (B) *CEO:* Pres. Samuel D. Cook
Enroll: 1898 (504) 283-8822

DOMESTIC HEALTH CARE INSTITUTE
4826 Jamestown Ave., Baton Rouge 70808 *Type:* Private *Calendar:* Courses of varying lengths *Degrees:* certificates, diplomas *Prof. Accred.:* Health Education *CEO:* Pres. Dan Chavis
(504) 925-5312

EASTERN COLLEGE OF HEALTH VOCATIONS
3540 I-10 Service Rd., S., Metairie 70001 *Type:* Private *Calendar:* Courses of varying lengths *Degrees:* diplomas *Prof. Accred.:* Health Education *CEO:* Pres. Susan Dalto
(504) 834-8644

ELAINE P. NUNEZ TECHNICAL INSTITUTE
3700 Lafontaine St., Chalmette 70043 *Type:* Public (state) *Accred.:* 1983/1988 (SACS-COEI) *Calendar:* Courses of varying lengths *Degrees:* certificates *CEO:* Dir. John J. Kane
Enroll: 282 (504) 278-7440

BRANCH CAMPUS
901 Delery St., New Orleans, LA 70117
CEO: Dir. John J. Kane
(504) 278-7440

BRANCH CAMPUS
P.O. Drawer 944, Port Sulphur, LA 70083
CEO: Dir. Martha McDaniel
(504) 564-2701

EVANGELINE TECHNICAL INSTITUTE
P.O. Box 68, 600 Martin Luther King, Jr. Dr, Martinville 70582 *Type:* Public (state) *Accred.:* 1974/1989 (SACS-COEI) *Calendar:* Courses of varying lengths *Degrees:* certificates *CEO:* Dir. Prosper Chretien
Enroll: 210 (318) 394-6466

FINED, SCHOOL OF FINANCIAL EDUCATION
5745 Essen La., Ste. 207, Baton Rouge 70809 *Type:* Private *Accred.:* 1991 (SACS-COEI) *Calendar:* Courses of varying lengths *Degrees:* certificates, diplomas *CEO:* Dir. Mark Reichel
Enroll: 7 (504) 767-7983

FISCHER TECHNICAL COLLEGE
8700 Lake Forest Blvd., Ste. 112, New Orleans 70127 *Type:* Private business *Accred.:* 1964/1986 (CCA-ACICS) *Calendar:* Qtr. plan *Degrees:* certificates, diplomas *CEO:* Dir. Don Brown
Enroll: 424 (504) 241-3404

FLORIDA PARISHES TECHNICAL INSTITUTE
P.O. Box 130, 100 College Dr., Greensburg 70441 *Type:* Public (state) *Accred.:* 1977/1988 (SACS-COEI) *Calendar:* Courses of varying lengths *Degrees:* certificates *CEO:* Dir. Jimmie Meadows
Enroll: 142 (504) 222-4251

FOLKES TECHNICAL INSTITUTE
Hwy. 10, E., P.O. Box 808, Jackson 70748 *Type:* Public (state) *Accred.:* 1981/1987 (SACS-COEI) *Calendar:* Courses of varying lengths *Degrees:* certificates *CEO:* Dir. James V. Soileau
Enroll: 194 (504) 634-2636

BRANCH CAMPUS
Dixon Correctional Inst., Hwy. 68, Jackson, LA 70748 *CEO:* Dir. George Clark
(504) 634-2636

BRANCH CAMPUS
Wakefield Abattoir, Hwy. 61, Wakefield, LA 70784 *CEO:* Dir. George Clark
(504) 634-2636

FRANKLIN COLLEGE OF COURT REPORTING
1200 S. Clearview Pkwy., New Orleans 70123 *Type:* Private *Accred.:* 1990 (SACS-COEI) *Calendar:* Courses of varying lengths

Degrees: certificates *CEO:* Pres. Mary Franklin
Enroll: 175   (504) 734-1000

GRAMBLING STATE UNIVERSITY
P.O. Drawer 607, Grambling 71245 *Type:* Public (state) liberal arts and professional *System:* Louisiana Board of Trustees for State Colleges and Universities *Accred.:* 1949/1990 (SACS-CC) *Calendar:* Sem. plan *Degrees:* A, B, M, D *Prof. Accred.:* Music, Nursing (B), Recreation Management, Social Work (B,M), Teacher Education (e,s,p), Theatre *CEO:* Pres. Harold W. Lundy
Enroll: 6132   (318) 274-2000

GRANTHAM COLLEGE OF ENGINEERING
34641 Grantham College Rd., P.O. Box 5700, Slidell 70469-5700 *Type:* Private home study *Accred.:* 1961/1991 (NHSC) *Calendar:* Courses of varying lengths *Degrees:* A, B *CEO:* Pres. Donald J. Grantham
(504) 649-4191

GULF AREA TECHNICAL INSTITUTE
1115 Clover St., P.O. Box 878, Abbeville 70528 *Type:* Public (state) *Accred.:* 1975/1990 (SACS-COEI) *Calendar:* Courses of varying lengths *Degrees:* certificates *CEO:* Dir. Ray Lavergne
Enroll: 221   (318) 893-4984

HAMMOND AREA VOCATIONAL SCHOOL
P.O. Box 489, Hwy. 190 and Pride Blvd., Hammond 70404 *Type:* Public (state) *Accred.:* 1975/1990 (SACS-COEI) *Calendar:* Courses of varying lengths *Degrees:* certificates *CEO:* Dir. Francis N. Bickham
Enroll: 150   (504) 549-5063

HUEY P. LONG TECHNICAL INSTITUTE
303 S. Jones St., Winnfield 71483 *Type:* Public (state) *Accred.:* 1977/1987 (SACS-COEI) *Calendar:* Courses of varying lengths *Degrees:* certificates *CEO:* Dir. Donald R. Purser
Enroll: 498   (318) 628-4342

BRANCH CAMPUS
E. Bradford St., Jena, LA 71342 *CEO:* Dir. Donald R. Purser
(318) 992-2910

INTERNATIONAL TECHNICAL INSTITUTE
13944 Airline Hwy., Baton Rouge 70817 *Type:* Private *Accred.:* 1981/1988 (CCA-ACTTS) *Calendar:* Courses of varying lengths *Degrees:* certificates *CEO:* Pres. Earl J. Martin, Jr.
Enroll: 261   (504) 752-4233

JEFF DAVIS BEAUTY COLLEGE
1103 N. Lake Arthur Ave., Jennings 70546 *Type:* Private *Accred.:* 1989 (SACS-COEI) *Calendar:* Courses of varying lengths *Degrees:* certificates *CEO:* Dir. Karine Folley
Enroll: 37   (318) 824-3371

JEFFERSON DAVIS TECHNICAL INSTITUTE
1230 N. Main St., P.O. Box 1327, Jennings 70546-1327 *Type:* Public (state) *Accred.:* 1976/1991 (SACS-COEI)*Calendar:* Courses of varying lengths *Degrees:* certificates *CEO:* Dir. Johnnie Smith
Enroll: 93   (318) 824-4811

JEFFERSON TECHNICAL INSTITUTE
5200 Blair Dr., Metairie 70001 *Type:* Public (state) *Accred.:* 1975/1989 (SACS-COEI) *Calendar:* Courses of varying lengths *Degrees:* certificates *CEO:* Dir. Justin LeMaitre
Enroll: 332   (504) 736-7076

JOCELYN DASPIT BEAUTY COLLEGE
3204 Independence St., Metairie 70006 *Type:* Private *Accred.:* 1987 (SACS-COEI) *Calendar:* Courses of varying lengths *Degrees:* certificates *CEO:* Dir. John A. Daspit
Enroll: 226   (504) 888-8983

BRANCH CAMPUS
507 W. Cypress St., Hammond, LA 70403 *CEO:* Dir. Jocelyn Fletcher
(504) 345-6307

BRANCH CAMPUS
1727 Airline Hwy., La Place, LA 70068 *CEO:* Dir. Lisa Bailey
(504) 652-6807

LAFAYETTE REGIONAL TECHNICAL INSTITUTE
1101 Bertrand Dr., P.O. Box 4909, Lafayette 70506 *Type:* Public (state) technical *Accred.:* 1981/1991 (SACS-COEI)*Calendar:* Courses

of varying lengths *Degrees:* certificates *Prof. Accred.:* Medical Laboratory Technology (AMA) *CEO:* Dir. Ted Ardoin
Enroll: 544 (318) 265-5962

LAMAR SALTER TECHNICAL INSTITUTE
Hwy. 171, S., Rte. 2, Box 25, Leesville 71446 *Type:* Public (state) *Accred.:* 1983/1988 (SACS-COEI) *Calendar:* Courses of varying lengths *Degrees:* certificates *CEO:* Dir. Tommy Cordova
Enroll: 165 (318) 537-3135

LOUISIANA ART INSTITUTE
3954 Florida Blvd., Baton Rouge 70806 *Type:* Private *Accred.:* 1988 (CCA-ACTTS) *Calendar:* Courses of varying lengths *Degrees:* certificates *CEO:* Dir. Norma Routt
(504) 383-7770

LOUISIANA COLLEGE
1140 College Dr., Pineville 71359 *Type:* Private (Southern Baptist) liberal arts *Accred.:* 1923/1991 (SACS-CC) *Calendar:* Sem. plan *Degrees:* A, B *Prof. Accred.:* Music, Nursing (B), Social Work (B-candidate) *CEO:* Pres. Robert L. Lynn
Enroll: 1008 (318) 487-7011

LOUISIANA INSTITUTE OF TECHNOLOGY
3412 Williams Blvd., Kenner 70065 *Type:* Private *Accred.:* 1983/1988 (SACS-COEI) *Calendar:* Courses of varying lengths *Degrees:* certificates *CEO:* Dir. Ralph White
Enroll: 404 (504) 443-3418

BRANCH CAMPUS
3349 Masonic Dr., Alexandria, LA 71301 *CEO:* Dir. Jackie Davis
(318) 442-1864

LOUISIANA STATE UNIVERSITY MEDICAL CENTER
433 Bolivar St., New Orleans 70112-2223 *Type:* Public (state) *System:* Louisiana State University System *Accred.:* 1931/1984 (SACS-CC) *Calendar:* Sem. plan *Degrees:* A, B, P, M, D *Prof. Accred.:* Audiology, Combined Prosthodontics, Dental Hygiene, Dental Laboratory Technology, Dentistry, Endodontics, General Dentistry, Medical Technology, Medicine, Nursing (A,B,M), Occupational Therapy, Oral and Maxillofacial Surgery, Orthodontics, Pediatric Dentistry, Periodontics, Physical Therapy, Respiratory Therapy, Speech-Language Pathology *CEO:* Chanc. Perry G. Rigby
Enroll: 1244 (504) 568-4808

LOUISIANA STATE UNIVERSITY AND AGRICULTURAL AND MECHANICAL COLLEGE
Baton Rouge 70803-2750 *Type:* Public (state) *System:* Louisiana State University System *Accred.:* 1913/1984 (SACS-CC) *Calendar:* Sem. plan *Degrees:* B, P, M, D *Prof. Accred.:* Architecture (B), Art, Business (B,M), Clinical Psychology, Construction Education, Engineering (agricultural, chemical, civil, computer, electrical, industrial, mechanical, petroleum), Forestry, Home Economics, Interior Design, Journalism, Landscape Architecture (B,M), Law, Librarianship, Music, Social Work (M), Speech-Language Pathology, Teacher Education (e,s,p) *CEO:* Chanc. William E. Davis
Enroll: 25223 (504) 388-3202

LOUISIANA STATE UNIVERSITY AT ALEXANDRIA
8100 Hwy. 71 S., Alexandria 71302-9633 *Type:* Public (state) *System:* Louisiana State University System *Accred.:* 1960/1984 (SACS-CC) *Calendar:* Sem. plan *Degrees:* A *Prof. Accred.:* Nursing (A) *CEO:* Chanc. Benjamin F. Martin
Enroll: 1977 (318) 445-3672

LOUISIANA STATE UNIVERSITY AT EUNICE
P.O. Box 1129, Eunice 70535 *Type:* Public (state) *System:* Louisiana State University System *Accred.:* 1967/1984 (SACS-CC) *Calendar:* Sem. plan *Degrees:* A *Prof. Accred.:* Respiratory Therapy Technology *CEO:* Chanc. Michael Smith
Enroll: 1424 (318) 457-7311

LOUISIANA STATE UNIVERSITY IN SHREVEPORT
One University Plaza, Shreveport 71115 *Type:* Public (state) *System:* Louisiana State University System *Accred.:* 1975/1984 (SACS-CC) *Calendar:* Sem. plan *Degrees:* B, P, M *Prof. Accred.:* Medicine, Radiogra-

phy, Teacher Education (e,s,p) *CEO:* Chanc. John R. Darling
Enroll: 3410 (318) 797-5000

LOUISIANA TECH UNIVERSITY
P.O. Box 3168, Tech Sta., Ruston 71272 *Type:* Public (state) *System:* Louisiana Board of Trustees for State Colleges and Universities *Accred.:* 1927/1984 (SACS-CC) *Calendar:* Qtr. plan *Degrees:* A, B, M, D *Prof. Accred.:* Accounting (Type A,B,C), Architecture (B), Art, Business (B,M), Computer Science, Engineering (bioengineering, chemical, civil, electrical, industrial, mechanical, petroleum), Engineering Technology (civil/construction, electrical), Forestry, Home Economics, Interior Design, Medical Record Administration, Medical Record Technology, Music, Nursing (A), Speech-Language Pathology, Teacher Education (e,s,p) *CEO:* Pres. Daniel D. Reneau
Enroll: 9024 (318) 257-0211

LOYOLA UNIVERSITY
6363 St. Charles Ave., New Orleans 70118 *Type:* Private (Roman Catholic) *Accred.:* 1929/1985 (SACS-CC) *Calendar:* Sem. plan *Degrees:* B, P, M, D *Prof. Accred.:* Business (B,M), Law, Music, Nursing (B) *CEO:* Pres. James C. Carter, S.J.
Enroll: 4541 (504) 865-2011

MCNEESE STATE UNIVERSITY
4100 Ryan St., Lake Charles 70609 *Type:* Public liberal arts *System:* Louisiana Board of Trustees for State Colleges and Universities *Accred.:* 1954/1986 (SACS-CC) *Calendar:* Sem. plan*Degrees:* A,B,M*Prof. Accred.:* Business (B,M), Engineering (general), Music, Nursing (B), Radiography, Teacher Education (e,s,p) *CEO:* Pres. Robert D. Hebert
Enroll: 6885 (318) 475-5000

NATCHITOCHES TECHNICAL INSTITUTE
220 Hwy. 3110, P.O. Box 657, Natchitoches 71458 *Type:* Public (state) *Accred.:* 1982/1987 (SACS-COEI) *Calendar:* Courses of varying lengths *Degrees:* certificates *CEO:* Dir. Dolores H. Tucker
Enroll: 181 (318) 357-3162

NATIONAL TRUCK DRIVER EDUCATION INSTITUTE
6963 Sullivan Rd., Greenwell Springs 70739 *Type:* Private *Accred.:* 1988 (CCA-ACTTS) *Calendar:* Courses of varying lengths *Degrees:* diplomas *CEO:* Dir. Carlos Gonzalez
(504) 261-1694

BRANCH CAMPUS
12170 Old Gentilly Rd., New Orleans, LA 70128 *CEO:* Dir. Carlos Padilla
(504) 246-3515

NEW ORLEANS BAPTIST THEOLOGICAL SEMINARY
3939 Gentilly Blvd., New Orleans 70126-4858 *Type:* Private (Southern Baptist) professional; graduate only *Accred.:* 1954/1986 (ATS); 1965/1986 (SACS-CC) *Calendar:* Sem. plan *Degrees:* A, P, M, D *Prof. Accred.:* Music *CEO:* Pres. Landrum P. Leavell, II
Enroll: 870 (504) 282-4455

NEW ORLEANS REGIONAL TECHNICAL INSTITUTE
980 Navarre Ave., New Orleans 70124 *Type:* Public (state) *Accred.:* 1988 (SACS-COEI) *Calendar:* Courses of varying lengths *Degrees:* certificates *CEO:* Dir. Simone Charbonnet
Enroll: 217 (504) 483-4666

NICHOLLS STATE UNIVERSITY
LA Hwy. 1, Thibodaux 70310 *Type:* Public liberal arts and teachers *System:* Louisiana Board of Trustees for State Colleges and Universities *Accred.:* 1964/1985 (SACS-CC) *Calendar:* Sem. plan *Degrees:* A, B, M *Prof. Accred.:* Business (B,M), Home Economics, Music, Nursing (A,B), Respiratory Therapy Technology, Teacher Education (e,s,p) *CEO:* Pres. Donald J. Ayo
Enroll: 6361 (504) 446-8111

NORTH CENTRAL AREA TECHNICAL INSTITUTE
605 N. Boundary, P.O. Box 548, Farmerville 71241 *Type:* Public (state) *Accred.:* 1979/

1984 (SACS-COEI) *Calendar:* Courses of varying lengths *Degrees:* certificates *CEO:* Dir. Johnny Bridges
Enroll: 76 (318) 368-3179

NORTHEAST LOUISIANA TECHNICAL INSTITUTE
1710 Warren St., Winnsboro 71295 *Type:* Public (state) *Accred.:* 1976/1987 (SACS-COEI) *Calendar:* Courses of varying lengths *Degrees:* certificates *CEO:* Dir. John Pinckard
Enroll: 122 (318) 435-2163

NORTHEAST LOUISIANA UNIVERSITY
700 University Avenue, Monroe 71209 *Type:* Public (state) *System:* Louisiana Board of Trustees for State Colleges and Universities *Accred.:* 1955/1989 (SACS-CC) *Calendar:* Sem. plan *Degrees:* A, B, M, D *Prof. Accred.:* Business (B,M), Computer Science, Construction Education, Counseling, Dental Hygiene, Home Economics, Music, Nursing (B), Occupational Therapy, Occupational Therapy Assisting, Pharmacy, Radiography, Social Work (B), Teacher Education (e,s,p) *CEO:* Pres. Lawson L. Swearingen, Jr.
Enroll: 11306 (318) 342-1000

NORTHWEST LOUISIANA TECHNICAL INSTITUTE
814 Constable, P.O. Box 835, Minden 71055 *Type:* Public (state) *Accred.:* 1975/1990 (SACS-COEI) *Calendar:* Courses of varying lengths *Degrees:* certificates *CEO:* Dir. Charles Strong
Enroll: 288 (318) 371-3035

NORTHWESTERN STATE UNIVERSITY
College Ave., Natchitoches 71497 *Type:* Public liberal arts and professional *System:* Louisiana Board of Trustees for State Colleges and Universities *Accred.:* 1941/1986 (SACS-CC) *Calendar:* Sem. plan *Degrees:* A, B, M, D *Prof. Accred.:* Music, Nursing (A,B,M), Radiography, Social Work (B), Teacher Education (e,s,p), Veterinary Technology (probational) *CEO:* Pres. Robert A. Alost
Enroll: 6252 (318) 357-6361

NOTRE DAME SEMINARY
2901 S. Carrollton Ave., New Orleans 70118-4391 *Type:* Private (Roman Catholic) graduate only *Accred.:* 1979/1986 (ATS); 1951/1986 (SACS-CC) *Calendar:* Qtr. plan *Degrees:* P, M *CEO:* Rector/Pres. Gregory M. Aymond
Enroll: 102 (504) 866-7426

OAKDALE TECHNICAL INSTITUTE
Old Pelican Hwy., P.O. Drawer EM, Oakdale 71463 *Type:* Public (state) *Accred.:* 1983/1991 (SACS-COEI)*Calendar:* Courses of varying lengths *Degrees:* certificates *CEO:* Dir. Darrell Rodriguez
Enroll: 227 (318) 335-3944

OCHSNER SCHOOL OF ALLIED HEALTH SCIENCES
1516 Jefferson Hwy., New Orleans 70121 *Type:* Private technical *Accred.:* 1978/1988 (SACS-COEI) *Calendar:* Courses of varying lengths *Degrees:* certificates *Prof. Accred.:* Blood Bank Technology, Diagnostic Medical Sonography, Medical Technology, Nuclear Medicine Technology, Perfusion, Radiation Therapy Technology, Radiography, Respiratory Therapy, Respiratory Therapy Technology, Surgical Technology *CEO:* Dir. George Porter
Enroll: 108 (504) 838-3232

OUR LADY OF THE HOLY CROSS COLLEGE
4123 Woodland Dr., New Orleans 70131-7399 *Type:* Private (Roman Catholic) liberal arts and teachers *Accred.:* 1972/1986 (SACS-CC) *Calendar:* Sem. plan *Degrees:* A, B, M *Prof. Accred.:* Nursing (B) *CEO:* Pres. Thomas E. Chambers
Enroll: 732 (504) 394-7744

PHILLIPS JUNIOR COLLEGE
822 S. Clearview Pkwy., New Orleans 70123 *Type:* Private junior *Accred.:* 1974/1986 (CCA-ACICS) *Calendar:* Courses of varying lengths *Degrees:* A, certificates, diplomas *Prof. Accred.:* Medical Assisting (AMA) *CEO:* Pres. Georjean R. Crosley
Enroll: 2017 (504) 734-0123

BRANCH CAMPUS
5001 Westbank Expy., Marrero, LA 70072 *Prof. Accred.:* Medical Assisting (AMA) *CEO:* Dir. Erik Brumme
(504) 348-1182

PROFESSIONAL CAREER CENTERS
3939 Veterans Blvd., Ste. 220, Metairie 70002 *Type:* Private *Accred.:* 1986 (CCA-ACTTS) *Calendar:* Courses of varying lengths *Degrees:* diplomas *CEO:* Dir. Carol Knight
Enroll: 265 (504) 887-8787

R.E.T.S. TRAINING CENTER
4323 Division St., Metairie 70002 *Type:* Private *Accred.:* 1990 (CCA-ACTTS) *Calendar:* Courses of varying lengths *Degrees:* certificates *CEO:* Treas. Garner Boulmay
(504) 888-6848

RIVER PARISHES TECHNICAL INSTITUTE
Airline Pkwy. at 10th St., P.O. Drawer AQ, Reserve 70084 *Type:* Public (state) *Accred.:* 1984/1989 (SACS-COEI)*Calendar:* Courses of varying lengths *Degrees:* certificates *CEO:* Dir. Jack Worrell
Enroll: 352 (504) 536-4418

ROBINSON BUSINESS COLLEGE
1517 Jackson St., Monroe 71201 *Type:* Private business *Accred.:* 1966/1991 (CCA-ACICS) *Calendar:* Sem. plan *Degrees:* certificates, diplomas *CEO:* Dir. Brent D. Henley
Enroll: 1125 (318) 323-7515

RUSTON TECHNICAL INSTITUTE
1010 James St., P.O. Box 1070, Ruston 71273-1070 *Type:* Public (state) *Accred.:* 1982/1988 (SACS-COEI)*Calendar:* Courses of varying lengths *Degrees:* certificates *CEO:* Dir. Donald Walsworth
Enroll: 134 (318) 251-4145

RUTLEDGE COLLEGE OF NEW ORLEANS
3030 Canal St., New Orleans 70119 *Type:* Private *Accred.:* 1986 (SACS-COEI) *Calendar:* Courses of varying lengths *Degrees:* certificates *CEO:* Dir. Stanley Davis
Enroll: 627 (504) 822-6111

SABINE VALLEY TECHNICAL INSTITUTEL SCHOOL
Hwy. 171 S., P.O. Box 790, Many 71449 *Type:* Public (state) *Accred.:* 1977/1988 (SACS-COEI) *Calendar:* Courses of varying lengths *Degrees:* certificates *CEO:* Dir. David B. Crittenden
Enroll: 108 (318) 256-5663

ST. BERNARD PARISH COMMUNITY COLLEGE
2500 Palmisano Blvd., Chalmette 70043 *Type:* Public junior *Accred.:* 1985 (SACS-CC) *Calendar:* Sem. plan *Degrees:* A *CEO:* Pres. Daniel D. Daste
Enroll: 902 (504) 277-1142

ST. JOSEPH SEMINARY COLLEGE
St. Benedict 70457-9990 *Type:* Private (Roman Catholic) liberal arts *Accred.:* 1956/1983 (SACS-CC) *Calendar:* Sem. plan *Degrees:* B *CEO:* Pres./Rector Ambrose G. Wathen
Enroll: 90 (504) 892-1800

SHREVEPORT-BOSSIER TECHNICAL INSTITUTE
2010 N. Market St., P.O. Box 78527, Shreveport 71137-8527 *Type:* Public (state) *Accred.:* 1976/1991 (SACS-COEI) *Calendar:* Courses of varying lengths *Degrees:* certificates *CEO:* Dir. Sam Merritt
Enroll: 472 (318) 226-7811

SIDNEY N. COLLIER TECHNICAL INSTITUTE
3727 Louisa St., New Orleans 70126 *Type:* Public (state) *Accred.:* 1977/1988 (SACS-COEI) *Calendar:* Courses of varying lengths *Degrees:* certificates *CEO:* Dir. Levi Lewis
Enroll: 226 (504) 942-8333

SLIDELL TECHNICAL INSTITUTE
1000 Canulette Rd., P.O. Box 827, Slidell 70459 *Type:* Public (state) *Accred.:* 1974/1989 (SACS-COEI) *Calendar:* Courses of varying lengths *Degrees:* certificates *CEO:* Dir. Kereigh Fallon
Enroll: 232 (504) 646-6430

SOUTH LOUISIANA BEAUTY COLLEGE
300 Howard Ave., Houma 70363 *Type:* Private *Accred.:* 1987 (SACS-COEI) *Calendar:*

Courses of varying lengths *Degrees:* certificates *CEO:* Dir. Catherine A. Nagy
Enroll: 26 (504) 873-8978

SOUTH LOUISIANA REGIONAL TECHNICAL INSTITUTE
201 St. Charles St., P.O. Box 5033, Houma 70360 *Type:* Public (state) *Accred.:* 1975/1990 (SACS-COEI) *Calendar:* Courses of varying lengths *Degrees:* certificates *CEO:* Dir. Kenneth Callahan
Enroll: 252 (504) 857-3655

BRANCH CAMPUS
310 E. 90th St., Cutoff, LA 70345 *CEO:* Dir. Kenneth Callahan
(504) 632-5177

BRANCH CAMPUS
331 Dixon Rd., Houma, LA 70363 *CEO:* Dir. Kenneth Callahan
(504) 857-3698

SOUTHEASTERN LOUISIANA UNIVERSITY
Western Ave., P.O. Box 784, Hammond 70402 *Type:* Public (state) liberal arts and professional *System:* Louisiana Board of Trustees for State Colleges and Universities *Accred.:* 1946/1984 (SACS-CC) *Calendar:* Sem. plan *Degrees:* A, B, M *Prof. Accred.:* Business (B,M), Music, Nursing (B), Respiratory Therapy Technology, Social Work (B), Teacher Education (e,s,p) *CEO:* Pres. G. Warren Smith
Enroll: 9668 (504) 549-2000

SOUTHERN TECHNICAL COLLEGE
303 Rue Louis XIV, Lafayette 70508 *Type:* Private business *Accred.:* 1988/1989 (CCA-ACICS) *Calendar:* Qtr. plan *Degrees:* A *CEO:* Dir. Joseph Gasper
Enroll: 1208 (318) 981-4010

SOUTHERN UNIVERSITY AND AGRICULTURAL AND MECHANICAL COLLEGE AT BATON ROUGE
Southern Branch Post Office, Box 96, Baton Rouge 70813 *Type:* Public (state) *System:* Southern University and Agricultural and Mechanical College System *Accred.:* 1938/1991 (SACS-CC) *Calendar:* Sem. plan *Degrees:* A, B, P, M, D *Prof. Accred.:* Architecture (B), Computer Science, Engineering (civil, electrical, mechanical), Home Economics, Law (ABA only), Music, Nursing (B), Social Work (B), Teacher Education (e,s) *CEO:* Pres. Marvin L. Yates
Enroll: 8374 (504) 771-4500

SOUTHERN UNIVERSITY AT NEW ORLEANS
6400 Press Dr., New Orleans 70126 *Type:* Public *System:* Southern University and Agricultural and Mechanical College System *Accred.:* 1958/1990 (SACS-CC) *Calendar:* Sem. plan *Degrees:* A, B, M *Prof. Accred.:* Social Work (B,M) *CEO:* Chanc. Robert B. Gex
Enroll: 3515 (504) 286-5000

SOUTHERN UNIVERSITY IN SHREVEPORT
3050 Martin Luther King Jr. Dr, Shreveport 71107 *Type:* Public *System:* Southern University and Agricultural and Mechanical College System *Accred.:* 1964/1991 (SACS-CC) *Calendar:* Sem. plan *Degrees:* A *Prof. Accred.:* Medical Laboratory Technology (AMA), Radiography, Respiratory Therapy *CEO:* Chanc. Robert H. Smith
Enroll: 1022 (318) 674-3300

SOUTHWEST LOUISIANA TECHNICAL INSTITUTE
1933 W. Huchinson Ave., P.O. Box 820, Crowley 70527-0820 *Type:* Public (state) *Accred.:* 1976/1991 (SACS-COEI) *Calendar:* Courses of varying lengths *Degrees:* certificates *CEO:* Dir. Richard A. Arnaud
Enroll: 253 (318) 788-7521

SOUTHWEST SCHOOL OF HEALTH CAREERS
Plaza 24 Ctr., 2424 Williams Blvd., Kenner 70062 *Type:* Private *Accred.:* 1988 (CCA-ACTTS) *Calendar:* Courses of varying lengths *Degrees:* certificates *CEO:* Dir. Debra Hoffman
(504) 465-9677

SOWELA REGIONAL TECHNICAL INSTITUTE
3820 Legion St., P.O. Box 16950, Lake Charles 70616 *Type:* Public (state) *Accred.:* 1971/1986 (SACS-COEI)*Calendar:* Courses

Accredited Institutions **Louisiana**

of varying lengths *Degrees:* certificates *CEO:* Dir. Stanley Leger
Enroll: 878 (318) 491-2698

BRANCH CAMPUS
P.O. Box 1056, DeQuincy, LA 70633 *CEO:* Asst. Dir. Colin Fake
(318) 491-2688

SPENCER COLLEGE
2902 Florida Blvd., Baton Rouge 70802 *Type:* Private business *Accred.:* 1966/1986 (CCA-ACICS) *Calendar:* Qtr. plan *Degrees:* certificates, diplomas *CEO:* Pres. Sharon B. Burke
Enroll: 959 (504) 383-7701

BRANCH CAMPUS
10555 Northwest Fwy., Ste. 100, Houston, TX 77092 *CEO:* Dir. Donald W. Myers
(713) 956-6996

SULLIVAN TECHNICAL INSTITUTE
1710 Sullivan Dr., Bogalusa 70427 *Type:* Public (state) *Accred.:* 1970/1988 (SACS-COEI) *Calendar:* Courses of varying lengths *Degrees:* certificates *CEO:* Dir. M.J. Murphy
Enroll: 371 (504) 732-6640

BRANCH CAMPUS
Washington Correctional Inst., Rte. 2, Box 500, Angie, LA 70426 *CEO:* Guidance Counselor Gary Ledet
(504) 732-6640

T.H. HARRIS TECHNICAL INSTITUTE
337 E. South St., P.O. Box 713, Opelousas 70570 *Type:* Public (state) *Accred.:* 1970/1990 (SACS-COEI) *Calendar:* Courses of varying lengths *Degrees:* certificates *CEO:* Dir. Ceasor Veazie
Enroll: 465 (318) 948-0239

TALLULAH TECHNICAL INSTITUTE
Old Hwy. 65 S., P.O. Drawer 1740, Tallulah 71284 *Type:* Public (state) *Accred.:* 1980/1990 (SACS-COEI) *Calendar:* Courses of varying lengths *Degrees:* certificates *CEO:* Dir. Patrick T. Murphy
Enroll: 164 (318) 574-4820

BRANCH CAMPUS
P.O. Box 368, Hwy. 883-I, Lake Providence, LA 71254 *CEO:* Asst. Dir. Ralph Moore
(318) 559-0864

TECHE AREA TECHNICAL INSTITUTE
P.O. Box 11057, Acadiana Airport, New Iberia 70561-1057 *Type:* Public (state) *Accred.:* 1976/1991 (SACS-COEI) *Calendar:* Courses of varying lengths *Degrees:* certificates *CEO:* Dir. Paul Fair
Enroll: 260 (318) 373-0011

THIBODAUX AREA TECHNICAL INSTITUTE
1425 Tiger Dr., Thibodaux 70302-1831 *Type:* Public (state) *Accred.:* 1988 (SACS-COEI) *Calendar:* Courses of varying lengths *Degrees:* certificates *CEO:* Dir. Joyce Viguerie
Enroll: 134 (504) 447-0924

TULANE UNIVERSITY
6823 St. Charles Ave., New Orleans 70118 *Type:* Private *Accred.:* 1903/1990 (SACS-CC) *Calendar:* Sem. plan *Degrees:* B, P, M, D *Prof. Accred.:* Architecture (B), Business (B,M), Computer Science, Engineering (bio-engineering, chemical, civil, electrical, mechanical), Health Services Administration, Law, Medicine, Psychology Internship, Public Health, Social Work (M) *CEO:* Pres. Eamon M. Kelly
Enroll: 10159 (504) 865-5000

TUMONVILLE MEMORIAL TECHNICAL INSTITUTE
Hospital Rd., P.O. Box 725, New Roads 70760 *Type:* Public (state) *Accred.:* 1976/1991 (SACS-COEI) *Calendar:* Courses of varying lengths *Degrees:* certificates *CEO:* Dir. George L. Grace
Enroll: 683 (504) 638-8613

BRANCH CAMPUS
Loiusiana State Penitentiary, Angola, LA 70712 *CEO:* Dir. George L. Grace
(504) 655-4411

BRANCH CAMPUS
3233 Rosedale Rd., Port Allen, LA 70767 *CEO:* Dir. George L. Grace

BRANCH CAMPUS
Louisiana Correctional Inst. for Women, St. Gabriel, LA 70776 *CEO:* Dir. George L. Grace
(504) 642-5529

BRANCH CAMPUS
Hunt Correctional Ctr., P.O. Box 40, St. Gabriel, LA 70776 *CEO:* Dir. George L. Grace
(504) 642-3306

UNIVERSITY OF NEW ORLEANS
Lake Front, New Orleans 70148 *Type:* Public *System:* Louisiana State University System *Accred.:* 1958/1984 (SACS-CC) *Calendar:* Sem. plan *Degrees:* A, B, M, D *Prof. Accred.:* Accounting (Type A,C), Art, Business (B,M), Computer Science, Counseling, Engineering (civil, electrical, mechanical, naval architecture/marine), Music, Planning (regional/urban), Teacher Education (e,s,p) *CEO:* Chanc. Gregory M. St. L. O'Brien
Enroll: 12440   (504) 286-6000

UNIVERSITY OF SOUTHWESTERN LOUISIANA
200 E. University Ave., Lafayette 70504 *Type:* Public (state) *System:* Louisiana Board of Trustees for State Colleges and Universities *Accred.:* 1925/1990 (SACS-CC) *Calendar:* Sem. plan *Degrees:* A, B, M, D *Prof. Accred.:* Architecture (B), Computer Science, Engineering (chemical, civil, electrical, mechanical, petroleum), Home Economics, Medical Record Administration, Music, Nursing (B), Speech-Language Pathology, Teacher Education (e,s,p) *CEO:* Pres. Ray P. Authement
Enroll: 13793   (318) 231-6000

VILLE PLATTE TECHNICAL INSTITUTE
One Vocaiton Dr., Industrial Park, Ward I, Ville Platte 70586 *Type:* Public (state) *Accred.:* 1981/1986 (SACS-COEI) *Calendar:* Courses of varying lengths *Degrees:* certificates *CEO:* Dir. C.B. Coreil
Enroll: 166   (318) 363-2197

WKG-TV VIDEO ELECTRONIC COLLEGE
9490 Airline Hwy., Baton Rouge 70815 *Type:* Private *Accred.:* 1984/1989 (SACS-COEI) *Calendar:* Courses of varying lengths *Degrees:* certificates *CEO:* Dir. William E. Murvin
Enroll: 85   (504) 928-0632

WEST JEFFERSON TECHNICAL INSTITUTE
475 Manhattan Blvd., Harvey 70058 *Type:* Public (state) *Accred.:* 1982/1988 (SACS-COEI) *Calendar:* Courses of varying lengths *Degrees:* certificates *Prof. Accred.:* Respiratory Therapy Technology *CEO:* Dir. Gerald Ayo
Enroll: 237   (504) 361-6464

WESTSIDE TECHNICAL INSTITUTE
1201 Bayou Rd., P.O. Box 733, Plaquemine 70765 *Type:* Public (state) *Accred.:* 1974/1991 (SACS-COEI) *Calendar:* Courses of varying lengths *Degrees:* certificates *CEO:* Dir. Alfred S. Bell
Enroll: 116   (504) 342-8228

XAVIER UNIVERSITY OF LOUISIANA
7325 Palmetto St., New Orleans 70125 *Type:* Private (Roman Catholic) *Accred.:* 1937/1990 (SACS-CC) *Calendar:* Sem. plan *Degrees:* B, M, D *Prof. Accred.:* Music, Nurse Anesthesia Education, Pharmacy *CEO:* Pres. Norman C. Francis
Enroll: 2710   (504) 486-7411

YOUNG MEMORIAL TECHNICAL INSTITUTE
900 Youngs Rd., P.O. Box 2148, Morgan City 70381 *Type:* Public (state) *Accred.:* 1976/1991 (SACS-COEI)*Calendar:* Courses of varying lengths *Degrees:* certificates *CEO:* Dir. Greg Garrett
Enroll: 25   (504) 380-2436

MAINE

ANDOVER COLLEGE
901 Washington Ave., Portland 04103 *Type:* Private junior *Accred.:* 1970/1986 (CCA-ACICS) *Calendar:* Qtr. plan *Degrees:* A, certificates, diplomas *CEO:* Pres. Lee C. Jenkins
Enroll: 787 (207) 774-6126

BANGOR THEOLOGICAL SEMINARY
300 Union St., Bangor 04401 *Type:* Private (United Church of Christ) professional; graduate only *Accred.:* 1974/1986 (ATS); 1968/1986 (NEASC-CIHE) *Calendar:* Sem. plan *Degrees:* P, M, D *CEO:* Pres. Malcolm L. Warford
Enroll: 97 (207) 942-6781

BATES COLLEGE
Lewiston 04240 *Type:* Private liberal arts *Accred.:* 1929/1990 (NEASC-CIHE) *Calendar:* Sem. plan *Degrees:* B *CEO:* Pres. Donald W. Harward
Enroll: 1552 (207) 786-6255

BEAL COLLEGE
629 Main St., Bangor 04401 *Type:* Private junior *Accred.:* 1966/1990 (CCA-ACICS) *Calendar:* Sem. and Tri. plans *Degrees:* A *Prof. Accred.:* Medical Assisting (AMA) *CEO:* Pres. Allen T. Stehle
Enroll: 443 (207) 947-4591

BOWDOIN COLLEGE
Brunswick 04011 *Type:* Private liberal arts *Accred.:* 1929/1987 (NEASC-CIHE) *Calendar:* Sem. plan *Degrees:* B, M *CEO:* Pres. Robert H. Edwards
Enroll: 1362 (207) 725-3000

CASCO BAY COLLEGE
477 Congress St., Portland 04101 *Type:* Private junior *Accred.:* 1968/1986 (CCA-ACICS) *Calendar:* Sem. and Tri. plans *Degrees:* A *CEO:* Pres. Gene F. Stearns
Enroll: 525 (207) 772-0196

CENTRAL MAINE MEDICAL CENTER SCHOOL OF NURSING
Lewiston 04240 *Type:* Private 2-year technical *Accred.:* 1978/1989 (NEASC-CVTCI) *Calendar:* Sem. plan *Degrees:* A *Prof. Accred.:* Nursing (A) *CEO:* Dir. Faye E. Ingersoll
Enroll: 76 (207) 795-2840

CENTRAL MAINE TECHNICAL COLLEGE
1250 Turner St., Auburn 04210 *Type:* Public (state) 2-year *Accred.:* 1976/1991 (NEASC-CVTCI) *Calendar:* Sem. plan *Degrees:* A, certificates *Prof. Accred.:* Engineering Technology (civil/construction), Nursing (A) *CEO:* Pres. William J. Hierstein
Enroll: 493 (207) 784-2385

COLBY COLLEGE
Waterville 04901 *Type:* Private liberal arts *Accred.:* 1929/1988 (NEASC-CIHE) *Calendar:* 4-1-4 plan *Degrees:* B, M *CEO:* Pres. William R. Cotter
Enroll: 1750 (207) 872-3000

COLLEGE OF THE ATLANTIC
103 Eden St., Bar Harbor 04609 *Type:* Private liberal arts *Accred.:* 1976/1988 (NEASC-CIHE) *Calendar:* Tri. plan *Degrees:* B, M *CEO:* Pres. Louis Rabineau
Enroll: 209 (207) 288-5015

EASTERN MAINE TECHNICAL COLLEGE
354 Hogan Rd., Bangor 04401 *Type:* Public (state) 2-year *Accred.:* 1973/1989 (NEASC-CVTCI) *Calendar:* Sem. plan *Degrees:* A *Prof. Accred.:* Medical Laboratory Technology (AMA), Radiography *CEO:* Pres. Darrel W. Staat
Enroll: 1690 (207) 941-4600

HANSON'S BARBER SCHOOL
219 Lisbon St., Lewiston 04240 *Type:* Private *Accred.:* 1986 (CCA-ACTTS) *Calendar:* Courses of varying lengths *Degrees:* diplomas *CEO:* Dir. D. Reginald Gousse
(207) 782-1471

HUSSON COLLEGE
Bangor 04401 *Type:* Private 4-year business and professional *Accred.:* 1974/1986 (NEASC-CIHE) *Calendar:* Sem. plan *De-

Maine

grees: A, B, M, certificates, diplomas *Prof. Accred.:* Nursing (B) *CEO:* Pres. William H. Beardsley
Enroll: 1203   (207) 947-1121

KENNEBEC VALLEY TECHNICAL COLLEGE
Fairfield 04937 *Type:* Public (state) 2-year *Accred.:* 1979/1989 (NEASC-CVTCI) *Calendar:* Sem. plan *Degrees:* A *Prof. Accred.:* Nursing (A), Respiratory Therapy Technology *CEO:* Pres. Barbara W. Woodlee
Enroll: 573   (207) 453-9762

THE LANDING SCHOOL OF BOATBUILDING AND DESIGN
P.O. Box 1490, Kennebunkport 04046 *Type:* Private *Accred.:* 1987 (CCA-ACTTS) *Calendar:* Courses of varying lengths *Degrees:* certificates *CEO:* Dir. John T. Burgess
Enroll: 56   (207) 985-7976

MAINE MARITIME ACADEMY
Castine 04420 *Type:* Public (state) professional *Accred.:* 1971/1986 (NEASC-CIHE) *Calendar:* Sem. plan *Degrees:* B, M *Prof. Accred.:* Engineering Technology (naval architecture/marine) *CEO:* Pres. Kenneth M. Curtis
Enroll: 610   (207) 326-4311

MID-STATE COLLEGE
88 E. Hardscrabble Rd., Auburn 04210 *Type:* Private business *Accred.:* 1970/1983 (CCA-ACICS) *Calendar:* Sem. plan *Degrees:* A, certificates, diplomas *CEO:* Pres. Mary E. Wells
Enroll: 1389   (207) 783-1478

BRANCH CAMPUS
218 Water St., Augusta, ME 04330 *CEO:* Dir. Valmond Ladry
          (207) 623-3962

NEW ENGLAND SCHOOL OF BROADCASTING
One College Cir., Bangor 04401 *Type:* Private *Accred.:* 1986 (CCA-ACTTS) *Calendar:* Courses of varying lengths *Degrees:* diplomas *CEO:* Pres. George E. Wildey
Enroll: 45   (207) 947-6083

NORTHERN MAINE TECHNICAL COLLEGE
33 Edgemont Dr., Presque Isle 04769 *Type:* Public (state) 2-year *Accred.:* 1975/1989 (NEASC-CVTCI) *Calendar:* Sem. plan *Degrees:* A *Prof. Accred.:* Nursing (A) *CEO:* Pres. Durward R. Huffman
Enroll: 988   (207) 769-2461

PORTLAND SCHOOL OF ART
Portland 04101 *Type:* Private 4-year professional *Accred.:* 1978/1985 (NEASC-CIHE) *Calendar:* Sem. plan *Degrees:* B *Prof. Accred.:* Art *CEO:* Pres. Roger Gilmore
Enroll: 286   (207) 775-3052

ST. JOSEPH'S COLLEGE
Windham 04062-1198 *Type:* Private (Roman Catholic) liberal arts *Accred.:* 1961/1985 (NEASC-CIHE) *Calendar:* Sem. plan *Degrees:* B, M *Prof. Accred.:* Nursing (B) *CEO:* Pres. Loring E. Hart
Enroll: 2033   (207) 892-6766

SOUTHERN MAINE TECHNICAL COLLEGE
Fort Rd., South Portland 04106 *Type:* Public (state) 2-year *Accred.:* 1974/1990 (NEASC-CVTCI) *Calendar:* Sem. plan *Degrees:* A *Prof. Accred.:* Nursing (A), Radiation Therapy Technology, Radiography, Respiratory Therapy *CEO:* Pres. Wayne H. Ross
Enroll: 1722   (207) 799-7303

THOMAS COLLEGE
Waterville 04901 *Type:* Private liberal arts and business *Accred.:* 1969/1986 (NEASC-CIHE probational) *Calendar:* Sem. plan *Degrees:* A, B, M *CEO:* Pres. George R. Spann
Enroll: 671   (207) 873-0771

UNITY COLLEGE
Unity 04988 *Type:* Private liberal arts *Accred.:* 1974/1987 (NEASC-CIHE probational) *Calendar:* Modular plan *Degrees:* A, B *CEO:* Pres. Wilson G. Hess
Enroll: 392   (207) 948-3131

UNIVERSITY OF MAINE
Orono 04469 *Type:* Public (state) *System:* University of Maine System *Accred.:* 1929/1988 (NEASC-CIHE) *Calendar:* Sem. plan *Degrees:* A, B, M, D *Prof. Accred.:* Animal

Medical Technology, Art, Business (B,M), Clinical Psychology, Dental Assisting, Dental Hygiene, Engineering (agricultural, chemical, civil, electrical, engineering physics/science, forest, mechanical, surveying), Engineering Technology (civil/construction, electrical, mechanical), Forestry, Medical Record Technology, Music, Nursing (B), Psychology Internship, Public Administration, Social Work (B,M), Speech-Language Pathology, Teacher Education (e,s,p) *CEO:* Pres. John C. Hitt
Enroll: 10604 (207) 581-1512

UNIVERSITY OF MAINE AT AUGUSTA
Augusta 04330 *Type:* Public (state) *System:* University of Maine System *Accred.:* 1973/1985 (NEASC-CIHE) *Calendar:* Sem. plan *Degrees:* A, B *Prof. Accred.:* Medical Laboratory Technology (AMA), Nursing (A) *CEO:* Pres. George P. Connick
Enroll: 1960 (207) 621-3403

UNIVERSITY OF MAINE AT FARMINGTON
86 Main St., Farmington 04938 *Type:* Public (state) liberal arts and teachers *System:* University of Maine System *Accred.:* 1958/1986 (NEASC-CIHE) *Calendar:* Sem. plan *Degrees:* A, B *Prof. Accred.:* Teacher Education (e,s) *CEO:* Pres. J. Michael Orenduff
Enroll: 2438 (207) 778-3501

UNIVERSITY OF MAINE AT FORT KENT
Pleasant St., Fort Kent 04743 *Type:* Public (state) liberal arts and teachers *System:* University of Maine System *Accred.:* 1970/1986 (NEASC-CIHE) *Calendar:* Sem. plan *Degrees:* A, B *Prof. Accred.:* Nursing (B) *CEO:* Pres. Richard G. Dumont
Enroll: 406 (207) 834-3162

UNIVERSITY OF MAINE AT MACHIAS
Machias 04654 *Type:* Public (state) liberal arts and teachers *System:* University of Maine System *Accred.:* 1970/1984 (NEASC-CIHE) *Calendar:* Sem. plan *Degrees:* A, B *Prof. Accred.:* Recreation Management *CEO:* Pres. Frederic A. Reynolds
Enroll: 676 (207) 255-3313

UNIVERSITY OF MAINE AT PRESQUE ISLE
181 Main St., Presque Isle 04769 *Type:* Public (state) liberal arts and teachers *System:* University of Maine System *Accred.:* 1968/1984 (NEASC-CIHE) *Calendar:* Sem. plan *Degrees:* A, B *Prof. Accred.:* Medical Laboratory Technology (AMA), Recreation and Leisure Services *CEO:* Pres. James R. Roach
Enroll: 981 (207) 764-0311

UNIVERSITY OF NEW ENGLAND
11 Hills Beach Rd., Biddeford 04005 *Type:* Private liberal arts and professional *Accred.:* 1966/1986 (NEASC-CIHE) *Calendar:* 4-1-4 plan *Degrees:* A, B, M, D *Prof. Accred.:* Nurse Anesthesia Education, Nursing (A), Occupational Therapy, Osteopathy, Physical Therapy, Social Work (M) *CEO:* Pres. Thomas H. Reynolds
Enroll: 1192 (207) 283-0171

UNIVERSITY OF SOUTHERN MAINE
96 Falmouth St., Portland 04103 *Type:* Public (state) liberal arts and professional *System:* University of Maine System *Accred.:* 1960/1981 (NEASC-CIHE) *Calendar:* Sem. plan *Degrees:* A, B, P, M, D *Prof. Accred.:* Art, Counseling, Law, Music, Nursing (B,M), Rehabilitation Counseling, Social Work (B), Teacher Education (e,s) *CEO:* Pres. Richard L. Pattenaude
Enroll: 6292 (207) 780-4141

WASHINGTON COUNTY VOCATIONAL-TECHNICAL INSTITUTE
Calais 04619 *Type:* Public (state) 2-year *Accred.:* 1976/1989 (NEASC-CVTCI) *Calendar:* Sem. plan *Degrees:* certificates *CEO:* Pres. Ronald P. Renaud
Enroll: 242 (207) 454-2144

WESTBROOK COLLEGE
Stevens Ave., Portland 04103 *Type:* Private liberal arts *Accred.:* 1934/1984 (NEASC-CIHE) *Calendar:* 4-1-4 plan *Degrees:* A, B *Prof. Accred.:* Dental Hygiene, Nursing (B) *CEO:* Pres. William D. Andrews
Enroll: 461 (207) 797-7261

MARYLAND

ABBIE BUSINESS INSTITUTE
186 Thomas Jefferson Dr., Ste. 203, Frederick 21701-4315 *Type:* Private business *Accred.:* 1984/1990 (CCA-ACICS) *Calendar:* Courses of varying lengths *Degrees:* certificates, diplomas *CEO:* Pres. Allan R. Short
Enroll: 172 (301) 694-0211

ALLEGANY COMMUNITY COLLEGE
Willowbrook Rd., Cumberland 21502 *Type:* Public (county) junior *System:* Maryland State Board for Community Colleges *Accred.:* 1965/1985 (MSA) *Calendar:* Sem. plan *Degrees:* A, certificates, diplomas *Prof. Accred.:* Dental Assisting, Dental Hygiene, Medical Laboratory Technology (AMA), Radiography, Respiratory Therapy *CEO:* Pres. Donald L. Alexander
Enroll: 2220 (301) 724-7700

ANNE ARUNDEL COMMUNITY COLLEGE
101 College Pkwy., Arnold 21012 *Type:* Public (county) junior *System:* Maryland State Board for Community Colleges *Accred.:* 1968/1989 (MSA) *Calendar:* Sem. plan *Degrees:* A *Prof. Accred.:* Nursing (A) *CEO:* Pres. Thomas E. Florestano
Enroll: 11664 (410) 647-7100

ARUNDEL INSTITUTE OF TECHNOLOGY
1808 Edison Hwy., Baltimore 21213 *Type:* Private *Accred.:* 1971/1988 (CCA-ACTTS) *Calendar:* Qtr. plan *Degrees:* diplomas *CEO:* Dir. Manfred Bloch
Enroll: 257 (410) 327-6640

AUTOMATION ACADEMY
17 S. Charles St., 2nd Fl., Baltimore 21201-3324 *Type:* Private *Accred.:* 1991 (CCA-ACTTS) *Calendar:* Courses of varying lengths *Degrees:* certificates *CEO:* Pres. Gerald W. Newman
(410) 727-3020

BALTIMORE HEBREW UNIVERSITY
5800 Park Heights Ave., Baltimore 21215 *Type:* Private professional and teachers *Accred.:* 1974/1984 (MSA) *Calendar:* Sem. plan *Degrees:* B, M, D *CEO:* Pres. Leivy Smolar
Enroll: 321 (410) 578-6900

BALTIMORE'S INTERNATIONAL CULINARY ARTS COLLEGE
25 S. Calvert St., Baltimore 21202-1503 *Type:* Private *Accred.:* 1991 (CCA-ACTTS); 1989 (MSA candidate) *Calendar:* Sem. plan *Degrees:* A *CEO:* Pres. Roger Chylinski
Enroll: 306 (410) 752-1087

BARCLAY CAREER SCHOOL
300 W. Lexington St., Ste. 700, Baltimore 21201 *Type:* Private *Accred.:* 1991 (CCA-ACTTS) *Calendar:* Courses of varying lengths *Degrees:* certificates *CEO:* Dir. John J. Pullen
(410) 547-0075

BOWIE STATE UNIVERSITY
14000 Jericho Park Rd., Bowie 20715 *Type:* Public (state) liberal arts and teachers *System:* University of Maryland System *Accred.:* 1961/1987 (MSA) *Calendar:* Sem. plan *Degrees:* B, M *Prof. Accred.:* Nursing (B), Social Work (B), Teacher Education (e,s,p) *CEO:* Pres. James E. Lyons, Sr.
Enroll: 3326 (301) 464-6500

BROADCASTING INSTITUTE OF MARYLAND
7200 Harford Rd., Baltimore 21234 *Type:* Private *Accred.:* 1980/1985 (CCA-ACTTS) *Calendar:* Sem. plan *Degrees:* diplomas *CEO:* Pres. John C. Jeppi
Enroll: 197 (800) 942-9246

CDI CAREER DEVELOPMENT INSTITUTE
10461 Mill Run Cir., Owings Mills 21117-5500 *Type:* Private *Accred.:* 1981/1988 (CCA-ACTTS) *Calendar:* Courses of varying lengths *Degrees:* certificates *CEO:* Dir. James Nesby
Enroll: 608 (410) 356-1600

Accredited Institutions — Maryland

CAPITOL COLLEGE
11301 Springfield Rd., Laurel 20708 *Type:* Private technological *Accred.:* 1976/1986 (MSA) *Calendar:* Sem. plan *Degrees:* A, B, certificates, diplomas *Prof. Accred.:* Engineering Technology (computer, electrical) *CEO:* Pres. G. William Troxler
Enroll: 777   (301) 953-0060

CATONSVILLE COMMUNITY COLLEGE
800 S. Rolling Rd., Catonsville 21228 *Type:* Public (county) junior *System:* Maryland State Board for Community Colleges *Accred.:* 1966/1986 (MSA) *Calendar:* Sem. plan *Degrees:* A, certificates, diplomas *Prof. Accred.:* Mortuary Science *CEO:* Pres. Frederick J. Walsh
Enroll: 11444   (410) 455-6050

CARROLL COUNTY COLLEGE
300 S. Center St., Westminster, MD 21157 *CEO:* Pres. Alan Shuman
  (410) 876-3880

CECIL COMMUNITY COLLEGE
1000 North East Rd., North East 21901 *Type:* Public (county) junior *System:* Maryland State Board for Community Colleges *Accred.:* 1974/1985 (MSA) *Calendar:* Sem. plan *Degrees:* A, certificates, diplomas *Prof. Accred.:* Nursing (A) *CEO:* Pres. Robert L. Gell
Enroll: 1447   (410) 287-6060

CHARLES COUNTY COMMUNITY COLLEGE
Mitchell Rd., P.O. Box 910, La Plata 20646 *Type:* Public (county) junior *System:* Maryland State Board for Community Colleges *Accred.:* 1969/1989 (MSA) *Calendar:* Sem. plan *Degrees:* A, certificates, diplomas *Prof. Accred.:* Nursing (A), Practical Nursing *CEO:* Pres. John M. Sine
Enroll: 4931   (301) 934-2251

CHESAPEAKE COLLEGE
P.O. Box 8, Wye Mills 21679 *Type:* Public (district) junior *System:* Maryland State Board for Community Colleges *Accred.:* 1970/1985 (MSA) *Calendar:* Sem. plan *Degrees:* A, certificates, diplomas *Prof. Accred.:* Radiography *CEO:* Pres. Robert C. Schleiger
Enroll: 2247   (410) 822-5400

COLLEGE OF NOTRE DAME OF MARYLAND
4701 N. Charles St., Baltimore 21210 *Type:* Private (Roman Catholic) liberal arts primarily for women *Accred.:* 1925/1987 (MSA) *Calendar:* Sem. plan *Degrees:* B, M *Prof. Accred.:* Nursing (B) *CEO:* Pres. Kathleen Feeley
Enroll: 2461   (410) 435-0100

COLUMBIA UNION COLLEGE
7600 Flower Ave., Takoma Park 20912 *Type:* Private (Seventh-Day Adventist) liberal arts *Accred.:* 1942/1989 (MSA) *Calendar:* Sem. plan *Degrees:* A, B, certificates, diplomas *Prof. Accred.:* Medical Laboratory Technology (AMA), Medical Technology, Nursing (B), Respiratory Therapy *CEO:* Pres. N. Clifford Sorenson
Enroll: 1204   (301) 891-4116

COPPIN STATE COLLEGE
2500 W. North Ave., Baltimore 21216 *Type:* Public (state) liberal arts *System:* University of Maryland System *Accred.:* 1962/1988 (MSA) *Calendar:* Sem. plan *Degrees:* B, M *Prof. Accred.:* Nursing (B), Rehabilitation Counseling, Social Work (B), Teacher Education (e,s) *CEO:* Pres. Calvin W. Burnett
Enroll: 2240   (410) 383-5910

DIESEL INSTITUTE OF AMERICA
Rte. 40, P.O. Box 69, Grantsville 21536 *Type:* Private *Accred.:* 1988 (CCA-ACTTS) *Calendar:* Courses of varying lengths *Degrees:* diplomas *CEO:* Dir. Bud Poland
Enroll: 76   (301) 895-5139

DUNDALK COMMUNITY COLLEGE
7200 Sollers Point Rd., Dundalk 21222 *Type:* Public (county) junior *System:* Maryland State Board for Community Colleges *Accred.:* 1975/1989 (MSA) *Calendar:* Sem. plan *Degrees:* A, certificates, diplomas *CEO:* Pres. Martha A. Smith
Enroll: 3206   (410) 282-6700

Maryland

EMERGENCY MANAGEMENT INSTITUTE
16825 S. Seton Ave., Emmitsburg 21727 *Type:* Private home study *Accred.:* 1988 (NHSC) *Calendar:* Courses of varying lengths *Degrees:* certificates *CEO:* Dir. Linda Straka
(301) 447-6771

ESSEX COMMUNITY COLLEGE
7201 Rossville Blvd., Baltimore 21237 *Type:* Public (county) junior *System:* Maryland State Board for Community Colleges *Accred.:* 1966/1987 (MSA) *Calendar:* Sem. plan *Degrees:* A *Prof. Accred.:* Medical Laboratory Technology (AMA), Medical Record Technology, Music, Nuclear Medicine Technology, Nursing (A), Physician Assisting, Radiation Therapy Technology, Radiography, Respiratory Therapy Technology, Theatre, Veterinary Technology *CEO:* Pres. Donald J. Slowinski
Enroll: 10218   (410) 682-6000

FLEET BUSINESS SCHOOL
2530 Riva Rd., Ste. 201, Annapolis 21401 *Type:* Private business *Accred.:* 1971/1989 (CCA-ACICS) *Calendar:* Qtr. plan *Degrees:* certificates, diplomas *CEO:* Dir. James H. Graves
Enroll: 277   (410) 266-8500

FREDERICK COMMUNITY COLLEGE
7932 Oppossumtown Pike, Frederick 21701 *Type:* Public (district) junior *System:* Maryland State Board for Community Colleges *Accred.:* 1971/1986 (MSA) *Calendar:* Sem. plan *Degrees:* A, certificates, diplomas *CEO:* Pres. Lee J. Betts
Enroll: 3483   (301) 694-5240

FROSTBURG STATE UNIVERSITY
Frostburg 21532-1099 *Type:* Public (state) liberal arts and teachers *System:* University of Maryland System *Accred.:* 1953/1986 (MSA) *Calendar:* Sem. plan *Degrees:* B, M, certificates, diplomas *Prof. Accred.:* Social Work (B-candidate) *CEO:* Pres. Catherine R. Gira
Enroll: 4525   (301) 689-4000

GARRETT COMMUNITY COLLEGE
Mosser Rd., P.O. Box 151, McHenry 21541 *Type:* Public (county) junior *System:* Maryland State Board for Community Colleges *Accred.:* 1975/1988 (MSA) *Calendar:* Sem. plan *Degrees:* A, certificates, diplomas *CEO:* Pres. Stephen J. Herman
Enroll: 612   (301) 387-6666

GOUCHER COLLEGE
Towson 21204 *Type:* Private liberal arts primarily for women *Accred.:* 1921/1989 (MSA) *Calendar:* Sem. plan *Degrees:* B, M *CEO:* Pres. Rhoda M. Dorsey
Enroll: 982   (410) 337-6000

HAGERSTOWN BUSINESS COLLEGE
1050 Crestwood Dr., Hagerstown 21740 *Type:* Private junior *Accred.:* 1968/1990 (CCA-ACICS) *Calendar:* Qtr. plan *Degrees:* A *CEO:* Dir. Cheryl M. Hyslop
Enroll: 680   (301) 739-2670

HAGERSTOWN JUNIOR COLLEGE
751 Robinwood Dr., Hagerstown 21740 *Type:* Public (county) junior *System:* Maryland State Board for Community Colleges *Accred.:* 1968/1989 (MSA) *Calendar:* Sem. plan *Degrees:* A *Prof. Accred.:* Radiography *CEO:* Pres. Norman P. Shea
Enroll: 2641   (301) 790-2800

HARFORD COMMUNITY COLLEGE
401 Thomas Run Rd., Bel Air 21014 *Type:* Public (county) junior *System:* Maryland State Board for Community Colleges *Accred.:* 1967/1987 (MSA) *Calendar:* Sem. plan *Degrees:* A *Prof. Accred.:* Histologic Technology, Nursing (A) *CEO:* Pres. Richard J. Pappas
Enroll: 4425   (410) 836-4000

HOME STUDY INTERNATIONAL
12501 Old Columbia Pike, P.O. Box 4437, Silver Spring 20914-4437 *Type:* Private home study *Accred.:* 1967/1988 (NHSC) *Calendar:* Courses of varying lengths *Degrees:* certificates *CEO:* Pres. Joseph E. Gurubatham
(301) 680-6570

HOOD COLLEGE
Rosemont Ave., Frederick 21701 *Type:* Private liberal arts primarily for women *Accred.:* 1922/1987 (MSA) *Calendar:* Sem. plan *Degrees:* B, M *Prof. Accred.:* Dietetics (coordinated), Home Economics, Social Work (B) *CEO:* Pres. Martha E. Church
Enroll: 1874 (301) 663-3131

HOWARD COMMUNITY COLLEGE
10901 Little Patuxent Pkwy., Columbia 21044 *Type:* Public (county) junior *System:* Maryland State Board for Community Colleges *Accred.:* 1975/1990 (MSA) *Calendar:* Sem. plan *Degrees:* A, certificates, diplomas *Prof. Accred.:* Nursing (A) *CEO:* Pres. Dwight A. Burrill
Enroll: 3926 (410) 992-4800

INTERNATIONAL ACADEMY OF HAIR DESIGN AND TECHNOLOGY
16 N. Dundalk Ave., Baltimore 21222-4221 *Type:* Private *Accred.:* 1991 (CCA-ACTTS) *Calendar:* Courses of varying lengths *Degrees:* certificates *CEO:* Pres. Simon V. Avara
(410) 285-7854

JOHNS HOPKINS UNIVERSITY
34th and Charles Sts., Baltimore 21218 *Type:* Private *Accred.:* 1921/1989 (MSA) *Calendar:* Sem. plan *Degrees:* B, P, M, D *Prof. Accred.:* Engineering (bioengineering, chemical, civil, electrical, engineering mechanics, materials), Medical Illustration, Medicine, Nursing (B,M), Public Health *CEO:* Pres. William C. Richardson
Enroll: 12651 (410) 516-8068

COLUMBIA CENTER
5457 Twin Knolls Rd., Ste. 202, Columbia, MD 21045 *CEO:* Dir. Elizabeth Mayotte
(410) 997-8045

PEABODY INSTITUTE OF MUSIC
One E. Mount Vernon Pl., Baltimore, MD 21202 *Prof. Accred.:* Music *CEO:* Dir. Robert O. Pierce
(410) 659-8100

SCHOOL OF ADVANCED INTERNATIONAL STUDIES
1740 Massachusetts Ave., N.W., Washington, DC 20036 *CEO:* Dir. George Packard
(202) 663-5600

LINCOLN TECHNICAL INSTITUTE
3200 Wilkens Ave., Baltimore 21229 *Type:* Private *Accred.:* 1968/1989 (CCA-ACTTS) *Calendar:* Courses of varying lengths *Degrees:* certificates, diplomas *CEO:* Dir. Craig Downs
Enroll: 957 (410) 646-5480

LINCOLN TECHNICAL INSTITUTE
7800 Central Ave., Landover 20785 *Type:* Private *Accred.:* 1968/1988 (CCA-ACTTS) *Calendar:* Courses of varying lengths *Degrees:* certificates, diplomas *CEO:* Dir. Joseph W. Fox
Enroll: 1289 (301) 336-7250

LOYOLA COLLEGE
4501 N. Charles St., Baltimore 21210 *Type:* Private (Roman Catholic) liberal arts *Accred.:* 1931/1990 (MSA) *Calendar:* Sem. plan *Degrees:* B, M, D *Prof. Accred.:* Accounting (Type A), Business (B,M), Computer Science, Counseling *CEO:* Pres. Joseph A. Sellinger, S.J.
Enroll: 5821 (410) 323-1010

THE MARYLAND COLLEGE OF ART AND DESIGN
10500 Georgia Ave., Silver Spring 20902 *Type:* Private 2-year professional *Calendar:* Qtr. plan *Degrees:* A, certificates *Prof. Accred.:* Art *CEO:* Pres. Edward Glynn
Enroll: 85 (301) 649-4454

MARYLAND DRAFTING INSTITUTE
2045 University Blvd. E., Langley Park 20783 *Type:* Private *Accred.:* 1974/1989 (CCA-ACTTS) *Calendar:* Courses of varying lengths *Degrees:* certificates, diplomas *CEO:* Admin. Dir. Carol B. Sawyer
Enroll: 514 (301) 439-7776

THE MARYLAND INSTITUTE COLLEGE OF ART
1300 W. Mount Royal Ave., Baltimore 21217 *Type:* Private professional *Accred.:*

1967/1988 (MSA) *Calendar:* Sem. plan *Degrees:* B, M, certificates, diplomas *Prof. Accred.:* Art *CEO:* Pres. Fred Lazarus, IV
Enroll: 1285 (410) 669-9200

MARYLAND INSTITUTE OF ULTRASOUND TECHNOLOGY
2712 N. Charles St., Baltimore 21218 *Type:* Private *Calendar:* 14-mo. plan *Degrees:* certificates *Prof. Accred.:* Diagnostic Medical Sonography *CEO:* Pres. Roy Soares
Enroll: 19 (410) 366-3480

THE MEDIX SCHOOL
1017 York Rd., Towson 21204 *Type:* Private *Accred.:* 1976/1988 (CCA-ACTTS) *Calendar:* Courses of varying lengths *Degrees:* certificates *Prof. Accred.:* Dental Assisting (prelim. provisional), Medical Assisting (AMA) *CEO:* Dir. Bernard E. Wilke
Enroll: 564 (410) 337-5155

MONTGOMERY COLLEGE—GERMANTOWN CAMPUS
20200 Observation Dr., Germantown 20874 *Type:* Public (county) junior *System:* Montgomery College Central Administration *Accred.:* 1980/1987 (MSA) *Calendar:* Sem. plan *Degrees:* A, certificates, diplomas *CEO:* Provost Stanley M. Dahlman
Enroll: 3124 (301) 972-2000

MONTGOMERY COLLEGE—ROCKVILLE CAMPUS
51 Mannakee St., Rockville 20850 *Type:* Public (county) junior *System:* Montgomery College Central Administration *Accred.:* 1968/1987 (MSA) *Calendar:* Sem. plan *Degrees:* A, certificates, diplomas *Prof. Accred.:* Engineering Technology (electrical), Music, Radiography *CEO:* Provost Antoinette P. Hastings
Enroll: 14119 (301) 279-5000

MONTGOMERY COLLEGE—TAKOMA PARK CAMPUS
Takoma Ave. and Fenton St., Takoma Park 20912 *Type:* Public (county) junior *System:* Montgomery College Central Administration *Accred.:* 1950/1987 (MSA) *Calendar:* Sem. plan *Degrees:* A, certificates, diplomas *Prof. Accred.:* Dental Assisting, Nursing (A) *CEO:* Provost O. Robert Brown
Enroll: 4328 (301) 587-4090

MORGAN STATE UNIVERSITY
Hillen Rd. and Cold Spring La., Baltimore 21239 *Type:* Public liberal arts *System:* Maryland Higher Education Commission *Accred.:* 1925/1988 (MSA) *Calendar:* Sem. plan *Degrees:* B, M, D *Prof. Accred.:* Architecture (M-candidate), Engineering (electrical), Medical Technology, Music, Planning (city/regional), Social Work (B), Teacher Education (e,s,p) *CEO:* Pres. Earl S. Richardson
Enroll: 4066 (410) 444-3333

MOUNT ST. MARY'S COLLEGE AND SEMINARY
Emmitsburg 21727-7797 *Type:* Private (Roman Catholic) liberal arts and theology *Accred.:* 1987 (ATS); 1922/1985 (MSA) *Calendar:* Sem. plan *Degrees:* B, P, M *CEO:* Pres. Robert J. Wickenheiser
Enroll: 1787 (301) 447-6122

NATIONAL CRYPTOLOGIC SCHOOL
Fort George G. Meade 20755-6000 *Type:* Public (federal) *Accred.:* 1990 (SACS-COEI) *Calendar:* Courses of varying lengths *Degrees:* certificates, diplomas *CEO:* Commanding Ofcr. Whitney Reed
Enroll: 1948 (410) 859-6136

NATIONAL EDUCATION CENTER—TEMPLE SCHOOL CAMPUS
3601 O'Donnell St., Baltimore 21224 *Type:* Private business *Accred.:* 1988 (CCA-ACICS) *Calendar:* Qtr. plan *Degrees:* certificates, diplomas *CEO:* Dir. Arthur Nelson
Enroll: 522 (410) 675-6000

NER ISRAEL RABBINICAL COLLEGE
400 Mount Wilson La., Baltimore 21208 *Type:* Private professional *Accred.:* 1974/1987 (AARTS) *Calendar:* Sem. plan *Degrees:* B, M, D *CEO:* Pres. Herman N. Neuberger
Enroll: 431 (410) 484-7200

Accredited Institutions **Maryland**

THE NEW COMMUNITY COLLEGE OF BALTIMORE
2901 Liberty Heights Ave., Baltimore 21215 *Type:* Public (city) junior *System:* Maryland State Board for Community Colleges *Accred.:* 1963/1980 (MSA) *Calendar:* Sem. plan *Degrees:* A *Prof. Accred.:* Dental Hygiene, Medical Record Technology, Nursing (A), Physical Therapy Assisting, Respiratory Therapy *CEO:* Interim Pres. James D. Tschechtelin
Enroll: 5254 (410) 396-0203

HARBOR CAMPUS
600 E. Lombard St., Baltimore, MD 21202 *CEO:* Dir. Mary Lynn Devlin
(410) 333-8348

PSI INSTITUTE
1310 Apple Ave., Silver Spring 20910 *Type:* Private *Accred.:* 1986 (CCA-ACTTS) *Calendar:* Courses of varying lengths *Degrees:* certificates *CEO:* Dir. Burl Dicken
Enroll: 683 (301) 589-0900

PSI INSTITUTE OF BALTIMORE
300 W. Lexington St., Ste. 500, Baltimore 21201 *Type:* Private *Accred.:* 1988 (CCA-ACTTS) *Calendar:* Courses of varying lengths *Degrees:* certificates *CEO:* Dir. Bernard DiPasquale
(410) 576-0060

PTC CAREER INSTITUTE
201 E. Baltimore St., Baltimore 21202 *Type:* Private *Accred.:* 1986 (CCA-ACTTS) *Calendar:* Courses of varying lengths *Degrees:* certificates *CEO:* Dir. Susan L. Sherwood
(410) 837-3270

PATRICIA STEVENS FASHION AND FINISHING SCHOOL
11301 Rockville Pike, 3rd Level, North Bethesda 20895 *Type:* Private *Accred.:* 1989 (CCA-ACICS) *Calendar:* Qtr. plan *Degrees:* certificates, diplomas *CEO:* Dir. Pearce Young
Enroll: 39 (301) 984-1252

PRINCE GEORGE'S COMMUNITY COLLEGE
301 Largo Rd., Largo 20772 *Type:* Public (county) junior *System:* Maryland State Board for Community Colleges *Accred.:* 1969/1985 (MSA) *Calendar:* Sem. plan *Degrees:* A *Prof. Accred.:* Engineering Technology (electrical), Medical Record Technology, Nuclear Medicine Technology, Nursing (A), Radiography, Respiratory Therapy *CEO:* Pres. Robert I. Bickford
Enroll: 13443 (301) 336-6000

BRANCH CAMPUS
Andrews A.F.B. Degree Ctr., Patrick Ave., Bldg. 3611, Andrews Air Force Base, MD 20331 *CEO:* Pres. Kathy Sexton
(301) 322-0778

R.E.T.S. ELECTRONIC SCHOOL
1520 S. Caton Ave., Baltimore 21227 *Type:* Private *Accred.:* 1973/1988 (CCA-ACTTS) *Calendar:* Courses of varying lengths *Degrees:* certificates, diplomas *CEO:* Pres. H.V. Leslie
Enroll: 2177 (410) 644-6400

ST. JOHN'S COLLEGE
60 College Ave., Annapolis 21404 *Type:* Private liberal arts *Accred.:* 1923/1989 (MSA) *Calendar:* Sem. plan *Degrees:* B, M *CEO:* Pres. Christopher Nelson
Enroll: 467 (410) 263-2371

ST. MARY'S COLLEGE OF MARYLAND
St. Mary's 20686 *Type:* Public (state) liberal arts *System:* Maryland Higher Education Commission *Accred.:* 1959/1984 (MSA) *Calendar:* Sem. plan *Degrees:* B *Prof. Accred.:* Music *CEO:* Pres. Edward T. Lewis
Enroll: 1585 (301) 862-0200

ST. MARY'S SEMINARY AND UNIVERSITY
5400 Roland Ave., Baltimore 21210 *Type:* Private (Roman Catholic) professional; graduate only *Accred.:* 1971/1981 (ATS); 1951/1987 (MSA) *Calendar:* Sem. plan *Degrees:* B, P, M *CEO:* Pres./Rector Robert F. Leavitt
Enroll: 413 (410) 323-3200

SALISBURY STATE UNIVERSITY
Salisbury 21801 *Type:* Public (state) liberal arts *System:* University of Maryland System *Accred.:* 1956/1986 (MSA) *Calendar:* Sem.

Maryland

plan *Degrees:* B, M *Prof. Accred.:* Medical Technology, Nursing (B,M), Respiratory Therapy, Social Work (B) *CEO:* Pres. Thomas E. Bellavance
Enroll: 5260   (410) 543-6000

SOJOURNER-DOUGLASS COLLEGE
500 N. Caroline St., Baltimore 21205 *Type:* Private *Accred.:* 1980/1985 (MSA) *Calendar:* Tri. plan *Degrees:* B *CEO:* Pres. Charles W. Simmons
Enroll: 353   (410) 276-0306

THE STRATFORD SCHOOL
705 York Rd., Towson 21204 *Type:* Private business *Accred.:* 1979/1982 (CCA-ACICS) *Calendar:* Courses of varying lengths *Degrees:* certificates, diplomas *CEO:* Admin. Dir. Sharon L. Hodge
Enroll: 281   (410) 825-2566

STRAYER BUSINESS COLLEGE
5 Light St., Baltimore 21202 *Type:* Private business *Accred.:* 1959/1987 (CCA-ACICS) *Calendar:* Courses of varying lengths *Degrees:* certificates, diplomas *CEO:* Dir. Ronald K. Bailey
Enroll: 470   (410) 539-5629

TESST ELECTRONICS AND COMPUTER INSTITUTE
5122 Baltimore Ave., Hyattsville 20781 *Type:* Private *Accred.:* 1975/1985 (CCA-ACTTS) *Calendar:* Sem. plan *Degrees:* diplomas *CEO:* Dir. Richard J. Armbruster
Enroll: 650   (301) 864-5750

TOWSON STATE UNIVERSITY
Towson 21204 *Type:* Public (state) liberal arts *System:* University of Maryland System *Accred.:* 1949/1989 (MSA) *Calendar:* Sem. plan *Degrees:* B, M *Prof. Accred.:* Dance, Music, Nursing (B), Occupational Therapy, Psychology Internship, Teacher Education (e,s,p) *CEO:* Pres. Hoke L. Smith
Enroll: 15169   (410) 321-2000

TRADITIONAL ACUPUNCTURE INSTITUTE
American City Bldg., Ste. 100, Columbia 21044 *Type:* Private *Calendar:* 3-yr. plan *Degrees:* M *Prof. Accred.:* Acupuncture *CEO:* Pres. Robert M. Duggan
    (301) 596-6006

UNIFORMED SERVICES UNIVERSITY OF THE HEALTH SCIENCES
4301 Jones Bridge Rd., Bethesda 20814 *Type:* Public (federal) professional *Accred.:* 1984 (MSA) *Calendar:* Courses of varying lengths *Degrees:* P, M, D *Prof. Accred.:* Community Health/Preventive Medicine, Medicine *CEO:* Pres. Jay P. Sanford
Enroll: 774   (301) 295-3030

UNITED STATES ARMY ORDNANCE CENTER AND SCHOOL
Aberdeen Proving Ground 21005-5201 *Type:* Public (federal) technical *Accred.:* 1978/1988 (SACS-COEI)*Calendar:* Courses of varying lengths *Degrees:* certificates *CEO:* Commandant James W. Ball
Enroll: 4258   (410) 278-3373

UNITED STATES NAVAL ACADEMY
Annapolis 21402-5000 *Type:* Public (federal) military *Accred.:* 1947/1986 (MSA) *Calendar:* Sem. plan *Degrees:* B *Prof. Accred.:* Computer Science, Engineering (aerospace, electrical, mechanical, naval architecture/marine, ocean, systems) *CEO:* Supt. Thomas C. Lynch
Enroll: 4557   (410) 267-6100

UNITED STATES NAVAL HEALTH SCIENCES EDUCATION AND TRAINING COMMAND
Naval Medical Command, National Capital Region, Bethesda 20889-5022 *Type:* Public (federal) technical *Accred.:* 1984/1990 (SACS-COEI) *Calendar:* Courses of varying lengths *Degrees:* certificates *Prof. Accred.:* Cytotechnology, Radiography *CEO:* Commanding Ofcr. David G. Kemp
Enroll: 4229   (301) 295-0203

UNITED STATES NAVAL AEROSPACE MEDICAL INSTITUTE
Pensacola, FL 32508-5600 *CEO:* Commandant Charles Bercier
    (904) 452-4554

Accredited Institutions   **Maryland**

UNITED STATES NAVAL DENTAL SCHOOL
National Naval Dental Ctr., Bethesda, MD 20889-5077 *Prof. Accred.:* Combined Prosthodontics, Combined Maxillofacial Prosthodontics, Endodontics, General Dentistry, Oral Pathology, Periodontics *CEO:* Commandant Francis J. Robertello
(301) 295-0064

UNITED STATES NAVAL HOSPITAL CORPS SCHOOL
Great Lakes, IL 60088-5275 *CEO:* Commandant C.W. Cote
(708) 688-5680

UNITED STATES NAVAL SCHOOL OF DENTAL ASSISTING AND TECHNOLOGY
Naval Sta., Box 147, San Diego, CA 92136-5147 *CEO:* Ofcr. in Charge Robert Flinton
(619) 556-8262

UNITED STATES NAVAL SCHOOL OF HEALTH SCIENCES—BETHESDA
Naval Medical Command, Bethesda, MD 20811-5033 *Prof. Accred.:* Medical Laboratory Technology (AMA), Nuclear Medicine Technology, Surgical Technology *CEO:* Commandant K.D. Gibson
(202) 295-1251

UNITED STATES NAVAL SCHOOL OF HEALTH SCIENCES—OAKLAND
San Diego Detachment, Oakland, CA 94627-5000 *Prof. Accred.:* Surgical Technology *CEO:* Ofcr. in Charge T. Bratton
(510) 633-6065

UNITED STATES NAVAL SCHOOL OF HEALTH SCIENCES—PORTSMOUTH
Portsmouth, VA 23708-5000 *Prof. Accred.:* Surgical Technology *CEO:* Commandant W.A. Nacrelli, U.S.N.
(804) 398-5032

UNITED STATES NAVAL SCHOOL OF HEALTH SCIENCES—SAN DIEGO
San Diego, CA 92134-6000 *Prof. Accred.:* Medical Laboratory Technology (AMA), Physician Assisting, Surgical Technology *CEO:* Commanding Ofcr. M. Iczkowski
(619) 532-7700

UNITED STATES NAVAL UNDERSEA MEDICAL INSTITUTE
Groton, CT 06349-5159 *CEO:* Ofcr. in Charge D.M. Sack
(203) 449-3365

UNITED STATES NAVY FIELD MEDICAL SERVICE SCHOOL
Camp Lejuene, NC 28542 *CEO:* Commandant A.E. Mataldi
(919) 451-0929

UNITED STATES NAVY FIELD MEDICAL SERVICE SCHOOL
Camp Pendelton, CA 92055-5008 *CEO:* Commanding Ofcr. George J. Hansel
(619) 725-7139

UNIVERSITY OF BALTIMORE
1420 N. Charles St., Baltimore 21201 *Type:* Public (state) liberal arts *System:* University of Maryland System *Accred.:* 1971/1987 (MSA) *Calendar:* Sem. plan *Degrees:* B, P, M, certificates, diplomas *Prof. Accred.:* Business (B,M), Law, Public Administration *CEO:* Pres. H. Mebane Turner
Enroll: 5228   (410) 625-3000

UNIVERSITY OF MARYLAND BALTIMORE COUNTY
5401 Wilkens Ave., Catonsville 21228 *Type:* Public (state) liberal arts *System:* University of Maryland System *Accred.:* 1966/1986 (MSA) *Calendar:* 4-1-4 plan *Degrees:* B, M, D *Prof. Accred.:* Clinical Psychology, Engineering (chemical, mechanical), Policy Science, Social Work (B) *CEO:* Pres. Michael K. Hooker
Enroll: 9868   (410) 455-1000

UNIVERSITY OF MARYLAND COLLEGE PARK
College Park 20742 *Type:* Public (state) liberal arts *System:* University of Maryland System *Accred.:* 1921/1986 (MSA) *Calendar:* Sem. plan *Degrees:* B, M, D, certificates, diplomas *Prof. Accred.:* Architecture (M), Audiology, Business (B,M), Clinical Psychology, Counseling, Counseling Psych-

Maryland

ology, Engineering (aerospace, agricultural, chemical, civil, electrical, fire protection, general, mechanical, nuclear), Journalism, Librarianship, Music, Planning (community), Psychology Internship, Recreation, Rehabilitation Counseling, School Psychology, Speech-Language Pathology, Teacher Education (e,s,p) *CEO:* Pres. William E. Kirwan
Enroll: 36681 (301) 405-1000

UNIVERSITY OF MARYLAND EASTERN SHORE
Princess Anne 21853 *Type:* Public (state) liberal arts *System:* University of Maryland System *Accred.:* 1937/1986 (MSA) *Calendar:* Sem. plan *Degrees:* B, M, D *Prof. Accred.:* Physical Therapy *CEO:* Pres. William P. Hytche
Enroll: 1559 (410) 651-2200

UNIVERSITY OF MARYLAND UNIVERSITY COLLEGE
University Blvd. at Adelphi Rd, College Park 20742-1600 *Type:* Public (state) liberal arts *System:* University of Maryland System *Accred.:* 1946/1986 (MSA) *Calendar:* Sem. plan *Degrees:* A, B, M, certificates, diplomas *CEO:* Pres. T. Benjamin Massey
Enroll: 36258 (301) 985-7000

UNIVERSITY OF MARYLAND AT BALTIMORE
520 W. Lombard St., Baltimore 21201 *Type:* Public (state) *System:* University of Maryland System *Accred.:* 1921/1986 (MSA) *Calendar:* 4-1-4 plan *Degrees:* B, P, M, D, certificates, diplomas *Prof. Accred.:* Combined Prosthodontics, Dental Hygiene, Dentistry, Endodontics, General Dentistry, General Practice Residency, Law, Medical Technology, Medicine, Nursing (B,M), Oral and Maxillofacial Surgery, Oral Pathology, Orthodontics, Pediatric Dentistry, Periodontics, Pharmacy, Physical Therapy, Social Work (B,M) *CEO:* Pres. Errol L. Reese
Enroll: 4563 (410) 328-3100

VILLA JULIE COLLEGE
1525 Green Spring Valley Rd., Stevenson 21153 *Type:* Private liberal arts *Accred.:* 1962/1988 (MSA) *Calendar:* Sem. plan *Degrees:* A, B *Prof. Accred.:* Medical Laboratory Technology (AMA) *CEO:* Pres. Carolyn Manuszak
Enroll: 1271 (410) 486-7000

WASHINGTON BIBLE COLLEGE
6511 Princess Garden Pkwy., Lanham 20706 *Type:* Private *Accred.:* 1962/1981 (AABC) *Calendar:* Sem. plan *Degrees:* A, B, M, certificates, diplomas *CEO:* Interim Pres. John A. Sproule
Enroll: 301 (301) 552-1400

WASHINGTON COLLEGE
Washington Ave., Chestertown 21620 *Type:* Private liberal arts *Accred.:* 1925/1988 (MSA) *Calendar:* Sem. plan *Degrees:* B, M, certificates, diplomas *CEO:* Pres. Charles H. Trout
Enroll: 988 (410) 778-2800

WASHINGTON THEOLOGICAL UNION
9001 New Hampshire Avenue, Silver Spring 20903-3699 *Type:* Private (Roman Catholic) professional; graduate only *Accred.:* 1973/1987 (ATS); 1973/1988 (MSA) *Calendar:* Sem. plan *Degrees:* P, M *CEO:* Pres. Vincent D. Cushing
Enroll: 339 (301) 439-0551

WESTERN MARYLAND COLLEGE
Westminster 21157 *Type:* Private liberal arts *Accred.:* 1922/1988 (MSA) *Calendar:* Sem. plan *Degrees:* B, M *Prof. Accred.:* Social Work (B) *CEO:* Pres. Robert Hunter Chambers, III
Enroll: 2002 (410) 848-7000

WOODBRIDGE BUSINESS INSTITUTE
309 E. Main St., Salisbury 21801 *Type:* Private business *Accred.:* 1982/1988 (CCA-ACICS) *Calendar:* Qtr. plan *Degrees:* certificates, diplomas *CEO:* Dir. Patricia L. Keeton
Enroll: 682 (410) 742-6700

BRANCH CAMPUS
14573-H Jefferson Davis Hwy., Woodbridge, VA 22191 *CEO:* Dir. Karen S. Pack
(703) 491-3715

Accredited Institutions **Maryland**

WOR-WIC TECH COMMUNITY COLLEGE
30 Wesley Dr., Salisbury 21801 *Type:* Public (district) junior *System:* Maryland State Board for Community Colleges *Accred.:* 1980/1985 (MSA) *Calendar:* Sem. plan *Degrees:* A *Prof. Accred.:* Radiography *CEO:* Pres. Arnold H. Maner
Enroll: 1032 (410) 749-8181

YORKTOWNE BUSINESS INSTITUTE
Landover Mall, 2121 Brightseat Rd., Landover 20785 *Type:* Private business *Accred.:* 1982/1988 (CCA-ACICS) *Calendar:* Courses of varying lengths *Degrees:* certificates, diplomas *CEO:* Dir. Catherine Hubert
Enroll: 651 (301) 386-3303

MASSACHUSETTS

AMERICAN INTERNATIONAL COLLEGE
1000 State St., Springfield 01109 *Type:* Private liberal arts and professional *Accred.:* 1933/1989 (NEASC-CIHE) *Calendar:* Sem. plan *Degrees:* B, M, D *Prof. Accred.:* Nursing (B) *CEO:* Pres. Harry J. Courniotes
Enroll: 1552 (413) 737-7000

AMHERST COLLEGE
Amherst 01002 *Type:* Private liberal arts *Accred.:* 1929/1988 (NEASC-CIHE) *Calendar:* Sem. plan *Degrees:* B *CEO:* Pres. Peter R. Pouncey
Enroll: 1601 (413) 542-2000

ANDOVER NEWTON THEOLOGICAL SCHOOL
210 Herrick Rd., Newton Centre 02159 *Type:* Private (United Church of Christ/Baptist); graduate only *Accred.:* 1938/1988 (ATS); 1978/1988 (NEASC-CIHE) *Calendar:* Sem. plan *Degrees:* P, M, D *CEO:* Pres. David T. Shannon
Enroll: 224 (617) 964-1100

ANNA MARIA COLLEGE
Paxton 01612 *Type:* Private (Roman Catholic) liberal arts *Accred.:* 1955/1989 (NEASC-CIHE) *Calendar:* Sem. plan *Degrees:* A, B, M *Prof. Accred.:* Medical Laboratory Technology (AMA), Music, Nursing (B), Social Work (B) *CEO:* Pres. Bernadette Madore, S.S.A.
Enroll: 897 (508) 757-4586

AQUINAS COLLEGE AT MILTON
303 Adams St., Milton 02186 *Type:* Private *Accred.:* 1975/1991 (NEASC-CVTCI) *Calendar:* Modular plan *Degrees:* A *Prof. Accred.:* Medical Assisting (AMA) *CEO:* Pres. Dorothy M. Oppenheim
Enroll: 225 (617) 696-3100

AQUINAS COLLEGE AT NEWTON
15 Walnut Park, Newton 02158 *Type:* Private *Accred.:* 1975/1991 (NEASC-CVTCI) *Calendar:* Sem. plan *Degrees:* A *CEO:* Pres. Marian Batho, C.S.J.
Enroll: 215 (617) 969-4400

THE ART INSTITUTE OF BOSTON
700 Beacon St., Boston 02215 *Type:* Private professional *Calendar:* Sem. plan *Degrees:* B, diplomas *Prof. Accred.:* Art *CEO:* Pres. Stan Trecker
Enroll: 350 (617) 262-1223

ARTHUR D. LITTLE MANAGEMENT EDUCATION INSTITUTE, INC.
Cambridge 02140-2390 *Type:* Private specialized graduate *Accred.:* 1976/1986 (NEASC-CIHE) *Calendar:* 10-month program *Degrees:* M *CEO:* Pres. Harland A. Riker, Jr.
Enroll: 66 (617) 864-5770

ASSOCIATED TECHNICAL INSTITUTE
345 W. Cummings Park, Woburn 01801 *Type:* Private *Accred.:* 1975/1989 (CCA-ACTTS) *Calendar:* Courses of varying lengths *Degrees:* certificates *CEO:* Dir. Brian Matza
Enroll: 495 (617) 935-3838

ASSUMPTION COLLEGE
500 Salisbury St., Worcester 01615-0005 *Type:* Private (Roman Catholic) liberal arts *Accred.:* 1949/1986 (NEASC-CIHE) *Calendar:* Sem. plan *Degrees:* A, B, M *Prof. Accred.:* Nursing (B), Rehabilitation Counseling *CEO:* Pres. Joseph H. Hagan
Enroll: 2209 (508) 752-5615

ATLANTIC UNION COLLEGE
P.O. Box 1000, South Lancaster 01561 *Type:* Private (Seventh-Day Adventist) liberal arts *Accred.:* 1945/1988 (NEASC-CIHE) *Calendar:* Sem. plan *Degrees:* A, B *Prof. Accred.:* Nursing (A,B), Social Work (B) *CEO:* Pres. Lawrence T. Geraty
Enroll: 635 (508) 368-2000

BABSON COLLEGE
Babson Park 02157 *Type:* Private professional *Accred.:* 1950/1982 (NEASC-CIHE) *Calendar:* Sem. plan *Degrees:* B, M *Prof.*

Accred.: Business (B,M) *CEO:* Pres. William F. Glavin
Enroll: 2299 (617) 235-1200

BANCROFT SCHOOL OF MASSAGE THERAPY
50 Franklin St., Worcester 01608 *Type:* Private *Accred.:* 1988 (CCA-ACTTS) *Calendar:* Courses of varying lengths *Degrees:* certificates *CEO:* Vice Pres. Stephen Tankanowge
Enroll: 85 (508) 757-7923

BAY PATH COLLEGE
Longmeadow 01106 *Type:* Private for women *Accred.:* 1965/1985 (NEASC-CIHE) *Calendar:* Sem. plan *Degrees:* A, B *CEO:* Pres. Jeanette T. Wright
Enroll: 557 (413) 567-0621

BAY STATE COLLEGE
122 Commonwealth Ave., Boston 02116 *Type:* Private *Accred.:* 1989 (NEASC-CVTCI) *Calendar:* Sem. plan *Degrees:* A, diplomas *Prof. Accred.:* Medical Assisting *CEO:* Pres. Frederick G. Pfannenstiehl
Enroll: 671 (617) 236-8000

BAY STATE SCHOOL OF APPLIANCES
15 Everett St., P.O. Box 598, Boston 02136 *Type:* Private *Accred.:* 1988 (CCA-ACTTS) *Calendar:* Courses of varying lengths *Degrees:* certificates *CEO:* Dir. Robert Mason
(617) 364-3434

BECKER COLLEGE
61 Sever St., Worcester 01615 *Type:* Private *Accred.:* 1976/1990 (NEASC-CVTCI) *Calendar:* Sem. plan *Degrees:* A *Prof. Accred.:* Nursing (A), Occupational Therapy Assisting, Physical Therapy Assisting *CEO:* Pres. Arnold C. Weller, Jr.
Enroll: 1737 (508) 791-9241

BRANCH CAMPUS
3 Paxton St., Leicester, MA 01524 *Prof. Accred.:* Veterinary Assisting (probational) *CEO:* Pres. Arnold C. Weller, Jr.
(508) 791-9241

BENTLEY COLLEGE
175 Forest St., Waltham 02154-4705 *Type:* Private professional *Accred.:* 1966/1981 (NEASC-CIHE) *Calendar:* Sem. plan *Degrees:* A, B, M *Prof. Accred.:* Business (B,M) *CEO:* Pres. Joseph M. Cronin
Enroll: 5530 (617) 891-2000

BERKLEE COLLEGE OF MUSIC
1140 Boylston St., Boston 02215 *Type:* Private professional *Accred.:* 1973/1987 (NEASC-CIHE) *Calendar:* Sem. plan *Degrees:* B *CEO:* Pres. Lee E. Berk
Enroll: 2541 (617) 266-1400

BERKSHIRE COMMUNITY COLLEGE
West St., Pittsfield 01201 *Type:* Public (state) junior *System:* Massachusetts Higher Education Coordinating Council *Accred.:* 1964/1989 (NEASC-CIHE) *Calendar:* Sem. plan *Degrees:* A *Prof. Accred.:* Nursing (A), Respiratory Therapy *CEO:* Pres. Cathryn L. Addy
Enroll: 1589 (413) 499-4660

BOSTON ARCHITECTURAL CENTER
320 Newbury St., Boston 02115 *Type:* Private professional *Accred.:* 1987 (NEASC-CIHE candidate) *Calendar:* Courses of varying lengths *Degrees:* B, certificates *Prof. Accred.:* Architecture (B) *CEO:* Pres. George B. Terrien
Enroll: 750 (617) 536-3170

BOSTON COLLEGE
Chestnut Hill 02167 *Type:* Private (Roman Catholic) *Accred.:* 1935/1986 (NEASC-CIHE) *Calendar:* Sem. plan *Degrees:* B, P, M, D *Prof. Accred.:* Business (B,M), Law, Nursing (B,M), Social Work (M), Teacher Education (e,s,p) *CEO:* Pres. J. Donald Monan, S.J.
Enroll: 12565 (617) 552-8000

BOSTON CONSERVATORY
Boston 02215 *Type:* Private *Accred.:* 1968/1988 (NEASC-CIHE) *Calendar:* Sem. plan *Degrees:* B, M *Prof. Accred.:* Music *CEO:* Pres. William A. Seymour
Enroll: 337 (617) 536-6340

Massachusetts

BOSTON UNIVERSITY
147 Bay State Rd., Boston 02215 *Type:* Private *Accred.:* 1938/1991 (ATS); 1929/1989 (NEASC-CIHE) *Calendar:* Sem. plan *Degrees:* B, P, M, D *Prof. Accred.:* Business (B,M), Clinical Psychology, Combined Prosthodontics (conditional), Counseling Psychology, Dentistry, Dental Public Health, Endodontics, Engineering (aerospace, bioengineering, computer, electrical, manufacturing, mechanical, systems), General Dentistry, Health Services Administration, Law, Medicine, Music, Nursing (B,M), Occupational Therapy, Ophthalmic Medical Technology, Oral and Maxillofacial Surgery, Orthodontics, Pediatric Dentistry, Periodontics, Physical Therapy, Psychology Internship, Public Health, Rehabilitation Counseling, Social Work (B,M), Speech-Language Pathology, Teacher Education (e,s,p) *CEO:* Pres. John Silber
Enroll: 21984 (617) 353-2000

BRADFORD COLLEGE
Bradford 01830-1835 *Type:* Private *Accred.:* 1931/1987 (NEASC-CIHE) *Calendar:* 4-1-4 plan *Degrees:* A, B *CEO:* Pres. Joseph Short
Enroll: 418 (508) 372-7161

BRANDEIS UNIVERSITY
Waltham 02254 *Type:* Private *Accred.:* 1953/1987 (NEASC-CIHE) *Calendar:* Sem. plan *Degrees:* B, M, D *Prof. Accred.:* Computer Science *CEO:* Pres. Samuel O. Thier
Enroll: 3689 (617) 736-2000

BRIDGEWATER STATE COLLEGE
Bridgewater 02324 *Type:* Public (state) liberal arts and teachers *System:* Massachusetts Higher Education Coordinating Council *Accred.:* 1953/1983 (NEASC-CIHE) *Calendar:* Sem. plan *Degrees:* B, M *Prof. Accred.:* Social Work (B), Teacher Education (e,s) *CEO:* Pres. Adrian Tinsley
Enroll: 6290 (508) 697-1200

BRISTOL COMMUNITY COLLEGE
777 Elsbree St., Fall River 02720 *Type:* Public (state) junior *System:* Massachusetts Higher Education Coordinating Council *Accred.:* 1970/1984 (NEASC-CIHE) *Calendar:* Sem. plan *Degrees:* A *Prof. Accred.:* Dental Hygiene, Medical Laboratory Technology (AMA), Nursing (A) *CEO:* Pres. Eileen T. Farley
Enroll: 3005 (508) 678-2811

BUNKER HILL COMMUNITY COLLEGE
Rutherford Ave., Boston 02129 *Type:* Public (state) junior *System:* Massachusetts Higher Education Coordinating Council *Accred.:* 1976/1990 (NEASC-CIHE) *Calendar:* Sem. plan *Degrees:* A *Prof. Accred.:* Dental Assisting, Nuclear Medicine Technology, Nursing (A), Radiography *CEO:* Interim Pres. Kathleen E. Assar
Enroll: 3185 (617) 241-8600

BURDETT SCHOOL
745 Boylston St., Boston 02116 *Type:* Private business *Accred.:* 1954/1990 (CCA-ACICS) *Calendar:* Courses of varying lengths *Degrees:* certificates, diplomas *CEO:* Pres. Maralin Manning
Enroll: 220 (617) 859-1900

BUTERA SCHOOL OF ART
111 Beacon St., Boston 02116 *Type:* Private *Accred.:* 1977/1989 (CCA-ACTTS) *Calendar:* Sem. plan *Degrees:* diplomas *CEO:* Dir. Joseph L. Butera
Enroll: 120 (617) 536-4623

CAMBRIDGE COLLEGE
15 Mifflin Pl., Cambridge 02138 *Type:* Private *Accred.:* 1981/1987 (NEASC-CIHE) *Calendar:* Sem. plan *Degrees:* M *CEO:* Pres. Eileen M. Brown
Enroll: 950 (617) 492-5108

CAPE COD COMMUNITY COLLEGE
Rte. 132, West Barnstable 02668 *Type:* Public (state) junior *System:* Massachusetts Higher Education Coordinating Council *Accred.:* 1967/1988 (NEASC-CIHE) *Calendar:* Sem. plan *Degrees:* A *Prof. Accred.:* Dental Hygiene, Nursing (A) *CEO:* Pres. Richard A. Kraus
Enroll: 2281 (508) 362-2131

Accredited Institutions — Massachusetts

CATHERINE E. HINDS INSTITUTE OF ESTHETICS
65 Riverside Pl., Medford 02155 *Type:* Private *Accred.:* 1987 (CCA-ACTTS) *Calendar:* Courses of varying lengths *Degrees:* certificates *CEO:* Dir. Catherine E. Hinds
Enroll: 35 (617) 391-3733

CATHERINE LABOURE COLLEGE
2120 Dorchester Ave., Boston 02124 *Type:* Private (Roman Catholic) 2-year *Accred.:* 1975/1991 (NEASC-CVTCI) *Calendar:* Sem. plan *Degrees:* A *Prof. Accred.:* Electroneurodiagnostic Technology, Medical Record Technology, Nursing (A), Radiation Therapy Technology *CEO:* Pres. Clarisse Correia, D.C.
Enroll: 367 (617) 296-8300

CHARLES H. MCCANN TECHNICAL SCHOOL
Hodges Crossroad, North Adams 01247 *Type:* Private *Calendar:* Courses of varying lengths *Degrees:* certificates *Prof. Accred.:* Dental Assisting *CEO:* Supt. Howard Brookner
(413) 663-5383

CLARK UNIVERSITY
Worcester 01610 *Type:* Private *Accred.:* 1929/1986 (NEASC-CIHE) *Calendar:* Mod. plan *Degrees:* B, M, D *Prof. Accred.:* Business (B,M), Clinical Psychology, Health Services Administration *CEO:* Pres. Richard P. Traina
Enroll: 2865 (508) 793-7711

COLLEGE OF OUR LADY OF THE ELMS
Chicopee 01013 *Type:* Private (Roman Catholic) liberal arts for women *Accred.:* 1942/1982 (NEASC-CIHE) *Calendar:* Sem. plan *Degrees:* B, M *Prof. Accred.:* Nursing (B), Social Work (B) *CEO:* Pres. Mary A. Dooley, S.S.J.
Enroll: 779 (413) 594-2761

COLLEGE OF THE HOLY CROSS
Worcester 01610-2395*Type:* Private (Roman Catholic) liberal arts *Accred.:* 1930/1990 (NEASC-CIHE) *Calendar:* Sem. plan *Degrees:* B, M *CEO:* Pres. John E. Brooks, S.J.
Enroll: 2648 (508) 793-2011

COMPUTER LEARNING CENTER
5 Middlesex Ave., Sommerville 02145 *Type:* Private business *Accred.:* 1982/1985 (CCA-ACICS) *Calendar:* Courses of varying lengths *Degrees:* certificates, diplomas *CEO:* Dir. Janet Gailun
Enroll: 1019 (617) 776-3500

COMPUTER PROCESSING INSTITUTE
615 Massachusetts Ave., Cambridge 02139 *Type:* Private business *Accred.:* 1982/1988 (CCA-ACICS) *Calendar:* Courses of varying lengths *Degrees:* certificates, diplomas *CEO:* Pres. Richard E. Brennan
Enroll: 936 (617) 354-6900

CONWAY SCHOOL OF LANDSCAPE DESIGN
Delabarre Ave., Conway 01341 *Type:* Private *Accred.:* 1989 (NEASC-CIHE) *Calendar:* Tri. plan *Degrees:* M *CEO:* Dir. Walt L. Cudnohufsky
Enroll: 18 (413) 369-4044

CURRY COLLEGE
Milton 02186 *Type:* Private liberal arts and teachers *Accred.:* 1970/1986 (NEASC-CIHE) *Calendar:* Sem. plan *Degrees:* B, M *Prof. Accred.:* Nursing (B) *CEO:* Pres. Catherine W. Ingold
Enroll: 1033 (617) 333-0500

DEAN JUNIOR COLLEGE
Franklin 02038 *Type:* Private *Accred.:* 1957/1986 (NEASC-CIHE) *Calendar:* Sem. plan *Degrees:* A *Prof. Accred.:* Medical Assisting (AMA) *CEO:* Pres. Frank B. Bruno
Enroll: 1596 (508) 528-9100

DUDLEY HALL CAREER INSTITUTE
16 Washington Sq., Worcester 01604 *Type:* Private *Accred.:* 1981/1987 (CCA-ACICS) *Calendar:* Qtr. plan *Degrees:* certificates, diplomas *CEO:* Pres. Curtis Riendeau
Enroll: 337 (508) 754-6699

EASTERN NAZARENE COLLEGE
23 E. Elm Ave., Quincy 02170 *Type:* Private (Nazarene) liberal arts *Accred.:* 1943/1990 (NEASC-CIHE) *Calendar:* 4-1-4 plan *De-*

Massachusetts

grees: A, B, M *Prof. Accred.:* Social Work (B) *CEO:* Pres. Cecil R. Paul
Enroll: 885   (617) 773-6350

EMERSON COLLEGE
100 Beacon St., Boston 02116 *Type:* Private liberal arts *Accred.:* 1950/1983 (NEASC-CIHE) *Calendar:* Sem. plan *Degrees:* B, M *Prof. Accred.:* Speech-Language Pathology *CEO:* Pres. John C. Zacharis
Enroll: 2080   (617) 578-8500

EMMANUEL COLLEGE
400 The Fenway, Boston 02115 *Type:* Private (Roman Catholic) liberal arts primarily for women *Accred.:* 1933/1983 (NEASC-CIHE) *Calendar:* Sem. plan *Degrees:* B, M *Prof. Accred.:* Nursing (B) *CEO:* Pres. Janet Eisner, S.N.D.
Enroll: 807   (617) 277-9430

ENDICOTT COLLEGE
Beverly 01915 *Type:* Private liberal arts for women *Accred.:* 1952/1987 (NEASC-CIHE) *Calendar:* Sem. plan *Degrees:* A, B *CEO:* Pres. Richard E. Wylie
Enroll: 1410   (508) 927-0585

EPISCOPAL DIVINITY SCHOOL
99 Brattle St., Cambridge 02138 *Type:* Private (Episcopal) professional; graduate only *Accred.:* 1938/1988 (ATS) *Calendar:* Sem. plan *Degrees:* P, M, D *CEO:* Dean Otis Charles
Enroll: 95   (617) 868-3450

ESSEX AGRICULTURAL AND TECHNICAL INSTITUTE
562 Maple St., Hathorne 01937 *Type:* Public (state) *System:* Massachusetts Higher Education Coordinating Council *Accred.:* 1979/1991 (NEASC-CVTCI) *Calendar:* Sem. plan *Degrees:* A, certificates *CEO:* Dir. Gustave D. Olson, Jr.
Enroll: 426   (508) 774-0050

FISHER COLLEGE
118 Beacon St., Boston 02116 *Type:* Private *Accred.:* 1970/1990 (NEASC-CIHE) *Cal-*

Accredited Institutions

endar: Sem. plan *Degrees:* A *CEO:* Pres. Scott A. Fisher
Enroll: 1453   (617) 262-3240

FITCHBURG STATE COLLEGE
160 Pearl St., Fitchburg 01420 *Type:* Public *System:* Massachusetts Higher Education Coordinating Council *Accred.:* 1953/1986 (NEASC-CIHE) *Calendar:* Sem. plan *Degrees:* B, M *Prof. Accred.:* Medical Technology, Nursing (B) *CEO:* Pres. Vincent J. Mara
Enroll: 3996   (508) 345-2151

FORSYTH SCHOOL OF DENTAL HYGIENISTS
140 The Fenway, Boston 02115 *Type:* Private *Calendar:* Courses of varying lengths *Degrees:* certificates *Prof. Accred.:* Dental Hygiene *CEO:* Dir. John W. Hein
                         (617) 262-5200

FRAMINGHAM STATE COLLEGE
100 State St., Framingham 01701-9101 *Type:* Public liberal arts and teachers *System:* Massachusetts Higher Education Coordinating Council *Accred.:* 1950/1984 (NEASC-CIHE) *Calendar:* Sem. plan *Degrees:* B, M *Prof. Accred.:* Dietetics (coordinated), Nursing (B) *CEO:* Pres. Paul F. Weller
Enroll: 4091   (508) 620-1220

FRANKLIN INSTITUTE OF BOSTON
Boston 02116 *Type:* Private 2-year technical *Accred.:* 1970/1990 (NEASC-CVTCI) *Calendar:* Sem. plan *Degrees:* A *Prof. Accred.:* Engineering Technology (architectural, civil/construction, computer, electrical, mechanical) *CEO:* Pres. Richard P. D'Onofrio
Enroll: 358   (617) 423-4630

GORDON COLLEGE
Wenham 01984 *Type:* Private liberal arts *Accred.:* 1961/1982 (NEASC-CIHE) *Calendar:* Tri. plan *Degrees:* B *Prof. Accred.:* Music, Social Work (B) *CEO:* Pres. Richard F. Gross
Enroll: 1119   (508) 927-2300

GORDON-CONWELL THEOLOGICAL SEMINARY
130 Essex St., South Hamilton 01982 *Type:* Private (interdenominational) professional; graduate only *Accred.:* 1964/1985 (ATS); 1985 (NEASC-CIHE) *Calendar:* Sem. plan *Degrees:* P, M, D *CEO:* Pres. Robert E. Cooley
Enroll: 479 (508) 468-7111

GREENFIELD COMMUNITY COLLEGE
One College Dr., Greenfield 01301 *Type:* Public (state) junior *System:* Massachusetts Higher Education Coordinating Council *Accred.:* 1966/1990 (NEASC-CIHE) *Calendar:* Sem. plan *Degrees:* A *Prof. Accred.:* Nursing (A) *CEO:* Pres. Katherine H. Sloan
Enroll: 1811 (413) 774-3131

HALLMARK INSTITUTE OF PHOTOGRAPHY
Turners Falls 01376 *Type:* Private *Accred.:* 1982/1987 (CCA-ACTTS) *Calendar:* Courses of varying lengths *Degrees:* certificates *CEO:* Dir. Paul R. Turnbull
Enroll: 49 (413) 863-2478

HAMPSHIRE COLLEGE
Amherst 01002 *Type:* Private liberal arts *Accred.:* 1974/1988 (NEASC-CIHE) *Calendar:* 4-1-4 plan *Degrees:* B *CEO:* Pres. Gregory S. Prince, Jr.
Enroll: 1261 (413) 549-4600

HARVARD UNIVERSITY
Cambridge 02138 *Type:* Private *Accred.:* 1940/1981 (ATS); 1929/1987 (NEASC-CIHE) *Calendar:* Sem. plan *Degrees:* A, B, P, M, D *Prof. Accred.:* Architecture (M), Business (M), Combined Prosthodontics, Dentistry, Dental Public Health, Engineering (engineering physics/science), Landscape Architecture (M), Law, Medicine, Oral Pathology (provisional), Orthodontics, Periodontics, Psychology Internship, Public Health *CEO:* Pres. Neil Rudenstine
Enroll: 18179 (617) 495-1000

HEBREW COLLEGE
Brookline 02146 *Type:* Private (Jewish) teachers *Accred.:* 1955/1988 (NEASC-CIHE) *Calendar:* Sem. plan *Degrees:* B, M *CEO:* Interim Pres. Barry Mesch
Enroll: 34 (617) 232-8710

HELLENIC COLLEGE/HOLY CROSS GREEK ORTHODOX THEOLOGICAL SCHOOL
Brookline 02146 *Type:* Private (Greek Orthodox) liberal arts and professional *Accred.:* 1974/1981 (ATS); 1974/1987 (NEASC-CIHE) *Calendar:* Sem. plan *Degrees:* B, P, M *CEO:* Pres. Methodios Tournas
Enroll: 133 (617) 731-3500

HICKOX SCHOOL
200 Tremont St., Boston 02116 *Type:* Private junior *Accred.:* 1968/1986 (CCA-ACICS) *Calendar:* Courses of varying lengths *Degrees:* A, certificates, diplomas *CEO:* Pres. S. Arthur Verenis
Enroll: 383 (617) 482-7655

HOLYOKE COMMUNITY COLLEGE
303 Homestead Ave., Holyoke 01040 *Type:* Public (state) junior *System:* Massachusetts Higher Education Coordinating Council *Accred.:* 1970/1990 (NEASC-CIHE) *Calendar:* Sem. plan *Degrees:* A *Prof. Accred.:* Medical Record Technology, Nursing (A), Radiography, Veterinary and Animal Science (probational) *CEO:* Pres. David M. Bartley
Enroll: 3138 (413) 538-7000

KATHARINE GIBBS SCHOOL
126 Newbury St., Boston 02116 *Type:* Private junior *Accred.:* 1967/1988 (CCA-ACICS) *Calendar:* Sem. plan *Degrees:* A, certificates, diplomas *CEO:* Dir. Jim Otten
Enroll: 827 (617) 578-7100

KINYON-CAMPBELL BUSINESS SCHOOL
59 Linden St., New Bedford 02740 *Type:* Private business *Accred.:* 1971/1988 (CCA-ACICS) *Calendar:* Qtr. plan *Degrees:* certificates, diplomas *CEO:* Dir. David B. Daganhardt
Enroll: 435 (508) 992-5448

Massachusetts   **Accredited Institutions**

LASELL COLLEGE
Newton 02166 *Type:* Private liberal arts for women *Accred.:* 1932/1987 (NEASC-CIHE) *Calendar:* Sem. plan *Degrees:* A, B *Prof. Accred.:* Physical Therapy Assisting *CEO:* Pres. Thomas E.J. de Witt
Enroll: 419   (617) 243-2000

LESLEY COLLEGE
29 Everett St., Cambridge 02138-2790 *Type:* Private teachers for women *Accred.:* 1952/1984 (NEASC-CIHE) *Calendar:* Sem. plan *Degrees:* A, B, M, D *CEO:* Pres. Margaret A. McKenna
Enroll: 2591   (617) 868-9600

LONGY SCHOOL OF MUSIC, INC.
One Follen St., Cambridge 02138 *Type:* Private professional *Calendar:* Courses of varying lengths *Degrees:* diplomas *Prof. Accred.:* Music *CEO:* Dir. Victor Rosenbaum
Enroll: 520   (617) 876-0956

MGH INSTITUTE OF HEALTH PROFESSIONS
15 River St., Boston 02108-3402 *Type:* Private professional *Accred.:* 1985/1990 (NEASC-CIHE) *Calendar:* Sem. plan *Degrees:* M *Prof. Accred.:* Nursing (M) *CEO:* Pres. Patrick E. McCarthy
Enroll: 147   (617) 726-8002

MARIAN COURT JUNIOR COLLEGE
35 Little's Point Rd., Swampscott 01907 *Type:* Private (Roman Catholic) *Accred.:* 1982 (NEASC-CVTCI) *Calendar:* Sem. plan *Degrees:* A *CEO:* Pres. Joanne Bibeau, R.S.M.
Enroll: 181   (617) 595-6768

MASSACHUSETTS BAY COMMUNITY COLLEGE
50 Oakland St., Wellesley Hills 02181 *Type:* Public (state) junior *System:* Massachusetts Higher Education Coordinating Council *Accred.:* 1967/1984 (NEASC-CIHE) *Calendar:* Sem. plan *Degrees:* A *Prof. Accred.:* Nursing (A), Radiography *CEO:* Pres. Roger A. Van Winkle
Enroll: 3358   (617) 237-1100

MASSACHUSETTS COLLEGE OF ART
621 Huntington Ave., Boston 02115 *Type:* Public (state) teachers and professional *System:* Massachusetts Higher Education Coordinating Council *Accred.:* 1954/1987 (NEASC-CIHE) *Calendar:* Sem. plan *Degrees:* B, M *Prof. Accred.:* Art *CEO:* Pres. William F. O'Neil
Enroll: 1269   (617) 232-1555

MASSACHUSETTS COLLEGE OF PHARMACY AND ALLIED HEALTH SCIENCES
179 Longwood Ave., Boston 02115 *Type:* Private professional *Accred.:* 1974/1987 (NEASC-CIHE) *Calendar:* Sem. plan *Degrees:* A, B, M, D *Prof. Accred.:* Nuclear Medicine Technology, Nursing (B), Pharmacy, Radiation Therapy Technology *CEO:* Pres. Louis P. Jeffrey
Enroll: 1041   (617) 732-2800

MASSACHUSETTS INSTITUTE OF TECHNOLOGY
Cambridge 02139 *Type:* Private *Accred.:* 1929/1989 (NEASC-CIHE) *Calendar:* Sem. plan *Degrees:* B, M, D *Prof. Accred.:* Architecture (M), Business (B,M), Engineering (aerospace, chemical, civil, computer, electrical, materials, mechanical, nuclear, ocean), Planning (city) *CEO:* Pres. Charles M. Vest
Enroll: 9628   (617) 253-1000

MASSACHUSETTS MARITIME ACADEMY
Academy Dr., Buzzards Bay 02532 *Type:* Public (state) professional *System:* Massachusetts Higher Education Coordinating Council *Accred.:* 1974/1990 (NEASC-CIHE) *Calendar:* Qtr. plan *Degrees:* B *CEO:* Pres. Peter Cressey, U.S.N.
Enroll: 798   (617) 759-5761

MASSACHUSETTS SCHOOL OF BARBERING AND MEN'S HAIRSTYLING
152 Packingway St., Quincy 02169 *Type:* Private *Accred.:* 1978/1985 (CCA-ACTTS) *Calendar:* Sem. plan *Degrees:* certificates *CEO:* Gen. Mgr. Richard Conragan
Enroll: 96   (617) 770-4444

MASSACHUSETTS SCHOOL OF PROFESSIONAL PSYCHOLOGY

322 Sprague St., Dedham 02026 *Type:* Private professional; graduate only *Accred.:* 1984 (NEASC-CIHE) *Calendar:* Sem. plan *Degrees:* D *Prof. Accred.:* Clinical Psychology (provisional) *CEO:* Pres. Bruce J. Weiss
Enroll: 133 (617) 329-6777

MASSASOIT COMMUNITY COLLEGE
One Massasoit Blvd., Brockton 02402 *Type:* Public (state) junior *System:* Massachusetts Higher Education Coordinating Council *Accred.:* 1971/1987 (NEASC-CIHE) *Calendar:* Sem. plan *Degrees:* A *Prof. Accred.:* Dental Assisting (conditional), Medical Laboratory Technology (AMA), Nursing (A), Radiography, Respiratory Therapy *CEO:* Pres. Gerard F. Burke
Enroll: 4182 (508) 588-9100

MERRIMACK COLLEGE
North Andover 01845 *Type:* Private (Roman Catholic) liberal arts *Accred.:* 1953/1986 (NEASC-CIHE) *Calendar:* Sem. plan *Degrees:* A, B *Prof. Accred.:* Engineering (civil, computer)*CEO:* Pres. John E. Deegan, O.S.A.
Enroll: 2512 (508) 683-7111

MIDDLESEX COMMUNITY COLLEGE
Springs Rd., Bedford 01730 *Type:* Public (state) junior *System:* Massachusetts Higher Education Coordinating Council *Accred.:* 1973/1987 (NEASC-CIHE) *Calendar:* Sem. plan *Degrees:* A *Prof. Accred.:* Dental Assisting, Dental Hygiene, Dental Laboratory Technology, Diagnostic Medical Sonography, Medical Assisting (AMA), Medical Laboratory Technology (AMA), Nursing (A), Radiography *CEO:* Pres. Carole Cowan
Enroll: 3951 (617) 275-8910

MONTSERRAT COLLEGE OF ART
Dunham Rd., Box 26, Beverly 01915 *Type:* Private 4-year professional *Accred.:* 1989 (NEASC-CIHE candidate); 1982 (NEASC-CVTCI) *Calendar:* Sem. plan *Degrees:* B, diplomas *Prof. Accred.:* Art *CEO:* Pres. Arthur Greenblatt
Enroll: 209 (508) 922-8222

MOUNT HOLYOKE COLLEGE
South Hadley 01075 *Type:* Private liberal arts for women*Accred.:* 1929/1988(NEASC-CIHE) *Calendar:* Sem. plan *Degrees:* B, M *CEO:* Pres. Elizabeth T. Kennan
Enroll: 1940 (413) 538-2000

MOUNT IDA COLLEGE
777 Dedham St., Newton Centre 02159 *Type:* Private primarily for women *Accred.:* 1970/1988 (NEASC-CIHE) *Calendar:* 12-6-12 plan *Degrees:* A, B *Prof. Accred.:* Dental Assisting, Funeral Service Education, Occupational Therapy Assisting, Veterinary Technology (probational) *CEO:* Pres. Bryan E. Carlson
Enroll: 1429 (617) 969-7000

MOUNT WACHUSETTS COMMUNITY COLLEGE
444 Green St., Gardner 01440 *Type:* Public (state) junior *System:* Massachusetts Higher Education Coordinating Council *Accred.:* 1968/1982 (NEASC-CIHE) *Calendar:* Sem. plan *Degrees:* A *Prof. Accred.:* Medical Laboratory Technology (AMA), Nursing (A) *CEO:* Pres. Daniel M. Asquino
Enroll: 2105 (508) 632-6600

NATIONAL EDUCATION CENTER—BRYMAN CAMPUS
323 Boylston St., Brookline 02146 *Type:* Private *Accred.:* 1973/1985 (CCA-ACTTS) *Calendar:* Courses of varying lengths *Degrees:* diplomas *CEO:* Dir. Robert Moon
Enroll: 522 (617) 232-6035

THE NEW ENGLAND BANKING INSTITUTE
One Lincoln Plaza, 89 South St., Boston 02111 *Type:* Private*Accred.:* 1985 (NEASC-CVTCI) *Calendar:* Sem. plan *Degrees:* A *CEO:* Pres. Robert A. Regan
Enroll: 343 (617) 951-2350

NEW ENGLAND COLLEGE OF OPTOMETRY
424 Beacon St., Boston 02115 *Type:* Private professional *Accred.:* 1976/1986 (NEASC-CIHE) *Calendar:* Sem. plan *Degrees:* B, P *Prof. Accred.:* Optometry *CEO:* Pres. Larry R. Clausen
Enroll: 371 (617) 266-2030

Massachusetts

NEW ENGLAND CONSERVATORY OF MUSIC
290 Huntington Ave., Boston 02115 *Type:* Private professional *Accred.:* 1951/1988 (NEASC-CIHE) *Calendar:* Sem. plan *Degrees:* B, M *Prof. Accred.:* Music *CEO:* Pres. Laurence Lesser
Enroll: 668 (617) 262-1120

NEW ENGLAND HAIR ACADEMY
492-500 Main St., Malden 02148 *Type:* Private *Accred.:* 1979/1989 (CCA-ACTTS) *Calendar:* Courses of varying lengths *Degrees:* certificates *CEO:* Pres. Anthony Clemente
Enroll: 35 (617) 324-6799

NEW ENGLAND SCHOOL OF ACCOUNTING
155 Ararat St., Worcester 01606 *Type:* Private business *Accred.:* 1969/1981 (CCA-ACICS) *Calendar:* Sem. plan *Degrees:* certificates, diplomas *CEO:* Controller Kevin Albano
Enroll: 90 (508) 853-8972

NEW ENGLAND SCHOOL OF ACUPUNCTURE
30 Common St., Watertown 02172 *Type:* Private *Calendar:* 3-year plan *Degrees:* M *Prof. Accred.:* Acupuncture *CEO:* Pres. Richard Feit
(617) 926-1788

NEW ENGLAND SCHOOL OF ART AND DESIGN
28 Newbury St., Boston 02116 *Type:* Private *Accred.:* 1968/1989 (CCA-ACTTS) *Calendar:* Sem. plan *Degrees:* diplomas *Prof. Accred.:* Interior Design *CEO:* Pres. Christy R. Rufo
Enroll: 186 (617) 536-0383

NEW ENGLAND SCHOOL OF LAW
154 Stuart St., Boston 02116 *Type:* Private professional *Calendar:* Sem. plan *Degrees:* P *Prof. Accred.:* Law (ABA only) *CEO:* Dean John F. O'Brien
Enroll: 1194 (617) 451-0010

NEW ENGLAND SCHOOL OF PHOTOGRAPHY
537 Commonwealth Ave., Boston 02215 *Type:* Private *Accred.:* 1981/1986 (CCA-ACTTS) *Calendar:* Sem. plan *Degrees:* diplomas *CEO:* Pres. John H. Carruthers
Enroll: 263 (617) 437-1868

NEW ENGLAND TRACTOR TRAILER TRAINING SCHOOL OF MASSACHUSETTS
1093 N. Montello St., Brockton 02401 *Type:* Private *Accred.:* 1982 (CCA-ACTTS) *Calendar:* 4-week program *Degrees:* diplomas *CEO:* Dir. Mark Greenberg
Enroll: 673 (508) 587-1100

BRANCH CAMPUS
1410 Bush St., Baltimore, MD 21230-9910 *CEO:* Exec. Dir. Frank Merritt
(410) 783-0100

NEWBURY COLLEGE
129 Fisher Ave., Brookline 02146 *Type:* Private *Accred.:* 1977/1989 (NEASC-CVTCI) *Calendar:* Sem. plan *Degrees:* A *Prof. Accred.:* Physical Therapy Assisting, Respiratory Therapy, Respiratory Therapy Technology *CEO:* Pres. Edward J. Tassinari
Enroll: 2276 (617) 739-0510

NICHOLS COLLEGE
Dudley 01570 *Type:* Private business *Accred.:* 1965/1984 (NEASC-CIHE) *Calendar:* Sem. plan *Degrees:* A, B, M *CEO:* Pres. Lowell C. Smith
Enroll: 1146 (508) 943-1560

NORTH ADAMS STATE COLLEGE
North Adams 01247 *Type:* Public teachers *System:* Massachusetts Higher Education Coordinating Council *Accred.:* 1953/1983 (NEASC-CIHE) *Calendar:* 4-1-4 plan *Degrees:* B, M *Prof. Accred.:* Teacher Education (e,s) *CEO:* Pres. Thomas D. Aceto
Enroll: 2119 (413) 664-4511

NORTH BENNET STREET SCHOOL
39 N. Bennet St., Boston 02113 *Type:* Private *Accred.:* 1982/1987 (CCA-ACTTS) *Calendar:* Courses of varying lengths *Degrees:* diplomas *CEO:* Dir. Thomas Williams
Enroll: 169 (617) 227-0155

Accredited Institutions   **Massachusetts**

NORTH SHORE COMMUNITY COLLEGE
3 Essex St., Beverly 01915 *Type:* Public (state) junior *System:* Massachusetts Higher Education Coordinating Council *Accred.:* 1969/1989 (NEASC-CIHE) *Calendar:* Sem. plan *Degrees:* A *Prof. Accred.:* Nursing (A), Occupational Therapy Assisting, Physical Therapy Assisting, Radiography, Respiratory Therapy *CEO:* Pres. George Traicoff
Enroll: 3192   (508) 922-6722

NORTHEAST BROADCASTING SCHOOL
142 Berkeley St., Boston 02116 *Type:* Private *Accred.:* 1972/1987 (CCA-ACTTS) *Calendar:* Sem. plan *Degrees:* certificates *CEO:* Pres. Howard E. Horton
Enroll: 180   (617) 267-7910

NORTHEAST INSTITUTE OF INDUSTRIAL TECHNOLOGY
41 Phillips St., Boston 02114 *Type:* Private *Accred.:* 1971/1987 (CCA-ACTTS) *Calendar:* Sem. plan *Degrees:* certificates, diplomas *CEO:* Dir. George M. Galvin
Enroll: 934   (617) 523-2869

NORTHEASTERN UNIVERSITY
360 Huntington Ave., Boston 02115-5095 *Type:* Private *Accred.:* 1940/1988 (NEASC-CIHE) *Calendar:* Qtr. plan *Degrees:* A, B, P, M, D *Prof. Accred.:* Audiology, Business (B,M), Computer Science, Engineering (chemical, civil, electrical, industrial, mechanical), Engineering Technology (electrical, mechanical), Law, Medical Laboratory Technology (AMA), Medical Record Administration, Medical Technology, Nursing (B,M), Perfusion, Pharmacy, Physical Therapy, Physician Assisting, Public Administration, Radiography, Recreation and Leisure Studies, Rehabilitation Counseling, Respiratory Therapy, Speech-Language Pathology *CEO:* Pres. John A. Curry
Enroll: 23378   (617) 437-2000

NORTHERN ESSEX COMMUNITY COLLEGE
100 Elliott Way, Haverhill 01830-2399 *Type:* Public (state) junior *System:* Massachusetts Higher Education Coordinating Council *Accred.:* 1969/1991 (NEASC-CIHE) *Calendar:* Sem. plan *Degrees:* A *Prof. Accred.:* Dental Assisting, Medical Record Technology, Nursing (A), Practical Nursing, Radiography, Respiratory Therapy, Respiratory Therapy Technology *CEO:* Pres. John R. Dimitry
Enroll: 4043   (508) 374-3900

PEDIGREE CAREER INSTITUTE
Harbor Mall, Rte. 1A, Lynnway, Lynn 01901 *Type:* Private *Accred.:* 1982/1987 (CCA-ACTTS) *Calendar:* Courses of varying lengths *Degrees:* certificates *CEO:* Dir. Russell L. Carriker
Enroll: 111   (617) 592-3647

PINE MANOR COLLEGE
400 Heath St., Chestnut Hill 02167 *Type:* Private liberal arts for women *Accred.:* 1939/1986 (NEASC-CIHE) *Calendar:* Sem. plan *Degrees:* A, B *CEO:* Pres. Rosemary Ashby
Enroll: 489   (617) 731-7000

POPE JOHN XXIII NATIONAL SEMINARY
558 South Ave., Weston 02193 *Type:* Private (Roman Catholic) professional; graduate only *Accred.:* 1983/1988 (ATS) *Calendar:* Sem. plan *Degrees:* P, M *CEO:* Pres. Cornelius McRae
Enroll: 44   (617) 899-5500

QUINCY COLLEGE
34 Coddington St., Quincy 02169 *Type:* Public (city) junior *System:* Massachusetts Higher Education Coordinating Council *Accred.:* 1980/1987 (NEASC-CIHE) *Calendar:* Sem. plan *Degrees:* A *Prof. Accred.:* Nursing (A), Practical Nursing, Surgical Technology *CEO:* Pres. O. Clayton Johnson
Enroll: 2123   (617) 984-1600

QUINSIGAMOND COMMUNITY COLLEGE
670 W. Boylston St., Worcester 01606 *Type:* Public (state) junior *System:* Massachusetts Higher Education Coordinating Council *Accred.:* 1967/1984 (NEASC-CIHE) *Calendar:* Sem. plan *Degrees:* A *Prof. Accred.:* Dental Hygiene, Nursing (A), Occupational

Massachusetts

Therapy Assisting, Radiography, Respiratory Therapy *CEO:* Pres. Clifford S. Peterson
Enroll: 2740 (508) 853-2300

R.E.T.S. ELECTRONIC SCHOOL
965 Commonwealth Ave., Boston 02215 *Type:* Private *Accred.:* 1974/1989 (CCA-ACTTS) *Calendar:* Courses of varying lengths *Degrees:* certificates, diplomas *CEO:* Dir. Don Harris
Enroll: 357 (617) 783-1197

RADCLIFFE COLLEGE
10 Garden St., Cambridge 02138 *Type:* Private primarily for women *Accred.:* 1929/1987 (NEASC-CIHE) *Calendar:* Sem. plan *Degrees:* A, B *CEO:* Pres. Linda S. Wilson
Enroll: 2692 (617) 495-8601

REGIS COLLEGE
Weston 02193 *Type:* Private (Roman Catholic) liberal arts for women *Accred.:* 1933/1986 (NEASC-CIHE) *Calendar:* Sem. plan *Degrees:* B *Prof. Accred.:* Nursing (B), Social Work (B) *CEO:* Pres. Therese Higgins, C.S.J.
Enroll: 927 (617) 893-1820

ROXBURY COMMUNITY COLLEGE
1234 Columbus Ave., Roxbury Crossing 02120-3400 *Type:* Public (state) junior *System:* Massachusetts Higher Education Coordinating Council *Accred.:* 1981/1986 (NEASC-CIHE) *Calendar:* Sem. plan *Degrees:* A *CEO:* Acting Admin. Alan Shepherd
Enroll: 1306 (617) 427-0060

ST. HYACINTH COLLEGE AND SEMINARY
Granby 01033 *Type:* Private (Roman Catholic Order of Friars Minor Conventual) for men *Accred.:* 1967/1988 (NEASC-CIHE) *Calendar:* Sem. plan *Degrees:* B *CEO:* Pres. Germain Kopaczynski, O.F.M.C.
Enroll: 23 (413) 467-7180

ST. JOHN'S SCHOOL OF BUSINESS
511 Main St., West Springfield 01090 *Type:* Private business *Accred.:* 1981/1990 (CCA-ACICS) *Calendar:* Qtr. plan *Degrees:* certificates, diplomas *CEO:* Dir. Kenneth C. Ballard
Enroll: 248 (413) 781-0390

ST. JOHN'S SEMINARY
127 Lake St., Brighton 02135 *Type:* Private (Roman Catholic)*Accred.:*1970/1989 (ATS); 1969/1989 (NEASC-CIHE) *Calendar:* Sem. plan *Degrees:* B,P,M *CEO:* Rector Timothy J. Moran
Enroll: 143 (617) 254-2610

SALEM STATE COLLEGE
352 Lafayette St., Salem 01970 *Type:* Public liberal arts and professional *System:* Massachusetts Higher Education Coordinating Council *Accred.:* 1953/1984 (NEASC-CIHE) *Calendar:* Sem. plan *Degrees:* B, M *Prof. Accred.:* Art, Nuclear Medicine Technology, Nursing (B,M), Social Work (B,M), Teacher Education (e,s,p) *CEO:* Pres. Nancy D. Harrington
Enroll: 6883 (508) 741-6000

SALTER SCHOOL
155 Ararat St., Worcester 01606 *Type:* Private business *Accred.:* 1953/1988 (CCA-ACICS) *Calendar:* Sem. plan *Degrees:* certificates, diplomas *CEO:* Dir. John F. Albano
Enroll: 362 (508) 853-1074

BRANCH CAMPUS
One Grove St., New Britain, CT 06053 *CEO:* Dir. Janet Cyr
(202) 224-8838

SCHOOL OF THE MUSEUM OF FINE ARTS, BOSTON
230 The Fenway, Boston 02115-9975 *Type:* Private professional *Calendar:* Sem. plan *Degrees:* B, M, diplomas *Prof. Accred.:* Art *CEO:* Dean Bruce K. Macdonald
(617) 267-6100

SIMMONS COLLEGE
Boston 02115 *Type:* Private liberal arts and professional for women *Accred.:* 1929/1990 (NEASC-CIHE) *Calendar:* Sem. plan *Degrees:* B, M, D *Prof. Accred.:* Librarianship, Nursing (B,M), Physical Therapy, Social Work (M) *CEO:* Pres. William J. Holmes, Jr.
Enroll: 2224 (617) 738-2000

Accredited Institutions **Massachusetts**

SIMON'S ROCK OF BARD COLLEGE
Great Barrington 01230 *Type:* Private liberal arts *Accred.:* 1974/1986 (NEASC-CIHE) *Calendar:* Sem. plan *Degrees:* A, B *CEO:* Pres. Leon Botstein
Enroll: 288 (413) 528-0771

SMITH COLLEGE
Northampton 01063 *Type:* Private liberal arts for women*Accred.:*1929/1988 (NEASC-CIHE) *Calendar:* Sem. plan *Degrees:* B, M, D *Prof. Accred.:* Social Work (M) *CEO:* Pres. Mary Maples Dunn
Enroll: 2641 (413) 584-2700

SOUTHEASTERN TECHNICAL INSTITUTE
250 Foundry St., South Easton 02375 *Type:* Private *Calendar:* Courses of varying lengths *Degrees:* certificates *Prof. Accred.:* Dental Assisting, Medical Laboratory Technology (AMA) *CEO:* Supt. Paul K. O'Leary
  (508) 238-4374

SPRINGFIELD COLLEGE
Springfield 01109 *Type:* Private liberal arts and professional *Accred.:* 1930/1989 (NEASC-CIHE) *Calendar:* Qtr. plan *Degrees:* B, M, D *Prof. Accred.:* Physical Therapy, Recreation and Leisure Services, Rehabilitation Counseling, Social Work (M-candidate) *CEO:* Interim Pres. Randolph W. Bromery
Enroll: 3300 (413) 788-3000

SPRINGFIELD TECHNICAL COMMUNITY COLLEGE
One Armory Sq., Springfield 01105 *Type:* Public (state) 2-year *System:* Massachusetts Higher Education Coordinating Council *Accred.:* 1971/1981 (NEASC-CIHE) *Calendar:* Sem. plan *Degrees:* A *Prof. Accred.:* Dental Assisting, Dental Hygiene, Medical Assisting (AMA), Medical Laboratory Technology (AMA), Nuclear Medicine Technology, Nursing (A), Physical Therapy Assisting, Radiation Therapy Technology, Radiography, Respiratory Therapy, Surgical Technology *CEO:* Pres. Andrew M. Scibelli
Enroll: 3498 (413) 781-7822

STONEHILL COLLEGE
North Easton 02357 *Type:* Private (Roman Catholic) liberal arts *Accred.:* 1959/1989 (NEASC-CIHE) *Calendar:* Sem. plan *Degrees:* B *Prof. Accred.:* Teacher Education (e) *CEO:* Pres. Bartley MacPhaidin, C.S.C.
Enroll: 2295 (508) 238-1081

SUFFOLK UNIVERSITY
8 Ashburton Pl., Beacon Hill, Boston 02108 *Type:* Private *Accred.:* 1952/1983 (NEASC-CIHE) *Calendar:* Sem. plan *Degrees:* A, B, P, M, D *Prof. Accred.:* Business (B,M), Law, Public Administration *CEO:* Pres. David J. Sargent
Enroll: 4307 (617) 723-4700

TAD TECHNICAL INSTITUTE
45 Spruce St., Chelsea 02150-2397 *Type:* Private *Accred.:* 1991 (CCA-ACTTS) *Calendar:* Courses of varying lengths *Degrees:* certificates *CEO:* Dir. Rod Kruse
  (617) 889-3600

TRAVEL EDUCATION CENTER
104 Mt. Auburn St., Harvard Sq., Cambridge 02138 *Type:* Private *Accred.:* 1979/1980 (CCA-ACTTS) *Calendar:* Courses of varying lengths *Degrees:* certificates *CEO:* Pres. Linda Paresky
Enroll: 301 (617) 547-7750

TRAVEL SCHOOL OF AMERICA
1047 Commonwealth Ave., Boston 02215 *Type:* Private *Accred.:* 1978/1988 (CCA-ACTTS) *Calendar:* Courses of varying lengths *Degrees:* certificates *CEO:* Dir. Bernard Garber
Enroll: 329 (617) 787-1214

TUFTS UNIVERSITY
Medford 02155 *Type:* Private liberal arts *Accred.:* 1929/1982 (NEASC-CIHE) *Calendar:* Sem. plan *Degrees:* B, P, M, D *Prof. Accred.:* Combined Prosthodontics, Dentistry, Endodontics, Engineering (chemical, civil, electrical, mechanical), General Practice Residency, Medicine, Occupational Therapy, Oral and Maxillofacial Surgery, Orthodontics, Pediatric Dentistry, Periodon-

tics, Psychology Internship (provisional) *CEO:* Pres. Jean Mayer
Enroll: 7463 (617) 628-5000

UNITED STATES ARMY INTELLIGENCE SCHOOL
Fort Devens 01433 *Type:* Public (federal) technological *Accred.:* 1976/1986 (NEASC-CVTCI) *Calendar:* Courses of varying lengths *Degrees:* certificates *CEO:* Commandant Michael E. Pheneger
Enroll: 2129 (508) 796-2293

UNITED TECHNICAL SCHOOLS
83 Worthen St., West Springfield 01089 *Type:* Private *Accred.:* 1973/1979 (CCA-ACTTS) *Calendar:* Courses of varying lengths *Degrees:* certificates *CEO:* Pres. John M. Dooley
Enroll: 100 (413) 733-0081

UNIVERSITY OF MASSACHUSETTS AT AMHERST
Amherst 01003 *Type:* Public (state) *System:* University of Massachusetts President's Office *Accred.:* 1932/1988 (NEASC-CIHE) *Calendar:* Sem. plan *Degrees:* A, B, P, M, D *Prof. Accred.:* Art, Audiology, Business (B,M), Clinical Psychology, Counseling Psychology, Engineering (chemical, civil, computer, electrical, environmental/sanitary, industrial, manufacturing, mechanical), Forestry, Interior Design, Landscape Architecture (B-initial,M), Leisure Studies and Resources, Music, Nursing (B,M), Planning (regional/urban), Psychology Internship, Public Administration, Public Health, Radiation Therapy Technology, Speech-Language Pathology, Teacher Education(e,s,p), Theatre *CEO:* Chanc. Richard D. O'Brien
Enroll: 21776 (413) 545-3171

UNIVERSITY OF MASSACHUSETTS AT BOSTON
Harbor Campus, Boston 02125 *Type:* Public (state) *System:* University of Massachusetts President's Office *Accred.:* 1972/1985 (NEASC-CIHE) *Calendar:* Sem. plan *Degrees:* B, M, D *Prof. Accred.:* Nursing (B,M), Rehabilitation Counseling (candidate) *CEO:* Chanc. Sherry H. Penney
Enroll: 8899 (617) 287-6800

UNIVERSITY OF MASSACHUSETTS AT DARTMOUTH
North Dartmouth 02747 *Type:* Public (state) *System:* University of Massachusetts President's Office *Accred.:* 1964/1990 (NEASC-CIHE) *Calendar:* Sem. plan *Degrees:* B, M *Prof. Accred.:* Art, Computer Science, Engineering (civil, computer, electrical, mechanical), Engineering Technology (electrical, mechanical), Medical Technology, Nursing (B) *CEO:* Interim Chanc. Joseph C. Deck
Enroll: 5819 (508) 999-8004

UNIVERSITY OF MASSACHUSETTS AT LOWELL
One University Ave., Lowell 01854 *Type:* Public (state) *System:* University of Massachusetts President's Office *Accred.:* 1975/1987 (NEASC-CIHE) *Calendar:* Sem. plan *Degrees:* A, B, M, D *Prof. Accred.:* Art, Business (B,M), Computer Science, Engineering (chemical, civil, electrical, mechanical, nuclear, plastics), Engineering Technology (civil/construction, electrical, mechanical), Medical Technology, Music, Nursing (B,M), Physical Therapy, Teacher Education (e,s,p) *CEO:* Chanc. William T. Hogan
Enroll: 10079 (508) 934-4000

UNIVERSITY OF MASSACHUSETTS AT WORCESTER
55 Lake Ave., N., Worcester 01655 *Type:* Public (state) *System:* University of Massachusetts President's Office *Calendar:* Sem. plan *Degrees:* B, P, M *Prof. Accred.:* Medicine, Nuclear Medicine Technology, Nursing (M), Radiation Therapy Technology *CEO:* Chanc. Aaron Lazare
Enroll: 407 (508) 856-2107

WELLESLEY COLLEGE
Wellesley 02181 *Type:* Private liberal arts for women *Accred.:* 1929/1989 (NEASC-CIHE) *Calendar:* 4-1-4 plan *Degrees:* B *CEO:* Pres. Nannerl O. Keohane
Enroll: 2181 (617) 235-0320

WENTWORTH INSTITUTE OF TECHNOLOGY
Boston 02115 *Type:* Private technological *Accred.:* 1967/1983 (NEASC-CIHE) *Calendar:* Sem. plan *Degrees:* A, B *Prof. Accred.:* Architecture (B-candidate), Engineering

Technology (aerospace, architectural, civil/construction, computer, electrical, manufacturing, mechanical) *CEO:* Pres. John F. Van Domelen
Enroll: 3310 (617) 442-9010

EAST COAST AERO TECHNICAL SCHOOL
Hanscom Field Box 426, Lexington, MA 02173 *Accred.:* 1967/1983 (NEASC-CIHE) *CEO:* Pres. Robert McTigue
(617) 274-6400

WENTWORTH TECHNICAL SCHOOL
191 Spring Ave., Lexington 02173 *Type:* Private *Accred.:* 1973/1988 (CCA-ACTTS) *Calendar:* Courses of varying lengths *Degrees:* diplomas *CEO:* Dir. Dorothy G. Pesek
Enroll: 1526 (617) 674-1000

WESTERN NEW ENGLAND COLLEGE
Springfield 01119 *Type:* Private liberal arts and professional *Accred.:* 1965/1985 (NEASC-CIHE) *Calendar:* Sem. plan *Degrees:* B, P, M, D *Prof. Accred.:* Engineering (electrical, industrial, mechanical), Law, Social Work (B) *CEO:* Pres. Beverly W. Miller
Enroll: 3612 (413) 782-3111

WESTFIELD STATE COLLEGE
Western Ave., Westfield 01086 *Type:* Public (state) liberal arts and teachers *System:* Massachusetts Higher Education Coordinating Council *Accred.:* 1957/1986 (NEASC-CIHE) *Calendar:* Sem. plan *Degrees:* B, M *Prof. Accred.:* Teacher Education (e,s) *CEO:* Pres. Ronald L. Applbaum
Enroll: 4041 (413) 568-3311

WESTON SCHOOL OF THEOLOGY
3 Phillips Pl., Cambridge 02138 *Type:* Private (Roman Catholic) professional; graduate only *Accred.:* 1968/1988 (ATS) *Calendar:* Sem. plan *Degrees:* P, M *CEO:* Pres. Edward M. O'Flaherty
Enroll: 159 (617) 492-1960

WHEATON COLLEGE
Norton 02766 *Type:* Private liberal arts for women *Accred.:* 1929/1989 (NEASC-CIHE) *Calendar:* Sem. plan *Degrees:* B *CEO:* Acting Pres. Hannah Goldberg
Enroll: 1243 (508) 285-7722

WHEELOCK COLLEGE
200 The Riverway, Boston 02215 *Type:* Private teachers for women *Accred.:* 1950/1985 (NEASC-CIHE) *Calendar:* Tri. plan *Degrees:* A, B, M *Prof. Accred.:* Social Work (B) *CEO:* Pres. Gerald Tirozzi
Enroll: 985 (617) 734-5200

WILLIAMS COLLEGE
Williamstown 01267 *Type:* Private liberal arts *Accred.:* 1929/1988 (NEASC-CIHE) *Calendar:* 4-1-4 plan *Degrees:* B, M *CEO:* Pres. Francis C. Oakley
Enroll: 2092 (413) 597-3131

WORCESTER POLYTECHNIC INSTITUTE
100 Institute Rd., Worcester 01609 *Type:* Private technological *Accred.:* 1937/1982 (NEASC-CIHE) *Calendar:* Sem. plan *Degrees:* B, M, D *Prof. Accred.:* Computer Science, Engineering (chemical, civil, electrical, mechanical) *CEO:* Pres. Jon C. Strauss
Enroll: 3356 (508) 831-5000

WORCESTER STATE COLLEGE
486 Chandler St., Worcester 01602 *Type:* Public (state) liberal arts and teachers *System:* Massachusetts Higher Education Coordinating Council *Accred.:* 1957/1984 (NEASC-CIHE) *Calendar:* Sem. plan *Degrees:* B, M *Prof. Accred.:* Nuclear Medicine Technology, Nursing (B), Occupational Therapy, Radiation Therapy Technology, Speech-Language Pathology *CEO:* Pres. Kalyan Ghosh
Enroll: 3763 (508) 793-8000

WORCESTER TECHNICAL INSTITUTE
251 Belmont St., Worcester 01605 *Type:* Public (state) technical *Accred.:* 1982/1985 (NEASC-CVTCI) *Calendar:* Sem. plan *Degrees:* certificates *Prof. Accred.:* Dental Assisting *CEO:* Dir. Janet M. Doe
Enroll: 372 (508) 799-1945

MICHIGAN

ACADEMY OF HEALTH CAREERS
21700 Greenfield Rd., Ste. 120, Oak Park 48237-2532 *Type:* Private *Accred.:* 1991 (CCA-ACTTS) *Calendar:* Courses of varying lengths *Degrees:* certificates *CEO:* Pres. Dale Saham
(313) 967-0404

ADRIAN COLLEGE
110 S. Madison St., Adrian 49221 *Type:* Private (United Methodist) liberal arts *Accred.:* 1916/1989 (NCA) *Calendar:* Sem. plan *Degrees:* A, B, certificates, diplomas *Prof. Accred.:* Teacher Education (e,s) *CEO:* Pres. Stanley P. Caine
Enroll: 1121   (517) 265-5161

ALBION COLLEGE
611 E. Porter St., Albion 49224 *Type:* Private (United Methodist) liberal arts *Accred.:* 1915/1981 (NCA) *Calendar:* Sem. plan *Degrees:* B *Prof. Accred.:* Music *CEO:* Pres. Melvin L. Vulgamore
Enroll: 1559   (517) 629-1000

ALMA COLLEGE
614 W. Superior St., Alma 48801 *Type:* Private (United Presbyterian) liberal arts *Accred.:* 1916/1990 (NCA) *Calendar:* 4-4-x plan *Degrees:* B *Prof. Accred.:* Music *CEO:* Pres. Alan J. Stone
Enroll: 1206   (517) 463-7111

ALPENA COMMUNITY COLLEGE
666 Johnson St., Alpena 49707 *Type:* Public (city) junior *System:* Michigan State Board of Education *Accred.:* 1963/1988 (NCA) *Calendar:* Sem. plan *Degrees:* A, certificates, diplomas *CEO:* Pres. Donald L. Newport
Enroll: 682   (517) 356-9021

AMERICAN TRAVEL SCHOOLS
26075 Woodward Ave., Huntington 48070 *Type:* Private *Accred.:* 1988 (CCA-ACTTS) *Calendar:* Courses of varying lengths *Degrees:* certificates *CEO:* Dir. Ruth K. Moss
(313) 399-5522

BRANCH CAMPUS
4339 Canal St., S.E., Grandville, MI 49418 *CEO:* Dir. Mary Joe Douwkamp
(616) 531-1600

ANDREWS UNIVERSITY
Berrien Springs 49104 *Type:* Private (Seventh-Day Adventist) liberal arts and professional *Accred.:* 1970/1989 (ATS); 1922/1989 (NCA) *Calendar:* Qtr. plan *Degrees:* A, B, P, M, D, certificates, diplomas *Prof. Accred.:* Architecture (B), Counseling, Dietetics (coordinated), Medical Technology, Music, Nursing (B,M), Physical Therapy, Social Work (B-candidate), Teacher Education (e,s,p) *CEO:* Pres. W. Richard Lesher
Enroll: 2357   (616) 471-3100

AQUINAS COLLEGE
1607 Robinson Rd., S.E., Grand Rapids 49506 *Type:* Private (Roman Catholic) liberal arts *Accred.:* 1946/1987 (NCA) *Calendar:* Sem. plan *Degrees:* A, B, M *CEO:* Pres. R. Paul Nelson
Enroll: 1794   (616) 459-8281

BAKER COLLEGE
G-1050 W. Bristol Rd., Flint 48507 *Type:* Private *Accred.:* 1985/1990 (NCA) *Calendar:* Qtr. plan *Degrees:* A, B, certificates, diplomas *Prof. Accred.:* Medical Assisting (AMA), Medical Record Technology *CEO:* Pres. Edward J. Kurtz
Enroll: 5948   (313) 767-7600

BAKER COLLEGE OF CADILLAC
9600 E. Thirty-Six Mile Rd., Cadillac, MI 49601 *CEO:* Dir. Maynard W. Thompson
(616) 775-8458

BAKER COLLEGE OF MOUNT CLEMENS
34950 Little Mack Ave., Mount Clemens, MI 48043 *CEO:* Dir. Elizabeth M. Haddad
(313) 791-6610

BAKER COLLEGE OF MUSKEGON
141 Hartford St., Muskegon, MI 49442 *Prof. Accred.:* Medical Assisting (AMA), Medical Record Technology *CEO:* Pres. Robert D. Jewell
(616) 726-4904

BAKER COLLEGE OF OWOSSO
1020 S. Washington St., Owosso, MI 48867 *Prof. Accred.:* Medical Assisting (AMA) *CEO:* Pres. Rick E. Amidon
(517) 723-5251

BAKER COLLEGE OF PONTIAC
76 Williams St., Pontiac, MI 48053 *CEO:* Dir. Timothy M. Yount
(313) 332-7000

BAKER COLLEGE OF PORT HURON
3403 Lapeer Rd., Port Huron, MI 48060 *CEO:* Dir. Lawrence Van Ness
(313) 985-7000

BAY DE NOC COMMUNITY COLLEGE
2001 N. Lincoln Rd., Escanaba 49829 *Type:* Public (district) junior *System:* Michigan State Board of Education *Accred.:* 1976/1991 (NCA) *Calendar:* Sem. plan *Degrees:* A, certificates, diplomas *CEO:* Pres. Dwight E. Link
Enroll: 1632   (906) 786-5802

BLACK FOREST HALL
2787 Quick Rd., P.O. Box 140, Harbor Springs 49740 *Type:* Private *Accred.:* 1988 (CCA-ACTTS) *Calendar:* Courses of varying lengths *Degrees:* certificates *CEO:* Dir. Ceejay Heckenberg
(616) 526-7066

CDI CAREER DEVELOPMENT INSTITUTE
21700 Northwestern Hwy., Tower 14, Ste. 1401, Southfield 48075 *Type:* Private *Accred.:* 1968/1989 (CCA-ACTTS) *Calendar:* Courses of varying lengths *Degrees:* certificates *CEO:* Dir. Norman L. Cohen
Enroll: 423   (313) 552-6600

CALVIN COLLEGE
3201 Burton St., S.E., Grand Rapids 49546 *Type:* Private (Christian Reformed) liberal arts *Accred.:* 1930/1985 (NCA) *Calendar:* 4-1-4 plan *Degrees:* B, M *Prof. Accred.:* Engineering (general), Music, Social Work (B-candidate), Teacher Education (e,s) *CEO:* Pres. Anthony J. Diekema
Enroll: 4126   (616) 957-6000

CALVIN THEOLOGICAL SEMINARY
Grand Rapids 49506 *Type:* Private (Christian Reformed) professional *Accred.:* 1944/1988 (ATS) *Calendar:* Qtr. plan *Degrees:* P, M *CEO:* Pres. James A. Dejong
Enroll: 182   (616) 949-6034

CAMBRIDGE BUSINESS SCHOOL
1505 Woodward Ave., Detroit 48226-2016 *Type:* Private business *Accred.:* 1977/1987 (CCA-ACICS) *Calendar:* Courses of varying lengths *Degrees:* certificates, diplomas *CEO:* Pres. Ted Jakub
Enroll: 646   (313) 961-5105

CARNEGIE INSTITUTE
550 Stephenson Hwy., Ste. 100, Troy 48083 *Type:* Private *Accred.:* 1968/1985 (CCA-ACTTS) *Calendar:* Qtr. plan *Degrees:* diplomas *Prof. Accred.:* Medical Assisting (AMA) *CEO:* Pres. James F. McEachern
Enroll: 454   (313) 589-1078

THE CENTER FOR CREATIVE STUDIES—COLLEGE OF ART AND DESIGN
245 E. Kirby St., Detroit 48202-4013 *Type:* Private professional *Accred.:* 1977/1982 (NCA) *Calendar:* Sem. plan *Degrees:* B *Prof. Accred.:* Art *CEO:* Pres. Josephine Kelsey, Ph.D.
Enroll: 770   (313) 872-3118

CENTER FOR HUMANISTIC STUDIES
40 E. Ferry Ave., Detroit 48202 *Type:* Private professional; graduate only *Accred.:* 1984/1989 (NCA) *Calendar:* Qtr. plan *Degrees:* P, M *CEO:* Pres. Clark Moustakas
Enroll: 70   (313) 875-7440

CENTRAL MICHIGAN UNIVERSITY
Mount Pleasant 48859 *Type:* Public (state) *System:* Michigan State Board of Education *Accred.:* 1915/1986 (NCA) *Calendar:* Sem. plan *Degrees:* B, M, D *Prof. Accred.:*

Michigan

Accounting (Type A), Audiology, Business (B,M), Clinical Psychology (provisional), Music, Recreation and Park Administration, Speech-Language Pathology, Teacher Education (e,s,p) *CEO:* Interim Pres. Leonard E. Plachta
Enroll: 15456 (517) 774-3131

CHARLES STEWART MOTT COMMUNITY COLLEGE
1401 E. Court St., Flint 48502 *Type:* Public (district) junior *System:* Michigan State Board of Education *Accred.:* 1926/1990 (NCA) *Calendar:* Sem. plan *Degrees:* A, certificates, diplomas *Prof. Accred.:* Dental Assisting, Dental Hygiene, Nursing (A), Respiratory Therapy *CEO:* Pres. David G. Moore
Enroll: 5433 (313) 762-0453

CHAUFFEURS TRAINING SCHOOL
14601 Dequindre St., Detroit 48212 *Type:* Private *Accred.:* 1985 (CCA-ACTTS) *Calendar:* Courses of varying lengths *Degrees:* certificates *CEO:* Dir. Joseph Labarge
(313) 883-2200

CHAUFFEURS TRAINING SCHOOL
G-6434 S. Dort Hwy., Grand Blanc 48439-8162 *Type:* Private *Accred.:* 1985 (CCA-ACTTS) *Calendar:* Courses of varying lengths *Degrees:* certificates *CEO:* Dir. Joseph Labarge
(313) 695-2900

CLEARY COLLEGE
2170 Washtenaw Ave., Ypsilanti 48197 *Type:* Private *Accred.:* 1988/1991 (NCA) *Calendar:* Qtr. plan *Degrees:* A, B, certificates, diplomas *Prof. Accred.:* Medical Record Technology *CEO:* Pres. Thomas P. Sullivan
Enroll: 758 (313) 483-4400

CONCORDIA COLLEGE
4090 Geddes Rd., Ann Arbor 48105 *Type:* Private (Lutheran-Missouri Synod) liberal arts *Accred.:* 1968/1986 (NCA) *Calendar:* Qtr. plan *Degrees:* A, B *CEO:* Pres. James Koerschen
Enroll: 599 (313) 995-7331

CRANBROOK ACADEMY OF ART
500 Lone Pine Rd., Box 801, Bloomfield Hills 48303-0801 *Type:* Private professional *Accred.:* 1960/1989 (NCA) *Calendar:* Sem. plan *Degrees:* M *Prof. Accred.:* Art *CEO:* Pres. Roy Slade
Enroll: 142 (313) 645-3300

DAVENPORT COLLEGE
415 E. Fulton St., Grand Rapids 49503 *Type:* Private *Accred.:* 1976/1988 (NCA) *Calendar:* Qtr. plan *Degrees:* A, B, certificates, diplomas *Prof. Accred.:* Medical Assisting (AMA) *CEO:* Pres. Donald W. Maine
Enroll: 5621 (616) 451-3511

BRANCH CAMPUS
3030 Eastern Ave., S.E., Grand Rapids, MI 49508 *CEO:* Dir. Vincent E. Norton
(616) 245-3030

BRANCH CAMPUS
4123 W. Main St., Kalamazoo, MI 49007 *Prof. Accred.:* Medical Assisting *CEO:* Dean C. Dexter Rohm
(616) 382-2835

BRANCH CAMPUS
220 E. Kalamazoo St., Lansing, MI 48933 *CEO:* Dir. Don Colizzi
(517) 484-2600

DELTA COLLEGE
University Center 48710 *Type:* Public (county and district) junior *System:* Michigan State Board of Education *Accred.:* 1968/1984 (NCA) *Calendar:* Sem. plan *Degrees:* A, certificates, diplomas *Prof. Accred.:* Dental Assisting, Dental Hygiene, Engineering Technology (electrical, mechanical), Nursing (A), Physical Therapy Assisting, Radiography, Respiratory Therapy, Surgical Technology *CEO:* Pres. Donald J. Carlyon
Enroll: 7580 (517) 686-9201

DETROIT BUSINESS INSTITUTE
115 State St., Detroit 48226 *Type:* Private business *Accred.:* 1961/1987 (CCA-ACICS) *Calendar:* Qtr. plan *Degrees:* certificates, diplomas *CEO:* Dir. Walter J. Stafford
Enroll: 634 (313) 962-6534

Accredited Institutions   **Michigan**

DETROIT BUSINESS INSTITUTE
21700 Northwestern Hwy., Southfield 48075 *Type:* Private business *Accred.:* 1986 (CCA-ACICS) *Calendar:* Qtr. plan *Degrees:* certificates, diplomas *CEO:* Dir. Leon D. Gust
Enroll: 283   (313) 557-5744

DETROIT BUSINESS INSTITUTE—DOWNRIVER
19100 Fort St., Riverview 48192 *Type:* Private business *Accred.:* 1983/1989 (CCA-ACICS) *Calendar:* Qtr. plan *Degrees:* certificates, diplomas *CEO:* Dir. Valentine Kolcheff
Enroll: 518   (313) 479-0660

DETROIT COLLEGE OF BUSINESS
4801 Oakman Blvd., Dearborn 48126 *Type:* Private *Accred.:* 1986/1991 (NCA) *Calendar:* Qtr. plan *Degrees:* A, B, certificates, diplomas *CEO:* Senior Vice Pres. James Mendola
Enroll: 3830   (313) 581-4400

DETROIT COLLEGE OF LAW
130 E. Elizabeth St., Detroit 48201 *Type:* Private professional *Calendar:* Sem. plan *Degrees:* P *Prof. Accred.:* Law *CEO:* Dean Arthur J. Lombard
Enroll: 713   (313) 965-0150

DETROIT INSTITUTE OF AERONAUTICS
Willow Run Airport, Ypsilanti 48198 *Type:* Private *Accred.:* 1976/1986 (CCA-ACTTS) *Calendar:* Sem. plan *Degrees:* diplomas *CEO:* Pres. Charles Hawes
Enroll: 100   (313) 483-3758

DETROIT INSTITUTE OF COMMERCE
4829 Woodward Ave., Detroit 48201 *Type:* Private business *Accred.:* 1971/1990 (CCA-ACICS) *Calendar:* Qtr. plan *Degrees:* certificates, diplomas *CEO:* Pres. G.M. Douglas
Enroll: 807   (313) 832-0200

DETROIT INSTITUTE OF OPHTHALMOLOGY
15415 E. Jefferson Ave., Grosse Pointe Park 48230 *Type:* Private *Calendar:* Courses of varying lengths *Degrees:* certificates *Prof. Accred.:* Ophthalmic Medical Technology *CEO:* Pres. Philip C. Hessburg, M.D.
                                  (313) 824-4800

DORSEY BUSINESS SCHOOL
30821 Barrington Ave., Madison Heights 48071 *Type:* Private business *Accred.:* 1984/1990 (CCA-ACICS) *Calendar:* Courses of varying lengths *Degrees:* certificates, diplomas *CEO:* Dir. Adrienne Lapish
Enroll: 259   (313) 585-9200

BRANCH CAMPUS
24901 Northwestern Hwy., Ste. 202, Southfield, MI 48075 *CEO:* Dir. Marchell McLean
                                  (313) 352-7830

DORSEY BUSINESS SCHOOL
31542 Gratiot Ave., Roseville 48066 *Type:* Private business *Accred.:* 1961/1990 (CCA-ACICS) *Calendar:* Qtr. plan *Degrees:* certificates, diplomas *CEO:* Managing Dir. Cheryl Steinmetz
Enroll: 368   (313) 296-3225

DORSEY BUSINESS SCHOOL
15755 Northline Rd., Southgate 48195 *Type:* Private business *Accred.:* 1972/1990 (CCA-ACICS) *Calendar:* Qtr. plan *Degrees:* certificates, diplomas *CEO:* Dir. Jack Peeples
Enroll: 344   (313) 285-5400

DORSEY BUSINESS SCHOOL
34841 Veteran's Plaza, Wayne 48184 *Type:* Private business *Accred.:* 1984/1990 (CCA-ACICS) *Calendar:* Courses of varying lengths *Degrees:* certificates, diplomas *CEO:* Managing Dir. Ledene Lewis
Enroll: 221   (313) 595-1540

ESI CAREER CENTER
1770 Fort St., Lincoln Park 48146-1988 *Type:* Private *Accred.:* 1991 (CCA-ACTTS) *Calendar:* Courses of varying lengths *Degrees:* certificates *CEO:* Dir. Guy D'Amico
                                  (313) 381-7800

EASTERN MICHIGAN UNIVERSITY
Ypsilanti 48197 *Type:* Public (state) *System:* Michigan State Board of Education *Accred.:* 1915/1991 (NCA) *Calendar:* Sem. plan *Degrees:* B, P, M, D, certificates, diplomas *Prof. Accred.:* Business (B,M), Construction Management, Counseling, Dietetics (coordi-

nated), Home Economics, Interior Design, Medical Technology, Music, Nursing (B), Occupational Therapy, Public Administration, Social Work (B), Speech-Language Pathology, Teacher Education (e,s,p) *CEO:* Pres. William E. Sheldon
Enroll: 18248   (313) 487-1849

EDUCATIONAL INSTITUTE OF THE AMERICAN HOTEL AND MOTEL ASSOCIATION
1407 S. Harrison Rd., P.O. Box 1240, East Lansing 48826 *Type:* Private home study *Accred.:* 1963/1988 (NHSC) *Calendar:* Courses of varying lengths *Degrees:* certificates, diplomas *CEO:* Pres. E. Ray Swan
     (517) 353-5500

ELECTRONIC SERVICING INSTITUTE
16900 W. Eight Mile Rd., Ste. 150, Southfield 48075 *Type:* Private *Accred.:* 1991 (CCA-ACTTS) *Calendar:* Courses of varying lengths *Degrees:* certificates *CEO:* Dir. Richard McIntire
     (313) 557-4100

FERRIS STATE UNIVERSITY
Big Rapids 49307 *Type:* Public professional and technical *System:* Michigan State Board of Education *Accred.:* 1959/1987 (NCA) *Calendar:* Qtr. plan *Degrees:* A, B, P, M, D, certificates, diplomas *Prof. Accred.:* Dental Assisting, Dental Hygiene, Dental Laboratory Technology, Medical Laboratory Technology (AMA), Medical Record Administration, Medical Record Technology, Medical Technology, Nuclear Medicine Technology, Nursing (B), Optometry, Pharmacy, Radiography, Respiratory Therapy, Social Work (B) *CEO:* Pres. Helen Popovich
Enroll: 10695   (616) 592-2000

FLINT INSTITUTE OF BARBERING
3214 Flushing Rd., Flint 48504 *Type:* Private *Accred.:* 1972/1988 (CCA-ACTTS) *Calendar:* Courses of varying lengths *Degrees:* diplomas *CEO:* Pres. John L. Ayre
Enroll: 61   (313) 232-4711

GMI ENGINEERING AND MANAGEMENT INSTITUTE
1700 W. Third Ave., Flint 48504 *Type:* Private technological *Accred.:* 1962/1988 (NCA) *Calendar:* Sem. plan *Degrees:* B, M *Prof. Accred.:* Engineering (electrical, industrial, manufacturing, mechanical) *CEO:* Pres. James E.A. John
Enroll: 2620   (313) 762-9864

GLEN OAKS COMMUNITY COLLEGE
62249 Shimmel Rd., Centreville 49032 *Type:* Public (district) junior *System:* Michigan State Board of Education *Accred.:* 1975/1983 (NCA) *Calendar:* Sem. plan *Degrees:* A, certificates, diplomas *CEO:* Pres. Philip G. Ward
Enroll: 788   (616) 467-9945

GOGEBIC COMMUNITY COLLEGE
E-4946 Jackson Rd., Ironwood 49938 *Type:* Public (county) junior *System:* Michigan State Board of Education *Accred.:* 1949/1986 (NCA) *Calendar:* Sem. plan *Degrees:* A, certificates, diplomas *CEO:* Pres. James R. Grote
Enroll: 835   (906) 932-4231

GRACE BIBLE COLLEGE
1011 Aldon St., P.O. Box 910, Wyoming 49509 *Type:* Private (Grace Gospel Fellowship) *Accred.:* 1964/1983 (AABC); 1990 (NCA) *Calendar:* Sem. plan *Degrees:* A, B, certificates, diplomas *CEO:* Pres. Bruce Kemper
Enroll: 114   (616) 538-2330

GRAND RAPIDS BAPTIST COLLEGE AND SEMINARY
1001 E. Beltline Ave., N.E., Grand Rapids 49505 *Type:* Private (Baptist) liberal arts and professional *Accred.:* 1977/1982 (NCA) *Calendar:* Sem. plan *Degrees:* A, B, M, certificates, diplomas *CEO:* Pres. Rex M. Rogers
Enroll: 769   (616) 949-5300

GRAND RAPIDS COMMUNITY COLLEGE
143 Bostwick St., N.E., Grand Rapids 49503 *Type:* Public (city) junior *System:* Michigan State Board of Education *Accred.:* 1917/1991 (NCA) *Calendar:* Sem. plan *Degrees:* A, certificates, diplomas *Prof. Accred.:* Dental Assisting, Dental Hygiene, Music, Nursing (A), Occupational Therapy Assisting,

Practical Nursing, Radiography *CEO:* Pres. Richard W. Calkins
Enroll: 7082 (616) 771-3900

GRAND RAPIDS EDUCATIONAL CENTER FOR MEDICAL AND DENTAL ASSISTANTS
2922 Fuller Ave., N.E., Northbrook Park, Bldg. 2, Grand Rapids 49505 *Type:* Private *Accred.:* 1978/1989 (CCA-ACTTS) *Calendar:* Courses of varying lengths *Degrees:* certificates *Prof. Accred.:* Health Education *CEO:* Admin. Robert J. Malone
(616) 364-8464

BRANCH CAMPUS
5349 W. Main St., Gulf Ridge Ctr., Kalamazoo, MI 49009 *Prof. Accred.:* Health Education *CEO:* Dir. Gloria Stender
(616) 381-6916

GRAND VALLEY STATE UNIVERSITY
One Campus Dr., Allendale 49401 *Type:* Public liberal arts *System:* Michigan State Board of Education *Accred.:* 1968/1989 (NCA) *Calendar:* Sem. plan *Degrees:* B, M *Prof. Accred.:* Art, Engineering (general), Music, Nursing (B,M), Physical Therapy, Social Work (B,M), Teacher Education (e,s,p) *CEO:* Pres. Arend D. Lubbers
Enroll: 8327 (616) 895-6611

GREAT LAKES BIBLE COLLEGE
6211 W. Willow Hwy., Lansing 48917 *Type:* Private (Christian Churches/Churches of Christ) *Accred.:* 1977/1987 (AABC) *Calendar:* Qtr. plan *Degrees:* A, B, certificates *CEO:* Pres. Philip H. Schlaegel
Enroll: 132 (517) 321-0242

GREAT LAKES JUNIOR COLLEGE OF BUSINESS
320 S. Washington Ave., Saginaw 48607 *Type:* Private junior *Accred.:* 1965/1985 (CCA-ACICS); 1991 (NCA candidate) *Calendar:* Qtr. plan *Degrees:* A, certificates, diplomas *CEO:* Pres. Angelo Guerriero
Enroll: 1853 (517) 755-3444

BRANCH CAMPUS
1231 Cleavor Rd., Caro, MI 48723 *CEO:* Dir. Pam Hensley
(517) 673-5857

BRANCH CAMPUS
3555 E. Patrick St., Midland, MI 48640 *CEO:* Dir. Lowell Thomas
(517) 835-5588

HEATHKIT EDUCATIONAL SYSTEMS
c/o Heath Company, 455 Riverview Dr., Benton Harbor 49023 *Type:* Private home study *Accred.:* 1979/1988 (NHSC) *Calendar:* Courses of varying lengths *Degrees:* certificates, diplomas *CEO:* Pres. William E. Johnson
(616) 925-3699

HENRY FORD COMMUNITY COLLEGE
5101 Evergreen Rd., Dearborn 48128 *Type:* Public (city) junior *System:* Michigan State Board of Education *Accred.:* 1949/1985 (NCA) *Calendar:* Sem. plan *Degrees:* A, certificates, diplomas *Prof. Accred.:* Medical Assisting (AMA), Medical Record Technology, Nursing (A), Respiratory Therapy *CEO:* Pres. Andrew A. Mazzara
Enroll: 8581 (313) 845-9650

HIGHLAND PARK COMMUNITY COLLEGE
Glendale Ave. at Third St., Highland Park 48203 *Type:* Public (city) junior *System:* Michigan State Board of Education *Accred.:* 1921/1987 (NCA) *Calendar:* Sem. plan *Degrees:* A, certificates, diplomas *Prof. Accred.:* Medical Laboratory Technology (AMA), Surgical Technology *CEO:* Acting Pres. Charles Mitchell
Enroll: 593 (313) 252-0436

HILLSDALE COLLEGE
33 E. College Ave., Hillsdale 49242 *Type:* Private liberal arts *Accred.:* 1915/1988 (NCA) *Calendar:* Sem. plan *Degrees:* B, certificates, diplomas *CEO:* Pres. George Charles Roche, III
Enroll: 1088 (517) 437-7341

HOPE COLLEGE
Holland 49423 *Type:* Private (Reformed Church in America) liberal arts *Accred.:* 1915/1984 (NCA) *Calendar:* Sem. plan *Degrees:* B *Prof. Accred.:* Art, Dance, Music,

Michigan   **Accredited Institutions**

Nursing (B), Theatre *CEO:* Pres. John H. Jacobson
Enroll: 2577   (616) 392-5111

ITT TECHNICAL INSTITUTE
3013 Eastern Ave., S.E., Grand Rapids 49508 *Type:* Private *Accred.:* 1972/1989 (CCA-ACTTS) *Calendar:* Qtr. plan *Degrees:* diplomas *CEO:* Dir. Dennis Hormel
    (616) 452-1458

ITT TECHNICAL INSTITUTE
1225 E. Big Beaver Rd., Troy 48083-1905 *Type:* Private *Accred.:* 1991 (CCA-ACTTS) *Calendar:* Qtr. plan *Degrees:* diplomas *CEO:* Dir. Robert Martin
    (313) 524-1800

JACKSON BUSINESS INSTITUTE
234 S. Mechanic St., Jackson 49201 *Type:* Private business *Accred.:* 1953/1987 (CCA-ACICS) *Calendar:* Qtr. plan *Degrees:* certificates, diplomas *CEO:* Pres. Jack D. Bunce
Enroll: 500   (517) 789-6123

JACKSON COMMUNITY COLLEGE
2111 Emmons Rd., Jackson 49201 *Type:* Public (district) junior *System:* Michigan State Board of Education *Accred.:* 1933/1986 (NCA) *Calendar:* Sem. plan *Degrees:* A, certificates, diplomas *Prof. Accred.:* Diagnostic Medical Sonography, Radiography *CEO:* Pres. Clyde E. LeTarte
Enroll: 3177   (517) 787-0800

KALAMAZOO COLLEGE
1200 Academy St., Kalamazoo 49007 *Type:* Private (Baptist) liberal arts *Accred.:* 1915/1983 (NCA) *Calendar:* Qtr. plan *Degrees:* B *CEO:* Pres. Lawrence D. Bryan
Enroll: 1265   (616) 383-8588

KALAMAZOO VALLEY COMMUNITY COLLEGE
6767 W. "O" Ave., Kalamazoo 49009 *Type:* Public (district) junior *System:* Michigan State Board of Education *Accred.:* 1972/1986 (NCA) *Calendar:* Sem. plan *Degrees:* A, certificates, diplomas *Prof. Accred.:* Dental Hygiene, Medical Assisting (AMA), Respiratory Therapy *CEO:* Pres. Marilyn J. Schlack
Enroll: 6036   (616) 372-5200

KELLOGG COMMUNITY COLLEGE
450 North Ave., Battle Creek 49017-3397 *Type:* Public (district) junior *System:* Michigan State Board of Education *Accred.:* 1965/1982 (NCA) *Calendar:* Sem. plan *Degrees:* A, certificates, diplomas *Prof. Accred.:* Dental Hygiene, Medical Laboratory Technology (AMA), Physical Therapy Assisting, Radiography *CEO:* Pres. Paul H. Ohm
Enroll: 3285   (616) 965-3931

KENDALL COLLEGE OF ART AND DESIGN
111 Division Ave., N., Grand Rapids 49503 *Type:* Private *Accred.:* 1981/1988 (NCA) *Calendar:* Sem. plan *Degrees:* A, B, certificates, diplomas *Prof. Accred.:* Art, Interior Design *CEO:* Pres. Charles L. Deihl
Enroll: 597   (616) 451-2787

KIRTLAND COMMUNITY COLLEGE
10775 N. St. Helen Rd., Roscommon 48653 *Type:* Public (district) junior *System:* Michigan State Board of Education *Accred.:* 1976/1989 (NCA) *Calendar:* Sem. plan *Degrees:* A, certificates, diplomas *CEO:* Pres. Dorothy N. Franke
Enroll: 846   (517) 275-5121

KRAINZ WOODS ACADEMY OF MEDICAL LABORATORY TECHNOLOGY
4327 E. Seven Mile Rd., Detroit 48234 *Type:* Private 2-year *Calendar:* Qtr. plan *Degrees:* diplomas *Prof. Accred.:* Medical Laboratory Technology *CEO:* Pres. Leophas Ford
Enroll: 72   (313) 366-5204

LAKE MICHIGAN COLLEGE
2755 E. Napier St., Benton Harbor 49022 *Type:* Public (county) junior *System:* Michigan State Board of Education *Accred.:* 1962/1989 (NCA) *Calendar:* Sem. plan *Degrees:* A, certificates, diplomas *Prof. Accred.:* Dental Assisting, Nursing (A), Radiography *CEO:* Pres. Anne E. Mulder
Enroll: 1645   (616) 927-3571

Accredited Institutions Michigan

LAKE SUPERIOR STATE UNIVERSITY
1000 College Dr., Sault Ste. Marie 49783 *Type:* Public liberal arts *System:* Michigan State Board of Education *Accred.:* 1968/1991 (NCA) *Calendar:* Qtr. plan *Degrees:* A, B, M, certificates, diplomas *Prof. Accred.:* Engineering Technology (automated systems, computer, electrical, mechanical, mechanical drafting/design), Nursing (B) *CEO:* Pres. H. Erik Shaar
Enroll: 2438   (906) 635-2202

LANSING COMMUNITY COLLEGE
521 N. Washington Sq., P.O. Box 40010, Lansing 48901-7210 *Type:* Public (district) junior *System:* Michigan State Board of Education *Accred.:* 1964/1984 (NCA) *Calendar:* Qtr. plan *Degrees:* A, certificates, diplomas *Prof. Accred.:* Dental Assisting, Dental Hygiene, EMT-Paramedic, Nursing (A), Radiation Therapy Technology, Radiography, Respiratory Therapy, Respiratory Therapy Technology *CEO:* Pres. Abel B. Sykes, Jr.
Enroll: 11385   (517) 483-1851

LANSING COMPUTER INSTITUTE
501 N. Marshall St., Ste. 101, Lansing 48912 *Type:* Private *Accred.:* 1985 (CCA-ACTTS) *Calendar:* Courses of varying lengths *Degrees:* certificates*CEO:* Dir. Virginia Hilbert
            (517) 482-8896

LAWRENCE TECHNOLOGICAL UNIVERSITY
21000 W. Ten Mile Rd., Southfield 48075 *Type:* Private professional and technological *Accred.:* 1967/1991 (NCA) *Calendar:* Qtr. plan *Degrees:* A, B, M *Prof. Accred.:* Architecture (B), Engineering (construction, electrical, mechanical), Engineering Technology (civil/construction, electrical, industrial, mechanical), Interior Design *CEO:* Pres. Richard E. Marburger
Enroll: 3625   (313) 356-0200

LAWTON SCHOOL
660 Plaza Dr., Ste. 2200, Detroit 48226-1207 *Type:* Private *Accred.:* 1991 (CCA-ACTTS) *Calendar:* Courses of varying lengths *Degrees:* certificates *CEO:* Exec. Dir. Audrey Gaylor
            (313) 961-3313

LEWIS COLLEGE OF BUSINESS
17370 Meyers Rd., Detroit 48235 *Type:* Private *Accred.:* 1978/1990 (NCA) *Calendar:* Tri. plan *Degrees:* A, certificates, diplomas *CEO:* Pres. Marjorie L. Harris
Enroll: 267   (313) 862-6300

MACOMB COMMUNITY COLLEGE
14500 E. Twelve Mile Rd., Warren 48093 *Type:* Public (district) junior *System:* Michigan State Board of Education *Accred.:* 1970/1987 (NCA) *Calendar:* Sem. plan *Degrees:* A, certificates, diplomas *Prof. Accred.:* Medical Assisting (AMA), Nursing (A), Physical Therapy Assisting, Respiratory Therapy, Veterinary Technology *CEO:* Pres. Albert L. Lorenzo
Enroll: 13069   (313) 445-7000

MADONNA UNIVERSITY
36600 Schoolcraft Rd., Livonia 48150 *Type:* Private(Roman Catholic) liberal arts*Accred.:* 1959/1988 (NCA) *Calendar:* Sem. plan *Degrees:* A, B, M, certificates, diplomas *Prof. Accred.:* Nursing (B), Social Work (B), Teacher Education (e,s) *CEO:* Pres. Mary Francilene
Enroll: 2719   (313) 591-5000

MARYGROVE COLLEGE
8425 W. McNichols Rd., Detroit 48221 *Type:* Private (Roman Catholic) liberal arts *Accred.:* 1926/1987 (NCA) *Calendar:* Sem. plan *Degrees:* A, B, M *Prof. Accred.:* Diagnostic Medical Sonography, Radiography, Respiratory Therapy, Social Work (B), Teacher Education (e,s,p) *CEO:* Pres. John E. Shay, Jr.
Enroll: 1031   (313) 862-8000

MICHIGAN BARBER SCHOOL
8990 Grand River Ave., Detroit 48204 *Type:* Private *Accred.:* 1988 (CCA-ACTTS) *Calendar:* Courses of varying lengths *Degrees:* certificates *CEO:* Dir. Forrest F. Green
Enroll: 58   (313) 894-2300

Michigan

MICHIGAN CAREER INSTITUTE
14520 Gratiot Ave., Detroit 48205 *Type:* Private *Accred.:* 1969/1989 (CCA-ACTTS) *Calendar:* Courses of varying lengths *Degrees:* diplomas *CEO:* Dir. Andrew Vigonne
Enroll: 533   (313) 526-6600

MICHIGAN CHRISTIAN COLLEGE
800 W. Avon Rd., Rochester 48063 *Type:* Private (Church of Christ) *Accred.:* 1974/1989 (NCA) *Calendar:* Sem. plan *Degrees:* A, B, certificates, diplomas *CEO:* Pres. Milton B. Fletcher
Enroll: 248   (313) 651-5800

MICHIGAN COMPUTER INSTITUTE
One Northland Plaza, 20755 Greenfield Rd., Southfield 48075 *Type:* Private business *Accred.:* 1986 (CCA-ACICS) *Calendar:* Courses of varying lengths *Degrees:* certificates, diplomas *CEO:* Dir. Bushra Hotaling
Enroll: 1116   (313) 443-5400

    BRANCH CAMPUS
    148 E. Second St., Flint, MI 48502 *CEO:* Dir. David Kirby
                               (313) 238-5400

    BRANCH CAMPUS
    64 W. Lawrence St., Pontiac, MI 48342 *CEO:* Dir. Deborah Squirewell
                               (313) 333-0404

MICHIGAN STATE UNIVERSITY
East Lansing 48824-1046 *Type:* Public *System:* Michigan State Board of Education *Accred.:* 1915/1986 (NCA) *Calendar:* Qtr. plan *Degrees:* B, P, M, D *Prof. Accred.:* Accounting (Type A,B), Audiology, Business (B,M), Clinical Psychology, Counseling Psychology, Engineering (agricultural, chemical, civil, electrical, materials, mechanical),Forestry(probational),Interior Design, Journalism, Landscape Architecture (B), Medical Technology, Medicine, Music, Nursing (B,M), Osteopathy, Planning (urban), Psychology Internship, Recreation and Park Administration, Rehabilitation Counseling, School Psychology, Social Work (B,M), Speech-Language Pathology, Teacher Education (e,s,p), Theatre, Veterinary Technology *CEO:* Pres. John DiBiaggio
Enroll: 38916   (517) 355-6560

MICHIGAN TECHNOLOGICAL UNIVERSITY
1400 Townsend Dr., Houghton 49931 *Type:* Public (state) *System:* Michigan State Board of Education *Accred.:* 1928/1988 (NCA) *Calendar:* Qtr. plan *Degrees:* A, B, M, D, certificates, diplomas *Prof. Accred.:* Engineering (chemical, civil, electrical, environmental/sanitary, general, geological/geophysical, materials, mechanical, mineral, mining), Engineering Technology (civil/construction, electrical, electromechanical, mechanical drafting/design), Forestry *CEO:* Pres. Curtis J. Tompkins
Enroll: 6162   (906) 487-1885

MID MICHIGAN COMMUNITY COLLEGE
1375 S. Clare Ave., Harrison 48625 *Type:* Public (district) junior *System:* Michigan State Board of Education *Accred.:* 1974/1982 (NCA) *Calendar:* Sem. plan *Degrees:* A, certificates, diplomas *Prof. Accred.:* Radiography *CEO:* Pres. Charles J. Corrigan, Ph.D.
Enroll: 1149   (517) 386-7792

MOTECH AUTOMOTIVE EDUCATION CENTER
35155 Industrial Rd., Livonia 48150 *Type:* Private *Accred.:* 1976/1985 (CCA-ACTTS) *Calendar:* Sem. plan *Degrees:* certificates *CEO:* Dir. Paul Alberts
Enroll: 437   (313) 522-9510

MONROE COUNTY COMMUNITY COLLEGE
1555 S. Raisinville Rd., Monroe 48161 *Type:* Public (district) junior *System:* Michigan State Board of Education *Accred.:* 1972/1990 (NCA) *Calendar:* Sem. plan *Degrees:* A, certificates, diplomas *Prof. Accred.:* Nursing (A), Respiratory Therapy, Respiratory Therapy Technology *CEO:* Pres. Gerald D. Welch
Enroll: 1667   (313) 242-7300

MONTCALM COMMUNITY COLLEGE
2800 College Dr., S.W., Sidney 48885 *Type:* Public (district) junior *System:* Michigan

State Board of Education *Accred.:* 1974/1986 (NCA) *Calendar:* Sem. plan *Degrees:* A, certificates, diplomas *CEO:* Pres. Donald C. Burns
Enroll: 1085 (517) 328-2111

MUSKEGON COMMUNITY COLLEGE
221 S. Quarterline Rd., Muskegon 49442 *Type:* Public (county) junior *System:* Michigan State Board of Education *Accred.:* 1929/1991 (NCA) *Calendar:* Sem. plan *Degrees:* A, certificates, diplomas *Prof. Accred.:* Respiratory Therapy, Respiratory Therapy Technology *CEO:* Pres. James L. Stevenson
Enroll: 1210 (616) 773-0311

NATIONAL EDUCATION CENTER—BRYMAN CAMPUS
4244 Oakman Blvd., Detroit 48204 *Type:* Private *Accred.:* 1987 (CCA-ACTTS) *Calendar:* Qtr. plan *Degrees:* diplomas *CEO:* Dir. Myra Martin
(313) 834-1400

NATIONAL EDUCATION CENTER—NATIONAL INSTITUTE OF TECHNOLOGY
15115 Deerfield Rd., East Detroit 48021 *Type:* Private *Accred.:* 1980/1985 (CCA-ACTTS) *Calendar:* Qtr. plan *Degrees:* certificates, diplomas *CEO:* Dir. Dolores Jurko
(313) 779-5530

NATIONAL EDUCATION CENTER—NATIONAL INSTITUTE OF TECHNOLOGY
18000 Newburgh Rd., Livonia 48152 *Type:* Private *Accred.:* 1970/1985 (CCA-ACTTS) *Calendar:* Qtr. plan *Degrees:* certificates, diplomas *CEO:* Dir. Grant C. Flemming
(313) 464-7387

NATIONAL EDUCATION CENTER—NATIONAL INSTITUTE OF TECHNOLOGY
2620/2630 Remico St., S.W., Wyoming 49509 *Type:* Private *Accred.:* 1980/1985 (CCA-ACTTS) *Calendar:* Qtr. plan *Degrees:* diplomas *CEO:* Dir. Bob Del Raso
(616) 538-3170

NATIONAL TECHNICAL INSTITUTE
144 W. Lafayette Blvd., Ste. 200, Detroit 48226 *Type:* Private *Calendar:* Courses of varying lengths *Degrees:* certificates, diplomas *Prof. Accred.:* Health Education *CEO:* C.E.O. David Kujawa
(313) 961-2240

NAZARETH COLLEGE*
3333 Gull Rd., Kalamazoo 49001 *Type:* Private (Roman Catholic) liberal arts *Accred.:* 1940/1989 (NCA) *Calendar:* Sem. plan *Degrees:* B, M *Prof. Accred.:* Nursing (B) *CEO:* Pres. Oliver H. Evans
Enroll: 486 (616) 349-4200

*Nazareth College will be closing in June 1992

NEW CAREERS OF LANSING
315 Grand Ave. S., Lansing 48933 *Type:* Private *Accred.:* 1991 (CCA-ACTTS) *Calendar:* Courses of varying lengths *Degrees:* certificates *CEO:* Dir. Robert Beckwith
(517) 484-9895

NORTH CENTRAL MICHIGAN COLLEGE
1515 Howard St., Petoskey 49770 *Type:* Public (district) junior *System:* Michigan State Board of Education *Accred.:* 1972/1985 (NCA) *Calendar:* Sem. plan *Degrees:* A, certificates, diplomas *Prof. Accred.:* Respiratory Therapy *CEO:* Pres. Robert B. Graham
Enroll: 975 (616) 348-6600

NORTHEASTERN SCHOOL OF COMMERCE
701 N. Madison Ave., P.O. Box 819, Bay City 48707 *Type:* Private business *Accred.:* 1953/1988 (CCA-ACICS) *Calendar:* Qtr. plan *Degrees:* certificates, diplomas *CEO:* Dir. Louis H. Bork
Enroll: 237 (517) 893-4502

NORTHERN MICHIGAN UNIVERSITY
Marquette 49855 *Type:* Public (state) *System:* Michigan State Board of Education *Accred.:* 1916/1985 (NCA) *Calendar:* Sem. plan *Degrees:* A, B, P, M, certificates, diplomas *Prof. Accred.:* Medical Laboratory Technology (AMA), Medical Technology, Music, Nursing (B,M), Social Work (B), Speech-Language Pathology, Teacher Edu-

cation (e,s,p) *CEO:* Interim Pres. William E. Vandament
Enroll: 6435 (906) 227-2920

NORTHWESTERN MICHIGAN COLLEGE
1701 E. Front St., Traverse City 49684 *Type:* Public (county) junior *System:* Michigan State Board of Education *Accred.:* 1961/1990 (NCA) *Calendar:* Qtr. plan *Degrees:* A, certificates, diplomas *Prof. Accred.:* Dental Assisting *CEO:* Pres. Timothy G. Quinn
Enroll: 2941 (616) 922-0650

NORTHWOOD INSTITUTE
3225 Cook Rd., Midland 48640 *Type:* Private business *Accred.:* 1974/1981 (NCA) *Calendar:* Qtr. plan *Degrees:* A, B *CEO:* Pres. David E. Fry
Enroll: 3604 (517) 837-4229

OAKLAND COMMUNITY COLLEGE
2480 Opdyke Rd., P.O. Box 812, Bloomfield Hills 48013-0812 *Type:* Public (district) junior *System:* Michigan State Board of Education *Accred.:* 1971/1988 (NCA) *Calendar:* Tri. plan *Degrees:* A, certificates, diplomas *Prof. Accred.:* Medical Assisting (AMA), Medical Laboratory Technology (AMA) *CEO:* Chanc. Patsy Fulton
Enroll: 13593 (313) 540-1500

AUBURN HILLS CAMPUS
2900 Featherstone Rd., Auburn Heights, MI 48057 *CEO:* Pres. Christine E. Gram
(313) 852-1000

HIGHLAND LAKES CAMPUS
7350 Cooley Lake Rd., Union Lake, MI 48085-2198 *Prof. Accred.:* Dental Hygiene, Medical Laboratory Technology (AMA) *CEO:* Pres. Richard T. Saunders
(313) 360-3032

ORCHARD RIDGE CAMPUS
27055 Orchard Lake Rd., Farmington Hills, MI 48334 *CEO:* Pres. Daniel A. Jaksen
(313) 471-7500

SOUTHFIELD CAMPUS
22322 Rutland Dr., Southfield, MI 48075 *Prof. Accred.:* Diagnostic Medical Sonography, Respiratory Therapy, Radiography *CEO:* Dean Joseph Macri
(313) 552-2600

OAKLAND UNIVERSITY
Rochester 48309 *Type:* Public (state) liberal arts and professional *System:* Michigan State Board of Education *Accred.:* 1966/1989 (NCA) *Calendar:* Tri. plan *Degrees:* B, P, M, D *Prof. Accred.:* Business (B,M), Computer Science, Engineering (computer, electrical, mechanical, systems), Nurse Anesthesia Education, Nursing (B,M), Physical Therapy, Public Administration, Teacher Education (e,s,p) *CEO:* Interim Pres. John De Carlo
Enroll: 8198 (313) 370-3500

OLIVET COLLEGE
Olivet 49076 *Type:* Private (United Church of Christ) liberal arts *Accred.:* 1913/1987 (NCA) *Calendar:* Sem. plan *Degrees:* B *Prof. Accred.:* Music *CEO:* Pres. Donald A. Morris
Enroll: 696 (616) 749-7641

PBS TRAINING CENTER
16250 Northland Dr., Ste. LL010, Southfield 48075-5225 *Type:* Private *Accred.:* 1991 (CCA-ACTTS) *Calendar:* Courses of varying lengths *Degrees:* certificates *CEO:* Dir. Sherre Kaigh
(313) 557-7757

PSI INSTITUTE FLINT
542 S. Saginaw St., Flint 48502-1804 *Type:* Private *Accred.:* 1991 (CCA-ACTTS) *Calendar:* Courses of varying lengths *Degrees:* certificates *CEO:* Dir. Ronald R. Murdock
(313) 235-1533

PSI INSTITUTE OF MICHIGAN
17000 W. Eight Mile Rd., Southfield 48075 *Type:* Private *Accred.:* 1988 (CCA-ACTTS) *Calendar:* Courses of varying lengths *Degrees:* certificates *CEO:* Dir. Paul Agosta
(313) 557-9055

Accredited Institutions — Michigan

PAYNE-PULLIAM SCHOOL OF TRADE AND COMMERCE
2345 Cass Ave., Detroit 48201 *Type:* Private business *Accred.:* 1978/1987 (CCA-ACICS) *Calendar:* Courses of varying lengths *Degrees:* certificates, diplomas *CEO:* Pres. Betty E. Pulliam
Enroll: 139 (313) 963-4710

PONTIAC BUSINESS INSTITUTE
18944 Grand River Ave., Detroit 48223 *Type:* Private business *Accred.:* 1986 (CCA-ACICS) *Calendar:* Qtr. plan *Degrees:* certificates, diplomas *CEO:* Dir. Richard McIntire
Enroll: 273 (313) 273-2022

PONTIAC BUSINESS INSTITUTE
6431 E. Twelve Mile Rd., Ste. C, Madison Heights 48071 *Type:* Private business *Accred.:* 1962/1986 (CCA-ACICS) *Calendar:* Qtr. plan *Degrees:* certificates, diplomas *CEO:* Dir. Tim Yount
Enroll: 420 (313) 545-7616

PONTIAC BUSINESS INSTITUTE
755 W. Drahner Rd., P.O. Box 459, Oxford 48371 *Type:* Private business *Accred.:* 1979/1986 (CCA-ACICS) *Calendar:* Qtr. plan *Degrees:* certificates, diplomas *CEO:* Dir. Patricia Fischer
Enroll: 371 (313) 628-4847

REFORMED BIBLE COLLEGE
3333 E. Beltline Ave., N.E., Grand Rapids 49505 *Type:* Private (Independent Reformed) *Accred.:* 1964/1984 (AABC) *Calendar:* Sem. plan *Degrees:* A, B, certificates *CEO:* Pres. Edwin D. Roels
Enroll: 160 (616) 363-2050

ROSS BUSINESS INSTITUTE
23400 Michigan Ave., Ste. 221, Dearborn 48124 *Type:* Private business *Accred.:* 1983 (CCA-ACICS) *Calendar:* Qtr. plan *Degrees:* certificates, diplomas *CEO:* Dir. Judith Sierota
Enroll: 140 (313) 563-0640

BRANCH CAMPUS
21165 Gratiot Ave., East Detroit, MI 48021 *CEO:* Dir. Jan Artushin
(313) 774-7880

BRANCH CAMPUS
1525 N. Telegraph Rd., Monroe, MI 48161 *Prof. Accred.:* Medical Assisting *CEO:* Dir. JoAnn Haedicke
(313) 243-5456

BRANCH CAMPUS
20820 Greenfield Rd., Oak Park, MI 48237 *CEO:* Dir. Valerie Penny
(313) 968-1970

ROSS BUSINESS INSTITUTE
1553 Woodward Ave., Ste. 750, Detroit 48226 *Type:* Private business *Accred.:* 1977/1983 (CCA-ACICS) *Calendar:* Qtr. plan *Degrees:* certificates, diplomas *CEO:* Dir. Deborah McMaster
Enroll: 245 (313) 965-2122

THE ROSS MEDICAL EDUCATION CENTER
1553 Woodward Ave., Ste. 650, Detroit 48226 *Type:* Private *Accred.:* 1979/1989 (CCA-ACTTS) *Calendar:* Courses of varying lengths *Degrees:* certificates *Prof. Accred.:* Health Education *CEO:* Exec. Dir. Nadine Lunsford
(313) 965-7451

BRANCH CAMPUS
15670 E. Eight Mile Rd., Detroit, MI 48205 *CEO:* Dir. Sandra Maniachi
(313) 371-2131

BRANCH CAMPUS
14110 Telegraph Rd., Detroit, MI 48239 *Prof. Accred.:* Health Education *CEO:* Dir. Karen Hamlin
(313) 532-2101

THE ROSS MEDICAL EDUCATION CENTER
1036 Gilbert Rd., Flint 48532 *Type:* Private *Accred.:* 1978 (CCA-ACTTS) *Calendar:* Courses of varying lengths *Degrees:* certificates *Prof. Accred.:* Health Education *CEO:* Exec. Dir. Margaret Scheneman
Enroll: 708 (313) 230-1100

Michigan **Accredited Institutions**

BRANCH CAMPUS
301 Francis St., 2nd Fl., Jackson, MI 49201 *Prof. Accred.:* Health Education *CEO:* Dir. Barbara Line
(517) 782-7677

BRANCH CAMPUS
950 W. Norton Ave., Roosevelt Park, MI 49441 *Prof. Accred.:* Health Education *CEO:* Dir. Melanie Jackson
(616) 739-1531

BRANCH CAMPUS
4054 Bay Rd., Saginaw, MI 48603 *Prof. Accred.:* Health Education *CEO:* Dir. Robin Thomas
(517) 793-9800

THE ROSS MEDICAL EDUCATION CENTER
913 W. Holmes Rd., Ste. 260, Lansing 48910 *Type:* Private *Accred.:* 1982/1987 (CCA-ACTTS) *Calendar:* Courses of varying lengths *Degrees:* certificates *Prof. Accred.:* Health Education *CEO:* Dir. Constance Monville
Enroll: 247   (517) 887-0180

BRANCH CAMPUS
2035 28th St., S.E., Ste. 0, Grand Rapids, MI 49508 *Prof. Accred.:* Health Education *CEO:* Dir. Milly Liles
(616) 243-3070

THE ROSS MEDICAL EDUCATION CENTER
20820 Greenfield Rd., 1st Fl., Oak Park 48237-3011 *Type:* Private *Accred.:* 1990 (CCA-ACTTS) *Calendar:* Courses of varying lengths *Degrees:* certificates *Prof. Accred.:* Health Education *CEO:* Exec. Dir. Julie Gadowski
Enroll: 245   (313) 967-3100

THE ROSS MEDICAL EDUCATION CENTER
26417 Hoover Rd., Warren 48089 *Type:* Private *Accred.:* 1981/1986 (CCA-ACTTS) *Calendar:* Courses of varying lengths *Degrees:* certificates *Prof. Accred.:* Health Education *CEO:* Exec. Dir. Beth Stirzinger
Enroll: 290   (313) 758-7200

THE ROSS MEDICAL EDUCATION CENTER
253 Summit Dr., Waterford 48328-3364 *Type:* Private *Accred.:* 1991 (CCA-ACTTS) *Calendar:* Courses of varying lengths *Degrees:* certificates *CEO:* Exec. Dir. Valerie Penny
(313) 683-1166

ROSS TECHNICAL INSTITUTE
23400 Michigan Ave., Ste. 225, Dearborn 48124-1915 *Type:* Private *Accred.:* 1991 (CCA-ACTTS) *Calendar:* Courses of varying lengths *Degrees:* certificates *CEO:* Dir. Judith Sierota
(313) 563-4220

SER BUSINESS AND TECHNICAL INSTITUTE
9301 Michigan Ave., Detroit 48210 *Type:* Private business *Accred.:* 1989 (CCA-ACICS) *Calendar:* Courses of varying lengths *Degrees:* certificates, diplomas *CEO:* Educ. Dir. Eva G. Dewaelsche
Enroll: 245   (313) 846-2240

SACRED HEART MAJOR SEMINARY
2701 Chicago Blvd., Detroit 48206 *Type:* Private (Roman Catholic) *Accred.:* 1991 (ATS); 1960/1984 (NCA) *Calendar:* Tri. plan *Degrees:* A, B, P, M *CEO:* Rector/Pres. John Nienstedt
Enroll: 112   (313) 883-8500

SAGINAW VALLEY STATE UNIVERSITY
2250 Pierce Rd., University Center 48710-4042 *Type:* Public (state) liberal arts *System:* Michigan State Board of Education *Accred.:* 1970/1987 (NCA) *Calendar:* Tri. plan *Degrees:* B, M *Prof. Accred.:* Nursing (B), Social Work (B) *CEO:* Pres. Eric R. Gilbertson
Enroll: 3900   (517) 790-4000

ST. CLAIR COUNTY COMMUNITY COLLEGE
323 Erie St., P.O. Box 5015, Port Huron 48061-5015 *Type:* Public (district) junior *System:* Michigan State Board of Education *Accred.:* 1930/1987 (NCA) *Calendar:* Sem. plan *Degrees:* A, certificates, diplomas *CEO:* Pres. R. Ernest Dear
Enroll: 2385   (313) 984-3881

ST. MARY'S COLLEGE
Orchard Lake Rd. at Commerce, Orchard Lake 48324 *Type:* Private (Roman Catholic) liberal arts *Accred.:* 1976/1987 (NCA) *Calendar:* Sem. plan *Degrees:* A, B, certificates, diplomas *CEO:* Pres. Edward D. Meyer
Enroll: 275 (313) 683-0504

SAWYER SCHOOL OF BUSINESS
26051 Hoover Rd., Warren 48089 *Type:* Private business *Accred.:* 1973/1985 (CCA-ACICS) *Calendar:* Courses of varying lengths *Degrees:* certificates, diplomas *CEO:* Pres. Joseph T. Belliotti
Enroll: 561 (313) 758-2300

SCHOOLCRAFT COLLEGE
18600 Haggerty Rd., Livonia 48152-2696 *Type:* Public (district) junior *System:* Michigan State Board of Education *Accred.:* 1968/1991 (NCA) *Calendar:* Sem. plan *Degrees:* A, certificates, diplomas *Prof. Accred.:* Medical Record Technology, Occupational Therapy Assisting *CEO:* Pres. Richard W. McDowell
Enroll: 5452 (313) 462-4400

SIENA HEIGHTS COLLEGE
1247 E. Siena Heights Dr., Adrian 49221 *Type:* Private (Roman Catholic) liberal arts *Accred.:* 1940/1981 (NCA) *Calendar:* Sem. plan *Degrees:* A,B,M, certificates, diplomas *Prof. Accred.:* Art *CEO:* Pres. Cathleen Real
Enroll: 1154 (517) 263-0731

SOUTHWESTERN MICHIGAN COLLEGE
58900 Cherry Grove Rd., Dowagiac 49047-9793 *Type:* Public (state) junior *System:* Michigan State Board of Education *Accred.:* 1971/1991 (NCA) *Calendar:* 4-1-4 plan *Degrees:* A, certificates, diplomas *CEO:* Pres. David C. Briegel
Enroll: 1890 (616) 782-5911

SPECS HOWARD SCHOOL OF BROADCAST ARTS
16900 W. Eight Mile Rd., Ste. 115, Southfield 48075 *Type:* Private *Accred.:* 1978/1985 (CCA-ACTTS) *Calendar:* Courses of varying lengths *Degrees:* diplomas *CEO:* Exec. Dir. Specs Howard
Enroll: 548 (313) 569-0101

SPRING ARBOR COLLEGE
Spring Arbor 49283 *Type:* Private (Free Methodist) liberal arts *Accred.:* 1960/1987 (NCA) *Calendar:* Sem. plan *Degrees:* A, B *Prof. Accred.:* Social Work (B-candidate) *CEO:* Pres. Allen Carden
Enroll: 1463 (517) 750-1200

SUOMI COLLEGE
601 Quincy St., Hancock 49930 *Type:* Private (Lutheran) junior *Accred.:* 1969/1989 (NCA) *Calendar:* Sem. plan *Degrees:* A, certificates, diplomas *CEO:* Pres. Robert A. Ubbelohde
Enroll: 496 (906) 482-5300

THOMAS M. COOLEY LAW SCHOOL
217 S. Capitol Ave., P.O. Box 13038, Lansing 48901 *Type:* Private professional *Calendar:* Sem. plan *Degrees:* P *Prof. Accred.:* Law (ABA only) *CEO:* Pres. Michael P. Cox
Enroll: 1028 (517) 371-5140

TRAVEL TRAINING CENTER
13234 Michigan Ave., Dearborn 48126-3539 *Type:* Private *Accred.:* 1991 (CCA-ACTTS) *Calendar:* Courses of varying lengths *Degrees:* certificates *CEO:* Dir. M.R. Younis
(313) 584-3823

UNIVERSITY OF DETROIT MERCY
4001 W. McNichols Rd., Detroit 48221 *Type:* Private (Roman Catholic) liberal arts *Accred.:* 1931/1985 (NCA) *Calendar:* Sem. plan *Degrees:* B, P, M, certificates, diplomas *Prof. Accred.:* Architecture (B), Business (B,M), Clinical Psychology (provisional), Dental Hygiene, Dentistry, Endodontics, Engineering (chemical, civil, electrical, mechanical), General Practice Residency, Law, Medical Record Administration, Medical Record Technology, Nurse Anesthesia Education, Nursing (B), Orthodontics, Physician Assisting, Social Work (B) *CEO:* Pres. Maureen A. Fay, O.P.
Enroll: 4312 (313) 927-1455

Michigan

UNIVERSITY OF MICHIGAN
Ann Arbor 48109 *Type:* Public (state) *System:* University of Michigan System *Accred.:* 1913/1990 (NCA) *Calendar:* Tri. plan *Degrees:* B, P, M, D, certificates, diplomas *Prof. Accred.:* Architecture (M), Art, Business (B,M), Clinical Psychology, Combined Prosthodontics, Dental Hygiene, Dentistry, Endodontics, Engineering (aerospace, chemical, civil, computer, electrical, industrial, materials, mechanical, naval architecture/marine, nuclear), Forestry, General Dentistry (prelim. provisional), General Practice Residency, Health Services Administration, Landscape Architecture (M), Law, Librarianship, Medical Illustration, Medicine, Music, Nursing (B,M), Oral and Maxillofacial Surgery, Oral Pathology, Orthodontics, Pediatric Dentistry, Periodontics, Pharmacy, Planning (urban), Psychology Internship, Public Health, Radiation Therapy Technology, Social Work (M), Teacher Education (e,s,p) *CEO:* Pres. James J. Duderstadt
Enroll: 34245   (313) 764-1817

UNIVERSITY OF MICHIGAN—DEARBORN
4901 Evergreen Rd., Dearborn 48128 *Type:* Public (state) *System:* University of Michigan System *Accred.:* 1970/1984 (NCA) *Calendar:* Tri. plan *Degrees:* B, M *Prof. Accred.:* Engineering (electrical, industrial, mechanical), Teacher Education (e,s) *CEO:* Chanc. Blenda J. Wilson
Enroll: 5128   (313) 593-5000

UNIVERSITY OF MICHIGAN—FLINT
Flint 48502-2186 *Type:* Public (state) *System:* University of Michigan System *Accred.:* 1970/1990 (NCA) *Calendar:* Sem. plan *Degrees:* B, M, certificates, diplomas *Prof. Accred.:* Business (B,M), Music, Physical Therapy, Teacher Education (e,s) *CEO:* Chanc. Clinton B. Jones
Enroll: 4226   (313) 762-3000

WALSH COLLEGE OF ACCOUNTANCY AND BUSINESS ADMINISTRATION
3838 Livernois Rd., P.O. Box 7006, Troy 48007-7006 *Type:* Private professional *Accred.:* 1975/1982 (NCA) *Calendar:* Sem. plan *Degrees:* B, M *CEO:* Pres. David Spencer
Enroll: 1779   (313) 689-8282

WASHTENAW COMMUNITY COLLEGE
4800 E. Huron River Dr., P.O. Box D-1, Ann Arbor 48106 *Type:* Public (district) junior *System:* Michigan State Board of Education *Accred.:* 1973/1990 (NCA) *Calendar:* Sem. plan *Degrees:* A, certificates, diplomas *Prof. Accred.:* Dental Assisting, Radiography, Respiratory Therapy *CEO:* Pres. Gundar A. Myran
Enroll: 6304   (313) 973-3300

WAYNE COUNTY COMMUNITY COLLEGE
801 W. Fort St., Detroit 48226 *Type:* Public (district) junior *System:* Michigan State Board of Education *Accred.:* 1976/1988 (NCA) *Calendar:* Sem. plan *Degrees:* A, certificates, diplomas *Prof. Accred.:* Dental Assisting, Dental Hygiene, Occupational Therapy Assisting, Veterinary Technology *CEO:* Pres. Rafael Cortada, Ph.D.
Enroll: 6608   (313) 496-2510

WAYNE STATE UNIVERSITY
Detroit 48202 *Type:* Public (state) *System:* Michigan State Board of Education *Accred.:* 1915/1987 (NCA) *Calendar:* Sem. plan *Degrees:* B, P, M, D, certificates, diplomas *Prof. Accred.:* Audiology, Business (B,M), Clinical Psychology, Cytotechnology, Dietetics (coordinated), Engineering (chemical, civil, electrical, industrial, mechanical, metallurgical), Law, Librarianship, Medical Technology, Medicine, Mortuary Science, Music, Nurse Anesthesia Education, Nursing (B,M), Occupational Therapy, Pharmacy, Physical Therapy, Public Administration, Radiation Therapy Technology, Social Work (B,M), Speech-Language Pathology, Teacher Education (e,s,p), Theatre *CEO:* Pres. David W. Adamany
Enroll: 21061   (313) 577-2230

WELDTECH WELDING EDUCATION CENTER
20201 Hoover Rd., Detroit 48205 *Type:* Private *Accred.:* 1982 (CCA-ACTTS) *Calen-

dar: Courses of varying lengths *Degrees:* certificates *CEO:* Dir. Glen Knight
Enroll: 132 (313) 267-3385

WELDOR TRAINING CENTER
520 W. Eight Mile Rd., Ferndale 48220 *Type:* Private *Accred.:* 1985 (CCA-ACTTS) *Calendar:* Courses of varying lengths *Degrees:* certificates *CEO:* Dir. Dennis Gilbert
Enroll: 137 (313) 399-3388

WEST SHORE COMMUNITY COLLEGE
3000 N. Stiles Rd., P.O. Box 277, Scottville 49454 *Type:* Public (district) junior *System:* Michigan State Board of Education *Accred.:* 1974/1986 (NCA) *Calendar:* Sem. plan *Degrees:* A, certificates, diplomas *CEO:* Pres. William M. Anderson
Enroll: 339 (616) 845-6211

WESTERN MICHIGAN UNIVERSITY
Kalamazoo 49008-5130 *Type:* Public (state) *System:* Michigan State Board of Education *Accred.:* 1915/1991 (NCA) *Calendar:* Tri. plan *Degrees:* B, P, M, D *Prof. Accred.:* Art, Audiology, Business (B,M), Computer Science, Counseling, Dance, Engineering (computer, electrical, industrial, mechanical), Engineering Technology (manufacturing), Music, Occupational Therapy, Physician Assisting, Social Work (B,M), Speech-Language Pathology, Teacher Education (e,s,p), Theatre *CEO:* Pres. Diether H. Haenicke
Enroll: 19212 (616) 387-2351

WESTERN THEOLOGICAL SEMINARY
Holland 49423 *Type:* Private professional; graduate only *Accred.:* 1940/1982 (ATS) *Calendar:* Sem.plan *Degrees:* P, M, D *CEO:* Pres. Marvin D. Hoff
Enroll: 91 (616) 392-8555

WESTWOOD EDUCATIONAL
2 Fountain Pl., N.E., Ste. 166, Grand Rapids 49503 *Type:* Private *Accred.:* 1988 (CCA-ACTTS) *Calendar:* Courses of varying lengths *Degrees:* certificates *CEO:* Pres. Anatoly Bidny
(616) 451-8844

WESTWOOD EDUCATIONAL
817 Cherry St., S.E., Grand Rapids 49503-3107 *Type:* Private *Accred.:* 1988 (CCA-ACTTS) *Calendar:* Courses of varying lengths *Degrees:* certificates *CEO:* Pres. Anatoly Bidny
(616) 451-8844

WESTWOOD EDUCATIONAL
205 N. Main St., Mount Pleasant 48858 *Type:* Private *Accred.:* 1988 (CCA-ACTTS) *Calendar:* Courses of varying lengths *Degrees:* certificates *CEO:* Pres. Anatoly Bidny
(517) 773-5329

WILLIAM TYNDALE COLLEGE
35700 W. Twelve Mile Rd., Farmington Hills 48331 *Type:* Independent liberal arts and professional *Accred.:* 1954/1984 (AABC); 1988 (NCA) *Calendar:* Sem. plan *Degrees:* A, B, certificates, diplomas *CEO:* Pres. James C. McHann, Jr.
Enroll: 239 (313) 553-7200

YESHIVA BETH YEHUDA-YESHIVA GEDOLAH OF GREATER DETROIT
24600 Greenfield St., Oak Park 48237 *Type:* Private professional *Accred.:* 1986/1991 (AARTS) *Degrees:* B, P, M, D *CEO:* Pres. S. Weingarden
Enroll: 38 (313) 557-9380

MINNESOTA

ACADEMY OF ACCOUNTANCY
4820 Excelsior Blvd., Ste. 123, Minneapolis 55416 *Type:* Private business *Accred.:* 1976/1986 (CCA-ACICS) *Calendar:* Qtr. plan *Degrees:* certificates, diplomas *CEO:* Dir. Mary Erickson
Enroll: 234 (612) 922-8900

ALEXANDRIA TECHNICAL COLLEGE
Alexandria 56308 *Type:* Public (state) 2-year *Accred.:* 1980/1984 (NCA) *Calendar:* Qtr. plan *Degrees:* A, certificates, diplomas *Prof. Accred.:* Interior Design, Medical Laboratory Technology (AMA) *CEO:* Pres. Frank Starke
Enroll: 1726 (612) 762-0221

ALFRED ADLER INSTITUTE OF MINNESOTA
1001 Hwy. 7, Ste. 344, Hopkins 55343 *Type:* Private professional; graduate only *Accred.:* 1991 (NCA) *Calendar:* Qtr. plan *Degrees:* M, certificates, diplomas *CEO:* Pres. Larry A. Hedberg
Enroll: 30 (612) 933-9363

ANOKA TECHNICAL COLLEGE
1355 W. Hwy. 10, Anoka 55303 *Type:* Private *Calendar:* Courses of varying lengths *Degrees:* A, certificates, diplomas *Prof. Accred.:* Electroneurodiagnostic Technology, Medical Assisting (AMA), Medical Record Technology, Occupational Therapy Assisting, Physical Therapy Assisting, Practical Nursing, Surgical Technology *CEO:* Pres. David Sayre
(612) 427-1880

ANOKA-RAMSEY COMMUNITY COLLEGE
11200 Mississippi Blvd., N.W., Coon Rapids 55433 *Type:* Public junior *System:* Minnesota Community College System *Accred.:* 1975/1987 (NCA) *Calendar:* Qtr. plan *Degrees:* A, certificates, diplomas *Prof. Accred.:* Nursing (A), Physical Therapy Assisting *CEO:* Pres. Patrick M. Johns
Enroll: 3182 (612) 427-2600

ART INSTRUCTION SCHOOLS
500 S. Fourth St., Minneapolis 55415 *Type:* Private home study *Accred.:* 1956/1991 (NHSC) *Calendar:* Courses of varying lengths *Degrees:* certificates *CEO:* Pres. Thomas R. Stuart
(612) 339-8721

AUGSBURG COLLEGE
731 21st Ave. S., Minneapolis 55454 *Type:* Private (Lutheran) liberal arts *Accred.:* 1954/1987 (NCA) *Calendar:* 4-1-4 plan *Degrees:* B, M *Prof. Accred.:* Music, Nursing (B), Social Work (B,M-candidate), Teacher Education (e,s) *CEO:* Pres. Charles S. Anderson
Enroll: 2577 (612) 330-1212

AUSTIN COMMUNITY COLLEGE
1600 8th Ave., N.W., Austin 55912 *Type:* Public junior *System:* Minnesota Community College System *Accred.:* 1971/1985 (NCA) *Calendar:* Qtr. plan *Degrees:* A, certificates, diplomas *Prof. Accred.:* Nursing (A), Occupational Therapy Assisting *CEO:* Pres. Steven R. Wallace
Enroll: 766 (507) 433-0508

BEMIDJI STATE UNIVERSITY
1500 Birchmont Dr., N.E., Bemidji 56601-2699 *Type:* Public liberal arts and teachers *System:* Minnesota State University System *Accred.:* 1943/1990 (NCA) *Calendar:* Qtr. plan *Degrees:* A, B, M *Prof. Accred.:* Music, Nursing (B), Social Work (B), Teacher Education (e,s,p) *CEO:* Pres. Leslie C. Duly
Enroll: 4460 (218) 755-2000

BEMIDJI TECHNICAL COLLEGE
905 Grant Ave., S.E, Bemidji 56601 *Type:* Private *Calendar:* Courses of varying lengths *Degrees:* certificates *Prof. Accred.:* Dental Assisting *CEO:* Pres. Melvin Salberge
(218) 759-3200

BETHANY LUTHERAN COLLEGE
734 Marsh St., Mankato 56001 *Type:* Private (Lutheran) junior *Accred.:* 1974/1989 (NCA)

Calendar: Sem. plan *Degrees:* A *CEO:* Pres. Marvin G. Meyer
Enroll: 289 (507) 625-2977

BETHEL COLLEGE
3900 Bethel Dr., St. Paul 55112 *Type:* Private (Baptist General Conference) liberal arts *Accred.:* 1959/1990 (NCA) *Calendar:* Sem. plan *Degrees:* A, B *Prof. Accred.:* Nursing (B), Social Work (B), Teacher Education (e,s) *CEO:* Pres. George K. Brushaber
Enroll: 1905 (612) 638-6400

BETHEL THEOLOGICAL SEMINARY
3949 Bethel Dr., St. Paul 55112 *Type:* Private (Baptist General Conference) professional *Accred.:* 1966/1991 (ATS); 1976/1991 (NCA) *Calendar:* Qtr. plan *Degrees:* P, M, D, certificates, diplomas *CEO:* Pres. George K. Brushaber
Enroll: 315 (612) 638-6180

BRAINERD COMMUNITY COLLEGE
501 W. College Dr., Brainerd 56401 *Type:* Public junior *System:* Clearwater Community College Region *Accred.:* 1977/1986 (NCA) *Calendar:* Qtr. plan *Degrees:* A *CEO:* Provost Sally Jane Ihne
Enroll: 1242 (218) 828-2510

BRAINERD TECHNICAL COLLEGE
300 Quince St., Brainerd 56401 *Type:* Private *Calendar:* Courses of varying lengths *Degrees:* certificates *Prof. Accred.:* Dental Assisting *CEO:* Dir. Craig Oliver
(218) 828-5344

CDI CAREER DEVELOPMENT INSTITUTE
1550 E. 78th St., Richfield 55423-4696 *Type:* Private *Accred.:* 1968/1988 (CCA-ACTTS) *Calendar:* Courses of varying lengths *Degrees:* certificates *CEO:* Dir. George E. Teagarden
Enroll: 1355 (612) 853-6100

CARLETON COLLEGE
One N. College St., Northfield 55057 *Type:* Private liberal arts *Accred.:* 1913/1989 (NCA) *Calendar:* 3-3 plan *Degrees:* B *Prof. Accred.:* Teacher Education (s) *CEO:* Pres. Stephen R. Lewis, Jr.
Enroll: 1841 (507) 663-4000

COLLEGE OF ASSOCIATED ARTS
344 Summit Ave., St. Paul 55102-2199 *Type:* Private *Accred.:* 1978/1988 (CCA-ACTTS) *Calendar:* Sem. plan *Degrees:* B, certificates *CEO:* Exec. Dir. Robert E. Hankey
Enroll: 104 (612) 224-3416

COLLEGE OF ST. BENEDICT
37 S. College Ave., St. Joseph 56374 *Type:* Private (Roman Catholic) liberal arts for women *Accred.:* 1933/1989 (NCA) *Calendar:* 4-1-4 plan *Degrees:* A, B *Prof. Accred.:* Dietetics (coordinated), Nursing (B), Social Work (B), Teacher Education (e,s) *CEO:* Pres. Colman O'Connell
Enroll: 1860 (612) 363-5505

COLLEGE OF ST. CATHERINE
2004 Randolph Ave., St. Paul 55105 *Type:* Private (Roman Catholic) liberal arts for women *Accred.:* 1916/1983 (NCA) *Calendar:* 4-1-4 plan *Degrees:* A, B, M, certificates, diplomas *Prof. Accred.:* Medical Record Technology, Music, Nursing (A,B), Occupational Therapy, Physical Therapy Assisting, Respiratory Therapy, Social Work (B,M-candidate), Teacher Education (e,s) *CEO:* Pres. Anita M. Pampusch
Enroll: 2692 (612) 690-6525

ST. MARY'S CAMPUS
2500 S. 6th St., Minneapolis, MN 55454 *Prof. Accred.:* Occupational Therapy Assisting *CEO:* Academic Dean/Chf. Admin. Mary E. Broderick
(612) 332-5521

COLLEGE OF ST. SCHOLASTICA
1200 Kenwood Ave., Duluth 55811 *Type:* Private (Roman Catholic) liberal arts *Accred.:* 1931/1983 (NCA) *Calendar:* Qtr. plan *Degrees:* B, M, certificates, diplomas *Prof. Accred.:* Medical Record Administration, Medical Technology, Nursing (B,M),

Physical Therapy, Social Work (B) *CEO:* Pres. Daniel H. Pilon
Enroll: 1766   (218) 723-6033

CONCORDE CAREER INSTITUTE
12 N. 12th St., Minneapolis 55403-1331 *Type:* Private *Accred.:* 1991 (CCA-ACTTS) *Calendar:* Courses of varying lengths *Degrees:* certificates *Prof. Accred.:* Dental Assisting *CEO:* Dir. Sally Mol
(612) 341-3850

CONCORDIA COLLEGE
901 S. 8th St., Moorhead 56560 *Type:* Private (Lutheran) liberal arts *Accred.:* 1927/1984 (NCA) *Calendar:* Tri. plan *Degrees:* B *Prof. Accred.:* Music, Social Work (B), Teacher Education (e,s,p) *CEO:* Pres. Paul J. Dovre
Enroll: 2910   (218) 299-3000

CONCORDIA COLLEGE
275 N. Syndicate St., St. Paul 55104 *Type:* Private (Lutheran-Missouri Synod) liberal arts and teachers *Accred.:* 1959/1988 (NCA) *Calendar:* Qtr. plan *Degrees:* A, B, M *Prof. Accred.:* Teacher Education (e,s) *CEO:* Pres. Robert A. Holst
Enroll: 1174   (612) 641-8211

CROWN COLLEGE
6425 County Rd. 30, St. Bonifacius 55375 *Type:* Private (Christian and Missionary Alliance) *Accred.:* 1950/1981 (AABC); 1980/1985 (NCA) *Calendar:* Sem. plan *Degrees:* A, B, certificates, diplomas *CEO:* Pres. Bill W. Lanpher
Enroll: 560   (612) 446-4100

DAKOTA COUNTY TECHNICAL COLLEGE
1300 145th St. E., Rosemont 55068 *Type:* Private *Calendar:* Courses of varying lengths *Degrees:* A, certificates *Prof. Accred.:* Interior Design, Practical Nursing *CEO:* Supervisor Wayne Davis
(612) 423-8414

DR. MARTIN LUTHER COLLEGE
1884 College Heights, New Ulm 56073 *Type:* Private (Evangelical Lutheran Synod) *Accred.:* 1980/1985 (NCA) *Calendar:* Sem. plan *Degrees:* B *CEO:* Pres. Lloyd O. Huebner
Enroll: 442   (507) 354-8221

DULUTH BUSINESS UNIVERSITY
412 W. Superior St., Duluth 55802 *Type:* Private business *Accred.:* 1970/1987 (CCA-ACICS) *Calendar:* Qtr. plan *Degrees:* certificates, diplomas *CEO:* Pres. James R. Gessner
Enroll: 121   (218) 722-3361

DULUTH TECHNICAL COLLEGE
2101 Trinity Rd., Duluth 55811 *Type:* Private *Calendar:* Courses of varying lengths *Degrees:* A *Prof. Accred.:* Medical Laboratory Technology (AMA), Occupational Therapy Assisting, Physical Therapy Assisting *CEO:* Dir. Harold Erickson, Ph.D.
(218) 722-2801

DUNWOODY INDUSTRIAL INSTITUTE
818 Dunwoody Blvd., Minneapolis 55403-1192 *Type:* Private *Accred.:* 1972/1988 (CCA-ACTTS) *Calendar:* Courses of varying lengths *Degrees:* diplomas *CEO:* Pres. M. James Bensen
Enroll: 1305   (612) 374-5800

EAST GRAND FORKS TECHNICAL COLLEGE
Hwy. 220 N., P.O. Box 111, East Grand Forks 56721 *Type:* Private *Calendar:* Courses of varying lengths *Degrees:* A, certificates, diplomas *Prof. Accred.:* Medical Assisting (AMA), Medical Laboratory Technology (AMA), Radiography, Respiratory Therapy, Respiratory Therapy Technology, Surgical Technology *CEO:* Pres. Gerald Folstrom
(218) 773-3441

FARIBAULT TECHNICAL COLLEGE
1225 S.W. Third St., Faribault 55021 *Type:* Private *Calendar:* Courses of varying lengths *Degrees:* certificates *Prof. Accred.:* Medical Laboratory Technology (AMA) *CEO:* Pres. Viril C. Layton
(507) 334-3965

FERGUS FALLS COMMUNITY COLLEGE
1414 College Way, Fergus Falls 56537 *Type:* Public junior *System:* Minnesota Community College System *Accred.:* 1972/1986 (NCA) *Calendar:* Qtr. plan *Degrees:* A, certificates, diplomas *Prof. Accred.:* Histologic Technology, Medical Laboratory Technology (AMA) *CEO:* Provost Daniel F. True
Enroll: 857 (218) 739-7500

GLOBE COLLEGE OF BUSINESS
289 E. Fifth St., St. Paul 55101 *Type:* Private business *Accred.:* 1953/1990 (CCA-ACICS) *Calendar:* Qtr. plan *Degrees:* certificates, diplomas *CEO:* Pres. Terry L. Myhre
Enroll: 607 (612) 224-4378

GUSTAVUS ADOLPHUS COLLEGE
St. Peter 56082 *Type:* Private (Lutheran) liberal arts *Accred.:* 1915/1983 (NCA) *Calendar:* 4-1-4 plan *Degrees:* B *Prof. Accred.:* Music, Nursing (B), Teacher Education (e,s) *CEO:* Pres. Axel D. Steuer
Enroll: 2342 (507) 931-8000

HAMLINE UNIVERSITY
1536 Hewitt Ave., St. Paul 55104 *Type:* Private (United Methodist) liberal arts *Accred.:* 1914/1988 (NCA) *Calendar:* 4-1-4 plan *Degrees:* B, M, D *Prof. Accred.:* Law, Music, Teacher Education (e,s) *CEO:* Pres. Larry G. Osnes
Enroll: 2267 (612) 641-2202

HENNEPIN TECHNICAL COLLEGE
9000 Brooklyn Blvd., Brooklyn Park 55455 *Type:* Private *Calendar:* Courses of varying lengths *Degrees:* certificates *Prof. Accred.:* Dental Assisting, Practical Nursing *CEO:* Dir. Marty Patterson
(612) 425-3800

HIBBING COMMUNITY COLLEGE
1515 E. 25th St., Hibbing 55746 *Type:* Public junior *System:* Arrowhead Community College Region *Accred.:* 1982/1989 (NCA) *Calendar:* Qtr. plan *Degrees:* A, certificates, diplomas *Prof. Accred.:* Radiography *CEO:* Provost Anthony Kuznik
Enroll: 2469 (218) 262-6700

HIBBING TECHNICAL COLLEGE
2900 E. Beltline, Hibbing 55746 *Type:* Private *Calendar:* Courses of varying lengths *Degrees:* A *Prof. Accred.:* Dental Assisting, Medical Laboratory Technology (AMA) *CEO:* Dir. Gerald Stuhr
(218) 262-6185

INVER HILLS COMMUNITY COLLEGE
8445 College Trail, Inver Grove Heights 55076 *Type:* Public junior *System:* Minnesota Community College System *Accred.:* 1976/1988 (NCA) *Calendar:* Qtr. plan *Degrees:* A, certificates, diplomas *Prof. Accred.:* Nursing (A) *CEO:* Acting Pres. Jerry Isaacs
Enroll: 2701 (612) 450-8634

ITASCA COMMUNITY COLLEGE
1851 E. Hwy. 169, Grand Rapids 55744 *Type:* Public junior *System:* Arrowhead Community College Region *Accred.:* 1982/1989 (NCA) *Calendar:* Qtr. plan *Degrees:* A *CEO:* Provost Lawrence Dukes
Enroll: 2469 (218) 327-4461

LAKELAND MEDICAL-DENTAL ACADEMY
1402 W. Lake St., Minneapolis 55408-1192 *Type:* Private *Accred.:* 1968/1989 (CCA-ACTTS) *Calendar:* Qtr. plan *Degrees:* diplomas *Prof. Accred.:* Dental Assisting, Medical Assisting (AMA), Medical Laboratory Technology (AMA) *CEO:* Dir. Lorrie Laurin
Enroll: 377 (800) 223-5157

LAKEWOOD COMMUNITY COLLEGE
3401 Century Ave., White Bear Lake 55110 *Type:* Public *System:* Minnesota Community College System *Accred.:* 1974/1986 (NCA) *Calendar:* Qtr. plan *Degrees:* A *Prof. Accred.:* Radiography *CEO:* Pres. Neil Christienson
Enroll: 3503 (612) 779-3200

LOWTHIAN COLLEGE
821 Marquette Ave., Ste. 300, Minneapolis 55402 *Type:* Private business *Accred.:* 1971/1989 (CCA-ACICS) *Calendar:* Courses of

Minnesota

varying lengths *Degrees:* A, certificates, diplomas *CEO:* Pres. Petrena Lowthian
Enroll: 185 (612) 332-3361

LUTHER NORTHWESTERN THEOLOGICAL SEMINARY
2481 Como Ave., W., St. Paul 55108 *Type:* Private (Evangelical Lutheran) professional; graduate only *Accred.:* 1979/1984 (NCA) *Calendar:* Sem. plan *Degrees:* P, M, D *CEO:* Pres. David L. Tiede
Enroll: 583 (612) 641-3456

MACALESTER COLLEGE
1600 Grand Ave., St. Paul 55105 *Type:* Private (United Presbyterian) liberal arts *Accred.:* 1913/1986 (NCA) *Calendar:* 4-1-4 plan *Degrees:* B *Prof. Accred.:* Teacher Education (e,s) *CEO:* Pres. Robert M. Gavin, Jr.
Enroll: 1780 (612) 696-6000

MANKATO AREA VOCATIONAL-TECHNICAL SCHOOL
1920 Lee Blvd., P.O. Box 1920, North Mankato 56001 *Type:* Private *Calendar:* Courses of varying lengths *Degrees:* certificates *Prof. Accred.:* Dental Assisting *CEO:* Pres. John Votca
(507) 625-3441

MANKATO STATE UNIVERSITY
Mankato 56001 *Type:* Public liberal arts and professional *System:* Minnesota State University System *Accred.:* 1916/1986 (NCA) *Calendar:* Qtr. plan *Degrees:* A, B, M *Prof. Accred.:* Art, Counseling, Dental Hygiene, Engineering (electrical), Engineering Technology (electrical, manufacturing), Music, Nursing (B), Recreation, Parks and Leisure Services, Rehabilitation Counseling, Social Work (B), Teacher Education (e,s,p) *CEO:* Pres. Margaret R. Preska
Enroll: 13603 (507) 389-1111

MAYO FOUNDATION
200 First St., S.W., Rochester 55905 *Type:* Private professional *System:* University of Minnesota System *Accred.:* 1984/1989 (NCA) *Calendar:* Sem. plan *Degrees:* M, D,

certificates, diplomas *Prof. Accred.:* Combined Prosthodontics, Cytotechnology, Diagnostic Medical Sonography, Medical Laboratory Technology (AMA), Medicine, Nuclear Medicine Technology, Nurse Anesthesia Education, Oral and Maxillofacial Surgery, Orthodontics, Periodontics, Physical Therapy, Radiation Therapy Technology, Radiography *CEO:* C.E.O. Robert R. Waller
Enroll: 1514 (507) 284-2511

MCCONNELL SCHOOL INC.
831 Second Ave. S., Minneapolis 55402-2861 *Type:* Private *Accred.:* 1967/1989 (CCA-ACTTS) *Calendar:* Courses of varying lengths *Degrees:* diplomas *CEO:* Dir. William McKay
Enroll: 752 (612) 332-4238

MEDICAL INSTITUTE OF MINNESOTA
2309 Nicollet Ave., Minneapolis 55404 *Type:* Private *Calendar:* Courses of varying lengths *Degrees:* certificates *Prof. Accred.:* Health Education, Medical Assisting (AMA), Medical Laboratory Technology (AMA), Veterinary Technology (probational) *CEO:* Exec. Dir. Phil Miller
(612) 871-8481

MESABI COMMUNITY COLLEGE
905 W. Chestnut St., Virginia 55792 *Type:* Public junior *System:* Arrowhead Community College Region *Accred.:* 1982/1989 (NCA) *Calendar:* Qtr. plan *Degrees:* A *CEO:* Provost Richard N. Kohlhase
Enroll: 2469 (218) 749-7700

METROPOLITAN STATE UNIVERSITY
121 Seventh Pl. E., Metro Sq., Ste. 121, St. Paul 55101 *Type:* Public liberal arts *System:* Minnesota State University System *Accred.:* 1975/1985 (NCA) *Calendar:* Qtr. plan *Degrees:* B, M *Prof. Accred.:* Nursing (B) *CEO:* Pres. Tobin G. Barrozo
Enroll: 2529 (612) 373-2727

MINNEAPOLIS BUSINESS COLLEGE
1711 W. County Rd. B, Roseville 55113 *Type:* Private business *Accred.:* 1962/1984 (CCA-ACICS) *Calendar:* Courses of vary-

ing lengths *Degrees:* certificates, diplomas *Prof. Accred.:* Medical Assisting (AMA) *CEO:* Pres. Robert Maxson
Enroll: 272 (612) 636-7406

MINNEAPOLIS COLLEGE OF ART AND DESIGN
2501 Stevens Ave. S., Minneapolis 55404 *Type:* Private professional *Accred.:* 1960/1988 (NCA) *Calendar:* Sem. plan *Degrees:* B *Prof. Accred.:* Art *CEO:* Pres. John S. Slorp
Enroll: 687 (612) 874-3700

MINNEAPOLIS COMMUNITY COLLEGE
1501 Hennepin Ave., Minneapolis 55403 *Type:* Public junior *System:* Minnesota Community College System *Accred.:* 1977/1986 (NCA) *Calendar:* Qtr. plan *Degrees:* A, certificates, diplomas *Prof. Accred.:* Nursing (A) *CEO:* Pres. Jacquelyn M. Belcher
Enroll: 2448 (612) 341-7055

MINNEAPOLIS DRAFTING SCHOOL
5700 West Broadway, Minneapolis 55428-3548 *Type:* Private *Accred.:* 1972/1988 (CCA-ACTTS) *Calendar:* Qtr. plan *Degrees:* certificates, diplomas *CEO:* Pres. Robert Casserly
Enroll: 256 (612) 535-8843

MINNEAPOLIS TECHNICAL COLLEGE
1415 Hennepin Ave. S., Room 446, Minneapolis 55403 *Type:* Private *Calendar:* Courses of varying lengths *Degrees:* certificates *Prof. Accred.:* Dental Assisting, Practical Nursing *CEO:* Pres. Harvey Rucker
(612) 370-9400

MINNESOTA BIBLE COLLEGE
920 Mayowood Rd, S.W., Rochester 55902 *Type:* Private (Christian Churches/Church of Christ) *Accred.:* 1948/1983 (AABC) *Calendar:* Qtr. plan *Degrees:* A, B *CEO:* Pres. Donald R. Lloyd
Enroll: 92 (507) 288-4563

MINNESOTA SCHOOL OF BARBERING
3615 E. Lake St., Minneapolis 55406 *Type:* Private *Accred.:* 1983/1988 (CCA-ACTTS) *Calendar:* Courses of varying lengths *Degrees:* certificates *CEO:* Dir. Margaret Schmidt
Enroll: 45 (612) 722-1996

MINNESOTA SCHOOL OF BUSINESS
11 S. Fifth St., Minneapolis 55402 *Type:* Private business *Accred.:* 1953/1985 (CCA-ACICS) *Calendar:* Qtr. plan *Degrees:* certificates, diplomas *CEO:* Dir. Patricia Peick
Enroll: 711 (612) 338-6721

BRANCH CAMPUS
6120 Earle Brown Dr., Brooklyn Center, MN 55430 *CEO:* Dir. Glenn Renick
(612) 566-7777

MOLER BARBER SCHOOL OF HAIRSTYLING
1411 Nicollet Ave., Minneapolis 55403-2666 *Type:* Private *Accred.:* 1983/1988 (CCA-ACTTS) *Calendar:* Courses of varying lengths *Degrees:* certificates *CEO:* Owner Delano Martinson
Enroll: 63 (612) 871-3754

MOORHEAD STATE UNIVERSITY
1104 7th Ave. S., Moorhead 56560 *Type:* Public liberal arts and teachers *System:* Minnesota State University System *Accred.:* 1916/1987 (NCA) *Calendar:* Qtr. plan *Degrees:* A, B, P, M *Prof. Accred.:* Art, Music, Nursing (B), Social Work (B), Teacher Education (e,s,p) *CEO:* Pres. Roland Dille
Enroll: 8128 (218) 236-2243

MOORHEAD TECHNICAL COLLEGE
1900 28th Ave. S., Moorhead 56560 *Type:* Private *Calendar:* Courses of varying lengths *Degrees:* A, certificates, diplomas *Prof. Accred.:* Dental Assisting, Medical Record Technology *CEO:* Dir. Nate Johnson
(218) 236-6277

MUSIC TECH
304 N. Washington Ave., Minneapolis 55401 *Type:* Private *Calendar:* Courses of varying lengths *Degrees:* diplomas *Prof. Accred.:* Music *CEO:* Educ. Dir. Douglas W. Smith
(612) 338-0175

Minnesota

NATIONAL EDUCATION CENTER—BROWN INSTITUTE CAMPUS
2225 E. Lake St., Minneapolis 55407-1900 *Type:* Private *Accred.:* 1967/1988 (CCA-ACTTS) *Calendar:* Courses of varying lengths *Degrees:* A, certificates, diplomas *CEO:* Pres. Steve Marks
Enroll: 2628 (612) 721-2481

NORMANDALE COMMUNITY COLLEGE
9700 France Ave. S., Bloomington 55431 *Type:* Public junior *System:* Minnesota Community College System *Accred.:* 1973/1983 (NCA) *Calendar:* Qtr. plan *Degrees:* A, certificates, diplomas *Prof. Accred.:* Dental Assisting, Dental Hygiene, Nursing (A) *CEO:* Pres. Thomas Horak
Enroll: 5621 (612) 832-6000

NORTH CENTRAL BIBLE COLLEGE
910 Elliot Ave. S., Minneapolis 55404 *Type:* Private (Assemblies of God) *Accred.:* 1964/1984 (AABC); 1986/1991 (NCA) *Calendar:* Sem. plan *Degrees:* A, B, certificates, diplomas *CEO:* Pres. Don H. Argue
Enroll: 1182 (612) 332-3491

NORTH HENNEPIN COMMUNITY COLLEGE
7411 85th Ave. N., Brooklyn Park 55445 *Type:* Public junior *System:* Minnesota Community College System *Accred.:* 1972/1986 (NCA) *Calendar:* Qtr. plan *Degrees:* A, certificates, diplomas *Prof. Accred.:* Nursing (A) *CEO:* Pres. Frederick W. Capshaw
Enroll: 3572 (612) 424-0811

NORTHEAST METRO TECHNICAL COLLEGE
3300 Century Ave. N., White Bear Lake 55110 *Type:* Private *Calendar:* Courses of varying lengths *Degrees:* diplomas *Prof. Accred.:* Dental Assisting, Dental Laboratory Technology, EMT-Paramedic, Medical Assisting (AMA) *CEO:* Supt. E. Dale Birkeland
(612) 770-2351

NORTHLAND COMMUNITY COLLEGE
Hwy. 1 E., Thief River Falls 56701 *Type:* Public junior *System:* Clearwater Community College Region *Accred.:* 1976/1986 (NCA) *Calendar:* Qtr. plan *Degrees:* A *CEO:* Acting Provost James Haviland
Enroll: 622 (218) 681-2181

NORTHWEST TECHNICAL INSTITUTE
11995 Singletree La., Eden Prairie 55344-5351 *Type:* Private *Accred.:* 1972/1988 (CCA-ACTTS) *Calendar:* Sem. plan *Degrees:* A *CEO:* Pres. Norris J. Nelson
Enroll: 70 (612) 944-0080

NORTHWESTERN COLLEGE
3003 N. Snelling Ave., St. Paul 55112 *Type:* Private liberal arts *Accred.:* 1978/1983 (NCA) *Calendar:* Qtr. plan *Degrees:* A, B, certificates, diplomas *Prof. Accred.:* Music *CEO:* Pres. Donald O. Ericksen
Enroll: 1024 (612) 631-5100

NORTHWESTERN COLLEGE OF CHIROPRACTIC
2501 West 84th Street, Bloomington 55431 *Type:* Private professional *Accred.:* 1988 (NCA) *Calendar:* Tri. plan *Degrees:* D *Prof. Accred.:* Chiropractic Education *CEO:* Pres. Donald M. Cassata
Enroll: 520 (612) 888-4777

NORTHWESTERN ELECTRONICS INSTITUTE
825 41st Ave., N.E., Columbia Heights 55421 *Type:* Private *Accred.:* 1968/1988 (CCA-ACTTS) *Calendar:* Qtr. plan *Degrees:* A, certificates, diplomas *CEO:* Pres. Charles R. Dettmann
Enroll: 1716 (612) 781-4881

OAK HILLS BIBLE COLLEGE
1600 Oak Hills Rd., S.W., Bemidji 56601 *Type:* Private professional *Accred.:* 1990 (AABC) *Calendar:* Sem. plan *Degrees:* A, B, certificates *CEO:* Pres. Mark Hovestol
Enroll: 102 (218) 751-8670

RAINY RIVER COMMUNITY COLLEGE
Hwy. 11-71 and 15th St., International Falls 56649 *Type:* Public junior *System:* Arrowhead Community College Region *Accred.:* 1982/1988 (NCA) *Calendar:* Qtr.plan *Degrees:* A *CEO:* Provost Karen Nagle
Enroll: 2469 (218) 285-7722

Accredited Institutions   **Minnesota**

RASMUSSEN BUSINESS COLLEGE
3500 Federal Dr., Eagan 55122 *Type:* Private business *Accred.:* 1953/1990 (CCA-ACICS) *Calendar:* Courses of varying lengths *Degrees:* A, certificates, diplomas *CEO:* Dir. Kristi Waite
Enroll: 722   (612) 687-9000

RASMUSSEN BUSINESS COLLEGE
Good Counsel Dr., Mankato 56001 *Type:* Private business *Accred.:* 1973/1986 (CCA-ACICS) *Calendar:* Courses of varying lengths *Degrees:* A, certificates, diplomas *CEO:* Dir. Brenda Page
Enroll: 480   (507) 625-6556

RASMUSSEN BUSINESS COLLEGE
12450 Wayzata Blvd., Minnetonka 55343-5602 *Type:* Private business *Accred.:* 1973/1980 (CCA-ACICS) *Calendar:* courses of varying lengths *Degrees:* A, certificates, diplomas *CEO:* Dir. Anne Scharff
Enroll: 722   (612) 545-2000

ROCHESTER COMMUNITY COLLEGE
851 30th Ave. S.E., Rochester 55904-4999 *Type:* Public junior *System:* Minnesota Community College System *Accred.:* 1923/1991 (NCA) *Calendar:* Qtr. plan *Degrees:* A, certificates, diplomas *Prof. Accred.:* Engineering Technology (civil/construction, electrical, mechanical), Medical Assisting (AMA), Nursing (A), Respiratory Therapy *CEO:* Pres. Geraldine A. Evans
Enroll: 2785   (507) 285-7216

ROCHESTER TECHNICAL COLLEGE
1926 College View Rd. E., Rochester 55904 *Type:* Private *Calendar:* Courses of varying lengths *Degrees:* diplomas *Prof. Accred.:* Dental Assisting, Practical Nursing, Surgical Technology *CEO:* Dir. Donald D. Supalla
           (507) 285-8616

ROFFLER HAIR DESIGN COLLEGE
1650 White Bear Ave., St. Paul 55106-1610 *Type:* Private *Accred.:* 1987 (CCA-ACTTS) *Calendar:* Courses of varying lengths *Degrees:* diplomas *CEO:* Dir. James Turner
           (612) 772-1417

ST. CLOUD BUSINESS COLLEGE
245 N. 37th Ave., St. Cloud 56303 *Type:* Private business *Accred.:* 1969/1981 (CCA-ACICS) *Calendar:* Qtr. plan *Degrees:* certificates, diplomas *CEO:* Dir. Judy Manetas
Enroll: 597   (612) 251-5600

ST. CLOUD STATE UNIVERSITY
740 Fourth Ave. S., St. Cloud 56301-4498 *Type:* Public liberal arts and professional *System:* Minnesota State University System *Accred.:* 1915/1988 (NCA) *Calendar:* Qtr. plan *Degrees:* A, B, P, M *Prof. Accred.:* Art, Business (B,M), Computer Science, Engineering (electrical), Engineering Technology (manufacturing), Journalism, Music, Rehabilitation Counseling, Social Work(B), Speech-Language Pathology, Teacher Education (e,s,p) *CEO:* Pres. Brendan J. McDonald
Enroll: 14011   (612) 255-2122

ST. CLOUD TECHNICAL COLLEGE
1540 Northway Dr., St. Cloud 56303 *Type:* Public 2-year *Accred.:* 1985 (NCA) *Calendar:* Qtr. plan *Degrees:* A, certificates, diplomas *Prof. Accred.:* Dental Assisting, Practical Nursing, Surgical Technology *CEO:* Pres. Larry Barnhardt
Enroll: 1650   (612) 252-0101

ST. JOHN'S UNIVERSITY
Collegeville 56321 *Type:* Private (Roman Catholic) liberal arts and seminary for men *Accred.:* 1969/1988 (ATS); 1950/1989 (NCA) *Calendar:* 4-1-4 plan *Degrees:* B, P, M, certificates, diplomas *Prof. Accred.:* Social Work (B) *CEO:* Pres. Dietrich Reinhart, O.S.B.
Enroll: 1986   (612) 363-2011

ST. MARY'S COLLEGE OF MINNESOTA
Terrace Heights, Winona 55987 *Type:* Private (Roman Catholic) liberal arts *Accred.:* 1934/1987 (NCA) *Calendar:* Sem. plan *Degrees:* B, M *Prof. Accred.:* Nuclear Medicine Technology, Nurse Anesthesia Education *CEO:* Pres. Louis De Thomasis
Enroll: 1899   (507) 457-1503

Minnesota

ST. OLAF COLLEGE
Northfield 55057 *Type:* Private (Lutheran) liberal arts *Accred.:* 1915/1983 (NCA) *Calendar:* 4-1-4 plan *Degrees:* B *Prof. Accred.:* Dance, Music, Nursing (B), Social Work (B), Teacher Education (s), Theatre *CEO:* Pres. Melvin D. George
Enroll: 3110 (507) 663-3000

ST. PAUL TECHNICAL COLLEGE
235 Marshall Ave., St. Paul 55102 *Type:* Public 2-year *Accred.:* 1983/1986 (NCA) *Calendar:* Qtr. plan *Degrees:* A, certificates, diplomas *Prof. Accred.:* Medical Laboratory Technology (AMA), Practical Nursing, Respiratory Therapy, Respiratory Therapy Technology *CEO:* Pres. Donovan Schwichtenberg
Enroll: 675 (612) 221-1364

SCHOOL OF COMMUNICATION ARTS, INC.
2526 27th Ave. S., Minneapolis 55406-1310 *Type:* Private *Accred.:* 1980/1985 (CCA-ACTTS) *Calendar:* Sem. plan *Degrees:* certificates *CEO:* Pres. Roger Klietz
Enroll: 320 (612) 721-5357

SOUTHWEST STATE UNIVERSITY
Marshall 56258 *Type:* Public liberal arts *System:* Minnesota State University System *Accred.:* 1972/1983 (NCA) *Calendar:* Qtr. plan *Degrees:* A, B *Prof. Accred.:* Music *CEO:* Pres. Oliver J. Ford
Enroll: 2598 (507) 537-6272

SOUTHWESTERN TECHNICAL COLLEGE
1593 11th Ave., Granite Falls 56241 *Type:* Private *Accred.:* 1991 (NCA) *Calendar:* Courses of varying lengths *Degrees:* A, certificates, diplomas *Prof. Accred.:* Dental Assisting *CEO:* Pres. Richard Pooley
(612) 564-4511

TWIN CITY SCHOOL OF PET GROOMING
2558 Hwy. 10, Mounds View 55112-4032 *Type:* Private *Accred.:* 1991 (CCA-ACTTS) *Calendar:* Courses of varying lengths *Degrees:* certificates *CEO:* Dir. Mary Bourke
(612) 755-9463

UNITED THEOLOGICAL SEMINARY OF THE TWIN CITIES
3000 Fifth St., N.W., New Brighton 55112 *Type:* Private (United Church of Christ) professional; graduate only *Accred.:* 1966/1982 (ATS); 1977/1982 (NCA) *Calendar:* Qtr. plan *Degrees:* P, M, D, certificates, diplomas *CEO:* Pres. Benjamin Griffin
Enroll: 120 (612) 633-4311

UNIVERSITY OF MINNESOTA—CROOKSTON
Crookston 56716 *Type:* Public (state) *System:* University of Minnesota System *Accred.:* 1971/1984 (NCA) *Calendar:* Qtr. plan *Degrees:* A *CEO:* Chanc. Donald G. Sargeant
Enroll: 1078 (218) 281-6510

UNIVERSITY OF MINNESOTA—DULUTH
Duluth 55812 *Type:* Public (state) *System:* University of Minnesota System *Accred.:* 1968/1988 (NCA) *Calendar:* Qtr. plan *Degrees:* A, B, P, M, certificates, diplomas *Prof. Accred.:* Computer Science, Dental Hygiene, Engineering (computer, industrial), Music, Social Work (M), Speech-Language Pathology, Teacher Education (e,s,p) *CEO:* Chanc. Lawrence A. Ianni
Enroll: 6345 (218) 726-8000

UNIVERSITY OF MINNESOTA—MORRIS
600 E. Fourth St., Morris 56267 *Type:* Public (state) *System:* University of Minnesota System *Accred.:* 1970/1990 (NCA) *Calendar:* Qtr. Plan *Degrees:* B *Prof. Accred.:* Teacher Education (e,s) *CEO:* Chanc. David C. Johnson
Enroll: 2021 (612) 589-2211

UNIVERSITY OF MINNESOTA—TWIN CITIES
100 Church St., S.E., Minneapolis 55455 *Type:* Public (state) *System:* University of Minnesota System *Accred.:* 1913/1986 (NCA) *Calendar:* Qtr. plan *Degrees:* A, B, P, M, D *Prof. Accred.:* Accounting (Type A), Architecture (B,M), Audiology (B,M), Business (B,M), Clinical Psychology, Combined Prosthodontics, Counseling Psychology, Dance, Dental Hygiene, Dentistry, Dietetics (coordinated), Endodontics, Engineering (aerospace, agricultural, chemical, civil, electrical, geological/geophysical, materials, mechanical, mineral), Forestry, General Dentistry, General Practice Residency, Health Services Administration, Interior

Design, Journalism, Landscape Architecture (B), Law, Medical Technology, Medicine, Mortuary Science, Music, Nurse Anesthesia Education, Nursing (B,M), Occupational Therapy, Oral and Maxillofacial Surgery, Oral Pathology, Orthodontics, Pediatric Dentistry, Periodontics, Pharmacy, Physical Therapy, Planning, Psychology Internship, Public Health, Radiation Therapy Technology, Radiography, Recreation, Park and Leisure Studies, School Psychology (M), Social Work (M), Speech-Language Pathology, Teacher Education (e,s,p), Theatre *CEO:* Pres. Nils Hasselmo
Enroll: 41471 (612) 625-5000

UNIVERSITY OF MINNESOTA—WASECA
1000 University Dr., S.W., Waseca 56093 *Type:* Public (state) *System:* University of Minnesota System *Accred.:* 1975/1990 (NCA) *Calendar:* Qtr. plan *Degrees:* A *Prof. Accred.:* Veterinary Technology *CEO:* Chanc. Nan Wilhelmson
Enroll: 766 (507) 835-9300

UNIVERSITY OF ST. THOMAS
2115 Summit Ave., St. Paul 55105 *Type:* Private (Roman Catholic) liberal arts *Accred.:* 1974/1984(ATS);1916/1984 (NCA) *Calendar:* 4-1-4 plan *Degrees:* B, P, M, D *Prof. Accred.:* Music, Nurse Anesthesia Education (B), Social Work (B,M-candidate), Teacher Education (e,s,p) *CEO:* Pres. Dennis J. Dease
Enroll: 6816 (612) 647-5000

VERMILION COMMUNITY COLLEGE
1900 E. Camp St., Ely 55731 *Type:* Public junior *System:* Arrowhead Community College Region *Accred.:* 1982/1989 (NCA) *Calendar:* Qtr. plan *Degrees:* A *CEO:* Provost Jon Harris
Enroll: 2469 (218) 365-7200

WALDEN UNIVERSITY
430 First Ave. N., Ste. 620, Minneapolis 55401 *Type:* Private graduate only *Accred.:* 1990 (NCA) *Calendar:* Tri. plan *Degrees:* D *CEO:* Pres. Glendon Drake
Enroll: 430 (612) 338-7224

WILLIAM MITCHELL COLLEGE OF LAW
875 Summit Ave., St. Paul 55105 *Type:* Private professional *Calendar:* Sem. plan *Degrees:* P *Prof. Accred.:* Law *CEO:* Pres./Dean James Hogg
Enroll: 329 (612) 227-9171

WILLMAR COMMUNITY COLLEGE
P.O. Box 797, Willmar 56201 *Type:* Public junior *System:* Minnesota Community College System *Accred.:* 1972/1985 (NCA) *Calendar:* Qtr. plan *Degrees:* A *CEO:* Pres. Harold G. Conradi
Enroll: 1091 (612) 231-5102

WILLMAR TECHNICAL COLLEGE
P.O. Box 1097, Willmar 56201 *Type:* Public (state) 2-year *Accred.:* 1976/1985 (NCA) *Calendar:* Tri. plan *Degrees:* A, certificates, diplomas *Prof. Accred.:* Medical Assisting (AMA), Practical Nursing *CEO:* Pres. Ronald A. Erpelding
Enroll: 388 (612) 235-5114

WINONA STATE UNIVERSITY
Winona 55987 *Type:* Public liberal arts and teachers *System:* Minnesota State University System *Accred.:* 1913/1991 (NCA) *Calendar:* Qtr. plan *Degrees:* A, B, P, M, certificates, diplomas *Prof. Accred.:* Music, Nursing (B,M), Social Work (B), Teacher Education (e,s,p) *CEO:* Pres. Darrell W. Krueger
Enroll: 6489 (507) 457-2017

WORTHINGTON COMMUNITY COLLEGE
1450 College Way, Worthington 56187 *Type:* Public junior *System:* Minnesota Community College System *Accred.:* 1973/1990 (NCA) *Calendar:* Qtr. plan *Degrees:* A *CEO:* Pres. C.W. Burchill
Enroll: 606 (507) 372-2107

MISSISSIPPI

ALCORN STATE UNIVERSITY
P.O. Box 359, Lorman 39096 *Type:* Public (state) teachers *System:* Mississippi Board of Trustees of State Institutions of Higher Learning *Accred.:* 1948/1991 (SACS-CC) *Calendar:* Sem. plan *Degrees:* A, B, M *Prof. Accred.:* Music, Nursing (A,B), Teacher Education (e,s) *CEO:* Pres. Walter Washington
Enroll: 2663 (601) 877-6100

AMHERST CAREER CENTER
201 W. Park Ave., Greenwood 38930 *Type:* Private *Accred.:* 1991 (SACS-COEI) *Calendar:* Courses of varying lengths *Degrees:* certificates *CEO:* Dir. Darryl Wiltshire
(601) 453-0480

BATESVILLE JOB CORPS CENTER
Rte. 3, Box 2J, Hwy. 51, S., Batesville 38606 *Type:* Public (state) *Accred.:* 1989 (SACS-COEI) *Calendar:* Courses of varying lengths *Degrees:* certificates *CEO:* Dir. Curtistene Eoff
Enroll: 360 (601) 563-4656

BELHAVEN COLLEGE
1500 Peachtree St., Jackson 39202 *Type:* Private (Presbyterian) liberal arts *Accred.:* 1946/1987 (SACS-CC) *Calendar:* Sem. plan *Degrees:* B *Prof. Accred.:* Art, Music *CEO:* Pres. Newton Wilson
Enroll: 713 (601) 968-5919

BLUE MOUNTAIN COLLEGE
P.O. Box 338, Blue Mountain 38610 *Type:* Private (Southern Baptist) liberal arts primarily for women *Accred.:* 1927/1984 (SACS-CC) *Calendar:* Sem. plan *Degrees:* B *CEO:* Pres. E. Harold Fisher
Enroll: 294 (601) 685-4771

BROCK'S HAIR DESIGN COLLEGE
116 Franklin St., Carthage 39051-3716 *Type:* Private *Accred.:* 1991 (CCA-ACTTS) *Calendar:* Courses of varying lengths *Degrees:* certificates *CEO:* Pres. Clinton E. Brock
(601) 267-3678

BRANCH CAMPUS
1508 S. Glouster St., Tupelo, MS 38801-6510 *CEO:* Dir. Michael Lee McBunch
(601) 680-4802

CAREER DEVELOPMENT INSTITUTE
813 Acme Plaza, Ste. 4, Meridian 39301 *Type:* Private *Accred.:* 1989/1990 (SACS-COEI) *Calendar:* Courses of varying lengths *Degrees:* certificates *CEO:* Dir. Joe Ivey
Enroll: 137 (601) 483-9773

COAHOMA COMMUNITY COLLEGE
Rte. 1, Box 616, Clarksdale 38614 *Type:* Public (state) junior *System:* Mississippi State Board for Community and Junior Colleges *Accred.:* 1975/1990 (SACS-CC) *Calendar:* Sem. plan *Degrees:* A *CEO:* Pres. McKinley C. Martin
Enroll: 1419 (601) 627-2571

COPIAH-LINCOLN COMMUNITY COLLEGE
P.O. Box 457, Wesson 39191-0091 *Type:* Public (district) junior *System:* Mississippi State Board for Community and Junior Colleges *Accred.:* 1936/1985 (SACS-CC) *Calendar:* Sem. plan *Degrees:* A *Prof. Accred.:* Medical Laboratory Technology (AMA), Radiography *CEO:* Pres. Billy B. Thames
Enroll: 2343 (601) 643-5101

DELTA STATE UNIVERSITY
Hwy. 8 W., Cleveland 38733 *Type:* Public liberal arts and teachers *System:* Mississippi Board of Trustees of State Institutions of Higher Learning *Accred.:* 1930/1984 (SACS-CC) *Calendar:* Sem. plan *Degrees:* B, M, D *Prof. Accred.:* Art, Home Economics, Music, Nursing (B), Social Work (B), Teacher Education (e,s,p) *CEO:* Pres. F. Kent Wyatt
Enroll: 4029 (601) 846-3000

DELTA TECHNICAL INSTITUTE
323 Central Ave., Cleveland 38732-2647 *Type:* Private *Accred.:* 1988 (CCA-ACTTS)

Calendar: Courses of varying lengths *Degrees:* certificates *CEO:* Dir. Van Carmicle
Enroll: 10 (601) 843-6063

DRAUGHON'S BUSINESS COLLEGE
502 North St., Jackson 39215 *Type:* Private business *Accred.:* 1968/1986 (CCA-ACICS) *Calendar:* Courses of varying lengths *Degrees:* certificates, diplomas *CEO:* Dir. Michael Anthony
Enroll: 329 (601) 353-3826

EAST CENTRAL COMMUNITY COLLEGE
P.O. Box 129, Decatur 39327-0129 *Type:* Public (district) junior *System:* Mississippi State Board for Community and Junior Colleges *Accred.:* 1939/1991 (SACS-CC) *Calendar:* Sem. plan *Degrees:* A *CEO:* Pres. Eddie M. Smith
Enroll: 1185 (601) 635-2111

EAST MISSISSIPPI COMMUNITY COLLEGE
P.O. Box 158, Scooba 39358 *Type:* Public (county) junior *System:* Mississippi State Board for Community and Junior Colleges *Accred.:* 1949/1987 (SACS-CC) *Calendar:* Sem. plan *Degrees:* A *Prof. Accred.:* Mortuary Science *CEO:* Pres. Thomas L. Davis, Jr.
Enroll: 1439 (601) 476-8442

GEIGER'S SCHOOL OF COSMETOLOGY
600 N. 26th Ave., Hattiesburg 39401 *Type:* Private *Accred.:* 1991 (SACS-COEI) *Calendar:* Courses of varying lengths *Degrees:* certificates *CEO:* Dir. Howard Steed
Enroll: 56 (601) 583-2523

GULFPORT JOB CORPS CENTER
3300 20th St., Gulfport 39501 *Type:* Public (state) *Accred.:* 1985/1987 (SACS-COEI) *Calendar:* Courses of varying lengths *Degrees:* certificates *CEO:* Dir. Bobbie Nunn
Enroll: 350 (601) 864-9691

HINDS COMMUNITY COLLEGE
Raymond 39154-0999 *Type:* Public (county) junior *System:* Mississippi State Board for Community and Junior Colleges *Accred.:* 1928/1986 (SACS-CC) *Calendar:* Sem. plan *Degrees:* A *Prof. Accred.:* Dental Assisting, Medical Laboratory Technology (AMA), Medical Record Technology, Nursing (A), Respiratory Therapy, Respiratory Therapy Technology, Surgical Technology, Veterinary Technology (provisional) *CEO:* Pres. V. Clyde Muse
Enroll: 8445 (601) 857-5261

HOLMES COMMUNITY COLLEGE
P.O. Box 369, Goodman 39079 *Type:* Public (district) junior *System:* Mississippi State Board for Community and Junior Colleges *Accred.:* 1934/1985 (SACS-CC) *Calendar:* Sem. plan *Degrees:* A *CEO:* Pres. Starkey A. Morgan, Sr.
Enroll: 1585 (601) 472-2312

ITAWAMBA COMMUNITY COLLEGE
Hwy. 78, Fulton 38843-1099 *Type:* Public (district) junior *System:* Mississippi State Board for Community and Junior Colleges *Accred.:* 1955/1988 (SACS-CC) *Calendar:* Sem. plan *Degrees:* A *Prof. Accred.:* Nursing (A), Radiography, Respiratory Therapy, Respiratory Therapy Technology *CEO:* Pres. Winston O. Benjamin
Enroll: 6399 (601) 862-3101

JACKSON ACADEMY OF BEAUTY
2525 Robinson Rd., Jackson 39209 *Type:* Private *Accred.:* 1990 (SACS-COEI) *Calendar:* Courses of varying lengths *Degrees:* certificates *CEO:* Dir. John Pitts, Jr.
Enroll: 97 (601) 352-3003

JACKSON HAIR DESIGN COLLEGE
2845 Suncrest Dr., Jackson 39212-2529 *Type:* Private *Accred.:* 1980/1985 (CCA-ACTTS) *Calendar:* Courses of varying lengths *Degrees:* diplomas *CEO:* Owner/Dir. Clovis V. Martin, Jr.
(601) 372-7667

BRANCH CAMPUS
852 W. Capitol St., Jackson, MS 39203 *CEO:* Dir. Susan M. Martin
(601) 353-8122

JACKSON STATE UNIVERSITY
1400 J.R. Lynch St., Jackson 39217 *Type:* Public (state) liberal arts and teachers *System:* Mississippi Board of Trustees of State

Mississippi

Institutions of Higher Learning *Accred.:* 1948/1991 (SACS-CC) *Calendar:* Sem. plan *Degrees:* B, M, D *Prof. Accred.:* Art, Journalism, Music, Public Policy, Rehabilitation Counseling, Social Work (B), Teacher Education (e,s,p) *CEO:* Interim Pres. Herman B. Smith, Jr.
Enroll: 6838 (601) 968-2323

JONES COUNTY JUNIOR COLLEGE
Ellisville 39437 *Type:* Public (district) junior *System:* Mississippi State Board for Community and Junior Colleges *Accred.:* 1940/1987 (SACS-CC) *Calendar:* Sem. plan *Degrees:* A *Prof. Accred.:* EMT-Paramedic, Nursing (A) *CEO:* Pres. Terrell Tisdale
Enroll: 3853 (601) 477-4000

MAGNOLIA BIBLE COLLEGE
P.O. Box 1109, Kosciusko 39090 *Type:* Private (Churches of Christ) *Accred.:* 1989 (AABC); 1990 (SACS-CC) *Calendar:* Sem. plan *Degrees:* B *CEO:* Pres. Cecil May, Jr.
Enroll: 33 (601) 289-2896

MARY HOLMES COLLEGE
Hwy. 50 W., P.O. Drawer 1257, West Point 39773 *Type:* Private (United Presbyterian) 2-year *Accred.:* 1973/1989 (SACS-CC) *Calendar:* Sem. plan *Degrees:* A *CEO:* Pres. Sammie Potts
Enroll: 797 (601) 494-6820

MERIDIAN COMMUNITY COLLEGE
910 Hwy. 19 N., Meridian 39307 *Type:* Public (city) junior *System:* Mississippi State Board for Community and Junior Colleges *Accred.:* 1942/1991 (SACS-CC) *Calendar:* Sem. plan *Degrees:* A *Prof. Accred.:* Dental Hygiene, Medical Laboratory Technology (AMA), Medical Record Technology, Nursing (A), Practical Nursing, Radiography, Respiratory Therapy Technology *CEO:* Pres. William F. Scaggs
Enroll: 2204 (601) 483-8241

MILLSAPS COLLEGE
1701 N. State St., Jackson 39210 *Type:* Private (United Methodist) liberal arts *Accred.:* 1912/1982 (SACS-CC) *Calendar:* Sem. plan *Degrees:* B, M *Prof. Accred.:* Business (B,M) *CEO:* Pres. George M. Harmon
Enroll: 1440 (601) 974-1000

MISSISSIPPI COLLEGE
P.O. Box 4086, Clinton 39058 *Type:* Private (Southern Baptist) liberal arts *Accred.:* 1922/1982 (SACS-CC) *Calendar:* Sem. plan *Degrees:* B, P, M, D *Prof. Accred.:* Law (ABA only), Music, Nursing (B), Teacher Education (e,s,p) *CEO:* Pres. Lewis Nobles
Enroll: 3056 (601) 925-3000

MISSISSIPPI DELTA COMMUNITY COLLEGE
Hwy. 3, P.O. Box 668, Moorhead 38761 *Type:* Public (county) junior *System:* Mississippi State Board for Community and Junior Colleges *Accred.:* 1930/1987 (SACS-CC) *Calendar:* Sem. plan *Degrees:* A *Prof. Accred.:* Medical Laboratory Technology (AMA), Nursing (A), Radiography *CEO:* Interim Pres. Harmon W. Boggs
Enroll: 4808 (601) 246-5631

MISSISSIPPI GULF COAST COMMUNITY COLLEGE
P.O. Box 67, Perkinston 39573 *Type:* Public (district) *System:* Mississippi State Board for Community and Junior Colleges *Accred.:* 1929/1989 (SACS-CC) *Calendar:* Sem. plan *Degrees:* A *Prof. Accred.:* EMT-Paramedic, Medical Laboratory Technology (AMA), Nursing (A), Radiography, Respiratory Therapy Technology *CEO:* Pres. Barry L. Mellinger
Enroll: 11641 (601) 928-5211

MISSISSIPPI JOB CORPS CENTER
501 Harmony Rd., P.O. Box 817, Crystal Springs 39059 *Type:* Public (state) *Accred.:* 1984/1989 (SACS-COEI) *Calendar:* Courses of varying lengths *Degrees:* certificates *CEO:* Dir. Hugh Webb
Enroll: 440 (601) 892-3348

MISSISSIPPI STATE UNIVERSITY
Mississippi State 39762 *Type:* Public (state) *System:* Mississippi Board of Trustees of State Institutions of Higher Learning *Accred.:* 1926/1983 (SACS-CC) *Calendar:* Sem. plan *Degrees:* B, M, D *Prof. Accred.:*

Accounting (Type A,C), Architecture (B), Art, Business (B,M), Computer Science, Counseling, Engineering (aerospace, agricultural, bioengineering, chemical, civil, computer, electrical, industrial, mechanical, nuclear, petroleum), Forestry, Home Economics, Landscape Architecture (B), Public Policy and Administration, Rehabilitation Counseling, Teacher Education (e,s,p) *CEO:* Pres. Donald W. Zacharias
Enroll: 25329 (601) 325-2323

MISSISSIPPI UNIVERSITY FOR WOMEN
P.O. Box W-1602, College St., Columbus 39701 *Type:* Public liberal arts and teachers for women *System:* Mississippi Board of Trustees of State Institutions of Higher Learning *Accred.:* 1921/1983 (SACS-CC) *Calendar:* Sem. plan *Degrees:* A, B, M *Prof. Accred.:* Art, Home Economics, Music, Nursing (A,B,M), Teacher Education (e,s,p) *CEO:* Pres. Clyda S. Rent
Enroll: 1791 (601) 329-4750

MISSISSIPPI VALLEY STATE UNIVERSITY
Hwy. 82 and Sunflower Rd., Itta Bena 38941 *Type:* Public (state) teachers *System:* Mississippi Board of Trustees of State Institutions of Higher Learning *Accred.:* 1968/1982 (SACS-CC) *Calendar:* Sem. plan *Degrees:* B, M *Prof. Accred.:* Art, Social Work (B), Teacher Education (e) *CEO:* Pres. William W. Sutton
Enroll: 1825 (601) 254-9041

MOORE CAREER COLLEGE
2460 Terry Rd., Jackson 39204 *Type:* Private *Accred.:* 1990 (CCA-ACICS); 1985/1990 (SACS-COEI) *Calendar:* Courses of varying lengths *Degrees:* certificates, diplomas *CEO:* Dir. Helen Pinkerton
Enroll: 685 (601) 932-8755

BRANCH CAMPUS
1500 N. 31st St., Hattiesburg, MS 39401 *CEO:* Dir. Linda Foley
(601) 583-4100

BRANCH CAMPUS
1500 Hwy. 19 N., Meridian, MS 39307 *CEO:* Dir. Mac LeBlanc
(601) 693-2900

BRANCH CAMPUS
880 Cliff Gookin Blvd., Tupelo, MS 38801 *CEO:* Dir. Joanna Schaffner
(601) 842-7600

NORTHEAST MISSISSIPPI COMMUNITY COLLEGE
Cunningham Blvd., Booneville 38829 *Type:* Public (district) junior *System:* Mississippi State Board for Community and Junior Colleges *Accred.:* 1956/1991 (SACS-CC) *Calendar:* Sem. plan *Degrees:* A *Prof. Accred.:* Dental Hygiene, Medical Assisting (AMA), Medical Laboratory Technology (AMA), Nursing (A), Respiratory Therapy Technology *CEO:* Pres. Joe M. Childers
Enroll: 2705 (601) 728-7751

NORTHWEST MISSISSIPPI COMMUNITY COLLEGE
510 N. Panola, Senatobia 38668 *Type:* Public (district) junior *System:* Mississippi State Board for Community and Junior Colleges *Accred.:* 1953/1988 (SACS-CC) *Calendar:* Sem. plan *Degrees:* A *Prof. Accred.:* Mortuary Science, Nursing (A), Respiratory Therapy *CEO:* Pres. David M. Haraway
Enroll: 4252 (601) 562-3200

PEARL RIVER COMMUNITY COLLEGE
Hwy. 11 S., Sta. A, Poplarville 39470 *Type:* Public (county) junior *System:* Mississippi State Board for Community and Junior Colleges *Accred.:* 1929/1985 (SACS-CC) *Calendar:* Sem. plan *Degrees:* A *Prof. Accred.:* Nursing (A), Respiratory Therapy Technology *CEO:* Pres. Ted J. Alexander
Enroll: 3157 (601) 795-6801

PHILLIPS JUNIOR COLLEGE
2680 Insurance Center Dr., Jackson 39216 *Type:* Private junior *Accred.:* 1975/1987 (CCA-ACICS); 1987 (SACS-CC) *Calendar:* Qtr. plan *Degrees:* A, certificates, diplomas *CEO:* Pres. Nan Thompson
Enroll: 1119 (601) 362-6341

Mississippi

PHILLIPS JUNIOR COLLEGE OF THE MISSISSIPPI GULF COAST
942 Beach Dr., Gulfport 39507 *Type:* Private junior *Accred.:* 1970/1987 (CCA-ACICS); 1987 (SACS-CC) *Calendar:* Qtr. plan *Degrees:* A, certificates, diplomas *CEO:* Pres. Harold R. Stones
Enroll: 950   (601) 896-6465

REFORMED THEOLOGICAL SEMINARY
5422 Clinton Blvd., Jackson 39209 *Type:* Private (interdenominational) professional; graduate only *Accred.:* 1977/1982 (ATS); 1977/1991 (SACS-CC) *Calendar:* 4-1-4 plan *Degrees:* P, M, D *CEO:* Pres. Luder G. Whitlock, Jr.
Enroll: 545   (601) 922-4988

RUST COLLEGE
150 E. Rust Ave., Holly Springs 38635-2328 *Type:* Private (United Methodist) liberal arts *Accred.:* 1970/1984 (SACS-CC) *Calendar:* Sem. plan *Degrees:* A, B *CEO:* Pres. W.A. McMillan
Enroll: 1021   (601) 252-4661

SOUTHEASTERN BAPTIST COLLEGE
P.O. Box 8276, Laurel 39440 *Type:* Private (Baptist Missionary Association) *Accred.:* 1988 (AABC) *Calendar:* Sem. plan *Degrees:* A, B, certificates, diplomas *CEO:* Pres. Gerald Kellar
Enroll: 53   (601) 426-6346

SOUTHERN DRIVER'S ACADEMY
1105 E. McDowell Rd., P.O. Box 8748, Jackson 39284-8748 *Type:* Private *Accred.:* 1990 (SACS-COEI) *Calendar:* Courses of varying lengths *Degrees:* certificates, diplomas *CEO:* Dir. Johnnie Twiner
Enroll: 31   (601) 371-1371

SOUTHERN TECHNICAL COLLEGE
2305 Lakeland Dr., Jackson 39208 *Type:* Private *Accred.:* 1981/1991 (SACS-COEI) *Calendar:* Courses of varying lengths *Degrees:* certificates *CEO:* Dir. Roy de Roza
Enroll: 212   (601) 366-9700

SOUTHWEST MISSISSIPPI COMMUNITY COLLEGE
College Dr., Summit 39666 *Type:* Public (district) junior *System:* Mississippi State Board for Community and Junior Colleges *Accred.:* 1958/1990 (SACS-CC) *Calendar:* Sem. plan *Degrees:* A *Prof. Accred.:* Nursing (A) *CEO:* Pres. Horace C. Holmes
Enroll: 1330   (601) 276-2000

TOUGALOO COLLEGE
500 E. County Line Rd., Tougaloo 39174 *Type:* Private liberal arts *Accred.:* 1953/1990 (SACS-CC) *Calendar:* Sem. plan *Degrees:* A, B *CEO:* Pres. Adib A. Shakir
Enroll: 985   (601) 977-7700

UNITED STATES NAVAL CONSTRUCTION TRAINING CENTER
Bldg. 343, Gulfport 39501 *Type:* Public (federal) technical *Accred.:* 1975/1990 (SACS-COEI) *Calendar:* Courses of varying lengths *Degrees:* certificates *CEO:* Commandant J.D. Hill
Enroll: 807   (601) 865-2531

UNITED STATES NAVAL TECHNICAL TRAINING CENTER
Naval Air Sta., Meridian 39309-5200 *Type:* Public (federal) technical *Accred.:* 1976/1991 (SACS-COEI) *Calendar:* Courses of varying lengths *Degrees:* certificates *CEO:* Commandant Lois Allen
Enroll: 1371   (601) 679-2724

UNIVERSITY OF MISSISSIPPI
University 38677 *Type:* Public (state) *System:* Mississippi Board of Trustees of State Institutions of Higher Learning *Accred.:* 1895/1989 (SACS-CC) *Calendar:* Sem. plan *Degrees:* B,P,M,D *Prof. Accred.:* Accounting (Type A,C), Art, Audiology, Business (B,M), Clinical Psychology, Computer Science, Engineering (chemical, civil, electrical, geological/geophysical, mechanical), Home Economics, Journalism, Law, Music, Nursing (B,M), Pharmacy, Physical Therapy, Psychology Internship, Public Administration, Social Work (B), Speech-Language

Pathology, Teacher Education (e,s,p) *CEO:* Chanc. R. Gerald Turner
Enroll: 10749　　　　　　(601) 232-7211

UNIVERSITY OF MISSISSIPPI MEDICAL CENTER
2500 N. State St., Jackson 39216-4505 *Type:* Public (state) *System:* Mississippi Board of Trustees of State Institutions of Higher Learning *Accred.:* 1991 (SACS-CC) *Calendar:* Qtr. plan *Degrees:* A, B, P, M *Prof. Accred.:* Cytotechnology, Dental Hygiene, Dentistry, EMT-Paramedic, General Dentistry (prelim. provisional), General Practice Residency, Medical Record Administration, Medical Technology, Medicine, Nuclear Medicine Technology, Occupational Therapy, Radiation Therapy Technology, Radiography, Respiratory Therapy, Respiratory Therapy Technology *CEO:* Vice Chanc. Norman Crooks Nelson, M.D.
Enroll: 1404　　　　　　(601) 984-1010

THE UNIVERSITY OF SOUTHERN MISSISSIPPI
Southern Sta., Box 5001, Hattiesburg 39406 *Type:* Public (state) *System:* Mississippi Board of Trustees of State Institutions of Higher Learning *Accred.:* 1929/1985 (SACS-CC) *Calendar:* Sem. plan *Degrees:* B, M, D *Prof. Accred.:* Art, Audiology, Business (B,M), Clinical Psychology, Computer Science, Counseling, Counseling Psychology, Dance, Dietetics (coordinated), Engineering Technology (architectural, civil/construction, computer, electrical, industrial, mechanical), Home Economics, Interior Design, Journalism, Librarianship, Medical Technology, Music, Nursing (B,M), Recreation, School Psychology, Social Work (B-candidate,M), Speech-Language Pathology, Teacher Education (e,s,p), Theatre *CEO:* Pres. Aubrey K. Lucas
Enroll: 13352　　　　　　(601) 266-5001

GULF PARK CAMPUS
E. Beach Blvd., Long Beach, MS 39560 *Prof. Accred.:* Engineering Technology (electrical) *CEO:* Dean Joseph Holloway
　　　　　　(601) 865-4500

WESLEY BIBLICAL SEMINARY
P.O. Box 9938, Jackson 39206 *Type:* Private (interdenominational) professional; graduate only *Accred.:* 1991 (ATS) *Calendar:* Sem. plan *Degrees:* P, M *CEO:* Pres. Harold Spann
Enroll: 34　　　　　　(601) 957-1314

WESLEY COLLEGE
P.O. Box 70, Florence 39073 *Type:* Private (Methodist) *Accred.:* 1979/1989 (AABC) *Calendar:* Sem. plan *Degrees:* B, certificates *CEO:* Pres. David Coker
Enroll: 54　　　　　　(601) 845-2265

WILLIAM CAREY COLLEGE
Tuscan Ave., Hattiesburg 39401 *Type:* Private (Southern Baptist) liberal arts *Accred.:* 1958/1990 (SACS-CC) *Calendar:* Sem. plan *Degrees:* B, M *Prof. Accred.:* Medical Technology, Music, Nursing (B) *CEO:* Pres. James W. Edwards
Enroll: 1300　　　　　　(601) 582-5051

WOOD JUNIOR COLLEGE
Wood College Rd., Mathiston 39752 *Type:* Private (United Methodist) junior *Accred.:* 1956/1990 (SACS-CC) *Calendar:* Sem. plan *Degrees:* A *CEO:* Pres. Doyce W. Gunter
Enroll: 411　　　　　　(601) 263-8128

MISSOURI

AERO MECHANICS SCHOOL
836 Richards Rd., Kansas City 64116-4237 *Type:* Private *Accred.:* 1991 (CCA-ACTTS) *Calendar:* Courses of varying lengths *Degrees:* certificates *CEO:* Dir. David E. Hochstein
(816) 221-7822

AL-MED ACADEMY
10963 St. Charles Rock Rd., St. Louis 63074 *Type:* Private *Calendar:* Courses of varying lengths *Degrees:* diplomas *Prof. Accred.:* Health Education, Medical Assisting *CEO:* Pres. Larkin Hicks
(314) 739-4450

AQUINAS INSTITUTE OF THEOLOGY
3642 Lindell Blvd., St. Louis 63108-3396 *Type:* Private (Roman Catholic) professional; graduate only *Accred.:* 1968/1986 (ATS); 1964/1986 (NCA) *Calendar:* 4-1-4 plan *Degrees:* P, M, D *CEO:* Pres. Charles E. Bouchard, O.P.
Enroll: 67 (314) 658-3882

ASSEMBLIES OF GOD THEOLOGICAL SEMINARY
1445 Boonville Ave., Springfield 65802 *Type:* Private (Assemblies of God) professional; graduate only *Accred.:* 1989 (ATS candidate); 1978/1988 (NCA) *Calendar:* 4-4-1-1 plan *Degrees:* P, M, D *CEO:* Pres. Delbert Tarr
Enroll: 238 (417) 862-3344

AVILA COLLEGE
11901 Wornall Rd., Kansas City 64145 *Type:* Private (Roman Catholic) liberal arts *Accred.:* 1946/1988 (NCA) *Calendar:* Sem. plan *Degrees:* A, B, M, certificates, diplomas *Prof. Accred.:* Medical Technology, Nursing (B), Radiography, Social Work (B) *CEO:* Pres. Larry Kramer
Enroll: 873 (816) 942-8400

BAPTIST BIBLE COLLEGE
628 E. Kearney St., Springfield 65803 *Type:* Private (Baptist Bible Fellowship) *Accred.:* 1978/1988 (AABC) *Calendar:* Sem. plan *Degrees:* A, B, M, certificates *CEO:* Pres. Leland R. Kennedy
Enroll: 819 (417) 869-6000

BASIC INSTITUTE OF TECHNOLOGY
4455 Chippewa Ave., St. Louis 63116-9990 *Type:* Private *Accred.:* 1974/1989 (CCA-ACTTS) *Calendar:* Qtr. plan *Degrees:* A, diplomas *CEO:* Dir. J.A. Zoeller
Enroll: 445 (314) 771-1200

BEREAN COLLEGE
1445 Boonville Ave., Springfield 65802 *Type:* Private home study *Accred.:* 1985 (NHSC) *Calendar:* Courses of varying lengths *Degrees:* certificates *CEO:* Pres. Zenas J. Bicket
(417) 862-2781

BRYAN INSTITUTE
12184 Natural Bridge Rd., Bridgeton 63044-2078 *Type:* Private *Accred.:* 1979/1989 (CCA-ACTTS) *Calendar:* Sem. plan *Degrees:* diplomas *Prof. Accred.:* Health Education *CEO:* Dir. John A. Howell
Enroll: 326 (314) 291-0241

BRYAN TRAVEL COLLEGE
500 W. University St., Ste. B, Springfield 65807 *Type:* Private *Accred.:* 1991 (CCA-ACICS) *Calendar:* Courses of varying lengths *Degrees:* certificates, diplomas *CEO:* Dir. Debra Lee
(417) 862-5700

CDI CAREER DEVELOPMENT INSTITUTE
9666 Olive Blvd., Ste. 700, St. Louis 63132-3020 *Type:* Private *Accred.:* 1971/1987 (CCA-ACTTS) *Calendar:* Courses of varying lengths *Degrees:* certificates *CEO:* Dir. Varghese Samuel
Enroll: 797 (314) 432-4400

CALVARY BIBLE COLLEGE
15800 Calvary Rd., Kansas City 64147-1341 *Type:* Private (Fundamentalist Churches of America) professional *Accred.:* 1961/1989

(AABC) *Calendar:* 4-1-4 plan *Degrees:* A, B, M, certificates *CEO:* Pres. Donald Urey
Enroll: 234 (816) 322-0110

CAPE GIRARDEAU AREA VOCATIONAL-TECHNICAL SCHOOL
301 N. Clark St., Cape Girardeau 63701 *Type:* Private *Calendar:* Courses of varying lengths *Degrees:* certificates *Prof. Accred.:* Respiratory Therapy Technology *CEO:* Dir. Gary K. Gilbert
(314) 334-3358

CENTRAL BIBLE COLLEGE
3000 N. Grant Ave., Springfield 65803 *Type:* Private (Assemblies of God) *Accred.:* 1948/1985 (AABC) *Calendar:* Sem. plan *Degrees:* A, B, certificates, diplomas *CEO:* Pres. H. Maurice Lednicky
Enroll: 1006 (417) 833-2551

CENTRAL CHRISTIAN COLLEGE OF THE BIBLE
911 Urbandale Dr., E., Moberly 65270 *Type:* Private (Christian Church/Church of Christ) *Accred.:* 1982/1987 (AABC) *Calendar:* Sem. plan *Degrees:* A, B *CEO:* Pres. Lloyd M. Pelfrey
Enroll: 67 (816) 263-3900

CENTRAL METHODIST COLLEGE
411 Central Methodist Sq., Fayette 65248 *Type:* Private (United Methodist) liberal arts *Accred.:* 1913/1981 (NCA) *Calendar:* 4-1-4 plan *Degrees:* A, B *Prof. Accred.:* Music *CEO:* Pres. Joe A. Howell
Enroll: 802 (816) 248-3391

CENTRAL MISSOURI STATE UNIVERSITY
Warrensburg 64093 *Type:* Public liberal arts and teachers *System:* Missouri Coordinating Board for Higher Education *Accred.:* 1915/1984 (NCA) *Calendar:* Qtr. plan *Degrees:* A, B, P, M, certificates, diplomas *Prof. Accred.:* Art, Audiology, Home Economics, Music, Nursing (B), Social Work (B), Speech-Language Pathology, Teacher Education (e,s,p) *CEO:* Pres. Ed M. Elliott
Enroll: 9575 (816) 429-4112

CLEVELAND CHIROPRACTIC COLLEGE
6401 Rockhill Rd., Kansas City 64131 *Type:* Public professional *Accred.:* 1984/1989 (NCA) *Calendar:* Tri. plan *Degrees:* D *Prof. Accred.:* Chiropractic Education *CEO:* Pres. Carl S. Cleveland, III
Enroll: 297 (816) 333-8230

COLLEGE OF THE OZARKS
Point Lookout 65726 *Type:* Private (Presbyterian) liberal arts *Accred.:* 1961/1981 (NCA) *Calendar:* Tri. plan *Degrees:* A, B *Prof. Accred.:* Music, Teacher Education (e,s) *CEO:* Pres. Jerry C. Davis
Enroll: 1456 (417) 334-6411

COLUMBIA COLLEGE
1001 Rogers St., Columbia 65216 *Type:* Private (Disciples of Christ) *Accred.:* 1918/1987 (NCA) *Calendar:* Sem. plan *Degrees:* A, B *Prof. Accred.:* Social Work (B-candidate) *CEO:* Pres. Donald B. Ruthenberg
Enroll: 2784 (314) 875-7200

CONCORDE CAREER INSTITUTE
3239 Broadway, Kansas City 64111-2407 *Type:* Private *Accred.:* 1990 (CCA-ACTTS) *Calendar:* Qtr. plan *Degrees:* diplomas *CEO:* Admin. Dir. John Clark
Enroll: 802 (816) 531-5223

CONCEPTION SEMINARY COLLEGE
Conception 64433 *Type:* Private (Roman Catholic) *Accred.:* 1960/1984 (NCA) *Calendar:* Sem. plan *Degrees:* B, certificates, diplomas *CEO:* Pres./Rector Gregory J. Polan
Enroll: 90 (816) 944-2218

CONCORDIA SEMINARY
801 De Mun Ave., St. Louis 63105 *Type:* Private (Lutheran-Missouri Synod) professional; graduate only *Accred.:* 1963/1983 (ATS); 1978/1984 (NCA) *Calendar:* Qtr. plan *Degrees:* P, M, D, certificates, diplomas *CEO:* Pres. John F. Johnson
Enroll: 481 (314) 721-5934

COTTEY COLLEGE
1000 West Austin St., Nevada 64772 *Type:* Private junior for women *Accred.:* 1918/

1983 (NCA) *Calendar:* Sem. plan *Degrees:* A *Prof. Accred.:* Music *CEO:* Pres. Helen R. Washburn
Enroll: 349 (417) 667-8181

COVENANT THEOLOGICAL SEMINARY
12330 Conway Rd., St. Louis 63141 *Type:* Private (Presbyterian) professional *Accred.:* 1988 (ATS); 1973/1988 (NCA) *Calendar:* Sem. plan *Degrees:* P, M, D *CEO:* Pres. Paul D. Kooistra
Enroll: 169 (314) 434-4044

CROWDER COLLEGE
Neosho 64850 *Type:* Public (district) junior *System:* Missouri Coordinating Board for Higher Education *Accred.:* 1977/1982 (NCA) *Calendar:* Sem. plan *Degrees:* A, certificates, diplomas *CEO:* Pres. Kent Farnsworth
Enroll: 1092 (417) 451-3223

CULVER-STOCKTON COLLEGE
Canton 63435 *Type:* Private (Disciples of Christ) liberal arts *Accred.:* 1924/1981 (NCA) *Calendar:* Sem. plan *Degrees:* A, B, certificates, diplomas *CEO:* Pres. Walter S. Reuling
Enroll: 1039 (314) 288-5221

DEACONESS COLLEGE OF NURSING
6150 Oakland Ave., St. Louis 63139 *Type:* Private professional *Accred.:* 1985/1990 (NCA) *Calendar:* Sem. plan *Degrees:* B, certificates, diplomas *CEO:* C.E.O./Provost Patricia A. Afshar
Enroll: 204 (314) 768-3040

DEVRY INSTITUTE OF TECHNOLOGY, KANSAS CITY
11224 Holmes Rd., Kansas City 64131 *Type:* Private *Accred.:* 1981/1987 (NCA) *Calendar:* Tri. plan *Degrees:* A, B, certificates *Prof. Accred.:* Engineering Technology (electrical) *CEO:* Pres. C. Robert Levalley
Enroll: 2805 (816) 941-0430

DIAMOND COUNCIL OF AMERICA
9140 Ward Pkwy., Kansas City 64114 *Type:* Private home study *Accred.:* 1984/1988 (NHSC) *Calendar:* Courses of varying lengths *Degrees:* certificates *CEO:* Exec. Dir. Jerry Fogel
(816) 444-3500

DICK HILL INTERNATIONAL FLIGHT SCHOOL
P.O. Box 10603, Springfield 65808-0603 *Type:* Private *Accred.:* 1988 (CCA-ACTTS) *Calendar:* Courses of varying lengths *Degrees:* certificates *CEO:* Dir. Marlene J. Hill
(417) 485-3474

DICKINSON BUSINESS SCHOOL
3822 Summit St., Kansas City 64111 *Type:* Private business *Accred.:* 1982(CCA-ACICS) *Calendar:* Qtr. plan *Degrees:* A, certificates, diplomas *CEO:* Dir. Fonda Hendrix
Enroll: 686 (816) 931-7600

DRAUGHON BUSINESS COLLEGE
P.O. Box 519, Joplin 64802 *Type:* Private business *Accred.:* 1988 (CCA-ACICS) *Calendar:* Courses of varying lengths *Degrees:* certificates *CEO:* Dir. Wilson Wood
Enroll: 478 (417) 642-3266

DRURY COLLEGE
900 N. Benton Ave., Springfield 65802 *Type:* Private (United Church of Christ) liberal arts *Accred.:* 1915/1991 (NCA) *Calendar:* Sem. plan *Degrees:* A, B, M *Prof. Accred.:* Art (B-candidate), Teacher Education (e,s) *CEO:* Pres. John E. Moore, Jr.
Enroll: 2397 (417) 865-8731

EAST CENTRAL COLLEGE
P.O. Box 529, Union 63084 *Type:* Public (district) junior *System:* Missouri Coordinating Board for Higher Education *Accred.:* 1976/1990 (NCA) *Calendar:* Sem. plan *Degrees:* A, certificates, diplomas *Prof. Accred.:* Dental Assisting *CEO:* Pres. Dale L. Gibson
Enroll: 1768 (314) 583-5193

EASTERN JACKSON COUNTY COLLEGE OF ALLIED HEALTH
808 S. 15th St., Blue Springs 64015 *Type:* Private *Calendar:* Courses of varying lengths *Degrees:* certificates *Prof. Accred.:*

Health Education *CEO:* Pres./Dir. Kathryn L. Harmon
(816) 229-4720

EDEN THEOLOGICAL SEMINARY
475 E. Lockwood Ave., St. Louis 63119 *Type:* Private (United Church of Christ) professional; graduate only *Accred.:* 1938/1988 (ATS); 1973/1989 (NCA) *Calendar:* 4-1-4 plan *Degrees:* P, M, D, certificates, diplomas *CEO:* Pres. Eugene S. Wehrli
Enroll: 127 (314) 961-3627

ELECTRONICS INSTITUTE
15329 Kensington Ave., Kansas City 64147-1212 *Type:* Private *Accred.:* 1971/1987 (CCA-ACTTS) *Calendar:* Qtr. plan *Degrees:* certificates *CEO:* Pres. Larry Fajen
Enroll: 604 (816) 331-5700

EVANGEL COLLEGE
1111 N. Glenstone Ave., Springfield 65802 *Type:* Private (Assemblies of God) liberal arts *Accred.:* 1965/1988 (NCA) *Calendar:* Sem. plan *Degrees:* A, B, certificates, diplomas *Prof. Accred.:* Music, Teacher Education (e,s) *CEO:* Pres. Robert H. Spence
Enroll: 1484 (417) 865-2811

FLORISSANT UPHOLSTERY SCHOOL
1420 N. Vandeventer St., St. Louis 63113-3416 *Type:* Private *Accred.:* 1988 (CCA-ACTTS) *Calendar:* Courses of varying lengths *Degrees:* certificates *CEO:* Dir. Charles S. Davis
(314) 534-1886

FONTBONNE COLLEGE
6800 Wydown Blvd., St. Louis 63105 *Type:* Private (Roman Catholic) liberal arts *Accred.:* 1926/1985 (NCA) *Calendar:* Sem. plan *Degrees:* B, M *Prof. Accred.:* Home Economics, Teacher Education (e,s) *CEO:* Pres. Meneve Dunham
Enroll: 776 (314) 889-1419

HANNIBAL AREA VOCATIONAL-TECHNICAL SCHOOL
4500 McMasters Ave., Hannibal 63401 *Type:* Private *Calendar:* Courses of varying lengths *Degrees:* certificates *Prof. Accred.:*

Respiratory Therapy Technology *CEO:* Dir. Harold D. Ward
(314) 221-4430

HANNIBAL-LAGRANGE COLLEGE
2800 Palmyra Rd., Hannibal 63401 *Type:* Private (Southern Baptist) liberal arts *Accred.:* 1958/1988 (NCA) *Calendar:* Sem. plan *Degrees:* A, B, certificates, diplomas *Prof. Accred.:* Nursing (A) *CEO:* Pres. Paul Brown
Enroll: 702 (314) 221-3675

HARRIS-STOWE STATE COLLEGE
3026 Laclede Ave., St. Louis 63103 *Type:* Public (state) teachers *System:* Missouri Coordinating Board for Higher Education *Accred.:* 1924/1991 (NCA) *Calendar:* Sem. plan *Degrees:* B *Prof. Accred.:* Teacher Education (e) *CEO:* Pres. Henry Givens, Jr.
Enroll: 901 (314) 533-3366

HEART OF THE OZARKS COMMUNITY TECHNICAL COLLEGE
P.O. Box 3757GS, Springfield 65808 *Type:* Private *Calendar:* Courses of varying lengths *Degrees:* certificates *Prof. Accred.:* Dental Assisting *CEO:* Pres. Norman K. Myers
(417) 863-0333

THE HICKEY SCHOOL
6710 Clayton Rd., St. Louis 63117 *Type:* Private business *Accred.:* 1968/1984 (CCA-ACICS) *Calendar:* Courses of varying lengths *Degrees:* A, certificates, diplomas *Prof. Accred.:* Medical Assisting (AMA) *CEO:* Pres. Steven M. Kinzer
Enroll: 491 (314) 644-2866

ITT TECHNICAL INSTITUTE
13505 Lakefront Dr., St. Louis 63045-1416 *Type:* Private *Accred.:* 1965/1988 (CCA-ACTTS) *Calendar:* Courses of varying lengths *Degrees:* certificates, diplomas *CEO:* Dir. L.D. Cunningham
(314) 298-7800

INTERNATIONAL HAIR INSTITUTE
415 S. Florissant Rd., Ferguson 63135-2715 *Type:* Private *Accred.:* 1984/1989 (CCA-

ACTTS) *Calendar:* Courses of varying lengths *Degrees:* diplomas *CEO:* Dir. Lawrence H. Coleman
Enroll: 29 (314) 524-3460

JEFFERSON COLLEGE
P.O. Box 1000, Hillsboro 63050-1000 *Type:* Public (district) junior *System:* Missouri Coordinating Board for Higher Education *Accred.:* 1969/1989 (NCA) *Calendar:* Sem. plan *Degrees:* A, certificates, diplomas *Prof. Accred.:* Animal Health Technology (probational) *CEO:* Pres. Gery C. Hochanadel
Enroll: 3286 (314) 789-3951

KANSAS CITY ART INSTITUTE
4415 Warwick Blvd., Kansas City 64111 *Type:* Private professional *Accred.:* 1964/1991 (NCA) *Calendar:* Sem. plan *Degrees:* B *Prof. Accred.:* Art *CEO:* Pres. Beatrice Rivas Sanchez
Enroll: 568 (816) 561-4852

KANSAS CITY BUSINESS COLLEGE
7910 Troost St., Kansas City 64131 *Type:* Private junior *Accred.:* 1964/1985 (CCA-ACICS) *Calendar:* Qtr. plan *Degrees:* A, certificates, diplomas *CEO:* Dir. Waunda M. Thomas
Enroll: 536 (816) 361-5444

KEMPER MILITARY SCHOOL AND COLLEGE
701 Third St., Boonville 65233 *Type:* Private junior for men *Accred.:* 1927/1986 (NCA) *Calendar:* Sem. plan *Degrees:* A *CEO:* Pres. Roger D. Harms
Enroll: 179 (816) 882-5623

KENRICK-GLENNON SEMINARY
5200 Glennon Dr., St. Louis 63119 *Type:* Private (Roman Catholic) professional; graduate only *Accred.:* 1973/1989 (ATS); 1973/1989 (NCA) *Calendar:* Sem. plan *Degrees:* P, M *CEO:* Pres./Rector Ronald Ramson, C.M.
Enroll: 70 (314) 644-0266

KIRKSVILLE COLLEGE OF OSTEOPATHIC MEDICINE
800 W. Jefferson Ave., Kirksville 63501 *Type:* Private professional *Calendar:* Qtr. plan *Degrees:* P *Prof. Accred.:* Osteopathy *CEO:* Pres. Fred C. Tinning, Ph.D.
Enroll: 531 (816) 626-2354

LINCOLN UNIVERSITY
820 Chestnut St., Jefferson City 65102-0029 *Type:* Public (state) liberal arts and professional *System:* Missouri Coordinating Board for Higher Education *Accred.:* 1926/1989 (NCA) *Calendar:* Sem. plan *Degrees:* A, B, M *Prof. Accred.:* Music, Nursing(A), Teacher Education (e,s,p) *CEO:* Pres. Wendell G. Rayburn
Enroll: 2392 (314) 681-5042

LINDENWOOD COLLEGE
209 S. Kingshighway Blvd., St. Charles 63301 *Type:* Private (United Presbyterian) liberal arts *Accred.:* 1918/1984 (NCA) *Calendar:* 4-1-4 plan *Degrees:* A, B, M *Prof. Accred.:* Teacher Education (e,s) *CEO:* Pres. Dennis C. Spellmann
Enroll: 1833 (314) 949-2000

LOGAN COLLEGE OF CHIROPRACTIC
1851 Schoettler Rd., P.O. Box 1065, Chesterfield 63006-1065 *Type:* Private professional *Accred.:* 1987 (NCA) *Calendar:* Sem. plan *Degrees:* B, D *Prof. Accred.:* Chiropractic Education *CEO:* Pres. Beatrice B. Hagen
Enroll: 679 (314) 227-2100

LONGVIEW COMMUNITY COLLEGE
500 Longview Rd., Lee's Summit 64063 *Type:* Public (district) junior *System:* Metropolitan Community College District *Accred.:* 1986 (NCA) *Calendar:* Sem. plan *Degrees:* A *CEO:* Pres. Aldo Leker
(816) 763-7777

MALLINCKRODT INSTITUTE OF RADIOLOGY
510 S. Kingshighway Blvd., St. Louis 63110 *Type:* Private *Calendar:* Courses of varying lengths *Degrees:* certificates *Prof. Accred.:* Radiation Therapy Technology, Radiography *CEO:* Dir. Ronald G. Evens, M.D.
(314) 362-7100

Accredited Institutions **Missouri**

MAPLE WOODS COMMUNITY COLLEGE
2601 N.E. Barny Rd., Kansas City 64156-1299 *Type:* Public (district) junior *System:* Metropolitan Community College District *Accred.:* 1986 (NCA) *Calendar:* Sem. plan *Degrees:* A *Prof. Accred.:* Veterinary Technology *CEO:* Pres. Stephen R. Brainard
(816) 436-6500

MARYVILLE UNIVERSITY OF ST. LOUIS
13550 Conway Rd., St. Louis 63141 *Type:* Private liberal arts *Accred.:* 1941/1985 (NCA) *Calendar:* 4-4-1 plan *Degrees:* A, B, M, certificates, diplomas *Prof. Accred.:* Interior Design, Nursing (B), Physical Therapy, Teacher Education (e,s) *CEO:* Pres. Claudius Pritchard
Enroll: 1940 (314) 576-9330

METRO BUSINESS COLLEGE
1732 N. Kingshighway Blvd., Cape Girardeau 63701 *Type:* Private *Accred.:* 1979/1981 (CCA-ACICS) *Calendar:* Courses of varying lengths *Degrees:* certificates, diplomas *CEO:* Dir. Mary Emmenderfer
Enroll: 317 (314) 334-9181

BRANCH CAMPUS
1407 Southwest Blvd., Jefferson City, MO 65109 *CEO:* Dir. Charles DeSha
(314) 635-6600

BRANCH CAMPUS
2233 Washington St., St. Louis, MO 63103 *CEO:* Dir. Doug Brinker
(314) 436-4400

METRO BUSINESS COLLEGE
2305 N. Bishop Ave., Hwy. 63 N., Rolla 65401 *Type:* Private business *Accred.:* 1985/1990 (CCA-ACICS) *Calendar:* Courses of varying lengths *Degrees:* certificates, diplomas *CEO:* Pres. Raymond Buchli
Enroll: 225 (314) 364-8464

MIDWEST INSTITUTE OF MEDICAL ASSISTANTS
112 W. Jefferson St., Ste. 120, Kirkwood 63122 *Type:* Private *Calendar:* Courses of varying lengths *Degrees:* diplomas *Prof. Accred.:* Health Education *CEO:* Dir. Elizabeth Shreffler
(314) 965-8363

MIDWESTERN BAPTIST THEOLOGICAL SEMINARY
5001 N. Oak St. Trafficway, Kansas City 64118 *Type:* Private (Southern Baptist) professional; graduate only *Accred.:* 1964/1981 (ATS); 1971/1981 (NCA) *Calendar:* Sem. plan *Degrees:* A, P, M, D *CEO:* Pres. Milton U. Ferguson
Enroll: 376 (816) 453-4600

MINERAL AREA COLLEGE
Flat River 63601 *Type:* Public (district) junior *System:* Missouri Coordinating Board for Higher Education *Accred.:* 1971/1988 (NCA) *Calendar:* Sem. plan *Degrees:* A, certificates, diplomas *Prof. Accred.:* Dental Assisting *CEO:* Pres. Dixie A. Kohn
Enroll: 1701 (314) 431-4593

MISSOURI BAPTIST COLLEGE
12542 Conway Rd., St. Louis 63141 *Type:* Private (Southern Baptist) liberal arts *Accred.:* 1978/1990 (NCA) *Calendar:* Sem. plan *Degrees:* A, B, certificates, diplomas *CEO:* Interim Pres. Thomas Field
Enroll: 658 (314) 434-1115

MISSOURI SCHOOL FOR DOCTORS' ASSISTANTS
10121 Manchester Rd., St. Louis 63122-1583 *Type:* Private *Accred.:* 1970/1988 (CCA-ACTTS) *Calendar:* Courses of varying lengths *Degrees:* certificates, diplomas *Prof. Accred.:* Medical Assisting *CEO:* Dir. Susan Day
Enroll: 346 (314) 821-7700

MISSOURI SCHOOL OF BARBERING AND HAIRSTYLING
3740 Noland Rd., Independence 64055-3343 *Type:* Private *Accred.:* 1987 (CCA-ACTTS) *Calendar:* Courses of varying lengths *Degrees:* diplomas *CEO:* Dir. Lana Jones
(816) 836-4118

MISSOURI SOUTHERN STATE COLLEGE
3950 Newman Rd., Joplin 64801 *Type:* Public liberal arts and teachers *System:* Missouri Coordinating Board for Higher Education

Missouri

Accred.: 1949/1988 (NCA) *Calendar:* Sem. plan *Degrees:* A,B*Prof. Accred.:* Dental Hygiene, Nursing (A,B), Radiography, Teacher Education (e,s) *CEO:* Pres. Julio S. Leon
Enroll: 4341 (417) 624-8181

MISSOURI TECHNICAL SCHOOL
1167 Corporate Lake Dr., St. Louis 63132-2907 *Type:* Private *Accred.:* 1985 (CCA-ACTTS) *Calendar:* Courses of varying lengths *Degrees:* diplomas *CEO:* Dir. Paul Dodge
Enroll: 165 (314) 569-3600

MISSOURI VALLEY COLLEGE
500 E. College Dr., Marshall 65340 *Type:* Private (Presbyterian) liberal arts *Accred.:* 1916/1987 (NCA) *Calendar:* Sem. plan *Degrees:* A, B *CEO:* Pres. Earl J. Reeves
Enroll: 1010 (816) 886-6924

MISSOURI VOCATIONAL CENTER
3839 Washington Blvd., St. Louis 63108 *Type:* Private *Accred.:* 1988 (CCA-ACTTS) *Calendar:* Courses of varying lengths *Degrees:* certificates *CEO:* Pres. Richard Scharlott
(314) 534-7581

BRANCH CAMPUS
1360 S. 5th St., Ste. 350, St. Charles, MO 63301-2447 *CEO:* Pres. Richard Scharlott
(314) 947-7066

MISSOURI WESTERN STATE COLLEGE
4525 Downs Dr., St. Joseph 64507 *Type:* Public *System:* Missouri Coordinating Board for Higher Education *Accred.:* 1919/1990 (NCA) *Calendar:* Sem. plan *Degrees:* A, B, certificates, diplomas *Prof. Accred.:* Music, Nursing (B), Social Work (B), Teacher Education (e,s) *CEO:* Pres. Janet G. Murphy
Enroll: 3534 (816) 271-4200

MISSOURI-NEBRASKA EXPRESS DRIVER TRAINING ACADEMY
P.O. Box 2848, Joplin 64803-2848 *Type:* Private *Accred.:* 1991 (CCA-ACTTS) *Calendar:* Courses of varying lengths *Degrees:* diplomas *CEO:* Pres. J. Michael Head
(417) 624-9101

MOBERLY AREA COMMUNITY COLLEGE
Moberly 65270 *Type:* Public (district) junior *System:* Missouri Coordinating Board for Higher Education *Accred.:* 1980/1985 (NCA) *Calendar:* Sem. plan *Degrees:* A, certificates, diplomas *CEO:* Pres. Andrew Komar, Jr.
Enroll: 1111 (816) 263-4110

NATIONAL CAREER INSTITUTE
17601-A E. 40 Hwy., Independence 64055 *Type:* Private business *Accred.:* 1985 (CCA-ACICS) *Calendar:* Courses of varying lengths *Degrees:* certificates, diplomas *CEO:* Dir. Jim Mullen
Enroll: 133 (816) 373-6292

BRANCH CAMPUS
1209 N. Seventh St., Harlingen, TX 78550 *CEO:* Dir. Alim Ansari
(512) 425-4183

NAZARENE THEOLOGICAL SEMINARY
1700 E. Meyer Blvd., Kansas City 64131 *Type:* Private (Nazarene) professional; graduate only *Accred.:* 1970/1989 (ATS) *Calendar:* Sem. plan *Degrees:* P, M, D *CEO:* Pres. Terrell C. Sanders, Jr.
Enroll: 313 (816) 333-6254

NICHOLS CAREER CENTER
609 Union St., Jefferson City 65101 *Type:* Private *Calendar:* Courses of varying lengths *Degrees:* certificates *Prof. Accred.:* Dental Assisting, Practical Nursing *CEO:* Dir. Harold Lynch
(314) 659-3000

NORTH CENTRAL MISSOURI COLLEGE
1301 Main St., Trenton 64683 *Type:* Public (district) junior *Accred.:* 1983/1987 (NCA) *Calendar:* Sem. plan *Degrees:* A, certificates, diplomas *CEO:* Pres. James E. Selby
Enroll: 590 (816) 359-3948

NORTHEAST MISSOURI STATE UNIVERSITY
Kirksville 63501 *Type:* Public liberal arts and teachers *System:* Missouri Coordinating Board for Higher Education *Accred.:* 1914/1985 (NCA) *Calendar:* Sem. plan *Degrees:* B, P, M, certificates, diplomas *Prof. Accred.:*

Home Economics, Music, Nursing (B), Speech-Language Pathology, Teacher Education (e,s,p) *CEO:* Pres. Russell G. Warren
Enroll: 5554 (816) 785-4000

NORTHWEST MISSOURI COMMUNITY COLLEGE
4315 Pickett Rd., St. Joseph 64503 *Type:* Private junior *Accred.:* 1980/1991 (NCA) *Calendar:* Qtr. plan *Degrees:* A, certificates, diplomas *CEO:* Pres. Stanley L. Shaver
Enroll: 710 (816) 364-5700

NORTHWEST MISSOURI STATE UNIVERSITY
Maryville 64468 *Type:* Public liberal arts and teachers *System:* Missouri Coordinating Board for Higher Education *Accred.:* 1921/1988 (NCA) *Calendar:* Sem. plan *Degrees:* A, B, P, M, certificates, diplomas *Prof. Accred.:* Home Economics, Music, Teacher Education (e,s,p) *CEO:* Pres. Dean L. Hubbard
Enroll: 5131 (816) 562-1110

OZARK CHRISTIAN COLLEGE
1111 N. Main St., Joplin 64801 *Type:* Private (Christian Churches/Churches of Christ) *Accred.:* 1988 (AABC) *Calendar:* Sem. plan *Degrees:* A, B, certificates *CEO:* Pres. Ken Idleman
Enroll: 482 (417) 624-2518

PARK COLLEGE
Parkville 64152 *Type:* Private (Latter-Day Saints) liberal arts *Accred.:* 1913/1990 (NCA) *Calendar:* 4-1-4 plan *Degrees:* A, B, M *CEO:* Pres. Donald J. Breckon
Enroll: 2468 (816) 741-2000

PATRICIA STEVENS COLLEGE
Forsythe Plaza at Union Sta., 1831 Chestnut St., St. Louis 63103 *Type:* Private business *Accred.:* 1968/1986 (CCA-ACICS) *Calendar:* Qtr. plan *Degrees:* certificates, diplomas *CEO:* Exec. Dir. Richard A. Harvey
Enroll: 306 (314) 421-0949

PENN VALLEY COMMUNITY COLLEGE
3201 S.W. Trafficway, Kansas City 64111 *Type:* Public (district) junior *System:* Metropolitan Community College District *Accred.:* 1986 (NCA) *Calendar:* Sem. plan *Degrees:* A *Prof. Accred.:* Medical Record Technology, Nursing (A), Occupational Therapy Assisting, Physical Therapy Assisting, Radiography *CEO:* Pres. E. Paul Williams
(816) 732-7600

PHILLIPS JUNIOR COLLEGE
625 N. Benton Ave., Springfield 65806 *Type:* Private junior *Accred.:* 1981/1987 (CCA-ACICS) *Calendar:* Qtr. plan *Degrees:* A *Prof. Accred.:* Medical Assisting (AMA) *CEO:* Dir. Barbara Loven
Enroll: 706 (417) 864-7220

PROFESSIONAL BUSINESS SCHOOL
1805 Grand Ave., Ste. 600, Kansas City 64108 *Type:* Private business *Accred.:* 1987 (CCA-ACICS) *Calendar:* Courses of varying lengths *Degrees:* certificates, diplomas *CEO:* Dir. Lorenzo Rice
Enroll: 866 (816) 842-1010

PROFESSIONAL BUSINESS SCHOOL
3115 S. Grand Blvd., 3rd Fl., St. Louis 63118 *Type:* Private business *Accred.:* 1987/1989 (CCA-ACICS) *Calendar:* Courses of varying lengths *Degrees:* certificates, diplomas *CEO:* Dir. Marilyn Morris
Enroll: 377 (314) 773-8040

PROFESSIONAL BUSINESS SCHOOL
1012 Locust St., Ste. 200, St. Louis 63101 *Type:* Private business *Accred.:* 1984/1990 (CCA-ACICS) *Calendar:* Courses of varying lengths *Degrees:* certificates, diplomas *CEO:* Exec. Dir. N.L. Baker
Enroll: 813 (314) 231-5266

BRANCH CAMPUS
702 Preston St., Ste. 200, Houston, TX 77002 *CEO:* Dir. Robert Reyes
(713) 247-9700

RANKEN TECHNICAL COLLEGE
4431 Finney Ave., St. Louis 63113 *Type:* Private *Accred.:* 1989 (NCA) *Calendar:* Tri. plan *Degrees:* A, certificates, diplomas *CEO:* Pres. Ben H. Ernst
Enroll: 710 (314) 371-0236

Missouri

RESEARCH COLLEGE OF NURSING
2316 E. Meyer Blvd., Kansas City 64132 *Type:* Private professional *Accred.:* 1987 (NCA) *Calendar:* Sem plan *Degrees:* B *Prof. Accred.:* Nursing (B) *CEO:* Pres./Dean Barbara A. Clemence
Enroll: 163 (816) 276-9300

ROCKHURST COLLEGE
1100 Rockhurst Rd., Kansas City 64110 *Type:* Private (Roman Catholic) liberal arts *Accred.:* 1934/1983 (NCA) *Calendar:* Sem. plan *Degrees:* A, B, M *Prof. Accred.:* Nursing (B), Physical Therapy *CEO:* Pres. Thomas J. Savage, S.J.
Enroll: 1782 (816) 926-4250

ROLLA AREA VOCATIONAL-TECHNICAL SCHOOL
1304 E. Tenth St., Rolla 65401-3699 *Type:* Private *Calendar:* Courses of varying lengths *Degrees:* certificates *Prof. Accred.:* Radiography *CEO:* Dir. Bob Chapman
(314) 364-3762

ST. CHARLES COUNTY COMMUNITY COLLEGE
102 Compass Point Dr., Ste. L, St. Charles 63301 *Type:* Public (county) junior *System:* Missouri Coordinating Board for Higher Education *Accred.:* 1991 (NCA) *Calendar:* Sem. plan *Degrees:* A, certificates, diplomas *Prof. Accred.:* Medical Record Technology *CEO:* Pres. Donald D. Shook
Enroll: 1742 (314) 723-1220

ST. LOUIS CHRISTIAN COLLEGE
1360 Grandview Dr., Florissant 63033 *Type:* Private (Christian Churches/Churches of Christ) *Accred.:* 1977/1987 (AABC) *Calendar:* Sem. plan *Degrees:* A, B, certificates *CEO:* Pres. Thomas W. McGee
Enroll: 122 (314) 837-6777

ST. LOUIS COLLEGE OF HEALTH CAREERS
4484 W. Pine Blvd., St. Louis 63108 *Type:* Private *Calendar:* Courses of varying lengths *Degrees:* certificates *Prof. Accred.:* Health Education *CEO:* Pres. Rush L. Robinson
(314) 652-0300

ST. LOUIS COLLEGE OF PHARMACY
4588 Parkview Pl., St. Louis 63110 *Type:* Private professional *Accred.:* 1967/1987 (NCA)*Calendar:* Sem. plan *Degrees:* B,M,D *Prof. Accred.:* Pharmacy *CEO:* Pres. Sumner M. Robinson
Enroll: 726 (314) 367-8700

ST. LOUIS COMMUNITY COLLEGE AT FLORISSANT VALLEY
3400 Pershall Rd., St. Louis 63135 *Type:* Public (district) junior *System:* St. Louis Community College District *Accred.:* 1988 (NCA) *Calendar:* Sem. plan *Degrees:* A, certificates, diplomas *Prof. Accred.:* Art, Engineering Technology (civil/construction, electrical, mechanical), Nursing (A) *CEO:* Pres. Michael T. Murphy
Enroll: 4789 (314) 595-4208

ST. LOUIS COMMUNITY COLLEGE AT FOREST PARK
5600 Oakland Ave., St. Louis 63110 *Type:* Public (district) junior *System:* St. Louis Community College District *Accred.:* 1988 (NCA) *Calendar:* Sem. plan *Degrees:* A, certificates, diplomas *Prof. Accred.:* Dental Assisting, Dental Hygiene, Diagnostic Medical Sonography, Funeral Service Education, Medical Assisting (AMA), Medical Laboratory Technology (AMA), Nursing (A), Radiography, Respiratory Therapy, Surgical Technology *CEO:* Acting Pres. Henry D. Shannon
Enroll: 5206 (314) 644-9743

ST. LOUIS COMMUNITY COLLEGE AT MERAMEC
11333 Big Bend Blvd., Kirkwood 63122 *Type:* Public (district) junior *System:* St. Louis Community College District *Accred.:* 1988 (NCA) *Calendar:* Sem. plan *Degrees:* A, certificates, diplomas *Prof. Accred.:* Dental Laboratory Technology, Nursing (A), Occupational Therapy Assisting, Physical Therapy Assisting *CEO:* Acting Pres. Richard A. Black
Enroll: 5940 (314) 984-7762

ST. LOUIS CONSERVATORY AND SCHOOLS FOR THE ARTS
560 Trinity Ave., St. Louis 63130 *Type:* Private professional *Calendar:* Sem. plan

Degrees: diplomas *Prof. Accred.:* Music *CEO:* Dean Shirley Bartzen
(314) 863-3033

ST. LOUIS TECH
4144 Cypress Rd., St. Ann 63074-1521 *Type:* Private *Accred.:* 1977/1988 (CCA-ACTTS) *Calendar:* Courses of varying lengths *Degrees:* certificates, diplomas *CEO:* Dir. Henry L. Kemp
Enroll: 192 (314) 427-3600

ST. LOUIS UNIVERSITY
221 N. Grand Blvd., St. Louis 63103 *Type:* Private (Roman Catholic) *Accred.:* 1916/1982 (NCA) *Calendar:* Sem. plan *Degrees:* A, B, P, M, D, certificates, diplomas *Prof. Accred.:* Business (B,M), Clinical Psychology, Community Health/Preventive Medicine, Dietetics (internship), Health Services Administration, Law, Medical Record Administration, Medical Technology, Medicine, Nuclear Medicine Technology, Nursing (B,M), Perfusion, Physical Therapy, Physician Assisting, Social Work (B,M), Speech-Language Pathology, Teacher Education (e,s,p) *CEO:* Pres. Lawrence Biondi, S.J.
Enroll: 9567 (314) 658-2474

ST. PAUL SCHOOL OF THEOLOGY
5123 Truman Rd., Kansas City 64127 *Type:* Private (United Methodist) professional; graduate only *Accred.:* 1964/1981 (ATS); 1976/1982 (NCA) *Calendar:* Sem. plan *Degrees:* P, M, D *CEO:* Pres. Lovett H. Weems, Jr.
Enroll: 153 (816) 483-9600

STE. GENEVIEVE BEAUTY COLLEGE
755 Market St., Ste. Genevieve 63670-1525 *Type:* Private *Accred.:* 1991 (CCA-ACTTS) *Calendar:* Courses of varying lengths *Degrees:* certificates *CEO:* Owner Donald Carron
(314) 883-5550

SANFORD-BROWN BUSINESS COLLEGE
12006 Manchester Dr., Des Peres 63131 *Type:* Private business *Accred.:* 1982 (CCA-ACICS); 1991 (NCA candidate) *Calendar:*

Qtr. plan *Degrees:* certificates, diplomas *CEO:* Dir. Bret Combs
(314) 822-7100

BRANCH CAMPUS
4100 Ashby Rd., St. Ann, MO 63074 *CEO:* Dir. Patricia Lanigan
Enroll: 417 (314) 427-7100

SOUTHEAST MISSOURI STATE UNIVERSITY
One University Plaza, Cape Girardeau 63701 *Type:* Public liberal arts and teachers *System:* Missouri Coordinating Board for Higher Education *Accred.:* 1915/1991 (NCA) *Calendar:* Sem. plan *Degrees:* A, B, P, M, certificates, diplomas *Prof. Accred.:* Music, Nursing (A,B), Social Work (B), Speech-Language Pathology, Teacher Education (e,s,p) *CEO:* Pres. Kala M. Stroup
Enroll: 7180 (314) 651-2000

SOUTHWEST BAPTIST UNIVERSITY
1601 S. Springfield St., Bolivar 65613 *Type:* Private (Southern Baptist) liberal arts *Accred.:* 1957/1990 (NCA) *Calendar:* Sem. plan *Degrees:* A, B, certificates, diplomas *Prof. Accred.:* Music *CEO:* Chanc. James L. Selles
Enroll: 2157 (417) 326-5281

SOUTHWEST MISSOURI STATE UNIVERSITY
901 S. National Ave., Springfield 65804 *Type:* Public liberal arts and teachers *System:* Missouri Coordinating Board for Higher Education *Accred.:* 1915/1986 (NCA) *Calendar:* Sem. plan *Degrees:* A, B, P, M, certificates, diplomas *Prof. Accred.:* Computer Science, Home Economics, Music, Nurse Anesthesia Education, Nursing (A,B), Recreation and Leisure Studies, Respiratory Therapy, Respiratory Therapy Technology, Social Work (B), Speech-Language Pathology, Teacher Education (e,s,p) *CEO:* Pres. Marshall Gordon
Enroll: 16336 (417) 836-5000

SOUTHWEST SCHOOL OF BROADCASTING
1031 E. Battlefield Rd., Ste. 212B, Springfield 65807-5083 *Type:* Private *Accred.:* 1988 (CCA-ACTTS) *Calendar:* Courses of

varying lengths *Degrees:* certificates *CEO:* Vice Pres. Johnie F. Jones
(417) 883-4060

STATE FAIR COMMUNITY COLLEGE
3201 W. 16th St., Sedalia 65301 *Type:* Public (district) junior *System:* Missouri Coordinating Board for Higher Education *Accred.:* 1977/1989 (NCA) *Calendar:* Sem. plan *Degrees:* A, certificates, diplomas *Prof. Accred.:* Respiratory Therapy Technology *CEO:* Pres. Marvin R. Fielding
Enroll: 1378   (816) 826-7100

STEPHENS COLLEGE
Columbia 65215 *Type:* Private liberal arts primarily for women *Accred.:* 1918/1988 (NCA) *Calendar:* Sem. plan *Degrees:* A, B, certificates, diplomas *Prof. Accred.:* Medical Record Administration *CEO:* Pres. Patsy H. Sampson
Enroll: 871   (314) 442-2211

SULLIVAN EDUCATIONAL CENTERS
1001 Harrison St., Kansas City 64106-3073 *Type:* Private *Accred.:* 1982/1987 (CCA-ACTTS) *Calendar:* Courses of varying lengths *Degrees:* diplomas *CEO:* Pres. Phillip C. Sullivan
Enroll: 662   (816) 471-1811

TAD TECHNICAL INSTITUTE
7910 Troost Ave., Kansas City 64131-1920 *Type:* Private *Accred.:* 1989 (CCA-ACTTS) *Calendar:* Qtr. plan *Degrees:* certificates, diplomas *CEO:* Pres. Waunda Thomas
Enroll: 175   (816) 765-0800

THREE RIVERS COMMUNITY COLLEGE
Three Rivers Blvd., Poplar Bluff 63901 *Type:* Public (district) junior *System:* Missouri Coordinating Board for Higher Education *Accred.:* 1974/1987 (NCA) *Calendar:* Sem. plan *Degrees:* A, certificates, diplomas *Prof. Accred.:* Medical Laboratory Technology (AMA), Nursing (A) *CEO:* Pres. Stephen M. Poort
Enroll: 1842   (314) 686-4101

TRANS WORLD TRAVEL ACADEMY
502 Earth City Plaza, Ste. 204, St. Louis 63045-1315 *Type:* Private home study *Accred.:* 1981/1987 (NHSC) *Calendar:* Courses of varying lengths *Degrees:* certificates *CEO:* Exec. Dir. Frank A. Bugler
(314) 291-6321

UNITED HEALTH CAREERS INSTITUTE
1100 Main St., 10th Fl., Kansas City 66105 *Type:* Private *Calendar:* Courses of varying lengths *Degrees:* certificates *Prof. Accred.:* Medical Assisting (AMA) *CEO:* Exec. Dir. Robert F. Brozman
(816) 474-4750

THE UNIVERSITY OF HEALTH SCIENCES
2105 Independence Blvd., Kansas City 64124 *Type:* Private professional *Calendar:* Tri. plan *Degrees:* P *Prof. Accred.:* Osteopathy *CEO:* Interim Pres. Clyde B. Jensen, Ph.D.
Enroll: 500   (816) 283-2000

UNIVERSITY OF MISSOURI—COLUMBIA
Columbia 65211 *Type:* Public *System:* University of Missouri System *Accred.:* 1913/1985 (NCA) *Calendar:* Sem. plan *Degrees:* B, P, M, D *Prof. Accred.:* Accounting (Type A,C), Business (B,M), Clinical Psychology, Counseling Psychology, Dietetics (coordinated), Engineering (agricultural, chemical, civil, computer, electrical, industrial, mechanical), Forestry, Health Services Administration, Home Economics, Interior Design, Journalism, Law, Librarianship, Medicine, Music, Nuclear Medicine Technology, Nurse Anesthesia Education, Nursing (B,M), Occupational Therapy, Parks Recreation and Tourism, Physical Therapy, Psychology Internship, Public Administration, Radiography, Rehabilitation Counseling, Respiratory Therapy, Social Work (B,M), Speech-Language Pathology, Teacher Education (e,s,p) *CEO:* Interim Chanc. Gerald Brouder
Enroll: 21010   (314) 882-3387

UNIVERSITY OF MISSOURI—KANSAS CITY
5100 Rockhill Rd., Kansas City 64110 *Type:* Public *System:* University of Missouri Sys-

tem *Accred.:* 1938/1990 (NCA) *Calendar:* Sem. plan *Degrees:* B, P, M, D, certificates, diplomas *Prof. Accred.:* Business (B,M), Combined Prosthodontics, Counseling Psychology, Dental Hygiene, Dentistry, Engineering (civil, electrical, mechanical), General Dentistry, Law, Maxillofacial Prosthodontics, Medicine, Music, Nurse Anesthesia Education, Nursing (B,M), Oral and Maxillofacial Surgery, Orthodontics, Pediatric Dentistry, Periodontics, Pharmacy, Psychology Internship (provisional), Public Administration, Teacher Education (e,s,p), Theatre *CEO:* Interim Chanc. Eleanor B. Schwartz
Enroll: 7448 (816) 235-1000

UNIVERSITY OF MISSOURI—ROLLA
Rolla 65401 *Type:* Public *System:* University of Missouri System *Accred.:* 1913/1989 (NCA) *Calendar:* Sem. plan *Degrees:* B, M, D *Prof. Accred.:* Computer Science, Engineering (aerospace, ceramic, chemical, civil, electrical, engineering management, geological/geophysical, mechanical, metallurgical, mining, nuclear, petroleum) *CEO:* Interim Chanc. John T. Park
Enroll: 4208 (314) 341-4114

UNIVERSITY OF MISSOURI—ST. LOUIS
8001 Natural Bridge Rd., St. Louis 63121 *Type:* Public *System:* University of Missouri System *Accred.:* 1960/1989 (NCA) *Calendar:* Sem. plan *Degrees:* B, M, D *Prof. Accred.:* Business (B,M), Clinical Psychology, Music, Nursing (B), Optometry, Public Policy Administration, Social Work (B), Teacher Education (e,s,p) *CEO:* Chanc. Blanche M. Touhill
Enroll: 8854 (314) 553-5000

THE VANDERSCHMIDT SCHOOL
4625 Lindell Blvd., St. Louis 63108 *Type:* Private business *Accred.:* 1985 (CCA-ACICS) *Calendar:* Courses of varying lengths *Degrees:* certificates, diplomas *CEO:* Exec. Dir. Nancy S. Rendleman
Enroll: 97 (314) 361-6000

VATTEROTT EDUCATIONAL CENTERS
3854 Washington Ave., St. Louis 63108-3406 *Type:* Private *Accred.:* 1976/1986 (CCA-ACTTS) *Calendar:* Courses of varying lengths *Degrees:* certificates, diplomas *CEO:* Pres. John C. Vatterott
(314) 534-2586

VATTEROTT EDUCATIONAL COLLEGE
3925 Industrial Dr., St. Ann 63074-1807 *Type:* Private *Accred.:* 1982/1987 (CCA-ACTTS) *Calendar:* Courses of varying lengths *Degrees:* certificates, diplomas *CEO:* Dir. J. Barry Mannion
(314) 428-5900

WASHINGTON UNIVERSITY
One Brooking Dr., St. Louis 63130 *Type:* Private *Accred.:* 1913/1984 (NCA) *Calendar:* Sem. plan *Degrees:* B, P, M, D, certificates, diplomas *Prof. Accred.:* Architecture (M), Art, Audiology, Business (B,M), Engineering (chemical, civil, computer, electrical, general, mechanical, systems), Health Services Administration, Law, Medicine, Music, Nurse Anesthesia Education, Occupational Therapy, Physical Therapy, Social Work (M), Teacher Education (e,s) *CEO:* Chanc. William H. Danforth
Enroll: 9758 (314) 889-5000

WATTERSON COLLEGE
6665 Delmar Blvd., University City 63130 *Type:* Private business *Accred.:* 1988 (CCA-ACICS) *Calendar:* Courses of varying lengths *Degrees:* certificates, diplomas *CEO:* Dir. James Canifax
Enroll: 288 (314) 721-3233

WEBSTER UNIVERSITY
470 E. Lockwood Ave., St. Louis 63119 *Type:* Private liberal arts *Accred.:* 1925/1989 (NCA) *Calendar:* Sem. plan *Degrees:* B, M, D, certificates, diplomas *Prof. Accred.:* Music, Nursing (B) *CEO:* Pres. Daniel H. Perlman
Enroll: 5541 (314) 968-6900

WENTWORTH MILITARY ACADEMY AND JUNIOR COLLEGE
Washington Ave., Lexington 64067 *Type:* Private junior primarily for men *Accred.:*

1930/1991 (NCA) *Calendar:* Sem. plan *Degrees:* A, certificates, diplomas *CEO:* Supt. Gerald Childress
Enroll: 331　　　　　　　　(816) 259-2221

WESTMINSTER COLLEGE
501 Westminster Ave., Fulton 65251-1299 *Type:* Private (Presbyterian) liberal arts *Accred.:* 1913/1985 (NCA) *Calendar:* Sem. plan*Degrees:*B*CEO:* Pres. J. Harvey Saunders
Enroll: 758　　　　　　　　(314) 642-3361

WILLIAM JEWELL COLLEGE
Liberty 64068 *Type:* Private (Southern Baptist) liberal arts *Accred.:* 1915/1991 (NCA) *Calendar:* 4-1-4 plan *Degrees:* B *Prof. Accred.:* Music, Nursing (B) *CEO:* Pres. J. Gordon Kingsley
Enroll: 1645　　　　　　　(816) 781-7700

WILLIAM WOODS COLLEGE
Fulton 65251 *Type:* Private (Disciples of Christ) liberal arts for women *Accred.:* 1919/1987 (NCA) *Calendar:* Sem. plan *Degrees:* B *Prof. Accred.:* Social Work (B), Teacher Education (e,s) *CEO:* Pres. Jahnae H. Barnett
Enroll: 738　　　　　　　　(314) 642-2251

WORLDSPAN TRAVEL ACADEMY
7310 Tiffany Springs Pkwy., Kansas City 64153-1387 *Type:* Private home study *Accred.:* 1991 (CCA-ACTTS); 1981/1987 (NHSC) *Calendar:* Courses of varying lenghts *Degrees:* certificates *CEO:* Dir. Frank LaRussa
　　　　　　　　　　　　(816) 891-5415

MONTANA

BIG SKY COLLEGE OF BARBER STYLING
750 Kensington Ave., Missoula 59801-5720 *Type:* Private *Accred.:* 1987 (CCA-ACTTS) *Calendar:* Courses of varying lengths *Degrees:* diplomas *CEO:* Pres. Gary T. Lucht
(406) 721-5588

BILLINGS SCHOOL OF BARBERING AND HAIRSTYLING
922-1/2 Grand Ave., Billings 59102-3302 *Type:* Private *Accred.:* 1985 (CCA-ACTTS) *Calendar:* Courses of varying lengths *Degrees:* diplomas *CEO:* Dir. Monte Krause
(406) 259-9369

BILLINGS VOCATIONAL-TECHNICAL CENTER
3803 Central Ave., Billings 59102 *Type:* Public (state) 2-year *System:* Montana Vocational-Technical System *Accred.:* 1979/1984 (NASC) *Calendar:* Sem. plan *Degrees:* A, certificates *CEO:* Dir. George E. Bell
Enroll: 351 (406) 255-3801

BLACKFEET COMMUNITY COLLEGE
Browning 59417 *Type:* Private tribal junior *Accred.:* 1985/1990 (NASC) *Calendar:* Qtr. plan *Degrees:* A *CEO:* Pres. Gordon Belcourt
Enroll: 275 (406) 338-5441

BUTTE VOCATIONAL-TECHNICAL CENTER
Basin Creek Rd., Butte 59701 *Type:* Public (state) 2-year *System:* Montana Vocational-Technical System *Accred.:* 1984/1989 (NASC) *Calendar:* Sem. plan *Degrees:* A, certificates *CEO:* Dir. Harrison J. Freebourn
Enroll: 434 (406) 494-2894

CARROLL COLLEGE
N. Benton Ave., Helena 59625 *Type:* Private (Roman Catholic) liberal arts *Accred.:* 1949/1990 (NASC) *Calendar:* Sem. plan *Degrees:* B *Prof. Accred.:* Medical Record Administration, Nursing (B), Social Work (B) *CEO:* Pres. Matthew J. Quinn
Enroll: 1248 (406) 442-3450

COLLEGE OF GREAT FALLS
Great Falls 59405 *Type:* Private (Roman Catholic) liberal arts *Accred.:* 1935/1989 (NASC) *Calendar:* Sem. plan *Degrees:* B, M *CEO:* Pres. William A. Shields
Enroll: 1096 (406) 761-8210

DAWSON COMMUNITY COLLEGE
Glendive 59330 *Type:* Public (district) junior *System:* Montana Community College System *Accred.:* 1969/1984 (NASC) *Calendar:* Sem. plan *Degrees:* A *CEO:* Pres. Donald H. Kettner
Enroll: 648 (406) 365-3396

EASTERN MONTANA COLLEGE
Billings 59101 *Type:* Public (state) liberal arts and teachers *System:* Montana University System *Accred.:* 1932/1988 (NASC) *Calendar:* Sem. plan *Degrees:* B, M *Prof. Accred.:* Art, Music, Rehabilitation Counseling, Teacher Education (e,s,p) *CEO:* Pres. Bruce H. Carpenter
Enroll: 4384 (406) 657-2011

FLATHEAD VALLEY COMMUNITY COLLEGE
Kalispell 59901 *Type:* Public (district) junior *System:* Montana Community College System *Accred.:* 1970/1982 (NASC) *Calendar:* Qtr. plan *Degrees:* A *CEO:* Pres. Howard L. Fryett
Enroll: 1824 (406) 756-3822

FORT PECK COMMUNITY COLLEGE
P.O. Box 1027, Poplar 59255 *Type:* Private tribal junior *Accred.:* 1991 (NASC) *Calendar:* Sem. plan *Degrees:* A *CEO:* Pres. James E. Shanley
Enroll: 226 (406) 768-5551

GREAT FALLS VOCATIONAL-TECHNICAL CENTER
2100 16th Ave., S., Great Falls 59405 *Type:* Public (state) 2-year *System:* Montana Vocational-Technical System *Accred.:* 1979/1984 (NASC) *Calendar:* Sem. plan *Degrees:* A, certificates *Prof. Accred.:* Dental Assisting, Occupational Therapy Assisting, Respiratory

Montana

Therapy, Respiratory Therapy Technology *CEO:* Dir. Willard R. Weaver
Enroll: 728 (406) 771-1240

HELENA VOCATIONAL-TECHNICAL CENTER
115 N. Roberts St., Helena 59620 *Type:* Public (state) 2-year *System:* Montana Vocational-Technical System *Accred.:* 1977/1982 (NASC) *Calendar:* Sem. plan *Degrees:* A, certificates *CEO:* Dir. Alex Capdeville
Enroll: 674 (406) 444-6800

LITTLE BIG HORN COLLEGE
P.O. Box 370, Crow Agency 59022 *Type:* Private tribal junior *Accred.:* 1990 (NASC) *Calendar:* Sem. plan *Degrees:* A *CEO:* Pres. Janine Pease-Windy Boy
Enroll: 260 (406) 638-7211

MAY TECHNICAL COLLEGE
1306 Central Ave., Billings 59102-5531 *Type:* Private *Accred.:* 1983/1988 (CCA-ACTTS) *Calendar:* Courses of varying lengths *Degrees:* diplomas *CEO:* Dir. Michael May
(406) 259-7000

BRANCH CAMPUS
1807 Third St., N.W., Great Falls, MT 59404-1922 *CEO:* Dir. Richard T. Norine
(406) 761-4000

MILES COMMUNITY COLLEGE
Miles City 59301 *Type:* Public (district) junior *System:* Montana Community College System *Accred.:* 1971/1986 (NASC) *Calendar:* Sem. plan *Degrees:* A *CEO:* Pres. Judson H. Flower
Enroll: 670 (406) 232-3031

MISSOULA VOCATIONAL-TECHNICAL CENTER
909 South Ave., W., Missoula 59801 *Type:* Public (state) 2-year *System:* Montana Vocational-Technical System *Accred.:* 1974/1989 (NASC) *Calendar:* Sem. plan *Degrees:* A, certificates *Prof. Accred.:* Respiratory Therapy Technology, Surgical Technology *CEO:* Dir. Dennis N. Lerum
Enroll: 574 (406) 542-6811

MONTANA COLLEGE OF MINERAL SCIENCE AND TECHNOLOGY
Butte 59701 *Type:* Public (state) technological *System:* Montana University System *Accred.:* 1932/1990 (NASC) *Calendar:* Sem. plan *Degrees:* B, M *Prof. Accred.:* Engineering (engineering physics/science, environmental/sanitary, geological/geophysical, metallurgical, mining, petroleum) *CEO:* Pres. Lindsay D. Norman, Jr.
Enroll: 1829 (406) 496-4101

MONTANA STATE UNIVERSITY
Bozeman 59717 *Type:* Public (state) *System:* Montana University System *Accred.:* 1932/1990 (NASC) *Calendar:* Sem. plan *Degrees:* B, M, D *Prof. Accred.:* Architecture (B), Art, Business (B), Engineering (agricultural, chemical, civil, electrical, industrial, mechanical), Engineering Technology (civil/construction, electrical, mechanical), Music, Nursing (B,M), Psychology Internship, Teacher Education (e,s,p) *CEO:* Pres. Michael Malone
Enroll: 10392 (406) 994-0211

NORTHERN MONTANA COLLEGE
P.O. Box 7751, Havre 59501 *Type:* Public (state) teachers *System:* Montana University System *Accred.:* 1932/1987 (NASC) *Calendar:* Qtr. plan *Degrees:* A, B, M *Prof. Accred.:* Nursing (B) *CEO:* Pres. William Daehling
Enroll: 1765 (406) 265-3221

ROCKY MOUNTAIN COLLEGE
1511 Poly Dr., Billings 59102 *Type:* Private liberal arts *Accred.:* 1949/1987 (NASC) *Calendar:* Sem. plan *Degrees:* A, B *CEO:* Pres. Arthur H. DeRosier
Enroll: 753 (406) 657-1020

SALISH KOOTENAI COLLEGE
P.O. Box 117, Pablo 59855 *Type:* Private tribal junior *Accred.:* 1984/1989 (NASC) *Calendar:* Qtr. plan *Degrees:* A *Prof. Accred.:* Dental Assisting (prelim. provisional) *CEO:* Pres. Joseph F. McDonald
Enroll: 685 (406) 675-4800

UNIVERSITY OF MONTANA
Missoula 59812 *Type:* Public (state) *System:* Montana University System *Accred.:* 1932/1989 (NASC) *Calendar:* Qtr. plan *Degrees:* A, B, M, D *Prof. Accred.:* Art, Business (B,M), Clinical Psychology, Forestry, Journalism, Law, Music, Pharmacy, Physical Therapy, Social Work (B), Teacher Education (e,s,p), Theatre *CEO:* Pres. George Dennison
Enroll: 10005 (406) 243-0211

WESTERN MONTANA COLLEGE
Dillon 59725 *Type:* Public (state) teachers *System:* Montana University System *Accred.:* 1932/1989 (NASC) *Calendar:* Sem. plan *Degrees:* A, B *CEO:* Provost W. Michael Easton
Enroll: 1011 (406) 683-7151

NEBRASKA

BELLEVUE COLLEGE
Galvin Rd. at Harvell Dr., Bellevue 68005 *Type:* Private liberal arts *Accred.:* 1977/1982 (NCA) *Calendar:* Sem. plan *Degrees:* B, M *CEO:* Pres. John B. Muller
Enroll: 1568 (402) 293-3703

BISHOP CLARKSON COLLEGE
333 S. 44th St., Omaha 68131 *Type:* Private professional *Accred.:* 1984/1989 (NCA) *Calendar:* Sem. plan *Degrees:* B, M, certificates, diplomas *Prof. Accred.:* Nursing (B) *CEO:* Pres. Fay Bower
Enroll: 175 (402) 559-2288

CENTRAL COMMUNITY COLLEGE
P.O. Box 4903, Grand Island 68802-4903 *Type:* Public 2-year technical *System:* Nebraska Coordinating Commission for Postsecondary Education *Accred.:* 1980 (NCA) *Calendar:* Qtr. plan *Degrees:* A, certificates, diplomas *Prof. Accred.:* Medical Assisting (AMA) *CEO:* Pres. Joseph W. Preusser
Enroll: 1103 (308) 384-5220

CENTRAL TECHNICAL COMMUNITY COLLEGE
P.O. Box 1024, Hastings 68902-1024 *Type:* Public 2-year technical *Calendar:* Courses of varying lengths *Degrees:* A, certificates, diplomas *Prof. Accred.:* Dental Assisting, Dental Hygiene, Dental Laboratory Technology *CEO:* Pres. Judy Dresser
(402) 463-9811

CHADRON STATE COLLEGE
10th and Maine Sts., Chadron 69337 *Type:* Public liberal arts and teachers *System:* Nebraska Coordinating Commission for Postsecondary Education *Accred.:* 1915/1987 (NCA) *Calendar:* Sem. plan *Degrees:* A, B, P, M *Prof. Accred.:* Social Work (B-candidate), Teacher Education (e,s,p) *CEO:* Pres. Samuel H. Rankin, Jr.
Enroll: 1843 (308) 432-4451

COLLEGE OF HAIR DESIGN
304 S. 11th St., Lincoln 68508-2199 *Type:* Private *Accred.:* 1977/1987 (CCA-ACTTS) *Calendar:* Qtr. plan *Degrees:* diplomas *CEO:* Pres. Alyce Howard
Enroll: 131 (402) 474-4244

COLLEGE OF ST. MARY
1901 S. 72nd St., Omaha 68124 *Type:* Private (Roman Catholic) liberal arts primarily for women *Accred.:* 1958/1989 (NCA) *Calendar:* Sem. plan *Degrees:* A, B, certificates, diplomas *Prof. Accred.:* Medical Record Administration, Medical Record Technology, Nursing (A,B) *CEO:* Pres. Kenneth R. Nielsen
Enroll: 885 (402) 399-2400

CONCORDIA TEACHERS COLLEGE
800 N. Columbia Ave., Seward 68434 *Type:* Private (Lutheran) *Accred.:* 1953/1988 (NCA) *Calendar:* Sem. plan *Degrees:* B, M, certificates, diplomas *Prof. Accred.:* Teacher Education (e,s,p) *CEO:* Pres. Orville C. Walz
Enroll: 781 (402) 643-3651

CREIGHTON UNIVERSITY
California St. at 24th Ave., Omaha 68178 *Type:* Private (Roman Catholic) *Accred.:* 1916/1987 (NCA) *Calendar:* Sem. plan *Degrees:* A, B, M, D, certificates, diplomas *Prof. Accred.:* Accounting (Type A), Business (B,M), Dentistry, EMT-Paramedic, General Dentistry, Law, Medicine, Nursing (B,M), Occupational Therapy, Pharmacy, Social Work (B-candidate), Teacher Education (e,s,p) *CEO:* Pres. Michael G. Morrison, S.J.
Enroll: 5434 (402) 280-2770

DANA COLLEGE
2848 College Dr., Blair 68008 *Type:* Private (Lutheran) liberal arts and professional *Accred.:* 1958/1982 (NCA) *Calendar:* 4-1-4 plan *Degrees:* B *Prof. Accred.:* Social Work (B), Teacher Education (e,s) *CEO:* Pres. Myrvin Christopherson
Enroll: 460 (402) 426-7200

DAVID'S HEAD COLLEGE OF HAIR DESIGN
798 Fort Crook Rd. S., Bellevue 68005-2964 *Type:* Private *Accred.:* 1991 (CCA-ACTTS) *Calendar:* Courses of varying lengths *Degrees:* diplomas *CEO:* Pres. Eugene L. White
(402) 291-9527

DOANE COLLEGE
1014 Boswell Ave., Crete 68333 *Type:* Private (United Church of Christ) liberal arts *Accred.:* 1913/1982 (NCA) *Calendar:* Sem. plan *Degrees:* B *Prof. Accred.:* Teacher Education (e,s) *CEO:* Pres. Frederic D. Brown
Enroll: 1049 (402) 826-2161

DR. WELBES COLLEGE OF MASSAGE THERAPY
3217 Leavenworth St., Omaha 68105-2015 *Type:* Private *Accred.:* 1991 (CCA-ACTTS) *Calendar:* Courses of varying lengths *Degrees:* certificates *CEO:* Owner John Welbes
(402) 341-9962

GATEWAY ELECTRONICS INSTITUTE
4862 S. 96th St., Omaha 68127-2048 *Type:* Private *Accred.:* 1973/1978 (CCA-ACTTS) *Calendar:* Qtr. plan *Degrees:* diplomas *CEO:* Dir. John E. Queen
Enroll: 373 (402) 593-9000

BRANCH CAMPUS
1033 O St., Lincoln, NE 68508-3621 *CEO:* Dir. Darwin Platt
(402) 434-6060

GRACE COLLEGE OF THE BIBLE
1515 S. Tenth St., Omaha 68108 *Type:* Private *Accred.:* 1948/1984 (AABC) *Calendar:* Sem. plan *Degrees:* A, B, certificates *CEO:* Pres. Warren E. Bathke
Enroll: 217 (402) 449-2800

HASTINGS COLLEGE
720 N. Turner Ave., P.O. Box 269, Hastings 68902 *Type:* Private (United Presbyterian) liberal arts *Accred.:* 1916/1985 (NCA) *Calendar:* 4-1-4 plan *Degrees:* B, M *Prof. Accred.:* Music, Teacher Education (e,s) *CEO:* Pres. Thomas J. Reeves
Enroll: 928 (402) 463-2402

INSTITUTE OF COMPUTER SCIENCE, LTD.
808 S. 74th Plaza, Ste. 200, Omaha 68114-4666 *Type:* Private *Accred.:* 1984/1989 (CCA-ACTTS) *Calendar:* Courses of varying lengths *Degrees:* certificates *CEO:* Owner Dave Weller
(402) 393-7064

LINCOLN SCHOOL OF COMMERCE
1821 K St., P.O. Box 82826, Lincoln 68501-2826 *Type:* Private junior *Accred.:* 1966/1989 (CCA-ACICS) *Calendar:* Sem. plan *Degrees:* A *CEO:* Dir. Joe Seewald
(402) 474-5315

MCCOOK COMMUNITY COLLEGE
McCook 69001 *Type:* Public 2-year technical *System:* Mid-Plains Community College Area *Accred.:* 1986 (NCA) *Calendar:* Sem. plan *Degrees:* A, certificates, diplomas *CEO:* Pres. Robert E. Smallfoot
(308) 345-6303

METROPOLITAN COMMUNITY COLLEGE
P.O. Box 3777, Omaha 68103-0777 *Type:* Public junior *System:* Nebraska Coordinating Commission for Postsecondary Education *Accred.:* 1979/1983 (NCA) *Calendar:* Qtr. plan *Degrees:* A, certificates, diplomas *Prof. Accred.:* Dental Assisting, Respiratory Therapy, Respiratory Therapy Technology, Surgical Technology *CEO:* Pres. J. Richard Gilliland
Enroll: 4473 (402) 449-8415

MID-PLAINS COMMUNITY COLLEGE
Rte. 4, Box 1, North Platte 69101 *Type:* Public 2-year technical *System:* Mid-Plains Community College Area *Accred.:* 1986 (NCA) *Calendar:* Sem. plan *Degrees:* A, certificates, diplomas *Prof. Accred.:* Dental Assisting, Medical Laboratory Technology (AMA) *CEO:* Pres. Kenneth L. Aten
(308) 532-8740

MIDLAND LUTHERAN COLLEGE
900 Clarkson St., Fremont 68025 *Type:* Private (Lutheran) liberal arts *Accred.:* 1947/1989 (NCA) *Calendar:* 4-1-4 plan *Degrees:*

Nebraska

A, B *Prof. Accred.:* Nursing (B) *CEO:* Pres. Carl L. Hansen
Enroll: 898 (402) 721-5480

NEBRASKA CHRISTIAN COLLEGE
1800 Syracuse St., Norfolk 68701 *Type:* Private (Christian Churches/Churches of Christ) professional *Accred.:* 1985/1990 (AABC) *Calendar:* Sem. plan *Degrees:* A, B *CEO:* Pres. Ray Stites
Enroll: 109 (402) 371-5960

NEBRASKA COLLEGE OF BUSINESS
3636 California St., Omaha 68131 *Type:* Private *Accred.:* 1968/1987 (CCA-ACICS) *Calendar:* Qtr. plan *Degrees:* A, certificates, diplomas *CEO:* Dir. Daniel A. Devere
Enroll: 1112 (402) 553-8500

NEBRASKA COLLEGE OF TECHNICAL AGRICULTURE
Curtis 69025 *Type:* Private *Calendar:* Sem. plan *Degrees:* A *Prof. Accred.:* Veterinary Technology *CEO:* Chrmn. Walter E. Long
(308) 367-4124

NEBRASKA CUSTOM DIESEL DRIVERS TRAINING
14243 C Cir., Omaha 68144-5600 *Type:* Private *Accred.:* 1986 (CCA-ACTTS) *Calendar:* Courses of varying lengths *Degrees:* certificates *CEO:* Dir. Charles H. Reece
Enroll: 266 (402) 393-7773

NEBRASKA INDIAN COMMUNITY COLLEGE
P.O. Box 752, Winnebago 68071 *Type:* Public (federal) 2-year *Accred.:* 1986/1989 (NCA) *Calendar:* Sem. plan *Degrees:* A, certificates, diplomas *CEO:* Pres. Thelma Thomas
Enroll: 191 (402) 878-2414

NEBRASKA METHODIST COLLEGE OF NURSING AND ALLIED HEALTH
8501 W. Dodge Rd., Omaha 68114 *Type:* Private *Accred.:* 1989 (NCA) *Calendar:* Sem. plan *Degrees:* A, B, certificates, diplomas *Prof. Accred.:* Nursing (B) *CEO:* Pres. Roger Koehler
Enroll: 313 (402) 390-4915

NEBRASKA WESLEYAN UNIVERSITY
5000 St. Paul Ave., Lincoln 68504 *Type:* Private (United Methodist) liberal arts *Accred.:* 1914/1990 (NCA) *Calendar:* Sem. plan *Degrees:* A, B *Prof. Accred.:* Music, Nursing (B), Social Work (B), Teacher Education (e,s) *CEO:* Pres. John W. White, Jr.
Enroll: 1479 (402) 466-2371

NORTHEAST COMMUNITY COLLEGE
801 E. Benjamin Ave., P.O. Box 469, Norfolk 68702-0469 *Type:* Public junior *System:* Nebraska Coordinating Commission for Postsecondary Education *Accred.:* 1979/1984 (NCA) *Calendar:* Sem. plan *Degrees:* A, certificates, diplomas *CEO:* Pres. Robert P. Cox
Enroll: 1519 (402) 371-2020

OMAHA COLLEGE OF BUSINESS
117 N. 32nd Ave., Omaha 68131 *Type:* Private business *Accred.:* 1981/1990 (CCA-ACICS) *Calendar:* Courses of varying lengths *Degrees:* certificates, diplomas *CEO:* Dir. Terry W. Murphy
Enroll: 138 (402) 346-4048

OMAHA COLLEGE OF HEALTH CAREERS
1052 Park Ave., Omaha 68105-2297 *Type:* Private *Accred.:* 1986 (CCA-ACTTS) *Calendar:* Qtr. plan *Degrees:* A, diplomas *Prof. Accred.:* Dental Assisting, Medical Assisting (AMA), Veterinary Technology (probational) *CEO:* Pres. William J. Stuckey
Enroll: 88 (402) 342-1818

OMAHA OPPORTUNITIES INDUSTRIALIZATION CENTER
2724 N. 24th St., Omaha 68110-2100 *Type:* Private *Accred.:* 1986 (CCA-ACTTS) *Calendar:* Courses of varying lengths *Degrees:* diplomas *CEO:* Exec. Dir. Bernice Dodd
Enroll: 233 (402) 457-4222

PERU STATE COLLEGE
Peru 68421 *Type:* Public liberal arts and teachers *Accred.:* 1915/1991 (NCA) *Calendar:* Sem. plan *Degrees:* A, B, M *Prof.*

Accred.: Teacher Education (e,s) *CEO:* Pres. Robert L. Burns
Enroll: 1198   (402) 872-3815

SOUTHEAST COMMUNITY COLLEGE—BEATRICE CAMPUS
Rte. 2, Box 35-A, Beatrice 68310 *Type:* Public 2-year technical *System:* Southeast Community College Area *Accred.:* 1983 (NCA) *Calendar:* Qtr. plan *Degrees:* A, certificates, diplomas *Prof. Accred.:* Practical Nursing *CEO:* Dir. Kenneth E. Shibata
(402) 228-3468

SOUTHEAST COMMUNITY COLLEGE—LINCOLN CAMPUS
8800 O St., Lincoln 68520 *Type:* Public 2-year technical *System:* Southeast Community College Area *Accred.:* 1983 (NCA) *Calendar:* Qtr. plan *Degrees:* A, certificates, diplomas *Prof. Accred.:* Dental Assisting, Medical Assisting (AMA), Medical Laboratory Technology (AMA), Practical Nursing, Radiography, Respiratory Therapy, Respiratory Therapy Technology, Surgical Technology *CEO:* Dir. Jack J. Huck, Ph.D.
(402) 471-3333

SOUTHEAST COMMUNITY COLLEGE—MILFORD CAMPUS
Rte. 2, Box D, Milford 68405 *Type:* Public 2-year technical *System:* Southeast Community College Area *Accred.:* 1983 (NCA) *Calendar:* Qtr. plan *Degrees:* A, certificates, diplomas *CEO:* Dir. Kenneth E. Shibata
(402) 761-2131

SPENCER SCHOOL OF BUSINESS
410 W. Second St., P.O. Box 399, Grand Island 68802 *Type:* Private business *Accred.:* 1972/1988 (CCA-ACICS) *Calendar:* Qtr. plan *Degrees:* A, certificates, diplomas *CEO:* Dir. Connie J. Collins
Enroll: 217   (308) 382-8044

UNION COLLEGE
3800 S. 48th St., Lincoln 68506 *Type:* Private (Seventh-Day Adventist) liberal arts *Accred.:* 1923/1990 (NCA) *Calendar:* Sem. plan *Degrees:* A, B, certificates, diplomas

Prof. Accred.: Nursing (B), Social Work (B), Teacher Education (e,s) *CEO:* Pres. John Kerbs
Enroll: 571   (402) 488-2331

UNIVERSAL TECHNICAL INSTITUTE
902 Capitol Ave., Omaha 68102-9954 *Type:* Private *Accred.:* 1967/1987 (CCA-ACTTS) *Calendar:* Courses of varying lengths *Degrees:* certificates, diplomas *CEO:* Dir. Ivan Abdouch
(402) 345-2422

UNIVERSITY OF NEBRASKA MEDICAL CENTER
42nd St. and Dewey Ave., Omaha 68105 *Type:* Public (state) *System:* University of Nebraska Central Administrative Office *Accred.:* 1913/1987 (NCA) *Calendar:* Sem. plan *Degrees:* A, B, M, D, certificates, diplomas *Prof. Accred.:* Medical Technology, Medicine, Nuclear Medicine Technology, Nursing (B,M), Pharmacy, Physical Therapy, Physician Assisting, Radiation Therapy Technology, Radiography *CEO:* Interim Chanc. William O. Berndt
Enroll: 2176   (402) 559-4000

UNIVERSITY OF NEBRASKA AT KEARNEY
905 W. 25th St., Kearney 68849 *Type:* Public (state) *System:* University of Nebraska Central Administrative Office *Accred.:* 1916/1984 (NCA) *Calendar:* Sem. plan *Degrees:* B, P, M *Prof. Accred.:* Music, Nursing (B), Social Work (B), Speech-Language Pathology, Teacher Education (e,s,p) *CEO:* Chanc. William R. Nester
Enroll: 7287   (308) 234-8208

UNIVERSITY OF NEBRASKA AT OMAHA
60th and Dodge Sts., Omaha 68182 *Type:* Public (state) *System:* University of Nebraska Central Administrative Office *Accred.:* 1939/1987 (NCA) *Calendar:* Sem. plan *Degrees:* B, P, M, certificates, diplomas *Prof. Accred.:* Business (B,M), Engineering (civil), Engineering Technology (civil/construction, electrical, manufacturing, mechanical drafting/design), Music, Public Administration, Recreation and Leisure Studies, Social Work (B,M), Speech-Language Pathology, Teach-

er Education (e,s,p) *CEO:* Chanc. Delbert D. Weber
Enroll: 11524 (402) 554-2311

UNIVERSITY OF NEBRASKA—LINCOLN
Lincoln 68588 *Type:* Public (state) *System:* University of Nebraska Central Administrative Office *Accred.:* 1913/1987 (NCA) *Calendar:* Sem. plan *Degrees:* A, B, P, M, D, certificates, diplomas *Prof. Accred.:* Accounting (Type A,C), Architecture (M), Art, Audiology, Business (B,M), Clinical Psychology, Construction Management, Dental Hygiene, Dentistry, Dietetics (internship), Endodontics, Engineering (agricultural, chemical, civil, electrical, industrial, mechanical), General Dentistry, General Practice Residency, Home Economics, Interior Design, Journalism, Law, Music, Oral and Maxillofacial Surgery, Orthodontics, Pediatric Dentistry, Periodontics, Planning (community/regional), Recreation and Leisure Studies, School Psychology, Speech-Language Pathology, Teacher Education (e,s,p), Theatre *CEO:* Chanc. Graham Spanier
Enroll: 21512 (402) 472-2116

WAYNE STATE COLLEGE
200 E. Tenth St., Wayne 68787 *Type:* Public liberal arts and teachers *System:* Nebraska Coordinating Commission for Postsecondary Education *Accred.:* 1917/1982 (NCA) *Calendar:* Sem. plan *Degrees:* B, P, M *Prof. Accred.:* Teacher Education (e,s,p) *CEO:* Pres. Donald J. Mash
Enroll: 2644 (402) 375-2200

WESTERN NEBRASKA COMMUNITY COLLEGE
1601 E. 27th St., Scottsbluff 69361 *Type:* Public junior *System:* Nebraska Coordinating Commission for Postsecondary Education *Accred.:* 1988/1990 (NCA) *Calendar:* Sem. plan *Degrees:* A, certificates, diplomas *Prof. Accred.:* Practical Nursing *CEO:* Pres. John N. Harms
Enroll: 537 (308) 635-3606

YORK COLLEGE
York 68467 *Type:* Private (Church of Christ) *Accred.:* 1970/1984 (NCA) *Calendar:* Sem. plan *Degrees:* A, B, certificates, diplomas *CEO:* Pres. Larry Roberts
Enroll: 318 (402) 362-4441

NEVADA

AMERICAN ACADEMY FOR CAREER EDUCATION
3120 E. Desert Inn Rd., Las Vegas 89121-3857 *Type:* Private *Accred.:* 1977/1987 (CCA-ACTTS) *Calendar:* Courses of varying lengths *Degrees:* certificates *CEO:* Dir. Grant Gailey
Enroll: 429 (702) 732-7748

CAREER COLLEGE OF NORTHERN NEVADA
1195-A Corporate Blvd., Reno 89502-2331 *Type:* Private *Accred.:* 1991 (CCA-ACTTS) *Calendar:* Courses of varying lengths *Degrees:* certificates *CEO:* Pres. Larry F. Clark
(702) 329-0904

COLUMBIA SCHOOL OF BROADCASTING
2840 E. Flamingo Rd., Ste. F, Las Vegas 89121 *Type:* Private home study *Accred.:* 1972/1987 (NHSC) *Calendar:* Courses of varying lengths *Degrees:* certificates *CEO:* Pres. Marcia Brock-Gandy
(702) 733-0003

COLUMBIA SCHOOL OF COMPUTER SCIENCE
2840 E. Flamingo Rd., Ste. F, Las Vegas 89121 *Type:* Private home study *Accred.:* 1988 (NHSC) *Calendar:* Courses of varying lengths *Degrees:* certificates *CEO:* Pres. Marcia Brock-Gandy
(702) 733-0003

COMMUNITY COLLEGE OF SOUTHERN NEVADA
3200 E. Cheyenne Ave., North Las Vegas 89030 *Type:* Public (district) junior *System:* University of Nevada System *Accred.:* 1975/1990 (NASC) *Calendar:* Sem. plan *Degrees:* A *Prof. Accred.:* Dental Hygiene, Medical Laboratory Technology (AMA), Medical Record Technology, Nursing (A), Practical Nursing, Respiratory Therapy, Respiratory Therapy Technology *CEO:* Pres. Paul E. Meacham
Enroll: 19555 (702) 643-6060

DANA MCKAY BUSINESS COLLEGE
953 E. Sahara Ave., Las Vegas 89104 *Type:* Private *Accred.:* 1985/1990 (CCA-ACICS) *Calendar:* Courses of varying lengths *Degrees:* certificates, diplomas *CEO:* Dir. Dana McKay
Enroll: 178 (702) 734-9449

EDUCATION DYNAMICS INSTITUTE
2635 N. Decatur Blvd., Las Vegas 89108-2913 *Type:* Private *Accred.:* 1973/1988 (CCA-ACTTS) *Calendar:* Courses of varying lengths *Degrees:* diplomas *CEO:* Controller Marge Ewing
Enroll: 573 (702) 648-1522

BRANCH CAMPUS
953 E. Sahara Ave., Bldg. 35-B, Ste. 102, Las Vegas, NV 89108-2906 *CEO:* Dir. Erick Mendoza
(702) 731-6421

INTERNATIONAL DEALERS SCHOOL
1030 E. Twain Ave., Las Vegas 89106-4212 *Type:* Private *Accred.:* 1983/1988 (CCA-ACTTS) *Calendar:* Courses of varying lengths *Degrees:* certificates, diplomas *CEO:* Dir. Toni Taylor
Enroll: 248 (702) 733-9133

BRANCH CAMPUS
1111 Las Vegas Blvd. S., Las Vegas, NV 89104-1305 *CEO:* Dir. Ron Handleman
(702) 385-7665

BRANCH CAMPUS
1055 S. Virginia St., Reno, NV 89502-2417 *CEO:* Dir. David Lee
(702) 322-8330

LAS VEGAS GAMING AND TECHNICAL SCHOOL
3030 S. Highland Dr., Las Vegas 89109-1047 *Type:* Private *Accred.:* 1991 (CCA-ACTTS) *Calendar:* Courses of varying lengths *Degrees:* certificates, diplomas *CEO:* Dir. Janice Welton
(702) 733-3030

MORRISON COLLEGE/RENO BUSINESS COLLEGE
140 Washington St., Reno 89503 *Type:* Private *Accred.:* 1983/1990 (CCA-ACICS) *Cal-*

Nevada *Accredited Institutions*

endar: Qtr. plan *Degrees:* A, B *CEO:* Vice Pres. Mary Morrison
Enroll: 885   (702) 323-4145

NATIONAL BROADCASTING SCHOOL
1771 E. Flamingo Rd., Ste. 109-B, Las Vegas 89119-5155 *Type:* Private *Accred.:* 1988 (CCA-ACTTS) *Calendar:* Courses of varying lengths *Degrees:* certificates *CEO:* Owner Todd J. Shipper
Enroll: 109   (702) 737-9400

NEVADA TECHNICAL INSTITUTE
3100 Sirius Rd., Las Vegas 89102-0401 *Type:* Private *Accred.:* 1976/1986 (CCA-ACTTS) *Calendar:* Courses of varying lengths *Degrees:* certificates, diplomas *CEO:* Pres. Carol B. Goodman
Enroll: 817   (702) 873-2345

NORTHERN NEVADA COMMUNITY COLLEGE
901 Elm St., Elko 89801 *Type:* Public (district) junior *System:* University of Nevada System *Accred.:* 1974/1984 (NASC) *Calendar:* Sem. plan *Degrees:* A *CEO:* Pres. Ronald Remington
Enroll: 2598   (702) 738-8493

PCI DEALERS SCHOOL
920 S. Valley View Blvd., Las Vegas 89107-4416 *Type:* Private *Accred.:* 1991 (CCA-ACTTS) *Calendar:* Courses of varying lengths *Degrees:* certificates *CEO:* Pres. Joel Lauer
                (702) 877-4724

PHILLIPS JUNIOR COLLEGE OF LAS VEGAS
3320 E. Flamingo Ave., Las Vegas 89121-4306 *Type:* Private *Accred.:* 1983/1990 (CCA-ACICS) *Calendar:* Qtr. plan *Degrees:* A *CEO:* Pres. Dennis Del Valle
Enroll: 958   (702) 434-0486

PROFESSIONAL CAREERS
2390 W. Spring Mountain Rd., Las Vegas 89109-3402 *Type:* Private *Accred.:* 1991 (CCA-ACTTS) *Calendar:* Courses of varying lengths *Degrees:* certificates *CEO:* Pres. Mathew Klabacka
                (702) 732-1304

SIERRA NEVADA COLLEGE
Incline Village 89450-4269 *Type:* Private liberal arts *Accred.:* 1977/1982 (NASC) *Calendar:* Sem. plan *Degrees:* B *CEO:* Pres. Benjamin J. Solomon
Enroll: 851   (702) 831-1314

STRIP DEALERS AND SLOT REPAIR SCHOOL
2121 Las Vegas Blvd. N., Las Vegas 89030 *Type:* Private *Accred.:* 1984/1989 (CCA-ACTTS) *Calendar:* Courses of varying lengths *Degrees:* certificates, diplomas *CEO:* Pres. Gary Mahoney
Enroll: 202   (702) 649-2929

TRUCKEE MEADOWS COMMUNITY COLLEGE
7000 Dandini Blvd., Reno 89512 *Type:* Public (district) junior *System:* University of Nevada System *Accred.:* 1980/1985 (NASC) *Calendar:* Sem. plan *Degrees:* A *Prof. Accred.:* Dental Assisting, Nursing (A), Radiography *CEO:* Pres. John W. Gwaltney
Enroll: 9803   (702) 673-7000

UNIVERSITY OF NEVADA, LAS VEGAS
4505 Maryland Pkwy., Las Vegas 89154 *Type:* Public (state) *System:* University of Nevada System *Accred.:* 1964/1990 (NASC) *Calendar:* Sem. plan *Degrees:* A, B, M, D *Prof. Accred.:* Accounting (Type A,C), Art, Business (B), Counseling, Engineering (civil, electrical, mechanical), Music, Nuclear Medicine Technology, Nursing (B,M), Public Administration, Radiography, Rehabilitation Counseling, Social Work (B,M-candidate), Teacher Education (e,s,p) *CEO:* Pres. Robert C. Maxson
Enroll: 18216   (702) 739-3201

UNIVERSITY OF NEVADA—RENO
Reno 89557 *Type:* Public (state) *System:* University of Nevada System *Accred.:* 1938/1988 (NASC) *Calendar:* Sem. plan *Degrees:* A, B, M, D *Prof. Accred.:* Business (B,M), Clinical Psychology, Engineering (chemical, civil, electrical, geological/geophysical, mechanical, metallurgical, mining), Journalism, Medical Laboratory Technology (AMA), Medical Technology, Medicine, Music, Nursing (B,M), Social Work (B,M-

candidate), Speech-Language Pathology, Teacher Education (e,s,p) *CEO:* Pres. Joseph N. Crowley
Enroll: 10753 (702) 784-4941

VEGAS DEALING SCHOOL
415 E. Carson Ave., Las Vegas 89101 *Type:* Private *Accred.:* 1991 (CCA-ACTTS) *Calendar:* Courses of varying lengths *Degrees:* certificates *CEO:* Owner Rudolph Bosko
(702) 477-7744

WESTERN NEVADA COMMUNITY COLLEGE
2201 W. Nye La., Carson City 89703 *Type:* Public (district) junior *System:* University of Nevada System *Accred.:* 1975/1990 (NASC) *Calendar:* Sem. plan *Degrees:* A *CEO:* Pres. Anthony D. Calabro
Enroll: 5320 (702) 887-3000

NEW HAMPSHIRE

CASTLE JUNIOR COLLEGE
Searles Rd., Windham 03087 *Type:* Private *Accred.:* 1985/1989 (NEASC-CVTCI) *Calendar:* Qtr. plan *Degrees:* A *CEO:* Pres. Sheila L. Garvey
Enroll: 277 (603) 893-6111

COLBY-SAWYER COLLEGE
New London 03257 *Type:* Private for women *Accred.:* 1933/1987 (NEASC-CIHE) *Calendar:* 4-1-4 plan *Degrees:* A, B *Prof. Accred.:* Nursing (B) *CEO:* Pres. Peggy Stock
Enroll: 493 (603) 526-2010

DANIEL WEBSTER COLLEGE
Nashua 03063 *Type:* Private *Accred.:* 1972/1986 (NEASC-CIHE) *Calendar:* Tri. plan *Degrees:* A, B *CEO:* Pres. Hannah M. McCarthy
Enroll: 829 (603) 883-3556

DARTMOUTH COLLEGE
Hanover 03755 *Type:* Private liberal arts *Accred.:* 1929/1989 (NEASC-CIHE) *Calendar:* Qtr. plan *Degrees:* P, M, D *Prof. Accred.:* Business (M), Engineering (general), Medicine, Psychology Internship, Theatre *CEO:* Pres. James O. Freedman
Enroll: 4892 (603) 646-1110

FRANKLIN PIERCE COLLEGE
College Rd., Rindge 03461 *Type:* Private liberal arts *Accred.:* 1968/1989 (NEASC-CIHE) *Calendar:* Sem. plan *Degrees:* B *CEO:* Pres. Walter R. Peterson
Enroll: 2827 (603) 899-5111

FRANKLIN PIERCE LAW CENTER
2 White St., Concord 03301 *Type:* Private professional *Calendar:* Sem. plan *Degrees:* P *Prof. Accred.:* Law (ABA only) *CEO:* Pres. Robert M. Viles
Enroll: 356 (603) 228-1541

HESSER COLLEGE
3 Sundial Ave., Manchester 03103 *Type:* Private junior business *Accred.:* 1985/1989 (NEASC-CVTCI) *Calendar:* Sem. plan *Degrees:* A *CEO:* Pres. Linwood W. Galeucia
Enroll: 1596 (603) 668-6660

KEENE STATE COLLEGE
229 Main St., Keene 03431 *Type:* Public (state) liberal arts and teachers *System:* University System of New Hampshire *Accred.:* 1949/1990 (NEASC-CIHE) *Calendar:* Sem. plan *Degrees:* A, B, M *Prof. Accred.:* Music, Teacher Education (e,s) *CEO:* Pres. Judith A. Sturnick
Enroll: 3709 (603) 352-1909

MCINTOSH COLLEGE
23 Cataract Ave., Dover 03820 *Type:* Private junior business *Accred.:* 1988 (NEASC-CVTCI) *Calendar:* Sem. plan *Degrees:* A, diplomas *CEO:* Pres. Robert J. DeColfmacker
Enroll: 534 (603) 742-1234

NEW ENGLAND COLLEGE
Henniker 03242 *Type:* Private liberal arts *Accred.:* 1967/1983 (NEASC-CIHE) *Calendar:* 4-1-4 plan *Degrees:* B, M *CEO:* Pres. William R. O'Connell, Jr.
Enroll: 1155 (603) 428-2211

NEW HAMPSHIRE COLLEGE
2500 N. River Rd., Manchester 03104 *Type:* Private *Accred.:* 1973/1985 (NEASC-CIHE) *Calendar:* Sem. plan *Degrees:* A, B, M *CEO:* Pres. Richard A. Gustafson
Enroll: 4031 (603) 668-2211

NEW HAMPSHIRE TECHNICAL COLLEGE AT BERLIN
2020 Riverside Dr., Berlin 03570 *Type:* Public (state) 2-year technical *Accred.:* 1974/1990 (NEASC-CVTCI) *Calendar:* Sem. plan *Degrees:* A *CEO:* Pres. Alex Easton
Enroll: 471 (603) 752-1113

NEW HAMPSHIRE TECHNICAL COLLEGE AT CLAREMONT
One College Dr., Claremont 03743-9707 *Type:* Public (state) 2-year technical *Accred.:* 1973/1989 (NEASC-CVTCI) *Cal-

endar: Sem. plan *Degrees:* A *Prof. Accred.:* Medical Assisting (AMA), Medical Laboratory Technology (AMA), Medical Record Technology, Occupational Therapy Assisting, Physical Therapy Assisting, Respiratory Therapy *CEO:* Pres. Willis Reed
Enroll: 489   (603) 542-7744

NEW HAMPSHIRE TECHNICAL COLLEGE AT LACONIA
Prescott Hill, Rte. 106, Laconia 03246 *Type:* Public (state) 2-year technical *Accred.:* 1974/1985 (NEASC-CVTCI) *Calendar:* Sem. plan *Degrees:* A *CEO:* Pres. Jane P. Kilcoyne
Enroll: 573   (603) 524-3207

NEW HAMPSHIRE TECHNICAL COLLEGE AT MANCHESTER
1066 Front St., Manchester 03102 *Type:* Public (state) 2-year technical *Accred.:* 1974/1985 (NEASC-CVTCI) *Calendar:* Sem. plan *Degrees:* A *CEO:* Pres. Richard E. Mandeville
Enroll: 1188   (603) 668-6706

NEW HAMPSHIRE TECHNICAL COLLEGE AT NASHUA
505 Amherst St., P.O. Box 2052, Nashua 03061 *Type:* Public (state) 2-year technical *Accred.:* 1974/1989 (NEASC-CVTCI) *Calendar:* Sem. plan *Degrees:* A *CEO:* Pres. Robert E. Bloomfield
Enroll: 710   (603) 882-6923

NEW HAMPSHIRE TECHNICAL COLLEGE AT STRATHAM
P.O. Box 365, Stratham 03885 *Type:* Public (state) 2-year technical *Accred.:* 1975/1990 (NEASC-CVTCI) *Calendar:* Sem. plan *Degrees:* A *CEO:* Pres. Charles H. Green
Enroll: 545   (603) 772-1194

NEW HAMPSHIRE TECHNICAL INSTITUTE
Institute Dr., P.O. Box 2039, Concord 03301-2039 *Type:* Public (state) 2-year technical *Accred.:* 1969/1991 (NEASC-CVTCI) *Calendar:* Sem. plan *Degrees:* A *Prof. Accred.:* Dental Assisting, Dental Hygiene (conditional), EMT-Paramedic, Engineering Technology (architectural, electrical, mechanical), Nursing (A), Radiography *CEO:* Pres. David E. Larrabee, Sr.
Enroll: 2951   (603) 225-1800

NORTHEAST CAREER SCHOOLS
P.O. Box 626, Londonderry 03053 *Type:* Private *Accred.:* 1988 (CCA-ACTTS) *Calendar:* Courses of varying lengths *Degrees:* certificates *CEO:* Dir. Chris Laponis
Enroll: 175   (603) 669-1151

NOTRE DAME COLLEGE
Manchester 03104 *Type:* Private (Roman Catholic) liberal arts *Accred.:* 1970/1986 (NEASC-CIHE) *Calendar:* Sem. plan *Degrees:* A, B, M *CEO:* Pres. Carol Descoteaux
Enroll: 875   (603) 669-4298

PLYMOUTH STATE COLLEGE
Plymouth 03264 *Type:* Public (state) liberal arts and professional *System:* University System of New Hampshire *Accred.:* 1955/1984 (NEASC-CIHE) *Calendar:* Sem. plan *Degrees:* A, B, M *Prof. Accred.:* Teacher Education (e,s,p) *CEO:* Pres. William J. Farrell
Enroll: 3796   (603) 535-5000

RIVIER COLLEGE
420 S. Main St., Nashua 03060 *Type:* Private (Roman Catholic) liberal arts primarily for women *Accred.:* 1948/1987 (NEASC-CIHE) *Calendar:* Sem. plan *Degrees:* A, B, M *Prof. Accred.:* Nursing (A) *CEO:* Pres. Jeanne Perreault
Enroll: 1594   (603) 888-1311

ST. ANSELM COLLEGE
Manchester 03102-1310 *Type:* Private (Roman Catholic) liberal arts *Accred.:* 1941/1989 (NEASC-CIHE) *Calendar:* Sem. plan *Degrees:* A, B *Prof. Accred.:* Nursing (B) *CEO:* Pres. Jonathan P. DeFelice, O.S.B.
Enroll: 1910   (603) 641-7000

SCHOOL FOR LIFELONG LEARNING
Durham 03824 *Type:* Public (state) *System:* University System of New Hampshire *Accred.:* 1980/1986 (NEASC-CIHE) *Calen-*

dar: Sem. plan *Degrees:* A, B *CEO:* Dean Victor B. Montana
Enroll: 657 (603) 862-1692

TRAVEL EDUCATION CENTER
402 Amherst St., Nashua 03063 *Type:* Private *Accred.:* 1985 (CCA-ACTTS) *Calendar:* Courses of varying lengths *Degrees:* certificates, diplomas *CEO:* Dir. Linda Paresky
Enroll: 155 (603) 880-7200

UNIVERSITY OF NEW HAMPSHIRE
Durham 03824 *Type:* Public (state) *System:* University System of New Hampshire *Accred.:* 1929/1985 (NEASC-CIHE) *Calendar:* Sem. plan *Degrees:* A, B, M, D *Prof. Accred.:* Computer Science, Engineering (chemical, civil, electrical, mechanical), Engineering Technology (electrical, mechanical), Forestry, Leisure Management and Tourism, Medical Technology, Music, Nursing (B,M), Occupational Therapy, Social Work (B), Speech-Language Pathology, Teacher Education (e,s,p) *CEO:* Pres. Dale F. Nitzschke
Enroll: 11794 (603) 862-1234

UNIVERSITY OF NEW HAMPSHIRE AT MANCHESTER
R.F.D. 4, Hackett Hill Rd., Manchester 03102 *Type:* Public (state) *System:* University System of New Hampshire *Accred.:* 1985 (NEASC-CIHE) *Calendar:* Sem. plan *Degrees:* A *CEO:* Dean Lewis Roberts, Jr.
Enroll: 354 (603) 668-0700

WHITE PINES COLLEGE
Chester 03036 *Type:* Private junior *Accred.:* 1975/1985 (NEASC-CIHE) *Calendar:* Sem. plan *Degrees:* A *CEO:* Pres. Faith Preston
Enroll: 62 (603) 887-4401

NEW JERSEY

ACADEMY OF PROFESSIONAL DEVELOPMENT
Park Plaza, 1131 Raritan Ave., Highland Park 08904 *Type:* Private business *Accred.:* 1986 (CCA-ACICS) *Calendar:* Courses of varying lengths *Degrees:* certificates, diplomas *CEO:* Pres. A. Roy Kirkley, Jr.
Enroll: 178 (201) 985-1100

BRANCH CAMPUS
Mercer County Airport Terminal, West Trenton, NJ 08628 *CEO:* Dir. Jean Battaglia
(609) 538-0400

AMERICAN BARTENDERS SCHOOL
398-412 Bloomfield Ave., Montclair 07042-2006 *Type:* Private *Accred.:* 1991 (CCA-ACTTS) *Calendar:* Courses of varying lengths *Degrees:* certificates *CEO:* Dir. Mark Salis
(201) 783-7100

AMERICAN BUSINESS ACADEMY
66 Moore St., Hackensack 07601 *Type:* Private business *Accred.:* 1976/1982 (CCA-ACICS) *Calendar:* Qtr. plan *Degrees:* certificates, diplomas *CEO:* Pres. Theodore S. Takvorian
Enroll: 332 (201) 488-9400

ASSUMPTION COLLEGE FOR SISTERS
Mallinckrodt Convent, Hilltop Rd., Mendham 07945 *Type:* Private (Roman Catholic) junior *Accred.:* 1965/1985 (MSA) *Calendar:* Sem. plan *Degrees:* A *CEO:* Pres. Mary Gerard Gebler, S.C.C.
Enroll: 24 (201) 543-6528

ATLANTIC COMMUNITY COLLEGE
Black Horse Pike, Mays Landing 08330 *Type:* Public (county) junior *System:* Office of Community Colleges *Accred.:* 1971/1986 (MSA) *Calendar:* Sem. plan *Degrees:* A *Prof. Accred.:* Engineering Technology (electrical), Nursing (A), Physical Therapy Assisting *CEO:* Pres. William A. Orth
Enroll: 4626 (609) 625-1111

AVIATION CAREER ACADEMY
Fostertown Rd., Medford 08055-9626 *Type:* Private *Accred.:* 1991 (CCA-ACTTS) *Calendar:* Courses of varying lengths *Degrees:* certificates *CEO:* Pres. Fred Trepper
(609) 267-1200

BARCLAY CAREER SCHOOL
28 S. Harrison St., East Orange 07018-1707 *Type:* Private *Accred.:* 1988 (CCA-ACTTS) *Calendar:* Courses of varying lengths *Degrees:* certificates *Prof. Accred.:* Medical Assisting (AMA) *CEO:* Dir. Virginia Kesting
Enroll: 362 (201) 673-0500

BERDAN INSTITUTE
265 Rte. 46 W., Totowa 07512-1819 *Type:* Private *Accred.:* 1980/1985 (CCA-ACTTS) *Calendar:* Courses of varying lengths *Degrees:* certificates, diplomas *Prof. Accred.:* Dental Assisting *CEO:* Dir. Rex D. Spaulding
Enroll: 125 (201) 256-3444

BERGEN COMMUNITY COLLEGE
400 Paramus Rd., Paramus 07652 *Type:* Public (county) junior *System:* Office of Community Colleges *Accred.:* 1972/1986 (MSA) *Calendar:* Sem. plan *Degrees:* A, certificates, diplomas *Prof. Accred.:* Dental Hygiene, Diagnostic Medical Sonography, Medical Assisting (AMA), Medical Laboratory Technology (AMA), Nursing (A), Radiography, Respiratory Therapy, Surgical Technology *CEO:* Pres. Jose Lopez-Isa
Enroll: 10919 (201) 447-7100

BERKELEY COLLEGE OF BUSINESS
44 Rifle Camp Rd., West Paterson 07424 *Type:* Private junior *Accred.:* 1983 (MSA) *Calendar:* Qtr. plan *Degrees:* A *CEO:* Pres. Kevin L. Luing
Enroll: 731 (201) 278-5400

BRANCH CAMPUS
100 W. Prospect St., Waldwick, NJ 07463 *CEO:* Dir. Harriett North
(201) 652-0388

New Jersey

BRANCH CAMPUS
430 Rahway Ave., Woodbridge, NJ 07095 *CEO:* Dir. David Baumol
(201) 750-1800

BETH MEDRASH GOVOHA
617 Sixth St., Lakewood 08701 *Type:* Private professional *Accred.:* 1974/1985 (AARTS) *Calendar:* Sem. plan *Degrees:* B, M *CEO:* Pres. M. Kotler
Enroll: 1394 (201) 367-1060

BILINGUAL INSTITUTE
685 Broad St., Newark 07102 *Type:* Private business *Accred.:* 1982/1988 (CCA-ACICS) *Calendar:* Courses of varying lengths *Degrees:* certificates, diplomas *CEO:* Dir. Antonio Cordoba
Enroll: 168 (201) 624-3883

BRANCH CAMPUS
2 W. Broadway, Paterson, NJ 07505 *CEO:* Dir. Eduardo L. Gonzalez
(201) 279-8988

BLOOMFIELD COLLEGE
229 Liberty St., Bloomfield 07003 *Type:* Private (Presbyterian) liberal arts *Accred.:* 1960/1987 (MSA) *Calendar:* 4-1-4 plan *Degrees:* B, certificates, diplomas *Prof. Accred.:* Nursing (B) *CEO:* Pres. John F. Noonan
Enroll: 1484 (201) 748-9000

BOARDWALK AND MARINA CASINO DEALERS SCHOOL
2709 Atlantic Ave., Atlantic City 08401-6401 *Type:* Private *Accred.:* 1991 (CCA-ACTTS) *Calendar:* Courses of varying lengths *Degrees:* certificates *CEO:* Vice Pres. Steven Edelblum
(609) 344-1986

BRICK COMPUTER SCIENCE INSTITUTE
515 Hwy. 70, Brick 08723-4043 *Type:* Private *Accred.:* 1974/1985 (CCA-ACTTS) *Calendar:* Courses of varying lengths *Degrees:* diplomas *CEO:* Dir. Robert H. Forsbee, Jr.
Enroll: 427 (201) 477-0975

BROOKDALE COMMUNITY COLLEGE
Newman Springs Rd., Lincroft 07738 *Type:* Public (district) junior *System:* Office of Community Colleges *Accred.:* 1972/1989 (MSA) *Calendar:* Sem. plan *Degrees:* A *Prof. Accred.:* Medical Laboratory Technology (AMA), Nursing (A), Respiratory Therapy *CEO:* Pres. Peter F. Burnham
Enroll: 10638 (908) 842-1900

BRANCH CAMPUS
Asbury Park Educ. Resource Ctr., Cookman St. and Grand Ave., Asbury Park, NJ 07712 *CEO:* Dir. Darrell Willis
(908) 842-1900

BRANCH CAMPUS
Freehold Community Learning Ctr., 47 Throckmorton St., Freehold, NJ 07728 *CEO:* Dir. Cheryl Lenon
(908) 842-1900

BRANCH CAMPUS
Long Branch Community Learning Ctr., Third Ave. and Broadway, Long Branch, NJ 07740 *CEO:* Dir. John Westbrook
(908) 842-1900

BRANCH CAMPUS
Bayshore Community Learning Ctr., 311 Laurel Ave., West Keansburg, NJ 07734 *CEO:* Dir. Judith Simon
(908) 842-1900

BURLINGTON COUNTY COLLEGE
Pemberton-Browns Mills Rd., Pemberton 08068 *Type:* Public (county) junior *System:* Office of Community Colleges *Accred.:* 1972/1989 (MSA) *Calendar:* Sem. plan *Degrees:* A, certificates, diplomas *Prof. Accred.:* Medical Laboratory Technology (AMA), Medical Record Technology *CEO:* Pres. Robert C. Messina, Jr.
Enroll: 6262 (609) 894-9311

BUSINESS TRAINING INSTITUTE
Forest and Spring Valley Aves., P.O. Box 9010, Paramus 07652 *Type:* Private business *Accred.:* 1985/1990 (CCA-ACICS) *Calendar:* Courses of varying lengths *Degrees:*

certificates, diplomas *CEO:* Pres. James P. Mellett, Jr.
Enroll: 392 (201) 845-9300

BRANCH CAMPUS
Village Square Shopping Ctr., 1909 E. Pass Rd., Ste. B, Gulfport, MS 39507 *CEO:* Dir. Susan Tasset
(601) 388-0991

CALDWELL COLLEGE
9 Ryerson Ave., Caldwell 07006 *Type:* Private (Roman Catholic) liberal arts *Accred.:* 1952/1985 (MSA) *Calendar:* Sem. plan *Degrees:* B, certificates, diplomas *CEO:* Pres. Vivien Jennings, O.P.
Enroll: 961 (201) 228-4424

CAMDEN COUNTY COLLEGE
P.O. Box 200, Blackwood 08012 *Type:* Public (county) junior *System:* Office of Community Colleges *Accred.:* 1972/1987 (MSA) *Calendar:* Sem. plan *Degrees:* A *Prof. Accred.:* Animal Science Technology, Dental Assisting, Dental Hygiene, Medical Laboratory Technology (AMA) *CEO:* Pres. Robert W. Ramsay
Enroll: 9363 (609) 227-7200

BRANCH CAMPUS
Seventh and Cooper Sts., Camden, NJ 08102 *CEO:* Dir. Dhamiri B. Abayomi
(609) 338-1817

CAMDEN COUNTY VOCATIONAL-TECHNICAL SCHOOL
Cross Keys Rd., P.O. Box 566, Sicklerville 08081 *Type:* Private *Calendar:* Courses of varying lengths *Degrees:* certificates *Prof. Accred.:* Dental Assisting, Medical Assisting (AMA) *CEO:* Supt. R. Sanders Haldeman
(609) 767-7000

CENTENARY COLLEGE
400 Jefferson St., Hackettstown 07840 *Type:* Private primarily for women *Accred.:* 1932/1987 (MSA) *Calendar:* Sem. plan *Degrees:* A, B *CEO:* Pres. Stephanie M. Bennett
Enroll: 807 (201) 852-1400

THE CHUBB INSTITUTE
8 Sylvan Way, Parsippany 07054-0342 *Type:* Private *Accred.:* 1972/1987 (CCA-ACTTS) *Calendar:* Courses of varying lengths *Degrees:* diplomas *CEO:* Dir. Todd Brown
Enroll: 1168 (201) 682-4900

BRANCH CAMPUS
40 Journal Sq., Jersey City, NJ 07306-4009 *CEO:* Dir. George C. Kiesel
(201) 656-0330

CITTONE INSTITUTE
1697 Oak Tree Rd., Edison 08820 *Type:* Private business *Accred.:* 1975/1990 (CCA-ACICS) *Calendar:* Courses of varying lengths *Degrees:* certificates, diplomas *CEO:* Dir. Simon Cittone
Enroll: 2217 (908) 548-8798

BRANCH CAMPUS
523 Fellowship Rd., Mount Laurel, NJ 08054 *CEO:* Dir. Matthew Cyrelson
(609) 722-9333

BRANCH CAMPUS
100 Canal Pointe Blvd., Princeton, NJ 08540 *CEO:* Dir. Michelle K. Avanzato
(609) 520-8798

CLAIRE DeMARZO INSTITUTE OF PROFESSIONAL ELECTROLOGY
5 Park Ave., Westwood 07675-2117 *Type:* Private *Accred.:* 1983/1988 (CCA-ACTTS) *Calendar:* Courses of varying lengths *Degrees:* certificates *CEO:* Pres. Claire DeMarzo
Enroll: 19 (201) 664-0171

COLLEGE OF ST. ELIZABETH
2 Convent Rd., Morristown 07960-6989 *Type:* Private (Roman Catholic) liberal arts for women *Accred.:* 1921/1988 (MSA) *Calendar:* Sem. plan *Degrees:* B, certificates, diplomas *Prof. Accred.:* Nursing (B) *CEO:* Pres. Jacqueline Burns
Enroll: 1040 (201) 292-6300

COMPUTER LEARNING CENTER
160 E. Rte. 4, Paramus 07652 *Type:* Private business *Accred.:* 1984 (CCA-ACICS) *Cal-*

endar: Courses of varying lengths *Degrees:* certificates, diplomas *CEO:* Pres./Dir. Graeme Dorras
Enroll: 850 (201) 845-6868

COUNTY COLLEGE OF MORRIS
214 Center Grove Rd., Randolph 07869 *Type:* Public (county) junior *System:* Office of Community Colleges *Accred.:* 1972/1988 (MSA) *Calendar:* Sem. plan *Degrees:* A, certificates, diplomas *Prof. Accred.:* Engineering Technology (electrical, mechanical), Medical Laboratory Technology (AMA), Nursing (A) *CEO:* Pres. Edward J. Yaw
Enroll: 9347 (201) 361-5000

CUMBERLAND COUNTY COLLEGE
College Dr., P.O. Box 517, Vineland 08360 *Type:* Public (county) junior *System:* Office of Community Colleges *Accred.:* 1970/1987 (MSA) *Calendar:* Sem. plan *Degrees:* A, certificates, diplomas *Prof. Accred.:* Nursing (A), Radiography *CEO:* Pres. Roland J. Chapdelaine
Enroll: 2266 (609) 691-8600

DEVRY TECHNICAL INSTITUTE, WOODBRIDGE
479 Green St., Woodbridge 07095-1489 *Type:* Private *Accred.:* 1971/1988 (CCA-ACTTS); 1981/1987 (NCA) *Calendar:* Tri. plan *Degrees:* certificates *Prof. Accred.:* Engineering Technology (electrical) *CEO:* Pres. Robert Bocchino
Enroll: 4233 (201) 634-3460

DIVERS ACADEMY OF THE EASTERN SEABOARD
2500 S. Broadway, Camden 08104-2431 *Type:* Private *Accred.:* 1981/1986 (CCA-ACTTS) *Calendar:* Courses of varying lengths *Degrees:* certificates, diplomas *CEO:* Dir. William M. Brown
Enroll: 106 (800) 238-3483

DOVER BUSINESS COLLEGE
15 E. Blackwell St., Dover 07801 *Type:* Private business *Accred.:* 1974/1986 (CCA-ACICS) *Calendar:* Qtr. plan *Degrees:* certificates, diplomas *CEO:* Dir. David H. Weaver
Enroll: 126 (201) 366-6700

DRAKE COLLEGE OF BUSINESS
9 Caldwell Pl., Elizabeth 07201 *Type:* Private business *Accred.:* 1982/1985 (CCA-ACICS) *Calendar:* Sem. plan *Degrees:* certificates, diplomas *CEO:* Pres. Freida Kay
Enroll: 108 (201) 352-5509

DRAKE SECRETARIAL COLLEGE
905 Bergen Ave., Jersey City 07306 *Type:* Private business *Accred.:* 1983/1986 (CCA-ACICS) *Calendar:* Sem. plan *Degrees:* certificates, diplomas *CEO:* Dir. Helen Poulos
Enroll: 438 (201) 653-2875

DREW UNIVERSITY
Madison Ave., Rte. 24, Madison 07940 *Type:* Private (United Methodist) *Accred.:* 1938/1991 (ATS); 1932/1985 (MSA) *Calendar:* Sem. plan *Degrees:* B, P, M, D *CEO:* Pres. Thomas H. Kean
Enroll: 2346 (201) 408-3000

DU CRET SCHOOL OF THE ARTS
1030 Central Ave., Plainfield 07060-2898 *Type:* Private *Accred.:* 1979/1989 (CCA-ACTTS) *Calendar:* Sem. plan *Degrees:* certificates, diplomas *CEO:* Dir. Frank J. Falotico
Enroll: 184 (908) 757-7171

EMPIRE TECHNICAL SCHOOLS OF NEW JERSEY
576 Central Ave., East Orange 07018-1983 *Type:* Private *Accred.:* 1969/1985 (CCA-ACTTS) *Calendar:* Courses of varying lengths *Degrees:* certificates *CEO:* Dir. Timothy M. Rodgers
Enroll: 723 (201) 675-0565

ENGINE CITY TECHNICAL INSTITUTE
Rte. 22 W., Box 3116, Union 07083-8517 *Type:* Private *Accred.:* 1984/1989 (CCA-ACTTS) *Calendar:* Courses of varying lengths *Degrees:* certificates *CEO:* Dir. Larry L. Berlin
Enroll: 361 (201) 964-1450

ESSEX COUNTY COLLEGE
303 University Ave., Newark 07102 *Type:* Public (county) junior *System:* Office of Community Colleges *Accred.:* 1974/1987 (MSA) *Calendar:* Sem. plan *Degrees:* A, certificates, diplomas *Prof. Accred.:* Physical

Accredited Institutions **New Jersey**

Therapy Assisting, Radiography *CEO:* Pres. A. Zachary Yamba
Enroll: 5664 (201) 877-3000

BRANCH CAMPUS
730 Bloomfield Ave., West Caldwell, NJ 07006 *CEO:* Dir. Elizabeth Porcelli
  (201) 228-3970

FAIRLEIGH DICKINSON UNIVERSITY
1000 River Rd., Teaneck 07666 *Type:* Private *Accred.:* 1948/1986 (MSA) *Calendar:* Sem. plan *Degrees:* A, B, P, M, D *Prof. Accred.:* Computer Science, Engineering (electrical) *CEO:* Pres. Francis J. Mertz
Enroll: 13087 (201) 692-2000

BRANCH CAMPUS
University Plaza 3, Hackensack, NJ 07840 *Prof. Accred.:* Clinical Psychology, Psychology Internship, Radiography, Respiratory Therapy *CEO:* Pres. Francis J. Mertz
  (201) 692-9170

FLORHAM-MADISON CAMPUS
285 Madison Ave., Madison, NJ 07940 *Prof. Accred.:* Physical Therapy Assisting *CEO:* Acting Pres. Walter T. Savage
  (201) 593-8500

RUTHERFORD CAMPUS
W. Passaic and Montross Aves., Rutherford, NJ 07070 *Prof. Accred.:* Nursing (B), Public Administration *CEO:* Pres. Francis J. Mertz
  (201) 460-5000

FELICIAN COLLEGE
260 S. Main St., Lodi 07644 *Type:* Private (Roman Catholic) liberal arts *Accred.:* 1974/1985 (MSA) *Calendar:* Sem. plan *Degrees:* A, B *Prof. Accred.:* Medical Laboratory Technology (AMA), Nursing (A,B) *CEO:* Pres. Theresa Mary Martin
Enroll: 647 (201) 778-1190

GENERAL TECHNICAL INSTITUTE WELDING TRADE SCHOOL
1118 Baltimore Ave., Linden 07036-1899 *Type:* Private *Accred.:* 1967/1987 (CCA-ACTTS) *Calendar:* Courses of varying lengths *Degrees:* certificates, diplomas *CEO:* Pres. Gregory G. Sytch
Enroll: 169 (201) 486-9353

GEORGIAN COURT COLLEGE
Lakewood Ave., Lakewood 08701 *Type:* Private (Roman Catholic) liberal arts primarily for women *Accred.:* 1922/1989 (MSA) *Calendar:* Sem. plan *Degrees:* B, M *Prof. Accred.:* Social Work (B-candidate) *CEO:* Pres. Barbara Williams
Enroll: 2054 (201) 364-2200

GLASSBORO STATE COLLEGE
Whitney Ave., Glassboro 08028 *Type:* Public (state) liberal arts and teachers *System:* Office of Senior Institutions *Accred.:* 1958/1989 (MSA) *Calendar:* Sem. plan *Degrees:* B, M, certificates, diplomas *Prof. Accred.:* Music, Teacher Education (e,s,p) *CEO:* Pres. Herman D. James
Enroll: 9500 (609) 863-5000

BRANCH CAMPUS
One Broadway, Camden, NJ 08102 *CEO:* Dir. Eric Clark
  (609) 757-2857

GLOBAL BUSINESS INSTITUTE
33 Journal Sq., Jersey City 07306 *Type:* Private business *Accred.:* 1988 (CCA-ACICS) *Calendar:* Courses of varying lengths *Degrees:* certificates, diplomas *CEO:* Dir. George P. Blount
  (201) 420-7900

GLOUCESTER COUNTY COLLEGE
Tanyard Rd., Deptford Twp., Sewell 08080 *Type:* Public (county) junior *System:* Office of Community Colleges *Accred.:* 1973/1988 (MSA) *Calendar:* Sem. plan *Degrees:* A, certificates, diplomas *Prof. Accred.:* Nuclear Medicine Technology, Nursing (A), Respiratory Therapy Technology *CEO:* Pres. Richard H. Jones
Enroll: 3702 (609) 468-5000

HARRIS SCHOOL OF BUSINESS
654 Longwood Ave., Cherry Hill 08002 *Type:* Private business *Accred.:* 1978/1987 (CCA-ACICS) *Calendar:* Courses of vary-

ing lengths *Degrees:* certificates, diplomas *CEO:* Dir. Joe Sowa
Enroll: 240 (609) 662-5300

THE HILL INSTITUTE
1719 Rte. 10, Bldg. B, Ste. 111, Parsippany 07054 *Type:* Private business *Accred.:* 1982/1985 (CCA-ACICS) *Calendar:* Qtr. plan *Degrees:* certificates, diplomas *CEO:* Dir. Philip A. Fishman
Enroll: 89 (201) 625-2660

HO-HO-KUS SCHOOL
27 S. Franklin Tpke., Ramsey 07446 *Type:* Private business *Accred.:* 1976/1985 (CCA-ACICS) *Calendar:* Courses of varying lengths *Degrees:* certificates, diplomas *CEO:* Dir. Thomas M. Eastwick
Enroll: 225 (201) 327-8877

HUDSON AREA SCHOOL OF RADIOLOGIC TECHNOLOGY
29 E. 29th St., Bayonne 07002 *Type:* Private *Calendar:* Courses of varying lengths *Degrees:* diplomas *Prof. Accred.:* Radiography *CEO:* Acting Chf. Operating Ofcr. Eugene Greenan
(201) 858-5202

HUDSON COUNTY COMMUNITY COLLEGE
901 Bergen Ave., Jersey City 07306 *Type:* Public (county) junior *System:* Office of Community Colleges *Accred.:* 1981/1986 (MSA) *Calendar:* Sem. plan *Degrees:* A *Prof. Accred.:* Engineering Technology (computer, electrical), Medical Assisting (AMA), Medical Record Technology *CEO:* Pres. Narcisa A. Polonio
Enroll: 2811 (201) 714-2100

IMMACULATE CONCEPTION SEMINARY OF SETON HALL UNIVERSITY
400 S. Orange Ave., South Orange 07079 *Type:* Private (Roman Catholic) *Accred.:* 1977/1982 (ATS) *Calendar:* Sem. plan *Degrees:* P, M *CEO:* Pres. Robert E. Harahan
Enroll: 164 (201) 761-9575

JERSEY CITY STATE COLLEGE
2039 Kennedy Blvd., Jersey City 07305 *Type:* Public (state) liberal arts and teachers *System:* Office of Senior Institutions *Accred.:* 1959/1985 (MSA) *Calendar:* Sem. plan *Degrees:* B, M, certificates, diplomas *Prof. Accred.:* Art, Music, Nursing (B), Teacher Education (e,s,p) *CEO:* Pres. William J. Maxwell
Enroll: 7552 (201) 547-6000

JOE KUBERT SCHOOL OF CARTOON AND GRAPHIC ART
37 Myrtle Ave., Dover 07801-4054 *Type:* Private *Accred.:* 1980/1985 (CCA-ACTTS) *Calendar:* Sem. plan *Degrees:* diplomas *CEO:* Owner Joe Kubert
Enroll: 139 (201) 361-1327

KANE BUSINESS INSTITUTE
206 Haddonfield Rd., Cherry Hill 08002 *Type:* Private business *Accred.:* 1985/1990 (CCA-ACICS) *Calendar:* Courses of varying lengths *Degrees:* certificates, diplomas *CEO:* Dir. Kathleen Mahaney
Enroll: 154 (609) 488-1166

KATHARINE GIBBS SCHOOL
33 Plymouth St., Montclair 07042 *Type:* Private junior *Accred.:* 1967/1988 (CCA-ACICS) *Calendar:* Sem. plan *Degrees:* A, certificates, diplomas *CEO:* Dir. Gloria Davis
Enroll: 770 (201) 744-2010

BRANCH CAMPUS
80 Kingsbridge Rd., Piscataway, NJ 08854 *CEO:* Dir. Terry Nighan
(908) 885-1580

KEAN COLLEGE OF NEW JERSEY
Morris Ave., Union 07083 *Type:* Public (state) liberal arts and teachers *System:* Office of Senior Institutions *Accred.:* 1960/1985 (MSA) *Calendar:* Sem. plan *Degrees:* B, M *Prof. Accred.:* Construction Education, Medical Record Administration, Music, Nursing (B), Occupational Therapy, Physical Therapy, Public Administration, Social Work (B), Teacher Education (e,p) *CEO:* Pres. Elsa Gomez
Enroll: 12372 (908) 527-2000

Accredited Institutions

New Jersey

LINCOLN TECHNICAL INSTITUTE
Haddonfield Rd. at Rte. 130N, Pennsauken 08110-1208 *Type:* Private *Accred.:* 1988 (CCA-ACTTS) *Calendar:* Courses of varying lengths *Degrees:* certificates *CEO:* Dir. Deborah M. Ramentol
Enroll: 1291   (609) 665-3010

LINCOLN TECHNICAL INSTITUTE
2299 Vauxhall Rd., Union 07083-5032 *Type:* Private *Accred.:* 1967/1988 (CCA-ACTTS) *Calendar:* Courses of varying lengths *Degrees:* certificates *CEO:* Dir. Robert P. Giocila
Enroll: 2397   (201) 964-7800

MERCER COUNTY COMMUNITY COLLEGE
1200 Old Trenton Rd., Trenton 08690 *Type:* Public (county) junior *System:* Office of Community Colleges *Accred.:* 1967/1985 (MSA) *Calendar:* Sem. plan *Degrees:* A, certificates, diplomas *Prof. Accred.:* Engineering Technology (civil/construction, electrical, mechanical), Funeral Service Education, Medical Laboratory Technology (AMA), Nursing (A), Radiography *CEO:* Pres. John P. Hanley
Enroll: 8651   (609) 586-4800

JAMES KERNEY CAMPUS
N. Broad and Academy Sts., Trenton, NJ 08690 *CEO:* Provost Beverly A. Richardson
    (609) 586-4800

METROPOLITAN TECHNICAL INSTITUTE
11 Daniel Rd., Fairfield 07004-2506 *Type:* Private *Accred.:* 1983/1988 (CCA-ACTTS) *Calendar:* Courses of varying lengths *Degrees:* certificates *CEO:* Dir. Frank Gergelyi
Enroll: 135   (201) 227-8191

MIDDLESEX COUNTY COLLEGE
155 Mill Rd., P.O. Box 3050, Edison 08818 *Type:* Public (county) junior *System:* Office of Community Colleges *Accred.:* 1970/1981 (MSA) *Calendar:* Sem. plan *Degrees:* A *Prof. Accred.:* Dental Hygiene, Engineering Technology (civil/construction, electrical, mechanical), Medical Laboratory Technology (AMA), Nursing (A), Radiography *CEO:* Pres. Flora Mancuso-Edwards
Enroll: 11218   (908) 548-6000

MONMOUTH COLLEGE
Norwood and Cedar Aves., West Long Branch 07764 *Type:* Private liberal arts *Accred.:* 1952/1986 (MSA) *Calendar:* Sem. plan *Degrees:* A, B, M *Prof. Accred.:* Engineering (electrical), Medical Technology, Nursing (B), Social Work (B) *CEO:* Pres. Samuel H. Magill
Enroll: 4430   (201) 571-3400

MONTCLAIR STATE COLLEGE
Valley Rd. and Normal Ave., Upper Montclair 07043 *Type:* Public (state) liberal arts and teachers *System:* Office of Senior Institutions *Accred.:* 1937/1987 (MSA) *Calendar:* Sem. plan *Degrees:* B, M *Prof. Accred.:* Art, Dance, Home Economics, Music, Recreation and Leisure Studies, Speech-Language Pathology, Teacher Education (s,p), Theatre *CEO:* Pres. Irvin D. Reid
Enroll: 12720   (201) 893-4000

THE NASH ACADEMY OF ANIMAL ARTS
595 Anderson Ave., Cliffside Park 07010-1830 *Type:* Private *Accred.:* 1982/1987 (CCA-ACTTS) *Calendar:* Courses of varying lengths *Degrees:* certificates, diplomas *CEO:* Dir. John Nash
Enroll: 76   (201) 945-2710

NATIONAL CENTER FOR LOGISTICS MANAGEMENT
819 Meetinghouse Rd., Cinnaminson 08077 *Type:* Private home study *Accred.:* 1990 (NHSC) *Calendar:* Courses of varying lengths *Degrees:* certificates *CEO:* Pres. Stanley C. Thomas, Jr.
    (609) 786-9112

NATIONAL EDUCATION CENTER—R.E.T.S. CAMPUS
103 Park Ave., Nutley 07110-3505 *Type:* Private *Accred.:* 1977/1988 (CCA-ACTTS) *Calendar:* Qtr. plan *Degrees:* certificates, diplomas *CEO:* Dir. Martin Klangasky
Enroll: 1050   (201) 661-0600

New Jersey

NEW BRUNSWICK THEOLOGICAL SEMINARY
17 Seminary Pl., New Brunswick 08901 *Type:* Private professional; graduate only *Accred.:* 1938/1986 (ATS) *Calendar:* Sem. plan *Degrees:* P, M *CEO:* Pres. Robert A. White
Enroll: 62   (908) 247-5241

NEW JERSEY INSTITUTE OF TECHNOLOGY
323 High St., Newark 07102 *Type:* Public (state and city) technological *System:* Office of Senior Institutions *Accred.:* 1934/1988 (MSA) *Calendar:* Sem. plan *Degrees:* B, M, D, certificates, diplomas *Prof. Accred.:* Architecture (B,M), Computer Science, Engineering (chemical, civil, electrical, industrial, mechanical), Engineering Technology (civil/construction, electrical, manufacturing, mechanical) *CEO:* Pres. Saul K. Fenster
Enroll: 7668   (201) 596-3000

OCEAN COUNTY COLLEGE
College Dr., Toms River 08753-2001 *Type:* Public (county) junior *System:* Office of Community Colleges *Accred.:* 1969/1989 (MSA) *Calendar:* Sem. plan *Degrees:* A, certificates, diplomas *Prof. Accred.:* Engineering Technology (electrical), Medical Laboratory Technology (AMA), Nursing (A) *CEO:* Pres. Milton Shaw
Enroll: 6214   (908) 255-4000

OMEGA INSTITUTE
Cinnaminson Mall, Rte. 130 S., Cinnaminson 08077 *Type:* Private business *Accred.:* 1982/1988 (CCA-ACICS) *Calendar:* Courses of varying lengths *Degrees:* certificates, diplomas *Prof. Accred.:* Medical Assisting *CEO:* Pres. Lee Cobleigh
Enroll: 424   (609) 786-2200

PTC CAREER INSTITUTE
200 Washington St., Newark 07102-2921 *Type:* Private *Accred.:* 1991 (CCA-ACTTS) *Calendar:* Courses of varying lengths *Degrees:* certificates *CEO:* Dir. Louis Monaco
   (201) 623-1100

PASSAIC COUNTY COMMUNITY COLLEGE
College Blvd., Paterson 07509 *Type:* Public (county) junior *System:* Office of Community Colleges *Accred.:* 1978/1984 (MSA) *Calendar:* Sem. plan *Degrees:* A, certificates, diplomas *Prof. Accred.:* Nursing (A), Radiography, Respiratory Therapy Technology *CEO:* Pres. Elliott Collins
Enroll: 2839   (201) 684-6800

PENNCO TECH
Erial Rd., P.O. Box 1427, Blackwood 08012-1427 *Type:* Private *Accred.:* 1980/1985 (CCA-ACTTS) *Calendar:* Courses of varying lengths *Degrees:* diplomas *CEO:* Dir. Donald S. VanDemark, Jr.
Enroll: 639   (609) 232-0310

PHILLIPS BUSINESS SCHOOL
60 Evergreen Pl., East Orange 07018 *Type:* Private business *Accred.:* 1986 (CCA-ACICS) *Calendar:* Courses of varying lengths *Degrees:* certificates, diplomas *CEO:* Dir. Catherine Palmer
Enroll: 661   (201) 673-6009

BRANCH CAMPUS
2844 Kennedy Blvd., Jersey City, NJ 07306 *CEO:* Dir. Gladys Beaty Foy
   (201) 659-1008

BRANCH CAMPUS
6-8 Mill St., Paterson, NJ 07505 *CEO:* Dir. Sylvester Lewis
   (201) 279-9800

THE PLAZA SCHOOL
The Bergen Mall, Paramus 07652 *Type:* Private *Accred.:* 1971/1988 (CCA-ACTTS) *Calendar:* Courses of varying lengths *Degrees:* diplomas *CEO:* Pres. Leslie Balter
Enroll: 217   (201) 843-0344

PRINCETON THEOLOGICAL SEMINARY
Princeton 08542 *Type:* Private (Presbyterian) professional; graduate only *Accred.:* 1938/1987 (ATS); 1968/1988 (MSA) *Calendar:* Sem. plan *Degrees:* P, M, D *CEO:* Pres. Thomas W. Gillespie
Enroll: 699   (609) 921-8300

Accredited Institutions

New Jersey

PRINCETON UNIVERSITY
Princeton 08544 *Type:* Private *Accred.:* 1921/1989 (MSA) *Calendar:* Sem. plan *Degrees:* B, P, M, D *Prof. Accred.:* Architecture (M), Engineering (aerospace, chemical, civil, electrical, engineering physics/science, geological/geophysical, mechanical), Public Affairs *CEO:* Pres. Harold T. Shapiro
Enroll: 6284   (609) 258-3000

RABBINICAL COLLEGE OF AMERICA
226 Sussex Ave., Morristown 07960 *Type:* Private professional *Accred.:* 1979/1990 (AARTS) *Calendar:* Sem. plan *Degrees:* B *CEO:* Pres. M. Herson
Enroll: 148   (201) 267-9404

RAMAPO COLLEGE OF NEW JERSEY
505 Ramapo Valley Rd., Mahwah 07430 *Type:* Public (state) liberal arts *System:* Office of Senior Institutions *Accred.:* 1975/1987 (MSA) *Calendar:* Sem. plan *Degrees:* B *Prof. Accred.:* Social Work (B) *CEO:* Pres. Robert A. Scott
Enroll: 4058   (201) 529-7500

RARITAN VALLEY COMMUNITY COLLEGE
P.O. Box 3300, Somerville 08876 *Type:* Public (county) junior *System:* Office of Community Colleges *Accred.:* 1972/1987 (MSA) *Calendar:* Sem. plan *Degrees:* A, certificates, diplomas *Prof. Accred.:* Nursing (A) *CEO:* Pres. Charles S. Irace
Enroll: 4844   (908) 526-1200

RICHARD STOCKTON STATE COLLEGE
Jimmy Leeds Rd., Pomona 08240 *Type:* Public (state) liberal arts *System:* Office of Senior Institutions *Accred.:* 1975/1988 (MSA) *Calendar:* Sem. plan *Degrees:* B *Prof. Accred.:* Nursing (B), Physical Therapy, Social Work (B) *CEO:* Pres. Vera King Farris
Enroll: 5297   (609) 652-1776

RIDER COLLEGE
2083 Lawrenceville Rd., Lawrenceville 08648 *Type:* Private liberal arts *Accred.:* 1955/1986 (MSA) *Calendar:* 4-1-4 plan *Degrees:* B, M *Prof. Accred.:* Teacher Education (e,s,p) *CEO:* Pres. J. Barton Luedeke
Enroll: 5352   (609) 896-5000

RUTGERS, THE STATE UNIVERSITY OF NEW JERSEY—CAMDEN
311 N. Fifth St., Camden 08102 *Type:* Public (state) *System:* Rutgers, The State University of New Jersey Central Office *Accred.:* 1950/1988 (MSA) *Calendar:* Sem. plan *Degrees:* B, P, M *Prof. Accred.:* Law, Nursing (B), Physical Therapy, Social Work (B,M) *CEO:* Provost Walter K. Gordon
Enroll: 5200   (609) 757-1766

RUTGERS, THE STATE UNIVERSITY OF NEW JERSEY—NEW BRUNSWICK
New Brunswick 08903 *Type:* Public (state) *System:* Rutgers, The State University of New Jersey Central Office *Accred.:* 1921/1988 (MSA) *Calendar:* Sem. plan *Degrees:* B, M, D *Prof. Accred.:* Accounting (Type A), Business (B), Clinical Psychology, Engineering (agricultural, ceramic, chemical, civil, electrical, industrial, mechanical), Landscape Architecture (B), Librarianship, Music, Pharmacy, Planning (city/regional), School Psychology, Social Work (B,M), Theatre *CEO:* Provost Paul D. Leath
Enroll: 32969   (908) 932-1766

RUTGERS, THE STATE UNIVERSITY OF NEW JERSEY—NEWARK
15 Washington St., Newark 07102 *Type:* Public (state) *System:* Rutgers, The State University of New Jersey Central Office *Accred.:* 1946/1988 (MSA) *Calendar:* Sem. plan *Degrees:* B, P, M, D *Prof. Accred.:* Business (B,M), Law, Music, Nursing (B,M), Public Administration, Social Work (B,M) *CEO:* Provost Norman Samuels
Enroll: 9730   (201) 648-1766

SCS BUSINESS AND TECHNICAL INSTITUTE
516 Main St., East Orange 07017 *Type:* Private business *Accred.:* 1988/1990 (CCA-ACICS) *Calendar:* Courses of varying lengths *Degrees:* certificates, diplomas *CEO:* Dir. Cheryl Dyer
Enroll: 528   (201) 675-4300

New Jersey

SCS BUSINESS AND TECHNICAL INSTITUTE
756 Broad St., Newark 07102 *Type:* Private business *Accred.:* 1986/1988 (CCA-ACICS) *Calendar:* Courses of varying lengths *Degrees:* certificates, diplomas *CEO:* Dir. Manuel Rios
Enroll: 1039 (201) 623-3939

BRANCH CAMPUS
714 Market St., Philadelphia, PA 19106 *CEO:* Dir. Alexandra Abramsky
(215) 592-8600

SCS BUSINESS AND TECHNICAL INSTITUTE
2200 Bergenline Ave., Union City 07087 *Type:* Private business *Accred.:* 1987/1990 (CCA-ACICS) *Calendar:* Courses of varying lengths *Degrees:* certificates, diplomas *CEO:* Dir. Judy Gacita
Enroll: 552 (201) 867-3500

ST. PETER'S COLLEGE
2641 Kennedy Blvd., Jersey City 07306 *Type:* Private (Roman Catholic) liberal arts *Accred.:* 1935/1988 (MSA) *Calendar:* Sem. plan *Degrees:* A, B, M, certificates, diplomas *Prof. Accred.:* Nursing (B) *CEO:* Pres. Daniel A. Degnan, S.J.
Enroll: 3346 (201) 915-9000

BRANCH CAMPUS
Hudson Terrace, Englewood Cliffs, NJ 07632 *CEO:* Dir. Katherine Restaino-Dick
(201) 568-7730

SALEM COMMUNITY COLLEGE
460 Hollywood Ave., Carneys Point 08069 *Type:* Public (district) junior *System:* Office of Community Colleges *Accred.:* 1979/1984 (MSA) *Calendar:* Sem. plan *Degrees:* A *CEO:* Pres. Philip O. Barry
Enroll: 1202 (609) 299-2100

SAWYER SCHOOL
664 Newark Ave., Elizabeth 07208 *Type:* Private business *Accred.:* 1972/1987 (CCA-ACICS) *Calendar:* Courses of varying lengths *Degrees:* certificates, diplomas *CEO:* Pres. George Vomacka
Enroll: 637 (201) 351-5150

SETON HALL UNIVERSITY
400 S. Orange Ave., South Orange 07079 *Type:* Private (Roman Catholic) *Accred.:* 1932/1989 (MSA) *Calendar:* Sem. plan *Degrees:* B, P, M, D, certificates, diplomas *Prof. Accred.:* Business (B,M), Nursing (B,M), Public Administration, Social Work (B), Teacher Education (e,s,p) *CEO:* Chanc. Thomas R. Peterson
Enroll: 8854 (201) 761-9000

SCHOOL OF LAW
1111 Raymond Blvd., Newark, NJ 07102 *Prof. Accred.:* Law *CEO:* Dean Ronald J. Riccio
Enroll: 1200 (201) 642-8500

STAR TECHNICAL INSTITUTE
2101 Ferry Ave., Ste. 217, Camden 08104-1910 *Type:* Private *Accred.:* 1991 (CCA-ACTTS) *Calendar:* Courses of varying lengths *Degrees:* diplomas *CEO:* Dir. B.J. Feider
(609) 963-7827

STAR TECHNICAL INSTITUTE
2224 U.S. Hwy., 130 Park Pl., Edgewater Park 08010-3105 *Type:* Private *Accred.:* 1985 (CCA-ACTTS) *Calendar:* Courses of varying lengths *Degrees:* diplomas *CEO:* Dir. Sharon Foley
(609) 877-2727

BRANCH CAMPUS
212 Wyoming Ave., Kingston, PA 18704 *CEO:* Dir. Jane M. Acri
(717) 287-9777

BRANCH CAMPUS
225 N. Washington Ave., Scranton, PA 18503-1514 *CEO:* Dir. Robert Wills
(717) 963-0144

STAR TECHNICAL INSTITUTE
Sommerdale Sq., Ste. 2, Sommerdale 08083-1345 *Type:* Private *Accred.:* 1985 (CCA-ACTTS) *Calendar:* Courses of varying lengths *Degrees:* diplomas *CEO:* Dir. Marcie Evans
Enroll: 263 (609) 435-7827

BRANCH CAMPUS
1255 Rte. 70, Ste. 12N, Lakewood, NJ 08701-5947 *CEO:* Dir. Charles Walker
(201) 901-0001

STAR TECHNICAL INSTITUTE
1386 S. Delsea Dr., Vineland 08360-6210 *Type:* Private *Accred.:* 1985 (CCA-ACTTS) *Calendar:* Courses of varying lengths *Degrees:* diplomas *CEO:* Dir. William J. Dougherty
Enroll: 61 (609) 696-0500

BRANCH CAMPUS
2105 Hwy. 35, Ocean Township, NJ 07712-7201 *CEO:* Dir. James Mannion
(201) 493-1660

STEVENS INSTITUTE OF TECHNOLOGY
Castle Point Sta., Hoboken 07030 *Type:* Private technical *Accred.:* 1927/1987 (MSA) *Calendar:* Sem. plan *Degrees:* B, M, D *Prof. Accred.:* Computer Science, Engineering (chemical, civil, computer, electrical, engineering physics/science, general, mechanical, metallurgical) *CEO:* Pres. Harold J. Raveche
Enroll: 3124 (201) 420-5100

STUART SCHOOL OF BUSINESS ADMINISTRATION
2400 Belmar Blvd., Wall 07719 *Type:* Private business *Accred.:* 1967/1979 (CCA-ACICS) *Calendar:* Sem. plan *Degrees:* certificates, diplomas *CEO:* Dir. Letitia M. Cooper
Enroll: 131 (201) 681-7200

TALMUDICAL ACADEMY OF NEW JERSEY
Rte. 524, Adelphia 07710 *Type:* Private professional *Accred.:* 1980/1986 (AARTS) *Calendar:* Sem. plan *Degrees:* B *CEO:* Pres. B. Leff
Enroll: 23 (201) 431-1600

TETERBORO SCHOOL OF AERONAUTICS
80 Moonachie Ave., Teterboro Airport, Teterboro 07608-1083 *Type:* Private *Accred.:* 1973/1989 (CCA-ACTTS) *Calendar:* Courses of varying lengths *Degrees:* certificates, diplomas *CEO:* Dir. Anthony DiStefano
Enroll: 609 (201) 288-6300

THOMAS A. EDISON STATE COLLEGE
101 W. State St., Trenton 08608 *Type:* Public (state) liberal arts *System:* Office of Senior Institutions *Accred.:* 1977/1987 (MSA) *Calendar:* Sem. plan *Degrees:* A, B, certificates, diplomas *Prof. Accred.:* Nursing (B) *CEO:* Pres. George A. Pruitt
Enroll: 6844 (609) 984-1100

TRENTON STATE COLLEGE
Hillwood Lakes, Trenton 08650 *Type:* Public (state) liberal arts and professional *System:* Office of Senior Institutions *Accred.:* 1939/1985 (MSA) *Calendar:* Sem. plan *Degrees:* B, M, certificates, diplomas *Prof. Accred.:* Engineering Technology (industrial, mechanical), Interior Design, Music, Nursing (B), Speech-Language Pathology, Teacher Education (e,s,p) *CEO:* Pres. Harold W. Eickhoff
Enroll: 7348 (609) 771-1855

ULTRASOUND DIAGNOSTIC SCHOOL
1030 Salem Rd., Union 07083 *Type:* Private *Calendar:* Courses of varying lengths *Degrees:* certificates *Prof. Accred.:* Health Education *CEO:* Admin. Estelle Wilchins
(201) 851-9150

UNION COUNTY COLLEGE
1033 Springfield Ave., Cranford 07016 *Type:* Public (county) junior *System:* Office of Community Colleges *Accred.:* 1957/1987 (MSA) *Calendar:* Sem. plan *Degrees:* A, certificates, diplomas *Prof. Accred.:* Dental Hygiene, Dental Laboratory Technology, Physical Therapy Assisting, Respiratory Therapy *CEO:* Pres. Thomas H. Brown, Ph.D.
Enroll: 8741 (908) 709-7000

BRANCH CAMPUS
12 W. Jersey St., Elizabeth, NJ 07206 *CEO:* Provost Marion Bonaparte
(908) 965-6090

New Jersey

BRANCH CAMPUS
232 E. Second St., Plainfield, NJ 07060 *CEO:* Pres. Thomas H. Brown, Ph.D.
(908) 889-8500

BRANCH CAMPUS
1776 Raritan Rd., Scotch Plains, NJ 07076 *Prof. Accred.:* Occupational Therapy Assisting, Practical Nursing *CEO:* Pres. Thomas H. Brown, Ph.D.
(908) 889-8000

UNITED STATES ARMY CHAPLAIN CENTER AND SCHOOL
Fort Monmouth 07703-5511 *Type:* Public (federal) professional *Accred.:* 1978/1988 (SACS-COEI) *Calendar:* Courses of varying lengths *Degrees:* certificates *CEO:* Commandant Bernard Windmiller
Enroll: 254   (201) 532-2266

UNITED STATES NAVAL AIR TECHNICAL TRAINING CENTER
Bldg. 150, Lakehurst 08733-5001 *Type:* Public (federal) *Accred.:* 1984/1989 (SACS-COEI) *Calendar:* Courses of varying lengths *Degrees:* certificates *CEO:* Commandant R.T. Wojcik
Enroll: 387   (908) 323-2684

BRANCH CAMPUS
Naval Air Sta., North Island, San Diego, CA 92135 *CEO:* Div. Head Kenneth Heinz
(619) 545-7952

UNIVERSITY OF MEDICINE AND DENTISTRY OF NEW JERSEY
30 Bergen St., Newark 07107 *Type:* Public (state) professional *System:* Office of Senior Institutions *Accred.:* 1979/1985 (MSA) *Calendar:* Sem. plan *Degrees:* A, B, P, M, D, certificates, diplomas *CEO:* Pres. Stanley S. Bergen, Jr.
Enroll: 2901   (201) 456-4300

GRADUATE SCHOOL OF BIOMEDICAL SCIENCES
185 S. Orange Ave., Newark, NJ 07103 *CEO:* Dean Vincent Lanzoni
Enroll: 681   (201) 456-4511

NEW JERSEY DENTAL SCHOOL
110 Bergen St., Newark, NJ 07103 *Accred.:* 1979/1985 (MSA) *Prof. Accred.:* Combined Prosthodontics, Dental Assisting, Dental Hygiene, Dentistry, Endodontics, Oral and Maxillofacial Surgery, Orthodontics, Pediatric Dentistry, Periodontics *CEO:* Dean Richard N. Buchanan
Enroll: 398   (201) 456-4633

NEW JERSEY MEDICAL SCHOOL
185 S. Orange Ave., Newark, NJ 07103 *Prof. Accred.:* Medicine, Psychology Internship *CEO:* Dean Ruy V. Lourenco
Enroll: 703   (201) 465-4539

ROBERT WOOD JOHNSON MEDICAL SCHOOL
675 Hoes La., Piscataway, NJ 08854 *Prof. Accred.:* Community Health/Preventive Medicine, Medicine, Physician Assisting, Psychology Internship *CEO:* Dean Norman H. Edelman
Enroll: 573   (908) 463-4557

SCHOOL OF HEALTH-RELATED PROFESSIONS
65 Bergen St., Newark, NJ 07107 *Prof. Accred.:* Cytotechnology, Diagnostic Medical Sonography, Dietetics (internship), Medical Technology, Nuclear Medicine Technology, Physical Therapy, Physical Therapy Assisting, Radiography, Respiratory Therapy, Respiratory Therapy Technology, Surgical Technology *CEO:* Acting Dean David M. Gibson
Enroll: 503   (201) 456-5453

SCHOOL OF OSTEOPATHIC MEDICINE
40 E. Laurel Rd., Stratford, NJ 08084 *Prof. Accred.:* Osteopathy *CEO:* Dean Frederick Humphrey, II
Enroll: 213   (609) 346-6990

UPSALA COLLEGE
Prospect St., East Orange 07019 *Type:* Private (Evangelical Lutheran) liberal arts *Accred.:* 1936/1984 (MSA) *Calendar:* Sem. plan *Degrees:* A, B, M *Prof. Accred.:* Social Work (B) *CEO:* Pres. Robert E. Karsten
Enroll: 1112   (201) 266-7000

WIRTHS CAMPUS
R.D. 3, Box 138-A, Sussex, NJ 07461
CEO: Dir. Edward Lawson
Enroll: 326 (201) 875-7187

WESTMINSTER CHOIR COLLEGE
Hamilton Ave. and Walnut La., Princeton 08540 *Type:* Private professional *Accred.:* 1966/1986 (MSA) *Calendar:* Sem. plan *Degrees:* B, M *Prof. Accred.:* Music *CEO:* C.E.O. Keith Spalding
Enroll: 347 (609) 921-7100

WILLIAM PATERSON COLLEGE OF NEW JERSEY
300 Pompton Rd., Wayne 07470 *Type:* Public (state) liberal arts and teachers *System:* Office of Senior Institutions *Accred.:* 1958/1988 (MSA) *Calendar:* Sem. plan *Degrees:* B, M *Prof. Accred.:* Music, Nursing (B), Speech-Language Pathology, Teacher Education (e,s,p) *CEO:* Pres. Arnold S. Speert
Enroll: 9230 (201) 595-2000

NEW MEXICO

ALBUQUERQUE BARBER COLLEGE
525 San Pedro Dr., N.E., Ste. 104, Albuquerque 87108 *Type:* Private *Accred.:* 1988 (CCA-ACTTS) *Calendar:* Courses of varying lengths *Degrees:* certificates *CEO:* Dir. Gene J. Varoz
(505) 266-4900

ALBUQUERQUE TECHNICAL-VOCATIONAL INSTITUTE
525 Buena Vista Dr., S.E., Albuquerque 87106 *Type:* Public 2-year *Accred.:* 1978/1983 (NCA) *Calendar:* Tri. plan *Degrees:* A, certificates, diplomas *Prof. Accred.:* Medical Laboratory Technology (AMA), Nursing (A), Practical Nursing, Respiratory Therapy Technology *CEO:* Pres. Ted F. Martinez
Enroll: 6225   (505) 768-0405

AMERICAN TRAVEL CENTRE
1130 Lomas Blvd., N.E., Albuquerque 87192 *Type:* Private home study *Accred.:* 1991 (NHSC) *Calendar:* Courses of varying lengths *Degrees:* certificates *CEO:* Pres. Kenneth G. Gabel
(505) 291-8100

CLOVIS COMMUNITY COLLEGE
417 Schepps Blvd., Clovis 88101 *Type:* Public (state) junior *System:* New Mexico Commission of Higher Education *Accred.:* 1987 (NCA) *Calendar:* Sem. plan *Degrees:* A, certificates, diplomas *Prof. Accred.:* Nursing (A), Radiography *CEO:* Provost Jay Gurley
Enroll: 596   (505) 769-2811

COLLEGE OF SANTA FE
St. Michael's Dr., Santa Fe 87501 *Type:* Private (Roman Catholic) liberal arts *Accred.:* 1965/1991 (NCA) *Calendar:* Sem. plan *Degrees:* A, B, M *Prof. Accred.:* Nursing (A) *CEO:* Pres. James A. Fries
Enroll: 851   (505) 473-6234

COLLEGE OF THE SOUTHWEST
6610 Lovington Hwy., Hobbs 88240 *Type:* Private liberal arts *Accred.:* 1980/1988 (NCA) *Calendar:* Sem. plan *Degrees:* B *CEO:* Pres. Joan M. Tucker
Enroll: 268   (505) 392-6561

DONA ANA BRANCH COMMUNITY COLLEGE
Box 30001, Las Cruces 88003 *Type:* Public 2-year *Calendar:* Courses of varying lengths *Degrees:* A, certificates, diplomas *Prof. Accred.:* Radiography *CEO:* Provost Donaciano Gonzalez
(505) 527-7510

EASTERN NEW MEXICO UNIVERSITY
Portales 88130 *Type:* Public (state) *System:* New Mexico Commission of Higher Education *Accred.:* 1947/1987 (NCA) *Calendar:* Sem. plan *Degrees:* A, B, M *Prof. Accred.:* Music, Teacher Education (e,s) *CEO:* Pres. Everett Frost
Enroll: 3123   (505) 562-2121

EASTERN NEW MEXICO UNIVERSITY—ROSWELL
P.O. Box 6000, Roswell 88202 *Type:* Public (state) *Accred.:* 1971/1987 (NCA) *Calendar:* Sem. plan *Degrees:* A, certificates, diplomas *Prof. Accred.:* Nursing (A) *CEO:* Provost Loyd R. Hughes
Enroll: 1077   (505) 624-7000

INSTITUTE OF AMERICAN INDIAN AND ALASKAN NATIVE CULTURE AND ARTS DEVELOPMENT
P.O. Box 20007, Santa Fe 87504 *Type:* Public (federal) *Accred.:* 1984/1990 (NCA) *Calendar:* Sem. plan *Degrees:* A, certificates, diplomas *Prof. Accred.:* Art *CEO:* Pres. Kathryn Harris Tijerina
Enroll: 227   (505) 988-6463

INTERNATIONAL BUSINESS COLLEGE
3200 N. White Sands Blvd., Alamogordo 88310 *Type:* Private business *Accred.:* 1982/1987 (CCA-ACICS) *Calendar:* Courses of varying lengths *Degrees:* certificates, diplomas *CEO:* Dir. Linda Wallace
Enroll: 301   (505) 437-1854

New Mexico

INTERNATIONAL BUSINESS COLLEGE
4223 Montgomery Blvd., N.E., Albuquerque 87109 *Type:* Private business *Accred.:* 1985/1987 (CCA-ACICS) *Calendar:* Courses of varying lengths *Degrees:* certificates, diplomas *CEO:* Dir. Andrea Gonzales
Enroll: 793   (505) 883-0696

BRANCH CAMPUS
221 San Pedro Dr., N.E., Albuquerque, NM 87108 *CEO:* Dir. David M. Loyd
          (505) 266-5591

INTERNATIONAL BUSINESS COLLEGE
650 E. Montana Ave., Ste. F, Las Cruces 88001 *Type:* Private business *Accred.:* 1981/1987 (CCA-ACICS) *Calendar:* Courses of varying lengths *Degrees:* certificates, diplomas *CEO:* Dir. Larry Madrid
Enroll: 648   (505) 526-5579

INTERNATIONAL INSTITUTE OF CHINESE MEDICINE
P.O. Box 4991, Santa Fe 87502 *Type:* Private *Calendar:* 3-year program *Degrees:* M *Prof. Accred.:* Acupuncture *CEO:* Pres. Michael Zeng
          (505) 473-5233

LUJAC BUSINESS SCHOOL
558 U.S. Hwy. 64, Farmington 87401 *Type:* Private business *Accred.:* 1988/1991 (CCA-ACICS) *Calendar:* Courses of varying lengths *Degrees:* certificates, diplomas *CEO:* Dir. Lucy C. Jacquez
Enroll: 48   (505) 326-6153

LUNA VOCATIONAL-TECHNICAL INSTITUTE
P.O. Drawer K, Las Vegas 87701 *Type:* Public 2-year *Accred.:* 1982/1987 (NCA) *Calendar:* Tri. plan *Degrees:* A, certificates, diplomas *CEO:* Pres. Samuel F. Vigil
Enroll: 571   (505) 454-2500

NEW MEXICO HIGHLANDS UNIVERSITY
National Ave., Las Vegas 87701 *Type:* Public (state) liberal arts and professional *System:* New Mexico Commission of Higher Education *Accred.:* 1926/1991 (NCA) *Calendar:* Sem. plan *Degrees:* A, B, P, M, certificates, diplomas *Prof. Accred.:* Social Work (B,M) *CEO:* Pres. Gilbert Sanchez
Enroll: 1990   (505) 425-7511

NEW MEXICO INSTITUTE OF MINING AND TECHNOLOGY
Socorro 87801 *Type:* Public (state) technological *System:* New Mexico Commission of Higher Education *Accred.:* 1949/1985 (NCA) *Calendar:* Sem. plan *Degrees:* A, B, M, D *Prof. Accred.:* Engineering (petroleum) *CEO:* Pres. Laurence H. Lattman
Enroll: 929   (505) 835-5600

NEW MEXICO JUNIOR COLLEGE
5317 Lovington Hwy., Hobbs 88240 *Type:* Public (district) junior *System:* New Mexico Commission of Higher Education *Accred.:* 1970/1986 (NCA) *Calendar:* Sem. plan *Degrees:* A, certificates, diplomas *Prof. Accred.:* Medical Laboratory Technology (AMA), Nursing (A) *CEO:* Pres. Charles D. Hays, Jr.
Enroll: 1265   (505) 392-4510

NEW MEXICO MILITARY INSTITUTE
100 W. College Blvd., Roswell 88201 *Type:* Public (state) junior *System:* New Mexico Commission of Higher Education *Accred.:* 1938/1991 (NCA) *Calendar:* Sem. plan *Degrees:* A *CEO:* Supt. Winfield W. Scott, Jr.
Enroll: 412   (505) 624-8000

NEW MEXICO STATE UNIVERSITY
Las Cruces 88003 *Type:* Public (state) *System:* New Mexico State University System *Accred.:* 1926/1988 (NCA) *Calendar:* Sem. plan *Degrees:* A, B, P, M, D, certificates, diplomas *Prof. Accred.:* Business (B,M), Computer Science, Dental Hygiene, Engineering (agricultural, chemical, civil, electrical, geological/geophysical, industrial, mechanical), Engineering Technology (civil/construction, electrical, mechanical), Music, Nursing (A,B), Public Administration, Social Work (B,M-candidate), Speech-Language Pathology, Teacher Education (e,s,p) *CEO:* Pres. James E. Halligan
Enroll: 11775   (505) 646-2035

New Mexico

NEW MEXICO STATE UNIVERSITY GRANTS
1500 3rd St., Grants, NM 87020 *CEO:* Provost William E. Sailer
(505) 287-7981

NEW MEXICO STATE UNIVERSITY AT ALAMOGORDO
P.O. Box 477, Alamogordo 88311-0477 *Type:* Public (state) *System:* New Mexico State University System *Accred.:* 1973/1983 (NCA) *Calendar:* Sem. plan *Degrees:* A *Prof. Accred.:* Medical Laboratory Technology (AMA) *CEO:* Provost Charles R. Reidlinger
Enroll: 950 (505) 437-6860

NEW MEXICO STATE UNIVERSITY AT CARLSBAD
1500 University Dr., Carlsbad 88220 *Type:* Public (state) *System:* New Mexico State University System *Accred.:* 1980/1985 (NCA) *Calendar:* Sem. plan *Degrees:* A, certificates, diplomas *Prof. Accred.:* Nursing (A) *CEO:* Provost Douglas Burgham
Enroll: 619 (505) 885-8831

NORTHERN NEW MEXICO COMMUNITY COLLEGE
1002 N. Onate St., Espanola 87532 *Type:* Public 2-year *System:* New Mexico Commission of Higher Education *Accred.:* 1982/1987 (NCA) *Calendar:* Sem. plan *Degrees:* A, certificates, diplomas *Prof. Accred.:* Radiography *CEO:* Pres. Connie Valdez
Enroll: 1005 (505) 753-7141

PARKS COLLEGE
1023 Tijeras Ave., N.W., Albuquerque 87102 *Type:* Private junior *Accred.:* 1981/1987 (CCA-ACICS) *Calendar:* Qtr. plan *Degrees:* A, certificates, diplomas *CEO:* Pres. Cynthia S. Welch
Enroll: 365 (505) 843-7500

BRANCH CAMPUS
6922 E. Broadway, Tucson, AZ 85710 *CEO:* Dir. Frank W. Welch
(602) 486-7979

PLAZA THREE ACADEMY
7200 Montgomery Blvd., N.E., No. 367, Albuquerque 87109-1581 *Type:* Private *Accred.:* 1988 (CCA-ACTTS) *Calendar:* Courses of varying lengths *Degrees:* certificates *CEO:* Dir. Christine Clear
(505) 884-8333

ST. JOHN'S COLLEGE
Santa Fe 87501-4599 *Type:* Private liberal arts *Accred.:* 1969/1989 (NCA) *Calendar:* Sem. plan *Degrees:* B, M *CEO:* Pres. John Agresto
Enroll: 463 (505) 982-3691

SAN JUAN COLLEGE
4601 College Blvd., Farmington 87402 *Type:* Public (state) 2-year *System:* New Mexico Commission of Higher Education *Accred.:* 1973/1984 (NCA) *Calendar:* Sem. plan *Degrees:* A, certificates, diplomas *Prof. Accred.:* Engineering Technology (mechanical drafting/design), Nursing (A) *CEO:* Pres. James C. Henderson
Enroll: 1634 (505) 326-3311

SANTA FE COMMUNITY COLLEGE
P.O. Box 4187, Santa Fe 87502 *Type:* Public (state) junior *Accred.:* 1988 (NCA) *Calendar:* Sem. plan *Degrees:* A *Prof. Accred.:* Nursing (A) *CEO:* Pres. William C. Witter
Enroll: 972 (505) 471-8200

SOUTHWEST ACUPUNCTURE COLLEGE
712 W. San Mateo, Santa Fe 87501 *Type:* Private *Calendar:* 3-year program *Degrees:* M *Prof. Accred.:* Acupuncture *CEO:* Pres. Anthony Abbate
(505) 988-3538

SOUTHWESTERN BUSINESS COLLEGE
100 N. Pennsylvania Ave., Roswell 88201 *Type:* Private business *Accred.:* 1978/1987 (CCA-ACICS) *Calendar:* Sem. plan *Degrees:* certificates, diplomas *CEO:* Exec. Vice Pres. Earliss D. Gleaton
Enroll: 110 (505) 622-8080

SOUTHWESTERN INDIAN POLYTECHNIC INSTITUTE
9169 Coors Blvd., N.W., Box 10146, Albuquerque 87184 *Type:* Public (federal) 2-year *Accred.:* 1975/1986 (NCA) *Calendar:* Qtr. plan *Degrees:* A, certificates, diplomas *CEO:* Pres. Carol Green
Enroll: 524 (505) 766-3197

THE UNIVERSITY OF NEW MEXICO
Albuquerque 87131 *Type:* Public (state) *System:* New Mexico Commission of Higher Education *Accred.:* 1922/1989 (NCA) *Calendar:* Sem. plan *Degrees:* A, B, P, M, D, certificates, diplomas *Prof. Accred.:* Architecture (M), Audiology, Business (B,M), Clinical Psychology, Computer Science, Counseling, Dance, Dental Assisting, Diagnostic Medical Sonography, EMT-Paramedic, Engineering (chemical, civil, computer, construction, electrical, mechanical, nuclear), Journalism, Law, Medical Technology, Medicine, Music, Nuclear Medicine Technology, Nursing (B,M), Parks and Recreation, Pharmacy, Physical Therapy, Planning (community/regional), Psychology Internship, Public Administration, Radiation Therapy Technology, Radiography, Respiratory Therapy, Speech-Language Pathology, Teacher Education (e,s,p), Theatre *CEO:* Pres. Richard E. Peck
Enroll: 18168 (505) 277-2626

GALLUP BRANCH
200 College Rd., Gallup, NM 87301 *Prof. Accred.:* Medical Laboratory Technology (AMA) *CEO:* Dir. John M. Phillips
(505) 722-7221

VALENCIA BRANCH
280 La Entrada, Los Lunas, NM 87031 *CEO:* Dir. Ralph Sigala
(505) 865-9596

WESTERN NEW MEXICO UNIVERSITY
1000 W. College Ave., P.O. Box 680, Silver City 88062 *Type:* Public (state) liberal arts and professional *System:* New Mexico Commission of Higher Education *Accred.:* 1926/1981 (NCA) *Calendar:* Sem. plan *Degrees:* A, B, M, certificates, diplomas *CEO:* Pres. Jerry L. Gallentine
Enroll: 1414 (505) 538-6238

NEW YORK

ACADEMY FOR CAREER EDUCATION
55-05 Myrtle Ave., Ridgewood 11385 *Type:* Private business *Accred.:* 1990 (CCA-ACICS) *Calendar:* Courses of varying lengths *Degrees:* certificates, diplomas *CEO:* Pres. Chana Schachner
(718) 497-4900

ADELPHI UNIVERSITY
South Ave., Garden City 11530 *Type:* Private *Accred.:* 1921/1988 (MSA) *Calendar:* Sem. plan *Degrees:* A, B, M, D, certificates, diplomas *Prof. Accred.:* Clinical Psychology, Nursing (B,M), Social Work (B,M), Speech-Language Pathology *CEO:* Pres. Peter Diamandopolous
Enroll: 9716 (516) 294-8700

ADIRONDACK COMMUNITY COLLEGE
Bay Rd., Glens Falls 12801 *Type:* Public (district) junior *System:* State University of New York Office of Community Colleges *Accred.:* 1971/1988 (MSA) *Calendar:* Sem. plan *Degrees:* A *CEO:* Pres. Roger C. Andersen
Enroll: 3096 (518) 793-4491

ADVANCED SOFTWARE ANALYSIS
5 Beekman St., Ste. 700, New York 10038 *Type:* Private business *Accred.:* 1987/1991 (CCA-ACICS) *Calendar:* Courses of varying lengths *Degrees:* certificates, diplomas *CEO:* Dir. Leon Rabinovch
(212) 349-9768

BRANCH CAMPUS
151 Lawrence St., 2nd Fl., Brooklyn, NY 11201 *CEO:* Dir. Alex Schegol
(718) 522-9073

ALBANY COLLEGE OF PHARMACY OF UNION UNIVERSITY
106 New Scotland Ave., Albany 12208 *Type:* Private professional *Accred.:* 1921/1987 (MSA) *Calendar:* Sem. plan *Degrees:* B, D *Prof. Accred.:* Pharmacy *CEO:* Pres. Kenneth W. Miller
Enroll: 652 (518) 445-7211

ALBANY LAW SCHOOL
80 New Scotland Ave., Albany 12208 *Type:* Private *Calendar:* Sem. plan *Degrees:* P, D *Prof. Accred.:* Law *CEO:* Dean John Baker
Enroll: 831 (518) 445-2321

ALBANY MEDICAL COLLEGE
47 New Scotland Ave., Albany 12208 *Type:* Private *Accred.:* 1921/1989 (MSA) *Calendar:* Sem. plan *Degrees:* P, M, D *Prof. Accred.:* Medicine, Nurse Anesthesia Education, Psychology Internship *CEO:* Acting Dean Anthony P. Tartaglia, M.D.
Enroll: 601 (518) 445-5544

ALFRED UNIVERSITY
Main St., Alfred 14802 *Type:* Private *Accred.:* 1921/1989 (MSA) *Calendar:* Sem. plan *Degrees:* B, M, D *Prof. Accred.:* Art, Business (B), Engineering (ceramic, industrial, mechanical), Nursing (B) *CEO:* Pres. Edward G. Coll, Jr.
Enroll: 2597 (607) 871-2111

ALLEN SCHOOL FOR PHYSICIANS' AIDES
188 Montague St., Brooklyn 11201 *Type:* Private *Accred.:* 1981/1986 (CCA-ACTTS) *Calendar:* Courses of varying lengths *Degrees:* certificates, diplomas *CEO:* Pres. Robert Trich
Enroll: 557 (718) 242-1700

ALVIN AILEY AMERICAN DANCE CENTER
211 W. 61st St., 3rd Fl., New York 10023 *Type:* Private *Calendar:* Courses of varying lengths *Degrees:* certificates *Prof. Accred.:* Dance *CEO:* Exec. Denise Jefferson
(212) 767-0940

AMERICAN ACADEMY MCALLISTER INSTITUTE OF FUNERAL SERVICE, INC.
450 W. 56th St., New York 10019 *Type:* Private professional *Calendar:* 1-year program *Degrees:* diplomas *Prof. Accred.:* Funeral Service Education *CEO:* Pres. Patrick J. O'Connor
(212) 757-1190

Accredited Institutions   **New York**

AMERICAN ACADEMY OF DRAMATIC ARTS
120 Madison Ave., New York 10016 *Type:* Private 2-year professional *Accred.:* 1983/1988 (MSA) *Calendar:* Sem. plan *Degrees:* A *Prof. Accred.:* Theatre *CEO:* Pres. George Cuttingham
Enroll: 469   (212) 686-9244

AMERICAN BALLET CENTER/JOFFREY BALLEY SCHOOL
434 Ave. of the Americas, New York 10011 *Type:* Private *Calendar:* Courses of varying lengths *Degrees:* certificates *Prof. Accred.:* Dance *CEO:* Exec. Dir. Edith D'Addario
(212) 254-8520

AMERICAN BARTENDERS SCHOOL
105-A Madison Ave., New York 10016-7418 *Type:* Private *Accred.:* 1988 (CCA-ACTTS) *Calendar:* Courses of varying lengths *Degrees:* certificates *CEO:* Pres. Jack Tiano
Enroll: 1583   (212) 532-4200

BRANCH CAMPUS
801 Motor Pkwy., Hauppauge, NY 11788-5200 *CEO:* Dir. Carmen Wolfe
(516) 234-0400

AMERICAN BUSINESS INSTITUTE
1657 Broadway, New York 10019 *Type:* Private business *Accred.:* 1978/1989 (CCA-ACICS) *Calendar:* Sem. plan *Degrees:* certificates, diplomas *CEO:* Dir. Danny L. Cesco
Enroll: 781   (212) 582-9040

AMERICAN CAREER SCHOOLS
466 Main St., New Rochelle 10801 *Type:* Private *Accred.:* 1981/1986 (CCA-ACTTS) *Calendar:* Courses of varying lengths *Degrees:* certificates *CEO:* Dir. Mary Kastenbaum
Enroll: 102   (914) 632-5800

BRANCH CAMPUS
130 Ontario St., Albany, NY 12206-2390 *CEO:* Pres. Carl P. Simmons, Ph.D.
(518) 462-6621

AMERICAN INSTITUTE OF MUSIC
M.P.O. Box 1706, Niagara Falls 14302-1706 *Type:* Private home study *Accred.:* 1988 (NHSC) *Calendar:* Courses of varying lengths *Degrees:* certificates *CEO:* Pres. Michael Freeman
(800) 950-8663

THE AMERICAN MUSICAL AND DRAMATIC ACADEMY
2109 Broadway, New York 10023 *Type:* Private *Calendar:* Courses of varying lengths *Degrees:* certificates *Prof. Accred.:* Theatre *CEO:* Exec. Dir. Jan Martin
(212) 787-5300

APEX TECHNICAL SCHOOL
635 Ave. of the Americas, New York 10011 *Type:* Private *Accred.:* 1968/1989 (CCA-ACTTS) *Calendar:* Courses of varying lengths *Degrees:* certificates *CEO:* Pres. Dorothy Cann
Enroll: 760   (212) 645-3300

BANK STREET COLLEGE OF EDUCATION
610 W. 112th St., New York 10025 *Type:* Private teachers; graduate only *Accred.:* 1960/1983 (MSA) *Calendar:* Sem. plan *Degrees:* M, certificates, diplomas *CEO:* Pres. Joseph Shenker
Enroll: 639   (212) 222-6700

BARD COLLEGE
Annandale-on-Hudson 12504 *Type:* Private liberal arts *Accred.:* 1922/1986 (MSA) *Calendar:* Sem. plan *Degrees:* B, M *CEO:* Pres. Leon Botstein
Enroll: 929   (914) 758-6822

BARNARD COLLEGE
3009 Broadway, New York 10027 *Type:* Private liberal arts for women *Accred.:* 1921/1986 (MSA) *Calendar:* Sem. plan *Degrees:* B *CEO:* Pres. Ellen V. Futter
Enroll: 2192   (212) 854-5262

BERK TRADE SCHOOL
311 W. 35th St., New York 10001-1725 *Type:* Private *Accred.:* 1973/1988 (CCA-ACTTS) *Calendar:* Courses of varying

lengths *Degrees:* certificates *CEO:* Dir. Irving Berk
Enroll: 3181 (212) 629-3736

THE BERKELEY SCHOOL
51-23 Terryville Rd., Port Jefferson Station 11776 *Type:* Private business *Accred.:* 1988 (CCA-ACICS) *Calendar:* Qtr. plan *Degrees:* certificates, diplomas *CEO:* Dir. Diane Case
(516) 474-3100

BERKELEY SCHOOL OF WESTCHESTER
W. Red Oak La., White Plains 10604 *Type:* Private *Accred.:* 1988 (MSA) *Calendar:* Qtr. plan *Degrees:* A *CEO:* Pres. Rose M. Healy-Dougherty
Enroll: 1003 (914) 694-1122

BERNARD M. BARUCH COLLEGE
17 Lexington Ave., New York 10010 *Type:* Public *System:* City University of New York Central Administration *Accred.:* 1968/1984 (MSA) *Calendar:* Sem. plan *Degrees:* B, M *Prof. Accred.:* Accounting (Type A,B), Business (B,M), Health Services Administration, Public Administration *CEO:* Pres. Matthew Goldstein
Enroll: 16475 (212) 447-3000

BETH HAMEDRASH SHAAREI YOSHER
4102 16th Ave., Brooklyn 11204 *Type:* Private professional *Accred.:* 1982/1990 (AARTS) *Calendar:* Sem. plan *Degrees:* Talmudic (1st and 2nd) *CEO:* Pres. J. Mayer
Enroll: 142 (718) 854-2900

BETH HATALMUD RABBINICAL COLLEGE
2127 82nd St., Brooklyn 11214 *Type:* Private professional *Accred.:* 1978/1990 (AARTS) *Calendar:* Sem. plan *Degrees:* Talmudic (1st and 2nd) *CEO:* Pres. Elozer Meyer
Enroll: 209 (718) 259-2525

BEXLEY HALL
1100 S. Goodman St., Rochester 14620 *Type:* Private (Episcopal) professional; graduate only *Accred.:* 1952/1982 (ATS) *Calendar:* Sem. plan *Degrees:* P, M, D *CEO:* Pres. James M. Evans, Jr.
(716) 271-1320

BLAKE BUSINESS SCHOOL
145-A Fourth Ave., New York 10003 *Type:* Private business *Accred.:* 1974/1987 (CCA-ACICS) *Calendar:* Courses of varying lengths *Degrees:* certificates, diplomas *CEO:* Pres. Barbara Marion
Enroll: 1181 (212) 254-1233

BORICUA COLLEGE
3755 Broadway, New York 10032 *Type:* Private liberal arts *Accred.:* 1980/1987 (MSA) *Calendar:* Tri. plan *Degrees:* A, B *CEO:* Pres. Victor G. Alicea
Enroll: 1127 (212) 694-1000

BRANCH CAMPUS
186 N. Sixth St., Brooklyn, NY 11211 *CEO:* Pres. Victor G. Alicea
(718) 782-2200

BOROUGH OF MANHATTAN COMMUNITY COLLEGE
199 Chambers St., New York 10007 *Type:* Public *System:* City University of New York Central Administration *Accred.:* 1964/1987 (MSA) *Calendar:* Sem. plan *Degrees:* A *Prof. Accred.:* Medical Record Technology, Nursing (A), Respiratory Therapy *CEO:* Pres. Augusta Souza Kappner
Enroll: 12642 (212) 618-1000

THE BRIARCLIFFE SCHOOL
55 N. Broadway, Hicksville 11801 *Type:* Private junior *Accred.:* 1977/1991 (CCA-ACICS); 1989 (MSA candidate) *Calendar:* Sem. plan *Degrees:* A, certificates, diplomas *CEO:* Dir. Carolyn Maher
Enroll: 600 (516) 681-1100

BRANCH CAMPUS
10 Peninsula Blvd., Lynbrook, NY 11563 *CEO:* Dir. Barbara Speier
(516) 596-1313

BRANCH CAMPUS
10 Lake St., Patchoque, NY 11772 *CEO:* Dir. Regina Cline
(516) 654-5300

BRONX COMMUNITY COLLEGE
University Ave. and W. 181st S, Bronx 10453 *Type:* Public *System:* City University

of New York Central Administration *Accred.:* 1961/1988 (MSA) *Calendar:* Sem. plan *Degrees:* A, certificates, diplomas *Prof. Accred.:* Engineering Technology (electrical), Nuclear Medicine Technology, Nursing (A), Radiography *CEO:* Pres. Roscoe C. Brown, Jr.
Enroll: 5730 (212) 220-6920

BROOKLYN COLLEGE
Bedford Ave. and Ave. H, Brooklyn 11210 *Type:* Public *System:* City University of New York Central Administration *Accred.:* 1933/1987 (MSA) *Calendar:* Sem. plan *Degrees:* B, P, M, certificates, diplomas *Prof. Accred.:* Audiology, Nurse Anesthesia Education, Speech-Language Pathology, Teacher Education (e,s,p) *CEO:* Acting Pres. James N. Loughran, S.J.
Enroll: 16550 (718) 780-5485

BROOKLYN LAW SCHOOL
250 Joralemon St., Brooklyn 11201 *Type:* Private professional *Calendar:* Sem. plan *Degrees:* P *Prof. Accred.:* Law *CEO:* Dean David G. Trager
Enroll: 1179 (718) 625-2200

BROOME COMMUNITY COLLEGE
Upper Front St., P.O. Box 1017, Binghamton 13902 *Type:* Public (county) junior *System:* State University of New York Office of Community Colleges *Accred.:* 1960/1985 (MSA) *Calendar:* Sem. plan *Degrees:* A *Prof. Accred.:* Dental Hygiene, Engineering Technology (chemical, civil/construction, electrical, mechanical), Medical Assisting (AMA), Medical Laboratory Technology (AMA), Medical Record Technology, Nursing (A), Physical Therapy Assisting, Radiography *CEO:* Pres. Donald A. Dellow
Enroll: 5819 (607) 771-5000

BRYANT AND STRATTON BUSINESS INSTITUTE
1259 Central Ave., Albany 12205 *Type:* Private business *Accred.:* 1953/1988 (CCA-ACICS) *Calendar:* Qtr. plan *Degrees:* A, certificates, diplomas *CEO:* Dir. Alan J. Hyers
Enroll: 515 (518) 437-1802

BRYANT AND STRATTON BUSINESS INSTITUTE
1028 Main St., Buffalo 14202 *Type:* Private business *Accred.:* 1978/1990 (CCA-ACICS) *Calendar:* Qtr. plan *Degrees:* A, certificates, diplomas *Prof. Accred.:* Medical Assisting (AMA) *CEO:* Dir. William B. Schatt
Enroll: 2950 (716) 884-9120

BRANCH CAMPUS
1214 Abbott Rd., Lackawanna, NY 14218 *CEO:* Dir. Doreen Justinger
(716) 821-9331

BRANCH CAMPUS
200 Bryant and Stratton Way, Williamsville, NY 14221 *CEO:* Dir. Nicholas J. DiMartina
(716) 631-0260

BRYANT AND STRATTON BUSINESS INSTITUTE
82 St. Paul St., Rochester 14604-1381 *Type:* Private business *Accred.:* 1975/1988 (CCA-ACICS) *Calendar:* Qtr. plan *Degrees:* A, certificates, diplomas *Prof. Accred.:* Medical Assisting (AMA) *CEO:* Dir. Jeffery Drojak
Enroll: 1247 (716) 325-6010

BRANCH CAMPUS
792 Calkins Rd., Rochester, NY 14623 *CEO:* Dir. Eric B. Donaldson
(716) 359-2130

BRYANT AND STRATTON BUSINESS INSTITUTE
400 Montgomery St., Syracuse 13202 *Type:* Private business *Accred.:* 1968/1987 (CCA-ACICS) *Calendar:* Qtr. plan *Degrees:* A, certificates, diplomas *Prof. Accred.:* Medical Assisting (AMA) *CEO:* Dir. Edward J. Heinrich
Enroll: 1203 (315) 472-6603

BRANCH CAMPUS
5775 S. Bay Rd., Cicero, NY 13039 *CEO:* Dir. Kenneth R. Sigmon
(315) 452-1105

BUSINESS INFORMATICS CENTER
134 S. Central Ave., Valley Stream 11580-5431 *Type:* Private *Accred.:* 1991 (CCA-ACTTS) *Calendar:* Courses of varying

lengths *Degrees:* certificates *CEO:* Dir. Joseph Brown
(516) 561-0050

CDI CAREER DEVELOPMENT INSTITUTE
19 W. 44th St., New York 10036-9991 *Type:* Private *Accred.:* 1980/1985 (CCA-ACTTS) *Calendar:* Courses of varying lengths *Degrees:* certificates *CEO:* Dir. Louis Cress
Enroll: 717 (212) 921-4646

CANISIUS COLLEGE
2001 Main St., Buffalo 14208 *Type:* Private liberal arts *Accred.:* 1921/1985 (MSA) *Calendar:* Sem. plan *Degrees:* A, B, M *Prof. Accred.:* Business (B,M), Computer Science, Teacher Education (s,p) *CEO:* Pres. James M. Demske, S.J.
Enroll: 4514 (716) 883-7000

CAREER INSTITUTE
500 Eighth Ave., 2nd Fl., New York 10018 *Type:* Private *Accred.:* 1991 (CCA-ACTTS) *Calendar:* Courses of varying lengths *Degrees:* certificates *CEO:* Owner Harry Lokos
(212) 564-0589

CASHIER TRAINING INSTITUTE
500 Eighth Ave., New York 10018-6504 *Type:* Private *Accred.:* 1985 (CCA-ACTTS) *Calendar:* Courses of varying lengths *Degrees:* certificates *CEO:* Pres. Harry Lokos
Enroll: 1581 (212) 564-0500

CAYUGA COUNTY COMMUNITY COLLEGE
Franklin St., Auburn 13021 *Type:* Public (city) junior *System:* State University of New York Office of Community Colleges *Accred.:* 1965/1986 (MSA) *Calendar:* Sem. plan *Degrees:* A, certificates, diplomas *Prof. Accred.:* Nursing (A) *CEO:* Pres. Lawrence H. Poole
Enroll: 2683 (315) 255-1743

CAZENOVIA COLLEGE
Seminary St., Cazenovia 13035 *Type:* Private junior for women *Accred.:* 1961/1986 (MSA) *Calendar:* Sem. plan *Degrees:* A, B *CEO:* Pres. Stephen M. Schneeweiss
Enroll: 905 (315) 655-8283

CENTER FOR THE MEDIA ARTS
226 W. 26th St., New York 10001-6786 *Type:* Private *Accred.:* 1969/1987 (CCA-ACTTS) *Calendar:* Courses of varying lengths *Degrees:* certificates *CEO:* Dir. David Sirota
Enroll: 2485 (212) 229-5900

CENTRAL YESHIVA TOMCHEI TMIMIM-LUBAVITCH
841-853 Ocean Pkwy., Brooklyn 11230 *Type:* Private professional *Accred.:* 1976/1988 (AARTS) *Calendar:* Sem. plan *Degrees:* Rabbinic (1st and 2nd), Talmudic (1st and 2nd) *CEO:* Pres. E. Sklar
Enroll: 525 (718) 434-0784

CHAUFFEURS TRAINING SCHOOL
12 Railroad Ave., Albany 12205-5727 *Type:* Private *Accred.:* 1980/1985 (CCA-ACTTS) *Calendar:* Courses of varying lengths *Degrees:* diplomas *CEO:* Dir. Albert V. Hanley
Enroll: 209 (518) 482-8601

CHERYL FELL'S SCHOOL OF BUSINESS
2541 Military Rd., Niagara Falls 14304 *Type:* Private business *Accred.:* 1984/1990 (CCA-ACICS) *Calendar:* Courses of varying lengths *Degrees:* certificates, diplomas *CEO:* Dir. Cheryl Anne Fell
Enroll: 35 (716) 297-2750

CHRIST THE KING SEMINARY
711 Knox Rd., P.O. Box 607, East Aurora 14052-0607 *Type:* Private (Roman Catholic) *Accred.:* 1977/1983 (ATS); 1974/1987 (MSA) *Calendar:* Sem. plan *Degrees:* P, M *CEO:* Pres./Rector Frederick D. Leising, Ph.D.
Enroll: 64 (716) 652-8900

CIRCLE IN THE SQUARE THEATRE SCHOOL
1633 Broadway, New York 10019 *Type:* Private *Calendar:* Courses of varying lengths *Degrees:* certificates *Prof. Accred.:* Theatre *CEO:* Exec. Dir. E. Colin O'Leary
(212) 307-3732

CITY COLLEGE
Convent Ave. at 138th St., New York 10031 *Type:* Public *System:* City University of New York Central Administration *Accred.:* 1921/1987 (MSA) *Calendar:* Sem. plan *Degrees:*

B, M, certificates, diplomas *Prof. Accred.:* Architecture (B), Clinical Psychology, Engineering (chemical, civil, electrical, mechanical), Engineering Technology (electromechanical), Landscape Architecture (B-provisional), Nursing (B), Physician Assisting, Teacher Education (e,s,p) *CEO:* Pres. Bernard W. Harleston
Enroll: 12780 (212) 690-6741

CLARKSON UNIVERSITY
Potsdam 13699 *Type:* Private technological *Accred.:* 1927/1988 (MSA) *Calendar:* Sem. plan *Degrees:* B, M, D *Prof. Accred.:* Business (B,M), Engineering (chemical, civil, electrical, mechanical) *CEO:* Pres. Richard H. Gallagher
Enroll: 3602 (315) 268-6400

CLINTON COMMUNITY COLLEGE
Bluff Point, Plattsburgh 12901 *Type:* Public (county) junior *System:* State University of New York Office of Community Colleges *Accred.:* 1975/1986 (MSA) *Calendar:* Sem. plan *Degrees:* A, certificates, diplomas *Prof. Accred.:* Medical Laboratory Technology (AMA) *CEO:* Pres. Jay L. Fennell
Enroll: 1812 (518) 561-6650

COLGATE ROCHESTER DIVINITY SCHOOL/CROZER THEOLOGICAL SEMINARY
1100 S. Goodman St., Rochester 14620 *Type:* Private (interdenominational) professional; graduate only *Accred.:* 1938/1982 (ATS) *Calendar:* Sem. plan *Degrees:* P, M, D *CEO:* Pres. James M. Evans, Jr.
Enroll: 118 (716) 271-1320

COLGATE UNIVERSITY
Hamilton 13346 *Type:* Private liberal arts *Accred.:* 1921/1988 (MSA) *Calendar:* Sem. plan *Degrees:* B, M *CEO:* Pres. Neil R. Grabois
Enroll: 2750 (315) 824-1000

COLLEGE FOR HUMAN SERVICES
345 Hudson St., New York 10014 *Type:* Private professional *Accred.:* 1984/1989 (MSA) *Calendar:* Sem. plan *Degrees:* A, B *CEO:* Pres. Audrey C. Cohen
Enroll: 728 (212) 989-2002

COLLEGE OF AERONAUTICS
La Guardia Airport, Flushing 11371 *Type:* Private technical *Accred.:* 1969/1987 (MSA) *Calendar:* Tri. plan *Degrees:* A, B *Prof. Accred.:* Engineering Technology (aerospace) *CEO:* Pres. Sam H. Frank
Enroll: 1255 (718) 429-6600

COLLEGE OF INSURANCE
101 Murray St., New York 10007 *Type:* Private professional *Accred.:* 1967/1988 (MSA) *Calendar:* Sem. plan *Degrees:* A, B, M, certificates, diplomas *CEO:* Pres. Ellen Thrower
Enroll: 651 (212) 962-4111

COLLEGE OF MOUNT ST. VINCENT
263rd St. and Riverdale Ave., Riverdale 10471 *Type:* Private liberal arts *Accred.:* 1921/1986 (MSA) *Calendar:* Sem. plan *Degrees:* A, B, M *Prof. Accred.:* Nursing (B) *CEO:* Pres. Doris Smith, S.C.
Enroll: 994 (212) 549-8000

COLLEGE OF NEW ROCHELLE
29 Castle Pl., New Rochelle 10805 *Type:* Private liberal arts *Accred.:* 1921/1987 (MSA) *Calendar:* Sem. plan *Degrees:* B, M, certificates, diplomas *Prof. Accred.:* Nursing (B,M), Social Work (B) *CEO:* Pres. Dorothy Ann Kelly, O.S.U.
Enroll: 4491 (914) 632-5300

BROOKLYN CAMPUS
1368 Fulton St., Brooklyn, NY 11216 *CEO:* Dir. James Wood
(718) 638-2500

CO-OP CITY CAMPUS
950 Baychester Ave., Bronx, NY 10475 *CEO:* Dir. Carolyn Wiggins
(212) 320-0300

DC 37 CAMPUS
125 Barclay St., New York, NY 10007 *CEO:* Dir. James Taaffle
(212) 815-1710

NEW YORK THEOLOGICAL SEMINARY CAMPUS
5 W. 29th St., New York, NY 10001
CEO: Dir. Louis DeSalle
(212) 689-6208

ROSA PARKS CAMPUS
144 W. 125th St., New York, NY 10024
CEO: Dir. Carolyn Tonge
(212) 662-7500

SOUTH BRONX CAMPUS
378 E. 151st St., Bronx, NY 10455 *CEO:* Dir. Celeste Ashe-Johnson
(212) 665-1310

COLLEGE OF ST. ROSE
432 Western Ave., Albany 12203 *Type:* Private liberal arts *Accred.:* 1928/1989 (MSA) *Calendar:* Sem. plan *Degrees:* B, M *Prof. Accred.:* Medical Technology *CEO:* Pres. Louis C. Vaccaro
Enroll: 3231 (518) 454-5111

COLLEGE OF STATEN ISLAND
130 Stuyvesant Pl., Staten Island 10301 *Type:* Public *System:* City University of New York Central Administration *Accred.:* 1963/1985 (MSA) *Calendar:* Sem. plan *Degrees:* A, B, M, certificates, diplomas *Prof. Accred.:* Computer Science, Engineering (engineering physics/science), Engineering Technology (civil/construction, electrical, electromechanical, industrial, mechanical), Medical Laboratory Technology (AMA), Nursing (A,B), Radiography *CEO:* Pres. Edmond L. Volpe
Enroll: 10683 (718) 390-7733

SUNNYSIDE CAMPUS
715 Ocean Terr., Staten Island, NY 10301
CEO: Dir. Felix Cardegna
(718) 390-7664

COLUMBIA UNIVERSITY
116th St. and Broadway, New York 10027 *Type:* Private *Accred.:* 1921/1985 (MSA) *Calendar:* Sem. plan *Degrees:* B, P, M, D, certificates, diplomas *Prof. Accred.:* Architecture (M), Business (M), Combined Prosthodontics, Dance, Dentistry, Endodontics, Engineering (chemical, civil, electrical, engineering mechanics, industrial, mechanical, metallurgical, mining), Journalism, Law, Librarianship, Medicine, Nurse Anesthesia Education, Nursing (B,M), Occupational Therapy, Orthodontics, Periodontics, Physical Therapy, Planning (urban), Public Health, Social Work (M) *CEO:* Pres. Michael I. Sovern
Enroll: 16540 (212) 854-1754

COLUMBIA-GREENE COMMUNITY COLLEGE
P.O. Box 1000, Hudson 12534 *Type:* Public (county) junior *System:* State University of New York Office of Community Colleges *Accred.:* 1975/1986 (MSA) *Calendar:* Sem. plan *Degrees:* A *Prof. Accred.:* Nursing (A) *CEO:* Pres. Terry A. Cline
Enroll: 1620 (518) 828-4181

COMMERCIAL DRIVER TRAINING
600 Patton Ave., West Babylon 11704-1421 *Type:* Private *Accred.:* 1984/1989 (CCA-ACTTS) *Calendar:* Courses of varying lengths *Degrees:* certificates *CEO:* Pres. John B. Rayne
Enroll: 876 (516) 249-1330

COMMUNITY COLLEGE OF THE FINGER LAKES
Lincoln Hill, Canandaigua 14424 *Type:* Public junior *System:* State University of New York Office of Community Colleges *Accred.:* 1977/1987 (MSA) *Calendar:* Sem. plan *Degrees:* A, certificates, diplomas *Prof. Accred.:* Nursing (A) *CEO:* Pres. Charles J. Meder
Enroll: 3355 (716) 394-3500

CONCORDIA COLLEGE
171 White Plains Rd., Bronxville 10708 *Type:* Private (Lutheran-Missouri Synod) *Accred.:* 1941/1985 (MSA) *Calendar:* Sem. plan *Degrees:* A, B *Prof. Accred.:* Social Work (B) *CEO:* Pres. Ralph C. Schultz
Enroll: 526 (914) 337-9300

CONTINENTAL HEALTH AND CAREER CENTER
49 Stone St., Rochester 14604 *Type:* Private *Calendar:* Courses of varying lengths *De-

grees: certificates *Prof. Accred.:* Health Education *CEO:* Pres. Arthur J. Resso
(716) 232-2222

THE COOPER UNION FOR THE ADVANCEMENT OF SCIENCE AND ART
41 Cooper Sq., New York 10003 *Type:* Private *Accred.:* 1946/1988 (MSA) *Calendar:* Sem. plan *Degrees:* B, M *Prof. Accred.:* Architecture (B), Art, Engineering (chemical, civil, electrical, mechanical) *CEO:* Pres. John J. Iselin
Enroll: 1001 (212) 254-6300

COPE INSTITUTE
425 McDonald Ave., Brooklyn 11218 *Type:* Private business *Accred.:* 1981/1987 (CCA-ACICS) *Calendar:* Qtr. plan *Degrees:* certificates, diplomas *CEO:* Dir. Yerachmiel Barash
Enroll: 448 (718) 436-1700

CORNELL UNIVERSITY
Ithaca 14853 *Type:* Private *Accred.:* 1921/1985 (MSA) *Calendar:* Sem. plan *Degrees:* B, P, M, D *Prof. Accred.:* Architecture (B), Business (M), Cytotechnology, Engineering (agricultural, chemical, civil, electrical, engineering physics/science, industrial, materials, mechanical), Health Services Administration, Interior Design, Landscape Architecture (B,M), Law, Medicine, Planning (city/regional), Radiography, Social Work (B), Surgeon Assisting *CEO:* Pres. Frank H. Rhodes
Enroll: 18131 (607) 255-2000

CORNING COMMUNITY COLLEGE
Spencer Hill, Corning 14830 *Type:* Public (city) junior *System:* State University of New York Office of Community Colleges *Accred.:* 1964/1985 (MSA) *Calendar:* Sem. plan *Degrees:* A, certificates, diplomas *Prof. Accred.:* Nursing (A) *CEO:* Pres. Donald H. Hangen
Enroll: 3230 (607) 962-9011

CULINARY INSTITUTE OF AMERICA
651 S. Albany Post Rd., Hyde Park 12538-1499 *Type:* Private *Accred.:* 1983/1988 (CCA-ACTTS) *Calendar:* Courses of varying lengths *Degrees:* diplomas *CEO:* Pres. Ferdinand E. Metz
Enroll: 1806 (914) 452-9600

D'YOUVILLE COLLEGE
320 Porter Ave., Buffalo 14201 *Type:* Private liberal arts primarily for women *Accred.:* 1928/1985 (MSA) *Calendar:* Sem. plan *Degrees:* B, M *Prof. Accred.:* Nursing (B,M), Occupational Therapy, Physical Therapy, Social Work (B) *CEO:* Pres. Denise A. Roche, G.N.S.H.
Enroll: 1075 (716) 881-3200

DAEMEN COLLEGE
4380 Main St., Amherst 14226 *Type:* Private liberal arts *Accred.:* 1956/1986 (MSA) *Calendar:* Sem. plan *Degrees:* B *Prof. Accred.:* Medical Record Administration, Medical Technology, Nursing (B), Physical Therapy, Social Work (B) *CEO:* Pres. Robert S. Marshall
Enroll: 1364 (716) 839-3600

DANCE THEATRE OF HARLEM, INC.
466 W. 152nd St., New York 10031 *Type:* Private *Calendar:* Courses of varying lengths *Degrees:* certificates *Prof. Accred.:* Dance *CEO:* Dir. Walter R. Raines
(212) 690-2800

DARKEI NO'AM RABBINICAL COLLEGE
2822 Ave. J, Brooklyn 11210 *Type:* Private professional *Accred.:* 1983/1988 (AARTS) *Calendar:* Tri. plan *Degrees:* Rabbinic (1st and 2nd) *CEO:* Pres. Joseph Sitorsky
Enroll: 102 (718) 338-6464

DOMINICAN COLLEGE OF BLAUVELT
10 Western Hwy., Orangeburg 10962 *Type:* Private liberal arts *Accred.:* 1972/1987 (MSA) *Calendar:* Sem. plan *Degrees:* A, B, certificates, diplomas *Prof. Accred.:* Nursing (B), Occupational Therapy, Social Work (B) *CEO:* Pres. Kathleen Sullivan
Enroll: 1443 (914) 359-7800

DOWLING COLLEGE
Idle Hour Blvd., Oakdale 11769 *Type:* Private liberal arts *Accred.:* 1971/1985 (MSA)

Calendar: Sem. plan *Degrees:* B, M *CEO:* Pres. Victor P. Meskill
Enroll: 4036 (516) 244-3000

DRAKE BUSINESS SCHOOL
2488 Grand Concourse, Bronx 10458 *Type:* Private business *Accred.:* 1974/1986 (CCA-ACICS) *Calendar:* Courses of varying lengths *Degrees:* certificates, diplomas *CEO:* Admin. Linda Levine
Enroll: 556 (212) 295-6200

DRAKE BUSINESS SCHOOL
36-09 Main St., 6th Fl., Flushing 11354 *Type:* Private business *Accred.:* 1974/1986 (CCA-ACICS) *Calendar:* Courses of varying lengths *Degrees:* certificates, diplomas *CEO:* Administrator Cheryl R. Caro
Enroll: 442 (718) 353-3535

DRAKE BUSINESS SCHOOL
225 Broadway, New York 10007 *Type:* Private business *Accred.:* 1974/1986 (CCA-ACICS) *Calendar:* Courses of varying lengths *Degrees:* certificates, diplomas *CEO:* Admin. Phyllis Haimson
Enroll: 805 (212) 349-7900

DRAKE BUSINESS SCHOOL
25 Victory Blvd., Staten Island 10301 *Type:* Private business *Accred.:* 1974/1986 (CCA-ACICS) *Calendar:* Courses of varying lengths *Degrees:* certificates, diplomas *CEO:* Admin. Richard DeCrescenzo
Enroll: 393 (718) 447-1515

DUTCHESS COMMUNITY COLLEGE
53 Pendell Rd., Poughkeepsie 12601 *Type:* Public (county) junior *System:* State University of New York Office of Community Colleges *Accred.:* 1964/1985 (MSA) *Calendar:* Sem. plan *Degrees:* A, certificates, diplomas *Prof. Accred.:* Medical Laboratory Technology (AMA), Nursing (A) *CEO:* Pres. Jerry A. Lee
Enroll: 6417 (914) 471-4500

BRANCH CAMPUS
Southern Dutchess Ext. Site, Blodgett House, Fishkill, NY 12524 *CEO:* Dir. Roger Fazzone
(914) 896-5775

BRANCH CAMPUS
Martha Lawrence Ext. Site, Spackenhill Rd., Poughkeepsie, NY 12603 *CEO:* Dir. Roger Fazzone
(914) 462-0063

ELMIRA BUSINESS INSTITUTE
180 Clemens Center Pkwy., Elmira 14901 *Type:* Private business *Accred.:* 1969/1986 (CCA-ACICS) *Calendar:* Sem. plan *Degrees:* certificates, diplomas *CEO:* Pres. Brad C. Phillips
Enroll: 377 (607) 733-7177

ELMIRA COLLEGE
Park Pl., Elmira 14901 *Type:* Private liberal arts *Accred.:* 1921/1989 (MSA) *Calendar:* Sem. plan *Degrees:* A, B, M *Prof. Accred.:* Nursing (B) *CEO:* Pres. Thomas K. Meier
Enroll: 1880 (607) 734-3911

EMPIRE STATE COLLEGE
One Union Ave., Saratoga Springs 12866 *Type:* Public (state) *System:* State University of New York System Office *Accred.:* 1974/1990 (MSA) *Calendar:* Sem. plan *Degrees:* A, B, M *CEO:* Pres. James W. Hall
Enroll: 6485 (518) 587-2100

BRANCH CAMPUS
Capital District Ctr., 845 Central Ave., Albany, NY 12206 *CEO:* Dir. Dennis Delong
(518) 485-5964

BRANCH CAMPUS
Niagara Frontier Regional Ctr., 564 Franklin St., Buffalo, NY 14202 *CEO:* Dir. Thomas Rocco
(716) 886-8020

BRANCH CAMPUS
Hudson Valley Regional Ctr., 200 N. Central Ave., Hartsdale, NY 10530 *CEO:* Dir. James Case
(914) 948-6208

BRANCH CAMPUS
Metropolitan Ctr., 666 Broadway, New York, NY 10012 *CEO:* Dir. Nancy Bunch
(212) 598-0640

BRANCH CAMPUS
Long Island Regional Ctr., Trainor House, P.O. Box 130, Old Westbury, NY 11568 *CEO:* Dir. Patricia Lefor
(516) 997-4700

BRANCH CAMPUS
Genessee Valley Regional Ctr., 8 Prince St., Rochester, NY 14607 *CEO:* Dir. James H. Matthews
(716) 244-3641

ERIE COMMUNITY COLLEGE
121 Ellicott St., Buffalo 14203 *Type:* Public *System:* State University of New York Office of Community Colleges *Accred.:* 1981/1984 (MSA) *Calendar:* Sem. plan *Degrees:* A, certificates, diplomas *Prof. Accred.:* Medical Assisting (AMA), Medical Laboratory Technology (AMA), Nursing (A), Occupational Therapy Assisting, Respiratory Therapy, Radiation Therapy Technology *CEO:* Vice Pres. John E. Baker
Enroll: 3019 (716) 842-2770

NORTH (AMHERST) CAMPUS
Main St. and Youngs Rd., Williamsville, NY 14221 *Accred.:* 1981/1984 (MSA) *Prof. Accred.:* Dental Hygiene, Engineering Technology (civil/construction, electrical, mechanical), Nursing (A) *CEO:* Vice Pres. James M. McDonnell
Enroll: 5871 (716) 634-0800

SOUTH CAMPUS
4140 Southwestern Blvd., Orchard Park, NY 14127 *Accred.:* 1981/1984 (MSA) *Prof. Accred.:* Dental Laboratory Technology *CEO:* Vice Pres. Kenneth Gubala
Enroll: 3433 (716) 648-5400

FEGS TRADES AND BUSINESS SCHOOL
62 W. 14th St., 2nd Fl., New York 10011-7593 *Type:* Private *Accred.:* 1986 (CCA-ACTTS) *Calendar:* Courses of varying lengths *Degrees:* certificates *CEO:* Vice Pres. Martin A. Hanfling
Enroll: 570 (212) 741-7583

NEW YORK CITY FURNITURE INSTITUTE
33-02 Skillman Ave., Long Island City, NY 11101 *CEO:* Dir. James Leggio
(718) 392-9819

FASHION INSTITUTE OF TECHNOLOGY
Seventh Ave. at 27th St., New York 10001 *Type:* Public (city) professional *System:* State University of New York System Office *Accred.:* 1957/1987 (MSA) *Calendar:* 4-1-4 plan *Degrees:* A, B, M, certificates, diplomas *Prof. Accred.:* Art, Interior Design *CEO:* Pres. Marvin J. Feldman
Enroll: 11944 (212) 760-7660

FIVE TOWNS COLLEGE
2165 Seaford Ave., Seaford 11783 *Type:* Private junior *Accred.:* 1988 (MSA) *Calendar:* Sem. plan *Degrees:* A *CEO:* Pres. Stanley G. Cohen
Enroll: 461 (516) 783-8800

FOLK ART INSTITUTE OF THE MUSEUM OF AMERICAN FOLK ART
61 W. 62nd St., New York 10023-7015 *Type:* Private *Calendar:* Courses of varying lengths *Degrees:* certificates *Prof. Accred.:* Art *CEO:* Dir. Barbara Kaufman-Cate
(212) 977-7170

FORDHAM UNIVERSITY
E. Fordham Rd., Bronx 10458 *Type:* Private liberal arts and professional *Accred.:* 1921/1985 (MSA) *Calendar:* Sem. plan *Degrees:* B, P, M, D, certificates, diplomas *Prof. Accred.:* Business (B,M), Clinical Psychology, Counseling Psychology (provisional), Law, School Psychology, Social Work (M), Teacher Education (e,s,p) *CEO:* Pres. Joseph A. O'Hare, S.J.
Enroll: 13036 (212) 579-2000

FRENCH CULINARY INSTITUTE
462 Broadway, New York 10013 *Type:* Private *Accred.:* 1985 (CCA-ACTTS) *Calendar:* Courses of varying lengths *Degrees:* certificates *CEO:* Pres. Dorothy Cann
Enroll: 97 (212) 219-8890

FRENCH FASHION ACADEMY
462 Broadway, 2nd Fl., New York 10013-2618 *Type:* Private *Accred.:* 1985 (CCA-ACTTS) *Calendar:* Courses of varying lengths *Degrees:* certificates *CEO:* Dir. John Klamar
Enroll: 376 (212) 219-9313

FULTON-MONTGOMERY COMMUNITY COLLEGE
Rte. 67, Johnstown 12095 *Type:* Public (county) junior *System:* State University of New York Office of Community Colleges *Accred.:* 1969/1986 (MSA) *Calendar:* Sem. plan *Degrees:* A *CEO:* Pres. John G. Boshart
Enroll: 1870 (518) 762-4651

THE GENERAL THEOLOGICAL SEMINARY
175 Ninth Ave., New York 10011 *Type:* Private (Episcopal) professional; graduate only *Accred.:* 1938/1983 (ATS) *Calendar:* Sem. plan *Degrees:* P, M, D *CEO:* Dean/Pres. James C. Fenhagen
Enroll: 108 (212) 243-5150

GENESEE COMMUNITY COLLEGE
One College Rd., Batavia 14020 *Type:* Public (district) junior *System:* State University of New York Office of Community Colleges *Accred.:* 1971/1986 (MSA) *Calendar:* Sem. plan *Degrees:* A, certificates, diplomas *Prof. Accred.:* Nursing (A) *CEO:* Pres. Stuart Steiner
Enroll: 3013 (716) 343-0055

GLOBAL BUSINESS INSTITUTE
1931 Mott Ave., Far Rockaway 11691 *Type:* Private business *Accred.:* 1984/1990 (CCA-ACICS) *Calendar:* Courses of varying lengths *Degrees:* certificates, diplomas *CEO:* Dir. Sandy Basso
Enroll: 291 (718) 327-2220

GLOBAL BUSINESS INSTITUTE
209 W. 125th St., New York 10027 *Type:* Private business *Accred.:* 1986 (CCA-ACICS) *Calendar:* Courses of varying lengths *Degrees:* certificates, diplomas *CEO:* Dir. Ethel Jones
(212) 663-1500

GRADUATE SCHOOL AND UNIVERSITY CENTER
33 W. 42nd St., New York 10036 *Type:* Public graduate only *System:* City University of New York Central Administration *Accred.:* 1961/1988 (MSA) *Calendar:* Sem. plan *Degrees:* M,D *CEO:* Pres. Frances D. Horowitz
Enroll: 4481 (212) 642-1600

GRUMMAN DATA SYSTEMS INSTITUTE
250 Crossways Park Dr., Woodbury 11797 *Type:* Private business *Accred.:* 1980/1986 (CCA-ACICS) *Calendar:* Courses of varying lengths *Degrees:* certificates, diplomas *CEO:* Dir. Jerry Agostisi
Enroll: 967 (516) 364-2055

HAMILTON COLLEGE
Clinton 13323 *Type:* Private liberal arts *Accred.:* 1921/1986 (MSA) *Calendar:* Sem. plan *Degrees:* B *CEO:* Pres. Harry C. Payne
Enroll: 1654 (315) 859-4011

HARTWICK COLLEGE
Oneonta 13820 *Type:* Private liberal arts *Accred.:* 1949/1989 (MSA) *Calendar:* 4-1-4 plan *Degrees:* B *Prof. Accred.:* Art, Music, Nursing (B) *CEO:* Pres. Philip S. Wilder, Jr.
Enroll: 1543 (607) 432-4200

HEBREW UNION COLLEGE—JEWISH INSTITUTE OF RELIGION
One W. Fourth St., New York 10012 *Type:* Private (Union of Hebrew Congregations) *Accred.:* 1960/1988 (MSA) *Calendar:* Sem. plan *Degrees:* P, M, D, certificates, diplomas *CEO:* Pres. Alfred Gottschalk
Enroll: 100 (212) 674-5300

HELENE FULD SCHOOL OF NURSING
1919 Madison Ave., New York 10035 *Type:* Private professional *Accred.:* 1988 (MSA) *Calendar:* Qtr. plan *Degrees:* A *Prof. Accred.:* Nursing (A) *CEO:* Dir./Dean Margaret Wines
Enroll: 172 (212) 650-4460

HERBERT H. LEHMAN COLLEGE
Bedford Park Blvd. W., Bronx 10468 *Type:* Public *System:* City University of New York Central Administration *Accred.:* 1968/1988 (MSA) *Calendar:* Sem. plan *Degrees:* B, M

Prof. Accred.: Nurse Anesthesia Education, Nursing (B,M), Social Work (B), Speech-Language Pathology, Teacher Education (e,s,p) *CEO:* Pres. Ricardo Fernandez
Enroll: 9498 (212) 960-8881

HERKIMER COUNTY COMMUNITY COLLEGE
100 Reservoir Rd., Herkimer 13350 *Type:* Public (county) junior *System:* State University of New York Office of Community Colleges *Accred.:* 1972/1988 (MSA) *Calendar:* Sem. plan *Degrees:* A, certificates, diplomas *Prof. Accred.:* Occupational Therapy Assisting *CEO:* Pres. Ronald F. Williams
Enroll: 2219 (315) 866-0300

HILBERT COLLEGE
5200 S. Park Ave., Hamburg 14075 *Type:* Private junior *Accred.:* 1976/1985 (MSA) *Calendar:* Sem. plan *Degrees:* A, certificates, diplomas *CEO:* Pres. Edmunette Paczesny
Enroll: 654 (716) 649-7900

HOBART AND WILLIAM SMITH COLLEGES
Geneva 14456 *Type:* Private liberal arts *Accred.:* 1921/1989 (MSA) *Calendar:* Tri. plan *Degrees:* B *CEO:* Pres. Richard H. Hersh
Enroll: 1966 (315) 789-5500

HOFSTRA UNIVERSITY
1000 Fulton St., Hempstead 11550 *Type:* Private *Accred.:* 1940/1989 (MSA) *Calendar:* Sem. plan *Degrees:* A, B, P, M, D, certificates, diplomas *Prof. Accred.:* Audiology, Business (B,M), Combined Professional-Scientific Psychology, Engineering (electrical, engineering physics/science, mechanical), Law, Rehabilitation Counseling, Speech-Language Pathology, Teacher Education (e,s,p) *CEO:* Pres. James M. Shuart
Enroll: 12333 (516) 560-6600

HOSTOS COMMUNITY COLLEGE
475 Grand Concourse, Bronx 10451 *Type:* Public *System:* City University of New York Central Administration *Accred.:* 1974/1985 (MSA) *Calendar:* Sem. plan *Degrees:* A

Prof. Accred.: Dental Hygiene, Radiography *CEO:* Pres. Isaura Santiago
Enroll: 3954 (212) 960-1200

HOUGHTON COLLEGE
Houghton 14744 *Type:* Private (Wesleyan) liberal arts *Accred.:* 1935/1985 (MSA) *Calendar:* Sem. plan *Degrees:* A, B *Prof. Accred.:* Music *CEO:* Pres. Daniel R. Chamberlain
Enroll: 1146 (716) 567-9200

BUFFALO SUBURBAN CAMPUS
910 Union Rd., West Seneca, NY 14224
CEO: Dean Clarence C. Bence
(716) 674-6363

HUDSON VALLEY COMMUNITY COLLEGE
80 Vandenburg Ave., Troy 12180 *Type:* Public (county) junior *System:* State University of New York Office of Community Colleges *Accred.:* 1969/1989 (MSA) *Calendar:* Sem. plan *Degrees:* A, certificates, diplomas *Prof. Accred.:* Dental Hygiene, Engineering Technology (civil/construction, electrical, mechanical), Medical Laboratory Technology (AMA), Mortuary Science, Nursing (A), Radiography, Respiratory Therapy *CEO:* Pres. Joseph J. Bulmer
Enroll: 8816 (518) 283-1100

HUNTER BUSINESS SCHOOL
3601 Hempstead Tpke., Levittown 11756 *Type:* Private business *Accred.:* 1982/1986 (CCA-ACICS) *Calendar:* Courses of varying lengths *Degrees:* certificates, diplomas *CEO:* Pres. Florence Kruman
Enroll: 198 (516) 935-7420

HUNTER COLLEGE
695 Park Ave., New York 10021 *Type:* Public *System:* City University of New York Central Administration *Accred.:* 1921/1987 (MSA) *Calendar:* Sem. plan *Degrees:* B, M, certificates, diplomas *Prof. Accred.:* Audiology, Community Health, Nursing (B,M), Physical Therapy, Planning (urban), Rehabilitation Counseling, Social Work (M),

Speech-Language Pathology *CEO:* Pres. Paul Le Clerc
Enroll: 20760 (212) 772-4000

INSTITUTE OF AUDIO RESEARCH
64 University Pl., New York 10003-4595 *Type:* Private *Accred.:* 1985 (CCA-ACTTS) *Calendar:* Courses of varying lengths *Degrees:* certificates *CEO:* Dir. Miriam Friedman
Enroll: 660 (212) 777-8550

INTERBORO INSTITUTE
450 W. 56th St., New York 10019 *Type:* Private business *Accred.:* 1968/1985 (CCA-ACICS) *Calendar:* Sem. plan *Degrees:* A *CEO:* Pres. Bruce R. Kalisch
Enroll: 983 (212) 399-0091

INTERNATIONAL CAREER INSTITUTE
120 W. 30th St., New York 10001 *Type:* Private business *Accred.:* 1978/1989 (CCA-ACICS); 1977/1987 (CCA-ACTTS) *Calendar:* Courses of varying lengths *Degrees:* certificates, diplomas *CEO:* Dir. Larry Stieglite
Enroll: 5954 (212) 244-5252

IONA COLLEGE
715 North Ave., New Rochelle 10801 *Type:* Private liberal arts *Accred.:* 1952/1986 (MSA) *Calendar:* Sem. plan *Degrees:* A, B, M, certificates, diplomas *Prof. Accred.:* Nursing (A), Practical Nursing, Social Work *CEO:* Pres. John G. Driscoll, C.F.C.
Enroll: 5987 (914) 633-2000

ROCKLAND CAMPUS
One Dutch Hill Rd., Orangeburg, NY 10962 *CEO:* Dir. Barbara Witchel
(914) 359-2252

YONKERS CAMPUS
1061 N. Broadway, Yonkers, NY 10701 *CEO:* Dir. Marian McGowan
(914) 378-8000

ISLAND DRAFTING AND TECHNICAL INSTITUTE
128 Broadway, Amityville 11701-2789 *Type:* Private *Accred.:* 1967/1987 (CCA-ACTTS) *Calendar:* Courses of varying lengths *Degrees:* diplomas *CEO:* Pres. Joseph P. DiLiberto
Enroll: 566 (516) 691-8733

ITHACA COLLEGE
Danby Rd., Ithaca 14850 *Type:* Private liberal arts and teachers *Accred.:* 1955/1987 (MSA) *Calendar:* Sem. plan *Degrees:* B, M *Prof. Accred.:* Audiology, Medical Record Administration, Music, Physical Therapy, Recreation and Leisure Studies, Speech-Language Pathology, Theatre *CEO:* Pres. James J. Whalen
Enroll: 6105 (607) 274-3013

JAMESTOWN BUSINESS COLLEGE
7 Fairmount Ave., P.O. Box 429, Jamestown 14702-0429 *Type:* Private business *Accred.:* 1968/1983 (CCA-ACICS) *Calendar:* Sem. plan *Degrees:* A *CEO:* Pres. Tyler C. Swanson
Enroll: 354 (716) 664-5100

JAMESTOWN COMMUNITY COLLEGE
525 Falconer St., Jamestown 14701 *Type:* Public (city) junior *System:* State University of New York Office of Community Colleges *Accred.:* 1956/1987 (MSA) *Calendar:* Sem. plan *Degrees:* A, certificates, diplomas *Prof. Accred.:* Nursing (A) *CEO:* Pres. Timothy G. Davies
Enroll: 4056 (716) 665-5220

BRANCH CAMPUS
244 N. Union St., Olean, NY 14760 *CEO:* Dean James J. Ross
(716) 372-1661

JEFFERSON COMMUNITY COLLEGE
Outer Coffeen St., Watertown 13601 *Type:* Public (county) junior *System:* State University of New York Office of Community Colleges *Accred.:* 1969/1985 (MSA) *Calendar:* Sem. plan *Degrees:* A, certificates, diplomas *Prof. Accred.:* Nursing (A) *CEO:* Pres. John W. Deans
Enroll: 2482 (315) 782-5250

JEWISH THEOLOGICAL SEMINARY OF AMERICA
3080 Broadway, New York 10027 *Type:* Private *Accred.:* 1954/1986 (MSA) *Calendar:*

Sem. plan *Degrees:* B, P, M, D *CEO:* Chanc. Ismar Schorsch
Enroll: 494 (212) 678-8000

JOHN JAY COLLEGE OF CRIMINAL JUSTICE
899 10th Ave., New York 10019 *Type:* Public *System:* City University of New York Central Administration *Accred.:* 1965/1988 (MSA) *Calendar:* Sem. plan *Degrees:* A, B, M, D *Prof. Accred.:* Public Administration *CEO:* Pres. Gerald W. Lynch
Enroll: 7312 (212) 237-8000

JOSEPH BULOVA SCHOOL
40-24 62nd St., Woodside 11377-4959 *Type:* Private *Accred.:* 1978/1988 (CCA-ACTTS) *Calendar:* Courses of varying lengths *Degrees:* certificates *CEO:* Dir. Richard M. Switzer
Enroll: 87 (718) 424-2929

THE JUILLIARD SCHOOL
Lincoln Center Plaza, New York 10023 *Type:* Private professional *Accred.:* 1956/1988 (MSA) *Calendar:* Sem. plan *Degrees:* B, M, D, certificates, diplomas *CEO:* Pres. Joseph W. Polisi
Enroll: 863 (212) 799-5000

KATHARINE GIBBS SCHOOL
535 Broad Hollow Rd., Melville 11747 *Type:* Private business *Accred.:* 1973/1985 (CCA-ACICS) *Calendar:* Sem. plan *Degrees:* A *CEO:* Dir. Patricia Martin
Enroll: 685 (516) 293-2460

KATHARINE GIBBS SCHOOL
200 Park Ave., New York 10017 *Type:* Private business *Accred.:* 1967/1985 (CCA-ACICS) *Calendar:* Courses of varying lengths *Degrees:* A, certificates, diplomas *CEO:* Dir. Mary J. Greco
Enroll: 1441 (212) 867-9300

KEHILLATH YAKOV RABBINICAL SEMINARY
206 Wilson St., Brooklyn 11211 *Type:* Private professional *Accred.:* 1981/1987 (AARTS) *Calendar:* Sem. plan *Degrees:* Rabbinic (1st and 2nd) *CEO:* Pres. Sandor Schwartz
Enroll: 102 (718) 963-3940

KEUKA COLLEGE
Keuka Park 14478 *Type:* Private liberal arts primarily for women *Accred.:* 1927/1988 (MSA) *Calendar:* 4-1-4 plan *Degrees:* B *Prof. Accred.:* Nursing (B), Social Work (B) *CEO:* Pres. Arthur F. Kirk, Jr.
Enroll: 600 (315) 536-4411

KING'S COLLEGE
Briarcliff Manor 10510 *Type:* Private liberal arts *Accred.:* 1968/1984 (MSA) *Calendar:* Sem. plan *Degrees:* A, B *CEO:* Pres. Friedhelm K. Radandt
Enroll: 508 (914) 941-7200

KINGSBOROUGH COMMUNITY COLLEGE
2001 Oriental Blvd., Manhattan Beach, Brooklyn 11235 *Type:* Public *System:* City University of New York Central Administration *Accred.:* 1964/1986 (MSA) *Calendar:* Sem. plan *Degrees:* A *Prof. Accred.:* Nursing (A) *CEO:* Pres. Leon M. Goldstein
Enroll: 12424 (718) 934-5000

KRISSLER BUSINESS INSTITUTE
166 Mansion Square Park, Poughkeepsie 12601 *Type:* Private business *Accred.:* 1975/1990 (CCA-ACICS) *Calendar:* Courses of varying lengths *Degrees:* certificates, diplomas *CEO:* Dir. Edgar H. Krissler
Enroll: 140 (914) 471-0330

LA GUARDIA COMMUNITY COLLEGE
31-10 Thomson Ave., Long Island City 11101 *Type:* Public *System:* City University of New York Central Administration *Accred.:* 1974/1984 (MSA) *Calendar:* Qtr. plan *Degrees:* A, certificates, diplomas *Prof. Accred.:* Animal Health Technology, Nursing (A), Occupational Therapy Assisting, Physical Therapy Assisting *CEO:* Pres. Raymond C. Bowen
Enroll: 8963 (718) 482-5700

LABAN/BARTENIEFF INSTITUTE OF MOVEMENT STUDIES, INC.
31 W. 27th St., New York 10001 *Type:* Private *Calendar:* Courses of varying lengths

Degrees: certificates *Prof. Accred.:* Dance *CEO:* Exec. Dir. Barbara Schaflin
(212) 689-0740

LABORATORY INSTITUTE OF MERCHANDISING
12 E. 53rd St., New York 10022 *Type:* Private *Accred.:* 1977/1986 (MSA) *Calendar:* 4-1-4 plan *Degrees:* A, B *CEO:* Pres. Adrian G. Marcuse
Enroll: 211 (212) 752-1530

LE MOYNE COLLEGE
Le Moyne Heights, Syracuse 13214 *Type:* Private liberal arts *Accred.:* 1953/1987 (MSA) *Calendar:* Sem. plan *Degrees:* B *CEO:* Pres. Kevin G. O'Connell, S.J.
Enroll: 2270 (315) 445-4100

LONG ISLAND BUSINESS INSTITUTE
6500 Jericho Tpke., Commack 11725 *Type:* Private business *Accred.:* 1984/1990 (CCA-ACICS) *Calendar:* Qtr. plan *Degrees:* certificates, diplomas *CEO:* Dir. Genevieve Baron
Enroll: 348 (516) 499-7100

LONG ISLAND UNIVERSITY
Greenvale 11548 *Type:* Private liberal arts and professional *Accred.:* 1955/1989 (MSA) *Calendar:* Sem. plan *Degrees:* A, B, M, D, certificates, diplomas *CEO:* Pres. David J. Steinberg
Enroll: 17433 (516) 299-0200

BRENTWOOD CAMPUS
Second Ave., Brentwood, NY 11717 *CEO:* Provost Dennis Payette
(516) 273-5112

BROOKLYN CAMPUS
One University Plaza, Brooklyn, NY 11201 *Prof. Accred.:* Nursing (A,B), Pharmacy, Physical Therapy *CEO:* Senior Vice Pres./Provost Gale Stevens-Haynes
(718) 403-1001

C.W. POST CAMPUS
Greenvale, NY 11548 *Prof. Accred.:* Clinical Psychology, Counseling, Medical Record Administration, Medical Technology, Nursing (B), Public Administration, Radiography, Respiratory Therapy *CEO:* Provost Doris Guidi
(516) 299-0200

ROCKLAND CAMPUS
Rte. 340, Orangeburg, NY 10962 *CEO:* Provost Joram Warmund
(914) 359-7200

SOUTHAMPTON CAMPUS
Southampton, NY 11968 *CEO:* Provost Timothy H. Bishop
(516) 283-4000

WESTCHESTER CAMPUS
555 Broadway, Dobbs Ferry, NY 10522 *CEO:* Provost Dennis Payette
(914) 693-4500

MAHANNA CAREER SCHOOL
1821 Broad St., Utica 13501-1196 *Type:* Private *Accred.:* 1986 (CCA-ACTTS) *Calendar:* Courses of varying lengths *Degrees:* certificates *CEO:* Dir. Justin J. Mahanna
Enroll: 57 (315) 738-0827

MANDL SCHOOL
254 W. 54th St., New York 10019-5516 *Type:* Private *Accred.:* 1987 (CCA-ACTTS) *Calendar:* Courses of varying lengths *Degrees:* certificates, diplomas *Prof. Accred.:* Health Education *CEO:* Pres. Melvyn P. Weiner
Enroll: 817 (212) 247-3434

MANHATTAN COLLEGE
Manhattan College Pkwy., Riverdale 10471 *Type:* Private liberal arts and professional *Accred.:* 1921/1986 (MSA) *Calendar:* Sem. plan *Degrees:* A, B, M *Prof. Accred.:* Engineering (chemical, civil, electrical, environmental/sanitary, mechanical), Nuclear Medicine Technology *CEO:* Pres. Thomas J. Scanlan
Enroll: 3961 (212) 920-0100

MANHATTAN SCHOOL OF MUSIC
120 Claremont Ave., New York 10027 *Type:* Private professional *Accred.:* 1956/1988 (MSA) *Calendar:* Sem. plan *Degrees:* B, M,

D, certificates, diplomas *CEO:* Pres. Peter C. Simon
Enroll: 782   (212) 749-2802

MANHATTAN SCHOOL OF PRINTING
88 W. Broadway, New York 10007 *Type:* Private *Calendar:* Courses of varying lengths *Degrees:* certificates *CEO:* Pres. John L. Kress, Jr.
Enroll: 367   (212) 962-4330

MANHATTAN TECHNICAL INSTITUTE
252 W. 29th St., New York 10001 *Type:* Private *Accred.:* 1983/1988 (CCA-ACTTS) *Calendar:* Courses of varying lengths *Degrees:* certificates *CEO:* Dir. Alan Shikowitz
Enroll: 781   (212) 967-6300

MANHATTANVILLE COLLEGE
125 Purchase St., Purchase 10577 *Type:* Private liberal arts *Accred.:* 1926/1980 (MSA) *Calendar:* Sem. plan *Degrees:* B, M *Prof. Accred.:* Music *CEO:* Pres. Marcia A. Savage
Enroll: 1570   (914) 694-2200

MARIA COLLEGE OF ALBANY
700 New Scotland Ave., Albany 12208 *Type:* Private junior for women *Accred.:* 1973/1988 (MSA) *Calendar:* Sem. plan *Degrees:* A *Prof. Accred.:* Nursing (A), Occupational Therapy Assisting, Physical Therapy Assisting *CEO:* Pres. Laureen Fitzgerald
Enroll: 927   (518) 438-7170

MARIST COLLEGE
82 North Rd., Poughkeepsie 12601 *Type:* Private liberal arts *Accred.:* 1964/1987 (MSA) *Calendar:* Sem. plan *Degrees:* B, M, certificates, diplomas *Prof. Accred.:* Medical Technology, Social Work (B) *CEO:* Pres. Dennis J. Murray
Enroll: 4545   (914) 471-3240

MARITIME COLLEGE
Fort Schuyler, Bronx 10465 *Type:* Public (state) *System:* State University of New York System Office *Accred.:* 1952/1986 (MSA) *Calendar:* Sem. plan *Degrees:* B, M *Prof. Accred.:* Engineering (electrical, naval architecture/marine) *CEO:* Pres. Floyd H. Miller, U.S.N. (Ret.)
Enroll: 847   (212) 409-7200

MARTHA GRAHAM SCHOOL OF CONTEMPORARY DANCE, INC.
316 E. 63rd St., New York 10021 *Type:* Private *Calendar:* Courses of varying lengths *Degrees:* certificates *Prof. Accred.:* Dance *CEO:* Dir. Diane Gray
         (212) 838-5886

MARYKNOLL SCHOOL OF THEOLOGY
Pinesbridge Rd., Maryknoll 10545 *Type:* Private (Roman Catholic) professional; graduate only *Accred.:* 1968/1983 (ATS); 1962/1988 (MSA) *Calendar:* Sem. plan *Degrees:* P, M *CEO:* Pres. John K. Halbert, M.M.
Enroll: 54   (914) 941-7590

MARYMOUNT COLLEGE
Tarrytown 10591 *Type:* Private liberal arts *Accred.:* 1927/1984 (MSA) *Calendar:* Sem. plan *Degrees:* B *Prof. Accred.:* Social Work (B) *CEO:* Pres. Brigid Driscoll, R.S.H.M.
Enroll: 1247   (914) 631-3200

MARYMOUNT MANHATTAN COLLEGE
221 E. 71st St., New York 10021 *Type:* Private liberal arts *Accred.:* 1961/1982 (MSA) *Calendar:* 4-1-4 plan *Degrees:* A, B *CEO:* Pres. Regina S. Peruggi
Enroll: 1306   (212) 517-0400

MATER DEI COLLEGE
Riverside Dr., Ogdensburg 13669 *Type:* Private *Accred.:* 1974/1984 (MSA) *Calendar:* Sem. plan *Degrees:* A, certificates, diplomas *CEO:* Pres. Carol A. Smith
Enroll: 525   (315) 393-5930

MEDAILLE COLLEGE
18 Agassiz Cir., Buffalo 14214 *Type:* Private liberal arts *Accred.:* 1951/1988 (MSA) *Calendar:* Sem. plan *Degrees:* A, B, certificates, diplomas *CEO:* Pres. Kevin I. Sullivan
Enroll: 1053   (716) 884-3281

MEDGAR EVERS COLLEGE
1150 Carroll St., Brooklyn 11225 *Type:* Public *System:* City University of New York

Central Administration *Accred.:* 1976/1987 (MSA) *Calendar:* Sem. plan *Degrees:* A, B, certificates, diplomas *Prof. Accred.:* Nursing (B) *CEO:* Pres. Edison O. Jackson
Enroll: 2434 (718) 270-4900

MERCE CUNNINGHAM STUDIO
463 West St., New York 10014 *Type:* Private *Calendar:* Courses of varying lengths *Degrees:* certificates *Prof. Accred.:* Dance *CEO:* Dir. Merce Cunningham
(212) 255-3130

MERCY COLLEGE
555 Broadway, Dobbs Ferry 10522 *Type:* Private liberal arts *Accred.:* 1968/1989 (MSA) *Calendar:* Sem. plan *Degrees:* A, B, M, certificates, diplomas *Prof. Accred.:* Nursing (B,M), Social Work (B), Veterinary Technology *CEO:* Pres. Jay Sexter
Enroll: 6117 (914) 693-4500

BRONX CAMPUS
50 Antin Pl., Bronx, NY 10462 *CEO:* Dean Marilyn Nielsen
(212) 798-8952

PEEKSKILL CAMPUS
Peekskill, NY 10566 *CEO:* Dean Wiley Dickerson
(914) 739-8300

WHITE PLAINS CAMPUS
Martine Ave. and S. Broadway, White Plains, NY 10601 *CEO:* Dean John McGrath
(914) 948-3666

YORKTOWN HEIGHTS CAMPUS
2651 Stang Blvd., Yorktown Heights, NY 10598 *CEO:* Dean Thomas Barry
(914) 245-6100

MESIVTA TIFERETH JERUSALEM OF AMERICA
141 E. Broadway, New York 10002 *Type:* Private professional *Accred.:* 1979/1989 (AARTS) *Calendar:* Sem. plan *Degrees:* Talmudic (1st and 2nd) *CEO:* Pres. D. Feinstein
Enroll: 86 (212) 964-2830

MESIVTA TORAH VODAATH SEMINARY
425 E. 9th St., Brooklyn 11218 *Type:* Private professional *Accred.:* 1976/1990 (AARTS) *Calendar:* Sem. plan *Degrees:* Talmudic (1st and 2nd) *CEO:* Dean Aaron Braun
Enroll: 320 (718) 941-8000

MESIVTA OF EASTERN PARKWAY RABBINICAL SEMINARY
510 Dahill Rd., Brooklyn 11218 *Type:* Private professional *Accred.:* 1980/1986 (AARTS) *Calendar:* Sem. plan *Degrees:* Talmudic (1st and 2nd) *CEO:* Pres. Joseph D. Epstein
Enroll: 48 (718) 438-1002

MIDTOWN SCHOOL OF BUSINESS
One E. 19th St., New York 10003 *Type:* Private business *Accred.:* 1974/1986 (CCA-ACICS) *Calendar:* Courses of varying lengths *Degrees:* certificates, diplomas *CEO:* Dir. Dale Wolkind Kramer
Enroll: 2192 (212) 995-9898

MILDRED ELLEY SCHOOL
1227 Quail St., Albany 12203 *Type:* Private business *Accred.:* 1982/1988 (CCA-ACICS) *Calendar:* Sem. plan *Degrees:* certificates, diplomas *CEO:* Pres. Faith Ann Takes
Enroll: 503 (518) 432-4534

MIRRER YESHIVA CENTRAL INSTITUTION
1795 Ocean Pkwy., Brooklyn 11223 *Type:* Private professional *Accred.:* 1975/1988 (AARTS) *Calendar:* Sem. plan *Degrees:* Talmudic (1st and 2nd) *CEO:* Pres. S.M. Kalmanowitz
Enroll: 202 (718) 645-0536

MODERN WELDING SCHOOL
1740 Broadway, Schenectady 12306-4998 *Type:* Private *Accred.:* 1984/1989 (CCA-ACTTS) *Calendar:* Courses of varying lengths *Degrees:* certificates *CEO:* Dir. Dana J. Gillenwalters
Enroll: 118 (518) 374-1216

MOHAWK VALLEY COMMUNITY COLLEGE
1101 Sherman Dr., Utica 13501 *Type:* Public (county) junior *System:* State University of New York Office of Community Colleges

Accred.: 1960/1988 (MSA) Calendar: Sem. plan Degrees: A Prof. Accred.: Engineering Technology (civil/construction, electrical, mechanical, surveying), Medical Record Technology, Nursing (A), Respiratory Therapy Technology CEO: Pres. Michael I. Schafer
Enroll: 6154 (315) 792-5400

BRANCH CAMPUS
Floyd Ave., Rome, NY 13440 CEO: Dean Michael B. Sewall
(315) 339-3470

MOLLOY COLLEGE
1000 Hempstead Ave., Rockville Centre 11570 Type: Private (Roman Catholic) liberal arts Accred.: 1967/1986 (MSA) Calendar: 4-1-4 plan Degrees: A, B Prof. Accred.: Nursing (B), Respiratory Therapy, Respiratory Therapy Technology, Social Work (B) CEO: Pres. Janet A. Fitzgerald, O.P.
Enroll: 1384 (516) 678-5000

MONROE COLLEGE
29 E. Fordham Rd., Bronx 10468 Type: Private junior Accred.: 1963/1990 (CCA-ACICS); 1987 (MSA candidate) Calendar: Sem. plan Degrees: A CEO: Pres. Stephen J. Jerome
Enroll: 2139 (212) 933-6700

BRANCH CAMPUS
434 Main St., New Rochelle, NY 10801 CEO: Dir. Peter Neigler
(914) 632-5400

MONROE COMMUNITY COLLEGE
1000 E. Henrietta Rd., Rochester 14623 Type: Public (county) junior System: State University of New York Office of Community Colleges Accred.: 1965/1986 (MSA) Calendar: Sem. plan Degrees: A Prof. Accred.: Dental Hygiene, Engineering Technology (electrical), Medical Record Technology, Nursing (A), Radiography CEO: Pres. Peter A. Spina
Enroll: 12768 (716) 424-5200

MOUNT ST. MARY COLLEGE
330 Powell Ave., Newburgh 12550 Type: Private liberal arts Accred.: 1968/1987 (MSA) Calendar: Sem. plan Degrees: B, M Prof. Accred.: Nursing (B) CEO: Pres. Ann Sakac
Enroll: 1226 (914) 561-0800

MOUNT SINAI SCHOOL OF MEDICINE
One Gustave L. Levy Pl., New York 10029 System: City University of New York Central Administration Calendar: Sem. plan Degrees: B, P, M, D Prof. Accred.: Health Services Administration, Medicine CEO: Dean John W. Rowe
Enroll: 483 (212) 650-6500

MUNSON-WILLIAMS-PROCTOR INSTITUTE
310 Genesee St., Utica 13502 Type: Private Calendar: Courses of varying lengths Degrees: A, diplomas Prof. Accred.: Art CEO: Dir. Clyde E. McCulley
(315) 797-8260

NASSAU COMMUNITY COLLEGE
Stewart Ave., Garden City 11530 Type: Public (county) junior System: State University of New York Office of Community Colleges Accred.: 1967/1984 (MSA) Calendar: Sem. plan Degrees: A Prof. Accred.: Engineering Technology (civil/construction), Music, Nursing (A), Physical Therapy Assisting, Radiation Therapy Technology, Radiography, Respiratory Therapy, Surgical Technology CEO: Pres. Sean A. Fanelli
Enroll: 20130 (516) 222-7205

NASSAU SCHOOL
40 E. 29th St., New York 10023-7911 Type: Private Accred.: 1978/1989 (CCA-ACTTS) Calendar: Courses of varying lengths Degrees: diplomas CEO: Dir. Daniel M. Greenfield
Enroll: 182 (212) 265-7790

NATIONAL SHAKESPEARE CONSERVATORY
591 Broadway, New York 10012 Type: Private Calendar: Courses of varying lengths

New York **Accredited Institutions**

Degrees: certificates *Prof. Accred.:* Theatre *CEO:* Dir. Albert Schoemann
(212) 219-9874

NATIONAL TAX TRAINING SCHOOL
4 Melnick Dr., P.O. Box 382, Monsey 10952 *Type:* Private home study *Accred.:* 1965/1991 (NHSC) *Calendar:* Courses of varying lengths *Degrees:* certificates *CEO:* Dir. Ben D. Eisenberg
(914) 352-3634

NATIONAL TRACTOR TRAILER SCHOOL
175 Katherine Street, Buffalo 14210-2007 *Type:* Private *Accred.:* 1991 (CCA-ACTTS) *Calendar:* Courses of varying lengths *Degrees:* certificates *CEO:* Dir. Judith A O'Brocta
(716) 849-6887

NATIONAL TRACTOR TRAILER SCHOOL
4650 Buckley Rd., P.O. Box 208, Liverpool 13088-0208 *Type:* Private *Accred.:* 1984/1989 (CCA-ACTTS) *Calendar:* Courses of varying lengths *Degrees:* certificates *CEO:* Pres. Harry Kowalchyk, Jr.
Enroll: 269 (315) 451-2430

NAZARETH COLLEGE OF ROCHESTER
4245 East Ave., Rochester 14610 *Type:* Private liberal arts *Accred.:* 1930/1986 (MSA) *Calendar:* Sem. plan *Degrees:* B, M *Prof. Accred.:* Music, Nursing (B), Social Work (B) *CEO:* Pres. Rose Marie Beston
Enroll: 2935 (716) 586-2525

NEW SCHOOL FOR SOCIAL RESEARCH
66 W. 12th St., New York 10011 *Type:* Private *Accred.:* 1960/1986 (MSA) *Calendar:* Sem. plan *Degrees:* A, B, M, D, certificates, diplomas *Prof. Accred.:* Art, Clinical Psychology, Urban Affairs and Policy Analysis *CEO:* Pres. Jonathan F. Fanton
Enroll: 7357 (212) 229-5500

NEW SCHOOL OF CONTEMPORARY RADIO
50 Colvin Ave., Albany 12206-1106 *Type:* Private *Accred.:* 1981/1986 (CCA-ACTTS) *Calendar:* Courses of varying lengths *Degrees:* certificates *CEO:* Dir. Thomas Brownlie, III
Enroll: 96 (518) 438-7682

NEW YORK BUSINESS SCHOOL
269 W. 40th St., New York 10018 *Type:* Private business *Accred.:* 1985/1991 (CCA-ACICS) *Calendar:* Courses of varying lengths *Degrees:* certificates, diplomas *CEO:* Pres. Irwin Mautner
Enroll: 1200 (212) 944-9200

NEW YORK CHIROPRACTIC COLLEGE
2360 Rte. 89, Seneca Falls 13148-0800 *Type:* Private professional *Accred.:* 1983 (MSA) *Calendar:* Tri. plan *Degrees:* P *Prof. Accred.:* Chiropractic Education *CEO:* Pres. Kenneth W. Padgett
Enroll: 757 (315) 568-3000

NEW YORK CITY TECHNICAL COLLEGE
300 Jay St., Brooklyn 11201 *Type:* Public *System:* City University of New York Central Administration *Accred.:* 1957/1987 (MSA) *Calendar:* Sem. plan *Degrees:* A, B, certificates, diplomas *Prof. Accred.:* Dental Hygiene, Dental Laboratory Technology, Engineering Technology (civil/construction, electrical, electromechanical, mechanical), Nursing (A), Radiography *CEO:* Pres. Charles W. Meredith
Enroll: 10323 (718) 643-4900

NEW YORK COLLEGE OF PODIATRIC MEDICINE
53 E. 124th St., New York 10035 *Type:* Private professional *Calendar:* Sem. plan *Degrees:* P *Prof. Accred.:* Podiatry *CEO:* Acting Pres. Monroe Seifer
Enroll: 554 (212) 410-8000

NEW YORK FOOD AND HOTEL MANAGEMENT SCHOOL
154 W. 14th St., New York 10011-7307 *Type:* Private *Accred.:* 1973/1989 (CCA-ACTTS) *Calendar:* Sem. plan *Degrees:* certificates *CEO:* Dir. Susan Flowerman
Enroll: 782 (212) 675-6655

NEW YORK INSTITUTE OF BUSINESS AND TECHNOLOGY
401 Park Ave. S., 2nd Fl., New York 10016 *Type:* Private business *Accred.:* 1985/1990

(CCA-ACICS) *Calendar:* Courses of varying lengths *Degrees:* certificates, diplomas *CEO:* Exec. Dir. Leith E. Yetman
Enroll: 1190 (212) 725-9400

NEW YORK INSTITUTE OF TECHNOLOGY
Wheatley Rd., Old Westbury 11568 *Type:* Private professional *Accred.:* 1969/1988 (MSA) *Calendar:* Sem. plan *Degrees:* A, B, P, M, certificates, diplomas *Prof. Accred.:* Architecture (B), Engineering (electrical, mechanical), Engineering Technology (computer), Interior Design, Medical Technology, Osteopathy *CEO:* Pres. Matthew Schure
Enroll: 12575 (516) 686-7516

CENTRAL ISLIP CAMPUS
211 Carleton Ave., Central Islip, NY 11722-7516 *CEO:* Dir. David J. Salten
(516) 348-3000

METROPOLITAN CAMPUS
61st St. and Broadway, New York, NY 10023 *CEO:* Dir. David J. Salten
(212) 399-8300

NEW YORK LAW SCHOOL
57 Worth St., New York 10013 *Type:* Private *Calendar:* Sem. plan *Degrees:* P *Prof. Accred.:* Law *CEO:* Dean James F. Simon
Enroll: 1250 (212) 431-2100

NEW YORK MEDICAL COLLEGE
Valhalla 10595 *Type:* Private professional *Calendar:* Sem. plan *Degrees:* P, D *Prof. Accred.:* Medicine *CEO:* Dean Karl P. Adler, M.D.
Enroll: 1283 (914) 347-5000

NEW YORK SCHOOL FOR MEDICAL AND DENTAL ASSISTANTS
116-16 Queens Blvd., Forest Hills 11375 *Type:* Private *Accred.:* 1973/1978 (CCA-ACTTS) *Calendar:* Courses of varying lengths *Degrees:* certificates, diplomas *CEO:* Pres. E. Richard Schwabach
Enroll: 355 (718) 793-2330

NEW YORK SCHOOL OF DOG GROOMING
248 E. 34th St., New York 10016-4873 *Type:* Private *Accred.:* 1973/1989 (CCA-ACTTS) *Calendar:* Courses of varying lengths *Degrees:* certificates *CEO:* Dir. Sam Kohl
Enroll: 219 (212) 685-3776

BRANCH CAMPUS
265-17 Union Tpke., New Hyde Park, NY 11040-1425 *CEO:* Dir. Sam Kohl
(718) 343-3130

NEW YORK SCHOOL OF INTERIOR DESIGN
155 E. 56th St., New York 10022 *Type:* Private *Calendar:* Courses of varying lengths *Degrees:* B, P *Prof. Accred.:* Interior Design *CEO:* Dean John Michael
Enroll: 136 (212) 753-5365

NEW YORK THEOLOGICAL SEMINARY
5 W. 29th St., New York 10001-4599 *Type:* Private (interdenominational) professional; graduate only *Accred.:* 1958/1984 (ATS) *Calendar:* 4-1-4 plan *Degrees:* P, M, D *CEO:* Pres. Keith A. Russell
Enroll: 230 (212) 532-4012

NEW YORK UNIVERSITY
70 Washington Sq. S., New York 10012 *Type:* Private *Accred.:* 1921/1984 (MSA) *Calendar:* Sem. plan *Degrees:* A, B, P, M, D, certificates, diplomas *Prof. Accred.:* Accounting (Type A,B,C), Business (B,M), Clinical Psychology, Community Health, Combined Prosthodontics, Counseling Psychology, Cytotechnology, Dance, Dental Assisting, Dental Hygiene, Dentistry, Diagnostic Medical Sonography, Endodontics, General Dentistry, Health Services Administration, Journalism, Law, Medicine, Music, Nuclear Medicine Technology, Nursing (B,M), Occupational Therapy, Oral and Maxillofacial Surgery (conditional), Orthodontics, Pediatric Dentistry, Periodontics, Physical Therapy, Physical Therapy Assisting, Planning (urban), Psychology Internship, Public Administration, Rehabilitation Counseling, Respiratory Therapy, School Psychology, Social Work (B,M), Speech-Language Pathology, Teacher Education (e,s,p) *CEO:* Pres. L. Jay Oliva
Enroll: 30735 (212) 998-1212

SCHOOL OF SOCIAL WORK BRANCH CAMPUS
10 Western Hwy., Orangeburg, NY 10962
CEO: Dean Shirley M. Ehrenkranz
(212) 998-5910

STERN SCHOOL OF BUSINESS
25 Purchase St., Rte. 120, Purchase, NY 10577 *CEO:* Dean Daniel E. Diamond
(914) 694-3375

NIAGARA COUNTY COMMUNITY COLLEGE
3111 Saunders Settlement Rd., Sanborn 14132 *Type:* Public (county) junior *System:* State University of New York Office of Community Colleges *Accred.:* 1970/1986 (MSA) *Calendar:* Sem. plan *Degrees:* A, certificates, diplomas *Prof. Accred.:* Electro-neurodiagnostic Technology, Engineering Technology (electrical, mechanical), Nursing (A), Surgical Technology *CEO:* Pres. Gerald L. Miller
Enroll: 4745 (716) 731-3271

NIAGARA UNIVERSITY
Niagara University 14109 *Type:* Private (Roman Catholic) liberal arts *Accred.:* 1922/1987 (MSA) *Calendar:* Sem. plan *Degrees:* A, B, M, certificates, diplomas *Prof. Accred.:* Nursing (B), Social Work (B), Teacher Education (s,p) *CEO:* Pres. Brian J. O'Connell
Enroll: 3048 (716) 285-1212

NIKOLAIS AND LOUIS DANCE LAB
375 W. Broadway, 5th Fl., New York 10012 *Type:* Private *Calendar:* Courses of varying lengths *Degrees:* certificates *Prof. Accred.:* Dance *CEO:* Dir. Lynn Lesniak Needle
(212) 226-7000

NORTH COUNTRY COMMUNITY COLLEGE
20 Winona Ave., P.O. Box 89, Saranac Lake 12983 *Type:* Public (county) junior *System:* State University of New York Office of Community Colleges *Accred.:* 1975/1990 (MSA) *Calendar:* Sem. plan *Degrees:* A *Prof. Accred.:* Radiography *CEO:* Pres. David W. Petty
Enroll: 1520 (518) 891-2915

BRANCH CAMPUS
College Ave., Malone, NY 12953 *CEO:* Dir. Wiley N. Kulia
(518) 483-4550

BRANCH CAMPUS
Montcalm St., Ticonderoga, NY 12883 *CEO:* Dir. Donna Condon
(518) 585-4454

NORTHEAST INSTITUTE
2643 Main St., Buffalo 14214-2015 *Type:* Private *Accred.:* 1991 (CCA-ACTTS) *Calendar:* Courses of varying lengths *Degrees:* certificates *CEO:* Dir. Michael Seifert
(716) 838-6984

NYACK COLLEGE
Nyack 10960 *Type:* Private (Christian Missionary Alliance) *Accred.:* 1990 (ATS); 1962/1978 (MSA) *Calendar:* Sem. plan *Degrees:* A, B, M *Prof. Accred.:* Music *CEO:* Pres. Rexford A. Boda
Enroll: 861 (914) 358-1710

OHR HAMEIR THEOLOGICAL SEMINARY
Furnace Woods Rd., P.O. Box 2130, Peekskill 10566 *Type:* Private professional *Accred.:* 1990 (AARTS) *Calendar:* Sem. plan *Degrees:* Talmudic (1st and 2nd) *CEO:* Pres. E. Kanarek
Enroll: 63 (914) 736-1500

OHR SOMAYACH-TANENBAUM EDUCATIONAL CENTER
P.O. Box 334, Monsey 0952 *Type:* Private professional *Accred.:* 1984/1989 (AARTS) *Calendar:* Tri. plan *Degrees:* Talmudic (1st and 2nd) *CEO:* Pres. A. Braun
Enroll: 52 (914) 425-1370

OLEAN BUSINESS INSTITUTE
301 N. Union St., Olean 14760 *Type:* Private business *Accred.:* 1969/1987 (CCA-ACICS) *Calendar:* Sem. plan *Degrees:* certificates, diplomas *CEO:* Dir. Patrick J. McCarthy
Enroll: 171 (716) 372-7978

ONONDAGA COMMUNITY COLLEGE
Rte. 173, Syracuse 13215 *Type:* Public (county) junior *System:* State University of

New York Office of Community Colleges *Accred.:* 1972/1989 (MSA) *Calendar:* Sem. plan *Degrees:* A *Prof. Accred.:* Dental Hygiene, Medical Record Technology, Nursing (A), Physical Therapy Assisting, Respiratory Therapy, Respiratory Therapy Technology, Surgical Technology *CEO:* Pres. Bruce H. Leslie
Enroll: 7148 (315) 469-7741

ORANGE COUNTY COMMUNITY COLLEGE
115 South St., Middletown 10940 *Type:* Public (county) junior *System:* State University of New York Office of Community Colleges *Accred.:* 1962/1988 (MSA) *Calendar:* Sem. plan *Degrees:* A, certificates, diplomas *Prof. Accred.:* Dental Hygiene, Engineering Technology (electrical), Medical Laboratory Technology (AMA), Nursing (A), Occupational Therapy Assisting, Physical Therapy Assisting, Radiography *CEO:* Pres. William F. Messner
Enroll: 4839 (914) 344-6222

OUR LADY OF VICTORY SECRETARIAL SCHOOL
146 S. Catherine St., Plattsburgh 12901 *Type:* Private business *Accred.:* 1981/1987 (CCA-ACICS) *Calendar:* Qtr. plan *Degrees:* certificates, diplomas *CEO:* Exec. Dir. Theresa Martel
Enroll: 82 (518) 563-0851

PSI INSTITUTE
269 W. 40th St., New York 10018-1502 *Type:* Private *Accred.:* 1971/1989 (CCA-ACTTS) *Calendar:* Courses of varying lengths *Degrees:* certificates, diplomas *CEO:* Dir. John Guzzardi
Enroll: 1575 (212) 944-9200

PACE BUSINESS SCHOOL
2433 E. Tremont Ave., Bronx 10461 *Type:* Private business *Accred.:* 1988 (CCA-ACICS) *Calendar:* Courses of varying lengths *Degrees:* certificates, diplomas *CEO:* Dir. Ted Amoruso
Enroll: 259 (212) 863-7400

PACE BUSINESS SCHOOL
45 Park Ave., Yonkers 10703 *Type:* Private business *Accred.:* 1980/1983 (CCA-ACICS) *Calendar:* Courses of varying lengths *Degrees:* certificates, diplomas *CEO:* Dir. Anita Vogel
Enroll: 226 (914) 963-7945

PACE UNIVERSITY
One Pace Plaza, New York 10038 *Type:* Private liberal arts and professional *Accred.:* 1957/1988 (MSA) *Calendar:* Sem. plan *Degrees:* A, B, P, M, D, certificates, diplomas *Prof. Accred.:* Clinical Psychology, Computer Science, School Psychology *CEO:* Pres. Patricia O'Donnell Ewers
Enroll: 9657 (212) 346-1200

PLEASANTVILLE/BRIARCLIFF CAMPUS
861 Bedford Rd., Pleasantville, NY 10570 *Prof. Accred.:* Nursing (A,B,M) *CEO:* Vice Pres. Richard S. Podgorski
(773) 769-3200

WHITE PLAINS CAMPUS
78 N. Broadway, White Plains, NY 10503 *Prof. Accred.:* Law *CEO:* Vice Pres. Margaret R. Gotti
(914) 773-3200

PAN AMERICAN SCHOOL
244 W. 14th St., New York 10011 *Type:* Private business *Accred.:* 1985 (CCA-ACICS) *Calendar:* Courses of varying lengths *Degrees:* certificates, diplomas *CEO:* Dir. Angelo P. Chavez
Enroll: 1038 (212) 675-6450

PAUL SMITH'S COLLEGE
Paul Smiths 12970 *Type:* Private *Accred.:* 1977/1988 (MSA) *Calendar:* Sem. plan *Degrees:* A *CEO:* Pres. H. David Chamberlain
Enroll: 813 (518) 327-6211

PHILLIPS BETH ISRAEL SCHOOL OF NURSING
310 E. 22nd St., New York 10010 *Type:* Private *Calendar:* Sem. plan *Degrees:* A *Prof. Accred.:* Nursing (A) *CEO:* Dean Julianne M. Hart
(212) 614-6104

New York

PLAZA BUSINESS INSTITUTE
74-09 37th Ave., Jackson Heights 11372
Type: Private junior *Accred.:* 1974/1980
(CCA-ACICS) *Calendar:* Tri. plan *Degrees:*
A *CEO:* Pres. Charles E. Callahan
Enroll: 1154 (718) 779-1430

POLYTECHNIC UNIVERSITY
6 Metrotech Ctr., Brooklyn 11201-2990
Type: Private liberal arts and technological
Accred.: 1927/1987 (MSA) *Calendar:* Sem.
plan *Degrees:* B, M, D *Prof. Accred.:* Computer Science, Engineering (aerospace, chemical, civil, electrical, industrial, mechanical, metallurgical) *CEO:* Pres. George Bugliarello
Enroll: 4219 (718) 260-3600

BRANCH CAMPUS
Long Island Ctr., Rte. 110, Farmingdale, NY 11735 *CEO:* Provost Ernest Racz
(516) 755-4400

BRANCH CAMPUS
Westchester Grad. Ctr., 36 Saw Mill River Rd., Hawthorne, NY 10532 *CEO:* Dir. Kathleen MacDonald
(914) 347-6940

PRACTICAL BIBLE TRAINING SCHOOL
P.O. Box 601, Bible School Park 13737
Type: Private (Independent Baptist) *Accred.:* 1985/1990 (AABC) *Calendar:* Sem. plan *Degrees:* A, certificates, diplomas *CEO:* Pres. Dale Linebaugh
Enroll: 131 (607) 729-1581

PRATT INSTITUTE
200 Willoughby Ave., Brooklyn 11205
Type: Private professional *Accred.:* 1950/1986 (MSA) *Calendar:* 4-1-4 plan *Degrees:* A, B, M, certificates, diplomas *Prof. Accred.:* Architecture (B), Art, Engineering (chemical, civil, electrical, mechanical), Interior Design, Librarianship, Planning (city/regional) *CEO:* Pres. Warren F. Ilchman
Enroll: 3639 (718) 636-3600

PRINTING TRADES SCHOOL
233 Park Ave. S., New York 10003-1690
Type: Private *Accred.:* 1975/1986 (CCA-ACTTS) *Calendar:* Courses of varying lengths *Degrees:* certificates *CEO:* Pres. Elizabeth G. Jenkins
Enroll: 595 (212) 671-0505

PROFESSIONAL BUSINESS INSTITUTE
125 Canal St., New York 10002 *Type:* Private business *Accred.:* 1985/1991 (CCA-ACICS) *Calendar:* Courses of varying lengths *Degrees:* certificates, diplomas *CEO:* Dir. Elayne S. Zinbarg
Enroll: 56 (212) 226-7300

QUEENS COLLEGE
65-30 Kissena Blvd., Flushing 11367 *Type:* Public *System:* City University of New York Central Administration *Accred.:* 1941/1986 (MSA) *Calendar:* Sem. plan *Degrees:* B, M *Prof. Accred.:* Audiology, Home Economics, Law (ABA only), Librarianship, Speech-Language Pathology *CEO:* Pres. Shirley Strum-Kenny
Enroll: 16948 (718) 520-7000

QUEENSBOROUGH COMMUNITY COLLEGE
56th Ave. and Springfield Blvd, Bayside 11364 *Type:* Public *System:* City University of New York Central Administration *Accred.:* 1963/1988 (MSA) *Calendar:* Sem. plan *Degrees:* A, certificates, diplomas *Prof. Accred.:* Engineering Technology (computer, electrical, mechanical), Nursing (A) *CEO:* Pres. Kurt R. Schmeller
Enroll: 11919 (718) 631-6262

RABBINICAL ACADEMY MESIVTA RABBI CHAIM BERLIN
1593 Coney Island Ave., Brooklyn 11230
Type: Private professional *Accred.:* 1975/1988 (AARTS) *Calendar:* Sem. plan *Degrees:* Talmudic (1st and 2nd) *CEO:* Pres. A.M. Schechter
Enroll: 300 (718) 377-0777

RABBINICAL COLLEGE BETH SHRAGA
28 Saddle River Rd., Monsey 10952 *Type:* Private professional *Accred.:* 1978/1991 (AARTS) *Calendar:* Sem. plan *Degrees:* Talmudic (1st and 2nd) *CEO:* Pres. S. Schiff
Enroll: 28 (914) 356-1980

RABBINICAL COLLEGE BOBOVER YESHIVA B'NEI ZION
1577 48th St., Brooklyn 11219 *Type:* Private professional *Accred.:* 1979/1984 (AARTS) *Calendar:* Sem. plan *Degrees:* Rabbinic (1st), Talmudic (1st and 2nd) *CEO:* Pres. N. Halberstam
Enroll: 309   (718) 438-2018

RABBINICAL COLLEGE CH'SAN SOFER
1876 50th St., Brooklyn 11204 *Type:* Private professional *Accred.:* 1979/1990 (AARTS) *Calendar:* Sem. plan *Degrees:* Talmudic (1st and 2nd) *CEO:* Pres. A. Ehrenfeld
Enroll: 75   (718) 236-1171

RABBINICAL COLLEGE OF LONG ISLAND
201 Magnolia Blvd., Long Beach 11561 *Type:* Private professional *Accred.:* 1979/1990 (AARTS) *Calendar:* Sem. plan *Degrees:* Talmudic (1st) *CEO:* Pres. Y. Feigelstock
Enroll: 65   (516) 431-7414

RABBINICAL SEMINARY ADAS YEREIM
185 Wilson St., Brooklyn 11211 *Type:* Private professional *Accred.:* 1979/1990 (AARTS) *Calendar:* Sem. plan *Degrees:* Talmudic (1st) *CEO:* Pres. A. Schonberger
Enroll: 99   (718) 388-1751

RABBINICAL SEMINARY M'KOR CHAIM
1571 55th St., Brooklyn 11219 *Type:* Private professional *Accred.:* 1979/1990 (AARTS) *Calendar:* Sem. plan *Degrees:* Talmudic (1st and 2nd) *CEO:* Pres. B. Paler
Enroll: 91   (718) 851-0183

RABBINICAL SEMINARY OF AMERICA
92-15 69th Ave., Forest Hills 11375 *Type:* Private professional *Accred.:* 1975/1988 (AARTS) *Calendar:* Sem. plan *Degrees:* Talmudic (1st and 2nd) *CEO:* Pres. A.H. Leibowitz
Enroll: 213   (718) 268-4700

RENSSELAER POLYTECHNIC INSTITUTE
110 Eighth St., Troy 12180 *Type:* Private *Accred.:* 1927/1986 (MSA) *Calendar:* Sem. plan *Degrees:* B, M, D *Prof. Accred.:* Architecture (B,M), Business (B,M), Engineering (aerospace, bioengineering, chemical, civil, computer, electrical, environmental/sanitary, industrial, materials, mechanical, nuclear) *CEO:* Pres. Roland W. Schmitt
Enroll: 6707   (518) 276-6000

RIDLEY-LOWELL SCHOOL OF BUSINESS
116 Front St., Binghamton 13905 *Type:* Private business *Accred.:* 1977/1990 (CCA-ACICS) *Calendar:* Courses of varying lengths *Degrees:* certificates, diplomas *CEO:* Dir. Richard Griffis, Jr.
Enroll: 296   (607) 724-2941

RIVERSIDE SCHOOL OF AERONAUTICS
Charlestown Complex, Ste. 100, 311 Turner St., Utica 13501-1785 *Type:* Private *Accred.:* 1972/1989 (CCA-ACTTS) *Calendar:* Qtr. plan *Degrees:* diplomas *CEO:* Vice Pres. Kathleen P. Guerino
Enroll: 124   (315) 724-7988

ROBERTS WESLEYAN COLLEGE
2301 Westside Dr., Rochester 14624 *Type:* Private (Methodist) liberal arts *Accred.:* 1963/1990 (MSA) *Calendar:* Sem. plan *Degrees:* A, B *Prof. Accred.:* Music, Nursing (B), Social Work (B) *CEO:* Pres. William C. Crothers
Enroll: 838   (716) 594-9471

ROCHESTER BUSINESS INSTITUTE
107 Clinton Ave. N., Rochester 14604 *Type:* Private business *Accred.:* 1966/1990 (CCA-ACICS) *Calendar:* Qtr. plan *Degrees:* A *CEO:* Exec. Dir. Tom Coute
Enroll: 808   (716) 325-7290

ROCHESTER INSTITUTE OF TECHNOLOGY
One Lomb Memorial Dr., P.O. Box 9887, Rochester 14623 *Type:* Private professional and technological *Accred.:* 1958/1987 (MSA) *Calendar:* Qtr. plan *Degrees:* A, B, M, certificates, diplomas *Prof. Accred.:* Art, Business (B,M), Computer Science, Diagnostic Medical Sonography, Dietetics (coordinated), Engineering (computer, electrical, industrial, mechanical), Engineering Technology (architectural, civil/construction, computer, electrical, electromechanical,

energy, manufacturing, mechanical, mechanical drafting/design), Medical Record Technology, Nuclear Medicine Technology, Social Work (B) *CEO:* Pres. M. Richard Rose
Enroll: 13181   (716) 475-2400

ROCKLAND COMMUNITY COLLEGE
145 College Rd., Suffern 10901 *Type:* Public (county) junior *System:* State University of New York Office of Community Colleges *Accred.:* 1968/1985 (MSA) *Calendar:* Sem. plan *Degrees:* A, certificates, diplomas *Prof. Accred.:* Medical Laboratory Technology (AMA), Medical Record Technology, Nursing (A), Occupational Therapy Assisting, Respiratory Therapy *CEO:* Pres. F. Thomas Clark
Enroll: 7644   (914) 356-4650

BRANCH CAMPUS
Haberstraw Learning Ctr., 36-39 Main St., Haberstraw, NY 10927 *CEO:* Dir. Julia Kolovchevich
        (914) 942-0624

BRANCH CAMPUS
New Square Learning Ctr., 766 N. Main St., New Square, NY 10977 *CEO:* Dir. Chaim Berger
        (914) 354-5973

BRANCH CAMPUS
Nyack Learning Ctr., 92-94 Main St., Nyack, NY 10960 *CEO:* Dir. Laurel Koras
        (914) 358-9392

BRANCH CAMPUS
Spring Valley Learning Ctr., 185 N. Main St., Spring Valley, NY 10977 *CEO:* Dir. Herman Stovall
        (914) 352-5535

ROYAL BARBER AND BEAUTY SCHOOL
108-112 Broadway, Schenectady 12305-2592 *Type:* Private *Accred.:* 1987 (CCA-ACTTS) *Calendar:* Courses of varying lengths *Degrees:* certificates *CEO:* Dir. Sondra Kaczmarek
Enroll: 28   (518) 346-2288

RUSSELL SAGE COLLEGE
45 Ferry St., Troy 12180 *Type:* Private liberal arts primarily for women *Accred.:* 1928/1986 (MSA) *Calendar:* 4-1-4 plan *Degrees:* A, B, M *Prof. Accred.:* Art, Nursing (A,B,M) *CEO:* Pres. Sara S. Chapman
Enroll: 3232   (518) 270-2000

RUSSELL SAGE JUNIOR COLLEGE OF ALBANY
140 New Scotland Ave., Albany, NY 12208 *Prof. Accred.:* Nursing (A), Physical Therapy *CEO:* Dean Sally A. Lawrence
        (518) 445-1711

SCS BUSINESS AND TECHNICAL INSTITUTE
2467 Jerome Ave., Bronx 10468 *Type:* Private business *Accred.:* 1986/1988 (CCA-ACICS) *Calendar:* Courses of varying lengths *Degrees:* certificates, diplomas *CEO:* Dir. Aaron Sultanik
Enroll: 1108   (212) 733-5200

SCS BUSINESS AND TECHNICAL INSTITUTE
394 Bridge St., Brooklyn 11201 *Type:* Private business *Accred.:* 1989 (CCA-ACICS) *Calendar:* Courses of varying lengths *Degrees:* certificates, diplomas *CEO:* Dir. Joseph Fuller
Enroll: 1091   (718) 802-9500

SCS BUSINESS AND TECHNICAL INSTITUTE
884 Flatbush Ave., Brooklyn 11226 *Type:* Private business *Accred.:* 1987/1988 (CCA-ACICS) *Calendar:* Courses of varying lengths *Degrees:* certificates, diplomas *CEO:* Dir. Seth Cohen
Enroll: 746   (718) 856-6100

SCS BUSINESS AND TECHNICAL INSTITUTE
163-02 Jamaica Ave., Jamaica 11432 *Type:* Private business *Accred.:* 1986/1988 (CCA-ACICS) *Calendar:* Courses of varying lengths *Degrees:* certificates, diplomas *CEO:* Dir. Charles Moorer
Enroll: 1236   (718) 658-8855

SCS BUSINESS AND TECHNICAL INSTITUTE
25 W. 17th St., New York 10011 *Type:* Private business *Accred.:* 1984/1990 (CCA-ACICS) *Calendar:* Courses of varying

lengths *Degrees:* certificates, diplomas *CEO:* Dir. Stephen Solomon
Enroll: 2219 (212) 366-1666

SYRIT COMPUTER SCHOOL SYSTEMS
1760 53rd St., Brooklyn 11204-9004 *Type:* Private *Accred.:* 1981/1986 (CCA-ACTTS) *Calendar:* Courses of varying lengths *Degrees:* diplomas *CEO:* Dir. Elliot Amsel
Enroll: 88 (718) 853-1212

ST. BERNARD'S INSTITUTE
1100 S. Goodman St., Rochester 14620-2545 *Type:* Private (Roman Catholic) professional; graduate only *Accred.:* 1970/1987 (ATS) *Calendar:* Sem. plan *Degrees:* P, M *CEO:* Pres. Sebastian A. Falcone
Enroll: 41 (716) 271-1320

ST. BONAVENTURE UNIVERSITY
Rte. 417, St. Bonaventure 14778 *Type:* Private *Accred.:* 1924/1989 (MSA) *Calendar:* Sem. plan *Degrees:* B, M *CEO:* Pres. Neil J. O'Connell, O.F.M.
Enroll: 2852 (716) 375-2000

ST. FRANCIS COLLEGE
180 Remsen St., Brooklyn 11201 *Type:* Private liberal arts *Accred.:* 1959/1984 (MSA) *Calendar:* Sem. plan *Degrees:* A, B, certificates, diplomas *CEO:* Pres. Donald Sullivan, O.S.F.
Enroll: 1929 (718) 522-2300

ST. JOHN FISHER COLLEGE
3690 East Ave., Rochester 14618 *Type:* Private liberal arts *Accred.:* 1957/1986 (MSA) *Calendar:* Sem. plan *Degrees:* B, M *CEO:* Pres. William L. Pickett
Enroll: 2357 (716) 385-8000

ST. JOHN'S UNIVERSITY
Grand Central and Utopia Pkwys, Jamaica 11439 *Type:* Private (Roman Catholic) *Accred.:* 1921/1986 (MSA) *Calendar:* Sem. plan *Degrees:* A, B, P, M, D, certificates, diplomas *Prof. Accred.:* Audiology, Business (B,M), Clinical Psychology, Law, Librarianship, Pharmacy, Speech-Language Pathology *CEO:* Pres. Donald J. Harrington, C.M.
Enroll: 19143 (718) 990-6161

BRANCH CAMPUS
300 Howard Ave., Staten Island, NY 10301 *CEO:* Senior Vice Pres. James F. Kiernan, C.M.
 (718) 390-4545

ST. JOSEPH'S COLLEGE
245 Clinton Ave., Brooklyn 11205 *Type:* Private liberal arts *Accred.:* 1928/1987 (MSA) *Calendar:* Sem. plan *Degrees:* B *Prof. Accred.:* Nursing (B) *CEO:* Pres. George Aquin O'Connor, C.S.J.
Enroll: 2560 (718) 636-6800

SUFFOLK CAMPUS
155 Roe Blvd., Patchogue, NY 11772 *CEO:* Pres. George Aquin O'Connor, C.S.J.
 (516) 654-3200

ST. JOSEPH'S SEMINARY
Dunwoodie, 201 Seminary Ave., Yonkers 10704 *Type:* Private (Roman Catholic) professional; graduate only *Accred.:* 1973/1983 (ATS); 1961/1988 (MSA) *Calendar:* Sem. plan *Degrees:* P, M *CEO:* Rector/Pres. Raymond T. Powers
Enroll: 90 (914) 968-6200

ST. LAWRENCE UNIVERSITY
Canton 13617 *Type:* Private liberal arts *Accred.:* 1921/1988 (MSA) *Calendar:* Sem. plan *Degrees:* B, M *Prof. Accred.:* Teacher Education(p) *CEO:* Pres. Patti McGill Peterson
Enroll: 2366 (315) 379-5011

ST. THOMAS AQUINAS COLLEGE
Rte. 340, Sparkill 10976 *Type:* Private liberal arts *Accred.:* 1972/1987 (MSA) *Calendar:* Sem. plan *Degrees:* A, B, M *CEO:* Pres. Donald T. McNelis
Enroll: 1983 (914) 359-9500

ST. VLADIMIR'S ORTHODOX THEOLOGICAL SEMINARY
Crestwood 10707 *Type:* Private (Orthodox Church in America) professional; graduate only *Accred.:* 1973/1983 (ATS) *Calendar:* Sem. plan *Degrees:* P, M, D *CEO:* Pres. Metropolitan Theodosius
Enroll: 73 (914) 961-8313

SARAH LAWRENCE COLLEGE
One Meadway, Bronxville 10708 *Type:* Private liberal arts *Accred.:* 1937/1987 (MSA) *Calendar:* Sem. plan *Degrees:* B, M *CEO:* Pres. Alice Stone Ilchman
Enroll: 1202 (914) 337-0700

SCHENECTADY COUNTY COMMUNITY COLLEGE
78 Washington Ave., Schenectady 12305 *Type:* Public (county) junior *System:* State University of New York Office of Community Colleges *Accred.:* 1974/1989 (MSA) *Calendar:* Sem. plan *Degrees:* A, certificates, diplomas *Prof. Accred.:* Music *CEO:* Interim Pres. Gabriel J. Basil
Enroll: 3115 (518) 346-6211

SCHOOL OF VISUAL ARTS
209 E. 23rd St., New York 10010 *Type:* Private professional *Accred.:* 1978/1986 (MSA) *Calendar:* Sem. plan *Degrees:* B, M *Prof. Accred.:* Art *CEO:* Pres. David J. Rhodes
Enroll: 4832 (212) 679-7350

SEMINARY OF THE IMMACULATE CONCEPTION
440 W. Neck Rd., Huntington 11743 *Type:* Private (Roman Catholic) professional; graduate only *Accred.:* 1976/1981 (ATS); 1976/1987 (MSA) *Calendar:* Sem. plan *Degrees:* P, M, D, certificates, diplomas *CEO:* Rector/Pres. John J. Strynkowski
Enroll: 104 (516) 423-0483

SH'OR YOSHUV RABBINICAL COLLEGE
1526 Central Ave., Far Rockaway 11691 *Type:* Private professional *Accred.:* 1979/1988 (AARTS) *Calendar:* Sem. plan *Degrees:* Talmudic (1st and 2nd) *CEO:* Pres. Maurice Friedman
Enroll: 110 (718) 327-2048

SIENA COLLEGE
515 Loudon Rd., Loudonville 12211-1462 *Type:* Private liberal arts *Accred.:* 1943/1989 (MSA) *Calendar:* Sem. plan *Degrees:* B *Prof. Accred.:* Social Work (B) *CEO:* Pres. William E. McConville, O.F.M.
Enroll: 3481 (518) 783-2300

SIMMONS INSTITUTE OF FUNERAL SERVICE
1828 South Ave., Syracuse 13207 *Type:* Private professional *Calendar:* 1-year plan *Degrees:* diplomas *Prof. Accred.:* Funeral Service Education *CEO:* Pres. Thomas R. Taggart
(315) 475-5142

SIMMONS SCHOOL
190 E. Post Rd., White Plains 10601 *Type:* Private business *Accred.:* 1983/1990 (CCA-ACICS) *Calendar:* Courses of varying lengths *Degrees:* certificates, diplomas *CEO:* Dir./Vice Pres. Peggy H. Simmons
Enroll: 113 (914) 761-2701

SKIDMORE COLLEGE
Saratoga Springs 12866 *Type:* Private liberal arts *Accred.:* 1925/1989 (MSA) *Calendar:* Sem. plan *Degrees:* B *Prof. Accred.:* Art, Social Work (B) *CEO:* Pres. David H. Porter
Enroll: 2595 (518) 584-5000

THE SONIA MOORE STUDIO OF THE THEATRE
485 Park Ave., No. 6A, New York 10022 *Type:* Private *Calendar:* Courses of varying lengths *Degrees:* certificates *Prof. Accred.:* Theatre *CEO:* Dir. Sonia Moore
(212) 755-5120

SOTHEBY'S EDUCATIONAL STUDIES
1334 York Ave., New York 10021 *Type:* Private *Calendar:* Courses of varying lengths *Degrees:* certificates *Prof. Accred.:* Art *CEO:* Vice Pres./Acting Dir. Elisabeth D. Garrett
(212) 606-7822

SPANISH-AMERICAN INSTITUTE
215 W. 43rd St., New York 10036 *Type:* Private business *Accred.:* 1986/1989 (CCA-ACICS) *Calendar:* Courses of varying lengths *Degrees:* certificates, diplomas *CEO:* Pres. Frank J. Ferraro
Enroll: 376 (212) 840-7111

SPENCER BUSINESS AND TECHNICAL INSTITUTE
200 State St., Schenectady 12305 *Type:* Private business *Accred.:* 1981/1987 (CCA-ACICS) *Calendar:* Courses of varying

lengths *Degrees:* certificates, diplomas *CEO:* Dir. Stephen Rall
Enroll: 206   (518) 374-7619

STATE UNIVERSITY OF NEW YORK COLLEGE AT BROCKPORT
Brockport 14420 *Type:* Public (state) *System:* State University of New York System Office *Accred.:* 1952/1987 (MSA) *Calendar:* Sem. plan *Degrees:* B, M, certificates, diplomas *Prof. Accred.:* Counseling, Dance, Nursing (B), Recreation and Leisure Studies, Social Work (B) *CEO:* Pres. John E. Van de Wetering
Enroll: 8840   (716) 395-2211

STATE UNIVERSITY OF NEW YORK COLLEGE AT BUFFALO
1300 Elmwood Ave., Buffalo 14222 *Type:* Public (state) *System:* State University of New York System Office *Accred.:* 1948/1986 (MSA) *Calendar:* Sem. plan *Degrees:* B, M, certificates, diplomas *Prof. Accred.:* Dietetics (coordinated), Engineering Technology (electrical, mechanical), Social Work (B), Speech-Language Pathology, Teacher Education (e,s) *CEO:* Pres. F.C. Richardson
Enroll: 12716   (716) 878-4000

STATE UNIVERSITY OF NEW YORK COLLEGE AT CORTLAND
P.O. Box 2000, Cortland 13045 *Type:* Public (state) *System:* State University of New York System Office *Accred.:* 1948/1987 (MSA) *Calendar:* Sem. plan *Degrees:* B, M, certificates, diplomas *Prof. Accred.:* Recreation and Leisure Studies *CEO:* Pres. James M. Clark
Enroll: 7263   (607) 753-2201

STATE UNIVERSITY OF NEW YORK COLLEGE AT FREDONIA
Fredonia 14063 *Type:* Public (state) *System:* State University of New York System Office *Accred.:* 1952/1986 (MSA) *Calendar:* Sem. plan *Degrees:* B, M, certificates, diplomas *Prof. Accred.:* Music *CEO:* Pres. Donald A. MacPhee
Enroll: 4994   (716) 673-3111

STATE UNIVERSITY OF NEW YORK COLLEGE AT GENESEO
Geneseo 14454 *Type:* Public (state) *System:* State University of New York System Office *Accred.:* 1952/1986 (MSA) *Calendar:* Sem. plan *Degrees:* B, M *Prof. Accred.:* Audiology, Speech-Language Pathology *CEO:* Pres. Carol C. Harter
Enroll: 5321   (716) 245-5211

STATE UNIVERSITY OF NEW YORK COLLEGE AT NEW PALTZ
New Paltz 12561 *Type:* Public (state) *System:* State University of New York System Office *Accred.:* 1950/1986 (MSA) *Calendar:* Sem. plan *Degrees:* B, M, certificates, diplomas *Prof. Accred.:* Engineering (electrical), Music, Nursing (B) *CEO:* Pres. Alice Chandler
Enroll: 8113   (914) 257-2121

STATE UNIVERSITY OF NEW YORK COLLEGE AT OLD WESTBURY
P.O. Box 210, Old Westbury 11568-0210 *Type:* Public (state) *System:* State University of New York System Office *Accred.:* 1976/1987 (MSA) *Calendar:* Sem. plan *Degrees:* B, certificates, diplomas *CEO:* Pres. L. Eudora Pettigrew
Enroll: 3923   (516) 876-3000

STATE UNIVERSITY OF NEW YORK COLLEGE AT ONEONTA
Oneonta 13820 *Type:* Public (state) *System:* State University of New York System Office *Accred.:* 1949/1988 (MSA) *Calendar:* Sem. plan *Degrees:* B, M, certificates, diplomas *Prof. Accred.:* Home Economics *CEO:* Pres. Alan B. Donovan
Enroll: 6017   (607) 431-3500

STATE UNIVERSITY OF NEW YORK COLLEGE AT OSWEGO
Oswego 13126 *Type:* Public (state) *System:* State University of New York System Office *Accred.:* 1950/1986 (MSA) *Calendar:* Sem. plan *Degrees:* B, M, certificates, diplomas *Prof. Accred.:* Music *CEO:* Pres. Stephen L. Weber
Enroll: 8697   (315) 341-2500

New York   **Accredited Institutions**

STATE UNIVERSITY OF NEW YORK COLLEGE AT PLATTSBURGH
Plattsburgh 12901 *Type:* Public (state) *System:* State University of New York System Office *Accred.:* 1952/1987 (MSA) *Calendar:* Sem. plan *Degrees:* B, M, certificates, diplomas *Prof. Accred.:* Computer Science, Counseling, Nursing (B) *CEO:* Pres. Charles O. Warren
Enroll: 6594   (518) 564-2000

STATE UNIVERSITY OF NEW YORK COLLEGE AT POTSDAM
Pierrepont Ave., Potsdam 13676 *Type:* Public (state) *System:* State University of New York System Office *Accred.:* 1952/1987 (MSA) *Calendar:* Sem. plan *Degrees:* B, M *Prof. Accred.:* Music *CEO:* Pres. William C. Merwin
Enroll: 4310   (315) 267-2000

STATE UNIVERSITY OF NEW YORK COLLEGE AT PURCHASE
735 Anderson Hill Rd., Purchase 10577 *Type:* Public (state) *System:* State University of New York System Office *Accred.:* 1976/1988 (MSA) *Calendar:* Sem. plan *Degrees:* B, M, certificates, diplomas *CEO:* Pres. Sheldon N. Grebstein
Enroll: 4143   (914) 251-6000

STATE UNIVERSITY OF NEW YORK COLLEGE OF AGRICULTURE AND TECHNOLOGY AT COBLESKI
Cobleskill 12043 *Type:* Public (state) *System:* State University of New York System Office *Accred.:* 1952/1986 (MSA) *Calendar:* Sem. plan *Degrees:* A, B *Prof. Accred.:* Histologic Technology *CEO:* Pres. Cornelius V. Robbins
Enroll: 2738   (518) 234-5011

STATE UNIVERSITY OF NEW YORK COLLEGE OF AGRICULTUTRE AND TECHNOLOGY AT MORRISV
Morrisville 13408 *Type:* Public (state) *System:* State University of New York System Office *Accred.:* 1952/1986 (MSA) *Calendar:* Sem. plan *Degrees:* A, certificates, diplomas *Prof. Accred.:* Engineering Technology (electrical, mechanical), Nursing (A) *CEO:* Pres. Frederick Woodward
Enroll: 3362   (315) 684-6000

STATE UNIVERSITY OF NEW YORK COLLEGE OF ENVIRONMENTAL SCIENCE AND FORESTRY
Syracuse 13210 *Type:* Public (state) *System:* State University of New York System Office *Accred.:* 1952/1987 (MSA) *Calendar:* Sem. plan *Degrees:* A, B, M, D *Prof. Accred.:* Engineering (forest), Forestry, Landscape Architecture (B,M) *CEO:* Pres. Ross S. Whaley
Enroll: 1518   (315) 470-6500

STATE UNIVERSITY OF NEW YORK COLLEGE OF OPTOMETRY
100 E. 24th St., New York 10010 *Type:* Public (state) *System:* State University of New York System Office *Accred.:* 1976/1987 (MSA) *Calendar:* Qtr. plan *Degrees:* P, M, D *Prof. Accred.:* Optometry *CEO:* Pres. Alden N. Haffner
Enroll: 284   (212) 420-4900

STATE UNIVERSITY OF NEW YORK COLLEGE OF TECHNOLOGY AT ALFRED
Alfred 14802 *Type:* Public (state) *System:* State University of New York System Office *Accred.:* 1952/1986 (MSA) *Calendar:* Sem. plan *Degrees:* A, certificates, diplomas *Prof. Accred.:* Engineering Technology (air conditioning, architectural, civil/construction, electrical, electromechanical, general drafting/design, mechanical, surveying), Medical Laboratory Technology (AMA), Medical Record Technology, Nursing (A) *CEO:* Pres. John O. Hunter
Enroll: 3775   (607) 587-4111

BRANCH CAMPUS
Wellsville, NY 14895 *CEO:* Dir. Albert Vanderline
    (607) 587-3105

STATE UNIVERSITY OF NEW YORK COLLEGE OF TECHNOLOGY AT CANTON
Cornell Dr., Canton 13617 *Type:* Public (state) *System:* State University of New York System Office *Accred.:* 1952/1986 (MSA)

Calendar: Sem. plan *Degrees:* A, certificates, diplomas *Prof. Accred.:* Engineering Technology (air conditioning, civil/construction, electrical, mechanical), Medical Laboratory Technology (AMA), Mortuary Science, Nursing (A), Veterinary Science Technology *CEO:* Pres. Earl W. MacArthur
Enroll: 2326 (315) 386-7204

STATE UNIVERSITY OF NEW YORK COLLEGE OF TECHNOLOGY AT DELHI
Delhi 13753 *Type:* Public (state) *System:* State University of New York System Office *Accred.:* 1952/1987 (MSA) *Calendar:* Sem. plan *Degrees:* A, certificates, diplomas *Prof. Accred.:* Veterinary Science Technology *CEO:* Pres. Mary Ellen Duncan
Enroll: 2453 (607) 746-4111

STATE UNIVERSITY OF NEW YORK COLLEGE OF TECHNOLOGY AT FARMINGDALE
Melville Rd., Farmingdale 11735 *Type:* Public (state) *System:* State University of New York System Office *Accred.:* 1952/1988 (MSA) *Calendar:* Sem. plan *Degrees:* A *Prof. Accred.:* Dental Hygiene, Engineering Technology (air conditioning, automotive, bioengineering, civil/construction, electrical, manufacturing, mechanical), Medical Laboratory Technology (AMA), Mortuary Science, Nursing (A), Veterinary Science Technology (probational) *CEO:* Pres. Frank A. Cipriani
Enroll: 10802 (516) 420-2000

STATE UNIVERSITY OF NEW YORK HEALTH SCIENCE CENTER AT BROOKLYN
450 Clarkson Ave., Brooklyn 11203 *Type:* Public (state) *System:* State University of New York System Office *Accred.:* 1952/1986 (MSA) *Calendar:* Courses of varying lengths *Degrees:* B, P, M, D, certificates, diplomas *Prof. Accred.:* Diagnostic Medical Sonography, Medical Record Administration, Medicine, Nuclear Medicine Technology, Nursing (B,M), Occupational Therapy, Physical Therapy *CEO:* Pres. Donald J. Scherl
Enroll: 1682 (718) 270-1000

STATE UNIVERSITY OF NEW YORK HEALTH SCIENCE CENTER AT BUFFALO
Capen Hall, Buffalo 14260 *Type:* Public (state) *System:* State University of New York System Office *Calendar:* Sem. plan *Degrees:* A, B, P, M, D, certificates, diplomas *Prof. Accred.:* Medical Technology, Nuclear Medicine Technology, Occupational Therapy *CEO:* Interim Pres. William R. Greiner
(716) 831-2000

STATE UNIVERSITY OF NEW YORK HEALTH SCIENCE CENTER AT STONY BROOK
Stony Brook 11794 *Type:* Public (state) *System:* State University of New York System Office *Calendar:* Sem. plan *Degrees:* B, M, D, certificates, diplomas *Prof. Accred.:* Cardiovascular Technology, Medical Technology, Physician Assisting, Respiratory Therapy *CEO:* Pres. John H. Marburger, III
(516) 444-2101

STATE UNIVERSITY OF NEW YORK HEALTH SCIENCE CENTER AT SYRACUSE
750 E. Adams St., Syracuse 13210 *Type:* Public (state) *System:* State University of New York System Office *Accred.:* 1952/1989 (MSA) *Calendar:* Courses of varying lengths *Degrees:* A, B, P, M, D *Prof. Accred.:* Blood Bank Technology, Cytotechnology, Medical Technology, Medicine, Nursing (A,B,M), Perfusion, Physical Therapy, Radiation Therapy Technology, Radiography, Respiratory Therapy *CEO:* Pres. John B. Henry
Enroll: 980 (315) 464-4570

STATE UNIVERSITY OF NEW YORK INSTITUTE OF TECHNOLOGY AT UTICA/ROME
P.O. Box 3050, Utica 13504-3050 *Type:* Public (state) *System:* State University of New York System Office *Accred.:* 1979/1983 (MSA) *Calendar:* Sem. plan *Degrees:* B, M *Prof. Accred.:* Engineering Technology (computer, electrical, industrial, mechanical), Medical Record Administration, Nursing (B) *CEO:* Pres. Peter J. Cayan
Enroll: 2620 (315) 792-7100

STATE UNIVERSITY OF NEW YORK AT ALBANY
1400 Washington Ave., Albany 12222 *Type:* Public (state) *System:* State University of New York System Office *Accred.:* 1938/1986 (MSA) *Calendar:* Sem. plan *Degrees:* B, M, D, certificates, diplomas *Prof. Accred.:* Business (B,M), Clinical Psychology, Computer Science, Counseling Psychology, Librarianship, Public Administration, Rehabilitation Counseling, Social Work (B,M) *CEO:* Pres. H. Patrick Swygert
Enroll: 16561 (518) 442-3300

STATE UNIVERSITY OF NEW YORK AT BINGHAMTON
Binghamton 13901 *Type:* Public (state) *System:* State University of New York System Office *Accred.:* 1952/1986 (MSA) *Calendar:* Sem. plan *Degrees:* B, M, D, certificates, diplomas *Prof. Accred.:* Business (B,M), Clinical Psychology, Computer Science, Engineering (electrical, mechanical), Engineering Technology (electrical, electromechanical, mechanical), Nursing (B,M) *CEO:* Pres. Lois B. DeFleur
Enroll: 12588 (607) 777-2000

STATE UNIVERSITY OF NEW YORK AT BUFFALO
Capen Hall, Buffalo 14260 *Type:* Public (state) *System:* State University of New York System Office *Accred.:* 1921/1989 (MSA) *Calendar:* Sem. plan *Degrees:* A, B, P, M, D, certificates, diplomas *Prof. Accred.:* Accounting (Type A,B), Architecture (M), Art, Audiology, Business (B,M), Clinical Psychology, Combined Prosthodontics, Counseling Psychology, Dental Assisting, Dentistry, Endodontics, Engineering (aerospace, chemical, civil, electrical, industrial, mechanical), General Dentistry (prelim. provisional), General Practice Residency, Law, Librarianship, Medicine, Music, Nurse Anesthesia Education, Nursing (B,M), Oral and Maxillofacial Surgery, Orthodontics, Periodontics, Pharmacy, Physical Therapy, Planning (urban), Psychology Internship, Rehabilitation Counseling, Social Work (M), Speech-Language Pathology *CEO:* Pres. William R. Greiner
Enroll: 28005 (716) 831-2000

STATE UNIVERSITY OF NEW YORK AT STONY BROOK
Stony Brook 11794 *Type:* Public (state) *System:* State University of New York System Office *Accred.:* 1957/1989 (MSA) *Calendar:* Sem. plan *Degrees:* B, M, D, certificates, diplomas *Prof. Accred.:* Clinical Psychology, Dentistry, Engineering (electrical, engineering physics/science, mechanical), General Dentistry, Medicine, Nursing (B,M), Physical Therapy, Psychology Internship, Social Work (B,M) *CEO:* Pres. John H. Marburger, III
Enroll: 14975 (516) 632-6000

STENOTOPIA, THE WORLD OF COURT REPORTING
380 N. Broadway, Penthouse W. 2, Jericho 11753 *Type:* Private business *Accred.:* 1990 (CCA-ACICS) *Calendar:* Courses of varying lengths *Degrees:* certificates, diplomas *CEO:* Pres. Randy Scheff Gordon
  (516) 932-5444

STENOTYPE ACADEMY
291 Broadway, New York 10007 *Type:* Private business *Accred.:* 1984/1990 (CCA-ACICS) *Calendar:* Courses of varying lengths *Degrees:* certificates, diplomas *CEO:* Pres. Ivan Londa
Enroll: 926 (212) 962-0002

SUBURBAN TECHNICAL SCHOOL
175 Fulton Ave., Hempstead 11550 *Type:* Private *Accred.:* 1972/1987 (CCA-ACTTS) *Calendar:* Courses of varying lengths *Degrees:* diplomas *CEO:* Pres. Randy S. Proto
Enroll: 1630 (516) 481-3771

BRANCH CAMPUS
2650 Sunrise Hwy., East Islip, NY 11730-1017 *CEO:* Dir. Jay Fund
  (516) 224-5001

SUFFOLK COMMUNITY COLLEGE AMMERMAN CAMPUS
533 College Rd., Selden 11784 *Type:* Public (county) junior *System:* Suffolk Community College System *Accred.:* 1966/1988 (MSA) *Calendar:* Sem. plan *Degrees:* A *Prof. Accred.:* Nursing (A), Physical Therapy

Assisting *CEO:* Exec. Dean William C. Hudson
Enroll: 11270 (516) 451-4110

SUFFOLK COMMUNITY COLLEGE EASTERN CAMPUS
Speonk-Riverhead Rd., Riverhead 11901 *Type:* Public (county) junior *System:* Suffolk Community College System *Accred.:* 1982/1988 (MSA) *Calendar:* Sem. plan *Degrees:* A *CEO:* Exec. Dean Steven T. Kenny
Enroll: 2101 (516) 369-2600

SUFFOLK COMMUNITY COLLEGE WESTERN CAMPUS
Crooked Hill Rd., Brentwood 11717 *Type:* Public (county) junior *System:* Suffolk Community College System *Accred.:* 1981/1987 (MSA) *Calendar:* Sem. plan *Degrees:* A *Prof. Accred.:* Nursing (A) *CEO:* Exec. Dean Salvatore LaLima
Enroll: 4759 (516) 434-6700

SUFFOLK TECHNICAL INSTITUTE
40 E. 29th St., New York 10016-7911 *Type:* Private *Accred.:* 1983 (CCA-ACTTS) *Calendar:* Courses of varying lengths *Degrees:* certificates, diplomas *CEO:* Dir. Muriel Adler
Enroll: 62 (212) 532-1660

SULLIVAN COUNTY COMMUNITY COLLEGE
College Rd., Loch Sheldrake 12759 *Type:* Public (county) junior *System:* State University of New York Office of Community Colleges *Accred.:* 1968/1987 (MSA) *Calendar:* 4-1-4 plan *Degrees:* A, certificates, diplomas *CEO:* Pres. John F. Walter
Enroll: 1890 (914) 434-5750

SUPERIOR CAREER INSTITUTE
116 W. 14th St., New York 10011-7395 *Type:* Private *Accred.:* 1983/1988 (CCA-ACTTS) *Calendar:* Courses of varying lengths *Degrees:* certificates *CEO:* Dir. Murray Bernstein
Enroll: 1356 (212) 675-2140

SUTTON BUSINESS SCHOOL
425 McDonald Ave., Brooklyn 11218 *Type:* Private business *Accred.:* 1981/1990 (CCA-ACICS) *Calendar:* Sem. plan *Degrees:* certificates, diplomas *CEO:* Pres. Frederick S. Hershinson
Enroll: 76 (718) 435-7800

BRANCH CAMPUS
300 N. Charles St., Baltimore, MD 21201 *CEO:* Dir. Gordon Weaver
(410) 752-0350

THE SWEDISH INSTITUTE
226 W. 26th St., 5th Fl., New York 10001-6700 *Type:* Private *Accred.:* 1981/1986 (CCA-ACTTS) *Calendar:* Sem. plan *Degrees:* diplomas *CEO:* Pres. Patricia J. Eckardt
Enroll: 609 (212) 924-5900

SYRACUSE UNIVERSITY
Syracuse 13244 *Type:* Private *Accred.:* 1921/1988 (MSA) *Calendar:* Sem. plan *Degrees:* A, B, P, M, D, certificates, diplomas *Prof. Accred.:* Architecture (B,M), Art, Audiology, Business (B,M), Clinical Psychology, Dietetics (coordinated), Engineering (aerospace, bioengineering, chemical, civil, computer, electrical, mechanical), Interior Design, Journalism, Law, Librarianship, Music, Nursing (B,M), Public Administration, Rehabilitation Counseling, School Psychology (provisional), Social Work (B,M), Speech-Language Pathology, Teacher Education (e,s,p) *CEO:* Pres./Chanc. Kenneth A. Shaw
Enroll: 22086 (315) 443-1870

UTICA COLLEGE OF SYRACUSE UNIVERSITY
1600 Burrstone Rd., Utica, NY 13502 *Accred.:* 1921/1988 (MSA) *Prof. Accred.:* Medical Technology, Nursing (B), Occupational Therapy *CEO:* Pres. Michael K. Simpson
Enroll: 2523 (315) 792-3111

TALMUDICAL SEMINARY OHOLEI TORAH
667 Eastern Pkwy., Brooklyn 11213 *Type:* Private professional *Accred.:* 1979/1990 (AARTS) *Calendar:* Sem. plan *Degrees:* Talmudic (1st) *CEO:* Pres. Teitelbaum
Enroll: 195 (718) 778-3340

New York   **Accredited Institutions**

TAYLOR BUSINESS INSTITUTE
One Penn Plaza, New York 10119 *Type:* Private business *Accred.:* 1981/1990 (CCA-ACICS) *Calendar:* Sem. plan *Degrees:* A *CEO:* Dir. David Schuchman
Enroll: 1111   (212) 279-0510

TEACHERS COLLEGE, COLUMBIA UNIVERSITY
525 W. 120th St., New York 10027 *Type:* Private professional; graduate only *Accred.:* 1921/1986 (MSA) *Calendar:* Sem. plan *Degrees:* M, D *Prof. Accred.:* Audiology, Clinical Psychology, Counseling Psychology, Nursing (M), School Psychology (provisional), Speech-Language Pathology *CEO:* Pres. Michael Timpane
Enroll: 4324   (212) 678-3000

TECHNICAL CAREER INSTITUTES
320 W. 31st St., New York 10001 *Type:* Private *Calendar:* Sem. plan *Degrees:* A *Prof. Accred.:* Engineering Technology (electrical) *CEO:* Pres. David M. Goodman
                              (212) 594-4000

TECHNO-DENTAL TRAINING CENTER
101 W. 31st St., 4th Fl., New York 10001-3507 *Type:* Private *Accred.:* 1983/1988 (CCA-ACTTS) *Calendar:* Tri. plan *Degrees:* certificates *CEO:* Pres. George A. Nossa
Enroll: 184   (212) 695-1818

TOBE-COBURN SCHOOL FOR FASHION CAREERS
686 Broadway, New York 10012-1107 *Type:* Private *Accred.:* 1972/1983 (CCA-ACTTS) *Calendar:* Tri. plan *Degrees:* certificates *CEO:* Dir. Ann Z. Wareham
Enroll: 601   (212) 460-9600

TOMPKINS CORTLAND COMMUNITY COLLEGE
170 North St., P.O. Box 139, Dryden 13053 *Type:* Public junior *System:* State University of New York Office of Community Colleges *Accred.:* 1973/1988 (MSA) *Calendar:* Sem. plan *Degrees:* A, certificates, diplomas *Prof. Accred.:* Nursing (A) *CEO:* Pres. Eduardo J. Marti
Enroll: 1595   (607) 844-8211

TOURO COLLEGE
844 Ave. of the Americas, New York 10001 *Type:* Private liberal arts *Accred.:* 1976/1987 (MSA) *Calendar:* Sem. plan *Degrees:* A, B, P, M *Prof. Accred.:* Law (ABA only), Medical Record Administration, Physical Therapy *CEO:* Pres. Bernard Lander
Enroll: 3913   (212) 447-0700

  BRANCH CAMPUS
  135 Carmen Rd., Bldg. 10, Dix Hills, NY 11746 *Prof. Accred.:* Occupational Therapy, Physician Assisting *CEO:* Dean Joseph Weisberg
                              (516) 673-3200

  BRANCH CAMPUS
  300 Nassau Rd., Huntington, NY 11743 *CEO:* Dean Howard Glickstein
                              (516) 421-2244

  BRANCH CAMPUS
  240 E. 123rd St., New York, NY 10035 *CEO:* Dir. Stephen Adolphus
                              (212) 722-1575

TRAPHAGEN SCHOOL OF FASHION
686 Broadway, New York 10012-1183 *Type:* Private *Accred.:* 1972/1988 (CCA-ACTTS) *Calendar:* Sem. plan *Degrees:* certificates *CEO:* Dir. William G. Coury
Enroll: 229   (212) 673-0300

TRAVEL INSTITUTE
15 Park Row No. 617, New York 10038-2301 *Type:* Private *Accred.:* 1991 (CCA-ACTTS) *Calendar:* Courses of varying lengths *Degrees:* certificates *CEO:* Owner/Dir. Robert Berger
                              (212) 349-3331

TROCAIRE COLLEGE
110 Red Jacket Pkwy., Buffalo 14220 *Type:* Private junior *Accred.:* 1974/1989 (MSA) *Calendar:* Sem. plan *Degrees:* A, certificates, diplomas *Prof. Accred.:* Medical Laboratory Technology (AMA), Nursing (A), Radiography, Surgical Technology *CEO:* Pres. Barbara Ciarico, R.S.N.
Enroll: 826   (716) 826-1200

Accredited Institutions New York

ULSTER COUNTY COMMUNITY COLLEGE
Stone Ridge 12484 *Type:* Public (county) junior *System:* State University of New York Office of Community Colleges *Accred.:* 1971/1986 (MSA) *Calendar:* Sem. plan *Degrees:* A, certificates, diplomas *CEO:* Pres. Robert T. Brown
Enroll: 2816 (914) 687-5000

ULTRASOUND DIAGNOSTIC SCHOOL
121 W. 27th St., New York 10001 *Type:* Private *Calendar:* Courses of varying lengths *Degrees:* certificates *Prof. Accred.:* Health Education *CEO:* Exec. Dir. William Spier, Ph.D.
(212) 645-9116

BRANCH CAMPUS
2760 E. Atlantic Blvd., Pompano Beach, FL 33062 *Prof. Accred.:* Health Education *CEO:* Admin. Irving Taffel
(305) 942-6551

BRANCH CAMPUS
5804 E. Breckenridge Pkwy., Tampa, FL 33610 *Prof. Accred.:* Health Education *CEO:* Admin. M. Lorraine Gittings
(813) 621-0072

BRANCH CAMPUS
13 Corp. Sq. Office Park, Ste. 140, Atlanta, GA 30329 *Prof. Accred.:* Health Education *CEO:* Admin. Vernita Branom
(404) 248-9070

BRANCH CAMPUS
1320 Fenwick La., Silver Spring, MD 20910 *Prof. Accred.:* Health Education *CEO:* Admin. Marilyn Lavender
(301) 588-0786

BRANCH CAMPUS
57 Providence Hwy., Norwood, MA 02062 *Prof. Accred.:* Health Education *CEO:* Admin. Dana Holland
(617) 551-0404

BRANCH CAMPUS
2269 Saw Mill River Rd., Elmsford, NY 10523 *Prof. Accred.:* Health Education *CEO:* Admin. Wayne Engel
(914) 347-6817

BRANCH CAMPUS
223 Jericho Tpke., Mineola, NY 11501 *Prof. Accred.:* Health Education *CEO:* Admin. Fran Wyrick
(516) 248-6060

BRANCH CAMPUS
3511 Cottman Ave., Philadelphia, PA 19149 *Prof. Accred.:* Health Education *CEO:* Admin. John F. O'Brien
(215) 624-8245

UNION COLLEGE
Schenectady 12308 *Type:* Private liberal arts *Accred.:* 1921/1985 (MSA) *Calendar:* Sem. plan *Degrees:* B, M, D *Prof. Accred.:* Engineering (civil, electrical, mechanical), Health Services Administration *CEO:* Pres. Roger H. Hull
Enroll: 2984 (518) 370-6000

BRANCH CAMPUS
249 Hooker Ave., Poughkeepsie, NY 12603 *CEO:* Dir. Armen Fisher
(914) 454-4490

UNION THEOLOGICAL SEMINARY
3041 Broadway, New York 10027 *Type:* Private (interdenominational) professional; graduate only *Accred.:* 1938/1988 (ATS); 1967/1989 (MSA) *Calendar:* Sem. plan *Degrees:* P, M, D *CEO:* Pres. Holland L. Hendrix
Enroll: 278 (212) 662-7100

UNITED STATES MERCHANT MARINE ACADEMY
Steamboat Rd., Kings Point 11024 *Type:* Public (federal) technological *Accred.:* 1949/1985 (MSA) *Calendar:* Qtr. plan *Degrees:* B *Prof. Accred.:* Engineering (naval architecture/marine) *CEO:* Supt. Paul L. Krinsky
Enroll: 878 (516) 773-5000

UNITED STATES MILITARY ACADEMY
West Point 10996 *Type:* Public (federal) professional *Accred.:* 1949/1989 (MSA) *Calendar:* Sem. plan *Degrees:* B *Prof. Accred.:* Engineering (civil, electrical, engineering management, mechanical) *CEO:* Supt. Howard D. Graves
Enroll: 4380 (914) 938-3122

New York

UNITED TALMUDICAL ACADEMY
82 Lee Ave., Brooklyn 11211 *Type:* Private professional *Accred.:* 1979/1987 (AARTS) *Calendar:* Sem. plan *Degrees:* Rabbinic (1st and 2nd) *CEO:* Pres. S. Deutsch
Enroll: 990   (718) 963-9260

UNIVERSITY OF ROCHESTER
Rochester 14627 *Type:* Private *Accred.:* 1921/1986 (MSA) *Calendar:* Sem. plan *Degrees:* B, P, M, D, certificates, diplomas *Prof. Accred.:* Business (M), Clinical Psychology, Community Health/Preventive Medicine, Engineering (chemical, electrical, mechanical), Medicine, Music, Nursing (B,M), Psychology Internship, Radiation Therapy Technology *CEO:* Pres. G. Dennis O'Brien
Enroll: 9195   (716) 275-2121

UNIVERSITY OF THE STATE OF NEW YORK REGENTS COLLEGE DEGREES
1450 Western Ave., Albany 12203 *Type:* Public (state) *Accred.:* 1977/1987 (MSA) *Calendar:* Sem. plan *Degrees:* A, B *Prof. Accred.:* Nursing (A,B) *CEO:* Pres. Thomas Sobol
Enroll: 14372   (518) 474-3703

UTICA SCHOOL OF COMMERCE
201 Bleecker St., Utica 13501 *Type:* Private business *Accred.:* 1969/1987 (CCA-ACICS) *Calendar:* Sem. plan *Degrees:* A *CEO:* Pres. Philip M. Williams
Enroll: 922   (315) 733-2307

VASSAR COLLEGE
Raymond Ave., Box 1, Poughkeepsie 12601 *Type:* Private liberal arts *Accred.:* 1921/1989 (MSA) *Calendar:* Sem. plan *Degrees:* B, M *CEO:* Pres. Frances D. Fergusson
Enroll: 2395   (914) 437-7000

VILLA MARIA COLLEGE OF BUFFALO
240 Pine Ridge Rd., Buffalo 14225 *Type:* Private junior *Accred.:* 1972/1988 (MSA) *Calendar:* Sem. plan *Degrees:* A, certificates, diplomas *CEO:* Pres. Marcella Maria Garus
Enroll: 567   (716) 896-0700

WADHAMS HALL SEMINARY/COLLEGE
R.D. 44, Box 80, Ogdensburg 13669 *Type:* Private (Roman Catholic) *Accred.:* 1972/1987 (MSA) *Calendar:* Sem. plan *Degrees:* B, certificates, diplomas *CEO:* Pres. Thomas Thottumkal
Enroll: 62   (315) 393-4231

WAGNER COLLEGE
Howard Ave. and Campus Rd., Staten Island 10301 *Type:* Private (Lutheran) liberal arts *Accred.:* 1931/1985 (MSA) *Calendar:* Sem. plan *Degrees:* B, M *Prof. Accred.:* Nursing (B,M) *CEO:* Pres. Norman R. Smith
Enroll: 1767   (718) 390-3100

WEBB INSTITUTE OF NAVAL ARCHITECTURE
Crescent Beach Rd., Glen Cove 11542 *Type:* Private technological *Accred.:* 1930/1985 (MSA) *Calendar:* Sem. plan *Degrees:* B *Prof. Accred.:* Engineering (naval architecture/marine) *CEO:* Pres. James J. Conti
Enroll: 80   (516) 671-2213

WELLS COLLEGE
Aurora 13026 *Type:* Private liberal arts for women *Accred.:* 1921/1984 (MSA) *Calendar:* 4-1-4 plan *Degrees:* B *CEO:* Pres. Robert Plane
Enroll: 419   (315) 364-3265

WESTCHESTER BUSINESS INSTITUTE
325 Central Ave., P.O. Box 710, White Plains 10602 *Type:* Private business *Accred.:* 1979/1990 (CCA-ACICS) *Calendar:* Qtr. plan *Degrees:* A, certificates, diplomas *CEO:* Exec. Vice Pres. Kenneth A. Gabbert
Enroll: 1792   (914) 948-4442

WESTCHESTER COMMUNITY COLLEGE
75 Grasslands Rd., Valhalla 10595 *Type:* Public junior *System:* State University of New York Office of Community Colleges *Accred.:* 1970/1985 (MSA) *Calendar:* Sem. plan *Degrees:* A *Prof. Accred.:* Radiography, Respiratory Therapy *CEO:* Pres. Joseph N. Hankin
Enroll: 8241   (914) 285-6600

Accredited Institutions **New York**

WESTCHESTER CONSERVATORY OF MUSIC
20 Soundview Ave., White Plains 10606 *Type:* Private professional *Calendar:* Courses of varying lengths *Degrees:* certificates *Prof. Accred.:* Music *CEO:* Exec. Dir. Laura Calzolari
Enroll: 639 (914) 761-3715

WOOD SCHOOL
8 E. 40th St., New York 10016 *Type:* Private business *Accred.:* 1967/1987 (CCA-ACICS) *Calendar:* Qtr. plan *Degrees:* A, certificates, diplomas *CEO:* Pres. Rosemary Duggan
Enroll: 552 (212) 686-9040

YESHIVA DERECH CHAIM
1573 39th St., Brooklyn 11218 *Type:* Private professional *Accred.:* 1984/1989 (AARTS) *Calendar:* Sem. plan *Degrees:* Talmudic (1st and 2nd) *CEO:* Pres. Mordechai Rennert
Enroll: 159 (718) 438-5476

YESHIVA KARLIN STOLIN BETH AARON V'ISRAEL RABBINICAL INSTITUTE
1818 54th St., Brooklyn 11204 *Type:* Private professional *Accred.:* 1975/1990 (AARTS) *Calendar:* Sem. plan *Degrees:* Talmudic (1st and 2nd) *CEO:* Pres. Israel Pilchick
Enroll: 65 (718) 232-7800

YESHIVA MIKDASH MELECH
1326 Ocean Pkwy., Brooklyn 11230-5655 *Type:* Private professional *Accred.:* 1990 (AARTS) *Calendar:* Sem. plan *Degrees:* Rabbinic *CEO:* Dean Haim Benoliel
Enroll: 31 (718) 339-1090

YESHIVA SHAAR HATORAH TALMUDIC RESEARCH INSTITUTE
83-96 117th St., Kew Gardens 11415 *Type:* Private professional *Accred.:* 1984/1991 (AARTS) *Calendar:* Sem. plan *Degrees:* Rabbinic (1st), Talmudic (1st and 2nd) *CEO:* Pres. Z. Epstein
Enroll: 59 (718) 846-1940

YESHIVA UNIVERSITY
500 W. 185th St., New York 10033 *Type:* Private *Accred.:* 1948/1986 (MSA) *Calendar:* Sem. plan *Degrees:* A, B, P, M, D, certificates, diplomas *Prof. Accred.:* Clinical Psychology, Law, Medicine, School Psychology (provisional), Social Work (M) *CEO:* Pres. Norman Lamm
Enroll: 4543 (212) 960-5400

YESHIVA OF NITRA—RABBINICAL COLLEGE YESHIVA FARM SETTLEMENT
194 Division Ave., Brooklyn 11211 *Type:* Private professional *Accred.:* 1980/1985 (AARTS) *Calendar:* Sem. plan *Degrees:* Rabbinic (1st and 2nd), Talmudic (1st and 2nd) *CEO:* Pres. Alexander Fischer
Enroll: 128 (718) 387-0422

YESHIVAH AND MESIVTA TORAH TEMIMAH TALMUDICAL SEMINARY
555 Ocean Pkwy., Brooklyn 11218 *Type:* Private professional *Accred.:* 1981/1991 (AARTS) *Calendar:* Sem. plan *Degrees:* Talmudic (1st and 2nd) *CEO:* Pres./Dean L. Margulies
Enroll: 165 (718) 853-8500

YESHIVATH VIZNITZ
P.O. Box 446, Monsey 10952 *Type:* Private professional *Accred.:* 1980/1986 (AARTS) *Calendar:* Sem. plan *Degrees:* Rabbinic (1st and 2nd) *CEO:* Pres. Gershon Neiman
Enroll: 331 (914) 356-1010

YESIVATH ZICHRON MOSHE
Laurel Park Rd., South Fallsburg 12779 *Type:* Private professional *Accred.:* 1979/1987 (AARTS) *Calendar:* Sem. plan *Degrees:* Talmudic (1st and 2nd) *CEO:* Pres. A. Gorelick
Enroll: 124 (914) 434-5240

YORK COLLEGE
94-20 Guy R. Brewer Blvd., Jamaica 11451 *Type:* Public *System:* City University of New York Central Administration *Accred.:* 1967/1987 (MSA) *Calendar:* Sem. plan *Degrees:* B *Prof. Accred.:* Nursing (B), Occupational Therapy, Social Work (B) *CEO:* Pres. Josephine D. Davis
Enroll: 4826 (718) 262-2000

YORK INSTITUTE
23 E. 15th St., New York 10003 *Type:* Private business *Accred.:* 1984/1990 (CCA-ACICS) *Calendar:* Courses of varying lengths *Degrees:* certificates, diplomas *CEO:* Pres. Kenneth F. Ostrom
Enroll: 1214 (212) 741-8820

NORTH CAROLINA

ACADEMY OF ARTISTIC HAIR DESIGN
314 10th St., North Wilkesboro 28659 *Type:* Private *Accred.:* 1987 (SACS-COEI) *Calendar:* Courses of varying lengths *Degrees:* certificates *CEO:* Dir. Hazel T. Mayes
Enroll: 50   (919) 838-4571

ADVANCE INSTITUTE
1330-B Patton Ave., Asheville 28806 *Type:* Private *Accred.:* 1990 (SACS-COEI) *Calendar:* Courses of varying lengths *Degrees:* certificates *CEO:* Dir. Grace Melton
Enroll: 23   (704) 251-1713

BRANCH CAMPUS
1005 Buncombe Rd., Mulberry Sq., Greenville, SC 29609 *CEO:* Dir. Jo Drucker
          (803) 233-5647

ALAMANCE COMMUNITY COLLEGE
P.O. Box 8000, Haw River 27253-8000 *Type:* Public (district) junior *System:* North Carolina State Board of Community Colleges *Accred.:* 1969/1983 (SACS-CC) *Calendar:* Qtr. plan *Degrees:* A *Prof. Accred.:* Dental Assisting, Engineering Technology (electrical), Medical Laboratory Technology (AMA) *CEO:* Pres. W. Ronald McCarter
Enroll: 4426   (919) 578-2002

ALLIANCE TRACTOR TRAILER TRAINING CENTER
P.O. Box 883, Arden 28704-0883 *Type:* Private *Accred.:* 1986 (CCA-ACTTS) *Calendar:* Courses of varying lengths *Degrees:* diplomas *CEO:* Vice Pres. R.W. Grassette
Enroll: 92   (704) 684-4454

AMERICAN BUSINESS AND FASHION INSTITUTE
1515 Mockingbird La., Ste. 600, Charlotte 28209 *Type:* Private business *Accred.:* 1978/1985 (CCA-ACICS) *Calendar:* Courses of varying lengths *Degrees:* certificates, diplomas *CEO:* Pres. Elizabeth M. Hummel
Enroll: 256   (704) 523-3738

ANSON COMMUNITY COLLEGE
P.O. Box 68, Ansonville 28007 *Type:* Public (district) junior *System:* North Carolina State Board of Community Colleges *Accred.:* 1977/1983 (SACS-CC) *Calendar:* Qtr. plan *Degrees:* A *CEO:* Pres. Edwin R. Chapman
Enroll: 987   (704) 826-8333

APPALACHIAN STATE UNIVERSITY
Boone 28608 *Type:* Public *System:* University of North Carolina General Administration *Accred.:* 1942/1982 (SACS-CC) *Calendar:* Sem. plan *Degrees:* B, M *Prof. Accred.:* Business (B,M), Computer Science, Counseling, Home Economics, Music, Social Work (B), Speech-Language Pathology, Teacher Education (e,s,p) *CEO:* Chanc. John E. Thomas
Enroll: 11090   (704) 262-2000

ARNOLD'S BEAUTY COLLEGE
3117 Shannon Rd., Durham 27707 *Type:* Private *Accred.:* 1989/1991 (SACS-COEI) *Calendar:* Courses of varying lengths *Degrees:* diplomas *CEO:* Dir. Arnold Braun
Enroll: 136   (919) 493-9557

ASHEVILLE-BUNCOMBE TECHNICAL COMMUNITY COLLEGE
340 Victoria Rd., Asheville 28801 *Type:* Public (district) junior *System:* North Carolina State Board of Community Colleges *Accred.:* 1969/1984 (SACS-CC) *Calendar:* Qtr. plan *Degrees:* A *Prof. Accred.:* Dental Assisting, Dental Hygiene, Medical Laboratory Technology (AMA), Radiography *CEO:* Pres. K. Ray Bailey
Enroll: 3927   (704) 254-1921

BARBER-SCOTIA COLLEGE
145 Cabarrus Ave., W., Concord 28025 *Type:* Private (Presbyterian) liberal arts and teachers *Accred.:* 1949/1984 (SACS-CC) *Calendar:* Sem. plan *Degrees:* B *CEO:* Pres. Joel O. Nwagbaraocha
Enroll: 482   (704) 786-5171

BARTON COLLEGE
College Sta., Wilson 27893 *Type:* Private (Disciples of Christ) liberal arts *Accred.:* 1955/1988 (SACS-CC) *Calendar:* Sem. plan

Degrees: B *Prof. Accred.:* Nursing (B) *CEO:* Pres. James B. Hemby, Jr.
Enroll: 1948 (919) 237-3161

BEAUFORT COUNTY COMMUNITY COLLEGE
P.O. Box 1069, Washington 27889 *Type:* Public (district) junior *System:* North Carolina State Board of Community Colleges *Accred.:* 1973/1988 (SACS-CC) *Calendar:* Qtr. plan *Degrees:* A *Prof. Accred.:* Medical Laboratory Technology (AMA) *CEO:* Pres. U. Ronald Champion
Enroll: 858 (919) 946-6194

BELMONT ABBEY COLLEGE
Belmont 28012-2795 *Type:* Private (Roman Catholic) liberal arts *Accred.:* 1957/1989 (SACS-CC) *Calendar:* Sem. plan *Degrees:* B *CEO:* Pres. Joseph S. Brosnan
Enroll: 954 (704) 825-6700

BENNETT COLLEGE
900 E. Washington St., Greensboro 27401-3239 *Type:* Private (United Methodist) liberal arts for women *Accred.:* 1935/1990 (SACS-CC) *Calendar:* Sem. plan *Degrees:* B *Prof. Accred.:* Social Work (B) *CEO:* Pres. Gloria Randall Scott
Enroll: 579 (919) 273-4431

BLACK WORLD COLLEGE OF HAIR DESIGN
1550 West Blvd., P.O. Box 669403, Charlotte 28266-9403 *Type:* Private *Accred.:* 1986 (CCA-ACTTS) *Calendar:* Courses of varying lengths *Degrees:* diplomas *CEO:* Dir. Luther Gore
Enroll: 70 (704) 372-8172

BLADEN COMMUNITY COLLEGE
P.O. Box 266, Dublin 28332 *Type:* Public (district) junior *System:* North Carolina State Board of Community Colleges *Accred.:* 1976/1982 (SACS-CC) *Calendar:* Qtr. plan *Degrees:* A *CEO:* Pres. Lynn G. King
Enroll: 743 (919) 862-2164

BLANTON'S COLLEGE
126 College St., Asheville 28801 *Type:* Private *Accred.:* 1972/1990 (CCA-ACICS) *Calendar:* Qtr. plan *Degrees:* A, certificates, diplomas *CEO:* Vice Pres. Wayne W. Blanton
Enroll: 2486 (704) 252-7346

BRANCH CAMPUS
145 N. Church St., Spartanburg, SC 29301 *CEO:* Dir. Lori Coggins
(803) 591-4246

BLUE RIDGE COMMUNITY COLLEGE
Rte. 2, Box 133A, Flat Rock 28731-9624 *Type:* Public (district) junior *System:* North Carolina State Board of Community Colleges *Accred.:* 1973/1988 (SACS-CC) *Calendar:* Qtr. plan *Degrees:* A *CEO:* Pres. David W. Sink, Jr.
Enroll: 2183 (704) 692-3572

BREVARD COLLEGE
N. Broad St., Brevard 28712 *Type:* Private (United Methodist) junior *Accred.:* 1949/1986 (SACS-CC) *Calendar:* Sem. plan *Degrees:* A *Prof. Accred.:* Music *CEO:* Pres. William T. Greer, Jr.
Enroll: 764 (704) 883-8292

BROOKSTONE COLLEGE OF BUSINESS
8307 Univ. Executive Park Dr., Ste. 240, Charlotte 28213 *Type:* Private business *Accred.:* 1984/1990 (CCA-ACICS) *Calendar:* Qtr. plan *Degrees:* certificates, diplomas *CEO:* Dir. Archie Cameron
Enroll: 434 (704) 547-8600

BRANCH CAMPUS
Airport W., 7815 National Service Rd., Greensboro, NC 27409 *CEO:* Dir. Michael Thompson
(919) 668-2627

BRUNSWICK COMMUNITY COLLEGE
P.O. Box 30, Supply 28462 *Type:* Public (district) junior *System:* North Carolina State Board of Community Colleges *Accred.:* 1983/1988 (SACS-CC) *Calendar:* Qtr. plan *Degrees:* A *CEO:* Pres. W. Michael Reaves
Enroll: 1493 (919) 754-6900

BURKE ACADEMY OF COSMETIC ART
304 W. Union St., Morganton 28655 *Type:* Private *Accred.:* 1991 (SACS-COEI) *Calen-

dar: Courses of varying lengths *Degrees:* certificates, diplomas *CEO:* Dir. Emily Lowe
Enroll: 4 (704) 437-1028

BRANCH CAMPUS
609 W. 29th St., Newton, NC 28658
CEO: Dir. Emily Lowe
(704) 465-7281

CALDWELL COMMUNITY COLLEGE AND TECHNICAL INSTITUTE
1000 Hickory Blvd., Hudson 28638 *Type:* Public (district) junior *System:* North Carolina State Board of Community Colleges *Accred.:* 1969/1986 (SACS-CC) *Calendar:* Qtr. plan *Degrees:* A *Prof. Accred.:* Diagnostic Medical Sonography, Occupational Therapy Assisting, Radiography *CEO:* Pres. Eric B. McKeithan
Enroll: 2817 (704) 726-2200

CAMPBELL UNIVERSITY
P.O. Box 127, Buies Creek 27506 *Type:* Private (Southern Baptist) liberal arts *Accred.:* 1941/1990 (SACS-CC) *Calendar:* Sem. plan *Degrees:* B, P, M, D *Prof. Accred.:* Law (ABA only), Pharmacy, Social Work (B-candidate) *CEO:* Pres. Norman A. Wiggins
Enroll: 4395 (919) 893-4111

CAPE FEAR COMMUNITY COLLEGE
411 N. Front St., Wilmington 28401-3993 *Type:* Public (district) junior *System:* North Carolina State Board of Community Colleges *Accred.:* 1971/1986 (SACS-CC) *Calendar:* Qtr. plan *Degrees:* A *CEO:* Pres. Richard C. Conrath
Enroll: 3269 (919) 343-0481

CAROLINA BEAUTY COLLEGE
801 English Rd., High Point 27262 *Type:* Private *Accred.:* 1984/1989 (SACS-COEI) *Calendar:* Courses of varying lengths *Degrees:* certificates *CEO:* Dir. Joylen Thomas
Enroll: 1283 (919) 886-4712

CARTERET COMMUNITY COLLEGE
3505 Arendell St., Morehead City 28557 *Type:* Public (district) junior *System:* North Carolina State Board of Community Colleges *Accred.:* 1974/1989 (SACS-CC) *Calendar:* Qtr. plan *Degrees:* A *Prof. Accred.:* Medical Assisting (AMA), Radiography, Respiratory Therapy, Respiratory Therapy Technology *CEO:* Pres. Donald W. Bryant
Enroll: 933 (919) 247-6000

CATAWBA COLLEGE
2300 W. Innes St., Salisbury 28144 *Type:* Private (United Church of Christ) liberal arts *Accred.:* 1928/1984 (SACS-CC) *Calendar:* Sem. plan *Degrees:* B, M *CEO:* Pres. Stephen H. Wurster
Enroll: 901 (704) 637-4111

CATAWBA VALLEY COMMUNITY COLLEGE
Rte. 3, P.O. Box 283, Hickory 28602-9699 *Type:* Public (district) junior *System:* North Carolina State Board of Community Colleges *Accred.:* 1969/1984 (SACS-CC) *Calendar:* Qtr. plan *Degrees:* A *Prof. Accred.:* EMT-Paramedic, Engineering Technology (architectural, electrical, industrial, mechanical) *CEO:* Pres. Cuyler A. Dunbar
Enroll: 3385 (704) 327-7000

CECILS JUNIOR COLLEGE OF BUSINESS
1567 Patton Ave., Asheville 28806 *Type:* Private *Accred.:* 1971/1991 (CCA-ACICS); 1984 (SACS-CC candidate) *Calendar:* Sem. plan *Degrees:* A *CEO:* Pres. John T. South, Jr.
Enroll: 149 (704) 258-9715

BRANCH CAMPUS
24 Pond Rd., Asheville, NC 28806 *CEO:* Dir. David Manning
(704) 258-9715

CENTRAL CAROLINA COMMUNITY COLLEGE
1105 Kelly Dr., Sanford 27330 *Type:* Public (district) junior *System:* North Carolina State Board of Community Colleges *Accred.:* 1972/1991 (SACS-CC) *Calendar:* Qtr. plan *Degrees:* A *Prof. Accred.:* Veterinary Medical Technology *CEO:* Pres. Marvin R. Joyner
Enroll: 3905 (919) 775-5401

CENTRAL PIEDMONT COMMUNITY COLLEGE
P.O. Box 35009, Charlotte 28235 *Type:* Public (district) junior *System:* North Carolina State Board of Community Colleges

Accred.: 1969/1983 (SACS-CC) *Calendar:* Qtr. plan *Degrees:* A *Prof. Accred.:* Dental Assisting, Dental Hygiene, Engineering Technology (architectural, civil/construction, computer, electrical, manufacturing, mechanical), Medical Assisting (AMA), Medical Record Technology, Physical Therapy Assisting, Respiratory Therapy *CEO:* Pres. Ruth G. Shaw
Enroll: 15624 (704) 342-6633

CHARLOTTE DIESEL DRIVING SCHOOL
6000 N. Tryon St., Charlotte 28213 *Type:* Private *Accred.:* 1991 (CCA-ACTTS) *Calendar:* Courses of varying lengths *Degrees:* diplomas *CEO:* Pres. J. Chris Watson
(704) 597-9550

CHOWAN COLLEGE
Murfreesboro 27855 *Type:* Private (Southern Baptist) junior *Accred.:* 1956/1988 (SACS-CC) *Calendar:* Sem. plan *Degrees:* A, B (candidate) *CEO:* Pres. Jerry F. Jackson
Enroll: 880 (919) 398-4101

CLEVELAND COMMUNITY COLLEGE
137 S. Post Rd., Shelby 28150 *Type:* Public (district) junior *System:* North Carolina State Board of Community Colleges *Accred.:* 1975/1991 (SACS-CC) *Calendar:* Qtr. plan *Degrees:* A *Prof. Accred.:* Radiography *CEO:* Pres. L. Steve Thornburg
Enroll: 1440 (704) 484-4000

COASTAL CAROLINA COMMUNITY COLLEGE
444 Western Blvd., Jacksonville 28546-6877 *Type:* Public (district) junior *System:* North Carolina State Board of Community Colleges *Accred.:* 1972/1987 (SACS-CC) *Calendar:* Qtr. plan *Degrees:* A *Prof. Accred.:* Dental Assisting, Dental Hygiene, Medical Laboratory Technology (AMA), Surgical Technology *CEO:* Pres. Ronald K. Lingle
Enroll: 4094 (919) 455-1221

THE COLLEGE OF THE ALBEMARLE
P.O. Box 2327, Elizabeth City 27906-2327 *Type:* Public (district) junior *System:* North Carolina State Board of Community Colleges *Accred.:* 1968/1983 (SACS-CC) *Calendar:* Qtr. plan *Degrees:* A *CEO:* Pres. J. Parker Chesson, Jr.
Enroll: 1838 (919) 335-0821

CRAVEN COMMUNITY COLLEGE
S. Glenburnie Rd. at College Ct., P.O. Box 885, New Bern 28563 *Type:* Public (district) junior *System:* North Carolina State Board of Community Colleges *Accred.:* 1971/1986 (SACS-CC) *Calendar:* Qtr. plan *Degrees:* A *CEO:* Pres. Lewis S. Redd
Enroll: 2070 (919) 638-4131

DAVIDSON COLLEGE
P.O. Box 1719, Davidson 28036-1719 *Type:* Private (Presbyterian) liberal arts *Accred.:* 1917/1986 (SACS-CC) *Calendar:* Sem. plan *Degrees:* B *CEO:* Pres. John W. Kuykendall
Enroll: 1508 (704) 892-2000

DAVIDSON COUNTY COMMUNITY COLLEGE
P.O. Box 1287, Lexington 27293-1287 *Type:* Public (district) junior *System:* North Carolina State Board of Community Colleges *Accred.:* 1968/1982 (SACS-CC) *Calendar:* Qtr. plan *Degrees:* A *Prof. Accred.:* Engineering Technology (electrical) *CEO:* Pres. J. Bryan Brooks
Enroll: 2830 (704) 249-8186

DUKE UNIVERSITY
Chapel Dr., Durham 27706 *Type:* Private liberal arts and professional *Accred.:* 1938/1984 (ATS); 1895/1988 (SACS-CC) *Calendar:* Sem. plan *Degrees:* A, B, P, M, D *Prof. Accred.:* Blood Bank Technology, Business (M), Clinical Psychology, Electroneurodiagnostic Technology, Engineering (bioengineering, civil, electrical, mechanical), Forestry, Health Services Administration, Law, Medical Technology, Medicine, Nursing (M), Ophthalmic Medical Technology, Physical Therapy, Physician Assisting, Psychology Internship *CEO:* Pres. H. Keith H. Brodie
Enroll: 10615 (919) 684-8111

DURHAM TECHNICAL COMMUNITY COLLEGE
P.O. Drawer 11307, Durham 27703 *Type:* Public (district) junior *System:* North Caroli-

na State Board of Community Colleges *Accred.:* 1971/1986 (SACS-CC) *Calendar:* Qtr. plan *Degrees:* A *Prof. Accred.:* Dental Laboratory Technology, Respiratory Therapy, Respiratory Therapy Technology *CEO:* Pres. Phail Wynn, Jr.
Enroll: 4056 (919) 598-9222

EAST CAROLINA UNIVERSITY
E. Fifth St., Greenville 27858-4353 *Type:* Public *System:* University of North Carolina General Administration *Accred.:* 1927/1982 (SACS-CC) *Calendar:* Sem. plan *Degrees:* B, P, M, D *Prof. Accred.:* Art, Audiology, Business (B,M), General Practice Residency (conditional), Home Economics, Leisure Systems Studies, Medical Record Administration, Medical Technology, Medicine, Music, Nursing (B,M), Occupational Therapy, Physical Therapy, Rehabilitation Counseling, Social Work (B,M), Speech-Language Pathology, Teacher Education (e,s,p) *CEO:* Chanc. Richard R. Eakin
Enroll: 15534 (919) 757-6131

EAST COAST BIBLE COLLEGE
6900 Wilkinson Blvd., Charlotte 28214 *Type:* Private (Church of God) *Accred.:* 1985/1990 (AABC); 1989 (SACS-CC) *Calendar:* Sem. plan *Degrees:* A, B *CEO:* Pres. Ronald D. Martin
Enroll: 211 (704) 394-2307

EDGECOMBE COMMUNITY COLLEGE
2009 W. Wilson St., Tarboro 27886 *Type:* Public (district) junior *System:* North Carolina State Board of Community Colleges *Accred.:* 1973/1988 (SACS-CC) *Calendar:* Qtr. plan *Degrees:* A *Prof. Accred.:* Radiography *CEO:* Pres. Charles B. McIntyre
Enroll: 2825 (919) 823-5166

ELIZABETH CITY STATE UNIVERSITY
Parkview Dr., Elizabeth City 27909 *Type:* Public liberal arts and teachers *System:* University of North Carolina General Administration *Accred.:* 1947/1991 (SACS-CC) *Calendar:* Sem. plan *Degrees:* B *CEO:* Chanc. Jimmy R. Jenkins
Enroll: 1677 (919) 335-3400

ELON COLLEGE
Elon College 27244 *Type:* Private (United Church of Christ) liberal arts *Accred.:* 1947/1982 (SACS-CC) *Calendar:* Sem. plan *Degrees:* B, M *CEO:* Pres. J. Fred Young
Enroll: 3019 (919) 584-9711

FAYETTEVILLE BEAUTY COLLEGE
2018 Ft. Bragg Rd., Fayetteville 28303 *Type:* Private *Accred.:* 1989 (SACS-COEI) *Calendar:* Courses of varying lengths *Degrees:* diplomas *CEO:* Dir. Bennie Dean
Enroll: 72 (919) 484-7191

FAYETTEVILLE STATE UNIVERSITY
1200 Murchison Rd., Newbold Sta., Fayetteville 28301-4298 *Type:* Public liberal arts and teachers *System:* University of North Carolina General Administration *Accred.:* 1947/1991 (SACS-CC) *Calendar:* Sem. plan *Degrees:* A, B, M *Prof. Accred.:* Teacher Education (e,s) *CEO:* Chanc. Lloyd V. Hackley
Enroll: 2875 (919) 486-1111

FAYETTEVILLE TECHNICAL COMMUNITY COLLEGE
2201 Hull Rd., P.O. Box 35236, Fayetteville 28303-0236 *Type:* Public (district) junior *System:* North Carolina State Board of Community Colleges *Accred.:* 1967/1991 (SACS-CC) *Calendar:* Qtr. plan *Degrees:* A *Prof. Accred.:* Dental Assisting, Dental Hygiene, Engineering Technology (civil/construction, electrical), Funeral Service Education, Nursing (A), Physical Therapy Assisting, Radiography, Respiratory Therapy, Surgical Technology *CEO:* Pres. Robert Craig Allen
Enroll: 4817 (919) 678-8400

FORSYTH TECHNICAL COMMUNITY COLLEGE
2100 Silas Creek Pkwy., Winston-Salem 27103-5197 *Type:* Public (district) junior *System:* North Carolina State Board of Community Colleges *Accred.:* 1968/1982 (SACS-CC) *Calendar:* Qtr. plan *Degrees:* A *Prof. Accred.:* Engineering Technology (electrical, manufacturing, mechanical drafting/design), Nuclear Medicine Technology, Radiation Therapy Technology, Radiogra-

phy, Respiratory Therapy *CEO:* Pres. Bob H. Greene
Enroll: 3646   (919) 723-0371

GARDNER-WEBB COLLEGE
P.O. Box 897, Boiling Springs 28017 *Type:* Private (Southern Baptist) liberal arts *Accred.:* 1948/1986 (SACS-CC) *Calendar:* Sem. plan *Degrees:* A, B, M *Prof. Accred.:* Music, Nursing (A,B) *CEO:* Pres. M. Christopher White
Enroll: 1817   (704) 434-2361

GASTON COLLEGE
201 Hwy. 321 S., Dallas 28034-1499 *Type:* Public (district) junior *System:* North Carolina State Board of Community Colleges *Accred.:* 1967/1991 (SACS-CC) *Calendar:* Qtr. plan *Degrees:* A *Prof. Accred.:* Engineering Technology (civil/construction, electrical, industrial, mechanical), Medical Assisting (AMA) *CEO:* Pres. W. Wayne Scott
Enroll: 3727   (704) 922-6200

GREENSBORO COLLEGE
815 W. Market St., Greensboro 27401-1875 *Type:* Private (United Methodist) liberal arts *Accred.:* 1926/1986 (SACS-CC) *Calendar:* Sem. plan *Degrees:* B *CEO:* Pres. William H. Likins
Enroll: 948   (919) 272-7102

GUILFORD COLLEGE
5800 W. Friendly Ave., Greensboro 27410 *Type:* Private liberal arts *Accred.:* 1926/1986 (SACS-CC) *Calendar:* Sem. plan *Degrees:* A, B *CEO:* Pres. William R. Rogers
Enroll: 1550   (919) 292-5511

GUILFORD TECHNICAL COMMUNITY COLLEGE
6300 High St., P.O. Box 309, Jamestown 27282 *Type:* Public (district) junior *System:* North Carolina State Board of Community Colleges *Accred.:* 1969/1984 (SACS-CC) *Calendar:* Qtr. plan *Degrees:* A *Prof. Accred.:* Dental Assisting, Dental Hygiene, Engineering Technology (civil/construction, electrical, mechanical drafting/design), Med-

ical Assisting (AMA) *CEO:* Pres. Donald W. Cameron
Enroll: 7844   (919) 334-4822

HAIRSTYLING INSTITUTE OF CHARLOTTE
209-B S. Kings Dr., Charlotte 28204-2621 *Type:* Private *Accred.:* 1983/1988 (CCA-ACTTS) *Calendar:* Courses of varying lengths *Degrees:* diplomas *CEO:* Pres. Costas Melissaris
Enroll: 88   (704) 334-5511

HALIFAX COMMUNITY COLLEGE
P.O. Drawer 809, Weldon 27890 *Type:* Public (district) junior *System:* North Carolina State Board of Community Colleges *Accred.:* 1975/1990 (SACS-CC) *Calendar:* Qtr. plan *Degrees:* A *Prof. Accred.:* Medical Laboratory Technology (AMA) *CEO:* Pres. Elton L. Newbern, Jr.
Enroll: 1117   (919) 536-2551

HAYWOOD COMMUNITY COLLEGE
Freedlander Dr., Clyde 28721 *Type:* Public (district) junior *System:* North Carolina State Board of Community Colleges *Accred.:* 1973/1988 (SACS-CC) *Calendar:* Qtr. plan *Degrees:* A *Prof. Accred.:* Medical Assisting (AMA) *CEO:* Pres. Dan W. Moore
Enroll: 1624   (704) 627-2821

HIGH POINT COLLEGE
933 Montlieu Ave., High Point 27262 *Type:* Private (United Methodist) liberal arts *Accred.:* 1951/1985 (SACS-CC) *Calendar:* Sem. plan *Degrees:* B *CEO:* Pres. Jacob C. Martinson, Jr.
Enroll: 2146   (919) 841-9000

ISOTHERMAL COMMUNITY COLLEGE
P.O. Box 804, Spindale 28160 *Type:* Public (district) junior *System:* North Carolina State Board of Community Colleges *Accred.:* 1970/1986 (SACS-CC) *Calendar:* Qtr. plan *Degrees:* A *CEO:* Pres. Willard L. Lewis, III
Enroll: 2121   (704) 286-3636

JAMES SPRUNT COMMUNITY COLLEGE
P.O. Box 398, Kenansville 28349-0398 *Type:* Public (district) junior *System:* North Carolina State Board of Community Coll-

eges *Accred.:* 1973/1988 (SACS-CC) *Calendar:* Qtr. plan *Degrees:* A *CEO:* Pres. Donald L. Reichard
Enroll: 1246 (919) 296-1341

JOHN WESLEY COLLEGE
2314 N. Centennial St., High Point 27265 *Type:* Private (Independent Wesleyan) *Accred.:* 1982/1987 (AABC) *Calendar:* Sem. plan *Degrees:* A, B, certificates *CEO:* Pres. Brian C. Donley
Enroll: 61 (919) 889-2262

JOHNSON C. SMITH UNIVERSITY
100 Beatties Ford Rd., Charlotte 28216 *Type:* Private (Presbyterian) liberal arts *Accred.:* 1933/1986 (SACS-CC) *Calendar:* Sem. plan *Degrees:* B *CEO:* Pres. Robert L. Albright
Enroll: 1170 (704) 378-1000

JOHNSTON COMMUNITY COLLEGE
P.O. Box 2350, Smithfield 27577 *Type:* Public (district) junior *System:* North Carolina State Board of Community Colleges *Accred.:* 1977/1982 (SACS-CC) *Calendar:* Qtr. plan *Degrees:* A *Prof. Accred.:* Radiography *CEO:* Pres. John L. Tart
Enroll: 2857 (919) 934-3051

KING'S COLLEGE
322 Lamar Ave., Charlotte 28204 *Type:* Private business *Accred.:* 1954/1986 (CCA-ACICS) *Calendar:* Qtr. plan *Degrees:* certificates, diplomas *Prof. Accred.:* Medical Assisting (AMA) *CEO:* Pres. C. Edward Arrington
Enroll: 501 (704) 372-0266

LEES-MCRAE COLLEGE
P.O. Box 128, Banner Elk 28604 *Type:* Private (Presbyterian) liberal arts *Accred.:* 1953/1985 (SACS-CC) *Calendar:* Sem. plan *Degrees:* A, B *CEO:* Pres. Bradford L. Crain
Enroll: 850 (704) 898-5241

LENOIR COMMUNITY COLLEGE
P.O. Box 188, Kinston 28502-0188 *Type:* Public (district) junior *System:* North Carolina State Board of Community Colleges *Accred.:* 1968/1983 (SACS-CC) *Calendar:* Qtr. plan *Degrees:* A *Prof. Accred.:* Surgical Technology *CEO:* Pres. Lonnie H. Blizzard
Enroll: 3573 (919) 527-6223

LENOIR-RHYNE COLLEGE
8th St. and 7th Ave., N.E, Hickory 28603 *Type:* Private (Lutheran) liberal arts *Accred.:* 1928/1982 (SACS-CC) *Calendar:* Sem. plan *Degrees:* B, M *Prof. Accred.:* Nursing (B), Teacher Education (e,s,p) *CEO:* Pres. John E. Trainer, Jr.
Enroll: 1484 (704) 328-1741

LIVINGSTONE COLLEGE
701 W. Monroe St., Salisbury 28144 *Type:* Private (African Methodist Episcopal) liberal arts *Accred.:* 1944/1991 (SACS-CC) *Calendar:* Sem. plan *Degrees:* B *Prof. Accred.:* Social Work (B) *CEO:* Pres. Bernard W. Franklin
Enroll: 737 (704) 638-5500

LOUISBURG COLLEGE
501 N. Main St., Louisburg 27549 *Type:* Private (United Methodist) junior *Accred.:* 1952/1986 (SACS-CC) *Calendar:* Sem. plan *Degrees:* A *CEO:* Pres. J. Allen Norris, Jr.
Enroll: 830 (919) 496-2521

MARS HILL COLLEGE
Main St., Mars Hill 28754 *Type:* Private (Southern Baptist) liberal arts *Accred.:* 1926/1991 (SACS-CC) *Calendar:* Sem. plan *Degrees:* B *Prof. Accred.:* Music, Social Work (B), Theatre *CEO:* Pres. Fred B. Bentley
Enroll: 1289 (704) 689-1111

MARTIN COMMUNITY COLLEGE
Kehukee Park Rd., Williamston 27892-9988 *Type:* Public (district) junior *System:* North Carolina State Board of Community Colleges *Accred.:* 1972/1988 (SACS-CC) *Calendar:* Qtr. plan *Degrees:* A *Prof. Accred.:* Physical Therapy Assisting *CEO:* Pres. Martin Nadelman
Enroll: 574 (919) 792-1521

MAYLAND COMMUNITY COLLEGE
P.O. Box 547, Spruce Pine 28777 *Type:* Public (district) junior *Accred.:* 1978/1984

Accredited Institutions

(SACS-CC) *Calendar:* Qtr. plan *Degrees:* A *CEO:* Pres. Virginia A. Foxx
Enroll: 608   (704) 765-7351

McDowell Technical Community College
Rte. 1, Box 170, Marion 28752 *Type:* Public (district) junior *System:* North Carolina State Board of Community Colleges *Accred.:* 1975/1990 (SACS-CC) *Calendar:* Qtr. plan *Degrees:* A *CEO:* Pres. Robert M. Boggs
Enroll: 1270   (704) 652-6021

Meredith College
3800 Hillborough St., Raleigh 27607-5298 *Type:* Private (Southern Baptist) liberal arts for women *Accred.:* 1921/1990 (SACS-CC) *Calendar:* Sem. plan *Degrees:* B, M *Prof. Accred.:* Music, Social Work (B), Teacher Education (e,s) *CEO:* Pres. John E. Weems
Enroll: 2049   (919) 829-6000

Methodist College
5400 Ramsey St., Fayetteville 28311-1499 *Type:* Private (United Methodist) liberal arts *Accred.:* 1964/1989 (SACS-CC) *Calendar:* Sem. plan *Degrees:* A, B *CEO:* Pres. M. Elton Hendricks
Enroll: 1158   (919) 488-7110

Miller-Motte Business College
606 S. College Rd., Wilmington 28403 *Type:* Private business *Accred.:* 1990 (SACS-COEI) *Calendar:* Courses of varying lengths *Degrees:* certificates, diplomas *CEO:* Pres. Richard Craig
Enroll: 252   (919) 392-0150

Miller-Motte Business College
647 W. Fifth St., Winston-Salem 27101-2704 *Type:* Private business *Accred.:* 1987/1990 (CCA-ACICS) *Calendar:* Qtr. plan *Degrees:* certificates, diplomas *CEO:* Dir. Bob Manor
Enroll: 440   (919) 724-7353

Mr. David's School of Hair Design
4248 Market St., Wilmington 28403 *Type:* Private *Accred.:* 1989 (SACS-COEI) *Calendar:* Courses of varying lengths *Degrees:* diplomas *CEO:* Dir. David Atkinson
Enroll: 76   (919) 763-4418

Mitchell Community College
500 W. Broad St., Statesville 28677-5293 *Type:* Public (district) junior *System:* North Carolina State Board of Community Colleges *Accred.:* 1955/1989 (SACS-CC) *Calendar:* Qtr. plan *Degrees:* A *CEO:* Pres. Douglas Eason
Enroll: 1862   (704) 878-3200

Montgomery Community College
P.O. Box 787, Troy 27371 *Type:* Public (district) junior *System:* North Carolina State Board of Community Colleges *Accred.:* 1978/1983 (SACS-CC) *Calendar:* Qtr. plan *Degrees:* A *CEO:* Pres. Benny B. Hampton
Enroll: 625   (919) 572-3691

Montreat-Anderson College
P.O. Box 1267, Montreat 28757 *Type:* Private (Presbyterian) liberal arts *Accred.:* 1960/1990 (SACS-CC) *Calendar:* Sem. plan *Degrees:* A, B *CEO:* Pres. Silas M. Vaughn
Enroll: 382   (704) 669-8011

Mount Olive College
209 N. Breazeale Ave., Mount Olive 28365 *Type:* Private (Free Will Baptist) liberal arts *Accred.:* 1960/1991 (SACS-CC) *Calendar:* Sem. plan *Degrees:* A, B *CEO:* Pres. W. Burkette Raper
Enroll: 756   (919) 658-2502

Nash Community College
P.O. Box 7488, Rocky Mount 27804-7488 *Type:* Public (district) junior *System:* North Carolina State Board of Community Colleges *Accred.:* 1976/1991 (SACS-CC) *Calendar:* Qtr. plan *Degrees:* A *Prof. Accred.:* Physical Therapy Assisting *CEO:* Pres. J. Reid Parrott
Enroll: 2109   (919) 443-4011

North Carolina Agricultural and Technical State University
1601 E. Market St., Greensboro 27411 *Type:* Public (state) *System:* University of North Carolina General Administration *Accred.:* 1936/1990 (SACS-CC) *Calendar:* Sem. plan *Degrees:* B, M *Prof. Accred.:* Accounting (Type A), Business (B), Engineering (archi-

tectural, electrical, industrial, mechanical), Home Economics, Nursing (B), Social Work (B), Teacher Education (e,s,p), Theatre *CEO:* Chanc. Edward B. Fort
Enroll: 6515 (919) 334-7500

NORTH CAROLINA CENTRAL UNIVERSITY
1801 Fayetteville St., Durham 27707 *Type:* Public (state) liberal arts and professional *System:* University of North Carolina General Administration *Accred.:* 1937/1989 (SACS-CC) *Calendar:* Sem. plan *Degrees:* B, P, M *Prof. Accred.:* Law (ABA only), Librarianship, Nursing (B), Teacher Education (e,s,p) *CEO:* Interim Chanc. Donna Benson
Enroll: 5481 (919) 560-6100

NORTH CAROLINA SCHOOL OF THE ARTS
200 Washington St., P.O. Box 12189, Winston-Salem 27117-2189 *Type:* Public (state) professional *System:* University of North Carolina General Administration *Accred.:* 1970/1985 (SACS-CC) *Calendar:* Tri. plan *Degrees:* B, M *CEO:* Chanc. Alexander C. Ewing
Enroll: 465 (919) 770-3399

NORTH CAROLINA STATE UNIVERSITY
P.O. Box 7001, Raleigh 27695 *Type:* Public (state) *System:* University of North Carolina General Administration *Accred.:* 1928/1984 (SACS-CC) *Calendar:* Sem. plan *Degrees:* A, B, M, D *Prof. Accred.:* Architecture (B,M), Computer Science, Counseling, Engineering (aerospace, agricultural, chemical, civil, computer, electrical, industrial, materials, mechanical, nuclear, textile), Forestry, Landscape Architecture (M), Public Affairs, Recreation Resources Administration, School Psychology, Social Work (B), Teacher Education (e,s,p) *CEO:* Chanc. Larry K. Monteith
Enroll: 22941 (919) 737-2011

NORTH CAROLINA WESLEYAN COLLEGE
3400 N. Wesleyan Blvd., Rocky Mount 27804 *Type:* Private (United Methodist) liberal arts *Accred.:* 1963/1990 (SACS-CC) *Calendar:* Sem. plan *Degrees:* B *CEO:* Pres. Leslie H. Garner, Jr.
Enroll: 1492 (919) 977-7171

OCONALUFTEE JOB CORPS CIVILIAN CONSERVATION CENTER
200 Park Cir., Cherokee 28719 *Type:* Public (federal) *Accred.:* 1984/1989 (SACS-COEI) *Calendar:* Courses of varying lengths *Degrees:* certificates *CEO:* Dir. Delmar P. Robinson
Enroll: 281 (704) 497-5411

PSI INSTITUTE OF CHARLOTTE
4 Woodlawn Green, Ste. 200, Charlotte 28217-2203 *Type:* Private *Accred.:* 1991 (CCA-ACTTS) *Calendar:* Courses of varying lengths *Degrees:* diplomas *CEO:* Dir. Richard Wilson
(704) 523-0555

PAMLICO COMMUNITY COLLEGE
Hwy. 306 S., P.O. Box 185, Grantsboro 28529 *Type:* Public (district) junior *System:* North Carolina State Board of Community Colleges *Accred.:* 1977/1982 (SACS-CC) *Calendar:* Qtr. plan *Degrees:* A *CEO:* Pres. E. Douglas Kearney, Jr.
Enroll: 226 (919) 249-1851

PEACE COLLEGE
15 E. Peace St., Raleigh 27604 *Type:* Private (Presbyterian) junior for women *Accred.:* 1947/1985 (SACS-CC) *Calendar:* Sem. plan *Degrees:* A *CEO:* Pres. Garrett Briggs
Enroll: 428 (919) 832-2881

PEMBROKE STATE UNIVERSITY
P.O. Box 1510, Pembroke 28372 *Type:* Public (state) liberal arts and teachers *System:* University of North Carolina General Administration *Accred.:* 1951/1990 (SACS-CC) *Calendar:* Sem. plan *Degrees:* B, M *Prof. Accred.:* Music, Social Work (B), Teacher Education (e,s,p) *CEO:* Chanc. Joseph B. Oxendine
Enroll: 2688 (919) 521-4214

PFEIFFER COLLEGE
Misenheimer 28109 *Type:* Private (United Methodist) liberal arts *Accred.:* 1959/1984

(SACS-CC) *Calendar:* Sem. plan *Degrees:* B, M *Prof. Accred.:* Music *CEO:* Pres. Zane E. Eargle
Enroll: 820   (704) 463-1360

PHILLIPS JUNIOR COLLEGE
4500 N. Tryon St., Charlotte 28213 *Type:* Private junior *Accred.:* 1991 (CCA-ACICS) *Calendar:* Qtr. plan *Degrees:* A, certificates, diplomas *CEO:* Dir. Brady Kraft
Enroll: 227   (704) 598-9000

  BRANCH CAMPUS
  610 E. Morehead St., Charlotte, NC 28202 *CEO:* Britt Dorman
    (704) 332-2625

PHILLIPS JUNIOR COLLEGE
603 Country Club Dr., Fayetteville 28301 *Type:* Private junior *Accred.:* 1973/1981 (CCA-ACICS) *Calendar:* Qtr. plan *Degrees:* A, certificates, diplomas *CEO:* Dir. Janis Schoonmaker
Enroll: 745   (919) 488-2527

PHILLIPS JUNIOR COLLEGE
617 W. Market St., Greensboro 27401 *Type:* Private junior *Accred.:* 1972/1989 (CCA-ACICS) *Calendar:* Qtr. plan *Degrees:* A, certificates, diplomas *CEO:* Dir. William M. Moore
Enroll: 502   (919) 275-6341

PHILLIPS JUNIOR COLLEGE
1920 North Blvd., Raleigh 27604 *Type:* Private junior *Accred.:* 1953/1988 (CCA-ACICS) *Calendar:* Qtr. plan *Degrees:* A, certificates, diplomas *CEO:* Dir. Wayne T. Thompson
Enroll: 1803   (919) 828-7291

PIEDMONT BIBLE COLLEGE
716 Franklin St., Winston-Salem 27101 *Type:* Private (Baptist) *Accred.:* 1956/1984 (AABC); 1985 (SACS-CC candidate) *Calendar:* Sem. plan *Degrees:* B *CEO:* Pres. Howard L. Wilburn
Enroll: 285   (919) 725-8344

PIEDMONT COMMUNITY COLLEGE
P.O. Box 1197, Roxboro 27573 *Type:* Public (district) junior *System:* North Carolina State Board of Community Colleges *Accred.:* 1977/1982 (SACS-CC) *Calendar:* Qtr. plan *Degrees:* A *CEO:* Pres. H. James Owen
Enroll: 1396   (919) 599-1181

PITT COMMUNITY COLLEGE
P.O. Drawer 7007, Greenville 27835-7007 *Type:* Public (district) junior *System:* North Carolina State Board of Community Colleges *Accred.:* 1969/1983 (SACS-CC) *Calendar:* Qtr. plan *Degrees:* A *Prof. Accred.:* Diagnostic Medical Sonography, Medical Assisting (AMA), Radiation Therapy Technology, Radiography, Respiratory Therapy *CEO:* Pres. Charles E. Russell
Enroll: 3581   (919) 355-4200

QUEENS COLLEGE
1900 Selwyn Ave., Charlotte 28274-0001 *Type:* Private (Presbyterian) liberal arts for women *Accred.:* 1932/1991 (SACS-CC) *Calendar:* Sem. plan *Degrees:* B, M *Prof. Accred.:* Music, Nursing (B) *CEO:* Pres. Billy O. Wireman
Enroll: 1068   (712) 337-2200

RANDOLPH COMMUNITY COLLEGE
P.O. Box 1009, Asheboro 27204-1009 *Type:* Public (district) junior *System:* North Carolina State Board of Community Colleges *Accred.:* 1974/1989 (SACS-CC) *Calendar:* Qtr. plan *Degrees:* A *CEO:* Pres. Larry K. Linker
Enroll: 2029   (919) 629-1471

RICHMOND COMMUNITY COLLEGE
P.O. Box 1189, Hamlet 28345 *Type:* Public (district) junior *System:* North Carolina State Board of Community Colleges *Accred.:* 1969/1983 (SACS-CC) *Calendar:* Qtr. plan *Degrees:* A *CEO:* Pres. Joseph W. Grimsley
Enroll: 779   (919) 582-7000

ROANOKE BIBLE COLLEGE
P.O. Box 387, Elizabeth City 27907-0387 *Type:* Private (Christian Churches/Churches of Christ) *Accred.:* 1979/1989 (AABC) *Cal-*

endar: Sem. plan *Degrees:* A, B *CEO:* Pres. William A. Griffin
Enroll: 106   (919) 338-5191

ROANOKE-CHOWAN COMMUNITY COLLEGE
Rte. 2, Box 46-A, Ahoskie 27910 *Type:* Public (district) junior *System:* North Carolina State Board of Community Colleges *Accred.:* 1976/1982 (SACS-CC) *Calendar:* Qtr. plan *Degrees:* A *CEO:* Pres. Harold E. Mitchell
Enroll: 619   (919) 332-5921

ROBESON COMMUNITY COLLEGE
P.O. Box 1420, Lumberton 28359 *Type:* Public (district) junior *System:* North Carolina State Board of Community Colleges *Accred.:* 1975/1990 (SACS-CC) *Calendar:* Qtr. plan *Degrees:* A *CEO:* Pres. Frederick G. Williams, Jr.
Enroll: 1561   (919) 738-7101

ROCKINGHAM COMMUNITY COLLEGE
P.O. Box 38, Wentworth 27375-0038 *Type:* Public (district) junior *System:* North Carolina State Board of Community Colleges *Accred.:* 1968/1983 (SACS-CC) *Calendar:* Qtr. plan *Degrees:* A *CEO:* Pres. N. Jerry Owens, Jr.
Enroll: 2745   (919) 342-4261

ROWAN-CABARRUS COMMUNITY COLLEGE
P.O. Box 1595, Salisbury 28144-1595 *Type:* Public (district) junior *System:* North Carolina State Board of Community Colleges *Accred.:* 1970/1985 (SACS-CC) *Calendar:* Qtr. plan *Degrees:* A *Prof. Accred.:* Dental Assisting, Radiography *CEO:* Pres. Richard L. Brownell
Enroll: 5580   (704) 637-0760

ST. ANDREWS PRESBYTERIAN COLLEGE
1700 Dogwood Mile Rd., Laurinburg 28352 *Type:* Private (Presbyterian) liberal arts *Accred.:* 1961/1990 (SACS-CC) *Calendar:* 4-1-4 plan *Degrees:* B *CEO:* Pres. Thomas L. Reuschling
Enroll: 764   (919) 276-3652

ST. AUGUSTINE'S COLLEGE
1315 Oakwood Ave., Raleigh 27610-2298 *Type:* Private (Episcopal) liberal arts *Accred.:* 1942/1991 (SACS-CC) *Calendar:* Sem. plan *Degrees:* B *CEO:* Pres. Prezell R. Robinson
Enroll: 2144   (919) 828-4451

ST. MARY'S COLLEGE
900 Hillsborough St., Raleigh 27603-1689 *Type:* Private (Episcopal) for women *Accred.:* 1927/1989 (SACS-CC) *Calendar:* Sem. plan *Degrees:* A *CEO:* Pres. Clauston L. Jenkins
Enroll: 300   (919) 828-2521

SALEM COLLEGE
Salem Sta., Winston-Salem 27108 *Type:* Private liberal arts for women *Accred.:* 1922/1990 (SACS-CC) *Calendar:* 4-1-4 plan *Degrees:* B, M *Prof. Accred.:* Music *CEO:* Pres. Julianne S. Thrift
Enroll: 601   (919) 721-2600

SALISBURY BUSINESS COLLEGE
129 Corriher Ave., Salisbury 28144 *Type:* Private business *Accred.:* 1975/1987 (CCA-ACICS) *Calendar:* Qtr. plan *Degrees:* certificates, diplomas *CEO:* Pres. Bill Hensley
Enroll: 220   (704) 636-4071

SAMPSON COMMUNITY COLLEGE
P.O. Drawer 318, Clinton 28328 *Type:* Public (district) junior *System:* North Carolina State Board of Community Colleges *Accred.:* 1977/1983 (SACS-CC) *Calendar:* Qtr. plan *Degrees:* A *CEO:* Pres. Clifton W. Paderick
Enroll: 1623   (919) 592-8081

SANDHILLS COMMUNITY COLLEGE
2200 Airport Rd., Pinehurst 28374 *Type:* Public (district) junior *System:* North Carolina State Board of Community Colleges *Accred.:* 1968/1983 (SACS-CC) *Calendar:* Qtr. plan *Degrees:* A *Prof. Accred.:* Medical Laboratory Technology (AMA), Nursing (A), Radiography, Respiratory Therapy, Surgical Technology *CEO:* Pres. John R. Dempsey
Enroll: 6418   (919) 692-6185

Accredited Institutions   **North Carolina**

SCHENCK CIVILIAN CONSERVATION CENTER
98 Schenck Dr., Pisgah Forest 28768 *Type:* Public (federal) *Accred.:* 1985/1991 (SACS-COEI) *Calendar:* Courses of varying lengths *Degrees:* certificates, diplomas *CEO:* Dir. John Henry Young
Enroll: 237   (704) 877-3291

SHAW UNIVERSITY
118 E. South St., Raleigh 27611 *Type:* Private liberal arts *Accred.:* 1943/1982 (SACS-CC) *Calendar:* Sem. plan *Degrees:* A, B *CEO:* Pres. Talbert O. Shaw
Enroll: 1590   (919) 546-8200

SHERRILLS ACADEMY
3421 Murchison Rd., Ste. M, Fayetteville 28311-9954 *Type:* Private *Accred.:* 1991 (CCA-ACTTS) *Calendar:* Courses of varying lengths *Degrees:* diplomas *CEO:* Dir. Van Michael Welch
     (919) 630-1140

SKYLAND ACADEMY OF COSMETIC ARTS
170 Rosscraggon Rd., Skyland 28776 *Type:* Private *Accred.:* 1988 (SACS-COEI) *Calendar:* Courses of varying lengths *Degrees:* certificates *CEO:* Dir. Luci Ratliff
Enroll: 133   (704) 687-1643

BRANCH CAMPUS
415 Seventh Ave., S.W., Hickory, NC 29601 *CEO:* Dir. Luci Ratliff
     (704) 327-2887

SOUTHEASTERN BAPTIST THEOLOGICAL SEMINARY*
P.O. Box 1889, Wake Forest 27587-1889 *Type:* Private (Southern Baptist) *Accred.:* 1958/1981 (ATS); 1978/1982 (SACS-CC warning) *Calendar:* Sem. plan *Degrees:* A, P, M, D *CEO:* Pres. Lewis A. Drummond
Enroll: 673   (919) 556-3101

*Accreditation on Warning (SACS-CC)

SOUTHEASTERN COMMUNITY COLLEGE
P.O. Box 151, Whiteville 28472 *Type:* Public (district) junior *System:* North Carolina State Board of Community Colleges *Accred.:* 1967/1991 (SACS-CC) *Calendar:* Qtr. plan *Degrees:* A *CEO:* Pres. Stephen C. Scott
Enroll: 1822   (919) 642-7141

SOUTHERN COLLEGE OF TECHNOLOGY
160 W. Franklin St., Gastonia 28052 *Type:* Private *Accred.:* 1987 (CCA-ACICS); 1989 (SACS-COEI) *Calendar:* Qtr. plan *Degrees:* certificates, diplomas *CEO:* Pres. Judy J. Reed
Enroll: 165   (704) 861-0833

BRANCH CAMPUS
546 S. Cherry Rd., Rock Hill, SC 29732 *CEO:* Pres. Ron Reed
     (803) 327-3106

SOUTHWESTERN COMMUNITY COLLEGE
275 Webster Rd., Sylva 28779 *Type:* Public (district) junior *System:* North Carolina State Board of Community Colleges *Accred.:* 1971/1986 (SACS-CC) *Calendar:* Qtr. plan *Degrees:* A *Prof. Accred.:* Medical Laboratory Technology (AMA), Radiography, Respiratory Therapy *CEO:* Pres. Barry W. Russell
Enroll: 1447   (704) 586-4091

STANLY COMMUNITY COLLEGE
Rte. 4, Box 55, Albemarle 28001 *Type:* Public (district) junior *System:* North Carolina State Board of Community Colleges *Accred.:* 1979/1984 (SACS-CC) *Calendar:* Qtr. plan *Degrees:* A *Prof. Accred.:* Occupational Therapy Assisting, Physical Therapy Assisting, Respiratory Therapy, Respiratory Therapy Technology *CEO:* Pres. Jan J. Crawford
Enroll: 1596   (704) 982-0121

SURRY COMMUNITY COLLEGE
P.O. Box 304, Dobson 27017 *Type:* Public (district) junior *System:* North Carolina State Board of Community Colleges *Accred.:* 1969/1984 (SACS-CC) *Calendar:* Qtr. plan *Degrees:* A *CEO:* Pres. Swanson Richards
Enroll: 3079   (919) 386-8121

TRI-COUNTY COMMUNITY COLLEGE
P.O. Box 40, Murphy 28906 *Type:* Public (district) junior *System:* North Carolina State Board of Community Colleges *Accred.:*

1975/1990 (SACS-CC) *Calendar:* Qtr. plan *Degrees:* A *CEO:* Pres. Vincent Crisp
Enroll: 977   (704) 837-6810

UNITED STATES ARMY JOHN F. KENNEDY SPECIAL WARFARE CENTER
Fort Bragg 28307-5000 *Type:* Public (federal) *Accred.:* 1976/1986 (SACS-COEI) *Calendar:* Courses of varying lengths *Degrees:* certificates *CEO:* Commandant Everett S. Deach, U.S.A.
Enroll: 1293   (919) 432-2949

THE UNIVERSITY OF NORTH CAROLINA AT ASHEVILLE
One University Heights, Asheville 28804-3299 *Type:* Public (state) *System:* University of North Carolina General Administration *Accred.:* 1958/1982 (SACS-CC) *Calendar:* Sem. plan *Degrees:* B, M (candidate) *Prof. Accred.:* Teacher Education (e,s) *CEO:* Chanc. Samuel Schuman
Enroll: 2645   (704) 251-6600

THE UNIVERSITY OF NORTH CAROLINA AT CHAPEL HILL
Chapel Hill 27599-9100 *Type:* Public (state) *System:* University of North Carolina General Administration *Accred.:* 1895/1985 (SACS-CC) *Calendar:* Sem. plan *Degrees:* B, P, M, D *Prof. Accred.:* Audiology, Business (B,M), Clinical Psychology, Combined Prosthodontics, Counseling, Counseling Psychology, Cytotechnology, Dental Assisting, Dental Hygiene, Dentistry, Dietetics (coordinated), Endodontics, Engineering (environmental/sanitary), General Dentistry, General Practice Residency, Health Services Administration, Journalism, Law, Librarianship, Medical Technology, Medicine, Nursing (B,M), Occupational Therapy, Oral and Maxillofacial Surgery, Orthodontics, Pediatric Dentistry, Periodontics, Pharmacy, Physical Therapy, Planning (city/regional), Psychology Internship, Public Administration, Public Health, Radiography, Recreation and Leisure Studies, Rehabilitation Counseling, School Psychology, Social Work (M), Speech-Language Pathology, Teacher Education (e,s,p) *CEO:* Chanc. Paul Hardin
Enroll: 20919   (919) 962-2211

THE UNIVERSITY OF NORTH CAROLINA AT CHARLOTTE
University City Blvd., Charlotte 28223 *Type:* Public (state) *System:* University of North Carolina General Administration *Accred.:* 1957/1982 (SACS-CC) *Calendar:* Sem. plan *Degrees:* B, M *Prof. Accred.:* Accounting (Type A), Architecture (B), Business (B,M), Engineering (civil, electrical, mechanical), Engineering Technology (civil/construction, electrical, mechanical), Nurse Anesthesia Education, Nursing (B,M), Teacher Education (e,s,p) *CEO:* Chanc. James H. Woodward, Jr.
Enroll: 12582   (704) 547-2000

THE UNIVERSITY OF NORTH CAROLINA AT GREENSBORO
1000 Spring Garden St., Greensboro 27412 *Type:* Public (state) *System:* University of North Carolina General Administration *Accred.:* 1921/1983 (SACS-CC) *Calendar:* Sem. plan *Degrees:* B, M, D *Prof. Accred.:* Business (B,M), Clinical Psychology, Counseling, Home Economics, Librarianship, Music, Nurse Anesthesia Education, Nursing (B,M), Recreation and Leisure Studies, Social Work (B), Speech-Language Pathology, Teacher Education (e,s,p), Theatre *CEO:* Chanc. William E. Moran
Enroll: 10884   (919) 334-5000

THE UNIVERSITY OF NORTH CAROLINA AT WILMINGTON
601 S. College Rd., Wilmington 28403-3297 *Type:* Public (state) *System:* University of North Carolina General Administration *Accred.:* 1952/1982 (SACS-CC) *Calendar:* Sem. plan *Degrees:* B, M *Prof. Accred.:* Music, Nursing (B), Parks and Recreation, Teacher Education (e,s,p) *CEO:* Chanc. James R. Leutze
Enroll: 6734   (919) 395-3000

VANCE-GRANVILLE COMMUNITY COLLEGE
Poplar Creek Rd., P.O. Box 917, Henderson 27536 *Type:* Public (district) junior *System:*

North Carolina State Board of Community Colleges *Accred.:* 1977/1983 (SACS-CC) *Calendar:* Qtr. plan *Degrees:* A *Prof. Accred.:* Radiography *CEO:* Pres. Benjamin F. Currin
Enroll: 2894 (919) 492-2061

WAKE FOREST UNIVERSITY
1834 Wake Forest Rd., Winston-Salem 27109 *Type:* Private (Southern Baptist) *Accred.:* 1921/1987 (SACS-CC) *Calendar:* Sem. plan *Degrees:* B, P, M, D *Prof. Accred.:* Accounting (Type A), Business (B,M), General Practice Residency, Law, Medical Technology, Medicine, Physician Assisting *CEO:* Pres. Thomas K. Hearn, Jr.
Enroll: 4368 (919) 759-5000

WAKE TECHNICAL COMMUNITY COLLEGE
9101 Fayetteville Rd., Raleigh 27603-5696 *Type:* Public (district) junior *System:* North Carolina State Board of Community Colleges *Accred.:* 1970/1985 (SACS-CC) *Calendar:* Qtr. plan *Degrees:* A, certificates *Prof. Accred.:* Dental Assisting, Engineering Technology (civil/construction, computer, electrical), Medical Assisting (AMA), Medical Laboratory Technology (AMA), Radiography *CEO:* Pres. Bruce I. Howell
Enroll: 7271 (919) 772-0551

WARREN WILSON COLLEGE
701 Warren Wilson Rd., Swannanoa 28778-2099 *Type:* Private (United Presbyterian) liberal arts *Accred.:* 1952/1984 (SACS-CC) *Calendar:* Sem. plan *Degrees:* B, M *Prof. Accred.:* Social Work (B) *CEO:* Pres. Douglas M. Orr, Jr.
Enroll: 569 (704) 298-3325

WAYNE COMMUNITY COLLEGE
Caller Box 8002, Goldsboro 27533-8002 *Type:* Public (district) junior *System:* North Carolina State Board of Community Colleges *Accred.:* 1970/1986 (SACS-CC) *Calendar:* Qtr. plan *Degrees:* A *Prof. Accred.:* Dental Assisting, Dental Hygiene *CEO:* Pres. G. Herman Porter
Enroll: 2948 (919) 735-5151

WESTERN CAROLINA UNIVERSITY
Cullowhee 28723 *Type:* Public (state) *System:* University of North Carolina General Administration *Accred.:* 1946/1986 (SACS-CC) *Calendar:* Sem. plan *Degrees:* B, M *Prof. Accred.:* Business (B,M), EMT-Paramedic, Engineering Technology (manufacturing), Home Economics, Medical Record Administration, Medical Technology, Music, Nursing (B), Social Work (B), Teacher Education (e,s,p) *CEO:* Chanc. Myron L. Coulter
Enroll: 5595 (704) 227-7211

WESTERN PIEDMONT COMMUNITY COLLEGE
1001 Burkemont Ave., Morganton 28655-9978 *Type:* Public (district) junior *System:* North Carolina State Board of Community Colleges *Accred.:* 1968/1983 (SACS-CC) *Calendar:* Qtr. plan *Degrees:* A *Prof. Accred.:* Dental Assisting, Medical Assisting (AMA), Medical Laboratory Technology (AMA), Nursing (A) *CEO:* Pres. James A. Richardson
Enroll: 2674 (704) 438-6000

WILKES COMMUNITY COLLEGE
Collegiate Dr., P.O. Box 120, Wilkesboro 28697-0120 *Type:* Public (district) junior *System:* North Carolina State Board of Community Colleges *Accred.:* 1970/1985 (SACS-CC) *Calendar:* Qtr. plan *Degrees:* A *Prof. Accred.:* Dental Assisting *CEO:* Pres. James R. Randolph
Enroll: 3639 (919) 651-8600

WILSON TECHNICAL COMMUNITY COLLEGE
P.O. Box 4305, Woodward Sta., Wilson 27893 *Type:* Public (district) junior *System:* North Carolina State Board of Community Colleges *Accred.:* 1969/1984 (SACS-CC) *Calendar:* Qtr. plan *Degrees:* A *CEO:* Pres. Frank L. Eagles
Enroll: 1758 (919) 291-1195

WINGATE COLLEGE
Wingate 28174-0157 *Type:* Private (Southern Baptist) liberal arts *Accred.:* 1951/1985 (SACS-CC) *Calendar:* Sem. plan *Degrees:* A, B, M *Prof. Accred.:* Medical Assisting

North Carolina

(AMA), Music, Nursing (B) *CEO:* Interim Pres. William Larry Ziglar, Jr.
Enroll: 1448 (704) 233-8000

WINSTON-SALEM BARBER SCHOOL
1531 Silas Creek Pkwy., Winston-Salem 27127-3757 *Accred.:* 1991 (CCA-ACTTS) *Degrees:* diplomas *CEO:* Pres. William Speece
(919) 724-1459

WINSTON-SALEM STATE UNIVERSITY
601 Martin Luther King Jr. Dr., Winston-Salem 27110 *Type:* Public liberal arts and teachers *System:* University of North Carolina General Administration *Accred.:* 1947/1990 (SACS-CC) *Calendar:* Sem. plan *Degrees:* B *Prof. Accred.:* Medical Technology, Music, Nursing (B), Teacher Education (e,s) *CEO:* Chanc. Cleon F. Thompson, Jr.
Enroll: 2517 (919) 750-2000

NORTH DAKOTA

AAKER'S BUSINESS COLLEGE
201 N. Third St., Post Office Box 876, Grand Forks 58203-0876 *Type:* Private business *Accred.:* 1966/1985 (CCA-ACICS) *Calendar:* Courses of varying lengths *Degrees:* certificates, diplomas *CEO:* Admin. Mark W. Hadlich
Enroll: 192 (701) 772-6646

BISMARK STATE COLLEGE
1500 Edwards Ave., Bismarck 58501 *Type:* Public (city) *System:* North Dakota University System *Accred.:* 1966/1988 (NCA) *Calendar:* Sem. plan *Degrees:* A, certificates, diplomas *Prof. Accred.:* Medical Laboratory Technology (AMA) *CEO:* Pres. Kermit Lidstrom
Enroll: 1794 (701) 224-5400

DICKINSON STATE UNIVERSITY
Dickinson 58601 *Type:* Public liberal arts and teachers *System:* North Dakota University System *Accred.:* 1928/1985 (NCA) *Calendar:* Sem. plan *Degrees:* A, B, certificates, diplomas *Prof. Accred.:* Nursing (B), Teacher Education (e,s) *CEO:* Pres. Albert A. Watrel, Dr.
Enroll: 1314 (701) 227-2507

FORT BERTHOLD COMMUNITY COLLEGE
P.O. Box 490, New Town 58763 *Type:* Public tribal *Accred.:* 1988/1991 (NCA) *Calendar:* Sem. plan *Degrees:* A, certificates, diplomas *CEO:* Pres. Phyllis Howard
Enroll: 136 (701) 627-4738

INTERSTATE BUSINESS COLLEGE
2720 32nd Avenue, S.W., Fargo 58103 *Type:* Private business *Accred.:* 1953/1990 (CCA-ACICS) *Calendar:* Courses of varying lengths *Degrees:* certificates, diplomas *CEO:* Dir. Tony Grindberg
Enroll: 744 (701) 232-2477

BRANCH CAMPUS
520 E. Main Ave., Bismarck, ND 58501 *CEO:* Dir. Rodney Wentz
(701) 255-0779

JAMESTOWN COLLEGE
Jamestown 58401 *Type:* Private (United Presbyterian) liberal arts *Accred.:* 1920/1991 (NCA) *Calendar:* 4-1-4 plan *Degrees:* B *Prof. Accred.:* Nursing (B) *CEO:* Pres. James S. Walker
Enroll: 865 (701) 252-3467

LITTLE HOOP COMMUNITY COLLEGE
P.O. Box 269, Fort Totten 58335 *Type:* Private tribal *Accred.:* 1990 (NCA) *Calendar:* Sem. plan *Degrees:* A, certificates, diplomas *CEO:* Pres. Merrill Berg
Enroll: 121 (701) 766-4415

MAYVILLE STATE UNIVERSITY
330 Third St., N.E., Mayville 58257 *Type:* Public liberal arts and teachers *System:* North Dakota University System *Accred.:* 1917/1986 (NCA) *Calendar:* Qtr. plan *Degrees:* A, B, certificates, diplomas *Prof. Accred.:* Teacher Education (e,s) *CEO:* Pres. James A. Schobel
Enroll: 732 (701) 786-2301

MEDCENTER ONE COLLEGE OF NURSING
512 N. Seventh St., Bismarck 58501 *Type:* Private professional *Accred.:* 1991 (NCA) *Calendar:* Sem. plan *Degrees:* B *Prof. Accred.:* Nursing (B) *CEO:* Provost/Dean Inez G. Hinsvark
Enroll: 94 (701) 224-6271

MEYER VOCATIONAL-TECHNICAL SCHOOL
P.O. Box 2126, Minot 58702-2126 *Type:* Private *Accred.:* 1991 (CCA-ACTTS) *Calendar:* Courses of varying lengths *Degrees:* certificates *CEO:* Dir. Scott Meyer
(701) 852-0427

MINOT SCHOOL FOR ALLIED HEALTH
20 Burdick Expy. W., Ste. 603, Minot 58701 *Type:* Private *Calendar:* Courses of varying lengths *Degrees:* certificates *Prof. Accred.:* Radiography *CEO:* C.E.O. Natalie Wagner
(701) 857-5620

North Dakota

MINOT STATE UNIVERSITY
Minot 58701 *Type:* Public liberal arts and teachers *System:* North Dakota University System *Accred.:* 1917/1988 (NCA) *Calendar:* Qtr. plan *Degrees:* A, B, M *Prof. Accred.:* Audiology, Music, Nursing (B), Social Work (B), Speech-Language Pathology, Teacher Education (e,s) *CEO:* Pres. Gordon B. Olson
Enroll: 3394 (701) 857-3300

NORTH DAKOTA STATE COLLEGE OF SCIENCE
800 N. Sixth St., Wahpeton 58075 *Type:* Public junior *System:* North Dakota University System *Accred.:* 1971/1981 (NCA) *Calendar:* Qtr. plan *Degrees:* A, certificates, diplomas *Prof. Accred.:* Dental Assisting, Dental Hygiene, Medical Record Technology, Occupational Therapy Assisting, Practical Nursing *CEO:* Pres. Jerry C. Olson
Enroll: 2093 (701) 671-2221

NORTH DAKOTA STATE UNIVERSITY
Fargo 58105 *Type:* Public *System:* North Dakota University System *Accred.:* 1915/1986 (NCA) *Calendar:* Qtr. plan *Degrees:* A, B, P, M, D *Prof. Accred.:* Architecture (B), Computer Science, Construction Education, Dietetics (coordinated), Engineering (agricultural, civil, construction, electrical, industrial, mechanical), Home Economics, Interior Design, Music, Nursing (B), Pharmacy, Respiratory Therapy, Teacher Education (s,p), Veterinary Technology *CEO:* Pres. Jim L. Ozbun
Enroll: 8379 (701) 237-7211

NORTH DAKOTA STATE UNIVERSITY—BOTTINEAU
First St. and Simrall Blvd., Bottineau 58318 *Type:* Public junior *System:* North Dakota University System *Accred.:* 1971/1989 (NCA) *Calendar:* Qtr. plan *Degrees:* A *CEO:* Dean J.W. Smith
Enroll: 487 (701) 228-2277

STANDING ROCK COLLEGE
Fort Yates 58538 *Type:* Public tribal *Accred.:* 1984/1991 (NCA) *Calendar:* Sem. plan *Degrees:* A, certificates, diplomas *CEO:* Pres. Dave Archambault
Enroll: 191 (701) 854-3861

TRAVEL CAREER INSTITUTE
855 Basin Ave., Bismarch 58504-9967 *Type:* Private *Accred.:* 1991 (CCA-ACTTS) *Calendar:* Courses of varying lengths *Degrees:* certificates *CEO:* Pres. W.P. Reisenauer
(701) 258-9419

TRI-COLLEGE UNIVERSITY
306 Ceres Hall, North Dakota State Univ., Fargo 58105 *Type:* Private *Accred.:* 1979/1984 (NCA) *Calendar:* Courses of varying lengths *Degrees:* B, P, M *Prof. Accred.:* Nursing (B), Teacher Education (p) *CEO:* Provost William Nelson
Enroll: 250 (701) 237-8170

TRINITY BIBLE COLLEGE
50 S. Sixth St., Ellendale 58436 *Type:* Private (Assemblies of God) *Accred.:* 1980/1990 (AABC); 1991 (NCA) *Calendar:* Sem. plan *Degrees:* A, B, certificates, diplomas *CEO:* Pres. Ray Trask
Enroll: 375 (701) 349-3621

TURTLE MOUNTAIN COMMUNITY COLLEGE
P.O. Box 340, Belcourt 58316-0340 *Type:* Private tribal *Accred.:* 1984/1989 (NCA) *Calendar:* Sem. plan *Degrees:* A, certificates, diplomas *CEO:* Pres. Gerald E. Monette
Enroll: 388 (701) 477-5605

TURTLE MOUNTAIN SCHOOL OF PARAMEDICAL TECHNIQUE
316 Okmer St., Box 203, Bottineau 58318 *Type:* Private *Calendar:* Courses of varying lengths *Degrees:* certificates *Prof. Accred.:* Medical Laboratory Technology *CEO:* Dean M. Gale Feland
(701) 228-3390

UNITED TRIBES TECHNICAL COLLEGE
3315 University Dr., Bismarck 58504 *Type:* Private tribal *Accred.:* 1982/1990 (NCA) *Calendar:* Qtr. plan *Degrees:* A, certificates, diplomas *CEO:* Pres. David M. Gipp
Enroll: 308 (701) 255-3285

University of Mary

7500 University Dr., Bismarck 58504 *Type:* Private (Roman Catholic) liberal arts *Accred.:* 1969/1983 (NCA) *Calendar:* 4-1-4 plan *Degrees:* A, B, M *Prof. Accred.:* Nurse Anesthesia Education, Nursing (B,M), Social Work (B) *CEO:* Pres. Thomas Welder
Enroll: 1291 (701) 255-7500

University of North Dakota

Box 8193, University Sta., Grand Forks 58202-8193 *Type:* Public *System:* North Dakota University System *Accred.:* 1913/1984 (NCA) *Calendar:* Sem. plan *Degrees:* A, B, P, M, D *Prof. Accred.:* Art, Business (B,M), Clinical Psychology, Computer Science, Counseling Psychology (provisional), Cytotechnology, Dietetics (coordinated), Engineering (chemical, civil, electrical, geological/geophysical, mechanical), Histologic Technology, Home Economics, Journalism, Law, Medical Technology, Medicine, Music, Nurse Anesthesia Education, Nursing (B,M), Occupational Therapy, Physical Therapy, Physician Assisting, Social Work (B,M-candidate), Speech-Language Pathology, Teacher Education (e,s,p), Theatre *CEO:* Pres. Thomas J. Clifford
Enroll: 10227 (701) 777-2121

University of North Dakota—Lake Region

N. College Dr., Devils Lake 58301 *Type:* Public *System:* North Dakota University System *Accred.:* 1974/1991 (NCA) *Calendar:* Sem. plan *Degrees:* A, certificates, diplomas *CEO:* Exec. Dean Sharon L. Etemad
Enroll: 660 (701) 662-8683

University of North Dakota—Williston

P.O. Box 1326, Williston 58801 *Type:* Public *System:* North Dakota University System *Accred.:* 1972/1990 (NCA) *Calendar:* Sem. plan *Degrees:* A, certificates, diplomas *CEO:* Exec. Dean Garvin L. Stevens
Enroll: 599 (701) 774-4200

Valley City State University

101 S.W. College St., Valley City 58072 *Type:* Public liberal arts and teachers *System:* North Dakota University System *Accred.:* 1915/1983 (NCA) *Calendar:* Qtr. plan *Degrees:* A, B, certificates, diplomas *Prof. Accred.:* Teacher Education (e,s) *CEO:* Pres. Charles B. House, Jr.
Enroll: 959 (701) 845-7100

OHIO

ACA COLLEGE OF DESIGN
2528 Kemper La., Cincinnati 45206-2014 *Type:* Private *Accred.:* 1979/1989 (CCA-ACTTS) *Calendar:* Qtr. plan *Degrees:* certificates *CEO:* Pres. Marion Allman
Enroll: 65   (513) 751-1206

ACADEMY OF COURT REPORTING
614 Superior Ave., N.W., Cleveland 44113 *Type:* Private business *Accred.:* 1980/1986 (CCA-ACICS) *Calendar:* Courses of varying lengths *Degrees:* A, certificates, diplomas *CEO:* Dir. Lynn Fisher
Enroll: 667   (216) 861-3222

BRANCH CAMPUS
26111 Evergreen Rd., Ste. 101, Southfield, MI 48076 *CEO:* Mgr. Kathryn Trauben
                                                 (313) 353-4880

BRANCH CAMPUS
2930 W. Market St., Akron, OH 44313 *CEO:* Dir. Michelle Endres
                                                 (216) 867-4030

BRANCH CAMPUS
630 E. Broad St., Columbus, OH 43215 *CEO:* Dir. Joseph A. Trocchio
                                                 (614) 221-7770

AIR FORCE INSTITUTE OF TECHNOLOGY
Wright-Patterson Air Force Base 45433 *Type:* Public (federal) technological; graduate only *Accred.:* 1960/1991 (NCA) *Calendar:* Qtr. plan *Degrees:* M, D *Prof. Accred.:* Engineering (aerospace, computer, electrical, engineering management, nuclear, systems) *CEO:* Commandant Stuart R. Boyd
Enroll: 938   (513) 255-4808

AKRON BARBER COLLEGE
3200 S. Arlington Rd., Ste. 2, Akron 44312-5269 *Type:* Private *Accred.:* 1986 (CCA-ACTTS) *Calendar:* Courses of varying lengths *Degrees:* diplomas *CEO:* Dir. Mary Jane Sabotin
Enroll: 49   (216) 644-9114

AKRON MACHINING INSTITUTE
2959 Barber Rd., Barberton 44203-1005 *Type:* Private *Accred.:* 1986 (CCA-ACTTS) *Calendar:* Courses of varying lengths *Degrees:* diplomas *CEO:* Dir. Daniel J. Lucas
Enroll: 165   (216) 745-1111

CLEVELAND MACHINING INSTITUTE
2500 Brookpark Rd., Cleveland, OH 44134-1407 *CEO:* Dir. Joan Cook
                                                 (216) 741-1100

AKRON MEDICAL-DENTAL INSTITUTE
733 W. Market St., Akron 44303-1078 *Type:* Private *Accred.:* 1977/1987 (CCA-ACTTS) *Calendar:* Qtr. plan *Degrees:* diplomas *Prof. Accred.:* Medical Assisting (AMA) *CEO:* Dir. Elizabeth Husk
Enroll: 341   (216) 762-9788

ALLSTATE HAIRSTYLING AND BARBER COLLEGE
2546 Lorain Ave., Cleveland 44113-3493 *Type:* Private *Accred.:* 1985 (CCA-ACTTS) *Calendar:* Courses of varying lengths *Degrees:* diplomas *CEO:* Dir. Phil D'Amico
Enroll: 84   (216) 241-6684

AMERICAN SCHOOL OF TECHNOLOGY
1120 Morse Rd., Ste. 120, Columbus 43229-6337 *Type:* Private *Accred.:* 1991 (CCA-ACTTS) *Calendar:* Courses of varying lengths *Degrees:* diplomas *CEO:* Dir. Doris L. Spratt
                                                 (614) 436-4820

ANTIOCH UNIVERSITY
795 Livermore St., Yellow Springs 45387 *Type:* Private liberal arts and professional *Accred.:* 1927/1989 (NCA) *Calendar:* Sem. plan *Degrees:* B, M, D, certificates, diplomas *Prof. Accred.:* Clinical Psychology (provisional) *CEO:* Pres. Alan E. Guskin
Enroll: 2601   (513) 767-7331

ANTONELLI INSTITUTE OF ART AND PHOTOGRAPHY
124 E. Seventh St., Cincinnati 45202-2592 *Type:* Private *Accred.:* 1975/1980 (CCA-

ACTTS) *Calendar:* Qtr. plan *Degrees:* A *CEO:* Pres. Mary Ann Davis
Enroll: 255   (513) 241-4338

ARISTOTLE INSTITUTE OF MEDICAL AND DENTAL TECHNOLOGY
5900 Westerville Rd., Westerville 43081 *Type:* Private *Calendar:* Courses of varying lengths *Degrees:* diplomas *Prof. Accred.:* Health Education *CEO:* Pres. Michael A. Walker
    (614) 891-1800

ART ACADEMY OF CINCINNATI
1125 St. Gregory St., Cincinnati 45202 *Type:* Private professional *Accred.:* 1990 (NCA) *Calendar:* Sem. plan *Degrees:* A, B, certificates, diplomas *Prof. Accred.:* Art *CEO:* Dir. Roger Williams
Enroll: 229   (513) 721-5205

ART ADVERTISING ACADEMY
4343 Bridgetown Rd., Cincinnati 45211-4427 *Type:* Private *Accred.:* 1984/1989 (CCA-ACTTS) *Calendar:* Courses of varying lengths *Degrees:* certificates *CEO:* Pres. Jerry E. Neff
Enroll: 34   (513) 574-1010

ASHLAND UNIVERSITY
401 College Ave., Ashland 44805 *Type:* Private (Brethren) liberal arts *Accred.:* 1969/1988 (ATS); 1930/1988 (NCA) *Calendar:* Sem. plan *Degrees:* A, B, M, D *Prof. Accred.:* Music, Nursing (B), Social Work (B), Teacher Education (e,s) *CEO:* Pres. Joseph R. Shultz
Enroll: 3564   (419) 289-4142

ATHENAEUM OF OHIO
6616 Beechmont Ave., Cincinnati 45230-2091 *Type:* Private (Roman Catholic) *Accred.:* 1972/1982 (ATS); 1959/1983 (NCA) *Calendar:* Qtr. plan *Degrees:* B, P, M *CEO:* Pres. Robert J. Mooney
Enroll: 221   (513) 231-2223

BALDWIN-WALLACE COLLEGE
275 Eastland Rd., Berea 44017 *Type:* Private (United Methodist) liberal arts *Accred.:* 1913/1988 (NCA) *Calendar:* Qtr. plan *Degrees:* B, M *Prof. Accred.:* Music, Teacher Education (e,s,p) *CEO:* Pres. Neal Malicky
Enroll: 3765   (216) 826-2424

BELMONT TECHNICAL COLLEGE
120 Fox-Shannon Pl., St. Clairsville 43950 *Type:* Public (state) 2-year *System:* Ohio Board of Regents *Accred.:* 1978/1988 (NCA) *Calendar:* Qtr. plan *Degrees:* A, certificates, diplomas *CEO:* Pres. Wesley R. Channell
Enroll: 1381   (614) 695-9500

BLISS COLLEGE
3770 N. High St., Columbus 43214 *Type:* Private business *Accred.:* 1961/1986 (CCA-ACICS) *Calendar:* Qtr. plan *Degrees:* A, certificates, diplomas *CEO:* Pres. Gene Blakenship
Enroll: 779   (614) 267-8355

BRANCH CAMPUS
95 Southland Mall, Columbus, OH 43207 *CEO:* Dir. Marion Smith
    (614) 491-4913

BRANCH CAMPUS
3035 W. Broad St., Columbus, OH 43204 *CEO:* Dir. James Towns
    (614) 276-8080

BLUFFTON COLLEGE
Bluffton 45817 *Type:* Private (Mennonite) liberal arts *Accred.:* 1953/1989 (NCA) *Calendar:* 4-1-4 plan *Degrees:* B *Prof. Accred.:* Music, Social Work (B) *CEO:* Pres. Elmer Neufeld
Enroll: 612   (419) 358-8015

BOHECKER'S BUSINESS COLLEGE
161 E. Main St., Ravenna 44266-9998 *Type:* Private business *Accred.:* 1985 (CCA-ACICS) *Calendar:* Courses of varying lengths *Degrees:* certificates, diplomas *CEO:* Dir. Peter Perkowski
Enroll: 367   (216) 297-7319

BRANCH CAMPUS
341 City Centre Mall, 2nd Fl., Middletown, OH 45045 *CEO:* Dir. Thomas Chappie
    (513) 423-6100

Ohio

BOWLING GREEN STATE UNIVERSITY
Bowling Green 43403 *Type:* Public (state) *System:* Ohio Board of Regents *Accred.:* 1916/1983 (NCA) *Calendar:* Sem. plan *Degrees:* A, B, P, M, D, certificates, diplomas *Prof. Accred.:* Art, Audiology, Business (B,M), Clinical Psychology, Journalism, Medical Record Technology, Medical Technology, Music, Nursing (B,M), Rehabilitation Counseling, Respiratory Therapy, Social Work (B), Speech-Language Pathology, Teacher Education (e,s,p), Theatre *CEO:* Pres. Paul J. Olscamp
Enroll: 16329 (419) 372-2211

FIRELANDS COLLEGE
910 Rye Beach Rd., Huron, OH 44839 *CEO:* Dean Robert Debard
(419) 433-5560

BRADFORD SCHOOL
6170 Busch Blvd., Columbus 43229 *Type:* Private business *Accred.:* 1960/1982 (CCA-ACICS) *Calendar:* Qtr. plan *Degrees:* A, certificates, diplomas *Prof. Accred.:* Medical Assisting (AMA) *CEO:* Pres. Tom Greenhouse
Enroll: 266 (614) 846-9410

BRYANT AND STRATTON BUSINESS INSTITUTE
26700 Brookpark Rd. Ext., North Olmstead 44070 *Type:* Private business *Accred.:* 1984/1990 (CCA-ACICS) *Calendar:* Qtr. plan *Degrees:* A, certificates, diplomas *CEO:* Dir. Elliot B. Jones
Enroll: 736 (216) 777-3151

BRANCH CAMPUS
Sears Bldg., 3rd Fl., 691 Richmond Rd., Richmond Heights, OH 44143 *CEO:* Dir. Ronald E. Nelson
(216) 461-3151

CAPITAL UNIVERSITY
2199 E. Main St., Columbus 43209 *Type:* Private (Lutheran) liberal arts and professional *Accred.:* 1921/1983 (NCA) *Calendar:* 4-1-4 plan *Degrees:* B, M, D, certificates, diplomas *Prof. Accred.:* Law, Music, Nursing (B), Social Work (B), Teacher Education (e,s) *CEO:* Pres. Josiah H. Blackmore
Enroll: 2546 (614) 236-6908

CAREERCOM COLLEGE OF BUSINESS
2572 Cleveland Ave., Columbus 43211 *Type:* Private business *Accred.:* 1985/1991 (CCA-ACICS) *Calendar:* Courses of varying lengths *Degrees:* A, certificates, diplomas *CEO:* Dir. James Tufts
Enroll: 772 (614) 268-8000

BRANCH CAMPUS
3375 E. Princess Anne Rd., Norfolk, VA 23504 *CEO:* Dir. Kenneth Sullivan
(804) 857-1667

CASE WESTERN RESERVE UNIVERSITY
2040 Adelbert Rd., Cleveland 44106-1712 *Type:* Private *Accred.:* 1913/1985 (NCA) *Calendar:* Sem. plan *Degrees:* B, M, D *Prof. Accred.:* Accounting (Type A,C), Anesthesiologist Assisting, Business (B,M), Clinical Psychology, Dentistry, Endodontics, Engineering (bioengineering, chemical, civil, computer, electrical, engineering physics/science, materials, mechanical, polymer, systems), General Dentistry, Law, Medicine, Music, Nurse Anesthesia Education, Nursing (B,M), Oral and Maxillofacial Surgery, Orthodontics, Pediatric Dentistry, Periodontics, Psychology Internship, Social Work (M), Speech-Language Pathology *CEO:* Pres. Agnar Pytte
Enroll: 6533 (216) 368-2000

CEDARVILLE COLLEGE
N. Main St., Box 601, Cedarville 45314-0601 *Type:* Private (Baptist) liberal arts *Accred.:* 1975/1987 (NCA) *Calendar:* Qtr. plan *Degrees:* A, B, certificates, diplomas *Prof. Accred.:* Nursing (B) *CEO:* Pres. Paul Dixon
Enroll: 1923 (513) 766-2211

CENTRAL OHIO TECHNICAL COLLEGE
University Dr., Newark 43055 *Type:* Public (district) 2-year *System:* Ohio Board of Regents *Accred.:* 1975/1988 (NCA) *Calendar:* Qtr. plan *Degrees:* A, certificates,

diplomas *Prof. Accred.:* Diagnostic Medical Sonography, Nursing (A), Physical Therapy Assisting, Radiography *CEO:* Pres. Julius S. Greenstein
Enroll: 1042 (614) 366-1351

CENTRAL STATE UNIVERSITY
1400 Brush Row Rd., Wilberforce 45384-3002 *Type:* Public (state) *System:* Ohio Board of Regents *Accred.:* 1949/1989 (NCA) *Calendar:* Qtr. plan *Degrees:* A, B, certificates, diplomas *Prof. Accred.:* Music *CEO:* Pres. Arthur E. Thomas
Enroll: 3051 (513) 376-6332

CHATFIELD COLLEGE
20918 State Rte. 251, St. Martin 45118 *Type:* Private liberal arts *Accred.:* 1971/1986 (NCA) *Calendar:* Sem. plan *Degrees:* A *CEO:* Pres. Ellen Doyle
Enroll: 97 (513) 875-3344

CHOFFIN CAREER CENTER
200 E. Wood St., Youngtown 44503 *Type:* Private *Calendar:* Courses of varying lengths *Degrees:* certificates *Prof. Accred.:* Dental Assisting (prelim. provisional), Practical Nursing *CEO:* Prin. Raymond Brown
(216) 744-8700

THE CHURCH OF GOD SCHOOL OF THEOLOGY
900 Walker St., N.E., P.O. Box 3330, Cleveland 37311 *Type:* Private (Church of God) professional; graduate only *Accred.:* 1989 (ATS); 1984/1989 (SACS-CC) *Calendar:* Sem. plan *Degrees:* P, M *CEO:* Pres. Cecil B. Knight
Enroll: 252 (615) 478-1131

CINCINNATI BIBLE COLLEGE
P.O. Box 043200, Cincinnati 45204 *Type:* Private (Christian Churches/Churches of Christ) *Accred.:* 1966/1986 (AABC); 1990 (NCA) *Calendar:* Sem. plan *Degrees:* A, B, M *CEO:* Pres. C. Barry McCarty
Enroll: 710 (513) 244-8100

CINCINNATI COLLEGE OF MORTUARY SCIENCE
Cohen Ctr., 3860 Pacific Ave., Cincinnati 45207-1033 *Type:* Private *Accred.:* 1982/1987 (NCA) *Calendar:* Qtr. plan *Degrees:* A, B, certificates, diplomas *Prof. Accred.:* Mortuary Science *CEO:* Pres. Dan L. Flory
Enroll: 118 (513) 745-3631

CINCINNATI METROPOLITAN COLLEGE
4320 Bertus St., St. Bernard 45217-1650 *Type:* Private business *Accred.:* 1973/1986 (CCA-ACICS) *Calendar:* Qtr. plan *Degrees:* A, certificates, diplomas *CEO:* Dir. Charles W. Stewart
Enroll: 714 (513) 242-0202

CINCINNATI SCHOOL OF COURT REPORTING AND BUSINESS
600 Executive Bldg., 35 E. Seventh St., Cincinnati 45202 *Type:* Private business *Accred.:* 1982 (CCA-ACICS) *Calendar:* Courses of varying lengths *Degrees:* certificates, diplomas *CEO:* Pres. Adeline M. Womack
Enroll: 219 (513) 241-1011

CINCINNATI TECHNICAL COLLEGE
3520 Central Pkwy., Cincinnati 45223 *Type:* Public (state) *System:* Ohio Board of Regents *Accred.:* 1976/1991 (NCA) *Calendar:* Qtr. plan *Degrees:* A, certificates, diplomas *Prof. Accred.:* Engineering Technology (bioengineering, civil/construction, computer, electrical, electromechanical, mechanical), Medical Assisting (AMA), Medical Laboratory Technology (AMA), Medical Record Technology, Occupational Therapy Assisting, Respiratory Therapy, Respiratory Therapy Technology, Surgical Technology *CEO:* Pres. James P. Long
Enroll: 2778 (513) 569-1500

CIRCLEVILLE BIBLE COLLEGE
P.O. Box 458, Circleville 43113 *Type:* Private (Church of Christ) *Accred.:* 1976/1986 (AABC) *Calendar:* Sem. plan *Degrees:* A, B *CEO:* Pres. David Van Hoose
Enroll: 158 (614) 474-8896

CLARK STATE COMMUNITY COLLEGE
570 E. Leffels La., Post Office Box 570, Springfield 45505 *Type:* Public (state) 2-year *System:* Ohio Board of Regents *Accred.:* 1974/1989 (NCA) *Calendar:* Qtr. plan *De-

grees: A, certificates, diplomas *Prof. Accred.:* Medical Laboratory Technology (AMA), Nursing (A) *CEO:* Pres. Albert A. Salerno
Enroll: 1574 (513) 325-0691

CLEVELAND COLLEGE OF JEWISH STUDIES
26500 Shaker Blvd., Beachwood 44122 *Type:* Private *Accred.:* 1988 (NCA) *Calendar:* Sem. plan *Degrees:* B, M *CEO:* Pres. David S. Ariel
Enroll: 110 (216) 464-4050

CLEVELAND INSTITUTE OF ART
11141 East Blvd., Cleveland 44106 *Type:* Private professional *Accred.:* 1970/1991 (NCA) *Calendar:* Sem. plan *Degrees:* B, certificates, diplomas *Prof. Accred.:* Art *CEO:* Pres. Robert A. Mayer
Enroll: 447 (216) 421-7000

CLEVELAND INSTITUTE OF DENTAL AND MEDICAL ASSISTANTS
1836 Euclid Ave., Rm. 401, Cleveland 44115-2285 *Type:* Private *Accred.:* 1989 (CCA-ACTTS) *Calendar:* Courses of varying lengths *Degrees:* certificates, diplomas *Prof. Accred.:* Health Education, Medical Assisting *CEO:* Pres. Beverly A. Davis
(216) 241-2930

BRANCH CAMPUS
5564 Mayfield Road, Lyndhurst, OH 44124-2928 *Prof. Accred.:* Health Education *CEO:* Exec. Vice Pres. Linda Carson McCafferty
(216) 473-6273

BRANCH CAMPUS
5733 Hopkins Rd., Mentor, OH 44060-2035 *Prof. Accred.:* Health Education *CEO:* Exec. Vice Pres. Linda Carson McCafferty
(216) 946-9530

CLEVELAND INSTITUTE OF ELECTRONICS
1776 E. 17th St., Cleveland 44114 *Type:* Private home study *Accred.:* 1956/1988 (NHSC) *Calendar:* Courses of varying lengths *Degrees:* A, certificates *CEO:* Pres. John R. Drinko
Enroll: 3876 (216) 781-9400

CLEVELAND INSTITUTE OF MUSIC
11021 East Blvd., Cleveland 44106 *Type:* Private professional *Accred.:* 1980/1986 (NCA) *Calendar:* Sem. plan *Degrees:* B, M, D *Prof. Accred.:* Music *CEO:* Pres. David Cerone
Enroll: 342 (216) 791-5000

CLEVELAND INSTITUTE OF TECHNOLOGY
6701 Rockside Rd., No. 102, Independence 44131-2316 *Type:* Private *Accred.:* 1974/1989 (CCA-ACTTS) *Calendar:* Courses of varying lengths *Degrees:* diplomas *CEO:* Owner Ronald Rozek
Enroll: 423 (216) 447-1095

BRANCH CAMPUS
2 Allegheny Ctr., Ste. 100, Pittsburgh, PA 15212-5403 *CEO:* Dir. Daniel K. Baker
(412) 359-8411

CLEVELAND STATE UNIVERSITY
Euclid Ave. at East 24th St., Cleveland 44115-2403 *Type:* Public (state) *System:* Ohio Board of Regents *Accred.:* 1940/1990 (NCA) *Calendar:* Qtr. plan *Degrees:* B, P, M, D *Prof. Accred.:* Accounting (Type A,C), Audiology, Business (B,M), Engineering (chemical, civil, electrical, industrial, mechanical), Health Services Administration, Law, Music (B), Nursing (B), Occupational Therapy, Physical Therapy, Public Administration, Social Work (B), Speech-Language Pathology, Teacher Education (e,s,p) *CEO:* Pres. John A. Flower
Enroll: 13129 (216) 687-2000

COLLEGE OF MOUNT ST. JOSEPH
Delphi and Neeb Rds., Mount St. Joseph 45051 *Type:* Private (Roman Catholic) liberal arts primarily for women *Accred.:* 1932/1989 (NCA) *Calendar:* Sem. plan *Degrees:* A, B, M *Prof. Accred.:* Music, Nursing (B) *CEO:* Pres. Francis Marie Thrailkill, O.S.U.
Enroll: 1573 (513) 244-4232

COLLEGE OF WOOSTER
Wooster 44691 *Type:* Private (United Presbyterian) liberal arts *Accred.:* 1915/1983 (NCA) *Calendar:* Qtr. plan *Degrees:* B *Prof.*

Accred.: Music *CEO:* Pres. Henry J. Copeland
Enroll: 1953 (216) 263-2311

COLUMBUS COLLEGE OF ART AND DESIGN
107 N. Ninth St., Columbus 43215 *Type:* Private professional *Accred.:* 1986/1991 (NCA) *Calendar:* Sem. plan *Degrees:* B *Prof. Accred.:* Art *CEO:* Pres. Joseph V. Canzani
Enroll: 1261 (614) 224-9101

COLUMBUS PARA-PROFESSIONAL INSTITUTE
1077 Lexington Ave., Columbus 43201 *Type:* Private *Accred.:* 1980 (CCA-ACTTS) *Calendar:* Qtr. plan *Degrees:* A, diplomas *CEO:* Dir. Ralph Rutledge
Enroll: 700 (614) 299-0200

COLUMBUS STATE COMMUNITY COLLEGE
550 E. Spring St., Post Office Box 1609, Columbus 43216-1609 *Type:* Public (state) 2-year *System:* Ohio Board of Regents *Accred.:* 1973/1990 (NCA) *Calendar:* Qtr. plan *Degrees:* A, certificates, diplomas *Prof. Accred.:* Dental Laboratory Technology, EMT-Paramedic, Engineering Technology (electrical), Histologic Technology, Medical Laboratory Technology (AMA), Nursing (A), Respiratory Therapy, Respiratory Therapy Technology, Veterinary Technology *CEO:* Pres. Harold M. Nestor
Enroll: 7260 (614) 227-2400

CUYAHOGA COMMUNITY COLLEGE
700 Carnegie Ave., Cleveland 44115 *Type:* Public (county) 2-year *System:* Ohio Board of Regents *Accred.:* 1979/1989 (NCA) *Calendar:* Qtr. plan *Degrees:* A, certificates, diplomas *Prof. Accred.:* Occupational Therapy Assisting *CEO:* Pres. Jerry S. Owens
Enroll: 11932 (216) 987-6000

EASTERN CAMPUS
4250 Richmond Rd., Highland Hills, OH 44122 *CEO:* Provost Grace Carolyn Brown
(216) 987-2000

METROPOLITAN CAMPUS
2900 Community College Ave., Cleveland, OH 44115 *Prof. Accred.:* Dental Assisting, Dental Hygiene, Dental Laboratory Technology, Nursing (A), Physical Therapy Assisting *CEO:* Provost Ronald R. Zambetti
(216) 987-4000

WESTERN CAMPUS
11000 W. Pleasant Valley Rd., Parma, OH 44130 *Prof. Accred.:* Nursing (A) *CEO:* Provost Ronald M. Sobel
(216) 987-5000

DAVIS COLLEGE
4747 Monroe St., Toledo 43623 *Type:* Private junior *Accred.:* 1953/1986 (CCA-ACICS); 1991 (NCA) *Calendar:* Qtr. plan *Degrees:* A *Prof. Accred.:* Medical Assisting (AMA) *CEO:* Pres. John M. Lambert
Enroll: 643 (419) 473-2700

DEVRY INSTITUTE OF TECHNOLOGY, COLUMBUS
1350 Alum Creek Dr., Columbus 43209-2764 *Type:* Private *Accred.:* 1981/1987 (NCA) *Calendar:* Courses of varying lengths *Degrees:* A, B, certificates *Prof. Accred.:* Engineering Technology (electrical) *CEO:* C.E.O. Dean Dugger
(614) 253-2791

THE DEFIANCE COLLEGE
701 N. Clinton St., Defiance 43512-1695 *Type:* Private (United Church of Christ) liberal arts *Accred.:* 1916/1983 (NCA) *Calendar:* 4-1-4 plan *Degrees:* A, B *Prof. Accred.:* Social Work (B) *CEO:* Pres. Marvin J. Ludwig
Enroll: 766 (419) 784-4010

DENISON UNIVERSITY
Granville 43023 *Type:* Private (Baptist) liberal arts *Accred.:* 1913/1990 (NCA) *Calendar:* Sem. plan *Degrees:* B *CEO:* Pres. Michele T. Myers
Enroll: 2019 (614) 587-0810

DYKE COLLEGE
112 Prospect Ave., S.E., Cleveland 44115-1096 *Type:* Private *Accred.:* 1978/1990 (NCA) *Calendar:* Tri. plan *Degrees:* A, B,

certificates, diplomas *CEO:* Pres. John C. Corfias
Enroll: 815 (216) 696-9000

ESI CAREER CENTER
25301 Euclid Ave., Euclid 44117-2609 *Type:* Private *Accred.:* 1981 (CCA-ACTTS) *Calendar:* Courses of varying lengths *Degrees:* certificates *CEO:* Pres. Thomas Strong
Enroll: 81 (216) 289-1299

BRANCH CAMPUS
1985 N. Ridge Rd., Lorain, OH 44055-9990 *CEO:* Pres. Thomas Strong
(216) 277-8832

ETI TECHNICAL COLLEGE
4300 Euclid Ave., Cleveland 44103-9932 *Type:* Private *Accred.:* 1969/1989 (CCA-ACTTS) *Calendar:* Qtr. plan *Degrees:* A, diplomas *CEO:* Pres. Alfred Jablonski
Enroll: 1770 (216) 391-9696

BRANCH CAMPUS
2076-86 Youngstown-Warren Rd., Niles, OH 44446-4398 *CEO:* Dir. Renee Zuzulo
(216) 652-9919

THE ETI TECHNICAL COLLEGE
1320 W. Maple St., N.W., North Canton 44720-2854 *Type:* Private *Accred.:* 1986 (CCA-ACTTS) *Calendar:* Qtr. plan *Degrees:* A, diplomas *CEO:* Dir. William LeWay
Enroll: 223 (216) 494-1214

EDISON STATE COMMUNITY COLLEGE
1973 Edison Dr., Piqua 45356-9253 *Type:* Public (state) 2-year *System:* Ohio Board of Regents *Accred.:* 1981/1987 (NCA) *Calendar:* Qtr. plan *Degrees:* A, certificates, diplomas *Prof. Accred.:* Nursing (A) *CEO:* Pres. Kenneth A. Yowell
Enroll: 1525 (513) 778-8600

FRANCISCAN UNIVERSITY OF STEUBENVILLE
Franciscan Way, Steubenville 43952 *Type:* Private (Roman Catholic) liberal arts *Accred.:* 1960/1985 (NCA) *Calendar:* Sem. plan *Degrees:* A, B, M *Prof. Accred.:* Nursing (B) *CEO:* Pres. Michael Scanlan
Enroll: 1413 (614) 283-6216

FRANKLIN UNIVERSITY
201 S. Grant Ave., Columbus 43215 *Type:* Private liberal arts and technical *Accred.:* 1976/1988 (NCA) *Calendar:* Tri. plan *Degrees:* A, B, certificates, diplomas *Prof. Accred.:* Engineering Technology (electrical, mechanical), Nursing (B) *CEO:* Pres. Paul J. Otte
Enroll: 2695 (614) 224-6237

GOD'S BIBLE COLLEGE
1810 Young St., Cincinnati 45210 *Type:* Private (Church of God Holiness) *Accred.:* 1986 (AABC) *Calendar:* Sem. plan *Degrees:* B, diplomas *CEO:* Pres. Bence Miller
Enroll: 175 (513) 721-7944

GREAT LAKES TECHNICAL INSTITUTE
1361 E. 55th St., Cleveland 44103-1389 *Type:* Private *Accred.:* 1971/1986 (CCA-ACTTS) *Calendar:* Courses of varying lengths *Degrees:* certificates *CEO:* Exec. Dir. Dennis J. Jacobs
Enroll: 903 (216) 431-1050

HAMMEL COLLEGE
885 E. Buchtel Ave., Akron 44305 *Type:* Private business *Accred.:* 1953/1982 (CCA-ACICS) *Calendar:* Courses of varying lengths *Degrees:* certificates, diplomas *CEO:* Dir. Mary F. Welch
Enroll: 464 (216) 762-7491

HAMRICK TRUCK DRIVING SCHOOL
1156 Medina Rd., Medina 44256-9615 *Type:* Private *Accred.:* 1988 (CCA-ACTTS) *Calendar:* Courses of varying lengths *Degrees:* certificates *CEO:* Pres. Denver Hamrick
Enroll: 286 (216) 239-2229

HARDING BUSINESS COLLEGE
1988 McCartney Rd., Youngstown 44505 *Type:* Private business *Accred.:* 1980/1989 (CCA-ACICS) *Calendar:* Qtr. plan *Degrees:* A, certificates, diplomas *CEO:* Dir. Nicol L. Burnett
Enroll: 74485 (216) 746-2424

HEBREW UNION COLLEGE—JEWISH INSTITUTE OF RELIGION
3101 Clifton Ave., Cincinnati 45220 *Type:* Private (Union of Hebrew Congregations)

primarily for men *Accred.:* 1960/1991 (NCA) *Calendar:* Qtr. plan *Degrees:* M, D *CEO:* Pres. Alfred Gottschalk
Enroll: 138 (513) 221-1875

HEIDELBERG COLLEGE
310 E. Market St., Tiffin 44883 *Type:* Private (United Church of Christ) liberal arts *Accred.:* 1913/1985 (NCA) *Calendar:* Sem. plan *Degrees:* B, M *Prof. Accred.:* Music *CEO:* Pres. William C. Cassell
Enroll: 1061 (419) 448-2202

HICKOK TECHNICAL INSTITUTE
5100 Pearl Rd., Cleveland 44129-1240 *Type:* Private *Accred.:* 1980/1985 (CCA-ACTTS) *Calendar:* Qtr. plan *Degrees:* diplomas *CEO:* Dir. Michael Kovalick
Enroll: 663 (216) 351-4600

HIRAM COLLEGE
Hiram 44234 *Type:* Private (Disciples of Christ) liberal arts *Accred.:* 1914/1990 (NCA) *Calendar:* Qtr. plan *Degrees:* B, certificates, diplomas *Prof. Accred.:* Music, Teacher Education (e,s) *CEO:* Pres. G. Benjamin Oliver
Enroll: 1253 (216) 569-3211

HOCKING TECHNICAL COLLEGE
3101 Hocking Pkwy., Nelsonville 45764 *Type:* Public (state) 2-year *System:* Ohio Board of Regents *Accred.:* 1976/1991 (NCA) *Calendar:* Qtr. plan *Degrees:* A, certificates, diplomas *Prof. Accred.:* Engineering Technology (ceramic), Medical Assisting (AMA), Medical Record Technology, Nursing (A), Practical Nursing *CEO:* Pres. John J. Light
Enroll: 3860 (614) 753-3591

HOSPITALITY TRAINING CENTER, INC.
220 N. Main St., Hudson 44236 *Type:* Private home study *Accred.:* 1986 (NHSC) *Calendar:* Courses of varying lengths *Degrees:* diplomas *CEO:* Pres. Duane R. Hills
(216) 653-9151

ITT TECHNICAL INSTITUTE
3325 Stop Eight Rd., Dayton 45414-9915 *Type:* Private *Accred.:* 1991 (CCA-ACTTS) *Calendar:* Courses of varying lengths *Degrees:* A, certificates, diplomas *CEO:* Dir. Dennis W. Alspaugh
(513) 454-2267

ITT TECHNICAL INSTITUTE
655 Wick Ave., Post Office Box 779, Youngstown 44501 *Type:* Private business *Accred.:* 1971/1989 (CCA-ACICS) *Calendar:* Courses of varying lengths *Degrees:* A, certificates, diplomas *CEO:* Dir. Michael Thompson
Enroll: 1026 (216) 747-5555

INSTITUTE OF MEDICAL AND DENTAL TECHNOLOGY
375 Glenspring Dr., Ste. 201, Cincinnati 45246 *Type:* Private *Calendar:* Courses of varing lengths *Degrees:* diplomas *Prof. Accred.:* Health Education *CEO:* Pres./Dir. Vincent J. Sofia
(513) 851-8500

THE INTERNATIONAL COLLEGE OF BROADCASTING
6 S. Smithville Rd., Dayton 45431-1833 *Type:* Private *Accred.:* 1976/1986 (CCA-ACTTS) *Calendar:* Courses of varying lengths *Degrees:* A, diplomas *CEO:* Pres. Michael A. Lemaster
Enroll: 80 (513) 258-8251

JEFFERSON TECHNICAL COLLEGE
4000 Sunset Blvd., Steubenville 43952 *Type:* Public (state) 2-year *System:* Ohio Board of Regents *Accred.:* 1973/1989 (NCA) *Calendar:* Qtr. plan *Degrees:* A, certificates, diplomas *Prof. Accred.:* Dental Assisting, Medical Assisting (AMA), Medical Laboratory Technology (AMA), Radiography, Respiratory Therapy *CEO:* Pres. Edward L. Florak
Enroll: 1117 (614) 264-5591

JOHN CARROLL UNIVERSITY
20700 N. Park Blvd., University Heights 44118 *Type:* Private (Roman Catholic) liberal arts and business *Accred.:* 1922/1984 (NCA) *Calendar:* Sem. plan *Degrees:* A, B, M, certificates, diplomas *Prof. Accred.:*

Business (B,M), Teacher Education (e,s,p) *CEO:* Pres. Michael J. Lavelle, S.J.
Enroll: 3896 (216) 397-1886

KENT STATE UNIVERSITY
Kent 44242 *Type:* Public *System:* Ohio Board of Regents *Accred.:* 1915/1984 (NCA) *Calendar:* Sem. plan *Degrees:* A, B, P, M, D *Prof. Accred.:* Architecture (B,M), Art, Audiology, Business (B,M), Clinical Psychology, Counseling Psychology (provisional), Interior Design, Journalism, Librarianship, Music, Nursing (A,B,M), Psychology Internship, Public Administration, Radiography, Rehabilitation Counseling, School Psychology, Speech-Language Pathology, Teacher Education (e,s,p) *CEO:* Pres. Carol A. Cartwright
Enroll: 19705 (216) 672-2210

ASHTABULA CAMPUS
3325 W. 13th St., Ashtabula, OH 44004 *Prof. Accred.:* Nursing (A) *CEO:* Dean John K. Mahan
(216) 964-3322

EAST LIVERPOOL CAMPUS
400 E. Fourth St., East Liverpool, OH 43920 *Prof. Accred.:* Nursing (A), Physical Therapy Assisting *CEO:* Dean Suzanne B. Fitzgerald
(216) 385-3805

GEUAGA CAMPUS
14111 Claridon-Troy Rd., Burton Township, OH 44021 *CEO:* Dean Larry Jones
(216) 834-4187

SALEM CAMPUS
2491 State Rte. 45 S., Salem, OH 44460 *CEO:* Dean James F. Cooney
(216) 332-0361

STARK CAMPUS
6000 Frank Ave., N.W., North Canton, OH 44720 *CEO:* Dean William G. Bittle
(216) 499-9600

TRUMBULL CAMPUS
4314 Mahoning Ave., N.W., Warren, OH 44483 *CEO:* Dean David Allen, Jr.
(216) 847-0571

TUSCARAWAS CAMPUS
University Dr., N.E., New Philadelphia, OH 44663 *Prof. Accred.:* Engineering Technology (electrical, electromechanical), Nursing (A) *CEO:* Dean Harold D. Shade
(216) 339-3391

KENYON COLLEGE
Gambier 43022-9623 *Type:* Private (Episcopal) liberal arts *Accred.:* 1913/1991 (NCA) *Calendar:* Sem. plan *Degrees:* B *CEO:* Pres. Philip Harding Jordan, Jr.
Enroll: 1509 (614) 427-5000

KETTERING COLLEGE OF MEDICAL ARTS
3737 Southern Blvd., Kettering 45429 *Type:* Private (Seventh-Day Adventist) junior *Accred.:* 1974/1990 (NCA) *Calendar:* Sem. plan *Degrees:* A, certificates, diplomas *Prof. Accred.:* Diagnostic Medical Sonography, Nursing (A), Physician Assisting, Radiography, Respiratory Therapy *CEO:* Provost Peter D.H. Bath
Enroll: 595 (513) 296-7218

LAKE ERIE COLLEGE
391 W. Washington St., Painesville 44077-3389 *Type:* Private liberal arts *Accred.:* 1913/1989 (NCA) *Calendar:* Courses of varying lengths *Degrees:* B, M *CEO:* Pres. Clodus R. Smith
Enroll: 776 (216) 352-3361

LAKELAND COMMUNITY COLLEGE
7700 Clocktower Dr., Mentor 44060 *Type:* Public (district) 2-year *System:* Ohio Board of Regents *Accred.:* 1973/1990 (NCA) *Calendar:* 4-1-4 plan *Degrees:* A, certificates, diplomas *Prof. Accred.:* Dental Hygiene, Medical Laboratory Technology (AMA), Nursing (A), Respiratory Therapy *CEO:* Pres. Ralph R. Doty
Enroll: 4121 (216) 953-7000

LIMA TECHNICAL COLLEGE
4240 Campus Dr., Lima 45804 *Type:* Public (state) 2-year *System:* Ohio Board of Regents *Accred.:* 1979/1984 (NCA) *Calendar:* Qtr. plan *Degrees:* A, certificates,

diplomas *Prof. Accred.:* Dental Hygiene, Nursing (A), Radiography, Respiratory Therapy, Respiratory Therapy Technology *CEO:* Pres. James J. Countryman
Enroll: 1766 (419) 222-8324

LORAIN BUSINESS COLLEGE
1907 N. Ridge Rd., Lorain 44055 *Type:* Private business *Accred.:* 1980 (CCA-ACICS) *Calendar:* Courses of varying lengths *Degrees:* A, certificates, diplomas *CEO:* Dir. Mary B. Kelleher
Enroll: 471 (216) 277-0021

BRANCH CAMPUS
4020 Milan Rd., Sandusky, OH 44870 *CEO:* Dir. Judith Shahan
(419) 627-8345

LORAIN COUNTY COMMUNITY COLLEGE
1005 Abbe Rd., Elyria 44035 *Type:* Public (district) 2-year *System:* Ohio Board of Regents *Accred.:* 1971/1984 (NCA) *Calendar:* Qtr. plan *Degrees:* A, certificates, diplomas *Prof. Accred.:* Medical Laboratory Technology, Nursing (A), Practical Nursing, Radiography *CEO:* Pres. Roy A. Church
Enroll: 4020 (216) 365-4191

LOURDES COLLEGE
6832 Convent Blvd., Sylvania 43560 *Type:* Private (Roman Catholic) liberal arts *Accred.:* 1964/1987 (NCA) *Calendar:* Sem. plan *Degrees:* A, B, certificates, diplomas *Prof. Accred.:* Nursing (B), Occupational Therapy Assisting, Social Work (B-candidate) *CEO:* Pres. Ann Francis Klimkowski
Enroll: 602 (419) 885-3211

MTA SCHOOL
3987 E. Main St., Columbus 43213-2952 *Type:* Private *Accred.:* 1985 (CCA-ACTTS) *Calendar:* Courses of varying lengths *Degrees:* certificates *CEO:* Dir. Samuel Lehman
Enroll: 2625 (614) 236-1972

BRANCH CAMPUS
4781 Hamilton Ave., Cincinnati, OH 45223-1596 *CEO:* Dir. Terry Queeno
(513) 681-0580

BRANCH CAMPUS
3405 N. Sixth St., Harrisburg, PA 17110 *CEO:* Dir. Dennis Shaeffer
(717) 232-3111

MTI BUSINESS SCHOOL
1901 E. 13th S., Ste. 310, Cleveland 44114 *Type:* Private business *Accred.:* 1980/1989 (CCA-ACICS) *Calendar:* Courses of varying lengths *Degrees:* A, certificates, diplomas *Prof. Accred.:* Medical Assisting (AMA) *CEO:* Pres. Charles M. Kramer
Enroll: 437 (216) 621-8228

MALONE COLLEGE
515 25th St., N.W., Canton 44709 *Type:* Private (Friends) liberal arts *Accred.:* 1964/1984 (NCA) *Calendar:* Sem. plan *Degrees:* A, B, M *Prof. Accred.:* Social Work (B) *CEO:* Pres. E. Arthur Self
Enroll: 1324 (216) 489-0800

MANSFIELD BUSINESS COLLEGE
3011 Mahoning Rd. N.E., Canton 44705 *Type:* Private business *Accred.:* 1984/1986 (CCA-ACICS) *Calendar:* Qtr. plan *Degrees:* A, certificates, diplomas *Prof. Accred.:* Medical Assisting (AMA) *CEO:* Dir. Russell O'Neill
Enroll: 547 (216) 452-8171

BRANCH CAMPUS
O'Neil's Plaza, 6th Fl., 222 S. Main St., Akron, OH 44308 *CEO:* Dir. George Dupey
(216) 762-3030

MARIETTA COLLEGE
Marietta 45750 *Type:* Private liberal arts *Accred.:* 1913/1986 (NCA) *Calendar:* Sem. plan *Degrees:* A, B, M, certificates, diplomas *Prof. Accred.:* Computer Science, Engineering (petroleum) *CEO:* Pres. Patrick D. McDonough
Enroll: 1175 (614) 373-4643

MARION TECHNICAL COLLEGE
1467 Mt. Vernon Ave., Marion 43302 *Type:* Public (state) 2-year *System:* Ohio Board of Regents *Accred.:* 1977/1987 (NCA) *Calendar:* Qtr. plan *Degrees:* A, certificates, diplomas *Prof. Accred.:* Medical Laboratory

Technology (AMA), Nursing (A) *CEO:* Pres. John Richard Bryson
Enroll: 965 (614) 389-4636

MCKIM TECHNICAL INSTITUTE
1791 S. Jacoby Rd., Akron 44321-2299 *Type:* Private *Accred.:* 1991 (CCA-ACTTS) *Calendar:* Courses of varying lengths *Degrees:* certificates *CEO:* Pres. Carol L. Swaney
(216) 666-4014

MEDICAL COLLEGE OF OHIO
P.O. Box 10008, Toledo 43699 *Type:* Public (state) professional *System:* Ohio Board of Regents *Accred.:* 1980/1991 (NCA) *Calendar:* Sem. plan *Degrees:* M, D, certificates, diplomas *Prof. Accred.:* General Practice Residency, Medicine, Nursing (B,M), Physical Therapy *CEO:* Pres. Richard D. Ruppert
Enroll: 711 (419) 381-4260

METHODIST THEOLOGICAL SCHOOL IN OHIO
3081 Columbus Pike, Delaware 43015-0931 *Type:* Private (United Methodist) professional; graduate only *Accred.:* 1965/1987 (ATS); 1976/1988 (NCA) *Calendar:* Qtr. plan *Degrees:* P,M,D *CEO:* Pres. Norman E. Dewire
Enroll: 195 (614) 363-1146

MIAMI UNIVERSITY
Oxford 45056 *Type:* Public (state) *System:* Ohio Board of Regents *Accred.:* 1913/1985 (NCA) *Calendar:* Sem. plan *Degrees:* A, B, P, M, D, certificates, diplomas *Prof. Accred.:* Accounting (Type A,C), Architecture (M), Art, Business (B,M), Clinical Psychology, Engineering (manufacturing), Home Economics, Interior Design, Music, Nursing, Speech-Language Pathology, Teacher Education (e,s,p) *CEO:* Pres. Paul G. Pearson
Enroll: 18131 (513) 529-2345

HAMILTON CAMPUS
1601 Peck Boulevard, Hamilton, OH 45011 *Prof. Accred.:* Nursing (A) *CEO:* Exec. Dir. Harriet V. Taylor
(513) 863-8833

MIDDLETOWN CAMPUS
4200 E. University Blvd., Middletown, OH 45042 *Accred.:* 1913/1985 (NCA) *Prof. Accred.:* Nursing (A) *CEO:* Exec. Dir. Michael P. Governanti
(513) 424-4444

MIAMI-JACOBS JUNIOR COLLEGE OF BUSINESS
400 E. Second St., Post Office Box 1433, Dayton 45401 *Type:* Private junior *Accred.:* 1957/1985 (CCA-ACICS) *Calendar:* Qtr. plan *Degrees:* A *CEO:* Pres. Charles G. Campbell
Enroll: 1274 (513) 461-5174

THE MICHAEL J. OWENS TECHNICAL COLLEGE
30335 Oregon Rd., Toledo 43699 *Type:* Public (state) 2-year *System:* Ohio Board of Regents *Accred.:* 1976/1991 (NCA) *Calendar:* Sem. plan *Degrees:* A, certificates, diplomas *Prof. Accred.:* Dental Hygiene, Diagnostic Medical Sonography, Engineering Technology (civil/construction, electrical, mechanical, mechanical drafting/design), Nursing (A), Radiation Therapy Technology, Radiography, Surgical Technology *CEO:* Pres. Daniel H. Brown
Enroll: 4149 (419) 666-0580

BRANCH CAMPUS
300 Davis St., Findlay, OH 45840 *CEO:* Exec. Dir. Kathleen Brubaker
(419) 423-6827

MOUNT UNION COLLEGE
1972 Clark Ave., Alliance 44601 *Type:* Private (United Methodist) liberal arts *Accred.:* 1913/1982 (NCA) *Calendar:* Sem. plan *Degrees:* B, certificates, diplomas *Prof. Accred.:* Music *CEO:* Pres. Harold M. Kolenbrander
Enroll: 1383 (216) 821-5320

MOUNT VERNON NAZARENE COLLEGE
800 Martinsburg Rd., Mount Vernon 43050 *Type:* Private (Nazarene) liberal arts *Accred.:* 1972/1989 (NCA) *Calendar:* 4-1-4 plan *Degrees:* A, B *CEO:* Pres. E. LeBron Fairbanks
Enroll: 997 (614) 397-1244

MUSKINGUM AREA TECHNICAL COLLEGE
1555 Newark Rd., Zanesville 43701 *Type:* Public (state) 2-year *System:* Ohio Board of Regents *Accred.:* 1975/1988 (NCA) *Calendar:* Qtr. plan *Degrees:* A, certificates, diplomas *Prof. Accred.:* Engineering Technology (electrical), Medical Assisting (AMA), Medical Laboratory Technology (AMA), Occupational Therapy Assisting, Radiography *CEO:* Pres. Lynn H. Willett
Enroll: 1339   (614) 454-2501

MUSKINGUM COLLEGE
New Concord 43762 *Type:* Private (United Presbyterian) liberal arts *Accred.:* 1919/1983 (NCA) *Calendar:* Sem. plan *Degrees:* B, M *Prof. Accred.:* Music *CEO:* Pres. Samuel W. Speck, Jr.
Enroll: 1101   (614) 826-8115

NHAW HOME STUDY INSTITUTE
1389 Dublin Rd., P.O. Box 16790, Columbus 43216 *Type:* Private home study *Accred.:* 1969/1991 (NHSC) *Calendar:* Courses of varying lengths *Degrees:* diplomas *CEO:* Dir. James H. Healy
                (614) 488-1835

NATIONAL EDUCATION CENTER—NATIONAL INSTITUTE OF TECHNOLGY CAMPUS
1225 Orlen Ave., Cuyahoga Falls 44221-2955 *Type:* Private *Accred.:* 1969/1985 (CCA-ACTTS) *Calendar:* Qtr. plan *Degrees:* diplomas *CEO:* Dir. Donald Miller
Enroll: 1417   (216) 923-9959

NORTH CENTRAL TECHNICAL COLLEGE
2441 Kenwood Cir., P.O. Box 698, Mansfield 44901-0698 *Type:* Public (state) 2-year *System:* Ohio Board of Regents *Accred.:* 1976/1988 (NCA) *Calendar:* Qtr. plan *Degrees:* A, certificates, diplomas *Prof. Accred.:* Nursing (A), Radiography, Respiratory Therapy *CEO:* Pres. Byron E. Kee
Enroll: 1412   (419) 755-4800

NORTHEASTERN OHIO UNIVERSITIES COLLEGE OF MEDICINE
4209 State Rte. 44, P.O. Box 95, Rootstown 44272-0095 *Type:* Public (state) professional *System:* Ohio Board of Regents *Calendar:* Sem. plan *Degrees:* P *Prof. Accred.:* Medicine, Psychology Internship *CEO:* Pres./Dean Colin Campbell
Enroll: 420   (216) 325-2511

NORTHSHORE TECHNICAL INSTITUTE
8815 Broadway Ave., Cleveland 44105-5191 *Type:* Private *Accred.:* 1988 (CCA-ACTTS) *Calendar:* Courses of varying lengths *Degrees:* certificates *CEO:* Pres. Donald Georgian
                (216) 883-2800

NORTHWEST TECHNICAL COLLEGE
Rte. 1, Box 246-A, Archbold 43502 *Type:* Public (state) 2-year *System:* Ohio Board of Regents *Accred.:* 1977/1989 (NCA) *Calendar:* Qtr. plan *Degrees:* A, certificates, diplomas *Prof. Accred.:* Nursing (A) *CEO:* Pres. Larry G. McDougle
Enroll: 966   (419) 267-5511

NORTHWESTERN COLLEGE
1441 N. Cable Rd., Lima 45805 *Type:* Private *Accred.:* 1987/1991 (NCA) *Calendar:* Qtr. plan *Degrees:* A *CEO:* Pres. Loren R. Jarvis
Enroll: 1024   (419) 227-3141

NOTRE DAME COLLEGE
4545 College Rd., Cleveland 44121 *Type:* Private (Roman Catholic) liberal arts for women *Accred.:* 1931/1991 (NCA) *Calendar:* Sem. plan *Degrees:* A, B, certificates, diplomas *CEO:* Pres. Marla Loehr, S.N.D.
Enroll: 656   (216) 381-1680

OBERLIN COLLEGE
Oberlin 44074 *Type:* Private liberal arts *Accred.:* 1913/1988 (NCA) *Calendar:* 4-1-4 plan *Degrees:* B, M, certificates, diplomas *Prof. Accred.:* Music *CEO:* Pres. Frederick S. Starr
Enroll: 2820   (216) 775-8121

OHIO AUTO/DIESEL TECHNICAL INSTITUTE
1421 E. 49th St., Cleveland 44103-1269 *Type:* Private *Accred.:* 1973/1988 (CCA-ACTTS) *Calendar:* Courses of varying

lengths *Degrees:* certificates *CEO:* Pres. Marc L. Brenner
Enroll: 642 (216) 881-1700

OHIO COLLEGE OF PODIATRIC MEDICINE
10515 Carnegie Ave., Cleveland 44106 *Type:* Private professional *Accred.:* 1987 (NCA) *Calendar:* Sem. plan *Degrees:* D *Prof. Accred.:* Podiatry *CEO:* Pres. Thomas V. Melillo
Enroll: 330 (216) 231-3300

OHIO DOMINICAN COLLEGE
1216 Sunbury Rd., Columbus 43219 *Type:* Private (Roman Catholic) liberal arts *Accred.:* 1934/1988 (NCA) *Calendar:* Sem. plan *Degrees:* A, B, certificates, diplomas *CEO:* Pres. Mary A. Matesich, O.P.
Enroll: 1086 (614) 253-2741

OHIO INSTITUTE OF PHOTOGRAPHY
2029 Edgefield Rd., Dayton 45439-1984 *Type:* Private *Accred.:* 1976/1986 (CCA-ACTTS) *Calendar:* Sem. plan *Degrees:* A, diplomas *CEO:* Pres. Terry Guthrie
Enroll: 308 (513) 294-6155

OHIO NORTHERN UNIVERSITY
S. Main St., Ada 45810 *Type:* Private (United Methodist) *Accred.:* 1958/1985 (NCA) *Calendar:* Qtr. plan *Degrees:* B, D *Prof. Accred.:* Engineering (civil, electrical, mechanical), Law, Music, Pharmacy *CEO:* Pres. DeBow Freed
Enroll: 2600 (419) 772-2000

OHIO SCHOOL OF BROADCAST TECHNOLOGY
5500 S. Marginal Rd., Cleveland 44103-1098 *Type:* Private *Accred.:* 1991 (CCA-ACTTS) *Calendar:* Courses of varying lengths *Degrees:* certificates *CEO:* Dir. Marjorie Bush
 (216) 431-5500

OHIO STATE COLLEGE OF BARBER STYLING
4390 Karl Rd., Columbus 43224-1107 *Type:* Private *Accred.:* 1989 (CCA-ACTTS) *Calendar:* Courses of varying lengths *Degrees:* diplomas *CEO:* Mgr. Kelly Fraley
Enroll: 171 (614) 267-4247

OHIO STATE COLLEGE OF BARBER STYLING
4602 E. Main St., Columbus 43213-3028 *Type:* Private *Accred.:* 1977/1987 (CCA-ACTTS) *Calendar:* Courses of varying lengths *Degrees:* diplomas *CEO:* Mgr. David Sears
Enroll: 155 (614) 868-1011

OHIO STATE COLLEGE OF BARBER STYLING
329 Superior St., Toledo 43604-1421 *Type:* Private *Accred.:* 1983/1988 (CCA-ACTTS) *Calendar:* Courses of varying lengths *Degrees:* diplomas *CEO:* Pres. Roger Bradley
Enroll: 58 (419) 241-5618

THE OHIO STATE UNIVERSITY
Columbus 43210 *Type:* Public (state) *System:* Ohio Board of Regents *Accred.:* 1913/1987 (NCA) *Calendar:* Qtr. plan *Degrees:* A, B, P, M, D, certificates, diplomas *Prof. Accred.:* Accounting (Type A,B), Architecture (M), Art, Audiology, Business (B,M), Clinical Psychology, Community Health/Preventive Medicine, Combined Prosthodontics, Counseling Psychology, Dance, Dental Hygiene, Dentistry, Dietetics (coordinated), Endodontics, Engineering (aerospace, agricultural, ceramic, chemical, civil, electrical, industrial, mechanical, metallurgical, welding), General Dentistry, General Practice Residency, Health Services Administration, Journalism, Landscape Architecture (B,M), Law, Medical Record Administration, Medical Technology, Medicine, Music, Nuclear Medicine Technology, Nursing (B,M), Occupational Therapy, Optometry, Oral and Maxillofacial Surgery, Oral Pathology, Orthodontics, Pediatric Dentistry, Perfusion, Periodontics, Pharmacy, Physical Therapy, Planning (city/regional), Psychology Internship, Public Administration, Radiography, Rehabilitation Counseling, Respiratory Therapy, Social Work (B,M), Speech-Language Pathology, Teacher Education (e,s,p), Theatre *CEO:* Pres. E. Gordon Gee
Enroll: 52946 (614) 292-2424

AGRICULTURAL TECHNICAL INSTITUTE
1328 Dover Rd., Wooster, OH 44691
Accred.: 1913/1987 (NCA) *CEO:* Dir.
Dan D. Garrison
(216) 264-3911

LIMA CAMPUS
4240 Campus Dr., Lima, OH 45804 *CEO:*
Dean/Dir. Violette J. Meek
(419) 221-2641

MANSFIELD CAMPUS
1680 University Dr., Mansfield, OH
44906 *CEO:* Dean/Dir. John O. Riedl
(419) 755-4221

MARION CAMPUS
1465 Mount Vernon Ave., Marion, OH
43302 *CEO:* Dean/Dir. Francis E. Hazard
(614) 389-2361

NEWARK CAMPUS
University Dr., Newark, OH 43055 *CEO:*
Dean/Dir. Julius S. Greenstein
(614) 366-9333

OHIO UNIVERSITY
Athens 45701 *Type:* Public (state) *System:*
Ohio Board of Regents *Accred.:* 1913/1984
(NCA) *Calendar:* Qtr. plan *Degrees:* A, B,
P, M, D, certificates, diplomas *Prof.
Accred.:* Audiology, Business (B,M), Clinical Psychology, Counseling, Dance, Engineering (chemical, civil, electrical, industrial, mechanical), Home Economics, Interior
Design, Journalism, Music, Nursing (B),
Osteopathy, Physical Therapy, Rehabilitation Counseling, Social Work (B), Speech-Language Pathology, Teacher Education
(e,s,p) *CEO:* Pres. Charles J. Ping
Enroll: 18738   (614) 593-1000

BELMONT CAMPUS
5425 National Rd., St. Clairsville, OH
43950 *CEO:* Dean James W. Newton
(614) 695-1720

CHILLICOTHE CAMPUS
P.O. Box 629, Chillicothe, OH 45601-
0629 *CEO:* Dean Delbert E. Meyer
(614) 774-7221

LANCASTER CAMPUS
1570 Granville Pike, Lancaster, OH 43130
CEO: Dean Raymond S. Wilkes
(614) 654-6711

SOUTHERN CAMPUS
1701 S. Seventh St., Ironton, OH 45638
CEO: Dean Bill W. Dingus
(614) 533-4600

ZANESVILLE CAMPUS
1425 Newark Rd., Zanesville, OH 43701
Prof. Accred.: Nursing (A) *CEO:* Dean
Craig D. Laubenthal
(614) 453-0762

OHIO VALLEY BUSINESS COLLEGE
500 Maryland Ave., P.O. Box 7000, East
Liverpool 43920 *Type:* Private *Accred.:*
1985 (CCA-ACICS) *Calendar:* Courses of
varying lengths *Degrees:* A *Prof. Accred.:*
Medical Assisting (AMA) *CEO:* Dir. Debra
Sanford
Enroll: 266   (216) 385-1070

OHIO WESLEYAN UNIVERSITY
61 S. Sanusky St., Delaware 43015 *Type:*
Private (United Methodist) liberal arts
Accred.: 1913/1989 (NCA) *Calendar:* 4-1-4
plan *Degrees:* B *Prof. Accred.:* Music, Nursing (B) *CEO:* Pres. David L. Warren
Enroll: 2008   (614) 368-3000

OTTERBEIN COLLEGE
Westerville 43081 *Type:* Private (United
Methodist) liberal arts *Accred.:* 1913/1985
(NCA) *Calendar:* 3-3 plan *Degrees:* A, B,
M, certificates, diplomas *Prof. Accred.:*
Music, Nursing (A,B), Teacher Education
(e,s) *CEO:* Pres. C. Brent DeVore
Enroll: 2016   (614) 898-1656

PSI INSTITUTE
1858 Euclid Ave., Cleveland 44115-2209
Type: Private *Accred.:* 1985 (CCA-ACTTS)
Calendar: Courses of varying lengths *Degrees:* diplomas *CEO:* Pres. Clifford L.
Scheer
Enroll: 798   (216) 771-6680

PSI INSTITUTE
340 E. Broad St., Columbus 43215-3249 *Type:* Private *Accred.:* 1991 (CCA-ACTTS) *Calendar:* Courses of varying lengths *Degrees:* diplomas *CEO:* Dir. David McGuire
(614) 224-3000

PTC CAREER INSTITUTE
1140 Euclid Ave., Cleveland 44115 *Type:* Private *Accred.:* 1991 (CCA-ACTTS) *Calendar:* Courses of varying lengths *Degrees:* certificates *CEO:* Dir. Richard Mills
(216) 575-1100

PENN-OHIO COLLEGE
3517 Market St., Youngstown 44507 *Type:* Private business *Accred.:* 1971/1989 (CCA-ACICS) *Calendar:* Sem. plan *Degrees:* certificates, diplomas *CEO:* Pres. William M. Clark, Jr.
Enroll: 227 (216) 788-5084

PONTIFICAL COLLEGE JOSEPHINUM
7625 N. High St., Columbus 43235 *Type:* Private (Roman Catholic) liberal arts and professional *Accred.:* 1970/1981 (ATS); 1977/1991 (NCA) *Calendar:* Sem. plan *Degrees:* B, P, M *CEO:* Pres./Rector Blase J. Cupich
Enroll: 133 (614) 885-5585

PROFESSIONAL SKILLS INSTITUTE
1232 Flaire Dr., Toledo 43615 *Type:* Private *Calendar:* Courses of varying lengths *Degrees:* certificates, diplomas *Prof. Accred.:* Health Education *CEO:* Dir. Patricia A. Finch
Enroll: 80 (419) 531-9610

PROGRESSIVE FASHION SCHOOL
2012 W. 25th St., Room 612, Cleveland 44113-4131 *Type:* Private *Accred.:* 1977/1987 (CCA-ACTTS) *Calendar:* Courses of varying lengths *Degrees:* certificates, diplomas *CEO:* Dir. Jean Dunn Salata
Enroll: 88 (216) 781-4595

R.E.T.S. INSTITUTE OF TECHNOLOGY
1606 W. Laskey Rd., Toledo 43612-2916 *Type:* Private *Accred.:* 1973/1985 (CCA-ACTTS) *Calendar:* Qtr. plan *Degrees:* certificates, diplomas *CEO:* Pres. Kevin Lambert
Enroll: 433 (419) 489-7387

R.E.T.S. TECH CENTER
P.O. Box 130, Centerville 45459-6120 *Type:* Private *Accred.:* 1974/1989 (CCA-ACTTS) *Calendar:* Qtr. plan *Degrees:* A, certificates *CEO:* Pres. Michael A. LeMaster
Enroll: 946 (513) 433-3410

RABBINICAL COLLEGE OF TELSHE
28400 Euclid Ave., Wickliffe 44092-2523 *Type:* Private professional *Accred.:* 1974/1989 (AARTS) *Calendar:* Sem. plan *Degrees:* M, D *CEO:* Pres. M. Gifter
Enroll: 220 (216) 943-5300

RAEDEL COLLEGE AND INDUSTRIAL WELDING SCHOOL
137 Sixth St., N.E., Canton 44702 *Type:* Private business *Accred.:* 1986 (CCA-ACICS) *Calendar:* Courses of varying length *Degrees:* certificates, diplomas *CEO:* Dir. Fred G. Holloway
Enroll: 186 (216) 454-9006

ROFFLER HAIR DESIGN COLLEGE
1440 Whipple Ave., Canton 44708 *Type:* Private *Accred.:* 1991 (CCA-ACTTS) *Calendar:* Courses of varying lengths *Degrees:* certificates *CEO:* Dir. Frank Ferren
(216) 477-6695

ST. MARY SEMINARY
1227 Ansel Rd., Cleveland 44108 *Type:* Private (Roman Catholic) professional; graduate only *Accred.:* 1970/1985 (ATS); 1981/1986 (NCA) *Calendar:* Qtr. plan *Degrees:* P, M *CEO:* Pres./Rector Allan R. Laubenthal
Enroll: 46 (216) 721-2100

SAWYER COLLEGE OF BUSINESS
13027 Lorain Ave., Cleveland 44111 *Type:* Private business *Accred.:* 1979/1988 (CCA-ACICS) *Calendar:* Qtr. plan *Degrees:* A, certificates, diplomas *CEO:* Dir. Betty Gray
Enroll: 287 (216) 941-7666

SAWYER COLLEGE OF BUSINESS
3150 Mayfield Rd., Cleveland Heights 44118 *Type:* Private business *Accred.:* 1973/1985 (CCA-ACICS) *Calendar:* Qtr. plan *Degrees:* A, certificates, diplomas *CEO:* Pres. Bruce T. Shields
Enroll: 647 (216) 932-0911

SCHOOL OF ADVERTISING ART
2900 Acosta St., Kettering 45420-3467 *Type:* Private *Accred.:* 1988 (CCA-ACTTS) *Calendar:* Courses of varying lengths *Degrees:* certificates *CEO:* Mgr. Terry Wilson
(513) 294-0592

SHAWNEE STATE UNIVERSITY
940 Second St., Portsmouth 45662 *Type:* Public (state) 2-year *System:* Ohio Board of Regents *Accred.:* 1975/1983 (NCA) *Calendar:* Qtr. plan *Degrees:* A, B, certificates, diplomas *Prof. Accred.:* Dental Hygiene, Medical Laboratory Technology (AMA), Occupational Therapy Assisting, Physical Therapy Assisting, Radiography, Respiratory Therapy *CEO:* Pres. Clive C. Veri
Enroll: 2431 (614) 355-2202

SINCLAIR COMMUNITY COLLEGE
444 W. Third St., Dayton 45402 *Type:* Public (district) 2-year *System:* Ohio Board of Regents *Accred.:* 1970/1988 (NCA) *Calendar:* Qtr. plan *Degrees:* A, certificates, diplomas *Prof. Accred.:* Dental Hygiene, Engineering Technology (electrical, industrial, mechanical), Medical Record Technology, Nursing (A), Occupational Therapy Assisting, Physical Therapy Assisting, Radiography, Respiratory Therapy, Surgical Technology *CEO:* Pres. David H. Ponitz
Enroll: 8723 (513) 226-2525

SOUTHEASTERN BUSINESS COLLEGE
1855 Western Ave., Chillicothe 45601 *Type:* Private business *Accred.:* 1976/1988 (CCA-ACICS) *Calendar:* Courses of varying lengths *Degrees:* A *CEO:* Exec. Dir. John T. Danicki
Enroll: 302 (614) 774-6300

BRANCH CAMPUS
420 E. Main St., Jackson, OH 45640 *CEO:* Dir. Zora Minor
(614) 286-1554

BRANCH CAMPUS
1522 Sheridan Dr., Lancaster, OH 43130 *CEO:* Dir. Alex Bosserman
(614) 687-6126

BRANCH CAMPUS
3879 Rhodes Ave., New Boston, OH 45662 *CEO:* Dir. Anita Thompson
(614) 456-4124

BRANCH CAMPUS
10 W. Broadway, Wellston, OH 45692 *CEO:* Dir. Ronaye Collins
(614) 384-2164

SOUTHEASTERN BUSINESS COLLEGE
529 Jackson Pike, Ste. 312, Gallipolis 45631 *Type:* Private business *Accred.:* 1983/1989 (CCA-ACICS) *Calendar:* Courses of varying lengths *Degrees:* A *CEO:* Dir. Teresa Whittington
Enroll: 196 (614) 446-4367

SOUTHERN OHIO COLLEGE
1055 Laidlaw Ave., Cincinnati 45237 *Type:* Private junior *Accred.:* 1964/1984 (CCA-ACICS); 1983/1986 (NCA) *Calendar:* Qtr. plan *Degrees:* A, certificates, diplomas *Prof. Accred.:* Medical Assisting (AMA) *CEO:* Pres. Ronald A. Rountree
Enroll: 1907 (513) 242-3791

NORTHERN KENTUCKY CAMPUS
309 Buttermilk Pike, Fort Mitchell, KY 41017 *CEO:* Dir. Don Underwood
(606) 341-5627

BRANCH CAMPUS
2791 Mogadore Rd., Akron, OH 44312 *Prof. Accred.:* Medical Assisting (AMA) *CEO:* Dir. Richard M. Thome
(216) 733-8766

Ohio

BRANCH CAMPUS
4641 Bacher La., Fairfield, OH 45014 *Prof. Accred.:* Medical Assisting (AMA) *CEO:* Dir. Burton Lipson
(513) 829-7100

SOUTHERN OHIO COLLEGE
4430 State Rd., Cleveland 44109 *Type:* Private business *Accred.:* 1983 (CCA-ACTTS) *Calendar:* Courses of varying lengths *Degrees:* certificates, diplomas *CEO:* Dir. Joseph C. Servick
(216) 661-4300

SOUTHERN OHIO COLLEGE
979 S. James Rd., Columbus 43227 *Type:* Private business *Accred.:* 1981 (CCA-ACTTS) *Calendar:* Courses of varying lengths *Degrees:* certificates, diplomas *CEO:* Dir. Susan Stella
(614) 231-8888

SOUTHERN STATE COMMUNITY COLLEGE
200 Hobart Dr., Hillsboro 45133 *Type:* Public (state) 2-year *System:* Ohio Board of Regents *Accred.:* 1981/1991 (NCA) *Calendar:* Qtr. plan *Degrees:* A, certificates, diplomas *Prof. Accred.:* Nursing (A) *CEO:* Pres. George R. McCormick
Enroll: 1006   (513) 393-3431

SOUTHWESTERN COLLEGE OF BUSINESS
225 W. First St., Dayton 45402 *Type:* Private business *Accred.:* 1973/1987 (CCA-ACICS) *Calendar:* Qtr. plan *Degrees:* A, certificates, diplomas *Prof. Accred.:* Medical Assisting *CEO:* Dir. Joan Koffenberger
Enroll: 772   (513) 224-0061

BRANCH CAMPUS
2929 S. Dixie Hwy., Crestview Hills, KY 41017 *Type:* Private. *Prof. Accred.:* Medical Assisting *CEO:* Dir. William Bradford
(606) 341-6633

BRANCH CAMPUS
717 Race St., Cincinnati, OH 45202 *Prof. Accred.:* Medical Assisting *CEO:* Dir. Clara Smith
(513) 421-3212

BRANCH CAMPUS
9910 Princeton-Glendale Rd., Cincinnati, OH 45246 *Prof. Accred.:* Medical Assisting *CEO:* Dir. Susan Hatfield
(513) 874-0432

BRANCH CAMPUS
631 S. Breiel Blvd., Middletown, OH 45044 *Prof. Accred.:* Medical Assisting *CEO:* Dir. Sharon Winstead
(513) 423-3346

STARK TECHNICAL COLLEGE
6200 Frank Ave., N.W., Canton 44720 *Type:* Public (state) 2-year *System:* Ohio Board of Regents *Accred.:* 1976/1991 (NCA) *Calendar:* Qtr. plan *Degrees:* A, certificates, diplomas *Prof. Accred.:* Engineering Technology (civil/construction, electrical, mechanical, mechanical drafting/design), Medical Assisting (AMA), Medical Laboratory Technology (AMA), Medical Record Technology, Occupational Therapy Assisting, Physical Therapy Assisting, Respiratory Therapy, Respiratory Therapy Technology *CEO:* Pres. John J. McGrath, Jr.
Enroll: 2423   (216) 494-6170

STAUTZENBERGER COLLEGE
1637 Tiffin Ave., Findlay 54840 *Type:* Private business *Accred.:* 1986/1989 (CCA-ACICS) *Calendar:* Courses of varying lengths *Degrees:* A, certificates, diplomas *Prof. Accred.:* Medical Assisting *CEO:* Dir. Craig Burnside
Enroll: 1031   (419) 423-2211

STAUTZENBERGER COLLEGE
5355 Southwyck Blvd., Toledo 43614 *Type:* Private business *Accred.:* 1962/1986 (CCA-ACICS) *Calendar:* Courses of varying lengths *Degrees:* diplomas *Prof. Accred.:* Medical Assisting *CEO:* Dir. Charles Hawes
Enroll: 1041   (419) 866-0261

STAUTZENBERGER COLLEGE—CENTRAL
1946 N. 13th St., Ste. 292, Toledo 43624 *Type:* Private business *Accred.:* 1987/1989 (CCA-ACICS) *Calendar:* Courses of varying lengths *Degrees:* A, certificates, diplo-

mas *Prof. Accred.:* Medical Assisting *CEO:* Dir. Sharon McDonald-Sims
Enroll: 655 (419) 248-3764

STAUTZENBERGER COLLEGE—EAST
4615 Woodville Rd., Toledo 43619 *Type:* Private business *Accred.:* 1984/1988 (CCA-ACICS) *Calendar:* Courses of varying lengths *Degrees:* A, certificates, diplomas *Prof. Accred.:* Medical Assisting *CEO:* Dir. Connie Buhr
Enroll: 374 (419) 693-9311

STAUTZENBERGER COLLEGE—WEST
4404 Secor Rd., Toledo 43623 *Type:* Private business *Accred.:* 1982/1988 (CCA-ACICS) *Calendar:* Courses of varying lengths *Degrees:* A, certificates, diplomas *Prof. Accred.:* Medical Assisting *CEO:* Dir. Larry Mitchell
Enroll: 1050 (419) 472-2115

TDDS
1688 N. Princetown Rd., Diamond 44412-9608 *Type:* Private *Accred.:* 1991 (CCA-ACTTS) *Calendar:* Courses of varying lengths *Degrees:* certificates *CEO:* Pres. Richard Rathburn
(216) 538-2216

TECHNOLOGY EDUCATION CENTER
288 S. Hamilton Rd., Columbus 43213-2087 *Type:* Private *Accred.:* 1980/1991 (CCA-ACTTS) *Calendar:* Courses of varying lengths *Degrees:* certificates *CEO:* Pres. Ronald H. Dooley
(614) 759-7700

TERRA TECHNICAL COLLEGE
2830 Napoleon Rd., Fremont 43420-9670 *Type:* Public (state) 2-year *System:* Ohio Board of Regents *Accred.:* 1975/1987 (NCA) *Calendar:* Qtr. plan *Degrees:* A, certificates, diplomas *CEO:* Pres. Richard M. Simon
Enroll: 1538 (419) 334-8400

TIFFIN UNIVERSITY
155 Miami St., Tiffin 44883 *Type:* Private *Accred.:* 1985/1990 (NCA) *Calendar:* Sem. plan *Degrees:* A, B, M, certificates, diplomas *CEO:* Pres. George Kidd, Jr.
Enroll: 693 (419) 447-6442

TOTAL TECHNICAL INSTITUTE
13505 W. 130th St., North Royalton 44133-4240 *Type:* Private *Accred.:* 1985 (CCA-ACTTS) *Calendar:* Courses of varying lengths *Degrees:* certificates *CEO:* Dir. David Mondi
Enroll: 841 (216) 237-0288

TRINITY LUTHERAN SEMINARY
2199 E. Main St., Columbus 43209 *Type:* Private (Lutheran) professional; graduate only *Accred.:* 1940/1982 (ATS); 1974/1982 (NCA) *Calendar:* Sem. plan *Degrees:* B, P, M, D *CEO:* Pres. Dennis A. Anderson
Enroll: 200 (614) 235-4136

TRUMBULL BUSINESS COLLEGE
3200 Ridge Rd., Warren 44484 *Type:* Private business *Accred.:* 1976/1988 (CCA-ACICS) *Calendar:* Courses of varying lengths *Degrees:* A, certificates, diplomas *CEO:* Pres. Dennis R. Griffith
Enroll: 282 (216) 369-3200

UNION INSTITUTE
440 E. McMillan St., Cincinnati 45206-1947 *Type:* Private *Accred.:* 1985/1990 (NCA) *Calendar:* Qtr. plan *Degrees:* B, D *CEO:* Pres. Robert T. Conley
Enroll: 1150 (513) 861-6400

UNITED THEOLOGICAL SEMINARY
1810 Harvard Blvd., Dayton 45406 *Type:* Private (United Methodist) professional; graduate only *Accred.:* 1938/1990 (ATS); 1975/1991 (NCA) *Calendar:* 4-1-4 plan *Degrees:* P, M, D *CEO:* Pres. Leonard I. Sweet
Enroll: 328 (513) 278-5817

THE UNIVERSITY OF AKRON
302 E. Buchtel Ave., Akron 44325 *Type:* Public (state) *System:* Ohio Board of Regents *Accred.:* 1914/1987 (NCA) *Calendar:* Sem. plan *Degrees:* A, B, P, M, D, certificates, diplomas *Prof. Accred.:* Accounting (Type A,B), Art, Audiology, Business (B,M), Clinical Psychology, Counseling,

Counseling Psychology, Dance, Dietetics (coordinated), Engineering (chemical, civil, electrical, mechanical), Engineering Technology (civil/construction, electrical, mechanical, surveying), Home Economics, Law, Medical Assisting (AMA), Music, Nursing (B,M), Respiratory Therapy, Social Work (B), Speech-Language Pathology, Surgical Technology, Teacher Education (e,s,p), Urban Studies and Public Administration *CEO:* Pres. William V. Muse
Enroll: 20341 (216) 972-7074

WAYNE COLLEGE
10470 Smucker Rd., Orrville, OH 44667 *Accred.:* 1914/1987 (NCA) *CEO:* Dean Tyrone M. Turning
(216) 683-2010

UNIVERSITY OF CINCINNATI
2624 Clifton Ave., Cincinnati 45221 *Type:* Public (state) *System:* Ohio Board of Regents *Accred.:* 1913/1989 (NCA) *Calendar:* Qtr. plan *Degrees:* A, B, P, M, D, certificates, diplomas *Prof. Accred.:* Architecture (B), Art, Audiology, Blood Bank Technology, Business (B,M), Clinical Psychology, Construction Education, Engineering (aerospace, chemical, civil, computer, electrical, engineering mechanics, environmental/sanitary, industrial, mechanical, metallurgical, nuclear), Interior Design, Law, Medical Technology, Music, Nuclear Medicine Technology, Nursing (B,M), Pharmacy, Physical Therapy Assisting, Planning (community/urban), Psychology Internship, School Psychology, Social Work (B,M), Speech-Language Pathology, Teacher Education (e,s,p) *CEO:* Pres. Joseph A. Steger
Enroll: 26707 (513) 556-2201

CLERMONT COLLEGE
725 College Dr., Batavia, OH 45103 *Accred.:* 1913/1989 (NCA) *CEO:* Acting Dean George A. Wolff
(513) 732-5200

OMI COLLEGE OF APPLIED SCIENCE
2220 Victory Pkwy., Cincinnati, OH 45206 *Prof. Accred.:* Engineering Technology (architectural, chemical, civil/construction, electrical, manufacturing, mechanical) *CEO:* Dean Fritz J. Krynan
(513) 556-6000

RAYMOND WALTERS COLLEGE
9555 Plainfield Rd., Cincinnati, OH 45236 *Accred.:* 1913/1989 (NCA) *Prof. Accred.:* Animal Health Technology, Dental Hygiene, Medicine, Nursing (A), Radiation Therapy Technology, Radiography *CEO:* Dean Neal A. Raisman
(513) 745-5661

UNIVERSITY OF DAYTON
300 College Park Ave., Dayton 45469 *Type:* Private (Roman Catholic) *Accred.:* 1928/1988 (NCA) *Calendar:* Tri. plan *Degrees:* A, B, M, D, certificates, diplomas *Prof. Accred.:* Business (B,M), Engineering (chemical, civil, electrical, mechanical), Engineering Technology (electrical, industrial, mechanical), Law, Medical Technology, Music, Social Work (B), Teacher Education (e,s,p) *CEO:* Pres. Raymond L. Fitz, S.M.
Enroll: 9423 (513) 229-4122

THE UNIVERSITY OF FINDLAY
1000 N. Main St., Findlay 45840 *Type:* Private (Churches of God) liberal arts *Accred.:* 1933/1984 (NCA) *Calendar:* Sem. plan *Degrees:* A, B, M *Prof. Accred.:* Nuclear Medicine Technology, Teacher Education (e,s) *CEO:* Pres. Kenneth E. Zirkle
Enroll: 1779 (419) 422-8313

UNIVERSITY OF RIO GRANDE
Rio Grande 45674 *Type:* Private liberal arts *Accred.:* 1969/1988 (NCA) *Calendar:* Qtr. plan *Degrees:* A, B, M, certificates, diplomas *Prof. Accred.:* Medical Laboratory Technology (AMA), Nursing (A), Social Work (B-candidate) *CEO:* Pres. Barry M. Dorsey
Enroll: 1639 (614) 245-5353

UNIVERSITY OF TOLEDO
2801 W. Bancroft St., Toledo 43606 *Type:* Public (state) *System:* Ohio Board of Regents *Accred.:* 1922/1983 (NCA) *Calen-*

dar: Qtr. plan *Degrees:* A, B, P, M, D, certificates, diplomas *Prof. Accred.:* Business (B,M), Clinical Psychology, Counseling, Engineering (chemical, civil, computer, electrical, engineering physics/science, industrial, mechanical), Engineering Technology (civil/construction, electrical, industrial, mechanical, mechanical drafting/design), Law, Medical Assisting (AMA), Music, Nursing (A,B), Pharmacy, Public Administration, Respiratory Therapy, Social Work (B), Teacher Education (e,s,p) *CEO:* Pres. Frank E. Horton
Enroll: 18851 (419) 537-2211

URBANA UNIVERSITY
One College Way, Urbana 43078 *Type:* Private (Swedenborgian) liberal arts *Accred.:* 1975/1991 (NCA) *Calendar:* Sem. plan *Degrees:* A, B *CEO:* Acting Pres. Harold Dickerscheid
Enroll: 669 (513) 652-1301

URSULINE COLLEGE
2550 Lander Rd., Pepper Pike 44124 *Type:* Private (Roman Catholic) liberal arts primarily for women *Accred.:* 1931/1981 (NCA) *Calendar:* Sem. plan *Degrees:* A, B, M, certificates, diplomas *Prof. Accred.:* Nursing (B) *CEO:* Pres. Anne Marie Diederich, O.S.U.
Enroll: 1194 (216) 449-4200

VIRGINIA MARTI SCHOOL OF FASHION AND ART
P.O. Box 580, Lakewood 44107-3002 *Type:* Private *Accred.:* 1975/1985 (CCA-ACTTS) *Calendar:* Courses of varying lengths *Degrees:* A, certificates, diplomas *CEO:* Dir. Virginia Marti
Enroll: 378 (216) 221-8584

WALSH COLLEGE
2020 Easton St., N.W., Canton 44720 *Type:* Private (Roman Catholic) liberal arts *Accred.:* 1970/1990 (NCA) *Calendar:* Sem. plan *Degrees:* A, B, M *Prof. Accred.:* Nursing (A,B) *CEO:* Pres. Francis Blouin
Enroll: 1275 (216) 499-7090

WASHINGTON STATE COMMUNITY COLLEGE
710 Colegate Dr., Marietta 45750 *Type:* Public (state) 2-year *System:* Ohio Board of Regents *Accred.:* 1979/1987 (NCA) *Calendar:* Qtr. plan *Degrees:* A, certificates, diplomas *Prof. Accred.:* Medical Laboratory Technology (AMA) *CEO:* Pres. Carson K. Miller
Enroll: 1080 (614) 374-8716

WEST SIDE INSTITUTE OF TECHNOLOGY
9801 Walford Ave., Cleveland 44102-4758 *Type:* Private *Accred.:* 1969/1988 (CCA-ACTTS) *Calendar:* Qtr. plan *Degrees:* A, certificates *CEO:* Dir. Richard R. Pountney
Enroll: 980 (216) 651-1656

WILBERFORCE UNIVERSITY
Wilberforce 45384 *Type:* Private (African Methodist Episcopal) liberal arts *Accred.:* 1939/1988 (NCA) *Calendar:* Tri. plan *Degrees:* B *CEO:* Pres. John L. Henderson
Enroll: 809 (513) 376-2911

WILMINGTON COLLEGE
P.O. Box 1185, Wilmington 45177 *Type:* Private (Friends) liberal arts *Accred.:* 1944/1988 (NCA) *Calendar:* Qtr. plan *Degrees:* A, B *CEO:* Pres. Neil A. Thorburn
Enroll: 1602 (513) 382-6661

WINEBRENNER THEOLOGICAL SEMINARY
701 E. Melrose Ave., P.O. Box 478, Findlay 45839 *Type:* Private (Churches of God) professional; graduate only *Accred.:* 1991 (ATS); 1986/1991 (NCA) *Calendar:* Sem. plan *Degrees:* P, M *CEO:* Pres. David E. Draper
Enroll: 29 (419) 422-4824

WITTENBERG UNIVERSITY
P.O. Box 720, Springfield 45501 *Type:* Private (Lutheran) *Accred.:* 1916/1987 (NCA) *Calendar:* 3-3 plan *Degrees:* B, certificates, diplomas *Prof. Accred.:* Music, Teacher Education (e,s) *CEO:* Pres. William Andrew Kinnison
Enroll: 2337 (513) 327-7916

Ohio

WOOSTER BUSINESS COLLEGE
11610 Euclid Ave., Cleveland 44106 *Type:* Private business *Accred.:* 1986/1990 (CCA-ACICS) *Calendar:* Courses of varying lengths *Degrees:* certificates, diplomas *CEO:* Dir. Phillip Drummond
Enroll: 1076 (216) 231-0000

WOOSTER BUSINESS COLLEGE
201 E. Liberty St., Wooster 44691 *Type:* Private business *Accred.:* 1986 (CCA-ACICS) *Calendar:* Courses of varying lengths *Degrees:* A *Prof. Accred.:* Medical Assisting (AMA) *CEO:* Dir. Richard T. Winner
Enroll: 291 (216) 264-4110

BRANCH CAMPUS
39 E. Market St., Akron, OH 44308 *CEO:* Dir. Rahmat O. Tavallali
(216) 434-0000

BRANCH CAMPUS
480 W. Tuscarawas Ave., Barberton, OH 44203 *CEO:* Dir. Farokh Rahimi
(216) 848-5000

BRANCH CAMPUS
14693 Lorain Ave., Cleveland, OH 44111 *CEO:* Dir. Chuck Catley
(216) 252-0000

WRIGHT STATE UNIVERSITY
9035 Colonel Glenn Hwy., Dayton 45435 *Type:* Public (state) *System:* Ohio Board of Regents *Accred.:* 1968/1986 (NCA) *Calendar:* Qtr. plan *Degrees:* A, B, P, M, D, certificates, diplomas *Prof. Accred.:* Rehabilitation Counseling (prelim.) *CEO:* Pres. Paige E. Mulhollan
Enroll: 12724 (513) 873-2312

LAKE CAMPUS
7600 State Rte. 703, Celina, OH 45822 *CEO:* Dean Donald A. Carlson
(419) 586-2365

XAVIER UNIVERSITY
3800 Victory Pkwy., Cincinnati 45207 *Type:* Private (Roman Catholic) *Accred.:* 1925/1989 (NCA) *Calendar:* Sem. plan *Degrees:* A, B, M *Prof. Accred.:* Health Services Administration, Nursing (B), Radiography, Social Work (B) *CEO:* Pres. James E. Hoff, S.J.
Enroll: 4489 (513) 745-3500

YOUNGSTOWN STATE UNIVERSITY
410 Wick Ave., Youngstown 44555 *Type:* Public (state) *System:* Ohio Board of Regents *Accred.:* 1945/1988 (NCA) *Calendar:* Qtr. plan *Degrees:* A, B, M, certificates, diplomas *Prof. Accred.:* Counseling, Dental Hygiene, Dietetics (coordinated), EMT-Paramedic, Engineering (chemical, civil, electrical, industrial, mechanical), Engineering Technology (civil/construction, electrical, mechanical), Medical Laboratory Technology (AMA), Music, Nursing (B), Respiratory Therapy, Social Work (B-candidate), Teacher Education (e,s,p) *CEO:* Pres. Neil D. Humphrey
Enroll: 11305 (216) 742-3101

OKLAHOMA

AAA WELDING SCHOOL
9363 E. 46th St., S., Tulsa 74145 *Type:* Private *Accred.:* 1982/1987 (CCA-ACTTS) *Calendar:* Courses of varying lengths *Degrees:* certificates *CEO:* Vice Pres. Frances A. Sells
Enroll: 99 (918) 627-2699

ACADEMY OF HAIR DESIGN
4320 S. Sunny La., P.O. Box 15157, Del City 73115 *Type:* Private *Accred.:* 1981/1986 (CCA-ACTTS) *Calendar:* Sem. plan *Degrees:* certificates, diplomas *CEO:* Pres. Gene Beavers
Enroll: 44 (405) 677-8311

AMERICAN COLLEGE
412 Summit Ave., P.O. Box 1007, Lawton 73502 *Type:* Private *Accred.:* 1988 (CCA-ACTTS) *Calendar:* Courses of varying lengths *Degrees:* certificates *CEO:* Dir. James P. Giles
Enroll: 273 (405) 357-7295

BACONE COLLEGE
99 Bacone Rd., Muskogee 74403-1597 *Type:* Private (Baptist) junior *Accred.:* 1965/1989 (NCA) *Calendar:* Sem. plan *Degrees:* A, certificates, diplomas *Prof. Accred.:* Nursing (A), Radiography *CEO:* Pres. Dennis Tanner
Enroll: 505 (918) 683-4581

BARTLESVILLE WESLEYAN COLLEGE
2201 Silver Lake Rd., Bartlesville 74006 *Type:* Private (Wesleyan) liberal arts *Accred.:* 1978/1991 (NCA) *Calendar:* Sem. plan *Degrees:* A, B, certificates, diplomas *CEO:* Pres. Paul R. Mills
Enroll: 411 (918) 333-6234

BRYAN INSTITUTE
2843 E. 51st St., Tulsa 74105 *Type:* Private *Accred.:* 1974/1989 (CCA-ACTTS) *Calendar:* Courses of varying lengths *Degrees:* diplomas *Prof. Accred.:* Medical Assisting *CEO:* Dir. Ed Gough
Enroll: 621 (918) 749-6891

CAMERON UNIVERSITY
2800 Gore Blvd., Lawton 73505 *Type:* Public (state) liberal arts and professional *System:* Oklahoma State Regents for Higher Education *Accred.:* 1973/1991 (NCA) *Calendar:* Sem. plan *Degrees:* A, B *Prof. Accred.:* Music, Nursing (A), Teacher Education (e,s,p) *CEO:* Pres. Don Davis
Enroll: 3730 (405) 581-2201

CARL ALBERT STATE COLLEGE
1507 S. McKenna, Poteau 74953-5208 *Type:* Public (state) junior *System:* Oklahoma State Regents for Higher Education *Accred.:* 1978/1983 (NCA) *Calendar:* Sem. plan *Degrees:* A, certificates, diplomas *Prof. Accred.:* Nursing (A) *CEO:* Pres. Joe E. White
Enroll: 1001 (918) 647-8660

CENTRAL OKLAHOMA AREA VOCATIONAL-TECHNICAL CENTER
3 CVT Cir., Drumright 74030 *Type:* Private *Calendar:* Courses of varying lengths *Degrees:* certificates *Prof. Accred.:* Practical Nursing *CEO:* Supt. John Hopper
(918) 352-2551

CLIMATE CONTROL INSTITUTE
708 S. Sheridan Rd., Tulsa 74112 *Type:* Private *Accred.:* 1978/1988 (CCA-ACTTS) *Calendar:* Qtr. plan *Degrees:* certificates *CEO:* Dir. Sue Kloehr
Enroll: 302 (918) 836-6656

CONNORS STATE COLLEGE
Rte. 1, Box 1000, Warner 74469 *Type:* Public (state) junior *System:* Oklahoma State Regents for Higher Education *Accred.:* 1963/1990 (NCA) *Calendar:* Sem. plan *Degrees:* A, certificates, diplomas *Prof. Accred.:* Nursing (A) *CEO:* Pres. Carl O. Westbrook
Enroll: 1469 (918) 463-2931

DRAUGHON COLLEGE
9301 S. Western Ave., Oklahoma City 73139 *Type:* Private business *Accred.:* 1960/

Oklahoma

1986 (CCA-ACICS) *Calendar:* Qtr. plan *Degrees:* certificates, diplomas *CEO:* Dir. Anita Bates
Enroll: 1754 (405) 682-2900

BRANCH CAMPUS
6202 S. Lewis Pl., Ste. 111, Tulsa, OK 74136 *CEO:* Dir. Ron Horne
(918) 749-7700

EAST CENTRAL UNIVERSITY
Ada 74820 *Type:* Public (state) liberal arts and teachers *System:* Oklahoma State Regents for Higher Education *Accred.:* 1922/1982 (NCA) *Calendar:* Sem. plan *Degrees:* B, M, certificates, diplomas *Prof. Accred.:* Medical Record Administration, Nursing (B), Social Work (B), Teacher Education (e,s) *CEO:* Pres. Bill S. Cole
Enroll: 3407 (405) 332-8000

EASTERN OKLAHOMA STATE COLLEGE
1301 W. Main St., Wilburton 74578 *Type:* Public (state) junior *System:* Oklahoma State Regents for Higher Education *Accred.:* 1954/1986 (NCA) *Calendar:* Sem. plan *Degrees:* A, certificates, diplomas *Prof. Accred.:* Nursing (A) *CEO:* Pres. Bill H. Hill
Enroll: 1707 (918) 465-2361

ENID BARBER STYLING COLLEGE
230 W. Broadway, Enid 73701 *Type:* Private *Accred.:* 1988 (CCA-ACTTS) *Calendar:* Courses of varying lengths *Degrees:* certificates *CEO:* Dir. Abe Preston
Enroll: 15 (405) 234-9133

FLAMING RAINBOW UNIVERSITY
419 N. Second St., Stilwell 74960 *Type:* Private *Accred.:* 1985/1990 (NCA probational) *Calendar:* Sem. plan *Degrees:* B *CEO:* Pres. George Poolaw
Enroll: 83 (918) 696-3644

FRANCIS TUTTLE VOCATIONAL-TECHNICAL CENTER
12777 N. Rockwell Ave., Oklahoma City 73142 *Type:* Private *Calendar:* Courses of varying lengths *Degrees:* certificates *Prof. Accred.:* Practical Nursing, Respiratory Therapy Technology *CEO:* Supt. Bruce Gray
(405) 722-7799

GREAT PLAINS AREA VOCATIONAL-TECHNICAL CENTER
4500 W. Lee Blvd., Lawton 73505 *Type:* Private *Calendar:* Courses of varying lengths *Degrees:* certificates *Prof. Accred.:* Practical Nursing, Radiography, Surgical Technology *CEO:* Supt. Kenneth Bridges
(405) 355-6371

INDIAN MERIDIAN VOCATIONAL-TECHNICAL CENTER
1312 S. Sangre St., Stillwater 74074 *Type:* Private *Calendar:* Courses of varying lengths *Degrees:* certificates *Prof. Accred.:* Radiography *CEO:* Supt. Fred A. Shultz
(405) 377-3333

LANGSTON UNIVERSITY
P.O. Box 907, Langston 73050-0907 *Type:* Public (state) liberal arts and professional *System:* Oklahoma State Regents for Higher Education *Accred.:* 1948/1988 (NCA) *Calendar:* Sem. plan *Degrees:* B, M *Prof. Accred.:* Nursing (B), Physical Therapy, Teacher Education (e,s) *CEO:* Pres. Ernest L. Holloway
Enroll: 2067 (405) 466-2231

MID-AMERICA BIBLE COLLEGE
3500 S.W. 119th St., Oklahoma City 73170 *Type:* Private (Church of God) *Accred.:* 1968/1988 (AABC); 1985/1989 (NCA) *Calendar:* Sem. plan *Degrees:* A, B *CEO:* Pres. Forrest Robinson
Enroll: 203 (405) 691-3800

MURRAY STATE COLLEGE
Tishomingo 73460 *Type:* Public (state) junior *System:* Oklahoma State Regents for Higher Education *Accred.:* 1964/1984 (NCA) *Calendar:* Sem. plan *Degrees:* A, certificates, diplomas *Prof. Accred.:* Nursing (A), Veterinary Technology *CEO:* Pres. Clyde R. Kindell
Enroll: 1002 (405) 371-2371

Accredited Institutions **Oklahoma**

NATIONAL EDUCATION CENTER—SPARTAN
SCHOOL OF AERONAUTICS CAMPUS
P.O. Box 582833, Tulsa 74158 *Type:* Private
Accred.: 1969/1986 (CCA-ACTTS) *Calendar:* Courses of varying lengths *Degrees:* A, certificates, diplomas *CEO:* Pres. Frank D. Iacobucci
Enroll: 4070 (918) 836-6886

NORTHEASTERN OKLAHOMA A&M COLLEGE
Second and I Sts., N.E., Miami 74354 *Type:* Public (state) junior *System:* Oklahoma State Regents for Higher Education *Accred.:* 1925/1987 (NCA) *Calendar:* Sem. plan *Degrees:* A, certificates, diplomas *Prof. Accred.:* Nursing (A) *CEO:* Pres. Bobby R. Wright
Enroll: 2268 (918) 542-8441

NORTHEASTERN STATE UNIVERSITY
Tahlequah 74464 *Type:* Public (state) liberal arts and teachers *System:* Oklahoma State Regents for Higher Education *Accred.:* 1922/1982 (NCA) *Calendar:* Sem. plan *Degrees:* B, M, D, certificates, diplomas *Prof. Accred.:* Nursing (B), Optometry, Social Work (B-candidate), Teacher Education (e,s,p) *CEO:* Pres. W. Roger Webb
Enroll: 6851 (918) 456-5511

NORTHERN OKLAHOMA COLLEGE
P.O. Box 310, Tonkawa 74653-0310 *Type:* Public (state) junior *System:* Oklahoma State Regents for Higher Education *Accred.:* 1948/1988 (NCA) *Calendar:* Sem. plan *Degrees:* A, certificates, diplomas *Prof. Accred.:* Nursing (A) *CEO:* Pres. Edward E. Vineyard
Enroll: 1388 (405) 628-2581

NORTHWESTERN STATE UNIVERSITY
705 Oklahoma Blvd., Alva 73717 *Type:* Public (state) liberal arts and teachers *System:* Oklahoma State Regents for Higher Education *Accred.:* 1922/1984 (NCA) *Calendar:* Sem. plan *Degrees:* B, M, certificates, diplomas *Prof. Accred.:* Nursing (B), Teacher Education (e,s) *CEO:* Pres. Joe J. Struckle
Enroll: 1587 (405) 327-1700

OKLAHOMA BAPTIST UNIVERSITY
Shawnee 74801 *Type:* Private (Southern Baptist) liberal arts and professional *Accred.:* 1952/1988 (NCA) *Calendar:* 4-1-4 plan *Degrees:* A, B, certificates, diplomas *Prof. Accred.:* Music, Nursing (B), Teacher Education (e,s) *CEO:* Pres. Bob R. Agee
Enroll: 1754 (405) 275-2850

OKLAHOMA CHRISTIAN UNIVERSITY OF SCIENCE AND ARTS
P.O. Box 11000, Oklahoma City 73136 *Type:* Private (Church of Christ) liberal arts *Accred.:* 1966/1986 (NCA) *Calendar:* Tri. plan *Degrees:* B, M *Prof. Accred.:* Teacher Education (e,s) *CEO:* Pres. J. Terry Johnson
Enroll: 1553 (405) 425-5000

OKLAHOMA CITY COMMUNITY COLLEGE
7777 S. May Ave., Oklahoma City 73159 *Type:* Public (district) junior *System:* Oklahoma State Regents for Higher Education *Accred.:* 1977/1982 (NCA) *Calendar:* 4-1-4 plan *Degrees:* A, certificates, diplomas *Prof. Accred.:* Nursing (A), Occupational Therapy Assisting, Physical Therapy Assisting *CEO:* Pres. Bob D. Gaines
Enroll: 3767 (405) 682-7503

OKLAHOMA CITY UNIVERSITY
2501 N. Blackwelder Ave., Oklahoma City 73106 *Type:* Private (United Methodist) *Accred.:* 1951/1983 (NCA) *Calendar:* Sem. plan *Degrees:* A, B, M, D *Prof. Accred.:* Law (ABA only), Music, Nursing (B) *CEO:* Pres. Jerald C. Walker
Enroll: 3398 (405) 521-5032

OKLAHOMA FARRIERS COLLEGE
Rte. 2, Box 88, Sperry 74073 *Type:* Private *Accred.:* 1980/1985 (CCA-ACTTS) *Calendar:* Courses of varying lengths *Degrees:* diplomas *CEO:* Pres. Bud Beaston
Enroll: 94 (918) 288-7221

OKLAHOMA HORSESHOEING SCHOOL, INC.
3000 N. Interstate 35, Oklahoma City 73111 *Type:* Private *Accred.:* 1988 (CCA-ACTTS)

Oklahoma

Calendar: Courses of varying lengths *Degrees:* certificates *CEO:* Dir. Jack Roth
(405) 424-3842

OKLAHOMA INSTITUTE OF HAIR DESIGN
5808 N.W. 36th St., Oklahoma City 73122 *Type:* Private *Accred.:* 1985 (CCA-ACTTS) *Calendar:* Courses of varying lengths *Degrees:* certificates *CEO:* Dir. Manly E. Jones
Enroll: 15 (405) 946-2297

OKLAHOMA JUNIOR COLLEGE
3232 N.W. 65th St., Oklahoma City 73116 *Type:* Private business *Accred.:* 1989 (CCA-ACICS); 1991 (NCA candidate) *Calendar:* Tri. plan *Degrees:* A, certificates, diplomas *CEO:* Dir. Cameron Faili
Enroll: 1554 (405) 848-3400

OKLAHOMA JUNIOR COLLEGE OF BUSINESS AND TECHNOLOGY
7370 E. 71st St., Tulsa 74133 *Type:* Private business *Accred.:* 1953/1985 (CCA-ACICS); 1990 (NCA candidate) *Calendar:* Sem. plan *Degrees:* A *Prof. Accred.:* Medical Assisting *CEO:* Pres. Joel D. Boyd
Enroll: 2356 (918) 459-0200

OKLAHOMA PANHANDLE STATE UNIVERSITY
P.O. Box 430, Goodwell 73939 *Type:* Public (state) liberal arts *System:* Oklahoma State Regents for Higher Education *Accred.:* 1926/1985 (NCA) *Calendar:* Sem. plan *Degrees:* B, certificates, diplomas *Prof. Accred.:* Teacher Education (e,s) *CEO:* Pres. Theodore W. Wischropp
Enroll: 1029 (405) 349-2610

OKLAHOMA STATE UNIVERSITY
Stillwater 74078 *Type:* Public (state) *System:* Oklahoma State University System *Accred.:* 1916/1986 (NCA) *Calendar:* Sem. plan *Degrees:* A, B, P, M, D, certificates, diplomas *Prof. Accred.:* Accounting (Type A,C), Architecture (B,M), Business (B,M), Clinical Psychology, Engineering (agricultural, architectural, chemical, civil, electrical, general, industrial, mechanical), Engineering Technology (civil/construction, electrical, fire protection/safety, manufacturing, mechanical, petroleum), Forestry, Home Economics, Interior Design, Journalism, Landscape Architecture (B-initial), Leisure Studies, Music, Speech-Language Pathology, Teacher Education (e,s,p) *CEO:* Pres. John R. Campbell
Enroll: 16013 (405) 744-6834

OKLAHOMA STATE UNIVERSITY COLLEGE OF OSTEOPATHIC MEDICINE
1111 W. 17th St., Tulsa 74107 *Type:* Public (state) professional *System:* Oklahoma State University System *Calendar:* Sem. plan *Degrees:* P *Prof. Accred.:* Osteopathy *CEO:* Provost/Dean Thomas Wesley Allen
Enroll: 271 (918) 582-1972

OKLAHOMA STATE UNIVERSITY—OKLAHOMA CITY
900 N. Portland Ave., Oklahoma City 73107 *Type:* Public (state) *System:* Oklahoma State University System *Accred.:* 1975/1990 (NCA) *Calendar:* Tri. plan *Degrees:* A, certificates, diplomas *Prof. Accred.:* Nursing (A) *CEO:* Dir. James E. Hooper
Enroll: 2153 (405) 947-4421

OKLAHOMA STATE UNIVERSITY—OKMULGEE
1801 E. Fourth St., Okmulgee 74447 *Type:* Public (state) *System:* Oklahoma State University System *Accred.:* 1975/1990 (NCA) *Calendar:* Tri. plan *Degrees:* A, certificates, diplomas *CEO:* Dir. Robert Klabenes
Enroll: 1683 (918) 756-6211

ORAL ROBERTS UNIVERSITY
7777 S. Lewis Pl., Tulsa 74171 *Type:* Private liberal arts and professional *Accred.:* 1980/1987 (ATS); 1971/1988 (NCA) *Calendar:* Sem. plan *Degrees:* B, M, D, certificates, diplomas *Prof. Accred.:* Music, Nursing (B,M), Social Work (B) *CEO:* Pres. G. Oral Roberts
Enroll: 3550 (918) 495-7349

PHILLIPS GRADUATE SEMINARY
102 University Dr., Enid 73702 *Type:* Private (Christian Church/Disciples of Christ) *Accred.:* 1952/1980 (ATS) *Calendar:* Sem.

plan *Degrees:* P, M, D *CEO:* Pres. William Tabbernee
Enroll: 95 (405) 237-4433

PHILLIPS UNIVERSITY
P.O. Box 2000, University Sta., Enid 73702 *Type:* Private (Christian Church/Disciples of Christ) *Accred.:* 1919/1989 (NCA) *Calendar:* Sem. plan *Degrees:* B, M *Prof. Accred.:* Music, Teacher Education (e,s) *CEO:* Pres. Robert D. Peck
Enroll: 719 (405) 237-4433

PLATT COLLEGE
4821 S. 72nd E. Ave., Tulsa 74145 *Type:* Private *Accred.:* 1985 (CCA-ACTTS) *Calendar:* Courses of varying lengths *Degrees:* certificates *CEO:* Dir. Jim Warren
Enroll: 637 (918) 663-9000

BRANCH CAMPUS
6125 W. Reno Ave., Ste. 300, Oklahoma City, OK 73127 *CEO:* Dir. Michael Pugliese
(405) 789-5052

REDLANDS COMMUNITY COLLEGE
P.O. Box 370, El Reno 73036-0370 *Type:* Public (state) junior *System:* Oklahoma State Regents for Higher Education *Accred.:* 1978/1991 (NCA) *Calendar:* Sem. plan *Degrees:* A, certificates, diplomas *Prof. Accred.:* Nursing (A) *CEO:* Pres. Larry F. Devane
Enroll: 863 (405) 262-2552

ROGERS STATE COLLEGE
Claremore 74017 *Type:* Public (state) junior *System:* Oklahoma State Regents for Higher Education *Accred.:* 1950/1987 (NCA) *Calendar:* Sem. plan *Degrees:* A, certificates, diplomas *Prof. Accred.:* Nursing (A) *CEO:* Pres. Richard H. Mosier
Enroll: 2151 (918) 341-7510

ROSE STATE COLLEGE
6420 S.E. 15th St., Midwest City 73110 *Type:* Public (state) junior *System:* Oklahoma State Regents for Higher Education *Accred.:* 1975/1988 (NCA) *Calendar:* Sem. plan *Degrees:* A, certificates, diplomas *Prof.*

Accred.: Dental Assisting, Dental Hygiene, Medical Laboratory Technology (AMA), Nursing (A), Radiography, Respiratory Therapy, Respiratory Therapy Technology *CEO:* Pres. Larry Nutter
Enroll: 5271 (405) 733-7300

ST. GREGORY'S COLLEGE
1900 W. MacArthur, Shawnee 74801-2499 *Type:* Private (Roman Catholic) junior *Accred.:* 1969/1989 (NCA) *Calendar:* Sem. plan *Degrees:* A *CEO:* Pres. Carmen A. Notaro
Enroll: 277 (405) 273-9870

SEMINOLE JUNIOR COLLEGE
P.O. Box 351, Seminole 74868-0351 *Type:* Public (state) junior *System:* Oklahoma State Regents for Higher Education *Accred.:* 1975/1990 (NCA) *Calendar:* Tri. plan *Degrees:* A, certificates, diplomas *Prof. Accred.:* Medical Laboratory Technology (AMA), Nursing (A) *CEO:* Pres. James J. Cook
Enroll: 1020 (405) 382-9950

SOONER COLLEGE OF TECHNOLOGY
3737 N. Portland Ave., Oklahoma City 73112 *Type:* Private *Accred.:* 1968/1989 (CCA-ACTTS) *Calendar:* Courses of varying lengths *Degrees:* diplomas *CEO:* Pres. Bob M. Culver
Enroll: 528 (405) 942-8683

SOUTHEASTERN OKLAHOMA STATE UNIVERSITY
Durant 74701 *Type:* Public (state) liberal arts and teachers *System:* Oklahoma State Regents for Higher Education *Accred.:* 1922/1984 (NCA) *Calendar:* Sem. plan *Degrees:* B, M, certificates, diplomas *Prof. Accred.:* Music, Teacher Education (e,s) *CEO:* Pres. Larry Williams
Enroll: 3409 (405) 924-0121

SOUTHERN NAZARENE UNIVERSITY
6729 N.W. 39th Expy., Bethany 73008 *Type:* Private (Nazarene) liberal arts *Accred.:* 1956/1990 (NCA) *Calendar:* Sem. plan *Degrees:* A, B, M, certificates, diplomas *Prof.*

Accred.: Nursing (B), Teacher Education (e,s) *CEO:* Pres. Loren P. Gresham, Ph.D.
Enroll: 1203   (405) 491-6304

SOUTHERN TECHNICAL COLLEGE
4233 Charter Ave., Oklahoma City 73108 *Type:* Private *Accred.:* 1979/1989 (CCA-ACTTS) *Calendar:* Courses of varying lengths *Degrees:* certificates, diplomas *CEO:* Dir. David Doolin
Enroll: 985   (405) 942-7700

SOUTHWEST TECHNICAL COLLEGE
1520 S. Central Ave., Oklahoma City 73129 *Type:* Private *Accred.:* 1967/1987 (CCA-ACTTS) *Calendar:* Courses of varying lengths *Degrees:* diplomas *CEO:* Dir. Anthony Marino
Enroll: 866   (405) 632-7785

SOUTHWESTERN COLLEGE OF CHRISTIAN MINISTRIES
7210 N.W. 39th Expy., P.O. Box 340, Bethany 73008-0340 *Type:* Private (Pentecostal Holiness) liberal arts *Accred.:* 1973/1991 (NCA) *Calendar:* Sem. plan *Degrees:* A, B *CEO:* Pres. Ronald Q. Moore
Enroll: 84   (405) 789-7661

SOUTHWESTERN OKLAHOMA STATE UNIVERSITY
100 Campus Dr., Weatherford 73096 *Type:* Public (state) liberal arts and professional *System:* Oklahoma State Regents for Higher Education *Accred.:* 1922/1991 (NCA) *Calendar:* Sem. plan *Degrees:* B, M, certificates, diplomas *Prof. Accred.:* Medical Record Administration, Music, Nursing (B), Pharmacy, Radiography, Teacher Education (e,s,p) *CEO:* Pres. Joe Anna Hibler
Enroll: 4517   (405) 772-6611

BRANCH CAMPUS
409 E. Mississippi, Sayre, OK 73662-1236 *Prof. Accred.:* Medical Laboratory Technology *CEO:* Dean Don Roberts
   (405) 928-5533

STATE BARBER AND HAIR DESIGN COLLEGE
2514 S. Agnew Ave., Oklahoma City 73108 *Type:* Private *Accred.:* 1988 (CCA-ACTTS) *Calendar:* Courses of varying lengths *Degrees:* certificates *CEO:* Dir. Bobby Lewis
Enroll: 95   (405) 631-8621

TULSA BARBER COLLEGE
1314 E. Third St., Tulsa 74120 *Type:* Private *Accred.:* 1985 (CCA-ACTTS) *Calendar:* Courses of varying lengths *Degrees:* certificates *CEO:* Dir. Manly E. Jones
Enroll: 21   (918) 599-0803

TULSA COUNTY AREA VOCATIONAL-TECHNICAL INSTITUTE
3420 S. Memorial Dr., Tulsa 74145 *Type:* Private *Calendar:* Courses of varying lengths *Degrees:* certificates *Prof. Accred.:* Practical Nursing *CEO:* Supt. Gene Callahan
   (918) 627-7200

TULSA JUNIOR COLLEGE
6111 E. Skelly Dr., Tulsa 74135-6101 *Type:* Public (state) junior *System:* Oklahoma State Regents for Higher Education *Accred.:* 1974/1989 (NCA) *Calendar:* Sem. plan *Degrees:* A, certificates, diplomas *Prof. Accred.:* Medical Assisting (AMA), Medical Laboratory Technology (AMA), Nursing (A), Physical Therapy Assisting, Radiography, Respiratory Therapy, Respiratory Therapy Technology *CEO:* Pres. Dean P. Van Trease
Enroll: 7829   (918) 622-5100

TULSA WELDING SCHOOL
3038 Southwest Blvd., P.O. Box 9829, Tulsa 74107 *Type:* Private *Accred.:* 1970/1985 (CCA-ACTTS) *Calendar:* Courses of varying lengths *Degrees:* diplomas *CEO:* Pres. Noel E. Adams
Enroll: 398   (918) 587-6789

UNITED STATES COAST GUARD INSTITUTE
P.O. Substation 18, Oklahoma City 73169-6999 *Type:* Public (federal) home study *Accred.:* 1981/1987 (NHSC) *Calendar:* Courses of varying lengths *Degrees:* certificates *CEO:* Commander Roland Isnor
   (405) 680-4262

Oklahoma

UNIVERSITY OF CENTRAL OKLAHOMA
100 N. University Dr., Edmond 73060 *Type:* Public liberal arts and teachers *System:* Oklahoma State Regents for Higher Education *Accred.:* 1921/1986 (NCA) *Calendar:* Sem. plan *Degrees:* B, M, certificates, diplomas *Prof. Accred.:* Funeral Service Education, Nursing (B), Teacher Education (e,s,p) *CEO:* Pres. William J. Lillard
Enroll: 9768 (405) 341-2980

UNIVERSITY OF OKLAHOMA
660 Parrington Oval, Norman 73019 *Type:* Public (state) *System:* University of Oklahoma Central Office *Accred.:* 1913/1982 (NCA) *Calendar:* Sem. plan *Degrees:* B, M, D, certificates, diplomas *Prof. Accred.:* Accounting (Type A,C), Architecture (B,M), Audiology, Business (B,M), Construction Education, Counseling Psychology, Engineering (aerospace, chemical, civil, electrical, engineering physics/science, general, industrial, mechanical, petroleum), Interior Design, Journalism, Law, Librarianship, Music, Psychology Internship, Public Health, Social Work (B,M), Speech-Language Pathology, Teacher Education (e,s,p) *CEO:* Pres. Richard L. Van Horn
Enroll: 17935 (405) 325-3916

UNIVERSITY OF OKLAHOMA HEALTH SCIENCES CENTER
P.O. Box 26901, Oklahoma City 73126-0901 *Type:* Public (state) *System:* University of Oklahoma Central Office *Calendar:* Sem. plan *Degrees:* A, B, P, M, D *Prof. Accred.:* Cytotechnology, Dental Hygiene, Dentistry, Diagnostic Medical Sonography, Dietetics (coordinated), General Dentistry (prelim. provisional), Medical Technology, Medicine, Nuclear Medicine Technology, Nursing (B,M), Occupational Therapy, Orthodontics, Periodontics, Pharmacy, Physical Therapy, Physician Assisting, Radiation Therapy Technology, Radiography *CEO:* Provost Clayton Rich
Enroll: 2313 (405) 271-4000

UNIVERSITY OF SCIENCE AND ARTS OF OKLAHOMA
P.O. Box 82345, Chickasha 73018 *Type:* Public (state) liberal arts and teachers *System:* Oklahoma State Regents for Higher Education *Accred.:* 1920/1989 (NCA) *Calendar:* Tri. plan *Degrees:* B *Prof. Accred.:* Music, Teacher Education (e,s) *CEO:* Pres. Roy Troutt
Enroll: 1105 (405) 224-3140

UNIVERSITY OF TULSA
600 S. College Ave., Tulsa 74104 *Type:* Private (United Presbyterian) *Accred.:* 1929/1988 (NCA) *Calendar:* 4-1-4 plan *Degrees:* B, M, D *Prof. Accred.:* Business (B,M), Computer Science, Engineering (chemical, electrical, engineering physics/science, mechanical, petroleum), Law, Music, Nursing (B), Speech-Language Pathology, Teacher Education (e,s,p) *CEO:* Pres. Robert H. Donaldson
Enroll: 4217 (918) 631-2000

WESTERN OKLAHOMA STATE COLLEGE
2801 N. Main St., Altus 73521 *Type:* Public (state) junior *System:* Oklahoma State Regents for Higher Education *Accred.:* 1976/1988 (NCA) *Calendar:* Sem. plan *Degrees:* A *Prof. Accred.:* Nursing (A) *CEO:* Pres. Stephen R. Hensley
Enroll: 1031 (405) 477-2000

WRIGHT BUSINESS SCHOOL
2219 S.W. 74th St., Ste. 122, Oklahoma City 73159 *Type:* Private business *Accred.:* 1986/1988 (CCA-ACICS) *Calendar:* Courses of varying lengths *Degrees:* certificates, diplomas *CEO:* Dir. Melissa Pickens
Enroll: 1050 (405) 681-2300

OREGON

APOLLO COLLEGE OF MEDICAL AND DENTAL CAREERS
2600 S.E. 98th St., Portland 97266-1302 *Type:* Private *Calendar:* Courses of varying lengths *Degrees:* certificates *Prof. Accred.:* Health Education *CEO:* Pres. Margaret M. Carlson
(503) 761-6100

BASSIST COLLEGE
2000 S.W. Fifth Ave., Portland 97201 *Type:* Private technical *Accred.:* 1977/1986 (NASC) *Calendar:* Qtr. plan *Degrees:* A, B *CEO:* Pres. Donald H. Bassist
Enroll: 151 (503) 228-6528

BLUE MOUNTAIN COMMUNITY COLLEGE
P.O. Box 100, Pendleton 97801 *Type:* Public (district) junior *System:* Oregon State Board of Education, Office of Community College Services *Accred.:* 1968/1984 (NASC) *Calendar:* Qtr. plan *Degrees:* A *Prof. Accred.:* Dental Assisting (conditional), Engineering Technology (electrical) *CEO:* Pres. Ronald L. Daniels
Enroll: 4423 (503) 276-1260

BRADFORD SCHOOL
921 S.W. Washington St., Ste. 200, Portland 97205-2820 *Type:* Private *Accred.:* 1982/1987 (CCA-ACTTS) *Calendar:* Courses of varying lengths *Degrees:* certificates *Prof. Accred.:* Dental Assisting, Medical Assisting (AMA) *CEO:* Dir. Carol Menck
Enroll: 390 (503) 242-9000

BROADCAST PROFESSIONALS, THE COMPLETE SCHOOL OF RADIO BROADCASTING
11505B S.W. Pacific Hwy., Portland 97223-8628 *Type:* Private *Accred.:* 1991 (CCA-ACTTS) *Calendar:* Courses of varying lengths *Degrees:* certificates *CEO:* Dir. Rosemary Reynolds
(503) 244-5113

CENTRAL OREGON COMMUNITY COLLEGE
Bend 97701-5998 *Type:* Public (district) junior *System:* Oregon State Board of Education, Office of Community College Services *Accred.:* 1966/1982 (NASC) *Calendar:* Qtr. plan *Degrees:* A *Prof. Accred.:* Medical Record Technology *CEO:* Pres. Robert Barber
Enroll: 3036 (503) 385-6112

CHEMEKETA COMMUNITY COLLEGE
P.O. Box 14007, Salem 97309 *Type:* Public (district) junior *System:* Oregon State Board of Education, Office of Community College Services *Accred.:* 1972/1987 (NASC) *Calendar:* Qtr. plan *Degrees:* A *Prof. Accred.:* Dental Assisting, Medical Assisting (AMA), Nursing (A) *CEO:* Pres. William E. Segura
Enroll: 20030 (503) 399-5000

CLACKAMAS COMMUNITY COLLEGE
19600 S. Molalla Ave., Oregon City 97045 *Type:* Public (district) junior *System:* Oregon State Board of Education, Office of Community College Services *Accred.:* 1971/1986 (NASC) *Calendar:* Qtr. plan *Degrees:* A *Prof. Accred.:* Nursing (A) *CEO:* Pres. John S. Keyser
Enroll: 12584 (503) 657-6958

CLATSOP COMMUNITY COLLEGE
1653 Jerome Ave., Astoria 97103 *Type:* Public (district) junior *System:* Oregon State Board of Education, Office of Community College Services *Accred.:* 1965/1991 (NASC) *Calendar:* Qtr. plan *Degrees:* A *CEO:* Pres. Doreen D. Dailey
Enroll: 6352 (503) 325-0910

COLLEGE OF LEGAL ARTS
527 S.W. Hall St., Ste. 415, Portland 97201 *Type:* Private business *Accred.:* 1978/1990 (CCA-ACICS) *Calendar:* Courses of varying lengths *Degrees:* certificates, diplomas *CEO:* Pres. Billy P. Ellis
Enroll: 381 (503) 223-5100

COLUMBIA CHRISTIAN COLLEGE
9101 E. Burnside St., Portland 97216-1515 *Type:* Private (Church of Christ) liberal arts *Accred.:* 1975/1980 (NASC) *Calendar:*

Sem. plan *Degrees:* A, B *CEO:* Acting Pres. William Free
Enroll: 280 (503) 257-1365

COMMERCIAL TRAINING SERVICES
2416 N. Marine Dr., Portland 97217-7741 *Type:* Private *Accred.:* 1973/1985 (CCA-ACTTS) *Calendar:* Courses of varying lengths *Degrees:* certificates *CEO:* Pres. Clifford Georgioff
Enroll: 155 (503) 285-7542

CONCORDE CAREER INSTITUTE
1827 N.E. 44th Ave., Portland 97213 *Type:* Private *Accred.:* 1991 (CCA-ACTTS) *Calendar:* Courses of varying lengths *Degrees:* certificates *CEO:* Dir. Larry W. Cartmill
(503) 281-4181

CONCORDIA COLLEGE
2811 N.E. Holman St., Portland 97211 *Type:* Private (Lutheran) liberal arts *Accred.:* 1962/1991 (NASC) *Calendar:* Qtr. plan *Degrees:* A, B *CEO:* Pres. Charles E. Schlimpert
Enroll: 817 (503) 288-9371

DIESEL TRUCK DRIVER TRAINING SCHOOL
90801 Hwy. 99 N., Eugene 97402-9624 *Type:* Private *Accred.:* 1991 (CCA-ACTTS) *Calendar:* Courses of varying lengths *Degrees:* certificates *CEO:* Dir. Curtis B. Olson
(503) 461-0400

EAST-WEST COLLEGE
812 S.W. Tenth Ave., Portland 97205-2593 *Type:* Private *Accred.:* 1991 (CCA-ACTTS) *Calendar:* Courses of varying lengths *Degrees:* certificates *CEO:* Pres. David Slawson
(503) 226-1127

EASTERN OREGON STATE COLLEGE
La Grande 97850 *Type:* Public (state) liberal arts and teachers *System:* Oregon State System of Higher Education *Accred.:* 1931/1988 (NASC) *Calendar:* Qtr. plan *Degrees:* A, B, M *Prof. Accred.:* Teacher Education (e,s) *CEO:* Pres. David E. Gilbert
Enroll: 2625 (503) 962-3512

EUGENE BIBLE COLLEGE
2155 Bailey Hill Rd., Eugene 97405 *Type:* Private *Accred.:* 1983/1988 (AABC) *Calendar:* Qtr. plan *Degrees:* B, certificates *CEO:* Pres. Jeffery Farmer
Enroll: 142 (503) 485-1780

GEORGE FOX COLLEGE
Newberg 97132 *Type:* Private liberal arts *Accred.:* 1959/1990 (NASC) *Calendar:* Sem. plan *Degrees:* B *Prof. Accred.:* Music *CEO:* Pres. Edward F. Stevens
Enroll: 1072 (503) 538-8383

ITT TECHNICAL INSTITUTE
6035 N.E. 78th Ct., Portland 97218-2854 *Type:* Private *Accred.:* 1973/1988 (CCA-ACTTS) *Calendar:* Courses of varying lengths *Degrees:* certificates, diplomas *CEO:* Dir. James Horner
Enroll: 1391 (503) 255-6500

LA GRANDE COLLEGE OF BUSINESS
10214 Wallow Lake Hwy., La Grande 97850 *Type:* Private business *Accred.:* 1979/1988 (CCA-ACICS) *Calendar:* Courses of varying lengths *Degrees:* certificates, diplomas *CEO:* Pres. Ronald L. Vincent
Enroll: 57 (503) 963-6485

LANE COMMUNITY COLLEGE
Eugene 97405 *Type:* Public (district) junior *System:* Oregon State Board of Education, Office of Community College Services *Accred.:* 1968/1984 (NASC) *Calendar:* Qtr. plan *Degrees:* A *Prof. Accred.:* Dental Assisting, Dental Hygiene, Nursing (A), Respiratory Therapy *CEO:* Pres. Jerry Moskus
Enroll: 8762 (503) 747-4501

LEWIS AND CLARK COLLEGE
0615 S.W. Palatine Hill Rd., Portland 97219 *Type:* Private (United Presbyterian) liberal arts *Accred.:* 1943/1990 (NASC) *Calendar:* Qtr. plan *Degrees:* B, M *Prof. Accred.:* Law, Music *CEO:* Pres. Michael J. Mooney
Enroll: 3658 (503) 293-2770

Oregon

LINFIELD COLLEGE
McMinnville 97128 *Type:* Private (Baptist) liberal arts *Accred.:* 1928/1988 (NASC) *Calendar:* 4-1-4 plan *Degrees:* B, M *Prof. Accred.:* Music, Nursing (B) *CEO:* Pres. Charles U. Walker
Enroll: 2242 (503) 472-4121

LINN-BENTON COMMUNITY COLLEGE
Albany 97321 *Type:* Public (district) junior *System:* Oregon State Board of Education, Office of Community College Services *Accred.:* 1972/1987 (NASC) *Calendar:* Qtr. plan *Degrees:* A *Prof. Accred.:* Dental Assisting, Nursing (A) *CEO:* Pres. Jon Carnahan
Enroll: 13196 (503) 967-6100

MARYLHURST COLLEGE FOR LIFELONG LEARNING
Marylhurst 97036 *Type:* Private (Roman Catholic) liberal arts *Accred.:* 1977/1986 (NASC) *Calendar:* Qtr. plan *Degrees:* B, M *Prof. Accred.:* Music *CEO:* Pres. Nancy A. Wilgenbusch
Enroll: 1036 (503) 636-8141

MOLER BARBER COLLEGE
517 S.W. Fourth St., Portland 97204-2118 *Type:* Private *Accred.:* 1988 (CCA-ACTTS) *Calendar:* Courses of varying lengths *Degrees:* certificates *CEO:* Pres. Gordon Scarbrough
(503) 223-9818

MOUNT ANGEL SEMINARY
St. Benedict 97373 *Type:* Private (Roman Catholic) *Accred.:* 1978/1985 (ATS); 1929/1987 (NASC) *Calendar:* Sem. plan *Degrees:* B, P, M *CEO:* Pres. Patrick Brennan
Enroll: 139 (503) 845-3030

MOUNT HOOD COMMUNITY COLLEGE
26000 S.E. Stark St., Gresham 97030 *Type:* Public (district) junior *System:* Oregon State Board of Education, Office of Community College Services *Accred.:* 1972/1987 (NASC) *Calendar:* Qtr. plan *Degrees:* A *Prof. Accred.:* Dental Hygiene, Funeral Service Education, Medical Assisting (AMA), Nursing (A), Occupational Therapy Assisting, Physical Therapy Assisting, Respiratory Therapy, Surgical Technology *CEO:* Pres. Paul E. Kreider
Enroll: 7631 (503) 667-6422

MULTNOMAH SCHOOL OF THE BIBLE
8435 N.E. Glisan St., Portland 97220 *Type:* Private *Accred.:* 1953/1983 (AABC) *Calendar:* Sem. plan *Degrees:* A, B, M, certificates *CEO:* Pres. Joseph C. Aldrich
Enroll: 553 (503) 255-0332

NATIONAL BROADCASTING SCHOOL
2501 S.W. First Ave., Ste. 101, Portland 97201-4797 *Type:* Private *Accred.:* 1991 (CCA-ACTTS) *Calendar:* Courses of varying lengths *Degrees:* certificates *CEO:* Dir. Terry Richard
(503) 242-3235

NORTHWEST CHRISTIAN COLLEGE
Eugene 97401 *Type:* Private (Disciples of Christ) liberal arts *Accred.:* 1962/1988 (NASC) *Calendar:* Qtr. plan *Degrees:* A, B, M *CEO:* Pres. James E. Womack
Enroll: 253 (503) 343-1641

OREGON COLLEGE OF ORIENTAL MEDICINE
11231 S.E. Market St., Portland 97216 *Type:* Private professional *Calendar:* 3-year program *Degrees:* M *Prof. Accred.:* Acupuncture *CEO:* Pres. Elizabeth Goldblatt
(503) 253-3443

OREGON DENTURIST COLLEGE
19001 S.E. Mcloughlin Blvd., Milwaukie 97268-0289 *Type:* Private *Accred.:* 1991 (CCA-ACTTS) *Calendar:* Courses of varying lengths *Degrees:* certificates *CEO:* Dean Joanne D. Thibert
(503) 655-7561

OREGON GRADUATE INSTITUTE OF SCIENCE AND TECHNOLOGY
19600 N.W. Von Neumann Dr., Beaverton 97006-1999 *Type:* Private graduate only *Accred.:* 1973/1988 (NASC) *Calendar:* Qtr. plan *Degrees:* M, D *CEO:* Pres. Dwight A. Sangrey
Enroll: 194 (503) 690-1020

Oregon

OREGON HEALTH SCIENCES UNIVERSITY
3181 S.W. Sam Jackson Park Rd., Portland 97201 *Type:* Public (state) professional *System:* Oregon State System of Higher Education *Accred.:* 1980/1985 (NASC) *Calendar:* Qtr. plan *Degrees:* A, B, M, D *Prof. Accred.:* Dental Hygiene, Dentistry, Dietetics (internship), EMT-Paramedic, Endodontics, Medical Technology, Medicine, Nursing (B,M), Oral and Maxillofacial Surgery, Oral Pathology, Orthodontics, Pediatric Dentistry, Periodontics, Psychology Internship, Radiation Therapy Technology *CEO:* Pres. Peter O. Kohler, M.D.
Enroll: 1453 (503) 494-8252

OREGON INSTITUTE OF TECHNOLOGY
Klamath Falls 97601-8801 *Type:* Public (state) technological *System:* Oregon State System of Higher Education *Accred.:* 1962/1982 (NASC) *Calendar:* Qtr. plan *Degrees:* A, B *Prof. Accred.:* Dental Hygiene, Engineering Technology (computer, electrical, manufacturing, mechanical), Medical Technology, Nursing (B), Radiography *CEO:* Pres. Lawrence J. Wolf
Enroll: 2784 (503) 885-1103

OREGON POLYTECHNIC INSTITUTE
900 S.E. Sandy Blvd., Portland 97214 *Type:* Private *Accred.:* 1977/1986 (CCA-ACTTS) *Calendar:* Qtr. plan *Degrees:* A *CEO:* Dir. Edward L. Yakimchick
Enroll: 661 (503) 234-9333

OREGON SCHOOL OF ARTS AND CRAFTS
8245 S.W. Barnes Rd., Portland 97225 *Type:* Private professional *Calendar:* Courses of varying lengths *Degrees:* certificates, diplomas *Prof. Accred.:* Art *CEO:* Pres. John W. Lottes
Enroll: 65 (503) 297-5544

OREGON STATE UNIVERSITY
Corvallis 97331 *Type:* Public (state) *System:* Oregon State System of Higher Education *Accred.:* 1924/1990 (NASC) *Calendar:* Qtr. plan *Degrees:* B, M, D *Prof. Accred.:* Accounting (Type A), Business (B,M), Construction Management, Counseling, Engineering (agricultural, chemical, civil, computer, electrical, industrial, mechanical), Engineering Technology (nuclear), Forestry, Home Economics, Music, Pharmacy, Teacher Education (e,s,p) *CEO:* Pres. John V. Byrne
Enroll: 16024 (503) 737-2565

PACIFIC NORTHWEST COLLEGE OF ART
1219 S.W. Park Ave., Portland 97205 *Type:* Private professional *Accred.:* 1961/1981 (NASC) *Calendar:* Sem. plan *Degrees:* B *Prof. Accred.:* Art *CEO:* Dir./C.E.O. Sally C. Lawrence
Enroll: 193 (503) 226-4391

PACIFIC UNIVERSITY
2043 College Way, Forest Grove 97116 *Type:* Private (United Church of Christ) *Accred.:* 1929/1987 (NASC) *Calendar:* Sem. plan *Degrees:* B, M, D *Prof. Accred.:* Clinical Psychology (provisional), Music, Occupational Therapy, Optometry, Physical Therapy *CEO:* Pres. Robert F. Duvall
Enroll: 1492 (503) 357-6151

PARAMEDIC TRAINING INSTITUTE
P.O. Box 1878, Beaverton 97075 *Type:* Private *Calendar:* Courses of varying lengths *Degrees:* certificates *Prof. Accred.:* EMT-Paramedic *CEO:* Dir. Louise A. Evans
(503) 226-1455

PORTLAND COMMUNITY COLLEGE
P.O. Box 19000, Portland 97219-0990 *Type:* Public (district) junior *System:* Oregon State Board of Education, Office of Community College Services *Accred.:* 1970/1985 (NASC) *Calendar:* Qtr. plan *Degrees:* A *Prof. Accred.:* Dental Assisting, Dental Hygiene, Dental Laboratory Technology, Engineering Technology (electrical), Medical Assisting (AMA), Medical Laboratory Technology (AMA), Medical Record Technology, Nursing (A), Radiography, Veterinary Technology (probational) *CEO:* Pres. Daniel F. Moriarty
Enroll: 23255 (503) 244-6111

Oregon

PORTLAND STATE UNIVERSITY
P.O. Box 751, Portland 97207 *Type:* Public (state) *System:* Oregon State System of Higher Education *Accred.:* 1955/1985 (NASC) *Calendar:* Qtr. plan *Degrees:* B, M, D *Prof. Accred.:* Accounting (Type A), Audiology, Business (B,M), Engineering (civil, electrical, mechanical), Music, Planning (urban), Public Administration, Social Work (M), Speech-Language Pathology, Teacher Education (e,s,p) *CEO:* Pres. Judith A. Ramaley
Enroll: 14758 (503) 725-4419

REED COLLEGE
3203 S.E. Woodstock Blvd., Portland 97202-8199 *Type:* Private liberal arts *Accred.:* 1920/1989 (NASC) *Calendar:* Sem. plan *Degrees:* B, M *CEO:* Acting Pres. William A. Haden
Enroll: 1348 (503) 771-1112

ROGUE COMMUNITY COLLEGE
3345 Redwood Hwy., Grants Pass 97527 *Type:* Public (district) junior *System:* Oregon State Board of Education, Office of Community College Services *Accred.:* 1976/1981 (NASC) *Calendar:* Qtr. plan *Degrees:* A *Prof. Accred.:* Respiratory Therapy, Respiratory Therapy Technology *CEO:* Pres. Harvey Bennett
Enroll: 5107 (503) 479-5541

SOUTHERN OREGON STATE COLLEGE
Ashland 97520 *Type:* Public (state) liberal arts and teachers *System:* Oregon State System of Higher Education *Accred.:* 1928/1987 (NASC) *Calendar:* Qtr. plan *Degrees:* B, M *Prof. Accred.:* Music, Nursing (B), Teacher Education (e,s) *CEO:* Pres. Joseph W. Cox
Enroll: 5196 (503) 552-6111

SOUTHWESTERN OREGON COMMUNITY COLLEGE
Coos Bay 97420 *Type:* Public (district) junior *System:* Oregon State Board of Education, Office of Community College Services *Accred.:* 1966/1982 (NASC) *Calendar:* Qtr. plan *Degrees:* A *CEO:* Pres. Steven Kridelbaugh
Enroll: 4729 (503) 888-2525

TARA LARA ACADEMY OF K-9 HAIR DESIGN
16552 S.E. Mcloughlin Blvd., Portland 97267-5134 *Type:* Private *Accred.:* 1991 (CCA-ACTTS) *Calendar:* Courses of varying lengths *Degrees:* certificates *CEO:* Dir. Arlene F. Steinle
(503) 653-7134

TREASURE VALLEY COMMUNITY COLLEGE
Ontario 97914 *Type:* Public (district) junior *System:* Oregon State Board of Education, Office of Community College Services *Accred.:* 1966/1990 (NASC) *Calendar:* Qtr. plan *Degrees:* A *CEO:* Pres. Glenn E. Mayle
Enroll: 3188 (503) 889-6493

TREND COLLEGE
1050 Green Acres Rd., Eugene 97401-6501 *Type:* Private business *Accred.:* 1974/1985 (CCA-ACICS) *Calendar:* Courses of varying lengths *Degrees:* certificates, diplomas *CEO:* Dir. Richard Lyons
Enroll: 543 (503) 342-5377

TREND COLLEGE
1950 S.W. Sixth Ave., Portland 97201 *Type:* Private business *Accred.:* 1966/1989 (CCA-ACICS) *Calendar:* Qtr. plan *Degrees:* certificates, diplomas *CEO:* Dir. Mary Mizrahi
Enroll: 652 (503) 224-6410

TREND COLLEGE
210 S.E. Liberty St., Salem 97301 *Type:* Private business *Accred.:* 1970/1986 (CCA-ACICS) *Calendar:* Courses of varying lengths *Degrees:* certificates, diplomas *CEO:* Dir. Greg H. Otter
Enroll: 660 (503) 581-1476

BRANCH CAMPUS
400 Earhart St., Medford, OR 97501 *CEO:* Dir. Thomas Miller
(503) 779-5581

UMPQUA COMMUNITY COLLEGE
Roseburg 97470 *Type:* Public (district) junior *System:* Oregon State Board of Education, Office of Community College Services *Accred.:* 1970/1985 (NASC) *Calendar:* Qtr.

plan *Degrees:* A *Prof. Accred.:* Nursing (A) *CEO:* Pres. James M. Kraby
Enroll: 2145 (503) 440-4600

UNIVERSITY OF OREGON
Eugene 97403-1226 *Type:* Public (state) *System:* Oregon State System of Higher Education *Accred.:* 1918/1987 (NASC) *Calendar:* Qtr. plan *Degrees:* B, M, D *Prof. Accred.:* Accounting (Type A), Architecture (B,M), Business (B,M), Clinical Psychology, Counseling, Counseling Psychology, Interior Design, Journalism, Landscape Architecture (B), Law, Leisure Services and Studies, Music, Planning (community/urban), Psychology Internship (provisional), Public Affairs, Speech-Language Pathology, Teacher Education (e,s,p) *CEO:* Pres. Myles Brand
Enroll: 17818 (503) 346-3036

UNIVERSITY OF PORTLAND
5000 N. Willamette Blvd., Portland 97203 *Type:* Private (Roman Catholic) *Accred.:* 1931/1990 (NASC) *Calendar:* Sem. plan *Degrees:* B, M *Prof. Accred.:* Business (B,M), Engineering (civil, electrical, mechanical), Nursing (B,M), Teacher Education (e,s) *CEO:* Pres. David T. Tyson
Enroll: 2889 (503) 283-7205

WARNER PACIFIC COLLEGE
2219 S.E. 68th Ave., Portland 97215 *Type:* Private (Church of God) liberal arts *Accred.:* 1961/1982 (NASC) *Calendar:* Sem. plan *Degrees:* A, B, M *CEO:* Pres. Marshall K. Christensen
Enroll: 510 (503) 775-4366

WEST COAST TRAINING
11919 N. Jensen Ave., Ste. 292, Portland 97217 *Type:* Private *Accred.:* 1986 (CCA-ACTTS) *Calendar:* Courses of varying lengths *Degrees:* certificates *CEO:* Dir. William Myer
(503) 289-8661

BRANCH CAMPUS
2525 S.E. Stubb St., Milwaukie, OR 97222-7323 *CEO:* Managing Dir. Charles Wertzbaugher
(503) 659-5181

WESTERN BAPTIST COLLEGE
5000 Deer Park Dr., S.E., Salem 97301 *Type:* Private *Accred.:* 1959/1980 (AABC); 1971/1985 (NASC) *Calendar:* Qtr. plan *Degrees:* A, B *CEO:* Pres. David F. Miller
Enroll: 417 (503) 581-8600

WESTERN BUSINESS COLLEGE
505 S.W. Sixth Ave., Portland 97204 *Type:* Private business *Accred.:* 1969/1987 (CCA-ACICS) *Calendar:* Qtr. plan *Degrees:* certificates, diplomas *CEO:* Exec. Dir. F. William King
Enroll: 1642 (503) 222-3225

BRANCH CAMPUS
6625 E. Mill Plain Blvd., Vancouver, WA 98661 *CEO:* Dir. Mary Durall-DuPree
(206) 694-3225

WESTERN CONSERVATIVE BAPTIST SEMINARY
5511 S.E. Hawthorne Blvd., Portland 97215 *Type:* Private (Baptist) *Accred.:* 1991 (ATS candidate); 1969/1983 (NASC) *Calendar:* Sem. plan *Degrees:* P, M, D *CEO:* Pres. John E. Vawter
Enroll: 541 (503) 233-8561

WESTERN CULINARY INSTITUTE
1316 S.W. 13th Ave., Portland 97201-3355 *Type:* Private *Accred.:* 1991 (CCA-ACTTS) *Calendar:* Courses of varying lengths *Degrees:* certificates *CEO:* Dir. Nick Fluge
(503) 223-2245

WESTERN EVANGELICAL SEMINARY
4200 S.E. Jennings Ave., Portland 97267 *Type:* Private (interdenominational) professional; graduate only *Accred.:* 1974/1981 (ATS); 1976/1981 (NASC) *Calendar:* Qtr. plan *Degrees:* P, M, D *CEO:* Interim Pres. James A. Field
Enroll: 155 (503) 654-5466

WESTERN MEDICAL COLLEGE OF ALLIED HEALTH CAREERS
560 Winter St., S.E., Ste. 5, Salem 97301 *Type:* Private *Calendar:* Courses of varying lengths *Degrees:* certificates *Prof. Accred.:* Health Education *CEO:* Dir. Marcella Arnold
(503) 363-4473

WESTERN OREGON STATE COLLEGE
Monmouth 97361 *Type:* Public (state) *System:* Oregon State System of Higher Education *Accred.:* 1924/1988 (NASC) *Calendar:* Qtr. plan *Degrees:* A, B, M *Prof. Accred.:* Counseling, Music, Rehabilitation Counseling, Teacher Education (e,s) *CEO:* Pres. Richard S. Meyers
Enroll: 4017   (503) 838-8215

WESTERN STATES CHIROPRACTIC COLLEGE
2900 N.E. 132nd Ave., Portland 97230 *Type:* Private professional *Accred.:* 1986/1990 (NASC) *Calendar:* Qtr. plan *Degrees:* B, P *Prof. Accred.:* Chiropractic Education *CEO:* Pres. William H. Dallas
Enroll: 418   (503) 256-3180

WESTERN TRUCK SCHOOL
10510 S.W. Industrial Way, Bldg. 1, Bay 1, P.O. Box 826, Tualatin 97062-0826 *Type:* Private *Accred.:* 1991 (CCA-ACTTS) *Calendar:* Courses of varying lengths *Degrees:* certificates *CEO:* Dir. John Petersen
(503) 691-0113

WILLAMETTE UNIVERSITY
Salem 97301 *Type:* Private (United Methodist) *Accred.:* 1924/1991 (NASC) *Calendar:* Sem. plan *Degrees:* B, M *Prof. Accred.:* Law, Music *CEO:* Pres. Jerry E. Hudson
Enroll: 2371   (503) 370-6200

PENNSYLVANIA

ACADEMY OF MEDICAL ARTS AND BUSINESS
279 Boas St., Harrisburg 17102-2944 *Type:* Private *Accred.:* 1983/1988 (CCA-ACTTS) *Calendar:* Courses of varying lengths *Degrees:* diplomas *Prof. Accred.:* Medical Assisting *CEO:* Dir. Gary Kay
Enroll: 145 (717) 233-2172

ACADEMY OF THE NEW CHURCH
P.O. Box 278, Bryn Athyn 19009 *Type:* Private (Church of New Jerusalem) liberal arts *Accred.:* 1952/1987 (MSA) *Calendar:* Tri. plan *Degrees:* A, B, P *CEO:* Pres. Geoffrey S. Childs
Enroll: 150 (215) 947-4200

ALBRIGHT COLLEGE
P.O. Box 15234, Reading 19612 *Type:* Private (United Methodist) liberal arts *Accred.:* 1926/1988 (MSA) *Calendar:* 4-1-4 plan *Degrees:* B *Prof. Accred.:* Nursing (B), Social Work (B) *CEO:* Pres. Marvin Wachman
Enroll: 2041 (215) 921-2381

ALL STATE CAREER SCHOOL
501 Seminole St., Lester 19029-1825 *Type:* Private *Accred.:* 1988 (CCA-ACTTS) *Calendar:* Courses of varying lengths *Degrees:* certificates *CEO:* Pres. Joseph Marino
Enroll: 347 (215) 521-1818

ALLEGHENY BUSINESS INSTITUTE
14 Wood St., 11th Fl., Pittsburgh 15222 *Type:* Private business *Accred.:* 1990 (CCA-ACICS) *Calendar:* Courses of varying lengths *Degrees:* certificates, diplomas *CEO:* Pres. James Rudolph
(412) 456-7100

ALLEGHENY COLLEGE
520 N. Main St., Meadville 16335 *Type:* Private (United Methodist) liberal arts *Accred.:* 1921/1984 (MSA) *Calendar:* Tri. plan *Degrees:* B, M *Prof. Accred.:* Computer Science *CEO:* Pres. Daniel F. Sullivan
Enroll: 1997 (814) 332-3100

ALLENTOWN COLLEGE OF ST. FRANCIS DE SALES
Station Ave., Center Valley 18034 *Type:* Private (Roman Catholic) liberal arts *Accred.:* 1970/1988 (MSA) *Calendar:* Sem. plan *Degrees:* B, M *Prof. Accred.:* Nursing (B,M) *CEO:* Pres. Daniel G. Gambet, O.S.F.S.
Enroll: 1691 (215) 282-1100

ALLIED MEDICAL CAREERS
Narrows Shopping Ctr., Rte. 11, Edwardsville 18704 *Type:* Private *Calendar:* Courses of varying lengths *Degrees:* certificates *Prof. Accred.:* Health Education *CEO:* Pres. Damon A. Young
(717) 288-8400

BRANCH CAMPUS
2901 Pittston Ave., Scranton, PA 18505 *Prof. Accred.:* Health Education *CEO:* Pres. Damon A. Young
(717) 342-8000

ALTOONA SCHOOL OF COMMERCE
508 58th St., Altoona 16602 *Type:* Private business *Accred.:* 1971/1989 (CCA-ACICS) *Calendar:* Qtr. plan *Degrees:* A *CEO:* Dir. J. William Laughlin
Enroll: 241 (814) 944-6134

ALVERNIA COLLEGE
Reading 19607 *Type:* Private (Roman Catholic) liberal arts *Accred.:* 1967/1987 (MSA) *Calendar:* Sem. plan *Degrees:* A, B *Prof. Accred.:* Nursing (A), Physical Therapy Assisting *CEO:* Pres. Daniel N. DeLucca
Enroll: 1060 (215) 777-5411

THE AMERICAN COLLEGE
270 Bryn Mawr Ave., Bryn Mawr 19010 *Type:* Private professional *Accred.:* 1978/1987 (MSA) *Calendar:* Sem. plan *Degrees:* M, certificates, diplomas *CEO:* Pres. Samuel H. Weese
Enroll: 24100 (215) 526-1000

AMERICAN INSTITUTE OF DESIGN
1616 Orthodox St., Philadelphia 19124-3706 *Type:* Private *Accred.:* 1972/1987 (CCA-

ACTTS) *Calendar:* Qtr. plan *Degrees:* A, certificates *CEO:* Pres. Peter Klein
Enroll: 413 (215) 288-8200

ANTONELLI INSTITUTE OF ART AND PHOTOGRAPHY
2910 Jolly Rd., P.O. Box 570, Plymouth Meeting 19462-0570 *Type:* Private *Accred.:* 1975/1985 (CCA-ACTTS) *Calendar:* Sem. plan *Degrees:* A *CEO:* Dir. Gilbert H. Weiss
Enroll: 414 (215) 275-3040

ANTONELLI MEDICAL AND PROFESSIONAL INSTITUTE
1700 Industrial Hwy., Pottstown 19464-3270 *Type:* Private *Accred.:* 1989 (CCA-ACTTS) *Calendar:* Courses of varying lengths *Degrees:* certificates, diplomas *CEO:* Dir. Michael Orthaus
(215) 323-7270

ART INSTITUTE OF PHILADELPHIA
1622 Chestnut St., Philadelphia 19103-5198 *Type:* Private *Accred.:* 1973/1988 (CCA-ACTTS) *Calendar:* Qtr. plan *Degrees:* A *CEO:* Pres. Max E. Tudor
Enroll: 1779 (215) 567-7080

ART INSTITUTE OF PITTSBURGH
526 Penn Ave., Pittsburgh 15222-3269 *Type:* Private *Accred.:* 1970/1985 (CCA-ACTTS) *Calendar:* Qtr. plan *Degrees:* A *CEO:* Pres. Saundra Van Dyke
Enroll: 2792 (412) 263-6600

AUTOMOTIVE TRAINING CENTER
114 Pickering Way, Exton 19341-1310 *Type:* Private *Accred.:* 1973/1988 (CCA-ACTTS) *Calendar:* Courses of varying lengths *Degrees:* certificates, diplomas *CEO:* Dir. Qamar A. Khan
Enroll: 359 (215) 363-6716

BAPTIST BIBLE COLLEGE
P.O. Box 800, Clarks Summit 18411 *Type:* Private *Accred.:* 1968/1984 (AABC); 1984 (MSA) *Calendar:* Sem. plan *Degrees:* A, B, M, certificates, diplomas *CEO:* Pres. Milo Thompson, Jr.
Enroll: 576 (717) 587-1172

BARBER STYLING INSTITUTE
3447 Simpson Ferry Rd., Camp Hill 17011-6485 *Type:* Private *Accred.:* 1983/1988 (CCA-ACTTS) *Calendar:* Courses of varying lengths *Degrees:* certificates *CEO:* Dir. Gregory Mekulski
Enroll: 64 (717) 763-4787

BEAVER COLLEGE
Easton and Church Rds., Glenside 19038 *Type:* Private (United Presbyterian) liberal arts *Accred.:* 1946/1989 (MSA) *Calendar:* 4-1-4 plan *Degrees:* A, B, M, certificates, diplomas *Prof. Accred.:* Art, Physical Therapy *CEO:* Pres. Bette E. Landman
Enroll: 2199 (215) 572-2900

BEREAN INSTITUTE
1901 W. Girard Ave., Philadelphia 19130-1599 *Type:* Private business *Accred.:* 1974/1987 (CCA-ACICS); 1990 (CCA-ACTTS) *Calendar:* Sem. plan *Degrees:* A *CEO:* Pres. Lucille P. Blondin
Enroll: 311 (215) 763-4833

BERKS TECHNICAL INSTITUTE
833 N. Park Rd., Wyomissing 19610-1341 *Type:* Private *Accred.:* 1991 (CCA-ACTTS) *Calendar:* Courses of varying lengths *Degrees:* certificates *CEO:* Pres. Kenneth Snyder
(215) 372-1722

BILL ALLEN'S POCONO INSTITUTE OF TAXIDERMY
R.D. 2, Box 2038, Whitehaven 18661-9633 *Type:* Private *Accred.:* 1991 (CCA-ACTTS) *Calendar:* Courses of varying lengths *Degrees:* certificates *CEO:* Dir. William Allen
(717) 443-9166

BLOOMSBURG UNIVERSITY OF PENNSYLVANIA
Bloomsburg 17815 *Type:* Public (state) liberal arts *System:* Pennsylvania State System of Higher Education *Accred.:* 1950/1989 (MSA) *Calendar:* Sem. plan *Degrees:* A, B, M, certificates, diplomas *Prof. Accred.:* Nursing (B,M), Social Work (B), Teacher Education (e,s) *CEO:* Pres. Harry Ausprich
Enroll: 6804 (717) 389-4000

Accredited Institutions   **Pennsylvania**

THE BOYD SCHOOL
One Chatham Ctr., Pittsburgh 15219 *Type:* Private home study *Accred.:* 1979/1990 (NHSC) *Calendar:* Courses of varying lengths *Degrees:* certificates *CEO:* Pres. Rod L. Piatt
                           (412) 456-1800

BRADFORD SCHOOL
355 Fifth Ave., Pittsburgh 15222 *Type:* Private business *Accred.:* 1970/1988 (CCA-ACICS) *Calendar:* Courses of varying lengths *Degrees:* certificates, diplomas *Prof. Accred.:* Medical Assisting (AMA) *CEO:* Pres. Vincent S. Graziano
Enroll: 602   (412) 391-6710

BRADLEY ACADEMY FOR THE VISUAL ARTS
625 E. Philadelphia St., York 17403-1625 *Type:* Private *Accred.:* 1983/1988 (CCA-ACTTS) *Calendar:* Sem. plan *Degrees:* A *CEO:* Dir. Loren H. Kroh
Enroll: 216   (717) 848-1447

BRYN MAWR COLLEGE
Bryn Mawr 19010 *Type:* Private liberal arts for women *Accred.:* 1921/1989 (MSA) *Calendar:* Sem. plan *Degrees:* B, M, D, certificates, diplomas *Prof. Accred.:* Social Work (M) *CEO:* Pres. Mary Patterson McPherson
Enroll: 1847   (215) 526-5000

BUCKNELL UNIVERSITY
Lewisburg 17837 *Type:* Private liberal arts *Accred.:* 1921/1988 (MSA) *Calendar:* 4-1-4 plan *Degrees:* B, M *Prof. Accred.:* Engineering (chemical, civil, electrical, mechanical), Music *CEO:* Pres. Gary A. Sojka
Enroll: 3519   (717) 523-1271

BUCKS COUNTY COMMUNITY COLLEGE
Swamp Rd., Newtown 18940 *Type:* Public (state) junior *System:* Pennsylvania State System of Higher Education *Accred.:* 1968/1987 (MSA) *Calendar:* Sem. plan *Degrees:* A, certificates, diplomas *Prof. Accred.:* Art, Nursing (A) *CEO:* Interim Pres. Charles E. Rollins
Enroll: 10029   (215) 968-8000

BUTLER COUNTY COMMUNITY COLLEGE
College Dr., Oak Hills, Butler 16001 *Type:* Public (state) junior *System:* Pennsylvania State System of Higher Education *Accred.:* 1971/1988 (MSA) *Calendar:* Sem. plan *Degrees:* A, certificates, diplomas *CEO:* Pres. Thaddeus H. Penar
Enroll: 2488   (412) 287-8711

CHI INSTITUTE
520 Street Rd., Southampton 18966-3787 *Type:* Private *Accred.:* 1985 (CCA-ACTTS) *Calendar:* Courses of varying lengths *Degrees:* certificates *CEO:* Dir. Glenn B. Murray
Enroll: 484   (215) 357-5100

CABRINI COLLEGE
Eagle and King of Prussia Rds., Radnor 19087 *Type:* Private (Roman Catholic) liberal arts for women *Accred.:* 1965/1985 (MSA) *Calendar:* Sem. plan *Degrees:* B, M *CEO:* Pres. Eileen Currie, M.S.C.
Enroll: 1263   (215) 971-8100

CALIFORNIA UNIVERSITY OF PENNSYLVANIA
Third St., California 15419 *Type:* Public (state) liberal arts *System:* Pennsylvania State System of Higher Education *Accred.:* 1951/1985 (MSA) *Calendar:* Sem. plan *Degrees:* A, B, M *Prof. Accred.:* Nurse Anesthesia Education, Nursing (B), Social Work (B), Teacher Education (e,s,p) *CEO:* Pres. John P. Watkins
Enroll: 6313   (412) 938-4000

CAMBRIA-ROWE BUSINESS COLLEGE
221 Central Ave., Johnstown 15902 *Type:* Private business *Accred.:* 1959/1990 (CCA-ACICS) *Calendar:* Qtr. plan *Degrees:* A *CEO:* Pres. Bill Coward
Enroll: 396   (814) 536-5168

THE CAREER INSTITUTE
1825 John F. Kennedy Blvd., Philadelphia 19103 *Type:* Private business *Accred.:* 1984/1990 (CCA-ACICS) *Calendar:* Qtr. plan *Degrees:* certificates, diplomas *CEO:* Exec. Dir. Eve M. Corey
Enroll: 321   (215) 561-7600

Pennsylvania

BRANCH CAMPUS
711 Market St. Mall, Wilmington, DE 19801 *CEO:* Exec. Dir. Eve Corey
(302) 575-1400

CAREER TRAINING ACADEMY
703 Fifth Ave., New Kensington 15068-6301 *Type:* Private *Accred.:* 1991 (CCA-ACTTS) *Calendar:* Courses of varying lengths *Degrees:* certificates *Prof. Accred.:* Medical Assisting (AMA) *CEO:* C.E.O. John M. Reddy
(412) 337-1000

CARLOW COLLEGE
3333 Fifth Ave., Pittsburgh 15213 *Type:* Private (Roman Catholic) liberal arts for women *Accred.:* 1935/1986 (MSA) *Calendar:* Sem. plan *Degrees:* B, M *Prof. Accred.:* Nursing (B) *CEO:* Pres. Grace Ann Geibel, R.S.M.
Enroll: 962 (412) 578-6000

CARNEGIE-MELLON UNIVERSITY
5000 Forbes Ave., Pittsburgh 15213 *Type:* Private *Accred.:* 1921/1988 (MSA) *Calendar:* Sem. plan *Degrees:* B, M, D *Prof. Accred.:* Architecture (B,M), Art, Business (B,M), Engineering (chemical, civil, computer, electrical, general, mechanical, metallurgical), Music, Public Management and Policy *CEO:* Pres. Robert Mehrabian
Enroll: 6993 (412) 268-2000

CEDAR CREST COLLEGE
100 College Dr., Allentown 18104 *Type:* Private (United Church of Christ) liberal arts for women *Accred.:* 1944/1983 (MSA) *Calendar:* Sem. plan *Degrees:* B *Prof. Accred.:* Nuclear Medicine Technology, Nursing (B), Social Work (B) *CEO:* Pres. Dorothy Gulbenkian Blaney
Enroll: 1039 (215) 437-4471

CENTRAL PENNSYLVANIA BUSINESS SCHOOL
College Hill Rd., Summerdale 17093 *Type:* Private *Accred.:* 1977/1987 (MSA) *Calendar:* Tri. plan *Degrees:* A *Prof. Accred.:* Medical Assisting (AMA), Physical Therapy Assisting *CEO:* Pres. Todd A. Milano
Enroll: 696 (717) 732-0702

CHATHAM COLLEGE
Woodland Rd., Pittsburgh 15232 *Type:* Private liberal arts for women *Accred.:* 1924/1988 (MSA) *Calendar:* 4-1-4 plan *Degrees:* B *CEO:* Pres. Esther Barazzone
Enroll: 686 (412) 365-1100

CHESTNUT HILL COLLEGE
Chestnut Hill, Philadelphia 19118-2695 *Type:* Private (Roman Catholic) liberal arts for women *Accred.:* 1930/1987 (MSA) *Calendar:* Sem. plan *Degrees:* A, B, M *CEO:* Pres. Matthew Anita MacDonald, S.S.J.
Enroll: 1022 (215) 248-7000

CHEYNEY UNIVERSITY OF PENNSYLVANIA
Cheney and Creek Rds., Cheyney 19319 *Type:* Public (state) liberal arts *System:* Pennsylvania State System of Higher Education *Accred.:* 1951/1989 (MSA) *Calendar:* Sem. plan *Degrees:* A, B, M *Prof. Accred.:* Teacher Education (e,s,p) *CEO:* Interim Pres. Valarie Swain Cade
Enroll: 1361 (215) 399-2000

CHUBB INSTITUTE—KEYSTONE SCHOOL
Baltimore Pike and Lincoln Ave, P.O. Box 252, Swarthmore 19081 *Type:* Private business *Accred.:* 1968/1986 (CCA-ACICS) *Calendar:* Sem. plan *Degrees:* A *CEO:* Dir. Charles A. Hamilton
Enroll: 600 (215) 543-1747

CHURCHMAN BUSINESS SCHOOL
355 Spring Garden St., Easton 18042 *Type:* Private business *Accred.:* 1954/1987 (CCA-ACICS) *Calendar:* Tri. plan *Degrees:* A *CEO:* Pres. Charles W. Churchman, Jr.
Enroll: 267 (215) 258-5345

CLARION UNIVERSITY OF PENNSYLVANIA
Clarion 16214 *Type:* Public (state) liberal arts *System:* Pennsylvania State System of Higher Education *Accred.:* 1948/1987 (MSA) *Calendar:* Sem. plan *Degrees:* A, B, M *Prof. Accred.:* Audiology, Librarianship,

Accredited Institutions — Pennsylvania

Speech-Language Pathology, Teacher Education (e,s) *CEO:* Pres. Diane L. Reinhard
Enroll: 6601 (814) 226-2000

VENANGO CAMPUS
W. First St., Oil City, PA 16301 *Prof. Accred.:* Nursing (A,B) *CEO:* Exec. Dean James W. Blake
(814) 676-6591

THE CLARISSA SCHOOL OF FASHION DESIGN
Warner Ctr., 332 Fifth Ave., Pittsburgh 15222-2411 *Type:* Private *Accred.:* 1976/1987 (CCA-ACTTS) *Calendar:* Sem. plan *Degrees:* certificates, diplomas *CEO:* Dir. Penelope M. Smith
Enroll: 75 (412) 471-4414

COLLEGE MISERICORDIA
Lake St., Dallas 18612 *Type:* Private (Roman Catholic) liberal arts primarily for women *Accred.:* 1935/1984 (MSA) *Calendar:* Sem. plan *Degrees:* A, B, M, certificates, diplomas *Prof. Accred.:* Nursing (B,M), Occupational Therapy, Radiography, Social Work (B) *CEO:* Pres. Pasquale DiPasquale
Enroll: 1114 (717) 675-2181

COMMUNITY COLLEGE OF ALLEGHENY COUNTY
ALLEGHENY CAMPUS
808 Ridge Ave., Pittsburgh 15212 *Type:* Public (state) junior *System:* Community College of Allegheny County *Accred.:* 1970/1984 (MSA) *Calendar:* Sem. plan *Degrees:* A, certificates, diplomas *Prof. Accred.:* Medical Assisting (AMA), Medical Laboratory Technology (AMA), Medical Record Technology, Nuclear Medicine Technology, Radiation Therapy Technology, Respiratory Therapy, Respiratory Therapy Technology *CEO:* Exec. Dean/Vice Pres. J. David Griffin
Enroll: 6928 (412) 237-2525

COMMUNITY COLLEGE OF ALLEGHENY COUNTY
BOYCE CAMPUS
595 Beatty Rd., Monroeville 15146 *Type:* Public (state) junior *System:* Community College of Allegheny County *Accred.:* 1970/1989 (MSA) *Calendar:* Sem. plan *Degrees:* A, certificates, diplomas *Prof. Accred.:* Diagnostic Medical Sonography, Occupational Therapy Assisting, Physical Therapy Assisting, Radiography, Surgical Technology *CEO:* Exec. Dean/Vice Pres. Carl A. DiSibio
Enroll: 4190 (412) 327-1327

COMMUNITY COLLEGE OF ALLEGHENY COUNTY
COLLEGE CENTER NORTH
111 Pines Plaza, 1130 Perry Hwy., Pittsburgh 15237 *Type:* Public (state) junior *System:* Community College of Allegheny County *Accred.:* 1979/1989 (MSA) *Calendar:* Sem. plan *Degrees:* A, certificates, diplomas *CEO:* Exec. Dean/Vice Pres. Fred F. Bartok
Enroll: 3112 (412) 366-7000

COMMUNITY COLLEGE OF ALLEGHENY COUNTY
SOUTH CAMPUS
1750 Clairton Rd., Rte. 885, West Mifflin 15122 *Type:* Public (state) junior *System:* Community College of Allegheny County *Accred.:* 1973/1989 (MSA) *Calendar:* Sem. plan *Degrees:* A, certificates, diplomas *Prof. Accred.:* Medical Laboratory Technology (AMA) *CEO:* Exec. Dean/Vice Pres. Thomas A. Juravich
Enroll: 4520 (412) 469-1100

COMMUNITY COLLEGE OF BEAVER COUNTY
College Dr., Monaca 15061 *Type:* Public (state) junior *System:* Pennsylvania State System of Higher Education *Accred.:* 1972/1989 (MSA) *Calendar:* Sem. plan *Degrees:* A, certificates, diplomas *Prof. Accred.:* Medical Laboratory Technology (AMA) *CEO:* Pres. Margaret J. Williams
Enroll: 2603 (412) 775-8561

COMMUNITY COLLEGE OF PHILADELPHIA
1700 Spring Garden St., Philadelphia 19130 *Type:* Public (state) junior *System:* Pennsylvania State System of Higher Education *Accred.:* 1968/1988 (MSA) *Calendar:* Sem. plan *Degrees:* A, certificates, diplomas *Prof. Accred.:* Dental Assisting, Dental Hygiene, Medical Assisting (AMA), Medical Laboratory Technology (AMA), Medical Record

Pennsylvania

Technology, Nursing (A), Radiography, Respiratory Therapy *CEO:* Pres. Ronald J. Temple
Enroll: 14215 (215) 751-8000

COMPUTER LEARNING CENTER
3600 Market St., University City 19104-2684 *Type:* Private business *Accred.:* 1981/1991 (CCA-ACICS) *Calendar:* Courses of varying lengths *Degrees:* certificates, diplomas *CEO:* Dir. Joseph F. Reichard
Enroll: 1068 (215) 222-6450

COMPUTER LEARNING NETWORK
3607 Rosemont Ave., Camp Hill 17011-6996 *Type:* Private *Accred.:* 1985 (CCA-ACTTS) *Calendar:* Courses of varying lengths *Degrees:* certificates *CEO:* Pres./Dir. G.L. Royer
Enroll: 298 (717) 761-1481

BRANCH CAMPUS
2900 Fairway Dr., Altoona, PA 16602-4457 *CEO:* Dir. Todd Fries
(814) 944-5643

COMPUTER TECH
107 Sixth St., Pittsburgh 15222 *Type:* Private business *Accred.:* 1971/1989 (CCA-ACICS) *Calendar:* Courses of varying lengths *Degrees:* A, certificates, diplomas *CEO:* Dir. Bruce Crowley
Enroll: 595 (412) 391-4197

BRANCH CAMPUS
Middletown Mall, I-79 and Rte. 250, Fairmont, WV 26554 *CEO:* Dir. Lawrence Grotstein
(304) 363-5100

CONSOLIDATED SCHOOL OF BUSINESS
1817 Olde Homestead La., Stes. I and J, Lancaster 17601 *Type:* Private business *Accred.:* 1987/1990 (CCA-ACICS) *Calendar:* Courses of varying lengths *Degrees:* A, certificates, diplomas *CEO:* Exec. Dir. Vincent P. Safran
Enroll: 255 (717) 394-6211

CONSOLIDATED SCHOOL OF BUSINESS
707 Loucks Rd., York 17404 *Type:* Private business *Accred.:* 1984/1990 (CCA-ACICS) *Calendar:* Courses of varying lengths *Degrees:* A, certificates, diplomas *CEO:* Exec. Dir. Betty J. Johnson
Enroll: 294 (717) 846-4076

THE CRAFT INSTITUTE
9 S. 12th St., Philadelphia 19107-3644 *Type:* Private *Accred.:* 1980/1985 (CCA-ACTTS) *Calendar:* Courses of varying lengths *Degrees:* certificates *CEO:* Dir. Gail Zukerman
Enroll: 411 (215) 665-8546

CURTIS INSTITUTE OF MUSIC
1726 Locust St., Philadelphia 19103 *Type:* Private professional *Accred.:* 1989 (MSA candidate) *Calendar:* Sem. plan *Degrees:* B, M *Prof. Accred.:* Music *CEO:* Dir. Gary Graffman
Enroll: 179 (215) 893-5252

DEAN INSTITUTE OF TECHNOLOGY
1501 W. Liberty Ave., Pittsburgh 15226-1197 *Type:* Private *Accred.:* 1969/1985 (CCA-ACTTS) *Calendar:* Qtr. plan *Degrees:* A, certificates, diplomas *CEO:* Dir. James S. Dean
Enroll: 468 (412) 531-4433

DELAWARE COUNTY COMMUNITY COLLEGE
Rte. 252 and Media Line Rd., Media 19063 *Type:* Public (state) junior *System:* Pennsylvania State System of Higher Education *Accred.:* 1970/1985 (MSA) *Calendar:* Sem. plan *Degrees:* A, certificates, diplomas *Prof. Accred.:* Medical Assisting (AMA), Nursing (A), Surgical Technology *CEO:* Pres. Richard D. DeCosmo
Enroll: 8273 (215) 359-5000

DELAWARE COUNTY INSTITUTE OF TRAINING
615 Ave. of the States, Chester 19013-6022 *Type:* Private *Accred.:* 1984/1989 (CCA-ACTTS) *Calendar:* Courses of varying lengths *Degrees:* certificates *CEO:* Dir. Howard R. Kauff
Enroll: 276 (215) 874-1888

Accredited Institutions   **Pennsylvania**

DELAWARE VALLEY ACADEMY OF MEDICAL AND DENTAL ASSISTANTS
6539-43 Roosevelt Blvd., Philadelphia 19149-2998 *Type:* Private *Calendar:* Courses of varying lengths *Degrees:* certificates *Prof. Accred.:* Health Education *CEO:* Dir. David M. Goldsmith
(215) 744-5300

DELAWARE VALLEY COLLEGE OF SCIENCE AND AGRICULTURE
Rte. 202 and New Britain Rd., Doylestown 18901 *Type:* Private professional primarily for men *Accred.:* 1962/1988 (MSA) *Calendar:* Sem. plan *Degrees:* A, B *CEO:* Acting Pres. George F. West
Enroll: 1654   (215) 345-1500

DICKINSON COLLEGE
Carlisle 17013 *Type:* Private liberal arts *Accred.:* 1921/1987 (MSA) *Calendar:* Sem. plan *Degrees:* B *CEO:* Pres. A. Lee Fritschler
Enroll: 2054   (717) 243-5121

DICKINSON SCHOOL OF LAW
150 S. College St., Carlisle 17013 *Type:* Private *Calendar:* Sem. plan *Degrees:* P *Prof. Accred.:* Law *CEO:* Dean John Maher
Enroll: 524   (717) 243-4611

DOUGLAS SCHOOL OF BUSINESS
130 Seventh St., Monessen 15062 *Type:* Private business *Accred.:* 1977/1986 (CCA-ACICS) *Calendar:* Tri. plan *Degrees:* A, certificates, diplomas *CEO:* Pres. Jeffrey D. Imbrescia
Enroll: 146   (412) 684-7644

DREXEL UNIVERSITY
32nd and Chestnut Sts., Philadelphia 19104 *Type:* Private *Accred.:* 1927/1987 (MSA) *Calendar:* Qtr. plan *Degrees:* B, M, D *Prof. Accred.:* Architecture (B), Business (B,M), Computer Science, Engineering (chemical, civil, electrical, materials, mechanical), Interior Design, Librarianship *CEO:* Pres. Richard D. Breslin
Enroll: 12265   (215) 895-2000

DUBOIS BUSINESS COLLEGE
One Beaver Dr., P.O. Box 0, DuBois 15801 *Type:* Private business *Accred.:* 1954/1988 (CCA-ACICS) *Calendar:* Tri. plan *Degrees:* A, certificates, diplomas *CEO:* Dir. Jackie Syktich
Enroll: 406   (814) 371-6920

DUFF'S BUSINESS INSTITUTE
110 Ninth St., Pittsburgh 15222 *Type:* Private business *Accred.:* 1961/1991 (CCA-ACICS) *Calendar:* Qtr. plan *Degrees:* A, certificates, diplomas *Prof. Accred.:* Medical Assisting (AMA) *CEO:* Dir. Mark Scott
Enroll: 1097   (412) 261-4520

DUQUESNE UNIVERSITY
600 Forbes Ave., Pittsburgh 15282 *Type:* Private (Roman Catholic) *Accred.:* 1935/1983 (MSA) *Calendar:* Sem. plan *Degrees:* A, B, P, M, D *Prof. Accred.:* Business (B,M), Law, Music, Nursing (B,M), Pharmacy *CEO:* Pres. John E. Murray, Jr.
Enroll: 6453   (412) 434-6000

EAST STROUDSBURG UNIVERSITY OF PENNSYLVANIA
East Stroudsburg 18301 *Type:* Public (state) liberal arts *System:* Pennsylvania State System of Higher Education *Accred.:* 1950/1987 (MSA) *Calendar:* Sem. plan *Degrees:* A, B, M *Prof. Accred.:* Community Health, Nursing (B), Recreation and Leisure Services, Teacher Education (e,s) *CEO:* Pres. James E. Gilbert
Enroll: 4910   (717) 424-3545

EASTERN BAPTIST THEOLOGICAL SEMINARY
City Line and Lancaster Aves., Philadelphia 19151-1495 *Type:* Private (Baptist) professional; graduate only *Accred.:* 1954/1984 (ATS); 1954/1985 (MSA) *Calendar:* 4-1-4 plan *Degrees:* P, M, D *CEO:* Pres. Manfred T. Brauch
Enroll: 173   (215) 896-5000

EASTERN COLLEGE
Fairview Dr., St. Davids 19087 *Type:* Private (Baptist) liberal arts *Accred.:* 1954/1989 (MSA) *Calendar:* Sem. plan *Degrees:* A, B,

M, certificates, diplomas *Prof. Accred.:* Nursing (B), Social Work (B) *CEO:* Pres. Roberta Hestenes
Enroll: 1155 (215) 341-5810

EDINBORO UNIVERSITY OF PENNSYLVANIA
Edinboro 16444 *Type:* Public (state) liberal arts *System:* Pennsylvania State System of Higher Education *Accred.:* 1949/1988 (MSA) *Calendar:* Sem. plan *Degrees:* A, B, M, certificates, diplomas *Prof. Accred.:* Dental Laboratory Technology, Dietetics (coordinated), Nurse Anesthesia Education, Nursing (B), Rehabilitation Counseling, Social Work (B), Teacher Education (e,s,p) *CEO:* Pres. Foster F. Diebold
Enroll: 7001 (814) 732-2000

ELECTRONIC INSTITUTES
19 Jamesway Plaza, Middletown 17057-4851 *Type:* Private *Accred.:* 1967/1987 (CCA-ACTTS) *Calendar:* Courses of varying lengths *Degrees:* A, certificates *CEO:* Dir. William F. Margut
Enroll: 334 (717) 944-2731

ELECTRONIC INSTITUTES
4634 Browns Hill Rd., Pittsburgh 15217-2919 *Type:* Private *Accred.:* 1971/1986 (CCA-ACTTS) *Calendar:* Courses of varying lengths *Degrees:* A, certificates *CEO:* Pres. Philip Chosky
Enroll: 473 (412) 521-8686

ELIZABETHTOWN COLLEGE
One Alpha Dr., Elizabethtown 17022 *Type:* Private (Church of Brethren) liberal arts *Accred.:* 1948/1989 (MSA) *Calendar:* Sem. plan *Degrees:* B *Prof. Accred.:* Music, Occupational Therapy, Social Work (B) *CEO:* Pres. Gerhard E. Spiegler
Enroll: 1773 (717) 367-1151

ERIE BUSINESS CENTER
246 W. Ninth St., Erie 16501 *Type:* Private business *Accred.:* 1989 (CCA-ACICS) *Calendar:* Courses of varying lengths *Degrees:* A, certificates, diplomas *CEO:* Exec. Dir. William G. Carver
Enroll: 573 (814) 456-7504

ERIE INSTITUTE OF TECHNOLOGY
2221 Peninsula Dr., Erie 16506-2954 *Type:* Private *Accred.:* 1979/1989 (CCA-ACTTS) *Calendar:* Courses of varying lengths *Degrees:* certificates *CEO:* Pres. Clinton L. Oviatt, Jr.
Enroll: 100 (814) 838-2711

EVANGELICAL SCHOOL OF THEOLOGY
121 S. College St., Myerstown 17067 *Type:* Private professional; graduate only *Accred.:* 1987 (ATS); 1984 (MSA) *Calendar:* Sem. plan *Degrees:* P, M *CEO:* Pres. Ray Seilhamer
Enroll: 53 (717) 866-5775

FRANKLIN AND MARSHALL COLLEGE
P.O. Box 3003, Lancaster 17604 *Type:* Private liberal arts *Accred.:* 1921/1989 (MSA) *Calendar:* Sem. plan *Degrees:* A, B *CEO:* Pres. A. Richard Kneedler
Enroll: 1896 (717) 291-3993

GANNON UNIVERSITY
University Sq., Erie 16541 *Type:* Private (Roman Catholic) liberal arts *Accred.:* 1951/1987 (MSA) *Calendar:* Sem. plan *Degrees:* A, B, M *Prof. Accred.:* Dietetics (coordinated), Engineering (electrical, mechanical), Medical Assisting (AMA), Nurse Anesthesia Education, Nursing (A,B,M), Physician Assisting, Radiography, Respiratory Therapy, Social Work (B) *CEO:* Pres. David Rubino
Enroll: 3687 (814) 871-7000

GARFIELD BUSINESS INSTITUTE
2590 Ridge Rd., Monaca 15061 *Type:* Private business *Accred.:* 1988 (CCA-ACICS) *Calendar:* Courses of varying lengths *Degrees:* certificates, diplomas *CEO:* Interim Dir. Ed Latagliata
Enroll: 47 (412) 728-4050

GATEWAY TECHNICAL INSTITUTE
100 Seventh St., Pittsburgh 15222-3404 *Type:* Private *Accred.:* 1969/1985 (CCA-ACTTS) *Calendar:* Tri. plan *Degrees:* diplomas *CEO:* Dir. Wayne D. Smith
Enroll: 715 (412) 281-4111

Accredited Institutions   **Pennsylvania**

GENEVA COLLEGE
College Ave., Beaver Falls 15010 *Type:* Private (Reformed Presbyterian) liberal arts *Accred.:* 1922/1988 (MSA) *Calendar:* Sem. plan *Degrees:* A, B, M *CEO:* Pres. Joseph McFarland
Enroll: 1192   (412) 846-5100

GETTYSBURG COLLEGE
North Washington St., Gettysburg 17325 *Type:* Private liberal arts *Accred.:* 1921/1988 (MSA) *Calendar:* Sem. plan *Degrees:* B *CEO:* Pres. Gordon Haaland
Enroll: 2074   (717) 337-6000

GRATZ COLLEGE
Old York Rd. and Melrose Ave., Melrose Park 19126 *Type:* Private *Accred.:* 1967/1987 (MSA) *Calendar:* Sem. plan *Degrees:* B, P, M, certificates, diplomas *CEO:* Pres. Gary S. Schiff
Enroll: 95   (215) 635-7300

GROVE CITY COLLEGE
Grove City 16127 *Type:* Private liberal arts *Accred.:* 1922/1985 (MSA) *Calendar:* Sem. plan *Degrees:* B *CEO:* Pres. Jerry H. Combee
Enroll: 2148   (412) 458-2000

GWYNEDD-MERCY COLLEGE
Gwynedd Valley 19437 *Type:* Private (Roman Catholic) liberal arts primarily for women *Accred.:* 1958/1986 (MSA) *Calendar:* Sem. plan *Degrees:* A, B, M, certificates, diplomas *Prof. Accred.:* Medical Record Technology, Nursing (A,B), Radiation Therapy Technology, Respiratory Therapy, Respiratory Therapy Technology *CEO:* Pres. Isabelle Keiss, R.S.M.
Enroll: 1812   (215) 646-7300

HAHNEMANN UNIVERSITY
Broad and Vine Sts., Philadelphia 19102 *Type:* Private *Accred.:* 1978/1989 (MSA) *Calendar:* Sem. plan *Degrees:* A, B, P, M, D *Prof. Accred.:* Medical Laboratory Technology (AMA), Medical Technology, Medicine, Nursing (A,B), Oral and Maxillofacial Surgery (provisional), Physical Therapy, Physical Therapy Assisting, Physician Assisting, Radiography *CEO:* Pres. Iqbal F. Paroo
Enroll: 386   (215) 448-7000

HARCUM JUNIOR COLLEGE
Morris and Montgomery Aves., Bryn Mawr 19010 *Type:* Private junior for women *Accred.:* 1970/1985 (MSA) *Calendar:* Sem. plan *Degrees:* A *Prof. Accred.:* Dental Assisting, Medical Assisting (AMA), Medical Laboratory Technology (AMA), Occupational Therapy Assisting, Physical Therapy Assisting, Veterinary Technology *CEO:* Pres. Norma Furst
Enroll: 762   (215) 525-4100

HARRISBURG AREA COMMUNITY COLLEGE
3300 Cameron Street Rd., Harrisburg 17110 *Type:* Public (state) junior *System:* Pennsylvania State System of Higher Education *Accred.:* 1967/1987 (MSA) *Calendar:* Sem. plan *Degrees:* A *Prof. Accred.:* Dental Assisting, EMT-Paramedic, Engineering Technology (electrical, mechanical), Medical Laboratory Technology (AMA), Nursing (A), Practical Nursing, Respiratory Therapy, Respiratory Therapy Technology *CEO:* Pres. Kenneth B. Woodbury, Jr.
Enroll: 7064   (717) 780-2300

HAVERFORD COLLEGE
370 Lancaster Ave., Haverford 19041 *Type:* Private liberal arts *Accred.:* 1921/1988 (MSA) *Calendar:* Sem. plan *Degrees:* B *CEO:* Pres. Tom G. Kessinger
Enroll: 1105   (215) 896-1000

HIRAM G. ANDREWS CENTER
727 Goucher St., Johnstown 15905-3092 *Type:* Private *Accred.:* 1987 (CCA-ACTTS) *Calendar:* Courses of varying lengths *Degrees:* certificates, diplomas *CEO:* Dir. Adele M. Sternberg
Enroll: 58   (814) 255-8200

HOLY FAMILY COLLEGE
Grant and Frankford Aves., Philadelphia 19114 *Type:* Private (Roman Catholic) liberal arts *Accred.:* 1961/1986 (MSA) *Calendar:*

Pennsylvania

Sem. plan *Degrees:* A, B *Prof. Accred.:* Nursing (B), Radiography *CEO:* Pres. M. Francesca Onley
Enroll: 1685 (215) 637-7700

HUSSIAN SCHOOL OF ART
1010 Arch St., Philadelphia 19107-3013 *Type:* Private *Accred.:* 1972/1989 (CCA-ACTTS) *Calendar:* Sem. plan *Degrees:* A *CEO:* Dir. Ronald Dove
Enroll: 166 (215) 238-9000

ICM SCHOOL OF BUSINESS
10 Wood St., Pittsburgh 15222 *Type:* Private business *Accred.:* 1967/1985 (CCA-ACICS) *Calendar:* Courses of varying lengths *Degrees:* A, certificates, diplomas *Prof. Accred.:* Medical Assisting (AMA) *CEO:* Dir. Carla M. Ryba
Enroll: 1246 (412) 261-2647

IMMACULATA COLLEGE
Immaculata 19345 *Type:* Private (Roman Catholic) liberal arts for women *Accred.:* 1928/1984 (MSA) *Calendar:* Sem. plan *Degrees:* A, B, M *Prof. Accred.:* Dietetics (coordinated), Music, Nursing (B) *CEO:* Pres. Marian William Hoben
Enroll: 2095 (215) 647-4400

INDIANA UNIVERSITY OF PENNSYLVANIA
Indiana 15705 *Type:* Public (state) liberal arts *System:* Pennsylvania State System of Higher Education *Accred.:* 1941/1987 (MSA) *Calendar:* Sem. plan *Degrees:* A, B, M, D, certificates, diplomas *Prof. Accred.:* Clinical Psychology, Music, Nursing (B), Respiratory Therapy, Teacher Education (e,s,p) *CEO:* Interim Pres. Charles R. Fuget
Enroll: 13650 (412) 357-2100

   ARMSTRONG COUNTY CAMPUS
   Kittanning, PA 16201 *CEO:* Dir. Robert H. Doerr
   (814) 543-1078

   PUNXSUTAWNEY CAMPUS
   Punxsutawney, PA 15767 *CEO:* Dir. Norman T. Storm
   (814) 938-6711

INFORMATION COMPUTER SYSTEMS INSTITUTE
2201 Hangar Pl., Allentown 18103-9504 *Type:* Private *Accred.:* 1984/1989 (CCA-ACTTS) *Calendar:* Courses of varying lengths *Degrees:* certificates *CEO:* Pres. William Barber
Enroll: 112 (215) 264-8029

INSTITUTE OF SECURITY AND TECHNOLOGY
319 S. 69th St., Upper Darby 19082-4297 *Type:* Private *Accred.:* 1984/1989 (CCA-ACTTS) *Calendar:* Courses of varying lengths *Degrees:* certificates *CEO:* Dir. Bill Wood
Enroll: 186 (215) 352-6100

INTERNATIONAL CORRESPONDENCE SCHOOL
925 Oak St., Scranton 18515 *Type:* Private home study *Accred.:* 1956/1989 (NHSC) *Calendar:* Courses of varying lengths *Degrees:* certificates *CEO:* Pres. Gary M. Keisling
(717) 342-7701

   BRANCH CAMPUS
   Ctr. for Degree Studies, 925 Oak St., Scranton, PA 18515 *CEO:* Dir. Gerald E. Burns
   (717) 342-7701

IVANHOE INSTITUTE LIMITED
244 Center Rd., Ste. 101, Monroeville 15146 *Type:* Private professional *Calendar:* Courses of varying lengths *Degrees:* certificates *Prof. Accred.:* Dental Assisting (prelim. provisional), Health Education *CEO:* Dir. Donna Warren
(412) 372-7997

J.H. THOMPSON'S ACADEMIES
2908 State St., Erie 16508-1832 *Type:* Private *Accred.:* 1979/1989 (CCA-ACTTS) *Calendar:* Courses of varying lengths *Degrees:* diplomas *CEO:* Dir. Jack Thompson
Enroll: 574 (814) 456-6217

JAMES MARTIN SCHOOL
Richmond and Ontario Sts., Philadelphia 19134 *Type:* Public (city) *Calendar:* Courses of varying lenghts *Degrees:* certificates *Prof. Accred.:* Medical Laboratory Technology,

Respiratory Therapy Technology *CEO:* Admin. Richard L. Brown
(215) 739-1891

JOHNSON TECHNICAL INSTITUTE
3427 N. Main Ave., Scranton 18508-1495 *Type:* Private *Accred.:* 1979/1989 (CCA-ACTTS) *Calendar:* Sem. plan *Degrees:* A *CEO:* Pres. Clair T. Kenny
Enroll: 562 (717) 342-6404

JOSEPH DONAHUE INTERNATIONAL SCHOOL OF HAIRSTYLING
2485 Grant Ave., Philadelphia 19114-1004 *Type:* Private *Accred.:* 1984/1989 (CCA-ACTTS) *Calendar:* Courses of varying lengths *Degrees:* certificates *CEO:* Owner/Pres. Nancy L. Johnson
Enroll: 24 (215) 969-1313

JUNIATA COLLEGE
1700 Moore St., Huntingdon 16652 *Type:* Private liberal arts *Accred.:* 1922/1987 (MSA) *Calendar:* Sem. plan *Degrees:* B *Prof. Accred.:* Social Work (B) *CEO:* Pres. Robert W. Neff
Enroll: 1137 (814) 643-4310

KALIX TRADE SCHOOL
439 N. 11th St., Philadelphia 19123-3715 *Type:* Private *Accred.:* 1988 (CCA-ACTTS) *Calendar:* Courses of varying lengths *Degrees:* certificates *CEO:* Dir. Thomas D. Treacy
Enroll: 314 (215) 765-7028

KATHARINE GIBBS SCHOOL
Land Title Bldg., Chestnut and Broad Sts., Philadelphia 19110 *Type:* Private business *Accred.:* 1979 (CCA-ACICS) *Calendar:* Courses of varying lengths *Degrees:* certificates, diplomas *CEO:* Dir. Jane Chadwick
Enroll: 461 (215) 564-5035

KEYSTONE JUNIOR COLLEGE
P.O. Box 50, La Plume 18440 *Type:* Private junior *Accred.:* 1936/1988 (MSA) *Calendar:* Sem. plan *Degrees:* A, certificates, diplomas *CEO:* Pres. Robert E. Mooney
Enroll: 1270 (717) 945-5141

KING'S COLLEGE
133 N. River St., Wilkes-Barre 18711 *Type:* Private (Roman Catholic) liberal arts *Accred.:* 1955/1989 (MSA) *Calendar:* Sem. plan *Degrees:* A, B, certificates, diplomas *Prof. Accred.:* Physician Assisting *CEO:* Pres. James R. Lackenmier, C.S.C.
Enroll: 2304 (717) 826-5900

KUTZTOWN UNIVERSITY OF PENNSYLVANIA
Kutztown 19530 *Type:* Public (state) liberal arts *System:* Pennsylvania State System of Higher Education *Accred.:* 1944/1988 (MSA) *Calendar:* Sem. plan *Degrees:* B, M *Prof. Accred.:* Nursing (B), Social Work (B-candidate), Teacher Education (e,s,p) *CEO:* Pres. David E. McFarland
Enroll: 7168 (215) 683-4000

LA ROCHE COLLEGE
9000 Babcock Blvd., Pittsburgh 15237 *Type:* Private (Roman Catholic) liberal arts *Accred.:* 1973/1988 (MSA) *Calendar:* Sem. plan *Degrees:* B, M *Prof. Accred.:* Interior Design, Nurse Anesthesia Education, Nursing (B) *CEO:* Pres. Margaret F. Huber, CDP
Enroll: 1852 (412) 367-9300

LA SALLE UNIVERSITY
Olney Ave. at 20th St., Philadelphia 19141 *Type:* Private (Roman Catholic) liberal arts *Accred.:* 1930/1986 (MSA) *Calendar:* Sem. plan *Degrees:* A, B, M *Prof. Accred.:* Nursing (B), Social Work (B) *CEO:* Pres. F. Patrick Ellis, F.S.C.
Enroll: 6364 (215) 951-1000

LACKAWANNA JUNIOR COLLEGE
901 Prospect Ave., Scranton 18505 *Type:* Private junior *Accred.:* 1973/1978 (MSA) *Calendar:* Sem. plan *Degrees:* A, certificates, diplomas *CEO:* Pres. Joseph G. Morelli
Enroll: 923 (717) 961-7810

LAFAYETTE COLLEGE
High St., Easton 18042 *Type:* Private liberal arts *Accred.:* 1921/1988 (MSA) *Calendar:* Sem. plan *Degrees:* B *Prof. Accred.:* Engi-

Pennsylvania

neering (chemical, civil, electrical, mechanical) *CEO:* Pres. Robert I. Rotberg
Enroll: 2352 (215) 250-5000

LANCASTER BIBLE COLLEGE
901 Eden Rd., Lancaster 17601 *Type:* Private *Accred.:* 1964/1984 (AABC); 1982/1987 (MSA) *Calendar:* Sem. plan *Degrees:* A, B, certificates, diplomas *CEO:* Pres. Gilbert A. Peterson
Enroll: 387 (717) 569-7071

LANCASTER THEOLOGICAL SEMINARY
555 W. James St., Lancaster 17603 *Type:* Private (United Church of Christ) professional; graduate only *Accred.:* 1938/1984 (ATS); 1978/1989 (MSA) *Calendar:* 3-1-3 plan *Degrees:* P, M, D *CEO:* Pres. Peter M. Schmiechen
Enroll: 103 (717) 393-0654

THE LANSDALE SCHOOL OF BUSINESS
201 Church Rd., North Wales 19454 *Type:* Private junior *Accred.:* 1967/1989 (CCA-ACICS) *Calendar:* Courses of varying lengths *Degrees:* A *CEO:* Pres. Marlon D. Keller
Enroll: 707 (215) 855-4212

THE LAUREL BUSINESS INSTITUTE
11-15 Penn St., Uniontown 15401 *Type:* Private business *Accred.:* 1987 (CCA-ACICS) *Calendar:* Courses of varying lengths *Degrees:* A, certificates, diplomas *CEO:* Pres. Christopher D. Decker
(412) 439-4900

LEARNING AND EVALUATION CENTER
515 Market St., P.O. Box 616, Bloomsburg 17815 *Type:* Private home study *Accred.:* 1985/1989 (NHSC) *Calendar:* Courses of varying lengths *Degrees:* certificates *CEO:* Pres./Dir. I.L. McCloskey
(717) 784-5220

LEBANON VALLEY COLLEGE
101 N. College Ave., Annville 17003-0501 *Type:* Private (United Methodist) liberal arts *Accred.:* 1922/1987 (MSA) *Calendar:* Sem.

Accredited Institutions

plan *Degrees:* A, B *Prof. Accred.:* Music *CEO:* Pres. John A. Synodinos
Enroll: 1248 (717) 867-6100

LEHIGH COUNTY COMMUNITY COLLEGE
2370 Main St., Schnecksville 18078 *Type:* Public (state) junior *System:* Pennsylvania State System of Higher Education *Accred.:* 1972/1988 (MSA) *Calendar:* Sem. plan *Degrees:* A, certificates, diplomas *Prof. Accred.:* Medical Assisting (AMA), Medical Record Technology, Occupational Therapy Assisting, Physical Therapy Assisting, Respiratory Therapy, Respiratory Therapy Technology *CEO:* Pres. Robert L. Barthlow
Enroll: 3487 (215) 799-2121

LEHIGH UNIVERSITY
Bethlehem 18015 *Type:* Private *Accred.:* 1921/1988 (MSA) *Calendar:* Sem. plan *Degrees:* B, M, D *Prof. Accred.:* Accounting (Type A), Business (B,M), Computer Science, Engineering (chemical, civil, computer, electrical, industrial, materials, mechanical), Teacher Education (e,s,p), Theatre *CEO:* Pres. Peter W. Likins
Enroll: 6569 (215) 758-3000

LIFETIME CAREER SCHOOLS, INC.
101 Harrison St., Archbald 18403 *Type:* Private home study *Accred.:* 1957/1990 (NHSC) *Calendar:* Courses of varying lengths *Degrees:* certificates *CEO:* Pres. Michael J. Zadarosni
(717) 876-6340

LINCOLN TECHNICAL INSTITUTE
5151 Tilghman St., Allentown 18104-3298 *Type:* Private *Accred.:* 1967/1988 (CCA-ACTTS) *Calendar:* Courses of varying lengths *Degrees:* A, diplomas *CEO:* Dir. Robert G. Milot
Enroll: 1903 (215) 398-5301

LINCOLN TECHNICAL INSTITUTE
9191 Torresdale Ave., Philadelphia 19136 *Type:* Private *Accred.:* 1969/1989 (CCA-ACTTS) *Calendar:* Courses of varying

lengths *Degrees:* A, diplomas *CEO:* Dir. Douglas M. Johnson
Enroll: 817   (215) 335-0080

LINCOLN UNIVERSITY
Lincoln University 19352 *Type:* Private (state) liberal arts *Accred.:* 1922/1988 (MSA) *Calendar:* Sem. plan *Degrees:* A, B, M, certificates, diplomas *Prof. Accred.:* Recreation *CEO:* Pres. Niara Sudarkasa
Enroll: 1251   (215) 932-8300

LOCK HAVEN UNIVERSITY OF PENNSYLVANIA
Lock Haven 17745 *Type:* Public (state) liberal arts *System:* Pennsylvania State System of Higher Education *Accred.:* 1949/1985 (MSA) *Calendar:* Sem. plan *Degrees:* A, B, M *Prof. Accred.:* Social Work (B), Teacher Education (e,s) *CEO:* Pres. Craig D. Willis
Enroll: 3012   (717) 893-2011

CLEARFIELD CAMPUS
Clearfield, PA 16830 *CEO:* Dir. Patrick Gerriero
   (814) 765-0559

LUTHERAN THEOLOGICAL SEMINARY AT GETTYSBURG
61 N.W. Confederate Ave., Gettysburg 17325 *Type:* Private professional; graduate only *Accred.:* 1938/1979 (ATS); 1971/1986 (MSA) *Calendar:* Qtr. plan *Degrees:* P, M, D *CEO:* Pres. Darold A. Beekmann
Enroll: 196   (717) 334-6286

LUTHERAN THEOLOGICAL SEMINARY AT PHILADELPHIA
7301 Germantown Ave., Philadelphia 19119 *Type:* Private professional; graduate only *Accred.:* 1938/1981 (ATS); 1971/1986 (MSA) *Calendar:* Sem. plan *Degrees:* P, M, D *CEO:* Interim Pres. D. Almen
Enroll: 145   (215) 248-4616

LUZERNE COUNTY COMMUNITY COLLEGE
Prospect St. and Middle Rd., Nanticoke 18634 *Type:* Public (state) junior *System:* Pennsylvania State System of Higher Education *Accred.:* 1975/1985 (MSA) *Calendar:* Tri. plan *Degrees:* A *Prof. Accred.:* Dental Hygiene, Nursing (A), Respiratory Therapy Technology *CEO:* Pres. Thomas J. Moran
Enroll: 5688   (717) 829-7300

LYCOMING COLLEGE
Academy St., Williamsport 17701 *Type:* Private (United Methodist) liberal arts *Accred.:* 1934/1986 (MSA) *Calendar:* Sem. plan *Degrees:* B *Prof. Accred.:* Nursing (B) *CEO:* Pres. James E. Douthat
Enroll: 1163   (717) 321-4000

MTA SCHOOL
1801 Oberlin Rd., Middletown 17057 *Type:* Private home study *Accred.:* 1973/1987 (NHSC) *Calendar:* Courses of varying lengths *Degrees:* certificates *CEO:* Dir. Arthur McMeans
   (717) 939-1981

MANOR JUNIOR COLLEGE
Fox Chase Rd. and Forrest Ave., Jenkintown 19046 *Type:* Private (Ukranian Catholic) for women *Accred.:* 1967/1988 (MSA) *Calendar:* Sem. plan *Degrees:* A, certificates, diplomas *Prof. Accred.:* Dental Assisting, Medical Laboratory Technology (AMA) *CEO:* Pres. Mary Cecilia Jurasinski
Enroll: 368   (215) 885-2360

MANSFIELD UNIVERSITY OF PENNSYLVANIA
Mansfield 16933 *Type:* Public (state) liberal arts *System:* Pennsylvania State System of Higher Education *Accred.:* 1942/1987 (MSA) *Calendar:* Sem. plan *Degrees:* A, B, M *Prof. Accred.:* Music, Radiography, Respiratory Therapy, Social Work (B), Teacher Education (e,s) *CEO:* Pres. Rodney C. Kelchner
Enroll: 2980   (717) 662-4000

MARYWOOD COLLEGE
2300 Adams Ave., Scranton 18509 *Type:* Private (Roman Catholic) liberal arts primarily for women *Accred.:* 1921/1986 (MSA) *Calendar:* Sem. plan *Degrees:* B, M *Prof. Accred.:* Art, Dietetics (coordinated), Music, Nursing (B), Social Work (B,M), Teacher Education (e,s) *CEO:* Pres. Mary Reap
Enroll: 3006   (717) 348-6231

MASTBAUM AREA VOCATIONAL-TECHNICAL SCHOOL
3120 Frankford Ave., Philadelphia 19134 *Type:* Private *Calendar:* Courses of varying lengths *Degrees:* certificates *Prof. Accred.:* Dental Laboratory Technology *CEO:* Prin. Charles Clark
(215) 291-4703

MCCANN SCHOOL OF BUSINESS
Main and Pine Sts., Mahanoy City 17948 *Type:* Private business *Accred.:* 1962/1985 (CCA-ACICS) *Calendar:* Tri. plan *Degrees:* A *CEO:* Dir. John J. Slodysko
Enroll: 293   (717) 773-1820

MCCARRIE SCHOOLS OF HEALTH SCIENCES AND TECHNOLOGY
512-20 S. Broad St., Philadelphia 19146-1695 *Type:* Private technical *Accred.:* 1973/1989 (CCA-ACTTS) *Calendar:* Courses of varying lengths *Degrees:* A, diplomas *Prof. Accred.:* Health Education, Medical Assisting, Medical Laboratory Technology *CEO:* Exec. Vice Pres. Robert J. Walder
Enroll: 783   (215) 545-7772

MEDIAN SCHOOL OF ALLIED HEALTH CAREERS
125 Seventh St., Pittsburgh 15222-3400 *Type:* Private *Accred.:* 1970/1986 (CCA-ACTTS) *Calendar:* Qtr. plan *Degrees:* A, certificates, diplomas *Prof. Accred.:* Dental Assisting, Medical Assisting (AMA) *CEO:* Pres. William Mosle
Enroll: 807   (412) 391-7021

MEDICAL COLLEGE OF PENNSYLVANIA
3300 Henry Ave., Philadelphia 19129 *Type:* Private professional *Accred.:* 1984 (MSA) *Calendar:* Sem. plan *Degrees:* P, M, D *Prof. Accred.:* General Practice Residency, Medicine, Nurse Anesthesia Education, Psychology Internship *CEO:* Pres. D. Walter Cohen
Enroll: 554   (215) 842-6000

MERCYHURST COLLEGE
501 E. 38th St., Erie 16546 *Type:* Private (Roman Catholic) liberal arts *Accred.:* 1931/1987 (MSA) *Calendar:* 4-2-4 plan *Degrees:* A, B, M *Prof. Accred.:* Dietetics (coordinated), Social Work (B) *CEO:* Pres. William P. Garvey
Enroll: 2044   (814) 825-0200

MESSIAH COLLEGE
Grantham 17027 *Type:* Private (Brethren) liberal arts *Accred.:* 1963/1988 (MSA) *Calendar:* Sem. plan *Degrees:* B *Prof. Accred.:* Music, Nursing (B), Social Work (B) *CEO:* Pres. D. Ray Hostetter
Enroll: 2179   (717) 766-2511

BRANCH CAMPUS
2026 N. Broad St., Philadelphia, PA 19121 *CEO:* Dir. Don Wingert
(215) 769-2526

MILLERSVILLE UNIVERSITY OF PENNSYLVANIA
Millersville 17551 *Type:* Public (state) liberal arts *System:* Pennsylvania State System of Higher Education *Accred.:* 1950/1985 (MSA) *Calendar:* Sem. plan *Degrees:* A, B, M *Prof. Accred.:* Music, Nursing (B), Respiratory Therapy, Social Work (B), Teacher Education (e,s,p) *CEO:* Pres. Joseph A. Caputo
Enroll: 6677   (717) 872-3011

MONTGOMERY COUNTY COMMUNITY COLLEGE
340 DeKalb Pike, Blue Bell 19422 *Type:* Public (state) junior *System:* Pennsylvania State System of Higher Education *Accred.:* 1970/1985 (MSA) *Calendar:* Sem. plan *Degrees:* A, certificates, diplomas *Prof. Accred.:* Dental Hygiene, Medical Laboratory Technology (AMA), Nursing (A) *CEO:* Pres. Edward M. Sweitzer
Enroll: 7170   (215) 641-6300

MOORE COLLEGE OF ART
The Parkway at 20th St., Philadelphia 19103 *Type:* Private professional for women *Accred.:* 1958/1984 (MSA) *Calendar:* Sem. plan *Degrees:* B *Prof. Accred.:* Art, Interior Design *CEO:* Pres. Mary-Linda Merriam
Enroll: 685   (215) 568-4515

MORAVIAN COLLEGE
1200 Main St., Bethlehem 18018 *Type:* Private (Moravian) liberal arts *Accred.:* 1954/1988 (ATS); 1922/1988 (MSA) *Calendar:* 4-

1-4 plan *Degrees:* B, P, M *CEO:* Pres. Roger H. Martin
Enroll: 1804 (215) 861-1300

BRANCH CAMPUS
60 W. Locust St., Bethlehem, PA 18018 *CEO:* Pres. Roger H. Martin
(215) 861-1516

MOUNT ALOYSIUS JUNIOR COLLEGE
William Penn Hwy., Cresson 16630 *Type:* Private (Roman Catholic) junior *Accred.:* 1943/1984 (MSA) *Calendar:* Sem. plan *Degrees:* A, certificates, diplomas *Prof. Accred.:* Medical Laboratory Technology (AMA), Nursing (A), Occupational Therapy Assisting, Surgical Technology *CEO:* Pres. Edward F. Pierce
Enroll: 943 (814) 886-4131

MUHLENBERG COLLEGE
24th and Chew Sts., Allentown 18104 *Type:* Private (Lutheran) liberal arts *Accred.:* 1921/1986 (MSA) *Calendar:* Sem. plan *Degrees:* A, B *CEO:* Pres. Jonathan C. Messerli
Enroll: 2084 (215) 821-3100

NATIONAL EDUCATION CENTER—ALLENTOWN CAMPUS
1501 Lehigh St., Allentown 18103 *Type:* Private business *Accred.:* 1968/1986 (CCA-ACICS) *Calendar:* Sem. plan *Degrees:* A, certificates, diplomas *CEO:* Dir. Virginia Carpenter
Enroll: 1469 (215) 791-5100

NATIONAL EDUCATION CENTER—THOMPSON CAMPUS
5650 Derry St., Harrisburg 17111-4112 *Type:* Private business *Accred.:* 1962/1985 (CCA-ACICS) *Calendar:* Qtr. plan *Degrees:* A, certificates, diplomas *CEO:* Dir. Rita A. Girondi
Enroll: 1077 (717) 564-8710

BRANCH CAMPUS
3440 Market St., Philadelphia, PA 19104 *CEO:* Dir. Robert L. Silsbe
(215) 387-1530

NATIONAL EDUCATION CENTER—VALE TECHNICAL INSTITUTE CAMPUS
135 W. Market St., Blairsville 15717-1389 *Type:* Private *Accred.:* 1967/1983 (CCA-ACTTS) *Calendar:* Courses of varying lengths *Degrees:* A *CEO:* Dir. Ronald G. Andersen
Enroll: 989 (412) 459-9500

BRANCH CAMPUS
14445 Broadway Ave., Cleveland, OH 44125 *CEO:* Exec. Dir. William Ewbank
(216) 475-7520

NATIONAL SCHOOLS
801 Arch St., 4th Fl., Philadelphia 19107-2419 *Type:* Private *Accred.:* 1979/1989 (CCA-ACTTS) *Calendar:* Courses of varying lengths *Degrees:* A, diplomas *Prof. Accred.:* Dental Assisting, Medical Assisting *CEO:* Pres. Diane Holland
Enroll: 901 (215) 574-0999

BRANCH CAMPUS
11000 Roosevelt Blvd., Philadelphia, PA 19116 *Prof. Accred.:* Dental Assisting *CEO:* Dir. Debbie Speille
(215) 676-2754

NEUMANN COLLEGE
Convent Rd., Aston 19014 *Type:* Private (Roman Catholic) liberal arts *Accred.:* 1972/1986 (MSA) *Calendar:* Sem. plan *Degrees:* A, B, M *Prof. Accred.:* Medical Technology, Nursing (B) *CEO:* Pres. Nan Hechenberger
Enroll: 1139 (215) 459-0905

NEW CASTLE BUSINESS SCHOOL
700 Moravia St., New Castle 16101 *Type:* Private business *Accred.:* 1986/1990 (CCA-ACICS) *Calendar:* Qtr. plan *Degrees:* A *CEO:* Dir. Norma Kelley
Enroll: 73 (412) 658-9066

NEW CASTLE SCHOOL OF TRADES
New Castle-Youngstown Rd., Rte. 422, R.D. 1, Pulaski 16143-9721 *Type:* Private *Accred.:* 1973/1988 (CCA-ACTTS) *Calendar:* Courses of varying lengths *Degrees:*

Pennsylvania

certificates, diplomas *CEO:* Dir. David Goehring
Enroll: 725 (412) 964-8811

NEW ENGLAND TRACTOR TRAINING SCHOOL
3715 E. Thompson St., Philadelphia 19137-1483 *Type:* Private *Accred.:* 1991 (CCA-ACTTS) *Calendar:* Courses of varying lengths *Degrees:* certificates *CEO:* Dir. James M. Lamers
(215) 288-7800

NEW KENSINGTON COMMERCIAL SCHOOL
945 Greensburg Rd., New Kensington 15068 *Type:* Private business *Accred.:* 1959/1981 (CCA-ACICS) *Calendar:* Qtr. plan *Degrees:* A *CEO:* Dir. J. Bryant Mullen
Enroll: 308 (412) 339-7542

NORTH HILLS SCHOOL OF HEALTH OCCUPATIONS
7805 McKnight Rd., Pittsburgh 15237 *Type:* Private *Calendar:* Courses of varying lengths *Degrees:* certificates *Prof. Accred.:* Health Education *CEO:* Exec. Dir. R. Gary Drent
Enroll: 426 (412) 367-8003

NORTHAMPTON COMMUNITY COLLEGE
3835 Green Pond Rd., Bethlehem 18017 *Type:* Public (state) junior *System:* Pennsylvania State System of Higher Education *Accred.:* 1970/1985 (MSA) *Calendar:* Sem. plan *Degrees:* A, certificates, diplomas *Prof. Accred.:* Dental Assisting, Dental Hygiene, Funeral Service Education, Medical Laboratory Technology (AMA), Nursing (A), Practical Nursing, Radiography *CEO:* Pres. Robert J. Kopecek
Enroll: 4712 (215) 861-5300

NORTHEAST INSTITUTE OF EDUCATION
527-535 Linden St., Scranton 18503 *Type:* Private business *Accred.:* 1982/1988 (CCA-ACICS) *Calendar:* Courses of varying lengths *Degrees:* A *CEO:* Pres. Gregory C. Walker
Enroll: 216 (717) 346-6666

BRANCH CAMPUS
1151 N. Ninth St., Stroudsburg, PA 18360 *CEO:* Dir. Anthony Iovacchini
(717) 476-4444

NORTHEASTERN CHRISTIAN JUNIOR COLLEGE
1860 Montgomery Ave., Villanova 19085 *Type:* Private (Church of Christ) junior *Accred.:* 1978/1986 (MSA) *Calendar:* Tri. plan *Degrees:* A *CEO:* Pres. John R. Hall
Enroll: 179 (215) 525-6780

OAKBRIDGE ACADEMY OF ARTS
401 Ninth St., New Kensington 15068-6470 *Type:* Private *Accred.:* 1980/1985 (CCA-ACTTS) *Calendar:* Courses of varying lengths *Degrees:* A, certificates, diplomas *CEO:* Dir. William H. Breyak
Enroll: 46 (412) 335-5336

ORLEANS TECHNICAL INSTITUTE
1330 Rhawn St., Philadelphia 19111-2899 *Type:* Private *Accred.:* 1981/1986 (CCA-ACTTS) *Calendar:* Courses of varying lengths *Degrees:* certificates, diplomas *CEO:* Dir. Jayne Siniari
Enroll: 491 (215) 728-4400

THE COURT REPORTING INSTITUTE
1845 Walnut St., Ste. 700, Philadelphia, PA 19103-4707 *CEO:* Dir. Marlyn DeWitt
(215) 854-1823

THE PJA SCHOOL
7900 W. Chester Pike, Upper Darby 19082-1926 *Type:* Private *Accred.:* 1985 (CCA-ACTTS) *Calendar:* Courses of varying lengths *Degrees:* diplomas *CEO:* Dir. David M. Hudiak
Enroll: 59 (215) 789-6700

PSI INSTITUTE
219 N. Broad St., Philadelphia 19107-5533 *Type:* Private *Accred.:* 1983/1988 (CCA-ACTTS) *Calendar:* Courses of varying lengths *Degrees:* diplomas *CEO:* Dir. William A. Hart
Enroll: 697 (215) 568-3140

PTC CAREER INSTITUTE
50 N. Second St., Philadelphia 19106 *Type:* Private *Accred.:* 1978/1988 (CCA-ACTTS) *Calendar:* Courses of varying lengths *Degrees:* diplomas *CEO:* Dir. Eugene Carboni
Enroll: 1966 (215) 922-4400

BRANCH CAMPUS
2209 Chestnut St., Philadelphia, PA 19103 *CEO:* Dir. Howard B. Patrick
(215) 567-3104

PACE INSTITUTE
606 Court St., Reading 19601 *Type:* Private business *Accred.:* 1984/1990 (CCA-ACICS) *Calendar:* Courses of varying lengths *Degrees:* A, certificates, diplomas *CEO:* Pres. Rhoda E. Dersh
Enroll: 289 (215) 375-1212

PALMER SCHOOL
1457 Manheim Pike, Lancaster 17601 *Type:* Private business *Accred.:* 1985 (CCA-ACICS) *Calendar:* Courses of varying lengths *Degrees:* A, certificates, diplomas *CEO:* Dir. Bob P. Sommers
Enroll: 490 (717) 392-1700

BRANCH CAMPUS
201 S. Arlington Ave., Baltimore, MD 21223 *CEO:* Dir. Sarah Muhammad
(410) 837-2626

PEIRCE JUNIOR COLLEGE
1420 Pine St., Philadelphia 19102 *Type:* Private junior *Accred.:* 1971/1987 (MSA) *Calendar:* Sem. plan *Degrees:* A, certificates, diplomas *CEO:* Pres. Arthur Lendo, Jr.
Enroll: 1197 (215) 545-6400

PENN COMMERCIAL INC.
82 S. Main St., Washington 15301 *Type:* Private business *Accred.:* 1960/1988 (CCA-ACICS) *Calendar:* Qtr. plan *Degrees:* A, certificates, diplomas *CEO:* Pres. Stanley S. Bazant, Sr.
Enroll: 199 (412) 222-5330

PENN TECHNICAL INSTITUTE
110 Ninth St., Pittsburgh 15222-3618 *Type:* Private *Accred.:* 1967/1983 (CCA-ACTTS) *Calendar:* Qtr. plan *Degrees:* A *CEO:* Dir. Louis A. Dimasi
Enroll: 730 (412) 355-0455

PENNCO TECH
3815 Otter St., Bristol 19007-3696 *Type:* Private *Accred.:* 1969/1985 (CCA-ACTTS) *Calendar:* Courses of varying lengths *Degrees:* A, certificates, diplomas *CEO:* Pres. John A. Hobyak
Enroll: 1427 (215) 824-3200

PENNSYLVANIA ACADEMY OF THE FINE ARTS
Broad and Cherry Sts., Philadelphia 19102 *Type:* Private professional *Calendar:* Courses of varying lengths *Degrees:* certificates *Prof. Accred.:* Art *CEO:* Dir. Frederick S. Osborne, Jr.
(215) 972-7623

PENNSYLVANIA BUSINESS INSTITUTE
Chestnut Professional Bldg., 13 Armand Hammer Blvd., Pottstown 19464 *Type:* Private business *Accred.:* 1983/1986 (CCA-ACICS) *Calendar:* Courses of varying lengths *Degrees:* A *CEO:* Pres. Eugene Speer
Enroll: 1113 (215) 326-6150

PENNSYLVANIA COLLEGE OF OPTOMETRY
1200 W. Godfrey Ave., Philadelphia 19141 *Type:* Private professional *Accred.:* 1954/1987 (MSA) *Calendar:* Sem. plan *Degrees:* B, P, M *Prof. Accred.:* Optometry *CEO:* Pres. Thomas L. Lewis
Enroll: 607 (215) 276-6200

PENNSYLVANIA COLLEGE OF PODIATRIC MEDICINE
Eighth and Race Sts., Philadelphia 19107 *Type:* Private professional *Accred.:* 1989 (MSA candidate) *Calendar:* Sem. plan *Degrees:* P *Prof. Accred.:* Podiatry *CEO:* Pres. James E. Bates
Enroll: 436 (215) 629-0300

PENNSYLVANIA COLLEGE OF TECHNOLOGY
One College Ave., Williamsport 17701 *Type:* Public (state) junior *System:* Pennsylvania State University Central Office *Accred.:* 1970/1988 (MSA) *Calendar:* Sem. plan *Degrees:* A *Prof. Accred.:* Dental Hygiene, Engineering Technology (civil/construction), Occupational Therapy Assisting, Radiography *CEO:* Pres. Robert L. Breuder
Enroll: 3720 (717) 326-3761

Pennsylvania

NORTH CAMPUS
Mansfield Rd., Wellsboro, PA 16901 *CEO:* Dean William J. Lex
(717) 724-7703

PENNSYLVANIA GUNSMITH SCHOOL
812 Ohio River Blvd., Pittsburgh 15202-2699 *Type:* Private *Accred.:* 1986 (CCA-ACTTS) *Calendar:* Courses of varying lengths *Degrees:* diplomas *CEO:* Dir. George Thacker
Enroll: 72   (412) 766-1812

PENNSYLVANIA INSTITUTE OF CULINARY ARTS
717 Liberty Ave., Pittsburgh 15222-3500 *Type:* Private *Accred.:* 1991 (CCA-ACTTS) *Calendar:* Courses of varying lengths *Degrees:* certificates, diplomas *CEO:* Pres. Nicholas Hoban
(412) 566-2433

PENNSYLVANIA INSTITUTE OF TAXIDERMY
R.D. 3, Box 188, Ebensburg 15931-8947 *Type:* Private *Accred.:* 1991 (CCA-ACTTS) *Calendar:* Courses of varying lengths *Degrees:* certificates *CEO:* Pres. Dan A. Bantley
(814) 472-4510

PENNSYLVANIA INSTITUTE OF TECHNOLOGY
800 Manchester Ave., Media 19063 *Type:* Private *Accred.:* 1983/1986 (MSA) *Calendar:* Qtr. plan *Degrees:* A, certificates, diplomas *CEO:* Pres. Edward R. D'Alessio
Enroll: 359   (215) 565-7900

PENNSYLVANIA SCHOOL OF ART AND DESIGN
204 N. Prince St., Lancaster 17603 *Type:* Private professional *Calendar:* Courses of varying lengths *Degrees:* diplomas *Prof. Accred.:* Art *CEO:* Pres. Robert Brummett
(717) 396-7833

PENNSYLVANIA STATE UNIVERSITY
201 Old Main, University Park 16802 *Type:* Public (state) *System:* Pennsylvania State University Central Office *Accred.:* 1921/1987 (MSA) *Calendar:* Sem. plan *Degrees:* A, B, M, D, certificates, diplomas *Prof. Accred.:* Accounting (Type A,B,C), Architecture (B,M), Art, Audiology, Business (B,M), Clinical Psychology, Counseling Psychology, Engineering (aerospace, agricultural, architectural, ceramic, chemical, civil, electrical, engineering physics/science, industrial, mechanical, metallurgical, mining, nuclear, petroleum), Forestry, Health Services Administration, Journalism, Landscape Architecture (B), Leisure Studies, Music, Nursing (B,M), Psychology Internship, Public Administration, Rehabilitation Counseling, School Psychology, Social Work (B), Speech-Language Pathology, Teacher Education (e,s,p), Theatre *CEO:* Exec. Vice Pres./Provost John A. Brighton
Enroll: 37269   (814) 865-4700

ALLENTOWN CAMPUS
6090 Mohr La., Fogelsville, PA 18051 *CEO:* Campus Exec. Ofcr. John V. Cooney
(215) 285-4811

ALTOONA CAMPUS
Ivyside Park, Altoona, PA 16601 *Prof. Accred.:* Engineering Technology (electrical, mechanical) *CEO:* Acting Campus Exec. Ofcr. Kjell Meling
(814) 949-5000

BEAVER CAMPUS
Brodhead Rd., Monaca, PA 15061 *Prof. Accred.:* Engineering Technology (electrical, mechanical, nuclear) *CEO:* Campus Exec. Ofcr. David B. Otto
(412) 773-3500

BERKS CAMPUS
Tulpehocken Rd., Reading, PA 19610 *Prof. Accred.:* Engineering Technology (electrical, mechanical) *CEO:* Campus Exec. Ofcr. Frederick H. Gaige
(215) 320-4800

DELAWARE COUNTY CAMPUS
25 Yearsley Mill Rd., Media, PA 19063 *Prof. Accred.:* Engineering Technology (electrical) *CEO:* Campus Exec. Ofcr. Edward S.J. Tomezsko
(215) 565-3300

DUBOIS CAMPUS
College Pl., DuBois, PA 15801 *Prof. Accred.:* Engineering Technology (electri-

Accredited Institutions — Pennsylvania

cal, mechanical) *CEO:* Campus Exec. Ofcr. Donald T. Hartman
(814) 375-4700

ERIE-BEHREND COLLEGE
5091 Station Rd., Erie, PA 16563 *Prof. Accred.:* Engineering Technology (electrical, mechanical) *CEO:* Provost/Dean John M. Lilley
(814) 898-6000

FAYETTE CAMPUS
P.O. Box 519, Rte. 119 N., Uniontown, PA 15401 *Prof. Accred.:* Engineering Technology (architectural, air conditioning, electrical) *CEO:* Campus Exec. Ofcr. John D. Sink
(412) 430-4100

GREAT VALLEY GRADUATE CENTER
30 E. Swedesford Rd., Malvern, PA 19355 *CEO:* Campus Exec. Ofcr. Lawrence S. Cote
(215) 889-1300

HARRISBURG-CAPITAL COLLEGE
Rte. 230, Middletown, PA 17057 *Prof. Accred.:* Engineering Technology (civil/construction, electrical, environmental/sanitary, mechanical), Public Administration *CEO:* Provost/Dean Ruth Leventhal
(717) 948-6100

HAZLETON CAMPUS
Highacres, Hazleton, PA 18201 *Prof. Accred.:* Engineering Technology (electrical, mechanical), Medical Laboratory Technology (AMA), Physical Therapy Assisting *CEO:* Campus Exec. Ofcr. James J. Staudenmeier
(717) 450-3000

HERSHEY MEDICAL CENTER
500 University Dr., Hershey, PA 17033 *Prof. Accred.:* Medicine, Perfusion, Radiography *CEO:* Senior Vice Pres./Dean C. McCollister Evarts
(717) 534-8521

MCKEESPORT CAMPUS
University Dr., McKeesport, PA 15132 *Prof. Accred.:* Engineering Technology (electrical, mechanical) *CEO:* Campus Exec. Ofcr. Casimir J. Kowalski
(412) 675-9000

MONT ALTO CAMPUS
Campus Dr., Mont Alto, PA 17237 *Prof. Accred.:* Physical Therapy Assisting *CEO:* Campus Exec. Ofcr. Corrinne A. Caldwell
(717) 749-3111

NEW KENSINGTON CAMPUS
3550 Seventh Street Rd., New Kensington, PA 15068 *Prof. Accred.:* Engineering Technology (bioengineering, electrical, mechanical), Medical Assisting (AMA), Medical Laboratory Technology (AMA) *CEO:* Campus Exec. Ofcr. Robert D. Arbuckle
(412) 339-5466

OGONTZ CAMPUS
1600 Woodland Rd., Abington, PA 19001 *Prof. Accred.:* Engineering Technology (electrical, mechanical) *CEO:* Campus Exec. Ofcr. Anthony Fusaro
(215) 886-9400

SCHUYLKILL CAMPUS
200 University Dr., Schuylkill Haven, PA 17972 *Prof. Accred.:* Engineering Technology (electrical), Radiography *CEO:* Campus Exec. Ofcr. Wayne D. Lammie
(717) 385-6000

SHENANGO CAMPUS
147 Shenango Ave., Sharon, PA 16146 *Prof. Accred.:* Engineering Technology (electrical, mechanical) *CEO:* Campus Exec. Ofcr. Albert N. Skamra
(412) 983-5800

WILKES-BARRE CAMPUS
P.O. Box PSU, Lehman, PA 18627 *Prof. Accred.:* Engineering Technology (bioengineering, electrical, mechanical, sur-

Pennsylvania	**Accredited Institutions**

veying) *CEO:* Acting Campus Exec. Ofcr. William A. Pearman
(717) 675-2171

WORTHINGTON-SCRANTON CAMPUS
120 Ridge View Dr., Dunmore, PA 18512 *Prof. Accred.:* Engineering Technology (architectural, electrical, mechanical) *CEO:* Campus Exec. Ofcr. James D. Gallagher
(717) 963-4757

YORK CAMPUS
1031 Edgecomb Ave., York, PA 17403 *Prof. Accred.:* Engineering Technology (electrical, mechanical) *CEO:* Campus Exec. Ofcr. John J. Romano
(717) 771-4000

PHILADELPHIA COLLEGE OF BIBLE
200 Manor Ave., Langhorne 19047 *Type:* Private *Accred.:* 1950/1986 (AABC); 1967/1986 (MSA) *Calendar:* Sem. plan *Degrees:* B *Prof. Accred.:* Music, Social Work (B) *CEO:* Pres. W. Sherrill Babb
Enroll: 591   (215) 752-5800

PHILADELPHIA COLLEGE OF OSTEOPATHIC MEDICINE
4150 City Ave., Philadelphia 19131 *Type:* Private professional *Accred.:* 1983 (MSA candidate) *Calendar:* Sem. plan *Degrees:* P, M, D *Prof. Accred.:* Osteopathy *CEO:* Pres. Leonard H. Finkelstein
Enroll: 808   (215) 871-2800

PHILADELPHIA COLLEGE OF PHARMACY AND SCIENCE
43rd St. and Woodland Ave., Philadelphia 19104 *Type:* Private professional *Accred.:* 1962/1988 (MSA) *Calendar:* Sem. plan *Degrees:* B, P, M, D *Prof. Accred.:* Pharmacy, Physical Therapy *CEO:* Pres. Allen Misher
Enroll: 1616   (215) 596-8800

PHILADELPHIA COLLEGE OF TEXTILES AND SCIENCE
School House La. and Henry Ave, Philadelphia 19144 *Type:* Private professional *Accred.:* 1955/1986 (MSA) *Calendar:* Sem.

plan *Degrees:* A, B, M *CEO:* Pres. James P. Gallagher
Enroll: 3417   (215) 951-2700

PHILADELPHIA WIRELESS TECHNICAL INSTITUTE
1533 Pine St., Philadelphia 19102-4693 *Type:* Private *Accred.:* 1985 (CCA-ACTTS) *Calendar:* Courses of varying lengths *Degrees:* certificates *CEO:* Dir. Peter Honczar
Enroll: 436   (215) 546-0745

PITTSBURGH INSTITUTE OF AERONAUTICS
P.O. Box 10897, Pittsburgh 15236-0897 *Type:* Private *Accred.:* 1970/1985 (CCA-ACTTS) *Calendar:* Qtr. plan *Degrees:* A, diplomas *CEO:* Pres. Ivan D. Livi
Enroll: 1197   (412) 462-9011

PITTSBURGH INSTITUTE OF MORTUARY SCIENCE
5808-10 Baum Blvd., Pittsburgh 15206 *Type:* Private *Calendar:* Courses of varying lengths *Degrees:* A, diplomas *Prof. Accred.:* Mortuary Science *CEO:* Pres. Eugene C. Ogrodnik
(412) 362-8500

PITTSBURGH TECHNICAL INSTITUTE
635 Smithfield St., Pittsburgh 15222-2560 *Type:* Private *Accred.:* 1976 (CCA-ACTTS) *Calendar:* Sem. plan *Degrees:* A *CEO:* Pres. J.R. McCartan
Enroll: 388   (412) 471-1011

PITTSBURGH THEOLOGICAL SEMINARY
616 N. Highland Ave., Pittsburgh 15206 *Type:* Private (Presbyterian) professional; graduate only *Accred.:* 1938/1982 (ATS); 1970/1987 (MSA) *Calendar:* Qtr. plan *Degrees:* P, M, D *CEO:* Pres. Carnegie Samuel Calian
Enroll: 291   (412) 362-5610

POINT PARK COLLEGE
201 Wood St., Pittsburgh 15222 *Type:* Private liberal arts *Accred.:* 1968/1989 (MSA) *Calendar:* Sem. plan *Degrees:* A, B, M, certificates, diplomas *Prof. Accred.:* Engineering Technology (civil/construction, electrical, mechanical) *CEO:* Pres. J. Matthew Simon
Enroll: 2793   (412) 391-4100

R.E.T.S. EDUCATION CENTER
2641 W. Chester Pike, Broomall 19008-1999 *Type:* Private *Accred.:* 1973/1988 (CCA-ACTTS) *Calendar:* Courses of varying lengths *Degrees:* diplomas *CEO:* Dir. James Lincke
Enroll: 1971   (215) 352-7630

RALPH AMODEI INTERNATIONAL INSTITUTE OF HAIR DESIGN AND TECHNOLOGY
4451 Frankford Ave., Philadelphia 19124-3636 *Type:* Private *Accred.:* 1986 (CCA-ACTTS) *Calendar:* Courses of varying lengths *Degrees:* certificates *CEO:* Pres. Ralph Amodei
Enroll: 35   (215) 289-4433

READING AREA COMMUNITY COLLEGE
P.O. Box 1706, Reading 19603 *Type:* Public (state) junior *System:* Pennsylvania State System of Higher Education *Accred.:* 1979/1988 (MSA) *Calendar:* Tri. plan *Degrees:* A, certificates, diplomas *Prof. Accred.:* Medical Laboratory Technology (AMA) *CEO:* Pres. Gust Zogas
Enroll: 1640   (215) 372-4721

THE RESTAURANT SCHOOL
4207 Walnut St., Philadelphia 19104 *Type:* Private *Accred.:* 1982/1987 (CCA-ACTTS) *Calendar:* Courses of varying lengths *Degrees:* diplomas *CEO:* Pres. Daniel Liberatoscioli
Enroll: 290   (215) 222-4200

ROBERT MORRIS COLLEGE
Narrows Run Rd., Coraopolis 15108 *Type:* Private liberal arts *Accred.:* 1968/1987 (MSA) *Calendar:* Tri. plan *Degrees:* A, B, M *Prof. Accred.:* Radiography *CEO:* Pres. Edward A. Nicholson
Enroll: 5596   (412) 262-8200

BRANCH CAMPUS
600 Fifth Ave., Pittsburgh, PA 15219 *CEO:* Dir. Daniel Pavlic
  (412) 227-6800

ROSEDALE TECHNICAL INSTITUTE
4634 Browns Hill Rd., Pittsburgh 15217-2919 *Type:* Private *Accred.:* 1979/1989 (CCA-ACTTS) *Calendar:* Qtr. plan *Degrees:* diplomas *CEO:* Exec. Vice Pres. David N. McCormick
Enroll: 766   (412) 521-6200

ROSEMONT COLLEGE
Rosemont 19010 *Type:* Private (Roman Catholic) liberal arts for women *Accred.:* 1930/1985 (MSA) *Calendar:* Sem. plan *Degrees:* B, M, certificates, diplomas *CEO:* Pres. Ofelia Garcia
Enroll: 651   (215) 527-0200

ST. CHARLES BORROMEO SEMINARY
1000 E. Wynnewood Rd., Philadelphia 19096-3099 *Type:* Private (Roman Catholic) *Accred.:* 1970/1986 (ATS); 1971/1986 (MSA) *Calendar:* Sem. plan *Degrees:* B, P, M, certificates, diplomas *CEO:* Pres. Daniel A. Murray
Enroll: 351   (215) 667-3394

ST. FRANCIS COLLEGE
Loretto 15940 *Type:* Private (Roman Catholic) liberal arts *Accred.:* 1939/1986 (MSA) *Calendar:* Sem. plan *Degrees:* A, B, M *Prof. Accred.:* Nursing (B), Physician Assisting, Social Work (B) *CEO:* Pres. Christian Oravec
Enroll: 1791   (814) 472-7000

ST. JOSEPH'S UNIVERSITY
5600 City Line Ave., Philadelphia 19131 *Type:* Private (Roman Catholic) liberal arts *Accred.:* 1922/1989 (MSA) *Calendar:* Sem. plan *Degrees:* A, B, M, certificates, diplomas *Prof. Accred.:* Nurse Anesthesia Education *CEO:* Pres. Nicholas S. Rashford, S.J.
Enroll: 5787   (215) 660-1000

ST. VINCENT COLLEGE
Latrobe 15650 *Type:* Private (Roman Catholic) liberal arts *Accred.:* 1984/1988 (ATS); 1921/1988 (MSA) *Calendar:* Sem. plan *Degrees:* B, P, M *CEO:* Pres. John F. Murtha, O.S.B.
Enroll: 1193   (412) 539-9761

SAWYER SCHOOL
717 Liberty Ave., Pittsburgh 15222 *Type:* Private business *Accred.:* 1973/1991 (CCA-

Pennsylvania   **Accredited Institutions**

ACICS) *Calendar:* Courses of varying lengths *Degrees:* A *Prof. Accred.:* Medical Assisting (AMA) *CEO:* Pres. Thomas B. Sapienza
Enroll: 845   (412) 261-5700

SCHUYLKILL BUSINESS INSTITUTE
2400 W. End Ave., Pottsville 17901 *Type:* Private business *Accred.:* 1980/1986 (CCA-ACICS) *Calendar:* Courses of varying lengths *Degrees:* A *CEO:* Pres. James Tarity, Jr.
Enroll: 156   (717) 622-4835

SETON HILL COLLEGE
Greensburg 15601 *Type:* Private (Roman Catholic) liberal arts for women *Accred.:* 1921/1987 (MSA) *Calendar:* Sem. plan *Degrees:* B *Prof. Accred.:* Dietetics (coordinated), Music *CEO:* Pres. JoAnne Boyle
Enroll: 870   (412) 834-2200

SHENANGO VALLEY SCHOOL OF BUSINESS
335 Boyd Dr., Sharon 16146 *Type:* Private business *Accred.:* 1977/1986 (CCA-ACICS) *Calendar:* Courses of varying lengths *Degrees:* A *CEO:* Dir. Patricia McMahon
Enroll: 360   (412) 983-0700

BRANCH CAMPUS
500 S. Mill St., New Castle, PA 16101 *CEO:* Dir. Richard P. McMahon
     (412) 654-1976

SHIPPENSBURG UNIVERSITY OF PENNSYLVANIA
Shippensburg 17257 *Type:* Public (state) liberal arts *System:* Pennsylvania State System of Higher Education *Accred.:* 1939/1989 (MSA) *Calendar:* Sem. plan *Degrees:* B, M *Prof. Accred.:* Business (B), Counseling, Social Work (B), Teacher Education (e,s,p) *CEO:* Pres. Anthony F. Ceddia
Enroll: 6352   (717) 532-9121

SHIRLEY ROCK SCHOOL OF THE PENNSYLVANIA BALLET
1101 S. Broad St., Philadelphia 19147 *Type:* Private *Calendar:* Courses of varying lengths *Degrees:* certificates *Prof. Accred.:* Dance *CEO:* Dir. Bojan Spassoff
     (215) 551-7000

SLIPPERY ROCK UNIVERSITY OF PENNSYLVANIA
Slippery Rock 16057 *Type:* Public (state) liberal arts *System:* Pennsylvania State System of Higher Education *Accred.:* 1943/1987 (MSA) *Calendar:* Sem. plan *Degrees:* B, M *Prof. Accred.:* Music, Nursing (B), Parks and Recreation, Physical Therapy, Social Work (B), Teacher Education (e,s,p) *CEO:* Pres. Robert N. Aebersold
Enroll: 7360   (412) 738-5425

SOUTH HILLS BUSINESS COLLEGE
480 Waupelani Dr., State College 16801-4516 *Type:* Private business *Accred.:* 1976/1985 (CCA-ACICS) *Calendar:* Tri. plan *Degrees:* A, certificates, diplomas *Prof. Accred.:* Medical Record Technology *CEO:* Dir. Maralyn J. Mazza
Enroll: 293   (814) 234-7755

SPRING GARDEN COLLEGE
7500 Germantown Ave., Philadelphia 19119 *Type:* Private *Accred.:* 1973/1984 (MSA) *Calendar:* Sem. plan *Degrees:* A, B, certificates, diplomas *Prof. Accred.:* Architecture (B-candidate), Engineering Technology (computer, mechanical) *CEO:* Acting Pres. Richard C. Ustick
Enroll: 1546   (215) 248-7900

SUSQUEHANNA UNIVERSITY
Selinsgrove 17870 *Type:* Private (Lutheran) liberal arts *Accred.:* 1930/1988 (MSA) *Calendar:* Sem. plan *Degrees:* A, B *Prof. Accred.:* Music *CEO:* Pres. Joel L. Cunningham
Enroll: 1697   (717) 374-0101

SWARTHMORE COLLEGE
Swarthmore 19081 *Type:* Private liberal arts *Accred.:* 1921/1989 (MSA) *Calendar:* Sem. plan *Degrees:* B, M *Prof. Accred.:* Engineering (general) *CEO:* Pres. Alfred H. Bloom
Enroll: 1334   (215) 328-8000

TALMUDICAL YESHIVA OF PHILADELPHIA
6063 Drexel Rd., Philadelphia 19131 *Type:* Private professional *Accred.:* 1875/1987 (AARTS) *Calendar:* Sem. plan *Degrees:*

Rabbinic (1st), Talmudic (1st and 2nd) *CEO:* Pres. E. Weinberg
Enroll: 109 (215) 473-1212

TEMPLE UNIVERSITY
Broad St. and Montgomery Ave., Philadelphia 19122 *Type:* Private (state) *System:* Pennsylvania State System of Higher Education *Accred.:* 1921/1989 (MSA) *Calendar:* Sem. plan *Degrees:* A, B, P, M, D, certificates, diplomas *Prof. Accred.:* Architecture (B), Art, Audiology, Business (B,M), Clinical Psychology, Community Health, Combined Prosthodontics, Counseling Psychology, Dance, Dentistry, Endodontics, Engineering (civil, electrical, mechanical), Engineering Technology (civil/construction, electrical, mechanical), General Dentistry (prelim. provisional), Health Services Administration, Journalism, Landscape Architecture (B-initial), Law, Medical Record Administration, Medicine, Music, Nursing (B), Occupational Therapy, Oral and Maxillofacial Surgery, Orthodontics, Periodontics, Pharmacy, Physical Therapy, Psychology Internship, Recreation and Leisure Studies, School Psychology, Social Work (B,M), Speech-Language Pathology, Teacher Education (e,s,p), Theatre *CEO:* Pres. Peter J. Liacouras
Enroll: 32139 (215) 787-7000

THIEL COLLEGE
75 College Ave., Greenville 16125 *Type:* Private (Lutheran) liberal arts *Accred.:* 1922/1987 (MSA) *Calendar:* Sem. plan *Degrees:* A, B *Prof. Accred.:* Nursing (B), Respiratory Therapy Technology *CEO:* Pres. C. Carlyle Haaland
Enroll: 956 (412) 589-2000

THOMAS JEFFERSON UNIVERSITY
11th and Walnut Sts., Philadelphia 19107 *Type:* Private liberal arts and professional *Accred.:* 1976/1987 (MSA) *Calendar:* Qtr. plan *Degrees:* A, B, P, M, D, certificates, diplomas *Prof. Accred.:* Cytotechnology, Dental Hygiene, Diagnostic Medical Sonography, Medical Technology, Medicine, Nursing (B), Occupational Therapy, Physical Therapy, Radiography *CEO:* Pres. Lewis W. Bluemle, Jr.
Enroll: 2112 (215) 928-6000

TRACEY-WARNER SCHOOL
401 N. Broad St., Philadelphia 19108-1001 *Type:* Private *Accred.:* 1972/1984 (CCA-ACTTS) *Calendar:* Sem. plan *Degrees:* A *CEO:* Pres. Joy Maxine Friedman
Enroll: 139 (215) 574-0402

TRI-CITY BARBER SCHOOL
128 E. Main St., Norristown 19401-4917 *Type:* Private *Accred.:* 1987 (CCA-ACTTS) *Calendar:* Courses of varying lengths *Degrees:* certificates *CEO:* Dir. Ann Marie Giuliani
(215) 279-4432

TRI-CITY BARBER SCHOOL
5901 N. Broad St., Philadelphia 19141-1801 *Type:* Private *Accred.:* 1986 (CCA-ACTTS) *Calendar:* Courses of varying lengths *Degrees:* certificates *CEO:* Exec. Dir. Marc S. Jacobs
(215) 927-3232

TRIANGLE TECH
P.O. Box 551, DuBois 15801-9990 *Type:* Private *Accred.:* 1981/1986 (CCA-ACTTS) *Calendar:* Courses of varying lengths *Degrees:* A, certificates *CEO:* Dir. Branda McCullough
(814) 371-2090

TRIANGLE TECH
2000 Liberty St., Erie 16502-9987 *Type:* Private *Accred.:* 1978/1988 (CCA-ACTTS) *Calendar:* Courses of varying lengths *Degrees:* A, certificates *CEO:* Dir. Kenneth Morrison
(814) 453-6016

TRIANGLE TECH
60 Blank School Rd., Greensburg 15601-9944 *Type:* Private *Accred.:* 1970/1985 (CCA-ACTTS) *Calendar:* Courses of varying lengths *Degrees:* A, certificates *CEO:* Pres. James R. Agras
(412) 832-1050

Pennsylvania

BUSINESS CAREERS INSTITUTE
33 W. Otterman St., Greensburg, PA 15601-2394 *CEO:* Dir. Jayne Kalp
(412) 834-1258

TRIANGLE TECH
1940 Perrysville Ave., Pittsburgh 15214-3897 *Type:* Private *Accred.:* 1970/1980 (CCA-ACTTS) *Calendar:* Courses of varying lengths *Degrees:* A, certificates *CEO:* Dir. Timothy McMahon
(412) 359-1000

MONROEVILLE SCHOOL OF BUSINESS
105 Mall Blvd., Expo Mart, 3rd Fl., Monroeville, PA 15146-2229 *CEO:* Dir. Marilyn McCarthy
(412) 856-8040

TRINITY EPISCOPAL SCHOOL FOR MINISTRY
311 11th St., Ambridge 15003 *Type:* Private (Episcopal) professional; graduate only *Accred.:* 1985/1990 (ATS) *Calendar:* Sem. plan *Degrees:* P, M *CEO:* Dean/Pres. William C. Frey
Enroll: 74 (412) 266-3838

UNITED STATES NAVAL DAMAGE CONTROL TRAINING CENTER
Naval Base, Philadelphia 19112-5082 *Type:* Public (federal) *Accred.:* 1985/1990 (SACS-COEI) *Calendar:* Courses of varying lengths *Degrees:* certificates *CEO:* Commanding Ofcr. W.A. Gottlieb
Enroll: 556 (215) 897-5677

UNIVERSITY OF PENNSYLVANIA
34th and Spruce Sts., Philadelphia 19104 *Type:* Private (state) *Accred.:* 1921/1989 (MSA) *Calendar:* Sem. plan *Degrees:* A, B, P, M, D, certificates, diplomas *Prof. Accred.:* Architecture (M), Business (B,M), Clinical Psychology, Combined Professional-Scientific Psychology, Dentistry, Endodontics, Engineering (bioengineering, chemical, civil, electrical, materials, mechanical, systems), General Dentistry, Health Services Administration, Landscape Architecture (M), Law, Medical Technology, Medicine, Nuclear Medicine Technology, Nursing (B,M), Oral and Maxillofacial Surgery, Orthodontics, Periodontics, Planning (city/regional), Psychology Internship, Social Work (M) *CEO:* Pres. F. Sheldon Hackney
Enroll: 22169 (215) 898-5000

UNIVERSITY OF PITTSBURGH
4200 Fifth Ave., Pittsburgh 15260 *Type:* Public (state) *System:* Pennsylvania State System of Higher Education *Accred.:* 1921/1986 (MSA) *Calendar:* Tri. plan *Degrees:* A, B, P, M, D, certificates, diplomas *Prof. Accred.:* Audiology, Business (B,M), Clinical Psychology, Combined Prosthodontics, Counseling, Counseling Psychology (provisional), Dental Hygiene, Dentistry, Dietetics (coordinated), Endodontics, Engineering (chemical, civil, electrical, industrial, materials, mechanical, metallurgical), General Dentistry (conditional), Health Services Administration, Law, Librarianship, Maxillofacial Prosthodontics, Medical Record Administration, Medical Technology, Medicine, Nurse Anesthesia Education, Nursing (B,M), Occupational Therapy, Oral and Maxillofacial Surgery, Orthodontics, Pediatric Dentistry, Periodontics, Pharmacy, Physical Therapy, Planning (regional/urban), Psychology Internship, Public Administration, Public Health, Rehabilitation Counseling, Social Work (B,M), Speech-Language Pathology, Teacher Education (e,s,p), Theatre *CEO:* Pres. Wesley W. Posvar
Enroll: 28524 (412) 624-4141

BRADFORD CAMPUS
Campus Dr., Bradford, PA 16701 *CEO:* Pres. Richard E. McDowell
(814) 362-7500

GREENSBURG CAMPUS
1150 Mount Pleasant Rd., Greensburg, PA 15601 *CEO:* Pres. George F. Chambers
(412) 837-7040

JOHNSTOWN CAMPUS
Johnstown, PA 15904 *Prof. Accred.:* Engineering Technology (civil/construction,

electrical, mechanical), Respiratory Therapy *CEO:* Pres. Frank H. Blackington, III
(814) 269-7000

TITUSVILLE CAMPUS
504 E. Main St., Titusville, PA 16354 *CEO:* Pres. Michael A. Worman
(814) 827-4400

UNIVERSITY OF SCRANTON
Scranton 18510 *Type:* Private (Roman Catholic) liberal arts *Accred.:* 1927/1988 (MSA) *Calendar:* 4-1-4 plan *Degrees:* A, B, M *Prof. Accred.:* Computer Science, Nursing (B), Physical Therapy, Rehabilitation Counseling, Teacher Education (s,p) *CEO:* Pres. Joseph A. Panuska, S.J.
Enroll: 4929 (717) 961-7400

UNIVERSITY OF THE ARTS
Broad and Pine Sts., Philadelphia 19102 *Type:* Private professional *Accred.:* 1969/1988 (MSA) *Calendar:* Sem. plan *Degrees:* A,B,M, certificates, diplomas *Prof. Accred.:* Art, Music *CEO:* Pres. Peter Solmssen
Enroll: 1371 (215) 875-4800

URSINUS COLLEGE
Main St., Collegeville 19426 *Type:* Private liberal arts *Accred.:* 1921/1989 (MSA) *Calendar:* Sem. plan *Degrees:* A, B *CEO:* Pres. Richard P. Richter
Enroll: 2286 (215) 489-4111

VALLEY FORGE CHRISTIAN COLLEGE
Charlestown Rd., Phoenixville 19460 *Type:* Private (Assemblies of God) *Accred.:* 1967/1987 (AABC) *Calendar:* Sem. plan *Degrees:* B, certificates, diplomas *CEO:* Pres. Wesley W. Smith
Enroll: 463 (215) 935-0450

VALLEY FORGE MILITARY JUNIOR COLLEGE
101 Eagle Rd., Wayne 19087 *Type:* Private for men *Accred.:* 1954/1980 (MSA) *Calendar:* 4-1-4 plan *Degrees:* A *CEO:* Supt. N. Ronald Thunman, U.S.N.
Enroll: 197 (215) 688-1800

VILLANOVA UNIVERSITY
Lancaster Pike, Villanova 19085 *Type:* Private (Roman Catholic) liberal arts *Accred.:* 1921/1986 (MSA) *Calendar:* Sem. plan *Degrees:* A,B,P,M,D *Prof. Accred.:* Accounting (Type A), Business (B,M), Counseling, Engineering (chemical, civil, electrical, mechanical), Law, Nursing (B,M) *CEO:* Pres. Edward J. Dobbin, O.S.A.
Enroll: 12055 (215) 645-4500

WASHINGTON INSTITUTE OF TECHNOLOGY
82 S. Main St., Washington 15301-6810 *Type:* Private *Accred.:* 1974/1989 (CCA-ACTTS) *Calendar:* Courses of varying lengths *Degrees:* certificates, diplomas *CEO:* Dir. Ron Davis
Enroll: 179 (412) 222-1942

WASHINGTON AND JEFFERSON COLLEGE
27 S. Lincoln St., Washington 15301 *Type:* Private liberal arts *Accred.:* 1921/1989 (MSA) *Calendar:* 4-1-4 plan *Degrees:* A, B, M *CEO:* Pres. Howard J. Burnett
Enroll: 1390 (412) 222-4400

WATTERSON SCHOOL OF BUSINESS AND TECHNOLOGY
5800 N. Marvine St., Philadelphia 19141 *Type:* Private business *Accred.:* 1988 (CCA-ACICS) *Calendar:* Courses of varying lengths *Degrees:* certificates, diplomas *CEO:* Dir. Jack Lidgaster
(215) 548-7200

WAYNESBURG COLLEGE
51 W. College St., Waynesburg 15370 *Type:* Private (United Presbyterian) liberal arts *Accred.:* 1950/1985 (MSA) *Calendar:* Sem. plan *Degrees:* A, B, M *Prof. Accred.:* Nursing (B) *CEO:* Pres. Timothy R. Thyreen
Enroll: 1031 (412) 627-8191

WELDER TRAINING AND TESTING INSTITUTE
729 E. Highland St., Allentown 18103-1263 *Type:* Private *Accred.:* 1973/1988 (CCA-ACTTS) *Calendar:* Courses of varying lengths *Degrees:* certificates *CEO:* Dir. Patrick F. Dorris
Enroll: 198 (215) 437-9720

Pennsylvania

WELDER TRAINING AND TESTING INSTITUTE
100 Penn Ave., Selinsgrove 17870-9339 *Type:* Private *Accred.:* 1985 (CCA-ACTTS) *Calendar:* Courses of varying lengths *Degrees:* certificates *CEO:* Dir. Jeffrey L. Kurtz
Enroll: 121   (717) 743-5500

WEST CHESTER UNIVERSITY OF PENNSYLVANIA
S. High St., West Chester 19383 *Type:* Public (state) liberal arts *System:* Pennsylvania State System of Higher Education *Accred.:* 1946/1981 (MSA) *Calendar:* Sem. plan *Degrees:* A, B, M *Prof. Accred.:* Music, Nursing (B), Respiratory Therapy, Social Work (B), Teacher Education (e,s,p) *CEO:* Interim Pres. Stanley J. Yarosewick
Enroll: 11475   (215) 436-1000

WESTERN SCHOOL OF HEALTH AND BUSINESS CAREERS
411 Seventh Ave., 2nd Fl., Pittsburgh 15219-1905 *Type:* Private *Accred.:* 1986 (CCA-ACTTS) *Calendar:* Courses of varying lengths *Degrees:* certificates *Prof. Accred.:* Histologic Technology, Medical Assisting *CEO:* Pres. Ross M. Perilman
     (412) 281-2600

 BRANCH CAMPUS
 One Monroeville Ctr., Ste. 250, Monroeville, PA 15146 *Prof. Accred.:* Medical Assisting *CEO:* Vice Pres. Karen Perilman
     (412) 373-6400

WESTMINSTER COLLEGE
S. Market St., New Wilmington 16172 *Type:* Private (United Presbyterian) liberal arts *Accred.:* 1921/1986 (MSA) *Calendar:* 4-1-4 plan *Degrees:* B, M *Prof. Accred.:* Music *CEO:* Pres. Oscar E. Remick
Enroll: 1475   (412) 946-8761

WESTMINSTER THEOLOGICAL SEMINARY
P.O. Box 27009, Philadelphia 19118 *Type:* Private (Presbyterian) professional; graduate only *Accred.:* 1986/1991 (ATS); 1954/1987 (MSA) *Calendar:* 4-1-4 plan *Degrees:* P, M, D *CEO:* Pres. Samuel T. Logan, Jr.
Enroll: 410   (215) 887-5511

WESTMORELAND COUNTY COMMUNITY COLLEGE
Ambrust Rd., Youngwood 15697 *Type:* Public (state) junior *System:* Pennsylvania State System of Higher Education *Accred.:* 1978/1988 (MSA) *Calendar:* Sem. plan *Degrees:* A, certificates, diplomas *CEO:* Pres. Daniel C. Krezenski
Enroll: 4570   (412) 925-4000

WIDENER UNIVERSITY
14th and Chestnut Sts., Chester 19013 *Type:* Private liberal arts *Accred.:* 1954/1986 (MSA) *Calendar:* Sem. plan *Degrees:* A, B, M, D, certificates, diplomas *Prof. Accred.:* Clinical Psychology, Engineering (chemical, electrical, mechanical), Health Services Administration, Nursing (B,M), Psychology Internship, Social Work (B,M-candidate) *CEO:* Pres. Robert J. Bruce
Enroll: 7894   (215) 499-4000

WILKES UNIVERSITY
170 S. Franklin St., Wilkes-Barre 18766 *Type:* Private liberal arts *Accred.:* 1937/1990 (MSA) *Calendar:* Sem. plan *Degrees:* B, M *Prof. Accred.:* Engineering (electrical, materials), Nursing (B) *CEO:* Pres. Christopher N. Breiseth
Enroll: 3848   (717) 824-4651

WILLIAMSON FREE SCHOOL OF MECHANICAL TRADES
106 S. New Middleton Rd., Media 19063-5299 *Type:* Private *Accred.:* 1970/1980 (CCA-ACTTS) *Calendar:* Sem. plan *Degrees:* A, diplomas *CEO:* Pres. Barry G. Schuler
Enroll: 225   (215) 566-1776

WILLIAMSPORT SCHOOL OF COMMERCE
941 W. Third St., Williamsport 17701 *Type:* Private business *Accred.:* 1963/1986 (CCA-ACICS) *Calendar:* Qtr. plan *Degrees:* A, certificates, diplomas *CEO:* Dir. Benjamin H. Comfort, III
Enroll: 222   (717) 326-2869

WILMA BOYD CAREER SCHOOLS
One Chatham Ctr., Pittsburgh 15219 *Type:* Private business *Accred.:* 1975/1990 (CCA-

ACICS) *Calendar:* Qtr. plan *Degrees:* certificates, diplomas *CEO:* Pres./Dir. Rod L. Piatt
Enroll: 1236 (412) 456-1800

BRANCH CAMPUS
Concourse Tower II, 2090 Palm Beach Lakes Blvd., West Palm Beach, FL 33409 *Accred.:* 1975/1990 (CCA-ACICS); 1991 (CCA-ACTTS) *CEO:* Dir. Sam A. Gentile
(407) 684-1222

WILSON COLLEGE
1015 Philadelphia Ave., Chambersburg 17201 *Type:* Private (United Presbyterian) liberal arts for women *Accred.:* 1922/1988 (MSA) *Calendar:* 4-1-4 plan *Degrees:* A, B, certificates, diplomas *Prof. Accred.:* Veterinary Medical Technology *CEO:* Pres. Gwendolyn E. Jensen
Enroll: 702 (717) 264-4141

YESHIVA BETH MOSHE
930 Hickory St., Scranton 18505 *Type:* Private professional *Accred.:* 1976/1989 (AARTS) *Calendar:* Sem. plan *Degrees:* Talmudic (1st and 2nd) *CEO:* Pres. David Fink
Enroll: 83 (717) 346-1747

YORK COLLEGE OF PENNSYLVANIA
Country Club Rd., York 17405-7199 *Type:* Private liberal arts *Accred.:* 1959/1985 (MSA) *Calendar:* Sem. plan *Degrees:* A, B, M *Prof. Accred.:* Medical Record Administration, Nursing (B), Recreation and Leisure Studies, Respiratory Therapy, Respiratory Therapy Technology *CEO:* Pres. George W. Waldner
Enroll: 4789 (717) 846-7788

YORK TECHNICAL INSTITUTE
3351 Whiteford Rd., York 17402-9017 *Type:* Private *Accred.:* 1979/1989 (CCA-ACTTS) *Calendar:* Courses of varying lengths *Degrees:* diplomas *CEO:* Dir. Harold L. Maley
Enroll: 164 (717) 757-1100

YORKTOWNE BUSINESS INSTITUTE
W. Seventh Ave., York 17404 *Type:* Private business *Accred.:* 1979/1985 (CCA-ACICS) *Calendar:* Courses of varying lengths *Degrees:* A, certificates, diplomas *CEO:* Dir. James P. Murphy
Enroll: 442 (717) 846-5111

PUERTO RICO

ABBYNELL BEAUTY ACADEMY
P.O. Box 7216, Caguas 00626 *Type:* Private *Accred.:* 1989 (CCA-ACTTS) *Calendar:* Courses of varying lengths *Degrees:* certificates, diplomas *CEO:* Pres. Magdalena Ortiz
Enroll: 88 (809) 743-3339

ACADEMIA ARCECIBENA DE BELLEZA
Jesus Cortes Torrex No. 102, P.O. Box 1106, Arecibo 00613 *Type:* Private *Accred.:* 1989 (CCA-ACTTS) *Calendar:* Courses of varying lengths *Degrees:* certificates *CEO:* Dir. Alfredo Torres
(809) 878-1020

ACADEMIA BERMUDEZ Y RIOS
Calle Betances No. 18, Bayamon 00619-6205 *Type:* Private *Accred.:* 1991 (CCA-ACTTS) *Calendar:* Courses of varying lengths *Degrees:* certificates *CEO:* Vice Pres. Aurelia Bermudez
(809) 780-5665

ACADEMIA LANIN
752 Andalucia St., Puerto Nuevo, Rio Piedras 00921 *Type:* Private *Accred.:* 1979/1989 (CCA-ACTTS) *Calendar:* Courses of varying lengths *Degrees:* certificates *CEO:* Owner Lanin A. de Santana
Enroll: 71 (809) 781-7960

ACADEMIA SINGER DEALER AUTORIZADO INC.
101 Comercio St., Ponce 00731 *Type:* Private *Accred.:* 1991 (CCA-ACTTS) *Calendar:* Courses of varying lengths *Degrees:* certificates *CEO:* Pres. Luis R. Perez De Ayala
(809) 848-4949

ACADEMIA DE BARBERIA Y COSMETOLOGIA
Ave. Quebradilla No. 185-A2, Isabela 00662-2006 *Type:* Private *Accred.:* 1991 (CCA-ACTTS) *Calendar:* Courses of varying lengths *Degrees:* certificates *CEO:* Dir. Wilfredo Ortiz
(809) 872-5154

AGUADILLA REGIONAL COLLEGE
Call Box 20000, Aguadilla 00605 *Type:* Private *System:* Universidad Interamericana de Puerto Rico Central Office *Accred.:* 1957/1983 (MSA) *Calendar:* Sem. plan *Degrees:* A, B, certificates, diplomas *CEO:* Dean/Dir. Hilda M. Baco
Enroll: 3426 (809) 891-0925

AGUADILLA REGIONAL COLLEGE
P.O. Box 160, Ramey 00604 *Type:* Public (state) *System:* University of Puerto Rico Regional Colleges Administration *Accred.:* 1976/1987 (MSA) *Calendar:* Sem. plan *Degrees:* A *CEO:* Dean/Dir. Miguel Gonzalez
Enroll: 1712 (809) 890-2681

ALLIED SCHOOLS OF PUERTO RICO
P.O. Box 1028, Bayamon 00619 *Type:* Private business *Accred.:* 1990 (CCA-ACICS) *Calendar:* Courses of varying lengths *Degrees:* certificates, diplomas *CEO:* Dir. Gustavo Sanchez
Enroll: 451 (809) 780-1612

AMERICAN EDUCATIONAL COLLEGE
P.O. Box 62, Carretera No. 2, KM 11 HM 8, Edificio Federal, Bayamon 00621 *Type:* Private business *Accred.:* 1985 (CCA-ACICS) *Calendar:* Courses of varying lengths *Degrees:* certificates, diplomas *CEO:* Pres. Joaquin E. Gonzalez Pinto
Enroll: 374 (809) 798-1199

AMERICAN UNIVERSITY OF PUERTO RICO
P.O. Box 2037, Bayamon 00621 *Type:* Private liberal arts *Accred.:* 1975/1988 (CCA-ACICS); 1982/1987 (MSA) *Calendar:* Sem. plan *Degrees:* A, B *CEO:* Pres. Juan B. Nazario-Negron
Enroll: 3126 (809) 798-2022

BRANCH CAMPUS
P.O. Box 929, Dorado, PR 00646 *CEO:* Dir. Juan Osorio
(809) 796-2169

Accredited Institutions   **Puerto Rico**

BRANCH CAMPUS
P.O. Box 1082, Manati, PR 00701 *CEO:* Dir. Jose Nazario
(809) 854-2835

ANTILLES SCHOOL OF TECHNICAL CAREERS
Calle Domenech No. 107, Hato Rey 00917 *Type:* Private *Calendar:* Courses of varying lengths *Degrees:* certificates, diplomas *Prof. Accred.:* Health Education, Practical Nursing *CEO:* Pres. Ignacio Acevedo Saenz
Enroll: 368   (809) 764-7576

ARECIBO TECHNOLOGICAL UNIVERSITY COLLEGE
P.O. Box A-4010, Arecibo 00613 *Type:* Public (state) *System:* University of Puerto Rico Regional Colleges Administration *Accred.:* 1967/1988 (MSA) *Calendar:* Sem. plan *Degrees:* A, B *Prof. Accred.:* Nursing (A) *CEO:* Interim Dean/Dir. Hector Otero Burgos
Enroll: 3742   (809) 878-2830

ARECIBO UNIVERSITY COLLEGE
Call Box UI, Arecibo 00613 *Type:* Private *System:* Universidad Interamericana de Puerto Rico Central Office *Accred.:* 1957/1983 (MSA) *Calendar:* Sem. plan *Degrees:* A, B, certificates, diplomas *CEO:* Dean/Dir. Maria De Los A. Ortiz
Enroll: 3483   (809) 878-5475

ART AND BUSINESS COLLEGE OF PUERTO RICO
P.O. Box 1269, Caguas 00626-1269 *Type:* Private *Accred.:* 1991 (CCA-ACTTS) *Calendar:* Courses of varying lengths *Degrees:* certificates *CEO:* Chrmn. of the Bd. Humberto Garcia
(809) 744-5493

ATLANTIC COLLEGE
P.O. Box 1774, Guaynabo 00651-1774 *Type:* Private junior *Accred.:* 1987 (CCA-ACICS) *Calendar:* Sem. plan *Degrees:* A, certificates, diplomas *CEO:* Pres. Teresa de Dios
Enroll: 552   (809) 720-1022

BARRANQUITAS REGIONAL COLLEGE
Barranquitas 00794 *Type:* Private *System:* Universidad Interamericana de Puerto Rico Central Office *Accred.:* 1957/1983 (MSA) *Calendar:* Sem. plan *Degrees:* A, B, certificates, diplomas *CEO:* Dir. Vidal Rivera-Garcia
Enroll: 1276   (809) 857-4040

BAYAMON CENTRAL UNIVERSITY
P.O. Box 1725, Bayamon 00621 *Type:* Private (Roman Catholic) liberal arts *Accred.:* 1971/1988 (MSA) *Calendar:* Sem. plan *Degrees:* A, B, M *CEO:* Pres. Vincent A.M. Van Rooij
Enroll: 2796   (809) 786-3030

BAYAMON TECHNICAL AND COMMERCIAL INSTITUTE
P.O. Box 6007, Sta. 1, Bayamon 00619 *Type:* Private business *Accred.:* 1984/1987 (CCA-ACICS) *Calendar:* Courses of varying lengths *Degrees:* certificates, diplomas *CEO:* Pres. Wilson Del Toro
Enroll: 572   (809) 787-8805

BAYAMON TECHNOLOGICAL UNIVERSITY COLLEGE
Bayamon 00619-1919 *Type:* Public (state) *System:* University of Puerto Rico Regional Colleges Administration *Accred.:* 1960/1987 (MSA) *Calendar:* Sem. plan *Degrees:* A, B *CEO:* Dean/Dir. Aida Canals de Bird
Enroll: 4302   (809) 786-2885

BAYAMON UNIVERSITY COLLEGE
Rd. 174, Minillas Industrial Park, Bayamon 00619 *Type:* Private *System:* Universidad Interamericana de Puerto Rico Central Office *Accred.:* 1981/1983 (MSA) *Calendar:* Sem. plan *Degrees:* A, B, certificates, diplomas *CEO:* Dean/Dir. Felix Torres-Leon
Enroll: 4427   (809) 780-4040

BENEDICT SCHOOL OF LANGUAGES AND COMMERCE
45 Munoz Rivera Ave., Hato Rey 00918 *Type:* Private business *Accred.:* 1982/1989 (CCA-ACICS) *Calendar:* Qtr. plan *Degrees:* certificates, diplomas *CEO:* Pres. Angel Lopez
Enroll: 735   (809) 754-1199

CARIBBEAN CENTER FOR ADVANCED STUDIES
Apartado 3711, Old San Juan Sta., San Juan 00904-3711 *Type:* Private *Accred.:* 1974/

Puerto Rico

1989 (MSA) *Calendar:* Sem. plan *Degrees:* M, D *CEO:* Pres. Salvador Santiago-Negron
Enroll: 237 (809) 725-6500

CARIBBEAN UNIVERSITY
P.O. Box 493, Bayamon 00621 *Type:* Private liberal arts *Accred.:* 1977/1987 (MSA) *Calendar:* Qtr. plan *Degrees:* A, B *CEO:* Pres. Angel E. Juan-Ortega
Enroll: 3136 (809) 780-0070

CAROLINA REGIONAL COLLEGE
P.O. Box 4800, Carolina 00984 *Type:* Public (state) *System:* University of Puerto Rico Regional Colleges Administration *Accred.:* 1978/1983 (MSA) *Calendar:* Sem. plan *Degrees:* A *CEO:* Dean/Dir. Andres Rodriguez Rubio
Enroll: 1923 (809) 757-2000

THE CATHOLIC UNIVERSITY OF PUERTO RICO
Las Americas Ave., Sta. 6, Ponce 00732 *Type:* Private (Roman Catholic) liberal arts *Accred.:* 1953/1983 (MSA) *Calendar:* Sem. plan *Degrees:* A, B, P, M, certificates, diplomas *Prof. Accred.:* Law (ABA only), Medical Technology, Nursing (B,M), Social Work(B) *CEO:* Pres. Tosello J. Gianciacomo
Enroll: 11551 (809) 844-4150

BRANCH CAMPUS
P.O. Box 495, Arecibo, PR 00613 *CEO:* Dean Epifania Bonilla
(809) 881-1212

BRANCH CAMPUS
P.O. Box 809, Guayama, PR 00654 *CEO:* Dean Felix Rosa-Crespo
(809) 864-0550

BRANCH CAMPUS
P.O. Box 1326, Mayaguez, PR 00709 *CEO:* Dean Jaime Ortiz-Vega
(809) 834-5151

CAYEY UNIVERSITY COLLEGE
Antonio R. Barcelo Ave., Cayey 00736 *Type:* Public (state) *System:* University of Puerto Rico Central Office *Accred.:* 1967/1989 (MSA) *Calendar:* Sem. plan *Degrees:* A, B *CEO:* Chanc. Margarita Benitez
Enroll: 3357 (809) 738-2161

CENTRO DE ESTUDIOS AVANZADOS DE PUERTO RICO Y EL CARIBE
Del Cristo St., No. 52, P.O. Box S 446, San Juan 00904 *Type:* Private *Accred.:* 1982/1987 (MSA) *Calendar:* Sem. plan *Degrees:* M *CEO:* Exec. Dir. Ricardo Alegria
Enroll: 154 (809) 723-4481

CENTRO DE ESTUDIOS MULTIDISCIPLINARIOS
6 Dr. Vidal St., Humacao 00661 *Type:* Private *Accred.:* 1981/1986 (CCA-ACTTS) *Calendar:* Courses of varying lengths *Degrees:* certificates *CEO:* Dir. Rivera Resto
Enroll: 174 (809) 852-5530

BRANCH CAMPUS
602 Barbosa Ave., 2nd Fl., Hato Rey, PR 00917 *Prof. Accred.:* Practical Nursing *CEO:* Dir. Juan Pagani
(809) 765-4210

COLEGIO BIBLICO PENTECOSTAL
P.O. Box 901, St. Just 00750-0901 *Type:* Private (Church of God) professional *Accred.:* 1990 (AABC) *Calendar:* Sem. plan *Degrees:* B, certificates *CEO:* Pres. Ernesto Rodriguez
Enroll: 143 (809) 761-0640

COLEGIO MAYOR DE TECNOLOGIA
Calle Morse No. 151, Arroyo 00615 *Type:* Private *Accred.:* 1988 (CCA-ACTTS) *Calendar:* Courses of varying lengths *Degrees:* certificates *CEO:* Dir. Mancio Vicente
Enroll: 45 (809) 839-5266

BRANCH CAMPUS
Calle Santiago Iglesias No. 7, Maunabo, PR 00707 *CEO:* Dir. Lind Ramas Cadiz
(809) 839-5266

COLLEGE OF PUERTO RICO
Calle Amedeo No. 14, Esq. Munoz Rivera, Carolina 00630-6209 *Type:* Private *Accred.:* 1991 (CCA-ACTTS) *Calendar:* Courses of

Accredited Institutions   **Puerto Rico**

varying lengths *Degrees:* certificates *CEO:* Dir. Ruben Rancano
(809) 726-3460

COLUMBIA COLLEGE
P.O. Box 8517, Carretera No. 183, KM 1.7, Caguas 00626 *Type:* Private *Accred.:* 1976/1990 (CCA-ACICS) *Calendar:* Tri. plan *Degrees:* A, B, certificates, diplomas *CEO:* Pres. Alex A. De Jorge
Enroll: 1203   (809) 743-4041

BRANCH CAMPUS
San Jose St. at Public Sq., Rio Grande, PR 00745 *CEO:* Dir. Jesus M. Rivera
(809) 887-3352

BRANCH CAMPUS
P.O. Box 3062, Yauco, PR 00768 *CEO:* Dir. Pablo Martinez
(809) 856-0845

CONSERVATORY OF MUSIC OF PUERTO RICO
P.O. Box 41227, Minillas Sta., Santurce 00940 *Type:* Public *Accred.:* 1975/1989 (MSA) *Calendar:* Sem. plan *Degrees:* B *CEO:* Chanc. Samuel Perez
Enroll: 264   (809) 751-0160

ELECTRONIC COLLEGE AND COMPUTER PROGRAMMING
Munoz Rivera No. 504 Altos, P.O. Box 202, Hato Rey 00918 *Type:* Private business *Accred.:* 1983/1986 (CCA-ACICS) *Calendar:* Courses of varying lengths *Degrees:* certificates, diplomas *CEO:* Pres. Chris Burgos
Enroll: 1457   (809) 753-1500

BRANCH CAMPUS
P.O. Box 1947, Arecibo, PR 00612 *CEO:* Dir. Madelana Vega
(809) 878-1500

BRANCH CAMPUS
Interior Rd. 923, P.O. Box 823, Humacao, PR 00661-0823 *CEO:* Dir. Moses Gonzales
(809) 852-6444

ELECTRONIC DATA PROCESSING COLLEGE
P.O. Box 2303, Hato Rey 00919 *Type:* Private *Accred.:* 1983/1990 (CCA-ACICS) *Calendar:* Courses of varying lengths *Degrees:* A, B *CEO:* Pres. Anibal N. Nieves
Enroll: 1315   (809) 765-3560

BRANCH CAMPUS
48 Betances St., P.O. Box 1647, San Sebastian, PR 00755 *CEO:* Dean Nelson Mender
(809) 896-2137

EVANGELICAL SEMINARY OF PUERTO RICO
Ave. Ponce de Leon, No. 776, Hato Rey 00918 *Type:* Private (interdenominational) professional; graduate only *Accred.:* 1982/1987 (ATS); 1989 (MSA candidate) *Calendar:* Sem. plan *Degrees:* P, M *CEO:* Pres. Luis Fidel Mercado
Enroll: 98   (809) 751-6483

FAJARDO REGIONAL COLLEGE
P.O. Box 1029, Fajardo 00648 *Type:* Private *System:* Universidad Interamericana de Puerto Rico Central Office *Accred.:* 1961/1983 (MSA) *Calendar:* Sem. plan *Degrees:* A, B, certificates, diplomas *CEO:* Dir. Yolanda Robles-Garcia
Enroll: 1851   (809) 863-2390

FASHION DESIGN COLLEGE
Calle Degetau No. 5, Esq. Betances, Bayamon 00619 *Type:* Private *Accred.:* 1988 (CCA-ACTTS) *Calendar:* Courses of varying lengths *Degrees:* certificates *CEO:* Pres. Arturo Aullis
(809) 785-2388

BRANCH CAMPUS
Centro Comercial 65 INF, Ave. 65, Esq. Barbosa, Bayamon, PR 00923 *CEO:* Pres. Arturo Aullis
(809) 765-0001

FASHION MERCHANDISING INSTITUTE
Chase Manhattan Bank Bldg., No. 402, Bayamon 00621 *Type:* Private *Accred.:* 1988 (CCA-ACTTS) *Calendar:* Courses of varying lengths *Degrees:* certificates *CEO:* Dir. Ralph James
Enroll: 160   (809) 798-8870

GUAYAMA REGIONAL COLLEGE
P.O. Box 1559, Guayama 00654 *Type:* Private *System:* Universidad Interamericana de Puerto Rico Central Office *Accred.:* 1957/1983 (MSA) *Calendar:* Sem. plan *Degrees:* A, certificates, diplomas *CEO:* Dir. Samuel Febres-Santiago
Enroll: 1444 (809) 864-2222

HUERTAS JUNIOR COLLEGE
P.O. Box 8429, Caguas 00625 *Type:* Private junior *Accred.:* 1977/1989 (CCA-ACICS) *Calendar:* Qtr. plan *Degrees:* A, certificates, diplomas *CEO:* Pres. Felix Rodriguez Matos
Enroll: 2306 (809) 743-2156

HUMACAO COMMUNITY COLLEGE
101-103 Cruz Ortiz Stella, P.O. Box 8948, Humacao 00661 *Type:* Private business *Accred.:* 1979/1988 (CCA-ACICS) *Calendar:* Courses of varying lengths *Degrees:* certificates, diplomas *CEO:* Pres. Jorge Mojica-Ramirez
Enroll: 430 (809) 852-1430

BRANCH CAMPUS
Garrido Morales No. 52, P.O. Box 1185, Fajardo, PR 00648 *CEO:* Exec. Vice Pres. Mario Francisquini
(809) 863-5210

HUMACAO UNIVERSITY COLLEGE
CUH Sta., Humacao 00661 *Type:* Public (state) *System:* University of Puerto Rico Central Office *Accred.:* 1962/1989 (MSA) *Calendar:* Sem. plan *Degrees:* A, B *Prof. Accred.:* Nursing (A), Occupational Therapy Assisting, Physical Therapy Assisting, Social Work (B) *CEO:* Chanc. Felix A. Castrodad
Enroll: 3825 (809) 850-0000

INSTITUCION CHAVIANO DE MAYAGUEZ
Calle Ramos Antonini, No. 116 Este, Mayaguez 00708 *Type:* Private *Accred.:* 1988 (CCA-ACTTS) *Calendar:* Courses of varying lengths *Degrees:* certificates *CEO:* Dir. Blanca L. Ortiz
(809) 833-2774

INSTITUTE OF MULTIPLE TECHNOLOGY
P.O. Box 209, Mayaguez 00709 *Type:* Private business *Accred.:* 1985 (CCA-ACICS) *Calendar:* Courses of varying lengths *Degrees:* certificates, diplomas *CEO:* Pres. Angel L. Negron
Enroll: 391 (809) 833-6305

BRANCH CAMPUS
163 Antonio R. Barcelo St., Esq. Mariano Vidal, Arecibo, PR 00612 *CEO:* Dir. Miriam Viruet
(809) 878-6844

INSTITUTO COMERCIAL DE PUERTO RICO JUNIOR COLLEGE
558 Munoz Rivera Ave., P.O. Box 304, Hato Rey 00919-0304 *Type:* Private *Accred.:* 1985 (MSA) *Calendar:* Tri. plan *Degrees:* A, certificates, diplomas *CEO:* Pres. Enrique Pineiro
Enroll: 963 (809) 763-7249

BRANCH CAMPUS
Rd. 2, KM 80.4, San Daniel Box 1606, Arecibo, PR 00612-1606 *CEO:* Dir. Angel Curbelo Soto
(809) 878-0524

BRANCH CAMPUS
Mendez Vigo No. 55, P.O. Box 1108, Mayaguez, PR 00708-1108 *CEO:* Dir. Genoveva Christian
(809) 832-2250

INSTITUTO TECNICO COMERCIAL JUNIOR COLLEGE
G.P.O. Box 2527, San Juan 00936 *Type:* Private junior *Accred.:* 1975/1985 (CCA-ACICS) *Calendar:* Courses of varying lengths *Degrees:* A, certificates, diplomas *CEO:* Pres. Carmen T. Ramirez de Jaime
Enroll: 326 (809) 767-4323

INSTITUTO DE BANCA Y COMERCIO
996 Munoz Rivera Ave., Rio Piedras 00926 *Type:* Private business *Accred.:* 1978/1989 (CCA-ACICS) *Calendar:* Courses of varying lengths *Degrees:* certificates, diplomas *CEO:* Pres. Fidel Alonso-Valls
Enroll: 2500 (809) 765-8687

Accredited Institutions Puerto Rico

BRANCH CAMPUS
Centro Industrial La Victoria, P.O. Box 1377, Carolina, PR 00628-1377 *CEO:* Dir. Rafael Jimenez
(809) 750-5200

BRANCH CAMPUS
164 Jose de Diego, P.O. Box K, Cayey, PR 00634 *CEO:* Dir. Angel Luis Lopez Galarza
(809) 738-5555

BRANCH CAMPUS
Edificio Iraola, St. No. 3, P.O. Box 6092, Guayama, PR 00654-9601 *CEO:* Dir. Edgardo Garcia Vasquez
(809) 864-3220

BRANCH CAMPUS
Calle Post No. 154 Norte, Mayaguez, PR 00708 *CEO:* Dir. William Ramirez
(809) 833-4690

BRANCH CAMPUS
Edificio Torre de Oro, Ave. Las Americas, Ponce, PR 00731 *CEO:* Dir. Jose Santiago
(809) 840-6119

INSTITUTO DE EDUCACION UNIVERSAL
P.O. Box 1027, Sabana Seca 00749 *Type:* Private *Accred.:* 1984 (CCA-ACTTS) *Calendar:* Courses of varying lengths *Degrees:* certificates *CEO:* Pres. Angel R. Rivera
Enroll: 1634   (809) 798-8606

BRANCH CAMPUS
Carretera No. 3, KM 11.0, No. 7, Carolina, PR 00628 *CEO:* Dir. Luis R. Diaz
(809) 752-4167

BRANCH CAMPUS
Ave. Barbosa No. 404, Edificio Alma, Hato Rey, PR 00917 *CEO:* Dir. Luis R. Diaz
(809) 758-6410

INSTITUTO DEL ARTE MODERNO
Ave. Monserrate FR-5, Carolina 00630 *Type:* Private *Accred.:* 1986 (CCA-ACTTS) *Calendar:* Courses of varying lengths *Degrees:* certificates *CEO:* Dir. Myriam Aporte
Enroll: 359   (809) 769-7636

INTERNATIONAL COLLEGE OF BUSINESS AND TECHNOLOGY
1612 Ponce de Leon Ave., P.O. Box 8245, San Juan 00910 *Type:* Private junior *Accred.:* 1984/1990 (CCA-ACICS) *Calendar:* Courses of varying lengths *Degrees:* A, certificates, diplomas *CEO:* Dir. Isabel Leon
Enroll: 501   (809) 725-8718

INTERNATIONAL TECHNICAL COLLEGE
1302 Central Ave., Puerto Nuevo, Rio Piedras 00921 *Type:* Private *Accred.:* 1988 (CCA-ACTTS) *Calendar:* Courses of varying lengths *Degrees:* certificates *CEO:* Dir. Roberto Rio Rivera
(809) 792-5620

LA MONTAÑA REGIONAL COLLEGE
P.O. Box 2500, Utuado 00761 *Type:* Public (state) *System:* University of Puerto Rico Regional Colleges Administration *Accred.:* 1981/1986 (MSA) *Calendar:* Sem. plan *Degrees:* A *CEO:* Dean/Dir. Felix Aponte Perez
Enroll: 608   (809) 894-2828

LICEO DE ARTE Y DISENOS
Calle Acosta No. 47, P.O. Box 1889, Caguas 00626-1889 *Type:* Private *Accred.:* 1991 (CCA-ACTTS) *Calendar:* Courses of varying lengths *Degrees:* certificates *CEO:* Exec. Dir. Sylvia Rodriguez Aponte
(809) 743-7447

LICEO DE ARTE Y TECNOLOGIA
405 Ponce de Leon Ave., Hato Rey 00918 *Type:* Private *Accred.:* 1978/1988 (CCA-ACTTS) *Calendar:* Courses of varying lengths *Degrees:* certificates *CEO:* Pres. Carlos M. Valencia
Enroll: 828   (809) 754-8250

MBTI BUSINESS TRAINING INSTITUTE
1257 Ponce de Leon Ave., Santurce 00907 *Type:* Private business *Accred.:* 1974/1986 (CCA-ACICS) *Calendar:* Courses of vary-

Puerto Rico

ing lengths *Degrees:* certificates, diplomas *CEO:* Dir. Carlos Vega
Enroll: 959 (809) 723-9402

MERLIX PROFESSIONAL AND TECHNICAL INSTITUTE
Calle Betances No. 24, P.O. Box 6241, Sta. 1, Bayamon 00619 *Type:* Private *Accred.:* 1988 (CCA-ACTTS) *Calendar:* Courses of varying lengths *Degrees:* certificates *CEO:* Dir. Felix Vargas
(809) 786-7035

NATIONAL COLLEGE OF BUSINESS AND TECHNOLOGY
Ramos Bldg., Hwy. No. 2, P.O. Box 2036, Bayamon 00621 *Type:* Private business *Accred.:* 1983 (CCA-ACICS) *Calendar:* Qtr. plan *Degrees:* certificates, diplomas *CEO:* Pres. Jesus Siverio Orta
Enroll: 3197 (809) 780-5134

BRANCH CAMPUS
Ave. Gonzalo Marin No. 109, Arecibo, PR 00612 *CEO:* Dir. Iride M. Dumatt
(809) 879-5044

NATIONAL COMPUTER COLLEGE
Calle Union No. 5, Fajardo 00648 *Type:* Private business *Accred.:* 1986/1990 (CCA-ACICS) *Calendar:* Courses of varying lengths *Degrees:* certificates, diplomas *CEO:* Pres. Antonio Caban
Enroll: 126 (809) 863-0593

PONCE COLLEGE OF TECHNOLOGY
Estrella St., No. 3, P.O. Box 1284, Ponce 00733 *Type:* Private *Accred.:* 1980/1985 (CCA-ACTTS) *Calendar:* Courses of varying lengths *Degrees:* certificates, diplomas *CEO:* Pres. Jose Cuevas
Enroll: 325 (809) 844-5325

PONCE PARAMEDICAL COLLEGE
Medical Bldg., P.O. Box 106, Coto Laurel 00644 *Type:* Private *Accred.:* 1988 (CCA-ACTTS) *Calendar:* Courses of varying lengths *Degrees:* certificates *CEO:* Dir. Alberto Aristizabal
Enroll: 92 (809) 848-1729

PONCE REGIONAL COLLEGE
Mercidita Sta., Ponce 00715 *Type:* Private *System:* Universidad Interamericana de Puerto Rico Central Office *Accred.:* 1962/1985 (MSA) *Calendar:* Sem. plan *Degrees:* A, B, certificates, diplomas *CEO:* Dean/Dir. Marilina L. Wayland
Enroll: 3379 (809) 840-9090

PONCE SCHOOL OF MEDICINE
Ponce 00732 *Type:* Private professional *Calendar:* Sem. plan *Degrees:* P *Prof. Accred.:* Medicine *CEO:* Dean Luis F. Sala, M.D.
Enroll: 177 (809) 843-8288

PONCE TECHNICAL SCHOOL
16 Salud St., Ponce 00731 *Type:* Private *Calendar:* Courses of varying lengths *Degrees:* certificates, diplomas *Prof. Accred.:* Health Education, Practical Nursing *CEO:* Pres. Fernando Torres
Enroll: 241 (809) 844-7940

PONCE TECHNOLOGICAL UNIVERSITY COLLEGE
P.O. Box 7186, Ponce 00731 *Type:* Public (state) *System:* University of Puerto Rico Regional Colleges Administration *Accred.:* 1970/1985 (MSA) *Calendar:* Sem. plan *Degrees:* A, B *Prof. Accred.:* Physical Therapy Assisting *CEO:* Dean/Dir. Pedro E. Laboy-Zengotita
Enroll: 2348 (809) 844-8181

PROFESSIONAL TRAINING ACADEMY OF ESTHETICS AND BEAUTY COURSES
Cristina No. 74, P.O. Box 7716, Ponce 00732-7716 *Type:* Private *Accred.:* 1991 (CCA-ACTTS) *Calendar:* Courses of varying lengths *Degrees:* certificates *CEO:* Pres. Carmen Molina
(809) 844-5960

BRANCH CAMPUS
Munoz Rivera No. 504, Hato Rey, PR 00917 *CEO:* Pres. Carmen Molina
(809) 766-2199

BRANCH CAMPUS
Mendez Vigo Corner to Pilar, Mayaguez, PR 00708 *CEO:* Pres. Carmen Molina
(809) 834-5210

Puerto Rico

PUERTO RICO BARBER COLLEGE
2018 Borinquen Ave., P.O. Box 14215, Obrero Sta., Santurce 00916-4215 *Type:* Private *Accred.:* 1988 (CCA-ACTTS) *Calendar:* Courses of varying lengths *Degrees:* certificates *CEO:* Dir. Sergio Cardona
Enroll: 82 (809) 726-6433

BRANCH CAMPUS
E52 Garrido Morales St., Fajardo, PR 00648 *CEO:* Dir. Jose Rivera
(809) 837-5050

PUERTO RICO JUNIOR COLLEGE
P.O. Box 21373, Rio Piedras 00928 *Type:* Private *System:* Ana G. Mendez Educational Foundation *Accred.:* 1959/1988 (MSA) *Calendar:* Sem. plan *Degrees:* A *Prof. Accred.:* Medical Record Technology *CEO:* Chanc. Alberto Maldonado
Enroll: 4589 (809) 758-7171

PUERTO RICO PROFESSIONAL COLLEGE
P.O. Box 8538, Bayamon 00621 *Type:* Private *Accred.:* 1990 (CCA-ACTTS) *Calendar:* Courses of varying lengths *Degrees:* certificates *CEO:* Pres. Ismael Hermandez
(809) 798-8200

PUERTO RICO TECHNOLOGY AND BEAUTY COLLEGE
P.O. Box 849, Bayamon 00621-0849 *Type:* Private *Accred.:* 1980/1985 (CCA-ACTTS) *Calendar:* Courses of varying lengths *Degrees:* certificates, diplomas *CEO:* Pres. Zenon T. Contes
Enroll: 869 (809) 787-0765

BRANCH CAMPUS
Calle Eugenio Maria de Hostos, No. 198, Arecibo, PR 00612 *CEO:* Pres. Zenon T. Contes
(809) 878-0164

BRANCH CAMPUS
Calle Mendez Vigo No. 11-E, Mayaguez, PR 00708 *CEO:* Pres. Efrain Cruz
(809) 833-6003

RAMIREZ COLLEGE OF BUSINESS AND TECHNOLOGY
103 Munoz Rivera Ave., P.O. Box 8074, Santurce 00910 *Type:* Private junior *Accred.:* 1975/1981 (CCA-ACICS) *Calendar:* Tri. plan *Degrees:* A *CEO:* Pres. Ludy G. Pinero
Enroll: 1410 (809) 763-3120

SAN JUAN CITY COLLEGE
501 Roberto H. Todd Ave., Call Box 9300, Santurce Sta., Santurce 00908 *Type:* Private *Accred.:* 1984/1990 (CCA-ACTTS) *Calendar:* Courses of varying lengths *Degrees:* certificates *CEO:* Pres. Americo Reyes-Morales
Enroll: 953 (809) 725-4949

BRANCH CAMPUS
P.O. Box 1821, Juana Diaz, PR 00665-1821 *CEO:* Dir. Juan Rivera
(809) 837-5050

TECHNOLOGICAL COLLEGE OF THE MUNICIPALITY OF SAN JUAN
Jose Oliver St., Hato Rey 00918 *Type:* Public *Accred.:* 1978/1987 (MSA) *Calendar:* Sem. plan *Degrees:* A *Prof. Accred.:* Nursing (A) *CEO:* Chanc. J.R.E. Perez-Lloveras
Enroll: 946 (809) 250-7111

UNIVERSIDAD ADVENTISTA DE LAS ANTILLAS
P.O. Box 118, Mayaguez 00709 *Type:* Private (Seventh-Day Adventist) liberal arts *Accred.:* 1978/1987 (MSA) *Calendar:* Sem. plan *Degrees:* A, B *CEO:* Pres. Moises Velazquez
Enroll: 813 (809) 834-9595

UNIVERSIDAD CENTRAL DEL CARIBE
P.O. Box 935, Cayey 00633 *Type:* Private professional *Calendar:* Courses of varying lengths *Degrees:* A, P *Prof. Accred.:* Medicine, Radiography *CEO:* Pres. Raul A. Marcial-Rojas, M.D.
(809) 798-3001

UNIVERSIDAD INTERAMERICANA DE PUERTO RICO
Harris Dr., Call Box 5100, San German 00753 *Type:* Private *System:* Universidad Interamericana de Puerto Rico Central Office *Accred.:* 1944/1987 (MSA) *Calendar:* Sem. plan *Degrees:* A, B, M *Prof.*

Puerto Rico

Accred.: Medical Technology *CEO:* Chanc. Federico Matheu
Enroll: 5711 (809) 892-1095

METROPOLITAN CAMPUS
P.O. Box 1293, Hato Rey, PR 00936 *Accred.:* 1944/1987 (MSA) *Prof. Accred.:* Medical Technology, Nursing (B), Optometry, Social Work (B) *CEO:* Chanc. Gamaliel Perez Santiago
Enroll: 12670 (809) 758-8000

SCHOOL OF LAW
P.O. Box 8897, Fernandez Juncos Sta., Santurce, PR 00910 *Prof. Accred.:* Law (ABA only) *CEO:* Dean Manuel J. Fernos
(809) 727-1930

UNIVERSIDAD METROPOLITANA
P.O. Box 2115, Rio Piedras 00928 *Type:* Private *System:* Ana G. Mendez Educational Foundation *Accred.:* 1980/1988 (MSA) *Calendar:* Sem. plan *Degrees:* A, B, M *Prof. Accred.:* Nursing (A,B), Respiratory Therapy *CEO:* Chanc. Rene L. Labarca
Enroll: 5711 (809) 766-1717

UNIVERSIDAD POLITECNICA DE PUERTO RICO
P.O. Box 2017, Hato Rey 00918 *Type:* Private *Accred.:* 1985 (MSA) *Calendar:* Qtr. plan *Degrees:* B *CEO:* Pres. Ernesto Vazquez-Torres
Enroll: 2721 (809) 754-8000

UNIVERSIDAD DEL TURABO
P.O. Box 3030, Gurabo 00658 *Type:* Private *System:* Ana G. Mendez Educational Foundation *Accred.:* 1974/1988 (MSA) *Calendar:* Sem. plan *Degrees:* A, B, M *CEO:* Chanc. Claudio R. Prieto
Enroll: 1720 (809) 743-7979

UNIVERSITY OF PUERTO RICO
Ponce de Leon Ave., P.O. Box 3300, U.P.R. Sta., Rio Piedras 00931 *Type:* Public (state) *System:* University of Puerto Rico Central Office *Accred.:* 1946/1985 (MSA) *Calendar:* Sem. plan *Degrees:* A, B, P, M, D, certificates, diplomas *Prof. Accred.:* Law, Librarianship, Planning, Rehabilitation Counseling, Social Work (B,M), Teacher Education (e,s,p) *CEO:* Chanc. Juan R. Fernandez
Enroll: 22524 (809) 764-0000

MAYAGUEZ CAMPUS
P.O. Box 5000, Mayaguez, PR 00608 *Accred.:* 1946/1985 (MSA) *Prof. Accred.:* Engineering (chemical, civil, electrical, industrial, mechanical), Nursing (A,B) *CEO:* Chanc. Alejandro Ruiz-Acevedo
Enroll: 9432 (809) 832-4040

MEDICAL SCIENCES CAMPUS
G.P.O. Box 5067, San Juan, PR 00936 *Accred.:* 1946/1985 (MSA) *Prof. Accred.:* Combined Prosthodontics, Dental Assisting, Dental Hygiene, Dentistry, Dietetics (coordinated), General Practice Residency, Health Services Administration, Medical Record Administration, Medical Technology, Medicine, Nuclear Medicine Technology, Nursing (B,M), Occupational Therapy, Ophthalmic Medical Technology, Oral and Maxillofacial Surgery, Pediatric Dentistry, Pharmacy, Physical Therapy, Public Health, Radiography, Speech-Language Pathology *CEO:* Chanc. Manuel Marina
Enroll: 3220 (809) 758-2525

SCHOOL OF ARCHITECTURE
San Juan, PR 00931 *Prof. Accred.:* Architecture (M) *CEO:* Dean Juan Marques
(809) 763-5101

UNIVERSITY OF THE SACRED HEART
Box 12383, Loiza Sta., Santurce 00914 *Type:* Private (Roman Catholic) liberal arts and teachers *Accred.:* 1950/1989 (MSA) *Calendar:* Sem. plan *Degrees:* A, B, M, certificates, diplomas *Prof. Accred.:* Medical Technology, Nursing (A,B), Social Work (B) *CEO:* Pres. Jose Alberto Morales
Enroll: 7480 (809) 728-1515

WORLD SUPREME TECHNICAL AND BEAUTY COLLEGE
P.O. Box 566, Caguas 00625-0566 *Type:* Private *Accred.:* 1991 (CCA-ACTTS) *Calendar:* Courses of varying lengths *Degrees:* certificates *CEO:* Pres. Abby Barrero
(809) 743-2464

Puerto Rico

YORK COLLEGE
P.O. Box 5183, San Juan 00906-5183 *Type:* Private *Accred.:* 1988 (CCA-ACTTS) *Calendar:* Courses of varying lengths *Degrees:* certificates *CEO:* Pres. Victor Vega
(809) 722-2000

RHODE ISLAND

BROWN UNIVERSITY
Providence 02912 *Type:* Private *Accred.:* 1929/1988 (NEASC-CIHE) *Calendar:* Sem. plan *Degrees:* B, P, M, D *Prof. Accred.:* Engineering (bioengineering, chemical, civil, electrical, materials, mechanical), Medicine, Psychology Internship *CEO:* Pres. Vartan Gregorian
Enroll: 7332 (401) 863-1000

BRYANT COLLEGE
1150 Douglas Pike, Smithfield 02917 *Type:* Private *Accred.:* 1964/1990 (NEASC-CIHE) *Calendar:* Sem. plan *Degrees:* A, B, M *CEO:* Pres. William E. Trueheart
Enroll: 3862 (401) 232-6000

COMMUNITY COLLEGE OF RHODE ISLAND
400 East Ave., Warwick 02886-1805 *Type:* Public (state) *System:* Rhode Island Office of Higher Education *Accred.:* 1969/1984 (NEASC-CIHE) *Calendar:* Sem. plan *Degrees:* A, certificates, diplomas *Prof. Accred.:* Dental Assisting, Dental Hygiene, Medical Laboratory Technology (AMA), Nursing (A), Practical Nursing, Radiography, Respiratory Therapy *CEO:* Pres. Edward J. Liston
Enroll: 8810 (401) 825-1000

HALL INSTITUTE OF TECHNOLOGY
120 High St., Pawtucket 02860 *Type:* Private technical *Accred.:* 1980/1985 (CCA-ACTTS) *Calendar:* Courses of varying lengths *Degrees:* certificates *CEO:* Dir. Charles K. Rogers
Enroll: 479 (401) 722-2003

JOHNSON AND WALES UNIVERSITY
8 Abbott Park Pl., Providence 02903 *Type:* Private *Accred.:* 1954/1981 (CCA-ACICS) *Calendar:* Tri. plan *Degrees:* A, B, P, M, certificates, diplomas *CEO:* Pres. Christopher T. Del Sesto
Enroll: 7903 (401) 456-1000

BRANCH CAMPUS
701 E. Bay St., Charleston, SC 29403 *CEO:* Dir. Paul W. Conco
(803) 723-4638

BRANCH CAMPUS
2428 Almeda Ave., Stes. 316-318, Norfolk, VA 23513 *CEO:* Dir. Debra C. Gray
(804) 853-3508

KATHARINE GIBBS SCHOOL
178 Butler Ave., Providence 02906 *Type:* Private business *Accred.:* 1967/1985 (CCA-ACICS) *Calendar:* Sem. plan *Degrees:* certificates, diplomas *CEO:* Dir. Elaine Carroll
Enroll: 553 (401) 861-1420

NASSON INSTITUTE
1080 Newport Ave., Pawtucket 02861 *Type:* Private business *Accred.:* 1989 (CCA-ACICS) *Calendar:* Courses of varying lengths *Degrees:* certificates, diplomas *CEO:* Dir. R.L. Newman
Enroll: 423 (401) 728-1570

NEW ENGLAND INSTITUTE OF TECHNOLOGY
2500 Post Rd., Warwick 02886 *Type:* Private *Accred.:* 1972/1989 (CCA-ACTTS); 1982 (NEASC-CVTCI) *Calendar:* Qtr. plan *Degrees:* A, B *CEO:* Pres. Richard I. Gouse
Enroll: 1863 (401) 739-5000

NEW ENGLAND TRACTOR TRAILER TRAINING OF RHODE ISLAND
10 Dunnell La., Pawtucket 02860 *Type:* Private *Accred.:* 1986 (CCA-ACTTS) *Calendar:* Courses of varying lengths *Degrees:* certificates *CEO:* Dir. Mark Greenburg
(401) 725-1220

OCEAN STATE BUSINESS INSTITUTE
140 Point Judith Rd., Unit 3A, Narragansett 02882 *Type:* Private business *Accred.:* 1979/1991 (CCA-ACICS) *Calendar:* Courses of varying lengths *Degrees:* certificates, diplomas *CEO:* Dir. Assunta G. Pouliot
Enroll: 186 (401) 789-0287

Rhode Island

PROVIDENCE COLLEGE
Providence 02918 *Type:* Private (Roman Catholic) liberal arts *Accred.:* 1933/1988 (NEASC-CIHE) *Calendar:* Sem. plan *Degrees:* B, M, D *Prof. Accred.:* Social Work (B) *CEO:* Pres. John F. Cunningham, O.P.
Enroll: 4343 (401) 865-1000

RHODE ISLAND COLLEGE
Providence 02908 *Type:* Public (state) liberal arts and teachers *System:* Rhode Island Office of Higher Education *Accred.:* 1958/1990 (NEASC-CIHE) *Calendar:* Sem. plan *Degrees:* B, M *Prof. Accred.:* Art, Music, Nursing (B), Rehabilitation Counseling, Social Work (B,M), Teacher Education (e,s,p) *CEO:* Pres. John Nazarian
Enroll: 6837 (401) 456-8000

RHODE ISLAND SCHOOL OF DESIGN
Providence 02903 *Type:* Private professional *Accred.:* 1949/1986 (NEASC-CIHE) *Calendar:* Sem. plan *Degrees:* B, M *Prof. Accred.:* Architecture (B), Art, Interior Design, Landscape Architecture (B) *CEO:* Pres. Thomas F. Schutte
Enroll: 2054 (401) 331-3511

RHODE ISLAND SCHOOL OF PHOTOGRAPHY
241 Webster Ave., Providence 02909 *Type:* Private *Accred.:* 1982/1987 (CCA-ACTTS) *Calendar:* Courses of varying lengths *Degrees:* diplomas *CEO:* Pres. Donald Folgo
Enroll: 139 (401) 943-7722

RHODE ISLAND TRADES SHOPS SCHOOL
361 W. Fountain St., Providence 02903 *Type:* Private *Accred.:* 1971/1988 (CCA-ACTTS) *Calendar:* Courses of varying lengths *Degrees:* diplomas *CEO:* Dir. Robert L. Newman
Enroll: 1024 (401) 331-3008

ROGER WILLIAMS COLLEGE
Bristol 02809 *Type:* Private liberal arts *Accred.:* 1972/1986 (NEASC-CIHE) *Calendar:* Sem. plan *Degrees:* A, B *Prof. Accred.:* Architecture (B), Engineering Technology (electrical, mechanical) *CEO:* Pres. Natale A. Sicuro
Enroll: 2804 (401) 253-1040

SALVE REGINA UNIVERSITY
100 Ochre Point Ave., Newport 02840 *Type:* Private (Roman Catholic) liberal arts *Accred.:* 1956/1986 (NEASC-CIHE) *Calendar:* Sem. plan *Degrees:* A, B, M *Prof. Accred.:* Art, Nursing (B), Social Work (B) *CEO:* Pres. Lucille McKillop, R.S.M.
Enroll: 1944 (401) 847-6650

SAWYER SCHOOL
101 Main St., Pawtucket 02860 *Type:* Private business *Accred.:* 1973/1985 (CCA-ACICS) *Calendar:* Courses of varying lengths *Degrees:* certificates, diplomas *CEO:* Pres. John F. Crowley
Enroll: 669 (401) 272-8400

BRANCH CAMPUS
1109 Warwick Ave., Warwick, RI 02888 *CEO:* Dir. Thomas W. Kirkpatrick
(401) 781-2887

SCHOOL OF MEDICAL AND LEGAL SECRETARIAL SCIENCES
60 Angell St., Providence 02906 *Type:* Private *Accred.:* 1981/1986 (CCA-ACTTS) *Calendar:* Courses of varying lengths *Degrees:* certificates *CEO:* Dir. Norma Casale
Enroll: 29 (401) 331-1711

UNITED STATES NAVAL WAR COLLEGE
Newport 02841-5010 *Type:* Public (federal) *Accred.:* 1989 (NEASC-CIHE) *Calendar:* Sem. plan *Degrees:* M *CEO:* Pres. Joseph C. Strasser
Enroll: 248 (401) 841-3089

UNIVERSITY OF RHODE ISLAND
Kingston 02881 *Type:* Public (state) *System:* Rhode Island Office of Higher Education *Accred.:* 1930/1987 (NEASC-CIHE) *Calendar:* Sem. plan *Degrees:* A, B, M, D *Prof. Accred.:* Audiology, Business (B,M), Clinical Psychology, Dental Hygiene, Engineering (chemical, civil, electrical, industrial, manufacturing, mechanical), Landscape Architecture (B-initial), Librarianship, Music, Nursing (B,M), Pharmacy, Physical Therapy, Planning (community/regional), School Psychology, Speech-Language Pathology, Teacher Education (p) *CEO:* Pres. Robert L. Carothers
Enroll: 12731 (401) 792-1000

SOUTH CAROLINA

AIKEN TECHNICAL COLLEGE
P.O. Box 696, Aiken 29802-0696 *Type:* Public (state) 2-year *System:* South Carolina State Board for Technical and Comprehensive Education *Accred.:* 1975/1990 (SACS-CC) *Calendar:* Qtr. plan *Degrees:* A *Prof. Accred.:* Dental Assisting (prelim. provisional) *CEO:* Pres. Paul L. Blowers
Enroll: 1719   (803) 593-9231

ALPHA BEAUTY SCHOOL
10 Liberty La., Greenville 29607-2315 *Type:* Private *Accred.:* 1986/1991 (SACS-COEI) *Calendar:* Courses of varying lengths *Degrees:* certificates *CEO:* Dir. Kenneth W. Lochridge
Enroll: 380   (803) 271-0020

BRANCH CAMPUS
Innsbruck Mall, Tunnel Rd., Asheville, NC 28805 *CEO:* Dir. Vera Hendricks
(704) 253-2875

BRANCH CAMPUS
2619 S. Main St., Anderson, SC 29624 *CEO:* Dir. Ethel Audrey
(803) 224-8338

BRANCH CAMPUS
112 E. North and Second Sts., Seneca, SC 29678 *CEO:* Dir. Deborah McCullough
(803) 882-0936

BRANCH CAMPUS
653 N. Church St., Spartanburg, SC 29301 *CEO:* Dir. Barbara Cash
(803) 585-6666

ANDERSON COLLEGE
316 Blvd., Anderson 29621 *Type:* Private (Southern Baptist) *Accred.:* 1959/1990 (SACS-CC) *Calendar:* Sem. plan *Degrees:* A, B (candidate) *Prof. Accred.:* Music *CEO:* Pres. Mark L. Hopkins
Enroll: 909   (803) 231-2000

BENEDICT COLLEGE
Harden and Blanding Sts., Columbia 29204 *Type:* Private liberal arts *Accred.:* 1946/1991 (SACS-CC) *Calendar:* Sem. plan *Degrees:* B *Prof. Accred.:* Social Work (B) *CEO:* Pres. Marshall C. Grigsby
Enroll: 1408   (803) 256-4220

BETTY STEVENS COSMETOLOGY INSTITUTE
301 Rainbow Dr., P.O. Box 3827, Florence 29501 *Type:* Private *Accred.:* 1985/1990 (SACS-COEI) *Calendar:* Courses of varying lengths *Degrees:* certificates *CEO:* Dir. Elizabeth Humphries
Enroll: 53   (803) 669-4452

CAMDEN SCHOOL OF HAIR DESIGN
2630 N. Broad St., Camden 29020 *Type:* Private *Accred.:* 1987 (SACS-COEI) *Calendar:* Courses of varying lengths *Degrees:* certificates *CEO:* Dir. Corliss Miller-Tomlin
Enroll: 10   (803) 425-1011

CENTRAL WESLEYAN COLLEGE
One Wesleyan Dr., Central 29630 *Type:* Private (Wesleyan Methodist) liberal arts and teachers *Accred.:* 1973/1989 (SACS-CC) *Calendar:* Sem. plan *Degrees:* A, B, M (candidate) *CEO:* Pres. John M. Newby
Enroll: 918   (803) 639-2453

CHARLESTON COSMETOLOGY INSTITUTE
8484 Dorchester Rd., Charleston 29420 *Type:* Private *Accred.:* 1986/1991 (SACS-COEI) *Calendar:* Courses of varying lengths *Degrees:* certificates *CEO:* Dir. Jerry R. Poer, Jr.
Enroll: 286   (803) 552-3670

CHARLESTON SOUTHERN UNIVERSITY
P.O. Box 10087, Charleston 29411 *Type:* Private (Southern Baptist) liberal arts and teachers *Accred.:* 1970/1986 (SACS-CC) *Calendar:* 4-1-4 plan *Degrees:* A, B, M *Prof. Accred.:* Music *CEO:* Pres. Jairy C. Hunter, Jr.
Enroll: 1824   (803) 863-7000

CHARLOTTE DIESEL DRIVING SCHOOL
550 Wilson Rd., Newberry 29108 *Type:* Private *Accred.:* 1989 (CCA-ACTTS) *Calen-

dar: Courses of varying lengths *Degrees:* certificates *CEO:* Dir. Richard Foster
Enroll: 24   (803) 276-7363

CHARZANNE BEAUTY COLLEGE
Rte. 2, Box 9, Greenwood 29649 *Type:* Private *Accred.:* 1986/1988 (SACS-COEI) *Calendar:* Courses of varying lengths *Degrees:* certificates *CEO:* Dir. Vance Kennedy
Enroll: 58   (803) 223-7321

CHESTERFIELD-MARLBORO TECHNICAL COLLEGE
1201 Chesterfield Hwy., No. 9 W., P.O. Drawer 1007, Cheraw 29520-1007 *Type:* Public (state) 2-year *System:* South Carolina State Board for Technical and Comprehensive Education *Accred.:* 1973/1988 (SACS-CC) *Calendar:* Qtr. plan *Degrees:* A *CEO:* Pres. Ronald W. Hampton
Enroll: 870   (803) 537-5286

CHRIS LOGAN CAREER COLLEGE
505 Seventh Ave., N., Myrtle Beach 29578 *Type:* Private *Accred.:* 1988 (SACS-COEI) *Calendar:* Courses of varying lengths *Degrees:* certificates *CEO:* Dir. Chris Logan
Enroll: 1094   (803) 448-6302

THE CITADEL
Citadel Sta., Charleston 29409 *Type:* Public (state) primarily for men *System:* South Carolina Commission on Higher Education *Accred.:* 1924/1984 (SACS-CC) *Calendar:* Sem. plan *Degrees:* B, M *Prof. Accred.:* Engineering (civil, electrical), Teacher Education (s,p) *CEO:* Pres. Claudius E. Watts, III
Enroll: 2864   (803) 792-5000

CLAFLIN COLLEGE
700 College Ave., Orangeburg 29115 *Type:* Private (United Methodist) liberal arts *Accred.:* 1947/1991 (SACS-CC) *Calendar:* Sem. plan *Degrees:* B *CEO:* Pres. Oscar A. Rogers, Jr.
Enroll: 899   (803) 534-2710

CLEMSON UNIVERSITY
Clemson 29634-5310 *Type:* Public (state) liberal arts *System:* South Carolina Commission on Higher Education *Accred.:* 1927/1991 (SACS-CC) *Calendar:* Sem. plan *Degrees:* B, M, D *Prof. Accred.:* Accounting (Type A,C), Architecture (M), Business (B,M), Computer Science, Construction Management, Engineering (agricultural, ceramic, chemical, civil, computer, electrical, environmental/sanitary, industrial, mechanical), Forestry, Nursing (B,M), Parks, Recreation and Tourism, Planning (city/regional), Teacher Education (e,s,p) *CEO:* Pres. Max A. Lennon
Enroll: 15834   (803) 656-3311

COKER COLLEGE
E. College Ave., Hartsville 29550 *Type:* Private liberal arts primarily for women *Accred.:* 1923/1985 (SACS-CC) *Calendar:* Sem. plan *Degrees:* B *Prof. Accred.:* Music *CEO:* Pres. James D. Daniels
Enroll: 778   (803) 383-8000

COLLEGE OF CHARLESTON
66 George St., Charleston 29424 *Type:* Public (state) liberal arts *System:* South Carolina Commission on Higher Education *Accred.:* 1916/1986 (SACS-CC) *Calendar:* Sem. plan *Degrees:* B, M *Prof. Accred.:* Business (B), Public Administration *CEO:* Pres. Harry M. Lightsey, Jr.
Enroll: 6612   (803) 792-5500

COLUMBIA BIBLE COLLEGE AND SEMINARY
P.O. Box 3122, Columbia 29230-3122 *Type:* Private *Accred.:* 1948/1982 (AABC); 1985/1990 (ATS); 1982/1991 (SACS-CC) *Calendar:* Tri. plan *Degrees:* A, B, P, M, D *CEO:* Pres. Johnny V. Miller
Enroll: 818   (803) 754-4100

COLUMBIA COLLEGE
1301 Columbia College Dr., Columbia 29203 *Type:* Private (United Methodist) liberal arts for women *Accred.:* 1938/1991 (SACS-CC) *Calendar:* Sem. plan *Degrees:* B, M *Prof. Accred.:* Music, Social Work (B) *CEO:* Pres. Peter T. Mitchell
Enroll: 1054   (803) 786-3012

COLUMBIA JUNIOR COLLEGE OF BUSINESS
3810 Main St., P.O. Box 1196, Columbia 29202 *Type:* Private junior *Accred.:* 1964/

South Carolina

1987 (CCA-ACICS) *Calendar:* Qtr. plan *Degrees:* A, certificates, diplomas *CEO:* Pres. Michael Gorman
Enroll: 771 (803) 799-9082

CONVERSE COLLEGE
580 E. Main St., Spartanburg 29302-0006 *Type:* Private liberal arts primarily for women *Accred.:* 1912/1986 (SACS-CC) *Calendar:* Sem. plan *Degrees:* B, M *Prof. Accred.:* Interior Design, Music *CEO:* Pres. Ellen Wood Hall
Enroll: 990 (803) 596-9000

DENMARK TECHNICAL COLLEGE
Solomon Blatt Blvd., P.O. Box 327, Denmark 29042-0327 *Type:* Public (state) 2-year *System:* South Carolina State Board for Technical and Comprehensive Education *Accred.:* 1979/1991 (SACS-CC) *Calendar:* Qtr. plan *Degrees:* A *CEO:* Pres. Curtis E. Bryan
Enroll: 617 (803) 793-3301

ERSKINE COLLEGE
Washington St., Due West 29639 *Type:* Private (Presbyterian) liberal arts *Accred.:* 1981/1985 (ATS); 1925/1982 (SACS-CC) *Calendar:* 4-1-4 plan *Degrees:* A, B, M, D *CEO:* Pres. James W. Strobel
Enroll: 600 (803) 379-2131

FARAH'S BEAUTY SCHOOL
520 Bush River Rd., Columbia 29210 *Type:* Private *Accred.:* 1987 (SACS-COEI) *Calendar:* Courses of varying lengths *Degrees:* certificates *CEO:* Dir. Rebecca Farah
Enroll: 46 (803) 772-0101

FARAH'S BEAUTY SCHOOL
107 Central Ave., Goose Creek 29445 *Type:* Private *Accred.:* 1985/1990 (SACS-COEI) *Calendar:* Courses of varying lengths *Degrees:* certificates *CEO:* Dir. Marilyn Farah
Enroll: 89 (803) 572-5705

FLORENCE-DARLINGTON TECHNICAL COLLEGE
P.O. Box 100548, Florence 29501-0548 *Type:* Public (state) 2-year *System:* South Carolina State Board for Technical and Comprehensive Education *Accred.:* 1970/

Accredited Institutions

1991 (SACS-CC) *Calendar:* Qtr. plan *Degrees:* A *Prof. Accred.:* Dental Assisting, Dental Hygiene, Engineering Technology (civil/construction, electrical, mechanical drafting/design), Medical Laboratory Technology (AMA), Medical Record Technology, Nursing (A), Radiography, Respiratory Therapy, Respiratory Therapy Technology, Surgical Technology *CEO:* Pres. Michael B. McCall
Enroll: 2543 (803) 661-8324

FORREST JUNIOR COLLEGE
601 E. River St., Anderson 29624 *Type:* Private business *Accred.:* 1982/1990 (CCA-ACICS) *Calendar:* Qtr. plan *Degrees:* A *CEO:* Dir. Carlene M. Shapiro
Enroll: 367 (803) 225-7653

FRANCIS MARION COLLEGE
P.O. Box 100547, Florence 29501-0547 *Type:* Public (state) liberal arts *System:* South Carolina Commission on Higher Education *Accred.:* 1972/1987 (SACS-CC) *Calendar:* Sem. plan *Degrees:* A, B, M *CEO:* Pres. Thomas C. Stanton
Enroll: 3213 (803) 661-1362

FURMAN UNIVERSITY
Poinsett Hwy., Greenville 29613 *Type:* Private (Southern Baptist) liberal arts *Accred.:* 1924/1987 (SACS-CC) *Calendar:* 3-2-3 plan *Degrees:* B, M *Prof. Accred.:* Music *CEO:* Pres. John E. Johns
Enroll: 2965 (803) 294-2000

GREENVILLE TECHNICAL COLLEGE
P.O. Box 5616, Sta. B, Greenville 29606-5616 *Type:* Public (state) 2-year *System:* South Carolina State Board for Technical and Comprehensive Education *Accred.:* 1968/1982 (SACS-CC) *Calendar:* Qtr. plan *Degrees:* A *Prof. Accred.:* Dental Assisting, Dental Hygiene, EMT-Paramedic, Engineering Technology (architectural, electrical, mechanical), Medical Laboratory Technology (AMA), Nursing (A), Optometric Technology, Physical Therapy Assisting, Radiography, Respiratory Therapy, Respiratory

Accredited Institutions   **South Carolina**

Therapy Technology, Surgical Technology *CEO:* Pres. Thomas E. Barton, Jr.
Enroll: 9387   (803) 250-8000

HORRY-GEORGETOWN TECHNICAL COLLEGE
P.O. Box 1966, Conway 29526 *Type:* Public (state) 2-year *System:* South Carolina State Board for Technical and Comprehensive Education *Accred.:* 1972/1991 (SACS-CC) *Calendar:* Qtr. plan *Degrees:* A *Prof. Accred.:* Engineering Technology (electrical) *CEO:* Pres. D. Kent Sharples
Enroll: 2341   (803) 347-3186

LANDER COLLEGE
Stanley Ave., Greenwood 29649 *Type:* Public (state) liberal arts *System:* South Carolina Commission on Higher Education *Accred.:* 1952/1986 (SACS-CC) *Calendar:* Sem. plan *Degrees:* B, M *Prof. Accred.:* Nursing (B) *CEO:* Pres. Larry A. Jackson
Enroll: 2359   (803) 229-8300

LIMESTONE COLLEGE
1115 College Dr., Gaffney 29340 *Type:* Private liberal arts *Accred.:* 1928/1990 (SACS-CC) *Calendar:* Sem. plan *Degrees:* B *Prof. Accred.:* Music *CEO:* Interim Pres. Dan Champion
Enroll: 777   (803) 489-7151

LUTHERAN THEOLOGICAL SOUTHERN SEMINARY
4201 N. Main St., Columbia 29203 *Type:* Private (Lutheran) professional; graduate only *Accred.:* 1944/1983 (ATS); 1983 (SACS-CC) *Calendar:* Sem. plan *Degrees:* M, D *CEO:* Pres. Mack C. Branham, Jr.
Enroll: 135   (803) 786-5150

LYNN WILEY'S HAIRSTYLING ACADEMY
4 Chick Spring Rd., Greenville 29609 *Type:* Private *Accred.:* 1987 (CCA-ACTTS) *Calendar:* Courses of varying lengths *Degrees:* diplomas *CEO:* Owner Lynn Wiley
         (803) 232-2676

MANGUM'S BARBER AND HAIRSTYLING COLLEGE
125 Hampton St., Rock Hill 29730 *Type:* Private *Accred.:* 1985 (CCA-ACTTS) *Calendar:* Courses of varying lengths *Degrees:* diplomas *CEO:* Dir. Richard Mangum
Enroll: 45   (803) 328-0807

MANSFIELD BUSINESS COLLEGE
6699 Two Notch Rd., Columbia 29223 *Type:* Private *Accred.:* 1989 (CCA-ACICS) *Calendar:* Courses of varying lengths *Degrees:* certificates, diplomas *CEO:* Dir. Elaine Cue
         (803) 754-0727

BRANCH CAMPUS
Post and Courier Bldg., 6296 Rivers Ave., North Charleston, SC 29148 *CEO:* Dir. Leo Dolan
         (803) 554-5453

BRANCH CAMPUS
4575 Bonney Rd., Virginia Beach, VA 23462 *CEO:* Dir. Sondra L. Abbott
         (804) 671-8583

MEDICAL UNIVERSITY OF SOUTH CAROLINA
171 Ashley Ave., Charleston 29425 *Type:* Public (state) professional *System:* South Carolina Commission on Higher Education *Accred.:* 1971/1986 (SACS-CC) *Calendar:* Sem. plan *Degrees:* B, M, D *Prof. Accred.:* Blood Bank Technology, Cytotechnology, Dentistry, General Dentistry (prelim. provisional), Health Services Administration, Histologic Technology, Medical Record Administration, Medical Technology, Medicine, Nurse Anesthesia Education, Nursing (B,M), Occupational Therapy, Ophthalmic Medical Technology, Oral and Maxillofacial Surgery, Pediatric Dentistry, Perfusion, Periodontics, Pharmacy, Physical Therapy, Psychology Internship, Radiation Therapy Technology *CEO:* Pres. James B. Edwards
Enroll: 1911   (803) 792-4196

MIDLANDS TECHNICAL COLLEGE
P.O. Box 2408, Columbia 29202 *Type:* Public (state) 2-year *System:* South Carolina State Board for Technical and Comprehensive Education *Accred.:* 1974/1989 (SACS-CC) *Calendar:* Qtr. plan *Degrees:* A *Prof. Accred.:* Dental Assisting, Dental Hygiene,

South Carolina

Engineering Technology (architectural, civil/construction, electrical, mechanical), Medical Laboratory Technology (AMA), Medical Record Technology, Nuclear Medicine Technology, Nursing (A), Practical Nursing, Radiography, Respiratory Therapy, Respiratory Therapy Technology, Surgical Technology *CEO:* Pres. James L. Hudgins
Enroll: 7074 (803) 738-1400

MORRIS COLLEGE
100 W. College St., Sumter 29150 *Type:* Private (Baptist) liberal arts *Accred.:* 1978/1983 (SACS-CC) *Calendar:* Sem. plan *Degrees:* B *CEO:* Pres. Luns C. Richardson
Enroll: 804 (803) 775-9371

NEWBERRY COLLEGE
2100 College St., Newberry 29108 *Type:* Private (Lutheran) liberal arts *Accred.:* 1936/1982 (SACS-CC) *Calendar:* Sem. plan *Degrees:* B *Prof. Accred.:* Music, Teacher Education (e,p) *CEO:* Pres. Hubert H. Setzler, Jr.
Enroll: 702 (803) 276-5010

NIELSEN ELECTRONICS INSTITUTE
1600 Meeting St., Charleston 29405 *Type:* Private *Accred.:* 1974/1979 (CCA-ACTTS) *Calendar:* Qtr. plan *Degrees:* A *CEO:* Pres. Stephen J. Anatalis
Enroll: 420 (803) 722-2344

NEI TRUCK DRIVER TRAINING
P.O. Box 400, Cowpens, SC 29330 *CEO:* Dir. Linda Cook
(803) 463-9344

NORTH AMERICAN INSTITUTE OF AVIATION
Conway-Horry County Airport, P.O. Box 680, Conway 29526 *Type:* Private *Accred.:* 1981/1986 (CCA-ACTTS) *Calendar:* Courses of varying lengths *Degrees:* certificates *CEO:* Pres. Douglas Beckner
Enroll: 241 (803) 397-9111

NORTH GREENVILLE COLLEGE
P.O. Box 1892, Tigerville 29688-1892 *Type:* Private (Southern Baptist) *Accred.:* 1957/1989 (SACS-CC) *Calendar:* Sem. plan *Degrees:* A *CEO:* Pres. James B. Epting
Enroll: 387 (803) 895-1410

Accredited Institutions

ORANGEBURG-CALHOUN TECHNICAL COLLEGE
3250 St. Mathews Rd., Orangeburg 29115 *Type:* Public (state) 2-year *System:* South Carolina State Board for Technical and Comprehensive Education *Accred.:* 1970/1991 (SACS-CC) *Calendar:* Qtr. plan *Degrees:* A *Prof. Accred.:* Medical Laboratory Technology (AMA), Nursing (A), Radiography, Respiratory Therapy Technology *CEO:* Pres. M. Rudolph Groomes
Enroll: 1668 (803) 536-0311

PRO DRIVE SOUTHEAST TRAINING CENTER
5110 Frontage Rd., Greenville 29615 *Type:* Private *Accred.:* 1991 (CCA-ACTTS) *Calendar:* Courses of varying lengths *Degrees:* certificates *CEO:* Dir. Tony Bannister
(803) 676-9262

PHILLIPS JUNIOR COLLEGE OF CHARLESTON
4639 Rivers Ave., North Charleston 29405 *Type:* Private junior *Accred.:* 1982 (CCA-ACICS) *Calendar:* Qtr. plan *Degrees:* A, certificates, diplomas *CEO:* Dir. W.D. John Almond
(803) 554-5091

PHILLIPS JUNIOR COLLEGE OF GREENVILLE
617 E. McBee Ave., Greenville 29615 *Type:* Private junior *Accred.:* 1981 (CCA-ACICS) *Calendar:* Qtr. plan *Degrees:* A *CEO:* Dir. Steven Mulder
Enroll: 417 (803) 232-8502

PHILLIPS JUNIOR COLLEGE OF SPARTANBURG
325 S. Church St., Spartanburg 29301 *Type:* Private junior *Accred.:* 1953/1987 (CCA-ACICS) *Calendar:* Qtr. plan *Degrees:* A *CEO:* Dir. John K. Mussetto
Enroll: 464 (803) 585-3446

BRANCH CAMPUS
533 Fourth Ave., Huntington, WV 25701 *CEO:* Dir. Darrell Chiles
(304) 525-5100

PIEDMONT TECHNICAL COLLEGE
P.O. Box 1467, Greenwood 29648 *Type:* Public (state) 2-year *System:* South Carolina State Board for Technical and Comprehensive Education *Accred.:* 1972/1991 (SACS-

CC) *Calendar:* Qtr. plan *Degrees:* A *Prof. Accred.:* Engineering Technology (electrical, general drafting/design), Radiography, Respiratory Therapy Technology *CEO:* Pres. Lex D. Walters
Enroll: 1594 (803) 223-8357

PRESBYTERIAN COLLEGE
503 S. Broad St., Clinton 29325 *Type:* Private (Presbyterian) liberal arts *Accred.:* 1949/1986 (SACS-CC) *Calendar:* Sem. plan *Degrees:* B *CEO:* Pres. Kenneth B. Orr
Enroll: 1114 (803) 833-2820

ROYAL ACADEMY OF HAIR DESIGN
Clinton Plaza, Clinton 29325 *Type:* Private *Accred.:* 1989 (SACS-COEI) *Calendar:* Courses of varying lengths *Degrees:* diplomas *CEO:* Dir. Darrell Whitsel
Enroll: 67 (803) 833-6976

RUSH INSTITUTE
560 King St., Charleston 29403 *Type:* Private *Accred.:* 1991 (SACS-COEI) *Calendar:* Courses of varying lengths *Degrees:* certificates *CEO:* Pres. Jerry Faulkenberry
Enroll: 121 (803) 723-8361

SHERMAN COLLEGE OF STRAIGHT CHIROPRACTIC
P.O. Box 1452, Spartanburg 29304 *Type:* Private professional *Accred.:* 1984 (SACS-CC probational) *Calendar:* Tri. plan *Degrees:* D *CEO:* Pres. T.A. Gelardi
Enroll: 164 (803) 578-8770

SOUTH CAROLINA STATE COLLEGE
300 College Ave., Orangeburg 29117 *Type:* Public (state) liberal arts *System:* South Carolina Commission on Higher Education *Accred.:* 1941/1990 (SACS-CC) *Calendar:* Sem. plan *Degrees:* B, M, D *Prof. Accred.:* Engineering Technology (civil/construction, electrical, mechanical), Home Economics, Social Work (B-candidate), Teacher Education (e,s,p) *CEO:* Interim Pres. Carl A. Carpenter
Enroll: 4956 (803) 536-7000

SOUTHERN TECHNICAL COLLEGE
2110 Beltline Blvd., Columbia 29204 *Type:* Private *Accred.:* 1988 (CCA-ACTTS) *Calendar:* Courses of varying lengths *Degrees:* certificates *CEO:* Dir. Robert C. McElhiney
Enroll: 83 (803) 782-5004

SPARTANBURG METHODIST COLLEGE
1200 Textile Rd., Spartanburg 29301-0009 *Type:* Private (United Methodist) *Accred.:* 1957/1988 (SACS-CC) *Calendar:* Sem. plan *Degrees:* A *CEO:* Pres. George D. Fields, Jr.
Enroll: 826 (803) 587-4000

SPARTANBURG TECHNICAL COLLEGE
P.O. Drawer 4386, Spartanburg 29305-4386 *Type:* Public (state) 2-year *System:* South Carolina State Board for Technical and Comprehensive Education *Accred.:* 1970/1991 (SACS-CC) *Calendar:* Qtr. plan *Degrees:* A *Prof. Accred.:* Dental Assisting, Engineering Technology (civil/construction, electrical, mechanical), Medical Laboratory Technology (AMA), Radiography, Respiratory Therapy, Respiratory Therapy Technology, Surgical Technology *CEO:* Pres. Jack A. Powers
Enroll: 2332 (803) 591-3600

SUMTER AREA TECHNICAL COLLEGE
506 N. Guignard Dr., Sumter 29150 *Type:* Public (state) 2-year *System:* South Carolina State Board for Technical and Comprehensive Education *Accred.:* 1970/1991 (SACS-CC) *Calendar:* Qtr. plan *Degrees:* A *Prof. Accred.:* Engineering Technology (civil/construction) *CEO:* Pres. Herbert C. Robbins
Enroll: 1624 (803) 778-1961

SUMTER BEAUTY COLLEGE
921 Carolina Ave., Sumter 29150 *Type:* Private *Accred.:* 1988 (SACS-COEI) *Calendar:* Courses of varying lengths *Degrees:* certificates *CEO:* Dir. Faye Smith
Enroll: 27 (803) 773-7311

TECHNICAL COLLEGE OF THE LOWCOUNTRY
100 S. Ribaut Rd., Beaufort 29902 *Type:* Public (state) 2-year *System:* South Carolina State Board for Technical and Comprehensive Education *Accred.:* 1978/1984 (SACS-CC) *Calendar:* Qtr. plan *Degrees:* A *Prof.*

South Carolina

Accred.: Nursing (A) *CEO:* Pres. Anne S. McNutt
Enroll: 858 (803) 525-8246

TRI-COUNTY TECHNICAL COLLEGE
Hwy. 76, P.O. Box 58, Pendleton 29670 *Type:* Public (state) 2-year *System:* South Carolina State Board for Technical and Comprehensive Education *Accred.:* 1971/1986 (SACS-CC) *Calendar:* Qtr. plan *Degrees:* A *Prof. Accred.:* Dental Assisting (conditional), Engineering Technology (electrical), Medical Laboratory Technology (AMA), Surgical Technology, Veterinary Technology *CEO:* Pres. Don C. Garrison
Enroll: 3774 (803) 646-8361

TRIDENT TECHNICAL COLLEGE
P.O. Box 10367, Charleston 29411 *Type:* Public (state) 2-year *System:* South Carolina State Board for Technical and Comprehensive Education *Accred.:* 1974/1990 (SACS-CC) *Calendar:* Qtr. plan *Degrees:* A *Prof. Accred.:* Dental Assisting, Engineering Technology (chemical, civil/construction, electrical, mechanical), Medical Assisting (AMA), Medical Laboratory Technology (AMA), Nursing (A), Occupational Therapy Assisting, Physical Therapy Assisting, Radiography, Respiratory Therapy *CEO:* Pres. Mary H. Dellamura
Enroll: 5606 (803) 572-6111

UNITED STATES NAVY FLEET AND MINE WARFARE TRAINING CENTER
Charleston 39408 *Type:* Public (federal) *Accred.:* 1988 (SACS-COEI) *Calendar:* Courses of varying lengths *Degrees:* certificates *CEO:* Commandant G.P. Lauzon, U.S.N.
Enroll: 330 (803) 743-4722

UNIVERSITY OF SOUTH CAROLINA—AIKEN
171 University Pkwy., Aiken 29801 *Type:* Public (state) *System:* University of South Carolina Central Office *Accred.:* 1961/1991 (SACS-CC) *Calendar:* Sem. plan *Degrees:* A, B *Prof. Accred.:* Nursing (A,B) *CEO:* Chanc. Robert E. Alexander
Enroll: 2507 (803) 648-6851

UNIVERSITY OF SOUTH CAROLINA—BEAUFORT
800 Carteret St., Beaufort 29902 *Type:* Public (state) *System:* University of South Carolina Central Office *Accred.:* 1959/1991 (SACS-CC) *Calendar:* Sem. plan *Degrees:* A *CEO:* Dean Chris Plyler
Enroll: 549 (803) 524-7112

UNIVERSITY OF SOUTH CAROLINA—COASTAL CAROLINA
P.O. Box 1954, Conway 29526 *Type:* Public (state) *System:* University of South Carolina Central Office *Accred.:* 1976/1991 (SACS-CC) *Calendar:* Sem. plan *Degrees:* A, B *Prof. Accred.:* Nursing (A) *CEO:* Chanc. Ronald G. Eaglin
Enroll: 3569 (803) 347-3161

UNIVERSITY OF SOUTH CAROLINA—COLUMBIA
Columbia 29208 *Type:* Public (state) *System:* University of South Carolina Central Office *Accred.:* 1917/1991 (SACS-CC) *Calendar:* Sem. plan *Degrees:* A, B, M, D *Prof. Accred.:* Accounting (Type A,C), Audiology, Business (B,M), Clinical Psychology, Computer Science, Counseling, Engineering (chemical, civil, electrical, mechanical), Journalism, Law, Librarianship, Medicine, Music, Nursing (B,M), Pharmacy, Psychology Internship, Public Administration, Public Health, Rehabilitation Counseling, School Psychology, Social Work (M), Speech-Language Pathology, Teacher Education (e,s,p), Theatre *CEO:* Pres. John M. Palms
Enroll: 21005 (803) 777-2001

UNIVERSITY OF SOUTH CAROLINA—LANCASTER
P.O. Box 889, Lancaster 29721 *Type:* Public (state) *System:* University of South Carolina Central Office *Accred.:* 1959/1991 (SACS-CC) *Calendar:* Sem. plan *Degrees:* A *CEO:* Dean John R. Arnold
Enroll: 700 (803) 285-7471

UNIVERSITY OF SOUTH CAROLINA—SALKEHATCHIE
P.O. Box 617, Allendale 29810 *Type:* Public (state) *System:* University of South Carolina Central Office *Accred.:* 1965/1991 (SACS-

CC) *Calendar:* Sem. plan *Degrees:* A *CEO:* Dean Carl A. Clayton
Enroll: 543 (803) 584-3446

UNIVERSITY OF SOUTH CAROLINA—SPARTANBURG
800 University Way, Spartanburg 29303 *Type:* Public (state) *System:* University of South Carolina Central Office *Accred.:* 1976/1991 (SACS-CC) *Calendar:* Sem. plan *Degrees:* A, B *Prof. Accred.:* Nursing (A,B) *CEO:* Chanc. Olin B. Sansbury, Jr.
Enroll: 2915 (803) 599-2000

UNIVERSITY OF SOUTH CAROLINA—SUMTER
200 Miller Rd., Sumter 29150 *Type:* Public (state) *System:* University of South Carolina Central Office *Accred.:* 1976/1991 (SACS-CC) *Calendar:* Sem. plan *Degrees:* A *CEO:* Dean Jack C. Anderson, Jr.
Enroll: 945 (803) 775-6341

UNIVERSITY OF SOUTH CAROLINA—UNION
P.O. Drawer 729, Union 29379 *Type:* Public (state) *System:* University of South Carolina Central Office *Accred.:* 1965/1991 (SACS-CC) *Calendar:* Sem. plan *Degrees:* A *CEO:* Dean Kenneth L. Davis
Enroll: 252 (803) 429-8728

VOORHEES COLLEGE
Voorhees Rd., Denmark 29042 *Type:* Private (Episcopal) liberal arts *Accred.:* 1946/1982 (SACS-CC) *Calendar:* Sem. plan *Degrees:* A, B *CEO:* Pres. Leonard E. Dawson
Enroll: 586 (803) 793-3351

WILLIAMSBURG TECHNICAL COLLEGE
601 Lane Rd., Kingstree 29556-4197 *Type:* Public (state) 2-year *System:* South Carolina State Board for Technical and Comprehensive Education *Accred.:* 1977/1982 (SACS-CC) *Calendar:* Qtr. plan *Degrees:* A *CEO:* Pres. John T. Wynn
Enroll: 784 (803) 354-7423

WINTHROP COLLEGE
701 Oakland Ave., Rock Hill 29733 *Type:* Public (state) liberal arts *System:* South Carolina Commission on Higher Education *Accred.:* 1923/1991 (SACS-CC) *Calendar:* Sem. plan *Degrees:* B, M *Prof. Accred.:* Art, Business (B,M), Computer Science, Interior Design, Music, Social Work (B), Teacher Education (e,s,p) *CEO:* Pres. Anthony J. DiGiorgio
Enroll: 5846 (803) 323-2211

WOFFORD COLLEGE
429 N. Church St., Spartanburg 29303-3840 *Type:* Private (United Methodist) liberal arts for men *Accred.:* 1917/1986 (SACS-CC) *Calendar:* 4-1-4 plan *Degrees:* B *CEO:* Pres. Joab M. Lesesne, Jr.
Enroll: 1050 (803) 585-4821

YORK TECHNICAL COLLEGE
452 S. Anderson Rd., Rock Hill 29730 *Type:* Public (state) 2-year *System:* South Carolina State Board for Technical and Comprehensive Education *Accred.:* 1970/1985 (SACS-CC) *Calendar:* Qtr. plan *Degrees:* A *Prof. Accred.:* Dental Assisting, Engineering Technology (electrical, mechanical drafting/design), Medical Laboratory Technology (AMA), Nursing (A), Radiography *CEO:* Pres. Dennis F. Merrell
Enroll: 2820 (803) 327-8000

SOUTH DAKOTA

AUGUSTANA COLLEGE
29th St. and Summit Ave., Sioux Falls 57197 *Type:* Private (Lutheran) liberal arts *Accred.:* 1931/1982 (NCA) *Calendar:* 4-1-4 plan *Degrees:* A, B, M *Prof. Accred.:* Music, Nursing (B), Social Work (B), Teacher Education (e,s) *CEO:* Pres. Lloyd Svendsbye
Enroll: 1871 (605) 336-4111

BLACK HILLS STATE UNIVERSITY
1200 University Ave., Spearfish 57799-9500 *Type:* Public (state) liberal arts and teachers *System:* South Dakota Board of Regents *Accred.:* 1928/1983 (NCA) *Calendar:* Sem. plan *Degrees:* A, B, M, certificates, diplomas *Prof. Accred.:* Music, Teacher Education (e,s) *CEO:* Pres. Clifford M. Trump
Enroll: 2241 (605) 642-6111

DAKOTA STATE UNIVERSITY
820 N. Washington St., Madison 57042 *Type:* Public (state) liberal arts and teachers *System:* South Dakota Board of Regents *Accred.:* 1920/1991 (NCA) *Calendar:* Sem. plan *Degrees:* A, B, certificates, diplomas *Prof. Accred.:* Medical Record Administration, Medical Record Technology, Respiratory Therapy, Teacher Education (e,s) *CEO:* Pres. Jerald A. Tunheim
Enroll: 880 (605) 256-5112

DAKOTA WESLEYAN UNIVERSITY
1200 W. Univ. Ave., Mitchell 57301 *Type:* Private (United Methodist) liberal arts *Accred.:* 1913/1987 (NCA) *Calendar:* Sem. plan *Degrees:* A, B, M, certificates, diplomas *Prof. Accred.:* Nursing (A) *CEO:* Pres. James B. Beddow
Enroll: 627 (605) 995-2600

HURON UNIVERSITY
333 Ninth St., S.W., Huron 57350 *Type:* Private liberal arts *Accred.:* 1915/1990 (NCA) *Calendar:* Sem. plan *Degrees:* A, B, M, certificates, diplomas *CEO:* Pres. R. John Reynolds
Enroll: 585 (605) 352-8721

KILIAN COMMUNITY COLLEGE
1600 S. Menlo Ave., Sioux Falls 57105 *Type:* Private *Accred.:* 1986/1990 (NCA) *Calendar:* Qtr. plan *Degrees:* A, certificates, diplomas *CEO:* Pres. Ronald F. MacDonald
Enroll: 133 (605) 336-1711

LAKE AREA VOCATIONAL-TECHNICAL INSTITUTE
230 11th St., N.E., Watertown 57201 *Type:* Public (district) *Accred.:* 1980/1990 (NCA) *Calendar:* Qtr. plan *Degrees:* certificates, diplomas *Prof. Accred.:* Dental Assisting, Medical Laboratory Technology (AMA), Practical Nursing *CEO:* Dir. Gary D. Williams
Enroll: 870 (605) 886-5872

MITCHELL VOCATIONAL-TECHNICAL SCHOOL
821 N. Capital St., Mitchell 57301 *Type:* Public (district) *Accred.:* 1980/1989 (NCA) *Calendar:* Sem. plan *Degrees:* A, certificates, diplomas *Prof. Accred.:* Medical Laboratory Technology (AMA) *CEO:* Dir. Chris A. Paustien
Enroll: 553 (605) 996-3024

MOUNT MARTY COLLEGE
1105 W. Eighth St., Yankton 57078 *Type:* Private (Roman Catholic) liberal arts *Accred.:* 1961/1983 (NCA) *Calendar:* Sem. plan *Degrees:* A, B, M, certificates, diplomas *Prof. Accred.:* Nurse Anesthesia Education, Nursing (B), Respiratory Therapy, Respiratory Therapy Technology *CEO:* Pres. Jacquelyn Ernster
Enroll: 709 (605) 668-1514

NATIONAL COLLEGE
321 Kansas City St., P.O. Box 1780, Rapid City 57701 *Type:* Private *Accred.:* 1985/1991 (NCA) *Calendar:* Qtr. plan *Degrees:* A, B, certificates, diplomas *Prof. Accred.:* Medical Record Technology, Veterinary Technology *CEO:* Pres. Vincent Zocco
Enroll: 1686 (605) 394-4800

South Dakota

NETTLETON COLLEGE
P.O. Box 924, Sioux Falls 57101 *Type:* Private junior *Accred.:* 1953/1988 (CCA-ACICS) *Calendar:* Courses of varying lengths *Degrees:* A, certificates, diplomas *CEO:* Pres. Diane Hoskins
Enroll: 807 (605) 336-1837

NORTH AMERICAN BAPTIST SEMINARY
1321 W. 22nd St., Sioux Falls 57105 *Type:* Private (Baptist) professional; graduate only *Accred.:* 1968/1984 (ATS); 1979/1984 (NCA) *Calendar:* Sem. plan *Degrees:* P, M, D, certificates, diplomas *CEO:* Pres. Charles M. Hiatt
Enroll: 139 (605) 336-6588

NORTHERN STATE UNIVERSITY
12th Ave. and Jay St., Aberdeen 57401 *Type:* Public (state) liberal arts and teachers *System:* South Dakota Board of Regents *Accred.:* 1918/1987 (NCA) *Calendar:* Sem. plan *Degrees:* A, B, M, certificates, diplomas *Prof. Accred.:* Music, Teacher Education (e,s,p) *CEO:* Pres. Terence Brown
Enroll: 2334 (605) 622-2521

OGLALA LAKOTA COLLEGE
P.O. Box 490, Kyle 57752 *Type:* Public tribal *Accred.:* 1983/1988 (NCA) *Calendar:* Sem. plan *Degrees:* A, B, certificates, diplomas *CEO:* Pres. Elgin Badwound
Enroll: 612 (605) 455-2321

PRESENTATION COLLEGE
1500 N. Main St., Aberdeen 57401 *Type:* Private (Roman Catholic) *Accred.:* 1971/1987 (NCA) *Calendar:* Sem. plan *Degrees:* A, B, certificates, diplomas *Prof. Accred.:* Medical Laboratory Technology (AMA), Nursing (A) *CEO:* Pres. Bernadette Bodine
Enroll: 439 (605) 225-0420

SINTE GLESKA COLLEGE
P.O. Box 490, Rosebud 57570 *Type:* Public tribal *Accred.:* 1983/1989 (NCA) *Calendar:* Sem. plan *Degrees:* A, B, M *CEO:* Pres. Lionel R. Bordeaux
Enroll: 407 (605) 747-2263

SIOUX FALLS COLLEGE
1501 S. Prairie Ave., Sioux Falls 57105 *Type:* Private (Baptist) liberal arts *Accred.:* 1931/1982 (NCA) *Calendar:* 4-1-4 plan *Degrees:* A, B, M *Prof. Accred.:* Social Work (B), Teacher Education (e,s) *CEO:* Pres. Thomas F. Johnson
Enroll: 751 (605) 331-6710

SISSETON-WAHPETON COMMUNITY COLLEGE
P.O. Box 689, Agency Village 57262 *Type:* Public tribal *Accred.:* 1990 (NCA) *Calendar:* Qtr. plan *Degrees:* A *CEO:* Pres. Gwen Hill
Enroll: 114 (605) 698-3966

SOUTH DAKOTA SCHOOL OF MINES AND TECHNOLOGY
501 E. St. Joseph St., Rapid City 57701 *Type:* Public (state) technological *System:* South Dakota Board of Regents *Accred.:* 1925/1986 (NCA) *Calendar:* Sem. plan *Degrees:* B, M, D *Prof. Accred.:* Engineering (chemical, civil, electrical, geological/geophysical, mechanical, metallurgical, mining) *CEO:* Pres. Richard J. Gowen
Enroll: 1850 (605) 394-2256

SOUTH DAKOTA STATE UNIVERSITY
P.O. Box 2201, University Sta., Brookings 57007 *Type:* Public (state) *System:* South Dakota Board of Regents *Accred.:* 1916/1990 (NCA) *Calendar:* Sem. plan *Degrees:* A, B, M, D *Prof. Accred.:* Engineering (agricultural, civil, electrical, mechanical), Home Economics, Journalism, Music, Nursing (B,M), Pharmacy, Teacher Education (s,p) *CEO:* Pres. Robert T. Wagner
Enroll: 6832 (605) 688-4173

SOUTHEAST VOCATIONAL-TECHNICAL INSTITUTE
2301 Career Pl., 1001 E. 14th St., Sioux Falls 57107 *Type:* Public (district) *Accred.:* 1981/1987 (NCA) *Calendar:* Qtr. plan *Degrees:* A, certificates, diplomas *CEO:* Dir. Terrence Sullivan
Enroll: 554 (605) 331-7624

South Dakota

STENOTYPE INSTITUTE OF SOUTH DAKOTA
705 West Ave. N., Sioux Falls 57104 *Type:* Private business *Accred.:* 1975/1988 (CCA-ACICS) *Calendar:* Courses of varying lengths *Degrees:* certificates, diplomas *CEO:* Pres. Linda Clauson
Enroll: 199 (605) 336-1442

UNIVERSITY OF SOUTH DAKOTA
414 E. Clark St., Vermillion 57069-2390 *Type:* Public (state) *System:* South Dakota Board of Regents *Accred.:* 1913/1991 (NCA) *Calendar:* Sem. plan *Degrees:* A, B, P, M, D *Prof. Accred.:* Art, Business (B,M), Clinical Psychology, Dental Hygiene, Law, Medicine, Music, Nurse Anesthesia Education, Nursing (A), Social Work (B), Speech-Language Pathology, Teacher Education (e,s,p), Theatre *CEO:* Pres. Betty Turner Asher
Enroll: 6105 (605) 677-5641

WESTERN DAKOTA VOCATIONAL-TECHNICAL INSTITUTE
1600 Sedivy La., Rapid City 57701-4178 *Type:* Public (district) *Accred.:* 1983/1988 (NCA) *Calendar:* Qtr. plan *Degrees:* A, certificates, diplomas *CEO:* Dir. Ken Gifford
Enroll: 427 (605) 394-4034

TENNESSEE

ALLIANCE TRACTOR TRAILER CENTER
P.O. Box 950, Lebanon 37088 *Type:* Private *Accred.:* 1986 (CCA-ACTTS) *Calendar:* Courses of varying lengths *Degrees:* certificates *CEO:* Dir. Jeff Carlton
(615) 449-6363

AMERICAN BAPTIST COLLEGE
1800 Baptist World Ctr., Nashville 37207 *Type:* Private (Baptist) *Accred.:* 1971/1982 (AABC) *Calendar:* Sem. plan *Degrees:* B, certificates *CEO:* Pres. Odell McGlothian, Sr.
Enroll: 193   (615) 228-7877

AMERICAN CAREER INSTITUTE
8415 Kingston Pike, Knoxville 37919-5352 *Type:* Private *Accred.:* 1987 (SACS-COEI) *Calendar:* Courses of varying lengths *Degrees:* certificates *CEO:* Dir. Sherry Sherrod
Enroll: 88   (615) 691-3900

AMERICAN TECHNICAL INSTITUTE
8760 Baylor Rd., Brunswick 38014 *Type:* Private *Accred.:* 1989 (SACS-CC) *Calendar:* Sem. plan *Degrees:* B *Prof. Accred.:* Engineering Technology (nuclear) *CEO:* Pres. D. Wayne Jones
Enroll: 29   (901) 382-4847

AQUINAS JUNIOR COLLEGE
4210 Harding Rd., Nashville 37205 *Type:* Private (Roman Catholic) *Accred.:* 1971/1986 (SACS-CC) *Calendar:* Sem. plan *Degrees:* A *Prof. Accred.:* Nursing (A) *CEO:* Pres. M. Inez Cabaniss, O.P.
Enroll: 334   (615) 297-7545

ARNOLD'S BEAUTY SCHOOL
1179 S. Second St., Milan 38358 *Type:* Private *Accred.:* 1983/1988 (SACS-COEI) *Calendar:* Courses of varying lengths *Degrees:* certificates *CEO:* Dir. Norma Arnold
Enroll: 31   (901) 686-7351

ARTISTE SCHOOL OF COSMETOLOGY
129 Springbrook Dr., Johnson City 37601 *Type:* Private *Accred.:* 1988 (CCA-ACTTS) *Calendar:* Courses of varying lengths *Degrees:* certificates *CEO:* Owner Phyllis Blair
(615) 282-6542

ATLANTIC CAREER INSTITUTE
1514 Church St., Nashville 37203 *Type:* Private *Accred.:* 1989 (SACS-COEI) *Calendar:* Courses of varying lengths *Degrees:* certificates *CEO:* Dir. Steven Dalton
Enroll: 313   (615) 320-0208

AUSTIN PEAY STATE UNIVERSITY
601 College St., Clarksville 37044 *Type:* Public (state) *System:* Tennessee Board of Regents *Accred.:* 1947/1984 (SACS-CC) *Calendar:* Sem. plan *Degrees:* A, B, M *Prof. Accred.:* Art, Medical Technology, Music, Nursing (B), Social Work (B), Teacher Education (e,s,p) *CEO:* Pres. Oscar C. Page
Enroll: 4922   (615) 648-7011

BELMONT COLLEGE
1900 Belmont Blvd., Nashville 37212-3757 *Type:* Private (Baptist) liberal arts *Accred.:* 1959/1990 (SACS-CC) *Calendar:* Sem. plan *Degrees:* A, B, M *Prof. Accred.:* Music *CEO:* Pres. William E. Troutt
Enroll: 2796   (615) 383-7001

BETHEL COLLEGE
Cherry St., McKenzie 38201 *Type:* Private (Presbyterian) liberal arts *Accred.:* 1952/1988 (SACS-CC) *Calendar:* Qtr. plan *Degrees:* B, M *CEO:* Pres. Bill Elkins
Enroll: 495   (901) 352-1000

BRANELL COLLEGE
2424 Hillsboro Pike, Nashville 37212 *Type:* Private business *Accred.:* 1986 (CCA-ACICS); 1988 (SACS-COEI) *Calendar:* Courses of varying lengths *Degrees:* certificates, diplomas *CEO:* Dir. Audrey Steed-Cline
Enroll: 452   (615) 297-1100

Tennessee

BRANCH CAMPUS
1700 Halstead Blvd., Bldg. 2, Ste. 2, Tallahassee, FL 32308 *CEO:* Dir. Shirley Pace
(904) 668-0200

BRANCH CAMPUS
500 N. Westshore Blvd., Ste. 820, Tampa, FL 33609 *CEO:* Dir. Renee M. Carey
(813) 287-0400

BRANCH CAMPUS
Hwy. 66, E., Grants, NM 87020 *CEO:* Dir. Brent Braum
(505) 287-2941

BRANCH CAMPUS
Rivergate Park Office Bldg., 1994 Gallatin Rd. N., Madison, TN 37115 *CEO:* Dir. Carl Zehner
(615) 851-1881

BRISTOL UNIVERSITY
2409 Volunteer Pkwy., P.O. Box 4366, Bristol 37625 *Type:* Private *Accred.:* 1970/1989 (CCA-ACICS) *Calendar:* Qtr. plan *Degrees:* A, B, M *CEO:* Pres. Craven H. Sumerell
Enroll: 266   (615) 968-1442

CAREERCOM COLLEGE OF BUSINESS
2200 Sutherland Ave., Ste. B-201, Knoxville 37919 *Type:* Private *Accred.:* 1990 (SACS-COEI) *Calendar:* Courses of varying lengths *Degrees:* certificates, diplomas *CEO:* Dir. Angela Green
Enroll: 91   (615) 524-0371

CARSON-NEWMAN COLLEGE
Russell Ave., P.O. Box 552, Jefferson City 37760 *Type:* Private (Southern Baptist) liberal arts *Accred.:* 1927/1983 (SACS-CC) *Calendar:* Sem. plan *Degrees:* B, M *Prof. Accred.:* Home Economics, Music, Nursing (B), Teacher Education (e,s) *CEO:* Pres. J. Cordell Maddox
Enroll: 2025   (615) 475-9061

CHATTANOOGA BARBER COLLEGE
409 Market St., Chattanooga 37402 *Type:* Private *Accred.:* 1987 (CCA-ACTTS) *Calendar:* Courses of varying lengths *Degrees:* diplomas *CEO:* Owner Judy Griggs
(615) 266-7013

CHATTANOOGA STATE TECHNICAL COMMUNITY COLLEGE
4501 Amnicola Hwy., Chattanooga 37406 *Type:* Public (state) 2-year *System:* Tennessee Board of Regents *Accred.:* 1967/1991 (SACS-CC) *Calendar:* Qtr. plan *Degrees:* A *Prof. Accred.:* Dental Assisting, Dental Hygiene, Engineering Technology (electrical, mechanical), Medical Record Technology, Nursing (A), Physical Therapy Assisting, Radiography, Respiratory Therapy *CEO:* Pres. James L. Catanzaro
Enroll: 5914   (615) 697-4400

CHRISTIAN BROTHERS UNIVERSITY
650 East Pkwy. S., Memphis 38104 *Type:* Private (Roman Catholic) liberal arts *Accred.:* 1958/1990 (SACS-CC) *Calendar:* Sem. plan *Degrees:* A, B, M *Prof. Accred.:* Engineering (chemical, civil, electrical, mechanical), Respiratory Therapy *CEO:* Pres. Theodore Drahmann
Enroll: 1526   (901) 722-0200

CLEVELAND STATE COMMUNITY COLLEGE
Adkisson Dr., P.O. Box 3570, Cleveland 37320-3570 *Type:* Public (state) junior *System:* Tennessee Board of Regents *Accred.:* 1969/1984 (SACS-CC) *Calendar:* Qtr. plan *Degrees:* A *Prof. Accred.:* Dental Laboratory Technology, Medical Laboratory Technology (AMA), Nursing (A) *CEO:* Pres. James W. Ford
Enroll: 2282   (615) 472-7141

COLUMBIA STATE COMMUNITY COLLEGE
P.O. Box 1315, Columbia 38402-1315 *Type:* Public (state) junior *System:* Tennessee Board of Regents *Accred.:* 1968/1983 (SACS-CC) *Calendar:* Qtr. plan *Degrees:* A *Prof. Accred.:* Medical Laboratory Technology (AMA), Nursing (A), Radiography, Respiratory Therapy, Veterinary Technology *CEO:* Pres. L. Paul Sands
Enroll: 3448   (615) 388-0120

CONCORDE CAREER INSTITUTE
5100 Poplar Ave., Ste. 132, Memphis 38137
Type: Private *Accred.:* 1980/1990 (SACS-COEI) *Calendar:* Courses of varying lengths *Degrees:* certificates *CEO:* Dir. Pamela Hammond
Enroll: 215 (901) 761-9494

COURT REPORTING INSTITUTE OF TENNESSEE
50 Century Blvd., Ste. 210, Nashville 37214
Type: Private *Accred.:* 1989 (CCA-ACTTS) *Calendar:* Courses of varying lengths *Degrees:* certificates, diplomas *CEO:* Dir. Donna Flowers
Enroll: 45 (615) 885-9770

CRICHTON COLLEGE
P.O. Box 757830, Memphis 38175-7830
Type: Private *Accred.:* 1986 (SACS-CC) *Calendar:* Sem. plan *Degrees:* B *CEO:* Chanc. James M. Latimer
Enroll: 303 (901) 367-9800

CUMBERLAND SCHOOL OF TECHNOLOGY
1065 E. Tenth St., Cookeville 38501 *Type:* Private 2-year *Accred.:* 1988 (SACS-COEI) *Calendar:* Courses of varying lengths *Degrees:* A, diplomas *Prof. Accred.:* Medical Laboratory Technology (AMA) *CEO:* Pres. Laverne Floyd
Enroll: 98 (615) 526-3660

BRANCH CAMPUS
4173 Government St., Baton Rouge, LA 70806 *CEO:* Dir. Laverne Floyd
(504) 338-9085

CUMBERLAND UNIVERSITY
S. Greenwood St., Lebanon 37087-3554
Type: Private *Accred.:* 1962/1990 (SACS-CC) *Calendar:* Sem. plan *Degrees:* A, B, M *CEO:* Pres. J. Thomas Mills, Jr.
Enroll: 574 (615) 444-2562

DAVID LIPSCOMB UNIVERSITY
3901 Granny White Pike, Nashville 37204-3951 *Type:* Private (Churches of Christ) liberal arts *Accred.:* 1954/1986 (SACS-CC) *Calendar:* Qtr. plan *Degrees:* B, M *Prof. Accred.:* Social Work (B-candidate), Teacher Education (e,s) *CEO:* Pres. Harold Hazelip
Enroll: 2353 (615) 269-1000

DAVIDSON TECHNICAL COLLEGE
212 Pavilion Blvd., Nashville 37217-1002
Type: Private *Accred.:* 1988 (SACS-COEI) *Calendar:* Courses of varying lengths *Degrees:* certificates *CEO:* Dir. Suzanne Davidson
Enroll: 189 (615) 360-3300

BRANCH CAMPUS
525 E. Main St., Jackson, TN 38301 *CEO:* Dir. Wanda Griffiths
(901) 424-6795

DRAUGHONS JUNIOR COLLEGE
1241 Volunteer Pkwy., Ste. 600, Bristol 37620 *Type:* Private *Accred.:* 1990 (CCA-ACICS) *Calendar:* Qtr. plan *Degrees:* A, certificates, diplomas *CEO:* Exec. Dir. Alex M. Biles
(615) 968-5000

DRAUGHONS JUNIOR COLLEGE
2220 College Dr., Johnson City 37602 *Type:* Private *Accred.:* 1985 (CCA-ACICS) *Calendar:* Qtr. plan *Degrees:* A, certificates, diplomas *CEO:* Dir. William McGuire
Enroll: 2108 (615) 282-3320

DRAUGHONS JUNIOR COLLEGE
315 Erin Dr., Knoxville 37919 *Type:* Private *Accred.:* 1984/1990 (CCA-ACICS) *Calendar:* Qtr. plan *Degrees:* A, certificates, diplomas *CEO:* Pres. DeWitt R. Shelton
Enroll: 1170 (615) 584-8621

BRANCH CAMPUS
202 W. Fourth St., Chattanooga, TN 37402 *CEO:* Dir. Pat Stevens
(615) 756-1431

DRAUGHONS JUNIOR COLLEGE
3200 Elvis Presley Blvd., Memphis 38116
Type: Private *Accred.:* 1984/1990 (CCA-ACICS) *Calendar:* Qtr. plan *Degrees:* A *CEO:* Exec. Dir. Ann Gibson
Enroll: 1127 (901) 332-7800

DRAUGHONS JUNIOR COLLEGE
Plus Park at Pavilion Blvd., Nashville 37217 *Type:* Private *Accred.:* 1954/1990 (CCA-ACICS) *Calendar:* Qtr. plan *Degrees:* A *CEO:* Chrmn. Charles W. Davidson
Enroll: 1238 (615) 361-7555

BRANCH CAMPUS
2424 Airway Dr. at Lover's La., Bowling Green, KY 42101 *CEO:* Dir. Peggy White
(502) 843-6750

BRANCH CAMPUS
1860 Guthrie Hwy., Clarksville, TN 37040 *CEO:* Dir. Jennie Stribling
(615) 552-7600

DYERSBURG STATE COMMUNITY COLLEGE
Lake Rd., Dyersburg 38024 *Type:* Public (state) junior *System:* Tennessee Board of Regents *Accred.:* 1971/1986 (SACS-CC) *Calendar:* Sem. plan *Degrees:* A *Prof. Accred.:* Nursing (A) *CEO:* Pres. Karen A. Bowyer
Enroll: 1313 (901) 286-3200

EAST TENNESSEE STATE UNIVERSITY
P.O. Box 19330, Johnson City 37614 *Type:* Public (state) *System:* Tennessee Board of Regents *Accred.:* 1927/1983 (SACS-CC) *Calendar:* Sem. plan *Degrees:* A, B, M, D *Prof. Accred.:* Accounting (Type A,C), Art, Business (B,M), Dental Assisting, Dental Hygiene, Dental Laboratory Technology, Engineering Technology (civil/construction, electrical, general drafting/design, manufacturing, surveying), Journalism, Medical Assisting (AMA), Medical Laboratory Technology (AMA), Medicine, Music, Nursing (A,B), Radiography, Respiratory Therapy Technology, Social Work (B), Surgical Technology, Teacher Education (e,s,p) *CEO:* Interim Pres. Bert C. Bach
Enroll: 11029 (615) 929-4112

EDMONDSON JUNIOR COLLEGE OF BUSINESS
3635 Brainerd Rd., Chattanooga 37411 *Type:* Private *Accred.:* 1954/1990 (CCA-ACICS) *Calendar:* Qtr. plan *Degrees:* A *Prof. Accred.:* Medical Assisting (AMA) *CEO:* Dir. Stan Banks
Enroll: 1494 (615) 698-3885

BRANCH CAMPUS
Exec. South Bldg., Ste. 200, 1161 Murfreesboro Rd., Nashville, TN 37217 *CEO:* Dir. Carol Trusty
(615) 366-1144

ELECTRONIC COMPUTER PROGRAMMING INSTITUTE
3805 Brainerd Rd., Chattanooga 37411 *Type:* Private *Accred.:* 1982/1987 (CCA-ACTTS) *Calendar:* Courses of varying lengths *Degrees:* certificates *CEO:* Dir. Jo A. Pearson
Enroll: 149 (615) 624-0077

EMMANUEL SCHOOL OF RELIGION
One Walker Dr., Johnson City 37601 *Type:* Private (Church of Christ) professional; graduate only *Accred.:* 1981/1986 (ATS); 1986 (SACS-CC) *Calendar:* Sem. plan *Degrees:* P, M *CEO:* Pres. Calvin L. Phillips
Enroll: 126 (615) 926-1186

FISK UNIVERSITY
1000 17th Ave. N., Nashville 37208-3051 *Type:* Private liberal arts *Accred.:* 1930/1989 (SACS-CC) *Calendar:* Sem. plan *Degrees:* B, M *Prof. Accred.:* Music *CEO:* Pres. Henry Ponder
Enroll: 1008 (615) 329-8676

FREE WILL BAPTIST BIBLE COLLEGE
P.O. Box 50117, Nashville 37205 *Type:* Private (Baptist) professional *Accred.:* 1958/1988 (AABC) *Calendar:* Sem. plan *Degrees:* A, B *CEO:* Pres. Tom Malone
Enroll: 230 (615) 383-1340

FREED-HARDEMAN UNIVERSITY
158 E. Main St., Henderson 38340-2399 *Type:* Private (Church of Christ) liberal arts *Accred.:* 1956/1991 (SACS-CC) *Calendar:* Sem. plan *Degrees:* B, M *Prof. Accred.:* Social Work (B), Teacher Education (e,s) *CEO:* Pres. Milton R. Sewell
Enroll: 1149 (901) 989-6000

Harding University Graduate School of Religion
1000 Cherry Rd., Memphis 38117 *Type:* Private professional *Accred.:* 1972/1987 (SACS-CC) *Calendar:* Sem. plan *Degrees:* P, M, D *CEO:* Dean C. Philip Slate
Enroll: 104 (901) 761-1350

Health Care Training Institute
1378 Union Ave., Memphis 38104 *Type:* Private *Accred.:* 1988 (SACS-COEI) *Calendar:* Courses of varying length. *Degrees:* diplomas *CEO:* Pres. Cheryl Horrell
Enroll: 229 (901) 722-2288

Hiwassee College
Hiwassee Rd., Madisonville 37354 *Type:* Private (United Methodist) junior *Accred.:* 1958/1990 (SACS-CC) *Calendar:* Qtr. plan *Degrees:* A *CEO:* Pres. Stephen E. Fritz
Enroll: 526 (615) 442-2001

ITT Technical Institute
441 Donelson Pike, P.O. Box 148029, Nashville 37214 *Type:* Private *Accred.:* 1985 (CCA-ACTTS) *Calendar:* Courses of varying lengths *Degrees:* diplomas *CEO:* Dir. Nathan Blaede
Enroll: 205 (615) 889-8700

Branch Campus
1637 Downtown West Blvd., Ste. 22, Knoxville, TN 37919 *CEO:* Dir. David Sollie
(615) 691-8111

International Barber and Style College
619 S. Gallatin Rd., Madison 37115 *Type:* Private *Accred.:* 1985 (CCA-ACTTS) *Calendar:* Courses of varying lengths *Degrees:* certificates, diplomas *CEO:* Dir. Edward L. Dunn
Enroll: 98 (615) 865-7233

Branch Campus
3709 Brainerd Rd., Chattanooga, TN 37411 *CEO:* Dir. Marilyn Beaman
(615) 624-6451

Jackson State Community College
2046 North Pkwy., Jackson 38301-3797 *Type:* Public (state) junior *System:* Tennessee Board of Regents *Accred.:* 1969/1984 (SACS-CC) *Calendar:* Sem. plan *Degrees:* A *Prof. Accred.:* EMT-Paramedic, Medical Laboratory Technology (AMA), Radiography, Respiratory Therapy *CEO:* Pres. Walter L. Nelms
Enroll: 2594 (901) 424-3520

Jacobs Creek Civilian Conservation Center
Cherokee National Forest, Drawer W, Bristol 37620 *Type:* Private *Accred.:* 1989 (SACS-COEI) *Calendar:* Courses of varying lengths *Degrees:* diplomas *CEO:* Dir. Willie Tarver
Enroll: 307 (615) 878-4021

Jett College of Cosmetology
3744 N. Watkins St., Memphis 38217 *Type:* Private *Accred.:* 1983/1989 (SACS-COEI) *Calendar:* Courses of varying lengths *Degrees:* certificates *CEO:* Dir. Charles Holland
Enroll: 149 (901) 358-5121

Jett College of Cosmetology
3740 N. Watkins St., Memphis 38127 *Type:* Private *Accred.:* 1989 (SACS-COEI) *Calendar:* Courses of varying lengths *Degrees:* certificates *CEO:* Dir. Mary Lou Holland
Enroll: 140 (901) 357-0388

Jett College of Cosmetology
524 S. Cooper St., Memphis 38104 *Type:* Private *Accred.:* 1989 (SACS-COEI) *Calendar:* Courses of varying lengths *Degrees:* certificates *CEO:* Dir. Notra Atchley
Enroll: 99 (901) 276-1721

Jett College of Cosmetology
1286 Southbrook Mall, Memphis 38116 *Type:* Private *Accred.:* 1989 (SACS-COEI) *Calendar:* Courses of varying lengths *Degrees:* certificates *CEO:* Dir. Delores Dunlap
Enroll: 127 (901) 332-7330

Jett College of Cosmetology
5016 Navy Rd., Millington 38053 *Type:* Private *Accred.:* 1989 (SACS-COEI) *Calendar:* Courses of varying lengths *Degrees:* certificates *CEO:* Dir. Barbara Lape
Enroll: 171 (901) 872-2208

Tennessee

JOHN A. GUPTON COLLEGE
2507 W. End Ave., Nashville 37203 *Type:* Private 2-year *Accred.:* 1971/1986 (SACS-CC) *Calendar:* Sem. plan *Degrees:* A *Prof. Accred.:* Mortuary Science *CEO:* Pres. John A. Gupton, III
Enroll: 44 (615) 327-3927

JOHNSON BIBLE COLLEGE
7900 Johnson Dr., Knoxville 37998 *Type:* Private (Church of Christ) *Accred.:* 1970/1990 (AABC); 1979/1985 (SACS-CC) *Calendar:* Sem. plan *Degrees:* A, B, M *CEO:* Pres. David L. Eubanks
Enroll: 552 (615) 573-4517

KING COLLEGE
1350 King College Rd., Bristol 37620 *Type:* Private (Presbyterian) liberal arts *Accred.:* 1947/1988 (SACS-CC) *Calendar:* 4-1-4 plan *Degrees:* B *CEO:* Acting Pres. Charles E. Cauthen
Enroll: 507 (615) 968-1187

KNOXVILLE BUSINESS COLLEGE
720 N. Fifth Ave., Knoxville 37917 *Type:* Private junior *Accred.:* 1955/1989 (CCA-ACICS) *Calendar:* Qtr. plan *Degrees:* A *CEO:* Pres. Stephen A. South
Enroll: 665 (615) 524-3043

KNOXVILLE COLLEGE
901 College St., Knoxville 37921 *Type:* Private (Presbyterian) liberal arts *Accred.:* 1948/1979 (SACS-CC) *Calendar:* Sem. plan *Degrees:* A, B *Prof. Accred.:* Medical Assisting (AMA) *CEO:* Pres. John B. Turner
Enroll: 1155 (615) 524-6500

KNOXVILLE INSTITUTE OF HAIR DESIGN
1221 N. Central Ave., Knoxville 37917 *Type:* Private *Accred.:* 1979/1989 (CCA-ACTTS) *Calendar:* Courses of varying lengths *Degrees:* certificates *CEO:* Dir. Jack Rogers
Enroll: 135 (615) 523-5541

KNOXVILLE JOB CORPS CENTER
621 Dale Ave., Knoxville 37921 *Type:* Private *Accred.:* 1990 (SACS-COEI) *Calendar:* Courses of varying lengths *Degrees:* certificates *CEO:* Dir. Rodney Chambers
Enroll: 273 (615) 544-5600

LAMBUTH COLLEGE
705 Lambuth Blvd., Jackson 38301 *Type:* Private (United Methodist) liberal arts *Accred.:* 1954/1989 (SACS-CC) *Calendar:* Sem. plan *Degrees:* B *CEO:* Pres. Thomas F. Boyd
Enroll: 696 (901) 425-2500

LANE COLLEGE
545 Lane Ave., Jackson 38301-4598 *Type:* Private (Christian Methodist Episcopal) liberal arts *Accred.:* 1949/1982 (SACS-CC) *Calendar:* Sem. plan *Degrees:* B *CEO:* Pres. Alex A. Chambers
Enroll: 697 (901) 426-7500

LEMOYNE-OWEN COLLEGE
807 Walker Ave., Memphis 38126 *Type:* Private (United Church of Christ/Baptist) liberal arts *Accred.:* 1960/1983 (SACS-CC) *Calendar:* Sem. plan *Degrees:* B *CEO:* Interim Pres. Doris W. Weathers
Enroll: 1013 (901) 774-9090

LEE COLLEGE
P.O. Box 3450, Cleveland 37320-3450 *Type:* Private (Churches of God) liberal arts *Accred.:* 1960/1984 (SACS-CC) *Calendar:* Sem. plan *Degrees:* B *CEO:* Pres. C. Paul Conn
Enroll: 1687 (615) 472-2111

LINCOLN MEMORIAL UNIVERSITY
Cumberland Gap Pkwy., Harrogate 37752-0901 *Type:* Private liberal arts *Accred.:* 1936/1991 (SACS-CC) *Calendar:* Qtr. plan *Degrees:* A, B, M *Prof. Accred.:* Medical Technology, Nursing (A), Veterinary Technology (probational) *CEO:* Pres. Scott D. Miller
Enroll: 1463 (615) 869-3611

MARTIN METHODIST COLLEGE
433 W. Madison St., Pulaski 38478 *Type:* Private (United Methodist) junior *Accred.:*

1952/1989 (SACS-CC) *Calendar:* Sem. plan *Degrees:* A *CEO:* Pres. George P. Miller
Enroll: 334 (615) 363-7456

MARYVILLE COLLEGE
800 S. Court St., Maryville 37801 *Type:* Private (United Presbyterian) liberal arts *Accred.:* 1922/1983 (SACS-CC) *Calendar:* Sem. plan *Degrees:* B *Prof. Accred.:* Music *CEO:* Pres. Richard I. Ferrin
Enroll: 677 (615) 981-8000

MCKENZIE COLLEGE
1000 Riverfront Pkwy., Chattanooga 37402 *Type:* Private junior *Accred.:* 1983/1990 (CCA-ACICS) *Calendar:* Qtr. plan *Degrees:* A, certificates, diplomas *CEO:* Pres. Jay Menuskin, Ph.D.
Enroll: 493 (615) 265-5343

MEDICAL CAREER COLLEGE
537 Main St., Nashville 37206 *Type:* Private *Accred.:* 1978/1988 (CCA-ACTTS); 1990 (SACS-COEI candidate) *Calendar:* Qtr. plan *Degrees:* diplomas *CEO:* Pres. Nollie Long
Enroll: 47 (615) 255-7531

MEHARRY MEDICAL COLLEGE
1005 D.B. Todd Blvd., Nashville 37208 *Type:* Private professional *Accred.:* 1972/1988 (SACS-CC) *Calendar:* Sem. plan *Degrees:* P, M, D *Prof. Accred.:* Dental Assisting (prelim. provisional), Dental Hygiene, Dentistry, General Dentistry (prelim. provisional), General Practice Residency, Health Services Administration, Medicine *CEO:* Pres. David Satcher
Enroll: 562 (615) 327-6000

MEMPHIS COLLEGE OF ART
Overton Park, Memphis 38112 *Type:* Private professional *Accred.:* 1963/1984 (SACS-CC) *Calendar:* Sem. plan *Degrees:* B, M *Prof. Accred.:* Art *CEO:* Pres. Jeffrey Nesin
Enroll: 256 (901) 726-4085

MEMPHIS STATE UNIVERSITY
Memphis 38152 *Type:* Public (state) *System:* Tennessee Board of Regents *Accred.:* 1927/1984 (SACS-CC) *Calendar:* Sem. plan *Degrees:* B, P, M, D *Prof. Accred.:* Accounting (Type A,B,C), Art, Audiology, Business (B,M), Clinical Psychology, Counseling Psychology (provisional), Engineering (civil, electrical, mechanical), Engineering Technology (architectural, computer, electrical, manufacturing), Home Economics, Journalism, Law (ABA only), Music, Nursing (B), Planning (city/regional), Psychology Internship (provisional), Public Administration, Rehabilitation Counseling, Social Work (B), Speech-Language Pathology, Teacher Education (e,s,p), Theatre *CEO:* Pres. V. Lane Rawlins
Enroll: 24487 (901) 678-2000

MEMPHIS THEOLOGICAL SEMINARY
168 East Pkwy. S., Memphis 38104 *Type:* Private (Presbyterian) professional; graduate only *Accred.:* 1973/1988 (ATS); 1988 (SACS-CC) *Calendar:* Sem. plan *Degrees:* P, M, D *CEO:* Pres. J. David Hester
Enroll: 111 (901) 458-8232

MID-AMERICA BAPTIST THEOLOGICAL SEMINARY
1255 Poplar Ave., Memphis 38104 *Type:* Private (Baptist) professional *Accred.:* 1981/1986 (SACS-CC) *Calendar:* Sem. plan *Degrees:* A,P,M,D *CEO:* Pres. B. Gray Allison
Enroll: 451 (901) 726-9171

MID-STATE BARBER STYLING COLLEGE
510 Jefferson St., Nashville 37208-2626 *Type:* Private *Accred.:* 1991 (CCA-ACTTS) *Calendar:* Courses of varying lengths *Degrees:* certificates *CEO:* Dir. James Oldham
(615) 242-9300

MIDSOUTH SCHOOL OF BEAUTY
3974 Elvis Presley Blvd., Memphis 38116 *Type:* Private *Accred.:* 1990 (SACS-COEI) *Calendar:* Courses of varying lengths *Degrees:* diplomas *CEO:* Dir. John Whisnant
Enroll: 96 (901) 332-6700

MIDDLE TENNESSEE SCHOOL OF ANESTHESIA
P.O. Box 6414, Madison 37116 *Type:* Private *Calendar:* Courses of varying lengths *Degrees:* certificates *Prof. Accred.:* Nurse

Tennessee

Anesthesia Education *CEO:* Dir. Mary Elizabeth DeVasher
(615) 865-2373

MIDDLE TENNESSEE STATE UNIVERSITY
Murfreesboro 37132 *Type:* Public (state) *System:* Tennessee Board of Regents *Accred.:* 1928/1985 (SACS-CC) *Calendar:* Sem. plan *Degrees:* A, B, P, M, D *Prof. Accred.:* Business (B,M), Home Economics, Journalism, Music, Nursing (B), Social Work (B), Teacher Education (e,s,p) *CEO:* Pres. James Walker
Enroll: 13037 (615) 898-2300

MILLER-HAWKINS BUSINESS COLLEGE
1399 Madison Ave., Memphis 38104 *Type:* Private business *Accred.:* 1965/1988 (CCA-ACICS) *Calendar:* Qtr. plan *Degrees:* certificates, diplomas *CEO:* Dir. Faith B. Barcroft
Enroll: 232 (901) 725-6614

MILLER-MOTTE BUSINESS COLLEGE
1820 Business Park Dr., Clarksville 37040 *Type:* Private *Accred.:* 1987 (CCA-ACICS); 1990 (SACS-COEI) *Calendar:* Courses of varying lengths *Degrees:* certificates, diplomas *CEO:* Dir. Raymond M. Green
Enroll: 288 (615) 553-0071

MILLIGAN COLLEGE
Milligan College 37682 *Type:* Private liberal arts *Accred.:* 1960/1982 (SACS-CC) *Calendar:* Sem. plan *Degrees:* A, B, M *Prof. Accred.:* Teacher Education (e,s) *CEO:* Pres. Marshall J. Leggett
Enroll: 776 (615) 461-8700

MR. WAYNE'S SCHOOL OF UNISEX HAIR DESIGN
170 S. Willow Ave., Cookeville 38501 *Type:* Private *Accred.:* 1985 (CCA-ACTTS) *Calendar:* Courses of varying lengths *Degrees:* diplomas *CEO:* Dir. Charles W. Fletcher
Enroll: 44 (615) 526-1478

MOTLOW STATE COMMUNITY COLLEGE
P.O. Box 88100, Tullahoma 37388-8100 *Type:* Public (state) junior *System:* Tennessee Board of Regents *Accred.:* 1971/1986 (SACS-CC) *Calendar:* Qtr. plan *Degrees:* A *Prof. Accred.:* Nursing (A) *CEO:* Pres. A. Frank Glass
Enroll: 2039 (615) 455-8511

MURFREESBORO BARBER AND STYLE COLLEGE
115 S. Maple St., Murfreesboro 37130-3569 *Type:* Private *Accred.:* 1991 (CCA-ACTTS) *Calendar:* Courses of varying lengths *Degrees:* certificates *CEO:* Dir. John Sloan
(615) 890-3515

NASHVILLE AUTO DIESEL COLLEGE
1524 Gallatin Rd., Nashville 37206 *Type:* Private *Accred.:* 1967/1985 (CCA-ACTTS) *Calendar:* Courses of varying lengths *Degrees:* diplomas *CEO:* Pres. Thomas W. Balls
Enroll: 1243 (615) 226-3990

NASHVILLE COLLEGE
402 Plaza Professional Bldg., Madison 37115 *Type:* Private *Accred.:* 1990 (CCA-ACTTS) *Calendar:* Courses of varying lengths *Degrees:* certificates *Prof. Accred.:* Medical Assisting *CEO:* Pres. A. Malek
Enroll: 170 (615) 868-2963

NASHVILLE STATE TECHNICAL INSTITUTE
120 White Bridge Rd., Nashville 37209 *Type:* Public (state) 2-year *System:* Tennessee Board of Regents *Accred.:* 1972/1987 (SACS-CC) *Calendar:* Qtr. plan *Degrees:* A *Prof. Accred.:* Engineering Technology (architectural, civil/construction, electrical, industrial, mechanical), Occupational Therapy Assisting *CEO:* Pres. Richard M. Turner, III
Enroll: 3047 (615) 353-3333

NORTHEAST STATE TECHNICAL COMMUNITY COLLEGE
2425 Hwy. 75, P.O. Box 246, Blountville 37617-0246 *Type:* Public (state) 2-year *System:* Tennessee Board of Regents *Accred.:* 1984/1991 (SACS-CC) *Calendar:* Qtr. plan *Degrees:* A *Prof. Accred.:* Engineering Technology (electrical, instrumentation) *CEO:* Pres. R. Wade Powers
Enroll: 2133 (615) 323-3191

Accredited Institutions **Tennessee**

NOSSI SCHOOL OF ART
620 Gallatin Rd. S., Madison 37115 *Type:* Private *Accred.:* 1988 (CCA-ACTTS) *Calendar:* Courses of varying lengths *Degrees:* diplomas *CEO:* Exec. Dir. Nossi Vatandoost
Enroll: 63 (615) 865-8095

O'MORE COLLEGE OF DESIGN
423 S. Margin St., P.O. Box 908, Franklin 37064 *Type:* Private professional *Calendar:* Sem. plan *Degrees:* B *Prof. Accred.:* Interior Design *CEO:* Pres. Eloise Pitts O'More
Enroll: 150 (615) 794-4254

PELLISSIPPI STATE TECHNICAL COMMUNITY COLLEGE
10915 Hardin Valley Rd., P.O. Box 22990, Knoxville 37933-0990 *Type:* Public (state) 2-year *System:* Tennessee Board of Regents *Accred.:* 1977/1982 (SACS-CC) *Calendar:* Sem. plan *Degrees:* A *Prof. Accred.:* Engineering Technology (chemical, civil/construction, electrical, mechanical, mechanical drafting/design) *CEO:* Pres. J.L. Goins
Enroll: 5103 (615) 694-6400

PHILLIPS JUNIOR COLLEGE OF MEMPHIS
1640 Sycamore View Rd., Memphis 38134 *Type:* Private *Accred.:* 1982/1988 (CCA-ACICS) *Calendar:* Qtr. plan *Degrees:* A, certificates, diplomas *CEO:* Dir. Jerriann Hix
Enroll: 682 (901) 377-1200

PRINCETON TECHNICAL INSTITUTE
1501 E. Fifth Ave., Knoxville 37917 *Type:* Private *Accred.:* 1979/1989 (CCA-ACTTS) *Calendar:* Courses of varying lengths *Degrees:* diplomas *CEO:* Pres. Jerry Rogers
(615) 546-5717

QUEEN CITY COLLEGE
1191 Fort Campbell Blvd., Clarksville 37042 *Type:* Private *Accred.:* 1987 (SACS-COEI) *Calendar:* Courses of varying lengths *Degrees:* certificates *CEO:* Dir. Laura S. Payne
Enroll: 48 (615) 645-2361

BRANCH CAMPUS
800 Hwy. One, S., Greenville, MS 38701 *CEO:* Dir. Ralph Payne
(601) 334-9120

RHODES COLLEGE
2000 North Pkwy., Memphis 38112 *Type:* Private (Presbyterian) liberal arts *Accred.:* 1911/1990 (SACS-CC) *Calendar:* Sem. plan *Degrees:* B *Prof. Accred.:* Music *CEO:* Pres. James H. Daughdrill, Jr.
Enroll: 1385 (901) 726-3000

RICE COLLEGE
2485 Union Ave., Memphis 38112 *Type:* Private business *Accred.:* 1952/1984 (CCA-ACICS); 1990 (SACS-COEI) *Calendar:* Courses of varying lengths *Degrees:* certificates, diplomas *CEO:* Pres. Rhonda Solomito
Enroll: 490 (901) 324-7423

BRANCH CAMPUS
5430 Norwood Ave., Jacksonville, FL 32208-5009 *CEO:* Dir. Frank Kello
(904) 765-7300

BRANCH CAMPUS
2525 Robinson Rd., Jackson, MS 39209 *CEO:* Dir. John Pitts
(601) 355-8100

BRANCH CAMPUS
1515 Magnolia Ave., Knoxville, TN 37917 *CEO:* Dir. James Babb
(615) 637-9899

ROANE STATE COMMUNITY COLLEGE
Patton La., Harriman 37748 *Type:* Public (state) 2-year *System:* Tennessee Board of Regents *Accred.:* 1974/1989 (SACS-CC) *Calendar:* Sem. plan *Degrees:* A *Prof. Accred.:* EMT-Paramedic, Medical Laboratory Technology (AMA), Medical Record Technology, Nursing (A), Physical Therapy Assisting, Radiography, Respiratory Therapy *CEO:* Pres. Sherry L. Hoppe
Enroll: 3680 (615) 354-3000

SEMINARY EXTENSION INDEPENDENT STUDY INSTITUTE
901 Commerce St., Ste. 500, Nashville 37203-3697 *Type:* Private home study *Accred.:* 1972/1988 (NHSC) *Calendar:* Courses of varying lengths *Degrees:* certificates *CEO:* Dir. Jack R. Cunningham
(615) 242-2453

SHELBY STATE COMMUNITY COLLEGE
P.O. Box 40568, Memphis 38174-0568 *Type:* Public (state) junior *System:* Tennessee Board of Regents *Accred.:* 1974/1989 (SACS-CC) *Calendar:* Sem. plan *Degrees:* A *Prof. Accred.:* EMT-Paramedic, Medical Laboratory Technology (AMA), Nursing (A), Physical Therapy Assisting, Radiography *CEO:* Pres. Lawrence M. Cox
Enroll: 3428   (901) 528-6700

SOUTHEAST COLLEGE OF TECHNOLOGY
2731 Nonconnah Blvd., Memphis 38132-2199 *Type:* Private *Accred.:* 1989 (CCA-ACTTS) *Calendar:* Courses of varying lengths *Degrees:* A, certificates, diplomas *CEO:* Dir. J. Matthews Bonnel
          (901) 345-1000

SOUTHEASTERN PARALEGAL INSTITUTE
2416 21st Ave. S., Ste. 300, Nashville 37212 *Type:* Private *Accred.:* 1985/1991 (SACS-COEI) *Calendar:* Courses of varying lengths *Degrees:* certificates *CEO:* Dir. Bruce Mallard
Enroll: 54   (615) 269-9900

SOUTHERN COLLEGE OF OPTOMETRY
1245 Madison Ave., Memphis 38104 *Type:* Private professional *Accred.:* 1967/1982 (SACS-CC) *Calendar:* Qtr. plan *Degrees:* P, D *Prof. Accred.:* Optometry *CEO:* Pres. William E. Cochran
Enroll: 345   (901) 722-3200

SOUTHERN COLLEGE OF SEVENTH-DAY ADVENTISTS
P.O. Box 370, Collegedale 37315-0370 *Type:* Private (Seventh-Day Adventist) liberal arts *Accred.:* 1950/1982 (SACS-CC) *Calendar:* Sem. plan *Degrees:* A, B *Prof. Accred.:* Music, Nursing (A,B), Teacher Education (e,s) *CEO:* Pres. Donald R. Sahly
Enroll: 1534   (615) 238-2111

STATE AREA VOCATIONAL-TECHNICAL SCHOOL—ATHENS
1634 Vo-Tech Dr., P.O. Box 848, Athens 37303 *Type:* Public (state) technical *Accred.:* 1971/1986 (SACS-COEI) *Calendar:* Courses of varying lengths *Degrees:* certificates *CEO:* Dir. Margaret H. Mahery
Enroll: 150   (615) 744-2814

STATE AREA VOCATIONAL-TECHNICAL SCHOOL—COVINGTON
1600 Hwy. 51 S., P.O. Box 249, Covington 38019 *Type:* Public (state) technical *Accred.:* 1972/1987 (SACS-COEI) *Calendar:* Courses of varying lengths *Degrees:* certificates *CEO:* Dir. Joe D. Martin
Enroll: 117   (901) 476-8634

STATE AREA VOCATIONAL-TECHNICAL SCHOOL—CROSSVILLE
715 N. Miller Ave., P.O. Box 2959, Crossville 38555 *Type:* Public (state) technical *Accred.:* 1971/1986 (SACS-COEI) *Calendar:* Courses of varying lengths *Degrees:* certificates *CEO:* Dir. James G. Purcell
Enroll: 226   (615) 484-7502

STATE AREA VOCATIONAL-TECHNICAL SCHOOL—DICKSON
740 Hwy. 46, Dickson 37055 *Type:* Public (state) technical *Accred.:* 1974/1989 (SACS-COEI) *Calendar:* Courses of varying lengths *Degrees:* certificates *CEO:* Dir. Robert Sullivan
Enroll: 151   (615) 446-4710

STATE AREA VOCATIONAL-TECHNICAL SCHOOL—ELIZABETHTON
1500 Arney St., P.O. Box 789, Elizabethton 37643 *Type:* Public (state) technical *Accred.:* 1973/1988 (SACS-COEI) *Calendar:* Courses of varying lengths *Degrees:* certificates *CEO:* Dir. Kelly C. Yates
Enroll: 162   (615) 542-4174

STATE AREA VOCATIONAL-TECHNICAL SCHOOL—HARRIMAN
Hwy. 27, N., P.O. Box 1109, Harriman 37748 *Type:* Public (state) technical *Accred.:* 1973/1988 (SACS-COEI) *Calendar:* Courses of varying lengths *Degrees:* certificates *CEO:* Dir. Farrell W. Kennedy
Enroll: 198   (615) 882-6703

STATE AREA VOCATIONAL-TECHNICAL SCHOOL—HARTSVILLE
716 McMurry Blvd., Hartsville 37074 *Type:* Public (state) technical *Accred.:* 1971/1986

Accredited Institutions — Tennessee

(SACS-COEI) *Calendar:* Courses of varying lengths *Degrees:* certificates *CEO:* Dir. H. Dean Ward
Enroll: 91   (615) 374-2147

STATE AREA VOCATIONAL-TECHNICAL SCHOOL—HOHENWALD
813 W. Main St., Hohenwald 38462 *Type:* Public (state) technical *Accred.:* 1972/1987 (SACS-COEI) *Calendar:* Courses of varying lengths *Degrees:* certificates *CEO:* Dir. Billy F. Tucker
Enroll: 100   (615) 796-5351

STATE AREA VOCATIONAL-TECHNICAL SCHOOL—JACKSBORO
Rte. 1, Elkins Rd., P.O. Box 419, Jacksboro 37757 *Type:* Public (state) technical *Accred.:* 1972/1987 (SACS-COEI) *Calendar:* Courses of varying lengths *Degrees:* certificates *CEO:* Dir. Coy Gibson
Enroll: 139   (615) 562-8648

STATE AREA VOCATIONAL-TECHNICAL SCHOOL—JACKSON
McKellar-Sipes Field, Jackson 38301 *Type:* Public (state) technical *Accred.:* 1972/1987 (SACS-COEI) *Calendar:* Courses of varying lengths *Degrees:* certificates *CEO:* Dir. Jo Evelyn Alred
Enroll: 252   (901) 424-0691

STATE AREA VOCATIONAL-TECHNICAL SCHOOL—KNOXVILLE
1100 Liberty St., Knoxville 37919 *Type:* Public (state) technical *Accred.:* 1971/1986 (SACS-COEI) *Calendar:* Courses of varying lengths *Degrees:* certificates *Prof. Accred.:* Dental Assisting *CEO:* Dir. Phillip W. Johnston
Enroll: 463   (615) 546-5567

STATE AREA VOCATIONAL-TECHNICAL SCHOOL—LIVINGSTON
Airport Rd., P.O. Box 219, Livingston 38570 *Type:* Public (state) technical *Accred.:* 1971/1986 (SACS-COEI) *Calendar:* Courses of varying lengths *Degrees:* certificates *CEO:* Dir. Ralph E. Robbins
Enroll: 226   (615) 823-5525

STATE AREA VOCATIONAL-TECHNICAL SCHOOL—MCKENZIE
Hwy. 22 N., P.O. Box 427, McKenzie 38201 *Type:* Public (state) technical *Accred.:* 1971/1986 (SACS-COEI) *Calendar:* Courses of varying lengths *Degrees:* certificates *CEO:* Dir. Kenneth D. Warren
Enroll: 130   (901) 352-5364

STATE AREA VOCATIONAL-TECHNICAL SCHOOL—MCMINNVILLE
1507 Vo-Tech Dr., McMinnville 37110 *Type:* Public (state) technical *Accred.:* 1971/1986 (SACS-COEI) *Calendar:* Courses of varying lengths *Degrees:* certificates *CEO:* Dir. Charles Nunley
Enroll: 150   (615) 473-5587

STATE AREA VOCATIONAL-TECHNICAL SCHOOL—MEMPHIS
620 Mosby Ave., Memphis 38105 *Type:* Public (state) technical *Accred.:* 1970/1990 (SACS-COEI) *Calendar:* Courses of varying lengths *Degrees:* certificates *Prof. Accred.:* Dental Assisting, Medical Laboratory Technology (AMA), Respiratory Therapy Technology, Surgical Technology *CEO:* Dir. Joseph Cornelius, Ph.D.
Enroll: 534   (901) 527-8455

BRANCH CAMPUS
2752 Winchester Rd., Memphis, TN 38116 *CEO:* Asst. Dir. Jay Clark
  (901) 345-1995

STATE AREA VOCATIONAL-TECHNICAL SCHOOL—MORRISTOWN
821 W. Louise Ave., P.O. Box 130, Morristown 37815 *Type:* Public (state) technical *Accred.:* 1971/1986 (SACS-COEI) *Calendar:* Courses of varying lengths *Degrees:* certificates *CEO:* Dir. Eugene G. Smith
Enroll: 401   (615) 586-5771

BRANCH CAMPUS
316 E. Main St., Rogersville, TN 37857 *CEO:* Asst. Dir. Dave Easterly
  (615) 272-2100

STATE AREA VOCATIONAL-TECHNICAL SCHOOL—MURFREESBORO
1303 Old Fort Pkwy., Murfreesboro 37129-3312 *Type:* Public (state) technical *Accred.:*

1980/1990 (SACS-COEI) *Calendar:* Courses of varying lengths *Degrees:* certificates *CEO:* Dir. Wallace E. Burke
Enroll: 162 (615) 898-8010

STATE AREA VOCATIONAL-TECHNICAL SCHOOL—NASHVILLE
100 White Bridge Rd., Nashville 37209 *Type:* Public (state) technical *Accred.:* 1972/1987 (SACS-COEI) *Calendar:* Courses of varying lengths *Degrees:* certificates *CEO:* Dir. Charles F. Malin
Enroll: 429 (615) 741-1241

BRANCH CAMPUS
7204 Cockrill Bend Rd., Nashville, TN 37209 *CEO:* Dir. Charles F. Malin
(615) 350-6224

STATE AREA VOCATIONAL-TECHNICAL SCHOOL—NEWBERN
340 Washington St., Newbern 38059 *Type:* Public (state) technical *Accred.:* 1972/1987 (SACS-COEI) *Calendar:* Courses of varying lengths *Degrees:* certificates *CEO:* Dir. Wallace E. Sexton
Enroll: 136 (901) 627-2511

STATE AREA VOCATIONAL-TECHNICAL SCHOOL—ONEIDA
120 Eli La., Oneida 37841 *Type:* Public (state) technical *Accred.:* 1973/1988 (SACS-COEI) *Calendar:* Courses of varying lengths *Degrees:* certificates *CEO:* Dir. Arvis Blakley
Enroll: 111 (615) 569-8338

STATE AREA VOCATIONAL-TECHNICAL SCHOOL—PARIS
312 S. Wilson St., Paris 38242 *Type:* Public (state) technical *Accred.:* 1974/1986 (SACS-COEI) *Calendar:* Courses of varying lengths *Degrees:* certificates *CEO:* Dir. Jimmie R. Pritchard
Enroll: 168 (901) 642-7552

STATE AREA VOCATIONAL-TECHNICAL SCHOOL—PULASKI
1233 E. College St., Pulaski 38478 *Type:* Public (state) technical *Accred.:* 1973/1988 (SACS-COEI) *Calendar:* Courses of varying lengths *Degrees:* certificates *CEO:* Dir. Henry H. Sims
Enroll: 144 (615) 363-1588

STATE AREA VOCATIONAL-TECHNICAL SCHOOL—RIPLEY
S. Industrial Park, Ripley 38063 *Type:* Public (state) technical *Accred.:* 1973/1988 (SACS-COEI) *Calendar:* Courses of varying lengths *Degrees:* certificates *CEO:* Dir. Jerry W. Little
Enroll: 47 (901) 635-3368

STATE AREA VOCATIONAL-TECHNICAL SCHOOL—SAVANNAH
Hwy. 64, W., P.O. Box 89, Crump 38327 *Type:* Public (state) technical *Accred.:* 1974/1987 (SACS-COEI) *Calendar:* Courses of varying lengths *Degrees:* certificates *CEO:* Dir. James King
Enroll: 126 (901) 632-3393

STATE AREA VOCATIONAL-TECHNICAL SCHOOL—SHELBYVILLE
1405 Madison St., Shelbyville 37160 *Type:* Public (state) technical *Accred.:* 1972/1987 (SACS-COEI) *Calendar:* Courses of varying lengths *Degrees:* certificates *CEO:* Dir. R.E. Holden
Enroll: 207 (615) 685-5013

STATE AREA VOCATIONAL-TECHNICAL SCHOOL—WHITEVILLE
Hwy. 100, W., P.O. Box 489, Whiteville 30875 *Type:* Public (state) technical *Accred.:* 1980/1990 (SACS-COEI) *Calendar:* Courses of varying lengths *Degrees:* certificates *CEO:* Dir. Russell Shelton
Enroll: 107 (901) 254-8521

STATE TECHNICAL INSTITUTE AT MEMPHIS
5983 Macon Cove, Memphis 38134-7693 *Type:* Public (state) 2-year *System:* Tennessee Board of Regents *Accred.:* 1969/1984 (SACS-CC) *Calendar:* Qtr. plan *Degrees:* A *Prof. Accred.:* Engineering Technology (architectural, bioengineering, chemical, civil/construction, computer, electrical,

industrial, mechanical) *CEO:* Pres. Charles M. Temple
Enroll: 5150 (901) 377-4100

TENNESSEE INSTITUTE OF ELECTRONICS
3203 Tazewell Pike, Knoxville 37918 *Type:* Private *Accred.:* 1967/1987 (CCA-ACTTS) *Calendar:* Qtr. plan *Degrees:* A, certificates, diplomas *CEO:* Pres. Ronald R. Rackley
Enroll: 347 (615) 688-9422

TENNESSEE STATE UNIVERSITY
3500 John Merritt Blvd., Nashville 37209-1561 *Type:* Public (state) *System:* Tennessee Board of Regents *Accred.:* 1946/1990 (SACS-CC) *Calendar:* Sem. plan *Degrees:* A, B, M, D *Prof. Accred.:* Engineering (architectural, civil, electrical, mechanical), Home Economics, Medical Record Administration, Medical Technology, Music, Nursing (A,B), Respiratory Therapy, Social Work (B), Speech-Language Pathology, Teacher Education (e,s,p) *CEO:* Pres. James A. Hefner
Enroll: 7679 (615) 320-3131

TENNESSEE TECHNOLOGICAL UNIVERSITY
N. Dixie Ave., Cookeville 38505 *Type:* Public (state) *System:* Tennessee Board of Regents *Accred.:* 1939/1985 (SACS-CC) *Calendar:* Qtr. plan *Degrees:* A, B, M, D *Prof. Accred.:* Accounting (Type A), Business (B,M), Engineering (chemical, civil, electrical, industrial, mechanical), Music, Nursing (B), Teacher Education (e,s,p) *CEO:* Pres. Angelo A. Volpe
Enroll: 13701 (615) 372-3101

TENNESSEE TEMPLE UNIVERSITY
1815 Union Ave., Chattanooga 37404 *Type:* Private (Baptist) *Accred.:* 1984/1989 (AABC) *Calendar:* Sem. plan *Degrees:* A, B, diplomas *CEO:* Pres. L.W. Nichols
Enroll: 1023 (615) 493-4100

TENNESSEE WESLEYAN COLLEGE
P.O. Box 40, Athens 37303 *Type:* Private (United Methodist) liberal arts *Accred.:* 1958/1990 (SACS-CC) *Calendar:* Qtr. plan *Degrees:* B *CEO:* Pres. James E. Cheek, II
Enroll: 539 (615) 745-7504

TOMLINSON COLLEGE
P.O. Box 3030, Cleveland 37320-3030 *Type:* Private (Church of God) junior *Accred.:* 1983/1988 (SACS-CC) *Calendar:* Sem. plan *Degrees:* A, B *CEO:* Pres. Perry E. Gillum
Enroll: 236 (615) 476-3271

TREVECCA NAZARENE COLLEGE
333 Murfreesboro Rd., Nashville 37210 *Type:* Private (Nazarene) liberal arts and teachers *Accred.:* 1969/1984 (SACS-CC) *Calendar:* Sem. plan *Degrees:* A, B, M *Prof. Accred.:* Medical Assisting (AMA), Music, Physician Assisting *CEO:* Pres. Millard Reed
Enroll: 1414 (615) 248-1200

TRI-CITY BARBER COLLEGE
113 S. Central St., Knoxville 37902 *Type:* Private *Accred.:* 1982/1987 (CCA-ACTTS) *Calendar:* Courses of varying lengths *Degrees:* diplomas *CEO:* Dir. Walter E. McGinnis
Enroll: 58 (615) 522-3736

TUSCULUM COLLEGE
P.O. Box 5035, Greeneville 37743 *Type:* Private (Presbyterian) liberal arts *Accred.:* 1926/1991 (SACS-CC) *Calendar:* Sem. plan *Degrees:* B, M *CEO:* Pres. Robert E. Knott
Enroll: 715 (615) 636-7300

UNION UNIVERSITY
2447 Hwy. 45 By-Pass, Jackson 38305 *Type:* Private (Southern Baptist) liberal arts *Accred.:* 1948/1987 (SACS-CC) *Calendar:* Sem. plan *Degrees:* A, B, M (candidate) *Prof. Accred.:* Music, Nursing (A,B) *CEO:* Pres. Hyran E. Barefoot
Enroll: 1814 (901) 668-1818

UNITED STATES NAVAL AIR TECHNICAL TRAINING CENTER
Naval Air Sta. Memphis, Millington 38054-5059 *Type:* Public (federal) *Accred.:* 1976/1991 (SACS-COEI) *Calendar:* Courses of varying lengths *Degrees:* certificates *CEO:* Commander T.W. Finta
Enroll: 7660 (901) 872-5306

UNIVERSITY OF BEAUTY
1703 S. Lee Hwy., Cleveland 37311 *Type:* Private *Accred.:* 1988/1990 (SACS-COEI) *Calendar:* Courses of varying lengths *Degrees:* certificates *CEO:* Dir. Barry Babb
Enroll: 36 (615) 683-6669

THE UNIVERSITY OF TENNESSEE AT CHATTANOOGA
615 McCallie Ave., Chattanooga 37403-2598 *Type:* Public (state) *System:* University of Tennessee System *Accred.:* 1910/1991 (SACS-CC) *Calendar:* Sem. plan *Degrees:* B, M *Prof. Accred.:* Business (B,M), Engineering (general), Music, Nursing (B), Social Work (B), Teacher Education (e,s,p) *CEO:* Chanc. Frederick W. Obear
Enroll: 6567 (615) 744-4111

THE UNIVERSITY OF TENNESSEE AT MARTIN
University Ave., Martin 38238 *Type:* Public (state) *System:* University of Tennessee System *Accred.:* 1951/1982 (SACS-CC) *Calendar:* Qtr. plan *Degrees:* A, B, M *Prof. Accred.:* Engineering Technology (civil/construction, electrical, mechanical), Home Economics, Music, Social Work (B), Teacher Education (e,s,p) *CEO:* Chanc. Margaret N. Perry
Enroll: 4823 (901) 587-7000

THE UNIVERSITY OF TENNESSEE, KNOXVILLE
527 Andy Holt Tower, Knoxville 37996-0150 *Type:* Public (state) *System:* University of Tennessee System *Accred.:* 1897/1981 (SACS-CC) *Calendar:* Qtr. plan *Degrees:* B, P, M, D *Prof. Accred.:* Accounting (Type A,B,C), Architecture (B), Art, Audiology, Business (B,M), Community Health/Preventive Medicine, Counseling, Counseling Psychology, Cytotechnology, Engineering (aerospace, agricultural, chemical, civil, electrical, engineering physics/science, industrial, materials, mechanical, nuclear), Forestry, Home Economics, Interior Design, Journalism, Law, Librarianship, Medical Technology, Music, Nuclear Medicine Technology, Nurse Anesthesia Education, Nursing (B,M), Planning, Psychology Internship, Radiography, Recreation and Leisure Studies, Rehabilitation Counseling, Social Work (B,M), Speech-Language Pathology, Teacher Education (e,s,p) *CEO:* Chanc. John J. Quinn
Enroll: 23005 (615) 974-1000

THE UNIVERSITY OF TENNESSEE, MEMPHIS
800 Madison Ave., Memphis 38163 *Type:* Public (state) *System:* University of Tennessee System *Accred.:* 1897/1983 (SACS-CC) *Calendar:* Qtr. plan *Degrees:* B, P, M, D *Prof. Accred.:* Cytotechnology, Dental Hygiene, Dentistry, Dietetics (internship), General Dentistry (prelim. provisional), Medical Record Administration, Medical Technology, Medicine, Nursing (B,M), Occupational Therapy, Oral and Maxillofacial Surgery, Orthodontics, Pediatric Dentistry, Periodontics, Pharmacy, Physical Therapy, Psychology Internship, Social Work (M) *CEO:* Chanc. James C. Hunt
Enroll: 1709 (901) 528-5500

THE UNIVERSITY OF THE SOUTH
University Ave., Sewanee 37375 *Type:* Private (Episcopal) liberal arts *Accred.:* 1958/1985 (ATS); 1895/1985 (SACS-CC) *Calendar:* Sem. plan *Degrees:* B, P, M, D *CEO:* Pres. Samuel R. Williamson, Jr.
Enroll: 1148 (615) 598-1000

VANDERBILT UNIVERSITY
W. End Ave., Nashville 37240 *Type:* Private *Accred.:* 1938/1983 (ATS); 1895/1986 (SACS-CC) *Calendar:* Sem. plan *Degrees:* B, P, M, D *Prof. Accred.:* Audiology, Business (M), Clinical Psychology, Counseling, Dietetics (internship), Engineering (chemical, civil, electrical, mechanical), General Practice Residency (prelim. provisional), Law, Medical Technology, Medicine, Music, Nuclear Medicine Technology, Nursing (M), Perfusion, Psychology Internship, Radiation Therapy Technology, Speech-Language Pathology, Teacher Education (e,s,p) *CEO:* Chanc. Joe B. Wyatt
Enroll: 8911 (615) 322-7311

VOLUNTEER STATE COMMUNITY COLLEGE
1360 Nashville Pike, Gallatin 37066-3188 *Type:* Public (state) 2-year *System:* Tenn-

essee Board of Regents *Accred.:* 1973/1989 (SACS-CC) *Calendar:* Qtr. plan *Degrees:* A *Prof. Accred.:* Dental Assisting, EMT-Paramedic, Medical Record Technology, Physical Therapy Assisting, Radiography, Respiratory Therapy Technology *CEO:* Pres. Hal R. Ramer
Enroll: 4248 (615) 452-8600

WALTERS STATE COMMUNITY COLLEGE
500 S. Davy Crockett Pkwy., Morristown 37813-6899 *Type:* Public (state) junior *System:* Tennessee Board of Regents *Accred.:* 1972/1987 (SACS-CC) *Calendar:* Qtr. plan *Degrees:* A *Prof. Accred.:* Nursing (A), Physical Therapy Assisting *CEO:* Pres. Jack E. Campbell
Enroll: 3146 (615) 587-9722

WEST TENNESSEE BUSINESS COLLEGE
1186 Hwy. 45 By-Pass, P.O. Box 1668, Jackson 38302-1668 *Type:* Private business *Accred.:* 1953/1991 (CCA-ACICS) *Calendar:* Tri. plan *Degrees:* certificates, diplomas *CEO:* Exec. Dir. Vicki Burch
Enroll: 711 (901) 668-7240

WILLIAM JENNINGS BRYAN COLLEGE
Box 7000, Dayton 37321-7000 *Type:* Private liberal arts *Accred.:* 1969/1984 (SACS-CC) *Calendar:* Sem. plan *Degrees:* A, B *CEO:* Pres. Kenneth G. Hanna
Enroll: 461 (615) 775-2041

WILLIAM R. MOORE SCHOOL OF TECHNOLOGY
1200 Poplar Ave., Memphis 38104 *Type:* Private *Accred.:* 1971/1991 (SACS-COEI) *Calendar:* Courses of varying lengths *Degrees:* certificates *CEO:* Dir. Gaylon S. Hall
Enroll: 76 (901) 726-1977

TEXAS

AIMS ACADEMY
Executive Tower, Ste. 305, 1106 N. Hwy. 360, Grand Prairie 75050 *Type:* Private technical *Accred.:* 1990 (SACS-COEI) *Calendar:* Courses of varying lengths *Degrees:* certificates, diplomas *CEO:* Dir. Crystal Hackling
Enroll: 53   (214) 988-3202

BRANCH CAMPUS
10830 N. Central Expy., Ste. 112, Dallas, TX 75231 *CEO:* Exec. Dir. Kenneth J. Carden
(214) 891-9672

ATDS—PRAIRIE HILL
FM Rd. 339, S. at Hwy. 84, Prairie Hill 76678 *Type:* Private *Accred.:* 1979/1991 (SACS-COEI) *Calendar:* Courses of varying lengths *Degrees:* certificates *CEO:* Dir. Dwight Tiedemann
(817) 344-2313

ATDS—TEXAS CITY
3524 First Ave., S., Texas City 77590 *Type:* Private *Accred.:* 1979/1989 (SACS-COEI) *Calendar:* Courses of varying lengths *Degrees:* certificates *CEO:* Dir. Ken Preston
Enroll: 220   (409) 945-5994

ATI
2449 W. Mockingbird La., Dallas 75235-5596 *Type:* Private *Accred.:* 1991 (CCA-ACTTS) *Calendar:* Courses of varying lengths *Degrees:* certificates *CEO:* Dir. John Hinkle
(214) 350-7557

ATI
6627 Maple Ave., Dallas 75235 *Type:* Private *Accred.:* 1975/1980 (CCA-ACTTS) *Calendar:* Courses of varying lengths *Degrees:* certificates, diplomas *CEO:* Pres. Joe Mehlmann
Enroll: 1077   (214) 352-2222

ATI
235 N.E. Loop 820, Ste. 300, Hurst 76053 *Type:* Private *Accred.:* 1986 (CCA-ACTTS) *Calendar:* Courses of varying lengths *Degrees:* certificates *CEO:* Dir. James W. Tisdale
Enroll: 384   (817) 284-1141

ATI COMPUTER TRAINING
2351 W. Northwest Hwy., Dallas 75220 *Type:* Private *Accred.:* 1987 (CCA-ACTTS) *Calendar:* Courses of varying lengths *Degrees:* certificates *CEO:* Dir. Gerald Parr
(214) 902-8191

ATI ELECTRONICS INSTITUTE
2345 W. Mockingbird La., Dallas 75235 *Type:* Private *Accred.:* 1987 (CCA-ACTTS) *Calendar:* Courses of varying lengths *Degrees:* certificates *CEO:* Dir. David Evans
(214) 350-7557

ATI GRAPHIC ARTS INSTITUTE
11034 Shady Trail, Dallas 75220 *Type:* Private *Accred.:* 1989 (CCA-ACTTS) *Calendar:* Courses of varying lengths *Degrees:* certificates *CEO:* Dir. Reza Nanbakhabi
(214) 353-9056

ATI HEALTH EDUCATION CENTER
8150 Brookriver Dr., 5th Fl., Dallas 75247 *Type:* Private *Accred.:* 1987 (CCA-ACTTS) *Calendar:* Courses of varying lengths *Degrees:* certificates *Prof. Accred.:* Health Education *CEO:* Dir. Barbara Monk
(214) 688-0467

ATI HEALTH EDUCATION CENTER
1200 Summit Ave., Ste. 200, Fort Worth 76102 *Type:* Private *Accred.:* 1989 (CCA-ACTTS) *Calendar:* Courses of varying lengths *Degrees:* certificates *Prof. Accred.:* Health Education *CEO:* Dir. Cindy Gordon
(817) 429-1045

ABILENE CHRISTIAN UNIVERSITY
1600 Campus Ct., Abilene 79699 *Type:* Private (Church of Christ) liberal arts *Accred.:*

1951/1991 (SACS-CC) *Calendar:* Sem. plan *Degrees:* A, B, P, M, D *Prof. Accred.:* Music, Social Work (B), Teacher Education (e,s) *CEO:* Pres. Royce Money
Enroll: 3657 (915) 674-2000

ACTION CAREER TRAINING
Rte. 3, Box 41, Merkel 79536-9803 *Type:* Private *Accred.:* 1989 (SACS-COEI) *Calendar:* Courses of varying lengths *Degrees:* certificates *CEO:* Dir. Betty Gregory
Enroll: 41 (915) 676-3136

ADVANCE CAREER TRAINING
6500 Greenville Ave., Ste. 180, Dallas 75206 *Type:* Private *Accred.:* 1989 (CCA-ACTTS) *Calendar:* Courses of varying lengths *Degrees:* certificates *CEO:* Pres. Harry Schmidlin
(214) 692-5400

ALLIED HEALTH CAREERS
5424 Hwy. 290 W., Austin 78735-8828 *Type:* Private *Accred.:* 1991 (CCA-ACTTS) *Calendar:* Courses of varying lengths *Degrees:* certificates *CEO:* Dir. Glynda Lee Bujanos
(512) 892-5210

ALVIN COMMUNITY COLLEGE
3110 Mustang Rd., Alvin 77511-4898 *Type:* Public (district) junior *System:* Texas Higher Education Coordinating Board *Accred.:* 1959/1990 (SACS-CC) *Calendar:* Sem. plan *Degrees:* A *Prof. Accred.:* Medical Laboratory Technology (AMA), Nursing (A), Respiratory Therapy, Respiratory Therapy Technology *CEO:* Pres. A. Rodney Allbright
Enroll: 3369 (713) 331-6111

AMARILLO AFFILIATED SCHOOL OF MEDICAL TECHNOLOGY
P.O. Box 1110, Amarillo 79115 *Type:* Private *Calendar:* Courses of varying lengths *Degrees:* certificates *Prof. Accred.:* Medical Technology *CEO:* Pres. James L. Goforth, M.D.
Enroll: 6 (806) 354-1756

AMARILLO COLLEGE
2201 S. Washington St., P.O. Box 447, Amarillo 79178 *Type:* Public (district) junior *System:* Texas Higher Education Coordinating Board *Accred.:* 1933/1982 (SACS-CC) *Calendar:* Sem. plan *Degrees:* A *Prof. Accred.:* Dental Hygiene, Engineering Technology (electrical), Medical Laboratory Technology, Music, Nursing (A), Physical Therapy Assisting, Radiation Therapy Technology, Radiography, Respiratory Therapy, Surgical Technology, Veterinary Technology (probational) *CEO:* Pres. George T. Miller
Enroll: 5385 (806) 371-5000

AMARILLO-WEST TEXAS BARBER STYLING COLLEGE
4001 Mockingbird La., Amarillo 79109 *Type:* Private *Accred.:* 1975/1985 (CCA-ACTTS) *Calendar:* Courses of varying lengths *Degrees:* certificates *CEO:* Vice Pres. James Watson
(806) 355-9426

AMBER UNIVERSITY
1700 Eastgate Dr., Garland 75041 *Type:* Private (Church of Christ) *Accred.:* 1981/1987 (SACS-CC) *Calendar:* Tri. plan *Degrees:* B, M *CEO:* Pres. Douglas W. Warner
Enroll: 1498 (214) 279-6511

AMERICAN CAREER TECH
6355 Grapevine Hwy., Fort Worth 76180 *Type:* Private *Accred.:* 1991 (CCA-ACTTS) *Calendar:* Courses of varying lengths *Degrees:* certificates *CEO:* Dir. Carl Negley
(800) 525-0496

AMERICAN CAREERS
410 S. Main St., Ste. 201, San Antonio 78204 *Type:* Private *Accred.:* 1989 (SACS-COEI) *Calendar:* Courses of varying lengths *Degrees:* certificates, diplomas *CEO:* Dir. Paul Herzig
Enroll: 53 (512) 271-7222

AMERICAN COMMERCIAL COLLEGE
402 Butternut St., Abilene 79602 *Type:* Private business *Accred.:* 1970/1987 (CCA-

ACICS) *Calendar:* Courses of varying lengths *Degrees:* certificates, diplomas *CEO:* Dir. Michael J. Otto
Enroll: 577 (915) 672-8495

AMERICAN COMMERCIAL COLLEGE
2007 34th St., Lubbock 79411 *Type:* Private business *Accred.:* 1982/1987 (CCA-ACICS) *Calendar:* Courses of varying lengths *Degrees:* certificates, diplomas *CEO:* Dir. Brent Sheets
Enroll: 754 (806) 747-4339

AMERICAN COMMERCIAL COLLEGE
2115 E. Eighth St., Odessa 79761 *Type:* Private business *Accred.:* 1970/1988 (CCA-ACICS) *Calendar:* Courses of varying lengths *Degrees:* certificates, diplomas *CEO:* Dir. Charles Vandiver
Enroll: 395 (915) 332-0768

AMERICAN COMMERCIAL COLLEGE
3177 Executive Dr., San Angelo 76904 *Type:* Private business *Accred.:* 1970/1988 (CCA-ACICS) *Calendar:* Courses of varying lengths *Degrees:* certificates, diplomas *CEO:* Dir. B.A. Reed
Enroll: 572 (915) 942-6797

AMERICAN INSTITUTE OF COMMERCE
5501 LBJ Fwy., Ste. 201, Dallas 75240 *Type:* Private business *Accred.:* 1989 (CCA-ACICS) *Calendar:* Courses of varying lengths *Degrees:* certificates, diplomas *CEO:* Dir. Mary Lou Gallagher
Enroll: 345 (214) 458-1225

AMERICAN TRAINING CENTER
1530 Main St., Ste. 300, Dallas 75201 *Type:* Private *Accred.:* 1987 (SACS-COEI) *Calendar:* Courses of varying lengths *Degrees:* certificates *CEO:* Dir. Gerald Newman
Enroll: 120 (214) 748-1278

AMHERST CAREER CENTER
2824 Terrell Rd., Ste. 500, Greenville 75401 *Type:* Private *Accred.:* 1988 (SACS-COEI) *Calendar:* Courses of varying lengths *Degrees:* certificates *CEO:* Dir. Marietta Page
Enroll: 282 (214) 455-7008

ANGELINA COLLEGE
Hwy. 59 S., Lufkin 75902 *Type:* Public (district) junior *System:* Texas Higher Education Coordinating Board *Accred.:* 1970/1985 (SACS-CC) *Calendar:* Sem. plan *Degrees:* A *Prof. Accred.:* Radiography *CEO:* Pres. Larry Phillips
Enroll: 2506 (409) 639-1301

ANGELO STATE UNIVERSITY
2601 West Ave. N., San Angelo 76909 *Type:* Public (state) liberal arts *System:* Texas State University System *Accred.:* 1936/1982 (SACS-CC) *Calendar:* Sem. plan *Degrees:* A, B, M *Prof. Accred.:* Music, Nursing (A,B) *CEO:* Pres. Lloyd D. Vincent
Enroll: 5549 (915) 942-2073

ARLINGTON BAPTIST COLLEGE
3001 W. Division St., Arlington 76012 *Type:* Private (Baptist) *Accred.:* 1981/1986 (AABC) *Calendar:* Sem. plan *Degrees:* B *CEO:* Pres. Wayne Martin
Enroll: 161 (817) 461-8741

ARLINGTON COURT REPORTING COLLEGE
1201 N. Watson Rd., Ste. 270, Arlington 76006 *Type:* Private *Accred.:* 1988 (CCA-ACTTS) *Calendar:* Courses of varying lengths *Degrees:* certificates *CEO:* Dir. Ronda Vecchio
Enroll: 129 (817) 640-8852

THE ART INSTITUTE OF DALLAS
2 NorthPark E., 8080 Park La., Dallas 75231 *Type:* Private professional *Accred.:* 1985 (CCA-ACTTS) *Calendar:* Qtr. plan *Degrees:* diplomas *CEO:* Pres. Deborah G. Wright
Enroll: 414 (800) 441-1577

ART INSTITUTE OF HOUSTON
3600 Yoakum Blvd., Houston 77006 *Type:* Private *Accred.:* 1979/1989 (CCA-ACTTS) *Calendar:* Qtr. plan *Degrees:* diplomas *CEO:* Dir. Steven Gregg
Enroll: 1476 (713) 523-2564

AUSTIN COLLEGE
900 N. Grand Ave., P.O. Box 1177, Sherman 75091-1177 *Type:* Private (Presbyterian) lib-

eral arts *Accred.:* 1947/1989 (SACS-CC) *Calendar:* 4-1-4 plan *Degrees:* B, M *CEO:* Pres. Harry E. Smith
Enroll: 1291 (214) 813-2000

AUSTIN COMMUNITY COLLEGE
P.O. Box 140526, Austin 78714 *Type:* Public (district) junior *System:* Texas Higher Education Coordinating Board *Accred.:* 1978/1983 (SACS-CC) *Calendar:* Sem. plan *Degrees:* A *Prof. Accred.:* Diagnostic Medical Sonography, EMT-Paramedic, Medical Laboratory Technology (AMA), Nursing (A), Occupational Therapy Assisting, Physical Therapy Assisting, Radiography, Surgical Technology *CEO:* Pres. Daniel D. Angel
Enroll: 16910 (512) 483-7000

AUSTIN PRESBYTERIAN THEOLOGICAL SEMINARY
100 E. 27th St., Austin 78705 *Type:* Private (Presbyterian) professional; graduate only *Accred.:* 1940/1989 (ATS); 1973/1989 (SACS-CC) *Calendar:* Sem. plan *Degrees:* P, M, D *CEO:* Pres. Jack L. Stotts
Enroll: 128 (512) 479-0738

AVALON VOCATIONAL-TECHNICAL INSTITUTE
4241 Tanglewood La., Odessa 79762 *Type:* Private *Accred.:* 1988 (SACS-COEI) *Calendar:* Courses of varying lengths *Degrees:* certificates *CEO:* Dir. Carole Paul
Enroll: 1555 (915) 367-2622

BRANCH CAMPUS
1407 Texas St., Fort Worth, TX 76102 *CEO:* Dir. Cheryl Parker
(817) 877-5511

BRANCH CAMPUS
3301 Marshall St., Longview, TX 76504 *CEO:* Dir. Bob Linthicum
(903) 295-2002

BRANCH CAMPUS
One Eureka Cir., Wichita Falls, TX 76308 *CEO:* Dir. Barbara Taylor
(817) 692-6513

BAPTIST MISSIONARY ASSOCIATION THEOLOGICAL SEMINARY
1410 E. Pine St., Jacksonville 75766 *Type:* Private (Baptist) professional; graduate only *Accred.:* 1986/1991 (SACS-CC) *Calendar:* Sem. plan *Degrees:* A, B, M *CEO:* Pres. Philip R. Bryan
Enroll: 51 (903) 586-2501

BAUDER FASHION COLLEGE
508 S. Center St., Arlington 76010 *Type:* Private *Accred.:* 1971/1984 (CCA-ACTTS); 1985/1990 (SACS-CC) *Calendar:* Qtr. plan *Degrees:* A *CEO:* Exec. Dir. Beverly Gooch
Enroll: 278 (817) 261-7586

BAYLOR COLLEGE OF DENTISTRY
3302 Gaston Ave., Dallas 75246 *Type:* Private professional; graduate only *Accred.:* 1976/1989 (SACS-CC) *Calendar:* Qtr. plan *Degrees:* M, D *Prof. Accred.:* Combined Prosthodontics, Dental Hygiene, Dentistry, Endodontics, General Dentistry (prelim. provisional), Oral and Maxillofacial Surgery, Orthodontics, Pediatric Dentistry, Periodontics *CEO:* Pres. Dominick P. DePaola
Enroll: 415 (214) 828-8100

BAYLOR COLLEGE OF MEDICINE
One Baylor Plaza, Houston 77030 *Type:* Private professional; graduate only *Accred.:* 1970/1985 (SACS-CC) *Calendar:* Qtr. plan *Degrees:* M, D *Prof. Accred.:* Medicine, Nuclear Medicine Technology, Nurse Anesthesia Education, Perfusion, Physician Assisting, Psychology Internship *CEO:* Pres. William T. Butler
Enroll: 999 (713) 798-4951

BAYLOR UNIVERSITY
1314 S. Seventh St., Waco 76798 *Type:* Private (Southern Baptist) *Accred.:* 1914/1986 (SACS-CC) *Calendar:* Sem. plan *Degrees:* B, P, M, D *Prof. Accred.:* Accounting (Type A), Business (B,M), Clinical Psychology, Computer Science, Engineering (general), Health Services Administration, Law, Music, Nursing (B), Physical Therapy, Radiation Therapy Technology, Radiography, Social Work (B), Speech-Language Pathology, Teacher Education (e,s,p) *CEO:* Pres. Herbert H. Reynolds
Enroll: 11541 (817) 755-1011

Texas

BAYTOWN TECHNICAL SCHOOL
112 S. Sixth St., Waco 76701 *Type:* Private *Accred.:* 1989 (SACS-COEI) *Calendar:* Courses of varying lengths *Degrees:* certificates *CEO:* Dir. Julia Carlile-Long
Enroll: 483   (817) 753-2525

BEE COUNTY COLLEGE
3800 Charco Rd., Beeville 78102 *Type:* Public (district) junior *System:* Texas Higher Education Coordinating Board *Accred.:* 1969/1984 (SACS-CC) *Calendar:* Sem. plan *Degrees:* A *Prof. Accred.:* Dental Hygiene *CEO:* Pres. Norman E. Wallace
Enroll: 1847   (512) 358-3130

BISH MATHIS INSTITUTE
710 S. Standard St., Longview 75604 *Type:* Private business *Accred.:* 1971/1987 (CCA-ACICS) *Calendar:* Courses of varying lengths *Degrees:* certificates, diplomas *CEO:* Dir. Renee Craft
Enroll: 346   (903) 759-0001

BRANCH CAMPUS
202 S. Alamo Blvd., Marshall, TX 75670 *CEO:* Dir. Sheri Wakefield
                                 (903) 935-2828

BRANCH CAMPUS
3111 W. Northwest Loop 323, Tyler, TX 75702 *CEO:* Dir. Paula Hughes
                                 (903) 593-0166

BLINN COLLEGE
902 College Ave., Brenham 77833 *Type:* Public (district) junior *System:* Texas Higher Education Coordinating Board *Accred.:* 1950/1984 (SACS-CC) *Calendar:* Sem. plan *Degrees:* A *Prof. Accred.:* Radiography *CEO:* Pres. Walter C. Schwartz
Enroll: 6514   (409) 830-4000

BRADFORD SCHOOL OF BUSINESS
4669 Southwest Fwy., Ste. 350, Houston 77027 *Type:* Private business *Accred.:* 1980 (CCA-ACICS) *Calendar:* Courses of varying lengths *Degrees:* certificates, diplomas *CEO:* Dir. Kathy Hughston
Enroll: 407   (713) 629-8940

BRAZOS BUSINESS COLLEGE
1702 S. Texas Ave., Bryan 77802 *Type:* Private business *Accred.:* 1986 (CCA-ACICS) *Calendar:* Courses of varying lengths *Degrees:* certificates, diplomas *CEO:* Dir. Steve Kalena
Enroll: 371   (409) 822-6423

BRANCH CAMPUS
2017 N. Frazier St., Conroe, TX 77301 *CEO:* Dir. Dale Inman
                                 (409) 539-4009

BRAZOSPORT COLLEGE
500 College Dr., Lake Jackson 77566 *Type:* Public (district) junior *System:* Texas Higher Education Coordinating Board *Accred.:* 1970/1985 (SACS-CC) *Calendar:* Sem. plan *Degrees:* A *CEO:* Pres. John R. Grable
Enroll: 2372   (409) 265-6131

BROOKHAVEN COLLEGE
3939 Valley View La., Farmers Branch 75244-4997 *Type:* Public (district) junior *System:* Dallas County Community College District *Accred.:* 1979/1983 (SACS-CC) *Calendar:* Sem. plan *Degrees:* A *CEO:* Pres. Walter G. Bumphus
Enroll: 9595   (214) 620-4700

BRYAN INSTITUTE
1719 W. Pioneer Pkwy., Arlington 76013-4799 *Type:* Private *Accred.:* 1982 (CCA-ACTTS) *Calendar:* Courses of varying lengths *Degrees:* certificates *Prof. Accred.:* Medical Assisting *CEO:* Dir. Richard Feldbush
                                 (817) 265-5588

BUSINESS SKILLS TRAINING CENTER
616 Fort Worth Dr., Ste. B, Denton 76201-7170 *Type:* Private *Accred.:* 1991 (CCA-ACTTS) *Calendar:* Courses of varying lengths *Degrees:* certificates *CEO:* Pres. Jane M. Hadley
                                 (817) 382-7922

CBM EDUCATION CENTER
406 W. Durango Blvd., San Antonio 78204 *Type:* Private *Accred.:* 1971/1982 (CCA-ACTTS) *Calendar:* Courses of varying

Accredited Institutions   Texas

lengths *Degrees:* A, diplomas *CEO:* Dir. Richard Jauregui
Enroll: 1268   (512) 224-9286

BRANCH CAMPUS
4115 Freidrich La., Austin, TX 78744
CEO: Dir. Chris Miteff
       (512) 442-3971

BRANCH CAMPUS
5555 Bear La., Corpus Christi, TX 78405
CEO: Dir. Ray Perrilloux
       (512) 289-1051

BRANCH CAMPUS
5904 West Dr., Ste. 7, Laredo, TX 78041
CEO: Dir. Doris Rodriguez
       (512) 725-4676

BRANCH CAMPUS
3201 N. Ware Rd., McAllen, TX 78501
CEO: Dir. William Kaltonback
       (512) 630-2800

BRANCH CAMPUS
203 W. Sheridan, San Antonio, TX 78204
CEO: Dir. Martin Burrell
       (512) 224-9834

BRANCH CAMPUS
2550 W. Hwy. 83, San Benito, TX 78586
CEO: Dir. Robert F. Stephens
       (512) 399-4007

CDI CAREER DEVELOPMENT INSTITUTE
8828 Stemmons Fwy., Ste. 300, Dallas 75247 *Type:* Private *Accred.:* 1968/1990 (CCA-ACTTS) *Calendar:* Courses of varying lengths *Degrees:* certificates *CEO:* Dir. Larry F. Sample
Enroll: 491   (214) 688-5900

CDI CAREER DEVELOPMENT INSTITUTE
2990 Richmond Ave., Ste. 600, Houston 77098 *Type:* Private *Accred.:* 1981/1986 (CCA-ACTTS) *Calendar:* Courses of varying lengths *Degrees:* certificates *CEO:* Dir. Robert Cheney
Enroll: 157   (713) 522-6000

CAPITOL CITY CAREERS
4630 Westgate Blvd., Austin 78745 *Type:* Private *Accred.:* 1989 (CCA-ACTTS); 1989 (SACS-COEI) *Calendar:* Courses of varying lengths *Degrees:* diplomas *CEO:* Dir. Wanda Bierschwale
Enroll: 397   (512) 892-4270

CAPITOL CITY TRADE AND TECHNICAL SCHOOL
205 E. Riverside Dr., Austin 78704 *Type:* Private *Accred.:* 1977/1989 (CCA-ACTTS); 1979/1989 (SACS-COEI) *Calendar:* Courses of varying lengths *Degrees:* diplomas *CEO:* Pres./Dir. George Hollowell
Enroll: 180   (512) 444-3257

CAREER ACADEMY
32 Oaklawn Village, Texarkana 75501 *Type:* Private *Accred.:* 1988 (SACS-COEI) *Calendar:* Courses of varying lengths *Degrees:* certificates *CEO:* Dir. Janet Windes
Enroll: 81   (214) 832-1021

CAREER CENTERS OF TEXAS—AUSTIN
4115 Freidrich La., Austin 78744-1895 *Type:* Private *Accred.:* 1991 (CCA-ACTTS) *Calendar:* Courses of varying lengths *Degrees:* certificates *CEO:* Dir. Harry Rumbaugh
       (512) 450-0101

CAREER CENTERS OF TEXAS—EL PASO
8375 Burnham Dr., El Paso 79907 *Type:* Private *Accred.:* 1988 (SACS-COEI) *Calendar:* Courses of varying lengths *Degrees:* certificates *Prof. Accred.:* Medical Assisting *CEO:* Dir. Comer Alden
Enroll: 131   (915) 595-1935

CAREER DEVELOPMENT CENTER
413 S. Chestnut St., Lufkin 75901 *Type:* Private *Accred.:* 1991 (SACS-COEI) *Calendar:* Courses of varying lengths *Degrees:* certificates *CEO:* Dir. Reed Amadon
Enroll: 71   (409) 637-1740

CAREER POINT BUSINESS SCHOOL
485 Spencer La., San Antonio 78201 *Type:* Private business *Accred.:* 1984/1989 (CCA-ACICS) *Calendar:* Courses of varying

Texas

lengths *Degrees:* certificates, diplomas *CEO:* Dir. Ardith K. Beckmann
Enroll: 1030   (512) 732-3000

CAREER TECHNICAL INSTITUTE
1406 S. Texas Ave., College Station 77840 *Type:* Private *Accred.:* 1985/1990 (SACS-COEI) *Calendar:* Courses of varying lengths *Degrees:* certificates *CEO:* Dir. Rodney Conwell
Enroll: 62   (409) 823-8223

CEDAR VALLEY COLLEGE
3030 N. Dallas Ave., Lancaster 75134 *Type:* Public (district) junior *System:* Dallas County Community College District *Accred.:* 1979/1983 (SACS-CC) *Calendar:* Sem. plan *Degrees:* A *Prof. Accred.:* Veterinary Technology *CEO:* Pres. Carol J. Spencer
Enroll: 2259   (214) 372-8200

CENTER FOR ADVANCED LEGAL STUDIES
3015 Richmond Ave., Houston 77098 *Type:* Private *Accred.:* 1989/1990 (SACS-COEI) *Calendar:* Courses of varying lengths *Degrees:* certificates *CEO:* Dir. Doyle Happe
Enroll: 119   (713) 529-2778

CENTRAL TEXAS COLLEGE
P.O. Box 1800, Killeen 76540-9990 *Type:* Public (district) junior *System:* Texas Higher Education Coordinating Board *Accred.:* 1969/1991 (SACS-CC) *Calendar:* Sem. plan *Degrees:* A *Prof. Accred.:* Medical Laboratory Technology (AMA), Nursing (A) *CEO:* Chanc. James R. Anderson
Enroll: 11115   (817) 526-7161

CENTRAL TEXAS COMMERCIAL COLLEGE
303 N. Center St., P.O. Box 1324, Brownwood 76804 *Type:* Private business *Accred.:* 1971/1989 (CCA-ACICS) *Calendar:* Qtr. plan *Degrees:* certificates, diplomas *CEO:* Dir. Kathy Day
Enroll: 235   (915) 646-0521

    BRANCH CAMPUS
    9400 N. Central Expy., Dallas, TX 75231 *CEO:* Dir. Dianne Day
          (214) 368-3680

CHENIER
6300 Richmond Ave., No. 300, Houston 77057 *Type:* Private *Accred.:* 1979/1989 (SACS-COEI) *Calendar:* Courses of varying lengths *Degrees:* certificates *CEO:* Dir. Sharon Ferrell
Enroll: 217   (409) 886-3102

CHENIER
845 Del Sasso, Orange 77630 *Type:* Private *Accred.:* 1990 (SACS-COEI) *Calendar:* Courses of varying lengths *Degrees:* certificates *CEO:* Dir. Melvin Broussard
Enroll: 19   (409) 886-5260

CHENIER BUSINESS SCHOOL
4320 Calder Ave., Beaumont 77706 *Type:* Private *Accred.:* 1979/1990 (SACS-COEI) *Calendar:* Courses of varying length *Degrees:* certificates *CEO:* Dir. John Wagliardo
Enroll: 154   (409) 899-3227

CHENIER BUSINESS SCHOOL
2819 Loop 306, San Angelo 76904 *Type:* Private *Accred.:* 1990 (SACS-COEI) *Calendar:* Courses of varying lengths *Degrees:* certificates *CEO:* Dir. Thomas Tyler
Enroll: 124   (915) 944-4404

CISCO JUNIOR COLLEGE
Rte. 3, Box 3, Cisco 76437 *Type:* Public (district) junior *System:* Texas Higher Education Coordinating Board *Accred.:* 1958/1989 (SACS-CC) *Calendar:* Sem. plan *Degrees:* A *Prof. Accred.:* Practical Nursing *CEO:* Pres. Roger C. Schustereit
Enroll: 3397   (817) 442-2567

CLARENDON COLLEGE
P.O. Box 968, Clarendon 79226 *Type:* Public (district) junior *System:* Texas Higher Education Coordinating Board *Accred.:* 1970/1985 (SACS-CC) *Calendar:* Sem. plan *Degrees:* A *CEO:* Pres. Jerry D. Stockton
Enroll: 697   (806) 874-3571

COLLEGE OF THE MAINLAND
1200 Amburn Rd., Texas City 77591 *Type:* Public (district) junior *System:* Texas Higher Education Coordinating Board *Accred.:* 1969/1984 (SACS-CC) *Calendar:* Sem. plan

Accredited Institutions   **Texas**

Degrees: A *Prof. Accred.:* Nursing (A) *CEO:* Pres. Larry L. Stanley
Enroll: 3995   (713) 938-1211

COLLIN COUNTY COMMUNITY COLLEGE
2200 W. University Dr., McKinney 75070 *Type:* Public (district) junior *System:* Texas Higher Education Coordinating Board *Accred.:* 1989 (SACS-CC) *Calendar:* Sem. plan *Degrees:* A *CEO:* Pres. John H. Anthony
Enroll: 5782   (214) 548-6790

COMMONWEALTH COLLEGE OF FUNERAL SERVICE
415 Barren Springs Dr., Houston 77090 *Type:* Private *Calendar:* Qtr. plan *Degrees:* A, diplomas *Prof. Accred.:* Funeral Service Education *CEO:* Exec. Dir. Terry McEnany
                         (713) 873-0262

COMPUTER CAREER CENTER
8201 Lockheed Dr., Ste. 100, El Paso 79925 *Type:* Private *Accred.:* 1989 (SACS-COEI) *Calendar:* Courses of varying lengths *Degrees:* certificates *CEO:* Dir. Lee Chayes
Enroll: 341   (915) 779-8031

CONCORDE CAREER INSTITUTE
4230 LBJ Fwy., Ste. 150, Dallas 75244-5804 *Type:* Private *Accred.:* 1991 (CCA-ACTTS) *Calendar:* Courses of varying lengths *Degrees:* certificates *CEO:* Dir. Barbara Puleio
                         (214) 387-8670

CONCORDE CAREER INSTITUTE
8866 Gulf Fwy., Ste. 105, Houston 77017-6528 *Type:* Private *Accred.:* 1991 (CCA-ACTTS) *Calendar:* Courses of varying lengths *Degrees:* certificates *CEO:* Dir. Ann H. Vollaro
                         (713) 943-3536

CONCORDE CAREER INSTITUTE
1919 North Loop W., Ste. 180, Houston 77008-1354 *Type:* Private *Accred.:* 1991 (CCA-ACTTS) *Calendar:* Courses of varying lengths *Degrees:* certificates *CEO:* Dir. Joseph T. Vollaro
                         (713) 863-0404

CONCORDIA LUTHERAN COLLEGE
3400 IH 35 N., Austin 78705 *Type:* Private (Lutheran) liberal arts *Accred.:* 1968/1988 (SACS-CC) *Calendar:* Sem. plan *Degrees:* A, B *CEO:* Pres. Ray F. Martens
Enroll: 634   (512) 452-7661

COOKE COUNTY COLLEGE
1525 W. California St., Gainesville 76240-4699 *Type:* Public (district) junior *System:* Texas Higher Education Coordinating Board *Accred.:* 1961/1991 (SACS-CC) *Calendar:* Sem. plan *Degrees:* A *Prof. Accred.:* Nursing (A) *CEO:* Pres. Luther Bud Joyner
Enroll: 2102   (817) 668-7731

CORPUS CHRISTI STATE UNIVERSITY
6300 Ocean Dr., Corpus Christi 78412 *Type:* Public (state) liberal arts *System:* Texas A&M University System *Accred.:* 1975/1990 (SACS-CC) *Calendar:* Sem. plan *Degrees:* B, M *Prof. Accred.:* Medical Technology, Music, Nursing (B,M) *CEO:* Pres. Robert R. Furgason
Enroll: 2571   (512) 991-6810

COURT REPORTING INSTITUTE OF DALLAS
8585 N. Stemmons Fwy., N. Tower, Ste. 200, Dallas 75247 *Type:* Private business *Accred.:* 1986 (CCA-ACICS) *Calendar:* Courses of varying lengths *Degrees:* certificates, diplomas *CEO:* Dir. Carolyn S. Willard
Enroll: 926   (214) 350-9722

THE CRISWELL COLLEGE
4010 Gaston Ave., Dallas 75246 *Type:* Private (Baptist) *Accred.:* 1985/1990 (SACS-CC) *Calendar:* Sem. plan *Degrees:* A, B, M *CEO:* Pres. L. Paige Patterson
Enroll: 310   (214) 821-5433

DALFORT AIRCRAFT TECH
7701 Lemmon Ave., Dallas 75209-3091 *Type:* Private *Accred.:* 1991 (CCA-ACTTS) *Calendar:* Courses of varying lengths *Degrees:* certificates *CEO:* Dir. Bryan Vinson, Jr.
                         (214) 358-7820

DALLAS BAPTIST UNIVERSITY
7777 W. Kiest Blvd., Dallas 75211-9800
Type: Private (Southern Baptist) liberal arts *Accred.:* 1959/1988 (SACS-CC) *Calendar:* 4-1-4 plan *Degrees:* B, M *Prof. Accred.:* Nursing (B) *CEO:* Pres. Gary R. Cook
Enroll: 1530 (214) 331-8311

DALLAS CHRISTIAN COLLEGE
2700 Christian Pkwy., Dallas 75234 *Type:* Private (Christian Church/Church of Christ) *Accred.:* 1978/1988 (AABC) *Calendar:* Sem. plan *Degrees:* A, B *CEO:* Pres. Gene Shepherd
Enroll: 84 (214) 241-3371

DALLAS INSTITUTE OF FUNERAL SERVICES
3909 S. Bruckner Blvd., Dallas 75227 *Type:* Private professional *Accred.:* 1974/1990 (SACS-COEI) *Calendar:* Qtr. plan *Degrees:* A, diplomas *Prof. Accred.:* Funeral Service Education *CEO:* Pres. Robert P. Kite
Enroll: 206 (214) 388-5466

DALLAS THEOLOGICAL SEMINARY
3909 Swiss Ave., Dallas 75204 *Type:* Private (interdenominational) professional *Accred.:* 1990 (ATS candidate); 1969/1984 (SACS-CC) *Calendar:* Sem. plan *Degrees:* P, M, D *CEO:* Pres. Donald K. Campbell
Enroll: 1038 (214) 824-3994

DEVRY INSTITUTE OF TECHNOLOGY, DALLAS
4250 N. Beltline Rd., Irving 75062 *Type:* Private *Accred.:* 1981/1987 (NCA) *Calendar:* Sem. plan *Degrees:* A, B, certificates *Prof. Accred.:* Engineering Technology (electrical) *CEO:* Acting Pres. Harry Overton
Enroll: 2322 (214) 258-6330

DEBBIE'S SCHOOL OF BEAUTY CULTURE
5206 Airline Dr., Houston 77002 *Type:* Private *Accred.:* 1988/1990 (SACS-COEI) *Calendar:* Courses of varying lengths *Degrees:* certificates *CEO:* Dir. Deborah Howell
Enroll: 64 (713) 699-2561

DEL MAR COLLEGE
101 Baldwin Blvd., Corpus Christi 78404-3897 *Type:* Public (district) junior *System:* Texas Higher Education Coordinating Board *Accred.:* 1946/1990 (SACS-CC) *Calendar:* Sem. plan *Degrees:* A *Prof. Accred.:* Art, Dental Assisting, Dental Hygiene, Diagnostic Medical Sonography, Engineering Technology (electrical), Medical Laboratory Technology (AMA), Music, Nursing (A), Radiography, Respiratory Therapy, Respiratory Therapy Technology, Surgical Technology *CEO:* Pres. Buddy R. Venters
Enroll: 8888 (512) 886-1203

DELTA CAREER INSTITUTE
1310 Pennsylvania Ave., Beaumont 77701 *Type:* Private business *Accred.:* 1990 (CCA-ACICS); 1990 (SACS-COEI candidate) *Calendar:* Qtr. plan *Degrees:* certificates, diplomas *CEO:* Dir. Willard R. Lively
Enroll: 780 (409) 833-6161

DIESEL SPECIALTY'S
615 S. Hwy. 80, 1104 N. Magnolia, Luling 78648 *Type:* Private *Accred.:* 1990 (SACS-COEI) *Calendar:* Courses of varying lengths *Degrees:* certificates *CEO:* Dir. Patty Chisolm
Enroll: 4 (512) 875-5648

DRAUGHON'S COLLEGE OF BUSINESS
2725 W. Seventh St., Fort Worth 76107 *Type:* Private *Accred.:* 1983/1988 (SACS-COEI) *Calendar:* Courses of varying lengths *Degrees:* certificates *CEO:* Dir. John L. Roberts
Enroll: 121 (817) 335-2381

DRAUGHON'S COLLEGE OF NURSING ASSISTANTS
1850 White Settlement Rd., Ste. 110, Fort Worth 76107 *Type:* Private *Accred.:* 1987/1990 (SACS-COEI) *Calendar:* Courses of varying lengths *Degrees:* certificates *CEO:* Dir. John L. Roberts
Enroll: 128 (817) 335-8400

DURHAM COLLEGE
1801 Wyoming St., El Paso 79902 *Type:* Private *Accred.:* 1990 (SACS-COEI) *Calendar:* Courses of varying lengths *Degrees:* certificates *CEO:* Dir. Perry Whitaker
Enroll: 289 (915) 533-9796

DURHAM COLLEGE
4618 San Pedro Ave., San Antonio 78212 *Type:* Private business *Accred.:* 1965/1988

(CCA-ACICS) *Calendar:* Courses of varying lengths *Degrees:* certificates, diplomas *CEO:* Dir. Isabel Alcala
Enroll: 623 (512) 736-1566

EAST TEXAS BAPTIST UNIVERSITY
1209 N. Grove Ave., Marshall 75670-1498 *Type:* Private (Southern Baptist) liberal arts *Accred.:* 1957/1989 (SACS-CC) *Calendar:* Sem. plan *Degrees:* A, B *Prof. Accred.:* Music *CEO:* Pres. Robert E. Craig
Enroll: 880 (214) 935-7963

EAST TEXAS STATE UNIVERSITY
ETSU Sta., Commerce 75429 *Type:* Public (state) *System:* Texas Higher Education Coordinating Board *Accred.:* 1925/1983 (SACS-CC) *Calendar:* Sem. plan *Degrees:* B, M, D *Prof. Accred.:* Business (B,M), Music, Social Work (B), Teacher Education (e,s,p) *CEO:* Pres. Jerry D. Morris
Enroll: 6271 (214) 886-5014

EAST TEXAS STATE UNIVERSITY AT TEXARKANA
P.O. Box 5518, Texarkana 75504 *Type:* Public (state) *System:* Texas Higher Education Coordinating Board *Accred.:* 1979/1985 (SACS-CC) *Calendar:* Sem. plan *Degrees:* B, M *CEO:* Pres. John F. Moss
Enroll: 822 (214) 838-6514

EASTFIELD COLLEGE
3737 Motley Dr., Mesquite 75150-2099 *Type:* Public (district) junior *System:* Dallas County Community College District *Accred.:* 1972/1983 (SACS-CC) *Calendar:* Sem. plan *Degrees:* A *CEO:* Pres. Justus Dan Sundermann
Enroll: 15362 (214) 324-7600

EL CENTRO COLLEGE
Main and S. Lamar Sts., Dallas 75202-3604 *Type:* Public (district) junior *System:* Dallas County Community College District *Accred.:* 1968/1983 (SACS-CC) *Calendar:* Sem. plan *Degrees:* A *Prof. Accred.:* Diagnostic Medical Sonography, Interior Design, Medical Laboratory Technology (AMA), Nursing (A), Radiography, Respiratory Therapy, Respiratory Therapy Technology, Surgical Technology *CEO:* Pres. Wright L. Lassiter, Jr.
Enroll: 7493 (214) 746-2010

EL PASO COMMUNITY COLLEGE
P.O. Box 20500, El Paso 79998 *Type:* Public (district) junior *System:* Texas Higher Education Coordinating Board *Accred.:* 1978/1983 (SACS-CC) *Calendar:* Sem. plan *Degrees:* A *Prof. Accred.:* Dental Assisting, Dental Hygiene, Diagnostic Medical Sonography, Medical Assisting (AMA), Medical Laboratory Technology (AMA), Medical Record Technology, Nursing (A), Radiation Therapy Technology, Radiography, Respiratory Therapy, Surgical Technology *CEO:* Pres. Leonardo de la Garza
Enroll: 8527 (915) 594-2000

EL PASO JOB CORPS CENTER
11155 Gateway W., El Paso 79935 *Type:* Private *Accred.:* 1986/1991 (SACS-COEI) *Calendar:* Courses of varying lengths *Degrees:* certificates *CEO:* Dir. Mary Young
Enroll: 451 (915) 594-0022

THE EPISCOPAL THEOLOGICAL SEMINARY OF THE SOUTHWEST
606 Rathervue Pl., P.O. Box 2247, Austin 78705 *Type:* Private (Episcopal) professional; graduate only *Accred.:* 1958/1983 (ATS); 1983 (SACS-CC) *Calendar:* 4-1-4 plan *Degrees:* P, M *CEO:* Dean Durstan R. McDonald
Enroll: 68 (512) 472-4133

EXECUTIVE SECRETARIAL SCHOOL
4849 Greenville Ave., Ste. 200, Dallas 75206-4125 *Type:* Private *Accred.:* 1969/1987 (CCA-ACICS); 1977/1987 (SACS-COEI) *Calendar:* Tri. plan *Degrees:* certificates, diplomas *CEO:* Chrmn. of the Bd. Jan B. Friedheim
Enroll: 391 (214) 369-9009

FORT WORTH TRADE SCHOOL
3617 Collinwood Ave., Fort Worth 76107 *Type:* Private *Accred.:* 1987 (SACS-COEI)

Calendar: Courses of varying lengths *Degrees:* certificates *CEO:* Dir. Larry Brosh
Enroll: 320   (817) 498-4655

FOUR-C COLLEGE
P.O. Box 4, Waco 76703 *Type:* Private business *Accred.:* 1973/1985 (CCA-ACICS) *Calendar:* Courses of varying lengths *Degrees:* certificates, diplomas *CEO:* Dir. Camilla M. McKenzie
Enroll: 483   (817) 756-7201

FRANK PHILLIPS COLLEGE
P.O. Box 5118, Borger 79008-5118 *Type:* Public (district) junior *System:* Texas Higher Education Coordinating Board *Accred.:* 1958/1989 (SACS-CC) *Calendar:* Sem. plan *Degrees:* A *CEO:* Pres. Vance W. Gipson
Enroll: 490   (806) 274-5311

GALVESTON COLLEGE
4015 Ave. Q, Galveston 77550 *Type:* Public (district) junior *System:* Texas Higher Education Coordinating Board *Accred.:* 1969/1984 (SACS-CC) *Calendar:* Sem. plan *Degrees:* A *Prof. Accred.:* Nuclear Medicine Technology, Nursing (A), Radiation Therapy Technology, Radiography, Respiratory Therapy, Surgical Technology *CEO:* Pres. Marc A. Nigliazzo
Enroll: 1480   (409) 763-6551

GARY JOB CORPS CENTER
Hwy. 21, P.O. Box 967, San Marcos 78667 *Type:* Public (federal) *Accred.:* 1985/1991 (SACS-COEI) *Calendar:* Courses of varying lengths *Degrees:* certificates *CEO:* Dir. Albert Perkins
Enroll: 1855   (512) 396-6652

GRAYSON COUNTY COLLEGE
6101 Grayson Dr., Denison 75020 *Type:* Public (district) junior *System:* Texas Higher Education Coordinating Board *Accred.:* 1967/1991 (SACS-CC) *Calendar:* Sem. plan *Degrees:* A *Prof. Accred.:* Dental Assisting, Medical Laboratory Technology (AMA), Nursing (A) *CEO:* Pres. James M. Williams, Jr.
Enroll: 3871   (214) 465-6030

GULF COAST TRADES CENTER
1375 FM Rd., P.O. Box 515, New Waverly 77358 *Type:* Private *Accred.:* 1984/1989 (SACS-COEI) *Calendar:* Courses of varying lengths *Degrees:* certificates *CEO:* Dir. Thomas M. Buzbee
Enroll: 199   (409) 344-6677

HALLMARK INSTITUTE OF TECHNOLOGY
1130 99th St., P.O. Box 14515, San Antonio 78214 *Type:* Private *Accred.:* 1971/1988 (CCA-ACTTS) *Calendar:* Courses of varying lengths *Degrees:* certificates *CEO:* Dir. Richard Fessler
Enroll: 513   (512) 924-8551

HALLMARK INSTITUTE OF TECHNOLOGY
10401 IH 10 W., San Antonio 78230 *Type:* Private *Accred.:* 1987 (CCA-ACTTS) *Calendar:* Courses of varying lengths *Degrees:* certificates *CEO:* Dir. Richard Fester
Enroll: 652   (512) 690-9000

HARDIN-SIMMONS UNIVERSITY
2200 Hickory St., Abilene 79698 *Type:* Private (Southern Baptist) *Accred.:* 1927/1987 (SACS-CC) *Calendar:* Sem. plan *Degrees:* A, B, M *Prof. Accred.:* Music, Social Work (B) *CEO:* Pres. Edwin L. Hall
Enroll: 1567   (915) 670-1000

HILL COLLEGE
112 Lamar Dr., P.O. Box 619, Hillsboro 76645 *Type:* Public (district) junior *System:* Texas Higher Education Coordinating Board *Accred.:* 1963/1990 (SACS-CC) *Calendar:* Sem. plan *Degrees:* A *CEO:* Pres. William R. Auvenshine
Enroll: 1143   (817) 582-2555

HOUSTON BALLET ACADEMY
1921 W. Bell St., P.O. Box 130487, Houston 77219-0487 *Type:* Private *Calendar:* Courses of varying lengths *Degrees:* certificates *Prof. Accred.:* Dance *CEO:* Admin. Kelli Walters Dunning
   (713) 523-6300

HOUSTON BAPTIST UNIVERSITY
7502 Fondren Rd., Houston 77074-3298 *Type:* Private (Southern Baptist) liberal arts

Accred.: 1968/1991 (SACS-CC) *Calendar:* Qtr. plan *Degrees:* A, B, M *Prof. Accred.:* Nursing (A,B) *CEO:* Pres. E. Douglas Hodo
Enroll: 2252 (713) 774-7661

HOUSTON COMMUNITY COLLEGE
22 Waugh Dr., P.O. Box 7849, Houston 77270-7849 *Type:* Public (district) junior *System:* Texas Higher Education Coordinating Board *Accred.:* 1977/1982 (SACS-CC) *Calendar:* Sem. plan *Degrees:* A *Prof. Accred.:* Dental Assisting, Engineering Technology (electrical), Medical Laboratory Technology (AMA), Medical Record Technology, Nuclear Medicine Technology, Occupational Therapy Assisting, Physical Therapy Assisting, Radiography, Respiratory Therapy, Respiratory Therapy Technology, Surgical Technology *CEO:* Pres. Charles A. Green
Enroll: 26830 (713) 869-5021

CENTRAL COLLEGE
1300 Holman Ave., Houston, TX 77004
CEO: Pres. James Engle
(713) 630-7205

COLLEGE WITHOUT WALLS
4310 Dunlavy St., Houston, TX 77006
CEO: Pres. Baltazar Acevedo
(713) 868-8797

NORTHEAST COLLEGE
4638 Airline Dr., Houston, TX 77022
CEO: Pres. Elaine Adams
(713) 699-1673

NORTHWEST COLLEGE
16360 Park Ten Pl., Houston, TX 77084
CEO: Pres. Judith K. Winn
(713) 492-7236

SOUTHEAST COLLEGE
6815 Rustic St., Houston, TX 77012
CEO: Pres. Sylvia Ramos
(713) 641-2725

SOUTHWEST COLLEGE
5407 Gulfton St., Houston, TX 77081
CEO: Pres. Sue Cox
(713) 661-4589

HOUSTON GRADUATE SCHOOL OF THEOLOGY
6910 Fannin St., Ste. 207, Houston 77030 *Type:* Private professional *Accred.:* 1986/1991 (SACS-CC) *Calendar:* Sem. plan *Degrees:* M *CEO:* Pres. Delbert P. Vaughn
Enroll: 159 (713) 791-9505

HOUSTON TRAINING SCHOOL
709 Shotwell St., Houston 77020 *Type:* Private *Accred.:* 1979/1988 (SACS-COEI) *Calendar:* Courses of varying lengths *Degrees:* certificates *CEO:* Dir. Diana Rodriguez
Enroll: 598 (713) 672-9607

BRANCH CAMPUS
6969 Gulf Fwy., Houston, TX 77087
CEO: Dir. Jay Martinez
(713) 649-5050

HOWARD COLLEGE
1001 Birdwell La., Big Spring 79720 *Type:* Public (district) junior *System:* Howard County Junior College District *Accred.:* 1955/1986 (SACS-CC) *Calendar:* Sem. plan *Degrees:* A *Prof. Accred.:* Dental Hygiene, Nursing (A) *CEO:* Pres. Bob E. Riley
Enroll: 1760 (915) 264-5000

HOWARD PAYNE UNIVERSITY
1000 Fisk Ave., Brownwood 76801 *Type:* Private (Southern Baptist) liberal arts *Accred.:* 1948/1984 (SACS-CC) *Calendar:* Sem. plan *Degrees:* B *Prof. Accred.:* Music *CEO:* Pres. Don Newbury, Jr.
Enroll: 1217 (915) 646-1084

HUSTON-TILLOTSON COLLEGE
1820 E. Eighth St., Austin 78702-2793 *Type:* Private (United Methodist/United Church of Christ) liberal arts *Accred.:* 1943/1990 (SACS-CC) *Calendar:* Sem. plan *Degrees:* B *CEO:* Pres. Joseph T. McMillan, Jr.
Enroll: 714 (512) 476-7421

ITT TECHNICAL INSTITUTE
2201 Arlington Downs Rd., Arlington 76011 *Type:* Private *Accred.:* 1983/1988 (CCA-ACTTS) *Calendar:* Qtr. plan *Degrees:* A, certificates *CEO:* Dir. Tommy D. Marley
Enroll: 530 (817) 640-7100

ITT TECHNICAL INSTITUTE
1821 Rutherford La., Austin 78754 *Type:* Private *Accred.:* 1986 (CCA-ACTTS) *Calendar:* Qtr. plan *Degrees:* A, certificates *CEO:* Dir. Margaret Harrison
Enroll: 660 (512) 339-8200

ITT TECHNICAL INSTITUTE
1640 Eastgate Dr., No. 100, Garland 75041 *Type:* Private *Accred.:* 1989 (CCA-ACTTS) *Calendar:* Qtr. plan *Degrees:* A, certificates *CEO:* Dir. Maureen K. Clements
(214) 279-0500

ITT TECHNICAL INSTITUTE
9421 W. Sam Houston Pkwy., Houston 77099 *Type:* Private *Accred.:* 1983/1988 (CCA-ACTTS) *Calendar:* Qtr. plan *Degrees:* A, certificates *CEO:* Dir. Louis Christensen
Enroll: 544 (713) 270-1634

ITT TECHNICAL INSTITUTE
15621 Blue Ash Dr., Ste. 160, Houston 77090 *Type:* Private *Accred.:* 1988 (CCA-ACTTS) *Calendar:* Qtr. plan *Degrees:* A, certificates *CEO:* Dir. Jeff Cochran
Enroll: 426 (713) 873-0512

ITT TECHNICAL INSTITUTE
4242 Piedras Dr. E., San Antonio 78228 *Type:* Private *Accred.:* 1988 (CCA-ACTTS) *Calendar:* Qtr. plan *Degrees:* A, certificates *CEO:* Dir. Barry Simich
(512) 737-1881

INCARNATE WORD COLLEGE
4301 Broadway, San Antonio 78209-6397 *Type:* Private (Roman Catholic) liberal arts *Accred.:* 1925/1985 (SACS-CC) *Calendar:* Sem. plan *Degrees:* B, M *Prof. Accred.:* Nuclear Medicine Technology, Nursing (B,M) *CEO:* Pres. Louis J. Agnese, Jr.
Enroll: 2080 (512) 828-1261

INSTITUTE FOR CHRISTIAN STUDIES
1909 University Ave., Austin 78705 *Type:* Private *Accred.:* 1987 (SACS-CC) *Calendar:* Sem. plan *Degrees:* B *CEO:* Pres. James W. Thompson
Enroll: 40 (512) 477-5701

INSTITUTE OF NURSING TECHNOLOGY
1575 W. Mockingbird La., Ste. 600, Dallas 75235 *Type:* Private *Accred.:* 1979/1989 (SACS-COEI) *Calendar:* Courses of varying lengths *Degrees:* certificates *CEO:* Dir. Horace Corley
Enroll: 120 (214) 630-4541

INTERACTIVE LEARNING SYSTEMS
8585 N. Stemmons Fwy., Twin Towers, No. M-50, Dallas 75247 *Type:* Private *Accred.:* 1989 (SACS-COEI) *Calendar:* Courses of varying lengths *Degrees:* certificates *CEO:* Dir. Martin Vogt
Enroll: 115 (214) 637-3377

BRANCH CAMPUS
10200 Richmond Ave., Houston, TX 77042 *CEO:* Dir. Harry Mauz
(713) 782-5161

INTERNATIONAL AVIATION AND TRAVEL ACADEMY
300 W. Arbrook Blvd., Arlington 76014-3105 *Type:* Private *Accred.:* 1988 (NHSC); 1979/1989 (SACS-COEI) *Calendar:* Courses of varying lengths *Degrees:* certificates *CEO:* Pres. Kenneth Woods
Enroll: 661 (817) 784-7000

BRANCH CAMPUS
9310 Max Conrad Dr., Spring, TX 77379 *CEO:* Dir. Jim Moore
(800) 627-4379

INTERNATIONAL BARBER SCHOOL OF EL PASO
9515 Gateway W., Ste. L, El Paso 79925-7250 *Type:* Private *Accred.:* 1991 (CCA-ACTTS) *Calendar:* Courses of varying lengths *Degrees:* certificates *CEO:* Owner Bob C. Lewis
(915) 594-9089

INTERNATIONAL BUSINESS COLLEGE
4121 Montana Ave., El Paso 79903 *Type:* Private business *Accred.:* 1969/1987 (CCA-ACICS) *Calendar:* Courses of varying lengths *Degrees:* certificates, diplomas *CEO:* Dir. Robert C. Brown
Enroll: 864 (915) 566-8644

INTERNATIONAL BUSINESS COLLEGE
3628 50th St., Lubbock 79413 *Type:* Private business *Accred.:* 1985/1987 (CCA-ACICS) *Calendar:* Courses of varying lengths *Degrees:* certificates, diplomas *CEO:* Dir. Dianna Wright
Enroll: 864 (806) 797-1933

BRANCH CAMPUS
1002 N. Walnut St., Sherman, TX 75090
CEO: Dir. Lee Ann Bubany
(806) 797-1933

INTERNATIONAL CAREER SCHOOL
7647 Bellfort St., Houston 77061-1707 *Type:* Private *Accred.:* 1991 (CCA-ACTTS) *Calendar:* Courses of varying lengths *Degrees:* certificates *CEO:* Dir. Sam Al-Rifai
(713) 649-0067

INTERNATIONAL CORRESPONDENCE INSTITUTE
6300 N. Belt Line Rd., Irving 75063 *Type:* Private home study *Accred.:* 1977/1988 (NHSC) *Calendar:* Courses of varying lengths *Degrees:* A, B *CEO:* Pres. George M. Flahery
(800) 444-0424

INTERNATIONAL TECHNICAL INSTITUTE
2121 Main St., Ste. 214, Dallas 75201 *Type:* Private *Accred.:* 1991 (CCA-ACTTS) *Calendar:* Courses of varying lengths *Degrees:* certificates *CEO:* Dir. Delores Kadlec
(214) 741-7503

IVERSON INSTITUTE OF COURT REPORTING
1200 Copeland Rd., Ste. 305, Arlington 76011 *Type:* Private *Accred.:* 1988 (SACS-COEI) *Calendar:* Coures of varying lengths *Degrees:* certificates *CEO:* Dir. Audrey Iveson
Enroll: 86 (817) 274-6465

JACKI NELL EXECUTIVE SECRETARY SCHOOL
2538 S. Congress Ave., Austin 78704 *Type:* Private business *Accred.:* 1978/1987 (CCA-ACICS) *Calendar:* Courses of varying lengths *Degrees:* certificates, diplomas *CEO:* Exec. Dir. Jackie Ward
Enroll: 295 (512) 447-9415

JACKSONVILLE COLLEGE
500 W. Pine St., Jacksonville 75766 *Type:* Private (Baptist) junior *Accred.:* 1974/1989 (SACS-CC) *Calendar:* Sem. plan *Degrees:* A *CEO:* Pres. Edwin Crank
Enroll: 257 (214) 586-2518

JARVIS CHRISTIAN COLLEGE
P.O. Drawer G, Hawkins 75765 *Type:* Private (Disciples of Christ) liberal arts *Accred.:* 1967/1983 (SACS-CC) *Calendar:* Sem. plan *Degrees:* A, B *CEO:* Pres. Sebetha Jenkins
Enroll: 589 (214) 769-2174

KD STUDIO
2600 Stemmons Fwy., No. 117, Dallas 75207 *Type:* Private *Calendar:* Courses of varying lengths *Degrees:* certificates *Prof. Accred.:* Theatre *CEO:* Pres. Kathy Tyner
(214) 638-0484

KEITH'S METRO HAIR ACADEMY
4123 W. 34th St., Amarillo 79109 *Type:* Private *Accred.:* 1988 (CCA-ACTTS) *Calendar:* Courses of varying lengths *Degrees:* certificates *CEO:* Dir. Frances Clark
Enroll: 49 (806) 355-7277

KILGORE COLLEGE
1100 Broadway Blvd., Kilgore 75662 *Type:* Public (district) junior *System:* Texas Higher Education Coordinating Board *Accred.:* 1939/1989 (SACS-CC) *Calendar:* Sem. plan *Degrees:* A *Prof. Accred.:* Medical Laboratory Technology (AMA), Nursing (A), Physical Therapy Assisting, Radiography *CEO:* Pres. Bert E. Woodruff
Enroll: 5717 (214) 984-8531

KINGWOOD COLLEGE
20000 Kingwood Dr., Kingwood 77339 *Type:* Public (district) junior *System:* North Harris Montgomery College District *Accred.:* 1976/1991 (SACS-CC) *Calendar:* Sem. plan *Degrees:* A *CEO:* Pres. Stephen Head
(713) 359-1600

LAMAR UNIVERSITY AT BEAUMONT
4400 Martin Luther King Pkwy., Beaumont 77710 *Type:* Public *System:* Lamar University System *Accred.:* 1955/1988 (SACS-CC) *Calendar:* Sem. plan *Degrees:* A, B, M, D *Prof. Accred.:* Audiology, Business (B,M), Dental Hygiene, Engineering (chemical, civil, electrical, industrial, mechanical), Music, Nursing (A,B), Radiography, Respiratory Therapy, Respiratory Therapy Technology, Social Work (B), Speech-Language Pathology, Teacher Education (e,s,p) *CEO:* Interim Pres. John P. Idoux
Enroll: 9350 (409) 880-8504

LAMAR UNIVERSITY AT ORANGE
410 Front St., Orange 77630 *Type:* Public *System:* Lamar University System *Accred.:* 1989 (SACS-CC) *Calendar:* Sem. plan *Degrees:* A *CEO:* Pres. Steve Maradian
Enroll: 970 (409) 883-7750

LAMAR UNIVERSITY AT PORT ARTHUR
P.O. Box 310, Port Arthur 77641-0310 *Type:* Public *System:* Lamar University System *Accred.:* 1988 (SACS-CC) *Calendar:* Sem. plan *Degrees:* A *CEO:* Pres. W. Sam Monroe
Enroll: 1457 (409) 983-4921

LAREDO JUNIOR COLLEGE
W. End Washington St., Laredo 78040-4395 *Type:* Public (district) junior *System:* Texas Higher Education Coordinating Board *Accred.:* 1957/1989 (SACS-CC) *Calendar:* Sem. plan *Degrees:* A *Prof. Accred.:* Medical Laboratory Technology (AMA), Nursing (A), Physical Therapy Assisting, Radiography *CEO:* Pres. Roger L. Worsley
Enroll: 6841 (512) 722-4395

LAREDO STATE UNIVERSITY
One W. End Washington St., Laredo 78040-9960 *Type:* Public (state) *System:* Texas A&M University System *Accred.:* 1970/1984 (SACS-CC) *Calendar:* Sem. plan *Degrees:* B, M *CEO:* Pres. Leo Sayavedra
Enroll: 837 (512) 722-8001

LARRY'S BARBER AND HAIR STYLING SCHOOL
1111 W. Ledbetter Dr., Ste. 500, Dallas 75224 *Type:* Private *Accred.:* 1991 (CCA-ACTTS) *Calendar:* Courses of varying lengths *Degrees:* certificates *CEO:* Dir. Larry S. Johnson
(214) 372-4871

LECHEF CULINARY ARTS SCHOOL
6020-B Dillard Cir., Austin 78752 *Type:* Private *Accred.:* 1990 (SACS-COEI) *Calendar:* Courses of varying lengths *Degrees:* certificates *CEO:* Dir. Ronald Boston
Enroll: 74 (512) 323-2511

LETOURNEAU UNIVERSITY
2100 Mobberly Ave., P.O. Box 7001, Longview 75607-7001 *Type:* Private liberal arts and professional *Accred.:* 1970/1986 (SACS-CC) *Calendar:* Sem. plan *Degrees:* A, B *Prof. Accred.:* Engineering (general) *CEO:* Pres. Alvin O. Austin
Enroll: 983 (214) 753-0231

LEE COLLEGE
511 S. Whiting St., Baytown 77520-4703 *Type:* Public (district) junior *System:* Texas Higher Education Coordinating Board *Accred.:* 1948/1985 (SACS-CC) *Calendar:* Sem. plan *Degrees:* A *Prof. Accred.:* Nursing (A) *CEO:* Interim Pres. J. B. Whitley
Enroll: 3805 (713) 427-5611

LINCOLN TECHNICAL INSTITUTE
2501 E. Arkansas La., Grand Prairie 75051 *Type:* Private *Accred.:* 1968/1988 (CCA-ACTTS) *Calendar:* Courses of varying lengths *Degrees:* diplomas *CEO:* Dir. E. Lynn Thacker
Enroll: 772 (214) 660-5701

LON MORRIS COLLEGE
822 College Ave., Jacksonville 75766 *Type:* Private (United Methodist) junior *Accred.:* 1927/1984 (SACS-CC) *Calendar:* Sem. plan *Degrees:* A *CEO:* Pres. Webb Faulk Landrum
Enroll: 323 (214) 586-2471

Accredited Institutions   **Texas**

LUBBOCK CHRISTIAN UNIVERSITY
5601 W. 19th St., Lubbock 79407-2099 *Type:* Private (Church of Christ) liberal arts *Accred.:* 1963/1988 (SACS-CC) *Calendar:* Sem. plan *Degrees:* A, B *Prof. Accred.:* Social Work (B), Teacher Education (e,s,p) *CEO:* Pres. Steven S. Lemley
Enroll: 951   (806) 796-8800

M&M WORD PROCESSING INSTITUTE
2650 Fountain View Dr., Ste. 127, Houston 77057-7611 *Type:* Private *Accred.:* 1991 (CCA-ACTTS) *Calendar:* Courses of varying lengths *Degrees:* certificates *CEO:* Owner Olgha Isid
(713) 781-4384

M. WEEKS WELDING LABORATORY TESTING AND SCHOOL
4405 Hwy. 347, Nederland 77627 *Type:* Private *Accred.:* 1991 (SACS-COEI) *Calendar:* Courses of varying lengths *Degrees:* certificates, diplomas *CEO:* Pres. Morris Weeks
Enroll: 20   (409) 727-7640

MTA SCHOOL
2227 Irving Blvd., Dallas 75207 *Type:* Private *Accred.:* 1988 (CCA-ACTTS) *Calendar:* Courses of varying lengths *Degrees:* certificates *CEO:* Dir. Richard Raymond
(214) 631-8113

MTA SCHOOL
723 Coliseum Rd., San Antonio 78219 *Type:* Private *Accred.:* 1991 (CCA-ACTTS) *Calendar:* Courses of varying lengths *Degrees:* certificates *CEO:* Dir. Cliff Phillips
(512) 233-8770

MANSFIELD BUSINESS COLLEGE
714 N. Watson Rd., Ste. 300, Arlington 76011 *Type:* Private business *Accred.:* 1968/1986 (CCA-ACICS) *Calendar:* Qtr. plan *Degrees:* certificates, diplomas *CEO:* Dir. Edward R. Murray
Enroll: 634   (817) 649-5166

BRANCH CAMPUS
2200 W. Alameda Ave., Denver, CO 80223 *CEO:* Dir. Douglas G. Bouche
(303) 936-5951

BRANCH CAMPUS
10325 Lake June Rd., Ste. 800, Dallas, TX 75217 *CEO:* Dir. Linda Smith
(214) 216-1996

MANSFIELD BUSINESS COLLEGE
4025 E. Belknap St., Fort Worth 76111 *Type:* Private business *Accred.:* 1989 (CCA-ACICS) *Calendar:* Courses of varying lengths *Degrees:* certificates, diplomas *CEO:* Dir. Michael Smith
Enroll: 1220   (817) 834-1926

BRANCH CAMPUS
Wynnewood Village Ctr., Ste. 740, Dallas, TX 75224 *CEO:* Dir. Skip Walls
(214) 943-7900

BRANCH CAMPUS
6101 Montana Ave., El Paso, TX 79925 *CEO:* Dir. James Laird
(915) 772-0555

BRANCH CAMPUS
129 Little York Rd., Houston, TX 77076 *CEO:* Dir. Annette Miller
(713) 692-0635

MANSFIELD BUSINESS COLLEGE
3615 Culebra Rd., San Antonio 78228 *Type:* Private business *Accred.:* 1986/1988 (CCA-ACICS) *Calendar:* Courses of varying lengths *Degrees:* certificates, diplomas *CEO:* Dir. Frank M. Jennings
Enroll: 1244   (512) 432-3668

BRANCH CAMPUS
2800 S. IH 35, Austin, TX 78704 *CEO:* Dir. John Weimer
(512) 440-8222

BRANCH CAMPUS
6994 S. Zarzamora St., San Antonio, TX 78224 *CEO:* Dir. Nancy Ellis
(512) 927-3924

BRANCH CAMPUS
807 Roosevelt Ave., San Antonio, TX 78210 *CEO:* Dir. John T. Lewis
(512) 533-2277

MASSEY BUSINESS COLLEGE
P.O. Box 630-444, Nacogdoches 75963 *Type:* Private business *Accred.:* 1984/1990 (CCA-ACICS) *Calendar:* Courses of varying lengths *Degrees:* certificates, diplomas *CEO:* Pres. Clarence E. Chandler
Enroll: 228 (409) 564-3788

MASSEY BUSINESS SCHOOL
2820 SPID, Ste. 180, Corpus Christi 78415 *Type:* Private business *Accred.:* 1990 (CCA-ACICS) *Calendar:* Qtr. plan *Degrees:* certificates, diplomas *CEO:* Dir. Manual Colomo
Enroll: 437 (512) 883-5700

MASSEY BUSINESS SCHOOL
4916 Main St., Houston 77002 *Type:* Private business *Accred.:* 1954/1985 (CCA-ACICS); 1984/1989 (SACS-COEI) *Calendar:* Qtr. plan *Degrees:* certificates, diplomas *CEO:* Pres. Paul E. Compton
Enroll: 485 (713) 521-0426

MCLENNAN COMMUNITY COLLEGE
1400 College Dr., Waco 76708 *Type:* Public (district) junior *System:* Texas Higher Education Coordinating Board *Accred.:* 1968/1982 (SACS-CC) *Calendar:* Sem. plan *Degrees:* A *Prof. Accred.:* Medical Laboratory Technology (AMA), Nursing (A), Physical Therapy Assisting, Radiography, Respiratory Therapy Technology *CEO:* Pres. Dennis Michaelis
Enroll: 4280 (817) 756-6551

MCMURRY UNIVERSITY
S. 14th St. and Sayles Blvd., Abilene 79697 *Type:* Private (United Methodist) liberal arts *Accred.:* 1949/1989 (SACS-CC) *Calendar:* Sem. plan *Degrees:* A,B *CEO:* Pres. Thomas K. Kim
Enroll: 1288 (915) 691-6200

METLS WELDING SCHOOL
7645 Gulf Fwy., P.O. Box 262585, Houston 77207 *Type:* Private *Accred.:* 1985/1990 (SACS-COEI) *Calendar:* Courses of varying lengths *Degrees:* certificates, diplomas *CEO:* Dir. Thomas C. Reed
Enroll: 287 (713) 641-0436

BRANCH CAMPUS
2302 N. Port Ave., Corpus Christi, TX 78469 *CEO:* Dir. Joe Morris
(512) 883-4357

METRO BUSINESS ACADEMY
3225-B Commerce St., P.O. Box 7609, Amarillo 79114 *Type:* Private *Accred.:* 1985 (CCA-ACTTS) *Calendar:* Courses of varying lengths *Degrees:* certificates *CEO:* Dir. Frances Clark
Enroll: 20 (806) 354-0580

METRO HAIR ACADEMY—LUBBOCK
2806 Ave. Q, Lubbock 79405 *Type:* Private *Accred.:* 1981/1986 (CCA-ACTTS) *Calendar:* Courses of varying lengths *Degrees:* certificates *CEO:* Dir. Janet M. Doe
Enroll: 61 (806) 744-8496

MICROCOMPUTER TECHNOLOGY INSTITUTE
7277 Regency Square Blvd., Houston 77036 *Type:* Private *Accred.:* 1983/1988 (CCA-ACTTS) *Calendar:* Courses of varying lengths *Degrees:* certificates, diplomas *CEO:* Pres. Robert Obenhaus
Enroll: 1033 (713) 974-7181

BRANCH CAMPUS
17164 Blackhawk Blvd., Friendswood, TX 77546 *CEO:* Dir. Robert Grenwelge
(713) 996-8180

MIDLAND COLLEGE
3600 N. Garfield St., Midland 79705 *Type:* Public (district) junior *System:* Texas Higher Education Coordinating Board *Accred.:* 1975/1990 (SACS-CC) *Calendar:* Sem. plan *Degrees:* A *Prof. Accred.:* Nursing (A), Radiography, Respiratory Therapy, Respiratory Therapy Technology *CEO:* Pres. David E. Daniel
Enroll: 2799 (915) 685-4500

MIDWESTERN STATE UNIVERSITY
3400 Taft Blvd., Wichita Falls 76308-2099 *Type:* Public (state) *System:* Texas Higher Education Coordinating Board *Accred.:* 1950/1982 (SACS-CC) *Calendar:* Sem. plan *Degrees:* A, B, M *Prof. Accred.:* Dental Hygiene, Engineering Technology (manu-

facturing), Music, Nursing (B), Radiography, Social Work (B-candidate), Teacher Education (e,s,p) *CEO:* Pres. Louis J. Rodriguez
Enroll: 4602 (817) 692-6611

MISS WADE'S FASHION MERCHANDISING COLLEGE
Apparel Mart, Ste. M5120, P.O. Box 586343, Dallas 75258 *Type:* Private *Accred.:* 1971/1987 (CCA-ACTTS); 1985/1990 (SACS-CC) *Calendar:* Tri. plan *Degrees:* A *CEO:* Pres. Frank J. Tortoriello, Jr.
Enroll: 321 (214) 637-3530

MODERN COLLEGE OF HAIR DESIGN
5555 N. Lamar Blvd., Bldg. J-103, Austin 78751 *Type:* Private *Accred.:* 1991 (SACS-COEI) *Calendar:* Courses of varying lengths *Degrees:* certificates *CEO:* Dir. David Meck
Enroll: 12 (512) 453-9019

MOUNTAIN VIEW COLLEGE
4849 W. Illinois Ave., Dallas 75211-6599 *Type:* Public (district) junior *System:* Dallas County Community College District *Accred.:* 1972/1983 (SACS-CC) *Calendar:* Sem. plan *Degrees:* A *CEO:* Pres. William H. Jordan
Enroll: 4821 (214) 333-8700

NATIONAL EDUCATION CENTER—BRYMAN CAMPUS
9724 Beechnut St., Ste. 300, Houston 77036 *Type:* Private *Accred.:* 1973/1988 (CCA-ACTTS) *Calendar:* Courses of varying lengths *Degrees:* diplomas *Prof. Accred.:* Medical Assisting *CEO:* Dir. Craig Wood
Enroll: 1578 (713) 776-3656

BRANCH CAMPUS
262 N. Sam Houston Pkwy. E., Ste. 400, Houston, TX 77060 *CEO:* Dir. Ed Rogan
(713) 447-6656

NATIONAL EDUCATION CENTER—FORT WORTH CAMPUS
300 E. Loop 820, Fort Worth 76112-1225 *Type:* Private *Accred.:* 1991 (CCA-ACTTS) *Calendar:* Courses of varying lengths *Degrees:* diplomas *CEO:* Dir. D. Lynn Johnson
(817) 451-0017

NATIONAL EDUCATION CENTER—NATIONAL INSTITUTE OF TECHNOLOGY CAMPUS
10945 Estates La., Dallas 75238 *Type:* Private *Accred.:* 1969/1988 (CCA-ACTTS) *Calendar:* Qtr. plan *Degrees:* diplomas *CEO:* Dir. Ron Sandler
Enroll: 673 (214) 503-9373

NATIONAL EDUCATION CENTER—NATIONAL INSTITUTE OF TECHNOLOGY CAMPUS
3622 Fredericksburg Rd., San Antonio 78201 *Type:* Private *Accred.:* 1985 (CCA-ACTTS) *Calendar:* Qtr. plan *Degrees:* diplomas *CEO:* Dir. Ed Howard
Enroll: 496 (512) 733-6000

NAVARRO COLLEGE
3200 W. Seventh Ave., Corsicana 75110 *Type:* Public (district) junior *System:* Texas Higher Education Coordinating Board *Accred.:* 1954/1985 (SACS-CC) *Calendar:* Sem. plan *Degrees:* A *Prof. Accred.:* Medical Laboratory Technology *CEO:* Pres. Gerald E. Burson
Enroll: 3049 (903) 874-6501

NORTH HARRIS COLLEGE
2700 W.W. Thorne Dr., Houston 77073 *Type:* Public (district) junior *System:* North Harris Montgomery College District *Accred.:* 1976/1991 (SACS-CC) *Calendar:* Sem. plan *Degrees:* A *Prof. Accred.:* Dental Assisting, Nursing (A), Respiratory Therapy, Respiratory Therapy Technology *CEO:* Pres. Sanford C. Shugart
(713) 443-5400

NORTH LAKE COLLEGE
5001 N. MacArthur Blvd., Irving 75038-3899 *Type:* Public (district) junior *System:* Dallas County Community College District *Accred.:* 1979/1983 (SACS-CC) *Calendar:* Sem. plan *Degrees:* A *CEO:* Pres. James F. Horton, Jr.
Enroll: 3727 (214) 659-5229

NORTHEAST TEXAS COMMUNITY COLLEGE
P.O. Drawer 1307, Mount Pleasant 75455-1307 *Type:* Public (district) junior *System:* Texas Higher Education Coordinating Board *Accred.:* 1987 (SACS-CC) *Calendar:* Sem. plan *Degrees:* A *CEO:* Pres. Michael C. Bruner
Enroll: 1281 (214) 572-1911

OBLATE SCHOOL OF THEOLOGY
285 Oblate Dr., San Antonio 78216-6693 *Type:* Private (Roman Catholic) *Accred.:* 1982/1989 (ATS); 1968/1989 (SACS-CC) *Calendar:* Sem. plan *Degrees:* P, M *CEO:* Pres. Patrick Guidon, O.M.I.
Enroll: 128 (512) 341-1366

OCCUPATIONAL SAFETY TRAINING INSTITUTE
9000 W. Bellfort St., Ste. 400, Houston 77031 *Type:* Private *Accred.:* 1991 (SACS-COEI) *Calendar:* Courses of varying lengths *Degrees:* certificates *CEO:* Dir. Eva Bonilla
Enroll: 10 (713) 270-6882

THE OCEAN CORPORATION
10840 Rockley Rd., Houston 77099-3416 *Type:* Private *Accred.:* 1991 (CCA-ACTTS) *Calendar:* Courses of varying lengths *Degrees:* certificates *CEO:* Pres. Les Joiner
(713) 530-0202

ODESSA COLLEGE
201 W. University Blvd., Odessa 79764 *Type:* Public (district) junior *System:* Texas Higher Education Coordinating Board *Accred.:* 1952/1982 (SACS-CC) *Calendar:* Sem. plan *Degrees:* A *Prof. Accred.:* Medical Laboratory Technology (AMA), Music, Nursing (A), Physical Therapy Assisting, Radiography, Respiratory Therapy, Respiratory Therapy Technology, Surgical Technology *CEO:* Pres. Philip T. Speegle
Enroll: 4350 (915) 335-6400

THE OFFICE CAREERS CENTRE
7904 N.E. Loop 820, No. D, Fort Worth 76180 *Type:* Private *Accred.:* 1988 (SACS-COEI) *Calendar:* Courses of varying lengths *Degrees:* certificates *CEO:* Dir. Susan Bauer
Enroll: 16 (817) 284-8107

OUR LADY OF THE LAKE UNIVERSITY
411 S.W. 24th St., San Antonio 78285 *Type:* Private (Roman Catholic) liberal arts *Accred.:* 1923/1982 (SACS-CC) *Calendar:* Sem. plan *Degrees:* B, M, D (candidate) *Prof. Accred.:* Social Work (B,M), Speech-Language Pathology *CEO:* Pres. Elizabeth Anne Sueltenfuss
Enroll: 1950 (512) 434-6711

PCI HEALTH TRAINING CENTER
8101 John Carpenter Fwy., Dallas 75247-4720 *Type:* Private *Accred.:* 1991 (CCA-ACTTS) *Calendar:* Courses of varying lengths *Degrees:* certificates *CEO:* Dir. Bobby Prince
(214) 630-0568

PALO ALTO COLLEGE
1400 W. Villaret Blvd., San Antonio 78224 *Type:* Public (district) junior *System:* Alamo Community College District *Accred.:* 1987 (SACS-CC) *Calendar:* Sem. plan *Degrees:* A *CEO:* Pres. Byron Skinner
Enroll: 3234 (512) 921-5000

PANOLA COLLEGE
1109 W. Panola St., Carthage 75633 *Type:* Public (district) junior *System:* Texas Higher Education Coordinating Board *Accred.:* 1960/1990 (SACS-CC) *Calendar:* Sem. plan *Degrees:* A *CEO:* Pres. Gary D. McDaniel
Enroll: 1278 (903) 693-2000

PARALEGAL TRAINING CENTER
711 Bay Area Blvd., Ste. 102, Webster 77598 *Type:* Private *Accred.:* 1990 (SACS-COEI) *Calendar:* Courses of varying lengths *Degrees:* certificates, diplomas *CEO:* Dir. Judy K. Hatfield
Enroll: 17 (713) 338-2668

PARIS JUNIOR COLLEGE
2400 Clarkville St., Paris 75460 *Type:* Public (district) junior *System:* Texas Higher Education Coordinating Board *Accred.:* 1934/1982 (SACS-CC) *Calendar:* Sem. plan *Degrees:* A *Prof. Accred.:* Nursing (A) *CEO:* Pres. Bobby R. Walters
Enroll: 1876 (903) 785-7661

PARKER COLLEGE OF CHIROPRACTIC
2500-2550 Walnut Hill La., Dallas 75229 *Type:* Private professional *Accred.:* 1987/1991 (SACS-CC) *Calendar:* Tri. plan *Degrees:* D *Prof. Accred.:* Chiropractic Education *CEO:* Pres. James W. Parker
Enroll: 646 (214) 438-6932

PAUL QUINN COLLEGE
3837 Simpson Stuart Rd., Dallas 75241 *Type:* Private (African Methodist Episcopal) liberal arts *Accred.:* 1972/1987 (SACS-CC probational) *Calendar:* Sem. plan *Degrees:* B *Prof. Accred.:* Social Work (B) *CEO:* Pres. Warren W. Morgan
Enroll: 1009 (214) 371-1015

PHARR VOCATIONAL SCHOOL
1006 E. Ferguson Rd., P.O. Box 750, Pharr 78577 *Type:* Private *Accred.:* 1982/1987 (SACS-COEI) *Calendar:* Courses of varying lengths *Degrees:* certificates *CEO:* Dir. David Coers, Jr.
Enroll: 614 (512) 783-1180

PHILLIPS SCHOOL OF BUSINESS AND TECHNOLOGY
119 W. Eighth St., Austin 78701 *Type:* Private business *Accred.:* 1967/1985 (CCA-ACICS) *Calendar:* Sem. plan *Degrees:* certificates, diplomas *CEO:* Pres. Karen Gautreau
Enroll: 695 (512) 478-3446

POLYTECHNIC INSTITUTE
4625 North Fwy., Houston 77022-2929 *Type:* Private *Accred.:* 1991 (CCA-ACTTS) *Calendar:* Courses of varying lengths *Degrees:* certificates *CEO:* Pres. Luis R. Cano
(713) 694-6027

PRAIRIE VIEW A&M UNIVERSITY
P.O. Box 188, Prairie View 77446 *Type:* Public (state) *System:* Texas A&M University System *Accred.:* 1934/1990 (SACS-CC) *Calendar:* Sem. plan *Degrees:* B, M *Prof. Accred.:* Architecture (B-candidate), Engineering Technology (computer, electrical), Home Economics, Nursing (B), Social Work (B), Teacher Education (e,s) *CEO:* Pres. Julius W. Becton, Jr.
Enroll: 4638 (409) 857-3311

PROFESSIONAL COURT REPORTING SCHOOL
250 E. Arapho Rd., No. 175, Richardson 75081 *Type:* Private *Accred.:* 1988 (CCA-ACTTS) *Calendar:* Courses of varying lengths *Degrees:* certificates *CEO:* Dir. Ardith Spies
Enroll: 147 (512) 231-9502

R.E.T.S. ELECTRONIC INSTITUTE
10900 Kingspoint Rd., Houston 77075-4103 *Type:* Private *Accred.:* 1991 (CCA-ACTTS) *Calendar:* Courses of varying lengths *Degrees:* certificates *CEO:* Dir. William Gresham
(713) 946-6366

R/S INSTITUTE
1111 N. Belt, E., Houston 77032 *Type:* Private *Accred.:* 1984/1989 (SACS-COEI) *Calendar:* Courses of varying lengths *Degrees:* certificates *CEO:* Dir. Douglas Watson
Enroll: 3 (713) 987-8991

R/S INSTITUTE
7122 Lawndale Ave., Houston 77023 *Type:* Private *Accred.:* 1984/1989 (SACS-COEI) *Calendar:* Courses of varying lengths *Degrees:* certificates *CEO:* Dir. Robert Saldivar
Enroll: 70 (713) 923-6968

RANGER JUNIOR COLLEGE
College Cir., Ranger 76470-3298 *Type:* Public (district) junior *System:* Texas Higher Education Coordinating Board *Accred.:* 1968/1982 (SACS-CC) *Calendar:* Sem. plan *Degrees:* A *CEO:* Pres. Joe Mills
Enroll: 829 (817) 647-3234

RICE AVIATION, A DIVISION OF A&J ENTERPRISES
8880 Telephone Rd., Houston 77061 *Type:* Private *Accred.:* 1988/1990 (SACS-COEI) *Calendar:* Courses of varying lengths *Degrees:* certificates *CEO:* Dir. Robert Doty
Enroll: 1372 (713) 644-6616

Texas

BRANCH CAMPUS
3201 E. Broad St., Phoenix, AZ 85040 *CEO:* Dir. Jim Garvey
(602) 243-6611

BRANCH CAMPUS
7811 N. Shepherd Dr., Bldg. E, Houston, TX 77088 *CEO:* Dir. Robert Taylor
(713) 591-2908

BRANCH CAMPUS
8333 Brownfield Hwy., Rte. 5, Lubbock, TX 79407 *CEO:* Dir. Lee Jackson
(806) 794-8435

BRANCH CAMPUS
124 Hopson Rd., Ashland, VA 23005 *CEO:* Dir. Tammy Gilbert
(804) 798-1638

BRANCH CAMPUS
5202 W. Military Hwy., Hangar 7, Chesapeake, VA 23321 *CEO:* Dir. Margaret Perry
(804) 465-2813

RICHLAND COLLEGE
12800 Abrams Rd., Dallas 75243-2199 *Type:* Public (district) junior *System:* Dallas County Community College District *Accred.:* 1974/1983 (SACS-CC) *Calendar:* Sem. plan *Degrees:* A *CEO:* Pres. Stephen K. Mittelstet
Enroll: 8656   (214) 238-6200

ROFFLER HAIR DESIGN COLLEGE
217 Pleasant Grove Ctr., Dallas 75217-1700 *Type:* Private *Accred.:* 1991 (CCA-ACTTS) *Calendar:* Courses of varying lengths *Degrees:* diplomas *CEO:* Dir. Daniel Ruidant
(214) 398-5905

ROFFLER HAIR DESIGN COLLEGE
505 Golden Triangle Ctr., Polk St. at Marvin D. Love Fwy, Dallas 75224-4425 *Type:* Private *Accred.:* 1991 (CCA-ACTTS) *Calendar:* Courses of varying lengths *Degrees:* diplomas *CEO:* Dir. Lori Ruidant
(214) 375-0592

ROFFLER HAIR DESIGN COLLEGE
1125 E. Seminary Dr., Fort Worth 76115 *Type:* Private *Accred.:* 1986 (CCA-ACTTS) *Calendar:* Courses of varying lengths *Degrees:* diplomas *CEO:* Dir. Thomas L. Campo
(817) 926-7555

ROFFLER HAIR DESIGN COLLEGE
2410 W. Walnut St., Garland 75042-6623 *Type:* Private *Accred.:* 1991 (CCA-ACTTS) *Calendar:* Courses of varying lengths *Degrees:* diplomas *CEO:* Dir. Daniel Ruidant
(214) 272-8995

ROFFLER HAIR DESIGN COLLEGE
3145 Denton Hwy., Haltom City 76117-3710 *Type:* Private *Accred.:* 1991 (CCA-ACTTS) *Calendar:* Courses of varying lengths *Degrees:* diplomas *CEO:* Dir. Thomas L. Campo
(817) 831-7261

S.W. SCHOOL OF BUSINESS AND TECHNICAL CAREERS
100 Main St., Eagle Pass 78852 *Type:* Private *Accred.:* 1989 (SACS-COEI) *Calendar:* Courses of varying lengths *Degrees:* certificates *CEO:* Dir. Marcia Limon
Enroll: 74   (512) 773-1373

S.W. SCHOOL OF BUSINESS AND TECHNICAL CAREERS
602 W. Southcross Blvd., San Antonio 78221 *Type:* Private *Accred.:* 1982/1987 (SACS-COEI) *Calendar:* Courses of varying lengths *Degrees:* certificates *CEO:* Dir. Al Salazar
Enroll: 217   (512) 921-0951

BRANCH CAMPUS
122 W. North St., Uvalde, TX 78801 *CEO:* Dir. Paulette Hahn
(512) 278-4103

S.W. SCHOOL OF BUSINESS AND TECHNICAL CAREERS
402 E. Travis St., San Antonio 78205 *Type:* Private *Accred.:* 1989 (SACS-COEI) *Calen-*

dar: Courses of varying lengths *Degrees:* certificates *CEO:* Dir. Mary Lou Cortinas
Enroll: 67 (512) 225-7287

ST. EDWARD'S UNIVERSITY
3001 S. Congress Ave., Austin 78704 *Type:* Private liberal arts and teachers *Accred.:* 1958/1987 (SACS-CC) *Calendar:* Sem. plan *Degrees:* B, M *Prof. Accred.:* Social Work (B) *CEO:* Pres. Patricia A. Hayes
Enroll: 2300 (512) 448-8400

ST. MARY'S UNIVERSITY
One Camino Santa Maria, San Antonio 78228-8507 *Type:* Private (Roman Catholic) *Accred.:* 1949/1984 (SACS-CC) *Calendar:* Sem. plan *Degrees:* B, M, D *Prof. Accred.:* Engineering (electrical, industrial), Law, Music *CEO:* Pres. John J. Moder
Enroll: 4077 (512) 436-3011

ST. PHILIP'S COLLEGE
2111 Nevada St., San Antonio 78203 *Type:* Public (district) junior *System:* Alamo Community College District *Accred.:* 1951/1985 (SACS-CC) *Calendar:* Sem. plan *Degrees:* A *Prof. Accred.:* Medical Laboratory Technology (AMA), Medical Record Technology, Occupational Therapy Assisting, Physical Therapy Assisting, Practical Nursing, Radiography, Respiratory Therapy Technology, Surgical Technology *CEO:* Pres. Stephen R. Mitchell
Enroll: 4685 (512) 531-3200

SAM HOUSTON STATE UNIVERSITY
Huntsville 77341 *Type:* Public (state) liberal arts and teachers *System:* Texas State University System *Accred.:* 1925/1989 (SACS-CC) *Calendar:* Sem. plan *Degrees:* B, M, D *Prof. Accred.:* Music, Teacher Education (e,s,p) *CEO:* Pres. Martin J. Anisman
Enroll: 11363 (409) 294-1111

SAN ANGELO HAIR ACADEMY
18 N. Chadbourne St., San Angelo 76903 *Type:* Private *Accred.:* 1986 (CCA-ACTTS) *Calendar:* Courses of varying lengths *Degrees:* diplomas *CEO:* Dir. Frances Clark
(915) 653-2615

SAN ANTONIO ART INSTITUTE
6000 N. New Braunfels Ave., P.O. Box 6092, San Antonio 78209-0092 *Type:* Private professional *Accred.:* 1988 (SACS-CC candidate) *Calendar:* Sem. plan *Degrees:* B *Prof. Accred.:* Art *CEO:* Pres. Russell A. Cargo
Enroll: 78 (512) 824-7224

SAN ANTONIO COLLEGE
1300 San Pedro Ave., San Antonio 78212 *Type:* Public (district) junior *System:* Alamo Community College District *Accred.:* 1952/1985 (SACS-CC) *Calendar:* Sem. plan *Degrees:* A *Prof. Accred.:* Dental Assisting, Medical Assisting (AMA), Mortuary Science, Nursing (A) *CEO:* Pres. Max Castillo
Enroll: 14493 (512) 733-2000

SAN ANTONIO COLLEGE OF MEDICAL AND DENTAL ASSISTANTS
4205 San Pedro Ave., San Antonio 78212-1899 *Type:* Private *Accred.:* 1970/1985 (CCA-ACTTS); 1984/1989 (SACS-COEI) *Calendar:* Courses of varying lengths *Degrees:* diplomas *Prof. Accred.:* Medical Assisting *CEO:* Dir. Esther Jones
Enroll: 320 (512) 733-0777

BRANCH CAMPUS
3900 N. 23rd St., McAllen, TX 78501 *Prof. Accred.:* Medical Assisting *CEO:* Dir. Bonito Mahannah
(512) 630-1499

BRANCH CAMPUS
5280 Medical Dr., Ste. 100, San Antonio, TX 78229 *CEO:* Dir. Denise Cordova
(512) 692-3829

SAN ANTONIO TRADE SCHOOL
120 Playmoor St., San Antonio 78210 *Type:* Private *Accred.:* 1982/1987 (SACS-COEI) *Calendar:* Courses of varying lengths *Degrees:* certificates *CEO:* Dir. Charles Lee
Enroll: 406 (512) 533-9126

BRANCH CAMPUS
117 W. Martin, Del Rio, TX 78840 *CEO:* Dir. Arnold Manchaca
(512) 774-5646

Texas

SAN ANTONIO TRAINING DIVISION
9350 S. Presa, San Antonio 78223-4799 *Type:* Private *Accred.:* 1984/1989 (SACS-COEI) *Calendar:* Courses of varying lengths *Degrees:* certificates *CEO:* Dir. James Partain
Enroll: 386   (512) 633-2893

BRANCH CAMPUS
Hemisfair Park, Bldg. 277, San Antonio, TX 78291-0040 *CEO:* Dir. Patricia Turner
(512) 227-8217

SAN JACINTO COLLEGE
4624 Fairmont Pkwy., Pasadena 77504 *Type:* Public (district) junior *System:* Texas Higher Education Coordinating Board *Accred.:* 1963/1989 (SACS-CC) *Calendar:* Sem. plan *Degrees:* A *Prof. Accred.:* Medical Laboratory Technology (AMA), Nursing (A), Radiography, Respiratory Therapy, Respiratory Therapy Technology, Surgical Technology *CEO:* Pres. Monte Blue
Enroll: 15406   (713) 998-6100

CENTRAL CAMPUS
8060 Spencer Hwy., Pasadena, TX 77505 *CEO:* Pres. Monte Blue
(713) 476-1501

NORTH CAMPUS
5800 Uvalde Rd., Houston, TX 77049 *CEO:* Pres. Edwin Lehr
(713) 458-4050

SOUTH CAMPUS
13735 Beamer Rd., Houston, TX 77089 *CEO:* Pres. Parker Williams
(713) 484-1900

SCHOOL OF AUTOMOTIVE MACHINISTS
1911 Antoine Dr., Houston 77055-1803 *Type:* Private *Accred.:* 1991 (CCA-ACTTS) *Calendar:* Courses of varying lengths *Degrees:* certificates *CEO:* Dir. Linda Massingill
(713) 683-3817

SCHREINER COLLEGE
2100 Memorial Blvd., Kerrville 78028 *Type:* Private (Presbyterian) *Accred.:* 1934/1989 (SACS-CC) *Calendar:* Sem. plan *Degrees:* A, B *CEO:* Pres. Sam M. Junkin
Enroll: 554   (512) 896-5411

SEBRING CAREER SCHOOLS
2212 Ave. I, Huntsville 77340 *Type:* Private *Accred.:* 1985/1990 (SACS-COEI) *Calendar:* Courses of Varying Lengths *Degrees:* certificates *CEO:* Dir. Reese Moore
Enroll: 269   (409) 291-6299

BRANCH CAMPUS
842-C W. Seventh St., Corsicana, TX 75110 *CEO:* Dir. Joe Taylor
(903) 874-7312

BRANCH CAMPUS
6672 Hwy. 6, S., Houston, TX 77083 *CEO:* Dir. M. Turner
(713) 561-6352

BRANCH CAMPUS
6715 Bissonnet St., Houston, TX 77074 *CEO:* Dir. Brooks Moore
(713) 772-6209

SEGUIN BEAUTY SCHOOL
102 E. Court St., Seguin 78155 *Type:* Private *Accred.:* 1987 (SACS-COEI) *Calendar:* Courses of varying lengths *Degrees:* certificates *CEO:* Dir. Joseph P. Evans
Enroll: 149   (512) 372-0935

BRANCH CAMPUS
214 W. San Antonio St., New Braunfels, TX 78130 *CEO:* Mgr. Maria Rosas
(512) 620-1301

SOUTH PLAINS COLLEGE
1401 College Ave., Levelland 79336 *Type:* Public (district) junior *System:* Texas Higher Education Coordinating Board *Accred.:* 1963/1983 (SACS-CC) *Calendar:* Sem. plan *Degrees:* A *Prof. Accred.:* Medical Record Technology, Radiography, Respiratory Therapy, Respiratory Therapy Technology, Surgical Technology *CEO:* Pres. Marvin L. Baker
Enroll: 4227   (806) 894-9611

SOUTH TEXAS COLLEGE OF LAW
1303 San Jacinto St., Houston 77002 *Type:* Private *Calendar:* Sem. plan *Degrees:* P *Prof. Accred.:* Law (ABA only) *CEO:* Pres./Dean William L. Wilks
Enroll: 1336 (713) 659-8040

SOUTH TEXAS VOCATIONAL-TECHNICAL INSTITUTE
2255 N. Coria St., Brownsville 78520 *Type:* Private *Accred.:* 1982/1987 (SACS-COEI) *Calendar:* Courses of varying lengths *Degrees:* certificates *CEO:* Dir. Maria Carrejo
Enroll: 163 (512) 546-0353

SOUTH TEXAS VOCATIONAL-TECHNICAL INSTITUTE
1812 S. 16th St., McAllen 78503 *Type:* Private *Accred.:* 1982/1987 (SACS-COEI) *Calendar:* Courses of varying lengths *Degrees:* certificates *CEO:* Dir. Elma G. Rodriguez
Enroll: 456 (512) 631-1107

SOUTH TEXAS VOCATIONAL-TECHNICAL INSTITUTE
2419 E. Haggar Ave., Weslaco 78596 *Type:* Private *Accred.:* 1982/1987 (SACS-COEI) *Calendar:* Courses of varying lengths *Degrees:* certificates *CEO:* Dir. Carlos Rodriguez, Jr.
Enroll: 438 (512) 969-1564

BRANCH CAMPUS
2255 N. Coria St., Brownsville, TX 78520
CEO: Dir. Terry Carrejo
(512) 546-0353

BRANCH CAMPUS
204 Northeast La., Cotulla, TX 78104
CEO: Dir. Hugo De Da Vina
(512) 879-3012

BRANCH CAMPUS
1812 S. 16th St., McAllen, TX 78503
CEO: Dir. Nina Garrett
(512) 631-1107

SOUTHEAST TEXAS TECHNICAL INSTITUTE
3101 McArdle Rd., Corpus Christi 78415 *Type:* Private *Accred.:* 1986/1990 (SACS-COEI) *Calendar:* Courses of varying lengths *Degrees:* certificates *CEO:* Dir. Barry Ballard
Enroll: 367 (512) 852-1888

SOUTHEASTERN PARALEGAL INSTITUTE
5440 Harvest Hill Rd., Ste. 200, Dallas 75230 *Type:* Private *Accred.:* 1989/1990 (SACS-COEI) *Calendar:* Courses of varying lengths *Degrees:* certificates *CEO:* Dir. Janice Bailey
Enroll: 51 (214) 385-1446

SOUTHERN INSTITUTE OF BUSINESS AND TECHNOLOGY
911 E. Arapaho Rd., Richardson 75081 *Type:* Private *Accred.:* 1988 (CCA-ACTTS) *Calendar:* Courses of varying lengths *Degrees:* certificates *CEO:* Dir. Wayne Paul
Enroll: 71 (214) 235-8400

SOUTHERN METHODIST UNIVERSITY
Dallas 75275 *Type:* Private (United Methodist) *Accred.:* 1938/1991 (ATS); 1921/1991 (SACS-CC) *Calendar:* Sem. plan *Degrees:* B, P, M, D *Prof. Accred.:* Business (B,M), Dance, Engineering (civil, computer, electrical, mechanical), Law, Music *CEO:* Pres. A. Kenneth Pye
Enroll: 7772 (214) 692-2000

SOUTHWEST INSTITUTE OF MERCHANDISING AND DESIGN
9611 Acer Ave., El Paso 79925 *Type:* Private *Accred.:* 1975/1985 (CCA-ACTTS) *Calendar:* Courses of varying lengths *Degrees:* diplomas *CEO:* Pres. Mary F. Simon
Enroll: 404 (915) 593-7328

SOUTHWEST SCHOOL OF COURT REPORTING
6851 Citizen's Pkwy., Ste. 100, San Antonio 78229 *Type:* Private *Accred.:* 1988 (CCA-ACTTS) *Calendar:* Courses of varying lengths *Degrees:* certificates *CEO:* Dir. Kathlin Holler
(512) 525-8595

SOUTHWEST SCHOOL OF ELECTRONICS
5424 Hwy. 290 W., Ste. 200, Austin 78735 *Type:* Private *Accred.:* 1978 (CCA-ACTTS) *Calendar:* Courses of varying lengths *De-*

grees: certificates, diplomas *CEO:* Dir. Barbara Butts
Enroll: 210 (512) 892-2640

SOUTHWEST SCHOOL OF MEDICAL ASSISTANTS
201 W. Sheridan, San Antonio 78204 *Type:* Private *Accred.:* 1974/1988 (CCA-ACTTS) *Calendar:* Courses of varying lengths *Degrees:* certificates *CEO:* Dir. Denise Jauregui
Enroll: 506 (512) 224-2296

SOUTHWEST TEXAS JUNIOR COLLEGE
Garner Field Rd., Uvalde 78801 *Type:* Public (district) junior *System:* Texas Higher Education Coordinating Board *Accred.:* 1964/1985 (SACS-CC) *Calendar:* Sem. plan *Degrees:* A *CEO:* Pres. Billy Word
Enroll: 1934 (512) 278-4401

SOUTHWEST TEXAS STATE UNIVERSITY
601 University Dr., San Marcos 78666-4616 *Type:* Public (state) liberal arts and teachers *System:* Texas State University System *Accred.:* 1925/1989 (SACS-CC) *Calendar:* Sem. plan *Degrees:* A, B, M *Prof. Accred.:* Health Services Administration, Home Economics, Interior Design, Medical Record Administration, Medical Technology, Music, Physical Therapy, Public Administration, Respiratory Therapy, Respiratory Therapy Technology, Social Work (B), Speech-Language Pathology, Teacher Education (e,s,p) *CEO:* Pres. Jerome H. Supple
Enroll: 18541 (512) 245-2111

SOUTHWESTERN ADVENTIST COLLEGE
College and Hillcrest, P.O. Box 567, Keene 76059-0567 *Type:* Private (Seventh-Day Adventist) liberal arts and teachers *Accred.:* 1958/1985 (SACS-CC) *Calendar:* Sem. plan *Degrees:* A, B, M *Prof. Accred.:* Nursing (A,B) *CEO:* Pres. Marvin E. Anderson
Enroll: 593 (817) 645-3921

SOUTHWESTERN ASSEMBLIES OF GOD COLLEGE
1200 Sycamore St., Waxahachie 75165 *Type:* Private (Assemblies of God) *Accred.:* 1948/1985 (AABC); 1968/1983 (SACS-CC) *Calendar:* Sem. plan *Degrees:* A, B *CEO:* Pres. Delmer R. Guynes
Enroll: 596 (214) 937-4010

SOUTHWESTERN BAPTIST THEOLOGICAL SEMINARY
2001 W. Seminary Dr., Fort Worth 76115 *Type:* Private (Southern Baptist) *Accred.:* 1944/1991 (ATS); 1969/1991 (SACS-CC) *Calendar:* Sem. plan *Degrees:* A, B, P, M, D *Prof. Accred.:* Music *CEO:* Pres. Russell H. Dilday, Jr.
Enroll: 4088 (817) 923-1921

SOUTHWESTERN CHRISTIAN COLLEGE
200 Bowser Cir., Terrell 75160 *Type:* Private (Church of Christ) liberal arts *Accred.:* 1973/1989 (SACS-CC) *Calendar:* Sem. plan *Degrees:* A, B *CEO:* Pres. Jack Evans, Sr.
Enroll: 230 (214) 563-3341

SOUTHWESTERN UNIVERSITY
University Ave. at Maple St., Georgetown 78626 *Type:* Private liberal arts *Accred.:* 1915/1982 (SACS-CC) *Calendar:* Sem. plan *Degrees:* B *Prof. Accred.:* Music *CEO:* Pres. Roy B. Shilling, Jr.
Enroll: 1221 (512) 863-6511

STEPHEN F. AUSTIN STATE UNIVERSITY
P.O. Box 6078, SFA Sta., Nacogdoches 75962-6078 *Type:* Public (state) liberal arts and teachers *System:* Texas Higher Education Coordinating Board *Accred.:* 1927/1990 (SACS-CC) *Calendar:* Sem. plan *Degrees:* B, M, D *Prof. Accred.:* Business (B,M), Forestry, Home Economics, Interior Design, Music, Nursing (B), Social Work (B), Teacher Education (e,s), Theatre *CEO:* Interim Pres. William J. Brophy
Enroll: 11907 (409) 568-2011

SUL ROSS STATE UNIVERSITY
Alpine 79832 *Type:* Public (state) liberal arts and teachers *System:* Texas State University System *Accred.:* 1929/1989 (SACS-CC) *Calendar:* Sem. plan *Degrees:* A, B, M *Prof. Accred.:* Veterinary Technology (probational) *CEO:* Pres. R. Victor Morgan
Enroll: 1848 (915) 837-8011

Accredited Institutions   **Texas**

BRANCH CAMPUS
Uvalde Study Ctr., Uvalde, TX 78801 *CEO:* Dean Frank Abbott
Enroll: 477   (512) 278-3339

SYSTEM ONE TRAVEL ACADEMY
652 E. North Belt Dr., Houston 77060 *Type:* Private business *Accred.:* 1988 (CCA-ACICS); 1991 (CCA-ACTTS) *Calendar:* Courses of varying lengths *Degrees:* certificates, diplomas *CEO:* Dir. Jeanne Guillen
Enroll: 797   (713) 878-3080

TARLETON STATE UNIVERSITY
1297 W. Washington St., Stephenville 76402 *Type:* Public (state) liberal arts and professional *System:* Texas A&M University System *Accred.:* 1926/1990 (SACS-CC) *Calendar:* Sem. plan *Degrees:* A, B, M *Prof. Accred.:* Medical Technology, Music, Social Work (B), Teacher Education (e,s,p) *CEO:* Pres. Dennis P. McCabe
Enroll: 5956   (817) 968-9100

TARRANT COUNTY JUNIOR COLLEGE
1500 Houston St., Fort Worth 76102-6599 *Type:* Public (district) junior *System:* Texas Higher Education Coordinating Board *Accred.:* 1969/1983 (SACS-CC) *Calendar:* Sem. plan *Degrees:* A *Prof. Accred.:* Dental Hygiene, Medical Laboratory Technology (AMA), Medical Record Technology, Nursing (A), Physical Therapy Assisting, Radiography, Respiratory Therapy, Surgical Technology *CEO:* Chanc. C.A. Roberson
Enroll: 20017   (817) 336-7851

NORTHEAST CAMPUS
828 Harwood Rd., Hurst, TX 76054 *CEO:* Pres. Herman Crow
    (817) 281-7860

NORTHWEST CAMPUS
4801 Marine Creek Pkwy., Fort Worth, TX 76179 *CEO:* Pres. Michael Saenz
    (817) 232-2900

SOUTH CAMPUS
5301 Campus Dr., Fort Worth, TX 76119 *CEO:* Pres. Jim Worden
    (817) 534-4861

TEMPLE ACADEMY OF COSMETOLOGY
5 S. First St., Temple 76501 *Type:* Private *Accred.:* 1986/1991 (SACS-COEI) *Calendar:* Courses of varying lengths *Degrees:* certificates *CEO:* Dir. Lenda Tuck
Enroll: 88   (817) 778-2221

BRANCH CAMPUS
1408 W. Marshall Ave., Longview, TX 75604 *CEO:* Dir. Shutona Vaughan
    (903) 753-4717

TEMPLE JUNIOR COLLEGE
2600 S. First St., Temple 76504-7435 *Type:* Public (district) junior *System:* Texas Higher Education Coordinating Board *Accred.:* 1959/1990 (SACS-CC) *Calendar:* Sem. plan *Degrees:* A *Prof. Accred.:* Medical Laboratory Technology (AMA), Music, Respiratory Therapy, Surgical Technology *CEO:* Pres. Marvin R. Felder
Enroll: 1728   (817) 773-9961

TEXARKANA COLLEGE
2500 N. Robison Rd., Texarkana 75501 *Type:* Public (district) junior *System:* Texas Higher Education Coordinating Board *Accred.:* 1931/1985 (SACS-CC) *Calendar:* Sem. plan *Degrees:* A *Prof. Accred.:* Nursing (A) *CEO:* Pres. Carl M. Nelson
Enroll: 3510   (214) 838-4541

TEXAS A&I UNIVERSITY
Campus Box 101, Kingsville 78363 *Type:* Public (state) *System:* Texas A&M University System *Accred.:* 1933/1984 (SACS-CC) *Calendar:* Sem. plan *Degrees:* B, M, D *Prof. Accred.:* Engineering (chemical, civil, electrical, mechanical, petroleum), Music *CEO:* Pres. Manuel L. Ibanez
Enroll: 5213   (512) 595-3207

TEXAS A&M UNIVERSITY
College Station 77843 *Type:* Public (state) *System:* Texas A&M University System *Accred.:* 1924/1983 (SACS-CC) *Calendar:* Sem. plan *Degrees:* B, M, D *Prof. Accred.:* Accounting (Type A,C), Architecture (M), Business (B,M), Clinical Psychology, Construction Education, Counseling Psychology,

Dietetics (internship), Engineering (aerospace, agricultural, bioengineering, chemical, civil, electrical, industrial, mechanical, mining, nuclear, ocean, petroleum, radiological health), Engineering Technology (electrical, manufacturing, mechanical), Forestry, Journalism, Landscape Architecture (B,M), Medicine, Planning (regional/urban), Psychology Internship, Public Administration, School Psychology, Teacher Education (e,s,p) *CEO:* Chanc. Herbert H. Richardson
Enroll: 38978 (409) 845-3211

TEXAS A&M UNIVERSITY AT GALVESTON
P.O. Box 1675, Galveston 77553 *Type:* Public (state) *System:* Texas A&M University System *Accred.:* 1978/1983 (SACS-CC) *Calendar:* Sem. plan *Degrees:* B *Prof. Accred.:* Engineering (naval architecture/marine) *CEO:* Pres. William J. Merrell, Jr.
Enroll: 1044 (409) 740-4400

TEXAS AERO TECH
6311 Lemmon Ave., Dallas 75209-3603 *Type:* Private *Accred.:* 1979/1989 (SACS-COEI) *Calendar:* Courses of varying lengths *Degrees:* certificates *CEO:* Dir. Thomas Stose
Enroll: 995 (214) 358-7295

TEXAS BARBER COLLEGE
531 W. Jefferson Blvd., Dallas 75208 *Type:* Private *Accred.:* 1988 (SACS-COEI) *Calendar:* Courses of varying lengths *Degrees:* certificates *CEO:* Dir. Helen Spears
Enroll: 63 (214) 943-7255

BRANCH CAMPUS
2406 Gus Thomasson Rd., Dallas, TX 75228 *CEO:* Dir. Helen Spears
(214) 324-2851

BRANCH CAMPUS
525 W. Arapaho Rd., Richardson, TX 75080 *CEO:* Dir. Helen Spears
(214) 644-4106

TEXAS CHIROPRACTIC COLLEGE
5912 Spencer Hwy., Pasadena 77505 *Type:* Private professional *Accred.:* 1984/1990 (SACS-CC) *Calendar:* Tri. plan *Degrees:* B, D *Prof. Accred.:* Chiropractic Education *CEO:* Pres. S.M. Elliott
Enroll: 333 (713) 487-1170

TEXAS CHRISTIAN UNIVERSITY
2800 S. University Dr., Fort Worth 76129 *Type:* Private (Christian Church/Disciples of Christ) *Accred.:* 1942/1989 (ATS); 1922/1984 (SACS-CC) *Calendar:* Sem. plan *Degrees:* B, M, D *Prof. Accred.:* Business (B,M), Computer Science, Dietetics (coordinated), Interior Design, Journalism, Music, Nursing (B), Social Work (B), Speech-Language Pathology, Teacher Education (e,s,p) *CEO:* Chanc. William E. Tucker
Enroll: 5855 (817) 921-7000

TEXAS COLLEGE
2404 N. Grand Ave., P.O. Box 4500, Tyler 75702-2404 *Type:* Private liberal arts and teachers *Accred.:* 1970/1984 (SACS-CC) *Calendar:* Sem. plan *Degrees:* B *CEO:* Pres. Maurice S. Cherry
Enroll: 471 (214) 593-8311

TEXAS COLLEGE OF OSTEOPATHIC MEDICINE
3500 Camp Bowie Blvd., Fort Worth 76107-2690 *Type:* Public (state) professional *System:* Texas Higher Education Coordinating Board *Calendar:* Sem. plan *Degrees:* P *Prof. Accred.:* Osteopathy *CEO:* Pres. David M. Richards, D.O.
Enroll: 372 (817) 735-2000

TEXAS DENTAL TECHNICAL SCHOOL
2414 Broadway, Houston 77102 *Type:* Private *Accred.:* 1989 (CCA-ACTTS) *Calendar:* Courses of varying lengths *Degrees:* certificates *CEO:* Dir. Albert Marquez
(713) 645-1612

TEXAS LUTHERAN COLLEGE
1000 W. Court St., Seguin 78155 *Type:* Private (Lutheran) liberal arts *Accred.:* 1953/1988 (SACS-CC) *Calendar:* Sem. plan *Degrees:* A, B *CEO:* Pres. Charles H. Oestreich
Enroll: 1043 (512) 372-8001

TEXAS SCHOOL OF BUSINESS
711 Airtex Blvd., Houston 77073 *Type:* Private business *Accred.:* 1985 (CCA-ACICS)

Calendar: Courses of varying lengths *Degrees:* certificates, diplomas *CEO:* Dir. Madeline Burillo
Enroll: 1797 (713) 876-2888

TEXAS SCHOOL OF BUSINESS—SOUTHWEST
10250 Bissonnet St., Houston 77036 *Type:* Private business *Accred.:* 1989 (CCA-ACICS) *Calendar:* Courses of varying lengths *Degrees:* certificates, diplomas *CEO:* Dir. Jody Hawk
(713) 771-1177

TEXAS SCHOOLS
524 E. 40th St., Lubbock 79404 *Type:* Private *Accred.:* 1983/1988 (SACS-COEI) *Calendar:* Courses of varying lengths *Degrees:* certificates *CEO:* Dir. Ron Stone
Enroll: 484 (806) 744-1300

TEXAS SOUTHERN UNIVERSITY
3100 Cleburne St., Houston 77004 *Type:* Public *System:* Texas Higher Education Coordinating Board *Accred.:* 1948/1990 (SACS-CC) *Calendar:* Sem. plan *Degrees:* B, M, D *Prof. Accred.:* Law (ABA only), Medical Record Administration, Medical Technology, Pharmacy, Respiratory Therapy, Social Work (B) *CEO:* Pres. William H. Harris
Enroll: 9427 (713) 527-7011

TEXAS SOUTHMOST COLLEGE
80 Fort Brown St., Brownsville 78520 *Type:* Public (district) junior *System:* Texas Higher Education Coordinating Board *Accred.:* 1930/1991 (SACS-CC) *Calendar:* Sem. plan *Degrees:* A *Prof. Accred.:* Medical Laboratory Technology (AMA), Nursing (A), Radiography, Respiratory Therapy, Respiratory Therapy Technology *CEO:* Pres. Juliet V. Garcia
Enroll: 5474 (512) 544-8200

TEXAS STATE TECHNICAL INSTITUTE—AMARILLO
P.O. Box 11197, Amarillo 79111 *Type:* Public (state) 2-year *System:* Texas State Technical Institute System *Accred.:* 1970/1985 (SACS-CC) *Calendar:* Qtr. plan *Degrees:* A *Prof. Accred.:* Interior Design *CEO:* Pres. Ronald L. DeSpain
Enroll: 946 (806) 335-2316

TEXAS STATE TECHNICAL INSTITUTE—HARLINGEN
P.O. Box 2628, Harlingen 78550 *Type:* Public (state) 2-year *System:* Texas State Technical Institute System *Accred.:* 1968/1985 (SACS-CC) *Calendar:* Qtr. plan *Degrees:* A *Prof. Accred.:* Medical Record Technology *CEO:* Pres. J. Gilbert Leal
Enroll: 2929 (512) 425-0600

TEXAS STATE TECHNICAL INSTITUTE—SWEETWATER
Rte. 3, P.O. Box 18, Sweetwater 79556 *Type:* Public (state) 2-year *System:* Texas State Technical Institute System *Accred.:* 1979/1984 (SACS-CC) *Calendar:* Qtr. plan *Degrees:* A *CEO:* Pres. Clay G. Johnson
Enroll: 1123 (915) 235-7300

TEXAS STATE TECHNICAL INSTITUTE—WACO
3801 Campus Dr., Waco 76705 *Type:* Public (state) 2-year *System:* Texas State Technical Institute System *Accred.:* 1968/1983 (SACS-CC) *Calendar:* Qtr. plan *Degrees:* A *Prof. Accred.:* Dental Assisting, Dental Laboratory Technology, Veterinary Technology *CEO:* Pres. Don E. Goodwin
Enroll: 3702 (817) 799-3611

TEXAS TECH UNIVERSITY
P.O. Box 4349, Lubbock 79409 *Type:* Public (state) *System:* Texas Higher Education Coordinating Board *Accred.:* 1928/1984 (SACS-CC) *Calendar:* Sem. plan *Degrees:* B, M, D *Prof. Accred.:* Accounting (Type A,C), Architecture (B), Art, Audiology, Business (B,M), Clinical Psychology, Counseling Psychology, Dietetics (internship), Engineering (agricultural, chemical, civil, electrical, engineering physics/science, industrial, mechanical, petroleum), Engineering Technology (civil/construction, electrical, mechanical), Home Economics, Interior Design, Journalism, Landscape Architecture (B), Law, Music, Psychology Internship, Public Administration, Social Work (B),

Speech-Language Pathology, Teacher Education (e,s,p) *CEO:* Pres. Robert W. Lawless
Enroll: 23391 (806) 742-2011

TEXAS TECH UNIVERSITY HEALTH SCIENCES CENTER
3601 Fourth St., Lubbock 79430 *Type:* Public (state) *System:* Texas Higher Education Coordinating Board *Calendar:* Sem. plan *Degrees:* B, M, D *Prof. Accred.:* EMT-Paramedic, Medical Technology, Medicine, Nursing (B), Occupational Therapy, Physical Therapy *CEO:* Pres. Robert W. Lawless
Enroll: 876 (806) 743-3111

TEXAS VOCATIONAL SCHOOL
Rte. 2, P.O. Box 791, Pharr 78577 *Type:* Private *Accred.:* 1982/1987 (SACS-COEI) *Calendar:* Courses of varying lengths *Degrees:* certificates *CEO:* Dir. Gene Calhoun
Enroll: 304 (512) 631-6181

TEXAS VOCATIONAL SCHOOL
1913 S. Flores St., San Antonio 78204 *Type:* Private *Accred.:* 1982 (CCA-ACTTS); 1982/1988 (SACS-COEI) *Calendar:* Courses of varying lengths *Degrees:* certificates *CEO:* Dir. Melvin Heitkemp
Enroll: 541 (512) 225-3253

TEXAS VOCATIONAL SCHOOLS
1921 E. Red River St., Victoria 77901 *Type:* Private *Accred.:* 1983/1988 (SACS-COEI) *Calendar:* Courses of varying lengths *Degrees:* certificates *CEO:* Dir. Angie S. Boone
Enroll: 368 (512) 575-4768

TEXAS WESLEYAN UNIVERSITY
1201 Wesleyan St., Fort Worth 76105-1536 *Type:* Private (United Methodist) liberal arts *Accred.:* 1949/1983 (SACS-CC) *Calendar:* Sem. plan *Degrees:* B, M *Prof. Accred.:* Music, Nurse Anesthesia Education, Teacher Education (e,s) *CEO:* Pres. Jake B. Schrum
Enroll: 1155 (817) 531-4444

TEXAS WOMAN'S UNIVERSITY
P.O. Box 23925, Denton 76204 *Type:* Public (state) for women *System:* Texas Higher Education Coordinating Board *Accred.:* 1923/1983 (SACS-CC) *Calendar:* Sem. plan *Degrees:* B, M, D *Prof. Accred.:* Dental Hygiene, Dietetics (internship), Librarianship, Medical Record Administration, Music, Nursing (B,M), Occupational Therapy, Physical Therapy, Psychology Internship, Social Work (B), Teacher Education (e,s,p) *CEO:* Pres. Shirley S. Chater
Enroll: 7356 (817) 898-2000

TOMBALL COLLEGE
30555 Tomball Pkwy., Tomball 77377 *Type:* Public (district) junior *System:* North Harris Montgomery College District *Accred.:* 1976/1991 (SACS-CC) *Calendar:* Sem. plan *Degrees:* A *Prof. Accred.:* Veterinary Technology (probational) *CEO:* Pres. Roy Lazenbey
(713) 351-3300

TRINITY UNIVERSITY
715 Stadium Dr., San Antonio 78212 *Type:* Private *Accred.:* 1946/1987 (SACS-CC) *Calendar:* Sem. plan *Degrees:* B, M *Prof. Accred.:* Engineering (engineering physics/science), Health Services Administration, Teacher Education (e,s,p) *CEO:* Pres. Ronald K. Calgaard
Enroll: 2376 (512) 736-7011

TRINITY VALLEY COMMUNITY COLLEGE
500 S. Prairieville, Athens 75751 *Type:* Public (district) junior *System:* Texas Higher Education Coordinating Board *Accred.:* 1952/1986 (SACS-CC) *Calendar:* Sem. plan *Degrees:* A *Prof. Accred.:* Nursing (A), Surgical Technology *CEO:* Pres. Ronald C. Baugh
Enroll: 5061 (214) 675-6200

TYLER JUNIOR COLLEGE
P.O. Box 9020, Tyler 75711 *Type:* Public (district) junior *System:* Texas Higher Education Coordinating Board *Accred.:* 1931/1990 (SACS-CC) *Calendar:* Sem. plan *Degrees:* A *Prof. Accred.:* Dental Hygiene, Medical Laboratory Technology (AMA), Radiography, Respiratory Therapy, Respiratory Therapy Technology *CEO:* Pres. Raymond M. Hawkins
Enroll: 8237 (903) 510-2306

Accredited Institutions   **Texas**

TYLER SCHOOL OF BUSINESS
621 E. Ferguson St., Tyler 75702 *Type:* Private business *Accred.:* 1986 (CCA-ACICS) *Calendar:* Courses of varying lengths *Degrees:* certificates, diplomas *CEO:* Pres. Marvin A. Gardner
Enroll: 304   (214) 566-3458

BRANCH CAMPUS
Rte. 14, Box 176, Hwy. 64E, Tyler, TX 75701 *CEO:* Dir. Wendell Gardner
(214) 566-1756

USA HAIR ACADEMY
2525 N. Laurent St., Victoria 77901 *Type:* Private *Accred.:* 1990 (SACS-COEI) *Calendar:* Courses of varying lengths *Degrees:* certificates *CEO:* Pres. Paul Piwonka
Enroll: 316   (512) 578-0035

BRANCH CAMPUS
9660 FM 1960 Bypass, Humble, TX 77338 *CEO:* Dir. David Wilbourn
(713) 548-1600

UNITED STATES ARMY ACADEMY OF HEALTH SCIENCES
Fort Sam Houston, San Antonio 78234-6100 *Type:* Public (federal) professional *Accred.:* 1983/1988 (SACS-COEI) *Calendar:* Courses of varying lengths *Degrees:* certificates *Prof. Accred.:* Dental Laboratory Technology, Occupational Therapy Assisting, Physician Assisting, Radiography, Respiratory Therapy Technology *CEO:* Commandant Frederick N. Bussey, U.S.A.
Enroll: 10840   (512) 221-8542

UNITED STATES ARMY SCHOOL OF AVIATION MEDICINE
Fort Rucker, AL 36362-5377 *CEO:* Commandant James Mitchell
(205) 255-7393

UNIVERSAL TECHNICAL INSTITUTE
721 Lockhaven Dr., Houston 77073 *Type:* Private *Accred.:* 1986 (CCA-ACTTS) *Calendar:* Courses of varying lengths *Degrees:* certificates *CEO:* Dir. Robert I. Sweet
Enroll: 1206   (713) 443-6262

UNIVERSITY OF CENTRAL TEXAS
U.S. Hwy. 190 W., P.O. Box 1416, Killeen 76540-1416 *Type:* Private *Accred.:* 1976/1985 (SACS-CC) *Calendar:* Sem. plan *Degrees:* B, M *CEO:* Pres. Jack W. Fuller
Enroll: 383   (817) 526-1277

THE UNIVERSITY OF DALLAS
1845 E. Northgate Dr., Irving 75062 *Type:* Private (Roman Catholic) *Accred.:* 1963/1984 (SACS-CC) *Calendar:* Sem. plan *Degrees:* B, M, D *CEO:* Pres. Robert F. Sasseen
Enroll: 3012   (214) 721-5000

UNIVERSITY OF HOUSTON—CLEAR LAKE
2700 Bay Area Blvd., Houston 77058-1050 *Type:* Public (state) *System:* University of Houston System *Accred.:* 1976/1982 (SACS-CC) *Calendar:* Sem. plan *Degrees:* B, M *Prof. Accred.:* Accounting (Type A,C), Business (B,M), Health Services Administration, Public Management, Teacher Education (e,s,p) *CEO:* Pres. Glenn A. Goerke
Enroll: 4886   (713) 283-7600

UNIVERSITY OF HOUSTON—DOWNTOWN
One Main St., Houston 77002 *Type:* Public (state) *System:* University of Houston System *Accred.:* 1976/1985 (SACS-CC) *Calendar:* Sem. plan *Degrees:* B *Prof. Accred.:* Engineering Technology (process/piping design) *CEO:* Interim Pres. George Magner
Enroll: 6063   (713) 221-8000

UNIVERSITY OF HOUSTON—UNIVERSITY PARK
4800 Calhoun Blvd., Houston 77204-2162 *Type:* Public (state) *System:* University of Houston System *Accred.:* 1954/1987 (SACS-CC) *Calendar:* Sem. plan *Degrees:* B, M, D *Prof. Accred.:* Accounting (Type A,B,C), Architecture (B,M), Business (B,M), Clinical Psychology, Computer Science, Counseling Psychology (provisional), Engineering (chemical, civil, electrical, industrial, mechanical), Engineering Technology (civil/construction, computer, electrical, manufacturing, mechanical drafting/design, surveying), Law, Music, Optometry, Pharmacy, Psychology Internship, Social Work

(M), Speech-Language Pathology, Teacher Education (e,s,p) *CEO:* Pres. Marguerite Ross Barnett
Enroll: 28831 (713) 749-2236

UNIVERSITY OF HOUSTON—VICTORIA
2302-C Red River St., Victoria 77901 *Type:* Public (state) *System:* University of Houston System *Accred.:* 1978/1983 (SACS-CC) *Calendar:* Sem. plan *Degrees:* B, M *CEO:* Interim Pres. Don Smith
Enroll: 746 (512) 576-3151

UNIVERSITY OF MARY HARDIN-BAYLOR
Box 8001, Belton 76513 *Type:* Private (Southern Baptist) liberal arts primarily for women *Accred.:* 1926/1983 (SACS-CC) *Calendar:* Sem. plan *Degrees:* B, M *Prof. Accred.:* Nursing (B) *CEO:* Pres. Jerry G. Bawcom
Enroll: 1504 (817) 939-8642

UNIVERSITY OF NORTH TEXAS
Denton 76203 *Type:* Public (state) *System:* Texas Higher Education Coordinating Board *Accred.:* 1925/1985 (SACS-CC) *Calendar:* Sem. plan *Degrees:* B, M, D *Prof. Accred.:* Accounting (Type A,C), Audiology, Business (B,M), Clinical Psychology, Computer Science, Counseling, Counseling Psychology, Interior Design, Journalism, Librarianship, Music, Public Administration, Recreation and Leisure Studies, Rehabilitation Counseling, Social Work (B), Speech-Language Pathology, Teacher Education (e,s,p) *CEO:* Chanc. Alfred F. Hurley
Enroll: 23172 (817) 565-2000

UNIVERSITY OF ST. THOMAS
3812 Montrose Blvd., Houston 77006 *Type:* Private (Roman Catholic) liberal arts *Accred.:* 1990 (ATS); 1954/1984 (SACS-CC) *Calendar:* Sem. plan *Degrees:* B, P, M, D *CEO:* Pres. Joseph M. McFadden
Enroll: 1484 (713) 522-7911

THE UNIVERSITY OF TEXAS HEALTH SCIENCE CENTER AT HOUSTON
P.O. Box 20036, Houston 77225-0036 *Type:* Public (state) *System:* University of Texas System *Accred.:* 1973/1990 (SACS-CC) *Calendar:* Sem. plan *Degrees:* B, M, D *Prof. Accred.:* Combined Prosthodontics, Dental Assisting, Dental Hygiene, Dentistry, Dietetics (coordinated), Endodontics, General Practice Residency, Medical Technology, Medicine, Nurse Anesthesia Education, Nursing (B,M), Oral and Maxillofacial Surgery, Orthodontics, Pediatric Dentistry, Perfusion, Periodontics, Psychology Internship, Public Health, Radiography, Respiratory Therapy *CEO:* Pres. M. David Low
Enroll: 2629 (713) 792-4975

THE UNIVERSITY OF TEXAS HEALTH SCIENCE CENTER AT SAN ANTONIO
7703 Floyd Curl Dr., San Antonio 78284-7834 *Type:* Public (state) *System:* University of Texas System *Accred.:* 1973/1989 (SACS-CC) *Calendar:* Sem. plan *Degrees:* B, M, D *Prof. Accred.:* Combined Prosthodontics, Dental Assisting, Dental Hygiene, Dental Laboratory Technology, Dentistry, EMT-Paramedic, Endodontics, General Dentistry, General Practice Residency, Medical Technology, Medicine, Nurse Anesthesia Education, Occupational Therapy, Pediatric Dentistry, Periodontics, Psychology Internship *CEO:* Pres. John P. Howe, III
Enroll: 2288 (512) 567-7000

THE UNIVERSITY OF TEXAS MEDICAL BRANCH AT GALVESTON
300 University Blvd., Galveston 77550 *Type:* Public (state) *System:* University of Texas System *Accred.:* 1973/1988 (SACS-CC) *Calendar:* Sem. plan *Degrees:* B, M, D *Prof. Accred.:* Blood Bank Technology, Medical Record Administration, Medical Technology, Medicine, Nursing (B,M), Occupational Therapy, Physical Therapy, Physician Assisting, Psychology Internship (provisional) *CEO:* Pres. Thomas N. James
Enroll: 1648 (409) 761-1687

THE UNIVERSITY OF TEXAS SOUTHWESTERN MEDICAL CENTER AT DALLAS
5323 Harry Hines Blvd., Dallas 75235-9002 *Type:* Public (state) *System:* University of Texas System *Accred.:* 1973/1989 (SACS-

CC) *Calendar:* Sem. plan *Degrees:* B, M, D *Prof. Accred.:* Blood Bank Technology, Clinical Psychology, Dietetics (coordinated), EMT-Paramedic, Medical Illustration, Medical Technology, Medicine, Physical Therapy, Physician Assisting, Psychology Internship *CEO:* Pres. C. Kern Wildenthal
Enroll: 1467 (214) 688-3111

The University of Texas at Arlington
P.O. Box 19125, Arlington 76019-0125 *Type:* Public (state) *System:* University of Texas System *Accred.:* 1964/1986 (SACS-CC) *Calendar:* Sem. plan *Degrees:* B, M, D *Prof. Accred.:* Accounting (Type A,B,C), Architecture (M), Business (B,M), Engineering (aerospace, civil, computer, electrical, industrial, mechanical), Music, Nursing (M), Planning (city/regional), Social Work (B,M) *CEO:* Pres. Wendell H. Nedderman
Enroll: 20409 (817) 273-2222

The University of Texas at Austin
University Sta., Austin 78712 *Type:* Public (state) *System:* University of Texas System *Accred.:* 1901/1988 (SACS-CC) *Calendar:* Sem. plan *Degrees:* B, M, D *Prof. Accred.:* Accounting (Type A,C), Architecture (B,M), Audiology, Business (B,M), Clinical Psychology, Counseling Psychology, Dietetics (coordinated), Engineering (aerospace, architectural, chemical, civil, computer, electrical, environmental/sanitary, mechanical, petroleum), Home Economics, Interior Design, Journalism, Law, Librarianship, Music, Nursing (B,M), Pharmacy, Planning (community/regional), Psychology Internship, Public Affairs, Rehabilitation Counseling, School Psychology, Social Work (B,M), Speech-Language Pathology, Teacher Education (e,s,p), Theatre *CEO:* Pres. William H. Cunningham
Enroll: 46221 (512) 471-3434

The University of Texas at Brownsville
1614 Ridgely Rd., Brownsville 78520-4991 *Type:* Public (state) *System:* University of Texas System *Accred.:* 1988 (SACS-CC) *Calendar:* Sem. plan *Degrees:* B, M *CEO:* Pres. Juliet V. Garcia
Enroll: 866 (512) 982-0100

The University of Texas at Dallas
P.O. Box 830688, Richardson 75083-0688 *Type:* Public (state) *System:* University of Texas System *Accred.:* 1972/1988 (SACS-CC) *Calendar:* Sem. plan *Degrees:* B, M, D *Prof. Accred.:* Audiology, Rehabilitation Counseling, Speech-Language Pathology *CEO:* Pres. Robert H. Rutford
Enroll: 5695 (214) 690-2111

The University of Texas at El Paso
500 W. University Ave., El Paso 79968 *Type:* Public (state) *System:* University of Texas System *Accred.:* 1936/1986 (SACS-CC) *Calendar:* Sem. plan *Degrees:* B, M, D *Prof. Accred.:* Accounting (Type A,C), Business (B,M), Computer Science, Engineering (civil, electrical, industrial, mechanical, metallurgical), Medical Technology, Music, Nursing (M) *CEO:* Pres. Diana S. Natalicio
Enroll: 14438 (915) 747-5000

The University of Texas at San Antonio
San Antonio 78285 *Type:* Public (state) *System:* University of Texas System *Accred.:* 1974/1990 (SACS-CC) *Calendar:* Sem. plan *Degrees:* B, M *Prof. Accred.:* Art, Business (B,M), Engineering (civil, electrical, mechanical), Music, Nursing (B,M), Physical Therapy *CEO:* Pres. Samuel A. Kirkpatrick
Enroll: 12337 (512) 691-4011

The University of Texas at Tyler
3900 University Blvd., Tyler 75701-6699 *Type:* Public (state) *System:* University of Texas System *Accred.:* 1974/1990 (SACS-CC) *Calendar:* Sem. plan *Degrees:* B, M *Prof. Accred.:* Medical Technology, Nursing (B) *CEO:* Pres. George F. Hamm
Enroll: 4485 (214) 566-7000

The University of Texas of the Permian Basin
4901 E. University Blvd., Odessa 79762 *Type:* Public (state) *System:* University of Texas System *Accred.:* 1975/1990 (SACS-

CC) *Calendar:* Sem. plan *Degrees:* B, M *CEO:* Interim Pres. Edwin R. Sharpe
Enroll: 1288   (915) 367-2011

THE UNIVERSITY OF TEXAS—PAN AMERICAN
1201 W. University Dr., Edinburg 78539-2999 *Type:* Public (state) liberal arts *System:* University of Texas System *Accred.:* 1956/1986 (SACS-CC) *Calendar:* Sem. plan *Degrees:* A, B, M *Prof. Accred.:* Business (B,M), Dietetics (coordinated), Medical Technology, Nursing (A,B), Physical Therapy Assisting, Social Work (B) *CEO:* Pres. Miguel A. Nevarez
Enroll: 10041   (512) 381-2111

VANGUARD INSTITUTE OF TECHNOLOGY
221 N. Eighth St., Edinburg 78539 *Type:* Private *Accred.:* 1990 (SACS-COEI) *Calendar:* Courses of varying lengths *Degrees:* certificates, diplomas *CEO:* Dir. Domingo Lopez
Enroll: 54   (512) 380-3264

VERNON REGIONAL JUNIOR COLLEGE
4400 College Dr., Vernon 76384 *Type:* Public (district) junior *System:* Texas Higher Education Coordinating Board *Accred.:* 1974/1989 (SACS-CC) *Calendar:* Sem. plan *Degrees:* A *CEO:* Pres. R. Wade Kirk
Enroll: 1686   (817) 552-6291

THE VICTORIA COLLEGE
2200 E. Red River St., Victoria 77901-4494 *Type:* Public (district) junior *System:* Texas Higher Education Coordinating Board *Accred.:* 1951/1983 (SACS-CC) *Calendar:* Sem. plan *Degrees:* A *Prof. Accred.:* Medical Laboratory Technology (AMA), Nursing (A), Respiratory Therapy Technology, Surgical Technology *CEO:* Pres. Jimmy L. Goodson
Enroll: 2560   (512) 573-3291

WAYLAND BAPTIST UNIVERSITY
1900 W. Seventh St., Plainview 79072 *Type:* Private (Southern Baptist) liberal arts *Accred.:* 1956/1989 (SACS-CC) *Calendar:* Sem. plan *Degrees:* A, B, M *CEO:* Pres. Wallace Davis, Jr.
Enroll: 1258   (806) 296-5521

WEATHERFORD COLLEGE
308 E. Park Ave., Weatherford 76086 *Type:* Public (district) junior *System:* Texas Higher Education Coordinating Board *Accred.:* 1956/1991 (SACS-CC) *Calendar:* Sem. plan *Degrees:* A *CEO:* Pres. E.W. Mince
Enroll: 2169   (817) 594-5471

WEST TEXAS STATE UNIVERSITY
2501 Fourth Ave., Canyon 79016 *Type:* Public (state) liberal arts and professional *System:* Texas A&M University System *Accred.:* 1925/1985 (SACS-CC) *Calendar:* Sem. plan *Degrees:* B, M *Prof. Accred.:* Music, Nursing (B,M), Social Work (B), Teacher Education (e,s,p) *CEO:* Pres. Barry B. Thompson
Enroll: 5290   (806) 656-2000

WESTERN TECHNICAL INSTITUTE
1000 Texas Ave., El Paso 79901 *Type:* Private *Accred.:* 1986 (CCA-ACTTS) *Calendar:* Courses of varying lengths *Degrees:* diplomas *Prof. Accred.:* Medical Assisting (AMA) *CEO:* Dir. Randy Kuykendall
Enroll: 887   (915) 532-3737

WESTERN TECHNICAL INSTITUTE
4710 Alabama St., El Paso 79930 *Type:* Private *Accred.:* 1990 (CCA-ACTTS) *Calendar:* Courses of varying lengths *Degrees:* diplomas *CEO:* Dir. James Bohanan
     (915) 566-9621

WESTERN TEXAS COLLEGE
6200 S. College Ave., Snyder 79549 *Type:* Public (district) junior *System:* Texas Higher Education Coordinating Board *Accred.:* 1973/1988 (SACS-CC) *Calendar:* Sem. plan *Degrees:* A *CEO:* Pres. Harry L. Krenek
Enroll: 1248   (915) 573-8511

WHARTON COUNTY JUNIOR COLLEGE
911 Boling Hwy., Wharton 77488 *Type:* Public (district) junior *System:* Texas Higher Education Coordinating Board *Accred.:* 1951/1988 (SACS-CC) *Calendar:* Sem. plan

Degrees: A *Prof. Accred.:* Dental Hygiene, Medical Laboratory Technology (AMA), Medical Record Technology, Physical Therapy Assisting, Radiography *CEO:* Pres. Elbert C. Hutchins
Enroll: 2774 (409) 532-4560

WILEY COLLEGE
711 Wiley Ave., Marshall 75670 *Type:* Private (United Methodist) liberal arts and teachers *Accred.:* 1933/1983 (SACS-CC) *Calendar:* Sem. plan *Degrees:* A, B *CEO:* Pres. David L. Beckley
Enroll: 477 (903) 927-3300

WILLIAM MARSH RICE UNIVERSITY
6100 S. Main St., P.O. Box 1892, Houston 77251 *Type:* Private *Accred.:* 1914/1985 (SACS-CC) *Calendar:* Sem. plan *Degrees:* B, M, D *Prof. Accred.:* Architecture (B,M), Engineering (chemical, civil, electrical, materials, mechanical) *CEO:* Pres. George Rupp
Enroll: 4597 (713) 527-8101

UTAH

AMERICAN INSTITUTE OF MEDICAL-DENTAL TECHNOLOGY
1675 N. Freedom Blvd., Bldg. 9-A, Provo 84604 *Type:* Private *Calendar:* Courses of varying lengths *Degrees:* certificates *Prof. Accred.:* Dental Assisting, Health Education, Medical Assisting (AMA) *CEO:* Admin. Keith T. Van Soest
Enroll: 124 (801) 377-2900

AMERICAN TECHNICAL CENTER
1144 W. 3300 S., Salt Lake City 84119 *Type:* Private *Accred.:* 1976/1982 (CCA-ACTTS) *Calendar:* Courses of varying lengths *Degrees:* certificates *CEO:* Dir. John S. Cowan
Enroll: 120 (801) 975-1000

BRIGHAM YOUNG UNIVERSITY
Provo 84602 *Type:* Private (Latter-Day Saints) *Accred.:* 1923/1986 (NASC) *Calendar:* Sem. plan *Degrees:* A, B, M, D *Prof. Accred.:* Animal Health Technology, Art, Audiology, Business (B,M), Clinical Psychology, Computer Science, Construction Management, Dance, Dietetics (coordinated), Engineering (chemical, civil, electrical, mechanical), Engineering Technology (electrical, manufacturing, mechanical drafting/design), Journalism, Law, Librarianship, Medical Technology, Music, Nursing (B,M), Public Administration, Recreation Management, Social Work (B,M), Speech-Language Pathology, Teacher Education (e,s,p), Theatre *CEO:* Pres. Rex E. Lee
Enroll: 37778 (801) 378-4668

THE BRYMAN SCHOOL
1144 W. 3300 S., Salt Lake City 84119 *Type:* Private *Accred.:* 1973/1989 (CCA-ACTTS) *Calendar:* Courses of varying lengths *Degrees:* certificates *Prof. Accred.:* Medical Assisting (AMA) *CEO:* Pres. John S. Cowan
Enroll: 722 (801) 975-7000

CERTIFIED CAREERS INSTITUTE
28 E. 2100 S., Ste. 208, Salt Lake City 84115 *Type:* Private *Accred.:* 1988 (CCA-ACTTS) *Calendar:* Courses of varying lengths *Degrees:* diplomas *CEO:* Dir. Gene Curtis
(801) 466-6593

BRANCH CAMPUS
2661 Washington Blvd., Ogden, UT 84401 *CEO:* Dir. Robert Johnson
(801) 621-4925

COLLEGE OF EASTERN UTAH
Price 84501 *Type:* Public (state) junior *System:* Utah System of Higher Education *Accred.:* 1945/1981 (NASC) *Calendar:* Qtr. plan *Degrees:* A *Prof. Accred.:* Nursing (A) *CEO:* Pres. Michael A. Petersen
Enroll: 2960 (801) 637-2120

DIXIE COLLEGE
St. George 84770 *Type:* Public (state) junior *System:* Utah System of Higher Education *Accred.:* 1945/1982 (NASC) *Calendar:* Qtr. plan *Degrees:* A *Prof. Accred.:* Nursing (A) *CEO:* Pres. Douglas D. Alder
Enroll: 2528 (801) 673-4811

ITT TECHNICAL INSTITUTE
920 W. LeVoy Dr., Murray 84123 *Type:* Private *Accred.:* 1985 (CCA-ACTTS) *Calendar:* Courses of varying lengths *Degrees:* certificates *CEO:* Pres. Larry Cammack
Enroll: 174 (801) 263-3313

INTERMOUNTAIN COLLEGE OF COURT REPORTING
5980 S. 300 E., Murray 84107 *Type:* Private business *Accred.:* 1981/1988 (CCA-ACICS) *Calendar:* Qtr. plan *Degrees:* certificates, diplomas *CEO:* Pres. Linda J. Smurthwaite
Enroll: 187 (801) 268-9271

LATTER-DAY SAINTS BUSINESS COLLEGE
411 E. South Temple St., Salt Lake City 84111 *Type:* Private (Latter-Day Saints) *Accred.:* 1977/1982 (NASC) *Calendar:* Qtr. plan *Degrees:* A *Prof. Accred.:* Medical

Assisting (AMA) *CEO:* Pres. Stephen Woodhouse
Enroll: 717 (801) 363-2765

LOGAN BUSINESS COLLEGE
75 S. 400 W., P.O. Box 745, Logan 84321-0745 *Type:* Private business *Accred.:* 1988 (CCA-ACICS) *Calendar:* Courses of varying lengths *Degrees:* certificates, diplomas *CEO:* Pres. June S. Welling
Enroll: 44 (801) 753-7520

PHILLIPS JUNIOR COLLEGE
3098 Highland Dr., Salt Lake City 84106 *Type:* Private junior *Accred.:* 1985/1990 (CCA-ACICS) *Calendar:* Courses of varying lengths *Degrees:* A, certificates, diplomas *CEO:* Pres. Wayne Wilson
Enroll: 1012 (801) 485-0221

PROVO COLLEGE
1275 N. University Ave., Ste. 2, Provo 84604 *Type:* Private *Accred.:* 1988 (CCA-ACTTS) *Calendar:* Courses of varying lengths *Degrees:* certificates *Prof. Accred.:* Dental Assisting *CEO:* Dir. Arda Molen
Enroll: 51 (801) 375-1861

SALT LAKE COMMUNITY COLLEGE
P.O. Box 30808, Salt Lake City 84130 *Type:* Public (state) junior *System:* Utah System of Higher Education *Accred.:* 1969/1984 (NASC) *Calendar:* Qtr. plan *Degrees:* A *Prof. Accred.:* Practical Nursing, Surgical Technology *CEO:* Pres. Frank W. Budd
Enroll: 13344 (801) 967-4111

SNOW COLLEGE
Ephraim 84627 *Type:* Public (state) junior *System:* Utah System of Higher Education *Accred.:* 1953/1982 (NASC) *Calendar:* Qtr. plan *Degrees:* A *CEO:* Pres. Gerald J. Day
Enroll: 1872 (801) 283-4021

SOUTHERN UTAH UNIVERSITY
Cedar City 84720 *Type:* Public (state) liberal arts and teachers *System:* Utah System of Higher Education *Accred.:* 1933/1983 (NASC) *Calendar:* Qtr. plan *Degrees:* A, B, M *Prof. Accred.:* Music, Nursing (A) *CEO:* Pres. Gerald R. Sherratt
Enroll: 4003 (801) 586-7710

THE STEVENS-HENAGER COLLEGE OF BUSINESS
2168 Washington Blvd., Ogden 84401-1467 *Type:* Private junior *Accred.:* 1962/1986 (CCA-ACICS) *Calendar:* Qtr. plan *Degrees:* A, certificates, diplomas *CEO:* Pres. Vicky Dewsnup
Enroll: 383 (801) 394-7791

THE STEVENS-HENAGER COLLEGE OF BUSINESS
25 E. 1700 S., Provo 84606-6157 *Type:* Private junior *Accred.:* 1989 (CCA-ACICS) *Calendar:* Qtr. plan *Degrees:* A, certificates, diplomas *CEO:* Dir. Robert J. Fox
Enroll: 452 (801) 375-5455

UNIVERSITY OF UTAH
Salt Lake City 84112 *Type:* Public (state) *System:* Utah System of Higher Education *Accred.:* 1933/1986 (NASC) *Calendar:* Qtr. plan *Degrees:* A, B, M, D *Prof. Accred.:* Accounting (Type A,C), Architecture (M), Audiology, Business (B,M), Clinical Psychology, Community Health/Preventive Medicine, Computer Science, Counseling Psychology, Cytotechnology, Dietetics (coordinated), Engineering (chemical, civil, electrical, geological/geophysical, materials, mechanical, metallurgical, mining), General Dentistry, General Practice Residency, Journalism, Law, Medical Technology, Medicine, Nuclear Medicine Technology, Nursing (B,M), Pharmacy, Physical Therapy, Physician Assisting, Psychology Internship, Public Administration, Radiation Therapy Technology, Radiography, Recreation and Leisure Studies, School Psychology, Social Work (M), Speech-Language Pathology *CEO:* Pres. Arthur K. Smith
Enroll: 25020 (801) 581-7200

UTAH STATE UNIVERSITY
Logan 84322-1400 *Type:* Public (state) *System:* Utah System of Higher Education *Accred.:* 1924/1988 (NASC) *Calendar:* Qtr. plan *Degrees:* A, B, M, D *Prof. Accred.:* Accounting (Type A,C), Audiology, Busi-

ness (B,M), Combined Professional-Scientific Psychology, Dietetics (coordinated), Engineering (agricultural, civil, electrical, manufacturing, mechanical), Forestry, Home Economics, Landscape Architecture (B,M), Music, Nursing (A), Social Work (B), Speech-Language Pathology, Teacher Education (e,s,p) *CEO:* Pres. Stanford Cazier
Enroll: 15156 (801) 750-1000

UTAH VALLEY COMMUNITY COLLEGE
800 W. 1200 S., Orem 84038 *Type:* Public (state) junior *System:* Utah System of Higher Education *Accred.:* 1969/1984 (NASC) *Calendar:* Qtr. plan *Degrees:* A *Prof. Accred.:* Engineering Technology (electrical), Nursing (A) *CEO:* Pres. Kerry D. Romesburg
Enroll: 7886 (801) 226-5000

WEBER STATE UNIVERSITY
3750 Harrison Blvd., Ogden 84408-1004 *Type:* Public (state) liberal arts and teachers *System:* Utah System of Higher Education *Accred.:* 1932/1984 (NASC) *Calendar:* Qtr. plan *Degrees:* A, B, M *Prof. Accred.:* Dental Hygiene, Diagnostic Medical Sonography, EMT-Paramedic, Engineering Technology (automotive, electrical, manufacturing, mechanical), Medical Laboratory Technology (AMA), Medical Record Technology, Medical Technology, Music, Nuclear Medicine Technology, Nursing (A,B), Practical Nursing, Radiation Therapy Technology, Radiography, Respiratory Therapy, Respiratory Therapy Technology, Social Work (B), Teacher Education (e,s) *CEO:* Pres. Paul H. Thompson
Enroll: 13449 (801) 626-6140

WESTMINSTER COLLEGE OF SALT LAKE CITY
1840 S. 1300 E., Salt Lake City 84105 *Type:* Private liberal arts and professional *Accred.:* 1936/1983 (NASC) *Calendar:* 4-1-4 plan *Degrees:* B, M *Prof. Accred.:* Nursing (B) *CEO:* Pres. Charles H. Dick
Enroll: 2054 (801) 488-4298

VERMONT

BENNINGTON COLLEGE
Bennington 05201 *Type:* Private liberal arts *Accred.:* 1935/1987 (NEASC-CIHE) *Calendar:* Courses of varying lengths *Degrees:* B, M *CEO:* Pres. Elizabeth Coleman
Enroll: 581 (802) 442-5401

BURLINGTON COLLEGE
Burlington 05401-8477 *Type:* Private *Accred.:* 1982/1987 (NEASC-CIHE) *Calendar:* Tri. plan *Degrees:* A, B *CEO:* Pres. Steward La Casce
Enroll: 138 (802) 862-9616

CASTLETON STATE COLLEGE
Castleton 05735 *Type:* Public (state) liberal arts and teachers *System:* Vermont State Colleges *Accred.:* 1960/1985 (NEASC-CIHE) *Calendar:* Sem. plan *Degrees:* A, B, M *Prof. Accred.:* Nursing (A), Social Work (B) *CEO:* Pres. Lyle A. Gray
Enroll: 2126 (802) 468-5611

CHAMPLAIN COLLEGE
P.O. Box 670, Burlington 05402-0670 *Type:* Private junior *Accred.:* 1991 (NEASC-CIHE) *Calendar:* Sem. plan *Degrees:* A *Prof. Accred.:* Engineering Technology (electrical), Radiography *CEO:* Pres. Robert A. Skiff
Enroll: 1510 (802) 658-0800

COLLEGE OF ST. JOSEPH
Rutland 05701 *Type:* Private (Roman Catholic) teachers *Accred.:* 1972/1986 (NEASC-CIHE) *Calendar:* Sem. plan *Degrees:* A, B, M *CEO:* Pres. Frank G. Miglorie, Jr.
Enroll: 334 (802) 773-5900

COMMUNITY COLLEGE OF VERMONT
Waterbury 05676 *Type:* Public (state) junior *System:* Vermont State Colleges *Accred.:* 1975/1982 (NEASC-CIHE) *Calendar:* Tri. plan *Degrees:* A *CEO:* Pres. Michael Holland
Enroll: 1571 (802) 241-3535

GODDARD COLLEGE
Plainfield 05667 *Type:* Private liberal arts *Accred.:* 1959/1986 (NEASC-CIHE) *Calendar:* Sem. plan *Degrees:* B, M *CEO:* Pres. Jackson Kytle
Enroll: 499 (802) 454-8311

GREEN MOUNTAIN COLLEGE
Poultney 05764 *Type:* Private (United Methodist) liberal arts *Accred.:* 1934/1987 (NEASC-CIHE) *Calendar:* 4-1-4 plan *Degrees:* A, B *Prof. Accred.:* Recreation and Leisure Studies *CEO:* Pres. James M. Pollock
Enroll: 781 (802) 287-9313

JOHNSON STATE COLLEGE
Johnson 05656 *Type:* Public (state) liberal arts and teachers *System:* Vermont State Colleges *Accred.:* 1961/1986 (NEASC-CIHE) *Calendar:* Sem. plan *Degrees:* A, B, M *CEO:* Interim Pres. Robert Hahn
Enroll: 1483 (802) 635-2356

LYNDON STATE COLLEGE
Vail Hill, Lyndonville 05851 *Type:* Public (state) liberal arts and teachers *System:* Vermont State Colleges *Accred.:* 1965/1989 (NEASC-CIHE) *Calendar:* Sem. plan *Degrees:* A, B, M *Prof. Accred.:* Recreation and Leisure Studies *CEO:* Pres. Margaret R. Williams
Enroll: 1173 (802) 626-9371

MARLBORO COLLEGE
Marlboro 05344 *Type:* Private liberal arts *Accred.:* 1965/1987 (NEASC-CIHE) *Calendar:* Courses of varying lengths *Degrees:* B, M *CEO:* Pres. Roderick M. Gander
Enroll: 233 (802) 257-4333

MIDDLEBURY COLLEGE
Middlebury 05753 *Type:* Private liberal arts *Accred.:* 1929/1990 (NEASC-CIHE) *Calendar:* Sem. plan *Degrees:* B, M, D *CEO:* Acting Pres. John McCardell
Enroll: 2244 (802) 388-3711

Vermont

NEW ENGLAND CULINARY INSTITUTE
250 Main St., P.O. Box 1255, Montpelier 05602 *Type:* Private *Accred.:* 1984/1989 (CCA-ACTTS) *Calendar:* Courses of varying lengths *Degrees:* certificates *CEO:* Pres. Francis Voigt
Enroll: 207   (802) 223-6324

BRANCH CAMPUS
Sullivan Hall, Ste. 230, 92 Ethan Allen, Colchester, VT 05446 *CEO:* Dir. John Turner
                            (802) 655-0808

NORWICH UNIVERSITY
Northfield 05663 *Type:* Private liberal arts *Accred.:* 1933/1990 (NEASC-CIHE) *Calendar:* Sem. plan *Degrees:* A, B, M, D *Prof. Accred.:* Engineering (civil, electrical, mechanical), Engineering Technology (environmental/sanitary) *CEO:* Pres. W. Russell Todd
Enroll: 2420   (802) 485-2000

VERMONT COLLEGE
College St., Montpelier, VT 05602 *Prof. Accred.:* Nursing (A,B) *CEO:* Vice Pres. Richard H. Hansen
                            (802) 485-2000

ST. MICHAEL'S COLLEGE
Winooski Park, Colchester 05439 *Type:* Private (Roman Catholic) *Accred.:* 1939/1990 (NEASC-CIHE) *Calendar:* Sem. plan *Degrees:* B, M *CEO:* Pres. Paul J. Reiss
Enroll: 2147   (802) 655-2000

SCHOOL FOR INTERNATIONAL TRAINING
P.O. Box 676, Brattleboro 05302 *Type:* Private liberal arts *Accred.:* 1974/1986 (NEASC-CIHE) *Calendar:* Sem. plan *Degrees:* B, M *CEO:* Pres. Neil Mangham
Enroll: 588   (802) 257-7751

SOUTHERN VERMONT COLLEGE
Bennington 05201 *Type:* Private *Accred.:* 1979/1989 (NEASC-CIHE) *Calendar:* Sem. plan *Degrees:* A, B, certificates, diplomas *CEO:* Pres. William A. Glasser
Enroll: 464   (802) 442-5427

STERLING COLLEGE
Craftsbury Common 05827 *Type:* Private 2-year *Accred.:* 1987/1991 (NEASC-CVTCI) *Calendar:* Qtr. plan *Degrees:* A *CEO:* Pres. Steve E. Wright
Enroll: 83   (802) 586-7711

TRINITY COLLEGE OF VERMONT
208 Colchester Ave., Burlington 05401 *Type:* Private (Roman Catholic) liberal arts for women *Accred.:* 1952/1985 (NEASC-CIHE) *Calendar:* Sem. plan *Degrees:* B *Prof. Accred.:* Social Work (B) *CEO:* Pres. Janice E. Ryan, R.S.M.
Enroll: 1100   (802) 658-0337

UNIVERSITY OF VERMONT
Burlington 05405-0160 *Type:* Public (state) *System:* Vermont State Colleges *Accred.:* 1929/1989 (NEASC-CIHE) *Calendar:* Sem. plan *Degrees:* A, B, P, M, D *Prof. Accred.:* Business (B,M), Clinical Psychology, Counseling, Dental Hygiene (conditional), Engineering (civil, electrical, mechanical), Forestry, Medical Technology, Medicine, Music, Nuclear Medicine Technology, Nursing (A,B), Physical Therapy, Radiation Therapy Technology, Social Work (B,M-candidate), Speech-Language Pathology, Teacher Education (e,s,p) *CEO:* Pres. Thomas Salmon
Enroll: 9307   (802) 656-3131

VERMONT LAW SCHOOL
Chelsea St., P.O. Box 96, South Royalton 05068 *Type:* Private professional *Accred.:* 1980/1985 (NEASC-CIHE) *Calendar:* Sem. plan *Degrees:* P *Prof. Accred.:* Law *CEO:* Dean Maximilian W. Kempner
Enroll: 490   (802) 763-8303

VERMONT TECHNICAL COLLEGE
Randolph Center 05061 *Type:* Public (state) 2-year *System:* Vermont State Colleges *Accred.:* 1970/1989 (NEASC-CVTCI) *Calendar:* Sem. plan *Degrees:* A *Prof. Accred.:* Engineering Technology (architectural, civil/construction, electrical, mechanical) *CEO:* Pres. Robert G. Clarke
Enroll: 859   (802) 728-3391

Accredited Institutions   **Vermont**

WOODBURY COLLEGE
660 Elm St., Montpelier 05602 *Type:* Private *Accred.:* 1984 (NEASC-CVTCI) *Calendar:* Sem. plan *Degrees:* certificates *CEO:* Pres. Lawrence H. Mandell *Enroll:* 104 (802) 229-0516

VIRGIN ISLANDS

UNIVERSITY OF THE VIRGIN ISLANDS
Charlotte Amalie, St. Thomas 00802 *Type:* Public liberal arts and professional *Accred.:* 1971/1986 (MSA) *Calendar:* Sem. plan *Degrees:* A, B, M *Prof. Accred.:* Nursing (A,B)
CEO: Pres. Orville E. Kean
Enroll: 2471 (809) 776-9200

BRANCH CAMPUS
St. Croix, VI 00850 *CEO:* Dir. Mary Savage
(809) 778-1620

VIRGINIA

ATI—HOLLYWOOD
3024 Trinkle Ave., Roanoke 24012 *Type:* Private *Accred.:* 1989 (SACS-COEI) *Calendar:* Courses of varying lengths *Degrees:* certificates *CEO:* Pres. Todd Rothrock
Enroll: 51 (703) 362-9338

BRANCH CAMPUS
1108 Brandon Ave., S.W., Roanoke, VA 24015 *CEO:* Dir. Marie Mullens
 (703) 343-0153

BRANCH CAMPUS
109 E. Main St., Salem, VA 24153 *CEO:* Dir. Priscilla Atkinson
 (703) 389-1500

ALLIANCE TRACTOR TRAILER TRAINING CENTER
610 Peppers Ferry Rd., P.O. Box 804, Wytheville 24382 *Type:* Private *Accred.:* 1988 (CCA-ACTTS) *Calendar:* Courses of varying lengths *Degrees:* certificates *CEO:* Dir. Richard W. Grassette
Enroll: 670 (703) 228-6101

ANTHONY'S BARBER COLLEGE
1307 Jefferson Ave., Newport News 23607 *Type:* Private *Accred.:* 1989 (CCA-ACTTS) *Calendar:* Courses of varying lengths *Degrees:* certificates *CEO:* Dir. Irene Anthony
 (804) 244-2311

APPRENTICE SCHOOL—NEWPORT NEWS SHIPBUILDING
4101 Washington Ave., Newport News 23607 *Type:* Private *Accred.:* 1982/1987 (SACS-COEI) *Calendar:* Courses of varying lengths *Degrees:* certificates *CEO:* Dir. James H. Hughes
Enroll: 637 (804) 380-2682

AVERETT COLLEGE
420 W. Main St., Danville 24541 *Type:* Private (Southern Baptist) liberal arts *Accred.:* 1928/1991 (SACS-CC) *Calendar:* Sem. plan *De-grees:* B, M *CEO:* Pres. Frank R. Campbell
Enroll: 1401 (804) 791-5600

BARCLAY CAREER SCHOOL
645 Church St., Norfolk 23510-1712 *Type:* Private *Accred.:* 1991 (CCA-ACTTS) *Calendar:* Courses of varying lengths *Degrees:* certificates *CEO:* Dir. Bob McNeeley
 (804) 533-9500

BLUE RIDGE COMMUNITY COLLEGE
P.O. Box 80, Weyers Cave 24486 *Type:* Public (state) junior *System:* Virginia Community College System *Accred.:* 1969/1984 (SACS-CC) *Calendar:* Sem. plan *Degrees:* A *Prof. Accred.:* Veterinary Technology *CEO:* Pres. James R. Perkins
Enroll: 1541 (703) 234-9261

BLUEFIELD COLLEGE
3000 College Dr., Bluefield 24605 *Type:* Private (Southern Baptist) liberal arts *Accred.:* 1949/1984 (SACS-CC) *Calendar:* Sem. plan *Degrees:* A, B *CEO:* Pres. Roy A. Dobyns
Enroll: 485 (703) 326-3682

THE BRAXTON SCHOOL
4917 Augusta Ave., P.O. Box 6508, Richmond 23230 *Type:* Private business *Accred.:* 1988 (CCA-ACICS) *Calendar:* Courses of varying lengths *Degrees:* certificates, diplomas *CEO:* Dir. Emily Swelnis
Enroll: 196 (804) 353-4458

BRIDGEWATER COLLEGE
Bridgewater 22812 *Type:* Private (Church of Brethren) liberal arts *Accred.:* 1925/1991 (SACS-CC) *Calendar:* 3-3-1-3 plan *De-grees:* B *CEO:* Pres. Wayne F. Geisert
Enroll: 981 (703) 828-2501

CDI CAREER DEVELOPMENT INSTITUTE
3717 Columbia Pike, Arlington 22204 *Type:* Private *Accred.:* 1968/1979 (CCA-ACTTS) *Calendar:* Courses of varying lengths *De-grees:* certificates *CEO:* Dir. Barbara Thomas
Enroll: 975 (703) 533-2050

Virginia

CAREER DEVELOPMENT CENTER
605 Thimble Shoals Blvd., No. 209, Newport News 23606 *Type:* Private *Accred.:* 1983/1988 (SACS-COEI) *Calendar:* Courses of varying lengths *Degrees:* certificates *CEO:* Dir. Patricia Ettus
Enroll: 111 (804) 873-2423

THE CATHOLIC HOME STUDY INSTITUTE
9 Loudoun St., S.E., Leesburg 22075 *Type:* Private home study *Accred.:* 1986/1991 (NHSC) *Calendar:* Courses of varying lengths *Degrees:* certificates *CEO:* Exec. Dir. Marianne E. Mount
 (703) 777-8388

CENTRAL VIRGINIA COMMUNITY COLLEGE
3506 Wards Rd., Lynchburg 24502 *Type:* Public (state) junior *System:* Virginia Community College System *Accred.:* 1969/1984 (SACS-CC) *Calendar:* Sem. plan *Degrees:* A *Prof. Accred.:* Medical Laboratory Technology (AMA), Medical Record Technology, Radiography, Respiratory Therapy Technology *CEO:* Pres. Johnnie E. Merritt
Enroll: 2316 (804) 386-4500

CHRISTENDOM COLLEGE
2101 Shenandoah Shores Rd., Front Royal 22630 *Type:* Private (Roman Catholic) liberal arts *Accred.:* 1987 (SACS-CC) *Calendar:* Sem. plan *Degrees:* A, B *CEO:* Pres. Damian P. Fedoryka
Enroll: 175 (703) 636-2900

CHRISTOPHER NEWPORT COLLEGE
50 Shoe La., Newport News 23606 *Type:* Public (state) liberal arts *System:* State Council of Higher Education for Virginia *Accred.:* 1971/1986 (SACS-CC) *Calendar:* Sem. plan *Degrees:* B *Prof. Accred.:* Nursing (B), Social Work (B) *CEO:* Pres. Anthony R. Santoro
Enroll: 3776 (804) 594-7000

CLINCH VALLEY COLLEGE OF THE UNIVERSITY OF VIRGINIA
College Ave., Wise 24293 *Type:* Public (state) liberal arts and teachers *System:* University of Virginia Central Office *Accred.:* 1970/1985 (SACS-CC) *Calendar:* Sem. plan *Degrees:* B *CEO:* Chanc. J.A. Knight
Enroll: 1263 (703) 328-0100

THE COLLEGE OF WILLIAM AND MARY
Williamsburg 23185 *Type:* Public (state) liberal arts *System:* State Council of Higher Education for Virginia *Accred.:* 1921/1985 (SACS-CC) *Calendar:* Sem. plan *Degrees:* A, B, M, D *Prof. Accred.:* Accounting (Type A), Business (B,M), Law, Teacher Education (e,s,p) *CEO:* Acting Pres. Melvyn D. Schiavelli
Enroll: 7092 (804) 221-4000

COMMONWEALTH COLLEGE
4160 Virginia Beach Blvd., Virginia Beach 23452 *Type:* Private *Accred.:* 1988/1990 (CCA-ACICS); 1984/1989 (SACS-COEI) *Calendar:* Courses of varying lengths *Degrees:* A, certificates, diplomas *CEO:* Pres. Julia Heffernan
Enroll: 1462 (804) 340-0222

BRANCH CAMPUS
1120 W. Mercury Blvd., Hampton, VA 23666-3319 *CEO:* Dir. Robin Rickenbach
Enroll: 739 (804) 838-2122

BRANCH CAMPUS
5579 Portsmouth Blvd., Norfolk, VA 23701 *CEO:* Dir. John H. Getgood
 (804) 488-7799

BRANCH CAMPUS
300 Boush St., Norfolk, VA 23510 *CEO:* Pres. Richard Heffernan
Enroll: 805 (804) 625-5891

BRANCH CAMPUS
4000 W. Broad St., Richmond, VA 23230 *CEO:* Pres. Ted Morris
Enroll: 518 (804) 353-2424

COMMUNITY HOSPITAL OF ROANOKE VALLEY COLLEGE OF HEALTH SCIENCES
P.O. Box 13186, Roanoke 24031-3186 *Type:* Private *Accred.:* 1986/1991 (SACS-CC) *Calendar:* Sem. plan *Degrees:* A *Prof. Accred.:* EMT-Paramedic, Physical Therapy Assist-

ing, Respiratory Therapy *CEO:* Pres. Harry C. Nickens
Enroll: 192 (703) 985-8483

COMPUTER DYNAMICS INSTITUTE
397 Little Neck Rd., 3000 South Bldg., No. 135, Virginia Beach 23452 *Type:* Private *Accred.:* 1990 (SACS-COEI) *Calendar:* Courses of varying lengths *Degrees:* certificates *CEO:* Dir. Deborah Carson
Enroll: 157 (804) 486-7300

COMPUTER LEARNING CENTER
6666 Commerce St., Springfield 22150 *Type:* Private business *Accred.:* 1979/1985 (CCA-ACICS); 1984/1989 (SACS-COEI) *Calendar:* Courses of varying lengths *Degrees:* certificates, diplomas *CEO:* Dir. Ronald Sandler
Enroll: 1710 (703) 971-0500

DABNEY S. LANCASTER COMMUNITY COLLEGE
Rte. 60 W., P.O. Box 1000, Clifton Forge 24422-1000 *Type:* Public (state) junior *System:* Virginia Community College System *Accred.:* 1969/1984 (SACS-CC) *Calendar:* Sem. plan *Degrees:* A *Prof. Accred.:* Nursing (A) *CEO:* Pres. John F. Backels
Enroll: 1051 (703) 862-4246

DANVILLE COMMUNITY COLLEGE
1008 S. Main St., Danville 24541 *Type:* Public (state) junior *System:* Virginia Community College System *Accred.:* 1970/1985 (SACS-CC) *Calendar:* Sem. plan *Degrees:* A *CEO:* Interim Pres. Robert Shaver
Enroll: 1898 (804) 797-3553

DEFENSE MAPPING SCHOOL
21st St. and Belvoir Rd., Fort Belvoir 22060-5828 *Type:* Public (federal) *Accred.:* 1975/1990 (SACS-COEI) *Calendar:* Courses of varying lengths *Degrees:* certificates *CEO:* Commandant Samuel Schwartz, U.S.A.
Enroll: 377 (703) 664-3673

DOMINION BUSINESS SCHOOL
4142-1 Melrose Ave., N.W., No. 1, Roanoke 24017 *Type:* Private business *Accred.:* 1972/1984 (CCA-ACICS) *Calendar:* Courses of varying lengths *Degrees:* certificates, diplomas *CEO:* Pres. Geraldine Hask
Enroll: 202 (703) 362-7738

BRANCH CAMPUS
933 Reservoir St., Harrisonburg, VA 22801 *CEO:* Dir. Jim Foster
(703) 433-6977

BRANCH CAMPUS
825 Richmond Rd., Staunton, VA 24401 *CEO:* Dir. Catherine E. Puffenberger
(703) 886-3596

ECPI COMPUTER INSTITUTE
4303 W. Broad St., Richmond 23230 *Type:* Private *Accred.:* 1986 (CCA-ACTTS); 1990 (SACS-COEI) *Calendar:* Courses of varying lengths *Degrees:* certificates *CEO:* Dir. F. Bruce Misiaszak
Enroll: 179 (804) 359-3535

BRANCH CAMPUS
4020 W. Chase Blvd., Ste. 500, Raleigh, NC 27606 *CEO:* Dir. Steve Hitchner
(919) 833-0400

BRANCH CAMPUS
1030 S. Jefferson St., S.E., Roanoke, VA 24016 *CEO:* Dir. Finn Pincus
(703) 342-0050

ECPI COMPUTER INSTITUTE
5555 Greenwich Rd., Ste. 300, Virginia Beach 23462 *Type:* Private *Accred.:* 1971/1986 (CCA-ACTTS); 1984/1989 (SACS-COEI) *Calendar:* Courses of varying lengths *Degrees:* certificates *CEO:* Dir. Alfred Dreyfus
Enroll: 1041 (804) 671-7171

BRANCH CAMPUS
1121 Wood Ridge Center Dr., No. 150, Charlotte, NC 28217 *CEO:* Dir. Paul Schultz
(704) 357-0077

BRANCH CAMPUS
7015 Albert Pick Rd., Greensboro, NC 27409 *CEO:* Dir. Peter Fay
(919) 665-1400

Virginia

BRANCH CAMPUS
1919 Commerce Dr., Ste. 200, Hampton, VA 23666 *CEO:* Dir. R.J. Ballance
(804) 838-9191

EASTERN MENNONITE COLLEGE AND SEMINARY
Harrisonburg 22801 *Type:* Private (Mennonite) liberal arts *Accred.:* 1986/1990 (ATS); 1959/1990 (SACS-CC) *Calendar:* Sem. plan *Degrees:* A, B, M *Prof. Accred.:* Nursing (B), Social Work (B), Teacher Education (e,s) *CEO:* Pres. Joseph L. Lapp
Enroll: 1019   (703) 432-2771

EASTERN SHORE COMMUNITY COLLEGE
Rte. 1, Box 6, Melfa 23410 *Type:* Public (state) junior *System:* Virginia Community College System *Accred.:* 1973/1988 (SACS-CC) *Calendar:* Sem. plan *Degrees:* A *CEO:* Pres. John C. Fiege
Enroll: 345   (804) 787-5900

EASTERN VIRGINIA MEDICAL SCHOOL
825 Fairfax Ave., Norfolk 23501 *Type:* Private professional *Accred.:* 1984/1990 (SACS-CC) *Calendar:* Sem. plan *Degrees:* M, D *Prof. Accred.:* Medicine, Psychology Internship *CEO:* Pres. Edward E. Brickell
Enroll: 483   (804) 446-5600

EMORY AND HENRY COLLEGE
Emory 24327 *Type:* Private (United Methodist) liberal arts *Accred.:* 1925/1987 (SACS-CC) *Calendar:* Sem. plan *Degrees:* B *CEO:* Interim Pres. Richard W. Trollinger
Enroll: 818   (703) 944-3121

FERRUM COLLEGE
Ferrum 24088 *Type:* Private (United Methodist) liberal arts *Accred.:* 1960/1991 (SACS-CC) *Calendar:* Sem. plan *Degrees:* A, B *Prof. Accred.:* Recreation and Leisure Studies, Social Work (B) *CEO:* Pres. Jerry M. Boone
Enroll: 1174   (703) 365-2121

FISCHER TECHNICAL INSTITUTE
5700 Southern Blvd., Virginia Beach 23462-2409 *Type:* Private *Accred.:* 1991 (CCA-ACTTS) *Calendar:* Courses of varying lengths *Degrees:* certificates *CEO:* Dir. George T. Elliott
(804) 490-1241

FLATWOODS CIVILIAN CONSERVATION CENTER
Rte. 1, Box 211, Coeburn 24230 *Type:* Private *Accred.:* 1989 (SACS-COEI) *Calendar:* Courses of varying lengths *Degrees:* certificates *CEO:* Dir. Lamar Carver
Enroll: 225   (703) 395-3384

GEORGE MASON UNIVERSITY
4400 University Dr., Fairfax 22030-4444 *Type:* Public (state) *System:* State Council of Higher Education for Virginia *Accred.:* 1957/1991 (SACS-CC) *Calendar:* Sem. plan *Degrees:* B, M, D *Prof. Accred.:* Accounting (Type A,C), Business (B,M), Clinical Psychology, Engineering (electrical), Law, Nursing (B,M), Public Administration, Social Work (B), Teacher Education (e,s,p) *CEO:* Pres. George W. Johnson
Enroll: 15553   (703) 993-8700

GERMANNA COMMUNITY COLLEGE
P.O. Box 339, Locust Grove 22508 *Type:* Public (state) junior *System:* Virginia Community College System *Accred.:* 1972/1987 (SACS-CC) *Calendar:* Sem. plan *Degrees:* A *Prof. Accred.:* Nursing (A) *CEO:* Pres. Frank S. Turnage
Enroll: 1457   (703) 399-1333

HAMPDEN-SYDNEY COLLEGE
P.O. Box 128, Hampden-Sydney 23943 *Type:* Private (Presbyterian) liberal arts for men *Accred.:* 1919/1986 (SACS-CC) *Calendar:* Sem. plan *Degrees:* B *CEO:* Pres. Ralph A. Rossum
Enroll: 956   (804) 223-4381

HAMPTON UNIVERSITY
Hampton 23668 *Type:* Private liberal arts *Accred.:* 1932/1988 (SACS-CC) *Calendar:* Sem. plan *Degrees:* B, M *Prof. Accred.:* Architecture (B), Computer Science, Music, Nursing (B,M), Social Work (B), Speech-Language Pathology, Teacher Education (e,s,p) *CEO:* Pres. William R. Harvey
Enroll: 4989   (804) 727-5000

Accredited Institutions   **Virginia**

HOLLINS COLLEGE
7916 Williamson Rd., Roanoke 24020 *Type:* Private liberal arts primarily for women *Accred.:* 1932/1986 (SACS-CC) *Calendar:* 4-1-4 plan *Degrees:* B, M *CEO:* Pres. Jane M. O'Brien
Enroll: 1007   (703) 362-6000

ITT TECHNICAL INSTITUTE
6465 College Park Sq., Virginia Beach 23464-3609 *Type:* Private *Accred.:* 1991 (CCA-ACTTS) *Calendar:* Courses of varying lengths *Degrees:* certificates *CEO:* Dir. Dennis McClosley
     (804) 424-0303

INSTITUTE OF TEXTILE TECHNOLOGY
P.O. Box 391, Charlottesville 22902 *Type:* Private *Accred.:* 1987 (SACS-CC) *Calendar:* Qtr. plan *Degrees:* M *CEO:* Pres. Charles G. Tewksbury
Enroll: 30   (804) 296-5511

J. SARGEANT REYNOLDS COMMUNITY COLLEGE
P.O. Box C-32040, Richmond 23261-2040 *Type:* Public (state) junior *System:* Virginia Community College System *Accred.:* 1974/1989 (SACS-CC) *Calendar:* Sem. plan *Degrees:* A *Prof. Accred.:* Dental Assisting, Dental Laboratory Technology, Medical Laboratory Technology (AMA), Nursing (A), Respiratory Therapy, Respiratory Therapy Technology *CEO:* Pres. S.A. Burnette
Enroll: 5640   (804) 371-3000

JAMES MADISON UNIVERSITY
Harrisonburg 22807 *Type:* Public (state) liberal arts and teachers *System:* State Council of Higher Education for Virginia *Accred.:* 1927/1982 (SACS-CC) *Calendar:* Sem. plan *Degrees:* B, M *Prof. Accred.:* Accounting (Type A,C), Art, Audiology, Business (B,M), Counseling, Music, Nursing (B), Social Work (B), Speech-Language Pathology, Teacher Education (e,s,p), Theatre *CEO:* Pres. Ronald E. Carrier
Enroll: 11892   (703) 568-6211

JOHN TYLER COMMUNITY COLLEGE
13101 Jefferson Davis Hwy., Chester 23831-5399 *Type:* Public (state) junior *System:* Virginia Community College System *Accred.:* 1969/1983 (SACS-CC) *Calendar:* Sem. plan *Degrees:* A *Prof. Accred.:* Engineering Technology (architectural, electrical), Funeral Service Education, Nursing (A) *CEO:* Pres. Marshall W. Smith
Enroll: 5780   (804) 796-4000

JUDGE ADVOCATE GENERAL'S SCHOOL
Charlottesville 22903-1781 *Type:* Public (federal) professional *Calendar:* Sem. plan *Degrees:* P *Prof. Accred.:* Law (ABA only) *CEO:* Dean Thomas M. Strassburg, U.S.A.
Enroll: 61   (804) 972-6301

LIBERTY UNIVERSITY
3765 Candlers Mountain Rd., P.O. Box 20000, Lynchburg 24506-8001 *Type:* Private (Baptist) liberal arts *Accred.:* 1980/1986 (SACS-CC) *Calendar:* Sem. plan *Degrees:* A, B, M *CEO:* Pres. A. Pierre Guillermin
Enroll: 10991   (804) 582-2000

LONGWOOD COLLEGE
Farmville 23901 *Type:* Public (state) liberal arts and teachers for women *System:* State Council of Higher Education for Virginia *Accred.:* 1927/1983 (SACS-CC) *Calendar:* Sem. plan *Degrees:* B, M *Prof. Accred.:* Music, Recreation, Social Work (B), Teacher Education (e,s,p) *CEO:* Pres. William F. Dorrill
Enroll: 3054   (804) 395-2000

LORD FAIRFAX COMMUNITY COLLEGE
Rte. 11 N., P.O. Box 47, Middletown 22645 *Type:* Public (state) junior *System:* Virginia Community College System *Accred.:* 1972/1987 (SACS-CC) *Calendar:* Sem. plan *Degrees:* A *CEO:* Pres. Marilyn C. Beck
Enroll: 1384   (703) 869-1120

LYNCHBURG COLLEGE
1501 Lakeside Dr., Lynchburg 24501-3199 *Type:* Private (Disciples of Christ) liberal arts *Accred.:* 1927/1983 (SACS-CC) *Calen-*

dar: Sem. plan *Degrees:* B, M *Prof. Accred.:* Nursing (B) *CEO:* Pres. George N. Rainsford
Enroll: 2053 (804) 522-8100

MARY BALDWIN COLLEGE
Staunton 24401 *Type:* Private (Presbyterian) liberal arts for women *Accred.:* 1931/1988 (SACS-CC) *Calendar:* 4-1-4 plan *Degrees:* B *CEO:* Pres. Cynthia H. Tyson
Enroll: 1096 (703) 887-7000

MARY WASHINGTON COLLEGE
Fredericksburg 22401-5358 *Type:* Public (state) liberal arts *System:* State Council of Higher Education for Virginia *Accred.:* 1930/1983 (SACS-CC) *Calendar:* Sem. plan *Degrees:* B, M *Prof. Accred.:* Music *CEO:* Pres. William M. Anderson, Jr.
Enroll: 3399 (703) 899-4100

MARYLAND DRAFTING INSTITUTE
8001 Forbes Pl., Springfield 22151 *Type:* Private *Accred.:* 1985 (CCA-ACTTS) *Calendar:* Courses of varying lengths *Degrees:* certificates *CEO:* Dir. Carol Sawyer
(703) 321-9777

MARYMOUNT UNIVERSITY
2807 N. Glebe Rd., Arlington 22207-4299 *Type:* Private for women *Accred.:* 1958/1988 (SACS-CC) *Calendar:* Sem. plan *Degrees:* A, B, M *Prof. Accred.:* Interior Design, Nursing (A,B,M), Teacher Education (e,s) *CEO:* Pres. M. Majella Berg
Enroll: 2219 (703) 522-5600

MORVEN PARK INTERNATIONAL EQUESTRIAN INSTITUTE
Rte. 4, Box 43, Leesburg 22075 *Type:* Private *Accred.:* 1975/1990 (SACS-COEI) *Calendar:* Courses of varying lengths *Degrees:* certificates *CEO:* Dir. Andrew Mouw
Enroll: 36 (703) 777-2414

MOUNTAIN EMPIRE COMMUNITY COLLEGE
P.O. Drawer 700, Big Stone Gap 24219 *Type:* Public (state) junior *System:* Virginia Community College System *Accred.:* 1974/1989 (SACS-CC) *Calendar:* Sem. plan *Degrees:* A *Prof. Accred.:* Nursing (A), Respiratory Therapy Technology *CEO:* Interim Pres. Donald E. Puyear
Enroll: 1729 (703) 523-2400

NATIONAL BUSINESS COLLEGE
1813 E. Main St., Salem 24153 *Type:* Private junior *Accred.:* 1954/1986 (CCA-ACICS) *Calendar:* Qtr. plan *Degrees:* A *Prof. Accred.:* Medical Assisting (AMA) *CEO:* Chrmn. Frank E. Longaker
Enroll: 691 (703) 986-1800

BRANCH CAMPUS
100 Logan St., Bluefield, VA 24605 *CEO:* Dir. Anna Marie Counts
(703) 326-3621

BRANCH CAMPUS
617 W. Main St., Charlottesville, VA 22901 *CEO:* Dir. Patricia O'Rourke
(804) 295-0136

BRANCH CAMPUS
734 Main St., Danville, VA 24541 *CEO:* Dir. Amy Atkins
(804) 793-6822

BRANCH CAMPUS
51B Burgess Rd., Harrisonburg, VA 22801 *CEO:* Dir. G.W. Nabers
(703) 432-0943

BRANCH CAMPUS
3024 Forest Hills Cir., Lynchburg, VA 24501 *CEO:* Dir. James Marshall
(804) 384-0400

BRANCH CAMPUS
10 Church St., Martinsville, VA 24114 *CEO:* Dir. Margaret Collins
(703) 632-5621

NATIONAL EDUCATION CENTER—KEE BUSINESS COLLEGE CAMPUS
803 Diligence Dr., Newport News 23606 *Type:* Private business *Accred.:* 1955/1982 (CCA-ACICS) *Calendar:* Qtr. plan *Degrees:* certificates, diplomas *CEO:* Dir. Kitty Heffington
Enroll: 897 (804) 873-1111

Accredited Institutions Virginia

NATIONAL EDUCATION CENTER—KEE BUSINESS COLLEGE CAMPUS
1510 Norview Ave., Norfolk 23513 *Type:* Private business *Accred.:* 1967/1985 (CCA-ACICS) *Calendar:* Qtr. plan *Degrees:* certificates, diplomas *Prof. Accred.:* Medical Assisting *CEO:* Dir. Joan L. Rhodes
Enroll: 936 (804) 855-3311

BRANCH CAMPUS
2106 County St., Portsmouth, VA 23704 *CEO:* Dir. Bettie Thomas
(804) 397-3800

BRANCH CAMPUS
6301 Midlothian Tpke., Richmond, VA 23225 *CEO:* Dir. Zoe S. Thompson
(804) 745-5660

NEW RIVER COMMUNITY COLLEGE
P.O. Drawer 1127, Dublin 24084 *Type:* Public (state) junior *System:* Virginia Community College System *Accred.:* 1972/1987 (SACS-CC) *Calendar:* Sem. plan *Degrees:* A *Prof. Accred.:* Nursing (A) *CEO:* Pres. Edwin L. Barnes
Enroll: 2430 (703) 674-3600

NORFOLK SKILLS CENTER
922 W. 21st St., Norfolk 23517-1516 *Type:* Private *Accred.:* 1988 (SACS-COEI) *Calendar:* Courses of varying lengths *Degrees:* certificates *CEO:* Dir. Raymond L. Murray
Enroll: 165 (804) 441-2665

NORFOLK STATE UNIVERSITY
2401 Corprew Ave., Norfolk 23504 *Type:* Public (state) liberal arts and teachers *System:* State Council of Higher Education for Virginia *Accred.:* 1967/1988 (SACS-CC) *Calendar:* Sem. plan *Degrees:* A, B, M *Prof. Accred.:* Business (B), Medical Record Administration, Medical Technology, Music, Nursing (A,B), Social Work (B,M), Teacher Education (e,s) *CEO:* Pres. Harrison B. Wilson
Enroll: 7397 (804) 683-8600

NORTHERN VIRGINIA COMMUNITY COLLEGE
4001 Wakefield Chapel Rd., Annandale 22003 *Type:* Public (state) junior *System:* Virginia Community College System *Accred.:* 1968/1982 (SACS-CC) *Calendar:* Sem. plan *Degrees:* A *Prof. Accred.:* Dental Hygiene, Dental Laboratory Technology, EMT-Paramedic, Medical Laboratory Technology (AMA), Medical Record Technology, Nursing (A), Physical Therapy Assisting, Radiography, Respiratory Therapy, Respiratory Therapy Technology *CEO:* Pres. Richard J. Ernst
Enroll: 20223 (703) 323-3000

BRANCH CAMPUS
3001 N. Beauregard St., Alexandria, VA 22311 *CEO:* Provost Jean Netherton
(703) 845-6200

BRANCH CAMPUS
6901 Sudley Rd., Manassas, VA 22110 *CEO:* Provost Gail Kettlewell
(703) 257-6600

BRANCH CAMPUS
1000 Harry Flood Byrd Hwy., Sterling, VA 22170 *Prof. Accred.:* Veterinary Technology *CEO:* Provost R. Neil Reynolds
(703) 450-2500

BRANCH CAMPUS
15200 Neabsco Mills Rd., Woodbridge, VA 22191 *CEO:* Provost Lionel Sylvas
(703) 878-5700

OLD DOMINION UNIVERSITY
5215 Hampton Blvd., Norfolk 23529 *Type:* Public (state) liberal arts and professional *System:* State Council of Higher Education for Virginia *Accred.:* 1961/1982 (SACS-CC) *Calendar:* Sem. plan *Degrees:* B, M, D *Prof. Accred.:* Accounting (Type A), Business (B,M), Computer Science, Cytotechnology, Dental Assisting, Dental Hygiene, Engineering (civil, computer, electrical, mechanical), Engineering Technology (civil/construction, electrical, mechanical), Medical Technology, Music, Nuclear Medicine Technology, Nursing (B,M), Ophthalmic Medical Technology, Physical Therapy, Public Administration, Recreation and Leisure Studies, Speech-Lan-

Virginia

guage Pathology, Teacher Education (e,s,p), Theatre *CEO:* Pres. James V. Koch
Enroll: 16342 (804) 683-3000

PATRICK HENRY COMMUNITY COLLEGE
P.O. Drawer 5311, Martinsville 24115-5311 *Type:* Public (state) junior *System:* Virginia Community College System *Accred.:* 1972/1987 (SACS-CC) *Calendar:* Qtr. plan *Degrees:* A *CEO:* Pres. Max F. Wingett
Enroll: 1144 (703) 638-8777

PAUL D. CAMP COMMUNITY COLLEGE
100 N. College Rd., P.O. Box 737, Franklin 23851 *Type:* Public (state) junior *System:* Virginia Community College System *Accred.:* 1973/1988 (SACS-CC) *Calendar:* Qtr. plan *Degrees:* A *CEO:* Interim Pres. Michael La Bouve
Enroll: 613 (804) 562-2171

PHILLIPS BUSINESS COLLEGE
1912 Memorial Ave., P.O. Box 169, Lynchburg 24505 *Type:* Private business *Accred.:* 1984/1990 (CCA-ACICS) *Calendar:* Qtr. plan *Degrees:* certificates, diplomas *CEO:* Vice Pres. Wynn F. Blanton
Enroll: 389 (804) 847-7701

PIEDMONT VIRGINIA COMMUNITY COLLEGE
Rte. 6, Box 1, Charlottesville 22901 *Type:* Public (state) junior *System:* Virginia Community College System *Accred.:* 1974/1989 (SACS-CC) *Calendar:* Qtr. plan *Degrees:* A *Prof. Accred.:* Nursing (A), Respiratory Therapy *CEO:* Pres. Deborah M. DiCroce
Enroll: 2126 (804) 977-3900

POTOMAC ACADEMY OF HAIR DESIGN
9101 Center St., Manassas 22110-5405 *Type:* Private *Accred.:* 1991 (CCA-ACTTS) *Calendar:* Courses of varying lengths *Degrees:* certificates *CEO:* Pres. Gail Donaway
  (703) 968-2910

PRESBYTERIAN SCHOOL OF CHRISTIAN EDUCATION
1205 Palmyra Ave., Richmond 23227 *Type:* Private (Presbyterian) *Accred.:* 1964/1988 (ATS); 1951/1988 (SACS-CC) *Calendar:* 4-1-4 plan *Degrees:* M, D *CEO:* Pres. Heath K. Rada
Enroll: 103 (804) 359-5031

PROTESTANT EPISCOPAL THEOLOGICAL SEMINARY IN VIRGINIA
Alexandria 22304 *Type:* Private (Episcopal) professional; graduate only *Accred.:* 1938/1983 (ATS) *Calendar:* Sem. plan *Degrees:* P, M, D *CEO:* Pres. Richard Reid
Enroll: 183 (703) 370-6600

RADFORD UNIVERSITY
Radford 24142 *Type:* Public (state) liberal arts and teachers *System:* State Council of Higher Education for Virginia *Accred.:* 1928/1983 (SACS-CC) *Calendar:* Sem. plan *Degrees:* B, M *Prof. Accred.:* Audiology, Music, Nursing (B,M), Recreation and Leisure Services, Social Work (B), Speech-Language Pathology, Teacher Education (e,s,p) *CEO:* Pres. Donald N. Dedmon
Enroll: 8242 (703) 831-5000

RANDOLPH-MACON COLLEGE
Ashland 23005 *Type:* Private (United Methodist) liberal arts *Accred.:* 1904/1987 (SACS-CC) *Calendar:* 4-1-4 plan *Degrees:* B *CEO:* Pres. Ladell Payne
Enroll: 1126 (804) 798-8372

RANDOLPH-MACON WOMAN'S COLLEGE
2500 Rivermont Ave., Lynchburg 24503-1526 *Type:* Private (United Methodist) liberal arts for women *Accred.:* 1902/1990 (SACS-CC) *Calendar:* Sem. plan *Degrees:* B *CEO:* Pres. Linda Koch Lorimer
Enroll: 658 (804) 846-7392

RAPPAHANNOCK COMMUNITY COLLEGE
P.O. Box 287, Glenns 23149 *Type:* Public (state) junior *System:* Virginia Community College System *Accred.:* 1973/1988 (SACS-CC) *Calendar:* Sem. plan *Degrees:* A *CEO:* Pres. John H. Upton
Enroll: 1021 (804) 758-5324

REGENT UNIVERSITY
1000 Centerville Tpke., Virginia Beach 23464-9800 *Type:* Private professional; graduate only *Accred.:* 1991 (ATS candi-

date); 1984/1989 (SACS-CC) *Calendar:* Qtr. plan *Degrees:* P, M, D *Prof. Accred.:* Law (ABA only) *CEO:* Pres. David J. Gyertson
Enroll: 800 (804) 523-7400

REPORTING ACADEMY OF VIRGINIA
Pembroke 5, Ste. 128, Virginia Beach 23462 *Type:* Private business *Accred.:* 1986 (CCA-ACICS) *Calendar:* Qtr. plan *Degrees:* certificates, diplomas *CEO:* Pres. Jane F. Braithwaite
Enroll: 244 (804) 499-5447

BRANCH CAMPUS
1001 Chinaberry Blvd., Ste. 305, Richmond, VA 23225 *CEO:* Dir. Bonnie Rathjen
(804) 323-1020

BRANCH CAMPUS
5501 Backlick Rd., Springfield, VA 22151 *CEO:* Dir. Trudi F. Terry
(703) 658-0588

RICHARD BLAND COLLEGE
Rte. 1, Box 77-A, Petersburg 23805 *Type:* Public (state) junior *System:* Virginia Community College System *Accred.:* 1961/1988 (SACS-CC) *Calendar:* Sem. plan *Degrees:* A *CEO:* Pres. Clarence Maze, Jr.
Enroll: 936 (804) 862-6213

ROANOKE COLLEGE
221 College La., Salem 24153 *Type:* Private (Lutheran) liberal arts *Accred.:* 1927/1981 (SACS-CC) *Calendar:* 4-1-4 plan *Degrees:* B *CEO:* Pres. David M. Gring
Enroll: 1588 (703) 375-2500

ST. PAUL'S COLLEGE
406 Winsor Ave., Lawrenceville 23868 *Type:* Private (Episcopal) liberal arts and teachers *Accred.:* 1950/1990 (SACS-CC) *Calendar:* Sem. plan *Degrees:* B *CEO:* Pres. Thomas M. Law
Enroll: 551 (804) 848-3111

SETON HOME STUDY SCHOOL
1350 Progress Dr., Front Royal 22630 *Type:* Private home study *Accred.:* 1990 (NHSC) *Calendar:* Courses of varying lengths *Degrees:* certificates, diplomas *CEO:* Dir. Mary K. Clark
(703) 636-9990

SHENANDOAH UNIVERSITY
1460 College Dr., Winchester 22601 *Type:* Private (United Methodist) *Accred.:* 1973/1989 (SACS-CC) *Calendar:* Sem. plan *Degrees:* A, B, M *Prof. Accred.:* Music, Nursing (A), Respiratory Therapy, Respiratory Therapy Technology *CEO:* Pres. James A. Davis
Enroll: 927 (703) 665-4505

SOUTHERN SEMINARY COLLEGE
Chestnut Ave., Buena Vista 24416 *Type:* Private for women *Accred.:* 1962/1983 (SACS-CC) *Calendar:* Sem. plan *Degrees:* A *CEO:* Pres. Joyce O. Davis
Enroll: 259 (703) 261-8400

SOUTHSIDE TRAINING SKILL CENTER
Hwy. 460, E., P.O. Box 258, Crewe 23930 *Type:* Private *Accred.:* 1988 (SACS-COEI) *Calendar:* Courses of varying lengths *Degrees:* certificates *CEO:* Dir. Gary Groneweg
Enroll: 41 (804) 645-7471

SOUTHSIDE VIRGINIA COMMUNITY COLLEGE
Rte. 1, Box 60, Alberta 23821 *Type:* Public (state) junior *System:* Virginia Community College System *Accred.:* 1972/1987 (SACS-CC) *Calendar:* Qtr. plan *Degrees:* A *CEO:* Pres. John J. Cavan
Enroll: 1655 (804) 949-7111

SOUTHWEST VIRGINIA COMMUNITY COLLEGE
P.O. Box SVCC, Richlands 24641 *Type:* Public (state) junior *System:* Virginia Community College System *Accred.:* 1970/1985 (SACS-CC) *Calendar:* Qtr. plan *Degrees:* A *Prof. Accred.:* Nursing (A), Radiography, Respiratory Therapy Technology *CEO:* Pres. Charles R. King
Enroll: 2453 (703) 964-2555

SWEET BRIAR COLLEGE
Sweet Briar 24595 *Type:* Private liberal arts for women *Accred.:* 1920/1990 (SACS-CC)

Calendar: Sem. plan *Degrees:* B *CEO:* Pres. Barbara A. Hill
Enroll: 527　　　　　　　　(804) 381-6100

TESST ELECTRONICS AND COMPUTER INSTITUTE
1400 Duke St., Alexandria 22314 *Type:* Private *Accred.:* 1986 (CCA-ACTTS) *Calendar:* Courses of varying lengths *Degrees:* certificates *CEO:* Dir. Clete Mehringer
Enroll: 225　　　　　　　　(703) 548-4800

THOMAS NELSON COMMUNITY COLLEGE
P.O. Box 9407, Hampton 23670 *Type:* Public (state) junior *System:* Virginia Community College System *Accred.:* 1970/1985 (SACS-CC) *Calendar:* Qtr. plan *Degrees:* A Prof. *Accred.:* Medical Laboratory Technology (AMA) *CEO:* Pres. Robert G. Templin
Enroll: 4197　　　　　　　　(804) 825-2700

TIDEWATER COMMUNITY COLLEGE
Rte. 135, Portsmouth 23703 *Type:* Public (state) junior *System:* Virginia Community College System *Accred.:* 1971/1986 (SACS-CC) *Calendar:* Qtr. plan *Degrees:* A Prof. *Accred.:* Medical Record Technology, Nursing (A), Physical Therapy Assisting, Radiography, Respiratory Therapy, Respiratory Therapy Technology *CEO:* Pres. Larry L. Whitworth
Enroll: 5771　　　　　　　　(804) 484-2121

TIDEWATER TECH
3313 Magic Hollow Blvd., Virginia Beach 23456 *Type:* Private *Accred.:* 1986 (CCA-ACTTS) *Calendar:* Courses of varying lengths *Degrees:* certificates *CEO:* Pres. Gerald Yagen
　　　　　　　　　　　　　　(804) 468-6348

BRANCH CAMPUS
2207 Executive Dr., Hampton, VA 23666 *CEO:* Dir. Tom Lowther
　　　　　　　　　　　　　　(804) 838-5433

BRANCH CAMPUS
1760 E. Little Creek Rd., Norfolk, VA 23518 *CEO:* Dir. Robert White
　　　　　　　　　　　　　　(804) 583-3200

UNION THEOLOGICAL SEMINARY IN VIRGINIA
3401 Brook Rd., Richmond 23227 *Type:* Private (Presbyterian) professional; graduate only *Accred.:* 1938/1986 (ATS); 1971/1986 (SACS-CC) *Calendar:* Courses of varying lengths *Degrees:* P, M, D *CEO:* Pres. T. Hartley Hall, IV
Enroll: 183　　　　　　　　(804) 355-0671

UNITED STATES ARMED FORCES SCHOOL OF MUSIC
Naval Amphibious Base, Bldg. 3602, Norfolk 23521-5240 *Type:* Public (federal) *Accred.:* 1983/1988 (SACS-COEI) *Calendar:* Courses of varying lengths *Degrees:* certificates *CEO:* Commanding Ofcr. William H. Phillips, U.S.N.
Enroll: 410　　　　　　　　(804) 464-7501

UNITED STATES ARMY INSTITUTE FOR PROFESSIONAL DEVELOPMENT
Fort Eustis 23604-5168 *Type:* Public (federal) home study *Accred.:* 1978/1989 (NHSC) *Calendar:* Courses of varying lengths *Degrees:* certificates *CEO:* Dir. Ned C. Motter
　　　　　　　　　　　　　　(804) 878-4774

UNITED STATES ARMY QUARTERMASTER SCHOOL
Bldg. P-5000, Fort Lee 23801-5041 *Type:* Public (federal) technical *Accred.:* 1975/1991 (SACS-COEI) *Calendar:* Courses of varying lengths *Degrees:* certificates *CEO:* Commander Paul Vanderploog, U.S.A.
Enroll: 4003　　　　　　　　(804) 734-2555

UNITED STATES ARMY TRANSPORTATION AND AVIATION LOGISTICS SCHOOL
ATZF-DOS-S, Fort Eustis 23604-5450 *Type:* Public (federal) technical *Accred.:* 1975/1987 (SACS-COEI) *Calendar:* Courses of varying lengths *Degrees:* certificates *CEO:* Commander Samuel Wakefield, U.S.A.
Enroll: 3217　　　　　　　　(804) 878-4400

UNITED STATES NAVAL GUIDED MISSILES SCHOOL
Dam Neck, Virginia Beach 23461-5250 *Type:* Public (federal) technical *Accred.:* 1983/1988 (SACS-COEI) *Calendar:* Cours-

es of varying lengths *Degrees:* certificates *CEO:* Commandant Leon F. King, U.S.N.
Enroll: 574 (804) 433-6628

UNITED STATES NAVY AND MARINE CORPS INTELLIGENCE TRAINING CENTER
Dam Neck, Bldg. 420, Virginia Beach 23461-5573 *Type:* Public (federal) *Accred.:* 1987 (SACS-COEI) *Calendar:* Courses of varying lengths *Degrees:* certificates *CEO:* Commandant Martin Higgins, U.S.N.
Enroll: 537 (804) 433-8001

UNIVERSITY OF RICHMOND
Richmond 23173 *Type:* Private (Southern Baptist) liberal arts *Accred.:* 1910/1988 (SACS-CC) *Calendar:* Sem. plan *Degrees:* A, B, M, D *Prof. Accred.:* Accounting (Type A), Business (B,M), Law, Music *CEO:* Pres. Richard L. Morill
Enroll: 3952 (804) 289-8000

UNIVERSITY OF VIRGINIA
P.O. Box 9011, Charlottesville 22906-9011 *Type:* Public (state) *System:* University of Virginia Central Office *Accred.:* 1904/1986 (SACS-CC) *Calendar:* Sem. plan *Degrees:* B, M, D *Prof. Accred.:* Accounting (Type A,C), Architecture (M), Audiology, Business (B,M), Clinical Psychology, Counseling, Dietetics (internship), Engineering (aerospace, chemical, civil, electrical, mechanical, nuclear, systems), Landscape Architecture (M), Law, Medical Technology, Medicine, Nuclear Medicine Technology, Nursing (B,M), Planning (city), Psychology Internship, Radiation Therapy Technology, Radiography, Speech-Language Pathology, Teacher Education (e,s,p) *CEO:* Pres. John T. Casteen, III
Enroll: 19348 (804) 924-3337

VIRGINIA COLLEGE
4142 Melrose Ave., N.W., Roanoke 24017 *Type:* Private junior *Accred.:* 1990 (CCA-ACICS) *Calendar:* Qtr. plan *Degrees:* A *CEO:* Pres. Craig H. Miller
 (703) 265-2895

VIRGINIA COMMONWEALTH UNIVERSITY
910 W. Franklin St., Richmond 23284 *Type:* Public (state) *System:* State Council of Higher Education for Virginia *Accred.:* 1953/1984 (SACS-CC) *Calendar:* Sem. plan *Degrees:* A, B, M, D *Prof. Accred.:* Accounting (Type A,C), Art, Business (B,M), Clinical Psychology, Combined Prosthodontics, Computer Science, Counseling Psychology, Dental Hygiene, Dentistry, Endodontics, General Practice Residency, Health Services Administration, Interior Design, Journalism, Medical Record Administration, Medical Technology, Medicine, Music, Nuclear Medicine Technology, Nurse Anesthesia Education, Nursing (B,M), Occupational Therapy, Oral and Maxillofacial Surgery, Orthodontics, Pediatric Dentistry, Periodontics, Pharmacy, Physical Therapy, Planning (regional/urban), Psychology Internship, Public Administration, Radiation Therapy Technology, Radiography, Recreation, Parks and Tourism, Rehabilitation Counseling, Social Work (B,M), Teacher Education (e,s,p) *CEO:* Pres. Eugene P. Trani
Enroll: 17700 (804) 367-0100

VIRGINIA HAIR ACADEMY
3312 Williamson Rd., N.W., Roanoke 24012 *Type:* Private *Accred.:* 1981/1986 (CCA-ACTTS) *Calendar:* Courses of varying lengths *Degrees:* certificates, diplomas *CEO:* Pres. Linwood Locklear
Enroll: 110 (703) 563-2015

VIRGINIA HIGHLANDS COMMUNITY COLLEGE
Rte. 372, P.O. Box 828, Abingdon 24210 *Type:* Public (state) junior *System:* Virginia Community College System *Accred.:* 1972/1987 (SACS-CC) *Calendar:* Sem. plan *Degrees:* A *Prof. Accred.:* Nursing (A) *CEO:* Pres. N. DeWitt Moore, Jr.
Enroll: 1475 (703) 628-6094

VIRGINIA INSTITUTE OF TECHNOLOGY
397 Little Neck Rd., Ste. 100, Virginia Beach 23452 *Type:* Private *Accred.:* 1980/1987 (CCA-ACTTS) *Calendar:* Qtr. plan *De-

grees: certificates, diplomas *CEO:* Vice Pres. J.D. Hall
Enroll: 745   (804) 498-9100

VIRGINIA INTERMONT COLLEGE
1013 Moore St., Bristol 24201 *Type:* Private (Southern Baptist) liberal arts *Accred.:* 1925/1987 (SACS-CC) *Calendar:* Sem. plan *Degrees:* A, B *CEO:* Pres. Gary M. Poulton
Enroll: 518   (703) 669-6101

VIRGINIA MILITARY INSTITUTE
Lexington 24450 *Type:* Public (state) for men *System:* State Council of Higher Education for Virginia *Accred.:* 1926/1986 (SACS-CC) *Calendar:* Sem. plan *Degrees:* B *Prof. Accred.:* Engineering (civil, electrical, mechanical) *CEO:* Supt. John W. Knapp
Enroll: 1352   (703) 464-7000

VIRGINIA POLYTECHNIC INSTITUTE AND STATE UNIVERSITY
Blacksburg 24061-0131 *Type:* Public (state) *System:* State Council of Higher Education for Virginia *Accred.:* 1923/1988 (SACS-CC) *Calendar:* Qtr. plan *Degrees:* A, B, M, D *Prof. Accred.:* Accounting (Type A,C), Architecture (B,M), Business (B,M), Clinical Psychology, Engineering (aerospace, agricultural, chemical, civil, computer, electrical, engineering mechanics, environmental/sanitary, industrial, materials, mechanical, mining, ocean), Forestry, Home Economics, Interior Design, Landscape Architecture (B,M), Planning (regional/urban), Teacher Education (e,s,p), Theatre *CEO:* Pres. James D. McComas
Enroll: 23467   (703) 231-6000

VIRGINIA SCHOOL OF COSMETOLOGY
1516 Willow Lawn Dr., Richmond 23230 *Type:* Private *Accred.:* 1987 (SACS-COEI) *Calendar:* Courses of varying lengths *Degrees:* certificates *CEO:* Dir. Francis Michael
Enroll: 51   (804) 288-7923

VIRGINIA STATE UNIVERSITY
Petersburg 23803 *Type:* Public (state) liberal arts and professional *System:* State Council of Higher Education for Virginia *Accred.:* 1933/1988 (SACS-CC) *Calendar:* Sem. plan *Degrees:* B, M *Prof. Accred.:* Music, Social Work (B), Teacher Education (e,s,p) *CEO:* Pres. Wesley Cornelious McClure
Enroll: 3988   (804) 524-5000

VIRGINIA UNION UNIVERSITY
1500 N. Lombardy St., Richmond 23220 *Type:* Private (Baptist) liberal arts *Accred.:* 1971/1987 (ATS); 1935/1990 (SACS-CC) *Calendar:* Sem. plan *Degrees:* B, P, M *Prof. Accred.:* Social Work (B) *CEO:* Pres. S. Dallas Simmons
Enroll: 1299   (804) 257-5600

VIRGINIA WESLEYAN COLLEGE
Wesleyan Dr., Norfolk 23502-5599 *Type:* Private (United Methodist) liberal arts and teachers *Accred.:* 1970/1985 (SACS-CC) *Calendar:* Sem. plan *Degrees:* B *Prof. Accred.:* Recreation and Leisure Services *CEO:* Pres. Lambuth M. Clarke
Enroll: 1219   (804) 455-3200

VIRGINIA WESTERN COMMUNITY COLLEGE
3095 Colonial Ave., S.W., Roanoke 24038 *Type:* Public (state) junior *System:* Virginia Community College System *Accred.:* 1969/1983 (SACS-CC) *Calendar:* Sem. plan *Degrees:* A *Prof. Accred.:* Dental Hygiene, Engineering Technology (electrical), Nursing (A), Radiography *CEO:* Pres. Charles L. Downs
Enroll: 3804   (703) 857-7311

WASHINGTON BUSINESS SCHOOL OF NORTHERN VIRGINIA
1980 Gallows Rd., Vienna 22182 *Type:* Private business *Accred.:* 1969/1984 (CCA-ACICS) *Calendar:* Qtr. plan *Degrees:* certificates, diplomas *CEO:* Dir. Katherine C. Embry
Enroll: 491   (703) 556-8888

WASHINGTON COUNTY ADULT SKILL CENTER
848 Thompson Dr., Abingdon 24210 *Type:* Public *Accred.:* 1990 (SACS-COEI) *Calen-*

dar: Courses of varying lengths *Degrees:* certificates, diplomas *CEO:* Dir. Jerry Crabtree
Enroll: 267 (703) 628-6641

WASHINGTON AND LEE UNIVERSITY
Lexington 24450 *Type:* Private liberal arts *Accred.:* 1895/1990 (SACS-CC) *Calendar:* 4-4-2 plan *Degrees:* B, D *Prof. Accred.:* Business (B), Journalism, Law *CEO:* Pres. John D. Wilson
Enroll: 1987 (703) 463-8400

WOODROW WILSON REHABILITATION CENTER
P.O. Box 81, Fishersville 22939 *Type:* Private *Accred.:* 1983/1988 (SACS-COEI) *Cal-endar:* Courses of varying lengths *Degrees:* certificates *CEO:* Dir. Paul Lavigne
Enroll: 314 (703) 332-7166

WYTHEVILLE COMMUNITY COLLEGE
1000 E. Main St., Wytheville 24382 *Type:* Public (state) junior *System:* Virginia Community College System *Accred.:* 1970/1985 (SACS-CC) *Calendar:* Qtr. plan *Degrees:* A *Prof. Accred.:* Dental Assisting, Dental Hygiene, Medical Laboratory Technology (AMA), Nursing (A), Physical Therapy Assisting *CEO:* Pres. William F. Snyder
Enroll: 1339 (703) 228-5541

WASHINGTON

ART INSTITUTE OF SEATTLE
2323 Elliott Ave., Seattle 98121 *Type:* Private *Accred.:* 1983 (CCA-ACTTS) *Calendar:* Qtr. plan *Degrees:* diplomas *CEO:* Dir. D.J. Pauldine
Enroll: 831 (206) 448-0900

BATES TECHNICAL COLLEGE
1101 S. Yakima Ave., Tacoma 98405 *Type:* Public (district) *Accred.:* 1988 (NASC) *Calendar:* Sem. plan *Degrees:* certificates *Prof. Accred.:* Dental Assisting, Dental Laboratory Technology *CEO:* Pres. William P. Mohler
Enroll: 54569 (206) 596-1500

BELLEVUE COMMUNITY COLLEGE
3000 Landerholm Cir., S.E., Bellevue 98007-6484 *Type:* Public (district) junior *System:* Washington State Board for Community College Education *Accred.:* 1970/1985 (NASC) *Calendar:* Qtr. plan *Degrees:* A *Prof. Accred.:* Diagnostic Medical Sonography, Nuclear Medicine Technology, Nursing (A), Radiation Therapy Technology, Radiography *CEO:* Pres. B. Jean Floten
Enroll: 14361 (206) 641-0111

BELLINGHAM VOCATIONAL-TECHNICAL INSTITUTE
3028 Lindburgh Ave., Bellingham 98225 *Type:* Public (district) *Calendar:* Courses of varying lengths *Degrees:* certificates *Prof. Accred.:* Dental Assisting, EMT-Paramedic *CEO:* Dir. Desmond McArdle
(206) 676-6490

BIG BEND COMMUNITY COLLEGE
7662 Chanute St., Moses Lake 98837-3299 *Type:* Public (district) junior *System:* Washington State Board for Community College Education *Accred.:* 1965/1982 (NASC) *Calendar:* Qtr. plan *Degrees:* A *CEO:* Pres. Gregory G. Fitch
Enroll: 2530 (509) 762-5351

CAPITOL BUSINESS COLLEGE
819 E. Olympia Ave., Olympia 98506 *Type:* Private business *Accred.:* 1972/1989 (CCA-ACICS) *Calendar:* Courses of varying lengths *Degrees:* certificates, diplomas *CEO:* Dir. Earle Tallman
Enroll: 389 (206) 357-9313

CAREER FLORAL DESIGN INSTITUTE
13200 Northup Way, Bellevue 98005 *Type:* Private *Accred.:* 1989 (CCA-ACTTS) *Calendar:* Courses of varying lengths *Degrees:* diplomas *CEO:* Admin. Roberta J. Chandler
(206) 746-8340

CENTRAL WASHINGTON UNIVERSITY
208 Bouillon, Ellensburg 98926 *Type:* Public (state) liberal arts and teachers *System:* Washington Higher Education Coordinating Board *Accred.:* 1918/1989 (NASC) *Calendar:* Qtr. plan *Degrees:* B, M *Prof. Accred.:* EMT-Paramedic, Engineering Technology (electrical), Leisure Services and Studies, Medical Technology, Music, Teacher Education (e,s,p) *CEO:* Interim Pres. James P. Pappas, Jr.
Enroll: 7660 (509) 963-1111

CENTRALIA COLLEGE
600 W. Locust St., Centralia 98531 *Type:* Public (district) junior *System:* Washington State Board for Community College Education *Accred.:* 1948/1990 (NASC) *Calendar:* Qtr. plan *Degrees:* A *CEO:* Pres. Henry P. Kirk
Enroll: 3441 (206) 736-9391

CITY UNIVERSITY
16661 Northup Way, Bellevue 98008 *Type:* Private *Accred.:* 1978/1990 (NASC) *Calendar:* Qtr. plan *Degrees:* A, B, M *CEO:* Pres. Michael A. Pastore
Enroll: 2619 (206) 643-2000

CLARK COLLEGE
1800 E. McLoughlin Blvd., Vancouver 98663 *Type:* Public (district) junior *System:* Washington State Board for Community

College Education *Accred.:* 1948/1989 (NASC) *Calendar:* Qtr. plan *Degrees:* A *Prof. Accred.:* Dental Hygiene, Nursing (A) *CEO:* Pres. Earl P. Johnson
Enroll: 9551   (206) 694-6521

CLOVER PARK VOCATIONAL-TECHNICAL INSTITUTE
4500 Steilacoom Blvd., S.W., Tacoma 98499 *Type:* Public (district) *Calendar:* Courses of varying lengths *Degrees:* certificates *Prof. Accred.:* Dental Assisting, Medical Laboratory Technology (AMA) *CEO:* Admin. Alson E. Green, Jr.
Enroll: 12   (206) 756-5500

COLUMBIA BASIN COLLEGE
2600 N. 20th Ave., Pasco 99302 *Type:* Public (district) junior *System:* Washington State Board for Community College Education *Accred.:* 1960/1990 (NASC) *Calendar:* Qtr. plan *Degrees:* A *CEO:* Pres. Marvin Weiss
Enroll: 6614   (509) 547-0511

COMMERCIAL TRAINING SERVICES
24325 Pacific Hwy. S., Des Moines 98198 *Type:* Private *Accred.:* 1973/1985 (CCA-ACTTS) *Calendar:* Courses of varying lengths *Degrees:* certificates *CEO:* Pres. Clifford Georgioff
Enroll: 136   (206) 824-3970

CORNISH COLLEGE OF THE ARTS
710 E. Roy St., Seattle 98102 *Type:* Private professional *Accred.:* 1977/1982 (NASC) *Calendar:* Sem. plan *Degrees:* B *CEO:* Pres. Robert N. Funk
Enroll: 598   (206) 323-1400

CROWN ACADEMY
607 S.E. Everett Mall Way, Everett 98204 *Type:* Private *Accred.:* 1979 (CCA-ACTTS) *Calendar:* Courses of varying lengths *Degrees:* diplomas *CEO:* Dir. John Wabel
Enroll: 58   (206) 259-6680

DIVERS INSTITUTE OF TECHNOLOGY, INC.
4315 11th Ave., N.W., P.O. Box 70667, Seattle 98107-0667 *Type:* Private *Accred.:* 1973/1988 (CCA-ACTTS) *Calendar:* Courses of varying lengths *Degrees:* certificates, diplomas *CEO:* Pres. John L. Ritter
Enroll: 219   (206) 783-5542

EASTERN WASHINGTON UNIVERSITY
Cheney 99004 *Type:* Public (state) liberal arts and teachers *System:* Washington Higher Education Coordinating Board *Accred.:* 1919/1988 (NASC) *Calendar:* Qtr. plan *Degrees:* B, M *Prof. Accred.:* Business (B,M), Computer Science, Counseling, Dental Hygiene, Dietetics (coordinated), Music, Nursing (B,M), Physical Therapy, Planning (regional/urban), Recreation and Leisure Services, Social Work (B,M), Speech-Language Pathology, Teacher Education (e,s,p) *CEO:* Pres. Marshall E. Drummond
Enroll: 8402   (509) 359-6200

EDMONDS COMMUNITY COLLEGE
20000 68th Ave. W., Lynnwood 98036 *Type:* Public (district) junior *System:* Washington State Board for Community College Education *Accred.:* 1973/1988 (NASC) *Calendar:* Qtr. plan *Degrees:* A *Prof. Accred.:* Medical Assisting (AMA) *CEO:* Pres. Thomas C. Nielsen
Enroll: 7704   (206) 771-1500

ETON TECHNICAL INSTITUTE
3649 Frontage Rd., Port Orchard 98366 *Type:* Private business *Accred.:* 1979/1988 (CCA-ACICS) *Calendar:* Courses of varying lengths *Degrees:* certificates, diplomas *CEO:* Dir. Ron Heit
Enroll: 342   (206) 479-3866

BRANCH CAMPUS
209 E. Casino Rd., Everett, WA 98208 *CEO:* Dir. Peggy Olason
  (206) 353-4888

BRANCH CAMPUS
31919 Sixth Ave. S., Federal Way, WA 98063 *CEO:* Dir. Dennis Palmer
  (206) 941-5800

EVERETT COMMUNITY COLLEGE
801 Wetmore Ave., Everett 98201-1327 *Type:* Public (district) junior *System:* Washington State Board for Community College

Education *Accred.:* 1948/1990 (NASC) *Calendar:* Qtr. plan *Degrees:* A *Prof. Accred.:* Nursing (A), Practical Nursing *CEO:* Pres. Robert J. Drewel
Enroll: 6105 (206) 259-7151

EVERGREEN STATE COLLEGE
Olympia 98505 *Type:* Public (state) liberal arts *System:* Washington Higher Education Coordinating Board *Accred.:* 1941/1989 (NASC) *Calendar:* Qtr. plan *Degrees:* B, M *CEO:* Interim Pres. L. Thomas Purce
Enroll: 3340 (206) 866-6000

GONZAGA UNIVERSITY
Spokane 99258 *Type:* Private (Roman Catholic) *Accred.:* 1927/1984 (NASC) *Calendar:* Sem. plan *Degrees:* B, M, D *Prof. Accred.:* Business (B,M), Engineering (civil, electrical, mechanical), Law (ABA only), Nurse Anesthesia Education, Nursing (B), Teacher Education (e,s,p) *CEO:* Pres. Bernard J. Coughlin, S.J.
Enroll: 4217 (509) 328-4220

GRAYS HARBOR COLLEGE
Aberdeen 98520 *Type:* Public (district) junior *System:* Washington State Board for Community College Education *Accred.:* 1948/1981 (NASC) *Calendar:* Qtr. plan *Degrees:* A *CEO:* Pres. Jewell C. Manspeaker
Enroll: 3141 (206) 532-9020

GREEN RIVER COMMUNITY COLLEGE
12401 S.E. 320th St., Auburn 98002 *Type:* Public (district) junior *System:* Washington State Board for Community College Education *Accred.:* 1967/1983 (NASC) *Calendar:* Qtr. plan *Degrees:* A *Prof. Accred.:* Occupational Therapy Assisting, Physical Therapy Assisting *CEO:* Pres. Richard A. Rutkowski
Enroll: 8048 (206) 833-9111

GRIFFIN COLLEGE
2505 Second Ave., Seattle 98121 *Type:* Private *Accred.:* 1972/1989 (CCA-ACICS) *Calendar:* Qtr. plan *Degrees:* A, B, certificates, diplomas *CEO:* Pres. Peggy Jacobson
Enroll: 1245 (206) 728-6800

BRANCH CAMPUS
10833 N.E. Eighth St., Bellevue, WA 98004 *CEO:* Dir. Michael Schledorn
(206) 455-3636

BRANCH CAMPUS
2111 90th St. S., Tacoma, WA 98444 *CEO:* Dir. Deanna Jiles
(206) 587-0833

HERITAGE COLLEGE
3240 Fort Rd., Toppenish 98948 *Type:* Private (Roman Catholic) liberal arts *Accred.:* 1986/1991 (NASC) *Calendar:* Sem. plan *Degrees:* A, B, M *CEO:* Pres. Kathleen Ross
Enroll: 966 (509) 865-2244

HIGHLINE COMMUNITY COLLEGE
P.O. Box 98000, Des Moines 98198-9800 *Type:* Public (district) junior *System:* Washington State Board for Community College Education *Accred.:* 1965/1983 (NASC) *Calendar:* Qtr. plan *Degrees:* A *Prof. Accred.:* Dental Assisting, Medical Assisting (AMA), Nursing (A), Respiratory Therapy *CEO:* Pres. Edward M. Command
Enroll: 9391 (206) 878-3710

ITT TECHNICAL INSTITUTE
130 Nickerson St., Ste. 200, Seattle 98109 *Type:* Private *Accred.:* 1977/1988 (CCA-ACTTS) *Calendar:* Qtr. plan *Degrees:* diplomas *CEO:* Dir. Thomas Hauser
Enroll: 932 (206) 244-3300

ITT TECHNICAL INSTITUTE
N. 1050 Argonne Rd., Spokane 99212 *Type:* Private *Accred.:* 1983/1988 (CCA-ACTTS) *Calendar:* Qtr. plan *Degrees:* diplomas *CEO:* Dir. William R. Miles
Enroll: 42 (800) 777-8324

INTERNATIONAL AIR ACADEMY
2901 E. Mill Plain Blvd., Vancouver 98661 *Type:* Private *Accred.:* 1983/1988 (CCA-ACTTS) *Calendar:* Courses of varying lengths *Degrees:* certificates *CEO:* Pres. Arch Miller
Enroll: 1273 (206) 695-2500

BRANCH CAMPUS
2326 Millpark Dr., Maryland Heights, MO 63043 *CEO:* Dir. Leo J. Appelbaum
(314) 429-7860

JOHN BASTYR COLLEGE
144 N.E. 54th St., Seattle 98105 *Type:* Private professional *Accred.:* 1989 (NASC) *Calendar:* Qtr. plan *Degrees:* B, M, D *CEO:* Pres. Joseph E. Pizzorno, Jr.
Enroll: 204 (206) 523-9585

LAKE WASHINGTON TECHNICAL COLLEGE
11605 132nd Ave., N.E., Kirkland 98034 *Type:* Public (district) *Accred.:* 1981/1986 (NASC) *Calendar:* Sem. plan *Degrees:* certificates *Prof. Accred.:* Dental Assisting *CEO:* Pres. Donald W. Fowler
Enroll: 8550 (206) 828-5600

LOWER COLUMBIA COLLEGE
P.O. Box 3010, Longview 98632-0310 *Type:* Public (district) junior *System:* Washington State Board for Community College Education *Accred.:* 1948/1990 (NASC) *Calendar:* Qtr. plan *Degrees:* A *Prof. Accred.:* Nursing (A), Practical Nursing *CEO:* Pres. Vernon R. Pickett
Enroll: 4338 (206) 577-2300

LUTHERAN BIBLE INSTITUTE OF SEATTLE
Providence Heights, Issaquah 98027 *Type:* Private (Lutheran) professional *Accred.:* 1982/1988 (NASC) *Calendar:* Qtr. plan *Degrees:* A, B *CEO:* Pres. Trygve R. Skarsten
Enroll: 148 (206) 392-0400

NATIONAL BROADCASTING SCHOOL
2615 Fourth Ave., No. 100, Seattle 98121 *Type:* Private *Accred.:* 1987 (CCA-ACTTS) *Calendar:* Courses of varying lengths *Degrees:* diplomas *CEO:* Pres. Bill Brock
(206) 728-2346

NORTH SEATTLE COMMUNITY COLLEGE
9600 College Way N., Seattle 98103 *Type:* Public (district) junior *System:* Washington State Community College District 6 *Accred.:* 1973/1988 (NASC) *Calendar:* Qtr. plan *Degrees:* A *Prof. Accred.:* Medical Assisting (AMA) *CEO:* Pres. Peter Ku
Enroll: 9296 (206) 527-3600

NORTHWEST COLLEGE OF ART
16464 State Hwy. 305, Poulsbo 98370 *Type:* Private *Accred.:* 1986 (CCA-ACTTS) *Calendar:* Courses of varying lengths *Degrees:* certificates, diplomas *CEO:* Dir. Craig Freeman
(206) 779-9993

NORTHWEST COLLEGE OF THE ASSEMBLIES OF GOD
P.O. Box 579, Kirkland 98033-0579 *Type:* Private (Assemblies of God) *Accred.:* 1952/1982 (AABC); 1973/1988 (NASC) *Calendar:* Sem. plan *Degrees:* A, B, certificates, diplomas *CEO:* Pres. Dennis A. Davis
Enroll: 681 (206) 822-8266

NORTHWEST INSTITUTE OF ACUPUNCTURE AND ORIENTAL MEDICINE
1307 N. 45th St., Seattle 98103 *Type:* Private *Calendar:* 3-year program *Degrees:* M *Prof. Accred.:* Acupuncture *CEO:* Pres. Frederick Lamphear
(206) 633-2419

OLYMPIC COLLEGE
1600 Chester Ave., Bremerton 98310 *Type:* Public (district) junior *System:* Washington State Board for Community College Education *Accred.:* 1948/1981 (NASC) *Calendar:* Qtr. plan *Degrees:* A *CEO:* Pres. Wallace A. Simpson
Enroll: 12321 (206) 478-4544

PACIFIC LUTHERAN UNIVERSITY
Tacoma 98447-0003 *Type:* Private (Lutheran) *Accred.:* 1936/1989 (NASC) *Calendar:* 4-1-4 plan *Degrees:* B, M *Prof. Accred.:* Accounting (Type A), Business (B,M), Computer Science, Music, Nursing (B), Social Work (B), Teacher Education (e,s,p) *CEO:* Pres. William O. Rieke
Enroll: 3654 (206) 531-6900

PACIFIC NORTHWEST BALLET SCHOOL
4649 Sunnyside Ave. N., Seattle 98103 *Type:* Private *Calendar:* Courses of varying

lengths *Degrees:* certificates *Prof. Accred.:* Dance *CEO:* Dir. Francia Russell
(206) 547-5910

PENINSULA COLLEGE
1502 E. Lauridsen Blvd., Port Angeles 98362 *Type:* Public (district) junior *System:* Washington State Board for Community College Education *Accred.:* 1965/1987 (NASC) *Calendar:* Qtr. plan *Degrees:* A *CEO:* Pres. Paul G. Cornaby
Enroll: 2954 (206) 452-9277

PERRY TECHNICAL INSTITUTE
2011 W. Washington Ave., Yakima 98903 *Type:* Private *Accred.:* 1969/1985 (CCA-ACTTS) *Calendar:* Courses of varying lengths *Degrees:* certificates *CEO:* Dir. Fred J. Iraola
Enroll: 469 (509) 453-0374

PIERCE COLLEGE
9401 Farwest Dr., S.W., Tacoma 98498 *Type:* Public (district) junior *System:* Washington State Board for Community College Education *Accred.:* 1972/1987 (NASC) *Calendar:* Qtr. plan *Degrees:* A *Prof. Accred.:* Dental Hygiene, Veterinary Technology *CEO:* Pres. Frank B. Brouillet
Enroll: 11015 (206) 964-6500

PUGET SOUND CHRISTIAN COLLEGE
410 Fourth Ave., N., Edmonds 98020 *Type:* Private (Christian Churches/Churches of Christ) *Accred.:* 1979/1989 (AABC) *Calendar:* Qtr. plan *Degrees:* B, certificates *CEO:* Pres. Glen Basey
Enroll: 57 (206) 775-8686

RENTON TECHNICAL COLLEGE
3000 Fourth St., N.E., Renton 98056 *Type:* Public (district) *Accred.:* 1978/1983 (NASC) *Calendar:* Sem. plan *Degrees:* certificates *Prof. Accred.:* Dental Assisting (prelim. provisional), Surgical Technology *CEO:* Pres. Robert C. Roberts
Enroll: 23194 (206) 235-2352

RESOURCE CENTER FOR THE HANDICAPPED
20150 45th Ave., N.E., Seattle 98155 *Type:* Private *Accred.:* 1987 (CCA-ACTTS) *Calendar:* Courses of varying lengths *Degrees:* certificates *CEO:* Dir. Paul Reich
(206) 362-2273

ST. MARTIN'S COLLEGE
Lacey 98503 *Type:* Private (Roman Catholic) liberal arts *Accred.:* 1933/1982 (NASC) *Calendar:* Sem. plan *Degrees:* A, B, M *Prof. Accred.:* Engineering (civil), Nursing (B) *CEO:* Pres. David R. Spangler
Enroll: 1156 (206) 491-4700

SEATTLE CENTRAL COMMUNITY COLLEGE
1701 Broadway, Seattle 98122 *Type:* Public (district) junior *System:* Washington State Community College District 6 *Accred.:* 1970/1985 (NASC) *Calendar:* Qtr. plan *Degrees:* A *Prof. Accred.:* Nursing (A), Respiratory Therapy, Surgical Technology *CEO:* Pres. Charles H. Mitchell
Enroll: 8768 (206) 587-3800

SEATTLE PACIFIC UNIVERSITY
3307 Third Ave. W., Seattle 98119 *Type:* Private (Methodist) liberal arts *Accred.:* 1933/1988 (NASC) *Calendar:* Qtr. plan *Degrees:* B, M *Prof. Accred.:* Engineering (electrical), Music, Nursing (B), Teacher Education (e,s,p) *CEO:* Provost Curtis A. Martin
Enroll: 11013 (206) 281-2000

SEATTLE UNIVERSITY
12th Ave. and E. Columbia St., Seattle 98122 *Type:* Private (Roman Catholic) *Accred.:* 1989 (ATS candidate); 1935/1989 (NASC) *Calendar:* Qtr. plan *Degrees:* B, M, D *Prof. Accred.:* Business (B,M), Diagnostic Medical Sonography, Engineering (civil, electrical, mechanical), Medical Record Administration, Nuclear Medicine Technology, Nursing (B), Rehabilitation Counseling, Teacher Education (e,s,p) *CEO:* Pres. William J. Sullivan, S.J.
Enroll: 4584 (206) 296-6000

SHORELINE COMMUNITY COLLEGE
16101 Greenwood Ave. N., Seattle 98133 *Type:* Public (district) junior *System:* Washington State Board for Community College

Education *Accred.:* 1966/1982 (NASC) *Calendar:* Qtr. plan *Degrees:* A *Prof. Accred.:* Dental Hygiene, Histologic Technology, Medical Laboratory Technology (AMA), Medical Record Technology, Nursing (A) *CEO:* Pres. Ronald E. Bell
Enroll: 7621 (206) 546-4101

SKAGIT BUSINESS COLLEGE
2021 E. College Way, Ste. 101, Mount Vernon 98273 *Type:* Private business *Accred.:* 1976/1982 (CCA-ACICS) *Calendar:* Courses of varying lengths *Degrees:* certificates, diplomas *CEO:* Pres. Karen A. Sather
Enroll: 118 (206) 336-3119

SKAGIT VALLEY COLLEGE
2405 College Way, Mount Vernon 98273 *Type:* Public (district) junior *System:* Washington State Board for Community College Education *Accred.:* 1948/1989 (NASC) *Calendar:* Qtr. plan *Degrees:* A *Prof. Accred.:* Practical Nursing *CEO:* Pres. James M. Ford
Enroll: 6010 (206) 428-1261

SOUTH PUGET SOUND COMMUNITY COLLEGE
2011 Mottman Rd., S.W., Olympia 98502 *Type:* Public (district) junior *System:* Washington State Board for Community College Education *Accred.:* 1975/1990 (NASC) *Calendar:* Qtr. plan *Degrees:* A *Prof. Accred.:* Dental Assisting, Nursing (A) *CEO:* Pres. Kenneth J. Minnaert
Enroll: 4684 (206) 754-7711

SOUTH SEATTLE COMMUNITY COLLEGE
6000 16th Ave., S.W., Seattle 98106 *Type:* Public (district) junior *System:* Washington State Community College District 6 *Accred.:* 1975/1990 (NASC) *Calendar:* Qtr. plan *Degrees:* A *CEO:* Pres. Jerry M. Brockey
Enroll: 6944 (206) 764-5300

SPOKANE COMMUNITY COLLEGE
N. 1810 Greene St., Spokane 99207 *Type:* Public (district) junior *System:* Washington State Community College District 17 *Accred.:* 1967/1983 (NASC) *Calendar:* Qtr. plan *Degrees:* A *Prof. Accred.:* Cardiovascular Technology, Dental Assisting, EMT-Paramedic, Medical Record Technology, Nursing (A), Respiratory Therapy, Surgical Technology *CEO:* Pres. Joseph Rich
Enroll: 5994 (509) 536-7000

SPOKANE FALLS COMMUNITY COLLEGE
W. 3410 Fort George Wright Dr., Spokane 99204 *Type:* Public (district) junior *System:* Washington State Community College District 17 *Accred.:* 1967/1983 (NASC) *Calendar:* Qtr. plan *Degrees:* A *CEO:* Pres. Vern Jerome Loland
Enroll: 5747 (509) 459-3500

TACOMA COMMUNITY COLLEGE
5900 S. 12th St., Tacoma 98465 *Type:* Public (district) junior *System:* Washington State Board for Community College Education *Accred.:* 1967/1984 (NASC) *Calendar:* Qtr. plan *Degrees:* A *Prof. Accred.:* EMT-Paramedic, Medical Record Technology, Nursing (A), Radiography, Respiratory Therapy, Respiratory Therapy Technology *CEO:* Pres. Raymond J. Needham
Enroll: 5454 (206) 566-5000

TREND COLLEGE
3311 W. Clearwater Ave., Ste. 1201, Kennewick 99336 *Type:* Private business *Accred.:* 1973/1989 (CCA-ACICS) *Calendar:* Courses of varying lengths *Degrees:* certificates, diplomas *CEO:* Dir. M. Dennis Way
Enroll: 580 (509) 735-8515

TREND COLLEGE
1260 Commerce St., Longview 98632 *Type:* Private business *Accred.:* 1973/1985 (CCA-ACICS) *Calendar:* Courses of varying lengths *Degrees:* certificates, diplomas *CEO:* Dir. Larry Ralphs
Enroll: 281 (206) 425-4790

TREND COLLEGE
N. 214 Wall St., Spokane 99201 *Type:* Private business *Accred.:* 1953/1986 (CCA-ACICS) *Calendar:* Courses of varying lengths *Degrees:* certificates, diplomas *Prof. Accred.:* Dental Assisting, Medical Assisting (AMA) *CEO:* Dir. Pamela Hartsoch
Enroll: 715 (509) 838-3521

Washington

BRANCH CAMPUS
230 Grant Rd., East Wenatchee, WA 98801 *CEO:* Dir. Marcia Henkle
(509) 884-1587

BRANCH CAMPUS
18023 Hwy. 99, Ste. A, Lynnwood, WA 98036-4404 *CEO:* Dir. Forrest Wetzel
(206) 771-8888

TREND COLLEGE
112 Pierce Ave., Yakima 98902 *Type:* Private business *Accred.:* 1972/1989 (CCA-ACICS) *Calendar:* Courses of varying lengths *Degrees:* certificates, diplomas *CEO:* Dir. Judy Pilger
Enroll: 537 (509) 248-4806

TRIDENT TRAINING FACILITY
Silverdale 98315-5400 *Type:* Public (federal) *Accred.:* 1991 (NASC) *Calendar:* Courses of varying lengths *Degrees:* certificates *CEO:* Commanding Ofcr. Gregory Bajuk
Enroll: 2196 (206) 396-4068

UNIVERSITY OF PUGET SOUND
Tacoma 98416 *Type:* Private (United Methodist) *Accred.:* 1923/1989 (NASC) *Calendar:* 4-1-4 plan *Degrees:* B, M *Prof. Accred.:* Law, Music, Occupational Therapy, Physical Therapy, Teacher Education (e,s) *CEO:* Pres. Philip M. Phibbs
Enroll: 4253 (206) 756-3100

UNIVERSITY OF WASHINGTON
Seattle 98195 *Type:* Public (state) *System:* Washington Higher Education Coordinating Board *Accred.:* 1918/1983 (NASC) *Calendar:* Qtr. plan *Degrees:* B, P, M, D *Prof. Accred.:* Accounting (Type A,C), Architecture (M), Audiology, Business (B,M), Clinical Psychology, Construction Education, Cytotechnology, Dentistry, EMT-Paramedic, Engineering (aerospace, ceramic, chemical, civil, computer, electrical, industrial, mechanical, metallurgical), Forestry, General Practice Residency, Health Services Administration, Journalism, Landscape Architecture (B,M), Law, Librarianship, Medical Technology, Medicine, Music, Nursing (B,M), Occupational Therapy, Pharmacy, Physical Therapy, Physician Assisting, Planning (urban), Psychology Internship, Public Health, Social Work (B,M), Speech-Language Pathology, Teacher Education (e,s,p), Theatre *CEO:* Pres. William P. Gerberding
Enroll: 33854 (206) 543-2100

WALLA WALLA COLLEGE
204 S. College Ave., College Place 99324 *Type:* Private (Seventh-Day Adventist) liberal arts *Accred.:* 1932/1982 (NASC) *Calendar:* Qtr. plan *Degrees:* A, B, M *Prof. Accred.:* Engineering (general), Music, Nursing (B), Social Work (B,M-candidate) *CEO:* Pres. Niels-Erik Andreasen
Enroll: 1651 (509) 527-2615

WALLA WALLA COMMUNITY COLLEGE
500 Tausick Way, Walla Walla 99362 *Type:* Public (district) junior *System:* Washington State Board for Community College Education *Accred.:* 1969/1985 (NASC) *Calendar:* Qtr. plan *Degrees:* A *Prof. Accred.:* Nursing (A), Respiratory Therapy *CEO:* Pres. Steven L. Van Ausdle
Enroll: 5591 (509) 522-2500

WASHINGTON STATE UNIVERSITY
Pullman 99164-1046 *Type:* Public (state) *System:* Washington Higher Education Coordinating Board *Accred.:* 1918/1990 (NASC) *Calendar:* Sem. plan *Degrees:* B, P, M, D *Prof. Accred.:* Accounting (Type A,C), Architecture (B), Business (B,M), Counseling Psychology, Dietetics (coordinated), Engineering (agricultural, chemical, civil, electrical, geological/geophysical, materials, mechanical), Forestry (probational), Interior Design, Landscape Architecture (B), Music, Nursing (B,M), Pharmacy, Psychology Internship, Recreation and Leisure Studies, Speech-Language Pathology, Teacher Education (e,s,p) *CEO:* Pres. Samuel H. Smith
Enroll: 16523 (509) 335-3564

WENATCHEE VALLEY COLLEGE
1300 Fifth St., Wenatchee 98801 *Type:* Public (district) junior *System:* Washington State Board for Community College Education

Accred.: 1948/1990 (NASC) *Calendar:* Qtr. plan *Degrees:* A *Prof. Accred.:* Medical Laboratory Technology (AMA), Radiography *CEO:* Pres. Arnold Heuchert
Enroll: 3367 (509) 662-1651

WESTERN WASHINGTON UNIVERSITY
Bellingham 98225 *Type:* Public (state) liberal arts and teachers *System:* Washington Higher Education Coordinating Board *Accred.:* 1921/1988 (NASC) *Calendar:* Qtr. plan *Degrees:* B, M *Prof. Accred.:* Audiology, Business (B,M), Computer Science, Engineering Technology (electrical, manufacturing), Music, Recreation and Park Management, Speech-Language Pathology, Teacher Education (e,s,p) *CEO:* Pres. Kenneth P. Mortimer
Enroll: 11495 (206) 676-3000

WHATCOM COMMUNITY COLLEGE
237 W. Kellogg Rd., Bellingham 98226 *Type:* Public (district) junior *System:* Washington State Board for Community College Education *Accred.:* 1976/1991 (NASC) *Calendar:* Qtr. plan *Degrees:* A *CEO:* Pres. Harold G. Heiner
Enroll: 2879 (206) 676-2170

WHITMAN COLLEGE
Walla Walla 99362 *Type:* Private liberal arts *Accred.:* 1918/1988 (NASC) *Calendar:* Sem. plan *Degrees:* B *CEO:* Pres. David E. Maxwell
Enroll: 1300 (509) 527-5111

WHITWORTH COLLEGE
Spokane 99251-0002 *Type:* Private (United Presbyterian) liberal arts *Accred.:* 1933/1978 (NASC) *Calendar:* 4-1-4 plan *Degrees:* B, M *Prof. Accred.:* Music, Nursing (B,M), Teacher Education (e,s) *CEO:* Pres. Arthur J. De Jong
Enroll: 1749 (509) 466-1000

YAKIMA VALLEY COMMUNITY COLLEGE
P.O. Box 1647, Yakima 98907 *Type:* Public (district) junior *System:* Washington State Board for Community College Education *Accred.:* 1948/1981 (NASC) *Calendar:* Qtr. plan *Degrees:* A, certificates *Prof. Accred.:* Dental Hygiene, Nursing (A), Occupational Therapy Assisting, Radiography *CEO:* Pres. V. Phillip Tullar
Enroll: 5082 (509) 575-2350

WEST VIRGINIA

ALDERSON-BROADDUS COLLEGE
Philippi 26416 *Type:* Private (Baptist) liberal arts *Accred.:* 1959/1991 (NCA) *Calendar:* Sem. plan *Degrees:* B, M *Prof. Accred.:* Nursing (B), Physician Assisting, Social Work (B) *CEO:* Pres. W. Christian Sizemore
Enroll: 711 (304) 457-1700

APPALACHIAN BIBLE COLLEGE
P.O. Box ABC, Bradley 25818 *Type:* Private (Baptist) *Accred.:* 1967/1987 (AABC) *Calendar:* Sem. plan *Degrees:* B, certificates, diplomas *CEO:* Pres. Daniel L. Anderson
Enroll: 174 (304) 877-6428

B.M. SPURR SCHOOL OF PRACTICAL NURSING
800 Wheeling Ave., Glen Dale 26038 *Type:* Public *Calendar:* Courses of varying lengths *Degrees:* certificates *Prof. Accred.:* Practical Nursing *CEO:* Dir. Dorothy McCulley
(304) 845-3211

BETHANY COLLEGE
Bethany 26031 *Type:* Private (Disciples of Christ) liberal arts *Accred.:* 1926/1989 (NCA) *Calendar:* Sem. plan *Degrees:* B *Prof. Accred.:* Social Work (B), Teacher Education (e,s) *CEO:* Pres. D. Duane Cummins
Enroll: 847 (304) 829-7111

BLUEFIELD STATE COLLEGE
219 Rock St., Bluefield 24701 *Type:* Public (state) liberal arts and teachers *System:* State College System of West Virginia *Accred.:* 1951/1982 (NCA) *Calendar:* Sem. plan *Degrees:* A, B, certificates, diplomas *Prof. Accred.:* Engineering Technology (architectural, civil/construction, electrical, mechanical, mining), Nursing (A), Radiography *CEO:* Pres. Gregory D. Adkins
Enroll: 1870 (304) 327-4030

BOONE COUNTY CAREER CENTER
P.O. Box 50 B, Danville 25053 *Type:* Private *Calendar:* Courses of varying lengths *Degrees:* certificates *Prof. Accred.:* Medical Laboratory Technology *CEO:* Dir. Jimmy H. Dolan
(304) 369-4585

THE COLLEGE OF WEST VIRGINIA
P.O. Box AG, Beckley 25802-2830 *Type:* Private *Accred.:* 1981/1985 (NCA) *Calendar:* Sem. plan *Degrees:* A, B *Prof. Accred.:* Respiratory Therapy *CEO:* Pres. Charles H. Polk
Enroll: 1548 (304) 253-7351

CONCORD COLLEGE
Athens 24712 *Type:* Public (state) liberal arts and teachers *System:* State College System of West Virginia *Accred.:* 1931/1988 (NCA) *Calendar:* Sem. plan *Degrees:* B *Prof. Accred.:* Social Work (B), Teacher Education (e,s) *CEO:* Pres. Jerry L. Beasley
Enroll: 2234 (304) 384-5223

DAVIS AND ELKINS COLLEGE
100 Sycamore St., Elkins 26241 *Type:* Private (Presbyterian) liberal arts *Accred.:* 1946/1990 (NCA) *Calendar:* 4-1-4 plan *Degrees:* A, B, certificates, diplomas *CEO:* Pres. Dorothy I. MacConkey
Enroll: 816 (304) 636-1900

FAIRMONT STATE COLLEGE
Locust Ave., Fairmont 26554 *Type:* Public (state) liberal arts and professional *System:* State College System of West Virginia *Accred.:* 1928/1982 (NCA) *Calendar:* Sem. plan *Degrees:* A, B, certificates, diplomas *Prof. Accred.:* Engineering Technology (civil/construction, electrical, mechanical, mechanical drafting/design, mining), Medical Laboratory Technology (AMA), Medical Record Technology, Nursing (A), Teacher Education (e,s), Veterinary Technology *CEO:* Pres. Robert J. Dillman
Enroll: 5152 (304) 367-4151

GLENVILLE STATE COLLEGE
200 High St., Glenville 26351 *Type:* Public (state) liberal arts and teachers *System:* State College System of West Virginia *Accred.:*

West Virginia

1949/1982 (NCA) *Calendar:* Sem. plan *Degrees:* A, B *Prof. Accred.:* Teacher Education (e,s) *CEO:* Pres. William K. Simmons
Enroll: 1776 (304) 462-4110

HUNTINGTON JUNIOR COLLEGE OF BUSINESS
900 Fifth Ave., Huntington 25701 *Type:* Private junior *Accred.:* 1969/1988 (CCA-ACICS) *Calendar:* Qtr. plan *Degrees:* A *CEO:* Dir. Carolyn Smith
Enroll: 823 (304) 697-7550

MARSHALL UNIVERSITY
Huntington 25701 *Type:* Public (state) *System:* University of West Virginia System *Accred.:* 1928/1986 (NCA) *Calendar:* Sem. plan *Degrees:* A, B, P, M, D, certificates, diplomas *Prof. Accred.:* Counseling, Journalism, Medical Laboratory Technology (AMA), Medical Record Technology, Medical Technology, Medicine, Music, Nursing (A,B), Social Work (B), Teacher Education (e,s,p) *CEO:* Pres. J. Wade Gilley
Enroll: 9430 (304) 696-2300

MOUNTAIN STATE COLLEGE
Spring at 16th St., Parkersburg 26101 *Type:* Private business *Accred.:* 1977/1989 (CCA-ACICS) *Calendar:* Qtr. plan *Degrees:* A, certificates, diplomas *CEO:* Dir. Judith Sutton
Enroll: 1515 (304) 485-5487

NATIONAL EDUCATION CENTER—NATIONAL INSTITUTE OF TECHNOLOGY CAMPUS
5514 Big Tyler Rd., Cross Lanes 25313 *Type:* Private *Accred.:* 1971/1986 (CCA-ACTTS) *Calendar:* Sem. plan *Degrees:* A, diplomas *CEO:* Pres. Hans Schmidt
Enroll: 656 (304) 776-6290

NEW CAREERS OF HUNTINGTON
338 Washington Ave., Huntington 25701 *Type:* Private *Accred.:* 1976/1985 (CCA-ACTTS) *Calendar:* Courses of varying lengths *Degrees:* diplomas *CEO:* Dir. Raymond R. Lindquist
Enroll: 57 (304) 523-6311

OHIO VALLEY COLLEGE
College Pwy., Parkersburg 26101 *Type:* Private *Accred.:* 1978/1983 (NCA) *Calendar:* Sem. plan *Degrees:* A, B *CEO:* Pres. E. Keith Stotts
Enroll: 205 (304) 485-7384

POTOMAC STATE COLLEGE OF WEST VIRGINIA UNIVERSITY
Keyser 26726 *Type:* Public (state) junior *System:* University of West Virginia System *Accred.:* 1926/1984 (NCA) *Calendar:* Sem. plan *Degrees:* A, certificates, diplomas *CEO:* Pres. Joseph M. Gratto
Enroll: 1167 (304) 788-3011

SALEM-TEIKYO UNIVERSITY
Salem 26426 *Type:* Private liberal arts *Accred.:* 1963/1990 (NCA) *Calendar:* Sem. plan *Degrees:* A, B, M *CEO:* Pres. Ronald E. Ohl
Enroll: 515 (304) 782-5011

SHEPHERD COLLEGE
Shepherdstown 25443 *Type:* Public (state) liberal arts and teachers *System:* State College System of West Virginia *Accred.:* 1950/1982 (NCA) *Calendar:* Sem. plan *Degrees:* A, B *Prof. Accred.:* Nursing (A), Social Work (B), Teacher Education (e,s) *CEO:* Pres. Michael P. Riccards
Enroll: 2923 (304) 876-2511

SOUTHERN WEST VIRGINIA COMMUNITY COLLEGE
Dempsey Branch Rd., P.O. Box 2900, Logan 25601-2900 *Type:* Public (state) junior *System:* State College System of West Virginia *Accred.:* 1971/1990 (NCA) *Calendar:* Sem. plan *Degrees:* A, certificates, diplomas *Prof. Accred.:* Nursing (A) *CEO:* Pres. Harry J. Boyer
Enroll: 1772 (304) 792-4300

BRANCH CAMPUS
Williamson, WV 25661 *CEO:* Provost William E. Barrett
(304) 235-2800

UNIVERSITY OF CHARLESTON
2300 MacCorkle Ave., Charleston 25304 *Type:* Private liberal arts *Accred.:* 1958/1988 (NCA) *Calendar:* Sem. plan *Degrees:* A, B, M *Prof. Accred.:* Nursing (A), Radiography,

Respiratory Therapy *CEO:* Pres. Edwin H. Welch
Enroll: 1055   (304) 357-4713

UNIVERSITY OF WEST VIRGINIA COLLEGE OF GRADUATE STUDIES
P.O. Box 1003, Institute 25112-1003 *Type:* Public (state) liberal arts and professional *System:* University of West Virginia System *Accred.:* 1972/1991 (NCA) *Calendar:* Sem. plan *Degrees:* M, certificates, diplomas *Prof. Accred.:* Teacher Education (e,s,p) *CEO:* Pres. Dennis P. Prisk
Enroll: 851   (304) 766-2000

WEBSTER COLLEGE
412 Fairmont Ave., Fairmont 26554 *Type:* Private business *Accred.:* 1968/1987 (CCA-ACICS) *Calendar:* Qtr. plan *Degrees:* A, certificates, diplomas *CEO:* Dir. Eldon A. Callen
Enroll: 371   (304) 363-8824

BRANCH CAMPUS
N. Bridge Plaza, 2192 N. U.S. Rte. 1, Fort Pierce, FL 34946 *CEO:* Dir. Lawrence Del Vecchio
(407) 464-7474

BRANCH CAMPUS
2002 N.W. 13th St., Gainesville, FL 32601 *CEO:* Exec. Dir. Deanne Tudor
(904) 375-8014

BRANCH CAMPUS
5623 U.S. Hwy. 19, Ste. 300, New Port Richey, FL 34652 *CEO:* Dir. William Polmear
(813) 849-4993

BRANCH CAMPUS
1530 S.W. Third Ave., Ocala, FL 32671 *CEO:* Dir. Kathryn Herold
(904) 629-1941

WEST LIBERTY STATE COLLEGE
West Liberty 26074 *Type:* Public (state) liberal arts and professional *System:* State College System of West Virginia *Accred.:* 1942/1988 (NCA) *Calendar:* Sem. plan *Degrees:* A, B *Prof. Accred.:* Dental Hygiene, Medical Technology, Music, Teacher Education (e,s) *CEO:* Pres. Clyde D. Campbell
Enroll: 2386   (304) 336-8000

WEST VIRGINIA BUSINESS COLLEGE
215 W. Main St., Clarksburg 26301 *Type:* Private business *Accred.:* 1990 (CCA-ACICS) *Calendar:* Qtr. plan *Degrees:* certificates, diplomas *CEO:* Dir. Marsha Shockey
Enroll: 222   (304) 624-7695

BRANCH CAMPUS
1052 Main St., Wheeling, WV 26003 *CEO:* Admin. Dir. Michelle Tomczyk
(304) 232-0631

WEST VIRGINIA CAREER COLLEGE
1000 Virginia St., E., Charleston 25301 *Type:* Private business *Accred.:* 1971/1989 (CCA-ACICS) *Calendar:* Qtr. plan *Degrees:* A, certificates, diplomas *CEO:* Vice Pres. Thomas A. Crouse
Enroll: 487   (304) 345-2820

BRANCH CAMPUS
Nova Village Market Plaza, 1104 Beville Rd., Daytona Beach, FL 32114 *CEO:* Dir. Nancy Whisenhaut
(904) 255-0175

WEST VIRGINIA CAREER COLLEGE
148 Willey St., Morgantown 26505 *Type:* Private business *Accred.:* 1953/1985 (CCA-ACICS) *Calendar:* Qtr. plan *Degrees:* A, certificates, diplomas *CEO:* Exec. Dir. Patricia A. Callen
Enroll: 656   (304) 296-8282

BRANCH CAMPUS
200 College Dr., Lemont Furnace, PA 15456 *CEO:* Dir. Trisha Gursky
(412) 437-4600

WEST VIRGINIA INSTITUTE OF TECHNOLOGY
Montgomery 25136 *Type:* Public (state) *System:* State College System of West Virginia *Accred.:* 1956/1989 (NCA) *Calendar:* Sem. plan *Degrees:* A, B, M, certificates, diplomas *Prof. Accred.:* Dental Hygiene, Engineering (chemical, civil, electrical, mechanical), Engineering Technology (civil/con-

struction, electrical, mechanical, mechanical drafting/design, mining), Teacher Education (s) *CEO:* Pres. Robert C. Gillespie
Enroll: 2654 (304) 442-3146

WEST VIRGINIA NORTHERN COMMUNITY COLLEGE
College Sq., Wheeling 26003 *Type:* Public (state) junior *System:* State College System of West Virginia *Accred.:* 1972/1986 (NCA) *Calendar:* Sem. plan *Degrees:* A, certificates, diplomas *Prof. Accred.:* Medical Laboratory Technology (AMA), Nursing (A), Respiratory Therapy, Surgical Technology *CEO:* Pres. Ronald M. Hutkin
Enroll: 1712 (304) 233-0272

WEST VIRGINIA SCHOOL OF OSTEOPATHIC MEDICINE
400 N. Lee St., Lewisburg 24901 *Type:* Public (state) professional *System:* University of West Virginia System *Calendar:* Sem. plan *Degrees:* P *Prof. Accred.:* Osteopathy *CEO:* Pres. Olen E. Jones, Jr.
Enroll: 233 (304) 645-6270

WEST VIRGINIA STATE COLLEGE
Institute 25112 *Type:* Public (state) liberal arts and professional *System:* State College System of West Virginia *Accred.:* 1927/1988 (NCA) *Calendar:* Sem. plan *Degrees:* A, B *Prof. Accred.:* Engineering Technology (electrical), Nuclear Medicine Technology, Recreation, Social Work (B), Teacher Education (e,s) *CEO:* Pres. Hazo W. Carter, Jr.
Enroll: 3277 (304) 766-3111

WEST VIRGINIA UNIVERSITY
Morgantown 26506 *Type:* Public (state) *System:* University of West Virginia System *Accred.:* 1926/1984 (NCA) *Calendar:* Sem. plan *Degrees:* B, P, M, D *Prof. Accred.:* Art, Audiology, Business (B,M), Clinical Psychology, Counseling Psychology (provisional), Dental Hygiene, Dentistry, Diagnostic Medical Sonography, Endodontics, Engineering (aerospace, chemical, civil, electrical, industrial, mechanical, mining, petroleum), Forestry, General Dentistry (prelim. provisional), General Practice Residency, Journalism, Landscape Architecture (B), Law, Medical Technology, Medicine, Music, Nuclear Medicine Technology, Nursing (B,M), Oral and Maxillofacial Surgery, Orthodontics, Pharmacy, Physical Therapy, Psychology Internship, Public Administration, Radiation Therapy Technology, Radiography, Recreation and Park Management, Rehabilitation Counseling, Social Work (B,M), Speech-Language Pathology, Teacher Education (e,s,p), Theatre *CEO:* Pres. Neil S. Bucklew
Enroll: 19135 (304) 293-0111

WEST VIRGINIA UNIVERSITY AT PARKERSBURG
Rte. 5, Box 167-A, Parkersburg 26101 *Type:* Public (state) junior *System:* University of West Virginia System *Accred.:* 1971/1987 (NCA) *Calendar:* Sem. plan *Degrees:* A, certificates, diplomas *Prof. Accred.:* Nursing (A) *CEO:* Pres. Eldon L. Miller
Enroll: 2194 (304) 424-8200

WEST VIRGINIA WESLEYAN COLLEGE
College Ave., Buckhannon 26201 *Type:* Private (United Methodist) liberal arts *Accred.:* 1927/1990 (NCA) *Calendar:* 4-1-4 plan *Degrees:* A, B, M *Prof. Accred.:* Music, Nursing (B), Social Work (B) *CEO:* Pres. Thomas B. Courtice
Enroll: 1497 (304) 473-8181

WHEELING BARBER COLLEGE
1107 Main St., Wheeling 26003 *Type:* Private *Accred.:* 1978/1988 (CCA-ACTTS) *Calendar:* Courses of varying lengths *Degrees:* certificates *CEO:* Mgr. Harry J. Adams
Enroll: 146 (304) 232-0100

WHEELING JESUIT COLLEGE
316 Washington Ave., Wheeling 26003 *Type:* Private (Roman Catholic) liberal arts *Accred.:* 1962/1989 (NCA) *Calendar:* Sem. plan *Degrees:* B, M *Prof. Accred.:* Nuclear Medicine Technology, Nursing (B), Respiratory Therapy *CEO:* Pres. Thomas S. Acker, S.J.
Enroll: 1113 (304) 243-2233

West Virginia

WOOD COUNTY VOCATIONAL SCHOOL
1511 Blizzard Dr., Parkersburg 26101 *Type:* Public *Calendar:* Courses of varying lengths *Degrees:* certificates *Prof. Accred.:* Practical Nursing *CEO:* Dir. William Gainer
(304) 420-9501

WISCONSIN

ACME INSTITUTE OF TECHNOLOGY
4638 S. 76th St., Greenfield 53220 *Type:* Private *Accred.:* 1967/1989 (CCA-ACTTS) *Calendar:* Courses of varying lengths *Degrees:* diplomas *CEO:* Dir. Shirle W. Miick
Enroll: 79 (414) 281-2111

ACME INSTITUTE OF TECHNOLOGY
1122 Washington St., Manitowoc 54220 *Type:* Private *Accred.:* 1967/1985 (CCA-ACTTS) *Calendar:* Courses of varying lengths *Degrees:* diplomas *CEO:* Dir. Bard Pitrowski
Enroll: 72 (414) 682-6144

ALVERNO COLLEGE
3401 S. 39th St., Milwaukee 53215 *Type:* Private (Roman Catholic) liberal arts primarily for women *Accred.:* 1951/1987 (NCA) *Calendar:* 4-1-4 plan *Degrees:* A, B, certificates, diplomas *Prof. Accred.:* Music, Nursing (B), Teacher Education (e,s) *CEO:* Pres. Joel Read, O.S.F.
Enroll: 1838 (414) 382-6064

BELLIN COLLEGE OF NURSING
929 Cass St., P.O. Box 1700, Green Bay 54305 *Type:* Private professional *Accred.:* 1989 (NCA) *Calendar:* 4-1-4 plan *Degrees:* B, certificates, diplomas *Prof. Accred.:* Nursing (B) *CEO:* Dean Joyce A. McCollum
Enroll: 176 (414) 433-3560

BELOIT COLLEGE
700 College St., Beloit 53511 *Type:* Private liberal arts *Accred.:* 1913/1987 (NCA) *Calendar:* Sem. plan *Degrees:* B, M, certificates, diplomas *CEO:* Pres. Victor E. Ferrall, Jr.
Enroll: 1088 (608) 363-2201

BLACKHAWK TECHNICAL COLLEGE
6004 Prairie Rd., P.O. Box 5009, Janesville 53547-5009 *Type:* Public (district) 2-year *Accred.:* 1978/1990 (NCA) *Calendar:* Sem. plan *Degrees:* A, certificates, diplomas *Prof. Accred.:* Dental Assisting, Nursing (A), Physical Therapy Assisting *CEO:* District Dir. James C. Catania
Enroll: 884 (608) 756-4121

CARDINAL STRITCH COLLEGE
6801 N. Yates Rd., Milwaukee 53217 *Type:* Private (Roman Catholic) liberal arts *Accred.:* 1953/1984 (NCA) *Calendar:* Sem. plan *Degrees:* A, B, M, certificates, diplomas *Prof. Accred.:* Nursing (A,B), Teacher Education (e,s) *CEO:* Pres. Mary Lee Schneider, O.S.F.
Enroll: 2848 (414) 352-5400

CARROLL COLLEGE
100 N. East Ave., Waukesha 53186 *Type:* Private (Presbyterian) liberal arts *Accred.:* 1913/1988 (NCA) *Calendar:* 4-1-4 plan *Degrees:* B, M *Prof. Accred.:* Nursing (B), Social Work (B) *CEO:* Pres. Dan C. West
Enroll: 1816 (414) 547-1211

CARTHAGE COLLEGE
2001 Alford Dr., Kenosha 53141 *Type:* Private (Lutheran) liberal arts *Accred.:* 1916/1985 (NCA) *Calendar:* 4-1-4 plan *Degrees:* B, M *Prof. Accred.:* Music, Social Work (B) *CEO:* Pres. F. Gregory Campbell
Enroll: 1369 (414) 551-8500

CHIPPEWA VALLEY TECHNICAL COLLEGE
620 W. Clairemont Ave., Eau Claire 54701 *Type:* Public (district) 2-year *Accred.:* 1973/1983 (NCA) *Calendar:* Sem. plan *Degrees:* A, certificates, diplomas *Prof. Accred.:* Diagnostic Medical Sonography, Histologic Technology, Medical Laboratory Technology (AMA), Medical Record Technology, Nursing (A), Radiography *CEO:* District Dir. Norbert Wurtzel
Enroll: 1260 (715) 833-6200

COLUMBIA COLLEGE OF NURSING
2121 E. Newport Ave., Milwaukee 53211 *Type:* Private *Accred.:* 1988 (NCA) *Calendar:* Sem. plan *Degrees:* B *CEO:* Dean/C.E.O. Marion H. Snyder
Enroll: 352 (414) 961-3890

Wisconsin

CONCORDIA UNIVERSITY WISCONSIN
12800 N. Lake Shore Rd., Mequon 53092 *Type:* Private (Lutheran) *Accred.:* 1964/1991 (NCA) *Calendar:* 4-1-4 plan *Degrees:* A, B, M *Prof. Accred.:* Nursing (B) *CEO:* Pres. R. John Buuck
Enroll: 1615 (414) 243-5700

DIESEL TRUCK DRIVER TRAINING SCHOOL
Hwy. 151 and Elder La., Rte. 2, Sun Prairie 53590 *Type:* Private *Accred.:* 1973/1988 (CCA-ACTTS) *Calendar:* Courses of varying lengths *Degrees:* certificates, diplomas *CEO:* Pres. Jerry Klabacka
Enroll: 1206 (608) 837-7800

EDGEWOOD COLLEGE
855 Woodrow St., Madison 53711 *Type:* Private (Roman Catholic) liberal arts *Accred.:* 1958/1988 (NCA) *Calendar:* Sem. plan *Degrees:* A, B, M *Prof. Accred.:* Nursing (B), Teacher Education (e,s) *CEO:* Pres. James A. Ebben
Enroll: 934 (608) 257-4861

FOX VALLEY TECHNICAL INSTITUTE
P.O. Box 2277, Appleton 54913-2277 *Type:* Public (district) 2-year *Accred.:* 1974/1986 (NCA) *Calendar:* Sem. plan *Degrees:* A, certificates, diplomas *Prof. Accred.:* Dental Assisting, Nursing (A) *CEO:* District Dir. Stanley J. Spanbauer
Enroll: 2661 (414) 735-5731

GATEWAY TECHNICAL COLLEGE
3520 30th Ave., P.O. Box 1486, Kenosha 53141-1486 *Type:* Public (district) 2-year *Accred.:* 1970/1990 (NCA) *Calendar:* Sem. plan *Degrees:* A, certificates, diplomas *Prof. Accred.:* Dental Assisting, Medical Assisting (AMA), Nursing (A), Surgical Technology *CEO:* Pres. John R. Birkholz
Enroll: 1825 (414) 656-6916

ITT TECHNICAL INSTITUTE
238 W. Wisconsin Ave., Ste. 908, Milwaukee 53203 *Type:* Private *Accred.:* 1989 (CCA-ACTTS) *Calendar:* Courses of varying lengths *Degrees:* certificates, diplomas *CEO:* Dir. Carmon Negron
(414) 277-9209

LAKELAND COLLEGE
P.O. Box 359, Sheboygan 53082-0359 *Type:* Private (United Church of Christ) liberal arts *Accred.:* 1961/1982 (NCA) *Calendar:* 4-1-4 plan *Degrees:* B, M *CEO:* Pres. David R. Black
Enroll: 1240 (414) 565-1201

LAKESHORE TECHNICAL COLLEGE
1290 North Ave., Cleveland 53015 *Type:* Public (district) 2-year *Accred.:* 1977/1982 (NCA) *Calendar:* Sem. plan *Degrees:* A, certificates, diplomas *Prof. Accred.:* Dental Assisting, Medical Assisting (AMA), Nursing (A) *CEO:* District Dir. Dennis Ladwig
Enroll: 846 (414) 458-4183

LAWRENCE UNIVERSITY
115 S. Drew St., Appleton 54912 *Type:* Private liberal arts *Accred.:* 1913/1989 (NCA) *Calendar:* Qtr. plan *Degrees:* B *Prof. Accred.:* Music *CEO:* Pres. Richard Warch
Enroll: 1235 (414) 739-3681

MBTI BUSINESS TRAINING INSTITUTE
820 N. Plankinton Ave., Milwaukee 53203 *Type:* Private *Accred.:* 1969/1987 (CCA-ACICS) *Calendar:* Courses of varying lengths *Degrees:* certificates, diplomas *CEO:* Pres. Sandra C. Suzuki
Enroll: 1172 (414) 272-2192

MADISON AREA TECHNICAL COLLEGE
3550 Anderson St., Madison 53703 *Type:* Public (district) 2-year *Accred.:* 1969/1983 (NCA) *Calendar:* Sem. plan *Degrees:* A, certificates, diplomas *Prof. Accred.:* Dental Assisting, Dental Hygiene, Medical Assisting (AMA), Medical Laboratory Technology (AMA), Nursing (A), Occupational Therapy Assisting, Radiography, Respiratory Therapy, Veterinary Technology *CEO:* District Dir. Beverly S. Simone
Enroll: 7128 (608) 246-6676

MADISON BUSINESS COLLEGE
1110 Spring Harbor Dr., Madison 53705
Type: Private junior *Accred.:* 1953/1984
(CCA-ACICS) *Calendar:* Tri. plan *Degrees:*
A, certificates, diplomas *CEO:* Pres. Stuart
E. Sears
Enroll: 417 (608) 238-4266

MARIAN COLLEGE OF FOND DU LAC
45 S. National Ave., Fond du Lac 54935
Type: Private (Roman Catholic) liberal arts
Accred.: 1960/1989 (NCA) *Calendar:* Sem.
plan *Degrees:* B, M *Prof. Accred.:* Nursing
(B), Social Work (B), Teacher Education
(e,s) *CEO:* Pres. Matthew G. Flanigan
Enroll: 1507 (414) 923-7600

MARQUETTE UNIVERSITY
615 N. 11th St., Milwaukee 53233 *Type:* Private (Roman Catholic) *Accred.:* 1922/1983
(NCA) *Calendar:* Sem. plan *Degrees:* A, B,
P, M, D *Prof. Accred.:* Accounting (Type
A), Business (B,M), Combined Prosthodontics, Dental Hygiene, Dentistry, Endodontics, Engineering (bioengineering, civil, electrical, industrial, mechanical), Journalism,
Law, Nursing (B,M), Orthodontics, Physical
Therapy, Social Work (B), Speech-Language
Pathology, Teacher Education (e,s) *CEO:*
Pres. Albert J. DiUlio, S.J.
Enroll: 10277 (414) 288-7223

MEDICAL COLLEGE OF WISCONSIN
8701 Watertown Plank Rd., Milwaukee
53226 *Type:* Private *Accred.:* 1922/1987
(NCA) *Calendar:* Sem. plan *Degrees:* B, M,
D, certificates, diplomas *Prof. Accred.:* Medicine, Oral and Maxillofacial Surgery, Radiation Therapy Technology *CEO:* Pres. T.
Michael Bolger
Enroll: 997 (414) 257-8225

MID-STATE TECHNICAL COLLEGE
500 32nd St. N., Wisconsin Rapids 54494
Type: Public (district) 2-year *Accred.:* 1979/
1984 (NCA) *Calendar:* Sem. plan *Degrees:*
A, certificates, diplomas *Prof. Accred.:* Medical Assisting (AMA), Respiratory Therapy,
Surgical Technology *CEO:* District Dir.
M.H. Schneeberg
Enroll: 1278 (715) 423-5650

MILWAUKEE AREA TECHNICAL COLLEGE
700 W. State St., Milwaukee 53233 *Type:*
Public (city) junior *Accred.:* 1959/1989
(NCA) *Calendar:* Sem. plan *Degrees:* A,
certificates, diplomas *Prof. Accred.:* Dental
Assisting, Dental Hygiene, Dental Laboratory Technology, Funeral Service Education,
Medical Assisting (AMA), Medical Laboratory Technology (AMA), Nursing (A),
Occupational Therapy Assisting, Physical
Therapy Assisting, Practical Nursing, Radiography, Respiratory Therapy, Respiratory
Therapy Technology, Surgical Technology
CEO: Pres. Barbara D. Holmes
Enroll: 12029 (414) 278-6320

MILWAUKEE INSTITUTE OF ART AND DESIGN
342 N. Water St., Milwaukee 53202 *Type:*
Private professional *Accred.:* 1987 (NCA)
Calendar: Sem. plan *Degrees:* B *Prof.
Accred.:* Art *CEO:* Pres. Terrence J. Coffman
Enroll: 413 (414) 276-7889

MILWAUKEE SCHOOL OF BUSINESS
161 W. Wisconsin Ave., Milwaukee 53203
Type: Private *Accred.:* 1969/1987 (CCA-ACICS) *Calendar:* Courses of varying
lengths *Degrees:* certificates, diplomas
CEO: Vice Pres./Dean Douglass Allen
Enroll: 449 (414) 272-4736

MILWAUKEE SCHOOL OF ENGINEERING
P.O. Box 644, Milwaukee 53201 *Type:* Private professional *Accred.:* 1971/1984 (NCA)
Calendar: Qtr. plan *Degrees:* A, B, M, certificates, diplomas *Prof. Accred.:* Engineering (architectural, bioengineering, computer,
electrical, industrial, mechanical), Engineering Technology (electrical, mechanical), Perfusion *CEO:* Pres. Hermann Viets
Enroll: 2203 (414) 277-7300

MORAINE PARK TECHNICAL COLLEGE
235 N. National Ave., P.O. Box 1940, Fond
du Lac 54936-1940 *Type:* Public (district) 2-year *Accred.:* 1975/1985 (NCA) *Calendar:*

Wisconsin

Sem. plan *Degrees:* A, certificates, diplomas *Prof. Accred.:* Medical Record Technology, Nursing (A), Practical Nursing *CEO:* Pres. John J. Shanahan
Enroll: 1322 (414) 922-8611

MOUNT MARY COLLEGE
2900 N. Menomonee River Pkwy., Milwaukee 53222 *Type:* Private (Roman Catholic) liberal arts primarily for women *Accred.:* 1926/1983 (NCA) *Calendar:* Sem. plan *Degrees:* B, M, certificates, diplomas *Prof. Accred.:* Dietetics (coordinated), Interior Design, Occupational Therapy, Social Work (B), Teacher Education (e,s) *CEO:* Pres. Ruth Hollenbach, S.S.N.D.
Enroll: 1088 (414) 258-4810

MOUNT SENARIO COLLEGE
1500 W. College Ave., Ladysmith 54848 *Type:* Private liberal arts *Accred.:* 1975/1990 (NCA) *Calendar:* Sem. plan *Degrees:* A, B *CEO:* Pres. John M. Cable
Enroll: 608 (715) 532-5511

NASHOTAH HOUSE
2777 Mission Rd., Nashotah 53058 *Type:* Private (Episcopal) professional; graduate only *Accred.:* 1954/1988 (ATS) *Calendar:* Sem. plan *Degrees:* P, M *CEO:* Dean Jack C. Knight
Enroll: 42 (414) 646-3371

NICOLET AREA TECHNICAL COLLEGE
P.O. Box 518, Rhinelander 54501 *Type:* Public (district) junior *Accred.:* 1975/1990 (NCA) *Calendar:* Sem. plan *Degrees:* A, certificates, diplomas *CEO:* District Dir. Adrian Lorbetske
Enroll: 482 (715) 369-4410

NORTHCENTRAL TECHNICAL COLLEGE
1000 Campus Dr., Wausau 54401 *Type:* Public (district) 2-year *Accred.:* 1970/1988 (NCA) *Calendar:* Sem. plan *Degrees:* A, certificates, diplomas *Prof. Accred.:* Dental Hygiene, Radiography, Surgical Technology *CEO:* District Dir. Donald L. Hagen
Enroll: 960 (715) 675-3331

NORTHEAST WISCONSIN TECHNICAL COLLEGE
2740 W. Mason St., P.O. Box 19042, Green Bay 54307 *Type:* Public (district) 2-year *Accred.:* 1976/1991 (NCA) *Calendar:* Sem. plan *Degrees:* A, certificates, diplomas *Prof. Accred.:* Dental Assisting, Dental Hygiene, Medical Assisting (AMA), Nursing (A), Physical Therapy Assisting, Respiratory Therapy, Surgical Technology *CEO:* Pres. Gerald Prindiville
Enroll: 1943 (414) 498-5411

NORTHLAND COLLEGE
1411 Ellis Ave., Ashland 54806 *Type:* Private (United Church of Christ) liberal arts *Accred.:* 1957/1991 (NCA) *Calendar:* 4-1-4 plan *Degrees:* B *CEO:* Pres. Robert R. Parsonage
Enroll: 728 (715) 682-4531

NORTHWESTERN COLLEGE
1300 Western Ave., Watertown 53094 *Type:* Private (Evangelical Lutheran) liberal arts *Accred.:* 1981/1984 (NCA) *Calendar:* Sem. plan *Degrees:* B *CEO:* Pres. Robert J. Voss
Enroll: 206 (414) 261-4352

PRO DRIVE, INC./AMERICAN TRAINING CENTER
13629 Hwy. K, Franksville 53126 *Type:* Private *Accred.:* 1988 (CCA-ACTTS) *Calendar:* Courses of varying lengths *Degrees:* certificates *CEO:* Pres. John Patterson
(800) 888-2128

RIPON COLLEGE
300 Seward St., P.O. Box 248, Ripon 54971-0248 *Type:* Private liberal arts *Accred.:* 1913/1990 (NCA) *Calendar:* Sem. plan *Degrees:* B *CEO:* Pres. William R. Stott, Jr.
Enroll: 825 (414) 748-8118

SACRED HEART SCHOOL OF THEOLOGY
7335 S. Hwy. 100, Hales Corners 53130-0429 *Type:* Private (Roman Catholic) professional; graduate only *Accred.:* 1981/1988 (ATS) *Calendar:* Sem. plan *Degrees:* P, M *CEO:* Pres. John A. Kasparek
Enroll: 142 (414) 425-8300

Accredited Institutions **Wisconsin**

ST. FRANCIS SEMINARY
3257 S. Lake Dr., Milwaukee 53207 *Type:* Private (Roman Catholic) professional; graduate only *Accred.:* 1976/1990 (ATS); 1963/1991 (NCA) *Calendar:* Sem. plan *Degrees:* P, M, certificates, diplomas *CEO:* Rector Daniel J. Pakenham
Enroll: 74   (414) 747-6400

ST. NORBERT COLLEGE
De Pere 54115 *Type:* Private (Roman Catholic) liberal arts *Accred.:* 1934/1982 (NCA) *Calendar:* Sem. plan *Degrees:* B, M *CEO:* Pres. Thomas A. Manion
Enroll: 1878   (414) 337-3949

SILVER LAKE COLLEGE
2406 S. Alverno Rd., Manitowoc 54220 *Type:* Private (Roman Catholic) liberal arts *Accred.:* 1959/1988 (NCA) *Calendar:* Sem. plan *Degrees:* A, B, M *Prof. Accred.:* Music, Nursing (B), Teacher Education (e,s) *CEO:* Pres. Barbara Belinske, O.S.F.
Enroll: 533   (414) 684-6691

SOUTHWEST WISCONSIN TECHNICAL COLLEGE
Bronson Blvd., Fennimore 53809 *Type:* Public (district) 2-year *Accred.:* 1976/1988 (NCA) *Calendar:* Sem. plan *Degrees:* A, certificates, diplomas *Prof. Accred.:* Nursing (A), Practical Nursing *CEO:* District Dir. Richard A. Rogers
Enroll: 897   (608) 822-3262

STRATTON COLLEGE
1300 N. Jackson St., Milwaukee 53202-2608 *Type:* Private junior *Accred.:* 1966/1987 (CCA-ACICS) *Calendar:* Qtr. plan *Degrees:* A, certificates, diplomas *CEO:* Dir. Edward B. Abrams
Enroll: 812   (414) 276-5200

TECHNICAL INSTITUTE OF MILWAUKEE
1748 N. Farwell Ave., Milwaukee 53202 *Type:* Private *Accred.:* 1985 (CCA-ACTTS) *Calendar:* Courses of varying lengths *Degrees:* diplomas *CEO:* Pres. Elmer F. Haas
Enroll: 2129   (414) 223-0223

TRANS AMERICAN SCHOOL OF BROADCASTING
600 Williamson St., Madison 53703 *Type:* Private *Accred.:* 1972/1987 (CCA-ACTTS) *Calendar:* Sem. plan *Degrees:* diplomas *CEO:* Dir. Chris Hutchings
Enroll: 142   (608) 257-4600

UNIVERSITY OF WISCONSIN CENTERS
150 E. Gilman St., P.O. Box 8680, Madison 53708-8680 *Type:* Public (state) *System:* University of Wisconsin System *Accred.:* 1913/1983 (NCA) *Calendar:* Sem. plan *Degrees:* A *CEO:* Acting Chanc. Arthur M. Kaplan
Enroll: 8003   (608) 262-1783

UNIVERSITY OF WISCONSIN CENTER—BARABOO-SAUK COUNTY
1006 Connie Rd., Baraboo, WI 53913 *CEO:* Dean Aural Umhoefer
    (608) 356-8351

UNIVERSITY OF WISCONSIN CENTER—BARRON COUNTY
1800 College Dr., Rice Lake, WI 54868 *CEO:* Dean Mary H. Somers
    (715) 234-8176

UNIVERSITY OF WISCONSIN CENTER—FOND DU LAC COUNTY
Campus Dr., Fond du Lac, WI 54935 *CEO:* Dean Bradley M. Gottfried
    (414) 929-3600

UNIVERSITY OF WISCONSIN CENTER—FOX VALLEY
1478 Midway Rd., P.O. Box 8002, Menasha, WI 54952-8002 *CEO:* Dean Robert E. Young
    (414) 832-2600

UNIVERSITY OF WISCONSIN CENTER—MANITOWOC COUNTY
705 Viebahn St., Manitowoc, WI 54220-6699 *CEO:* Dean Roland A. Baldwin
    (414) 683-4700

UNIVERSITY OF WISCONSIN CENTER—MARATHON COUNTY
518 S. Seventh Ave., Wausau, WI 54401 *CEO:* Dean G. Dennis Massey
    (715) 845-9602

Wisconsin

UNIVERSITY OF WISCONSIN CENTER—MARINETTE COUNTY
750 W. Bay Shore St., Marinette, WI 54143 *CEO:* Dean William A. Schmidtke
(715) 735-7477

UNIVERSITY OF WISCONSIN CENTER—MARSHFIELD-WOOD COUNTY
P.O. Box 150, Marshfield, WI 54449 *CEO:* Dean Carol L. McCart
(715) 387-1147

UNIVERSITY OF WISCONSIN CENTER—RICHLAND COUNTY
Hwy. 14 W., Richland Center, WI 53581 *CEO:* Dean Dion Q. Kempthorne
(608) 647-6186

UNIVERSITY OF WISCONSIN CENTER—ROCK COUNTY
2909 Kellogg Ave., Janesville, WI 53546 *CEO:* Dean Jane E. Crisler
(608) 755-2811

UNIVERSITY OF WISCONSIN CENTER—SHEBOYGAN COUNTY
One University Dr., Sheboygan, WI 53081 *CEO:* Dean Barbara P. Losty
(414) 459-6600

UNIVERSITY OF WISCONSIN CENTER—WASHINGTON COUNTY
400 University Dr., West Bend, WI 53095 *CEO:* Dean Joel M. Rodney
(414) 335-5200

UNIVERSITY OF WISCONSIN CENTER—WAUKESHA COUNTY
1500 University Dr., Waukesha, WI 53188 *CEO:* Dean Mary S. Knudten
(414) 521-5200

UNIVERSITY OF WISCONSIN—EAU CLAIRE
Eau Claire 54701 *Type:* Public (state) liberal arts and teachers *System:* University of Wisconsin System *Accred.:* 1950/1990 (NCA) *Calendar:* Sem. plan *Degrees:* A, B, P, M *Prof. Accred.:* Business (B), Journalism, Music, Nursing (B,M), Social Work (B), Speech-Language Pathology *CEO:* Chanc. Larry G. Schnack
Enroll: 9595   (715) 836-2326

UNIVERSITY OF WISCONSIN—GREEN BAY
2420 Nicolet Dr., Green Bay 54311-7001 *Type:* Public (state) liberal arts and teachers *System:* University of Wisconsin System *Accred.:* 1972/1988 (NCA) *Calendar:* Sem. plan *Degrees:* A, B, M *Prof. Accred.:* Music, Nursing (B), Social Work (B) *CEO:* Chanc. David L. Outcalt
Enroll: 4004   (414) 465-2207

UNIVERSITY OF WISCONSIN—LA CROSSE
1725 State St., La Crosse 54601 *Type:* Public (state) liberal arts and teachers *System:* University of Wisconsin System *Accred.:* 1928/1986 (NCA) *Calendar:* Sem. plan *Degrees:* A, B, M *Prof. Accred.:* Business (B,M), Music, Nurse Anesthesia Education, Physical Therapy, Recreation and Park Administration, Social Work (B), Teacher Education (e,s,p) *CEO:* Chanc. Judith L. Kuipers
Enroll: 8218   (608) 785-8000

UNIVERSITY OF WISCONSIN—MADISON
500 Lincoln Dr., Madison 53706 *Type:* Public (state) liberal arts and teachers *System:* University of Wisconsin System *Accred.:* 1913/1989 (NCA) *Calendar:* Sem. plan *Degrees:* B, P, M, D, certificates, diplomas *Prof. Accred.:* Accounting (Type A,B,C), Art, Audiology, Business (B,M), Clinical Psychology, Construction Education, Counseling Psychology, Dietetics (coordinated), Dietetics (internship), Engineering (agricultural, chemical, civil, electrical, engineering mechanics, industrial, mechanical, metallurgical, nuclear, surveying), Forestry, Health Services Administration, Interior Design, Journalism, Landscape Architecture (B-provisional), Law, Librarianship, Medical Technology, Medicine, Music, Nursing (B,M), Occupational Therapy, Pharmacy, Physical Therapy, Physician Assisting, Planning (regional/urban), Psychology Internship, Public Policy and Administration, Rehabilitation Counseling, School Psychology,

Social Work (B,M), Speech-Language Pathology *CEO:* Chanc. Donna E. Shalala
Enroll: 37721 (608) 262-9946

UNIVERSITY OF WISCONSIN—MILWAUKEE
P.O. Box 413, Milwaukee 53201 *Type:* Public (state) liberal arts and teachers *System:* University of Wisconsin System *Accred.:* 1969/1985 (NCA) *Calendar:* Sem. plan *Degrees:* B, P, M, D, certificates, diplomas *Prof. Accred.:* Architecture (M), Business (B,M), Clinical Psychology, Engineering (civil, electrical, industrial, materials, mechanical), Librarianship, Medical Record Administration, Medical Technology, Music, Nursing (B,M), Occupational Therapy, Planning (urban), Rehabilitation Counseling, Social Work (B,M), Speech-Language Pathology, Teacher Education (p) *CEO:* Chanc. John H. Schroeder
Enroll: 17264 (414) 229-4331

UNIVERSITY OF WISCONSIN—OSHKOSH
800 Algoma Blvd., Oshkosh 54901 *Type:* Public (state) liberal arts and teachers *System:* University of Wisconsin System *Accred.:* 1915/1987 (NCA) *Calendar:* Sem. plan *Degrees:* A, B, M *Prof. Accred.:* Business (B,M), Journalism, Music, Nursing (B,M), Social Work (B) *CEO:* Chanc. John E. Kerrigan
Enroll: 9632 (414) 424-0200

UNIVERSITY OF WISCONSIN—PARKSIDE
Box 2000, Kenosha 53141-2000 *Type:* Public (state) liberal arts and teachers *System:* University of Wisconsin System *Accred.:* 1972/1983 (NCA) *Calendar:* Sem. plan *Degrees:* B, M *CEO:* Chanc. Sheila Kaplan
Enroll: 3643 (414) 553-2211

UNIVERSITY OF WISCONSIN—PLATTEVILLE
One University Plaza, Platteville 53818 *Type:* Public (state) liberal arts and teachers *System:* University of Wisconsin System *Accred.:* 1918/1987 (NCA) *Calendar:* Sem. plan *Degrees:* A, B, M *Prof. Accred.:* Engineering (civil, electrical, industrial, mechani-cal), Music, Teacher Education (e,s,p) *CEO:* Chanc. William W. Chmurny
Enroll: 4857 (608) 342-1234

UNIVERSITY OF WISCONSIN—RIVER FALLS
River Falls 54022 *Type:* Public (state) liberal arts and teachers *System:* University of Wisconsin System *Accred.:* 1935/1988 (NCA) *Calendar:* Qtr. plan *Degrees:* A, B, M *Prof. Accred.:* Journalism, Music, Social Work (B-candidate), Speech-Language Pathology, Teacher Education (e,s,p) *CEO:* Chanc. Gary A. Thibodeau
Enroll: 4619 (715) 425-3843

UNIVERSITY OF WISCONSIN—STEVENS POINT
Stevens Point 54481 *Type:* Public (state) liberal arts and teachers *System:* University of Wisconsin System *Accred.:* 1916/1988 (NCA) *Calendar:* Sem. plan *Degrees:* A, B, M *Prof. Accred.:* Art, Audiology, Dance, Forestry, Music, Speech-Language Pathology, Theatre *CEO:* Chanc. Keith R. Sanders
Enroll: 7992 (715) 346-2123

UNIVERSITY OF WISCONSIN—STOUT
Menomonie 54751 *Type:* Public (state) liberal arts and teachers *System:* University of Wisconsin System *Accred.:* 1928/1986 (NCA) *Calendar:* Sem. plan *Degrees:* B, P, M *Prof. Accred.:* Art, Teacher Education (e,s,p) *CEO:* Chanc. Charles W. Sorensen
Enroll: 6965 (715) 232-2441

UNIVERSITY OF WISCONSIN—SUPERIOR
1800 Grand Ave., Superior 54880 *Type:* Public (state) liberal arts and teachers *System:* University of Wisconsin System *Accred.:* 1916/1983 (NCA) *Calendar:* Sem. plan *Degrees:* A, B, P, M *Prof. Accred.:* Music, Social Work (B) *CEO:* Acting Chanc. Betty J. Youngblood
Enroll: 2088 (715) 394-8223

UNIVERSITY OF WISCONSIN—WHITEWATER
800 W. Main St., Whitewater 53190 *Type:* Public (state) liberal arts and teachers *System:* University of Wisconsin System *Accred.:* 1915/1986 (NCA) *Calendar:* Sem. plan *Degrees:* A, B, M *Prof. Accred.:* Busi-

ness (B,M), Music, Social Work (B), Speech-Language Pathology, Teacher Education (e,s,p) *CEO:* Chanc. H. Gaylon Greenhill
Enroll: 8787 (414) 472-1918

VITERBO COLLEGE
815 S. Ninth St., La Crosse 54601 *Type:* Private (Roman Catholic) liberal arts *Accred.:* 1954/1989 (NCA) *Calendar:* Sem. plan *Degrees:* B, M *Prof. Accred.:* Dietetics (coordinated), Music, Nursing (B), Teacher Education (e,s) *CEO:* Pres. William J. Medland
Enroll: 876 (608) 784-0040

WAUKESHA COUNTY TECHNICAL COLLEGE
800 Main St., Pewaukee 53072 *Type:* Public (district) 2-year *Accred.:* 1975/1980 (NCA) *Calendar:* Sem. plan *Degrees:* A, certificates, diplomas *Prof. Accred.:* Medical Assisting (AMA), Nursing (A), Surgical Technology *CEO:* District Dir. Richard Todd Anderson
Enroll: 1398 (414) 691-5201

WESTERN WISCONSIN TECHNICAL COLLEGE
304 N. Sixth St., P.O. Box 908, La Crosse 54602 *Type:* Public (district) 2-year *Accred.:* 1972/1982 (NCA) *Calendar:* Qtr. plan *Degrees:* A, certificates, diplomas *Prof. Accred.:* Dental Assisting, Electroneurodiagnostic Technology, Medical Assisting (AMA), Medical Laboratory Technology (AMA), Medical Record Technology, Nursing (A), Radiography, Respiratory Therapy, Surgical Technology *CEO:* District Dir. James Lee Rasch
Enroll: 2961 (608) 785-9101

WISCONSIN CONSERVATORY OF MUSIC
1584 N. Prospect Ave., Milwaukee 53202 *Type:* Private *Calendar:* Courses of varying lengths *Degrees:* certificates, diplomas *Prof. Accred.:* Music *CEO:* Dir. Florence L. Ponzi
(414) 276-5760

WISCONSIN INDIANHEAD TECHNICAL COLLEGE
HCR 69, Box 10B, Shell Lake 54871 *Type:* Public (district) 2-year *Accred.:* 1979/1984 (NCA) *Calendar:* Sem. plan *Degrees:* A, certificates, diplomas *Prof. Accred.:* Medical Assisting (AMA), Nursing (A) *CEO:* District Dir. David R. Hildebrand
Enroll: 2095 (715) 468-2815

WISCONSIN LUTHERAN COLLEGE
8830 W. Bluemond Rd., Milwaukee 53226 *Type:* Private (Lutheran) *Accred.:* 1987/1990 (NCA) *Calendar:* Sem. plan *Degrees:* B *CEO:* Pres. Gary J. Greenfield
Enroll: 268 (414) 774-8620

WISCONSIN SCHOOL OF ELECTRONICS
1601 N. Sherman Ave., Madison 53704 *Type:* Private *Accred.:* 1970/1980 (CCA-ACTTS) *Calendar:* Qtr. plan *Degrees:* certificates *CEO:* Dir. Donald G. Madelung
Enroll: 650 (608) 249-6611

WISCONSIN SCHOOL OF PROFESSIONAL PSYCHOLOGY
9120 W. Hampton Ave., Ste. 212, Milwaukee 53225 *Type:* Private professional *Accred.:* 1987/1990 (NCA) *Calendar:* Sem. plan *Degrees:* D *CEO:* Pres. Samuel H. Friedman
Enroll: 31 (414) 281-3580

WYOMING

CASPER COLLEGE
125 College Dr., Casper 82601 *Type:* Public (district) junior *System:* Wyoming Community College Commission *Accred.:* 1960/1989 (NCA) *Calendar:* Sem. plan *Degrees:* A, certificates, diplomas *Prof. Accred.:* Music, Nursing (A), Practical Nursing, Radiography *CEO:* Pres. Leroy Strausner
Enroll: 3101 (307) 268-2548

CENTRAL WYOMING COLLEGE
2660 Peck Ave., Riverton 82501 *Type:* Public (district) junior *System:* Wyoming Community College Commission *Accred.:* 1976/1988 (NCA) *Calendar:* Sem. plan *Degrees:* A, certificates, diplomas *Prof. Accred.:* Nursing (A) *CEO:* Pres. Jo Anne McFarland
Enroll: 1126 (307) 856-9291

CERTIFIED WELDING AND TRADE SCHOOL
7030 Salt Creek Rte., Box 7, Casper 82601 *Type:* Private *Accred.:* 1980/1989 (CCA-ACTTS) *Calendar:* Courses of varying lengths *Degrees:* certificates, diplomas *CEO:* Pres./Dir. David Long
Enroll: 101 (307) 266-2066

CHEYENNE AERO TECH
3801 Morrie Ave., Cheyenne 82001 *Type:* Private *Accred.:* 1983/1988 (CCA-ACTTS) *Calendar:* Courses of varying lengths *Degrees:* certificates *CEO:* Pres. Thomas Stose
Enroll: 685 (800) 366-2376

EASTERN WYOMING COLLEGE
3200 W. C St., Torrington 82240 *Type:* Public (district) junior *System:* Wyoming Community College Commission *Accred.:* 1976/1991 (NCA) *Calendar:* Sem. plan *Degrees:* A, certificates, diplomas *Prof. Accred.:* Veterinary Technology *CEO:* Pres. Roy B. Mason
Enroll: 1022 (307) 532-7111

LARAMIE COUNTY COMMUNITY COLLEGE
1400 E. College Dr., Cheyenne 82007 *Type:* Public (district) junior *System:* Wyoming Community College Commission *Accred.:* 1975/1990 (NCA) *Calendar:* Sem. plan *Degrees:* A, certificates, diplomas *Prof. Accred.:* Nursing (A), Practical Nursing, Radiography *CEO:* Interim Pres. Ed Boenisch
Enroll: 2574 (307) 778-5222

NORTHWEST COLLEGE
231 W. Sixth St., Powell 82435 *Type:* Public (district) junior *System:* Wyoming Community College Commission *Accred.:* 1964/1991 (NCA) *Calendar:* Sem. plan *Degrees:* A, certificates, diplomas *Prof. Accred.:* Practical Nursing *CEO:* Pres. John P. Hanna
Enroll: 1776 (307) 754-6200

SHERIDAN COLLEGE
P.O. Box 1500, Sheridan 82801 *Type:* Public (district) junior *System:* Wyoming Community College Commission *Accred.:* 1968/1988 (NCA) *Calendar:* Sem. plan *Degrees:* A, certificates, diplomas *Prof. Accred.:* Dental Assisting, Dental Hygiene, Nursing (A), Practical Nursing *CEO:* Pres. Stephen J. Maier
Enroll: 1647 (307) 674-6446

UNIVERSITY OF WYOMING
P.O. Box 3434, University Sta., Laramie 82071 *Type:* Public (state) *Accred.:* 1915/1990 (NCA) *Calendar:* Sem. plan *Degrees:* B, M, D *Prof. Accred.:* Audiology, Business (B,M), Clinical Psychology, Counseling, Engineering (agricultural, architectural, chemical, civil, electrical, mechanical, petroleum), Law, Medical Technology, Music, Nursing (B,M), Pharmacy, Social Work (B), Speech-Language Pathology, Teacher Education (e,s,p) *CEO:* Pres. Terry P. Roark
Enroll: 10321 (307) 766-4121

WESTERN WYOMING COLLEGE
P.O. Box 428, Rock Springs 82902 *Type:* Public (district) junior *System:* Wyoming Community College Commission *Accred.:* 1976/1987 (NCA) *Calendar:* Sem. plan *Degrees:* A, certificates, diplomas *Prof. Accred.:* Radiography, Respiratory Therapy,

Wyoming

Respiratory Therapy Technology *CEO:* Pres. Tex Boggs
Enroll: 1593 (307) 382-1600

WYOMING TECHNICAL INSTITUTE
P.O. Box 906, Laramie 82070 *Type:* Private *Accred.:* 1969/1989 (CCA-ACTTS) *Calendar:* Courses of varying lengths *Degrees:* diplomas *CEO:* Pres. Ray Gauthier
Enroll: 1094 (307) 742-3776

OUTSIDE THE UNITED STATES

BAHAMAS

BAHAMAS HOTEL TRAINING COLLEGE
College Ave., P.O. Box N-4896, Nassau *Type:* Public technical *Accred.:* 1977/1990 (SACS-COEI) *Calendar:* Courses of varying lengths *Degrees:* certificates *CEO:* Dir. Michael A. Pinchbeck
Enroll: 82 (809) 323-8175

BRANCH CAMPUS
Settler's Way W., P.O. Box F-1679, Freeport *CEO:* Dir. Iva Dahl-Brown
(809) 352-2896

CANADA

ACADIA DIVINITY COLLEGE
Wolfville, Nova Scotia B0P 1X0 *Type:* Private (Baptist) professional; graduate only *Accred.:* 1984/1990 (ATS) *Calendar:* Sem. plan *Degrees:* P, M, D *CEO:* Prin. Andrew D. MacRae
Enroll: 86 (902) 542-2285

ATLANTIC SCHOOL OF THEOLOGY
640 Francklyn St., Halifax, Nova Scotia B3H 3B5 *Type:* Private (interdenominational) professional; graduate only *Accred.:* 1976/1983 (ATS) *Calendar:* Sem. plan *Degrees:* P, M *CEO:* Pres. Gordon MacDermid
Enroll: 69 (902) 423-6801

BETHANY BIBLE COLLEGE—CANADA
26 Western St., Sussex, New Brunswick E0E 1P0 *Type:* Private (Wesleyan) professional *Accred.:* 1987 (AABC) *Calendar:* Sem. plan *Degrees:* B, certificates, diplomas *CEO:* Pres. David Medders
Enroll: 145 (506) 433-3668

BRIERCREST BIBLE COLLEGE
510 College Dr., Caronport, Saskatchewan S0H 0S0 *Type:* Private *Accred.:* 1976/1986 (AABC) *Calendar:* Sem. plan *Degrees:* A, B, M, certificates *CEO:* Pres. John Barkman
Enroll: 810 (306) 756-3200

CANADIAN BIBLE COLLEGE AND THEOLOGICAL SEMINARY
4400 Fourth Ave., Regina, Saskatchewan S4T 0H8 *Type:* Private *Accred.:* 1961/1980 (AABC); 1989 (ATS) *Calendar:* Sem. plan *Degrees:* A,B,P,M *CEO:* Pres. Robert Rose
Enroll: 474 (306) 545-1515

DALHOUSIE UNIVERSITY
Halifax, Nova Scotia B3H 3J5 *Type:* Private *Calendar:* Sem. plan *Degrees:* B, P, M, D *Prof. Accred.:* Dentistry, Librarianship, Medicine *CEO:* Pres./Vice Chanc. Howard C. Clark, Ph.D.
Enroll: 11046 (902) 424-2211

DAWSON COLLEGE
2120 Sherbrooke St. E., Montreal, Quebec H2K 1C1 *Type:* Private *Calendar:* Sem. plan *Degrees:* diplomas *Prof. Accred.:* Interior Design *CEO:* Chrmn. Sally Nelson
(514) 931-8371

EASTERN PENTECOSTAL BIBLE COLLEGE
780 Argyle St., Peterborough, Ontario K9H 5T2 *Type:* Private (Pentacostal Assemblies of Canada) *Accred.:* 1989 (AABC) *Calendar:* Sem. plan *Degrees:* B, certificates, diplomas *CEO:* Pres. Robert Taitinger
Enroll: 509 (705) 748-9111

EMMANUEL BIBLE COLLEGE
100 Fergus Ave., Kitchener, Ontario N2A 2H2 *Type:* Private (Missionary Church) *Accred.:* 1982/1987 (AABC) *Calendar:* Sem. plan *Degrees:* B, diplomas *CEO:* Pres. Thomas Dow
Enroll: 159 (519) 894-8900

EMMANUEL COLLEGE OF VICTORIA UNIVERSITY
75 Queen's Park Crescent, E., Toronto, Ontario M5S 1K7 *Type:* Private (United Church of Canada) professional; graduate only *Accred.:* 1938/1991 (ATS) *Calendar:* Sem. plan *Degrees:* P, M, D *CEO:* Prin. John C. Hoffman
Enroll: 137 (416) 585-4539

HILLCREST CHRISTIAN COLLEGE
2801 13th Ave., S.E., Medicine Hat, Alberta T1A 3R1 *Type:* Private (Evangelical Lutheran) *Accred.:* 1989 (AABC) *Calendar:* Sem. plan *Degrees:* A, B, diplomas *CEO:* Pres. Kervin Raugust
Enroll: 57 (403) 526-6951

HURON COLLEGE FACULTY OF THEOLOGY
1349 Western Rd., London, Ontario N6G 1H3 *Type:* Private (Anglican) professional; graduate only *Accred.:* 1981/1985 (ATS) *Calendar:* Sem. plan *Degrees:* P, M *CEO:* Prin. Charles Jago
Enroll: 23 (519) 438-7224

JOINT BOARD OF THEOLOGICAL COLLEGES
3473 University St., Montreal, Quebec H3A 2A8 *Type:* Private (interdenominational) professional; graduate only *Accred.:* 1989 (ATS) *Calendar:* Sem. plan *Degrees:* P, M *CEO:* Pres. Pierre Goldberger
Enroll: 16 (514) 849-8511

KNOX COLLEGE
59 St. George St., Toronto, Ontario M5S 2E6 *Type:* Private (Presbyterian) professional; graduate only *Accred.:* 1948/1980 (ATS) *Calendar:* Sem. plan *Degrees:* P, M, D *CEO:* Interim Pres. James Ferris
Enroll: 89 (416) 978-4500

LUTHERAN THEOLOGICAL SEMINARY
114 Seminary Crescent, Saskatoon, Saskatchewan S7N 0X3 *Type:* Private (Lutheran) professional; graduate only *Accred.:* 1976/1988 (ATS) *Calendar:* Sem. plan *Degrees:* P, M *CEO:* Pres. Roger Nostbakken
Enroll: 67 (306) 975-0084

MCGILL UNIVERSITY
845 Sherbrooke St. W., Montreal, Quebec H3A 2T5 *Type:* Private *Accred.:* 1952/1990 (ATS) *Calendar:* Sem. plan *Degrees:* B, P, M, D *Prof. Accred.:* Clinical Psychology, Dentistry, Librarianship, Medicine, Physical Therapy, Psychology Internship *CEO:* Prin./Vice Chanc. D.L. Johnston
Enroll: 30314 (514) 398-4455

MCMASTER UNIVERSITY
Hamilton, Ontario L8S 4L8 *Type:* Private *Accred.:* 1954/1987 (ATS) *Calendar:* Sem. plan *Degrees:* P, M, D *Prof. Accred.:* Medicine *CEO:* Pres. William H. Brackney
Enroll: 16628 (416) 525-9140

MEMORIAL UNIVERSITY OF NEWFOUNDLAND
St. John's, Newfoundland A1B 3V6 *Type:* Public *Calendar:* Sem. plan *Degrees:* B, P, M, D *Prof. Accred.:* Medicine *CEO:* Pres. Arthur May
Enroll: 15606 (709) 737-8000

MOUNT ROYAL COLLEGE
4825 Richard Rd., S.W., Calgary, Alberta T3E 6K6 *Type:* Private *Calendar:* Sem. plan *Degrees:* diplomas *Prof. Accred.:* Interior Design *CEO:* Chrmn. Janice Smith
(403) 240-6100

NER ISRAEL YESHIVA COLLEGE OF TORONTO
8950 Bathurst St., P.O. Box 5002, Thornhill, Ontario L3T 6K1 *Type:* Private professional *Accred.:* 1980/1989 (AARTS) *Calendar:* Sem. plan *Degrees:* B *CEO:* Pres. S. Hofstadter
Enroll: 20 (416) 731-1224

NORTH AMERICAN BAPTIST COLLEGE
11525 23rd Ave., Edmonton, Alberta T6J 4T3 *Type:* Private (Baptist) *Accred.:* 1969/1989 (AABC) *Calendar:* Sem. plan *Degrees:* A, B, M, certificates, diplomas *CEO:* Pres. Paul Siewert
Enroll: 303 (403) 437-1960

NORTHWEST BAPTIST THEOLOGICAL COLLEGE
P.O. Box 790, Langley, British Columbia V3A 8B8 *Type:* Private *Accred.:* 1989 (AABC) *Calendar:* Sem. plan *Degrees:* A, B, M, certificates *CEO:* Pres. Doug Harris
Enroll: 129 (604) 888-3310

ONTARIO BIBLE COLLEGE
25 Ballyconnor Ct., Willowdale, Ontario M2M 4B3 *Type:* Private *Accred.:* 1966/1988 (AABC); 1989 (ATS) *Calendar:* Sem. plan *Degrees:* B, P, M, certificates, diplomas *CEO:* Pres. William McRae
Enroll: 605 (416) 226-6380

Accredited Institutions **Outside the United States**

QUEEN'S UNIVERSITY
Kingston, Ontario K7L 3N6 *Type:* Private *Accred.:* 1986/1991 (ATS) *Calendar:* Sem. plan *Degrees:* B, P, M, D *Prof. Accred.:* Medicine *CEO:* Prin./Vice Chanc. Clifford G. Hospital
Enroll: 16586   (613) 545-2000

REGENT COLLEGE
5800 University Blvd., Vancouver, British Columbia V6T 2E4 *Type:* Private (interdenominational) professional; graduate only *Accred.:* 1985/1990 (ATS) *Calendar:* Sem. plan *Degrees:* P, M *CEO:* Pres. Walter C. Wright, Jr.
Enroll: 222   (604) 224-3245

REGIS COLLEGE
15 St. Mary St., Toronto, Ontario M4Y 2R5 *Type:* Private (Roman Catholic) professional; graduate only *Accred.:* 1970/1990 (ATS) *Calendar:* Sem. plan *Degrees:* P, M, D *CEO:* Pres. John Costello
Enroll: 126   (416) 922-5474

RYERSON POLYTECHNICAL INSTITUTE
350 Victoria St., Toronto, Ontario M5B 2K3 *Degrees:* B *Prof. Accred.:* Interior Design *CEO:* Chrmn. Lorna Kelly
     (416) 979-5188

ST. AUGUSTINE'S SEMINARY OF TORONTO
2661 Kingston Rd., Scarborough, Ontario M1M 1M3 *Type:* Private (Roman Catholic) professional; graduate only *Accred.:* 1980/1991 (ATS) *Calendar:* Sem. plan *Degrees:* P, M *CEO:* Pres. James Wingle
Enroll: 86   (416) 261-7207

ST. PETER'S SEMINARY
1040 Waterloo St., London, Ontario N6A 3Y1 *Type:* Private (Roman Catholic) professional; graduate only *Accred.:* 1986/1991 (ATS) *Calendar:* Sem. plan *Degrees:* P, M *CEO:* Rector Patrick Fuerth
Enroll: 67   (519) 432-1824

TORONTO SCHOOL OF THEOLOGY
47 Queen's Park Crescent, E., Toronto, Ontario M5S 2C3 *Type:* Private (interdenominational) professional; graduate only *Accred.:* 1980/1991 (ATS) *Calendar:* Sem. plan *Degrees:* P, M, D *CEO:* Dir. E. James Reed
     (416) 978-4039

TRINITY COLLEGE
6 Hoskin Ave., Toronto, Ontario M5S 1H8 *Type:* Private *Accred.:* 1938/1991 (ATS) *Calendar:* Sem. plan *Degrees:* P, M, D *CEO:* Provost Robert H. Painter
Enroll: 114   (416) 978-2522

TRITONE MUSIC
56 Chadwick Crescent, Richmond Hill, Ontario L4B 2V9 *Type:* Private home study *Accred.:* 1988 (NHSC) *Calendar:* Courses of varying lengths *Degrees:* certificates *CEO:* Pres. Michael Freeman
     (416) 225-1001

UNIVÉRSITÉ LAVAL
Cite Universitaire, Quebec, Quebec G1K 7P4 *Type:* Private *Calendar:* Sem. plan *Degrees:* B, P, M, D *Prof. Accred.:* Dentistry, Medicine, Oral and Maxillofacial Surgery *CEO:* Rector Michel Gervais
Enroll: 35373   (418) 656-2131

UNIVÉRSITÉ DE MONTRÉAL
Case Postal 6128, Succursale A, Montreal, Quebec H3C 3J7 *Type:* Private *Calendar:* Sem. plan *Degrees:* B, P, M, D *Prof. Accred.:* Dentistry, Health Services Administration, Librarianship, Medicine, Optometry, Planning (urban) *CEO:* Rector G.G. Cloutier
Enroll: 49837   (514) 343-6111

UNIVÉRSITÉ DE SHERBROOKE
2500 Blvd. de l'Universite, Sherbrooke, Quebec J1K 2R1 *Type:* Private *Calendar:* Sem. plan *Degrees:* B,P,M,D *Prof. Accred.:* Medicine *CEO:* Rector A. Cabana, Ph.D.
Enroll: 17411   (819) 821-7000

UNIVERSITY OF ALBERTA
Edmonton, Alberta T6G 2E1 *Type:* Public *Calendar:* Sem. plan *Degrees:* B, P, M, D *Prof. Accred.:* Dentistry, Health Services Administration, Librarianship, Medicine,

Outside the United States   **Accredited Institutions**

Orthodontics *CEO:* Pres./Vice Chanc. P. Davenport, Ph.D.
Enroll: 29536   (403) 492-3111

UNIVERSITY OF BRITISH COLUMBIA
2075 Westbrook Mall, Vancouver, British Columbia V6T 1W5 *Type:* Public *Calendar:* Sem. plan *Degrees:* B, P, M, D *Prof. Accred.:* Clinical Psychology, Counseling, Dentistry, Health Services Administration, Librarianship, Medicine, Periodontics, Planning (community/regional), Psychology Internship *CEO:* Pres./Vice Chanc. D.W. Strangway, Ph.D.
Enroll: 28461   (604) 228-2375

UNIVERSITY OF CALGARY
2500 University Dr., N.W., Calgary, Alberta T2N 1N4 *Type:* Public *Calendar:* Sem. plan *Degrees:* B, P, M, D *Prof. Accred.:* Business (B), Medicine *CEO:* Prin. Toni Prediger
Enroll: 20541   (403) 220-5110

UNIVERSITY OF GUELPH
Guelph, Ontario N1G 2W1 *Type:* Public *Calendar:* Sem. plan *Degrees:* B, M *Prof. Accred.:* Landscape Architecture (B,M) *CEO:* Pres./Vice Chanc. B. Segal
Enroll: 12723   (519) 824-4120

UNIVERSITY OF MANITOBA
Winnipeg, Manitoba R3T 2N2 *Type:* Public *Calendar:* Sem. plan *Degrees:* B, P, M, D *Prof. Accred.:* Clinical Psychology, Dentistry, Interior Design, Medicine, Oral and Maxillofacial Surgery, Orthodontics, Psychology Internship *CEO:* Pres./Vice Chanc. Arnold Naimark
Enroll: 23462   (204) 474-8880

UNIVERSITY OF OTTAWA
Ottawa, Ontario K1N 6N5 *Type:* Public *Calendar:* Sem. plan *Degrees:* B, P, M, D *Prof. Accred.:* Clinical Psychology, Health Services Administration, Medicine, Psychology Internship (provisional) *CEO:* Rector/Vice Chanc. M. Hamelin
Enroll: 23694   (613) 564-3311

UNIVERSITY OF ST. MICHAEL'S COLLEGE
81 St. Mary St., Toronto, Ontario M5S 1J4 *Type:* Private (Roman Catholic) professional; graduate only *Accred.:* 1972/1991 (ATS) *Calendar:* Sem. plan *Degrees:* P, M, D *CEO:* Dean Michael A. Fahey
Enroll: 221   (416) 926-7140

UNIVERSITY OF SASKATCHEWAN
Saskatoon, Saskatchewan S7N 0W0 *Type:* Public *Calendar:* Sem. plan *Degrees:* B, P, M, D *Prof. Accred.:* Clinical Psychology, Dentistry *CEO:* Pres./Vice Chanc. J.W.G. Ivany
Enroll: 15546   (306) 244-4343

UNIVERSITY OF TORONTO
Toronto, Ontario M5S 1A1 *Type:* Public *Calendar:* Sem. plan *Degrees:* B, P, M, D *Prof. Accred.:* Dentistry, Health Services Administration, Landscape Architecture (B), Librarianship, Medicine *CEO:* Pres. J.R.S Prichard
Enroll: 53313   (416) 978-2011

UNIVERSITY OF WATERLOO
University Ave., Waterloo, Ontario N2L 3G1 *Type:* Private *Calendar:* Sem. plan *Degrees:* B, P, M *Prof. Accred.:* Clinical Psychology, Optometry, Psychology Internship *CEO:* Pres./Vice Chanc. D.T. Wright
Enroll: 25337   (519) 885-1211

UNIVERSITY OF WESTERN ONTARIO
London, Ontario N6A 3K7 *Type:* Private *Calendar:* Sem. plan *Degrees:* B, P, M, D *Prof. Accred.:* Clinical Psychology, Dentistry, Librarianship, Medicine *CEO:* Pres./Vice Chanc. K.G. Pedersen
Enroll: 22450   (519) 679-2111

UNIVERSITY OF WINDSOR
Windsor, Ontario N9B 3P4 *Type:* Public *Calendar:* Sem. plan *Degrees:* B, P, M, D *Prof. Accred.:* Clinical Psychology *CEO:* Pres./Vice Chanc. R.W. Ianni
Enroll: 14079   (519) 253-4232

VANCOUVER SCHOOL OF THEOLOGY
6000 Iona Dr., Vancouver, British Columbia V6T 1L4 *Type:* Private (interdenomination-

al) professional; graduate only *Accred.:* 1976/1980 (ATS) *Calendar:* Sem. plan *Degrees:* P, M *CEO:* Prin. Arthur Van Seters
Enroll: 90 (604) 228-9031

WATERLOO LUTHERAN SEMINARY
75 University Ave., W., Waterloo, Ontario N2L 3C5 *Type:* Private professional; graduate only *Accred.:* 1982/1987 (ATS) *Calendar:* Sem. plan *Degrees:* P, M *CEO:* Pres. Richard C. Crossman
Enroll: 93 (519) 884-1970

WESTERN PENTECOSTAL BIBLE COLLEGE
Box 1000, Clayburn, British Columbia V0X 1E0 *Type:* Private *Accred.:* 1980/1990 (AABC) *Calendar:* Sem. plan *Degrees:* B, certificates, diplomas *CEO:* Pres. James Richards
Enroll: 180 (604) 853-7491

WINNIPEG BIBLE COLLEGE
Otterburne, Manitoba R0A 1G0 *Type:* Private *Accred.:* 1973/1983 (AABC); 1989 (ATS candidate) *Calendar:* Sem. plan *Degrees:* B, P, M, certificates, diplomas *CEO:* Pres. William R. Eichhorst
Enroll: 407 (204) 433-7488

WYCLIFFE COLLEGE
5 Hoskin Ave., Toronto, Ontario M5S 1H7 *Type:* Private (Anglican) professional; graduate only *Accred.:* 1978/1991 (ATS) *Calendar:* Sem. plan *Degrees:* P, M, D *CEO:* Prin. Peter Mason
Enroll: 102 (416) 979-2870

CAYMAN ISLANDS

INTERNATIONAL COLLEGE
P.O. Box Savannah, Newlands, Grand Cayman *Type:* Private *Accred.:* 1984/1990 (CCA-ACICS) *Calendar:* Qtr. plan *Degrees:* A, B, M, certificates, diplomas *CEO:* Pres. Elsa M. Cummings
Enroll: 303 (809) 947-1100

EGYPT

AMERICAN UNIVERSITY IN CAIRO
113 Sharia Dasr El Aini, Cairo *Type:* Private liberal arts *Accred.:* 1982/1988 (MSA) *Calendar:* Sem. plan *Degrees:* B, M *CEO:* Pres. Donald McDonald
Enroll: 3146 [20] 354-1830

FRANCE

THE AMERICAN UNIVERSITY OF PARIS
31 Ave. Bosquet, 75007 Paris *Type:* Private liberal arts *Accred.:* 1973/1988 (MSA) *Calendar:* Sem. plan *Degrees:* B *CEO:* Pres. Catherine W. Ingold
Enroll: 932 [33] (14) 555-9173

CESAR RITZ INSTITUTE OF HOTEL MANAGEMENT
Hotelconsult SHCC, Le Bouveret CH-1897 *Type:* Private *Accred.:* 1989 (CCA-ACICS) *Calendar:* Courses of varying length *Degrees:* certificates, diplomas *CEO:* Dir. Martin Kisselef
Enroll: 467 [41] (25) 813-0150

SCHILLER INTERNATIONAL UNIVERSITY
Chateau Pourtales, 161 rue Melanie, 6700 Strasbourg *Type:* Private *Accred.:* 1983 (CCA-ACICS) *Calendar:* Sem. plan *Degrees:* A, B, M *CEO:* Pres. Allen Ason
Enroll: 118 [33] (8) 831-0107

SCHILLER INTERNATIONAL UNIVERSITY
32 Blvd. de Vaugirard, 75015 Paris *Type:* Private *Accred.:* 1983/1987 (CCA-ACICS) *Calendar:* Sem. plan *Degrees:* A, B, M *CEO:* Dir. Joseph Tomchak
Enroll: 343 [33] (14) 538-5601

GERMANY

SCHILLER INTERNATIONAL UNIVERSITY
Bergstrasse 106, 6900 Heidelberg *Type:* Private *Accred.:* 1983 (CCA-ACICS) *Calendar:* Sem. plan *Degrees:* A, B, M *CEO:* Dir. Dieter Andreas
[49] (62) 211-2046

BRANCH CAMPUS
453 Edgewater Dr., Dunedin, FL 34698-4964 *CEO:* Dir. Jeanette Brock
Enroll: 62 (813) 736-5082

GREECE

DEREE COLLEGE
P.O. Box 60018 GR-153, 10 Agnia, Paraskevi Attikis *Type:* Private liberal arts *Accred.:* 1981/1986 (NEASC-CIHE) *Calendar:* 4-1-4 plan *Degrees:* A, B *CEO:* Pres. John S. Bailey
Enroll: 2554 [30] (1) 639-3250

MARSHALL ISLANDS

COLLEGE OF THE MARSHALL ISLANDS
P.O. Box 1258, Majuro RMI 96960 *Type:* Public junior *System:* College of Micronesia *Accred.:* 1991 (WASC-Jr.) *Calendar:* Sem. plan *Degrees:* A *CEO:* Admin. Hilda Heine-Jetnil
Enroll: 278 (692) 9-3394

COMMUNITY COLLEGE OF MICRONESIA
P.O. Box 159, Kolonia, Pohnpei FSM 96941 *Type:* Public junior *System:* College of Micronesia *Accred.:* 1978/1987 (WASC-Jr.) *Calendar:* Sem. plan *Degrees:* A *CEO:* Pres. Paul Gallen
Enroll: 368 (691) 320-2840

MEXICO

FUNDACION UNIVERSIDAD DE LAS AMERICAS
Apartado Postal 100, Sta. Catarina Mart, Puebla 72820 *Type:* Private *Accred.:* 1959/1984 (SACS-CC) *Calendar:* Sem. plan *Degrees:* B, M *CEO:* Rector Enrique Cardenas
Enroll: 5295 [52] (22) 47-00-00

INSTITUTO TECNOLOGICO Y DE ESTUDIOS SUPERIORES DE MONTERREY
Ave. Eugenio Garza Sada, 2501 Sur, Monterrey, N.L. 64849 *Type:* Private *Accred.:* 1950/1989 (SACS-CC) *Calendar:* Sem. plan *Degrees:* B,M,D *CEO:* Pres. Rafael Rangel-Sostmann
Enroll: 30654 [52] (83) 58-20-33

UNIVERSIDAD DE LAS AMERICAS, A.C.
Calle Puebla No. 223, Col. Roma, Mexico D.F. 06700 *Type:* Private *Accred.:* 1991 (SACS-CC) *Calendar:* Sem. plan *Degrees:* B, M *CEO:* Pres. Margarita Gomez-Palacio
Enroll: 1454 [52] (11) 525-40-66

NIGERIA

THE NIGERIAN BAPTIST THEOLOGICAL SEMINARY
P.O. Box 30, Ogbomoso *Type:* Private (Southern Baptist) professional *Accred.:* 1983/1988 (SACS-CC) *Calendar:* Sem. plan *Degrees:* B *CEO:* Prin. Osadolor Imasogie
Enroll: 267 [234] (38) 710011

NORTHERN MARIANAS ISLANDS

NORTHERN MARIANAS COLLEGE
P.O. Box 1250, Saipan CNMI 96950 *Type:* Public junior *System:* College of Micronesia *Accred.:* 1985/1990 (WASC-Jr.) *Calendar:* Sem. plan *Degrees:* A *CEO:* Pres. Agnes M. McPhetres
Enroll: 444 (670) 234-6932

PALAU

MICRONESIAN OCCUPATIONAL COLLEGE
P.O. Box 9, Koror RP 96940 *Type:* Public professional *Accred.:* 1977/1987 (WASC-Jr.) *Calendar:* Sem. plan *Degrees:* A *CEO:* Pres. Francis M. Matsutaro
Enroll: 391 (680) 9-488-2471

PANAMA

PANAMA CANAL COLLEGE
DoDDS, Panama Region, A.P.O. Miami 34002 *Type:* Public (federal) junior *Accred.:* 1941/1983 (MSA) *Calendar:* Sem. plan *Degrees:* A *CEO:* Dean Joseph F. Shields
Enroll: 1390 [507] 52-3107

SPAIN

SCHILLER INTERNATIONAL UNIVERSITY
Calle de Rodriguez San Pedro, 28015 Madrid *Type:* Private *Accred.:* 1983 (CCA-

ACICS) *Calendar:* Sem. plan *Degrees:* A, B, M *CEO:* Dir. Lynn Bergunde
Enroll: 201 [34] (1) 446-2349

SWITZERLAND

FRANKLIN COLLEGE
Via Ponte Tresa 29, 6924 Sorengo, Lugano *Type:* Private liberal arts *Accred.:* 1975/1983 (MSA) *Calendar:* Sem. plan *Degrees:* A, B *CEO:* Pres. Theodore E. Brenner
Enroll: 182 [41] (91) 550-101

HOTEL INSTITUTE FOR MANAGEMENT
15 Ave. des Alpes, Montreux CH-1820 *Type:* Private *Accred.:* 1990 (CCA-ACICS) *Calendar:* Courses of varying lengths *Degrees:* certificates, diplomas *CEO:* Managing Dir. Edward Dandrieux
[41] (21) 963-7404

HOTEL MANAGEMENT SCHOOL, "LES ROCHES"
Bluche Crans-Montana, Valais CH-3975 *Type:* Private *Accred.:* 1991 (NEASC-CVTCI) *Calendar:* Courses of varying lengths *Degrees:* diplomas *CEO:* Prin. Hans von Rotz
Enroll: 995

UNITED KINGDOM

IMC-INTERNATIONAL MANAGEMENT CENTERS
Castle St., Buckingham, England MK18 1BP *Type:* Private home study *Accred.:* 1989 (NHSC) *Calendar:* Courses of varying lengths *Degrees:* certificates *CEO:* Prin. Gordon Wills
[44] (28) 081-7222

RICHMOND COLLEGE
Queens Rd., Richmond, Surrey, England TW10 6JP *Type:* Private liberal arts *Accred.:* 1981/1986 (MSA) *Calendar:* Sem. plan *Degrees:* A, B *CEO:* Pres. William J. Petrek
Enroll: 1019 [44] (11) 940-9762

SCHILLER INTERNATIONAL UNIVERSITY
51-55 Waterloo Rd., London, England SEI 8TX *Type:* Private *Accred.:* 1983 (CCA-ACICS) *Calendar:* Sem. plan *Degrees:* A, B, P, M *CEO:* Dir. Richard Taylor
Enroll: 674 [44] (1) 928-1372

BRANCH CAMPUS
Wickham Ct., W. Wickham, Kent, England BR4 9HW *CEO:* Dir. Louise Cody
[44] (81) 777-8069

Major Changes

Atlanta University and Clark College, GA, merged to become Clark Atlanta University (summer 1990)
Atlantic Christian College, NC, changed its name to Barton College (summer 1991)
Beckley College, WV, changed its name to College of West Virginia (summer 1991)
CBN University, VA, changed its name to Regent University (summer 1990)
Central State University, OK, changed its name to University of Central Oklahoma (summer 1991)
Chapman College, CA, changed its name to Chapman University (summer 1991)
Clark County Community College, NV, changed its name to Community College of Southern Nevada (summer 1991)
College of Boca Raton, FL, changed its name to Lynn University (summer 1991)
College of Idaho, ID, changed its name to Albertson College (summer 1991)
College of St. Teresa, MN, closed (winter 1990)
College of St. Thomas, MN, changed its name to University of St. Thomas (fall 1990)
Colorado Christian College, CO, changed its name to Colorado Christian University (summer 1990)
Concordia College, IL, changed its name to Concordia University (winter 1990)
Don Bosco College, NJ, closed (summer 1990)
Eastern New Mexico University—Clovis, NM, changed its name to Clovis Community College (summer 1991)
El Reno Junior College, OK, changed its name to Redlands Community College (summer 1991)
Feather River Community College, CA, changed its name to Feather River College (summer 1991)
Friends Bible College, KS, changed its name to Barclay College (summer 1990)
Grand Rapids Junior College, MI, changed its name to Grand Rapids Community College (summer 1991)
Kearney State College, NE, changed its name to University of Nebraska at Kearney (summer 1991)
Loma Linda University's Riverside Campus, CA, became La Sierra University (summer 1991)
Madonna College, MI, changed its name to Madonna University (summer 1991)
Martin Center College, IN, changed its name to Martin University (summer 1991)
Marycrest College, IA, changed its name to Teikyo Marycrest University (summer 1991)
Medical College of Hampton Roads, VA, changed its name to Eastern Virginia Medical School (summer 1991)
Mercy College of Detroit and University of Detroit, MI, merged to become University of Detroit Mercy (spring 1990)
Midwest College of Engineering, IL, closed (summer 1990)
Mundelein College, IL, merged into Loyola University of Chicago (summer 1991)
National College of Education, IL, changed its name to National-Louis University (summer 1990)
Nazareth College, MI, will be closing (summer 1992)
Northrop University, CA, will be closing (summer 1992)
Oklahoma Christian College, OK, changed its name to Oklahoma Christian University of Science and Arts (spring 1990)
Pan American University, TX, became a member of the University of Texas System and changed its name to University of Texas-Pan American and University of Texas at Brownsville (spring 1990)
Post College, CT, changed its name to Teikyo Post University (spring 1990)
Prospersi Institute of Art, CT, changed its name to Connecticut Institute of Art (summer 1991)
Regis College, CO, changed its name to Regis University (summer 1991)
St. Alphonse College, CT, closed (summer 1990)
St. Paul Bible College, MN, changed its name to Crown College (summer 1991)
School of the Ozarks, MO, changed its name to College of the Ozarks (summer 1990)
Sierra Community College, CA, changed its name to Sierra College (summer 1991)
Southeastern Massachusetts University, MA, changed its name to University of Massachusetts at Dartmouth (summer 1991)
Southern Baptist College, AR, changed its name to Williams Baptist College (summer 1990)
University of Lowell, MA, changed its name to University of Massachusetts at Lowell (summer 1991)
University of Massachusetts Medical Center, MA, changed its name to University of Massachusetts at Worcester (summer 1991)
Westmar College, IA, changed its name to Teikyo Westmar College (spring 1990)

Candidates

Candidates for Accreditation

Candidate for Accreditation is a status of affiliation with a recognized accrediting commission which indicates that an institution has achieved initial recognition and is progressing toward, but does not assure, accreditation.

The Candidate for Accreditation classification is designed for postsecondary institutions which may or may not be fully operative. In either case the institution must provide evidence of sound planning, the resources to implement these plans, and appear to have the potential for attaining its goals within a reasonable time.

To be considered for Candidate for Accreditation status the applicant organization must be a postsecondary educational institution with the following characteristics:

1. Have a charter and/or formal authority from an appropriate governmental agency to award a certificate, diploma, or degree.
2. Have a governing board which includes representation reflecting the public interest.
3. Have employed a chief administrative officer.
4. Offer, or plan to offer, one or more educational programs of at least one academic year in length, or the equivalent at the postsecondary level, with clearly defined and published educational objectives, as well as a clear statement of the means for achieving them.
5. Include general education at the postsecondary level as a prerequisite to or an essential element in its principal educational programs.
6. Have admission policies compatible with its stated objectives.
7. Have developed a preliminary survey or evidence of basic planning for the development of the institution.
8. Have established an adequate financial base of funding commitments and have available a summary of its latest audited financial statement.

ALABAMA

PHILLIPS COLLEGE OF MOBILE
3446 Demetropolis Rd., Mobile 36693 *Type:* Private business *Accred.:* 1990 (CCA-ACICS candidate) *Calendar:* Qtr. plan *Degrees:* A *CEO:* Dir. Jay Lambeth
Enroll: 849   (205) 666-9696

ARKANSAS

NORTHWEST ARKANSAS COMMUNITY COLLEGE
Bentonville 72712 *Type:* Public junior *Accred.:* 1991 (NCA candidate) *Degrees:* A *CEO:* Pres. Bob Burns, Ph.D.
          (501) 636-7202

CALIFORNIA

AMERICAN ARMENIAN INTERNATIONAL COLLEGE
1950 Third St., La Verne 91750 *Type:* Independent *Accred.:* 1986 (WASC-Sr. candidate) *Calendar:* 4-1-4 plan *Degrees:* B *CEO:* Pres. Garbis Der Yeghiayan
Enroll: 106   (714) 593-0432

AMERICAN COLLEGE OF TRADITIONAL CHINESE MEDICINE
455 Arkansas St., San Francisco 94107 *Type:* Private professional *Calendar:* 3-year plan *Degrees:* M *Prof. Accred.:* Acupuncture (candidate) *CEO:* Pres. Kevin Ergil
          (415) 282-7600

CALIFORNIA STATE UNIVERSITY, SAN MARCOS
820 W. Los Vallecitos, San Marcos 92069 *Type:* Public (state) *System:* California State University System *Accred.:* 1990 (WASC-Sr. candidate) *Calendar:* Sem. plan *Degrees:* B, M *CEO:* Pres. Bill W. Stacy
Enroll: 250   (619) 471-4100

NEW COLLEGE FOR ADVANCED CHRISTIAN STUDIES, BERKELEY
2600 Dwight Way, Berkeley 94704 *Type:* Independent *Accred.:* 1988 (WASC-Sr. candidate) *Calendar:* Sem. plan *Degrees:* M *CEO:* Acting Pres. Richard Benner
Enroll: 25 (510) 841-9386

SAN JOAQUIN COLLEGE OF LAW
3385 E. Shields Ave., Fresno 93726 *Type:* Independent professional *Accred.:* 1987 (WASC-Sr. candidate) *Calendar:* Sem. plan *Degrees:* P, M, certificates *CEO:* Dean Janice Pearson
Enroll: 145 (209) 225-4953

UNITED STATES NAVAL FLEET ANTI-SUBMARINE WARFARE TRAINING CENTER
San Diego 92547-5000 *Type:* Public (federal) technical *Accred.:* 1991 (SACS-COEI candidate) *Calendar:* Courses of varying lengths *Degrees:* certificates *CEO:* Commandant J.R. Tinsley, III
(619) 524-1665

COLORADO

COLLEGE FOR FINANCIAL PLANNING
4695 S. Monaco St., Denver 80237 *Type:* Private professional *Accred.:* 1991 (NCA candidate) *Calendar:* Courses of varying lengths *Degrees:* M, certificates *CEO:* Pres. William L. Anthes
Enroll: 7959 (303) 220-1200

NATIONAL THEATRE CONSERVATORY
1050 13th St., Denver 80204 *Type:* Private *Accred.:* 1987 (NCA candidate) *Calendar:* Courses of varying lengths *Degrees:* M *CEO:* Exec. Dir. Kevin Maifield
Enroll: 43 (303) 893-4000

FLORIDA

BUSINESS AND TECHNOLOGY INSTITUTE
42 N.W. 27th Ave., Miami 33125 *Type:* Private *Accred.:* 1990 (SACS-COEI candidate) *Calendar:* Courses of varying lengths *Degrees:* diplomas *CEO:* Dir. Fernando N. Llerena
Enroll: 8 (305) 541-4463

TRINITY COLLEGE OF FLORIDA
P.O. Box 9000, Holiday 34690 *Type:* Independent *Accred.:* 1990 (AABC candidate) *Calendar:* Sem. plan *Degrees:* A, B, certificates, diplomas *CEO:* Pres. Richard Williams
Enroll: 119 (813) 376-6911

GEORGIA

ALTAMAHA TECHNICAL INSTITUTE
1777 W. Cherry St., Jesup 31545 *Type:* Public (state) *Accred.:* 1990 (SACS-COEI candidate) *Calendar:* Courses of varying lengths *Degrees:* diplomas *CEO:* Pres. C. Paul Scott
Enroll: 91 (912) 427-5800

BRANCH CAMPUS
P.O. Box 571, Cromatie St., Hazlhurst, GA 31319 *CEO:* Dir. Molly Hinson
(912) 375-5480

NORTH METRO TECHNICAL INSTITUTE
5198 Ross Rd., Acworth 30101 *Type:* Public (state) *Accred.:* 1990 (SACS-COEI candidate) *Calendar:* Courses of varying lengths *Degrees:* diplomas *CEO:* Pres. Kenneth Allen
Enroll: 312 (404) 975-4010

OGEECHEE TECHNICAL INSTITUTE
One Joe Kennedy Blvd., Statesboro 30458 *Type:* Public (state) *Accred.:* 1990 (SACS-COEI candidate) *Calendar:* Courses of varying lengths *Degrees:* diplomas *CEO:* Pres. Robert C. Ernst
Enroll: 18 (912) 764-8530

SOUTHEASTERN FLIGHT ACADEMY
Herbert Smart Airport, Macon 31201 *Type:* Private *Accred.:* 1989 (SACS-COEI candidate) *Calendar:* Courses of varying lengths *Degrees:* certificates, diplomas *CEO:* Pres. Jim Miresse
Enroll: 173 (800) 423-7510

HAWAII

TAI HSUAN FOUNDATION COLLEGE OF
ACUPUNCTURE AND HERBAL MEDICINE
2600 S. King St., No. 206, Honolulu 96826
Type: Private *Calendar:* 3-year plan *Prof. Accred.:* Acupuncture (candidate) *CEO:* Pres. Lily Siou
(808) 947-4788

ILLINOIS

INSTITUTE FOR CLINICAL SOCIAL WORK
30 N. Michigan Ave., Ste. 420, Chicago 60602 *Type:* Private professional *Accred.:* 1990 (NCA candidate) *Calendar:* Sem. plan *Degrees:* D *CEO:* Pres. Arnold M. Levin
Enroll: 60 (312) 726-8480

LAKEVIEW COLLEGE OF NURSING
812 N. Logan Ave., Danville 61832 *Type:* Private professional *Accred.:* 1991 (NCA candidate) *Calendar:* Sem. plan *Degrees:* B *CEO:* Pres. Irene A. Steward
Enroll: 51 (217) 443-5238

LEXINGTON INSTITUTE OF HOSPITALITY CAREERS
10840 S. Western Ave., Chicago 60643 *Type:* Private *Accred.:* 1987 (NCA candidate) *Calendar:* Sem. plan *Degrees:* A *CEO:* Dir. Ana Maria Boza
Enroll: 34 (312) 779-3800

MIDWEST CENTER FOR THE STUDY OF ORIENTAL MEDICINE
4334 N. Hazel St., Ste. 206, Chicago 60613 *Type:* Private *Calendar:* 3-year program *Degrees:* M *Prof. Accred.:* Acupuncture (candidate) *CEO:* Pres. William Dunbar
(312) 975-1295

ST. JOSEPH COLLEGE OF NURSING
290 N. Springfield Ave., Joliet 60435 *Type:* Private *Accred.:* 1990 (NCA candidate) *Calendar:* Qtr. plan *Degrees:* B *CEO:* Pres. Lois K. Benich
Enroll: 94 (815) 725-7133

INDIANA

LUTHERAN COLLEGE OF HEALTH PROFESSIONS
535 Home Ave., Fort Wayne 46807 *Type:* Private *Accred.:* 1990 (NCA candidate) *Calendar:* Qtr. plan *Degrees:* A, B, certificates, diplomas *CEO:* Dean Marilyn R. Wilson
Enroll: 325 (219) 458-2451

KENTUCKY

KENTUCKY CAREER INSTITUTE
8095 Connector Dr., Florence 41042 *Type:* Private *Accred.:* 1989 (SACS-COEI candidate) *Calendar:* Courses of varying lengths *Degrees:* certificates, diplomas *CEO:* Pres. Harry Beck
Enroll: 57 (606) 371-9393

KENTUCKY MOUNTAIN BIBLE COLLEGE
Box 10, Vancleve 41385 *Type:* Private (Kentucky Mountain Holiness Asscociation) *Accred.:* 1989 (AABC candidate) *Calendar:* Sem. plan *Degrees:* A, B *CEO:* Pres. Wilfred Fisher
Enroll: 51 (606) 666-5000

LOUISIANA

ABBEVILLE BEAUTY ACADEMY
1828 Veterans Memorial Dr., Abbeville 70510 *Type:* Private *Accred.:* 1990 (SACS-COEI candidate) *Calendar:* Courses of varying lengths *Degrees:* certificates *CEO:* Dir. Hazel Doucet
Enroll: 41 (318) 893-1228

CLOYD'S BEAUTY SCHOOL No. 2
407 DeSiard St., P.O. Box 603, West Monroe 71294-0603 *Type:* Private *Accred.:* 1989 (SACS-COEI candidate) *Calendar:* Courses of varying lengths *Degrees:* certificates, diplomas *CEO:* Dir. William R. Mathieu
Enroll: 25 (318) 322-5314

CLOYD'S BEAUTY SCHOOL No. 3
2514 Ferrand St., Monroe 71203 *Type:* Private *Accred.:* 1989 (SACS-COEI candidate) *Calendar:* Courses of varying lengths *De-

grees: certificates, diplomas *CEO:* Dir. William R. Mathieu
Enroll: 59 (318) 322-5314

JOHN JAY BEAUTY COLLEGE
540 Robert E. Lee Blvd., New Orleans 70124 *Type:* Private *Accred.:* 1988 (SACS-COEI candidate) *Calendar:* Courses of varying lengths *Degrees:* certificates *CEO:* Dir. John Grissafi
Enroll: 113 (504) 282-4907

BRANCH CAMPUS
3144 Ponchartrain Dr., Slidell, LA 70458 *CEO:* Dir. John Grissafi
(504) 643-9894

MANSFIELD VOCATIONAL-TECHNICAL SCHOOL
1001 Oxford Rd., P.O. Box 1236, Mansfield 71052 *Type:* Public *Accred.:* 1989 (SACS-COEI candidate) *Calendar:* Courses of varying lengths *Degrees:* certificates, diplomas *CEO:* Dir. Ronald E. Wright
Enroll: 75 (318) 872-2243

ROBERTS BEAUTY COLLEGE
502 N. Columbia St., Covington 70433 *Type:* Private *Accred.:* 1989 (SACS-COEI candidate) *Calendar:* Courses of varying lengths *Degrees:* certificates, diplomas *CEO:* Dir. Mary Dale Roberts
Enroll: 23 (504) 892-3826

WORLD EVANGELISM BIBLE COLLEGE AND SEMINARY
P.O. Box 38000, 7200 Bluebonnet Rd., Baton Rouge 70828-8000 *Type:* Private *Accred.:* 1991 (SACS-CC candidate) *Calendar:* Sem. plan *Degrees:* A, B, M *CEO:* Pres. Michael W. Haley
Enroll: 466 (504) 768-3662

MASSACHUSETTS

GORDON INSTITUTE
Audubon Rd., Wakefield 01880-1201 *Type:* Private professional *Accred.:* 1990 (NEASC-CIHE candidate) *Calendar:* Sem. plan *Degrees:* M *CEO:* Pres. Peter E. Hexner
Enroll: 13 (617) 246-4750

MICHIGAN

BAY MILLS COMMUNITY COLLEGE
Rte. 1, Brimley 49715 *Type:* Public (district) junior *Accred.:* 1991 (NCA candidate) *Calendar:* Sem. plan *Degrees:* A, certificates, diplomas *CEO:* Pres. Martha McLeod
(906) 248-3354

JORDAN COLLEGE
360 W. Pine St., Cedar Springs 49319 *Type:* Private *Accred.:* 1990 (NCA candidate) *Calendar:* Sem. plan *Degrees:* A, B *CEO:* Pres. Lexie K. Coxon
Enroll: 2047 (616) 696-1180

MINNESOTA

PILLSBURY BAPTIST BIBLE COLLEGE
315 Groove St., Owatonna 55060 *Type:* Private *Accred.:* 1990 (NCA candidate) *Calendar:* Sem. plan *Degrees:* B *CEO:* Pres. Alan L. Potter
Enroll: 345 (507) 451-2710

MONTANA

DULL KNIFE MEMORIAL COLLEGE
P.O. Box 98, Lame Deer 59043 *Type:* Private tribal junior *Accred.:* 1990 (NASC candidate) *Degrees:* A *CEO:* Pres. Arthur L. McDonald
Enroll: 345 (406) 477-6215

FORT BELKNAP COLLEGE
P.O. Box 39, Harlem 59526 *Type:* Private tribal junior *Accred.:* 1989 (NASC candidate) *Calendar:* Sem. plan *Degrees:* A *CEO:* Pres. Margaret C. Perez
Enroll: 125 (406) 353-2205

STONE CHILD COMMUNITY COLLEGE
Box Elder 59532 *Type:* Private tribal junior *Accred.:* 1989 (NASC candidate) *Calendar:* Sem. plan *Degrees:* A *CEO:* Pres. Margaret Nagel
Enroll: 138 (406) 395-4313

NEW HAMPSHIRE

THE THOMAS MORE COLLEGE OF LIBERAL ARTS
6 Manchester St., Merrimack 03054-3805 *Type:* Private *Accred.:* 1990 (NEASC-CIHE candidate) *Calendar:* Sem. plan *Degrees:* B *CEO:* Pres. Peter V. Sampo
Enroll: 72 (603) 880-8308

NEW JERSEY

SUSSEX COUNTY COMMUNITY COLLEGE COMMISSION
College Hill, Newton 07860 *Type:* Public (county) junior *System:* Office of Community Colleges *Accred.:* 1988 (MSA candidate) *Calendar:* Sem. plan *Degrees:* A *CEO:* Pres. William A. Connor
Enroll: 1759 (201) 579-5400

WARREN COUNTY COMMUNITY COLLEGE COMMISSION
P.O. Box 168, Rte. 57, Washington 07882 *Type:* Public (county) junior *System:* Office of Community Colleges *Accred.:* 1987 (MSA candidate) *Calendar:* Sem. plan *Degrees:* A *CEO:* Pres. Vincent DeSanctis
Enroll: 954 (908) 689-1090

NEW YORK

BAIS MEDRASH L'TORAH RABBINICAL COLLEGE
118 W. Central Ave., Spring Valley 10977 *Type:* Private professional *Accred.:* 1990 (AARTS candidate) *Calendar:* Courses of varying lengths *Degrees:* Talmudic (1st and 2nd) *CEO:* Pres. S. Faivelson
Enroll: 40 (914) 352-5150

THE BERKELEY SCHOOL OF NEW YORK
3 E. 43rd St., New York 10017 *Type:* Private 2-year *Accred.:* 1988 (MSA candidate) *Calendar:* Sem. plan *Degrees:* A *CEO:* Pres. Louis Cress
Enroll: 709 (212) 986-4343

FRIENDS WORLD COLLEGE
Plover La., Huntington 11743 *Type:* Private liberal arts *Accred.:* 1984 (MSA candidate) *Calendar:* Sem. plan *Degrees:* B *CEO:* Pres. Leo Barrington
Enroll: 194 (516) 549-5000

KOL YAAKOV TORAH CENTER
29 W. Maple Ave., Monsey 10952 *Type:* Private professional *Accred.:* 1990 (AARTS candidate) *Calendar:* Sem. plan *Degrees:* Rabbinic (1st) *CEO:* Pres. Leib Tropper
Enroll: 38 (914) 425-3863

MACHZIKEI HADATH RABBINICAL COLLEGE
5407 16th Ave., Brooklyn 11204 *Type:* Private professional *Accred.:* 1989 (AARTS candidate) *Calendar:* Sem. plan *Degrees:* Talmudic (1st and 2nd) *CEO:* Pres. Ari Klein
Enroll: 96 (718) 331-6613

TALMUDICAL INSTITUTE OF UPSTATE NEW YORK
769 Park Ave., Rochester 14607 *Type:* Private professional *Accred.:* 1988 (AARTS candidate) *Calendar:* Sem. plan *Degrees:* Talmudic (1st and 2nd) *CEO:* Pres. M. Lebovics
Enroll: 23 (716) 473-2810

UNIFICATION THEOLOGICAL SEMINARY
10 Dock Rd., Barrytown 12507 *Type:* Private (Unification Church) *Accred.:* 1988 (MSA candidate) *Calendar:* Sem. plan *Degrees:* P, M *CEO:* Pres. David S.C. Kim
Enroll: 102 (914) 758-6881

YESHIVA GEDOLAH BAIS YISROEL
1719 Ave. P, Brooklyn 11229 *Type:* Private professional *Accred.:* 1985 (AARTS candidate) *Calendar:* Sem. plan *Degrees:* Talmudic (1st and 2nd) *CEO:* Pres. S. Miller
Enroll: 39 (718) 376-3838

YESHIVA GEDOLAH IMREI YOSEF D'SPINKA
1460 56th St., Brooklyn 11219 *Type:* Private professional *Accred.:* 1989 (AARTS candidate) *Calendar:* Sem. plan *Degrees:* Talmudic (1st) *CEO:* Pres. Mordechai Majerowitz
Enroll: 69 (718) 851-1653

YESHIVA AND KOLEL BAIS MEDRASH ELYON
73 Main St., Monsey 10952 *Type:* Private professional *Accred.:* 1989 (AARTS candi-

date) *Calendar:* Sem. plan *Degrees:* Rabbinic (1st), Talmudic (1st) *CEO:* Pres. I. Falk
Enroll: 59   (914) 356-7064

YESHIVA AND KOLLEL HARBOTZAS TORAH
1049 E. 15th St., Brooklyn 11230 *Type:* Private professional *Accred.:* 1991 (AARTS candidate) *Calendar:* Sem. plan *Degrees:* Rabbinic (1st), Talmudic (1st and 2nd) *CEO:* Pres. Y. Bittersfeld
Enroll: 44   (718) 692-0208

YESHIVA AND MESIVTA KOL TORAH
4823 48th St., Brooklyn 11224 *Type:* Private professional *Accred.:* 1989 (AARTS candidate) *Calendar:* Sem. plan *Degrees:* Talmudic (1st and 2nd) *CEO:* Pres. B. Klein
Enroll: 36   (718) 265-5840

NORTH CAROLINA

LYNDON B. JOHNSON CIVILIAN CONSERVATION CENTER
466 Job Corps Dr., Franklin 29734 *Type:* Public (state) *Accred.:* 1988 (SACS-COEI candidate) *Calendar:* Courses of varying lengths *Degrees:* certificates *CEO:* Dir. Edward Washington
Enroll: 234   (704) 524-4446

MTA SCHOOL
1155 Hwy. 66, S., Kernersville 27284-3534 *Type:* Private *Accred.:* 1989 (SACS-COEI candidate) *Calendar:* Courses of varying lengths *Degrees:* certificates *CEO:* Dir. Katherine Sharpe
Enroll: 2142   919-37197200

OHIO

MOUNT CARMEL COLLEGE OF NURSING
127 S. Davis Ave., Columbus 43222 *Type:* Private (Roman Catholic) *Accred.:* 1991 (NCA candidate) *Calendar:* Sem. plan *Degrees:* B *CEO:* Pres. Ann Schiele
Enroll: 49   (614) 225-5800

OKLAHOMA

SPARTAN SCHOOL OF AERONAUTICS
8820 E. Pine St., Tulsa 74115 *Type:* Private *Accred.:* 1991 (NCA candidate) *Calendar:* Sem. plan *Degrees:* A, certificates, diplomas *CEO:* Pres. Frank D. Iacobucci
Enroll: 2668   (918) 836-6886

PENNSYLVANIA

BIBLICAL THEOLOGICAL SEMINARY
200 N. Main St., Hatfield 19440 *Type:* Private (interdenominational) professional *Accred.:* 1983 (MSA candidate) *Degrees:* P, M, certificates, diplomas *CEO:* Pres. David G. Dunbar
Enroll: 195   (215) 368-5000

PINEBROOK JUNIOR COLLEGE
600 S. Main St., Coopersburg 18036 *Type:* Private *Accred.:* 1989 (AABC candidate) *Calendar:* 4-1-4 plan *Degrees:* A *CEO:* Pres. Carl C. Cassel
Enroll: 109   (215) 282-4000

RECONSTRUCTIONIST RABBINICAL COLLEGE
Greenwood Ave. and Church Rd., Wyncote 19095 *Type:* Private professional *Accred.:* 1984 (MSA candidate) *Calendar:* Sem. plan *Degrees:* P, M *CEO:* Pres. Arthur Green
Enroll: 50   (215) 576-0800

REFORMED PRESBYTERIAN THEOLOGICAL SEMINARY
7418 Penn Ave., Pittsburgh 15208 *Type:* Private (Presbyterian) professional; graduate only *Accred.:* 1991 (ATS candidate) *Calendar:* Sem. plan *Degrees:* P, M *CEO:* Pres. Bruce Stewart
Enroll: 40   (412) 731-8690

THADDEUS STEVENS STATE SCHOOL OF TECHNOLOGY
750 E. King St., Lancaster 17602 *Type:* Public (state) junior *Accred.:* 1983 (MSA candidate) *Calendar:* Sem. plan *Degrees:* A, certificates, diplomas *CEO:* Pres. Alan K. Cohen
Enroll: 389   (717) 299-7730

PUERTO RICO

ESCUELA DE ARTES PLASTICAS INSTITUTO DE CULTURA PUERTORRIQUENA
Apartado 4184, San Juan 00905 *Type:* Public (state) *Accred.:* 1988 (MSA candidate) *Cal-*

endar: Sem. plan *Degrees:* B *CEO:* Chanc. Margarita Fernandez Zavala
Enroll: 166   (809) 725-8120

SOUTH CAROLINA

ALLEN UNIVERSITY
1530 Harden St., Columbia 29204 *Type:* Private (African Methodist Episcopal) liberal arts and teachers *Accred.:* 1990 (SACS-CC candidate) *Calendar:* Sem. plan *Degrees:* B *CEO:* Pres. Collie Coleman
Enroll: 188   (803) 254-4165

SOUTH CAROLINA CRIMINAL JUSTICE TRAINING ACADEMY
5400 Broad River Rd., Columbia 29210 *Type:* Public (state) professional *Accred.:* 1990 (SACS-COEI candidate) *Calendar:* Courses of varying lengths *Degrees:* certificates, diplomas *CEO:* Dir. Walter J. Johnson, Jr.
Enroll: 437   (803) 737-8400

TENNESSEE

BOBBIE'S SCHOOL OF BEAUTY ARTS
108 Decatur Pike, P.O. Box 688, Athens 37303 *Type:* Private *Accred.:* 1991 (SACS-COEI candidate) *Calendar:* Courses of varying lengths *Degrees:* certificates *CEO:* Dir. Bobbie Wallace
Enroll: 28   (615) 744-7251

FORT SANDERS SCHOOL OF NURSING
1915 White Ave., Knoxville 37916 *Type:* Private *Accred.:* 1990 (SACS-COEI candidate) *Calendar:* Courses of varying lengths *Degrees:* diplomas *CEO:* Dir. Margaret Heins
Enroll: 38   (615) 541-1290

TEXAS

ALL STATE BUSINESS COLLEGE
6200 Maple Ave., Dallas 75235 *Type:* Private *Accred.:* 1989 (SACS-COEI candidate) *Calendar:* Courses of varying lengths *Degrees:* diplomas *CEO:* Dir. Thomas Graham
Enroll: 196   (214) 357-8453

BAY RIDGE CHRISTIAN COLLEGE
P.O. Box 726, Kendleton 77451 *Type:* Private (Church of God) professional *Accred.:* 1989 (AABC candidate) *Calendar:* Sem. plan *Degrees:* A, B, certificates *CEO:* Pres. Robert Williams
Enroll: 29   (409) 532-3982

TECHNICAL TRAINING INSTITUTE
2616 Southloop, W., Ste. 400, Houston 77054 *Type:* Private *Accred.:* 1989 (SACS-COEI candidate) *Calendar:* Courses of varying lengths *Degrees:* certificates, diplomas *CEO:* Pres. Ruthie Hebert
Enroll: 25   (713) 661-3653

VERMONT

LANDMARK COLLEGE
Putney 05346 *Type:* Private junior *Accred.:* 1987 (NEASC-CIHE candidate) *Calendar:* Sem. plan *Degrees:* A *CEO:* Pres. Gene Cesari
Enroll: 20   (802) 387-4767

VIRGINIA

CAREER TRAINING CENTER
4000 W. Broad St., Richmond 23230 *Type:* Private *Accred.:* 1990 (SACS-COEI candidate) *Calendar:* Courses of varying lengths *Degrees:* certificates *CEO:* Dir. Jacalyn Adams
Enroll: 57   (804) 342-1190

BRANCH CAMPUS
2600 Memorial Ave., No. 201, Lynchburg, VA 24501 *CEO:* Dir. Donna Barrette
    (804) 845-7949

NOTRE DAME APOSTOLIC CATECHETICAL INSTITUTE
200 N. Glebe Rd., Arlington 22203 *Type:* Private *Accred.:* 1990 (SACS-CC candidate) *Calendar:* Sem. plan *Degrees:* M *CEO:* Pres. Franklyn M. McAfee
Enroll: 114   (703) 841-9730

WASHINGTON

NORTHWEST INDIAN COLLEGE
2522 Kwina Rd., Bellingham 98226 *Type:* Private (tribal) junior *Accred.:* 1990 (NASC candidate) *Calendar:* Sem. plan *Degrees:* A *CEO:* Pres. Robert J. Lorence
Enroll: 979   (206) 676-2772

WISCONSIN

LAC COURTE OREILLES OJIBWA COMMUNITY COLLEGE
Rte. 2, Box 2357, Hayward 54843 *Type:* Public (tribal) junior *Accred.:* 1989 (NCA candidate) *Calendar:* Sem. plan *Degrees:* A, certificates, diplomas *CEO:* Pres. Jasjit S. Minhas
Enroll: 239   (715) 634-4790

MARANTHA BAPTIST BIBLE COLLEGE
745 W. Main St., P.O. Box 438, Watertown 53094 *Type:* Private *Accred.:* 1991 (NCA candidate) *Calendar:* Sem. plan *Degrees:* A, B, certificates, diplomas *CEO:* Pres. Arno Q. Weniger
Enroll: 431   (414) 261-9300

OUTSIDE THE UNITED STATES

CANADA

CATHERINE BOOTH BIBLE COLLEGE
447 Webb Pl., Winnipeg, Manitoba R3B 2P2 *Type:* Private *Accred.:* 1987 (AABC candidate) *Calendar:* Sem. plan *Degrees:* A, B, certificates *CEO:* Pres. Maj. Earl Robinson
Enroll.: 62   (204) 947-6701

NEWMAN THEOLOGICAL COLLEGE
R.R. 8, Edmonton, Alberta T5L 4H8 *Type:* Private (Roman Catholic) professional; graduate only *Accred.:* 1988 (ATS candidate) *Calendar:* Sem. plan *Degrees:* P, M *CEO:* Pres. Don Macdonald
Enroll.: 125   (403) 447-2993

STEINBACH BIBLE COLLEGE
P.O. Box 1420, Steinbach, Manitoba R0A 2A0 *Type:* Private *Accred.:* 1987 (AABC candidate) *Calendar:* Sem. plan *Degrees:* B, diplomas *CEO:* Pres. Ben Eidse
Enroll.: 77   (204) 326-6451

Public Systems of Higher Education

ALABAMA

**The Alabama College System
(Two-Year Institutions)**
401 Adams Ave., Montgomery 36104
Chanc. Fred J. Gainous
(205) 242-2900

Bishop State Community College
351 N. Broad St., Mobile 36690
Pres. Yvonne Kennedy
(205) 690-6416

Brewer State Junior College
2631 Temple Ave., N., Fayette 35555
Pres. Wayland K. DeWitt
(205) 932-3221

Central Alabama Community College
P.O. Box 699, 908 Cherokee Rd., Alexander City 35010
Pres. James H. Cornell
(205) 234-6346

Chattahoochee Valley State Community College
2602 College Dr., Phenix City 36867
Pres. James E. Owen
(205) 291-4900

Enterprise State Junior College
600 Plaza Dr., Enterprise 36330-1300
Pres. Joseph D. Talmadge
(205) 347-2623

Gadsden State Community College
P.O. Box 227, Gadsden 35902-0227
Pres. Victor B. Ficker
(205) 549-8200

George C. Wallace State Community College
Napier Field, Dothan 36303
Interim Pres. Imogene Mixson
(205) 983-3521

George Corley Wallace State Community College
3000 Range Line Rd., P.O. Box 1049, Selma 36702-1049
Pres. Julius R. Brown
(205) 875-2634

James H. Faulkner State Junior College
Hwy. 31 S., Bay Minette 36507
Pres. Gary L. Branch
(205) 937-9581

Jefferson Davis State Junior College
220 Aleo Dr., Brewton 36426
Pres. Sandra K. McCleod
(205) 867-4832

Jefferson State Community College
2601 Carson Rd., Birmingham 35215-3098
Pres. Judy M. Merritt
(205) 853-1200

John C. Calhoun State Community College
P.O. Box 2216, Decatur 35609-2216
Interim Pres. Jack Sasser
(205) 353-3102

Lawson State Community College
3060 Wilson Rd., S.W., Birmingham 35221
Pres. Perry W. Ward
(205) 925-2515

Lurleen B. Wallace State Junior College
Hwy. 84 E., P.O. Box 1418, Andalusia 36420
Pres. Seth Hammett
(205) 222-6591

Northeast Alabama State Junior College
Hwy. 35, P.O. Box 159, Rainsville 35986
Pres. Charles M. Pendley
(205) 638-4418

Northwest Alabama Community College
Rte. 3, P.O. Box 77, Phil Campbell 35581
Pres. Charles W. Britnell
(205) 993-5331

Patrick Henry State Junior College
P.O. Box 2000, Monroeville 36461
Pres. John A. Johnson
(205) 575-3158

Public Systems of Higher Education — Alabama

Shelton State Community College
202 Skyland Blvd., Tuscaloosa
35405
Pres. Thomas E. Umphrey
(205) 759-1541

Shoals Community College
George Wallace Blvd., P.O. Box 2545,
Muscle Shoals 35662
Pres. Larry McCoy
(205) 381-2813

Snead State Junior College
200 Walnut St., P.O. Drawer D, Boaz
35957
Pres. William H. Osborn
(205) 593-5120

Southern Union State Junior College
Roberts St., Wadley 36276
Pres. Richard J. Federinko
(205) 395-2211

Wallace State Community College
801 Main St., Hanceville 35077
Pres. James C. Bailey
(205) 352-6403

Alabama Commission on Higher Education
One Court Sq., Ste. 221, Montgomery
36197
Exec. Dir. Henry J. Hector
(205) 269-2700

Alabama Agricultural and Mechanical University
P.O. Box 285, 4107 Meridian St.,
Normal 35762
Interim Pres. Alan L. Keyes
(205) 851-5000

Alabama State University
915 S. Jackson St., Montgomery
36101-0271
Interim Pres. C.C. Baker
(205) 293-4100

Athens State College
Beaty St., Athens 35611
Pres. Jerry Bartlett
(205) 233-1800

Auburn University Central Office
Auburn University 36849-5113
Pres. James E. Martin
(205) 826-4000

Auburn University
Auburn University 36849-5113
Pres. James E. Martin
(205) 844-4000

Auburn University at Montgomery
7300 University Dr.,
Montgomery 36117-3596
Chanc. James O. Williams
(205) 244-3000

Jacksonville State University
N. Pelham Rd., Jacksonville 36265
Pres. Harold J. McGee
(205) 782-5781

Livingston University
Hwy. 11, Livingston 35470
Pres. Asa N. Green
(205) 652-9661

Troy State University System
University Ave., Troy 36082
Pres. Jack Hawkins, Jr.
(205) 566-8112

Troy State University
University Ave., Troy 36082
Chanc. Jack Hawkins, Jr.,PhD.
(205) 566-8112

Troy State University at Dothan
3601 U.S. Hwy. 231 N., Dothan
36304
Pres. Thomas E. Harrison
(205) 983-6556

Troy State University in Montgomery
231 Montgomery St.,
Montgomery 36103
Pres. Millard E. Elrod
(205) 834-1400

University of Alabama System
401 Queen City Ave., Tuscaloosa
35401
Chanc. Philip E. Austin
(205) 348-5121

Alabama

The University of Alabama
Tuscaloosa 35487
Pres. Roger Sayers
(205) 348-6010

The University of Alabama at Birmingham
UAB Sta., Birmingham 35294
Pres. Charles A. McCallum, Jr.
(205) 934-4011

University of Montevallo
Sta. 6001, Montevallo 35115-6001
Pres. John W. Stewart
(205) 665-6001

University of North Alabama
Florence 35632-0001
Pres. Robert L. Potts
(205) 760-4100

University of South Alabama
307 University Blvd., Mobile 36688
Pres. Frederick P. Whiddon
(205) 460-6101

ALASKA

University of Alaska System
Butrovich Bldg., Ste. 202, 910 Yukon Dr.,
Fairbanks 99775
Pres. Jerome Komisar
(907) 474-7311

Prince William Sound Community College
P.O. Box 97, Valdez 99686
Pres. John M. Devens
(907) 835-2421

University of Alaska Anchorage
3211 Providence Dr., Anchorage 99508
Chanc. Donald Behrend
(907) 786-1437

University of Alaska Anchorage—Kenai Peninsula College
34820 College Dr., Soldotna 99669
Dir. Ginger Steffy
(907) 262-5801

University of Alaska Anchorage—Kodiak College
Kodiak 99615
Dir. Carol Hagel
(907) 486-4161

University of Alaska Anchorage—Matanuska-Susitna College
Palmer 99645
Dir. Glenn Massay, Ph.D.
(907) 745-9774

University of Alaska Fairbanks
320 Signers' Hall, Fairbanks 99775
Chanc. Joan Wadlow
(907) 474-7112

University of Alaska Fairbanks—Chukchi
P.O. Box 297, Kotzebue 99752
Dir. Lynn Johnson
(907) 442-3400

University of Alaska Fairbanks—Kuskokwim
Bethel 99559
Pres. Linwood Laughy
(907) 543-4502

University of Alaska Fairbanks—Northwest
P.O. Box 1023, Nome 99762
Dir. Nancy Mendenhall
(907) 443-2201

University of Alaska Southeast
11120 Glacier Hwy., Juneau 99801
Chanc. Marshall L. Lind
(907) 789-4509

University of Alaska Southeast—Ketchikan
Ketchikan 99901
Dir. Francis Feinerman
(907) 225-6177

University of Alaska Southeast—Sitka
1332 Seward Ave., Sitka 99835
Dir. Richard Griffin
(907) 747-6653

ARIZONA

Arizona Board of Regents
3030 N. Central Ave., Suite 1400,
Phoenix 85004
Interim Exec. Dir. Frank H. Besnette
(602) 255-4082

Arizona State University
Tempe 85287-2203
Pres. Lattie F. Coor
(602) 965-5606

Northern Arizona University
Box 4092, Flagstaff 86011
Pres. Eugene M. Hughes
(602) 523-3232

University of Arizona
Tucson 85721
Pres. Manuel T. Pacheco
(602) 621-2211

Arizona State Board of Directors for Community Colleges
3325 N. Central Ave., Century Plaza, Ste. 1220, Phoenix 85012
Exec. Dir. Wayne M. McGrath
(602) 255-4037

Arizona Western College
P.O. Box 929, Yuma 85366
Pres. James Carruthers
(602) 726-1000

Central Arizona College
8470 N. Overfield Rd., Coolidge 85228
Pres. John J. Klein
(602) 723-4141

Cochise College
Douglas 85607
Pres. Dan Rehurek
(602) 364-7943

Eastern Arizona College
600 Church St., Thatcher 85552-0769
Pres. Gherald L. Hoopes, Jr.
(602) 428-8233

Maricopa County Community College District
3910 E. Washington St., Phoenix 85034
Chanc. Paul A. Elsner
(602) 731-8000

Gateway Community College
108 N. 40th St., Phoenix 85034
Pres. Phil D. Randolph
(602) 275-8500

Glendale Community College
6000 W. Olive Ave., Glendale 85302-3090
Pres. John R. Waltrip
(602) 435-3000

Mesa Community College
1833 W. Southern Ave., Mesa 85202
Pres. Larry K. Christiansen
(602) 461-7000

Paradise Valley Community College
18401 N. 32nd St., Phoenix 85032
Pres. John A. Cordova
(602) 493-2600

Phoenix College
1202 W. Thomas Rd., Phoenix 85013
Pres. Myrna Harrison
(602) 285-7433

Rio Salado Community College
640 N. First Ave., Phoenix 85003
Pres. Linda M. Thor
(602) 243-4000

Scottsdale Community College
9000 E. Chaparral Rd., Scottsdale 85256
Pres. Arthur W. DeCabooter
(602) 423-6000

South Mountain Community College
7050 S. 24th St., Phoenix 85040
Pres. Raul Cardenas
(602) 243-8000

Public Systems of Higher Education   **Arizona**

Mohave Community College
 1971 Jagerson Ave., Kingman 86401
 Pres. Charles W. Hall
 (602) 757-4331

Northland Pioneer College
 1200 E. Hermosa Dr., P.O. Box 610,
  Holbrook 86025-1993
 Pres. John H. Anderson
 (602) 524-6111

Pima County Community College District
 200 N. Stone Ave., P.O. Box 3010,
  Tucson 85702
 Pres. Johnas F. Hockaday
 (602) 884-6047

Yavapai College
 1100 E. Sheldon St., Prescott 86301
 Pres. Paul D. Walker
 (602) 445-7300

ARKANSAS

Arkansas Department of Higher Education
1220 W. 3rd St., Little Rock 72201
Dir. Diane S. Gilleland
(501) 324-9300

Arkansas State University System Office
P.O. Box 76, State University 72467
Pres. Eugene W. Smith
(501) 972-3030

Arkansas State University
P.O. Box 76, State University 72467
Pres. Eugene W. Smith
(501) 972-3030

Arkansas State University—Beebe
Drawer H, Beebe 72012
Chanc. William H. Owen, Jr.
(501) 882-6452

Arkansas Tech University
Russellville 72801
Pres. Kenneth G. Kersh
(501) 968-0237

Henderson State University
1100 Henderson St., Arkadelphia 71923
Pres. Charles D. Dunn
(501) 246-5511

University of Central Arkansas
Conway 72032
Pres. Winfred Thompson
(501) 329-2931

University of Arkansas System
601 University Tower Bldg., 1123 South University Ave., Little Rock 72204
Pres. B. Alan Sugg
(501) 686-2505

University of Arkansas at Little Rock
2801 S. University Ave., Little Rock 72204
Chanc. James H. Young
(501) 569-3200

University of Arkansas at Monticello
Monticello 71655
Chanc. Fred J. Taylor
(501) 460-1020

University of Arkansas at Pine Bluff
Pine Bluff 71601
Interim Chanc. Carolyn Blakely
(501) 541-6512

University of Arkansas for Medical Sciences
4301 W. Markham St., Little Rock 72205
Chanc. Harry P. Ward
(501) 686-5680

University of Arkansas, Fayetteville
Fayetteville 72701
Chanc. Daniel E. Ferritor
(501) 575-4148

CALIFORNIA

**California Community Colleges
(Board of Governors)**
1107 Ninth St., 6th Fl., Sacramento 95814
Chanc. David Mertes
(916) 322-4005

Allan Hancock Joint Community College District
800 S. College Dr., Santa Maria 93454
Supt. Gary R. Edelbrock
(805) 922-6966

Allan Hancock College
800 S. College Dr., Santa Maria 93454
Interim Pres. Frances Conn
(805) 922-6966

Antelope Valley Community College District
3041 W. Ave. K, Lancaster 93536
Supt. Allan W. Kurki
(805) 943-3241

Antelope Valley College
3041 W. Ave. K, Lancaster 93536
Pres. Allan W. Kurki
(805) 943-3241

Barstow Community College District
2700 Barstow Rd., Barstow 92311
Supt. John C. Menzie
(619) 252-2411

Barstow College
2700 Barstow Rd., Barstow 92311
Pres. John C. Menzie
(619) 252-2411

Butte Community College District
3536 Butte Campus Dr., Oroville 95965
Supt. Betty M. Dean
(916) 895-2511

Butte College
3536 Butte Campus Dr., Oroville 95965
Pres. Betty M. Dean
(916) 895-2511

Cabrillo Community College District
6500 Soquel Dr., Aptos 95003
Supt. John D. Hurd
(408) 479-6100

Cabrillo College
6500 Soquel Dr., Aptos 95003
Pres. John D. Hurd
(408) 479-6100

Cerritos Community College District
11110 E. Alondra Blvd., Norwalk 90650
Supt. Ernest A. Martinez
(213) 860-2451

Cerritos College
11110 E. Alondra Blvd., Norwalk 90650
Pres. Ernest A. Martinez
(310) 860-2451

Chabot-Las Positas Community College District
5673 Gibraltar Dr., Ste. 100, Pleasanton 94588
Chanc. Terry L. DiCianna
(415) 460-5334

Chabot College
25555 Hesperian Blvd., Hayward 94545
Pres. Raul Cardoza
(510) 786-6600

Las Positas College
3033 Collier Canyon Rd., Livermore 94550
Pres. Barbara A. Adams
(415) 373-5800

Chaffey Community College District
5885 Haven Ave., Rancho Cucamonga 91701
Supt. Jerry W. Young
(714) 987-1737

California — Public Systems of Higher Education

Chaffey College
5885 Haven Ave., Rancho Cucamonga 91701
Pres. Jerry W. Young
(714) 987-1737

Citrus Community College District
1000 W. Foothill Blvd., Glendora 91740
Supt. Louis E. Zellers
(818) 963-0323

Citrus College
1000 W. Foothill Blvd., Glendora 91740
Pres. Louis E. Zellers
(818) 963-0323

Coast Community College District
1370 Adams Ave., Costa Mesa 92626
Chanc. Alfred P. Fernandez
(714) 432-5813

Coastline Community College
11460 Warner Ave., Fountain Valley 92708
Pres. William M. Vega
(714) 546-7600

Golden West College
15744 Golden West St., Huntington Beach 92647
Pres. Judith Valles
(714) 892-7711

Orange Coast College
2701 Fairview Rd., Box 5005, Costa Mesa 92628
Pres. David A. Grant
(714) 432-0202

Compton Community College District
1111 E. Artesia Blvd., Compton 90221
Supt. Warren A. Washington
(213) 637-2660

Compton Community College
1111 E. Artesia Blvd., Compton 90221
Pres. Warren A. Washington
(310) 637-2660

Contra Costa Community College District
500 Court St., Martinez 94553
Chanc. Robert D. Jensen
(510) 229-1000

Contra Costa College
2600 Mission Bell Dr., San Pablo 94806
Pres. D. Candy Rose
(510) 235-7800

Diablo Valley College
321 Golf Club Rd., Pleasant Hill 94523
Pres. Phyllis L. Peterson
(510) 685-1230

Los Medanos College
2700 E. Leland Rd., Pittsburg 94565
Pres. Stanley Chin
(510) 798-3500

Desert Community College District
43-500 Monterey Ave., Palm Desert 92260
Supt. David A. George
(619) 346-8041

College of the Desert
43-500 Monterey Ave., Palm Desert 92260
Pres. David A. George
(619) 346-8041

El Camino Community College District
16007 Crenshaw Blvd., Torrance 90506
Supt. Sam Schauerman
(213) 532-3670

El Camino College
16007 S. Crenshaw Blvd., Torrance 90506
Pres. Sam Schauerman
(310) 715-3111

Feather River Community College District
570 Golden Eagle Ave., Quincy 95971
Supt. Donald J. Donato
(916) 283-0202

Public Systems of Higher Education — California

Feather River College
570 Golden Eagle Ave., Quincy
95971
Pres. Donald J. Donato
(916) 283-0202

Foothill-DeAnza Community College District
12345 El Monte Rd., Los Altos Hills
94022
Chanc. Thomas W. Fryer, Jr.
(415) 949-6100

DeAnza College
21250 Stevens Creek Blvd.,
Cupertino 95014
Pres. A. Robert DeHart
(408) 996-4760

Foothill College
12345 El Monte Rd., Los Altos
Hills 94022
Pres. Thomas H. Clements
(415) 960-4600

Fremont-Newark Community College District
43600 Mission Blvd., P.O. Box 3909,
Fremont 94539
Supt. Peter Blomerley
(510) 659-6000

Ohlone College
43600 Mission Blvd., Fremont
94539
Pres. Peter Blomerley
(510) 659-6000

Gavilan Community College District
5055 Santa Teresa Blvd., Gilroy
95020
Supt. John J. Holleman
(408) 847-1400

Gavilan College
5055 Santa Teresa Blvd., Gilroy
95020
Pres. John J. Holleman
(408) 848-4712

Glendale Community College District
1500 N. Verdugo Rd., Glendale
91208
Supt. John A. Davitt
(818) 240-1000

Glendale Community College
1500 N. Verdugo Rd., Glendale
91208
Pres. John A. Davitt
(818) 240-1000

Grossmont-Cuyamaca Community College District
8800 Grossmont College Dr.,
El Cajon 92020
Chanc. Donald E. Walker
(619) 697-9090

Cuyamaca College
2950 Jamacha Rd., El Cajon
92019
Pres. Samuel M. Ciccati
(619) 670-1980

Grossmont College
8800 Grossmont College Dr.,
El Cajon 92020
Pres. Richard Sanchez
(619) 465-1700

Hartnell Community College District
156 Homestead Ave., Salinas 93901
Supt. James R. Hardt
(408) 755-6700

Hartnell College
156 Homestead Ave., Salinas
93901
Pres. James R. Hardt
(408) 755-6700

Imperial Community College District
P.O. Box 158, Imperial 92251-0158
Supt. John A. DePaoli, Jr.
(619) 352-8320

Imperial Valley College
380 E. Ira Aten Rd., P.O. Box
158, Imperial 92251
Pres. John A. DePaoli, Jr.
(619) 352-8320

California   **Public Systems of Higher Education**

Kern Community College District
2100 Chester Ave., Bakersfield 93301
Chanc. James C. Young
(805) 395-4104

Bakersfield College
1801 Panorama Dr., Bakersfield 93305
Pres. Richard L. Wright
(805) 395-4011

Cerro Coso Community College
3000 College Heights Blvd., Ridgecrest 93555
Pres. Raymond A. McCue
(619) 375-5001

Porterville College
900 S. Main St., Porterville 93257
Pres. Paul D. Alcantra
(209) 781-3130

Lake Tahoe Community College District
One College Dr., P.O. Box 14445, South Lake Tahoe 95702
Supt. James W. Duke
(916) 541-4660

Lake Tahoe Community College
One College Dr., P.O. Box 14445, South Lake Tahoe 95702
Pres. Guy F. Lease
(916) 541-4660

Lassen Community College District
Hwy. 139, P.O. Box 3000, Susanville 96130
Supt. Larry J. Blake
(916) 257-6181

Lassen College
Hwy. 139, P.O. Box 3000, Susanville 96130
Supt./Pres. Larry J. Blake
(916) 257-6181

Long Beach Community College District
4901 E. Carson St., Long Beach 90808
Supt. Beverly L. O'Neill
(213) 420-4111

Long Beach City College
4901 E. Carson St., Long Beach 90808
Pres. Beverly L. O'Neill
(310) 420-4111

Los Angeles Community College District
617 W. Seventh St., Los Angeles 90017
Chanc. Donald G. Phelps
(213) 891-2201

East Los Angeles College
1301 Brooklyn Ave., Monterey Park 91754
Pres. Omero Suarez
(213) 265-8650

Los Angeles City College
855 N. Vermont Ave., Los Angeles 90029
Acting Pres. Jose Robledo
(213) 669-4000

Los Angeles Harbor College
1111 Figueroa Pl., Wilmington 90744
Pres. James Heinselman
(310) 518-1000

Los Angeles Mission College
13356 Eldridge Ave., Sylmar 91342
Pres. Jack Fujimoto
(818) 364-7600

Los Angeles Pierce College
6201 Winnetka Ave., Woodland Hills 91371
Pres. Daniel G. Means
(818) 347-0551

Los Angeles Southwest College
1600 W. Imperial Hwy., Los Angeles 90047
Interim Pres. Patricia Wainwright
(310) 777-2225

Los Angeles Trade-Technical College
400 W. Washington Blvd.,
Los Angeles 90015
Pres. Thomas L. Stevens, Jr.
(213) 744-9500

Los Angeles Valley College
5800 Fulton Ave., Van Nuys
91401
Pres. Mary E. Lee
(818) 781-1200

West Los Angeles College
4800 Freshman Dr., Culver City
90230
Pres. Evelyn C. Wong
(310) 836-7110

Los Rios Community College District
1919 Spanos Ct., Sacramento
95825
Chanc. Marjorie K. Blaha
(916) 920-7821

American River College
4700 College Oak Dr.,
Sacramento 95841
Pres. Queen F. Randall
(916) 484-8011

Cosumnes River College
8401 Center Pkwy., Sacramento
95823
Pres. Marc E. Hall
(916) 686-7300

Sacramento City College
3835 Freeport Blvd.,
Sacramento 95822
Pres. Robert M. Harris
(916) 449-7111

Marin Community College District
Kentfield 94904
Supt. Myrna R. Miller
(415) 457-8811

College of Marin
College Ave., Kentfield 94904
Pres. Myrna R. Miller
(415) 457-8811

Mendocino Lake Community College District
1000 Hensley Creek Rd., Ukiah
95482
Supt. Carl J. Ehmann
(707) 468-3002

Mendocino College
P.O. Box 3000, Ukiah 95482
Pres. Carl J. Ehmann
(707) 468-3100

Merced Community College District
3600 M St., Merced 95348-2898
Supt. E. Jan Moser
(209) 384-6000

Merced College
3600 M St., Merced 95348
Pres. E. Jan Moser
(209) 384-6000

MiraCosta Community College District
One Barnard Dr., Oceanside 92056
Supt. H. Deon Holt
(619) 757-2121

MiraCosta College
One Barnard Dr., Oceanside
92056
Pres. H. Deon Holt
(619) 757-2121

Monterey Peninsula Community College District
980 Freemont Blvd., Monterey
93940
Supt. David W. Hopkins, Jr.
(408) 646-4010

Monterey Peninsula College
980 Fremont St., Monterey
93940
Pres. David W. Hopkins, Jr.
(408) 646-4010

Mount San Antonio Community College District
1100 N. Grand Ave., Walnut 91789
Supt. William H. Feddersen
(714) 594-5611

California

Mount San Antonio College
1100 N. Grand Ave., Walnut
91789
Pres. William H. Feddersen
(714) 594-5611

Mount San Jacinto Community College District
1499 N. State St., San Jacinto 92383
Supt. Richard H. Lowe
(714) 654-8011

Mount San Jacinto College
1499 N. State St., San Jacinto
92383
Pres. Richard H. Lowe
(714) 654-8011

Napa Valley Community College District
2277 Napa-Vallejo Hwy., Napa 94558
Supt. William H. Feddersen
(707) 253-3095

Napa Valley College
2277 Napa-Vallejo Hwy., Napa
94558
Pres. William H. Feddersen
(707) 253-3095

North Orange County Community College District
1000 N. Lemon St., Fullerton 92634
Chanc. Tom K. Harris, Jr.
(714) 871-4030

Cypress College
9200 Valley View St., Cypress
90630
Pres. Kirk Avery
(714) 826-2220

Fullerton College
321 E. Chapman Ave., Fullerton
92634
Pres. Philip W. Borst
(714) 992-7000

Palo Verde Community College District
811 W. Chanslor Way, Blythe 92225
Supt. Wilford J. Beumel
(619) 922-6168

Palo Verde College
811 W. Chanslor Way, Blythe
92225
Pres. Wilford J. Beumel
(619) 922-6168

Palomar Community College District
1140 W. Mission Rd., San Marcos
92069
Supt. George R. Boggs
(619) 744-1150

Palomar College
1140 W. Mission Rd., San
Marcos 92069
Pres. George R. Boggs
(619) 744-1150

Pasadena Area Community College District
1570 E. Colorado Blvd., Pasadena
91106
Supt. Jack A. Scott
(818) 585-7547

Pasadena City College
1570 E. Colorado Blvd.,
Pasadena 91106
Pres. Jack A. Scott
(818) 585-7123

Peralta Community College District
333 E. Eighth St., Oakland 94606
Chanc./Supt. Robert J. Scannell
(510) 466-7200

College of Alameda
555 Atlantic Ave., Alameda
94501
Pres. Marie Smith
(510) 522-7221

Laney College
900 Fallon St., Oakland 94607
Pres. Odell Johnson
(510) 834-5740

Merritt College
12500 Campus Dr., Oakland
94619
Pres. Donald R. Hongisto
(510) 531-4911

Vista College
2020 Milvia St., Berkeley 94704
Pres. Barbara A. Beno
(510) 841-8431

Rancho Santiago Community College District
17th and Bristol Sts., Santa Ana 92706
Supt. Lincoln G. Hall
(714) 667-3000

Rancho Santiago Community College
17th and Bristol Sts., Santa Ana 92706
Chanc. Vivian B. Blevins
(714) 667-3000

Redwoods Community College District
7351 Tompkins Hill Rd., Eureka 95501
Supt. Cedric A. Sampson
(707) 443-8411

College of the Redwoods
7351 Tompkins Hill Rd., Eureka 95501
Pres. Cedric A. Sampson
(707) 445-6700

Rio Hondo Community College District
3600 Workman Mill Rd., Whittier 90608
Supt. Alex A. Sanchez
(310) 692-0921

Rio Hondo College
3600 Workman Mill Rd., Whittier 90608
Pres. Alex A. Sanchez
(310) 692-0921

Riverside Community College District
4800 Magnolia Ave., Riverside 92506
Supt. Charles A. Kane
(714) 684-3240

Riverside Community College
4800 Magnolia Ave., Riverside 92506
Pres. Charles A. Kane
(714) 684-3240

Saddleback Community College District
28000 Marguerite Pkwy., Mission Viejo 92692
Chanc. Richard Sneed
(714) 831-4840

Irvine Valley College
5500 Irvine Center Dr., Irvine 92720
Pres. Anna L. McFarlin
(714) 559-9300

Saddleback College
28000 Marguerite Pkwy., Mission Viejo 92692
Pres. Constance M. Carroll
(714) 582-4500

San Bernardino Community College District
441 W. 8th St., San Bernardino 92401
Chanc. Stuart M. Bundy
(714) 884-2533

Crafton Hills College
11711 Sand Canyon Rd., Yucaipa 92399
Acting Pres. Luis S. Gomez
(714) 794-2161

San Bernardino Valley College
701 S. Mt. Vernon Ave., San Bernardino 92410
Pres. Donald L. Singer
(714) 888-6511

San Diego Community College District
3375 Camino del Rio S., San Diego 92108
Chanc. Augustine P. Gallego
(619) 584-6957

San Diego City College
1313 12th Ave., San Diego 92101
Pres. Jeanne L. Atherton
(619) 230-2400

San Diego Mesa College
7250 Mesa College Dr., San Diego 92111
Pres. Allen Brooks
(619) 560-2600

San Diego Miramar College
10440 Black Mountain Rd., San Diego 92126
Pres. Jerome Hunter, Ed.D.
(619) 693-6800

San Francisco Community College District
50 Phelan Ave., San Francisco 94112
Supt. Evan S. Dobelle
(415) 239-3000

City College of San Francisco
50 Phelan Ave., San Francisco 94112
Chanc. Evan S. Dobelle
(415) 239-3000

San Joaquin Delta Community College District
5151 Pacific Ave., Stockton 95207
Supt. L.H. Horton, Jr.
(209) 474-5151

San Joaquin Delta College
5151 Pacific Ave., Stockton 95207
Pres. L.H. Horton, Jr.
(209) 474-5625

San Jose-Evergreen Community College District
4750 San Felipe Rd., San Jose 95135
Chanc. Ronald A. Kong
(408) 270-6402

Evergreen Valley College
3095 Yerba Buena Rd., San Jose 95135
Pres. Richard G. Carpenter
(408) 274-7900

San Jose City College
2100 Moorpark Ave., San Jose 95128
Pres. Del Anderson
(408) 298-2181

San Luis Obispo Community College District
P.O. Box 8106, San Luis Obispo 93403-8106
Supt. Grace N. Mitchell
(805) 544-2943

Cuesta College
P.O. Box 8106, San Luis Obispo 93403
Pres. Grace N. Mitchell
(805) 546-3101

San Mateo County Community College District
3401 CSM Dr., San Mateo 94402
Chanc./Supt. Lois A. Callahan
(415) 574-6550

Canada College
4200 Farm Hill Blvd., Redwood City 94061
Pres. Miles D. Ketcher
(415) 364-1212

College of San Mateo
1700 W. Hillsdale Blvd., San Mateo 94402
Interim Pres. Richard A. Jones
(415) 574-6161

Skyline College
3300 College Dr., San Bruno 94066
Pres. Linda Graef Salter
(415) 355-7000

Santa Barbara Community College District
721 Cliff Dr., Santa Barbara 93109
Supt. Peter R. MacDougall
(805) 965-0581

Santa Barbara City College
721 Cliff Dr., Santa Barbara 93109
Pres. Peter R. MacDougall
(805) 965-0581

Santa Clarita Community College District
26455 N. Rockwell Canyon Rd., Valencia 91355
Supt. Diane G. Van Hook
(805) 259-7800

College of the Canyons
26455 N. Rockwell Canyon Rd., Santa Clarita 91355
Pres. Dianne G. Van Hook
(805) 259-7800

Santa Monica Community College District
1900 Pico Blvd., Santa Monica 90405
Supt. Richard L. Moore
(310) 450-5150

Santa Monica College
1900 Pico Blvd., Santa Monica 90405
Pres. Richard L. Moore
(310) 450-5150

Sequoias Community College District
915 S. Monney Blvd., Visalia 93277
Supt. Robert A. Lombardi
(209) 733-2050

College of the Sequoias
915 S. Mooney Blvd., Visalia 93277
Pres. Robert A. Lombardi
(209) 730-3700

Shasta-Tehama Trinity Joint Community College District
1065 N. Old Oregon Trail, Redding 96049
Supt. Kenneth B. Cerreta
(916) 225-4600

Shasta College
P.O. Box 496006, Redding 96049
Pres. Kenneth B. Cerreta
(916) 225-4600

Sierra Joint Community College District
5000 Rocklin Rd., Rocklin 95677
Supt. Gerald C. Angove
(916) 624-3333

Sierra College
5000 Rocklin Rd., Rocklin 95677
Pres. Gerald C. Angove
(916) 624-3333

Siskiyous Joint Community College District
800 College Ave., Weed 96094
Supt. Eugene Schumacher
(916) 938-4461

College of the Siskiyous
800 College Ave., Weed 96094
Pres. Eugene Schumacher
(916) 938-4461

Solano County Community College District
4000 Suisun Valley Rd., Suisun 94585
Interim Supt. Otto Reimmich
(707) 864-7112

Solano Community College
4000 Suisun Valley Rd., Suisun 94585
Pres. Virginia L. Holten
(707) 864-7000

Sonoma County Junior College District
1501 Mendocino Ave., Santa Rosa 95401
Supt. Roy G. Mikalson
(707) 527-4431

Santa Rosa Junior College
1501 Mendocino Ave., Santa Rosa 95401
Pres. Robert F. Agrella
(707) 527-4443

Southwestern Community College District
900 Otay Lakes Rd., Chula Vista 92010
Supt. Joseph M. Conte
(619) 421-6700

Southwestern College
900 Otay Lakes Rd., Chula Vista 91910
Pres. Joseph M. Conte
(619) 421-6700

California

State Center Community College District
1525 E. Weldon Ave., Fresno 93704
Chanc. William F. Stewart
(209) 226-0720

Fresno City College
1101 E. University Ave., Fresno 93741
Pres. Brice W. Harris
(209) 442-4600

Kings River Community College
995 N. Reed Ave., Reedley 93654
Pres. Richard J. Giese
(209) 638-3641

Ventura County Community College District
71 Day Rd., Ventura 93003
Chanc. Thomas G. Lakin
(805) 654-6412

Moorpark College
7075 Campus Rd., Moorpark 93021
Acting Pres. Roger Boedecker
(805) 378-1400

Oxnard College
4000 S. Rose Ave., Oxnard 93033
Pres. Elise D. Schneider
(805) 488-0911

Ventura College
4667 Telegraph Rd., Ventura 93003
Pres. Robert W. Long
(805) 642-3211

Victor Valley Community College District
18422 Bear Valley Rd., Victorville 92392
Supt. Ed Gould
(619) 245-4271

Victor Valley College
18422 Bear Valley Rd., Victorville 92392
Pres. Ed Gould
(619) 245-4271

West Hills Community College District
300 Cherry La., Coalinga 93210
Supt. Dale A. Miller
(209) 935-0801

West Hills Community College
300 Cherry La., Coalinga 93210
Pres. Stan Arterberry
(209) 935-0801

West Kern Community College District
29 Emmons Park Dr., Taft 93268
Supt. David Cothrun
(805) 763-4282

Taft College
29 Emmons Park Dr., Taft 93268
Pres. David Cothrun
(805) 763-4282

West Valley-Mission Community College District
14000 Fruitvale Ave., Saratoga 95070
Chanc. Gustavo A. Mellander
(408) 741-2011

Mission College
3000 Mission College Blvd., Santa Clara 95054
Pres. Floyd M. Hogue
(408) 988-2200

West Valley College
14000 Fruitvale Ave., Saratoga 95070
Pres. Leo Chavez
(408) 867-2200

Yosemite Community College District
P.O. Box 4065, Modesto 95352
Chanc. Tom Van Groningen
(209) 575-6508

Columbia College
P.O. Box 1849, Columbia 95310
Pres. W. Dean Cunningham
(209) 533-5100

Modesto Junior College
435 College Ave., Modesto 95350
Pres. Stanley Hodges
(209) 575-6067

Public Systems of Higher Education

California

Yuba Community College District
2088 N. Beale Rd., Marysville 95901
Supt. Patricia L. Wirth
(916) 741-6471

Yuba College
2088 N. Beale Rd., Marysville 95901
Pres. Patricia L. Wirth
(916) 741-6700

The California State University System
400 Golden Shore Dr., Long Beach 90802-4275
Chanc. Barry Munitz
(213) 590-5506

California Polytechnic State University, San Luis Obispo
San Luis Obispo 93407
Pres. Warren J. Baker
(805) 756-1111

California State Polytechnic University, Pomona
3801 W. Temple Ave., Pomona 91768
Pres. Bob H. Suzuki
(714) 869-7659

California State University, Bakersfield
9001 Stockdale Hwy., Bakersfield 93311-1099
Pres. Tomas A. Arciniega
(805) 664-2011

California State University, Chico
First and Normal Sts., Chico 95929-0110
Pres. Robin S. Wilson
(916) 898-4636

California State University, Dominguez Hills
1000 E. Victoria St., Carson 90747
Pres. Robert C. Detweiler
(213) 516-3300

California State University, Fresno
5241 N. Maple Ave., Fresno 93740
Pres. John D. Welty
(209) 278-4240

California State University, Fullerton
800 N. State College Blvd., Fullerton 92634
Pres. Milton A. Gordon
(714) 773-2011

California State University, Hayward
Hayward 94542
Pres. Norma Rees
(510) 881-3000

California State University, Long Beach
1250 Bellflower Blvd., Long Beach 90840
Pres. Curtis McCray
(213) 985-4111

California State University, Los Angeles
5151 State University Dr., Los Angeles 90032-8508
Pres. James M. Rosser
(213) 343-3000

California State University, Northridge
18111 Nordhoff St., Northridge 91330
Pres. James W. Cleary
(818) 885-1200

California State University, Sacramento
6000 J St., Sacramento 95819-2694
Pres. Donald R. Gerth
(916) 278-6011

California State University, San Bernardino
5500 State University Pkwy., San Bernardino 92407
Pres. Anthony H. Evans
(714) 880-5000

California State University, Stanislaus
801 W. Monte Vista Ave., Turlock 95380
Pres. John W. Moore
(209) 667-3122

Humboldt State University
Arcata 95521
Pres. Alistair W. McCrone
(707) 826-3011

California

San Diego State University
5300 Campanile Dr., San Diego
92182
Pres. Thomas B. Day
(619) 594-5200

San Francisco State University
1600 Holloway Ave., San Francisco
94132
Pres. Robert A. Corrigan
(415) 338-1111

San Jose State University
One Washington Sq., San Jose 95192
Interim Pres. J. Handel Evans
(408) 924-1000

Sonoma State University
Rohnert Park 94928
Pres. David W. Benson
(707) 664-2880

University of California Office of the President
300 Lakeside Dr., Oakland 94612-3550
Pres. David P. Gardner
(510) 987-0700

University of California, Berkeley
Berkeley 94720
Chanc. Chang-Lin Tien
(510) 642-6000

University of California, Davis
Davis 95616
Chanc. Theodore L. Hullar
(916) 752-1011

University of California, Hastings College of the Law
200 McAllister St., San Francisco 94102
Dean Frank T. Read
(415) 565-4600

University of California, Irvine
Irvine 92717
Chanc. Jack W. Peltason
(714) 856-6345

University of California, Los Angeles
405 Hilgard Ave., Los Angeles
90024
Chanc. Charles E. Young
(213) 825-4321

University of California, Riverside
Riverside 92502-9879
Chanc. Rosemary Schraer, SJ
(714) 787-1012

University of California, San Diego
La Jolla 92092
Chanc. Richard C. Atkinson
(619) 534-2230

University of California, San Francisco
Third and Parnassus Aves., San Francisco 94143
Chanc. Julius R. Krevans, M.D.
(415) 476-9000

University of California, Santa Barbara
Santa Barbara 93106
Chanc. Barbara S. Uehling
(805) 893-2231

University of California, Santa Cruz
Santa Cruz 95064
Interim Chanc. Karl S. Piester
(408) 459-0111

COLORADO

Colorado Commission on Higher Education
Colorado History Museum, 1300
  Broadway, 2nd Fl., Denver 80203
Exec. Dir. David A. Longanecker
(303) 866-2723

Colorado State University System
Fort Collins 80523
Chanc. Philip E. Austin
(303) 491-6216

Colorado State University
Fort Collins 80523
Pres. Albert C. Yates
(303) 491-6211

Fort Lewis College
Durango 81301
Pres. Joel M. Jones
(303) 247-7100

University of Southern Colorado
2200 Bonforte Blvd., Pueblo 81001
Pres. Robert C. Shirley
(719) 549-2306

University of Colorado System
Boulder 80309
Pres. Judith E.N. Albino
(303) 492-6201

University of Colorado Health Sciences Center
4200 E. Ninth Ave., Denver 80262
Chanc. Bernard W. Nelson
(303) 270-7682

University of Colorado at Boulder
Boulder 80309
Chanc. James N. Corbridge, Jr.
(303) 492-8908

University of Colorado at Colorado Springs
P.O. Box 7150, Colorado Springs 80933
Chanc. Dwayne C. Nuzum
(719) 593-3119

University of Colorado at Denver
1200 Larimer St., Denver 80204
Chanc. John C. Buechner
(303) 556-3279

Colorado Community College and Occupational Education System
1391 N. Speer Blvd., Ste. 600, Denver 80204-2554
Pres. Jerome F. Wartgow
(303) 620-4000

Aims Community College
5401 W. 20th St., P.O. Box 69, Greeley 80632
Pres. George R. Conger
(303) 330-8008

Arapahoe Community College
2500 W. College Dr., P.O. Box 9002, Littleton 80160-9002
Pres. James F. Weber
(303) 794-1550

Colorado Mountain College
215 9th St., Glenwood Springs 81602
Pres. Dennis Mayer
(303) 945-8691

Colorado Northwestern Community College
500 Kennedy Dr., Rangely 81648
Pres. Aubrey Holderness
(303) 675-2261

Community College of Aurora
16000 E. Centretech Pkwy., Aurora 80011
Pres. Larry D. Carter
(303) 360-4700

Community College of Denver
1111 W. Colfax Ave., Denver 80204
Pres. Byron N. McClenney
(303) 556-2411

Front Range Community College
3645 W. 112th Ave., Westminster 80030
Pres. Thomas Gonzales
(303) 466-8811

Colorado

Lamar Community College
2401 S. Main St., Lamar 81052
Pres. Marvin E. Lane
(719) 336-2248

Morgan Community College
17800 Rd. 20, Fort Morgan 80701
Pres. Richard Bond
(303) 867-3081

Northeastern Junior College
Sterling 80751
Pres. Henry M. Milander
(303) 522-6600

Otero Junior College
La Junta 81050
Pres. William L. McDivitt
(719) 384-8721

Pikes Peak Community College
5675 S. Academy Blvd., Colorado Springs 80906
Pres. Marijane A. Paulsen
(719) 540-7551

Pueblo Community College
900 W. Orman Ave., Pueblo 81004
Pres. P. Anthony Zeiss
(719) 549-3213

Red Rocks Community College
13300 W. Sixth Ave., Lakewood 80401
Pres. Dorothy Horrell
(303) 988-6160

Trinidad State Junior College
600 Prospect St., Trinidad 81082
Pres. Harold Deselms
(719) 846-5541

State Colleges in Colorado
1580 Lincoln St., Ste. 750, Denver 80203
Pres. Glenn Burnham
(303) 866-2588

Adams State College
Alamosa 81102
Pres. William Fulkerson, Jr.
(719) 589-7341

Mesa State College
P.O. Box 2647, Grand Junction 81502
Pres. Raymond N. Kieft
(303) 248-1498

Metropolitan State College of Denver
1006 11th St., P.O. Box 173362, Denver 80217-3362
Pres. Thomas B. Brewer
(303) 556-3022

Western State College of Colorado
Gunnison 81231
Pres. Kaye Howe
(303) 943-2114

CONNECTICUT

Connecticut Board of Governers for Higher Education
61 Woodland St., Hartford 06105
Commissioner Norma F. Glasgow
(203) 566-5766

Connecticut Community-Technical Colleges
61 Woodland St., Hartford 06105
Exec. Dir. Andrew C. McKirdy
(203) 566-8760

Asnuntuck Community College
Enfield 06082
Pres. Harvey S. Irlen
(203) 253-3000

Greater Hartford Community College
Hartford 06105
Pres. Conrad L. Mallett
(203) 520-7800

Greater New Haven State Technical College
88 Bassett Rd., North Haven 06473
Pres. George D. Harris
(203) 234-3300

Hartford State Technical College
401 Flatbush Ave., Hartford 06106
Pres. John E. Arnet
(203) 527-4111

Housatonic Community College
510 Barnum Ave., Bridgeport 06608
Pres. Vincent S. Darnowski
(203) 579-6400

Manchester Community College
P.O. Box 1046, P.P. Sta., Manchester 06040
Pres. Jonathan M. Daube
(203) 647-6000

Mattatuck Community College
Waterbury 06708
Pres. Richard L. Sanders
(203) 575-0328

Middlesex Community College
Middletown 06457
Pres. Leila G. Sullivan
(203) 344-3011

Mohegan Community College
Norwich 06360
Interim Pres. Diann Williams
(203) 886-1931

Northwestern Connecticut Community College
Winsted 06098
Pres. Booker T. DeVaughn
(203) 738-6300

Norwalk Community College
Norwalk 06854
Pres. William H. Schwab
(203) 853-2040

Norwalk State Technical College
181 Richards Ave., Norwalk 06850
Pres. John K. Fisher
(203) 855-6600

Quinebaug Valley Community College
724 Upper Maple St., Danielson 06239
Pres. Robert E. Miller
(203) 774-1130

South Central Community College
60 Sargent Dr., New Haven 06511
Pres. Antonio Perez
(203) 789-7071

Thames Valley State Technical College
574 New London Tpke., Norwich 06360
Pres. R. Eileen Baccus
(203) 886-0177

Tunxis Community College
Farmington 06032
Pres. Marilyn Menack
(203) 677-7701

Connecticut

Waterbury State Technical College
750 Chase Pkwy., Waterbury
06708
Pres. Charles A. Ekstrom
(203) 575-8082

Connecticut State University Central Office
P.O. Box 2008, New Britain 06050
Pres. Dallas K. Beal
(203) 827-7700

Central Connecticut State University
New Britain 06050
Pres. John W. Shumaker
(203) 827-7000

Eastern Connecticut State University
Willimantic 06226
Pres. David G. Carter
(203) 456-2231

Southern Connecticut State University
New Haven 06515
Pres. Michael J. Adanti
(203) 397-4000

Public Systems of Higher Education

Western Connecticut State University
Danbury 06810
Pres. Stephen Feldman
(203) 797-4347

University of Connecticut System
Storrs 06269
Pres. Harry J. Hartley
(203) 486-2000

The University of Connecticut
Storrs 06269
Pres. Harry J. Hartley
(203) 486-2000

The University of Connecticut Health Center
263 Farmington Ave., Farmington 06032
Interim Pres. Harry J. Hartley
(203) 679-2000

DELAWARE

Delaware Postsecondary Education Commission
Carvel St. Office Bldg., 820 N. French St., Wilmington 19801
Exec. Dir. John F. Corrozi
(302) 571-3240

Delaware State College
1200 N. Dupont Hwy., Dover 19901
Pres. William DeLauder
(302) 736-4901

Delaware Technical and Community College President's Office
P.O. Box 897, Dover 19903
Pres. John R. Kotula
(302) 739-4621

Delaware Technical and Community College Southern
P.O. Box 610, Georgetown 19947
Vice Pres./Dir. Jack F. Owens
(302) 856-5422

Delaware Technical and Community College Stanton
400 Christiana-Stanton Rd., Newark 19713
Vice Pres./Dir. Lawrence Miller
(302) 454-3917

Delaware Technical and Community College Terry
1832 N. Dupont Pkwy., Dover 19903
Vice Pres./Dir. Linda C. Jolly
(302) 736-5321

Delaware Technical and Community College Wilmington
333 Shipley St., Wilmington 19801
Vice Pres./Dir. Orlando J. George
(302) 573-5481

University of Delaware
Newark 19716
Pres. David P. Roselle
(302) 831-2000

FLORIDA

Florida State Board of Community Colleges
1314 Florida Educ. Ctr., 325 W. Gaines St.,
Tallahassee 32399
Exec. Dir. Clark Maxwell, Jr.
(904) 488-1721

Brevard Community College
1519 Clearlake Rd., Cocoa 32922
Pres. Maxwell C. King
(407) 632-1111

Broward Community College
225 E. Las Olas Blvd., Fort Lauderdale 33301
Pres. Willis N. Holcombe
(305) 761-7400

Central Florida Community College
3001 S.W. College Rd., Ocala 32678
Pres. William J. Campion
(904) 237-2111

Chipola Junior College
1200 College St., Marianna 32446
Pres. Jerry W. Kandzer
(904) 526-2761

Daytona Beach Community College
1200 Volusia Ave., P.O. Box 2811, Daytona Beach 32114
Pres. Philip R. Day, Jr.
(904) 255-8131

Edison Community College
8099 College Pkwy., P.O. Box 06210, Fort Myers 33906-6210
Pres. Kenneth P. Walker
(813) 489-9300

Florida Community College at Jacksonville
501 W. State St., Jacksonville 32202
Pres. Charles C. Spence
(904) 632-3224

Florida Keys Community College
5901 W. Junior College Rd., Key West 33040
Pres. William A. Seeker
(305) 296-9081

Gulf Coast Community College
5230 W. Hwy. 98, Panama City 32401
Pres. Robert L. McSpadden
(904) 872-3800

Hillsborough Community College
P.O. Box 31127, Tampa 33631-3127
Pres. Andreas A. Paloumpis
(813) 253-7000

Indian River Community College
3209 Virginia Ave., Fort Pierce 34981-5599
Pres. Edwin R. Massey
(407) 468-4700

Lake City Community College
Rte. 3, Box 7, Lake City 32055
Pres. Muriel K. Heimer
(904) 752-1822

Lake-Sumter Community College
9501 U.S. Hwy. 441, Leesburg 34788
Pres. Carl C. Andersen
(904) 787-3747

Manatee Community College
5840 26th St., W., Bradenton 34206
Pres. Stephen J. Korcheck
(813) 755-1511

Miami-Dade Community College
300 N.E. Second Ave., Miami 33132
Pres. Robert H. McCabe
(305) 237-3100

North Florida Junior College
1000 Turner Davis Dr., Madison 32340
Pres. William H. McCoy
(904) 973-2288

Okaloosa-Walton Community College
100 College Blvd., Niceville 32578
Pres. James R. Richburg
(904) 729-5360

Public Systems of Higher Education — Florida

Palm Beach Community College
4200 Congress Ave., Lake Worth 33461-4796
Pres. Edward M. Eissey
(407) 439-8000

Pasco-Hernando Community College
2401 State Hwy. 41, N., Dade City 33525-7599
Pres. Milton O. Jones
(904) 567-6701

Pensacola Junior College
1000 College Blvd., Pensacola 32504
Pres. Horace E. Hartsell
(904) 484-1000

Polk Community College
999 Ave. H, N.E., Winter Haven 33881-4299
Pres. Maryly V. Peck
(813) 297-1000

St. Johns River Community College
5001 St. Johns Ave., Palatka 32177
Pres. Robert L. McLendon, Jr.
(904) 328-1571

St. Petersburg Junior College
P.O. Box 13489, St. Petersburg 33733
Pres. Carl M. Kuttler, Jr.
(813) 341-3600

Santa Fe Community College
3000 N.W. 83rd St., Gainesville 32606
Pres. Lawrence W. Tyree
(904) 395-5000

Seminole Community College
100 Weldon Blvd., Sanford 32773-6199
Pres. Earl S. Weldon
(407) 323-1450

South Florida Community College
600 W. College Dr., Avon Park 33825
Pres. Catherine P. Cornelius
(813) 453-6661

Tallahassee Community College
444 Appleyard Dr., Tallahassee 32304
Pres. James H. Hinson, Jr.
(904) 488-9200

Valencia Community College
P.O. Box 3028, Orlando 32802
Pres. Paul C. Gianini, Jr.
(407) 299-5000

State University System of Florida
325 W. Gaines St., Ste. 1514, Tallahassee 32399-1950
Chanc. Charles B. Reed
(904) 488-4234

Florida Agricultural and Mechanical University
Tallahassee 32307
Pres. Frederick S. Humphries
(904) 599-3000

Florida Atlantic University
500 N.W. 20th St., Boca Raton 33431
Pres. Anthony J. Catanese
(407) 367-3000

Florida International University
University Park, Miami 33199
Pres. Modesto A. Maidique
(305) 348-2000

Florida State University
Tallahassee 32306-1037
Pres. Dale W. Lick
(904) 644-2525

University of Central Florida
4000 Central Florida Blvd., Orlando 32816
Interim Pres. Robert A. Bryan
(407) 823-2000

University of Florida
Gainesville 32611
Pres. John V. Lombardi
(904) 392-3261

University of North Florida
4567 St. Johns Bluff Rd., S., Jacksonville 32216
Pres. Adam W. Herbert, Jr.
(904) 646-2666

Florida

University of South Florida
4202 E. Fowler Ave., Tampa 33620-6100
Pres. Francis T. Borkowski
(813) 974-2011

The University of West Florida
11000 University Pkwy., Pensacola 32514-5750
Pres. Morris L. Marx
(904) 474-2000

GEORGIA

Board of Regents, University System of Georgia
244 Washington St., S.W., Atlanta 30334
Chanc. H. Dean Propst
(404) 656-2202

Abraham Baldwin Agricultural College
P.O. Box 1, ABAC Sta., Tifton 31794-2693
Pres. Harold J. Loyd
(912) 386-3236

Albany State College
504 College Dr., Albany 31705-2794
Pres. Billy C. Black
(912) 430-4600

Armstrong State College
11935 Abercorn Ext., Savannah 31419-1997
Pres. Robert A. Burnett
(912) 927-5211

Atlanta Metropolitan College
1630 Stewart Ave., S.W., Atlanta 30310
Pres. Edwin A. Thompson
(404) 756-4441

Augusta College
2500 Walton Way, Augusta 30910
Pres. Richard S. Wallace
(404) 737-1401

Bainbridge College
Highway 84 E., Bainbridge 31717
Pres. Edward D. Mobley
(912) 248-2500

Brunswick College
Altama at Fourth St., Brunswick 31523
Pres. Dorothy L. Lord
(912) 264-7235

Clayton State College
5900 Lee St., Morrow 30260
Pres. Harry S. Downs
(404) 961-3400

Columbus College
Algonquin Dr., Columbus 31993-2399
Pres. Frank D. Brown
(404) 568-2001

Dalton College
213 N. College Dr., Dalton 30720
Pres. Derrell C. Roberts
(404) 272-4436

Darton College
2400 Gillionville Rd., Albany 31707-3098
Pres. Peter J. Sireno
(912) 888-8888

East Georgia College
237 Thigpen Dr., Swainsboro 30401
Pres. Willie D. Gunn
(919) 237-7831

Floyd College
P.O. Box 1864, Rome 30162-1864
Acting Pres. Richard W. Trimble
(404) 295-6328

Fort Valley State College
1005 State College Dr., Fort Valley 31030-3298
Pres. Oscar L. Prater
(912) 825-6315

Gainesville College
Mundy Mill Rd., P.O. Box 1358, Gainesville 30503
Pres. J. Foster Watkins
(404) 535-6239

Georgia College
231 W. Hancock St., Milledgeville 31061
Pres. Edwin G. Speir, Jr.
(912) 453-5350

Georgia Institute of Technology
225 North Ave., N.W., Atlanta 30332-0325
Pres. John P. Crecine
(404) 894-2000

Georgia

Georgia Southern University
Landrum Box 8033, Statesboro
30460-8033
Pres. Nicholas Henry
(912) 681-5611

Georgia Southwestern College
Americus 31709
Pres. William H. Capitan
(912) 928-1278

Georgia State University
Univ. Plaza, Atlanta 30303-3083
Acting Pres. Sherman R. Day
(404) 651-2000

Gordon College
103 College Dr., Barnesville 30204
Pres. Jerry M. Williamson
(404) 358-5016

Kennesaw State College
P.O. Box 444, Marietta 30061
Pres. Betty L. Siegel
(404) 423-6000

Macon College
College Station Dr., Macon 31298
Pres. S. Aaron Hyatt
(912) 471-2700

Medical College of Georgia
1120 15th St., Augusta 30912
Pres. Francis J. Tedesco
(407) 721-0211

Middle Georgia College
Sarah St., Cochran 31014
Pres. Joe B. Welch
(912) 934-6221

North Georgia College
College Ave., Dahlonega 30597
Pres. John H. Owen
(404) 864-1600

Savannah State College
State Coll. Branch, Savannah 31404
Acting Pres. Annette K. Brock
(912) 356-2186

South Georgia College
Douglas 31533-5098
Pres. Edward D. Jackson, Jr.
(912) 383-4220

Southern College of Technology
S. Marietta Pkwy., Marietta 30060-2896
Pres. Stephen R. Cheshier
(404) 528-7230

The University of Georgia
Athens 30602
Pres. Charles B. Knapp
(404) 542-3000

Valdosta State College
Patterson St., Valdosta 31698
Pres. Hugh C. Bailey
(912) 333-5800

Waycross College
2001 Francis St., Waycross 31501
Pres. James M. Dye
(912) 285-6130

West Georgia College
Carrollton 30118-0001
Pres. Maurice K. Townsend
(404) 836-6500

HAWAII

University of Hawaii System
2444 Dole St., Honolulu 96822
Pres. Albert J. Simone
(808) 948-8207

University of Hawaii Community Colleges
2327 Dole St., Honolulu 96822
Chanc. Joyce S. Tsunoda
(808) 948-7313

Hawaii Community College
523 W. Lanikaula St., Hilo 96720-4091
Provost Sandra Sakaguchi
(808) 933-3311

Honolulu Community College
874 Dillingham Blvd., Honolulu 96817
Provost Peter R. Kessinger
(808) 845-9225

Kapiolani Community College
4303 Diamond Head Rd., Honolulu 96816
Provost John E. Morton
(808) 734-9111

Kauai Community College
3-1901 Kaumualii Hwy., Lihue, Kauai 96766
Provost David Iha
(808) 245-8311

Leeward Community College
96-045 Ala Ike, Pearl City 96782
Provost Barbara Polk
(808) 455-0011

Maui Community College
310 Kaahumanu Ave., Kahului 96732
Provost Clyde Sakamoto
(808) 244-9181

Windward Community College
45-720 Keaahala Rd., Kaneohe, Oahu 96744
Provost Peter T. Dyer
(808) 235-0077

University of Hawaii at Hilo
Hilo 96720-4091
Chanc. Edward J. Kormondy
(808) 933-3311

University of Hawaii at Manoa
2444 Dole St., Honolulu 96822
Chanc. Albert J. Simone
(808) 956-8111

University of Hawaii at West Oahu
96-043 Ala Ike, Pearl City 96782
Chanc. Edward J. Kormondy
(808) 456-5921

IDAHO

State Board of Education and Board of Regents of the University of Idaho
L.B. Jordan Bldg., Room 307, 650 W. State St., Boise 83720
Exec. Dir. Rayburn Barton
(208) 334-2270

Boise State University
Boise 83725
Interim Pres. Larry Selland
(208) 385-1491

College of Southern Idaho
315 Falls Ave., P.O. Box 1238, Twin Falls 83303-1238
Pres. Gerald R. Meyerhoeffer
(208) 733-9554

Idaho State University
Pocatello 83209-0009
Pres. Richard L. Bowen
(208) 236-3340

Lewis-Clark State College
Lewiston 83501
Pres. Lee A. Vickers
(208) 799-2216

North Idaho College
Coeur d'Alene 83814
Pres. C. Robert Bennett
(208) 769-3300

University of Idaho
Moscow 83843
Pres. Elisabeth A. Zinser
(208) 885-6365

ILLINOIS

Illinois Board of Governors of State Colleges and Universities
700 E. Adams St., Ste. 200, Springfield 62701-1601
Chanc. Thomas D. Layzell
(217) 782-6392

Chicago State University
9501 S. Martin Luther King Dr., Chicago 60628
Pres. Dolores E. Cross
(312) 995-2000

Eastern Illinois University
Charleston 61920
Pres. Stanley G. Rives
(217) 581-2011

Governors State University
University Park 60466
Pres. Leo Goodman-Malamuth, II
(708) 534-5000

Northeastern Illinois University
5500 N. St. Louis Ave., Chicago 60625
Pres. Gordon H. Lamb
(312) 583-4050

Western Illinois University
900 W. Adams St., Macomb 61455
Pres. Ralph H. Wagoner
(309) 295-1414

Illinois Community College Board
509 S. Sixth St., Rm. 400, Springfield 62701-1874
Exec. Dir. Cary A. Israel
(217) 785-0123

Belleville Area College
2500 Carlyle Rd., Belleville 62221
Pres. Joseph J. Cipfl
(618) 235-2700

Black Hawk College—East
Rtes. 34 and 78, P.O. Box 489, Kewanee 61443-0489
Pres. Charles E. Warthen
(309) 852-5671

Black Hawk College—Quad Citites
6600 34th Ave., Moline 61265-5899
Pres. Herbert C. Lyon
(309) 796-1311

Carl Sandburg College
2232 S. Lake Storey Rd., Galesburg 61401
Interim Pres. Donald Christ
(309) 344-2518

City Colleges of Chicago
226 W. Jackson Blvd., Chicago 60606
Chanc. Nelvia M. Brady
(312) 641-2595

Chicago City-Wide College
226 W. Jackson Blvd., Chicago 60606
Pres. Martha S. Bazik
(312) 641-2595

Harold Washington College
30 E. Lake St., Chicago 60601
Pres. Bernice J. Miller
(312) 781-9430

Harry S Truman College
1145 W. Wilson Ave., Chicago 60640
Pres. Wallace B. Appelson
(312) 989-6125

Kennedy-King College
6800 S. Wentworth Ave., Chicago 60621
Pres. Harold Pates
(312) 962-3200

Malcolm X College
1900 W. Van Buren St., Chicago 60612
Pres. Milton F. Brown
(312) 942-3000

Olive-Harvey College
10001 S. Woodlawn Ave., Chicago 60628
Pres. Homer D. Franklin
(312) 568-3700

Illinois

Public Systems of Higher Education

Richard J. Daley College
7500 S. Pulaski Rd., Chicago 60652
Pres. William P. Conway
(312) 735-3000

Wilbur Wright College
3400 N. Austin Ave., Chicago 60634
Pres. Raymond F. Le Fevour
(312) 794-3182

College of Du Page
22nd St. and Lambert Rd., Glen Ellyn 60137
Pres. Harold D. McAninch
(708) 858-2800

College of Lake County
19351 W. Washington St., Grayslake 60030
Pres. Daniel J. LaVista
(708) 223-6601

Danville Area Community College
2000 E. Main St., Danville 61832
Pres. Harry J. Braun
(217) 443-1811

Elgin Community College
1700 Spartan Dr., Elgin 60123
Pres. Paul R. Heath
(708) 697-1000

Highland Community College
2998 W. Pearl City Rd., Freeport 61032
Pres. Ruth M. Smith
(815) 235-6121

Illinois Central College
One College Dr., East Peoria 61635
Pres. Thomas K. Thomas
(309) 694-5431

Illinois Eastern Community College System
233 E. Chestnut St., Olney 62450-2298
Chanc. Harry V. Smith, Jr.
(618) 393-2982

Frontier Community College
Frontier Dr., Rural Rte. 1, Fairfield 62837-9701
Pres. Richard L. Mason
(618) 842-3711

Lincoln Trail College
Rte. 3, Box 82A, Robinson 62454-9524
Pres. Donald E. Donnay
(618) 544-8657

Olney Central College
305 N. West St., Olney 62450-1099
Pres. Judith Hansen
(618) 395-4351

Wabash Valley College
2200 College Dr., Mount Carmel 62863-2699
Pres. Harry K. Benson
(618) 262-8641

Illinois Valley Community College
2578 E. 350th Rd., Oglesby 61348
Pres. Alfred E. Wisgoski
(815) 224-2720

John A. Logan College
Rte. 2, Carterville 62918
Pres. J. Ray Hancock
(618) 985-3741

John Wood Community College
150 S. 48th St., Quincy 62301
Pres. Robert C. Keys
(217) 224-6500

Joliet Junior College
1216 Houbolt Ave., Joliet 60436
Pres. Raymond A. Pietak
(815) 729-9020

Kankakee Community College
P.O. Box 888, Kankakee 60901
Pres. Lawrence D. Huffman
(815) 933-0211

Kaskaskia College
Shattuc Rd., Centralia 62801
Pres. Raymond D. Woods
(618) 532-1981

Public Systems of Higher Education — Illinois

Kishwaukee College
21193 Malta Rd., Malta 60150
Pres. Norman J. Jenkins
(815) 825-2086

Lake Land College
5001 Lake Land Blvd., Mattoon 61938
Pres. Robert K. Luther
(217) 235-3131

Lewis and Clark Community College
5800 Godfrey Rd., Godfrey 62035
Pres. J. Neil Admire
(618) 466-3411

Lincoln Land Community College
Shepherd Rd., Springfield 62794
Pres. William D. Law, Jr.
(217) 786-2268

McHenry County College
Rte. 14 and Lucas Rd., Crystal Lake 60012
Pres. Robert C. Bartlett
(815) 455-3700

Moraine Valley Community College
10900 S. 88th Ave., Palos Hills 60465
Pres. Vernon O. Crawley
(708) 974-4300

Morton College
3801 S. Central Ave., Cicero 60650
Pres. Charles P. Ferro
(708) 656-8000

Oakton Community College
1600 E. Golf Rd., Des Plaines 60016
Pres. Thomas TenHoeve
(708) 635-1600

Parkland College
2400 W. Bradley Ave., Champaign 61821
Pres. Zelema M. Harris
(217) 351-2200

Prairie State College
202 S. Halsted St., Chicago Heights 60411
Pres. E. Timothy Lightfield
(708) 756-3110

Rend Lake College
Rural Rte. 1, Ina 62846
Pres. Mark Kern
(618) 437-5321

Richland Community College
One College Park, Decatur 62521
Pres. Charles R. Novak
(217) 875-7200

Rock Valley College
3301 N. Mulford Rd., Rockford 61111
Pres. Karl J. Jacobs
(815) 654-4260

Sauk Valley Community College
173 Illinois Rte. 2, Dixon 61021
Pres. Richard L. Behrendt
(815) 288-5511

Shawnee Community College
Shawnee College Rd., Ullin 62992
Pres. Jack D. Hill
(618) 634-2242

South Suburban College of Cook County
15800 S. State St., South Holland 60473
Pres. Richard W. Fonte
(708) 596-2000

Southeastern Illinois College
Rural Rte. 4, Box 510, Harrisburg 62946
Pres. Harry W. Abell
(618) 252-4411

Spoon River College
Rural Rte. 1, Canton 61520
Pres. Felix T. Haynes, Jr.
(309) 647-4645

State Community College of East St. Louis
601 James R. Thompson Blvd., East St. Louis 62201
Pres. Cunthia O. Pace
(618) 583-2500

Triton College
2000 Fifth Ave., River Grove 60171
Pres. Michael J. Bakalis
(708) 456-0300

Illinois

Waubonsee Community College
Rte. 47 at Harter Rd., Sugar Grove 60554
Pres. John J. Swalec
(708) 466-4811

William Rainey Harper College
1200 W. Algonquin Rd., Palatine 60067-7398
Pres. Paul N. Thompson
(708) 397-3000

Regency Universities System
616 Myers Bldg., Springfield 62701
Chanc. Roderick T. Groves
(217) 782-3770

Illinois State University
Normal 61761
Pres. Thomas Wallace
(309) 438-5677

Northern Illinois University
De Kalb 60115
Pres. John E. LaTourette
(815) 753-1271

Sangamon State University
Springfield 62794
Pres. Naomi D. Lynn
(217) 786-6634

Southern Illinois University System
Colyer Hall, Carbondale 62901-6801
Interim Chanc. James M. Brown
(618) 536-3331

Southern Illinois University at Carbondale
Carbondale 62901
Pres. John C. Guyon
(618) 453-2341

Southern Illinois University at Edwardsville
Edwardsville 62026
Pres. Earl E. Lazerson
(618) 692-2475

University of Illinois System
506 S. Wright St., Urbana 61801
Pres. Stanley O. Ikenberry
(217) 333-1000

University of Illinois at Chicago
P.O. Box 4348, Chicago 60680
Chanc. James J. Stuckel
(312) 996-3000

University of Illinois at Urbana—Champaign
601 E. John St., Champaign 61820
Chanc. Morton W. Weir
(217) 333-1000

INDIANA

Indiana Commission for Higher Education
101 W. Ohio St., Ste. 550, Indianapolis 46204
Commissioner Clyde R. Ingle
(317) 232-1900

Ball State University
2000 University Ave., Muncie 47306
Pres. John E. Worthen
(317) 285-5555

Indiana State University
Terre Haute 47809
Pres. Richard G. Landini
(812) 237-6311

Indiana University System
Bryan Hall, Room 200, Bloomington 47405
Pres. Thomas Ehrlich
(812) 332-0211

Indiana University Bloomington
Bloomington 47405
Chanc. Kenneth R. Gros Louis
(812) 855-4602

Indiana University East
2325 N. Chester Blvd., Richmond 47374
Chanc. Charlie Nelms
(317) 973-8200

Indiana University Northwest
3400 Broadway, Gary 46408
Chanc. Peggy Elliott
(219) 980-6700

Indiana University Southeast
4201 Grant Line Rd., New Albany 47150
Chanc. Leon Rand
(812) 941-2000

Indiana University at Kokomo
P.O. Box 9003, Kokomo 46904-9003
Chanc. Emita B. Hill
(317) 455-9225

Indiana University at South Bend
1700 Mishawaka Ave., South Bend 46634
Chanc. H. Daniel Cohen
(219) 237-4181

Indiana University-Purdue University at Fort Wayne
2101 Coliseum Blvd. E., Fort Wayne 46805
Chanc. Joanne B. Lantz
(219) 481-6100

Indiana University-Purdue University at Indianapolis
355 N. Lansing St., Indianapolis 46202
Chanc. Gerald L. Bepko
(317) 264-4417

Purdue University System
West Lafayette 47907
Pres. Steven C. Beering
(317) 494-4600

Purdue University
West Lafayette 47907
Pres. Steven C. Beering
(317) 494-4600

Purdue University—Calumet
Hammond 46323
Chanc. James W. Yackel
(219) 989-2203

Purdue University—North Central
1401 S. U.S. Hwy. 421, Westville 46391
Chanc. Dale W. Alspaugh
(219) 785-5200

University of Southern Indiana
8600 University Blvd., Evansville 47712
Pres. David L. Rice
(812) 464-1756

Vincennes University
1002 N. First St., Vincennes 47591
Pres. Phillip M. Summers
(812) 882-3350

Indiana

Indiana Vocational-Technical College Executive Headquarters
One W. 26th St., Indianapolis 46206
Pres. Gerald I. Lamkin
(317) 872-3210

Indiana Vocational-Technical College—Central Indiana Technical Institute
One W. 26th St., P.O. Box 1763, Indianapolis 46206
Vice Pres./Chanc. Meredith L. Carter
(317) 921-4882

Indiana Vocational-Technical College—Columbus Technical Institute
4475 Central Ave., Columbus 47203
Vice Pres./Chanc. Homer B. Smith
(812) 372-9925

Indiana Vocational-Technical College—Eastcentral Technical Institute
4301 S. Cowan Rd., P.O. Box 3100, Muncie 47307
Vice Pres./Chanc. Judith A. Redwine
(317) 289-2291

Indiana Vocational-Technical College—Kokomo Technical Institute
1815 E. Morgan St., Kokomo 46901
Vice Pres./Chanc. Carl F. Lutz
(317) 459-0561

Indiana Vocational-Technical College—Lafayette Technical Institute
3208 Ross Rd., P.O. Box 6299, Lafayette 47903
Vice Pres./Chanc. H. Victor Baldi
(317) 477-9138

Indiana Vocational-Technical College—Northcentral Technical Institute
1534 W. Sample St., South Bend 46619
Vice Pres./Chanc. Carl F. Lutz
(219) 289-7001

Indiana Vocational-Technical College—Northeast Technical Institute
3800 N. Anthony Blvd., Fort Wayne 46805
Vice Pres./Dean Jon L. Rupright
(219) 482-9171

Indiana Vocational-Technical College—Northwest Technical Institute
1440 E. 35th Ave., Gary 46409
Vice Pres./Chanc. Ernest Jones
(219) 981-1111

Indiana Vocational-Technical College—Southcentral Technical Institute
8204 Hwy. 311, Sellersburg 47171
Vice Pres./Chanc. Homer B. Smith
(812) 246-3301

Indiana Vocational-Technical College—Southeast Technical Institute
Hwy. 62 and Ivy Tech Dr., Madison 47250
Vice Pres. Homer B. Smith
(812) 265-2580

Indiana Vocational-Technical College—Southwest Technical Institute
3501 First Ave., Evansville 47710
Vice Pres./Chanc. H. Victor Baldi
(812) 426-2865

Indiana Vocational-Technical College—Wabash Valley Technical Institute
7377 S. Dixie Bee Hwy., Terre Haute 47802
Vice Pres./Dean Sam Borden
(812) 299-1121

Indiana Vocational-Technical College—Whitewater Technical Institute
2325 Chester Blvd., Richmond 47374
Vice Pres./Chanc. Judith A. Redwine
(317) 966-2656

IOWA

Iowa Community Colleges and Vocational Schools
Grimes State Ofc. Bldg., Des Moines 50319-0146
Admin. Joann Horton
(515) 281-8260

Des Moines Area Community College
2006 S. Ankeny Blvd., Ankeny 50021
Pres. Joseph A. Borgen, Ph.D.
(515) 964-6260

Eastern Iowa Community College District
306 W. River Dr., Davenport 52801
Chanc. John T. Blong
(319) 322-5015

Clinton Community College
1000 Lincoln Blvd., Clinton 52732
Pres. Desna I. Wallin
(319) 242-6841

Muscatine Community College
152 Colorado St., Muscatine 52761
Pres. Victor G. McAvoy
(319) 263-8250

Scott Community College
500 Belmont Rd., Bettendorf 52722
Pres. Lenny E. Stone
(319) 359-7531

Hawkeye Institute of Technology
1501 E. Orange Rd., Waterloo 50704
Pres. John E. Hawse
(319) 296-2320

Indian Hills Community College
525 Grandview Ave., Ottumwa 52501
Pres. Lyle Adrian Hellyer
(515) 683-5111

Iowa Central Community College
330 Ave. M, Fort Dodge 50501
Pres. Jack Bottenfield
(515) 576-7201

Iowa Lakes Community College
19 S. 7th St., Estherville 51334
Pres. Richard H. Blacker
(712) 362-2601

Iowa Valley Community College District
Marshalltown 50158
Pres. Paul Tambrino
(515) 752-4643

Ellsworth Community College
1100 College Ave., Iowa Falls 50126
Dean Duane R. Lloyd
(515) 648-4611

Marshalltown Community College
3700 S. Center St., P.O. Box 430, Marshalltown 50158
Dean William M. Simpson
(515) 752-7106

Iowa Western Community College
2700 College Rd., Council Bluffs 51501
Pres. Carl L. Heinrich
(712) 325-3201

Kirkwood Community College
6301 Kirkwood Blvd., S.W., Cedar Rapids 52406
Pres. Norman R. Nielsen
(319) 398-5411

North Iowa Area Community College
500 College Dr., Mason City 50401
Pres. David L. Buettner
(515) 423-1264

Northeast Iowa Community College
Box 400, Calmar 52132
Pres. Don Roby
(319) 562-3263

Northwest Iowa Technical College
Hwy. 18 W., Sheldon 51201
Pres. Carl H. Rolf
(712) 324-5061

Southeastern Community College
    1015 S. Gear Ave., Drawer F, West
        Burlington 52655
    Pres. R. Gene Gardner
    (319) 752-2731

Southwestern Community College
    1501 Townline St., Creston 50801
    Supt./Pres. Richard L. Byerly
    (515) 782-7081

Western Iowa Tech Community College
    4647 Stone Ave., P.O. Box 265,
        Sioux City 51102
    Pres. Robert Dunker
    (712) 274-6400

Iowa State Board of Regents
    Old Historical Bldg., Des Moines 50319
    Exec. Dir. R. Wayne Richey
    (515) 281-3934

Iowa State University
    Ames 50011
    Pres. Martin Jischke
    (515) 294-2042

University of Iowa
    Iowa City 52242
    Pres. Hunter J. Rawlings, III
    (319) 335-3549

University of Northern Iowa
    Cedar Falls 50614
    Pres. Constantine W. Curris
    (319) 273-2566

KANSAS

Kansas Board of Regents
Capitol Tower, Ste. 609, 400 S.W. Eighth St., Topeka 66603-3911
Exec. Dir. Stanley Z. Koplik
(913) 296-3421

Emporia State University
1200 Commercial St., Emporia 66801
Pres. Robert E. Glennen, Jr.
(316) 343-1200

Fort Hays State University
600 Park St., Hays 67601
Pres. Edward H. Hammond
(913) 628-5880

Kansas State University
Manhattan 66506-0113
Pres. Jon Wefald
(913) 532-6222

Pittsburg State University
1701 S. Broadway, Pittsburg 66762
Pres. Donald W. Wilson
(316) 231-7000

University of Kansas
Lawrence 66045
Chanc. Gene A. Budig
(913) 864-2700

Wichita State University
1845 Fairmont St., Wichita 67208
Pres. Warren B. Armstrong
(316) 689-3001

Kansas State Board of Education
120 E. Tenth St., Topeka 66612-1103
Dir. John Hanna
(913) 296-2635

Allen County Community College
1801 N. Central, Iola 66749
Pres. William A. Griffin, Jr.
(316) 365-5116

Barton County Community College
Rural Rte. 3, Box 136Z, Great Bend 67530
Pres. Jimmie L. Downing
(316) 792-2701

Butler County Community College
901 Haverhill Rd., El Dorado 67042
Pres. Rodney V. Cox
(316) 321-5083

Cloud County Community College
2221 Campus Dr., P.O. Box 1002, Concordia 66901-1002
Pres. James P. Ihrig
(913) 243-1435

Coffeyville Community College
11th and Willow, Coffeyville 67337
Pres. Dan D. Kinney
(316) 251-7700

Colby Community College
1255 S. Range, Colby 67701
Pres. Mikel V. Ary
(913) 462-3984

Cowley County Community College
125 S. Second St., P.O. Box 1147, Arkansas City 67005
Pres. Patrick J. McAtee
(316) 442-0430

Dodge City Community College
2501 N. 14th St., Dodge City 67801
Pres. Thomas E. Gamble
(316) 225-1321

Fort Scott Community College
2108 S. Horton St., Fort Scott 66701
Pres. Laura Meeks
(316) 223-2700

Garden City Community College
801 Campus Dr., Garden City 67846
Pres. James H. Tangeman
(316) 276-7611

Highland Community College
Box 68, Highland 66035
Pres. Eric M. Priest
(913) 442-3236

Hutchinson Community College
1300 N. Plum St., Hutchinson 67501
Pres. James H. Stringer
(316) 665-3500

Kansas *Public Systems of Higher Education*

Independence Community College
College Ave. and Brookside Dr.,
Independence 67301
Pres. Jo Ann C. McDowell
(316) 331-4100

Johnson County Community College
12345 College Blvd. at Quivira,
Overland Park 66210
Pres. Charles J. Carlsen
(913) 469-8500

Kansas City Kansas Community College
7250 State Ave., Kansas City 66112
Pres. Bill R. Spencer
(913) 334-1100

Labette Community College
200 S. 14th St., Parsons 67357
Interim Pres. John Patterson
(316) 421-6700

Neosho County Community College
1000 S. Allen, Chanute 66720
Pres. George H. Van Allen
(316) 431-2820

Pratt Community College
Hwy. 61, Pratt 67124
Pres. William A. Wojciechowski
(316) 672-5641

Seward County Community College
1801 N. Kansas St., Liberal 67901
Pres. Donald E. Guild
(316) 624-1951

KENTUCKY

Kentucky Council on Higher Education
1050 U.S. 127 S., Ste. 101, Frankfort 40601-4395
Exec. Dir. Gary S. Cox
(502) 564-3553

Eastern Kentucky University
Richmond 40475-3101
Pres. Hanly Funderburk
(606) 622-1000

Kentucky State University
Frankfort 40601-2355
Pres. Mary L. Smith
(502) 227-6000

Morehead State University
Morehead 40351-1663
Pres. C. Nelson Grote
(606) 783-2221

Murray State University
Murray 42071-3305
Pres. Ronald J. Kurth
(502) 762-3011

Northern Kentucky University
Highland Heights 41076-1448
Pres. Leon E. Boothe
(606) 572-5100

University of Kentucky
Lexington 40506-0032
Pres. Charles T. Wethington, Jr.
(606) 257-9000

University of Louisville
Louisville 40292-0001
Pres. Donald C. Swain
(502) 588-5555

Western Kentucky University
Bowling Green 42101-3576
Pres. Thomas C. Meredith
(502) 745-0111

University of Kentucky Community College System
Breckinridge Hall, Lexington 40506-0056
Chanc. Ben W. Carr, Jr.
(606) 257-8607

Ashland Community College
1400 College Dr., Ashland 41101-3617
Pres. Anthony Newberry
(606) 329-2999

Elizabethtown Community College
600 College Street Rd., Elizabethtown 42701
Pres. Charles E. Stebbins
(502) 769-2371

Hazard Community College
One Community College Dr., Hazard 41701-2402
Pres. G. Edward Hughes
(606) 436-5721

Henderson Community College
2660 S. Green St., Henderson 42420
Pres. Patrick R. Lake
(502) 827-1867

Hopkinsville Community College
P.O. Box 2100, Hopkinsville 42241-2100
Pres. A. James Kerley
(502) 886-3921

Jefferson Community College
109 E. Broadway, Louisville 40202-2005
Pres. Ronald J. Horvath
(502) 584-0181

Lexington Community College
Oswald Bldg., Cooper Dr., Lexington 40506-0235
Pres. Allen G. Edwards
(606) 257-4831

Madisonville Community College
2000 College Dr., Madisonville 42431
Pres. Arthur D. Stumpf
(502) 821-2250

Maysville Community College
Rte. 2, Maysville 41056
Pres. James C. Shires
(606) 759-7141

Kentucky — Public Systems of Higher Education

Owensboro Community College
4800 New Hartford Rd., Owensboro 42303
Pres. John M. McGuire
(502) 686-4400

Paducah Community College
Alben Barkley Dr., P.O. Box 7380, Paducah 42002-7380
Pres. Leonard O'Hara
(502) 554-9200

Prestonsburg Community College
One Bert T. Combs Dr., Prestonsburg 41653
Pres. Deborah Lee Floyd
(606) 886-3863

Somerset Community College
808 Monticello Rd., Somerset 42501
Pres. Rollin J. Watson
(606) 679-8501

Southeast Community College
300 College Rd., Cumberland 40823-1099
Pres. W. Bruce Ayers
(606) 589-2145

Vocational Education Region 1 (Purchase)
1400 H.C. Mathis Dr., Paducah 42002-7769
Regional Dir. Sandra Parks
(502) 444-8356

Kentucky Tech—Fulton County Area Vocational Education Center
Rte. 4, Hickman 42050
Coord. Larry Lynch
(502) 236-2517

Kentucky Tech—Mayfield Area Vocational Education Center
710 Doughtit Rd., Mayfield 42066
Coord. Jim Lawson
(502) 247-4710

Kentucky Tech—Murray Area Vocational Education Center
18th and Sycamore Sts., Murray 42071
Prin. Lynn Tackett
(502) 753-1870

Kentucky Tech—Paducah Area Vocational Education Center
2400 Adams St., Paducah 42001
Prin. Robert Rouff
(502) 443-6592

Kentucky Tech—West Kentucky State Vocational-Technical School
Blandville Rd., P.O. Box 7408, Paducah 42002-7408
Prin. William D. Houston
(502) 554-4991

Vocational Education Region 2 (Pennyrile)
100 School Ave., P.O. Box 608, Madisonville 42431
Regional Dir. Bill M. Hatley
(502) 825-6546

Kentucky Tech—Caldwell County Area Vocational Education Center
P.O. Box 350, Princeton 42445
Coord. Arthur Dunn
(502) 365-5563

Kentucky Tech—Christian County Area Vocational Education Center
109 Hamond Plaza, Ste. 2, Fort Campbell Blvd., Hopkinsville 42240
Coord. Ann Claxton
(502) 887-2524

Kentucky Tech—Eddyville Vocational Education Center
P.O. Box 128, Eddyville 42038-0128
Coord. Jim Creekmur
(502) 388-2211

Kentucky Tech—Madisonville Health Occupations Center
701 N. Laffoon, Madisonville 42431
Coord. Mary Stanley
(502) 825-6552

Kentucky Tech—Madisonville State Vocational-Technical School
150 School Ave., Madisonville 42431
Prin. James Pfeffer
(502) 825-6544

Kentucky Tech—Muhlenberg County Area Vocational Education Center
R.R. Box 67, Greenville 42345
Coord. Andrew Swansey
(502) 338-1271

Kentucky Tech—Webster County Area Vocational Education Center
P.O. Box 188, Dixon 42409
Coord. Claude Hicks
(502) 639-5035

Vocational Education Region 3 (Green River)
1905 Southeastern Pkwy., P.O. Box 1677, Owensboro 42302
Regional Dir. W.O. Jackson
(502) 686-3321

Kentucky Tech—Daviess County State Vocational-Technical School
P.O. Box 1677, Owensboro 42303-1677
Prin. Ray Gillaspie
(502) 686-3321

Kentucky Tech—Henderson County Area Vocational Education Center
2440 Zion Rd., Henderson 42420
Prin. Dennis Harrell
(502) 827-3810

Kentucky Tech—Ohio County Area Vocational Education Center
P.O. Box 1406, U.S. 231 S., Hartford 42347
Coord. Ray Price
(502) 274-9612

Kentucky Tech—Owensboro Vocational-Technical School
1501 Frederica St., Owensboro 42301
Prin. Tara Parker
(502) 686-3255

Kentucky Tech—Union County Area Vocational Education Center
Rte. 4, Morganfield 42437
Coord. Michael Helm
(502) 389-3120

Vocational Education Region 4 (Barren River)
1845 Loop Dr., P.O. Box 1868, Bowling Green 42102-1868
Regional Dir. Joe D. Hunt
(502) 843-5467

Kentucky Tech—Barren County Area Vocational Education Center
491 Trojan Tr., Glasgow 42141
Coord. Max Doty
(502) 651-2196

Kentucky Tech—Bowling Green State Transportation Center
6198 Nashville Rd., Bowling Green 42101
Coord. Robert Bierman
(502) 781-0711

Kentucky Tech—Bowling Green State Vocational-Technical School
1845 Loop Dr., Bowling Green 42101
Prin. Donald R. Williams
(502) 843-5461

Kentucky Tech—Glasgow School for Health Occupations
1215 N. Race St., Glasgow 42141
Coord. Rebecca Forrest
(502) 651-5673

Kentucky Tech—Kentucky Advanced Technology Center
1845 Loop Dr., Bowling Green 42101
Coord. Jack Thomas
(502) 843-5807

Kentucky Tech—Monroe County Area Vocational Education Center
4th and Emmerton Sts., Tompkinsville 42167
Coord. Bill Polland
(502) 487-8261

Kentucky Tech—Russellville Area Vocational Education Center
1103 W. 9th St., Russellville 42276
Coord. Maurice Grayson
(502) 726-8433

Kentucky — Public Systems of Higher Education

Vocational Education Region 5 (Elizabethtown)
505 University Dr., Elizabethtown 42701
Regional Dir. Roye S. Wilson
(502) 769-2326

Kentucky Tech—Breckinridge County Area Vocational Education Center
P.O. Box 68, Harnet 40144
Coord. Wayne A. Spencer
(502) 756-2138

Kentucky Tech—Elizabethtown State Vocational-Technical School
505 University Dr., Elizabethtown 42701
Prin. Neil Ramer
(502) 765-2104

Kentucky Tech—Marion County Area Vocational Education Center
Rte. 3, Box 100, Lebanon 40033
Coord. John Coyle
(502) 692-3155

Kentucky Tech—Meade County Area Vocational Education Center
Old State Rd., Brandenburg 40108
Coord. William Whalen
(502) 422-3955

Kentucky Tech—Nelson County Area Vocational Education Center
1060 Bloomfield Rd., Bardstown 40004
Coord. John T. Kromer
(502) 348-9096

Vocational Education Regions 6 and 8 (Jefferson)
9127 E. Galene Dr., Louisville 40299
Regional Dir. Bill L. Evans
(502) 267-9187

Kentucky Tech—Bullitt County Area Vocational Education Center
395 High School Dr., Sheperdsville 40165
Coord. Robert Hazelrigg
(502) 543-7018

Kentucky Tech—Fairdale Vocational Education Center
907 Fairdale Rd., Fairdale 40118
Coord. David Schalk
(502) 473-8249

Kentucky Tech—Jefferson State Vocational-Technical School
727 W. Chestnut St., Louisville 40203
Prin. James Woodrow
(502) 588-4223

Kentucky Tech—Jeffersontown Vocational Education Center
9127-E Galene Dr., Louisville 40299
Coord. Jim Floyd
(502) 267-9187

Kentucky Tech—LaGrange Vocational Education Center
3001 W. Hwy. 146, LaGrange 40031
Coord. Margaret Moore
(502) 222-9441

Kentucky Tech—Luckett Vocational Education Center
1612 Dawkins Rd., Box 6, LaGrange 40031
Coord. David Visel
(502) 222-0363

Kentucky Tech—Oldham County Vocational Education Center
P.O. Box 127, Hwy. 393, Buckner 40065
Prin. Jeanette Stratton
(502) 222-0131

Kentucky Tech—Peewee Valley Education Center
P.O. Box 337, Peewee Valley 40056
Prin. Vivian Whitehouse
(502) 241-8454

Kentucky Tech—Shelby County Area Vocational Education Center
Rte. 7, Box 331, Shelbyville 40065
Coord. Ruth Bunch
(502) 633-6554

Public Systems of Higher Education — Kentucky

Vocational Education Region 7 (Northern Kentucky)
1025 Amsterdam Rd., Covington 41018
Regional Dir. John G. Corwin
(606) 292-6423

Kentucky Tech—Boone County Area Vocational Education Center
3320 Cougar Path, Hebron 41048
Coord. Stephanie Rottman
(606) 689-7855

Kentucky Tech—Campbell County Area Vocational Education Center
50 Orchard La., Alexandria 41001
Coord. Kenneth McCormick
(606) 635-4101

Kentucky Tech—Carroll County Area Vocational Education Center
1704 Highland Ave., Carrollton 41008
Coord. Donald W. Garner
(502) 732-4479

Kentucky Tech—Northern Campbell County Vocational-Technical School
Campbell Dr., Highland Heights 41076
Coord. Earl Wittenrock
(606) 441-2010

Kentucky Tech—Northern Kentucky Health Occupations Center
790 Thomas More Pkwy., Edgewood 41017
Coord. Wade Halsey
(606) 341-5200

Kentucky Tech—Northern Kentucky State Vocational-Technical School
1025 Amsterdam Rd., Covington 41011
Prin. Edward Burton
(606) 431-2700

Kentucky Tech—Patton Vocational Education Center
3234 Turkeyfoot Rd., Fort Mitchell 41017
Coord. Eugene Penn
(606) 341-2266

Vocational Education Region 9 (Buffalo Trace)
32 S. Christy St., P.O. Box 1098, Morehead 40351
Regional Dir. Karen B. Hamilton
(606) 784-7541

Kentucky Tech—Maysville Area Vocational Education Center
646 Kent Station Rd., Maysville 41056
Coord. Glenn Collins
(606) 759-7101

Kentucky Tech—Montgomery County Area Vocational Education Center
682 Woodford Dr., Mount Sterling 40353
Coord. Norma Willoughby
(606) 498-1103

Kentucky Tech—Morehead Treatment Center
100 Pine Crest Rd., Morehead 40351
Acting Supt. Jamie Brown
(606) 784-6421

Kentucky Tech—Morgan County Area Vocational Education Center
P.O. Box 249, West Liberty 41472
Coord. Willis Lyon
(606) 743-4321

Kentucky Tech—Rowan State Vocational-Technical School
100 Vo-Tech Dr., Morehead 40351
Prin. Jamie Brown
(606) 783-1538

Kentucky Tech—Woodsbend Boys' Camp
Rte. 1, Box 765, West Liberty 41472
Prin. Willis Lyon
(606) 743-3177

Vocational Education Region 10 (Fivco)
4818 Roberts Dr., Ashland 41102
Regional Dir. Howard Moore
(606) 928-6427

Kentucky

Public Systems of Higher Education

Kentucky Tech—Ashland State
Vocational-Technical School
4818 Roberts Dr., Ashland 41102-9046
Prin. Howard Moore
(606) 928-6427

Kentucky Tech—Greenup County Area
Vocational Education Center
P.O. Box 7, South Shore 41175
Coord. Helen Spears
(606) 932-3107

Kentucky Tech—Russell Area Vocational
Education Center
705 Red Devil La., Russell 41169
Coord. Michael Chapman
(606) 836-1256

Vocational Education Region 11 (Big Sandy)
513 Third St., Paintsville 41240
Regional Dir. Bronelle Skaggs
(606) 789-3115

Kentucky Tech—Belfry Area Vocational
Education Center
P.O. Box 280, Belfry 41514
Prin. Brad W. May
(606) 353-4951

Kentucky Tech—Garth Area Vocational
Education Center
HC 79, Box 205, Martin 41649
Prin. Ronald Turner
(606) 285-3088

Kentucky Tech—Martin County Area
Vocational Education Center
HC 68, Box 2177, Inez 41224
Coord. Robert L. Allen
(606) 298-3879

Kentucky Tech—Mayo State Vocational-
Technical School
Third St., Paintsville 41240
Prin. Gary Coleman
(606) 789-5321

Kentucky Tech—Millard Area Vocational
Education Center
430 Millard Hwy., Pikeville 41501
Prin. William Justice
(606) 437-6059

Kentucky Tech—Phelps Area Vocational
Education Center
HC 67, No. 1002, Phelps 41553
Prin. Curtis Akers
(606) 456-8136

**Vocational Education Region 12
(Kentucky River)**
101 Vo-Tech Dr., Hazard 41701
Regional Dir. Finley Begley
(606) 439-2500

Kentucky Tech—Breathitt County Area
Vocational Education Center
P.O. Box 786, Jackson 41339
Coord. Fred Deaton
(606) 666-5153

Kentucky Tech—Hazard State Vocational-
Technical School
101 Vo-Tech Dr., Hazard 41701
Prin. Connie W. Johnson
(606) 436-3101

Kentucky Tech—Knott County Area
Vocational Education Center
HCR 60, Box 1100, Hindman 41822
Coord. Sonny Smith
(606) 785-5350

Kentucky Tech—Lee County Area
Vocational Education Center
P.O. Box B, Beattyville 41311
Coord. Fred Kincaid
(606) 464-2475

Kentucky Tech—Leslie County Area
Vocational Education Center
P.O. Box 902, Hyden 41749
Coord. Betty Huff
(606) 672-2859

Kentucky Tech—Letcher County Area
Vocational Education Center
610 Circle Dr., Whitesburg 41858
Coord. James G. Estep
(606) 633-5053

**Vocational Education Region 13
(Cumberland Valley)**
333 N. Main St., Ste. One, London 40741
Regional Dir. Stuart Hodges
(606) 878-9555

Public Systems of Higher Education   **Kentucky**

Kentucky Tech—Bell County Area Vocational Education Center
Box 199-A, Rte. 7, Pineville 40977
Coord. Ron Mason
(606) 337-3094

Kentucky Tech—Clay County Area Vocational Education Center
Rte. 2, Box 256, Manchester 40962
Coord. Charles McWhorter
(606) 598-2194

Kentucky Tech—Corbin Area Vocational Education Center
1909 S. Snyder Ave., Corbin 40701
Coord. Ronnie Partin
(606) 528-5338

Kentucky Tech—Cumberland Valley Health Occupations Center
U.S. 25E S., P.O. Box 187, Pineville 40977
Coord. Mildred Winkler
(606) 337-3106

Kentucky Tech—Harlan State Vocational-Technical School
21 Ballpark Rd., Harlan 40831
Prin. Harve J. Couch
(606) 573-1506

Kentucky Tech—Knox County Area Vocational Education Center
210 Wall St., Barbourville 40906
Coord. Charles Frasier
(606) 546-5320

Kentucky Tech—Laurel County State Vocational-Technical School
235 S. Laurel Rd., London 40741
Prin. Donnie Robinson
(606) 864-7311

Kentucky Tech—Rockcastle County Area Vocational Education Center
P.O. Box 275, Mount Vernon 40456
Coord. Donna Hopkins
(606) 256-4346

Vocational Education Region 14 (Lake Cumberland)
P.O. Box 110, Somerset 42501
Regional Dir. W.L. Ford
(606) 679-2225

Kentucky Tech—Casey County Area Vocational Education Center
Rte. 4, Box 49, Liberty 42539
Coord. J.D. Shugars
(606) 787-6241

Kentucky Tech—Clinton County Area Vocational Education Center
Rte. 3, Box 8, Albany 42602
Coord. Preston Sparks
(606) 387-6448

Kentucky Tech—Green County Area Vocational Education Center
P.O. Box H, Greensburg 42743
Coord. Jerry O. Rogers
(502) 932-4263

Kentucky Tech—Russell County Area Vocational Education Center
P.O. Box 599, Russell Springs 42642
Prin. Chester Taylor
(502) 866-6175

Kentucky Tech—Somerset State Vocational-Technical School
714 Airport Rd., Somerset 42501
Prin. J.P. McCarty
(606) 679-4303

Kentucky Tech—Wayne County Area Vocational Education Center
Rte. 4, Box 1B, Monticello 42633
Coord. Sharon Tiller
(606) 348-8424

Vocational Education Region 15 (Bluegrass)
1093 S. Broadway, Ste. 9, Lexington 40504
Regional Dir. Ann C. Vescio
(606) 252-3418

Kentucky Tech—Blackburn Correctional Complex
3111 Spurr Rd., Lexington 40511
Coord. Clyde Carroll
(606) 254-2791

Kentucky Tech—Central Kentucky State Vocational-Technical School
104 Vo-Tech Rd., Lexington 40510
Prin. Patrick White
(606) 255-8500

Kentucky

Kentucky Tech—Clark County Area Vocational Education Center
650 Boone Ave., Winchester 40391
Coord. William Lockhart
(606) 744-1250

Kentucky Tech—Danville School of Health Occupations
448 S. Third St., Danville 40422
Coord. Sandra Houston
(606) 236-2053

Kentucky Tech—Garrad County Area Vocational Education Center
306 W. Maple Ave., Lancaster 40444
Coord. James Spurlin
(606) 792-2144

Kentucky Tech—Harrison County Area Vocational Education Center
551 Webster Ave., Cynthiana 41031
Coord. James Plummer
(606) 234-5286

Kentucky Tech—Harrodsburg Area Vocational Education Center
661 Tapt Rd., P.O. Box 628, Harrodsburg 40330
Coord. L. Hughes Jones
(606) 734-9329

Kentucky Tech—Madison County Area Vocational Education Center
P.O. Box 809, 703 N. Second St., Richmond 40476-0809
Coord. Evelyn Watson
(606) 623-4061

Kentucky Tech—Northpoint Education Center
P.O. Box 479, Burgin 40310
Coord. Luther Spotts
(606) 236-9012

LOUISIANA

Louisiana Board of Trustees for State Colleges and Universities
150 Riverside Mall, 3rd Fl., Baton Rouge 70801
Acting Pres. David McCormick
(504) 342-6950

Grambling State University
P.O. Drawer 607, Grambling 71245
Pres. Harold W. Lundy
(318) 274-2000

Louisiana Tech University
P.O. Box 3168, Tech Sta., Ruston 71272
Pres. Daniel D. Reneau
(318) 257-0211

McNeese State University
4100 Ryan St., Lake Charles 70609
Pres. Robert D. Hebert
(318) 475-5000

Nicholls State University
LA Hwy. 1, Thibodaux 70310
Pres. Donald J. Ayo
(504) 446-8111

Northeast Louisiana University
700 University Avenue, Monroe 71209
Pres. Lawson L. Swearingen, Jr.
(318) 342-1000

Northwestern State University
College Ave., Natchitoches 71497
Pres. Robert A. Alost
(318) 357-6361

Southeastern Louisiana University
Western Ave., P.O. Box 784, Hammond 70402
Pres. G. Warren Smith
(504) 549-2000

University of Southwestern Louisiana
200 E. University Ave., Lafayette 70504
Pres. Ray P. Authement
(318) 231-6000

Louisiana State University System
Baton Rouge 70803-8402
Pres. Allen A. Copping
(504) 388-3202

Louisiana State University Medical Center
433 Bolivar St., New Orleans 70112
Chanc. Perry G. Rigby
(504) 568-4808

Louisiana State University and Agricultural and Mechanical College
Baton Rouge 70803-2750
Chanc. William E. Davis
(504) 388-3202

Louisiana State University at Alexandria
8100 Hwy. 71 S., Alexandria 71302
Chanc. Benjamin F. Martin
(318) 445-3672

Louisiana State University at Eunice
P.O. Box 1129, Eunice 70535
Chanc. Michael Smith
(318) 457-7311

Louisiana State University in Shreveport
One University Plaza, Shreveport 71115
Chanc. John R. Darling
(318) 797-5000

University of New Orleans
Lake Front, New Orleans 70148
Chanc. Gregory M. St. L. O'Brien
(504) 286-6000

Southern University and Agricultural and Mechanical College System
Baton Rouge 70813
Pres. Dolores R. Spikes
(504) 771-4500

Southern University and Agricultural and Mechanical College at Baton Rouge
Southern Branch Post Office, Box 96, Baton Rouge 70813
Pres. Marvin L. Yates
(504) 771-4500

Louisiana   **Public Systems of Higher Education**

Southern University at New Orleans
   6400 Press Dr., New Orleans 70126
   Chanc. Robert B. Gex
   (504) 286-5000

Southern University in Shreveport
   3050 Martin Luther King Jr. Dr,
   Shreveport 71107
   Chanc. Robert H. Smith
   (318) 674-3300

MAINE

University of Maine System
107 Maine Ave., Bangor 04401-1805
Chanc. Robert L. Woodbury
(207) 947-0336

University of Maine
Orono 04469
Pres. John C. Hitt
(207) 581-1512

University of Maine at Augusta
Augusta 04330
Pres. George P. Connick
(207) 621-3403

University of Maine at Farmington
86 Main St., Farmington 04938
Pres. J. Michael Orenduff
(207) 778-3501

University of Maine at Fort Kent
Pleasant St., Fort Kent 04743
Pres. Richard G. Dumont
(207) 834-3162

University of Maine at Machias
Machias 04654
Pres. Frederic A. Reynolds
(207) 255-3313

University of Maine at Presque Isle
181 Main St., Presque Isle 04769
Pres. James R. Roach
(207) 764-0311

University of Southern Maine
96 Falmouth St., Portland 04103
Pres. Richard L. Pattenaude
(207) 780-4141

MARYLAND

Maryland Higher Education Commission
16 Francis St., Annapolis 21401
Secy. Shaila Aery
(410) 974-2971

   Morgan State University
      Hillen Rd. and Cold Spring La.,
      Baltimore 21239
      Pres. Earl S. Richardson
      (410) 444-3333

   St. Mary's College of Maryland
      St. Mary's 20686
      Pres. Edward T. Lewis
      (301) 862-0200

Maryland State Board for Community Colleges
914 Bay Ridge Rd., Ste. 210, Annapolis 21403
Exec. Dir. Jean E. Hunter
(410) 974-2881

   Allegany Community College
      Willowbrook Rd., Cumberland 21502
      Pres. Donald L. Alexander
      (301) 724-7700

   Anne Arundel Community College
      101 College Pkwy., Arnold 21012
      Pres. Thomas E. Florestano
      (410) 647-7100

   Catonsville Community College
      800 S. Rolling Rd., Catonsville 21228
      Pres. Frederick J. Walsh
      (410) 455-6050

   Cecil Community College
      1000 North East Rd., North East 21901
      Pres. Robert L. Gell
      (410) 287-6060

   Charles County Community College
      Mitchell Rd., P.O. Box 910, La Plata 20646
      Pres. John M. Sine
      (301) 934-2251

   Chesapeake College
      P.O. Box 8, Wye Mills 21679
      Pres. Robert C. Schleiger
      (410) 822-5400

   Dundalk Community College
      7200 Sollers Point Rd., Dundalk 21222
      Pres. Martha A. Smith
      (410) 282-6700

   Essex Community College
      7201 Rossville Blvd., Baltimore 21237
      Pres. Donald J. Slowinski
      (410) 682-6000

   Frederick Community College
      7932 Oppossumtown Pike, Frederick 21701
      Pres. Lee J. Betts
      (301) 694-5240

   Garrett Community College
      Mosser Rd., P.O. Box 151, McHenry 21541
      Pres. Stephen J. Herman
      (301) 387-6666

   Hagerstown Junior College
      751 Robinwood Dr., Hagerstown 21740
      Pres. Norman P. Shea
      (301) 790-2800

   Harford Community College
      401 Thomas Run Rd., Bel Air 21014
      Pres. Richard J. Pappas
      (410) 836-4000

   Howard Community College
      10901 Little Patuxent Pkwy., Columbia 21044
      Pres. Dwight A. Burrill
      (410) 992-4800

Montgomery College Central Administration
51 Mannakee St., Rockville 20850
Pres. Robert E. Parilla
(301) 279-5000

Public Systems of Higher Education — Maryland

Montgomery College—Germantown Campus
20200 Observation Dr., Germantown 20874
Provost Stanley M. Dahlman
(301) 972-2000

Montgomery College—Rockville Campus
51 Mannakee St., Rockville 20850
Provost Antoinette P. Hastings
(301) 279-5000

Montgomery College—Takoma Park Campus
Takoma Ave. and Fenton St., Takoma Park 20912
Provost O. Robert Brown
(301) 587-4090

The New Community College of Baltimore
2901 Liberty Heights Ave., Baltimore 21215
Interim Pres. James D. Tschechtelin
(410) 396-0203

Prince George's Community College
301 Largo Rd., Largo 20772
Pres. Robert I. Bickford
(301) 336-6000

Wor-Wic Tech Community College
30 Wesley Dr., Salisbury 21801
Pres. Arnold H. Maner
(410) 749-8181

University of Maryland System
3330 Metzerott Rd., Adelphi 20783
Chanc. Donald N. Langenberg
(301) 853-3601

Bowie State University
14000 Jericho Park Rd., Bowie 20715
Pres. James E. Lyons, Sr.
(301) 464-6500

Coppin State College
2500 W. North Ave., Baltimore 21216
Pres. Calvin W. Burnett
(410) 383-5910

Frostburg State University
Frostburg 21532-1099
Pres. Catherine R. Gira
(301) 689-4000

Salisbury State University
Salisbury 21801
Pres. Thomas E. Bellavance
(410) 543-6000

Towson State University
Towson 21204
Pres. Hoke L. Smith
(410) 321-2000

University of Baltimore
1420 N. Charles St., Baltimore 21201
Pres. H. Mebane Turner
(410) 625-3000

University of Maryland Baltimore County
5401 Wilkens Ave., Catonsville 21228
Pres. Michael K. Hooker
(410) 455-1000

University of Maryland College Park
College Park 20742
Pres. William E. Kirwan
(301) 405-1000

University of Maryland Eastern Shore
Princess Anne 21853
Pres. William P. Hytche
(410) 651-2200

University of Maryland University College
University Blvd. at Adelphi Rd, College Park 20742-1600
Pres. T. Benjamin Massey
(301) 985-7000

University of Maryland at Baltimore
520 W. Lombard St., Baltimore 21201
Pres. Errol L. Reese
(410) 328-3100

MASSACHUSETTS

The Massachusetts Higher Education Coordinating Council
One Ashburton Pl., 1401 McCormack Bldg., Boston 02108
Interim Chanc. Rudolph W. Bromery
(617) 727-7785

Berkshire Community College
West St., Pittsfield 01201
Pres. Cathryn L. Addy
(413) 499-4660

Bridgewater State College
Bridgewater 02324
Pres. Adrian Tinsley
(508) 697-1200

Bristol Community College
777 Elsbree St., Fall River 02720
Pres. Eileen T. Farley
(508) 678-2811

Bunker Hill Community College
Rutherford Ave., Boston 02129
Interim Pres. Kathleen E. Assar
(617) 241-8600

Cape Cod Community College
Rte. 132, West Barnstable 02668
Pres. Richard A. Kraus
(508) 362-2131

Essex Agricultural and Technical Institute
562 Maple St., Hathorne 01937
Dir. Gustave D. Olson, Jr.
(508) 774-0050

Fitchburg State College
160 Pearl St., Fitchburg 01420
Pres. Vincent J. Mara
(508) 345-2151

Framingham State College
100 State St., Framingham 01701
Pres. Paul F. Weller
(508) 620-1220

Greenfield Community College
One College Dr., Greenfield 01301
Pres. Katherine H. Sloan
(413) 774-3131

Holyoke Community College
303 Homestead Ave., Holyoke 01040
Pres. David M. Bartley
(413) 538-7000

Massachusetts Bay Community College
50 Oakland St., Wellesley Hills 02181
Pres. Roger A. Van Winkle
(617) 237-1100

Massachusetts College of Art
621 Huntington Ave., Boston 02115
Pres. William F. O'Neil
(617) 232-1555

Massachusetts Maritime Academy
Academy Dr., Buzzards Bay 02532
Pres. Peter Cressey, U.S.N.
(617) 759-5761

Massasoit Community College
One Massasoit Blvd., Brockton 02402
Pres. Gerard F. Burke
(508) 588-9100

Middlesex Community College
Springs Rd., Bedford 01730
Pres. Carole Cowan
(617) 275-8910

Mount Wachusetts Community College
444 Green St., Gardner 01440
Pres. Daniel M. Asquino
(508) 632-6600

North Adams State College
North Adams 01247
Pres. Thomas D. Aceto
(413) 664-4511

North Shore Community College
3 Essex St., Beverly 01915
Pres. George Traicoff
(508) 922-6722

Northern Essex Community College
100 Elliott Way, Haverhill 01830-2399
Pres. John R. Dimitry
(508) 374-3900

Quincy College
34 Coddington St., Quincy 02169
Pres. O. Clayton Johnson
(617) 984-1600

Quinsigamond Community College
670 W. Boylston St., Worcester 01606
Pres. Clifford S. Peterson
(508) 853-2300

Roxbury Community College
1234 Columbus Ave., Roxbury Crossing 02120-3400
Acting Admin. Alan Shepherd
(617) 427-0060

Salem State College
352 Lafayette St., Salem 01970
Pres. Nancy D. Harrington
(508) 741-6000

Springfield Technical Community College
One Armory Sq., Springfield 01105
Pres. Andrew M. Scibelli
(413) 781-7822

Westfield State College
Western Ave., Westfield 01086
Pres. Ronald L. Applbaum
(413) 568-3311

Worcester State College
486 Chandler St., Worcester 01602
Pres. Kalyan Ghosh
(508) 793-8000

University of Massachusetts President's Office
250 Stuart St., Boston 02116
Pres. E.K. Fretwell, Jr.
(617) 287-7000

University of Massachusetts at Amherst
Amherst 01003
Chanc. Richard D. O'Brien
(413) 545-3171

University of Massachusetts at Boston
Harbor Campus, Boston 02125
Chanc. Sherry H. Penney
(617) 287-6800

University of Massachusetts at Dartmouth
North Dartmouth 02747
Interim Chanc. Joseph C. Deck
(508) 999-8004

University of Massachusetts at Lowell
One University Ave., Lowell 01854
Chanc. William T. Hogan
(508) 934-4000

University of Massachusetts at Worcester
55 Lake Ave., N., Worcester 01655
Chanc. Aaron Lazare
(508) 856-2107

MICHIGAN

Michigan State Board of Education
P.O. Box 30008, Lansing 48909
Pres. Cherry Jacobus
(517) 373-3900

Alpena Community College
666 Johnson St., Alpena 49707
Pres. Donald L. Newport
(517) 356-9021

Bay de Noc Community College
2001 N. Lincoln Rd., Escanaba 49829
Pres. Dwight E. Link
(906) 786-5802

Central Michigan University
Mount Pleasant 48859
Interim Pres. Leonard E. Plachta
(517) 774-3131

Charles Stewart Mott Community College
1401 E. Court St., Flint 48502
Pres. David G. Moore
(313) 762-0453

Delta College
University Center 48710
Pres. Donald J. Carlyon
(517) 686-9201

Eastern Michigan University
Ypsilanti 48197
Pres. William E. Sheldon
(313) 487-1849

Ferris State University
Big Rapids 49307
Pres. Helen Popovich
(616) 592-2000

Glen Oaks Community College
62249 Shimmel Rd., Centreville 49032
Pres. Philip G. Ward
(616) 467-9945

Gogebic Community College
E-4946 Jackson Rd., Ironwood 49938
Pres. James R. Grote
(906) 932-4231

Grand Rapids Community College
143 Bostwick St., N.E., Grand Rapids 49503
Pres. Richard W. Calkins
(616) 771-3900

Grand Valley State University
One Campus Dr., Allendale 49401
Pres. Arend D. Lubbers
(616) 895-6611

Henry Ford Community College
5101 Evergreen Rd., Dearborn 48128
Pres. Andrew A. Mazzara
(313) 845-9650

Highland Park Community College
Glendale Ave. at Third St., Highland Park 48203
Acting Pres. Charles Mitchell
(313) 252-0436

Jackson Community College
2111 Emmons Rd., Jackson 49201
Pres. Clyde E. LeTarte
(517) 787-0800

Kalamazoo Valley Community College
6767 W. "O" Ave., Kalamazoo 49009
Pres. Marilyn J. Schlack
(616) 372-5200

Kellogg Community College
450 North Ave., Battle Creek 49017-3397
Pres. Paul H. Ohm
(616) 965-3931

Kirtland Community College
10775 N. St. Helen Rd., Roscommon 48653
Pres. Dorothy N. Franke
(517) 275-5121

Lake Michigan College
2755 E. Napier St., Benton Harbor 49022
Pres. Anne E. Mulder
(616) 927-3571

Lake Superior State University
 1000 College Dr., Sault Ste. Marie
  49783
 Pres. H. Erik Shaar
 (906) 635-2202

Lansing Community College
 521 N. Washington Sq., P.O. Box
  40010, Lansing 48901-7210
 Pres. Abel B. Sykes, Jr.
 (517) 483-1851

Macomb Community College
 14500 E. Twelve Mile Rd., Warren
  48093
 Pres. Albert L. Lorenzo
 (313) 445-7000

Michigan State University
 East Lansing 48824-1046
 Pres. John A. DiBiaggio
 (517) 355-6560

Michigan Technological University
 1400 Townsend Dr., Houghton
  49931
 Pres. Curtis J. Tompkins
 (906) 487-1885

Mid Michigan Community College
 1375 S. Clare Ave., Harrison 48625
 Pres. Charles J. Corrigan, Ph.D.
 (517) 386-7792

Monroe County Community College
 1555 S. Raisinville Rd., Monroe
  48161
 Pres. Gerald D. Welch
 (313) 242-7300

Montcalm Community College
 2800 College Dr., S.W., Sidney
  48885
 Pres. Donald C. Burns
 (517) 328-2111

Muskegon Community College
 221 S. Quarterline Rd., Muskegon
  49442
 Pres. James L. Stevenson
 (616) 773-0311

North Central Michigan College
 1515 Howard St., Petoskey 49770
 Pres. Robert B. Graham
 (616) 348-6600

Northern Michigan University
 Marquette 49855
 Interim Pres. William E.
  Vandament
 (906) 227-2920

Northwestern Michigan College
 1701 E. Front St., Traverse City
  49684
 Pres. Timothy G. Quinn
 (616) 922-0650

Oakland Community College
 2480 Opdyke Rd., P.O. Box 812,
  Bloomfield Hills 48013-0812
 Chanc. Patsy Fulton
 (313) 540-1500

Oakland University
 Rochester 48309
 Interim Pres. John De Carlo
 (313) 370-3500

Saginaw Valley State University
 2250 Pierce Rd., University Center
  48710-4042
 Pres. Eric R. Gilbertson
 (517) 790-4000

St. Clair County Community College
 323 Erie St., P.O. Box 5015, Port
  Huron 48061-5015
 Pres. R. Ernest Dear
 (313) 984-3881

Schoolcraft College
 18600 Haggerty Rd., Livonia 48152-
  2696
 Pres. Richard W. McDowell
 (313) 462-4400

Southwestern Michigan College
 58900 Cherry Grove Rd., Dowagiac
  49047-9793
 Pres. David C. Briegel
 (616) 782-5911

Michigan — Public Systems of Higher Education

University of Michigan System
Ann Arbor 48109
Pres. James J. Duderstadt
(313) 764-1817

University of Michigan
Ann Arbor 48109
Pres. James J. Duderstadt
(313) 764-1817

University of Michigan—Dearborn
4901 Evergreen Rd., Dearborn 48128
Chanc. Blenda J. Wilson
(313) 593-5000

University of Michigan—Flint
Flint 48502-2186
Chanc. Clinton B. Jones
(313) 762-3000

Washtenaw Community College
4800 E. Huron River Dr., P.O. Box D-1, Ann Arbor 48106
Pres. Gundar A. Myran
(313) 973-3300

Wayne County Community College
801 W. Fort St., Detroit 48226
Pres. Rafael Cortada, Ph.D.
(313) 496-2510

Wayne State University
Detroit 48202
Pres. David W. Adamany
(313) 577-2230

West Shore Community College
3000 N. Stiles Rd., P.O. Box 277, Scottville 49454
Pres. William M. Anderson
(616) 845-6211

Western Michigan University
Kalamazoo 49008-5130
Pres. Diether H. Haenicke
(616) 387-2351

MINNESOTA

Minnesota Community College System
203 Capitol Square Bldg., 550 Cedar St.,
St. Paul 55101
Pres. Gerald W. Christenson
(612) 296-3990

Anoka-Ramsey Community College
11200 Mississippi Blvd., N.W., Coon
Rapids 55433
Pres. Patrick M. Johns
(612) 427-2600

Arrowhead Community College Region
1855 E. Hwy. 169, Grand Rapids
55744
Pres. Philip J. Anderson
(218) 327-4380

Hibbing Community College
1515 E. 25th St., Hibbing 55746
Provost Anthony Kuznik
(218) 262-6700

Itasca Community College
1851 E. Hwy. 169, Grand
Rapids 55744
Provost Lawrence Dukes
(218) 327-4461

Mesabi Community College
905 W. Chestnut St., Virginia
55792
Provost Richard N. Kohlhase
(218) 749-7700

Rainy River Community College
Hwy. 11-71 and 15th St.,
International Falls 56649
Provost Karen Nagle
(218) 285-7722

Vermilion Community College
1900 E. Camp St., Ely 55731
Provost Jon Harris
(218) 365-7200

Austin Community College
1600 8th Ave., N.W., Austin 55912
Pres. Steven R. Wallace
(507) 433-0508

Clearwater Community College Region
1414 College Way, Fergus Falls
56537
Pres. Alex Easton
(218) 739-7500

Brainerd Community College
501 W. College Dr., Brainerd
56401
Provost Sally Jane Ihne
(218) 828-2510

Northland Community College
Hwy. 1 E., Thief River Falls
56701
Acting Provost James Haviland
(218) 681-2181

Fergus Falls Community College
1414 College Way, Fergus Falls
56537
Provost Daniel F. True
(218) 739-7500

Inver Hills Community College
8445 College Trail, Inver Grove
Heights 55076
Acting Pres. Jerry Isaacs
(612) 450-8634

Lakewood Community College
3401 Century Ave., White Bear Lake
55110
Pres. Neil Christienson
(612) 779-3200

Minneapolis Community College
1501 Hennepin Ave., Minneapolis
55403
Pres. Jacquelyn M. Belcher
(612) 341-7055

Normandale Community College
9700 France Ave. S., Bloomington
55431
Pres. Thomas Horak
(612) 832-6000

Minnesota

North Hennepin Community College
7411 85th Ave. N., Brooklyn Park 55445
Pres. Frederick W. Capshaw
(612) 424-0811

Rochester Community College
851 30th Ave. S.E., Rochester 55904
Pres. Geraldine A. Evans
(507) 285-7216

Willmar Community College
P.O. Box 797, Willmar 56201
Pres. Harold G. Conradi
(612) 231-5102

Worthington Community College
1450 College Way, Worthington 56187
Pres. C.W. Burchill
(507) 372-2107

Minnesota State University System
555 Park St., 230 Park Office Bldg., St. Paul 55103
Chanc. Terrence J. MacTaggart
(612) 296-2844

Bemidji State University
1500 Birchmont Dr., N.E., Bemidji 56601-2699
Pres. Leslie C. Duly
(218) 755-2000

Mankato State University
Mankato 56001
Pres. Margaret R. Preska
(507) 389-1111

Metropolitan State University
121 Seventh Pl. E., Metro Sq., Ste. 121, St. Paul 55101
Pres. Tobin G. Barrozo
(612) 373-2727

Moorhead State University
1104 7th Ave. S., Moorhead 56560
Pres. Roland Dille
(218) 236-2243

St. Cloud State University
740 Fourth Ave. S., St. Cloud 56301
Pres. Brendan J. McDonald
(612) 255-2122

Southwest State University
Marshall 56258
Pres. Oliver J. Ford
(507) 537-6272

Winona State University
Winona 55987
Pres. Darrell W. Krueger
(507) 457-2017

University of Minnesota System
100 Church St., S.E., Minneapolis 55455-0110
Pres. Nils Hasselmo
(612) 625-5000

Mayo Foundation
200 First St., S.W., Rochester 55905
C.E.O. Robert R. Waller
(507) 284-2511

University of Minnesota—Crookston
Crookston 56716
Chanc. Donald G. Sargeant
(218) 281-6510

University of Minnesota—Duluth
Duluth 55812
Chanc. Lawrence A. Ianni
(218) 726-8000

University of Minnesota—Morris
600 E. Fourth St., Morris 56267
Chanc. David C. Johnson
(612) 589-2211

University of Minnesota—Twin Cities
100 Church St., S.E., Minneapolis 55455
Pres. Nils Hasselmo
(612) 625-5000

University of Minnesota—Waseca
1000 University Dr., S.W., Waseca 56093
Chanc. Nan Wilhelmson
(507) 835-9300

MISSISSIPPI

Mississippi Board of Trustees of State Institutions of Higher Learning
3825 Ridgewood Rd., Jackson 39211
Commissioner W. Ray Cleere
(601) 982-6611

Alcorn State University
P.O. Box 359, Lorman 39096
Pres. Walter Washington
(601) 877-6100

Delta State University
Hwy. 8 W., Cleveland 38733
Pres. F. Kent Wyatt
(601) 846-3000

Jackson State University
1400 J.R. Lynch St., Jackson 39217
Interim Pres. Herman B. Smith, Jr.
(601) 968-2323

Mississippi State University
Mississippi State 39762
Pres. Donald W. Zacharias
(601) 325-2323

Mississippi University for Women
P.O. Box W-1602, College St., Columbus 39701
Pres. Clyda S. Rent
(601) 329-4750

Mississippi Valley State University
Hwy. 82 and Sunflower Rd., Itta Bena 38941
Pres. William W. Sutton
(601) 254-9041

University of Mississippi
University 38677
Chanc. R. Gerald Turner
(601) 232-7211

University of Mississippi Medical Center
2500 N. State St., Jackson 39216-4505
Vice Chanc. Norman Crooks Nelson, M.D.
(601) 984-1010

The University of Southern Mississippi
Southern Sta., Box 5001, Hattiesburg 39406
Pres. Aubrey K. Lucas
(601) 266-5001

Mississippi State Board for Community and Junior Colleges
3825 Ridgewood Rd., No. 3, Jackson 39211
Dir. Olon E. Ray
(601) 982-6518

Coahoma Community College
Rte. 1, Box 616, Clarksdale 38614
Pres. McKinley C. Martin
(601) 627-2571

Copiah-Lincoln Community College
P.O. Box 457, Wesson 39191-0091
Pres. Billy B. Thames
(601) 643-5101

East Central Community College
P.O. Box 129, Decatur 39327-0129
Pres. Eddie M. Smith
(601) 635-2111

East Mississippi Community College
P.O. Box 158, Scooba 39358
Pres. Thomas L. Davis, Jr.
(601) 476-8442

Hinds Community College
Raymond 39154-0999
Pres. V. Clyde Muse
(601) 857-5261

Holmes Community College
P.O. Box 369, Goodman 39079
Pres. Starkey A. Morgan, Sr.
(601) 472-2312

Itawamba Community College
Hwy. 78, Fulton 38843-1099
Pres. Winston O. Benjamin
(601) 862-3101

Jones County Junior College
Ellisville 39437
Pres. Terrell Tisdale
(601) 477-4000

Mississippi

Meridian Community College
910 Hwy. 19 N., Meridian 39307
Pres. William F. Scaggs
(601) 483-8241

Mississippi Delta Community College
Hwy. 3, P.O. Box 668, Moorhead 38761
Interim Pres. Harmon W. Boggs
(601) 246-5631

Mississippi Gulf Coast Community College
P.O. Box 67, Perkinston 39573
Pres. Barry L. Mellinger
(601) 928-5211

Northeast Mississippi Community College
Cunningham Blvd., Booneville 38829
Pres. Joe M. Childers
(601) 728-7751

Northwest Mississippi Community College
510 N. Panola, Senatobia 38668
Pres. David M. Haraway
(601) 562-3200

Pearl River Community College
Hwy. 11 S., Sta. A, Poplarville 39470
Pres. Ted J. Alexander
(601) 795-6801

Southwest Mississippi Community College
College Dr., Summit 39666
Pres. Horace C. Holmes
(601) 276-2000

MISSOURI

Missouri Coordinating Board for Higher Education
101 Adams St., Jefferson City 65101
Commissioner Charles J. McClain
(314) 751-2361

Central Missouri State University
Warrensburg 64093
Pres. Ed M. Elliott
(816) 429-4112

Crowder College
Neosho 64850
Pres. Kent Farnsworth
(417) 451-3223

East Central College
P.O. Box 529, Union 63084
Pres. Dale L. Gibson
(314) 583-5193

Harris-Stowe State College
3026 Laclede Ave., St. Louis 63103
Pres. Henry Givens, Jr.
(314) 533-3366

Jefferson College
P.O. Box 1000, Hillsboro 63050-1000
Pres. Gery C. Hochanadel
(314) 789-3951

Lincoln University
820 Chestnut St., Jefferson City 65102-0029
Pres. Wendell G. Rayburn
(314) 681-5042

Metropolitan Community College District
3200 Broadway, Kansas City 64111
Chanc. William J. Mann
(816) 756-0220

Longview Community College
500 Longview Rd., Lee's Summit 64063
Pres. Aldo Leker
(816) 763-7777

Maple Woods Community College
2601 N.E. Barny Rd., Kansas City 64156-1299
Pres. Stephen R. Brainard
(816) 436-6500

Penn Valley Community College
3201 S.W. Trafficway, Kansas City 64111
Pres. E. Paul Williams
(816) 732-7600

Mineral Area College
Flat River 63601
Pres. Dixie A. Kohn
(314) 431-4593

Missouri Southern State College
3950 Newman Rd., Joplin 64801
Pres. Julio S. Leon
(417) 624-8181

Missouri Western State College
4525 Downs Dr., St. Joseph 64507
Pres. Janet G. Murphy
(816) 271-4200

Moberly Area Community College
Moberly 65270
Pres. Andrew Komar, Jr.
(816) 263-4110

Northeast Missouri State University
Kirksville 63501
Pres. Russell G. Warren
(816) 785-4000

Northwest Missouri State University
Maryville 64468
Pres. Dean L. Hubbard
(816) 562-1110

St. Charles County Community College
102 Compass Point Dr., Ste. L, St. Charles 63301
Pres. Donald D. Shook
(314) 723-1220

Missouri

St. Louis Community College District
300 S. Broadway, St. Louis 63102-1708
Pres. Gwendolyn W. Stephenson
(314) 539-5150

St. Louis Community College at Florissant Valley
3400 Pershall Rd., St. Louis 63135
Pres. Michael T. Murphy
(314) 595-4208

St. Louis Community College at Forest Park
5600 Oakland Ave., St. Louis 63110
Acting Pres. Henry D. Shannon
(314) 644-9743

St. Louis Community College at Meramec
11333 Big Bend Blvd., Kirkwood 63122
Acting Pres. Richard A. Black
(314) 984-7762

Southeast Missouri State University
One University Plaza, Cape Girardeau 63701
Pres. Kala M. Stroup
(314) 651-2000

Southwest Missouri State University
901 S. National Ave., Springfield 65804
Pres. Marshall Gordon
(417) 836-5000

State Fair Community College
3201 W. 16th St., Sedalia 65301
Pres. Marvin R. Fielding
(816) 826-7100

Three Rivers Community College
Three Rivers Blvd., Poplar Bluff 63901
Pres. Stephen M. Poort
(314) 686-4101

University of Missouri System
Columbia 65211
Pres. George A. Russell
(314) 882-2011

University of Missouri—Columbia
Columbia 65211
Interim Chanc. Gerald Brouder
(314) 882-3387

University of Missouri—Kansas City
5100 Rockhill Rd., Kansas City 64110
Interim Chanc. Eleanor B. Schwartz
(816) 235-1000

University of Missouri—Rolla
Rolla 65401
Interim Chanc. John T. Park
(314) 341-4114

University of Missouri—St. Louis
8001 Natural Bridge Rd., St. Louis 63121
Chanc. Blanche M. Touhill
(314) 553-5000

MONTANA

Montana Community College System
33 S. Last Chance Gulch, Helena 59620-2602
Coord. David L. Toppen
(406) 444-6570

Dawson Community College
Glendive 59330
Pres. Donald H. Kettner
(406) 365-3396

Flathead Valley Community College
Kalispell 59901
Pres. Howard L. Fryett
(406) 756-3822

Miles Community College
Miles City 59301
Pres. Judson H. Flower
(406) 232-3031

Montana University System
33 S. Last Chance Gulch, Helena 59620-2602
Commissioner John Hutchinson
(406) 444-6570

Eastern Montana College
Billings 59101
Pres. Bruce H. Carpenter
(406) 657-2011

Montana College of Mineral Science and Technology
Butte 59701
Pres. Lindsay D. Norman, Jr.
(406) 496-4101

Montana State University
Bozeman 59717
Pres. Michael Malone
(406) 994-0211

Northern Montana College
P.O. Box 7751, Havre 59501
Pres. William Daehling
(406) 265-3221

University of Montana
Missoula 59812
Pres. George Dennison
(406) 243-0211

Western Montana College
Dillon 59725
Provost W. Michael Easton
(406) 683-7151

Montana Vocational-Technical System
33 S. Last Chance Gulch, Helena 406-444-6570
Deputy Commissioner Brady J. Vardemann

Billings Vocational-Technical Center
3803 Central Ave., Billings 59102
Dir. George E. Bell
(406) 255-3801

Butte Vocational-Technical Center
Basin Creek Rd., Butte 59701
Dir. Harrison J. Freebourn
(406) 494-2894

Great Falls Vocational-Technical Center
2100 16th Ave., S., Great Falls 59405
Dir. Willard R. Weaver
(406) 771-1240

Helena Vocational-Technical Center
115 N. Roberts St., Helena 59620
Dir. Alex Capdeville
(406) 444-6800

Missoula Vocational-Technical Center
909 South Ave., W., Missoula 59801
Dir. Dennis N. Lerum
(406) 542-6811

NEBRASKA

Nebraska Coordinating Commission for Postsecondary Education
Capitol Bldg., 6th Fl., P.O. Box 95005, Lincoln 68509-5005
Exec. Dir. Bruce G. Stahl
(402) 471-2847

Central Community College
P.O. Box 4903, Grand Island 68802-4903
Pres. Joseph W. Preusser
(308) 384-5220

Chadron State College
10th and Maine Sts., Chadron 69337
Pres. Samuel H. Rankin, Jr.
(308) 432-4451

Metropolitan Community College
P.O. Box 3777, Omaha 68103-0777
Pres. J. Richard Gilliland
(402) 449-8415

Mid-Plains Community College Area
416 N. Jeffers, North Platte 69101
Pres. William G. Hasemeyer
(308) 534-9265

McCook Community College
McCook 69001
Pres. Robert E. Smallfoot
(308) 345-6303

Mid-Plains Community College
Rte. 4, Box 1, North Platte 69101
Pres. Kenneth L. Aten
(308) 532-8740

Northeast Community College
801 E. Benjamin Ave., P.O. Box 469, Norfolk 68702-0469
Pres. Robert P. Cox
(402) 371-2020

Southeast Community College Area
8800 O St., Lincoln 68520
Pres. Robert S. Eicher
(402) 471-3413

Southeast Community College—Beatrice Campus
Rte. 2, Box 35-A, Beatrice 68310
Dir. Kenneth E. Shibata
(402) 228-3468

Southeast Community College—Lincoln Campus
8800 O St., Lincoln 68520
Dir. Jack J. Huck, Ph.D.
(402) 471-3333

Southeast Community College—Milford Campus
Rte. 2, Box D, Milford 68405
Dir. Kenneth E. Shibata
(402) 761-2131

University of Nebraska Central Administrative Office
3835 Holdrege St., Lincoln 68583
Pres. Martin A. Massengale
(402) 472-2111

University of Nebraska Medical Center
42nd St. and Dewey Ave., Omaha 68105
Interim Chanc. William O. Berndt
(402) 559-4000

University of Nebraska at Kearney
905 W. 25th St., Kearney 68849
Chanc. William R. Nester
(308) 234-8208

University of Nebraska at Omaha
60th and Dodge Sts., Omaha 68182
Chanc. Delbert D. Weber
(402) 554-2311

University of Nebraska—Lincoln
Lincoln 68588
Chanc. Graham Spanier
(402) 472-2116

Public Systems of Higher Education **Nebraska**

Wayne State College
200 E. Tenth St., Wayne 68787
Pres. Donald J. Mash
(402) 375-2200

Western Nebraska Community College
1601 E. 27th St., Scottsbluff 69361
Pres. John N. Harms
(308) 635-3606

NEVADA

University of Nevada System
 2601 Enterprise Rd., Reno 89512
 Chanc. Mark H. Dawson
 (702) 784-4901

 Community College of Southern Nevada
  3200 E. Cheyenne Ave., North Las Vegas 89030
  Pres. Paul E. Meacham
  (702) 643-6060

 Northern Nevada Community College
  901 Elm St., Elko 89801
  Pres. Ronald Remington
  (702) 738-8493

 Truckee Meadows Community College
  7000 Dandini Blvd., Reno 89512
  Pres. John W. Gwaltney
  (702) 673-7000

 University of Nevada, Las Vegas
  4505 Maryland Pkwy., Las Vegas 89154
  Pres. Robert C. Maxson
  (702) 739-3201

 University of Nevada—Reno
  Reno 89557
  Pres. Joseph N. Crowley
  (702) 784-4941

 Western Nevada Community College
  2201 W. Nye La., Carson City 89703
  Pres. Anthony D. Calabro
  (702) 887-3000

NEW HAMPSHIRE

University System of New Hampshire
Dunlap Ctr., Durham 03824-3563
Chanc. Claire A. Van Ummersen
(603) 868-1800

Keene State College
229 Main St., Keene 03431
Pres. Judith A. Sturnick
(603) 352-1909

Plymouth State College
Plymouth 03264
Pres. William J. Farrell
(603) 535-5000

School for Lifelong Learning
Durham 03824
Dean Victor B. Montana
(603) 862-1692

University of New Hampshire
Durham 03824
Pres. Dale F. Nitzschke
(603) 862-1234

University of New Hampshire at Manchester
R.F.D. 4, Hackett Hill Rd.,
Manchester 03102
Dean Lewis Roberts, Jr.
(603) 668-0700

NEW JERSEY

New Jersey Department of Higher Education
20 W. State St., Trenton 08625
Chanc. Edward D. Goldberg
(609) 292-4310

Office of Community Colleges
20 W. State St., Trenton 08625
Dir. Marguerite A. Beardsley
(609) 984-2676

Atlantic Community College
Black Horse Pike, Mays Landing 08330
Pres. William A. Orth
(609) 625-1111

Bergen Community College
400 Paramus Rd., Paramus 07652
Pres. Jose Lopez-Isa
(201) 447-7100

Brookdale Community College
Newman Springs Rd., Lincroft 07738
Pres. Peter F. Burnham
(908) 842-1900

Burlington County College
Pemberton-Browns Mills Rd., Pemberton 08068
Pres. Robert C. Messina, Jr.
(609) 894-9311

Camden County College
P.O. Box 200, Blackwood 08012
Pres. Robert W. Ramsay
(609) 227-7200

County College of Morris
214 Center Grove Rd., Randolph 07869
Pres. Edward J. Yaw
(201) 361-5000

Cumberland County College
College Dr., P.O. Box 517, Vineland 08360
Pres. Roland J. Chapdelaine
(609) 691-8600

Essex County College
303 University Ave., Newark 07102
Pres. A. Zachary Yamba
(201) 877-3000

Gloucester County College
Tanyard Rd., Deptford Twp., Sewell 08080
Pres. Richard H. Jones
(609) 468-5000

Hudson County Community College
901 Bergen Ave., Jersey City 07306
Pres. Narcisa A. Polonio
(201) 714-2100

Mercer County Community College
1200 Old Trenton Rd., Trenton 08690
Pres. John P. Hanley
(609) 586-4800

Middlesex County College
155 Mill Rd., P.O. Box 3050, Edison 08818
Pres. Flora Mancuso-Edwards
(908) 548-6000

Ocean County College
College Dr., Toms River 08753
Pres. Milton Shaw
(908) 255-4000

Passaic County Community College
College Blvd., Paterson 07509
Pres. Elliott Collins
(201) 684-6800

Raritan Valley Community College
P.O. Box 3300, Somerville 08876
Pres. Charles S. Irace
(908) 526-1200

Salem Community College
460 Hollywood Ave., Carneys Point 08069
Pres. Philip O. Barry
(609) 299-2100

Public Systems of Higher Education — New Jersey

Union County College
1033 Springfield Ave., Cranford 07016
Pres. Thomas H. Brown, Ph.D.
(908) 709-7000

Office of Senior Institutions
20 W. State St., Trenton 08625
Dir. Sarah Kleinman
(609) 292-7170

Glassboro State College
Whitney Ave., Glassboro 08028
Pres. Herman D. James
(609) 863-5000

Jersey City State College
2039 Kennedy Blvd., Jersey City 07305
Pres. William J. Maxwell
(201) 547-6000

Kean College of New Jersey
Morris Ave., Union 07083
Pres. Elsa Gomez
(908) 527-2000

Montclair State College
Valley Rd. and Normal Ave., Upper Montclair 07043
Pres. Irvin D. Reid
(201) 893-4000

New Jersey Institute of Technology
323 High St., Newark 07102
Pres. Saul K. Fenster
(201) 596-3000

Ramapo College of New Jersey
505 Ramapo Valley Rd., Mahwah 07430
Pres. Robert A. Scott
(201) 529-7500

Richard Stockton State College
Jimmy Leeds Rd., Pomona 08240
Pres. Vera King Farris
(609) 652-1776

Rutgers, The State University of New Jersey Central Office
P.O. Box 2101, New Brunswick 08903
Pres. Francis L. Lawrence
(908) 932-1766

Rutgers, The State University of New Jersey—Camden
311 N. Fifth St., Camden 08102
Provost Walter K. Gordon
(609) 757-1766

Rutgers, The State University of New Jersey—New Brunswick
New Brunswick 08903
Provost Paul D. Leath
(908) 932-1766

Rutgers, The State University of New Jersey—Newark
15 Washington St., Newark 07102
Provost Norman Samuels
(201) 648-1766

Thomas A. Edison State College
101 W. State St., Trenton 08608
Pres. George A. Pruitt
(609) 984-1100

Trenton State College
Hillwood Lakes, Trenton 08650
Pres. Harold W. Eickhoff
(609) 771-1855

University of Medicine and Dentistry of New Jersey
30 Bergen St., Newark 07107
Pres. Stanley S. Bergen, Jr.
(201) 456-4300

William Paterson College of New Jersey
300 Pompton Rd., Wayne 07470
Pres. Arnold S. Speert
(201) 595-2000

NEW MEXICO

New Mexico Commission of Higher Education
1068 Cerrillos Rd., Santa Fe 87501-4295
Exec. Dir. Kathleen M. Kies
(505) 827-8300

Clovis Community College
417 Schepps Blvd., Clovis 88101
Provost Jay Gurley
(505) 769-2811

Eastern New Mexico University
Portales 88130
Pres. Everett Frost
(505) 562-2121

New Mexico Highlands University
National Ave., Las Vegas 87701
Pres. Gilbert Sanchez
(505) 425-7511

New Mexico Institute of Mining and Technology
Socorro 87801
Pres. Laurence H. Lattman
(505) 835-5600

New Mexico Junior College
5317 Lovington Hwy., Hobbs 88240
Pres. Charles D. Hays, Jr.
(505) 392-4510

New Mexico Military Institute
100 W. College Blvd., Roswell 88201
Supt. Winfield W. Scott, Jr.
(505) 624-8000

New Mexico State University System
Las Cruces 88003-0105
Pres. James E. Halligan
(505) 646-2035

New Mexico State University
Las Cruces 88003
Pres. James E. Halligan
(505) 646-2035

New Mexico State University at Alamogordo
P.O. Box 477, Alamogordo 88311-0477
Provost Charles R. Reidlinger
(505) 437-6860

New Mexico State University at Carlsbad
1500 University Dr., Carlsbad 88220
Provost Douglas Burgham
(505) 885-8831

Northern New Mexico Community College
1002 N. Onate St., Espanola 87532
Pres. Connie Valdez
(505) 753-7141

San Juan College
4601 College Blvd., Farmington 87402
Pres. James C. Henderson
(505) 326-3311

The University of New Mexico
Albuquerque 87131
Pres. Richard E. Peck
(505) 277-2626

Western New Mexico University
1000 W. College Ave., P.O. Box 680, Silver City 88062
Pres. Jerry L. Gallentine
(505) 538-6238

NEW YORK

City University of New York Central Administration
535 E. 80th St., New York 10021
Chanc. W. Ann Reynolds
(212) 794-5414

Bernard M. Baruch College
17 Lexington Ave., New York 10010
Pres. Matthew Goldstein
(212) 447-3000

Borough of Manhattan Community College
199 Chambers St., New York 10007
Pres. Augusta Souza Kappner
(212) 618-1000

Bronx Community College
University Ave. and W. 181st S,
Bronx 10453
Pres. Roscoe C. Brown, Jr.
(212) 220-6920

Brooklyn College
Bedford Ave. and Ave. H, Brooklyn 11210
Acting Pres. James N. Loughran, S.J.
(718) 780-5485

City College
Convent Ave. at 138th St., New York 10031
Pres. Bernard W. Harleston
(212) 690-6741

College of Staten Island
130 Stuyvesant Pl., Staten Island 10301
Pres. Edmond L. Volpe
(718) 390-7733

Graduate School and University Center
33 W. 42nd St., New York 10036
Pres. Frances D. Horowitz
(212) 642-1600

Herbert H. Lehman College
Bedford Park Blvd. W., Bronx 10468
Pres. Ricardo Fernandez
(212) 960-8881

Hostos Community College
475 Grand Concourse, Bronx 10451
Pres. Isaura Santiago
(212) 960-1200

Hunter College
695 Park Ave., New York 10021
Pres. Paul Le Clerc
(212) 772-4000

John Jay College of Criminal Justice
899 10th Ave., New York 10019
Pres. Gerald W. Lynch
(212) 237-8000

Kingsborough Community College
2001 Oriental Blvd., Manhattan Beach, Brooklyn 11235
Pres. Leon M. Goldstein
(718) 934-5000

La Guardia Community College
31-10 Thomson Ave., Long Island City 11101
Pres. Raymond C. Bowen
(718) 482-5700

Medgar Evers College
1150 Carroll St., Brooklyn 11225
Pres. Edison O. Jackson
(718) 270-4900

Mount Sinai School of Medicine
One Gustave L. Levy Pl., New York 10029
Dean John W. Rowe
(212) 650-6500

New York City Technical College
300 Jay St., Brooklyn 11201
Pres. Charles W. Meredith
(718) 643-4900

Queens College
65-30 Kissena Blvd., Flushing 11367
Pres. Shirley Strum-Kenny
(718) 520-7000

New York — Public Systems of Higher Education

Queensborough Community College
56th Ave. and Springfield Blvd,
Bayside 11364
Pres. Kurt R. Schmeller
(718) 631-6262

York College
94-20 Guy R. Brewer Blvd., Jamaica 11451
Pres. Josephine D. Davis
(718) 262-2000

State University of New York System Office
State University Plaza, Albany 12246
Chanc. D. Bruce Johnstone
(518) 443-5355

Empire State College
One Union Ave., Saratoga Springs 12866
Pres. James W. Hall
(518) 587-2100

Fashion Institute of Technology
Seventh Ave. at 27th St., New York 10001
Pres. Marvin J. Feldman
(212) 760-7660

Maritime College
Fort Schuyler, Bronx 10465
Pres. Floyd H. Miller, USN(Ret)
(212) 409-7200

State University of New York College at Brockport
Brockport 14420
Pres. John E. Van de Wetering
(716) 395-2211

State University of New York College at Buffalo
1300 Elmwood Ave., Buffalo 14222
Pres. F.C. Richardson
(716) 878-4000

State University of New York College at Cortland
P.O. Box 2000, Cortland 13045
Pres. James M. Clark
(607) 753-2201

State University of New York College at Fredonia
Fredonia 14063
Pres. Donald A. MacPhee
(716) 673-3111

State University of New York College at Geneseo
Geneseo 14454
Pres. Carol C. Harter
(716) 245-5211

State University of New York College at New Paltz
New Paltz 12561
Pres. Alice Chandler
(914) 257-2121

State University of New York College at Old Westbury
P.O. Box 210, Old Westbury 11568-0210
Pres. L. Eudora Pettigrew
(516) 876-3000

State University of New York College at Oneonta
Oneonta 13820
Pres. Alan B. Donovan
(607) 431-3500

State University of New York College at Oswego
Oswego 13126
Pres. Stephen L. Weber
(315) 341-2500

State University of New York College at Plattsburgh
Plattsburgh 12901
Pres. Charles O. Warren
(518) 564-2000

State University of New York College at Potsdam
Pierrepont Ave., Potsdam 13676
Pres. William C. Merwin
(315) 267-2000

Public Systems of Higher Education — New York

State University of New York College at Purchase
735 Anderson Hill Rd., Purchase 10577
Pres. Sheldon N. Grebstein
(914) 251-6000

State University of New York College of Agriculture and Technology at Cobleski
Cobleskill 12043
Pres. Cornelius V. Robbins
(518) 234-5011

State University of New York College of Agricultutre and Technology at Morrisv
Morrisville 13408
Pres. Frederick Woodward
(315) 684-6000

State University of New York College of Environmental Science and Forestry
Syracuse 13210
Pres. Ross S. Whaley
(315) 470-6500

State University of New York College of Optometry
100 E. 24th St., New York 10010
Pres. Alden N. Haffner
(212) 420-4900

State University of New York College of Technology at Alfred
Alfred 14802
Pres. John O. Hunter
(607) 587-4111

State University of New York College of Technology at Canton
Cornell Dr., Canton 13617
Pres. Earl W. MacArthur
(315) 386-7204

State University of New York College of Technology at Delhi
Delhi 13753
Pres. Mary Ellen Duncan
(607) 746-4111

State University of New York College of Technology at Farmingdale
Melville Rd., Farmingdale 11735
Pres. Frank A. Cipriani
(516) 420-2000

State University of New York Health Science Center at Brooklyn
450 Clarkson Ave., Brooklyn 11203
Pres. Donald J. Scherl
(718) 270-1000

State University of New York Health Science Center at Buffalo
Capen Hall, Buffalo 14260
Interim Pres. William R. Greiner
(716) 831-2000

State University of New York Health Science Center at Stony Brook
Stony Brook 11794
Pres. John H. Marburger, III
(516) 444-2101

State University of New York Health Science Center at Syracuse
750 E. Adams St., Syracuse 13210
Pres. John B. Henry
(315) 464-4570

State University of New York Institute of Technology at Utica/Rome
P.O. Box 3050, Utica 13504-3050
Pres. Peter J. Cayan
(315) 792-7100

State University of New York Office of Community Colleges
SUNY Plaza, Rm. T-705, Albany 12246
Deputy to Chanc. Thomas S. Kubala
(518) 443-5134

Adirondack Community College
Bay Rd., Glens Falls 12801
Pres. Roger C. Andersen
(518) 793-4491

Broome Community College
Upper Front St., P.O. Box 1017, Binghamton 13902
Pres. Donald A. Dellow
(607) 771-5000

Cayuga County Community College
Franklin St., Auburn 13021
Pres. Lawrence H. Poole
(315) 255-1743

New York

Public Systems of Higher Education

Clinton Community College
Bluff Point, Plattsburgh 12901
Pres. Jay L. Fennell
(518) 561-6650

Columbia-Greene Community College
P.O. Box 1000, Hudson 12534
Pres. Terry A. Cline
(518) 828-4181

Community College of the Finger Lakes
Lincoln Hill, Canandaigua 14424
Pres. Charles J. Meder
(716) 394-3500

Corning Community College
Spencer Hill, Corning 14830
Pres. Donald H. Hangen
(607) 962-9011

Dutchess Community College
53 Pendell Rd., Poughkeepsie 12601
Pres. Jerry A. Lee
(914) 471-4500

Erie Community College
121 Ellicott St., Buffalo 14203
Vice Pres. John E. Baker
(716) 842-2770

Fulton-Montgomery Community College
Rte. 67, Johnstown 12095
Pres. John G. Boshart
(518) 762-4651

Genesee Community College
One College Rd., Batavia 14020
Pres. Stuart Steiner
(716) 343-0055

Herkimer County Community College
100 Reservoir Rd., Herkimer 13350
Pres. Ronald F. Williams
(315) 866-0300

Hudson Valley Community College
80 Vandenburg Ave., Troy 12180
Pres. Joseph J. Bulmer
(518) 283-1100

Jamestown Community College
525 Falconer St., Jamestown 14701
Pres. Timothy G. Davies
(716) 665-5220

Jefferson Community College
Outer Coffeen St., Watertown 13601
Pres. John W. Deans
(315) 782-5250

Mohawk Valley Community College
1101 Sherman Dr., Utica 13501
Pres. Michael I. Schafer
(315) 792-5400

Monroe Community College
1000 E. Henrietta Rd., Rochester 14623
Pres. Peter A. Spina
(716) 424-5200

Nassau Community College
Stewart Ave., Garden City 11530
Pres. Sean A. Fanelli
(516) 222-7205

Niagara County Community College
3111 Saunders Settlement Rd., Sanborn 14132
Pres. Gerald L. Miller
(716) 731-3271

North Country Community College
20 Winona Ave., P.O. Box 89, Saranac Lake 12983
Pres. David W. Petty
(518) 891-2915

Onondaga Community College
Rte. 173, Syracuse 13215
Pres. Bruce H. Leslie
(315) 469-7741

Orange County Community College
 115 South St., Middletown
 10940
 Pres. William F. Messner
 (914) 344-6222

Rockland Community College
 145 College Rd., Suffern 10901
 Pres. F. Thomas Clark
 (914) 356-4650

Schenectady County Community College
 78 Washington Ave.,
  Schenectady 12305
 Interim Pres. Gabriel J. Basil
 (518) 346-6211

Suffolk Community College System
 533 College Rd., Selden 11784
 Pres. John F. Cooper
 (516) 451-4110

  Suffolk Community College Ammerman Campus
   533 College Rd., Selden 11784
   Exec. Dean William C. Hudson
   (516) 451-4110

  Suffolk Community College Eastern Campus
   Speonk-Riverhead Rd., Riverhead 11901
   Exec. Dean Steven T. Kenny
   (516) 369-2600

  Suffolk Community College Western Campus
   Crooked Hill Rd., Brentwood 11717
   Exec. Dean Salvatore LaLima
   (516) 434-6700

Sullivan County Community College
 College Rd., Loch Sheldrake 12759
 Pres. John F. Walter
 (914) 434-5750

Tompkins Cortland Community College
 170 North St., P.O. Box 139, Dryden 13053
 Pres. Eduardo J. Marti
 (607) 844-8211

Ulster County Community College
 Stone Ridge 12484
 Pres. Robert T. Brown
 (914) 687-5000

Westchester Community College
 75 Grasslands Rd., Valhalla 10595
 Pres. Joseph N. Hankin
 (914) 285-6600

State University of New York at Albany
 1400 Washington Ave., Albany 12222
 Pres. H. Patrick Swygert
 (518) 442-3300

State University of New York at Binghamton
 Binghamton 13901
 Pres. Lois B. DeFleur
 (607) 777-2000

State University of New York at Buffalo
 Capen Hall, Buffalo 14260
 Pres. William R. Greiner
 (716) 831-2000

State University of New York at Stony Brook
 Stony Brook 11794
 Pres. John H. Marburger, III
 (516) 632-6000

NORTH CAROLINA

North Carolina State Board of Community Colleges
200 W. Jones St., Raleigh 27603-1337
Pres. Robert W. Scott
(919) 733-7051

Alamance Community College
P.O. Box 8000, Haw River 27253-8000
Pres. W. Ronald McCarter
(919) 578-2002

Anson Community College
P.O. Box 68, Ansonville 28007
Pres. Edwin R. Chapman
(704) 826-8333

Asheville-Buncombe Technical Community College
340 Victoria Rd., Asheville 28801
Pres. K. Ray Bailey
(704) 254-1921

Beaufort County Community College
P.O. Box 1069, Washington 27889
Pres. U. Ronald Champion
(919) 946-6194

Bladen Community College
P.O. Box 266, Dublin 28332
Pres. Lynn G. King
(919) 862-2164

Blue Ridge Community College
Rte. 2, Box 133A, Flat Rock 28731-9624
Pres. David W. Sink, Jr.
(704) 692-3572

Brunswick Community College
P.O. Box 30, Supply 28462
Pres. W. Michael Reaves
(919) 754-6900

Caldwell Community College and Technical Institute
1000 Hickory Blvd., Hudson 28638
Pres. Eric B. McKeithan
(704) 726-2200

Cape Fear Community College
411 N. Front St., Wilmington 28401-3993
Pres. Richard C. Conrath
(919) 343-0481

Carteret Community College
3505 Arendell St., Morehead City 28557
Pres. Donald W. Bryant
(919) 247-6000

Catawba Valley Community College
Rte. 3, P.O. Box 283, Hickory 28602-9699
Pres. Cuyler A. Dunbar
(704) 327-7000

Central Carolina Community College
1105 Kelly Dr., Sanford 27330
Pres. Marvin R. Joyner
(919) 775-5401

Central Piedmont Community College
P.O. Box 35009, Charlotte 28235
Pres. Ruth G. Shaw
(704) 342-6633

Cleveland Community College
137 S. Post Rd., Shelby 28150
Pres. L. Steve Thornburg
(704) 484-4000

Coastal Carolina Community College
444 Western Blvd., Jacksonville 28546-6877
Pres. Ronald K. Lingle
(919) 455-1221

The College of the Albemarle
P.O. Box 2327, Elizabeth City 27906-2327
Pres. J. Parker Chesson, Jr.
(919) 335-0821

Craven Community College
S. Glenburnie Rd. at Coll. Ct., P.O. Box 885, New Bern 28563
Pres. Lewis S. Redd
(919) 638-4131

Public Systems of Higher Education — North Carolina

Davidson County Community College
P.O. Box 1287, Lexington 27293-1287
Pres. J. Bryan Brooks
(704) 249-8186

Durham Technical Community College
P.O. Drawer 11307, Durham 27703
Pres. Phail Wynn, Jr.
(919) 598-9222

Edgecombe Community College
2009 W. Wilson St., Tarboro 27886
Pres. Charles B. McIntyre
(919) 823-5166

Fayetteville Technical Community College
2201 Hull Rd., P.O. Box 35236, Fayetteville 28303-0236
Pres. Robert Craig Allen
(919) 678-8400

Forsyth Technical Community College
2100 Silas Creek Pkwy., Winston-Salem 27103-5197
Pres. Bob H. Greene
(919) 723-0371

Gaston College
201 Hwy. 321 S., Dallas 28034-1499
Pres. W. Wayne Scott
(704) 922-6200

Guilford Technical Community College
6300 High St., P.O. Box 309, Jamestown 27282
Pres. Donald W. Cameron
(919) 334-4822

Halifax Community College
P.O. Drawer 809, Weldon 27890
Pres. Elton L. Newbern, Jr.
(919) 536-2551

Haywood Community College
Freedlander Dr., Clyde 28721
Pres. Dan W. Moore
(704) 627-2821

Isothermal Community College
P.O. Box 804, Spindale 28160
Pres. Willard L. Lewis, III
(704) 286-3636

James Sprunt Community College
P.O. Box 398, Kenansville 28349-0398
Pres. Donald L. Reichard
(919) 296-1341

Johnston Community College
P.O. Box 2350, Smithfield 27577
Pres. John L. Tart
(919) 934-3051

Lenoir Community College
P.O. Box 188, Kinston 28502-0188
Pres. Lonnie H. Blizzard
(919) 527-6223

Martin Community College
Kehukee Park Rd., Williamston 27892-9988
Pres. Martin Nadelman
(919) 792-1521

McDowell Technical Community College
Rte. 1, Box 170, Marion 28752
Pres. Robert M. Boggs
(704) 652-6021

Mitchell Community College
500 W. Broad St., Statesville 28677-5293
Pres. Douglas Eason
(704) 878-3200

Montgomery Community College
P.O. Box 787, Troy 27371
Pres. Benny B. Hampton
(919) 572-3691

Nash Community College
P.O. Box 7488, Rocky Mount 27804-7488
Pres. J. Reid Parrott
(919) 443-4011

Pamlico Community College
Hwy. 306 S., P.O. Box 185, Grantsboro 28529
Pres. E. Douglas Kearney, Jr.
(919) 249-1851

Piedmont Community College
P.O. Box 1197, Roxboro 27573
Pres. H. James Owen
(919) 599-1181

Pitt Community College
P.O. Drawer 7007, Greenville 27835-7007
Pres. Charles E. Russell
(919) 355-4200

Randolph Community College
P.O. Box 1009, Asheboro 27204-1009
Pres. Larry K. Linker
(919) 629-1471

Richmond Community College
P.O. Box 1189, Hamlet 28345
Pres. Joseph W. Grimsley
(919) 582-7000

Roanoke-Chowan Community College
Rte. 2, Box 46-A, Ahoskie 27910
Pres. Harold E. Mitchell
(919) 332-5921

Robeson Community College
P.O. Box 1420, Lumberton 28359
Pres. Frederick G. Williams, Jr.
(919) 738-7101

Rockingham Community College
P.O. Box 38, Wentworth 27375-0038
Pres. N. Jerry Owens, Jr.
(919) 342-4261

Rowan-Cabarrus Community College
P.O. Box 1595, Salisbury 28144-1595
Pres. Richard L. Brownell
(704) 637-0760

Sampson Community College
P.O. Drawer 318, Clinton 28328
Pres. Clifton W. Paderick
(919) 592-8081

Sandhills Community College
2200 Airport Rd., Pinehurst 28374
Pres. John R. Dempsey
(919) 692-6185

Southeastern Community College
P.O. Box 151, Whiteville 28472
Pres. Stephen C. Scott
(919) 642-7141

Southwestern Community College
275 Webster Rd., Sylva 28779
Pres. Barry W. Russell
(704) 586-4091

Stanly Community College
Rte. 4, Box 55, Albemarle 28001
Pres. Jan J. Crawford
(704) 982-0121

Surry Community College
P.O. Box 304, Dobson 27017
Pres. Swanson Richards
(919) 386-8121

Tri-County Community College
P.O. Box 40, Murphy 28906
Pres. Vincent Crisp
(704) 837-6810

Vance-Granville Community College
Poplar Creek Rd., P.O. Box 917, Henderson 27536
Pres. Benjamin F. Currin
(919) 492-2061

Wake Technical Community College
9101 Fayetteville Rd., Raleigh 27603
Pres. Bruce I. Howell
(919) 772-0551

Wayne Community College
Caller Box 8002, Goldsboro 27533
Pres. G. Herman Porter
(919) 735-5151

Western Piedmont Community College
1001 Burkemont Ave., Morganton 28655-9978
Pres. James A. Richardson
(704) 438-6000

Wilkes Community College
Collegiate Dr., P.O. Box 120, Wilkesboro 28697-0120
Pres. James R. Randolph
(919) 651-8600

Wilson Technical Community College
P.O. Box 4305, Woodward Sta., Wilson 27893
Pres. Frank L. Eagles
(919) 291-1195

North Carolina

The University of North Carolina General Administration
P.O. Box 2688, Chapel Hill 27515-2688
Pres. C.D. Spangler, Jr.
(919) 962-1000

Appalachian State University
Boone 28608
Chanc. John E. Thomas
(704) 262-2000

East Carolina University
E. Fifth St., Greenville 27858-4353
Chanc. Richard R. Eakin
(919) 757-6131

Elizabeth City State University
Parkview Dr., Elizabeth City 27909
Chanc. Jimmy R. Jenkins
(919) 335-3400

Fayetteville State University
1200 Murchison Rd., Newbold Sta., Fayetteville 28301-4298
Chanc. Lloyd V. Hackley
(919) 486-1111

North Carolina Agricultural and Technical State University
1601 E. Market St., Greensboro 27411
Chanc. Edward B. Fort
(919) 334-7500

North Carolina Central University
1801 Fayetteville St., Durham 27707
Interim Chanc. Donna Benson
(919) 560-6100

North Carolina School of the Arts
200 Washington St., P.O. Box 12189, Winston-Salem 27117-2189
Chanc. Alexander C. Ewing
(919) 770-3399

North Carolina State University
P.O. Box 7001, Raleigh 27695
Chanc. Larry K. Monteith
(919) 737-2011

Pembroke State University
P.O. Box 1510, Pembroke 28372
Chanc. Joseph B. Oxendine
(919) 521-4214

The University of North Carolina at Asheville
One University Heights, Asheville 28804-3299
Chanc. Samuel Schuman
(704) 251-6600

The University of North Carolina at Chapel Hill
Chapel Hill 27599-9100
Chanc. Paul Hardin
(919) 962-2211

The University of North Carolina at Charlotte
University City Blvd., Charlotte 28223
Chanc. James H. Woodward, Jr.
(704) 547-2000

The University of North Carolina at Greensboro
1000 Spring Garden St., Greensboro 27412
Chanc. William E. Moran
(919) 334-5000

The University of North Carolina at Wilmington
601 S. College Rd., Wilmington 28403-3297
Chanc. James R. Leutze
(919) 395-3000

Western Carolina University
Cullowhee 28723
Chanc. Myron L. Coulter
(704) 227-7211

Winston-Salem State University
601 Martin Luther King Jr. Dr., Winston-Salem 27110
Chanc. Cleon F. Thompson, Jr.
(919) 750-2000

NORTH DAKOTA

North Dakota State Board of Higher Education
State Capitol Bldg., Bismarck 58505-0154
Pres. Sarlene Leinen
(701) 224-2960

North Dakota University System
State Capitol Bldg., 600 East Blvd., Bismarck 58505
Pres. Douglas Treadway
(701) 224-2960

Bismark State College
1500 Edwards Ave., Bismarck 58501
Pres. Kermit Lidstrom
(701) 224-5400

Dickinson State University
Dickinson 58601
Pres. Albert A. Watrel, Dr.
(701) 227-2507

Mayville State University
330 Third St., N.E., Mayville 58257
Pres. James A. Schobel
(701) 786-2301

Minot State University
Minot 58701
Pres. Gordon B. Olson
(701) 857-3300

North Dakota State College of Science
800 N. Sixth St., Wahpeton 58075
Pres. Jerry C. Olson
(701) 671-2221

North Dakota State University
Fargo 58105
Pres. Jim L. Ozbun
(701) 237-7211

North Dakota State University—Bottineau
First St. and Simrall Blvd., Bottineau 58318
Dean J.W. Smith
(701) 228-2277

University of North Dakota
Box 8193, University Sta., Grand Forks 58202-8193
Pres. Thomas J. Clifford
(701) 777-2121

University of North Dakota—Lake Region
N. College Dr., Devils Lake 58301
Exec. Dean Sharon L. Etemad
(701) 662-8683

University of North Dakota—Williston
P.O. Box 1326, Williston 58801
Exec. Dean Garvin L. Stevens
(701) 774-4200

Valley City State University
101 S.W. College St., Valley City 58072
Pres. Charles B. House, Jr.
(701) 845-7100

OHIO

Ohio Board of Regents
30 E. Broad St., 36th Fl., Columbus
43266-0417
Chanc. Elaine H. Hairston
(614) 466-6000

Belmont Technical College
120 Fox-Shannon Pl., St. Clairsville
43950
Pres. Wesley R. Channell
(614) 695-9500

Bowling Green State University
Bowling Green 43403
Pres. Paul J. Olscamp
(419) 372-2211

Central Ohio Technical College
University Dr., Newark 43055
Pres. Julius S. Greenstein
(614) 366-1351

Central State University
1400 Brush Row Rd., Wilberforce
45384-3002
Pres. Arthur E. Thomas
(513) 376-6332

Cincinnati Technical College
3520 Central Pkwy., Cincinnati 45223
Pres. James P. Long
(513) 569-1500

Clark State Community College
570 E. Leffels La., Post Office Box
570, Springfield 45505
Pres. Albert A. Salerno
(513) 325-0691

Cleveland State University
Euclid Ave. at East 24th St.,
Cleveland 44115-2403
Pres. John A. Flower
(216) 687-2000

Columbus State Community College
550 E. Spring St., Post Office Box
1609, Columbus 43216-1609
Pres. Harold M. Nestor
(614) 227-2400

Cuyahoga Community College
700 Carnegie Ave., Cleveland 44115
Pres. Jerry S. Owens
(216) 987-6000

Edison State Community College
1973 Edison Dr., Piqua 45356-9253
Pres. Kenneth A. Yowell
(513) 778-8600

Hocking Technical College
3101 Hocking Pkwy., Nelsonville
45764
Pres. John J. Light
(614) 753-3591

Jefferson Technical College
4000 Sunset Blvd., Steubenville 43952
Pres. Edward L. Florak
(614) 264-5591

Kent State University
Kent 44242
Pres. Carol A. Cartwright
(216) 672-2210

Lakeland Community College
7700 Clocktower Dr., Mentor 44060
Pres. Ralph R. Doty
(216) 953-7000

Lima Technical College
4240 Campus Dr., Lima 45804
Pres. James J. Countryman
(419) 222-8324

Lorain County Community College
1005 Abbe Rd., Elyria 44035
Pres. Roy A. Church
(216) 365-4191

Marion Technical College
1467 Mt. Vernon Ave., Marion 43302
Pres. John Richard Bryson
(614) 389-4636

Medical College of Ohio
P.O. Box 10008, Toledo 43699
Pres. Richard D. Ruppert
(419) 381-4260

Ohio

Miami University
  Oxford 45056
  Pres. Paul G. Pearson
  (513) 529-2345

The Michael J. Owens Technical College
  30335 Oregon Rd., Toledo 43699
  Pres. Daniel H. Brown
  (419) 666-0580

Muskingum Area Technical College
  1555 Newark Rd., Zanesville 43701
  Pres. Lynn H. Willett
  (614) 454-2501

North Central Technical College
  2441 Kenwood Cir., P.O. Box 698,
    Mansfield 44901-0698
  Pres. Byron E. Kee
  (419) 755-4800

Northeastern Ohio Universities College of
    Medicine
  4209 State Rte. 44, P.O. Box 95,
    Rootstown 44272-0095
  Pres./Dean Colin Campbell
  (216) 325-2511

Northwest Technical College
  Rte. 1, Box 246-A, Archbold 43502
  Pres. Larry G. McDougle
  (419) 267-5511

The Ohio State University
  Columbus 43210
  Pres. E. Gordon Gee
  (614) 292-2424

Ohio University
  Athens 45701
  Pres. Charles J. Ping
  (614) 593-1000

Shawnee State University
  940 Second St., Portsmouth 45662
  Pres. Clive C. Veri
  (614) 355-2202

Sinclair Community College
  444 W. Third St., Dayton 45402
  Pres. David H. Ponitz
  (513) 226-2525

Southern State Community College
  200 Hobart Dr., Hillsboro 45133
  Pres. George R. McCormick
  (513) 393-3431

Stark Technical College
  6200 Frank Ave., N.W., Canton
    44720
  Pres. John J. McGrath, Jr.
  (216) 494-6170

Terra Technical College
  2830 Napoleon Rd., Fremont 43420-
    9670
  Pres. Richard M. Simon
  (419) 334-8400

The University of Akron
  302 E. Buchtel Ave., Akron 44325
  Pres. William V. Muse
  (216) 972-7074

University of Cincinnati
  2624 Clifton Ave., Cincinnati 45221
  Pres. Joseph A. Steger
  (513) 556-2201

University of Toledo
  2801 W. Bancroft St., Toledo 43606
  Pres. Frank E. Horton
  (419) 537-2211

Washington State Community College
  710 Colegate Dr., Marietta 45750
  Pres. Carson K. Miller
  (614) 374-8716

Wright State University
  9035 Colonel Glenn Hwy., Dayton
    45435
  Pres. Paige E. Mulhollan
  (513) 873-2312

Youngstown State University
  410 Wick Ave., Youngstown 44555
  Pres. Neil D. Humphrey
  (216) 742-3101

OKLAHOMA

Oklahoma State Regents for Higher Education
500 Education Bldg., State Capitol Complex, Oklahoma City 73105-4503
Chanc. Hans Brisch
(405) 524-9100

Cameron University
2800 Gore Blvd., Lawton 73505
Pres. Don Davis
(405) 581-2201

Carl Albert State College
1507 S. McKenna, Poteau 74953-5208
Pres. Joe E. White
(918) 647-8660

Connors State College
Rte. 1, Box 1000, Warner 74469
Pres. Carl O. Westbrook
(918) 463-2931

East Central University
Ada 74820
Pres. Bill S. Cole
(405) 332-8000

Eastern Oklahoma State College
1301 W. Main St., Wilburton 74578
Pres. Bill H. Hill
(918) 465-2361

Langston University
P.O. Box 907, Langston 73050-0907
Pres. Ernest L. Holloway
(405) 466-2231

Murray State College
Tishomingo 73460
Pres. Clyde R. Kindell
(405) 371-2371

Northeastern Oklahoma A&M College
Second and I Sts., N.E., Miami 74354
Pres. Bobby R. Wright
(918) 542-8441

Northeastern State University
Tahlequah 74464
Pres. W. Roger Webb
(918) 456-5511

Northern Oklahoma College
P.O. Box 310, Tonkawa 74653-0310
Pres. Edward E. Vineyard
(405) 628-2581

Northwestern State University
705 Oklahoma Blvd., Alva 73717
Pres. Joe J. Struckle
(405) 327-1700

Oklahoma City Community College
7777 S. May Ave., Oklahoma City 73159
Pres. Bob D. Gaines
(405) 682-7503

Oklahoma Panhandle State University
P.O. Box 430, Goodwell 73939
Pres. Theodore W. Wischropp
(405) 349-2610

Oklahoma State University System
Stillwater 74078
Pres. John R. Campbell
(405) 744-6834

Oklahoma State University
Stillwater 74078
Pres. John R. Campbell
(405) 744-6834

Oklahoma State University College of Osteopathic Medicine
1111 W. 17th St., Tulsa 74107
Provost/Dean Thomas Wesley Allen
(918) 582-1972

Oklahoma State University— Oklahoma City
900 N. Portland Ave., Oklahoma City 73107
Dir. James E. Hooper
(405) 947-4421

Oklahoma — Public Systems of Higher Education

Oklahoma State University—Okmulgee
1801 E. Fourth St., Okmulgee 74447
Dir. Robert Klabenes
(918) 756-6211

Redlands Community College
P.O. Box 370, El Reno 73036-0370
Pres. Larry F. Devane
(405) 262-2552

Rogers State College
Claremore 74017
Pres. Richard H. Mosier
(918) 341-7510

Rose State College
6420 S.E. 15th St., Midwest City 73110
Pres. Larry Nutter
(405) 733-7300

Seminole Junior College
P.O. Box 351, Seminole 74868-0351
Pres. James J. Cook
(405) 382-9950

Southeastern Oklahoma State University
Durant 74701
Pres. Larry Williams
(405) 924-0121

Southwestern Oklahoma State University
100 Campus Dr., Weatherford 73096
Pres. Joe Anna Hibler
(405) 772-6611

Tulsa Junior College
6111 E. Skelly Dr., Tulsa 74135-6101
Pres. Dean P. Van Trease
(918) 622-5100

University of Central Oklahoma
100 N. University Dr., Edmond 73060
Pres. William J. Lillard
(405) 341-2980

University of Oklahoma Central Office
660 Parrington Oval, Norman 73019
Pres. Richard L. Van Horn
(405) 325-3916

University of Oklahoma
660 Parrington Oval, Norman 73019
Pres. Richard L. Van Horn
(405) 325-3916

University of Oklahoma Health Sciences Center
P.O. Box 26901, Oklahoma City 73126-0901
Provost Clayton Rich
(405) 271-4000

University of Science and Arts of Oklahoma
P.O. Box 82345, Chickasha 73018
Pres. Roy Troutt
(405) 224-3140

Western Oklahoma State College
2801 N. Main St., Altus 73521
Pres. Stephen R. Hensley
(405) 477-2000

Public Systems of Higher Education Oregon

OREGON

Oregon State Board of Education, Office of Community College Services
700 Pringle Pkwy., S.E., Salem 97310
Commissioner Mike Holland
(503) 378-8515

Blue Mountain Community College
P.O. Box 100, Pendleton 97801
Pres. Ronald L. Daniels
(503) 276-1260

Central Oregon Community College
Bend 97701-5998
Pres. Robert Barber
(503) 385-6112

Chemeketa Community College
P.O. Box 14007, Salem 97309
Pres. William E. Segura
(503) 399-5000

Clackamas Community College
19600 S. Molalla Ave., Oregon City 97045
Pres. John S. Keyser
(503) 657-6958

Clatsop Community College
1653 Jerome Ave., Astoria 97103
Pres. Doreen D. Dailey
(503) 325-0910

Lane Community College
Eugene 97405
Pres. Jerry Moskus
(503) 747-4501

Linn-Benton Community College
Albany 97321
Pres. Jon Carnahan
(503) 967-6100

Mount Hood Community College
26000 S.E. Stark St., Gresham 97030
Pres. Paul E. Kreider
(503) 667-6422

Portland Community College
P.O. Box 19000, Portland 97219-0990
Pres. Daniel F. Moriarty
(503) 244-6111

Rogue Community College
3345 Redwood Hwy., Grants Pass 97527
Pres. Harvey Bennett
(503) 479-5541

Southwestern Oregon Community College
Coos Bay 97420
Pres. Steven Kridelbaugh
(503) 888-2525

Treasure Valley Community College
Ontario 97914
Pres. Glenn E. Mayle
(503) 889-6493

Umpqua Community College
Roseburg 97470
Pres. James M. Kraby
(503) 440-4600

Oregon State System of Higher Education
P.O. Box 3175, Eugene 97403-0175
Chanc. Thomas A. Bartlett
(503) 346-5700

Eastern Oregon State College
La Grande 97850
Pres. David E. Gilbert
(503) 962-3512

Oregon Health Sciences University
3181 S.W. Sam Jackson Park Rd., Portland 97201
Pres. Peter O. Kohler, M.D.
(503) 494-8252

Oregon Institute of Technology
Klamath Falls 97601-8801
Pres. Lawrence J. Wolf
(503) 885-1103

Oregon State University
Corvallis 97331
Pres. John V. Byrne
(503) 737-2565

Portland State University
P.O. Box 751, Portland 97207
Pres. Judith A. Ramaley
(503) 725-4419

Oregon　　　　　　　　　　　　　　　　　　　　　　　**Public Systems of Higher Education**

Southern Oregon State College
Ashland 97520
Pres. Joseph W. Cox
(503) 552-6111

University of Oregon
Eugene 97403-1226
Pres. Myles Brand
(503) 346-3036

Western Oregon State College
Monmouth 97361
Pres. Richard S. Meyers
(503) 838-8215

PENNSYLVANIA

Pennsylvania State System of Higher Education
301 Market St., P.O. Box 809, Harrisburg 17108
Chanc. James H. McCormick
(717) 783-8887

Bloomsburg University of Pennsylvania
Bloomsburg 17815
Pres. Harry Ausprich
(717) 389-4000

Bucks County Community College
Swamp Rd., Newtown 18940
Interim Pres. Charles E. Rollins
(215) 968-8000

Butler County Community College
College Dr., Oak Hills, Butler 16001
Pres. Thaddeus H. Penar
(412) 287-8711

California University of Pennsylvania
Third St., California 15419
Pres. John P. Watkins
(412) 938-4000

Cheyney University of Pennsylvania
Cheney and Creek Rds., Cheyney 19319
Interim Pres. Valarie Swain Cade
(215) 399-2000

Clarion University of Pennsylvania
Clarion 16214
Pres. Diane L. Reinhard
(814) 226-2000

Community College of Allegheny County
800 Allegheny Ave., Pittsburgh 15233
Pres. John M. Kingsmore
(412) 323-2323

Community College of Allegheny County Allegheny Campus
808 Ridge Ave., Pittsburgh 15212
Exec. Dean/Vice Pres. J. David Griffin
(412) 237-2525

Community College of Allegheny County Boyce Campus
595 Beatty Rd., Monroeville 15146
Exec. Dean/Vice Pres. Carl A. DiSibio
(412) 327-1327

Community College of Allegheny County College Center North
111 Pines Plaza, 1130 Perry Hwy., Pittsburgh 15237
Exec. Dean/Vice Pres. Fred F. Bartok
(412) 366-7000

Community College of Allegheny County South Campus
1750 Clairton Rd., Rte. 885, West Mifflin 15122
Exec. Dean/Vice Pres. Thomas A. Juravich
(412) 469-1100

Community College of Beaver County
College Dr., Monaca 15061
Pres. Margaret J. Williams
(412) 775-8561

Community College of Philadelphia
1700 Spring Garden St., Philadelphia 19130
Pres. Ronald J. Temple
(215) 751-8000

Delaware County Community College
Rte. 252 and Media Line Rd., Media 19063
Pres. Richard D. DeCosmo
(215) 359-5000

East Stroudsburg University of Pennsylvania
East Stroudsburg 18301
Pres. James E. Gilbert
(717) 424-3545

Edinboro University of Pennsylvania
Edinboro 16444
Pres. Foster F. Diebold
(814) 732-2000

Pennsylvania

Harrisburg Area Community College
3300 Cameron Street Rd., Harrisburg 17110
Pres. Kenneth B. Woodbury, Jr.
(717) 780-2300

Indiana University of Pennsylvania
Indiana 15705
Interim Pres. Charles R. Fuget
(412) 357-2100

Kutztown University of Pennsylvania
Kutztown 19530
Pres. David E. McFarland
(215) 683-4000

Lehigh County Community College
2370 Main St., Schnecksville 18078
Pres. Robert L. Barthlow
(215) 799-2121

Lock Haven University of Pennsylvania
Lock Haven 17745
Pres. Craig D. Willis
(717) 893-2011

Luzerne County Community College
Prospect St. and Middle Rd., Nanticoke 18634
Pres. Thomas J. Moran
(717) 829-7300

Mansfield University of Pennsylvania
Mansfield 16933
Pres. Rodney C. Kelchner
(717) 662-4000

Millersville University of Pennsylvania
Millersville 17551
Pres. Joseph A. Caputo
(717) 872-3011

Montgomery County Community College
340 DeKalb Pike, Blue Bell 19422
Pres. Edward M. Sweitzer
(215) 641-6300

Northampton Community College
3835 Green Pond Rd., Bethlehem 18017
Pres. Robert J. Kopecek
(215) 861-5300

Public Systems of Higher Education

Pennsylvania State University Central Office
308 Old Main, University Park 16802
Pres. Joab L. Thomas
(814) 865-4700

Pennsylvania College of Technology
One College Ave., Williamsport 17701
Pres. Robert L. Breuder
(717) 326-3761

Pennsylvania State University
201 Old Main, University Park 16802
Exec. Vice Pres./Provost John A. Brighton
(814) 865-4700

Reading Area Community College
P.O. Box 1706, Reading 19603
Pres. Gust Zogas
(215) 372-4721

Shippensburg University of Pennsylvania
Shippensburg 17257
Pres. Anthony F. Ceddia
(717) 532-9121

Slippery Rock University of Pennsylvania
Slippery Rock 16057
Pres. Robert N. Aebersold
(412) 738-5425

Temple University
Broad St. and Montgomery Ave., Philadelphia 19122
Pres. Peter J. Liacouras
(215) 787-7000

University of Pittsburgh
4200 Fifth Ave., Pittsburgh 15260
Pres. Wesley W. Posvar
(412) 624-4141

West Chester University of Pennsylvania
S. High St., West Chester 19383
Interim Pres. Stanley J. Yarosewick
(215) 436-1000

Westmoreland County Community College
Ambrust Rd., Youngwood 15697
Pres. Daniel C. Krezenski
(412) 925-4000

PUERTO RICO

Universidad Interamericana de Puerto Rico Central Office
G.P.O. Box 3255, San Juan 00936
Pres. Jose A. Gonzalez
(809) 766-1912

Aguadilla Regional College
Call Box 20000, Aguadilla 00605
Dean/Dir. Hilda M. Baco
(809) 891-0925

Arecibo University College
Call Box UI, Arecibo 00613
Dean/Dir. Maria De Los A. Ortiz
(809) 878-5475

Barranquitas Regional College
Barranquitas 00794
Dir. Vidal Rivera-Garcia
(809) 857-4040

Bayamon University College
Rd. 174, Minillas Industrial Park, Bayamon 00619
Dean/Dir. Felix Torres-Leon
(809) 780-4040

Fajardo Regional College
P.O. Box 1029, Fajardo 00648
Dir. Yolanda Robles-Garcia
(809) 863-2390

Guayama Regional College
P.O. Box 1559, Guayama 00654
Dir. Samuel Febres-Santiago
(809) 864-2222

Ponce Regional College
Mercidita Sta., Ponce 00715
Dean/Dir. Marilina L. Wayland
(809) 840-9090

Universidad Interamericana de Puerto Rico
Harris Dr., Call Box 5100, San German 00753
Chanc. Federico Matheu
(809) 892-1095

University of Puerto Rico Central Office
G.P.O. Box 4984, San Juan 00936-4984
Pres. Jose M. Saldana
(809) 250-0000

Cayey University College
Antonio R. Barcelo Ave., Cayey 00736
Chanc. Margarita Benitez
(809) 738-2161

Humacao University College
CUH Sta., Humacao 00661
Chanc. Felix A. Castrodad
(809) 850-0000

University of Puerto Rico
Ponce de Leon Ave., P.O. Box 3300, U.P.R. Sta., Rio Piedras 00931
Chanc. Juan R. Fernandez
(809) 764-0000

University of Puerto Rico Regional Colleges Administration
P.O. Box 21876, U.P.R. Sta., San Juan 00931-1876
Chanc. Ivette Ramos Buonomo
(809) 758-3454

Aguadilla Regional College
P.O. Box 160, Ramey 00604
Dean/Dir. Miguel Gonzalez
(809) 890-2681

Arecibo Technological University College
P.O. Box A-4010, Arecibo 00613
Interim Dean/Dir. Hector Otero Burgos
(809) 878-2830

Bayamon Technological University College
Bayamon 00619-1919
Dean/Dir. Aida Canals de Bird
(809) 786-2885

Carolina Regional College
P.O. Box 4800, Carolina 00984
Dean/Dir. Andres Rodriguez Rubio
(809) 757-2000

Puerto Rico   **Public Systems of Higher Education**

La Montaña Regional College
  P.O. Box 2500, Utuado 00761
  Dean/Dir. Felix Aponte Perez
  (809) 894-2828

Ponce Technological University College
  P.O. Box 7186, Ponce 00731
  Dean/Dir. Pedro E. Laboy-Zengotita
  (809) 844-8181

RHODE ISLAND

Rhode Island Office of Higher Education
301 Promenade St., Providence 02908
Commissioner Americo W. Petrocelli, Ph.D.
(401) 277-6560

Community College of Rhode Island
400 East Ave., Warwick 02886-1805
Pres. Edward J. Liston
(401) 825-1000

Rhode Island College
Providence 02908
Pres. John Nazarian
(401) 456-8000

University of Rhode Island
Kingston 02881
Pres. Robert L. Carothers
(401) 792-1000

SOUTH CAROLINA

South Carolina Commission on Higher Education
1333 Main St., Ste. 300, Columbia 29201
Commissioner Fred R. Sheheen
(803) 253-6260

The Citadel
Citadel Sta., Charleston 29409
Pres. Claudius E. Watts, III
(803) 792-5000

Clemson University
Clemson 29634-5310
Pres. Max A. Lennon
(803) 656-3311

College of Charleston
66 George St., Charleston 29424
Pres. Harry M. Lightsey, Jr.
(803) 792-5500

Francis Marion College
P.O. Box 100547, Florence 29501-0547
Pres. Thomas C. Stanton
(803) 661-1362

Lander College
Stanley Ave., Greenwood 29649
Pres. Larry A. Jackson
(803) 229-8300

Medical University of South Carolina
171 Ashley Ave., Charleston 29425
Pres. James B. Edwards
(803) 792-4196

South Carolina State College
300 College Ave., Orangeburg 29117
Interim Pres. Carl A. Carpenter
(803) 536-7000

University of South Carolina Central Office
Columbia 29208
Pres. John M. Palms
(803) 777-7000

University of South Carolina—Aiken
171 University Pkwy., Aiken 29801
Chanc. Robert E. Alexander
(803) 648-6851

University of South Carolina—Beaufort
800 Carteret St., Beaufort 29902
Dean Chris Plyler
(803) 524-7112

University of South Carolina—Coastal Carolina
P.O. Box 1954, Conway 29526
Chanc. Ronald G. Eaglin
(803) 347-3161

University of South Carolina—Columbia
Columbia 29208
Pres. John M. Palms
(803) 777-2001

University of South Carolina—Lancaster
P.O. Box 889, Lancaster 29721
Dean John R. Arnold
(803) 285-7471

University of South Carolina—Salkehatchie
P.O. Box 617, Allendale 29810
Dean Carl A. Clayton
(803) 584-3446

University of South Carolina—Spartanburg
800 University Way, Spartanburg 29303
Chanc. Olin B. Sansbury, Jr.
(803) 599-2000

University of South Carolina—Sumter
200 Miller Rd., Sumter 29150
Dean Jack C. Anderson, Jr.
(803) 775-6341

Public Systems of Higher Education   **South Carolina**

University of South Carolina—Union
P.O. Drawer 729, Union 29379
Dean Kenneth L. Davis
(803) 429-8728

Winthrop College
701 Oakland Ave., Rock Hill 29733
Pres. Anthony J. DiGiorgio
(803) 323-2211

South Carolina State Board for Technical and Comprehensive Education
111 Executive Center Dr., Columbia 29210
Exec. Dir. James R. Morris, Jr.
(803) 737-9320

Aiken Technical College
P.O. Box 696, Aiken 29802-0696
Pres. Paul L. Blowers
(803) 593-9231

Chesterfield-Marlboro Technical College
1201 Chesterfield Hwy., No. 9 W., P.O. Drawer 1007, Cheraw 29520-1007
Pres. Ronald W. Hampton
(803) 537-5286

Denmark Technical College
Solomon Blatt Blvd., P.O. Box 327, Denmark 29042-0327
Pres. Curtis E. Bryan
(803) 793-3301

Florence-Darlington Technical College
P.O. Box 100548, Florence 29501-0548
Pres. Michael B. McCall
(803) 661-8324

Greenville Technical College
P.O. Box 5616, Sta. B, Greenville 29606-5616
Pres. Thomas E. Barton, Jr.
(803) 250-8000

Horry-Georgetown Technical College
P.O. Box 1966, Conway 29526
Pres. D. Kent Sharples
(803) 347-3186

Midlands Technical College
P.O. Box 2408, Columbia 29202
Pres. James L. Hudgins
(803) 738-1400

Orangeburg-Calhoun Technical College
3250 St. Mathews Rd., Orangeburg 29115
Pres. M. Rudolph Groomes
(803) 536-0311

Piedmont Technical College
P.O. Box 1467, Greenwood 29648
Pres. Lex D. Walters
(803) 223-8357

Spartanburg Technical College
P.O. Drawer 4386, Spartanburg 29305-4386
Pres. Jack A. Powers
(803) 591-3600

Sumter Area Technical College
506 N. Guignard Dr., Sumter 29150
Pres. Herbert C. Robbins
(803) 778-1961

Technical College of the Lowcountry
100 S. Ribaut Rd., Beaufort 29902
Pres. Anne S. McNutt
(803) 525-8246

Tri-County Technical College
Hwy. 76, P.O. Box 58, Pendleton 29670
Pres. Don C. Garrison
(803) 646-8361

Trident Technical College
P.O. Box 10367, Charleston 29411
Pres. Mary H. Dellamura
(803) 572-6111

Williamsburg Technical College
601 Lane Rd., Kingstree 29556-4197
Pres. John T. Wynn
(803) 354-7423

York Technical College
452 S. Anderson Rd., Rock Hill 29730
Pres. Dennis F. Merrell
(803) 327-8000

SOUTH DAKOTA

South Dakota Board of Regents
207 E. Capitol Ave., Pierre 57501-2291
Exec. Dir. Howell W. Todd
(605) 773-3455

Black Hills State University
1200 University Ave., Spearfish 57799-9500
Pres. Clifford M. Trump
(605) 642-6111

Dakota State University
820 N. Washington St., Madison 57042
Pres. Jerald A. Tunheim
(605) 256-5112

Northern State University
12th Ave. and Jay St., Aberdeen 57401
Pres. Terence Brown
(605) 622-2521

South Dakota School of Mines and Technology
501 E. St. Joseph St., Rapid City 57701
Pres. Richard J. Gowen
(605) 394-2256

South Dakota State University
P.O. Box 2201, University Sta., Brookings 57007
Pres. Robert T. Wagner
(605) 688-4173

University of South Dakota
414 E. Clark St., Vermillion 57069-2390
Pres. Betty Turner Asher
(605) 677-5641

TENNESSEE

Tennessee Board of Regents
1415 Murfreesboro Rd., Ste. 350,
Nashville 37219
Chanc. Otis L. Floyd
(615) 366-4403

Austin Peay State University
601 College St., Clarksville 37044
Pres. Oscar C. Page
(615) 648-7011

Chattanooga State Technical Community College
4501 Amnicola Hwy., Chattanooga 37406
Pres. James L. Catanzaro
(615) 697-4400

Cleveland State Community College
Adkisson Dr., P.O. Box 3570, Cleveland 37320-3570
Pres. James W. Ford
(615) 472-7141

Columbia State Community College
P.O. Box 1315, Columbia 38402-1315
Pres. L. Paul Sands
(615) 388-0120

Dyersburg State Community College
Lake Rd., Dyersburg 38024
Pres. Karen A. Bowyer
(901) 286-3200

East Tennessee State University
P.O. Box 19330, Johnson City 37614
Interim Pres. Bert C. Bach
(615) 929-4112

Jackson State Community College
2046 North Pkwy., Jackson 38301-3797
Pres. Walter L. Nelms
(901) 424-3520

Memphis State University
Memphis 38152
Pres. V. Lane Rawlins
(901) 678-2000

Middle Tennessee State University
Murfreesboro 37132
Pres. James Walker
(615) 898-2300

Motlow State Community College
P.O. Box 88100, Tullahoma 37388-8100
Pres. A. Frank Glass
(615) 455-8511

Nashville State Technical Institute
120 White Bridge Rd., Nashville 37209
Pres. Richard M. Turner, III
(615) 353-3333

Northeast State Technical Community College
2425 Hwy. 75, P.O. Box 246, Blountville 37617-0246
Pres. R. Wade Powers
(615) 323-3191

Pellissippi State Technical Community College
10915 Hardin Valley Rd., P.O. Box 22990, Knoxville 37933-0990
Pres. J.L. Goins
(615) 694-6400

Roane State Community College
Patton La., Harriman 37748
Pres. Sherry L. Hoppe
(615) 354-3000

Shelby State Community College
P.O. Box 40568, Memphis 38174-0568
Pres. Lawrence M. Cox
(901) 528-6700

State Technical Institute at Memphis
5983 Macon Cove, Memphis 38134-7693
Pres. Charles M. Temple
(901) 377-4100

Tennessee

Tennessee State University
3500 John Merritt Blvd., Nashville
37209-1561
Pres. James A. Hefner
(615) 320-3131

Tennessee Technological University
N. Dixie Ave., Cookeville 38505
Pres. Angelo A. Volpe
(615) 372-3101

Volunteer State Community College
1360 Nashville Pike, Gallatin 37066-3188
Pres. Hal R. Ramer
(615) 452-8600

Walters State Community College
500 S. Davy Crockett Pkwy., Morristown 37813-6899
Pres. Jack E. Campbell
(615) 587-9722

The University of Tennessee System
Knoxville 37916
Pres. Joseph E. Johnson
(615) 974-1000

The University of Tennessee at Chattanooga
615 McCallie Ave., Chattanooga
37403-2598
Chanc. Frederick W. Obear
(615) 744-4111

The University of Tennessee at Martin
University Ave., Martin 38238
Chanc. Margaret N. Perry
(901) 587-7000

The University of Tennessee, Knoxville
527 Andy Holt Tower, Knoxville
37996-0150
Chanc. John J. Quinn
(615) 974-1000

The University of Tennessee, Memphis
800 Madison Ave., Memphis 38163
Chanc. James C. Hunt
(901) 528-5500

TEXAS

Texas Higher Education Coordinating Board
P.O. Box 12788, Capitol Sta., Austin 78711
Commissioner Kenneth H. Ashworth
(512) 483-6100

Alamo Community College District
811 W. Houston St., San Antonio 78284
Chanc. Ivory V. Nelson
(512) 220-1500

Palo Alto College
1400 W. Villaret Blvd., San Antonio 78224
Pres. Byron Skinner
(512) 921-5000

St. Philip's College
2111 Nevada St., San Antonio 78203
Pres. Stephen R. Mitchell
(512) 531-3200

San Antonio College
1300 San Pedro Ave., San Antonio 78212
Pres. Max Castillo
(512) 733-2000

Alvin Community College
3110 Mustang Rd., Alvin 77511-4898
Pres. A. Rodney Allbright
(713) 331-6111

Amarillo College
2201 S. Washington St., P.O. Box 447, Amarillo 79178
Pres. George T. Miller
(806) 371-5000

Angelina College
Hwy. 59 S., Lufkin 75902
Pres. Larry Phillips
(409) 639-1301

Austin Community College
P.O. Box 140526, Austin 78714
Pres. Daniel D. Angel
(512) 483-7000

Bee County College
3800 Charco Rd., Beeville 78102
Pres. Norman E. Wallace
(512) 358-3130

Blinn College
902 College Ave., Brenham 77833
Pres. Walter C. Schwartz
(409) 830-4000

Brazosport College
500 College Dr., Lake Jackson 77566
Pres. John R. Grable
(409) 265-6131

Central Texas College
P.O. Box 1800, Killeen 76540-9990
Chanc. James R. Anderson
(817) 526-7161

Cisco Junior College
Rte. 3, Box 3, Cisco 76437
Pres. Roger C. Schustereit
(817) 442-2567

Clarendon College
P.O. Box 968, Clarendon 79226
Pres. Jerry D. Stockton
(806) 874-3571

College of the Mainland
1200 Amburn Rd., Texas City 77591
Pres. Larry L. Stanley
(713) 938-1211

Collin County Community College
2200 W. University Dr., McKinney 75070
Pres. John H. Anthony
(214) 548-6790

Cooke County College
1525 W. California St., Gainesville 76240-4699
Pres. Luther Bud Joyner
(817) 668-7731

Dallas County Community College District
701 Elm St., Dallas 75202-3299
Chanc. J. William Wenrich
(214) 746-2125

Brookhaven College
3939 Valley View La., Farmers Branch 75244-4997
Pres. Walter G. Bumphus
(214) 620-4700

Cedar Valley College
3030 N. Dallas Ave., Lancaster 75134
Pres. Carol J. Spencer
(214) 372-8200

Eastfield College
3737 Motley Dr., Mesquite 75150-2099
Pres. Justus Dan Sundermann
(214) 324-7600

El Centro College
Main and S. Lamar Sts., Dallas 75202-3604
Pres. Wright L. Lassiter, Jr.
(214) 746-2010

Mountain View College
4849 W. Illinois Ave., Dallas 75211-6599
Pres. William H. Jordan
(214) 333-8700

North Lake College
5001 N. MacArthur Blvd., Irving 75038-3899
Pres. James F. Horton, Jr.
(214) 659-5229

Richland College
12800 Abrams Rd., Dallas 75243-2199
Pres. Stephen K. Mittelstet
(214) 238-6200

Del Mar College
101 Baldwin Blvd., Corpus Christi 78404-3897
Pres. Buddy R. Venters
(512) 886-1203

East Texas State University
ETSU Sta., Commerce 75429
Pres. Jerry D. Morris
(214) 886-5014

East Texas State University at Texarkana
P.O. Box 5518, Texarkana 75504
Pres. John F. Moss
(214) 838-6514

El Paso Community College
P.O. Box 20500, El Paso 79998
Pres. Leonardo de la Garza
(915) 594-2000

Frank Phillips College
P.O. Box 5118, Borger 79008-5118
Pres. Vance W. Gipson
(806) 274-5311

Galveston College
4015 Ave. Q, Galveston 77550
Pres. Marc A. Nigliazzo
(409) 763-6551

Grayson County College
6101 Grayson Dr., Denison 75020
Pres. James M. Williams, Jr.
(214) 465-6030

Hill College
112 Lamar Dr., P.O. Box 619, Hillsboro 76645
Pres. William R. Auvenshine
(817) 582-2555

Houston Community College
22 Waugh Dr., P.O. Box 7849, Houston 77270-7849
Pres. Charles A. Green
(713) 869-5021

Howard County Junior College District
1001 Birdwell La., Big Spring 79720
Pres. Bob E. Riley
(915) 267-6311

Howard College
1001 Birdwell La., Big Spring 79720
Pres. Bob E. Riley
(915) 264-5000

Kilgore College
1100 Broadway Blvd., Kilgore 75662
Pres. Bert E. Woodruff
(214) 984-8531

Public Systems of Higher Education — Texas

Lamar University System
P.O. Box 11900, Lamar Sta.,
Beaumont 77710
Chanc. George McLaughlin
(409) 880-2304

> *Lamar University at Beaumont*
> 4400 Martin Luther King
>   Pkwy., Beaumont 77710
> Interim Pres. John P. Idoux
> (409) 880-8504

> *Lamar University at Orange*
> 410 Front St., Orange 77630
> Pres. Steve Maradian
> (409) 883-7750

> *Lamar University at Port Arthur*
> P.O. Box 310, Port Arthur
>   77641-0310
> Pres. W. Sam Monroe
> (409) 983-4921

Laredo Junior College
W. End Washington St., Laredo
  78040-4395
Pres. Roger L. Worsley
(512) 722-4395

Lee College
511 S. Whiting St., Baytown 77520-
  4703
Interim Pres. J. B. Whitley
(713) 427-5611

McLennan Community College
1400 College Dr., Waco 76708
Pres. Dennis Michaelis
(817) 756-6551

Midland College
3600 N. Garfield St., Midland 79705
Pres. David E. Daniel
(915) 685-4500

Midwestern State University
3400 Taft Blvd., Wichita Falls
  76308-2099
Pres. Louis J. Rodriguez
(817) 692-6611

Navarro College
3200 W. Seventh Ave., Corsicana
  75110
Pres. Gerald E. Burson
(903) 874-6501

North Harris Montgomery College District
250 Sam Houston Pkwy. E., Houston
  77060
Chanc. John E. Pickelman
(713) 591-3500

> *Kingwood College*
> 20000 Kingwood Dr.,
>   Kingwood 77339
> Pres. Stephen Head
> (713) 359-1600

> *North Harris College*
> 2700 W.W. Thorne Dr.,
>   Houston 77073
> Pres. Sanford C. Shugart
> (713) 443-5400

> *Tomball College*
> 30555 Tomball Pkwy., Tomball
>   77377
> Pres. Roy Lazenbey
> (713) 351-3300

Northeast Texas Community College
P.O. Drawer 1307, Mount Pleasant
  75455-1307
Pres. Michael C. Bruner
(214) 572-1911

Odessa College
201 W. University Blvd., Odessa
  79764
Pres. Philip T. Speegle
(915) 335-6400

Panola College
1109 W. Panola St., Carthage 75633
Pres. Gary D. McDaniel
(903) 693-2000

Paris Junior College
2400 Clarkville St., Paris 75460
Pres. Bobby R. Walters
(903) 785-7661

Texas

Public Systems of Higher Education

Ranger Junior College
College Cir., Ranger 76470-3298
Pres. Joe Mills
(817) 647-3234

San Jacinto College
4624 Fairmont Pkwy., Pasadena 77504
Pres. Monte Blue
(713) 998-6100

South Plains College
1401 College Ave., Levelland 79336
Pres. Marvin L. Baker
(806) 894-9611

Southwest Texas Junior College
Garner Field Rd., Uvalde 78801
Pres. Billy Word
(512) 278-4401

Stephen F. Austin State University
P.O. Box 6078, SFA Sta.,
Nacogdoches 75962-6078
Interim Pres. William J. Brophy
(409) 568-2011

Tarrant County Junior College
1500 Houston St., Fort Worth 76102-6599
Chanc. C.A. Roberson
(817) 336-7851

Temple Junior College
2600 S. First St., Temple 76504-7435
Pres. Marvin R. Felder
(817) 773-9961

Texarkana College
2500 N. Robison Rd., Texarkana 75501
Pres. Carl M. Nelson
(214) 838-4541

The Texas A&M University System
College Station 77843-1122
Chanc. Herbert H. Richardson
(409) 845-4331

Corpus Christi State University
6300 Ocean Dr., Corpus Christi 78412
Pres. Robert R. Furgason
(512) 991-6810

Laredo State University
One W. End Washington St.,
Laredo 78040-9960
Pres. Leo Sayavedra
(512) 722-8001

Prairie View A&M University
P.O. Box 188, Prairie View 77446
Pres. Julius W. Becton, Jr.
(409) 857-3311

Tarleton State University
1297 W. Washington St.,
Stephenville 76402
Pres. Dennis P. McCabe
(817) 968-9100

Texas A&I University
Campus Box 101, Kingsville 78363
Pres. Manuel L. Ibanez
(512) 595-3207

Texas A&M University
College Station 77843
Chanc. Herbert H. Richardson
(409) 845-3211

Texas A&M University at Galveston
P.O. Box 1675, Galveston 77553
Pres. William J. Merrell, Jr.
(409) 740-4400

West Texas State University
2501 Fourth Ave., Canyon 79016
Pres. Barry B. Thompson
(806) 656-2000

Texas College of Osteopathic Medicine
3500 Camp Bowie Blvd., Fort Worth 76107-2690
Pres. David M. Richards, D.O.
(817) 735-2000

Texas Southern University
3100 Cleburne St., Houston 77004
Pres. William H. Harris
(713) 527-7011

Public Systems of Higher Education — Texas

Texas Southmost College
80 Fort Brown St., Brownsville 78520
Pres. Juliet V. Garcia
(512) 544-8200

Texas State University System
505 Sam Houston Bldg., Austin 78701
Dir. Lamar Urbanovsky
(512) 463-1808

    Angelo State University
    2601 West Ave. N., San Angelo 76909
    Pres. Lloyd D. Vincent
    (915) 942-2073

    Sam Houston State University
    Huntsville 77341
    Pres. Martin J. Anisman
    (409) 294-1111

    Southwest Texas State University
    601 University Dr., San Marcos 78666-4616
    Pres. Jerome H. Supple
    (512) 245-2111

    Sul Ross State University
    Alpine 79832
    Pres. R. Victor Morgan
    (915) 837-8011

Texas Tech University
P.O. Box 4349, Lubbock 79409
Pres. Robert W. Lawless
(806) 742-2011

Texas Tech University Health Sciences Center
3601 Fourth St., Lubbock 79430
Pres. Robert W. Lawless
(806) 743-3111

Texas Woman's University
P.O. Box 23925, Denton 76204
Pres. Shirley S. Chater
(817) 898-2000

Trinity Valley Community College
500 S. Prairieville, Athens 75751
Pres. Ronald C. Baugh
(214) 675-6200

Tyler Junior College
P.O. Box 9020, Tyler 75711
Pres. Raymond M. Hawkins
(903) 510-2306

The University of Houston System
1600 Smith St., Ste. 3400, Houston 77002
Chanc. Alexander F. Schilt
(713) 754-7404

    University of Houston—Clear Lake
    2700 Bay Area Blvd., Houston 77058-1050
    Pres. Glenn A. Goerke
    (713) 283-7600

    University of Houston—Downtown
    One Main St., Houston 77002
    Interim Pres. George Magner
    (713) 221-8000

    University of Houston—University Park
    4800 Calhoun Blvd., Houston 77204-2162
    Pres. Marguerite Ross Barnett
    (713) 749-2236

    University of Houston—Victoria
    2302-C Red River St., Victoria 77901
    Interim Pres. Don Smith
    (512) 576-3151

University of North Texas
Denton 76203
Chanc. Alfred F. Hurley
(817) 565-2000

The University of Texas System
601 Colorado St., Austin 78701
Chanc. Hans Michael Mark
(512) 471-3434

    The University of Texas Health Science Center at Houston
    P.O. Box 20036, Houston 77225-0036
    Pres. M. David Low
    (713) 792-4975

The University of Texas Health Science Center at San Antonio
7703 Floyd Curl Dr., San Antonio 78284-7834
Pres. John P. Howe, III
(512) 567-7000

The University of Texas Medical Branch at Galveston
300 University Blvd., Galveston 77550
Pres. Thomas N. James
(409) 761-1687

The University of Texas Southwestern Medical Center at Dallas
5323 Harry Hines Blvd., Dallas 75235-9002
Pres. C. Kern Wildenthal
(214) 688-3111

The University of Texas at Arlington
P.O. Box 19125, Arlington 76019-0125
Pres. Wendell H. Nedderman
(817) 273-2222

The University of Texas at Austin
University Sta., Austin 78712
Pres. William H. Cunningham
(512) 471-3434

The University of Texas at Brownsville
1614 Ridgely Rd., Brownsville 78520-4991
Pres. Juliet V. Garcia
(512) 982-0100

The University of Texas at Dallas
P.O. Box 830688, Richardson 75083-0688
Pres. Robert H. Rutford
(214) 690-2111

The University of Texas at El Paso
500 W. University Ave., El Paso 79968
Pres. Diana S. Natalicio
(915) 747-5000

The University of Texas at San Antonio
San Antonio 78285
Pres. Samuel A. Kirkpatrick
(512) 691-4011

The University of Texas at Tyler
3900 University Blvd., Tyler 75701-6699
Pres. George F. Hamm
(214) 566-7000

The University of Texas of the Permian Basin
4901 E. University Blvd., Odessa 79762
Interim Pres. Edwin R. Sharpe
(915) 367-2011

The University of Texas—Pan American
1201 W. University Dr., Edinburg 78539-2999
Pres. Miguel A. Nevarez
(512) 381-2111

Vernon Regional Junior College
4400 College Dr., Vernon 76384
Pres. R. Wade Kirk
(817) 552-6291

The Victoria College
2200 E. Red River St., Victoria 77901-4494
Pres. Jimmy L. Goodson
(512) 573-3291

Weatherford College
308 E. Park Ave., Weatherford 76086
Pres. E.W. Mince
(817) 594-5471

Western Texas College
6200 S. College Ave., Snyder 79549
Pres. Harry L. Krenek
(915) 573-8511

Wharton County Junior College
911 Boling Hwy., Wharton 77488
Pres. Elbert C. Hutchins
(409) 532-4560

Public Systems of Higher Education — Texas

Texas State Technical Institute System
Waco 76705
Chanc. Cecil B. Groves
(817) 799-3611

Texas State Technical Institute—Amarillo
P.O. Box 11197, Amarillo 79111
Pres. Ronald L. DeSpain
(806) 335-2316

Texas State Technical Institute—Harlingen
P.O. Box 2628, Harlingen 78550
Pres. J. Gilbert Leal
(512) 425-0600

Texas State Technical Institute—Sweetwater
Rte. 3, P.O. Box 18, Sweetwater 79556
Pres. Clay G. Johnson
(915) 235-7300

Texas State Technical Institute—Waco
3801 Campus Dr., Waco 76705
Pres. Don E. Goodwin
(817) 799-3611

UTAH

Utah System of Higher Education
355 W. North Temple St., 3 Triad Ctr.,
 Ste. 550, Salt Lake City 84180-1205
Commissioner William R. Kerr
(801) 538-5247

College of Eastern Utah
Price 84501
Pres. Michael A. Petersen
(801) 637-2120

Dixie College
St. George 84770
Pres. Douglas D. Alder
(801) 673-4811

Salt Lake Community College
P.O. Box 30808, Salt Lake City 84130
Pres. Frank W. Budd
(801) 967-4111

Snow College
Ephraim 84627
Pres. Gerald J. Day
(801) 283-4021

Southern Utah University
Cedar City 84720
Pres. Gerald R. Sherratt
(801) 586-7710

University of Utah
Salt Lake City 84112
Pres. Arthur K. Smith
(801) 581-7200

Utah State University
Logan 84322-1400
Pres. Stanford Cazier
(801) 750-1000

Utah Valley Community College
800 W. 1200 S., Orem 84038
Pres. Kerry D. Romesburg
(801) 226-5000

Weber State University
3750 Harrison Blvd., Ogden 84408-1004
Pres. Paul H. Thompson
(801) 626-6140

VERMONT

Vermont State Colleges
P.O. Box 359, Waterbury 05676-0359
Chanc. Charles I. Bunting
(802) 241-2520

Castleton State College
Castleton 05735
Pres. Lyle A. Gray
(802) 468-5611

Community College of Vermont
Waterbury 05676
Pres. Michael Holland
(802) 241-3535

Johnson State College
Johnson 05656
Interim Pres. Robert Hahn
(802) 635-2356

Lyndon State College
Vail Hill, Lyndonville 05851
Pres. Margaret R. Williams
(802) 626-9371

University of Vermont
Burlington 05405-0160
Pres. Thomas Salmon
(802) 656-3131

Vermont Technical College
Randolph Center 05061
Pres. Robert G. Clarke
(802) 728-3391

VIRGINIA

State Council of Higher Education for Virginia
James Monroe Bldg., 101 N. 14th St., Richmond 23219
Dir. Gordon K. Davies
(804) 225-2600

Christopher Newport College
50 Shoe La., Newport News 23606
Pres. Anthony R. Santoro
(804) 594-7000

The College of William and Mary
Williamsburg 23185
Acting Pres. Melvyn D. Schiavelli
(804) 221-4000

George Mason University
4400 University Dr., Fairfax 22030
Pres. George W. Johnson
(703) 993-8700

James Madison University
Harrisonburg 22807
Pres. Ronald E. Carrier
(703) 568-6211

Longwood College
Farmville 23901
Pres. William F. Dorrill
(804) 395-2000

Mary Washington College
Fredericksburg 22401-5358
Pres. William M. Anderson, Jr.
(703) 899-4100

Norfolk State University
2401 Corprew Ave., Norfolk 23504
Pres. Harrison B. Wilson
(804) 683-8600

Old Dominion University
5215 Hampton Blvd., Norfolk 23529
Pres. James V. Koch
(804) 683-3000

Radford University
Radford 24142
Pres. Donald N. Dedmon
(703) 831-5000

University of Virginia Central Office
Charlottesville 22903
Pres. John T. Casteen, III
(804) 924-0311

Clinch Valley College of the University of Virginia
College Ave., Wise 24293
Chanc. J.A. Knight
(703) 328-0100

University of Virginia
P.O. Box 9011, Charlottesville 22906-9011
Pres. John T. Casteen, III
(804) 924-3337

Virginia Commonwealth University
910 W. Franklin St., Richmond 23284
Pres. Eugene P. Trani
(804) 367-0100

Virginia Military Institute
Lexington 24450
Supt. John W. Knapp
(703) 464-7000

Virginia Polytechnic Institute and State University
Blacksburg 24061-0131
Pres. James D. McComas
(703) 231-6000

Virginia State University
Petersburg 23803
Pres. Wesley Cornelious McClure
(804) 524-5000

Virginia Community College System
James Monroe Bldg., 101 N. 14th St., Richmond 23219
Chanc. Arnold R. Oliver
(804) 225-2118

Blue Ridge Community College
P.O. Box 80, Weyers Cave 24486
Pres. James R. Perkins
(703) 234-9261

Public Systems of Higher Education — Virginia

Central Virginia Community College
3506 Wards Rd., Lynchburg 24502
Pres. Johnnie E. Merritt
(804) 386-4500

Dabney S. Lancaster Community College
Rte. 60 W., P.O. Box 1000, Clifton Forge 24422-1000
Pres. John F. Backels
(703) 862-4246

Danville Community College
1008 S. Main St., Danville 24541
Interim Pres. Robert Shaver
(804) 797-3553

Eastern Shore Community College
Rte. 1, Box 6, Melfa 23410
Pres. John C. Fiege
(804) 787-5900

Germanna Community College
P.O. Box 339, Locust Grove 22508
Pres. Frank S. Turnage
(703) 399-1333

J. Sargeant Reynolds Community College
P.O. Box C-32040, Richmond 23261-2040
Pres. S.A. Burnette
(804) 371-3000

John Tyler Community College
13101 Jefferson Davis Hwy., Chester 23831-5399
Pres. Marshall W. Smith
(804) 796-4000

Lord Fairfax Community College
Rte. 11 N., P.O. Box 47, Middletown 22645
Pres. Marilyn C. Beck
(703) 869-1120

Mountain Empire Community College
P.O. Drawer 700, Big Stone Gap 24219
Interim Pres. Donald E. Puyear
(703) 523-2400

New River Community College
P.O. Drawer 1127, Dublin 24084
Pres. Edwin L. Barnes
(703) 674-3600

Northern Virginia Community College
4001 Wakefield Chapel Rd., Annandale 22003
Pres. Richard J. Ernst
(703) 323-3000

Patrick Henry Community College
P.O. Drawer 5311, Martinsville 24115-5311
Pres. Max F. Wingett
(703) 638-8777

Paul D. Camp Community College
100 N. College Rd., P.O. Box 737, Franklin 23851
Interim Pres. Michael La Bouve
(804) 562-2171

Piedmont Virginia Community College
Rte. 6, Box 1, Charlottesville 22901
Pres. Deborah M. DiCroce
(804) 977-3900

Rappahannock Community College
P.O. Box 287, Glenns 23149
Pres. John H. Upton
(804) 758-5324

Richard Bland College
Rte. 1, Box 77-A, Petersburg 23805
Pres. Clarence Maze, Jr.
(804) 862-6213

Southside Virginia Community College
Rte. 1, Box 60, Alberta 23821
Pres. John J. Cavan
(804) 949-7111

Southwest Virginia Community College
P.O. Box SVCC, Richlands 24641
Pres. Charles R. King
(703) 964-2555

Thomas Nelson Community College
P.O. Box 9407, Hampton 23670
Pres. Robert G. Templin, Jr.
(804) 825-2700

Tidewater Community College
Rte. 135, Portsmouth 23703
Pres. Larry L. Whitworth
(804) 484-2121

Virginia

Virginia Highlands Community College
Rte. 372, P.O. Box 828, Abingdon
24210
Pres. N. DeWitt Moore, Jr.
(703) 628-6094

Virginia Western Community College
3095 Colonial Ave., S.W., Roanoke
24038
Pres. Charles L. Downs
(703) 857-7311

Wytheville Community College
1000 E. Main St., Wytheville 24382
Pres. William F. Snyder
(703) 228-5541

WASHINGTON

Washington Higher Education Coordinating Board
917 Lakeridge Way, Olympia 98504
Exec. Dir. Ann Daley
(206) 753-3241

Central Washington University
208 Bouillon, Ellensburg 98926
Interim Pres. James P. Pappas, Jr.
(509) 963-1111

Eastern Washington University
Cheney 99004
Pres. Marshall E. Drummond
(509) 359-6200

Evergreen State College
Olympia 98505
Interim Pres. L. Thomas Purce
(206) 866-6000

University of Washington
Seattle 98195
Pres. William P. Gerberding
(206) 543-2100

Washington State University
Pullman 99164-1046
Pres. Samuel H. Smith
(509) 335-3564

Western Washington University
Bellingham 98225
Pres. Kenneth P. Mortimer
(206) 676-3000

Washington State Board for Community College Education
319 Seventh Ave., Olympia 98504
Exec. Dir. Earl Hale
(206) 753-7412

Bellevue Community College
3000 Landerholm Cir., S.E., Bellevue 98007-6484
Pres. B. Jean Floten
(206) 641-0111

Big Bend Community College
7662 Chanute St., Moses Lake 98837-3299
Pres. Gregory G. Fitch
(509) 762-5351

Centralia College
600 W. Locust St., Centralia 98531
Pres. Henry P. Kirk
(206) 736-9391

Clark College
1800 E. McLoughlin Blvd., Vancouver 98663
Pres. Earl P. Johnson
(206) 694-6521

Columbia Basin College
2600 N. 20th Ave., Pasco 99302
Pres. Marvin Weiss
(509) 547-0511

Edmonds Community College
20000 68th Ave. W., Lynnwood 98036
Pres. Thomas C. Nielsen
(206) 771-1500

Everett Community College
801 Wetmore Ave., Everett 98201-1327
Pres. Robert J. Drewel
(206) 259-7151

Grays Harbor College
Aberdeen 98520
Pres. Jewell C. Manspeaker
(206) 532-9020

Green River Community College
12401 S.E. 320th St., Auburn 98002
Pres. Richard A. Rutkowski
(206) 833-9111

Highline Community College
P.O. Box 98000, Des Moines 98198-9800
Pres. Edward M. Command
(206) 878-3710

Washington — Public Systems of Higher Education

Lower Columbia College
P.O. Box 3010, Longview 98632-0310
Pres. Vernon R. Pickett
(206) 577-2300

Olympic College
1600 Chester Ave., Bremerton 98310
Pres. Wallace A. Simpson
(206) 478-4544

Peninsula College
1502 E. Lauridsen Blvd., Port Angeles 98362
Pres. Paul G. Cornaby
(206) 452-9277

Pierce College
9401 Farwest Dr.,S.W., Tacoma 98498
Pres. Frank B. Brouillet
(206) 964-6500

Shoreline Community College
16101 Greenwood Ave., Seattle 98133
Pres. Ronald E. Bell
(206) 546-4101

Skagit Valley College
2405 College Way, Mount Vernon 98273
Pres. James M. Ford
(206) 428-1261

South Puget Sound Community College
2011 Mottman Rd., S.W., Olympia 98502
Pres. Kenneth J. Minnaert
(206) 754-7711

Tacoma Community College
5900 S. 12th St., Tacoma 98465
Pres. Raymond J. Needham
(206) 566-5000

Walla Walla Community College
500 Tausick Way, Walla Walla 99362
Pres. Steven L. Van Ausdle
(509) 522-2500

Washington State Community College District 17
N. 2000 Greene St., Spokane 99207
C.E.O. Terrance R. Brown
(509) 536-7401

Spokane Community College
N. 1810 Greene St., Spokane 99207
Pres. Joseph Rich
(509) 536-7000

Spokane Falls Community College
W. 3410 Fort George Wright Dr., Spokane 99204
Pres. Vern Jerome Loland
(509) 459-3500

Washington State Community College District 6
1500 Harvard St., Seattle 98122
Interim C.E.O. Otto Roemmich
(206) 587-3872

North Seattle Community College
9600 College Way N., Seattle 98103
Pres. Peter Ku
(206) 527-3600

Seattle Central Community College
1701 Broadway, Seattle 98122
Pres. Charles H. Mitchell
(206) 587-3800

South Seattle Community College
6000 16th Ave., S.W., Seattle 98106
Pres. Jerry M. Brockey
(206) 764-5300

Wenatchee Valley College
1300 Fifth St., Wenatchee 98801
Pres. Arnold Heuchert
(509) 662-1651

Whatcom Community College
237 W. Kellogg Rd., Bellingham 98226
Pres. Harold G. Heiner
(206) 676-2170

Yakima Valley Community College
P.O. Box 1647, Yakima 98907
Pres. V. Phillip Tullar
(509) 575-2350

WEST VIRGINIA

State College System of West Virginia
1018 Kanawha Blvd., E., Charleston 25301
Chanc. Paul B. Marion
(304) 348-0699

Bluefield State College
219 Rock St., Bluefield 24701
Pres. Gregory D. Adkins
(304) 327-4030

Concord College
Athens 24712
Pres. Jerry L. Beasley
(304) 384-5223

Fairmont State College
Locust Ave., Fairmont 26554
Pres. Robert J. Dillman
(304) 367-4151

Glenville State College
200 High St., Glenville 26351
Pres. William K. Simmons
(304) 462-4110

Shepherd College
Shepherdstown 25443
Pres. Michael P. Riccards
(304) 876-2511

Southern West Virginia Community College
Dempsey Branch Rd., P.O. Box 2900, Logan 25601-2900
Pres. Harry J. Boyer
(304) 792-4300

University of West Virginia System
1018 Kanawha Blvd., E., Charleston 25301
Chanc. Charles Manning
(304) 348-0267

Marshall University
Huntington 25701
Pres. J. Wade Gilley
(304) 696-2300

Potomac State College of West Virginia University
Keyser 26726
Pres. Joseph M. Gratto
(304) 788-3011

University of West Virginia College of Graduate Studies
P.O. Box 1003, Institute 25112-1003
Pres. Dennis P. Prisk
(304) 766-2000

West Virginia School of Osteopathic Medicine
400 N. Lee St., Lewisburg 24901
Pres. Olen E. Jones, Jr.
(304) 645-6270

West Virginia University
Morgantown 26506
Pres. Neil S. Bucklew
(304) 293-0111

West Virginia University at Parkersburg
Rte. 5, Box 167-A, Parkersburg 26101
Pres. Eldon L. Miller
(304) 424-8200

West Liberty State College
West Liberty 26074
Pres. Clyde D. Campbell
(304) 336-8000

West Virginia Institute of Technology
Montgomery 25136
Pres. Robert C. Gillespie
(304) 442-3146

West Virginia Northern Community College
College Sq., Wheeling 26003
Pres. Ronald M. Hutkin
(304) 233-0272

West Virginia State College
Institute 25112
Pres. Hazo W. Carter, Jr.
(304) 766-3111

WISCONSIN

University of Wisconsin System
1220 Linden Dr., Madison 53706
Acting Pres. Katharine C. Lyall
(608) 262-2321

University of Wisconsin Centers
150 E. Gilman St., P.O. Box 8680,
Madison 53708-8680
Acting Chanc. Arthur M. Kaplan
(608) 262-1783

University of Wisconsin—Eau Claire
Eau Claire 54701
Chanc. Larry G. Schnack
(715) 836-2326

University of Wisconsin—Green Bay
2420 Nicolet Dr., Green Bay 54311-7001
Chanc. David L. Outcalt
(414) 465-2207

University of Wisconsin—La Crosse
1725 State St., La Crosse 54601
Chanc. Judith L. Kuipers
(608) 785-8000

University of Wisconsin—Madison
500 Lincoln Dr., Madison 53706
Chanc. Donna E. Shalala
(608) 262-9946

University of Wisconsin—Milwaukee
P.O. Box 413, Milwaukee 53201
Chanc. John H. Schroeder
(414) 229-4331

University of Wisconsin—Oshkosh
800 Algoma Blvd., Oshkosh 54901
Chanc. John E. Kerrigan
(414) 424-0200

University of Wisconsin—Parkside
Box 2000, Kenosha 53141-2000
Chanc. Sheila Kaplan
(414) 553-2211

University of Wisconsin—Platteville
One University Plaza, Platteville 53818
Chanc. William W. Chmurny
(608) 342-1234

University of Wisconsin—River Falls
River Falls 54022
Chanc. Gary A. Thibodeau
(715) 425-3843

University of Wisconsin—Stevens Point
Stevens Point 54481
Chanc. Keith R. Sanders
(715) 346-2123

University of Wisconsin—Stout
Menomonie 54751
Chanc. Charles W. Sorensen
(715) 232-2441

University of Wisconsin—Superior
1800 Grand Ave., Superior 54880
Acting Chanc. Betty J. Youngblood
(715) 394-8223

University of Wisconsin—Whitewater
800 W. Main St., Whitewater 53190
Chanc. H. Gaylon Greenhill
(414) 472-1918

WYOMING

Wyoming Community College Commission
122 W. 25th St., Cheyenne 82002
Exec. Dir. James Meznek
(307) 777-7763

Casper College
125 College Dr., Casper 82601
Pres. Leroy Strausner
(307) 268-2548

Central Wyoming College
2660 Peck Ave., Riverton 82501
Pres. Jo Anne McFarland
(307) 856-9291

Eastern Wyoming College
3200 W. C St., Torrington 82240
Pres. Roy B. Mason
(307) 532-7111

Laramie County Community College
1400 E. College Dr., Cheyenne 82007
Interim Pres. Ed Boenisch
(307) 778-5222

Northwest College
231 W. Sixth St., Powell 82435
Pres. John P. Hanna
(307) 754-6200

Sheridan College
P.O. Box 1500, Sheridan 82801
Pres. Stephen J. Maier
(307) 674-6446

Western Wyoming College
P.O. Box 428, Rock Springs 82902
Pres. Tex Boggs
(307) 382-1600

OUTSIDE THE UNITED STATES

MARSHALL ISLANDS

College of Micronesia
P.O. Drawer F, Kolonia, Pohnpei,
Micronesia FSM 96941
Exec. Dir. Singeru Sigeo
(691) 320-2462

College of the Marshall Islands
P.O. Box 1258, Majuro RMI 96960
Admin. Hilda Heine-Jetnil
(692) 9-3394

Community College of Micronesia
P.O. Box 159, Kolonia, Pohnpei
FSM 96941
Pres. Paul Gallen
(691) 320-2840

Northern Marianas College
P.O. Box 1250, Saipan CNMI 96950
Pres. Agnes M. McPhetres
(670) 234-6932

Appendices

Appendices

A. The Accrediting Process

Accreditation is a system for recognizing educational institutions and professional programs affiliated with those institutions for a level of performance, integrity, and quality which entitles them to the confidence of the educational community and the public they serve. In the United States, this recognition is extended primarily through nongovernmental, voluntary institutional or professional associations. These groups establish criteria for accreditation, arrange site visits, evaluate those institutions and professional programs which desire accredited status, and publicly designate those which meet their criteria.

In most other countries, the establishment and maintenance of educational standards are the responsibilities of a central government bureau. In the United States, however, public authority in education is constitutionally reserved to the states. The system of voluntary nongovernmental evaluation, called accreditation, has evolved to promote both regional and national approaches to the determination of educational quality. While accreditation is basically a private, voluntary process, accrediting decisions are used as a consideration in many formal actions—by governmental funding agencies, scholarship commissions, foundations, employers, counselors, and potential students. Accrediting bodies have, therefore, come to be viewed as quasi-public entities with certain responsibilities to the many groups which interact with the educational community.

In America, accreditation at the postsecondary level performs a number of important functions, including the encouragement of efforts toward maximum educational effectiveness. The accrediting process requires institutions and programs to examine their goals, activities, and achievements; to consider the expert criticism and suggestions of a visiting team; and to determine internal procedures for action on recommendations from the accrediting body. Since accreditation status is reviewed on a periodic basis, recognized institutions and professional programs are encouraged to maintain continuous self-study and improvement mechanisms.

Types of Accreditation

Institutional accreditation is granted by the regional and national accrediting commissions of schools and colleges, which collectively serve most of the institutions chartered or licensed in the United States and its possessions. These commissions and associations accredit total operating units only.

Specialized accreditation of professional or occupational schools and programs is granted by national professional organizations in such fields as business, dentistry, engineering, and law. Each of these groups has its distinctive definitions of eligibility, criteria for accreditation, and operating procedures, but all have undertaken accreditation activities primarily to provide quality assurances concerning educational preparation of members of the profession or occupation. Many of the specialized accrediting bodies will consider requests for accreditation reviews only from programs affiliated with institutions holding comprehensive accreditation. Some specialized agencies, however, accredit professional programs at institutions not otherwise accredited. These are generally independent institutions which offer only the particular specified discipline or course of study in question.

Procedures in Accreditation

The accrediting process is continuously evolving. The trend has been qualitative criteria, from the early days of simple checklists to an increasing interest and emphasis on measuring the outcomes of educational experiences.

The process begins with the institutional or programmatic self-study, a comprehensive effort to measure progress according to previously accepted objectives. The self-study considers the interests of a broad cross-section of constituencies—students, faculty, administrators, alumni, trustees, and, in some circumstances, the local community.

Appendices

The resulting report is reviewed by the appropriate commission and serves as the basis for evaluation by a site-visit team from the accrediting group. The site-visit team normally consists of professional educators (faculty and administrators), specialists selected according to the nature of the institution, and members representing specific interests. The visiting team assesses the institution or program in light of the self-study and adds judgments based on its own expertise and its external perspective. The team prepares an evaluation report, which is reviewed by the institution or program for factual accuracy.

The original self-study, the team report, and any response the institution or program may wish to make are forwarded to the accreditation commission. The review body uses these materials as the basis for action regarding the accreditation status of the institution or program. Negative actions may be appealed according to established procedures of the accrediting body.

Although accreditation is generally granted for a specific term (e.g., five or ten years), accrediting bodies reserve the right to review member institutions or programs at any time for cause. They also reserve the right to review any substantive change, such as an expansion from undergraduate to graduate offerings. Such changes may require prior approval and/or review upon implementation. In this way, accrediting bodies hold their member institutions and programs continually responsible to their educational peers, to the constituents they serve, and to the public.

Accreditation's Purposes

Throughout the evolution of its procedures, postsecondary accreditation's aims have been and are to:

- foster excellence in postsecondary education through the development of uniform national criteria and guidelines for assessing educational effectiveness;
- encourage improvement through continuous self-study and review;
- assure the educational community, the general public, and other agencies or organizations that an institution or program has clearly defined and appropriate objectives, maintains conditions under which their achievement can reasonably be expected, is in fact accomplishing them substantially, and can be expected to continue to do so;
- provide counsel and assistance to established and developing institutions and programs; and
- endeavor to protect institutions against encroachments which might jeopardize their educational effectiveness or academic freedom.

Postsecondary education in the United States derives its strength and excellence from the unique and diverse character of its many individual institutions. Such qualities are best sustained and extended by the freedom of these institutions to determine their own objectives and to experiment in the ways and means of education within the framework of their respective authority and responsibilities.

Public as well as educational needs must be served simultaneously in determining and fostering standards of quality and integrity in the institutions and such specialized programs as they offer. Accreditation, through nongovernmental institutional and specialized agencies, provides a major means for meeting those needs.

Role of the Council on Postsecondary Accreditation

The Council on Postsecondary Accreditation (COPA) is a nongovernmental organization that works to foster and facilitate the role of accrediting bodies in promoting and insuring the quality and diversity of American postsecondary education. The accrediting bodies, while established and supported by their membership, are intended to serve the broader interests of society as well. To promote these ends, COPA recognizes, coordinates, and periodically reviews the work of its member accrediting bodies, and the appropriateness of existing or proposed accrediting bodies and their activities, through its granting of recognition and performance of other related functions.

Appendices

B. Accrediting Groups Recognized by COPA

COPA periodically evaluates the accrediting activities of institutional and professional associations. Upon determining that those activities meet or exceed COPA provisions, the accrediting organizations are publicly recognized through this listing. Groups that are regional in nature are identified with their geographical areas; all others are national in their activities.

NATIONAL INSTITUTIONAL ACCREDITING BODIES

AMERICAN ASSOCIATION OF BIBLE COLLEGES
Randall E. Bell, *Executive Director*
Commission on Accrediting
P.O. Box 1523
Fayetteville, AR 72702
(501) 521-8164, Fax: (501) 521-9202

ASSOCIATION OF ADVANCED RABBINICAL AND TALMUDIC SCHOOLS
Dr. Bernard Fryshman, *Executive Vice President*
Accreditation Commission
175 Fifth Avenue
Suite 711
New York, NY 10010
(212) 477-0950, Fax: (212) 533-5335

THE ASSOCIATION OF THEOLOGICAL SCHOOLS IN THE UNITED STATES AND CANADA
James L. Waits, *Executive Director*
Commission on Accrediting
10 Summit Park Drive
Pittsburgh, PA 15275-1103
(412) 788-6505, Fax: (412) 788-6510

CAREER COLLEGE ASSOCIATION
750 First Street, N.E.
Suite 900
Washington, DC 20002
(202) 336-6700, Fax: (202) 337-0566
James Phillips, *Director*
Accrediting Commission for Independent Colleges and Schools
Debbie Wolfe, *Director*
Accrediting Commission for Trade and Technical Schools

NATIONAL HOME STUDY COUNCIL
William A. Fowler, *Executive Secretary*
Accrediting Commission
1601 18th Street, N.W.
Washington, DC 20009
(202) 234-5100, Fax: (202) 332-1386

REGIONAL INSTITUTIONAL ACCREDITING BODIES

MIDDLE STATES ASSOCIATION OF COLLEGES AND SCHOOLS
Delaware, District of Columbia, Maryland, New Jersey, New York, Pennsylvania, Puerto Rico, Virgin Islands
   Howard L. Simmons, *Executive Director*
   The Commission on Higher Education
   3624 Market Street
   Philadelphia, PA 19104
   (215) 662-5606, Fax: (215) 662-5950

NEW ENGLAND ASSOCIATION OF SCHOOLS AND COLLEGES, INC.
Connecticut, Maine, Massachusetts, New Hampshire, Rhode Island, Vermont
   The Sanborn House
   15 High Street
   Winchester, MA 01890
   (617) 729-6762, Fax: (617) 729-0924
   Charles M. Cook, *Director*
   Commission on Institutions of Higher Education
   Daniel S. Maloney, *Director*
   Commission on Vocational, Technical, and Career Institutions

NORTH CENTRAL ASSOCIATION OF COLLEGES AND SCHOOLS
Arizona, Arkansas, Colorado, Illinois, Indiana, Iowa, Kansas, Michigan, Minnesota, Missouri, Nebraska, New Mexico, North Dakota, Ohio, Oklahoma, South Dakota, West Virginia, Wisconsin, Wyoming
   Dr. Patricia A. Thrash, *Executive Director*
   Commission on Institutions of Higher Education
   159 North Dearborn Street
   Chicago, IL 60601
   (312) 263-0456, Fax: (312) 263-7462

THE NORTHWEST ASSOCIATION OF SCHOOLS AND COLLEGES
Alaska, Idaho, Montana, Nevada, Oregon, Utah, Washington
   Joseph A. Malik, *Executive Director*
   Commission on Colleges
   3700-B University Way, N.E.
   Seattle, WA 98105
   (206) 543-0195

SOUTHERN ASSOCIATION OF COLLEGES AND SCHOOLS
Alabama, Florida, Georgia, Kentucky, Louisiana, Mississippi, North Carolina, South Carolina, Tennessee, Texas, Virginia
   1866 Southern Lane
   Decatur, GA 30033-4097
   (404) 329-6500, Fax: (404) 329-6598
   James T. Rogers, *Executive Director*
   Commission on Colleges
   Kenneth W. Tidwell, *Executive Director*
   Commission on Occupational Education Institutions
   (404) 329-6530, Fax: (404) 329-6598

WESTERN ASSOCIATION OF SCHOOLS AND COLLEGES
California, Guam, Hawaii
   Stephen S. Weiner, *Executive Director*
   Accrediting Commission for Senior Colleges and Universities
   P.O. Box 9990
   Mills College
   Oakland, CA 94613-0990
   (415) 632-5000, Fax: (415) 632-8361

   John C. Petersen, *Executive Director*
   Accrediting Commission for Community and Junior Colleges
   P.O. Box 70
   3060 Valencia Avenue
   Aptos, CA 95003
   (408) 688-7575, Fax: (408) 688-1841

Appendices

SPECIALIZED ACCREDITING BODIES

ACCREDITATION BOARD FOR ENGINEERING AND TECHNOLOGY, INC.
Professional engineering programs at the baccalaureate and master's levels preparing for entry into the engineering profession; baccalaureate and two-year programs (including those leading to the associate degree) in engineering technology; programs in industrial hygiene at the master's level; programs in occupational health and safety at the baccalaureate and master's level; and programs in surveying or surveying and mapping at the baccalaureate level.
Engineering Accreditation Commission
David R. Reyes-Guerra, *Executive Director*
345 East 47th Street
New York, NY 10017-2397
(212) 705-7685, Fax: (212) 838-8062

ACCREDITING BUREAU OF HEALTH EDUCATION SCHOOLS
Private postsecondary institutions offering educational programs exclusively in allied health, medical assistant programs in private institutions, and medical laboratory technician programs in private and public institutions.
Jeanne Glankler, *Administrator*
Oak Manor Offices
29089 U.S. 20 West
Elkhart, IN 46514
(219) 293-0124, Fax: (219) 295-8564

ACCREDITING COMMISSION ON EDUCATION FOR HEALTH SERVICES ADMINISTRATION
Graduate programs at the master's degree level or the equivalent in health services administration, health planning, and health policy analysis.
Sherril B. Gelmon, DrPH, *Executive Director*
1911 North Fort Myer Drive
Suite 503
Arlington, VA 22209
(703) 524-0511, Fax: (703) 525-4791

ACCREDITING COUNCIL ON EDUCATION IN JOURNALISM AND MASS COMMUNICATIONS
Units within institutions, a major part of the unit's activities being to offer professional programs preparing students at the bachelor's and master's levels for careers in journalism and mass communications.
Susanne Shaw, *Executive Director*
Stauffer-Flint Hall
University of Kansas
Lawrence, KS 66045
(913) 864-3973, Fax: (913) 864-4755

AMERICAN ASSEMBLY OF COLLEGIATE SCHOOLS OF BUSINESS
Baccalaureate and master's degree programs in business administration and management and baccalaureate and master's degree programs in accounting.
Accreditation Council
Milton Blood, *Director of Accreditation*
605 Old Ballas Road
Suite 220
St. Louis, MO 63141-7077
(314) 872-8481, Fax: (314) 872-8495

AMERICAN ASSOCIATION FOR COUNSELING AND DEVELOPMENT
Master's degree programs designed to prepare individuals for community counseling, mental health counseling, school counseling, and student affairs practice in higher education; and doctoral level programs in counselor education and supervision.
Council for Accreditation of Counseling and Related Educational Programs
Dr. Carol L. Bobby, *Executive Director*
5999 Stevenson Avenue
Alexandria, VA 22304
(703) 823-9800, Fax: (703) 823-0252

AMERICAN BAR ASSOCIATION/ASSOCIATION OF AMERICAN LAW SCHOOLS
Programs leading to the first professional degree and advanced degrees in law.
Council of the Section of Legal Education and Admissions to the Bar
James P. White, *Consultant on Legal Education*
American Bar Association
550 West North Street
Indianapolis, IN 46202
(317) 264-8340, Fax: (317) 264-8355

Appendices

Programs leading to the first professional degree.
Betsy Levin, *Executive Vice President*
Association of American Law Schools
1201 Connecticut Avenue, N.W.
Suite 800
Washington, DC 20036
(202) 296-8851, Fax: (202) 296-8869

AMERICAN BOARD OF FUNERAL SERVICE EDUCATION, INC.
Institutions and programs offering diplomas, associate and baccalaureate degrees in funeral service education and mortuary science education.
Committee on Accreditation
Gordon S. Bigelow, *Executive Director*
14 Crestwood Road
Cumberland, ME 04021
(207) 829-5715, Fax: (207) 829-4443

AMERICAN COUNCIL FOR CONSTRUCTION EDUCATION
Associate degree programs in construction, and baccalaureate programs in construction, construction science, construction management, and construction technology.
Daniel E. Dupree, *Executive Vice President*
901 Hudson Lane
Monroe, LA 71201
(318) 328-2413, Fax: (318) 323-2413

THE AMERICAN COUNCIL ON PHARMACEUTICAL EDUCATION
First professional degree programs (baccalaureate or doctoral) in pharmacy. Programs in planning at the baccalaureate and master's levels.
Daniel A. Nona, *Executive Director*
311 West Superior Street
Suite 512
Chicago, IL 60610
(312) 664-3575, Fax: (312) 664-4652

AMERICAN DENTAL ASSOCIATION
First professional degree programs in dental education; degree, certificate, and diploma programs in allied dental education (dental assisting, dental hygiene, and dental laboratory technology); and advanced degrees and certificate programs in dental education (dental public health, endodontics, oral pathology; oral and maxillofacial surgery, orthodontics, pediatric dentistry, periodontics, prosthodontics, general practice residency and general dentistry).
Commission on Dental Accreditation
Mario V. Santangelo, DDS, *Secretary*
211 East Chicago Avenue
Chicago, IL 60611
(312) 440-2719, Fax: (312) 440-2915

AMERICAN DIETETIC ASSOCIATION
Coordinated bachelor's degree programs, post-baccalaureate dietetic internship programs, and coordinated master's degree programs in dietetics.
Department of Education
Beverly Mitchell, *Administrator*
216 West Jackson Boulevard
Suite 800
Chicago, IL 60606-6995
(312) 899-4872, Fax: (312) 899-1758

AMERICAN HOME ECONOMICS ASSOCIATION
Baccalaureate programs in home economics.
Council for Professional Development
Karl G. Weddle, *Director of Accreditation*
1555 King Street
Alexandria, VA 22314
(703) 706-4600, Fax: (703) 706-HOME

AMERICAN LIBRARY ASSOCIATION
First professional degree programs at the master's level in librarianship.
Committee on Accreditation
June Lester, *Accreditation Officer*
50 East Huron Street
Chicago, IL 60611
(312) 280-2432, Fax: (312) 280-3258

AMERICAN MEDICAL ASSOCIATION
COPA recognizes the Committee on Allied Health Education and Accreditation (CAHEA) as an umbrella agency for 20 review committees representing professional organizations collaborating in the accreditation of programs in the following areas of allied health. All questions concerning accreditation of these programs should be directed to CAHEA at the address given. The review committees are:
• Accreditation Review Committee of Education for the *Anesthesiologist Assistant*;

Appendices

- Committee on *Athletic Trainer* Education;
- Committee on Accreditation (AABB), *Specialist in Blood Bank Technology*;
- Joint Review Committee on Education in *Cardiovascular Technology*;
- *Cytotechnology* Programs Review Committee;
- Joint Review Committee on Education in *Diagnostic Medical Sonography*;
- Joint Review Committee on Education in *Electroneurodiagnostic Technology*;
- Joint Review Committee on Educational Programs for the *EMT-Paramedic*;
- National Accrediting Agency for Clinical Laboratory Science, *Histologic Technician/Technologist, Medical Laboratory Technician (associate degree), Medical Laboratory Technician (certificate), Medical Technologist*;
- Curriculum Review Board (AAMA), *Medical Assistant*;
- Accreditation Review Committee for the *Medical Illustrator*;
- Council on Education (AMRA), *Medical Record Technician, Medical Record Administrator*;
- Joint Review Committee on Educational Programs in *Nuclear Medicine Technology*;
- Accreditation Committee (AOTA), *Occupational Therapy, Occupational Therapy Assistant*;
- Joint Review Committee on Education Programs for the *Ophthalmic Medical Technician/Technologist*;
- Joint Review Committee for *Perfusion Education*;
- Accreditation Review Committee on Education for the *Physician Assistant, Surgeon's Assistant*;
- Joint Review Committee on Education in Radiologic Technology, *Radiologic Technology, Radiation Therapy Technologist, Radiographer*;
- Joint Review Committee for Respiratory Therapy Education, *Respiratory Therapist, Respiratory Therapy Technician*;
- Accreditation Review Committee on Educational Programs for the *Surgical Technologist*.

Committee on Allied Health Education and Accreditation
Division of Allied Health Education and Accreditation
John J. Fauser, Ph.D., *Director*
515 North State Street
Chicago, IL 60610
(312) 464-4660, Fax: (312) 464-5830

AMERICAN MEDICAL ASSOCIATION/ASSOCIATION OF AMERICAN MEDICAL COLLEGES
Programs leading to the professional degree in medicine (Doctor of Medicine) and to post-baccalaureate programs in the basic medical sciences.

Liaison Committee on Medical Education
(in odd-numbered years beginning July 1st)
Harry S. Jonas, M.D., *Secretary*
American Medical Association
515 North State Street
Chicago, IL 60610
(312) 464-4933, Fax: (312) 464-5830

(in even-numbered years beginning July 1st)
Donald G. Kassebaum, M.D., *Secretary*
Association of American Medical Colleges
2450 N Street, N.W.
Washington, DC 20037
(202) 828-0596, Fax: (202) 785-5027

AMERICAN OPTOMETRIC ASSOCIATION
Optometric technician associate degree programs, professional optometric doctoral degree programs, and optometric post-doctoral residency programs.

Council on Optometric Education
Joyce Urbek, *Manager*
243 North Lindbergh Boulevard
St. Louis, MO 63141
(314) 991-4100, Fax: (314) 991-4101

AMERICAN OSTEOPATHIC ASSOCIATION
Programs leading to the Doctor of Osteopathy degree.

Bureau of Professional Education
Department of Education
W. Douglas Ward, Ph.D., *Director*
142 East Ontario Street
Chicago, IL 60611-2864
(312) 280-5840, Fax: (312) 280-5893

Appendices

AMERICAN PHYSICAL THERAPY ASSOCIATION
Physical therapist assistant programs at the associate degree level and physical therapist programs at the baccalaureate, post-baccalaureate certificate, and master's degree levels.
Commission on Accreditation in Physical Therapy Education
Virginia M. Nieland, *Director*
1111 North Fairfax Street
Alexandria, VA 22314
(703) 706-3245, Fax: (703) 684-7343

AMERICAN PODIATRIC MEDICAL ASSOCIATION
Programs leading to the degree of Doctor of Podiatric Medicine.
Council on Podiatric Medical Education
Jay Levrio, *Director*
9312 Old Georgetown Road
Bethesda, MD 20814-1621
(301) 571-9200, Fax: (301) 530-2752

AMERICAN PSYCHOLOGICAL ASSOCIATION
Doctoral programs in professional specialties of psychology and pre-doctoral internship training programs in professional psychology.
Committee on Accreditation
Paul D. Nelson, *Director*
1200 17th Street, N.W.
Washington, DC 20036
(202) 955-7670

AMERICAN SOCIETY OF LANDSCAPE ARCHITECTS
First professional programs at the bachelor's or master's level in landscape architecture.
Landscape Architecture Accreditation Board
Ronald C. Leighton, *Accreditation Manager*
4401 Connecticut Avenue, N.W., 5th Floor
Washington, DC 20008-2302
(202) 686-2752, Fax: (202) 686-1001

AMERICAN SPEECH-LANGUAGE-HEARING ASSOCIATION
Master's degree programs in speech-language pathology and/or audiology.
Educational Standards Board
Sharon Goldsmith, *Director*
10801 Rockville Pike
Rockville, MD 20852
(301) 897-5700, Fax: (301) 571-0457

AMERICAN VETERINARY MEDICAL ASSOCIATION
First professional degree programs in veterinary medicine.
Council on Education
Edward R. Ames, *Director*
930 North Meacham Road
Schaumburg, IL 60196
(708) 605-8070, Fax: (708) 330-2862

ASSOCIATION OF COLLEGIATE SCHOOLS OF PLANNING
Programs in planning at the baccalaureate and master's level.
Planning Accreditation Board
Beatrice Clupper, *Director*
2501 North Loop Drive
Suite 800
Iowa State University Research Park
Ames, IA 50010
(515) 296-7030, Fax: (515) 296-9910

COMPUTING SCIENCES ACCREDITATION BOARD
Baccalaureate degree programs designated as computer science programs which prepare students for entry into the computer science profession.
Computer Science Accreditation Commission
Patrick M. LaMalva, *Executive Director*
345 East 47th Street
New York, NY 10017
(212) 705-7314, Fax: (212) 371-9622

COUNCIL ON ACCREDITATION OF NURSE ANESTHESIA EDUCATIONAL PROGRAMS
Generic nurse anesthesia educational programs.
Betty J. Horton, CRNA, MA, *Director of Accreditation*
216 Higgins Road
Park Ridge, IL 60068-5790
(708) 692-7050, Fax: (708) 692-6968

THE COUNCIL ON CHIROPRACTIC EDUCATION
Institutions offering the doctor of chiropractic degree.
Commission on Accreditation
Ralph G. Miller, *Executive Vice President*
4401 Westown Parkway, Suite 120
West Des Moines, IA 50265
(515) 226-9001, Fax: (515) 226-9031

Appendices

THE COUNCIL ON EDUCATION FOR PUBLIC HEALTH
Graduate schools of public health and graduate programs outside schools of public health in community health education and community health/preventive medicine.
  Patricia P. Evans, *Executive Director*
  1015 15th Street, N.W.
  Suite 403
  Washington, DC 20005
  (202) 789-1050, Fax: (202) 289-8274

COUNCIL ON REHABILITATION EDUCATION
Master's degree programs in rehabilitation counselor education.
  Commission on Standards and Accreditation
  Emer D. Broadbent, *Executive Director*
  P.O. Box 1680
  Champaign, IL 61824-1680
  (217) 333-6688, Fax: (217) 244-6784

COUNCIL ON SOCIAL WORK EDUCATION
Baccalaureate and master's degree programs in social work education.
  Commission on Accreditation
  Nancy Randolph, *Director*
  1600 Duke Street
  Alexandria, VA 22314-3421
  (703) 683-8080, Fax: (703) 683-8099

FOUNDATION FOR INTERIOR DESIGN EDUCATION RESEARCH
Programs from the junior college through the graduate level in interior design.
  Kayem Dunn, *Executive Director*
  60 Monroe Center, N.W.
  Grand Rapids, MI 49503
  (616) 458-0400

NATIONAL ACCREDITATION COMMISSION FOR SCHOOLS AND COLLEGES OF ACUPUNCTURE AND ORIENTAL MEDICINE
First professional master's degree programs and professional master's level certificate or diploma programs in acupuncture that are based upon the theory of Oriental medicine, that are at least three academic years in length, and that follow at least two years of college level general education.
  Penelope Ward, *Executive Director*
  1424 16th Street, N.W.
  Suite 501
  Washington, DC 20036
  (202) 265-3370

NATIONAL ARCHITECTURAL ACCREDITING BOARD
Professional (bachelor's and master's) degree programs in architecture.
  John M. Maudlin-Jeronimo, *Executive Director*
  1735 New York Avenue, N.W.
  Washington, DC 20006
  (202) 783-2007, Fax: (202) 626-7421

NATIONAL ASSOCIATION OF SCHOOLS OF ART AND DESIGN
Institutions and units within institutions which offer associate, baccalaureate, and/or graduate degree programs in art, design, and art/design related disciplines; also nondegree-granting institutions having programs in these areas.
  Commission on Accreditation
  Samuel Hope, *Executive Director*
  11250 Roger Bacon Drive
  Suite 21
  Reston, VA 22090
  (703) 437-0700

NATIONAL ASSOCIATION OF SCHOOLS OF DANCE
Institutions and units within institutions which offer associate, baccalaureate, and/or graduate degree programs in dance and dance-related disciplines; and nondegree-granting institutions having programs in these areas.
  Commission on Accreditation
  Samuel Hope, *Director*
  11250 Roger Bacon Drive
  Suite 21
  Reston, VA 22090
  (703) 437-0700

NATIONAL ASSOCIATION OF SCHOOLS OF MUSIC
Institutions and units within institutions which offer associate, baccalaureate, and/or degree

programs in music and/or music-related disciplines, and nondegree-granting institutions having programs in these areas.
Commission on Accreditation
Samuel Hope, *Executive Director*
11250 Roger Bacon Drive
Suite 21
Reston, VA 22090
(703) 437-0700

NATIONAL ASSOCIATION OF SCHOOLS OF PUBLIC AFFAIRS AND ADMINISTRATION
Master's degree programs in public affairs and administration.
Commission on Peer Review and Accreditation
Alfred M. Zuck, *Executive Director*
1120 G Street, N.W.
Suite 730
Washington, DC 20005
(202) 628-8965, Fax: (202) 626-4978

NATIONAL ASSOCIATION OF SCHOOLS OF THEATRE
Institutions and units within institutions which offer associate, baccalaureate and/or graduate degree programs in theatre and theatre-related disciplines; and nondegree-granting institutions having programs in these areas.
Commission on Accreditation
Samuel Hope, *Executive Director*
11250 Roger Bacon Drive
Suite 21
Reston, VA 22090
(703) 437-0700

NATIONAL COUNCIL FOR ACCREDITATION OF TEACHER EDUCATION
Units within institutions offering professional education programs at the basic and advanced levels.
Arthur E. Wise, *President*
2010 Massachusetts Avenue, N.W.
Suite 200
Washington, DC 20036
(202) 466-7496, Fax: (202) 296-6620

NATIONAL LEAGUE FOR NURSING
Practical nurse, diploma, associate, baccalaureate, and higher degree programs.
Division of Education and Accreditation
Patricia Moccia, Ph.D., *Executive Vice President*
350 Hudson Street
New York, NY 10014
(212) 989-9393, Fax: (212) 989-3710

NATIONAL RECREATION AND PARK ASSOCIATION
Programs in recreation, park resources, and leisure services at the baccalaureate level.
Council on Accreditation
Michelle Park, *Professional Services Director*
3101 Park Center Drive
Alexandria, VA 22302
(703) 820-4940, Fax: (703) 671-6772

SOCIETY OF AMERICAN FORESTERS
First professional degree programs, baccalaureate or graduate, in forestry education.
Committee on Accreditation
P. Gregory Smith, *Associate Director*
5400 Grosvenor Lane
Bethesda, MD 20814-2198
(301) 897-9720, Fax: (301) 897-3690

Appendices

C. Joint Statement on Transfer and Award of Academic Credit

The following set of guidelines originally was developed by three national associations in higher education whose member institutions are directly involved in the transfer and award of academic credit. In 1990, a fourth national association joined the original three by officially approving the statement. It is one in a series of policy guidelines developed through the American Council on Education to respond to issues in higher education by means of voluntary self-regulation. Each statement is developed through a process of wide review among representatives of different types of institutions and professional responsibilities in higher education. They are intended to summarize general principles of good practice that can be adapted to the specific circumstances of each college and university.

Transfer of credit is a concept that now involves transfer between dissimilar institutions and curricula and recognition of extra-institutional learning, as well as transfer between institutions and curricula of similar characteristics. As their personal circumstances and educational objectives change, students seek to have their learning, wherever and however attained, recognized by educational institutions where they enroll for further study. It is important for reasons of social equity and educational effectiveness, as well as the wide use of resources, for all institutions to develop reasonable and definitive policies and procedures for acceptance of transfer credit. Such policies and procedures should provide maximum consideration for the individual student who has changed institutions or objectives. It is the receiving institution's responsibility to provide reasonable and definitive policies and procedures for determining a student's knowledge in required subject areas. All institutions have a responsibility to furnish transcripts and other documents necessary for a receiving institution to judge the quality and quantity of the work. Institutions also have a responsibility to advise the students that the work *reflected* on the transcript *may or may not* be accepted by a receiving institution.

Inter-Institutional Transfer of Credit

Transfer of credit from one institution to another involves at least three considerations:

(1) the educational quality of the institution from which the student transfers;
(2) the comparability of the nature, content, and level of credit earned to that offered by the receiving institution; and
(3) the appropriateness and applicability of the credit earned to the programs offered by the receiving institution, in light of the student's educational goals.

Accredited Institutions

Accreditation speaks primarily to the first of these considerations, serving as the basic indicator that an institution meets certain minimum standards. Users of accreditation are urged to give careful attention to the accreditation conferred by accrediting bodies recognized by the Council on Postsecondary Accreditation (COPA). COPA has a formal process of recognition which requires that any accrediting body so recognized must meet the same standards. Under these standards, COPA has recognized a number of accrediting bodies, including:

(1) regional accrediting commissions (which historically accredited the more traditional colleges and universities, but which now accredit proprietary, vocational-technical, and single-purpose institutions as well);
(2) national accrediting bodies that accredit various kinds of specialized institutions; and
(3) certain professional organizations that accredit free-standing professional schools, in addition to programs within multi-purpose institutions. (COPA annually publishes a list of recognized accrediting bodies, and the American Council on Education publishes for COPA a directory of institutions accredited by these organizations.)

Although accrediting agencies vary in the ways they are organized and in their statements of scope and mission, all accrediting bodies that meet COPA's provisions for recognition function to assure that the institutions or programs they accredit have met generally accepted minimum standards for accreditation.

Accreditation affords reason for confidence in an institution's or a program's purposes, in the appropriateness of its resources and plans for carrying out these purposes, and in its effectiveness in accomplishing its goals, insofar as these things can be judged. Accreditation speaks to the probability, but does not guarantee, that students have met acceptable standards of educational accomplishment.

Comparability and Applicability

Comparability of the nature, content, and level of transfer credit and the appropriateness and applicability of the credit earned to programs offered by the receiving institution are as important in the evaluation process as the accreditation status of the institution at which the transfer credit was awarded. Since accreditation does not address these questions, this information must be obtained from catalogues and other materials and from direct contact between knowledgeable and experienced faculty and staff at both the receiving and sending institutions. When such considerations as comparability and appropriateness of credit are satisfied, however, the receiving institution should have reasonable confidence that students from accredited institutions are qualified to undertake the receiving institution's educational program.

Admissions and Degree Purposes

At some institutions there may be differences between the acceptance of credit for admission purposes and applicability of credit for degree purposes. A receiving institution may accept previous work, place a credit value on it, and enter it on the transcript. However, that previous work, because of its nature and not its inherent quality, may be determined to have no applicability to a specific degree to be pursued by the student.

Institutions have a responsibility to make this distinction and its implications clear to students before they decide to enroll. This should be a matter of full disclosure, with the best interests of the student in mind. Institutions also should make every reasonable effort to reduce the gap between credits accepted and credits applied toward an educational credential.

Unaccredited Institutions

Institutions of postsecondary education that are not accredited by COPA-recognized accrediting bodies may lack that status for reasons unrelated to questions of quality. Such institutions, however, cannot provide a reliable, third-party assurance that they meet or exceed minimum standards. That being the case, students transferring from such institutions may encounter special problems in gaining acceptance and transferring credits to accredited institutions. Institutions admitting students from unaccredited institutions should take steps to validate credits previously earned.

Foreign Institutions

In most cases, foreign institutions are chartered and authorized by their national governments, usually through a ministry of education. Although this provides for a standardization within a country, it does not produce useful information about comparability from one country to another. No other nation has a system comparable to voluntary accreditation. At the operational level, three organizations—the National Council on the Evaluation of Foreign Student Credentials (CEC), the National Association for Foreign Student Affairs (NAFSA), and the National Liaison Committee on Foreign Student Admissions (NLC)—often can assist institutions by distributing general or specific guidelines on admission and placement of foreign students. Equivalency or placement recommendations are to be evaluated in terms of the programs and policies of the individual receiving institution.

Appendices

Validation of Extra-Institutional and Experiential Learning for Transfer Purposes

Transfer-of-credit policies should encompass educational accomplishment attained in extra-institutional settings as well as at accredited postsecondary institutions. In deciding on the award of credit for extra-institutional learning, institutions will find the service of the American Council on Education's Center for Adult Learning and Educational Credentials helpful. One of the Center's functions is to operate and foster programs to determine credit equivalencies for various modes of extra-institutional learning. The Center maintains evaluation programs for formally structured courses offered by the military and civilian noncollegiate sponsors such as businesses, corporations, government agencies, and labor unions. Evaluation services are also available for examination programs, for occupations with validated job proficiency evaluation systems, and for correspondence courses offered by schools accredited by the National Home Study Council. The results are published in a *Guide* series. Another resource is the General Educational Development (GED) Testing Program, which provides a means for assessing high school equivalency.

For learning that has not been validated through the ACE formal credit recommendation process or through credit-by-examination programs, institutions are urged to explore the Council for Adult and Experiential Learning (CAEL) procedures and processes. Pertinent CAEL publications designed for this purpose are available from CAEL National Headquarters, 223 West Jackson Boulevard, Suite 510, Chicago, IL 60606.

Uses of this Statement

This statement has been endorsed by the four national associations most concerned with practices in the area of transfer and awarding of credit—the American Association of Collegiate Registrars and Admissions Officers, the American Council on Education/Commission on Educational Credit and Credentials, the Council on Postsecondary Accreditation, and the American Association of Community and Junior Colleges.

Institutions are encouraged to use this statement as a basis for discussions in developing or reviewing institutional policies with regard to transfer. If the statement reflects an institution's policies, that institution might want to use this publication to inform faculty, staff, and students.

It is recommended that accrediting bodies reflect the essential precepts of this statement in their criteria.

Approved by the COPA Board
October 10, 1978; Reaffirmed April 25, 1990

Approved by the American Council on Education/Commission on Educational Credit
December 5, 1978; Reaffirmed by the Commission on Educational Credit and Credentials
September 26, 1990

Approved by the Executive Committee, American Association of Collegiate Registrars and Admission Officers
November 21, 1978; Reaffirmed February 1989

Approved by the Board of Directors, American Association of Community and Junior Colleges
April 1990

Institutional Index

Institutional Index

A

A B Inst. 31
AAA Welding Sch. 399
ABC Tech 32
ABC Tech. and Trade Sch. 18
ABC Welding Sch. 18
ABS Training Ctr. 31
ACA Coll. of Design 378
AIMS Acad. 478
ATDS—Prairie Hill 478
ATDS—Texas City 478
ATI 478
ATI Career Training Ctr. 101
ATI Computer Training 478
ATI Electronics Inst. 478
ATI Graphic Arts Inst. 478
ATI Health Ed. Ctr. 101 (FL); 478 (TX)
ATI—Hollywood 519
Aaker's Bus. Coll. 375
Abbeville Beauty Acad. 566
Abbie Bus. Inst. 224
Abbynell Beauty Acad. 440
Abilene Christian Univ. 478
Abraham Baldwin Agricultural Coll. 124, 601
Academia Arecicbena de Belleza 440
Academia Bermudez y Rios 440
Academia de Barberia y Cosmetologia 440
Academia Lanin 440
Academia Singer Dealer Autorizado Inc. 440
Acad. for Career Ed. 324
Acad. of Accountancy 264
Acad. of Allied Health Careers 145
Acad. of Art Coll. 31
Acad. of Artistic Hair Design 360
Acad. of Bus. Coll. 18
Acad. of Court Reporting 378
Acad. of Floral Design 79
Acad. of Hair Design 165 (IN); 399 (OK)
Acad. of Health Careers 248
Acad. of Medical Arts and Bus. 413
Acad. of Prof. Development 307
Acad. of the New Church 413
Acad. Pacific Bus. and Travel Coll. 31
Acadia Divinity Coll. 555
Acadiana Tech. Coll. 208
Acme Inst. of Tech. 545
Action Career Training 479
Adams State Coll. 79, 594
Adelphi Univ. 324
Adirondack Comm. Coll. 324, 649
Adler Inst. of Minnesota (see: Alfred Adler Inst. of Minnesota)

Adler Sch. of Prof. Psychology 145
Adolphus Coll. (see: Gustavus Adolphus Coll.)
Adrian Coll. 248
Advance Career Training 479
Advance Inst. 360
Advance Sch. of Driving 31
Advanced International Studies Sch. (see: Sch. of Advanced International Studies)
Advanced Legal Studies Ctr. (see: Ctr. for Advanced Legal Studies)
Advanced Software Analysis 324
Advertising Art Sch. (see: Sch. of Advertising Art)
Aero Mechanics Sch. 280
Aeronautics Coll. (see: Coll. of Aeronautics)
Agnes Scott Coll. 124
Aguadilla Regional Coll. 440, 665
Aiken Tech. Coll. 452, 669
Ailey American Dance Ctr. (see: Alvin Ailey American Dance Ctr.)
Aims Comm. Coll. 79, 593
Air Force Acad. (see: U.S. Air Force Acad.)
Air Force Comm. Coll. (see: Comm. Coll. of the Air Force)
Air Force Inst. of Tech. 378
Akron Barber Coll. 378
Akron Machining Inst. 378
Akron Medical-Dental Inst. 378
Al Collins Graphic Design Sch. 18
Al-Med Acad. 280
Alabama Agricultural and Mechanical Univ. 3, 575
Alabama Aviation and Tech. Coll. 3
Alabama Christian Sch. of Religion 3
Alabama Coll. System (Two-Year Insts.) 574
Alabama Commission on Higher Ed. 575
Alabama State Coll. of Barber Styling 3
Alabama State Univ. 3, 575
Alamance Comm. Coll. 360, 652
Alameda Coll. (see: Coll. of Alameda)
Alamo Comm. Coll. Dist. 673
Alaska Bible Coll. 15
Alaska Jr. Coll. 15
Alaska Pacific Univ. 15
Albany Coll. of Pharmacy of Union Univ. 324
Albany Law Sch. 324
Albany Medical Coll. 324
Albany State Coll. 124, 601

Albany State Univ. (see: State Univ. of New York at Albany)
Albany Tech. Inst. 124
Albemarle Coll. (see: Coll. of the Albemarle)
Albert I. Prince Regional Vo-Tech Sch. 88
Albert State Coll. (see: Carl Albert State Coll.)
Albertson Coll. 143
Albertus Magnus Coll. 88
Albion Coll. 248
Albright Coll. 413
Albuquerque Barber Coll. 320
Albuquerque Tech.-Voc. Inst. 320
Alcorn State Univ. 274, 635
Alderson-Broaddus Coll. 540
Alexandria Regional Tech. Inst. 208
Alexandria Tech. Coll. 264
Alfred Adler Inst. of Minnesota 264
Alfred Coll. of Tech. (see: State Univ. of New York Coll. of Tech. at Alfred)
Alfred Univ. 324
Alice Lloyd Coll. 190
All Points Travel Sch. 101
All State Bus. Coll. 570
All State Career Sch. 413
Allan Hancock Coll. 31, 581
Allan Hancock Joint Comm. Coll. Dist. 581
Allegany Comm. Coll. 224, 626
Allegheny Bus. Inst. 413
Allegheny Coll. 413
Allegheny Co. Comm. Coll. (see: Comm. Coll. of Allegheny Co.)
Allen Co. Comm. Coll. 183, 613
Allen Sch. for Physicians' Aides 324
Allen Univ. 570
Allen's Pocono Inst. of Taxidermy (see: Bill Allen's Pocono Inst. of Taxidermy)
Allentown Coll. of St. Francis De Sales 413
Alliance Tractor Trailer Ctr. 463
Alliance Tractor Trailer Training 124
Alliance Tractor Trailer Training Ctr. 360 (NC); 519 (VA)
Allied Health Careers 479
Allied Medical Careers 413
Allied Schs. of Puerto Rico 440
Allstate Hairstyling and Barber Coll. 378
Allstate Tractor Trailer Training Sch. 88
Alma Coll. 248
Alpena Comm. Coll. 248, 630
Alpha Beauty Sch. 452

1991-92 / Accredited Institutions of Postsecondary Education   707

Institutional Index

Altamaha Tech. Inst. 565
Altoona Sch. of Commerce 413
Alvernia Coll. 413
Alvemo Coll. 545
Alvin Ailey American Dance Ctr. 324
Alvin Comm. Coll. 479, 673
Amarillo Affiliated Sch. of Medical Tech. 479
Amarillo Coll. 479, 673
Amarillo-West Texas Barber Styling Coll. 479
Amber Univ. 479
American Acad. for Career Ed. 31 (CA); 301 (NV)
American Acad. McAllister Inst. of Funeral Service, Inc. 324
American Acad. of Art 145
American Acad. of Dramatic Arts 325
American Acad. of Dramatic Arts West 31
American Acad. of Nutrition 31
American Armenian International Coll. 564
American Ballet Ctr./Joffrey Balley Sch. 325
American Baptist Coll. 463
American Baptist Sem. of the West 31
American Bartenders Sch. 307 (NJ); 325 (NY)
American Bus. Acad. 307
American Bus. and Fashion Inst. 360
American Bus. Coll. 31
American Bus. Inst. 325
American Career Coll. 183
American Career Inst. 463
American Career Schs. 325
American Career Tech 479
American Careers 479
American Coll. 18 (AZ); 208 (LA); 399 (OK); 413 (PA)
American Coll. for the Applied Arts 124
American Coll. of Electrology 32
American Coll. of Optics 32
American Coll. of Tech. 145
American Coll. of Traditional Chinese Medicine 564
American Commercial Coll. 479-480
American Conservatory of Music 145
American Conservatory Theatre 32
American Diesel and Automotive Coll. 79
American Educational Coll. 440
American Educational Inst. 88

American Film Inst. Ctr. for Advanced Film and Television Studies 32
American Grad. Sch. of International Management 18
American Indian Arts Inst. (see: Inst. of American Indian and Alaskan Native Culture and Arts Development)
American Indian Bible Coll. 18
American Inst. 18
American Inst. of Bus. 176
American Inst. of Commerce 176 (IA); 480 (TX)
American Inst. of Design 413
American Inst. of Medical-Dental Tech. 512
American Inst. of Music 325
American Inst. of Tech. 18
American International Coll. 234
American Medical Record Association 145
American Medical Training Inst. 101
American Musical and Dramatic Acad. 325
American River Coll. 32, 585
American Samoa Comm. Coll. 17
American Sch. 145
American Sch. of Bus. 208
American Sch. of Tech. 378
American Schs. of Prof. Psychology 145
American Tech. Ctr. 18 (AZ); 512 (UT)
American Tech. Coll. for Career Training 32
American Tech. Inst. 463
American Teller Schs. 18
American Training Ctr. 480
American Travel Centre 320
American Travel Schs. 248
American Univ. 98
American Univ. in Cairo 559
American Univ. of Paris 559
American Univ. of Puerto Rico 440
Americo Tech. Career Inst. 208
Ameritech Coll. 32
Ameritech Coll. of Bakersfield 32
Amherst Career Ctr. 274 (MS); 480 (TX)
Amherst Coll. 234
Amodei International Inst. of Hair Design and Tech. (see: Ralph Amodei International Inst. of Hair Design and Tech.)
Amtech Inst. 183
Ancilla Coll. 165
Anderson Coll. 452
Anderson Univ. 165
Andon Coll. at Modesto 32

Andon Coll. at Stockton 32
Andover Coll. 221
Andover Newton Theol. Sch. 234
Andrew Coll. 124
Andrews Ctr. (see: Hiram G. Andrews Ctr.)
Andrews Univ. 248
Angelina Coll. 480, 673
Angelo State Univ. 480, 677
Anjons Sch. of Cosmetology 32
Anna Maria Coll. 234
Anne Arundel Comm. Coll. 224, 626
Anoka Tech. Coll. 264
Anoka-Ramsey Comm. Coll. 264, 633
Anson Comm. Coll. 360, 652
Antelope Valley Coll. 33, 581
Antelope Valley Comm. Coll. Dist. 581
Anthony's Barber Coll. 519
Antilles Sch. of Tech. Careers 441
Antioch Univ. 378
Antonelli Inst. of Art and Photography 378 (OH); 414 (PA)
Antonelli Medical and Prof. Inst. 414
Apex Tech. Sch. 325
Apollo Coll. of Medical and Dental Careers 19 (AZ); 406 (OR)
Appalachian Bible Coll. 540
Appalachian State Univ. 360, 655
Apprentice Sch.—Newport News Shipbuilding 519
Aquinas Coll. (see: Thomas Aquinas Coll.)
Aquinas Coll. 248
Aquinas Coll. at Milton 234
Aquinas Coll. at Newton 234
Aquinas Inst. of Theol. 280
Aquinas Jr. Coll. 463
Arapahoe Comm. Coll. 79, 593
Arecibo Tech. Univ. Coll. 441, 665
Arecibo Univ. Coll. 441, 665
Aristotle Coll. of Medical and Dental Tech. 165
Aristotle Inst. of Medical and Dental Tech. 379
Arizona Acad. of Medical and Dental Assistants 19
Arizona Board of Regents 578
Arizona Coll. of the Bible 19
Arizona Inst. of Bus. and Tech. 19
Arizona Inst. of Electrolysis 71
Arizona State Board of Directors for Comm. Colls. 578
Arizona State Univ. 19, 578
Arizona Western Coll. 20, 578
Arkansas Baptist Coll. 26
Arkansas Coll. 26

Institutional Index

Arkansas Coll. of Barbering and Hair Design 26
Arkansas Department of Higher Ed. 580
Arkansas State Univ. 26, 580
Arkansas State Univ. System Office 580
Arkansas State Univ.—Beebe 26, 580
Arkansas Tech Univ. 26, 580
Arkansas Valley Vo-Tech Sch. 26
Arlington Baptist Coll. 480
Arlington Court Reporting Coll. 480
Armed Forces Sch. of Music (see: U.S. Armed Forces Sch. of Music)
Armstrong Coll. 33
Armstrong State Coll. 124, 601
Armstrong Univ. of Beauty 124
Army Acad. of Health Scis. (see: U.S. Army Acad. of Health Scis.)
Army Chaplain Ctr. and Sch. (see: U.S. Army Chaplain Ctr. Sch.)
Army Command and General Staff Coll. (see: U.S. Army Command and General Staff Coll.)
Army Inst. for Prof. Development (see: U.S. Army Inst. for Prof. Development)
Army Intelligence Ctr. and Sch. (see: U.S. Army Intelligence Ctr. and Sch.)
Army Intelligence Sch. (see: U.S. Army Intelligence Sch.)
Army John F. Kennedy Special Warfare Ctr. (see: U.S. Army John F. Kennedy Special Warfare Ctr.)
Army Ordnance Ctr. and Sch. (see: U.S. Army Ordnance Ctr. Sch.)
Army Ordnance Missile and Munitions Ctr. and Sch. (see: U.S. Army Ordnance Missile and Munitions Ctr. and Sch.)
Army Quartermaster Sch. (see: U.S. Army Quartermaster Sch.)
Army Sch. of Aviation Medicine (see: U.S. Army Sch. of Aviation Medicine)
Army Signal Ctr. and Sch. (see: U.S. Army Signal Ctr. and Sch.)
Army Soldier Support Ctr. (see: U.S. Army Soldier Support Ctr.)
Army Transportation and Aviation Logistics Sch. (see: U.S. Army Transportation and Aviation Logistics Sch.)
Arnold's Beauty Coll. 360
Arnold's Beauty Sch. 463
Arrowhead Comm. Coll. Region 633
Art Acad. of Cincinnati 379
Art Advertising Acad. 379
Art and Bus. Coll. of Puerto Rico 441
Art Ctr. Coll. of Design 33
Art Inst. of Atlanta 124
Art Inst. of Boston 234
Art Inst. of Chicago Sch. (see: Sch. of the Art Inst. of Chicago)
Art Inst. of Dallas 480
Art Inst. of Fort Lauderdale 101
Art Inst. of Houston 480
Art Inst. of Philadelphia 414
Art Inst. of Pittsburgh 414
Art Inst. of Seattle 532
Art Inst. of Southern California 33
Art Instruction Schs. 264
Arthur D. Little Management Ed. Inst., Inc. 234
Artiste Sch. of Cosmetology 463
Artistic Beauty Coll. 124
Arundel Inst. of Tech. 224
Asbury Coll. 190
Asbury Theol. Sem. 190
Ascension Coll. 208
Ascension Tech. Inst. 208
Asher Sch. of Bus. 125
Asheville-Buncombe Tech. Comm. Coll. 360, 652
Ashland Comm. Coll. 190, 615
Ashland State Vo-Tech Sch. (see: Kentucky Tech—Ashland State Vo-Tech Sch.)
Ashland Univ. 379
Asnuntuck Comm. Coll. 88, 595
Assemblies of God Theol. Sem. 280
Associated Arts Coll. (see: Coll. of Associated Arts)
Associated Tech. Coll. 33
Associated Tech. Inst. 234
Assumption Coll. 234
Assumption Coll. for Sisters 307
Athenaeum of Ohio 379
Athens Area Tech. Inst. 125
Athens State Coll. 3, 575
Atlanta Area Tech. Sch. 125
Atlanta Christian Coll. 125
Atlanta Coll. of Art 125
Atlanta Coll. of Medical and Dental Careers 125
Atlanta Job Corps Ctr. 125
Atlanta Metropolitan Coll. 125, 601
Atlanta Sch. of Massage 125
Atlantic Career Inst. 463
Atlantic Coll. (see: Coll. of the Atlantic)
Atlantic Coll. 441
Atlantic Comm. Coll. 307, 644
Atlantic Sch. of Theol. 555
Atlantic Union Coll. 234
Atlantic Vo-Tech Ctr. 101
Atmore State Tech. Coll. 3
Auburn Univ. 3, 575
Auburn Univ. at Montgomery 3, 575
Auburn Univ. Central Office 575
Augsburg Coll. 264
Augusta Coll. 125, 601
Augusta Tech. Inst. 126
Augustana Coll. 145 (IL); 460 (SD)
Aurora Comm. Coll. (see: Comm. Coll. of Aurora)
Aurora Univ. 145
Austin Coll. 480
Austin Comm. Coll. 264, 633 (MN); 481, 673 (TX)
Austin Peay State Univ. 463, 671
Austin Presbyterian Theol. Sem. 481
Austin State Univ. (see: Stephen F. Austin State Univ.)
Automation Acad. 98 (DC); 224 (MD)
Automotive Machinists Sch. (see: Sch. of Automotive Machinists)
Automotive Tech. Inst. 145
Automotive Training Ctr. 414
Automotive Transmission Sch. 101
Avalon Vo-Tech Inst. 481
Averett Coll. 519
Aviation Career Acad. 307
Avila Coll. 280
Avoyelles Tech. Inst. 208
Ayers Inst. 208
Ayers State Tech. Coll. (see: Harry M. Ayers State Tech. Coll.)
AzTech Coll. 20
Azusa Pacific Univ. 33

B

B.M. Spurr Sch. of Practical Nursing 540
Babson Coll. 234
Bacone Coll. 399
Bahamas Hotel Training Coll. 555
Bailey Fashion Coll. (see: Mable Bailey Fashion Coll.)
Bainbridge Coll. 126, 601
Bais Medrash L'Torah Rabbinical Coll. 568
Baker Aviation Sch. (see: George T. Baker Aviation Sch.)
Baker Coll. 248
Baker Coll. of Cadillac 248
Baker Coll. of Mount Clemens 248
Baker Coll. of Muskegon 249
Baker Coll. of Owosso 249
Baker Coll. of Pontiac 249
Baker Coll. of Port Huron 249
Baker Univ. 183
Bakersfield Coll. 33, 584

Institutional Index

Baldwin Agricultural Coll. (see: Abraham Baldwin Agricultural Coll.)
Baldwin Coll. (see: Mary Baldwin Coll.)
Baldwin-Wallace Coll. 379
Balin Inst. 126
Ball State Univ. 165, 609
Ballard Co. Area Voc. Ed. Ctr. 190
Baltimore Comm. Coll. (see: New Comm. Coll. of Baltimore)
Baltimore Hebrew Univ. 224
Baltimore's International Culinary Arts Coll. 224
Bancroft Sch. of Massage Therapy 235
Bangor Theol. Sem. 221
Bank Street Coll. of Ed. 325
Baptist Bible Coll. 280 (MO); 414 (PA)
Baptist Missionary Association Theol. Sem. 481
Barat Coll. 145
Barber Styling Inst. 414
Barber-Scotia Coll. 360
Barclay Career Sch. 98 (DC); 101 (FL); 224 (MD); 307 (NJ); 519 (VA)
Barclay Coll. 33 (CA); 183 (KS)
Bard Coll. 325
Barna Inst. 101
Barnard Coll. 325
Barnes Bus. Coll. 79
Barranquitas Regional Coll. 441, 665
Barren Co. Area Voc. Ed. Ctr. (see: Kentucky Tech—Barren Co. Area Voc. Ed. Ctr.)
Barrett & Company Sch. of Hair Design 190
Barry Univ. 101
Barstow Coll. 34, 581
Barstow Comm. Coll. Dist. 581
Bartlesville Wesleyan Coll. 399
Barton Coll. 360
Barton Co. Comm. Coll. 183, 613
Baruch Coll. (see: Bernard M. Baruch Coll.)
Basic Inst. of Tech. 280
Bassist Coll. 406
Bastrop Tech. Inst. 208
Bastyr Coll. (see: John Bastyr Coll.)
Bates Coll. 221
Bates Tech. Coll. 532
Batesville Job Corps Ctr. 274
Baton Rouge Sch. of Computers 209
Baton Rouge Tech. Inst. 209
Bauder Fashion Coll. 481
Bauder Fashion Coll.—Atlanta 126
Bay Area Legal Acad. 102
Bay Area Vo-Tech Sch. 102

Bay de Noc Comm. Coll. 249, 630
Bay Medical Ctr. Sch. of Nurse Anesthesia 102
Bay Mills Comm. Coll. 567
Bay Path Coll. 235
Bay Ridge Christian Coll. 570
Bay State Coll. 235
Bay State Sch. of Appliances 235
Bayamon Central Univ. 441
Bayamon Tech. and Commercial Inst. 441
Bayamon Tech. Univ. Coll. 441, 665
Bayamon Univ. Coll. 441, 665
Baylor Coll. of Dentistry 481
Baylor Coll. of Medicine 481
Baylor Univ. 481
Bayou Tech. Inst. 209
Baytown Tech. Sch. 209 (LA); 482 (TX)
Beacon Career Inst. 102
Beal Coll. 221
Beaufort Co. Comm. Coll. 361, 652
Beauty Schs. of America 102
Beaver Coll. 414
Beaver Co. Comm. Coll. (see: Comm. Coll. of Beaver Co.)
Becker Coll. 235
Bee Co. Coll. 482, 673
Bel-Rea Inst. of Animal Tech. 79
Belfry Area Voc. Ed. Ctr. (see: Kentucky Tech—Belfry Area Voc. Ed. Ctr.)
Belhaven Coll. 274
Bell Co. Area Voc. Ed. Ctr. (see: Kentucky Tech—Bell Co. Area Voc. Ed. Ctr.)
Bellarmine Coll. 190
Belleville Area Coll. 146, 605
Belleville Barber Coll. 146
Bellevue Coll. 296
Bellevue Comm. Coll. 532, 685
Bellflower Bus. Coll. 34
Bellin Coll. of Nursing 545
Bellingham Vo-Tech Inst. 532
Belmont Abbey Coll. 361
Belmont Coll. 463
Belmont Tech. Coll. 379, 657
Beloit Coll. 545
Bemidji State Univ. 264, 634
Bemidji Tech. Coll. 264
Ben Hill-Irwin Area Vo-Tech Sch. 126
Benedict Coll. 452
Benedict Sch. of Languages and Commerce 441
Benedictine Coll. 183
Bennett Coll (see: Sue Bennett Coll.)
Bennett Coll. 361
Bennington Coll. 515
Bentley Coll. 235

Berdan Inst. 307
Berea Coll. 190
Berean Coll. 280
Berean Inst. 414
Bergen Comm. Coll. 307, 644
Berk Trade Sch. 325
Berkeley Coll. of Bus. 307
Berkeley Divinity Sch. 88
Berkeley Sch. 326
Berkeley Sch. of New York 568
Berkeley Sch. of Westchester 326
Berklee Coll. of Music 235
Berks Tech. Inst. 414
Berkshire Comm. Coll. 235, 628
Bernard M. Baruch Coll. 326, 647
Berry Coll. 126
Bessemer State Tech. Coll. 4
Beth Benjamin Acad. of Connecticut 88
Beth HaMedrash Shaarei Yosher 326
Beth HaTalmud Rabbinical Coll. 326
Beth Medrash Govoha 308
Beth-El Coll. of Nursing 79
Bethany Bible Coll.—Canada 555
Bethany Coll. 183 (KS); 540 (WV)
Bethany Coll. of the Assemblies of God 34
Bethany Lutheran Coll. 264
Bethany Theol. Sem. 146
Bethel Coll. 165 (IN); 183 (KS); 265 (MN); 463 (TN)
Bethel Theol. Sem. 265
Bethune-Cookman Coll. 102
Betty Stevens Cosmetology Inst. 452
Bexley Hall 326
Biblical Theol. Sem. 569
Big Bend Comm. Coll. 532, 685
Big Sky Coll. of Barber Styling 293
Bilingual Inst. 308
Bill Allen's Pocono Inst. of Taxidermy 414
Billings Sch. of Barbering and Hairstyling 293
Billings Vo-Tech Ctr. 293, 639
Binghamton State Univ. (see: State Univ. of New York at Binghamton)
Biola Univ. 34
Birmingham-Southern Coll. 4
Bish Mathis Inst. 482
Bishop Clarkson Coll. 296
Bishop State Comm. Coll. 4, 574
Bismark State Coll. 375, 656
Black Forest Hall 249
Black Hawk Coll.—East 146, 605
Black Hawk Coll.—Quad Cities 146, 605
Black Hills State Univ. 460, 670
Black River Vo-Tech Sch. 26

Institutional Index

Black World Coll. of Hair Design 361
Blackburn Coll. 146
Blackburn Correctional Complex (see: Kentucky Tech—Blackburn Correctional Complex)
Blackfeet Comm. Coll. 293
Blackhawk Tech. Coll. 545
Bladen Comm. Coll. 361, 652
Blair Jr. Coll. 79
Blake Bus. Sch. 326
Bland Coll.(see: Richard Bland Coll.)
Blanton's Coll. 361
Blessing-Rieman Coll. of Nursing 146
Blinn Coll. 482, 673
Bliss Coll. 379
Bloomfield Coll. 308
Bloomington-Normal Sch. of Radiography 146
Bloomsburg Univ. of Pennsylvania 414, 663
Blue Mountain Coll. 274
Blue Mountain Comm. Coll. 406, 661
Blue Ridge Comm. Coll. 361, 652 (NC); 519, 682 (VA)
Bluefield Coll. 519
Bluefield State Coll. 540, 687
Bluffton Coll. 379
Board of Regents, Univ. System of Georgia 601
Boardwalk and Marina Casino Dealers Sch. 308
Bobbie's Sch. of Beauty Arts 570
Bohecker's Bus. Coll. 379
Boise Bible Coll. 143
Boise State Univ. 143, 604
Bolton Avenue Beauty Sch. 209
Boone Co. Area Voc. Ed. Ctr. (see: Kentucky Tech—Boone Co. Area Voc. Ed. Ctr.)
Boone Co. Career Ctr. 540
Booth Bible Coll. (see: Catherine Booth Bible Coll.)
Boricua Coll. 326
Borough of Manhattan Comm. Coll. 326, 647
Bosco Tech. Inst. (see: Don Bosco Tech. Inst.)
Bossier Parish Comm. Coll. 209
Boston Architectural Ctr. 235
Boston Coll. 235
Boston Conservatory 235
Boston Museum of Fine Arts Sch. (see: Sch. of the Museum of Fine Arts, Boston)
Boston Univ. 236
Boulder Sch. of Massage Therapy 79

Boulder Valley Area Vo-Tech Ctr. 79
Bowdoin Coll. 221
Bowie State Univ. 224, 627
Bowling Green State Transportation Ctr. (see: Kentucky Tech—Bowling Green State Transportation Ctr.)
Bowling Green State Univ. 380, 657
Bowling Green State Vo-Tech Sch. (see: Kentucky Tech—Bowling Green State Vo-Tech Sch.)
Boyd Career Schs. (see: Wilma Boyd Career Schs.)
Boyd Sch. 415
Bradford Coll. 236
Bradford Sch. 380 (OH); 406 (OR); 415 (PA)
Bradford Sch. of Bus. 482
Bradley Acad. for the Visual Arts 415
Bradley Univ. 146
Brainerd Comm. Coll. 265, 633
Brainerd Tech. Coll. 265
Brandeis Univ. 236
Branell Coll. 126 (GA); 463 (TN)
Branford Hall Sch. of Bus. 88
Brannon Bus. Sch. 190
Braxton Sch. 519
Brazos Bus. Coll. 482
Brazosport Coll. 482, 673
Breathitt Co. Area Voc. Ed. Ctr. (see: Kentucky Tech—Breathitt Co. Area Voc. Ed. Ctr.)
Breckinridge Co. Area Voc. Ed. Ctr. (see:Kentucky Tech—Breckinridge Co. Area Voc. Ed. Ctr.)
Brenau Coll. 126
Brescia Coll. 190
Brevard Coll. 361
Brevard Comm. Coll. 102, 598
Brewer State Jr. Coll. 4, 574
Brewster Vo-Tech Ctr. (see: Henry W. Brewster Vo-Tech Ctr.)
Brewton-Parker Coll. 126
Briar Cliff Coll. 176
Briarcliff Coll. 102
Briarcliffe Sch. 326
Briarwood Coll. 88
Brick Computer Sci. Inst. 308
Bridgeport Engineering Inst. 88
Bridgewater Coll. 519
Bridgewater State Coll. 236, 628
Briercrest Bible Coll. 555
Brigham Young Univ. 512
Brigham Young Univ.—Hawaii Campus 140
Bristol Comm. Coll. 236, 628
Bristol Univ. 464

Broadcast Profs., The Complete Sch. of Radio Broadcasting 406
Broadcasting Inst. of Maryland 224
Brock's Hair Design Coll. 274
Brockport Coll. (see: State Univ. of New York Coll. at Brockport)
Bronx Comm. Coll. 326, 647
Brookdale Comm. Coll. 308, 644
Brookhaven Coll. 482, 674
Brookline Tech. Inst. 34
Brooklyn Coll. 327, 647
Brooklyn Health Sci. Ctr. (see: State Univ. of New York Health Sci. Ctr. at Brooklyn)
Brooklyn Law Sch. 327
Brooks Coll. 34
Brooks Inst. of Photography 34
Brookstone Coll. of Bus. 361
Broome Comm. Coll. 327, 649
Broward Comm. Coll. 102, 598
Brown Coll. (see: Morris Brown Coll.)
Brown Coll. of Court Reporting and Bus. 127
Brown Mackie Coll. 183
Brown Univ. (see:John Brown Univ.)
Brown Univ. 450
Brown's Bus. Coll. 146
Brunswick Coll. 127, 601
Brunswick Comm. Coll. 361, 652
Bryan Coll. (see: William Jennings Bryan Coll.)
Bryan Coll. of Court Reporting 34
Bryan Inst. 183 (KS); 280 (MO); 399 (OK); 482 (TX)
Bryan Travel Coll. 183 (KS); 280 (MO)
Bryant and Stratton Bus. Inst. 327 (NY); 380 (OH)
Bryant Coll. 450
Bryman Sch. 21 (AZ); 512 (UT)
Bryn Mawr Coll. 415
Bucknell Univ. 415
Bucks Co. Comm. Coll. 415, 663
Buena Vista Coll. 176
Buffalo Coll. (see: State Univ. of New York Coll. at Buffalo)
Buffalo Health Sci. Ctr. (see: State Univ. of New York Health Sci. Ctr. at Buffalo)
Buffalo State Univ. (see: State Univ. of New York at Buffalo)
Bullitt Co. Area Voc. Ed. Ctr. (see: Kentucky Tech—Bullitt Co. Area Voc. Ed. Ctr.)
Bulova Sch.(see:Joseph Bulova Sch.)
Bunker Hill Comm. Coll. 236, 628
Burdett Sch. 236
Burke Acad. of Cosmetic Art 361
Burlington Coll. 515

Institutional Index

Burlington Co. Coll. 308, 644
Bus. and Tech. Inst. 565
Bus. Careers Inst. 88 (CT); 436 (PA)
Bus. Industry Sch. 34
Bus. Informatics Ctr. 327
Bus. Skills Training Ctr. 482
Bus. Training Inst. 102-103 (FL); 308 (NJ)
Butera Sch. of Art 236
Butler Bus. Sch. 88
Butler Co. Comm. Coll. 184, 613 (KS); 415, 663 (PA)
Butler Univ. 165
Butte Coll. 34, 581
Butte Comm. Coll. Dist. 581
Butte Vo-Tech Ctr. 293, 639

C

CARTI Sch. of Radiation Therapy Tech. 26
CBM Ed. Ctr. 482
CCI Travel Careers 146
CDI Career Development Inst. 34 (CA); 79 (CO); 127 (GA); 147 (IL); 224 (MD); 249 (MI); 265 (MN); 280 (MO); 328 (NY); 483 (TX); 519 (VA)
CHI Inst. 415
Cabrillo Coll. 35, 581
Cabrillo Comm. Coll. Dist. 581
Cabrini Coll. 415
Caldwell Coll. 309
Caldwell Comm. Coll. and Tech. Inst. 362, 652
Caldwell Co. Area Voc. Ed. Ctr. (see: Kentucky Tech—Caldwell Co. Area Voc. Ed. Ctr.)
Calhoun State Comm. Coll. (see: John C. Calhoun State Comm. Coll.)
California Baptist Coll. 35
California Career Sch. 35
California Coll. for Health Scis. 35
California Coll. of Arts and Crafts 35
California Coll. of Podiatric Medicine 35
California Comm. Colls. (Board of Governors) 581
California Culinary Acad. 35
California Family Study Ctr. 35
California Inst. of Integral Studies 35
California Inst. of Tech. 35
California Inst. of the Arts 35
California Lutheran Univ. 36
California Maritime Acad. 36
California Nannie Coll. 36

California Paramedical and Tech. Coll. 36
California Paramedical and Tech. Sch. 36
California Polytechnic State Univ., San Luis Obispo 36, 591
California Sch. of Court Reporting 36
California Sch. of Prof. Psychology, Berkeley/Alameda 36
California Sch. of Prof. Psychology, Fresno 36
California Sch. of Prof. Psychology, Los Angeles 37
California Sch. of Prof. Psychology, San Diego 37
California State Polytechnic Univ., Pomona 37, 591
California State Univ., Bakersfield 37, 591
California State Univ., Chico 37, 591
California State Univ., Dominguez Hills 37, 591
California State Univ., Fresno 37, 591
California State Univ., Fullerton 37, 591
California State Univ., Hayward 38, 591
California State Univ., Long Beach 38, 591
California State Univ., Los Angeles 38, 591
California State Univ., Northridge 38, 591
California State Univ., Sacramento 38, 591
California State Univ., San Bernardino 38, 591
California State Univ., San Marcos 564
California State Univ., Stanislaus 38, 591
California State Univ. System 591
California Univ. of Pennsylvania 415, 663
California Western Sch. of Law 39
Calumet Coll. of Saint Joseph 165
Calvary Bible Coll. 280
Calvin Coll. 249
Calvin Theol. Sem. 249
Cambria-Rowe Bus. Coll. 415
Cambridge Acad. 103
Cambridge Bus. Sch. 249
Cambridge Coll. 236
Camden Co. Coll. 309, 644
Camden Co. Vo-Tech Sch. 309
Camden Sch. of Hair Design 452
Camelot Career Coll. 209

Cameron Coll. 209
Cameron Univ. 399
Camp Comm. Coll. (see: Paul D. Camp Comm. Coll.)
Campbell Co. Area Voc. Ed. Ctr. (see: Kentucky Tech—Campbell Co. Area Voc. Ed. Ctr.)
Campbell Univ. 362
Campbellsville Coll. 190
Cañada Coll. 39, 588
Canadian Bible Coll. and Theol. Sem. 555
Canisius Coll. 328
Cannon's International Bus. Coll. of Honolulu 140
Canton Coll. of Tech. (see: State Univ. of New York Coll. of Tech. at Canton)
Canyons Coll. (see: Coll. of the Canyons)
Cape Cod Comm. Coll. 236, 628
Cape Fear Comm. Coll. 362, 652
Cape Girardeau Area Vo-Tech Sch. 281
Capital City Bus. Coll. 26
Capital City Jr. Coll. 26
Capital Univ. 380
Capitol Bus. Coll. 532
Capitol City Barber Coll. 80 (CO); 184 (KS)
Capitol City Careers 483
Capitol City Trade and Tech. Sch. 483
Capitol Coll. 225
Capps Coll. 4
Capri Cosmetology Coll. 176
Cardinal Stritch Coll. 545
Career Acad. 483
Career Ctrs. of Texas—Austin 483
Career Ctrs. of Texas—El Paso 483
Career City Coll. 103
Career Coll. of Northern Nevada 301
Career Development Ctr. 4 (AL); 483 (TX); 520 (VA)
Career Development Inst. 4 (AL); 274 (MS)
Career Floral Design Inst. 532
Career Inst. 39 (CA); 209 (LA); 328 (NY); 415, 428 (PA)
Career Inst. of America 103
Career Point Bus. Sch. 483
Career Tech. Inst. 484
Career Training Acad. 416
Career Training Ctr. 570
Career Training International 20
Career Training Specialists 209
CareerCom Coll. of Bus. 39 (CA); 380 (OH); 464 (TN)
CareerCom Jr. Coll. of Bus. 190

Institutional Index

Carey Coll. (see: William Carey Coll.)
Caribbean Ctr. for Advanced Studies 441
Caribbean Univ. 442
Carl Albert State Coll. 399
Carl D. Perkins Job Corps Ctr. 191
Carl Sandburg Coll. 147, 605
Carleton Coll. 265
Carlow Coll. 416
Carnegie Inst. 249
Carnegie-Mellon Univ. 416
Carolina Beauty Coll. 362
Carolina Regional Coll. 442, 665
Carroll Coll. 293 (MT); 545 (WI)
Carroll Co. Area Voc. Ed. Ctr. (see: Kentucky Tech—Carroll Co. Area Voc. Ed. Ctr.)
Carroll Co. Coll. 225
Carroll Tech. Inst. 127
Carroll Univ. (see: John Carroll Univ.)
Carson-Newman Coll. 464
Carteret Comm. Coll. 362, 652
Carthage Coll. 545
Carver State Tech. Coll. 4
Casa Loma Coll. 39
Casco Bay Coll. 221
Case Western Reserve Univ. 380
Casey Co. Area Voc. Ed. Ctr. (see: Kentucky Tech—Casey Co. Area Voc. Ed. Ctr.)
Cashier Training Inst. 328
Casper Coll. 553, 689
Castle Jr. Coll. 304
Castleton State Coll. 515, 681
Catawba Coll. 362
Catawba Valley Comm. Coll. 362, 652
Catherine Booth Bible Coll. 571
Catherine Coll. 39 (CA); 147 (IL)
Catherine E. Hinds Inst. of Esthetics 237
Catherine Laboure Coll. 237
Catholic Home Study Inst. 520
Catholic Theol. Union 147
Catholic Univ. of America 98
Catholic Univ. of Puerto Rico 442
Catonsville Comm. Coll. 225, 626
Cave Tech. Inst. 147
Cayey Univ. Coll. 442, 665
Cayuga Co. Comm. Coll. 328, 649
Cazenovia Coll. 328
Cecil Comm. Coll. 225, 626
Cecils Jr. Coll. of Bus. 362
Cedar Crest Coll. 416
Cedar Rapids Sch. of Hairstyling 176
Cedar Valley Coll. 484, 674
Cedarville Coll. 380
Centenary Coll. 309

Centenary Coll. of Louisiana 209
Ctr. for Advanced Legal Studies 484
Ctr. for Creative Studies—Coll. of Art and Design 249
Ctr. for Humanistic Studies 249
Ctr. for the Media Arts 328
Ctr. for Training in Bus. and Industry 184
Central Alabama Comm. Coll. 5, 574
Central Alabama Skills Ctr. 5
Central Arizona Coll. 20, 578
Central Baptist Coll. 27
Central Baptist Theol. Sem. 184
Central Bible Coll. 281
Central Bus. Coll. 184
Central Carolina Comm. Coll. 362, 652
Central Christian Coll. of the Bible 281
Central Coll. 176 (IA); 184 (KS); 489 (TX)
Central Comm. Coll. 296, 640
Central Connecticut State Univ. 89, 596
Central Florida Comm. Coll. 103, 598
Central Indiana Tech. Inst. (see: Indiana Vo-Tech Coll.—Central Indiana Tech. Inst.)
Central Kentucky State Vo-Tech Sch. (see: Kentucky Tech—Central Kentucky State Vo-Tech Sch.)
Central Maine Medical Ctr. Sch. of Nursing 221
Central Maine Tech. Coll. 221
Central Methodist Coll. 281
Central Michigan Univ. 249, 630
Central Missouri State Univ. 281, 637
Central Ohio Tech. Coll. 380, 657
Central Oklahoma Area Vo-Tech Ctr. 399
Central Oregon Comm. Coll. 406, 661
Central Pennsylvania Bus. Sch. 416
Central Piedmont Comm. Coll. 362, 652
Central State Univ. 381, 657
Central Tech. Comm. Coll. 296
Central Texas Coll. 484, 673
Central Texas Commercial Coll. 484
Central Virginia Comm. Coll. 520, 683
Central Washington Univ. 532, 685
Central Wesleyan Coll. 452
Central Wyoming Coll. 553, 689
Central Yeshiva Tomchei Tmimim-Lubavitch 328
Centralia Coll. 532, 685

Centre Coll. 191
Centro de Estudios Avanzados de Puerto Rico y El Caribe 442
Centro de Estudios Multidisciplinarios 442
Century Schs. 39
Cerritos Coll. 39, 581
Cerritos Comm. Coll. Dist. 581
Cerro Coso Comm. Coll. 39, 584
Certified Careers Inst. 512
Certified Welding and Trade Sch. 553
Cesar Ritz Inst. of Hotel Management 559
Chabot Coll. 40, 581
Chabot-Las Positas Comm. Coll. Dist. 581
Chadron State Coll. 296, 640
Chaffey Coll. 40, 582
Chaffey Comm. Coll. Dist. 581
Chaminade Univ. of Honolulu 140
Champlain Coll. 515
Chaparral Career Coll. 20
Chapman Sch. of Seamanship 103
Chapman Univ. 40
Charles Co. Comm. Coll. 225, 626
Charles H. McCann Tech. Sch. 237
Charles R. Drew Univ. 40
Charles Stewart Mott Comm. Coll. 250, 630
Charleston Coll. (see: Coll. of Charleston)
Charleston Cosmetology Inst. 452
Charleston Southern Univ. 452
Charlotte Diesel Driving Sch. 363 (NC); 452 (SC)
Charlotte Vo-Tech Ctr. 103
Charter Coll. 15
Charter Oak Coll. 89
Charterway Coll. 40
Charzanne Beauty Coll. 453
Chatfield Coll. 381
Chatham Coll. 416
Chattahochee Tech. Inst. 127
Chattahoochee Valley State Comm. Coll. 5, 574
Chattanooga Barber Coll. 464
Chattanooga State Tech. Comm. Coll. 464, 671
Chauffeurs Training Sch. 250 (MI); 328 (NY)
Chemeketa Comm. Coll. 406, 661
Chenier 484
Chenier Bus. Sch. 484
Cheryl Fell's Sch. of Bus. 328
Chesapeake Coll. 225, 626
Chesterfield-Marlboro Tech. Coll. 453, 669
Chestnut Hill Coll. 416
Cheyenne Aero Tech 553

Institutional Index

Cheyney Univ. of Pennsylvania 416, 663
Chicago City-Wide Coll. 147, 605
Chicago Coll. of Commerce 147
Chicago Coll. of Osteopathic Medicine 147
Chicago Sch. of Prof. Psychology 147
Chicago State Univ. 147, 605
Chicago Theol. Sem. 147
Chicago Truck Driving Sch. 148
Chipola Jr. Coll. 103, 598
Chippewa Valley Tech. Coll. 545
Choctaw Training Inst. 5
Choffin Career Ctr. 381
Chowan Coll. 363
Chris Logan Career Coll. 453
Christ Coll., Irvine 40
Christ the King Sem. 328
Christendom Coll. 520
Christian Brothers Univ. 464
Christian Co. Area Voc. Ed. Ctr. (see: Kentucky Tech—Christian Co. Area Voc. Ed. Ctr.)
Christian Heritage Coll. 40
Christian Theol. Sem. 165
Christopher Newport Coll. 520, 682
Chubb Inst. 309
Chubb Inst.—Keystone Sch. 416
Church Divinity Sch. of the Pacific 40
Church of God Sch. of Theol. 381
Churchman Bus. Sch. 416
Cincinnati Bible Coll. 381
Cincinnati Coll. of Mortuary Sci. 381
Cincinnati Metropolitan Coll. 381
Cincinnati Sch. of Court Reporting and Bus. 381
Cincinnati Tech. Coll. 381, 657
Circle in the Square Theatre Sch. 328
Circleville Bible Coll. 381
Cisco Jr. Coll. 484, 673
Citadel 453, 668
Citizens' High Sch. 127
Citrus Coll. 40, 582
Citrus Comm. Coll. Dist. 582
Cittone Inst. 309
City Coll. 328, 647
City Coll. of San Francisco 40, 588
City Colls. of Chicago 605
City Univ. 532
City Univ. of New York Central Administration 647
Clackamas Comm. Coll. 406, 661
Claflin Coll. 453
Claiborne Tech. Inst. 209
Claire DeMarzo Inst. of Prof. Electrology 309
Claremont Grad. Sch. 41
Claremont McKenna Coll. 41

Claremont Sch. of Theol. (see: Sch. of Theol. at Claremont)
Clarendon Coll. 484, 673
Clarion Univ. of Pennsylvania 416, 663
Clarissa Sch. of Fashion Design 417
Clark Atlanta Univ. 127
Clark Coll. 165 (IN); 209 (LA); 532, 685 (WA)
Clark Co. Area Voc. Ed. Ctr. (see: Kentucky Tech—Clark Co. Area Voc. Ed. Ctr.)
Clark State Comm. Coll. 381, 657
Clark Univ. 237
Clarke Coll. 176
Clarkson Univ. 329
Clatsop Comm. Coll. 406, 661
Clay Co. Area Voc. Ed. Ctr. (see: Kentucky Tech—Clay Co. Area Voc. Ed. Ctr.)
Clayton State Coll. 127, 601
Clear Creek Baptist Bible Coll. 191
Clearwater Christian Coll. 103
Clearwater Comm. Coll. Region 633
Cleary Coll. 250
Clements Job Corps Ctr. (see: Earle C. Clements Job Corps Ctr.)
Clemson Univ. 453, 668
Clermont Coll. 396
Cleveland Chiropractic Coll. 281
Cleveland Chiropractic Coll. of Cleveland Univ. Los Angeles 41
Cleveland Coll. of Jewish Studies 382
Cleveland Comm. Coll. 363, 652
Cleveland Inst. of Art 382
Cleveland Inst. of Dental and Medical Assistants 382
Cleveland Inst. of Electronics 382
Cleveland Inst. of Music 382
Cleveland Inst. of Tech. 382
Cleveland Machining Inst. 378
Cleveland State Comm. Coll. 464, 671
Cleveland State Univ. 382, 657
Climate Control Inst. 184 (KS); 399 (OK)
Clinch Valley Coll. of the Univ. of Virginia 520, 682
Clinton Comm. Coll. 176, 611 (IA); 329, 650 (NY)
Clinton Co. Area Voc. Ed. Ctr. (see: Kentucky Tech—Clinton Co. Area Voc. Ed. Ctr.)
Clinton Tech. Inst./Motorcycle Mechanics Inst. 20
Cloud Co. Comm. Coll. 184, 613
Clover Park Vo-Tech Inst. 533
Clovis Comm. Coll. 320, 646
Cloyd's Beauty Sch. No.2 566

Cloyd's Beauty Sch. No.3 566
Coahoma Comm. Coll. 274, 635
Coast Comm. Coll. Dist. 582
Coast Guard Acad. (see: U.S. Coast Guard Acad.)
Coast Guard Inst. (see: U.S. Coast Guard Inst.)
Coastal Carolina Comm. Coll. 363, 652
Coastal Coll. 210
Coastline Comm. Coll. 41, 582
Cobleskill Coll. of Agriculture and Tech. (see: State Univ. of New York Coll. of Agriculture and Tech. at Cobleski)
Cochise Coll. 20, 578
Coe Coll. 176
Coffeyville Comm. Coll. 184, 613
Cogswell Polytechnical Coll. 41
Coker Coll. 453
Colby Coll. 221
Colby Comm. Coll. 184, 613
Colby-Sawyer Coll. 304
Colegio Biblico Pentecostal 442
Colegio Mayor de Tech. 442
Coleman Coll. 41
Colgate Rochester Divinity Sch./Crozer Theol. Sem. 329
Colgate Univ. 329
Coll. for Financial Planning 565
Coll. for Human Services 329
Coll. Misericordia 417
Coll. of Aeronautics 329
Coll. of Alameda 41, 586
Coll. of Associated Arts 265
Coll. of Charleston 453, 668
Coll. of Court Reporting 166
Coll. of Du Page 148, 606
Coll. of Eastern Utah 512, 680
Coll. of Great Falls 293
Coll. of Hair Design 296
Coll. of Insurance 329
Coll. of Lake Co. 148, 606
Coll. of Legal Arts 406
Coll. of Marin 41, 585
Coll. of Micronesia 690
Coll. of Mount St. Joseph 382
Coll. of Mount St. Vincent 329
Coll. of New Rochelle 329
Coll. of Notre Dame 41
Coll. of Notre Dame Maryland 225
Coll. of Oceaneering 41
Coll. of Office Tech. 148
Coll. of Osteopathic Medicine of the Pacific 41
Coll. of Our Lady of the Elms 237
Coll. of Puerto Rico 442
Coll. of Recording Arts 41
Coll. of St. Benedict 265
Coll. of St. Catherine 265

Institutional Index

Coll. of St. Elizabeth 309
Coll. of St. Francis 148
Coll. of St. Joseph 515
Coll. of St. Mary 296
Coll. of St. Rose 330
Coll. of St. Scholastica 265
Coll. of San Mateo 42, 588
Coll. of Santa Fe 320
Coll. of Southern Idaho 143, 604
Coll. of Staten Island 330, 647
Coll. of the Albemarle 363, 652
Coll. of the Atlantic 221
Coll. of the Canyons 42, 589
Coll. of the Desert 42, 582
Coll. of the Holy Cross 237
Coll. of the Mainland 484, 673
Coll. of the Marshall Islands 560, 690
Coll. of the Ozarks 281
Coll. of the Palm Beaches 103
Coll. of the Redwoods 42, 587
Coll. of the Sequoias 42, 589
Coll. of the Siskiyous 42, 589
Coll. of the Southwest 320
Coll. of West Virginia 540, 687
Coll. of William and Mary 520, 682
Coll. of Wooster 382
Coll. Without Walls 489
Collier Tech. Inst. (see: Sidney N. Collier Tech. Inst.)
Collin Co. Comm. Coll. 485, 673
Collins Graphic Design Sch. (see: Al Collins Graphic Design Sch.)
Colorado Aero Tech 80
Colorado Christian Univ. 80
Colorado Coll. 80
Colorado Commission on Higher Ed. 593
Colorado Comm. Coll. and Occupational Ed. System 593
Colorado Inst. of Art 80
Colorado Mountain Coll. 80, 593
Colorado Northwestern Comm. Coll. 80, 593
Colorado Sch. of Dog Grooming 80
Colorado Sch. of Mines 80
Colorado Sch. of Trades 81
Colorado Sch. of Travel 81
Colorado State Univ. 81, 593
Colorado State Univ. System 593
Colorado Tech. Coll. 81
Columbia Basin Coll. 533, 685
Columbia Bible Coll. and Sem. 453
Columbia Christian Coll. 406
Columbia Coll. 42, 590 (CA); 148 (IL); 281 (MO); 443 (PR); 453 (SC)
Columbia Coll. Hollywood 42
Columbia Coll. of Nursing 545
Columbia Jr. Coll. of Bus. 453
Columbia Sch. of Broadcasting 301

Columbia Sch. of Computer Sci. 301
Columbia State Comm. Coll. 464, 671
Columbia Theol. Sem. 127
Columbia Union Coll. 225
Columbia Univ. 330
Columbia-Greene Comm. Coll. 330, 650
Columbus Coll. 127, 601
Columbus Coll. of Art and Design 383
Columbus Para-Prof. Inst. 383
Columbus State Comm. Coll. 383, 657
Columbus Tech. Inst. (see: Indiana Vo-Tech Coll.—Columbus Tech. Inst.)
Columbus Tech. Inst. 128
Commercial Coll. of Baton Rouge 210
Commercial Coll. of Shreveport 210
Commercial Driver Training 330
Commercial Training Services 407 (OR); 533 (WA)
Commonwealth Bus. Coll. 166
Commonwealth Coll. 520
Commonwealth Coll. of Funeral Service 485
Communication Arts Sch. (see: Sch. of Communication Arts)
Communication Electronics Sch. (see: Sch. of Communication Electronics)
Comm. Coll. of Allegheny Co. 663
Comm. Coll. of Allegheny Co. Allegheny Campus 417, 663
Comm. Coll. of Allegheny Co. Boyce Campus 417, 663
Comm. Coll. of Allegheny Co. Coll. Ctr. North 417, 663
Comm. Coll. of Allegheny Co. South Campus 417, 663
Comm. Coll. of Aurora 81, 593
Comm. Coll. of Beaver Co. 417, 663
Comm. Coll. of Denver 81, 593
Comm. Coll. of Micronesia 560, 690
Comm. Coll. of Philadelphia 417, 663
Comm. Coll. of Rhode Island 450, 667
Comm. Coll. of Southern Nevada 301, 642
Comm. Coll. of the Air Force 5
Comm. Coll. of the Finger Lakes 330, 650
Comm. Coll. of Vermont 515, 681
Comm. Hospital of Roanoke Valley Coll. of Health Scis. 520
Compton Comm. Coll. 42, 582

Compton Comm. Coll. Dist. 582
Computer Career Ctr. 485
Computer Dynamics Inst. 521
Computer Learning Ctr. 42 (CA); 148 (IL); 237 (MA); 309 (NJ); 418 (PA); 521 (VA)
Computer Learning Network 418
Computer Processing Inst. 89 (CT); 237 (MA)
Computer Sci. Inst. (see: Inst. of Computer Sci., Ltd.)
Computer Tech 418
Conception Sem. Coll. 281
Concord Coll. 540, 687
ConCorde Career Inst. 43 (CA); 81 (CO); 103-104 (FL); 266 (MN); 281 (MO); 407 (OR); 465 (TN); 485 (TX)
Concordia Coll. 5 (AL); 250 (MI); 266 (MN); 330 (NY); 407 (OR)
Concordia Lutheran Coll. 485
Concordia Sem. 281
Concordia Teachers Coll. 296
Concordia Tech. Inst. 210
Concordia Theol. Sem. 166
Concordia Univ. 148
Concordia Univ. Wisconsin 546
Connecticut Board of Governers for Higher Ed. 595
Connecticut Bus. Inst. 89
Connecticut Ctr. for Massage Therapy, Inc. 89
Connecticut Coll. 89
Connecticut Comm.-Tech. Colls. 595
Connecticut Inst. of Art 89
Connecticut Inst. of Hair Design 89
Connecticut Sch. of Electronics 89
Connecticut State Univ. Central Office 596
Connors State Coll. 399
Conservatory of Music of Puerto Rico 443
Conservatory of Recording Arts and Scis. 20
Consolidated Sch. of Bus. 418
Consolidated Welding Schs. 43
Continental Health and Career Ctr. 330
Contra Costa Coll. 43, 582
Contra Costa Comm. Coll. Dist. 582
Converse Coll. 454
Conway Sch. of Landscape Design 237
Cooke Co. Coll. 485, 673
Cooking and Hospitality Inst. of Chicago 148
Cooley Law Sch. (see: Thomas M. Cooley Law Sch.)
Cooper Acad. of Court Reporting 104

Institutional Index

Cooper Union for the Advancement of Sci. and Art 331
Coosa Valley Tech. Inst. 128
Cope Inst. 331
Copiah-Lincoln Comm. Coll. 274, 635
Coppin State Coll. 225, 627
Corbin Area Voc. Ed. Ctr. (see: Kentucky Tech—Corbin Area Voc. Ed. Ctr.)
Corcoran Sch. of Art 98
Cornell Coll. 176
Cornell Univ. 331
Corning Comm. Coll. 331, 650
Cornish Coll. of the Arts 533
Corpus Christi State Univ. 485, 676
Cortland Coll. (see: State Univ. of New York Coll. at Cortland)
Cosumnes River Coll. 43, 585
Cottey Coll. 281
Cotton Boll Vo-Tech Sch. 27
Co. Coll. of Morris 310, 644
Co. Schs., Inc. 89
Court Reporting Careers, Inc. 104
Court Reporting Coll. (see: Coll. of Court Reporting)
Court Reporting Inst. 428
Court Reporting Inst. of Dallas 485
Court Reporting Inst. of Tennessee 465
Covenant Coll. 128
Covenant Theol. Sem. 282
Cowley Co. Comm. Coll. 184, 613
Coyne-American Inst. 148
Craft Inst. 418
Crafton Hills Coll. 43, 587
Cranbrook Acad. of Art 250
Crandall Jr. Coll. 128
Cranford Coll. 185
Craven Comm. Coll. 363, 652
Creative Sch. of Beauty 104
Creighton Univ. 296
Crenshaw Tech. Inst. 44
Crescent City Tech 210
Crichton Coll. 465
Criswell Coll. 485
Crowder Coll. 282, 637
Crown Acad. 533
Crown Bus. Inst. 104
Crown Coll. 266
Cuesta Coll. 44, 588
Culinary Inst. of America 331
Culver-Stockton Coll. 282
Cumberland Coll. 191
Cumberland Co. Coll. 310, 644
Cumberland Sch. of Tech. 465
Cumberland Univ. 465

Cumberland Valley Health Occupations Ctr. (see: Kentucky Tech—Cumberland Valley Health Occupations Ctr.)
Cummins Sch. of Anesthesia (see: Manley L. Cummins Sch. of Anesthesia)
Cunningham Studio (see: Merce Cunningham Studio)
Curry Coll. 237
Curtis Inst. of Music 418
Cuyahoga Comm. Coll. 383, 657
Cuyamaca Coll. 44, 583
Cypress Coll. 44, 586

D

D'Youville Coll. 331
D-Q Univ. 44
Dabney S. Lancaster Comm. Coll. 521, 683
Daemen Coll. 331
Dakota Co. Tech. Coll. 266
Dakota State Univ. 460, 670
Dakota Wesleyan Univ. 460
Daley Coll. (see: Richard J. Daley Coll.)
Dalfort Aircraft Tech 485
Dalhousie Univ. 555
Dallas Baptist Univ. 486
Dallas Christian Coll. 486
Dallas Co. Comm. Coll. Dist. 673
Dallas Inst. of Funeral Services 486
Dallas Theol. Sem. 486
Dalton Coll. 128, 601
Dalton Voc. Sch. of Health Occupations 128
Dana Coll. 296
Dana McKay Bus. Coll. 301
Dance Theatre of Harlem, Inc. 331
Daniel Webster Coll. 304
Danville Area Comm. Coll. 148, 606
Danville Comm. Coll. 521, 683
Danville Sch. of Health Occupations (see: Kentucky Tech—Danville Sch. of Health Occupations)
Darkei No'am Rabbinical Coll. 331
Dartmouth Coll. 304
Darton Coll. 128, 601
Daspit Beauty Coll. (see: Jocelyn Daspit Beauty Coll.)
Data Inst. 90
Data Processing Inst. (see: Inst. of Data Processing)
Davenport Barber Coll. 177
Davenport Coll. 166 (IN); 250 (MI)
David G. Erwin Tech. Ctr. 104
David Lipscomb Univ. 465

David's Head Coll. of Hair Design 297
David's Sch. of Hair Design (see: Mr. David's Sch. of Hair Design)
Davidson Coll. 363
Davidson Co. Comm. Coll. 363, 653
Davidson Tech. Coll. 465
Daviess Co. State Vo-Tech Sch. (see: Kentucky Tech—Daviess Co. State Vo-Tech Sch.)
Davis and Elkins Coll. 540
Davis Beauty Coll. (see: Jeff Davis Beauty Coll.)
Davis Coll. 383
Davis State Jr. Coll. (see: Jefferson Davis State Jr. Coll.)
Davis Tech. Inst. (see: Jefferson Davis Tech. Inst.)
Dawn Aeronautics 96
Dawson Coll. 555
Dawson Comm. Coll. 293, 639
Daytona Beach Comm. Coll. 104, 598
De Sales Sch. of Theol. 98
Deaconess Coll. of Nursing 282
Dean Inst. of Tech. 418
Dean Jr. Coll. 237
DeAnza Coll. 44, 583
Debbie's Sch. of Beauty Culture 5 (AL); 486 (TX)
Deep Springs Coll. 44
Defense Equal Opportunity Management Inst. 104
Defense Information Sch. 166
Defense Intelligence Coll. 98
Defense Language Inst. 44
Defense Mapping Sch. 521
Defiance Coll. 383
DeKalb Beauty Coll. 128
DeKalb Coll. 128
DeKalb Co. Occupational Ed. Ctr.—Central 128
DeKalb Co. Occupational Ed. Ctr.—North 128
DeKalb Co. Occupational Ed. Ctr.—South 128
DeKalb Tech. Inst. 129
Del Mar Coll. 486, 674
Delaware Co. Comm. Coll. 418, 663
Delaware Co. Inst. of Training 418
Delaware Postsecondary Ed. Commission 597
Delaware State Coll. 96, 597
Delaware Tech. and Comm. Coll. President's Office 597
Delaware Tech. and Comm. Coll. Southern 96, 597
Delaware Tech. and Comm. Coll. Stanton 96, 597

Institutional Index

Delaware Tech. and Comm. Coll. Terry 96, 597
Delaware Tech. and Comm. Coll. Wilmington 96, 597
Delaware Valley Acad. of Medical and Dental Assistants 419
Delaware Valley Coll. of Sci. and Agriculture 419
Delgado Comm. Coll. 210
Delhi Coll. of Tech. (see: State Univ. of New York Coll. of Tech. at Delhi)
Dell'Arte Sch. of Physical Theatre 44
Delta Career Coll. 27 (AR); 210-211 (LA)
Delta Career Inst. 486
Delta Coll. 250, 630
Delta Jr. Coll. 211
Delta Sch. of Bus. and Tech. 211
Delta Schs. 211
Delta State Univ. 274, 635
Delta Tech. Inst. 274
Delta-Ouachita Tech. Inst. 211
DeMarzo Inst. of Prof. Electrology (see: Claire DeMarzo Inst. of Prof. Electrology)
Denham Springs Beauty Coll. 211
Denison Univ. 383
Denmark Tech. Coll. 454, 669
Dental Tech. Inst. 44
Denver Acad. of Court Reporting 81
Denver Automotive and Diesel Coll. 81
Denver Bus. Coll. 81
Denver Comm. Coll. (see: Comm. Coll. of Denver)
Denver Conservative Baptist Sem. 82
Denver Inst. of Tech. 82
Denver Paralegal Inst. 82
Denver Tech. Coll. 82
DePaul Univ. 149
DePauw Univ. 166
Deree Coll. 560
DermaClinic Acad. of Make-Up and Skin Care for Estheticians 129
Des Moines Area Comm. Coll. 177, 611
Desert Coll. (see: Coll. of the Desert)
Desert Comm. Coll. Dist. 582
Desert Inst. of the Healing Arts 20
Design Inst. of San Diego 45
Detroit Bus. Inst. 250-251
Detroit Bus. Inst.—Downriver 251
Detroit Coll. of Bus. 251
Detroit Coll. of Law 251
Detroit Inst. of Aeronautics 251
Detroit Inst. of Commerce 251
Detroit Inst. of Ophthalmology 251

DeVry Inst. of Tech., Atlanta 129
DeVry Inst. of Tech., Columbus 383
DeVry Inst. of Tech., Dallas 486
DeVry Inst. of Tech., Kansas City 282
DeVry Inst. of Tech., Lombard 149
DeVry Inst. of Tech., Los Angeles 44
DeVry Inst. of Tech., Phoenix 20
DeVry Insts. 149
DeVry Tech. Inst., Woodbridge 310
Diablo Valley Coll. 45, 582
Diamond Council of America 282
Diana Ramsay's Specialty Beauty Sch. 104
Dick Hill International Flight Sch. 282
Dickinson Bus. Sch. 282
Dickinson Coll. 419
Dickinson Sch. of Law 419
Dickinson State Univ. 375, 656
Dickinson-Warren Bus. Coll. 45
Diesel Driving Acad. 211
Diesel Inst. of America 104 (FL); 225 (MD)
Diesel Specialty's 486
Diesel Tech. Inst. 90
Diesel Truck Driver Training Sch. 407 (OR); 546 (WI)
Dillard Univ. 212
Dist. of Columbia Sch. of Law 98
Divers Acad. of the Eastern Seaboard 310
Divers Inst. of Tech., Inc. 533
Divine Word Coll. 177
Dixie Coll. 512, 680
Doane Coll. 297
Dr. Martin Luther Coll. 266
Dr. Welbes Coll. of Massage Therapy 297
Dr. William M. Scholl Coll. of Podiatric Medicine 149
Dodge City Comm. Coll. 185, 613
Doggie Mat 20
Domestic Health Care Inst. 212
Dominican Coll. of Blauvelt 331
Dominican Coll. of San Rafael 45
Dominican House of Studies 98
Dominican Sch. of Philosophy and Theol. 45
Dominion Bus. Sch. 521
Don Bosco Tech. Inst. 45
Dona Ana Branch Comm. Coll. 320
Donahue International Sch. of Hairstyling (see: Joseph Donahue International Sch. of Hairstyling)
Donnelly Coll. 185
Dootson Sch. of Trucking 45
Dordt Coll. 177

Dorsey Bus. Sch. 251
Douglas MacArthur State Tech. Coll. 5
Douglas Sch. of Bus. 419
Dover Bus. Coll. 310
Dowling Coll. 331
Drake Bus. Sch. 332
Drake Coll. of Bus. 310
Drake Secretarial Coll. 310
Drake State Tech. Coll. (see: J.F. Drake State Tech. Coll.)
Drake Univ. 177
Draughon Bus. Coll. 27 (AR); 282 (MO)
Draughon Coll. 399
Draughon's Bus. Coll. 275
Draughon's Coll. of Bus. 486
Draughon's Coll. of Nursing Assistants 486
Draughons Coll. 129
Draughons Jr. Coll. 5 (AL); 465-466 (TN)
Drew Univ. (see: Charles R. Drew Univ.)
Drew Univ. 310
Drexel Univ. 419
Drury Coll. 282
du Cret Sch. of the Arts 310
Du Page Coll.(see: Coll. of Du Page)
DuBois Bus. Coll. 419
Dudley Hall Career Inst. 237
Duff's Bus. Inst. 419
Duke Univ. 363
Dull Knife Memorial Coll. 567
Duluth Bus. Univ. 266
Duluth Tech. Coll. 266
Dundalk Comm. Coll. 225, 626
Dunwoody Industrial Inst. 266
Duquesne Univ. 419
Durham Coll. 486
Durham Tech. Comm. Coll. 363, 653
Dutchess Comm. Coll. 332, 650
Dyersburg State Comm. Coll. 466, 671
Dyke Coll. 383

E

ECPI Computer Inst. 521
ESI Career Ctr. 251 (MI); 384 (OH)
ETI Tech. Coll. 384
Earle C. Clements Job Corps Ctr. 191
Earlham Coll. 166
East Alabama Skills Ctr. 5
East Arkansas Comm. Coll. 27
East Carolina Univ. 364, 655
East Central Coll. 282, 637
East Central Comm. Coll. 275, 635

Institutional Index

East Central Univ. 400
East Coast Aero Tech. Sch. 247
East Coast Bible Coll. 364
East Georgia Coll. 129, 601
East Grand Forks Tech. Coll. 266
East Los Angeles Coll. 45, 584
East Los Angeles Occupational Ctr. 45
East Mississippi Comm. Coll. 275, 635
East St. Louis Comm. Coll. (see: State Comm. Coll. of East St. Louis)
East Stroudsburg Univ. of Pennsylvania 419, 663
East Tennessee State Univ. 466, 671
East Texas Baptist Univ. 487
East Texas State Univ. 487, 674
East Texas State Univ. at Texarkana 487, 674
East-West Coll. 407
East-West Univ. 149
Eastcentral Tech. Inst. (see: Indiana Vo-Tech Coll.— Eastcentral Tech. Inst.)
Eastern Arizona Coll. 21, 578
Eastern Baptist Theol. Sem. 419
Eastern Coll. 419
Eastern Coll. of Health Vocations 27 (AR); 212 (LA)
Eastern Connecticut State Univ. 90, 596
Eastern Idaho Tech. Coll. 143
Eastern Illinois Univ. 149, 605
Eastern Iowa Comm. Coll. Dist. 611
Eastern Jackson Co. Coll. of Allied Health 282
Eastern Kentucky Univ. 191, 615
Eastern Maine Tech. Coll. 221
Eastern Mennonite Coll. and Sem. 522
Eastern Michigan Univ. 251, 630
Eastern Montana Coll. 293, 639
Eastern Nazarene Coll. 237
Eastern New Mexico Univ. 320, 646
Eastern New Mexico Univ.— Roswell 320
Eastern Oklahoma State Coll. 400
Eastern Oregon State Coll. 407, 661
Eastern Pentecostal Bible Coll. 555
Eastern Shore Comm. Coll. 522, 683
Eastern Utah Coll. (see: Coll. of Eastern Utah)
Eastern Virginia Medical Sch. 522
Eastern Washington Univ. 533, 685
Eastern Wyoming Coll. 553, 689
Eastfield Coll. 487, 674
Echols International Hotel Sch. 149
Eckerd Coll. 104

Eddyville Voc. Ed. Ctr. (see: Kentucky Tech—Eddyville Voc. Ed. Ctr.)
Eden Area Voc. Ctr. (see: John Pope Eden Area Voc. Ed. Ctr.)
Eden Theol. Sem. 283
Edgecombe Comm. Coll. 364, 653
Edgewood Coll. 546
Edinboro Univ. of Pennsylvania 420, 663
Edison Comm. Coll. 105, 598
Edison State Coll. (see: Thomas A. Edison State Coll.)
Edison State Comm. Coll. 384, 657
Edmonds Comm. Coll. 533, 685
Edmondson Jr. Coll. of Bus. 466
Ed. Dynamics Inst. 301
Educational Inst. of the American Hotel and Motel Association 252
Educorp Career Coll./Rosston Sch. 45
Eduplex Career Ctr. 45
Edward Waters Coll. 105
El Camino Coll. 45, 582
El Camino Comm. Coll. Dist. 582
El Centro Coll. 487, 674
El Paso Comm. Coll. 487, 674
El Paso Job Corps Ctr. 487
Elaine P. Nunez Tech. Inst. 212
Eldorado Coll. 46
Electronic Coll. and Computer Programming 443
Electronic Computer Programming Inst. 466
Electronic Data Processing Coll. 443
Electronic Insts. 420
Electronic Servicing Inst. 252
Electronic Tech. Inst. 46
Electronics Inst. 283
Elegance International 46
Elgin Comm. Coll. 149, 606
Eli Whitney Regional Vo-Tech Sch. 90
Elinor Smith Sch. 105
Elizabeth City State Univ. 364, 655
Elizabethtown Coll. 420
Elizabethtown Comm. Coll. 191, 615
Elizabethtown State Vo-Tech Sch. (see: Kentucky Tech—Elizabethtown State Vo-Tech Sch.)
Elkins Inst. of Jacksonville 105
Elley Sch. (see: Mildred Elley Sch.)
Ellsworth Comm. Coll. 177, 611
Elmhurst Coll. 149
Elmira Bus. Inst. 332
Elmira Coll. 332
Elon Coll. 364
Embry-Riddle Aeronautical Univ. 105
Emergency Management Inst. 226

Emerson Coll. 238
Emily Griffith Opportunity Sch. 82
Emmanuel Bible Coll. 555
Emmanuel Coll. 129 (GA); 238 (MA)
Emmanuel Coll. of Victoria Univ. 555
Emmanuel Sch. of Religion 466
Emmaus Bible Coll. 177
Emory and Henry Coll. 522
Emory Univ. 129
Emperor's Coll. of Traditional Oriental Medicine 46
Empire Bus. Coll. 82
Empire Coll. 46
Empire State Coll. 332, 648
Empire Tech. Schs. of New Jersey 310
Emporia State Univ. 185, 613
Endicott Coll. 238
Engine City Tech. Inst. 310
Engine Tech. Inst./Pratt and Whitney Aircraft 105
English Language Inst. of America 149
Enid Barber Styling Coll. 400
Enterprise State Jr. Coll. 5, 574
Environmental Sci. and Forestry Coll. (see: State Univ. of New York Coll. of Environmental Sci. and Forestry)
Environmental Tech. Sch. 149
Episcopal Divinity Sch. 238
Episcopal Theol. Sem. of the Southwest 487
Erie Bus. Ctr. 420
Erie Comm. Coll. 333, 650
Erie Inst. of Tech. 420
Erie-Behrend Coll. 431
Erskine Coll. 454
Erwin Tech. Ctr. (see: David G. Erwin Tech. Ctr.)
Escuela de Artes Plasticas Instituto de Cultura Puertorriquena 569
Essex Agricultural and Tech. Inst. 238, 628
Essex Comm. Coll. 226, 626
Essex Co. Coll. 310, 644
Estelle Harman Actors' Workshop 46
Eton Tech. Inst. 533
Eugene Bible Coll. 407
Eureka Coll. 150
Evangel Coll. 283
Evangelical Sch. of Theol. 420
Evangelical Sem. of Puerto Rico 443
Evangeline Tech. Inst. 212
Everett Comm. Coll. 533, 685
Evergreen State Coll. 534, 685
Evergreen Valley Coll. 46, 588

Institutional Index

Evers Coll.(see:Medgar Evers Coll.)
Executive Secretarial Sch. 487
Executive Security International, Ltd. 82
Extension Course Inst. of the U.S. Air Force 6

F

FAA Ctr. for Management Development 105
FEGS Trades and Bus. Sch. 333
Fairdale Voc. Ed. Ctr. (see: Kentucky Tech—Fairdale Voc. Ed. Ctr.)
Fairfax Comm. Coll. (see: Lord Fairfax Comm. Coll.)
Fairfield Univ. 90
Fairleigh Dickinson Univ. 311
Fairmont State Coll. 540, 687
Faith Baptist Bible Coll. and Theol. Sem. 177
Fajardo Regional Coll. 443, 665
Farah's Beauty Sch. 454
Faribault Tech. Coll. 266
Farmingdale Coll. of Tech. (see: State Univ. of New York Coll. of Tech. at Farmingdale)
Fashion Careers of California 46
Fashion Design Coll. 443
Fashion Inst. of Design and Merchandising 46
Fashion Inst. of Tech. 333, 648
Fashion Merchandising Inst. 443
Faulkner Area Voc. Ctr. 6
Faulkner State Jr. Coll. (see: James H. Faulkner State Jr. Coll.)
Faulkner Univ. 6
Fayetteville Beauty Coll. 364
Fayetteville State Univ. 364, 655
Fayetteville Tech. Comm. Coll. 364, 653
Feather River Coll. 47, 583
Feather River Comm. Coll. Dist. 582
Federal Correctional Inst. 105
Felician Coll. 311
Fell's Sch. of Bus. (see: Cheryl Fell's Sch. of Bus.)
Fergus Falls Comm. Coll. 267, 633
Ferris State Univ. 252, 630
Ferrum Coll. 522
Fielding Inst. 47
Financial Planning Coll. (see: Coll. for Financial Planning)
FinEd, Sch. of Financial Ed. 212
Finger Lakes Comm. Coll. (see: Comm. Coll. of the Finger Lakes)

Firelands Coll. 380
Fischer Tech. Coll. 212
Fischer Tech. Inst. 522
Fisher Coll. 238
Fisk Univ. 466
Fitchburg State Coll. 238, 628
Five Towns Coll. 333
Flagler Career Inst.—Jacksonville 105
Flagler Career Inst.—Miami 105
Flagler Coll. 105
Flaming Rainbow Univ. 400
Flathead Valley Comm. Coll. 293, 639
Flatwoods Civilian Conservation Ctr. 522
Fleet Bus. Sch. 226
Flight Safety International 106
Flint Hills Tech. Sch. 185
Flint Inst. of Barbering 252
Florence-Darlington Tech. Coll. 454, 669
Florida Agricultural and Mechanical Univ. 106, 599
Florida Atlantic Univ. 106, 599
Florida Baptist Theol. Coll. 106
Florida Bible Coll. 106
Florida Career Inst. 106
Florida Christian Coll. 106
Florida Coll. 106
Florida Comm. Coll. at Jacksonville 106, 598
Florida Computer and Bus. Coll. 106
Florida Inst. of Massage Therapy 106
Florida Inst. of Tech. 107
Florida Inst. of Ultrasound 107
Florida International Univ. 107, 599
Florida Keys Comm. Coll. 107, 598
Florida Memorial Coll. 107
Florida National Coll. 107
Florida Parishes Tech. Inst. 212
Florida Sch. of Bus. 107
Florida Southern Coll. 107
Florida State Board of Comm. Colls. 598
Florida State Univ. 107, 599
Florida Tech. Coll. 108
Florissant Upholstery Sch. 283
Floyd Coll. 129, 601
Folk Art Inst. of the Museum of American Folk Art 333
Folkes Tech. Inst. 212
Fontbonne Coll. 283
Foothill Coll. 47, 583
Foothill-DeAnza Comm. Coll. Dist. 583
Ford Comm. Coll. (see: Henry Ford Comm. Coll.)
Fordham Univ. 333

Forest Inst. of Prof. Psychology 150
Forrest Jr. Coll. 454
Forsyth Sch. of Dental Hygienists 238
Forsyth Tech. Comm. Coll. 364, 653
Fort Belknap Coll. 567
Fort Berthold Comm. Coll. 375
Fort Hays State Univ. 185, 613
Fort Lauderdale Coll. 108
Fort Lewis Coll. 82, 593
Fort Peck Comm. Coll. 293
Fort Sanders Sch. of Nursing 570
Fort Scott Comm. Coll. 185, 613
Fort Valley State Coll. 129, 601
Fort Wayne Sch. of Radiography 166
Fort Worth Trade Sch. 487
Four-C Coll. 488
Fox Coll. (see: George Fox Coll.)
Fox Secretarial Coll. 150
Fox Valley Tech. Inst. 546
Framingham State Coll. 238, 628
Francis Marion Coll. 454, 668
Francis Tuttle Vo-Tech Ctr. 400
Franciscan Sch. of Theol. 47
Franciscan Univ. of Steubenville 384
Frank Lloyd Wright Sch. of Architecture 21
Frank Phillips Coll. 488, 674
Franklin and Marshall Coll. 420
Franklin Coll. 191 (KY); 561 (Switzerland)
Franklin Coll. of Court Reporting 212
Franklin Coll. of Indiana 166
Franklin Inst. of Boston 238
Franklin Pierce Coll. 304
Franklin Pierce Law Ctr. 304
Franklin Univ. 384
Fredd State Tech. Coll. 6
Frederick Comm. Coll. 226, 626
Fredonia Coll. (see: State Univ. of New York Coll. at Fredonia)
Free Will Baptist Bible Coll. 466
Freed-Hardeman Univ. 466
Fremont-Newark Comm. Coll. Dist. 583
French Culinary Inst. 333
French Fashion Acad. 334
Fresno City Coll. 47, 590
Fresno Pacific Coll. 47
Friends Univ. 185
Friends World Coll. 568
Front Range Comm. Coll. 82, 593
Frontier Comm. Coll. 150, 606
Frostburg State Univ. 226, 627
Fugazzi Coll. 191
Fuld Sch. of Nursing (see: Helene Fuld Sch. of Nursing)

Institutional Index

Full Sail Ctr. for the Recording Arts 108
Fuller Theol. Sem. 47
Fullerton Coll. 47, 586
Fulton Co. Area Voc. Ed. Ctr. (see: Kentucky Tech—Fulton Co. Area Voc. Ed. Ctr.)
Fulton-Montgomery Comm. Coll. 334, 650
Fundacion Universidad de las Americas 560
Furman Univ. 454
Futures in Ed., Inc. 47

G

GMI Engineering and Management Inst. 252
Gadsden Bus. Coll. 6
Gadsden State Comm. Coll. 6, 574
Gainesville Coll. 129, 601
Galen Coll. of Medical and Dental Assistants 47
Gallaudet Univ. 98
Galveston Coll. 488, 674
Gannon Univ. 420
Garces Commercial Coll. 108
Garden City Comm. Coll. 185, 613
Gardner-Webb Coll. 365
Garfield Bus. Inst. 420
Garland Co. Comm. Coll. 27
Garrad Co. Area Voc. Ed. Ctr. (see: Kentucky Tech—Garrad Co. Area Voc. Ed. Ctr.)
Garrett Comm. Coll. 226, 626
Garrett-Evangelical Theol. Sem. 150
Garth Area Voc. Ed. Ctr. (see: Kentucky Tech—Garth Area Voc. Ed. Ctr.)
Gary Job Corps Ctr. 488
Gaston Coll. 365, 653
Gateway Comm. Coll. 21, 578
Gateway Electronics Inst. 297
Gateway Tech. Coll. 546
Gateway Tech. Inst. 420
Gavilan Coll. 48, 583
Gavilan Comm. Coll. Dist. 583
Geiger's Sch. of Cosmetology 275
Gem City Coll. 150
Gemological Inst. of America 48
General Tech. Inst. Welding Trade Sch. 311
General Theol. Sem. 334
Genesee Comm. Coll. 334, 650
Geneseo Coll. (see: State Univ. of New York Coll. at Geneseo)
Geneva Coll. 421
George C. Wallace State Comm. Coll. 6, 574

George Corley Wallace State Comm. Coll. 6, 574
George Fox Coll. 407
George Mason Univ. 522, 682
George Stone Vo-Tech Ctr. 108
George T. Baker Aviation Sch. 108
George Washington Univ. 98
Georgetown Coll. 192
Georgetown Univ. 99
Georgia Coll. 129, 601
Georgia Inst. of Tech. 130, 601
Georgia Medical Coll. (see: Medical Coll. of Georgia)
Georgia Medical Inst. 130
Georgia Military Coll. 130
Georgia Southern Univ. 130, 602
Georgia Southwestern Coll. 130, 602
Georgia State Univ. 130, 602
Georgian Court Coll. 311
Germanna Comm. Coll. 522, 683
Gettysburg Coll. 421
Gibbs Sch. (see: Katharine Gibbs Sch.)
Glasgow Sch. for Health Occupations (see: Kentucky Tech—Glasgow Sch. for Health Occupations)
Glassboro State Coll. 311, 645
Glen Oaks Comm. Coll. 252, 630
Glendale Career Coll. 48
Glendale Comm. Coll. 21, 578 (AZ); 48, 583 (CA)
Glendale Comm. Coll. Dist. 583
Glenville State Coll. 540, 687
Global Bus. Inst. 311 (NJ); 334 (NY)
Globe Coll. of Bus. 267
Gloucester Co. Coll. 311, 644
God's Bible Coll. 384
Goddard Coll. 515
Gogebic Comm. Coll. 252, 630
Golden Gate Baptist Theol. Sem. 48
Golden Gate Univ. 48
Golden State Sch. 48
Golden West Coll. 48, 582
Goldey Beacom Coll. 96
Golf Acad. of San Diego 48
Golf Acad. of the South 49
Gonzaga Univ. 534
Gordon Coll. 130, 602 (GA); 238 (MA)
Gordon Inst. 567
Gordon-Conwell Theol. Sem. 239
Goshen Biblical Sem. 166
Goshen Coll. 167
Goucher Coll. 226
Governors State Univ. 150, 605
Grace Bible Coll. 252
Grace Coll. 167
Grace Coll. of the Bible 297
Grace Theol. Sem. 167

Graceland Coll. 177
Grad. Sch. and Univ. Ctr. 334, 647
Grad. Sch. of Biomedical Scis. 318
Grad. Theol. Union 49
Graham Sch. of Contemporary Dance (see: Martha Graham Sch. of Contemporary Dance)
Grambling State Univ. 213, 623
Grand Canyon Univ. 21
Grand Rapids Baptist Coll. and Sem. 252
Grand Rapids Comm. Coll. 252, 630
Grand Rapids Educational Ctr. for Medical and Dental Assts. 253
Grand Valley State Univ. 253, 630
Grand View Coll. 177
Grantham Coll. of Engineering 213
Gratz Coll. 421
Grays Harbor Coll. 534, 685
Grayson Co. Coll. 488, 674
Great Falls Coll. (see: Coll. of Great Falls)
Great Falls Vo-Tech Ctr. 293, 639
Great Lakes Bible Coll. 253
Great Lakes Jr. Coll. of Bus. 253
Great Lakes Tech. Inst. 384
Great Plains Area Vo-Tech Ctr. 400
Greater Hartford Comm. Coll. 90, 595
Greater New Haven State Tech. Coll. 90, 595
Green Co. Area Voc. Ed. Ctr. (see: Kentucky Tech—Green Co. Area Voc. Ed. Ctr.)
Green Mountain Coll. 515
Green River Comm. Coll. 534, 685
Greenfield Comm. Coll. 239, 628
Greensboro Coll. 365
Greenup Co. Area Voc. Ed. Ctr. (see: Kentucky Tech—Greenup Co. Area Voc. Ed. Ctr.)
Greenville Coll. 150
Greenville Tech. Coll. 454, 669
Griffin Coll. 534
Griffin Tech. Inst. 130
Grinnell Coll. 177
Grossmont Coll. 49, 583
Grossmont-Cuyamaca Comm. Coll. Dist. 583
Grove City Coll. 421
Grove Sch. of Music 49
Grumman Data Systems Inst. 334
Guam Comm. Coll. 139
Guayama Regional Coll. 444, 665
Guilford Coll. 365
Guilford Tech. Comm. Coll. 365, 653
Gulf Area Tech. Inst. 213
Gulf Coast Comm. Coll. 108, 598
Gulf Coast Trades Ctr. 488

Gulfport Job Corps Ctr. 275
Gupton Coll. (see: John A. Gupton Coll.)
Gupton-Jones Coll. of Funeral Service 131
Gustavus Adolphus Coll. 267
Gwinnett Coll. 131
Gwinnett Tech. Inst. 131
Gwynedd-Mercy Coll. 421

H

Hadley Sch. for the Blind 150
Hagerstown Bus. Coll. 226
Hagerstown Jr. Coll. 226, 626
Hahnemann Univ. 421
Hair Design Coll. (see: Coll. of Hair Design)
Hairstyling Inst. of Charlotte 365
Halifax Comm. Coll. 365, 653
Hall Career Inst. (see: Dudley Hall Career Inst.)
Hall Inst. of Tech. 450
Hallmark Inst. of Photography 239
Hallmark Inst. of Tech. 488
Hamilton Bus. Coll. 177
Hamilton Coll. 334
Hamilton Tech. Coll. 178
Hamline Univ. 267
Hammel Coll. 384
Hammond Area Voc. Sch. 213
Hampden-Sydney Coll. 522
Hampshire Coll. 239
Hampton Univ. 522
Hamrick Truck Driving Sch. 384
Hancock Coll. (see: Allan Hancock Coll.)
Haney Vo-Tech Ctr. (see: Tom P. Haney Vo-Tech Ctr.)
Hannah Harrison Career Sch. 99
Hannibal Area Vo-Tech Sch. 283
Hannibal-LaGrange Coll. 283
Hanover Coll. 167
Hanson's Barber Sch. 221
Harcum Jr. Coll. 421
Hardin-Simmons Univ. 488
Harding Bus. Coll. 384
Harding Univ. 27
Harding Univ. Grad. Sch. of Religion 467
Harford Comm. Coll. 226, 626
Harlan State Vo-Tech Sch. (see: Kentucky Tech—Harlan State Vo-Tech Sch.)
Harman Actors' Workshop (see: Estelle Harman Actors' Workshop)
Harold Washington Coll. 151, 605

Harper Coll. (see: William Rainey Harper Coll.)
Harrington Inst. of Interior Design 151
Harris Sch. of Bus. 311
Harris Tech. Inst. (see: T.H. Harris Tech. Inst.)
Harris-Stowe State Coll. 283, 637
Harrisburg Area Comm. Coll. 421, 664
Harrisburg-Capital Coll. 431
Harrison Career Sch. (see: Hannah Harrison Career Sch.)
Harrison Co. Area Voc. Ed. Ctr. (see: Kentucky Tech—Harrison Co. Area Voc. Ed. Ctr.)
Harrodsburg Area Voc. Ed. Ctr. (see: Kentucky Tech—Harrodsburg Area Voc. Ed. Ctr.)
Harry M. Ayers State Tech. Coll. 6
Harry S Truman Coll. 151, 605
Hartford Ballet Sch. (see: Sch. of the Hartford Ballet)
Hartford Camerata Conservatory 90
Hartford Coll. for Women 90
Hartford Grad. Ctr. 90
Hartford Secretarial Sch. 90
Hartford Sem. 90
Hartford State Tech. Coll. 90, 595
Hartford Tech. Inst. 91
Hartnell Coll. 49, 583
Hartnell Comm. Coll. Dist. 583
Hartwick Coll. 334
Harvard Univ. 239
Harvey Mudd Coll. 49
Haskell Indian Jr. Coll. 185
Hastings Coll. 297
Hastings Coll. of the Law (see: Univ. of California, Hastings Coll. of the Law)
Haverford Coll. 421
Hawaii Bus. Coll. 140
Hawaii Comm. Coll. 140, 603
Hawaii Inst. of Hair Design 140
Hawaii Loa Coll. 140
Hawaii Pacific Univ. 140
Hawaii Transportation System 140
Hawkeye Inst. of Tech. 178, 611
Haywood Comm. Coll. 365, 653
Hazard Comm. Coll. 192, 615
Hazard State Vo-Tech Sch. (see: Kentucky Tech—Hazard State Vo-Tech Sch.)
Heald 4C's Coll. 49
Heald Bus. Coll.—Hayward 49
Heald Bus. Coll.—Oakland 49
Heald Bus. Coll.—Rohnert Park 49
Heald Bus. Coll.—Sacramento 49
Heald Bus. Coll.—Salinas 49
Heald Bus. Coll.—San Francisco 49

Heald Bus. Coll.—San Jose 49
Heald Bus. Coll.—Stockton 50
Heald Bus. Coll.—Walnut Creek 50
Heald Inst. of Tech.—Hayward 50
Heald Inst. of Tech.—Martinez 50
Heald Inst. of Tech.—Sacramento 50
Heald Inst. of Tech.—San Francisco 50
Heald Inst. of Tech.—San Jose 50
Health Care Training Inst. 467
Health Careers Occupations Sch. 192
Health Staff Training Inst. 50
Heart of Georgia Tech. Inst. 131
Heart of the Ozarks Comm. Tech. Coll. 283
Heathkit Educational Systems 253
Hebrew Coll. 239
Hebrew Union Coll.—Jewish Inst. of Religion 50 (CA); 334 (NY); 384 (OH)
Heidelberg Coll. 385
Helena Vo-Tech Ctr. 294, 639
Helene Fuld Sch. of Nursing 334
Hellenic Coll./Holy Cross Greek Orthodox Theol. Sch. 239
Hemphill Schs. 50
Henderson Comm. Coll. 192, 615
Henderson Co. Area Voc. Ed. Ctr. (see: Kentucky Tech—Henderson Co. Area Voc. Ed. Ctr.)
Henderson State Univ. 27, 580
Hendrix Coll. 27
Hennepin Tech. Coll. 267
Henry Comm. Coll. (see: Patrick Henry Comm. Coll.)
Henry Ford Comm. Coll. 253, 630
Henry State Jr. Coll. (see: Patrick Henry State Jr. Coll.)
Henry W. Brewster Vo-Tech Ctr. 109
Herbert H. Lehman Coll. 334, 647
Heritage Coll. 534
Heritage Coll. of Health Careers 82
Herkimer Co. Comm. Coll. 335, 650
Herzing Inst. 6
Hesser Coll. 304
Hesston Coll. 185
Hibbing Comm. Coll. 267, 633
Hibbing Tech. Coll. 267
Hickey Sch. 283
Hickok Tech. Inst. 385
Hickox Sch. 239
High Point Coll. 365
High-Tech Inst. 21
Highland Comm. Coll. 151, 606 (IL); 186, 613 (KS)
Highland Park Comm. Coll. 253, 630
Highline Comm. Coll. 534, 685

Institutional Index

Hilbert Coll. 335
Hill Coll. 488, 674
Hill Inst. 312
Hill International Flight Sch. (see: Dick Hill International Flight Sch.)
Hillcrest Christian Coll. 556
Hillsborough Comm. Coll. 109, 598
Hillsdale Coll. 253
Hinds Comm. Coll. 275, 635
Hinds Inst. of Esthetics (see: Catherine E. Hinds Inst. of Esthetics)
Hiram Coll. 385
Hiram G. Andrews Ctr. 421
Hiwassee Coll. 467
Ho-Ho-Kus Sch. 312
Hobart and William Smith Colls. 335
Hobe Sound Bible Coll. 109
Hobson State Tech. Coll. 7
Hocking Tech. Coll. 385, 657
Hofstra Univ. 335
Hollins Coll. 523
Hollywood Scriptwriting Inst. 50
Holmes Coll. (see: Mary Holmes Coll.)
Holmes Comm. Coll. 275, 635
Holy Apostles Coll. and Sem. 91
Holy Cross Coll. (see: Coll. of the Holy Cross)
Holy Cross Coll. 167
Holy Family Coll. 421
Holy Names Coll. 50
Holyoke Comm. Coll. 239, 628
Home Study International 226
Honolulu Comm. Coll. 140, 603
Hood Coll. 227
Hope Coll. 253
Hopkins Tech. Ed. Ctr. (see: Lindsey Hopkins Tech. Ed. Ctr.)
Hopkinsville Comm. Coll. 192, 615
Horry-Georgetown Tech. Coll. 455, 669
Hospitality Training Ctr., Inc. 385
Hostos Comm. Coll. 335, 647
Hotel Inst. for Management 561
Hotel Management Sch., "Les Roches" 561
Houghton Coll. 335
Housatonic Comm. Coll. 91, 595
Houston Aeronautical Coll. 131
Houston Ballet Acad. 488
Houston Baptist Univ. 488
Houston Comm. Coll. 489, 674
Houston Grad. Sch. of Theol. 489
Houston State Univ. (see: Sam Houston State Univ.)
Houston Training Sch. 489
Howard Coll. 489, 674
Howard Comm. Coll. 227, 626

Howard Co. Jr. Coll. Dist. 674
Howard Payne Univ. 489
Howard Sch. of Broadcast Arts (see: Specs Howard Sch. of Broadcast Arts)
Howard Univ. 99
Hudson Area Sch. of Radiologic Tech. 312
Hudson Co. Comm. Coll. 312, 644
Hudson Valley Comm. Coll. 335, 650
Huertas Jr. Coll. 444
Huey P. Long Tech. Inst. 213
Humacao Comm. Coll. 444
Humacao Univ. Coll. 444, 665
Human Services Coll. (see: Coll. for Human Services)
Humana Health Inst. 192
Humanities Ctr. Sch. of Therapuetic Massage 109
Humboldt State Univ. 50, 591
Humphreys Coll. 51
Hunter Bus. Sch. 335
Hunter Coll. 335, 647
Huntingdon Coll. 7
Huntington Coll. 167
Huntington Coll. of Dental Tech. 51
Huntington Inst. 91
Huntington Jr. Coll. of Bus. 541
Huntsville Bus. Inst. Sch. of Court Reporting 7
Huron Coll. Faculty of Theol. 556
Huron Univ. 460
Hussian Sch. of Art 422
Husson Coll. 221
Huston-Tillotson Coll. 489
Hutchinson Comm. Coll. 186, 613
Hypnosis Motivation Inst. 51

I

ICM Sch. of Bus. 422
IMC-International Management Ctrs. 561
ITT Tech. Inst. 21 (AZ); 51 (CA); 82 (CO); 109 (FL); 143 (ID); 167 (IN); 254 (MI); 283 (MO); 385 (OH); 407 (OR); 467 (TN); 489-490 (TX); 512 (UT); 523 (VA); 534 (WA); 546 (WI)
Idaho State Univ. 143, 604
Iliff Sch. of Theol. 83
Illinois Benedictine Coll. 151
Illinois Board of Governors of State Colls. and Univs. 605
Illinois Central Coll. 151, 606
Illinois Coll. 151, 607
Illinois Coll. of Optometry 151
Illinois Comm. Coll. Board 605

Illinois Eastern Comm. Coll. System 606
Illinois Inst. of Tech. 151
Illinois Medical Training Ctr. 151
Illinois State Univ. 151, 608
Illinois Valley Comm. Coll. 152, 606
Illinois Wesleyan Univ. 152
Immaculata Coll. 422
Immaculate Conception Sem. of Seton Hall Univ. 312
Imperial Comm. Coll. Dist. 583
Imperial Valley Coll. 51, 583
Incarnate Word Coll. 490
Independence Comm. Coll. 186, 614
Indian Hills Comm. Coll. 178, 611
Indian Meridian Vo-Tech Ctr. 400
Indian River Comm. Coll. 109, 598
Indiana Barber/Stylist Coll. 167
Indiana Bus. Coll. 167-168
Indiana Inst. of Tech. 168
Indiana State Univ. 168, 609
Indiana Univ. at Kokomo 168, 609
Indiana Univ. at South Bend 169, 609
Indiana Univ. Bloomington 168, 609
Indiana Univ. East 168, 609
Indiana Univ. Northwest 168, 609
Indiana Univ. of Pennsylvania 422, 664
Indiana Univ. Southeast 168, 609
Indiana Univ. System 609
Indiana Univ.-Purdue Univ. at Fort Wayne 169, 609
Indiana Univ.-Purdue Univ. at Indianapolis 169, 609
Indiana Vo-Tech Coll. Executive Headquarters 610
Indiana Vo-Tech Coll.—Central Indiana Tech. Inst. 169, 610
Indiana Vo-Tech Coll.—Columbus Tech. Inst. 169, 610
Indiana Vo-Tech Coll.—Eastcentral Tech. Inst. 169, 610
Indiana Vo-Tech Coll.—Kokomo Tech. Inst. 170, 610
Indiana Vo-Tech Coll.—Lafayette Tech. Inst. 170, 610
Indiana Vo-Tech Coll.—Northcentral Tech. Inst. 170, 610
Indiana Vo-Tech Coll.—Northeast Tech. Inst. 170, 610
Indiana Vo-Tech Coll.—Northwest Tech. Inst. 170, 610
Indiana Vo-Tech Coll.—Southcentral Tech. Inst. 170, 610
Indiana Vo-Tech Coll.—Southeast Tech. Inst. 170, 610
Indiana Vo-Tech Coll.—Southwest Tech. Inst. 171, 610
Indiana Vo-Tech Coll.—Wabash Valley Tech. Inst. 171, 610

Institutional Index

Indiana Vo-Tech Coll.—
 Whitewater Tech. Inst. 171, 610
Indiana Wesleyan Univ. 171
Information Computer Systems
 Inst. 422
Institucion Chaviano de Mayaguez 444
Inst. for Bus. and Tech. 51
Inst. for Christian Studies 490
Inst. for Clinical Social Work 566
Inst. of American Indian and
 Alaskan Native Culture and
 Arts Development 320
Inst. of Audio Research 336
Inst. of AudioVisual Engineering 51
Inst. of Computer Sci., Ltd. 297
Inst. of Computer Tech. 51
Inst. of Data Processing 171
Inst. of Development Tech 51
Inst. of Electronic Tech. 192
Inst. of Medical and Dental Tech. 385
Inst. of Medical-Dental Tech. at Mesa 21
Inst. of Multiple Tech. 444
Inst. of Nursing Tech. 490
Inst. of Paper Sci. and Tech. 131
Inst. of Security and Tech. 109 (FL); 422 (PA)
Inst. of Textile Tech. 523
Instituto Comercial de Puerto Rico Jr. Coll. 444
Instituto de Banca y Comercio 444
Instituto de Educacion Universal 445
Instituto del Arte Moderno 445
Instituto Tecnico Comercial Jr. Coll. 444
Instituto Tecnologico y de Estudios Superiores de Monterrey 560
Insurance Coll. (see: Coll. of Insurance)
Inter American Univ. of Puerto Rico (see: Universidad Interamericana de Puerto Rico)
Interactive Learning Systems 131 (GA); 490 (TX)
Interboro Inst. 336
Interdenominational Theol. Ctr. 131
Interior Design Inst. of Denver 83
Interior Designers Inst. 52
Intermountain Coll. 83
Intermountain Coll. of Court Reporting 512
International Acad. of Hair Design and Tech. 227
International Acad. of Merchandising and Design 109 (FL); 152 (IL)

International Air Acad. 52 (CA); 534 (WA)
International Aviation and Travel Acad. 490
International Barber and Style Coll. 467
International Barber Sch. of El Paso 490
International Bible Coll. 7
International Bus. Coll. 320-321 (NM); 490-491 (TX)
International Bus. Coll. of Guam 139
International Bus. Coll.—Fort Wayne 171
International Bus. Coll.— Indianapolis 171
International Career Inst. 7 (AL); 109 (FL); 336 (NY)
International Career Sch. 491
International Coll. 110, 564 (FL); 559 (Cayman Islands)
International Coll. of Broadcasting 385
International Coll. of Bus. and Tech. 445
International Correspondence Inst. 491
International Correspondence Sch. 422
International Dealers Sch. 52 (CA); 301 (NV)
International Fine Arts Coll. 110
International Hair Inst. 283
International Inst. of Chinese Medicine 321
International Sch. of Skin and Nailcare 132
International Tech. Coll. 445
International Tech. Inst. 110 (FL); 213 (LA); 491 (TX)
International Training Sch. (see: Sch. for International Training)
International Univ. (see: U.S. International Univ.)
Interstate Bus. Coll. 375
Inver Hills Comm. Coll. 267, 633
Iona Coll. 336
Iowa Central Comm. Coll. 178, 611
Iowa Comm. Colls. and Voc. Schs. 611
Iowa Lakes Comm. Coll. 178, 611
Iowa Sch. of Barbering and Hairstyling 178
Iowa State Board of Regents 612
Iowa State Univ. 178, 612
Iowa Valley Comm. Coll. Dist. 611
Iowa Wesleyan Coll. 178
Iowa Western Comm. Coll. 179, 611
Irvine Coll. of Bus. 52

Irvine Valley Coll. 52, 587
Island Drafting and Tech. Inst. 336
Isothermal Comm. Coll. 365, 653
Itasca Comm. Coll. 267, 633
Itawamba Comm. Coll. 275, 635
Ithaca Coll. 336
Ivanhoe Inst. Limited 422
Iverson Inst. of Court Reporting 491

J

J. Sargeant Reynolds Comm. Coll. 523, 683
J.F. Drake State Tech. Coll. 7
J.F. Ingram State Tech. Coll. 7
J.H. Thompson's Acads. 422
J.R. Pittard Area Voc. Sch. 7
Jacki Nell Executive Secretary Sch. 491
Jackson Acad. of Beauty 275
Jackson Bus. Inst. 254
Jackson Comm. Coll. 254, 630
Jackson Hair Design Coll. 275
Jackson State Comm. Coll. 467, 671
Jackson State Univ. 275, 635
Jacksonville Coll. 491
Jacksonville State Univ. 7, 575
Jacksonville Univ. 110
Jacobs Creek Civilian Conservation Ctr. 467
James H. Faulkner State Jr. Coll. 7, 574
James L. Walker Vo-Tech Ctr. 110
James Madison Univ. 523, 682
James Martin Sch. 422
James Sprunt Comm. Coll. 365, 653
Jamestown Bus. Coll. 336
Jamestown Coll. 375
Jamestown Comm. Coll. 336, 650
Jarvis Christian Coll. 491
Jay Beauty Coll. (see: John Jay Beauty Coll.)
Jay Coll. of Criminal Justice (see: John Jay Coll. of Criminal Justice)
Jay's Hair Acad. (see: Mr. Jay's Hair Acad.)
Jeff Davis Beauty Coll. 213
Jefferson Coll. 284, 637
Jefferson Comm. Coll. 192, 615 (KY); 336, 650 (NY)
Jefferson Davis State Jr. Coll. 7, 574
Jefferson Davis Tech. Inst. 213
Jefferson State Comm. Coll. 8, 574
Jefferson State Vo-Tech Sch. (see: Kentucky Tech—Jefferson State Vo-Tech Sch.)
Jefferson Tech. Coll. 385, 657

Institutional Index

Jefferson Tech. Inst. 213
Jefferson Univ. (see: Thomas Jefferson Univ.)
Jeffersontown Voc. Ed. Ctr. (see: Kentucky Tech—Jeffersontown Voc. Ed. Ctr.)
Jersey City State Coll. 312, 645
Jesuit Sch. of Theol. at Berkeley 52
Jett Coll. of Cosmetology 467
Jewell Coll. (see: William Jewell Coll.)
Jewish Theol. Sem. of America 336
Jocelyn Daspit Beauty Coll. 213
Joe Kubert Sch. of Cartoon and Graphic Art 312
Joffrey Ballet Sch. (see: American Ballet Ctr./Joffrey Balley Sch.)
John A. Gupton Coll. 468
John A. Logan Coll. 152, 606
John B. Stetson Univ. 110
John Bastyr Coll. 535
John Brown Univ. 27
John C. Calhoun State Comm. Coll. 8, 574
John Carroll Univ. 385
John F. Kennedy Univ. 52
John Jay Beauty Coll. 567
John Jay Coll. of Criminal Justice 337, 647
John M. Patterson State Tech. Coll. 8
John Marshall Law Schoool 152
John Pope Eden Area Voc. Ed. Ctr. 8
John Tracy Clinic 52
John Tyler Comm. Coll. 523, 683
John Wesley Coll. 366
John Wood Comm. Coll. 152, 606
Johns Hopkins Univ. 227
Johnson and Wales Univ. 450
Johnson Bible Coll. 468
Johnson C. Smith Univ. 366
Johnson Civilian Conservation Ctr. (see: Lyndon B. Johnson Civilian Conservation Ctr.)
Johnson Co. Comm. Coll. 186, 614
Johnson Medical Sch. (see: Robert Wood Johnson Medical Sch.)
Johnson State Coll. 515, 681
Johnson Tech. Inst. 423
Johnston Comm. Coll. 366, 653
Joint Board of Theol. Colls. 556
Joliet Jr. Coll. 152, 606
Jones Coll. 110
Jones Co. Jr. Coll. 276, 635
Jordan Coll. 567
Joseph Bulova Sch. 337
Joseph Donahue International Sch. of Hairstyling 423
Judge Advocate General's Sch. 523

Judson Coll. 8 (AL); 152 (IL)
Juilliard Sch. 337
Juniata Coll. 423

K

KD Studio 491
Kalamazoo Coll. 254
Kalamazoo Valley Comm. Coll. 254, 630
Kalix Trade Sch. 423
Kane Bus. Inst. 312
Kankakee Comm. Coll. 152, 606
Kansai Gaidai-Hawaii Coll. 140
Kansas Board of Regents 613
Kansas City Art Inst. 284
Kansas City Bus. Coll. 284
Kansas City Kansas Comm. Coll. 186, 614
Kansas Coll. of Tech. 186
Kansas Newman Coll. 186
Kansas Sch. of Hairstyling 186
Kansas State Board of Ed. 613
Kansas State Univ. 186, 613
Kansas Wesleyan Univ. 187
Kapiolani Comm. Coll. 140, 603
Kaskaskia Coll. 152, 606
Katharine Gibbs Sch. 91 (CT); 239 (MA); 312 (NJ); 337 (NY); 423 (PA); 450 (RI)
Kauai Comm. Coll. 141, 603
Kean Coll. of New Jersey 312, 645
Kee Bus. Coll. (see: National Ed. Ctr.—Kee Bus. Coll. Campus)
Keene State Coll. 304, 643
Kehillath Yakov Rabbinical Sem. 337
Keiser Coll. of Tech. 111
Keith's Metro Hair Acad. 491
Keller Grad. Sch. of Mgmt. 153
Kellogg Comm. Coll. 254, 630
Kelsey-Jenny Bus. Coll. 52
Kemper Military Sch. and Coll. 284
Kenai Peninsula Coll. (see: Univ. of Alaska Anchorage—Kenai Peninsula Coll.)
Kendall Coll. 153
Kendall Coll. of Art and Design 254
Kennebec Valley Tech. Coll. 222
Kennedy Special Warfare Ctr. (see: U.S. Army John F. Kennedy Special Warfare Ctr.)
Kennedy Univ. (see: John F. Kennedy Univ.)
Kennedy-King Coll. 153, 605
Kennesaw State Coll. 132, 602
Kenrick-Glennon Sem. 284
Kent State Univ. 386, 657

Kentucky Advanced Tech. Ctr. (see: Kentucky Tech—Kentucky Advanced Tech. Ctr.)
Kentucky Career Inst. 566
Kentucky Christian Coll. 192
Kentucky Coll. of Barbering and Hairstyling 192
Kentucky Coll. of Bus. 193
Kentucky Coll. of Tech. (see: National Ed. Ctr.—Kentucky Coll. of Tech.)
Kentucky Council on Higher Ed. 615
Kentucky Mountain Bible Coll. 566
Kentucky Polytechnic Inst. 193
Kentucky Sch. of Financial Ed. 193
Kentucky State Univ. 193, 615
Kentucky Tech—Ashland State Vo-Tech Sch. 193, 620
Kentucky Tech—Barren Co. Area Voc. Ed. Ctr. 193, 617
Kentucky Tech—Belfry Area Voc. Ed. Ctr. 193, 620
Kentucky Tech—Bell Co. Area Voc. Ed. Ctr. 193, 621
Kentucky Tech—Blackburn Correctional Complex 193, 621
Kentucky Tech—Boone Co. Area Voc. Ed. Ctr. 194, 619
Kentucky Tech—Bowling Green State Transp. Ctr. 194, 617
Kentucky Tech—Bowling Green State Vo-Tech Sch. 194, 617
Kentucky Tech—Breathitt Co. Area Voc. Ed. Ctr. 194, 620
Kentucky Tech—Breckinridge Co. Area Voc. Ed. Ctr. 194, 618
Kentucky Tech—Bullitt Co. Area Voc. Ed. Ctr. 194, 618
Kentucky Tech—Caldwell Co. Area Voc. Ed. Ctr. 194, 616
Kentucky Tech—Campbell Co. Area Voc. Ed. Ctr. 194, 619
Kentucky Tech—Carroll Co. Area Voc. Ed. Ctr. 194, 619
Kentucky Tech—Casey Co. Area Voc. Ed. Ctr. 195, 621
Kentucky Tech—Central Kentucky State Vo-Tech Sch. 195, 621
Kentucky Tech—Christian Co. Area Voc. Ed. Ctr. 195, 616
Kentucky Tech—Clark Co. Area Voc. Ed. Ctr. 195, 622
Kentucky Tech—Clay Co. Area Voc. Ed. Ctr. 195, 621
Kentucky Tech—Clinton Co. Area Voc. Ed. Ctr. 195, 621
Kentucky Tech—Corbin Area Voc. Ed. Ctr. 195, 621

Institutional Index

Kentucky Tech—Cumberland Valley Health Occupations Ctr. 195, 621
Kentucky Tech—Danville Sch. of Health Occupations 195, 622
Kentucky Tech—Daviess Co. State Vo-Tech Sch. 195, 617
Kentucky Tech—Eddyville Voc. Ed. Ctr. 196, 616
Kentucky Tech—Elizabethtown State Vo-Tech Sch. 196, 618
Kentucky Tech—Fairdale Voc. Ed. Ctr. 196, 618
Kentucky Tech—Fulton Co. Area Voc. Ed. Ctr. 196, 616
Kentucky Tech—Garrad Co. Area Voc. Ed. Ctr. 196, 622
Kentucky Tech—Garth Area Voc. Ed. Ctr. 196, 620
Kentucky Tech—Glasgow Sch. for Health Occupations 196, 617
Kentucky Tech—Green Co. Area Voc. Ed. Ctr. 196, 621
Kentucky Tech—Greenup Co. Area Voc. Ed. Ctr. 196, 620
Kentucky Tech—Harlan State Vo-Tech Sch. 196, 621
Kentucky Tech—Harrison Co. Area Voc. Ed. Ctr. 197, 622
Kentucky Tech—Harrodsburg Area Voc. Ed. Ctr. 197, 622
Kentucky Tech—Hazard State Vo-Tech Sch. 197, 620
Kentucky Tech—Henderson Co. Area Voc. Ed. Ctr. 197, 617
Kentucky Tech—Jefferson State Vo-Tech Sch. 197, 618
Kentucky Tech—Jeffersontown Voc. Ed. Ctr. 197, 618
Kentucky Tech—Kentucky Advanced Tech. Ctr. 197, 617
Kentucky Tech—Knott Co. Area Voc. Ed. Ctr. 197, 620
Kentucky Tech—Knox Co. Area Voc. Ed. Ctr. 197, 621
Kentucky Tech—LaGrange Voc. Ed. Ctr. 197, 618
Kentucky Tech—Laurel Co. State Vo-Tech Sch. 198, 621
Kentucky Tech—Lee Co. Area Voc. Ed. Ctr. 198, 620
Kentucky Tech—Leslie Co. Area Voc. Ed. Ctr. 198, 620
Kentucky Tech—Letcher Co. Area Voc. Ed. Ctr. 198, 620
Kentucky Tech—Luckett Voc. Ed. Ctr. 198, 618
Kentucky Tech—Madison Co. Area Voc. Ed. Ctr. 198, 622
Kentucky Tech—Madisonville Health Occupations Ctr. 198, 616
Kentucky Tech—Madisonville State Vo-Tech Sch. 198, 616
Kentucky Tech—Marion Co. Area Voc. Ed. Ctr. 198, 618
Kentucky Tech—Martin Co. Area Voc. Ed. Ctr. 198, 620
Kentucky Tech—Mayfield Area Voc. Ed. Ctr. 199, 616
Kentucky Tech—Mayo State Vo-Tech Sch. 199, 620
Kentucky Tech—Maysville Area Voc. Ed. Ctr. 199, 619
Kentucky Tech—Meade Co. Area Voc. Ed. Ctr. 199, 618
Kentucky Tech—Millard Area Voc. Ed. Ctr. 199, 620
Kentucky Tech—Monroe Co. Area Voc. Ed. Ctr. 199, 617
Kentucky Tech—Montgomery Co. Area Voc. Ed. Ctr. 199, 619
Kentucky Tech—Morehead Treatment Ctr. 199, 619
Kentucky Tech—Morgan Co. Area Voc. Ed. Ctr. 199, 619
Kentucky Tech—Muhlenberg Co. Area Voc. Ed. Ctr. 199, 617
Kentucky Tech—Murray Area Voc. Ed. Ctr. 200, 616
Kentucky Tech—Nelson Co. Area Voc. Ed. Ctr. 200, 618
Kentucky Tech—Northern Campbell Co. Vo-Tech Sch. 200, 619
Kentucky Tech—Northern Kentucky Health Occupations Ctr. 200, 619
Kentucky Tech—Northern Kentucky State Vo-Tech Sch. 200, 619
Kentucky Tech—Northpoint Ed. Ctr. 200, 622
Kentucky Tech—Ohio Co. Area Voc. Ed. Ctr. 200, 617
Kentucky Tech—Oldham Co. Voc. Ed. Ctr. 200, 618
Kentucky Tech—Owensboro Vo-Tech Sch. 200, 617
Kentucky Tech—Paducah Area Voc. Ed. Ctr. 200, 616
Kentucky Tech—Patton Voc. Ed. Ctr. 201, 619
Kentucky Tech—Peewee Valley Ed. Ctr. 201, 618
Kentucky Tech—Phelps Area Voc. Ed. Ctr. 201, 620
Kentucky Tech—Rockcastle Co. Area Voc. Ed. Ctr. 201, 621
Kentucky Tech—Rowan State Vo-Tech Sch. 201, 619
Kentucky Tech—Russell Area Voc. Ed. Ctr. 201, 620
Kentucky Tech—Russell Co. Area Voc. Ed. Ctr. 201, 621
Kentucky Tech—Russellville Area Voc. Ed. Ctr. 201, 617
Kentucky Tech—Shelby Co. Area Voc. Ed. Ctr. 201, 618
Kentucky Tech—Somerset State Vo-Tech Sch. 202, 621
Kentucky Tech—Union Co. Area Voc. Ed. Ctr. 202, 617
Kentucky Tech—Wayne Co. Area Voc. Ed. Ctr. 202, 621
Kentucky Tech—Webster Co. Area Voc. Ed. Ctr. 202, 617
Kentucky Tech—West Kentucky State Vo-Tech Sch. 202, 616
Kentucky Tech—Woodsbend Boys' Camp 202, 619
Kentucky Wesleyan Coll. 202
Kenyon Coll. 386
Kern Comm. Coll. Dist. 584, 590
Kerr Bus. Coll. 132
Kettering Coll. of Medical Arts 386
Keuka Coll. 337
Keystone Jr. Coll. 423
Keystone Sch. (see: Chubb Inst.—Keystone Sch.)
Kilgore Coll. 491, 674
Kilian Comm. Coll. 460
King Coll. 468
King's Coll. 337 (NY); 366 (NC); 423 (PA)
Kings River Comm. Coll. 52, 590
Kingsborough Comm. Coll. 337, 647
Kingwood Coll. 491, 675
Kinyon-Campbell Bus. Sch. 239
Kirksville Coll. of Osteopathic Medicine 284
Kirkwood Comm. Coll. 179, 611
Kirtland Comm. Coll. 254, 630
Kishwaukee Coll. 153, 607
Knott Co. Area Voc. Ed. Ctr. (see: Kentucky Tech—Knott Co. Area Voc. Ed. Ctr.)
Knowledge Systems Inst. 153
Knox Coll. 153 (IL); 556 (Canada)
Knox Co. Area Voc. Ed. Ctr. (see: Kentucky Tech—Knox Co. Area Voc. Ed. Ctr.)
Knoxville Bus. Coll. 468
Knoxville Coll. 468
Knoxville Inst. of Hair Design 468
Knoxville Job Corps Ctr. 468
Kodiak Coll. (see: Univ. of Alaska Anchorage—Kodiak Coll.)

Institutional Index

Kokomo Tech. Inst. (see: Indiana Vo-Tech Coll.—Kokomo Tech. Inst.)
Kol Yaakov Torah Ctr. 568
Krainz Woods Acad. of Medical Laboratory Tech. 254
Krissler Bus. Inst. 337
Kubert Sch. of Cartoon and Graphic Art (see: Joe Kubert Sch. of Cartoon and Graphic Art)
Kutztown Univ. of Pennsylvania 423, 664

L

L.I.F.E. Bible Coll. 52
La Grande Coll. of Bus. 407
La Guardia Comm. Coll. 337, 647
La Jolla Acad. of Advertising Arts 52
La Montaña Regional Coll. 445, 666
La Roche Coll. 423
La Salle Univ. 423
La Sierra Univ. 52
Laban/Bartenieff Inst. of Movement Studies, Inc. 337
Labette Comm. Coll. 187, 614
Laboratory Inst. of Merchandising 338
Laboure Coll. (see: Catherine Laboure Coll.)
Lac Courte Oreilles Ojibwa Comm. Coll. 571
Lackawanna Jr. Coll. 423
Lafayette Coll. 423
Lafayette Regional Tech. Inst. 213
Lafayette Tech. Inst. (see: Indiana Vo-Tech Coll.—Lafayette Tech. Inst.)
LaGrange Coll. 132
LaGrange Voc. Ed. Ctr. (see: Kentucky Tech—LaGrange Voc. Ed. Ctr.)
Lake Area Vo-Tech Inst. 460
Lake City Comm. Coll. 111, 598
Lake Co. Area Vo-Tech Ctr. 111
Lake Co. Coll. (see: Coll. of Lake Co.)
Lake Erie Coll. 386
Lake Forest Coll. 153
Lake Forest Grad. Sch. of Management 153
Lake Land Coll. 153, 607
Lake Michigan Coll. 254, 630
Lake Superior State Univ. 255, 631
Lake Tahoe Comm. Coll. 53, 584
Lake Tahoe Comm. Coll. Dist. 584
Lake Washington Tech. Coll. 535
Lake-Sumter Comm. Coll. 111, 598

Lakeland Coll. 546
Lakeland Comm. Coll. 386, 657
Lakeland Medical-Dental Acad. 267
Lakeshore Tech. Coll. 546
Lakeview Coll. of Nursing 566
Lakewood Comm. Coll. 267, 633
Lamar Comm. Coll. 83, 594
Lamar Salter Tech. Inst. 214
Lamar Univ. at Beaumont 492, 675
Lamar Univ. at Orange 492, 675
Lamar Univ. at Port Arthur 492, 675
Lamar Univ. System 675
Lambuth Coll. 468
Lamson Bus. Coll. 21
Lamson Jr. Coll. 21-22
Lancaster Bible Coll. 424
Lancaster Comm. Coll. (see: Dabney S. Lancaster Comm. Coll.)
Lancaster Theol. Sem. 424
Lander Coll. 455, 668
Landing Sch. of Boatbuilding and Design 222
Landmark Coll. 570
Lane Coll. 468
Lane Comm. Coll. 407, 661
Laney Coll. 53, 586
Langston Univ. 400
Lanier Tech. Inst. 132
Lansdale Sch. of Bus. 424
Lansing Comm. Coll. 255, 631
Lansing Computer Inst. 255
Laramie Co. Comm. Coll. 553, 689
Laredo Jr. Coll. 492, 675
Laredo State Univ. 492, 676
Larry's Barber and Hair Styling Sch. 492
Las Positas Coll. 53, 581
Las Vegas Gaming and Tech. Sch. 301
Lasell Coll. 240
Lassen Coll. 53, 584
Lassen Comm. Coll. Dist. 584
Latter-Day Saints Bus. Coll. 512
Laural Sch. 22 '
Laurel Bus. Inst. 424
Laurel Co. State Vo-Tech Sch. (see: Kentucky Tech—Laurel Co. State Vo-Tech Sch.)
Lawrence Coll. (see: Sarah Lawrence Coll.)
Lawrence Tech. Univ. 255
Lawrence Univ. 546
Lawson State Comm. Coll. 8, 574
Lawton Sch. 53 (CA); 255 (MI)
Le Moyne Coll. 338
Learning and Evaluation Ctr. 424
Lebanon Valley Coll. 424
LeChef Culinary Arts Sch. 492
Lederwolff Culinary Acad. 53
Lee Coll. 468 (TN); 492, 675 (TX)

Lee Co. Area Voc. Ed. Ctr. (see: Kentucky Tech—Lee Co. Area Voc. Ed. Ctr.)
Lee Co. Area Vo-Tech Sch. 111
Lees Coll. 202
Lees-McRae Coll. 366
Leeward Comm. Coll. 141, 603
Legal Arts Coll. (see: Coll. of Legal Arts)
Legal Career Inst. 111
Lehigh Co. Comm. Coll. 424, 664
Lehigh Univ. 424
Lehman Coll. (see: Herbert H. Lehman Coll.)
LeMoyne-Owen Coll. 468
Lenoir Comm. Coll. 366, 653
Lenoir-Rhyne Coll. 366
Lesley Coll. 240
Leslie Co. Area Voc. Ed. Ctr. (see: Kentucky Tech—Leslie Co. Area Voc. Ed. Ctr.)
Letcher Co. Area Voc. Ed. Ctr. (see: Kentucky Tech—Letcher Co. Area Voc. Ed. Ctr.)
LeTourneau Univ. 492
Levine Sch. of Music 99
Lewis and Clark Coll. 407
Lewis and Clark Comm. Coll. 153, 607
Lewis Coll. of Bus. 255
Lewis Univ. 153
Lewis-Clark State Coll. 143, 604
Lexington Comm. Coll. 202, 615
Lexington Inst. of Hospitality Careers 566
Lexington Theol. Sem. 202
Liberty Univ. 523
Liceo de Arte y Disenos 445
Liceo de Arte y Tecnologia 445
Life Chiropractic Coll.—West 53
Life Coll. 132
Lifelong Learning Sch. (see: Sch. for Lifelong Learning)
Lifetime Career Schs., Inc. 424
Lima Tech. Coll. 386, 657
Limestone Coll. 455
Lincoln Christian Coll. 153
Lincoln Coll. 154
Lincoln Land Comm. Coll. 154, 607
Lincoln Memorial Univ. 468
Lincoln Sch. of Commerce 297
Lincoln Tech. Inst. 154 (IL); 171 (IN); 179 (IA); 227 (MD); 313 (NJ); 424 (PA); 492 (TX)
Lincoln Trail Coll. 154, 606
Lincoln Univ. 53 (CA); 284, 637 (MO); 425 (PA)
Lindenwood Coll. 284
Lindsey Hopkins Tech. Ed. Ctr. 111
Lindsey Wilson Coll. 203

Institutional Index

Linfield Coll. 408
Linn-Benton Comm. Coll. 408, 661
Lipscomb Univ. (see: David Lipscomb Univ.)
Little Big Horn Coll. 294
Little Hoop Comm. Coll. 375
Little Management Ed. Inst., Inc. (see: Arthur D. Little Management Ed. Inst., Inc.)
Lively Area Vo-Tech Ctr. 111
Livingston Univ. 8, 575
Livingstone Coll. 366
Lloyd Coll. (see: Alice Lloyd Coll.)
Lock Haven Univ. of Pennsylvania 425, 664
Locklin Vo-Tech Ctr. (see: Radford M. Locklin Vo-Tech Ctr.)
Lockyear Coll. 171
Logan Bus. Coll. 513
Logan Career Coll. (see: Chris Logan Career Coll.)
Logan Coll. (see: John A. Logan Coll.)
Logan Coll. of Chiropractic 284
Loma Linda Univ. 53
Lon Morris Coll. 492
Long Beach City Coll. 54, 584
Long Beach Coll. of Bus. 54
Long Beach Comm. Coll. Dist. 584
Long Island Bus. Inst. 338
Long Island Univ. 338
Long Medical Inst. 22
Long Tech. Inst. (see: Huey P. Long Tech. Inst.)
Longview Comm. Coll. 284, 637
Longwood Coll. 523, 682
Longy Sch. of Music, Inc. 240
Lorain Bus. Coll. 387
Lorain Co. Comm. Coll. 387, 657
Loras Coll. 179
Lord Fairfax Comm. Coll. 523, 683
Los Angeles City Coll. 54, 584
Los Angeles Coll. of Chiropractic 54
Los Angeles Comm. Coll. Dist. 584
Los Angeles Harbor Coll. 54, 584
Los Angeles Mission Coll. 54, 584
Los Angeles ORT Tech. Inst. 54
Los Angeles Pierce Coll. 54, 584
Los Angeles Southwest Coll. 54, 584
Los Angeles Trade-Tech. Coll. 54, 585
Los Angeles Valley Coll. 54, 585
Los Medanos Coll. 55, 582
Los Rios Comm. Coll. Dist. 585
Louisburg Coll. 366
Louise Salinger Acad. Fashion 55
Louisiana Art Inst. 214
Louisiana Board of Trustees for State Colls. and Univs. 623
Louisiana Coll. 214

Louisiana Inst. of Tech. 214
Louisiana State Univ. and Agricultural and Mechanical Coll. 214, 623
Louisiana State Univ. at Alexandria 214, 623
Louisiana State Univ. at Eunice 214, 623
Louisiana State Univ. in Shreveport 214, 623
Louisiana State Univ. Medical Ctr. 214, 623
Louisiana State Univ. System 623
Louisiana Tech Univ. 215, 623
Louisville Presbyterian Theol. Sem. 203
Louisville Tech. Inst. 203
Lourdes Coll. 387
Lower Columbia Coll. 535, 686
Lowthian Coll. 267
Loyola Coll. 227
Loyola Marymount Univ. 55
Loyola Univ. 215
Loyola Univ. of Chicago 154
Lubbock Christian Univ. 493
Luckett Voc. Educaiton Ctr. (see: Kentucky Tech—Luckett Voc. Ed. Ctr.)
Lujac Bus. Sch. 321
Luna Vo-Tech Inst. 321
Lurleen B. Wallace State Jr. Coll. 8, 574
Luther Coll. 179
Luther Northwestern Theol. Sem. 268
Lutheran Bible Inst. of Seattle 535
Lutheran Coll. of Health Professions 566
Lutheran Sch. of Theol. at Chicago 154
Lutheran Theol. Sem. 556
Lutheran Theol. Sem. at Gettysburg 425
Lutheran Theol. Sem. at Philadelphia 425
Lutheran Theol. Southern Sem. 455
Luzerne Co. Comm. Coll. 425, 664
Lycoming Coll. 425
Lynchburg Coll. 523
Lyndon B. Johnson Civilian Conservation Ctr. 569
Lyndon State Coll. 515, 681
Lynn Univ. 111
Lynn Wiley's Hairstyling Acad. 455

M

M&M Word Processing Inst. 493

M. Weeks Welding Laboratory Testing and Sch. 493
MBTI Bus. Training Inst. 445 (PR); 546 (WI)
MGH Inst. of Health Professions 240
MTA Sch. 111 (FL); 171, 569 (IN); 569 (NC); 387 (OH); 425 (PA); 493, 569 (TX)
MTI Bus. Coll. of Stockton 55
MTI Bus. Sch. 387
MTI Coll. 55
MTI-Western Bus. Coll. 55
Mable Bailey Fashion Coll. 132
Macalester Coll. 268
MacArthur State Tech. Coll. (see: Douglas MacArthur State Tech. Coll.)
MacCormac Jr. Coll. 154
Machzikei Hadath Rabbinical Coll. 568
MacMurray Coll. 154
Macomb Comm. Coll. 255, 631
Macon Beauty Sch. 132
Macon Coll. 132, 602
Macon Tech. Inst. 132
Madison Area Tech. Coll. 546
Madison Bus. Coll. 547
Madison Co. Area Voc. Ed. Ctr. (see: Kentucky Tech—Madison Co. Area Voc. Ed. Ctr.)
Madison Univ. (see: James Madison Univ.)
Madisonville Comm. Coll. 203, 615
Madisonville Health Occupations Ctr. (see: Kentucky Tech—Madisonville Health Occupations Ctr.)
Madisonville State Vo-Tech Sch. (see: Kentucky Tech—Madisonville State Vo-Tech Sch.)
Madonna Univ. 255
Magnolia Bible Coll. 276
Magnus Coll. (see: Albertus Magnus Coll.)
Mahanna Career Sch. 338
Maharishi International Univ. 179
Maine Maritime Acad. 222
Mainland Coll. (see: Coll. of the Mainland)
Malcolm X Coll. 154, 605
Mallinckrodt Inst. of Radiology 284
Malone Coll. 387
Manatee Area Vo-Tech Ctr. 112
Manatee Comm. Coll. 112, 598
Manchester Coll. 171
Manchester Comm. Coll. 91, 595
Mandl Sch. 338
Mangum's Barber and Hairstyling Coll. 455
Manhattan Christian Coll. 187

Institutional Index

Manhattan Coll. 338
Manhattan Comm. Coll. (see: Borough of Manhattan Comm. Coll.)
Manhattan Sch. of Music 338
Manhattan Sch. of Printing 339
Manhattan Tech. Inst. 339
Manhattanville Coll. 339
Mankato Area Vo-Tech Sch. 268
Mankato State Univ. 268, 634
Manley L. Cummins Sch. of Anesthesia 8
Manor Fashion Inst. 55
Manor Jr. Coll. 425
Mansfield Bus. Coll. 387 (OH); 455 (SC); 493 (TX)
Mansfield Univ. of Pennsylvania 425, 664
Mansfield Vo-Tech Sch. 567
Maple Woods Comm. Coll. 285, 637
Marantha Baptist Bible Coll. 571
Margaret Murray Washington Voc. Sch. 99
Maria Coll. of Albany 339
Marian Coll. 172
Marian Coll. of Fond du Lac 547
Marian Court Jr. Coll. 240
Maric Coll. of Medical Careers 55
Maricopa Co. Comm. Coll. Dist. 578
Marietta Coll. 387
Marietta Univ. of Cosmetology 133
Marin Ballet Sch. 55
Marin Coll. (see: Coll. of Marin)
Marin Comm. Coll. Dist. 585
Marine Corps Inst. (see: U.S. Marine Corps Inst.)
Marine Corps Intelligence Training Ctr. (see: U.S. Navy and Marine Corps Intelligence Training Ctr.)
Marion Coll. (see: Francis Marion Coll.)
Marion Co. Area Voc. Ed. Ctr. (see: Kentucky Tech—Marion Co. Area Voc. Ed. Ctr.)
Marion Co. Sch. of Radiologic Tech. 112
Marion Military Inst. 8
Marion Tech. Coll. 387, 657
Marist Coll. 339
Maritime Coll. 339, 648
Marlboro Coll. 515
Marquette Univ. 547
Mars Hill Coll. 366
Marshall Co. Area Voc. Ed. Ctr. 203
Marshall Islands Coll. (see: Coll. of the Marshall Islands)
Marshall Law Sch. (see: John Marshall Law Schoool)
Marshall Univ. 541, 687

Marshalltown Comm. Coll. 179, 611
Martha Graham Sch. of Contemporary Dance, Inc. 339
Marti Sch. pf Fashion and Art (see: Virginia Marti Sch. of Fashion and Art)
Martin Comm. Coll. 366, 653
Martin Co. Area Voc. Ed. Ctr. (see: Kentucky Tech—Martin Co. Area Voc. Ed. Ctr.)
Martin Luther Coll. (see: Dr. Martin Luther Coll.)
Martin Methodist Coll. 468
Martin Sch. (see: James Martin Sch.)
Martin Tech. Coll. 112
Martin Univ. 172
Mary Baldwin Coll. 524
Mary Holmes Coll. 276
Mary Washington Coll. 524, 682
Marycrest Coll. 155
Marygrove Coll. 255
Maryknoll Sch. of Theol. 339
Maryland Coll. of Art and Design 227
Maryland Drafting Inst. 227 (MD); 524 (VA)
Maryland Higher Ed. Commission 626
Maryland Inst. Coll. of Art 227
Maryland Inst. of Ultrasound Tech. 228
Maryland State Board for Comm. Colls. 626
Marylhurst Coll. for Lifelong Learning 408
Marymount Coll. 55 (CA); 339 (NY)
Marymount Manhattan Coll. 339
Marymount Univ. 524
Maryville Coll. 469
Maryville Univ. of St. Louis 285
Marywood Coll. 425
Mason Univ. (see: George Mason Univ.)
Massachusetts Bay Comm. Coll. 240, 628
Massachusetts Coll. of Art 240, 628
Massachusetts Coll. of Pharmacy and Allied Health Scis. 240
Massachusetts Higher Ed. Coordinating Council 628
Massachusetts Inst. of Tech. 240
Massachusetts Maritime Acad. 240, 628
Massachusetts Sch. of Barbering and Men's Hairstyling 240
Massachusetts Sch. of Prof. Psychology 240
Massasoit Comm. Coll. 241, 628
Massey Bus. Coll. 133 (GA); 494 (TX)

Massey Bus. Sch. 494
Mastbaum Area Vo-Tech Sch. 426
Master Sch. of Bartending 112
Master's Coll. 56
Masters Inst. 56
Matanuska-Susitna Coll. (see: Univ. of Alaska Anchorage—Matanuska-Susitna Coll.)
Mater Dei Coll. 339
Mathis Inst. (see: Bish Mathis Inst.)
Mattatuck Comm. Coll. 91, 595
Maui Comm. Coll. 141, 603
May Tech. Coll. 294
Mayfield Area Voc. Ed. Ctr. (see: Kentucky Tech—Mayfield Area Voc. Ed. Ctr.)
Mayland Comm. Coll. 366
Mayo Foundation 268, 634
Mayo State Vo-Tech Sch. (see: Kentucky Tech—Mayo State Vo-Tech Sch.)
Maysville Area Voc. Ed. Ctr. (see: Kentucky Tech—Maysville Area Voc. Ed. Ctr.)
Maysville Comm. Coll. 203, 615
Mayville State Univ. 375, 656
McCann Sch. of Bus. 426
McCann Tech. Sch. (see: Charles H. McCann Tech. Sch.)
McCarrie Schs. of Health Scis. and Tech. 426
McConnell Coll. (see: Truett McConnell Coll.)
McConnell Sch. Inc. 268
McCook Comm. Coll. 297, 640
McCormick Theol. Sem. 155
McDowell Tech. Comm. Coll. 367, 653
McFatter Vo-Tech Ctr. (see: William T. McFatter Vo-Tech Ctr.)
McGill Univ. 556
McGraw-Hill Continuing Ed. Ctr. 99
McHenry Co. Coll. 155, 607
McIntosh Coll. 304
McKay Bus. Coll. (see: Dana McKay Bus. Coll.)
McKendree Coll. 155
McKenzie Coll. 469
McKim Tech. Inst. 388
McLennan Comm. Coll. 494, 675
McMaster Univ. 556
McMurry Univ. 494
McNeese State Univ. 215, 623
McPherson Coll. 187
Meade Co. Area Voc. Ed. Ctr. (see: Kentucky Tech—Meade Co. Area Voc. Ed. Ctr.)
Meadows Coll. of Bus. 133

Institutional Index

Meadville/Lombard Theol. Sch. 155
Med-Assist Sch. of Hawaii 141
Med-Help Training Sch. 56
Medaille Coll. 339
Medcenter One Coll. of Nursing 375
Medgar Evers Coll. 339, 647
Media Arts Ctr. (see: Ctr. for the Media Arts)
Median Sch. of Allied Health Careers 426
Medical and Legal Secretarial Scis. Sch. (see: Sch. of Medical and Legal Secretarial Scis.)
Medical Arts Training Ctr. 112
Medical Career Coll. 469
Medical Careers Inst. 155
Medical Careers Training Ctr. 83
Medical Coll. of Georgia 133, 602
Medical Coll. of Ohio 388, 657
Medical Coll. of Pennsylvania 426
Medical Coll. of Wisconsin 547
Medical Inst. of Minnesota 268
Medical Univ. of South Carolina 455, 668
Medix Sch. 133 (GA); 228 (MD)
Meharry Medical Coll. 469
Memorial Univ. of Newfoundland 556
Memphis Coll. of Art 469
Memphis State Univ. 469, 671
Memphis Theol. Sem. 469
Mendocino Coll. 56, 585
Mendocino Lake Comm. Coll. Dist. 585
Menlo Coll. 56
Mennonite Biblical Sem. 172
Mennonite Brethren Biblical Sem. 56
Mennonite Coll. of Nursing 155
Merce Cunningham Studio 340
Merced Coll. 56, 585
Merced Comm. Coll. Dist. 585
Mercer Co. Comm. Coll. 313, 644
Mercer Univ. 133
Merchant Marine Acad. (see: U.S. Merchant Marine Acad.)
Mercy Coll. 340
Mercyhurst Coll. 426
Meredith Coll. 367
Meridian Comm. Coll. 276, 636
Merit Coll. 56
Merlix Prof. and Tech. Inst. 446
Merrimack Coll. 241
Merritt Coll. (see: Samuel Merritt Coll.)
Merritt Coll. 56, 586
Mesa Comm. Coll. 22, 578
Mesa State Coll. 83, 594
Mesabi Comm. Coll. 268, 633
Mesivta of Eastern Parkway Rabbinical Sem. 340

Mesivta Tifereth Jerusalem of America 340
Mesivta Torah Vodaath Sem. 340
Messiah Coll. 426
Methodist Coll. 367
Methodist Theol. Sch. in Ohio 388
Metils Welding Sch. 494
Metro Bus. Acad. 494
Metro Bus. Coll. 285
Metro Hair Acad.—Lubbock 494
Metropolitan Bus. Coll. 155
Metropolitan Coll. of Bus. 133
Metropolitan Comm. Coll. 297, 640
Metropolitan Comm. Coll. Dist. 637
Metropolitan Sch. of Hair Design 133
Metropolitan State Coll. of Denver 83, 594
Metropolitan State Univ. 268, 634
Metropolitan Tech. Inst. 313
Meyer Vo-Tech Sch. 375
Miami Christian Coll. 112
Miami Inst. of Psychology 112
Miami Job Corps Ctr. 112
Miami Lakes Tech. Ed. Ctr. 112
Miami Tech. Coll. 112-113
Miami Univ. 388, 658
Miami-Dade Comm. Coll. 113, 598
Miami-Jacobs Jr. Coll. of Bus. 388
Michael J. Owens Tech. Coll. 388, 658
Michiana Coll. 172
Michigan Barber Sch. 255
Michigan Career Inst. 256
Michigan Christian Coll. 256
Michigan Computer Inst. 256
Michigan State Board of Ed. 630
Michigan State Univ. 256, 631
Michigan Tech. Univ. 256, 631
Microcomputer Tech. Inst. 494
Micronesia Comm. Coll. (see: Comm. Coll. of Micronesia)
Micronesian Occupational Coll. 560
Mid Michigan Comm. Coll. 256, 631
Mid-America Baptist Theol. Sem. 469
Mid-America Bible Coll. 400
Mid-America Coll. of Funeral Service 172
Mid-Continent Baptist Bible Coll. 203
Mid-Florida Tech. Inst. 113
Mid-Plains Comm. Coll. 297, 640
Mid-Plains Comm. Coll. Area 640
Mid-State Barber Styling Coll. 469
Mid-State Coll. 222
Mid-State Tech. Coll. 547
MidAmerica Nazarene Coll. 187
Middle Georgia Coll. 133, 602
Middle Georgia Tech. Inst. 134

Middle Tennessee Sch. of Anesthesia 469
Middle Tennessee State Univ. 470, 671
Middlebury Coll. 515
Middlesex Comm. Coll. 91, 595 (CT); 241, 628 (MA)
Middlesex Co. Coll. 313, 644
Midland Coll. 494, 675
Midland Lutheran Coll. 297
Midlands Tech. Coll. 455, 669
MidSouth Sch. of Beauty 469
Midstate Coll. 155
Midtown Sch. of Bus. 340
Midway Coll. 203
Midwest Ctr. for the Study of Oriental Medicine 566
Midwest Inst. of Medical Assistants 285
Midwest Travel Inst. 179
Midwestern Baptist Theol. Sem. 285
Midwestern State Univ. 494, 675
Mildred Elley Sch. 340
Mile Hi Coll. 83
Miles Coll. 8
Miles Comm. Coll. 294, 639
Military Acad. (see: U.S. Military Acad.)
Miller-Hawkins Bus. Coll. 470
Miller-Motte Bus. Coll. 367 (NC); 470 (TN)
Millersville Univ. of Pennsylvania 426, 664
Milligan Coll. 470
Millikin Univ. 155
Mills Coll. 56
Millsaps Coll. 276
Milwaukee Area Tech. Coll. 547
Milwaukee Inst. of Art and Design 547
Milwaukee Sch. of Bus. 547
Milwaukee Sch. of Engineering 547
Mineral Area Coll. 285, 637
Minneapolis Bus. Coll. 268
Minneapolis Coll. of Art and Design 269
Minneapolis Comm. Coll. 269, 633
Minneapolis Drafting Sch. 269
Minneapolis Tech. Coll. 269
Minnesota Bible Coll. 269
Minnesota Comm. Coll. System 633
Minnesota Sch. of Barbering 269
Minnesota Sch. of Bus. 269
Minnesota State Univ. System 634
Minot Sch. for Allied Health 375
Minot State Univ. 376, 656
MiraCosta Coll. 56, 585
MiraCosta Comm. Coll. Dist. 585
Mirrer Yeshiva Central Inst. 340

Institutional Index

Misericordia Coll. (see: Coll. Misericordia)
Miss Wade's Fashion Merchandising Coll. 495
Mission Coll. 54, 590
Mississippi Bd. of Trustees of State Insts. of Higher Learning 635
Mississippi Coll. 276
Mississippi Co. Comm. Coll. 27
Mississippi Delta Comm. Coll. 276, 636
Mississippi Gulf Coast Comm. Coll. 276, 636
Mississippi Job Corps Ctr. 276
Mississippi State Board for Comm. and Jr. Colls. 635
Mississippi State Univ. 276, 635
Mississippi Univ. for Women 277, 635
Mississippi Valley State Univ. 277, 635
Missoula Vo-Tech Ctr. 294, 639
Missouri Baptist Coll. 285
Missouri Coordinating Board for Higher Ed. 637
Missouri Sch. for Doctors' Assistants 285
Missouri Sch. of Barbering and Hairstyling 285
Missouri Southern State Coll. 285, 637
Missouri Tech. Sch. 286
Missouri Valley Coll. 286
Missouri Voc. Ctr. 286
Missouri Western State Coll. 286, 637
Missouri-Nebraska Express Driver Training Acad. 286
Mr. David's Sch. of Hair Design 367
Mr. Jay's Hair Acad. 172
Mr. Wayne's Sch. of Unisex Hair Design 470
Mitchell Coll. 91
Mitchell Coll. of Law (see: William Mitchell Coll. of Law)
Mitchell Comm. Coll. 367, 653
Mitchell Vo-Tech Sch. 460
Moberly Area Comm. Coll. 286, 637
Mobile Coll. 8
Modern Coll. of Hair Design 495
Modern Schs. of America, Inc. 22
Modern Tech. Sch. X-Ray 56
Modern Welding Sch. 340
Modesto Jr. Coll. 57, 590
Mohave Comm. Coll. 22, 579
Mohawk Valley Comm. Coll. 340, 650
Mohegan Comm. Coll. 91, 595

Moler Barber Coll. 57 (CA); 408 (OR)
Moler Barber Sch. of Hairstyling 269
Moler Hairstyling Coll. 155
Molloy Coll. 341
Monmouth Coll. 156 (IL); 313 (NJ)
Monroe Coll. 341
Monroe Comm. Coll. 341, 650
Monroe Co. Area Voc. Ed. Ctr. (see: Kentucky Tech—Monroe Co. Area Voc. Ed. Ctr.)
Monroe Co. Comm. Coll. 256, 631
Monroeville Sch. of Bus. 436
Montana Coll. of Mineral Sci. and Tech. 294, 639
Montana Comm. Coll. System 639
Montana State Univ. 294, 639
Montana Univ. System 639
Montana Vo-Tech System 639
Montay Coll. 156
Montcalm Comm. Coll. 256, 631
Montclair State Coll. 313, 645
Monterey Inst. of International Studies 57
Monterey Peninsula Coll. 57, 585
Monterey Peninsula Comm. Coll. Dist. 585
Montgomery Coll. Central Administration 626
Montgomery Coll.—Germantown Campus 228, 627
Montgomery Coll.—Rockville Campus 228, 627
Montgomery Coll.—Takoma Park Campus 228, 627
Montgomery Comm. Coll. 367, 653
Montgomery Co. Area Voc. Ed. Ctr. (see: Kentucky Tech—Montgomery Co. Area Voc. Ed. Ctr.)
Montgomery Co. Comm. Coll. 426, 664
Montreat-Anderson Coll. 367
Montserrat Coll. of Art 241
Moody Bible Inst. 156
Moore Career Coll. 277
Moore Coll. of Art 426
Moore Sch. of Tech. (see: William R. Moore Sch. of Tech.)
Moore Studio of the Theatre (see: Sonia Moore Studio of the Theatre)
Moorhead State Univ. 269, 634
Moorhead Tech. Coll. 269
Moorpark Coll. 57, 590
Moraine Park Tech. Coll. 547
Moraine Valley Comm. Coll. 156, 607
Moravian Coll. 426
More Coll. (see: Thomas More Coll.)

More Coll. of Liberal Arts (see: Thomas More Coll. of Liberal Arts)
Morehead State Univ. 203, 615
Morehead Treatment Ctr. (see: Kentucky Tech—Morehead Treatment Ctr.)
Morehouse Coll. 134
Morehouse Sch. of Medicine 134
Morgan Comm. Coll. 83, 594
Morgan Co. Area Voc. Ed. Ctr. (see: Kentucky Tech—Morgan Co. Area Voc. Ed. Ctr.)
Morgan State Univ. 228, 626
Morgan Vo-Tech Inst. (see: Robert Morgan Vo-Tech Inst.)
Morningside Coll. 179
Morris Brown Coll. 134
Morris Coll. (see: Lon Morris Coll.)
Morris Coll. (see: Robert Morris Coll.)
Morris Coll. 456
Morris Co. Coll. (see: Co. Coll. of Morris)
Morrison Coll./Reno Bus. Coll. 301
Morrison Inst. of Tech. 156
Morrisville Coll. of Agriculture and Tech. (see: State Univ. of New York Coll. of Agricultutre and Tech. at Morrisv)
Morse Sch. of Bus. 91
Morton Coll. 156, 607
Morven Park International Equestrian Inst. 524
MoTech Automotive Ed. Ctr. 256
Motlow State Comm. Coll. 470, 671
Mott Comm. Coll. (see: Charles Stewart Mott Comm. Coll.)
Moultrie Area Tech. Inst. 134
Mount Aloysius Jr. Coll. 427
Mount Angel Sem. 408
Mount Carmel Coll. of Nursing 569
Mount Holyoke Coll. 241
Mount Hood Comm. Coll. 408, 661
Mount Ida Coll. 241
Mount Marty Coll. 460
Mount Mary Coll. 548
Mount Mercy Coll. 179
Mount Olive Coll. 367
Mount Royal Coll. 556
Mount St. Clare Coll. 180
Mount St. Joseph Coll. (see: Coll. of Mount St. Joseph)
Mount St. Mary Coll. 341
Mount St. Mary's Coll. 57
Mount St. Mary's Coll. and Sem. 228
Mount St. Vincent Coll. (see: Coll. of Mount St. Vincent)
Mount San Antonio Coll. 57, 586

Institutional Index

Mount San Antonio Comm. Coll. Dist. 585
Mount San Jacinto Coll. 58, 586
Mount San Jacinto Comm. Coll. Dist. 586
Mount Senario Coll. 548
Mount Sinai Sch. of Medicine 341, 647
Mount Union Coll. 388
Mount Vernon Coll. 99
Mount Vernon Nazarene Coll. 388
Mount Wachusetts Comm. Coll. 241, 628
Mountain Empire Comm. Coll. 524, 683
Mountain State Coll. 541
Mountain States Tech. Inst. 22
Mountain View Coll. 495, 674
Muhlenberg Coll. 427
Muhlenberg Co. Area Voc. Ed. Ctr. (see: Kentucky Tech—Muhlenberg Co. Area Voc. Ed.)
Multnomah Sch. of the Bible 408
Mundus Inst. 22
Munson-Williams-Proctor Inst. 341
Murfreesboro Barber and Style Coll. 470
Murray Area Voc. Edcuation Ctr. (see: Kentucky Tech—Murray Area Voc. Ed. Ctr.)
Murray State Coll. 400
Murray State Univ. 203, 615
Murray Washington Voc. Sch. (see: Margaret Murray Washington Voc. Sch.)
Muscatine Comm. Coll. 180, 611
Music Ctr. of the North Shore 156
Music Tech 269
Musicians Inst. 58
Muskegon Comm. Coll. 257, 631
Muskingum Area Tech. Coll. 389, 658
Muskingum Coll. 389

N

NEI Truck Driver Training 456
NHAW Home Study Inst. 389
Naes Coll. 156
Napa Valley Coll. 58, 586
Napa Valley Comm. Coll. Dist. 586
Napoleon Hill Foundation 156
Naropa Inst. 83
Nash Acad. of Animal Arts 313
Nash Comm. Coll. 367, 653
Nashotah House 548
Nashville Auto Diesel Coll. 470
Nashville Coll. 470
Nashville State Tech. Inst. 470, 671

Nassau Comm. Coll. 341, 650
Nassau Sch. 341
Nasson Inst. 450
Natchitoches Tech. Inst. 215
National Aviation Acad. 113
National Barber Coll. 156
National Broadcasting Sch. 58 (CA); 302 (NV); 408 (OR); 535 (WA)
National Bus. Coll. 524
National Bus. Inst. 134
National Career Coll. 9
National Career Inst. 113 (FL); 286 (MO)
National Ctr. for Logistics Management 313
National Coll. 460
National Coll. of Bus. and Tech. 446
National Coll. of Chiropractic 156
National Computer Coll. 446
National Conservatory of Dramatic Arts 99
National Cryptologic Sch. 228
National Ed. Ctr.—Allentown Campus 427
National Ed. Ctr.—Arizona Automotive Inst. Campus 22
National Ed. Ctr.—Arkansas Coll. of Tech. 28
National Ed. Ctr.—Bauder Fashion Coll. 113
National Ed. Ctr.—Brown Inst. Campus 270
National Ed. Ctr.—Bryman Campus 58 (CA); 134 (GA); 156-157 (IL); 241 (MA); 257 (MI); 495 (TX)
National Ed. Ctr.—Capitol Hill Campus 100
National Ed. Ctr.—Fort Worth Campus 495
National Ed. Ctr.—Kee Bus. Coll. Campus 524-525
National Ed. Ctr.—Kentucky Coll. of Tech. 203
National Ed. Ctr.—National Inst. of Tech. 59 (CA); 180 (IA); 257 (MI)
National Ed. Ctr.—National Inst. of Tech. Campus 9 (AL); 389 (OH); 495 (TX); 541 (WV)
National Ed. Ctr.—R.E.T.S. Campus 313
National Ed. Ctr.—Sawyer Campus 59
National Ed. Ctr.—Skadron Campus 59
National Ed. Ctr.—Spartan Sch. of Aeronautics Campus 401

National Ed. Ctr.—Temple Sch. Campus 228
National Ed. Ctr.—Thompson Campus 427
National Ed. Ctr.—Vale Tech. Inst. Campus 427
National Safety Council Safety Training Inst. 157
National Sch. of Tech., Inc. 113
National Schs. 427
National Shakespeare Conservatory 341
National Tax Training Sch. 342
National Tech. Inst. 257
National Tech. Univ. 83
National Theatre Conservatory 565
National Tractor Trailer Sch. 342
National Training, Inc. 114
National Truck Driver Ed. Inst. 215
National Univ. 59
National-Louis Univ. 157
Navajo Comm. Coll. 22
Naval Acad. (see: U.S. Naval Acad.)
Naval Aerospace Medical Inst. (see: U.S. Naval Aerospace Medical Inst.)
Naval Air Tech. Training Ctr. (see: U.S. Naval Air Tech. Training Ctr.)
Naval Amphibious Sch. (see: U.S. Naval Amphibious Sch.)
Naval Construction Training Ctr. (see: U.S. Naval Construction Training Ctr.)
Naval Damage Control Training Ctr. (see: U.S. Naval Damage Control Training Ctr.)
Naval Dental Sch. (see: U.S. Naval Dental Sch.)
Naval Diving and Salvage Training Ctr. (see: U.S. Naval Diving and Salvage Training Ctr.)
Naval Fleet Anti-Submarine Warfare Training Ctr. (see: U.S. Naval Fleet Anti-Submarine Warfare Training Ctr.)
Naval Guided Missiles Sch. (see: U.S. Naval Guided Missiles Sch.)
Naval Health Scis. Ed. and Training Command (see: U.S. Naval Health Scis. Ed. and Training Command)
Naval Hospital Corps Sch. (see: U.S. Naval Hospital Corps Sch.)
Naval Postgraduate Sch. (see: U.S. Naval Postgraduate Sch.)
Naval Sch. of Dental Assisting and Tech. (see: U.S. Naval Sch. of Dental Assisting and Tech.)

Institutional Index

Naval Sch. of Health Scis.—Bethesda (see: U.S. Naval Sch. of Health Scis.—Bethesda)
Naval Sch. of Health Scis.—Oakland (see: U.S. Naval Sch. of Health Scis.—Oakland)
Naval Sch. of Health Scis.—Portsmouth (see: U.S. Naval Sch. of Health Scis.—Portsmouth)
Naval Sch. of Health Scis.—San Diego (see: U.S. Naval Sch. of Health Scis.—San Diego)
Naval Service Sch. Command (see: U.S. Naval Service Sch. Command)
Naval Tech. Training Ctr. (see: U.S. Naval Tech. Training Ctr.)
Naval Tech. Training Ctr.—Corry Station (see: U.S. Naval Tech. Training Ctr.—Corry Station)
Naval Transportation Management Sch. (see: U.S. Naval Transp. Management Sch.)
Naval Undersea Medical Inst. (see: U.S. Naval Undersea Medical Inst.)
Naval War Coll. (see: U.S. Naval War Coll.)
Navarro Coll. 495, 675
Navy and Marine Corps Intelligence Training Ctr. (see: U.S. Navy and Marine Corps Intelligence Training Ctr.)
Navy Combat Systems Tech. Schs. Command (see: U.S. Navy Combat Systems Tech. Schs. Command)
Navy Field Medical Service Sch. (see: U.S. Navy Field Medical Service Sch.)
Navy Fleet and Mine Warfare Training Ctr. (see: U.S. Navy Fleet and Mine Warfare Training Ctr.)
Navy Service Sch. Command (see: U.S. Navy Service Sch. Command)
Navy Supply Corps Sch. (see: U.S. Navy Supply Corps Sch.)
Nazarene Bible Coll. 83
Nazarene Theol. Sem. 286
Nazareth Coll. 257
Nazareth Coll. of Rochester 342
Nebraska Christian Coll. 298
Nebraska Coll. of Bus. 298
Nebraska Coll. of Tech. Agriculture 298
Nebraska Coordinating Commission for Postsecondary Ed. 640
Nebraska Custom Diesel Drivers Training 298
Nebraska Indian Comm. Coll. 298
Nebraska Methodist Coll. of Nursing and Allied Health 298
Nebraska Wesleyan Univ. 298
Nell Executive Secretary Sch. (see: Jacki Nell Exec. Secretary Sch.)
Nelson Comm. Coll. (see: Thomas Nelson Comm. Coll.)
Nelson Co. Area Voc. Ed. Ctr. (see: Kentucky Tech—Nelson Co. Area Voc. Ed. Ctr.)
Neosho Co. Comm. Coll. 187, 614
Ner Israel Rabbinical Coll. 228
Ner Israel Yeshiva Coll. of Toronto 556
Nettleton Coll. 461
Neumann Coll. 427
Nevada Tech. Inst. 302
New Brunswick Theol. Sem. 314
New Careers of Huntington 541
New Careers of Lansing 257
New Castle Bus. Sch. 427
New Castle Sch. of Trades 427
New Coll. for Advanced Christian Studies, Berkeley 565
New Coll. of California 59
New Comm. Coll. of Baltimore 229, 627
New England Banking Inst. 241
New England Coll. 304
New England Coll. of Optometry 241
New England Conservatory of Music 242
New England Culinary Inst. 516
New England Hair Acad. 242
New England Inst. of Tech. 450
New England Inst. of Tech. at Palm Beach 114
New England Sch. of Accounting 242
New England Sch. of Acupuncture 242
New England Sch. of Art and Design 242
New England Sch. of Broadcasting 222
New England Sch. of Law 242
New England Sch. of Photography 242
New England Tech. Inst. of Connecticut 92
New England Tractor Trailer Training 92
New England Tractor Trailer Training of Rhode Island 450
New England Tractor Trailer Training Sch. of Massachusetts 242
New England Tractor Training Sch. 428
New Hampshire Coll. 304
New Hampshire Tech. Coll. at Berlin 304
New Hampshire Tech. Coll. at Claremont 304
New Hampshire Tech. Coll. at Laconia 305
New Hampshire Tech. Coll. at Manchester 305
New Hampshire Tech. Coll. at Nashua 305
New Hampshire Tech. Coll. at Stratham 305
New Hampshire Tech. Inst. 305
New Image Coll. of Cosmetology 204
New Jersey Dental Sch. 318
New Jersey Department of Higher Ed. 644
New Jersey Inst. of Tech. 314, 645
New Jersey Medical Sch. 318
New Kensington Commercial Sch. 428
New Mexico Commission of Higher Ed. 646
New Mexico Highlands Univ. 321, 646
New Mexico Inst. of Mining and Tech. 321, 646
New Mexico Jr. Coll. 321, 646
New Mexico Military Inst. 321, 646
New Mexico State Univ. 321, 646
New Mexico State Univ. at Alamogordo 322, 646
New Mexico State Univ. at Carlsbad 322, 646
New Mexico State Univ. System 646
New Orleans Baptist Theol. Sem. 215
New Orleans Regional Tech. Inst. 215
New Paltz Coll. (see: State Univ. of New York Coll. at New Paltz)
New River Comm. Coll. 525, 683
New Rochelle Coll. (see: Coll. of New Rochelle)
New Sch. for Social Research 342
New Sch. of Architecture 59
New Sch. of Contemporary Radio 342
New Tyler Barber Coll. 28
New World Coll. of Bus. 9
New York Bus. Sch. 342
New York Chiropractic Coll. 342

Institutional Index

New York City Furniture Inst. 333
New York City Tech. Coll. 342, 647
New York Coll. of Podiatric Medicine 342
New York Food and Hotel Management Sch. 342
New York Inst. of Bus. and Tech. 342
New York Inst. of Tech. 343
New York Law Sch. 343
New York Medical Coll. 343
New York Sch. for Medical and Dental Assistants 343
New York Sch. of Dog Grooming 343
New York Sch. of Interior Design 343
New York Tech. Inst. of Hawaii 141
New York Theol. Sem. 343
New York Univ. 343
Newberry Coll. 456
Newbridge Coll. 59
Newbury Coll. 242
Newman Theol. Coll. 571
Newport Coll. (see: Christopher Newport Coll.)
Niagara Co. Comm. Coll. 344, 650
Niagara Univ. 344
Nicholls State Univ. 215, 623
Nichols Career Ctr. 286
Nichols Coll. 242
Nicolet Area Tech. Coll. 548
Nielsen Electronics Inst. 456
Nigerian Baptist Theol. Sem. 560
Nikolais and Louis Dance Lab 344
Norfolk Skills Ctr. 525
Norfolk State Univ. 525, 682
Normandale Comm. Coll. 270, 633
North Adams State Coll. 242, 628
North Alabama Coll. of Commerce 9
North Alabama Skills Ctr. 9
North American Baptist Coll. 556
North American Baptist Sem. 461
North American Coll. 22
North American Inst. of Aviation 456
North Arkansas Comm. Coll. 28
North Bennet Street Sch. 242
North Carolina Agricultural and Tech. State Univ. 367, 655
North Carolina Central Univ. 368, 655
North Carolina Sch. of the Arts 368, 655
North Carolina State Board of Comm. Colls. 652
North Carolina State Univ. 368, 655
North Carolina Wesleyan Coll. 368
North Central Area Tech. Inst. 215

North Central Bible Coll. 270
North Central Coll. 157
North Central Kansas Area Vo-Tech Sch. 187
North Central Michigan Coll. 257, 631
North Central Missouri Coll. 286
North Central Tech. Coll. 389, 658
North Country Comm. Coll. 344, 650
North Dakota State Board of Higher Ed. 656
North Dakota State Coll. of Sci. 376, 656
North Dakota State Univ. 376, 656
North Dakota State Univ.—Bottineau 376, 656
North Dakota Univ. System 656
North Florida Jr. Coll. 114, 598
North Georgia Coll. 134, 602
North Georgia Tech. Inst. 134
North Greenville Coll. 456
North Harris Coll. 495, 675
North Harris Montgomery Coll. Dist. 675
North Hennepin Comm. Coll. 270, 634
North Hills Sch. of Health Occupations 428
North Idaho Coll. 143, 604
North Iowa Area Comm. Coll. 180, 611
North Lake Coll. 495, 674
North Metro Tech. Inst. 565
North Orange Co. Comm. Coll. Dist. 586
North Park Coll. 59
North Park Coll. and Theol. Sem. 157
North Seattle Comm. Coll. 535, 686
North Shore Comm. Coll. 243, 628
North Tech. Ed. Ctr. 114
North Valley Occupational Ctr. 59
Northampton Comm. Coll. 428, 664
Northcentral Tech. Coll. 548
Northcentral Tech. Inst. (see: Indiana Vo-Tech Coll.—Northcentral Tech. Inst.)
Northeast Alabama State Jr. Coll. 9, 574
Northeast Broadcasting Sch. 243
Northeast Career Schs. 305
Northeast Coll. 489
Northeast Comm. Coll. 298, 640
Northeast Inst. 344
Northeast Inst. of Ed. 428
Northeast Inst. of Industrial Tech. 243
Northeast Iowa Comm. Coll. 180, 611

Northeast Louisiana Tech. Inst. 216
Northeast Louisiana Univ. 216, 623
Northeast Metro Tech. Coll. 270
Northeast Mississippi Comm. Coll. 277, 636
Northeast Missouri State Univ. 286, 637
Northeast State Tech. Comm. Coll. 470, 671
Northeast Tech. Inst. (see: Indiana Vo-Tech Coll.—Northeast Tech. Inst.)
Northeast Texas Comm. Coll. 496, 675
Northeast Wisconsin Tech. Coll. 548
Northeastern Christian Jr. Coll. 428
Northeastern Illinois Univ. 157, 605
Northeastern Jr. Coll. 84, 594
Northeastern Ohio Univs. Coll. of Medicine 389, 658
Northeastern Oklahoma A&M Coll. 401
Northeastern Sch. of Commerce 257
Northeastern State Univ. 401
Northeastern Univ. 243
Northern Arizona Inst. of Tech. 22
Northern Arizona Univ. 23, 578
Northern Baptist Theol. Sem. 157
Northern Campbell Co. Vo-Tech Sch. (see: Kentucky Tech—Northern Campbell Co. Vo-Tech Sch.)
Northern Essex Comm. Coll. 243, 628
Northern Illinois Univ. 157, 608
Northern Kentucky Health Occupations Ctr. (see: Kentucky Tech—Northern Kentucky Health Occupations Ctr.)
Northern Kentucky State Vo-Tech Sch. (see: Kentucky Tech—Northern Kentucky State Vo-Tech Sch.)
Northern Kentucky Univ. 204, 615
Northern Maine Tech. Coll. 222
Northern Marianas Coll. 560, 690
Northern Michigan Univ. 257, 631
Northern Montana Coll. 294, 639
Northern Nevada Career Coll. (see: Career Coll. of Northern Nevada)
Northern Nevada Comm. Coll. 302, 642
Northern New Mexico Comm. Coll. 322, 646
Northern Oklahoma Coll. 401
Northern State Univ. 461, 670
Northern Virginia Comm. Coll. 525, 683
Northland Coll. 548

Institutional Index

Northland Comm. Coll. 270, 633
Northland Pioneer Coll. 23, 579
Northpoint Ed. Ctr. (see: Kentucky Tech—Northpoint Ed. Ctr.)
Northrop Univ. 59
Northshore Tech. Inst. 389
Northwest Alabama Comm. Coll. 9, 574
Northwest Arkansas Comm. Coll. 564
Northwest Baptist Theol. Coll. 556
Northwest Christian Coll. 408
Northwest Coll. 489 (TX); 553, 689 (WY)
Northwest Coll. of Art 535
Northwest Coll. of Medical and Dental Assistants 60
Northwest Coll. of the Assemblies of God 535
Northwest Indian Coll. 571
Northwest Inst. of Acupuncture and Oriental Medicine 535
Northwest Iowa Tech. Coll. 180, 611
Northwest Louisiana Tech. Inst. 216
Northwest Mississippi Comm. Coll. 277, 636
Northwest Missouri Comm. Coll. 287
Northwest Missouri State Univ. 287, 637
Northwest Nazarene Coll. 144
Northwest Tech. Coll. 389, 658
Northwest Tech. Inst. (see: Indiana Vo-Tech Coll.—Northwest Tech. Inst.)
Northwest Tech. Inst. 270
Northwestern Bus. Coll. 157
Northwestern Coll. 180 (IA); 270 (MN); 389 (OH); 548 (WI)
Northwestern Coll. of Chiropractic 270
Northwestern Connecticut Comm. Coll. 92, 595
Northwestern Electronics Inst. 270
Northwestern Michigan Coll. 258, 631
Northwestern State Univ. 216, 623 (LA); 401 (OK)
Northwestern Univ. 157
Northwood Inst. 258
Norwalk Comm. Coll. 92, 595
Norwalk State Tech. Coll. 92, 595
Norwich Univ. 516
Nossi Sch. of Art 471
Notre Dame Apostolic Catechetical Inst. 570
Notre Dame Coll. (see: Coll. of Notre Dame)
Notre Dame Coll. 305 (NH); 389 (OH)

Notre Dame Coll. of Maryland (see: Coll. of Notre Dame of Maryland)
Notre Dame Sem. 216
Nova Inst. of Health Tech. 60
Nova Univ. 114
Nu-Tek Acad. of Beauty 204
Nunez Tech. Inst. (see: Elaine P. Nunez Tech. Inst.)
Nyack Coll. 344

O

OMI Coll. of Applied Sci. 396
O'More Coll. of Design 471
Oak Hills Bible Coll. 270
Oakbridge Acad. of Arts 428
Oakdale Tech. Inst. 216
Oakland City Coll. 172
Oakland Coll. of Court Reporting 60
Oakland Comm. Coll. 258, 631
Oakland Univ. 258, 631
Oakton Comm. Coll. 158, 607
Oakwood Coll. 9
Oberlin Coll. 389
Oblate Coll. 100
Oblate Sch. of Theol. 496
Occidental Coll. 60
Occupational Ed. Ctr.—Central 128
Occupational Ed. Ctr.—North 128
Occupational Ed. Ctr.—South 128
Occupational Safety Training Inst. 496
Ocean Corporation 496
Ocean Co. Coll. 314, 644
Ocean State Bus. Inst. 450
Oceaneering Coll. (see: Coll. of Oceaneering)
Ochsner Sch. of Allied Health Scis. 216
Oconaluftee Job Corps Civilian Conservation Ctr. 368
Odessa Coll. 496, 675
Office Careers Centre 496
Office of Comm. Colls. 644, 649
Office of Sr. Insts. 645
Office Tech. Coll. (see: Coll. of Office Tech.)
Ogeechee Tech. Inst. 565
Oglala Lakota Coll. 461
Oglethorpe Univ. 135
Ohio Auto/Diesel Tech. Inst. 389
Ohio Board of Regents 657
Ohio Coll. of Podiatric Medicine 390
Ohio Co. Area Voc. Ed. Ctr. (see: Kentucky Tech—Ohio Co. Area Voc. Ed. Ctr.)
Ohio Dominican Coll. 390

Ohio Inst. of Photography 390
Ohio Northern Univ. 390
Ohio Sch. of Broadcast Tech. 390
Ohio State Coll. of Barber Styling 390
Ohio State Univ. 390, 658
Ohio Univ. 391, 658
Ohio Valley Bus. Coll. 391
Ohio Valley Coll. 541
Ohio Wesleyan Univ. 391
Ohlone Coll. 60, 583
Ohr HaMeir Theol. Sem. 344
Ohr Somayach-Tanenbaum Educational Ctr. 344
Okaloosa-Walton Comm. Coll. 114, 598
Okefenokee Tech. Inst. 135
Oklahoma Baptist Univ. 401
Oklahoma Christian Univ. of Sci. and Arts 401
Oklahoma City Comm. Coll. 401
Oklahoma City Univ. 401
Oklahoma Farriers Coll. 401
Oklahoma Horseshoeing Sch. 401
Oklahoma Inst. of Hair Design 402
Oklahoma Jr. Coll. 402
Oklahoma Jr. Coll. of Bus. and Tech. 402
Oklahoma Panhandle State Univ. 402
Oklahoma State Regents for Higher Ed. 659
Oklahoma State Univ. 402
Oklahoma State Univ. Coll. of Osteopathic Medicine 402
Oklahoma State Univ. System 659
Oklahoma State Univ.—Oklahoma City 402
Oklahoma State Univ.—Okmulgee 402
Old Dominion Univ. 525, 682
Old Westbury Coll. (see: State Univ. of New York Coll. at Old Westbury)
Oldham Co. Voc. Ed. Ctr. (see: Kentucky Tech—Oldham Co. Voc. Ed. Ctr.)
Olean Bus. Inst. 344
Olive-Harvey Coll. 158, 605
Olivet Coll. 258
Olivet Nazarene Univ. 158
Olney Central Coll. 158, 606
Olympic Coll. 535, 686
Omaha Coll. of Bus. 298
Omaha Coll. of Health Careers 298
Omaha Opportunities Industrialization Ctr. 298
Omar Rivas Acad. of Barber Arts and Sci. 158
Omega Inst. 314

Institutional Index

Oneonta Coll. (see: State Univ. of New York Coll. at Oneonta)
Onondaga Comm. Coll. 344, 650
Ontario Bible Coll. 556
Opelika State Tech. Coll. 9
Oral Roberts Univ. 402
Orange Coast Coll. 60, 582
Orange Co. Bus. Coll. 60
Orange Co. Comm. Coll. 345, 651
Orangeburg-Calhoun Tech. Coll. 456, 669
Oregon Coll. of Oriental Medicine 408
Oregon Denturist Coll. 408
Oregon Grad. Inst. of Sci. and Tech. 408
Oregon Health Scis. Univ. 409, 661
Oregon Inst. of Tech. 409, 661
Oregon Polytechnic Inst. 409
Oregon Sch. of Arts and Crafts 409
Oregon State Board of Ed., Office of Comm. Coll. Services 661
Oregon State System of Higher Ed. 661
Oregon State Univ. 409, 661
Orlando Coll. 114
Orlando Vo-Tech Ctr. 114
Orleans Tech. Inst. 428
Osteopathic Medicine Coll. (see: Coll. of Osteopathic Medicine of the Pacific)
Oswego Coll. (see: State Univ. of New York Coll. at Oswego)
Otero Jr. Coll. 84, 594
Otis Art Inst. of Parsons Sch. of Design 60
Ottawa Univ. 187
Otterbein Coll. 391
Ouachita Baptist Univ. 28
Our Lady of the Elms Coll. (see: Coll. of Our Lady of the Elms)
Our Lady of the Holy Cross Coll. 216
Our Lady of the Lake Univ. 496
Our Lady of Victory Secretarial Sch. 345
Owens Tech. Coll. (see: Michael J. Owens Tech. Coll.)
Owensboro Comm. Coll. 204, 616
Owensboro Jr. Coll. of Bus. 204
Owensboro Vo-Tech Sch. (see: Kentucky Tech—Owensboro Vo-Tech Sch.)
Oxnard Coll. 61, 590
Ozark Christian Coll. 287
Ozarks Coll. (see: Coll. of the Ozarks)

P

PBS Training Ctr. 158 (IL); 258 (MI)
PCI Dealers Sch. 302
PCI Health Training Ctr. 496
PJ's Coll. of Cosmetology 204
PJA Sch. 428
PPI Health Careers Sch. 84
PRO DRIVE Southeast Training Ctr. 456
PRO Drive, Inc./American Training Ctr. 548
PRS Career Acad. 114
PSI Inst. 172 (IN); 229 (MD); 345 (NY); 391-392 (OH); 428 (PA)
PSI Inst. Flint 258
PSI Inst. of Baltimore 229
PSI Inst. of Charlotte 368
PSI Inst. of Miami 114
PSI Inst. of Michigan 258
PTC Career Inst. 100 (DC); 158 (IL); 229 (MD); 314 (NJ); 392 (OH); 428 (PA)
Pace Bus. Sch. 345
Pace Inst. 429
Pace Univ. 345
Pacific Christian Coll. 61
Pacific Coast Coll. 61
Pacific Coast Tech. Inst. 61
Pacific Coll. of Oriental Medicine 61
Pacific Grad. Sch. of Psychology 61
Pacific Lutheran Theol. Sem. 61
Pacific Lutheran Univ. 535
Pacific Northwest Ballet Sch. 535
Pacific Northwest Coll. of Art 409
Pacific Oaks Coll. 61
Pacific Sch. of Religion 61
Pacific Travel Sch. 61
Pacific Union Coll. 61
Pacific Univ. 409
Paducah Area Voc. Ed. Ctr. (see: Kentucky Tech—Paducah Area Voc. Ed. Ctr.)
Paducah Comm. Coll. 204, 616
Paier Coll. of Art, Inc. 92
Paine Coll. 135
Palm Beach Atlantic Coll. 114
Palm Beach Comm. Coll. 115, 599
Palm Beaches Coll. (see: Coll. of the Palm Beaches)
Palmer Coll. of Chiropractic 180
Palmer Coll. of Chiropractic—West 61
Palmer Sch. 429
Palo Alto Coll. 496, 673
Palo Verde Coll. 61, 586
Palo Verde Comm. Coll. Dist. 586
Palomar Coll. 62, 586
Palomar Comm. Coll. Dist. 586

Pamlico Comm. Coll. 368, 653
Pan American Sch. 345
Pan American Univ. (see: Univ. of Texas—Pan American)
Panama Canal Coll. 115 (FL); 560 (Panama)
Panola Coll. 496, 675
Paper Sci. and Tech. Inst. (see: Inst. of Paper Sci. and Tech.)
Paradise Valley Comm. Coll. 23, 578
Paralegal Careers 115
Paralegal Inst., Inc. 23
Paralegal Training Ctr. 496
Paramedic Training Inst. 409
Paris Jr. Coll. 496, 675
Park Coll. 287
Parker Coll. of Chiropractic 497
Parkland Coll. 158, 607
Parks Coll. 322
Parks Coll. of St. Louis Univ. 158
Parks Jr. Coll. 84
Pasadena Area Comm. Coll. Dist. 586
Pasadena City Coll. 62, 586
Pasco-Hernando Comm. Coll. 115, 599
Passaic Co. Comm. Coll. 314, 644
Paterson Coll. of New Jersey (see: William Paterson Coll. of New Jersey)
Patricia Stevens Coll. 287
Patricia Stevens Fashion and Finishing Sch. 229
Patrick Henry Comm. Coll. 526, 683
Patrick Henry State Jr. Coll. 10, 574
Patten Coll. 62
Patterson State Tech. Coll. (see: John M. Patterson State Tech. Coll.)
Patton Voc. Ed. Ctr. (see: Kentucky Tech—Patton Voc. Ed. Ctr.)
Paul D. Camp Comm. Coll. 526, 683
Paul Quinn Coll. 497
Paul Smith's Coll. 345
Payne Univ. (see: Howard Payne Univ.)
Payne-Pulliam Sch. of Trade and Commerce 259
Peabody Inst. of Music 227
Peace Coll. 368
Pearl River Comm. Coll. 277, 636
Pedigree Career Inst. 23 (AZ); 243 (MA)
Peewee Valley Ed. Ctr. (see: Kentucky Tech—Peewee Valley Ed. Ctr.)
Peirce Jr. Coll. 429
Pellissippi State Tech. Comm. Coll. 471, 671

Institutional Index

Pembroke State Univ. 368, 655
Peninsula Coll. 536, 686
Penn Coll. (see: William Penn Coll.)
Penn Commercial Inc. 429
Penn Tech. Inst. 429
Penn Valley Comm. Coll. 287, 637
Penn-Ohio Coll. 392
Pennco Tech 314
Pennco Tech 429
Pennsylvania Acad. of the Fine Arts 429
Pennsylvania Ballet Sch. (see: Shirley Rock Sch. of the Pennsylvania Ballet)
Pennsylvania Bus. Inst. 429
Pennsylvania Coll. of Optometry 429
Pennsylvania Coll. of Podiatric Medicine 429
Pennsylvania Coll. of Tech. 429, 664
Pennsylvania Gunsmith Sch. 430
Pennsylvania Inst. of Culinary Arts 430
Pennsylvania Inst. of Taxidermy 430
Pennsylvania Inst. of Tech. 430
Pennsylvania Sch. of Art and Design 430
Pennsylvania State System of Higher Ed. 663
Pennsylvania State Univ. 430, 664
Pennsylvania State Univ. Central Office 664
Pensacola Jr. Coll. 115, 599
Pepperdine Univ. 62
Peralta Comm. Coll. Dist. 586
Perkins Job Corps Ctr. (see: Carl D. Perkins Job Corps Ctr.)
Perry Tech. Inst. 536
Peru State Coll. 298
Pfeiffer Coll. 368
Pharr Voc. Sch. 497
Phelps Area Voc. Ed. Ctr. (see: Kentucky Tech—Phelps Area Voc. Ed. Ctr.)
Philadelphia Art Inst. (see: Art Inst. of Philadelphia)
Philadelphia Coll. of Bible 432
Philadelphia Coll. of Osteopathic Medicine 432
Philadelphia Coll. of Pharmacy and Sci. 432
Philadelphia Coll. of Textiles and Sci. 432
Philadelphia Comm. Coll. (see: Comm. Coll. of Philadelphia)
Philadelphia Wireless Tech. Inst. 432
Philander Smith Coll. 28
Phillips Beth Israel Sch. of Nursing 345

Phillips Bus. Coll. 526
Phillips Bus. Sch. 314
Phillips Coll. (see: Frank Phillips Coll.)
Phillips Coll. 62 (CA); 205 (KY)
Phillips Coll. of Atlanta 135
Phillips Coll. of Chicago 159
Phillips Coll. of Mobile 564
Phillips Co. Comm. Coll. 28
Phillips Grad. Sem. 402
Phillips Jr. Coll. 62 (CA); 115 (FL); 135 (GA); 216 (LA); 277 (MS); 287 (MO); 369 (NC); 513 (UT)
Phillips Jr. Coll. of Charleston 456
Phillips Jr. Coll. of Greenville 456
Phillips Jr. Coll. of Las Vegas 302
Phillips Jr. Coll. of Memphis 471
Phillips Jr. Coll. of Spartanburg 456
Phillips Jr. Coll. of the Mississippi Gulf Coast 278
Phillips Sch. of Bus. and Tech. 497
Phillips Univ. 403
Phoenix Coll. 10 (AL); 23, 578 (AZ)
Phoenix Educational Systems 115
Phoenix Inst. of Tech. 23
Pickens Tech. Ctr. (see: T.H. Pickens Tech. Ctr.)
Pickens Tech. Inst. 135
Piedmont Bible Coll. 369
Piedmont Coll. 135
Piedmont Comm. Coll. 369, 653
Piedmont Tech. Coll. 456, 669
Piedmont Virginia Comm. Coll. 526, 683
Pierce Coll. (see: Franklin Pierce Coll.)
Pierce Coll. 536, 686
Pierce Law Ctr. (see: Franklin Pierce Law Ctr.)
Pikes Peak Comm. Coll. 84, 594
Pikeville Coll. 205
Pillsbury Baptist Bible Coll. 567
Pima Co. Comm. Coll. Dist. 23, 579
Pima Medical Inst. 23
Pine Manor Coll. 243
Pinebrook Jr. Coll. 569
Pinellas Tech. Ed. Ctr.—Clearwater 115
Pinellas Tech. Ed. Ctr.—St. Petersburg Campus 115
Pitt Comm. Coll. 369, 654
Pittard Area Voc. Sch. (see: J.R. Pittard Area Voc. Sch.)
Pittsburg State Univ. 187, 613
Pittsburgh Art Inst. (see: Art Inst. of Pittsburgh)
Pittsburgh Inst. of Aeronautics 432
Pittsburgh Inst. of Mortuary Sci. 432
Pittsburgh Tech. Inst. 432
Pittsburgh Theol. Sem. 432

Pitzer Coll. 62
Platt Coll. 62 (CA); 84 (CO); 403 (OK)
Plattsburgh Coll. (see: State Univ. of New York Coll. at Plattsburgh)
Plaza Bus. Inst. 346
Plaza Sch. 314
Plaza Three Acad. 322
Plymouth State Coll. 305, 643
Point Loma Nazarene Coll. 63
Point Park Coll. 432
Politechnical Inst. 116
Polk Comm. Coll. 116, 599
Polytechnic Inst. 497
Polytechnic Univ. 346
Pomona Coll. 63
Ponce Coll. of Tech. 446
Ponce Paramedical Coll. 446
Ponce Regional Coll. 446, 665
Ponce Sch. of Medicine 446
Ponce Tech. Sch. 446
Ponce Tech. Univ. Coll. 446, 666
Pontiac Bus. Inst. 172 (IN); 259 (MI)
Pontifical Coll. Josephinum 392
Pope John XXIII National Sem. 243
Porter and Chester Inst. 92
Porterville Coll. 63, 584
Portfolio Ctr. 135
Portland Comm. Coll. 409, 661
Portland Sch. of Art 222
Portland State Univ. 410, 661
Potomac Acad. of Hair Design 526
Potomac State Coll. of West Virginia Univ. 541, 687
Potsdam Coll. (see: State Univ. of New York Coll. at Potsdam)
Poynter Inst. for Media Studies 116
Practical Bible Training Sch. 346
Practical Schs. 63
Prairie State Coll. 159, 607
Prairie View A&M Univ. 497, 676
Pratt Comm. Coll. 187, 614
Pratt Inst. 346
Presbyterian Coll. 457
Presbyterian Sch. of Christian Ed. 526
Presbyterian-St. Luke Ctr. for Health Sci. Ed. 84
Prescott Coll. 24
Presentation Coll. 461
Prestonsburg Comm. Coll. 205, 616
Prince George's Comm. Coll. 229, 627
Prince Inst. of Prof. Studies 10
Prince Regional Vo-Tech Sch. (see: Albert I. Prince Regional Vo-Tech Sch.)

Institutional Index

Prince William Sound Comm. Coll. 15, 577
Princeton Tech. Inst. 471
Princeton Theol. Sem. 314
Princeton Univ. 315
Principia Coll. 159
Printing Trades Sch. 346
Pro-Way Hair Sch. 135
Prof. Bus. Inst. 346
Prof. Bus. Sch. 287
Prof. Career Ctrs. 217
Prof. Career Coll. 63
Prof. Careers 302
Prof. Careers Inst., Inc. 172
Prof. Court Reporting Sch. 497
Prof. Hair Design Acad. 116
Prof. Skills Inst. 392
Prof. Training Acad. of Esthetics and Beauty Courses 446
Progressive Fashion Sch. 392
Prospect Hall Coll. 116
Protestant Episcopal Theol. Sem. in Virginia 526
Providence Coll. 451
Provo Coll. 513
Pueblo Coll. of Bus. and Tech. 84
Pueblo Comm. Coll. 84, 594
Puerto Rico Barber Coll. 447
Puerto Rico Coll. (see: Coll. of Puerto Rico)
Puerto Rico Conservatory of Music (see: Conservatory of Music of Puerto Rico)
Puerto Rico Jr. Coll. 447
Puerto Rico Prof. Coll. 447
Puerto Rico Tech. and Beauty Coll. 447
Puget Sound Christian Coll. 536
Pulaski Vo-Tech Sch. 28
Purchase Coll. (see: State Univ. of New York Coll. at Purchase)
Purchase Training Ctr. 202
Purdue Univ. 172, 609
Purdue Univ. System 609
Purdue Univ.—Calumet 173, 609
Purdue Univ.—North Central 173, 609

Q

QUALTEC Inst. for Competitive Advantage 116
Quality Plus Office Skills and Motivational Training Ctr. 135
Queen City Coll. 471
Queen of the Holy Rosary Coll. 63
Queen's Univ. 557
Queens Coll. 346, 647 (NY); 369 (NC)
Queensborough Comm. Coll. 346, 648
Quincy Coll. 159 (IL); 243, 629 (MA)
Quincy Tech. Schs. 159
Quinebaug Valley Comm. Coll. 92, 595
Quinn Coll. (see: Paul Quinn Coll.)
Quinnipiac Coll. 93
Quinsigamond Comm. Coll. 243, 629

R

R.E.T.S. Ed. Ctr. 433
R.E.T.S. Electronic Inst. 10 (AL); 205 (KY); 497 (TX)
R.E.T.S. Electronic Sch. 229 (MD); 244 (MA)
R.E.T.S. Inst. of Tech. 392
R.E.T.S. Tech Ctr. 392
R.E.T.S. Training Ctr. 217
R/S Inst. 497
Rabbinical Acad. Mesivta Rabbi Chaim Berlin 346
Rabbinical Coll. Beth Shraga 346
Rabbinical Coll. Bobover Yeshiva B'nei Zion 347
Rabbinical Coll. Ch'san Sofer 347
Rabbinical Coll. of America 315
Rabbinical Coll. of Long Island 347
Rabbinical Coll. of Telshe 392
Rabbinical Sem. Adas Yereim 347
Rabbinical Sem. M'kor Chaim 347
Rabbinical Sem. of America 347
Radcliffe Coll. 244
Radford M. Locklin Vo-Tech Ctr. 116
Radford Univ. 526, 682
Raedel Coll. and Industrial Welding Sch. 392
Rainy River Comm. Coll. 270, 633
Ralph Amodei International Inst. of Hair Design and Tech. 433
Ramapo Coll. of New Jersey 315, 645
Ramirez Coll. of Bus. and Tech. 447
Ramsay's Specialty Beauty Sch. (see: Diana Ramsay's Specialty Beauty Sch.)
Rancho Santiago Comm. Coll. 63, 587
Rancho Santiago Comm. Coll. Dist. 587
Rand Grad. Sch. of Policy Studies 63
Randolph Comm. Coll. 369, 654
Randolph-Macon Coll. 526
Randolph-Macon Woman's Coll. 526
Ranger Jr. Coll. 497, 676
Ranken Tech. Coll. 287
Rappahannock Comm. Coll. 526, 683
Raritan Valley Comm. Coll. 315, 644
Rasmussen Bus. Coll. 271
Ray Coll. of Design 159
Raymond Walters Coll. 396
Reading Area Comm. Coll. 433, 664
Reconstructionist Rabbinical Coll. 569
Recording Arts Coll. (see: Coll. of Recording Arts)
Recreational Vehicle Service Acad. 116
Red River Vo-Tech Sch. 28
Red Rocks Comm. Coll. 85, 594
Redlands Comm. Coll. 403
Redwoods Coll. (see: Coll. of the Redwoods)
Redwoods Comm. Coll. Dist. 587
Reed Coll. 410
Reese Inst. Sch. of Massage Therapy 116
Reformed Bible Coll. 259
Reformed Presbyterian Theol. Sem. 569
Reformed Theol. Sem. 278
Refrigeration Sch. 24
Regency Univs. System 608
Regent Coll. 557
Regent Univ. 526
Regent's Coll. (see: Univ. of the State of New York Regents Coll. Degrees)
Regional Sem. of St. Vincent de Paul 116
Regis Coll. 244 (MA); 557 (Canada)
Regis Univ. 85
Reid State Tech. Coll. 10
Reinhardt Coll. 135
Rend Lake Coll. 159, 607
Reno Bus. Coll. (see: Morrison Coll./Reno Bus. Coll.)
Rensselaer Polytechnic Inst. 347
Renton Tech. Coll. 536
Reporting Acad. of Virginia 527
Research Coll. of Nursing 288
Resource Ctr. for the Handicapped 536
Restaurant Sch. 433
Reynolds Comm. Coll. (see: J. Sargeant Reynolds Comm. Coll.)
Rhode Island Coll. 451, 667
Rhode Island Comm. Coll. (see: Comm. Coll. of Rhode Island)
Rhode Island Office of Higher Ed. 667
Rhode Island Sch. of Design 451

Institutional Index

Rhode Island Sch. of Photography 451
Rhode Island Trades Shops Sch. 451
Rhodes Coll. 471
Rice Aviation, A Div. of A&J Enterprises 497
Rice Coll. 10 (AL); 471 (TN)
Rice Univ. (see: William Marsh Rice Univ.)
Rich Mountain Comm. Coll. 28
Richard Bland Coll. 527, 683
Richard J. Daley Coll. 159, 606
Richard Stockton State Coll. 315, 645
Richland Coll. 498, 674
Richland Comm. Coll. 159, 607
Richmond Coll. 561
Richmond Comm. Coll. 369, 654
Ricks Coll. 144
Rider Coll. 315
Ridge Vo-Tech Ctr. 116
Ridley-Lowell Bus. and Tech. Inst. 93
Ridley-Lowell Sch. of Bus. 347
Riley Coll. 10
Ringling Sch. of Art and Design 116
Rio Hondo Coll. 63, 587
Rio Hondo Comm. Coll. Dist. 587
Rio Salado Comm. Coll. 24, 578
Ripon Coll. 548
Ritz Inst. of Hotel Management (see: Cesar Ritz Inst. of Hotel Management)
Rivas Acad. of Barber Arts and Sci. (see: Omar Rivas Acad. of Barber Arts and Sci.)
River Parishes Tech. Inst. 217
Riverside Comm. Coll. 64, 587
Riverside Comm. Coll. Dist. 587
Riverside Sch. of Aeronautics 347
Rivier Coll. 305
Roane State Comm. Coll. 471, 671
Roanoke Bible Coll. 369
Roanoke Coll. 527
Roanoke Valley Comm. Hospital Coll. of Health Scis. (see: Comm. Hospital of Roanoke Valley Coll. of Health Scis.)
Roanoke-Chowan Comm. Coll. 370, 654
Robert Morgan Vo-Tech Inst. 117
Robert Morris Coll. 159 (IL); 433 (PA)
Robert Wood Johnson Medical Sch. 318
Roberto-Venn Sch. of Luthiery 24
Roberts Beauty Coll. 567
Roberts Univ. (see: Oral Roberts Univ.)
Roberts Wesleyan Coll. 347
Robeson Comm. Coll. 370, 654
Robinson Bus. Coll. 217
Rochester Bus. Inst. 347
Rochester Comm. Coll. 271, 634
Rochester Inst. of Tech. 347
Rochester Tech. Coll. 271
Rock Valley Coll. 159, 607
Rockcastle Co. Area Voc. Ed. Ctr. (see: Kentucky Tech—Rockcastle Co. Area Voc. Ed. Ctr.)
Rockford Bus. Coll. 159
Rockford Coll. 160
Rockhurst Coll. 288
Rockingham Comm. Coll. 370, 654
Rockland Comm. Coll. 348, 651
Rocky Mountain Coll. 294
Rocky Mountain Coll. of Art and Design 85
Roffler Acad. for Hairstylists 93
Roffler Hair Design Coll. 117 (FL); 271 (MN); 392 (OH); 498 (TX)
Roffler Tech. Inst. 117
Roffler-Moler Hairstyling 136
Roger Williams Coll. 451
Rogers State Coll. 403
Rogue Comm. Coll. 410, 661
Rolla Area Vo-Tech Sch. 288
Rollins Coll. 117
Romar Hairstyling Acad. 117
Roosevelt Univ. 160
Rosary Coll. 160
Rose State Coll. 403
Rose-Hulman Inst. of Tech. 173
Rosedale Tech. Inst. 433
Rosemont Coll. 433
Ross Bus. Inst. 259
Ross Medical Ed. Ctr. 259-260
Ross State Univ. (see: Sul Ross State Univ.)
Ross Tech. Inst. 117-118 (FL); 260 (MI)
Rosston Sch. of Men's Hair Design 64
Rouse Sch. of Special Detective Training 64
Rowan State Vo-Tech Sch. (see: Kentucky Tech—Rowan State Vo-Tech Sch.)
Rowan-Cabarrus Comm. Coll. 370, 654
Roxbury Comm. Coll. 244, 629
Roy's of Louisville Beauty Acad. 205
Royal Acad. of Hair Design 457
Royal Barber and Beauty Sch. 348
Royal Hair Inst. 64
Rush Inst. 136 (GA); 457 (SC)
Rush Univ. 160
Russell Area Voc. Ed. Ctr. (see: Kentucky Tech—Russell Area Voc. Ed. Ctr.)
Russell Co. Area Voc. Ed. Ctr. (see: Kentucky Tech—Russell Co. Area Voc. Ed. Ctr.)
Russell Sage Coll. 348
Russell Sage Jr. Coll. of Albany 348
Russellville Area Voc. Ed. Ctr. (see: Kentucky Tech—Russellville Area Voc. Ed. Ctr.)
Rust Coll. 278
Ruston Tech. Inst. 217
Rutgers, The State Univ. of New Jersey Central Office 645
Rutgers, The State Univ. of New Jersey—Camden 315, 645
Rutgers, The State Univ. of New Jersey—New Brunswick 315, 645
Rutgers, The State Univ. of New Jersey—Newark 315, 645
Rutledge Coll. of New Orleans 217
Ryerson Polytechnical Inst. 557

S

S.W. Sch. of Bus. and Tech. Careers 498
SCS Bus. and Tech. Inst. 315-316 (NJ); 348 (NY)
SER Bus. and Tech. Inst. 260
SER-IBM Bus. Inst. 118
SYRIT Computer Sch. Systems 349
Sabine Valley Tech. Inst. Sch. 217
Sacramento City Coll. 64, 585
Sacred Heart Major Sem. 260
Sacred Heart Sch. of Theol. 548
Sacred Heart Univ. 93
Saddleback Coll. 64, 587
Saddleback Comm. Coll. Dist. 587
Sage Coll. (see: Russell Sage Coll.)
Sage Jr. Coll. of Albany (see: Russell Sage Jr. Coll. of Albany)
Saginaw Valley State Univ. 260, 631
St. Ambrose Univ. 180
St. Andrews Presbyterian Coll. 370
St. Anselm Coll. 305
St. Augustine Coll. 160
St. Augustine Tech. Ctr. 118
St. Augustine's Coll. 370
St. Augustine's Sem. of Toronto 557
St. Benedict Coll. (see: Coll. of St. Benedict)
St. Bernard Parish Comm. Coll. 217
St. Bernard's Inst. 349
St. Bonaventure Univ. 349
St. Catharine Coll. 205

Institutional Index

St. Catherine Coll. (see: Coll. of St. Catherine)
St. Charles Borromeo Sem. 433
St. Charles Co. Comm. Coll. 288, 637
St. Clair Co. Comm. Coll. 260, 631
St. Cloud Bus. Coll. 271
St. Cloud State Univ. 271, 634
St. Cloud Tech. Coll. 271
St. Edward's Univ. 499
St. Elizabeth Coll. (see: Coll. of St. Elizabeth)
St. Francis Coll. (see: Coll. of St. Francis)
St. Francis Coll. 173 (IN); 349 (NY); 433 (PA)
St. Francis De Sales Coll. (see: Allentown Coll. of St. Francis De Sales)
St. Francis Medical Ctr. Coll. of Nursing 160
St. Francis Sem. 549
St. Gregory's Coll. 403
St. Hyacinth Coll. and Sem. 244
St. John Fisher Coll. 349
St. John Vianney Coll. Sem. 118
St. John's Coll. 229 (MD); 322 (NM)
St. John's Sch. of Bus. 244
St. John's Sem. 64 (CA); 244 (MA)
St. John's Sem. Coll. 64
St. John's Univ. 271 (MN); 349 (NY)
St. Johns River Comm. Coll. 118, 599
St. Joseph Coll. (see: Coll. of St. Joseph)
St. Joseph Coll. 93
St. Joseph Coll. of Nursing 566
St. Joseph Sem. Coll. 217
St. Joseph's Coll. 64 (CA); 173 (IN); 222 (ME); 349 (NY)
St. Joseph's Sem. 349
St. Joseph's Univ. 433
St. Lawrence Univ. 349
St. Leo Coll. 118
St. Louis Christian Coll. 288
St. Louis Coll. of Health Careers 288
St. Louis Coll. of Pharmacy 288
St. Louis Comm. Coll. at Florissant Valley 288, 638
St. Louis Comm. Coll. at Forest Park 288, 638
St. Louis Comm. Coll. at Meramec 288, 638
St. Louis Comm. Coll. Dist. 638
St. Louis Conservatory and Schs. for the Arts 288
St. Louis Tech 289
St. Louis Univ. 289
St. Martin's Coll. 536

St. Mary Coll. (see: Coll. of St. Mary)
St. Mary Coll. 187
St. Mary of the Lake Univ. (see: Univ. of St. Mary of the Lake, Mundelein Sem.)
St. Mary of the Plains Coll. 188
St. Mary Sem. 392
St. Mary's Coll. 173 (IN); 261 (MI); 370 (NC)
St. Mary's Coll. of California 64
St. Mary's Coll. of Maryland 229, 626
St. Mary's Coll. of Minnesota 271
St. Mary's Sem. and Univ. 229
St. Mary's Univ. 499
St. Mary-of-the-Woods Coll. 173
St. Meinrad Coll. 173
St. Meinrad Sch. of Theol. 173
St. Michael's Coll. 516
St. Norbert Coll. 549
St. Olaf Coll. 272
St. Patrick's Sem. 64
St. Paul Sch. of Theol. 289
St. Paul Tech. Coll. 272
St. Paul's Coll. 527
St. Peter's Coll. 316
St. Peter's Sem. 557
St. Petersburg Jr. Coll. 118, 599
St. Philip's Coll. 499, 673
St. Rose Coll. (see: Coll. of St. Rose)
St. Scholastica Coll. (see: Coll. of St. Scholastica)
St. Thomas Aquinas Coll. 349
St. Thomas Theol. Sem. 85
St. Thomas Univ. 118
St. Vincent Coll. 433
St. Vladimir's Orthodox Theol. Sem. 349
St. Xavier Coll. 160
Ste. Genevieve Beauty Coll. 289
Salem Coll. 370
Salem Comm. Coll. 316, 644
Salem State Coll. 244, 629
Salem-Teikyo Univ. 541
Salinger Acad. of Fashion (see: Louise Salinger Acad. of Fashion)
Salisbury Bus. Coll. 370
Salisbury State Univ. 229, 627
Salish Kootenai Coll. 294
Salt Lake Comm. Coll. 513, 680
Salter Sch. 244
Salter Tech. Inst. (see: Lamar Salter Tech. Inst.)
Salvation Army Sch. for Officers' Training 65
Salve Regina Univ. 451
Sam Houston State Univ. 499, 677

Samford Univ. 10
Sampson Comm. Coll. 370, 654
Samra Univ. of Oriental Medicine 65
Samuel Merritt Coll. 65
San Angelo Hair Acad. 499
San Antonio Art Inst. 499
San Antonio Coll. 499, 673
San Antonio Coll. of Medical and Dental Assistants 499
San Antonio Trade Sch. 499
San Antonio Training Div. 500
San Bernardino Comm. Coll. Dist. 587
San Bernardino Valley Coll. 65, 587
San Diego City Coll. 65, 587
San Diego Coll. for Medical and Dental Careers 65
San Diego Comm. Coll. Dist. 587
San Diego Mesa Coll. 65, 588
San Diego Miramar Coll. 65, 588
San Diego State Univ. 65, 592
San Francisco Art Inst. 65
San Francisco Ballet Sch. 66
San Francisco Barber Coll. 66
San Francisco Coll. of Mortuary Sci. 66
San Francisco Comm. Coll. Dist. 588
San Francisco Conservatory of Music 66
San Francisco State Univ. 66, 592
San Francisco Theol. Sem. 66
San Jacinto Coll. 500, 676
San Joaquin Coll. of Law 565
San Joaquin Delta Coll. 66, 588
San Joaquin Delta Comm. Coll. Dist. 588
San Joaquin Valley Coll. 66
San Jose Christian Coll. 66
San Jose City Coll. 66, 588
San Jose State Univ. 67, 592
San Jose-Evergreen Comm. Coll. Dist. 588
San Juan City Coll. 447
San Juan Coll. 322, 646
San Luis Obispo Comm. Coll. Dist. 588
San Mateo Coll. (see: Coll. of San Mateo)
San Mateo Co. Comm. Coll. Dist. 588
Sandburg Coll. (see: Carl Sandburg Coll.)
Sandhills Comm. Coll. 370, 654
Sanford-Brown Bus. Coll. 289
Sangamon State Univ. 160, 608
Santa Barbara Bus. Coll. 67
Santa Barbara City Coll. 67, 588

Institutional Index

Santa Barbara Comm. Coll. Dist. 588
Santa Clara Univ. 67
Santa Clarita Comm. Coll. Dist. 589
Santa Fe Coll. (see: Coll. of Santa Fe)
Santa Fe Comm. Coll. 118, 599 (FL); 322 (NM)
Santa Monica Coll. 67, 589
Santa Monica Comm. Coll. Dist. 589
Santa Rosa Jr. Coll. 67, 589
Sarah Lawrence Coll. 350
Sarasota Co. Vo-Tech Ctr. 118
Sauk Valley Comm. Coll. 160, 607
Savannah Coll. of Art and Design 136
Savannah State Coll. 136, 602
Savannah Tech. Inst. 136
Sawyer Coll. 67 (CA); 173 (IN)
Sawyer Coll. at Pomona 67
Sawyer Coll. at Ventura 68
Sawyer Coll. of Bus. 68 (CA); 392-393 (OH)
Sawyer Sch. 316 (NJ); 433 (PA); 451 (RI)
Sawyer Sch. of Bus. 261
Saybrook Inst. 68
Schenck Civilian Conservation Ctr. 371
Schenectady Co. Comm. Coll. 350, 651
Schiller International Univ. 559 (FL); 559 (France); 559 (Germany); 560 (Spain); 561 (United Kingdom)
Scholl Coll. of Podiatric Medicine (see: Dr. William M. Scholl Coll. of Podiatric Medicine)
Sch. for International Training 516
Sch. for Lifelong Learning 305, 643
Sch. of Advanced International Studies 227
Sch. of Advertising Art 393
Sch. of Automotive Machinists 500
Sch. of Communication Arts 272
Sch. of Communication Electronics 68
Sch. of Health-Related Professions 318
Sch. of Medical and Legal Secretarial Scis. 451
Sch. of Osteopathic Medicine 318
Sch. of the Art Inst. of Chicago 160
Sch. of the Hartford Ballet 93
Sch. of the Museum of Fine Arts, Boston 244
Sch. of Theol. at Claremont 68
Sch. of Visual Arts 350
Schoolcraft Coll. 261, 631

Schreiner Coll. 500
Schuylkill Bus. Inst. 434
Scott Coll. (see: Agnes Scott Coll.)
Scott Comm. Coll. 180, 611
Scottsdale Comm. Coll. 24, 578
Scottsdale Culinary Inst. 24
Scripps Coll. 68
Seabury-Western Theol. Sem. 160
Seattle Central Comm. Coll. 536, 686
Seattle Pacific Univ. 536
Seattle Univ. 536
Sebring Career Schs. 500
Segal Inst. of Court Reporting 119
Seguin Beauty Sch. 500
Selma Univ. 11
Sem. Extension Independent Study Inst. 471
Sem. of the Immaculate Conception 350
Seminole Comm. Coll. 119, 599
Seminole Jr. Coll. 403
Sequoia Automotive Inst. 68
Sequoias Coll. (see: Coll. of the Sequoias)
Sequoias Comm. Coll. Dist. 589
Seton Hall Univ. 316
Seton Hill Coll. 434
Seton Home Study Sch. 527
Seward Co. Comm. Coll. 188, 614
Sh'or Yoshuv Rabbinical Coll. 350
Shasta Coll. 68, 589
Shasta-Tehama Trinity Joint Comm. Coll. Dist. 589
Shaw Univ. 371
Shawnee Comm. Coll. 161, 607
Shawnee State Univ. 393, 658
Shelby Co. Area Voc. Ed. Ctr. (see: Kentucky Tech—Shelby Co. Area Voc. Ed. Ctr.)
Shelby State Comm. Coll. 472, 671
Sheldon Jackson Coll. 15
Shelton State Comm. Coll. 11, 575
Shenandoah Univ. 527
Shenango Valley Sch. of Bus. 434
Shepherd Coll. 541, 687
Sheridan Coll. 553, 689
Sheridan Vo-Tech Ctr. 119
Sherman Coll. of Straight Chiropractic 457
Sherrills Acad. 371
Shimer Coll. 161
Shippensburg Univ. of Pennsylvania 434, 664
Shirley Rock Sch. of the Pennsylvania Ballet 434
Shoals Comm. Coll. 11, 575
Shoreline Comm. Coll. 536, 686
Shorter Coll. 28 (AR); 136 (GA)
Shreveport-Bossier Tech. Inst. 217

Sidney N. Collier Tech. Inst. 217
Siena Coll. 350
Siena Heights Coll. 261
Sierra Acad. of Aeronautics Tech. Inst. 68
Sierra Coll. 68, 589
Sierra Joint Comm. Coll. Dist. 589
Sierra Nevada Coll. 302
Sierra Valley Bus. Coll. 68
Silver Lake Coll. 549
Simi Valley Adult Sch. 68
Simmons Coll. 244
Simmons Inst. of Funeral Service 350
Simmons Sch. 350
Simon's Rock of Bard Coll. 245
Simpson Coll. 69 (CA); 180 (IA)
Sinclair Comm. Coll. 393, 658
Sinte Gleska Coll. 461
Sioux City Barber Coll. 181
Sioux Falls Coll. 461
Siskiyous Coll. (see: Coll. of the Siskiyous)
Siskiyous Joint Comm. Coll. Dist. 589
Sisseton-Wahpeton Comm. Coll. 461
Skagit Bus. Coll. 537
Skagit Valley Coll. 537, 686
Skidmore Coll. 350
Skyland Acad. of Cosmetic Arts 371
Skyline Coll. 69, 588
Slidell Tech. Inst. 217
Slippery Rock Univ. of Pennsylvania 434, 664
Smith Bus. Sch. 100
Smith Coll. 245
Smith Sch. (see: Elinor Smith Sch.)
Smith Univ. (see: Johnson C. Smith Univ.)
Smith's Coll. (see: Paul Smith's Coll.)
Snead State Jr. Coll. 11, 575
Snow Coll. 513, 680
Sojourner-Douglass Coll. 230
Solano Comm. Coll. 69, 589
Solano Co. Comm. Coll. Dist. 589
Somerset Comm. Coll. 205, 616
Somerset State Vo-Tech Sch. (see: Kentucky Tech—Somerset State Vo-Tech Sch.)
Sonia Moore Studio of the Theatre 350
Sonoma Co. Jr. Coll. Dist. 589
Sonoma State Univ. 69, 592
Sooner Coll. of Tech. 403
Sotheby's Educational Studies 350
South Alabama Skills Ctr. 11
South Carolina Commission on Higher Ed. 668

Institutional Index

South Carolina Criminal Justice Training Acad. 570
South Carolina State Board for Tech. and Comprehensive Ed. 669
South Carolina State Coll. 457, 668
South Central Career Coll. 28
South Central Comm. Coll. 93, 595
South Coast Coll. of Court Reporting 69
South Coll. 136
South Dakota Board of Regents 670
South Dakota Sch. of Mines and Tech. 461, 670
South Dakota State Univ. 461, 670
South Florida Comm. Coll. 119, 599
South Georgia Coll. 136, 602
South Georgia Tech. Inst. 136
South Hills Bus. Coll. 434
South Louisiana Beauty Coll. 217
South Louisiana Regional Tech. Inst. 218
South Mountain Comm. Coll. 24, 578
South Plains Coll. 500, 676
South Puget Sound Comm. Coll. 537, 686
South Seattle Comm. Coll. 537, 686
South Suburban Coll. of Cook Co. 161, 607
South Tech. Ed. Ctr. 119
South Texas Coll. of Law 501
South Texas Vo-Tech Inst. 501
South West Acad. of Tech. 24
Southcentral Tech. Inst. (see: Indiana Vo-Tech Coll.—Southcentral Tech. Inst.)
Southeast Alabama Skills Ctr. 11
Southeast Coll. 489
Southeast Coll. of Tech. 11
Southeast Coll. of Tech. 472
Southeast Comm. Coll. 205, 616
Southeast Comm. Coll. Area 640
Southeast Comm. Coll.—Beatrice Campus 299, 640
Southeast Comm. Coll.—Lincoln Campus 299, 640
Southeast Comm. Coll.—Milford Campus 299, 640
Southeast Missouri State Univ. 289, 638
Southeast Tech. Inst. (see: Indiana Vo-Tech Coll.—Southeast Tech. Inst.)
Southeast Texas Tech. Inst. 501
Southeast Vo-Tech Inst. 461
Southeastern Acad. 119
Southeastern Baptist Coll. 278
Southeastern Baptist Theol. Sem. 371
Southeastern Bible Coll. 11
Southeastern Bus. Coll. 393
Southeastern Ctr. for the Arts 136
Southeastern Coll. of the Assemblies of God 119
Southeastern Comm. Coll. 181, 612 (IA); 371, 654 (NC)
Southeastern Flight Acad. 565
Southeastern Illinois Coll. 161, 607
Southeastern Louisiana Univ. 218, 623
Southeastern Oklahoma State Univ. 403
Southeastern Paralegal Inst. 472 (TN); 501 (TX)
Southeastern Tech. Inst. 245
Southeastern Univ. 100
Southeastern Univ. of Health Scis. 119
Southern Arkansas Univ. 29
Southern Arkansas Univ. Tech 29
Southern Arkansas Univ.—El Dorado 29
Southern Baptist Theol. Sem. 205
Southern California Coll. 69
Southern California Coll. of Optometry 69
Southern California Inst. of Architecture 69
Southern Career Inst. 119
Southern Coll. 119
Southern Coll. of Optometry 472
Southern Coll. of Seventh-Day Adventists 472
Southern Coll. of Tech. 137, 602 (GA); 371 (NC)
Southern Connecticut State Univ. 93, 596
Southern Driver's Acad. 278
Southern Idaho Coll. (see: Coll. of Southern Idaho)
Southern Illinois Univ. at Carbondale 161, 608
Southern Illinois Univ. at Edwardsville 161, 608
Southern Illinois Univ. System 608
Southern Inst. of Bus. and Tech. 501
Southern Jr. Coll. 11
Southern Maine Tech. Coll. 222
Southern Methodist Univ. 501
Southern Nazarene Univ. 403
Southern Nevada Comm. Coll. (see: Comm. Coll. of Southern Nevada)
Southern Ohio Coll. 393-394
Southern Oregon State Coll. 410, 662
Southern Sem. Coll. 527
Southern State Comm. Coll. 394, 658
Southern Tech. Coll. 11 (AL); 29 (AR); 188 (KS); 218(LA); 278 (MS); 404 (OK); 457 (SC)
Southern Union State Jr. Coll. 12, 575
Southern Univ. and Agricultural and Mechanical Coll. at Baton Rouge 218, 623
Southern Univ. and Agricultural and Mechanical Coll. System 623
Southern Univ. at New Orleans 218, 624
Southern Univ. in Shreveport 218, 624
Southern Utah Univ. 513, 680
Southern Vermont Coll. 516
Southern Voc. Coll. 12
Southern West Virginia Comm. Coll. 541, 687
Southside Training Skill Ctr. 527
Southside Virginia Comm. Coll. 527, 683
Southwest Acupuncture Coll. 322
Southwest Baptist Univ. 289
Southwest Coll. (see: Coll. of the Southwest)
Southwest Coll. 69 (CA); 489 (TX)
Southwest Inst. of Merchandising and Design 501
Southwest Louisiana Tech. Inst. 218
Southwest Mississippi Comm. Coll. 278, 636
Southwest Missouri State Univ. 289, 638
Southwest Sch. of Broadcasting 289
Southwest Sch. of Court Reporting 501
Southwest Sch. of Electronics 501
Southwest Sch. of Health Careers 218
Southwest Sch. of Medical Assistants 502
Southwest State Univ. 272, 634
Southwest Tech. Coll. 404
Southwest Tech. Inst. (see: Indiana Vo-Tech Coll.—Southwest Tech. Inst.)
Southwest Texas Jr. Coll. 502, 676
Southwest Texas State Univ. 502, 677
Southwest Virginia Comm. Coll. 527, 683
Southwest Wisconsin Tech. Coll. 549
Southwestern Adventist Coll. 502
Southwestern Assemblies of God Coll. 502
Southwestern Baptist Theol. Sem. 502

Institutional Index

Southwestern Bus. Coll. 322
Southwestern Christian Coll. 502
Southwestern Coll. 25 (AZ); 69, 589 (CA); 188 (KS)
Southwestern Coll. of Bus. 394
Southwestern Coll. of Christian Ministries 404
Southwestern Comm. Coll. 181, 612 (IA); 371, 654 (NC)
Southwestern Comm. Coll. Dist. 589
Southwestern Indian Polytechnic Inst. 322
Southwestern Michigan Coll. 261, 631
Southwestern Oklahoma State Univ. 404
Southwestern Oregon Comm. Coll. 410, 661
Southwestern Tech. Coll. 272
Southwestern Univ. 502
Southwestern Univ. Sch. of Law 70
Sowela Regional Tech. Inst. 218
Spalding Univ. 205
Spanish-American Inst. 350
Sparks Coll. 161
Sparks State Tech. Coll. 12
Spartan Sch. of Aeronautics (see: National Ed. Ctr.—Spartan Sch. of Aeronautics Campus)
Spartan Sch. of Aeronautics 569
Spartanburg Methodist Coll. 457
Spartanburg Tech. Coll. 457, 669
Specs Howard Sch. of Broadcast Arts 261
Spelman Coll. 137
Spencer Bus. and Tech. Inst. 350
Spencer Coll. 219
Spencer Sch. of Bus. 181 (IA); 299 (NE)
Spencerian Coll. 206
Spertus Coll. of Judaica 161
Spokane Comm. Coll. 537, 686
Spokane Falls Comm. Coll. 537, 686
Spoon River Coll. 161, 607
Sports Acad. (see: U.S. Sports Acad.)
Spring Arbor Coll. 261
Spring Garden Coll. 434
Spring Hill Coll. 12
Springfield Coll. 245
Springfield Coll. in Illinois 161
Springfield Tech. Comm. Coll. 245, 629
Sprunt Comm. Coll. (see: James Sprunt Comm. Coll.)
Spurr Sch. of Practical Nursing (see: B.M. Spurr Sch. of Practical Nursing)

Standing Rock Coll. 376
Stanford Univ. 70
Stanly Comm. Coll. 371, 654
Star Tech. Inst. 96 (DE); 316-317 (NJ)
Stark Tech. Coll. 394, 658
Starr King Sch. for the Ministry 70
State Area Vo-Tech Sch.—Athens 472
State Area Vo-Tech Sch.—Covington 472
State Area Vo-Tech Sch.—Crossville 472
State Area Vo-Tech Sch.—Dickson 472
State Area Vo-Tech Sch.—Elizabethton 472
State Area Vo-Tech Sch.—Harriman 472
State Area Vo-Tech Sch.—Hartsville 472
State Area Vo-Tech Sch.—Hohenwald 473
State Area Vo-Tech Sch.—Jacksboro 473
State Area Vo-Tech Sch.—Jackson 473
State Area Vo-Tech Sch.—Knoxville 473
State Area Vo-Tech Sch.—Livingston 473
State Area Vo-Tech Sch.—McKenzie 473
State Area Vo-Tech Sch.—McMinnville 473
State Area Vo-Tech Sch.—Memphis 473
State Area Vo-Tech Sch.—Morristown 473
State Area Vo-Tech Sch.—Murfreesboro 473
State Area Vo-Tech Sch.—Nashville 474
State Area Vo-Tech Sch.—Newbern 474
State Area Vo-Tech Sch.—Oneida 474
State Area Vo-Tech Sch.—Paris 474
State Area Vo-Tech Sch.—Pulaski 474
State Area Vo-Tech Sch.—Ripley 474
State Area Vo-Tech Sch.—Savannah 474
State Area Vo-Tech Sch.—Shelbyville 474
State Area Vo-Tech Sch.—Whiteville 474

State Barber and Hair Design Coll. 404
State Barber/Styling Coll. 144
State Board of Ed. and Bd. of Regents of the Univ. of Idaho 604
State Ctr. Comm. Coll. Dist. 590
State Coll. System of West Virginia 687
State Colls. in Colorado 594
State Comm. Coll. of East St. Louis 162, 607
State Council of Higher Ed. for Virginia 682
State Fair Comm. Coll. 290, 638
State Tech. Inst. at Memphis 474, 671
State Univ. of New York at Albany 354, 651
State Univ. of New York at Binghamton 354, 651
State Univ. of New York at Buffalo 354, 651
State Univ. of New York at Stony Brook 354, 651
State Univ. of New York Coll. at Brockport 351, 648
State Univ. of New York Coll. at Buffalo 351, 648
State Univ. of New York Coll. at Cortland 351, 648
State Univ. of New York Coll. at Fredonia 351, 648
State Univ. of New York Coll. at Geneseo 351, 648
State Univ. of New York Coll. at New Paltz 351, 648
State Univ. of New York Coll. at Old Westbury 351, 648
State Univ. of New York Coll. at Oneonta 351, 648
State Univ. of New York Coll. at Oswego 351, 648
State Univ. of New York Coll. at Plattsburgh 352, 648
State Univ. of New York Coll. at Potsdam 352, 648
State Univ. of New York Coll. at Purchase 352, 649
State Univ. of New York Coll. of Agriculture and Tech. at Cobleski 352, 649
State Univ. of New York Coll. of Agricultutre and Tech. at Morrisv 352, 649
State Univ. of New York Coll. of Environmental Sci. and Forestry 352, 649
State Univ. of New York Coll. of Optometry 352, 649

Institutional Index

State Univ. of New York Coll. of Tech. at Alfred 352, 649
State Univ. of New York Coll. of Tech. at Canton 352, 649
State Univ. of New York Coll. of Tech. at Delhi 353, 649
State Univ. of New York Coll. of Tech. at Farmingdale 353, 649
State Univ. of New York Health Sci. Ctr. at Brooklyn 353, 649
State Univ. of New York Health Sci. Ctr. at Buffalo 353, 649
State Univ. of New York Health Sci. Ctr. at Stony Brook 353, 649
State Univ. of New York Health Sci. Ctr. at Syracuse 353, 649
State Univ. of New York Inst. of Tech. at Utica/Rome 353, 649
State Univ. of New York Office of Comm. Colls. 649
State Univ. of New York System Office 648
State Univ. System of Florida 599
Staten Island Coll. (see: Coll. of Staten Island)
Stautzenberger Coll. 394
Stautzenberger Coll.—Central 394
Stautzenberger Coll.—East 395
Stautzenberger Coll.—West 395
Steinbach Bible Coll. 571
Stenotopia, The World of Court Reporting 354
Stenotype Acad. 354
Stenotype Inst. of Jacksonville 119
Stenotype Inst. of South Dakota 462
Stephen F. Austin State Univ. 502, 676
Stephens Coll. 290
Sterling Coll. 188 (KS); 516 (VT)
Sterling Sch. 25
Stetson Univ. (see: John B. Stetson Univ.)
Stevens Coll. (see: Patricia Stevens Coll.)
Stevens Cosmetology Inst. (see: Betty Stevens Cosmetology Inst.)
Stevens Fashion and Finishing Sch. (see: Patricia Stevens Fashion and Finishing Sch.)
Stevens Inst. of Tech. 317
Stevens State Sch. of Tech. (see: Thaddeus Stevens State Sch. of Tech.)
Stevens-Henager Coll. of Bus. 513
Stillman Coll. 12
Stockton State Coll. (see: Richard Stockton State Coll.)
Stone Acad. 93
Stone Child Comm. Coll. 567

Stone Vo-Tech Ctr. (see: George Stone Vo-Tech Ctr.)
Stonehill Coll. 245
Stony Brook State Univ. (see: State Univ. of New York at Stony Brook)
Storey's Sch. of Taxidermy 181
Stratford Sch. 230
Stratton Coll. 549
Strayer Bus. Coll. 230
Strayer Coll. 100
Strich Coll. (see: Cardinal Stritch Coll.)
Strip Dealers and Slot Repair Sch. 302
Stuart Sch. of Bus. Admin. 317
Studio Seven Fashion Career Coll. 70
Suburban Tech. Sch. 354
Sue Bennett Coll. 206
Suffolk Comm. Coll. Ammerman Campus 354, 651
Suffolk Comm. Coll. Eastern Campus 355, 651
Suffolk Comm. Coll. System 651
Suffolk Comm. Coll. Western Campus 355, 651
Suffolk Tech. Inst. 355
Suffolk Univ. 245
Sul Ross State Univ. 502, 677
Sullivan Coll. 206
Sullivan Co. Comm. Coll. 355, 651
Sullivan Educational Ctrs. 290
Sullivan Tech. Inst. 219
Summit Christian Coll. 174
Sumter Area Tech. Coll. 457, 669
Sumter Beauty Coll. 457
Suncoast Sch. of Massage Therapy 119
Sunstate Coll. of Hair Design 120
Suomi Coll. 261
Superior Career Inst. 355
Superior Sch. 120
Surry Comm. Coll. 371, 654
Susquehanna Univ. 434
Sussex Co. Comm. Coll. Commission 568
Sutton Bus. Sch. 355
Suwanee-Hamilton Area Voc., Tech. and Adult Ctr. 120
Swainsboro Tech. Inst. 137
Swarthmore Coll. 434
Swedish Inst. 355
Sweet Briar Coll. 527
Syracuse Health Sci. Ctr. (see: State Univ. of New York Health Sci. Ctr. at Syracuse)
Syracuse Univ. 355
System One Travel Acad. 503

Systems Programming Development Inst. 70

T

T.H. Harris Tech. Inst. 219
T.H. Pickens Tech. Ctr. 85
TAD Tech. Inst. 245 (MA); 290 (MO)
TDDS 395
TESST Electronics and Computer Inst. 230 (MD); 528 (VA)
Tabor Coll. 188
Tacoma Comm. Coll. 537, 686
Taft Coll. 70, 590
Tai Hsuan Foundation Coll. of Acupuncture and Herbal Medicine 566
Talladega Coll. 12
Tallahassee Comm. Coll. 120, 599
Tallapoosa-Alexander City Area Voc. Ctr. 12
Tallulah Tech. Inst. 219
Talmudic Coll. of Florida 120
Talmudical Acad. of New Jersey 317
Talmudical Inst. of Upstate New York 568
Talmudical Sem. Oholei Torah 355
Talmudical Yeshiva of Philadelphia 434
Tampa Coll. 120
Tampa Tech. Inst. 120
Tara Lara Acad. of K-9 Hair Design 410
Tarleton State Univ. 503, 676
Tarrant Co. Jr. Coll. 503, 676
Taylor Bus. Inst. 162 (IL); 356 (NY)
Taylor Univ. 174
Teachers Coll., Columbia Univ. 356
Teche Area Tech. Inst. 219
Tech. Career Insts. 356
Tech. Careers Inst. 93
Tech. Coll. of the Lowcountry 457, 669
Tech. Health Careers Sch. 70
Tech. Inst. of Milwaukee 549
Tech. Trades Inst. 85
Tech. Training Ctr. 70
Tech. Training Inst. 570
Techno-Dental Training Ctr. 356
Tech. Coll. of the Municipality of San Juan 447
Tech. Ed. Ctr. 395
Teikyo Marycrest Univ. 181
Teikyo Post Univ. 94
Teikyo Westmar Univ. 181
Telshe Yeshiva-Chicago 162
Temple Acad. of Cosmetology 503

Institutional Index

Temple Jr. Coll. 503, 676
Temple Univ. 435, 664
Tennessee Board of Regents 671
Tennessee Inst. of Electronics 475
Tennessee State Univ. 475, 672
Tennessee Tech. Univ. 475, 672
Tennessee Temple Univ. 475
Tennessee Wesleyan Coll. 475
Terra Tech. Coll. 395, 658
Teterboro Sch. of Aeronautics 317
Texarkana Coll. 503, 676
Texas A&I Univ. 503, 676
Texas A&M Univ. 503, 676
Texas A&M Univ. at Galveston 504, 676
Texas A&M Univ. System 676
Texas Aero Tech 504
Texas Barber Coll. 504
Texas Chiropractic Coll. 504
Texas Christian Univ. 504
Texas Coll. 504
Texas Coll. of Osteopathic Medicine 504, 676
Texas Dental Tech. Sch. 504
Texas Higher Ed. Coordinating Board 673
Texas Lutheran Coll. 504
Texas Sch. of Bus. 504
Texas Sch. of Bus.—Southwest 505
Texas Schs. 505
Texas Southern Univ. 505, 676
Texas Southmost Coll. 505, 677
Texas State Tech. Inst. System 679
Texas State Tech. Inst.—Amarillo 505, 679
Texas State Tech. Inst.—Harlingen 505, 679
Texas State Tech. Inst.—Sweetwater 505, 679
Texas State Tech. Inst.—Waco 505, 679
Texas State Univ. System 677
Texas Tech Univ. 505, 677
Texas Tech Univ. Health Scis. Ctr. 506, 677
Texas Voc. Sch. 506
Texas Voc. Schs. 506
Texas Wesleyan Univ. 506
Texas Woman's Univ. 506, 677
Textile Tech. Inst. (see: Inst. of Textile Tech.)
Thaddeus Stevens State Sch. of Tech. 569
Thames Valley State Tech. Coll. 94, 595
Thibodaux Area Tech. Inst. 219
Thiel Coll. 435
Thomas A. Edison State Coll. 317, 645
Thomas Aquinas Coll. 70

Thomas Coll. 137 (GA); 222 (ME)
Thomas Jefferson Univ. 435
Thomas M. Cooley Law Sch. 261
Thomas More Coll. 206
Thomas More Coll. of Liberal Arts 568
Thomas Nelson Comm. Coll. 528, 683
Thomas Tech. Inst. 137
Thompson's Acads. (see: J.H. Thompson's Acads.)
Three Rivers Comm. Coll. 290, 638
Tidewater Comm. Coll. 528, 683
Tidewater Tech 528
Tiffin Univ. 395
Tobe-Coburn Sch. for Fashion Careers 356
Toccoa Falls Coll. 137
Tom P. Haney Vo-Tech Ctr. 120
Tomball Coll. 506, 675
Tomlinson Coll. 475
Tompkins Cortland Comm. Coll. 356, 651
Topeka Sch. of Medical Tech. 188
Topeka Tech. Coll. 188
Toronto Sch. of Theol. 557
Total Tech. Inst. 395
Tougaloo Coll. 278
Touro Coll. 356
Towson State Univ. 230, 627
Tracey-Warner Sch. 435
Tracy Clinic (see: John Tracy Clinic)
Traditional Acupuncture Inst. 230
Trans American Sch. of Broadcasting 549
Trans World Travel Acad. 290
Transylvania Univ. 206
Traphagen Sch. of Fashion 356
Travel Acad. 15
Travel and Trade Career Inst. 70
Travel Career Inst. 376
Travel Ed. Ctr. 245 (MA); 306 (NH)
Travel Inst. 356
Travel Inst. of the Pacific 141
Travel Sch. of America 245
Travel Training Ctr. 261
Travel Univ. International 70 (CA); 141 (HI)
Traviss Vo-Tech Ctr. 121
Treasure Valley Comm. Coll. 410, 661
Trend Coll. 410 (OR);537-538 (WA)
Trenholm State Tech. Coll. 12
Trenton State Coll. 317, 645
Trevecca Nazarene Coll. 475
Tri-City Barber Coll. 475
Tri-City Barber Sch. 435
Tri-Coll. Univ. 376
Tri-Co. Comm. Coll. 371, 654
Tri-Co. Tech. Coll. 458, 669

Tri-State Beauty Acad. 206
Tri-State Univ. 174
Triangle Tech 435-436
Trident Tech. Coll. 458, 669
Trident Training Facility 538
Trinidad State Jr. Coll. 85, 594
Trinity Bible Coll. 376
Trinity Christian Coll. 162
Trinity Coll. 94 (CT); 100 (DC); 162, 565 (IL); 557 (Canada)
Trinity Coll. of Florida 565
Trinity Coll. of Vermont 516
Trinity Episcopal Sch. for Ministry 436
Trinity Evangelical Divinity Sch. 162
Trinity Lutheran Sem. 395
Trinity Univ. 506
Trinity Valley Comm. Coll. 506, 677
Triton Coll. 162, 607
Tritone Music 557
Trocaire Coll. 356
Troy State Univ. 12, 575
Troy State Univ. at Dothan 12, 575
Troy State Univ. in Montgomery 12, 575
Troy State Univ. System 575
Truck Driver Sch. (see: U.S. Truck Driver Sch.)
Truck Driving Acad. 71
Truck Driving Sch. (see: U.S. Truck Driving Sch.)
Truck Marketing Inst. 71
Truckee Meadows Comm. Coll. 302, 642
Truett McConnell Coll. 137
Truman Coll. (see: Harry S Truman Coll.)
Trumbull Bus. Coll. 395
Tucson Coll. of Bus. 25
Tufts Univ. 245
Tulane Univ. 219
Tulsa Barber Coll. 404
Tulsa Co. Area Vo-Tech Inst. 404
Tulsa Jr. Coll. 404
Tulsa Welding Sch. 404
Tumonville Memorial Tech. Inst. 219
Tunxis Comm. Coll. 94, 595
Turner Job Corps Ctr. 137
Turtle Mountain Comm. Coll. 376
Turtle Mountain Sch. of Paramedical Technique 376
Tusculum Coll. 475
Tuskegee Univ. 12
Tuttle Vo-Tech Ctr. (see: Francis Tuttle Vo-Tech Ctr.)
Twentieth Century Coll. 13

Institutional Index

Twin City Sch. of Pet Grooming 272
Tyler Comm. Coll. (see: John Tyler Comm. Coll.)
Tyler Jr. Coll. 506, 677
Tyler Sch. of Bus. 507
Tyler Sch. of Secretarial Scis. 162
Tyndale Coll. (see: William Tyndale Coll.)

U

USA Hair Acad. 507
USA Training Acad., Inc. 96
Ulster Co. Comm. Coll. 357, 651
Ultrasound Diagnostic Sch. 317 (NJ); 357 (NY)
Umpqua Comm. Coll. 410, 661
Unification Theol. Sem. 568
Unified Schs. of America 71
Uniformed Services Univ. of the Health Scis. 230
Union Coll. 206 (KY); 299 (NE); 357 (NY)
Union Co. Area Voc. Ed. Ctr. (see: Kentucky Tech—Union Co. Area Voc. Ed. Ctr.)
Union Co. Coll. 317, 645
Union Inst. 395
Union Theol. Sem. 357
Union Theol. Sem. in Virginia 528
Union Univ. 475
United Electronics Inst. 121
United Health Careers Inst. 71 (CA); 290 (MO)
U.S. Air Force Acad. 85
U.S. Armed Forces Sch. of Music 528
U.S. Army Acad. of Health Scis. 507
U.S. Army Chaplain Ctr. and Sch. 318
U.S. Army Command and General Staff Coll. 188
U.S. Army Inst. for Prof. Development 528
U.S. Army Intelligence Ctr. and Sch. 25
U.S. Army Intelligence Sch. 246
U.S. Army John F. Kennedy Special Warfare Ctr. 372
U.S. Army Ordnance Ctr. and Sch. 230
U.S. Army Ordnance Missile and Munitions Ctr. and Sch. 13
U.S. Army Quartermaster Sch. 528
U.S. Army Sch. of Aviation Medicine 507
U.S. Army Signal Ctr. and Sch. 137

U.S. Army Soldier Support Ctr. 174
U.S. Army Transportation and Aviation Logistics Sch. 528
U.S. Coast Guard Acad. 94
U.S. Coast Guard Inst. 404
U.S. International Univ. 71
U.S. Marine Corps Inst. 100
U.S. Merchant Marine Acad. 357
U.S. Military Acad. 357
U.S. Naval Acad. 230
U.S. Naval Aerospace Medical Inst. 230
U.S. Naval Air Tech. Training Ctr. 318 (NJ); 475 (TN)
U.S. Naval Amphibious Sch. 71
U.S. Naval Construction Training Ctr. 72 (CA); 278 (MS)
U.S. Naval Damage Control Training Ctr. 436
U.S. Naval Dental Sch. 231
U.S. Naval Diving and Salvage Training Ctr. 121
U.S. Naval Fleet Anti-Submarine Warfare Training Ctr. 565
U.S. Naval Guided Missiles Sch. 528
U.S. Naval Health Scis. Ed. and Training Command 230
U.S. Naval Hospital Corps Sch. 231
U.S. Naval Postgraduate Sch. 72
U.S. Naval Sch. of Dental Assisting and Tech. 231
U.S. Naval Sch. of Health Scis.—Bethesda 231
U.S. Naval Sch. of Health Scis.—Oakland 231
U.S. Naval Sch. of Health Scis.—Portsmouth 231
U.S. Naval Sch. of Health Scis.—San Diego 231
U.S. Naval Service Sch. Command 72
U.S. Naval Tech. Training Ctr. 72 (CA); 278 (MS)
U.S. Naval Tech. Training Ctr.—Corry Station 121
U.S. Naval Transportation Management Sch. 72
U.S. Naval Undersea Medical Inst. 231
U.S. Naval War Coll. 451
U.S. Navy and Marine Corps Intelligence Training Ctr. 529
U.S. Navy Combat Systems Tech. Schs. Command 72
U.S. Navy Field Medical Service Sch. 231 (CA); 231 (NC)
U.S. Navy Fleet and Mine Warfare Training Ctr. 458

U.S. Navy Service Sch. Command 121
U.S. Navy Supply Corps Sch. 137
U.S. Schs. 121
U.S. Sports Acad. 13
U.S. Truck Driver Sch. 72
U.S. Truck Driving Sch. 85
United Talmudical Acad. 358
United Tech. Schs. 246
United Theol. Sem. 395
United Theol. Sem. of the Twin Cities 272
United Training Inst., Inc. 72
United Tribes Tech. Coll. 376
Unity Coll. 222
Universal Tech. Inst. 25 (AZ); 299 (NE); 507 (TX)
Universidad Adventista de las Antillas 447
Universidad Central del Caribe 447
Universidad de las Americas, A.C. 560
Universidad del Turabo 448
Universidad Interamericana de Puerto Rico 447, 665
Universidad Interamericana de Puerto Rico Central Office 665
Universidad Metropolitana 448
Universidad Politecnica de Puerto Rico 448
Univ. de Montréal 557
Univ. de Sherbrooke 557
Univ. Laval 557
Univ. of Akron 395, 658
Univ. of Alabama 13, 576
Univ. of Alabama at Birmingham 13, 576
Univ. of Alabama in Huntsville 13
Univ. of Alabama System 575
Univ. of Alaska Anchorage 15, 577
Univ. of Alaska Anchorage—Kenai Peninsula Coll. 15, 577
Univ. of Alaska Anchorage—Kodiak Coll. 15, 577
Univ. of Alaska Anchorage—Matanuska-Susitna Coll. 15, 577
Univ. of Alaska Fairbanks 15, 577
Univ. of Alaska Fairbanks—Chukchi 16, 577
Univ. of Alaska Fairbanks—Kuskokwim 16, 577
Univ. of Alaska Fairbanks—Northwest 16, 577
Univ. of Alaska Southeast 16, 577
Univ. of Alaska Southeast—Ketchikan 16, 577
Univ. of Alaska Southeast—Sitka 16, 577
Univ. of Alaska System 577
Univ. of Alberta 557

Institutional Index

Univ. of Arizona 25, 578
Univ. of Arkansas at Little Rock 29, 580
Univ. of Arkansas at Monticello 29, 580
Univ. of Arkansas at Pine Bluff 29, 580
Univ. of Arkansas for Medical Scis. 29, 580
Univ. of Arkansas System 580
Univ. of Arkansas, Fayetteville 29, 580
Univ. of Baltimore 231, 627
Univ. of Beauty 476
Univ. of Bridgeport 94
Univ. of British Columbia 558
Univ. of Calgary 558
Univ. of California Office of the President 592
Univ. of California, Berkeley 72, 592
Univ. of California, Davis 72, 592
Univ. of California, Hastings Coll. of the Law 73, 592
Univ. of California, Irvine 73, 592
Univ. of California, Los Angeles 73, 592
Univ. of California, Riverside 73, 592
Univ. of California, San Diego 73, 592
Univ. of California, San Francisco 73, 592
Univ. of California, Santa Barbara 73, 592
Univ. of California, Santa Cruz 74, 592
Univ. of Central Arkansas 30, 580
Univ. of Central Florida 121, 599
Univ. of Central Oklahoma 405
Univ. of Central Texas 507
Univ. of Charleston 541
Univ. of Chicago 162
Univ. of Cincinnati 396, 658
Univ. of Colorado at Boulder 86, 593
Univ. of Colorado at Colorado Springs 86, 593
Univ. of Colorado at Denver 86, 593
Univ. of Colorado Health Scis. Ctr. 86, 593
Univ. of Colorado System 593
Univ. of Connecticut 94, 596
Univ. of Connecticut Health Ctr. 94, 596
Univ. of Connecticut System 596
Univ. of Dallas 507
Univ. of Dayton 396
Univ. of Delaware 96, 597

Univ. of Denver 86
Univ. of Detroit Mercy 261
Univ. of Dubuque 181
Univ. of Dubuque—Theol. Sem. 181
Univ. of Evansville 174
Univ. of Findlay 396
Univ. of Florida 121, 599
Univ. of Georgia 137, 602
Univ. of Guam 139
Univ. of Guelph 558
Univ. of Hartford 94
Univ. of Hawaii at Hilo 141, 603
Univ. of Hawaii at Manoa 141, 603
Univ. of Hawaii at West Oahu 141, 603
Univ. of Hawaii Comm. Colls. 603
Univ. of Hawaii System 603
Univ. of Health Scis. 290
Univ. of Health Scis./The Chicago Medical Sch. 162
Univ. of Houston System 677
Univ. of Houston—Clear Lake 507, 677
Univ. of Houston—Downtown 507, 677
Univ. of Houston—Univ. Park 507, 677
Univ. of Houston—Victoria 508, 677
Univ. of Idaho 143-144, 604
Univ. of Illinois at Chicago 163, 608
Univ. of Illinois at Urbana—Champaign 163, 608
Univ. of Illinois System 608
Univ. of Indianapolis 174
Univ. of Iowa 181, 612
Univ. of Judaism 74
Univ. of Kansas 188, 613
Univ. of Kansas Medical Ctr. 188
Univ. of Kentucky 206, 615
Univ. of Kentucky Comm. Coll. System 615
Univ. of La Verne 74
Univ. of Louisville 206, 615
Univ. of Maine 222, 625
Univ. of Maine at Augusta 223, 625
Univ. of Maine at Farmington 223, 625
Univ. of Maine at Fort Kent 223, 625
Univ. of Maine at Machias 223, 625
Univ. of Maine at Presque Isle 223, 625
Univ. of Maine System 625
Univ. of Manitoba 558
Univ. of Mary 377
Univ. of Mary Hardin-Baylor 508

Univ. of Maryland at Baltimore 232, 627
Univ. of Maryland Baltimore Co. 231, 627
Univ. of Maryland College Park 231, 627
Univ. of Maryland Eastern Shore 232, 627
Univ. of Maryland System 627
Univ. of Maryland Univ. Coll. 232, 627
Univ. of Massachusetts at Amherst 246, 629
Univ. of Massachusetts at Boston 246, 629
Univ. of Massachusetts at Dartmouth 246, 629
Univ. of Massachusetts at Lowell 246, 629
Univ. of Massachusetts at Worcester 246, 629
Univ. of Massachusetts President's Office 629
Univ. of Medicine and Dentistry of New Jersey 318, 645
Univ. of Miami 122
Univ. of Michigan 262, 632
Univ. of Michigan System 632
Univ. of Michigan—Dearborn 262, 632
Univ. of Michigan—Flint 262, 632
Univ. of Minnesota System 634
Univ. of Minnesota—Crookston 272, 634
Univ. of Minnesota—Duluth 272, 634
Univ. of Minnesota—Morris 272, 634
Univ. of Minnesota—Twin Cities 272, 634
Univ. of Minnesota—Waseca 273, 634
Univ. of Mississippi 278, 635
Univ. of Mississippi Medical Ctr. 279, 635
Univ. of Missouri System 638
Univ. of Missouri—Columbia 290, 638
Univ. of Missouri—Kansas City 290, 638
Univ. of Missouri—Rolla 291, 638
Univ. of Missouri—St. Louis 291, 638
Univ. of Montana 295, 639
Univ. of Montevallo 13, 576
Univ. of Nebraska at Kearney 299, 640
Univ. of Nebraska at Omaha 299, 640

Institutional Index

Univ. of Nebraska Central Administrative Office 640
Univ. of Nebraska Medical Ctr. 299, 640
Univ. of Nebraska—Lincoln 300, 640
Univ. of Nevada System 642
Univ. of Nevada, Las Vegas 302, 642
Univ. of Nevada—Reno 302, 642
Univ. of New England 223
Univ. of New Hampshire 306, 643
Univ. of New Hampshire at Manchester 306, 643
Univ. of New Haven 95
Univ. of New Mexico 323, 646
Univ. of New Orleans 220, 623
Univ. of North Alabama 14, 576
Univ. of North Carolina at Asheville 372, 655
Univ. of North Carolina at Chapel Hill 372, 655
Univ. of North Carolina at Charlotte 372, 655
Univ. of North Carolina at Greensboro 372, 655
Univ. of North Carolina at Wilmington 372, 655
Univ. of North Carolina General Administration 655
Univ. of North Dakota 377, 656
Univ. of North Dakota—Lake Region 377, 656
Univ. of North Dakota—Williston 377, 656
Univ. of North Florida 122, 599
Univ. of North Texas 508, 677
Univ. of Northern Colorado 86
Univ. of Northern Iowa 182, 612
Univ. of Notre Dame 174
Univ. of Oklahoma 405
Univ. of Oklahoma Central Office 660
Univ. of Oklahoma Health Scis. Ctr. 405
Univ. of Oregon 411, 662
Univ. of Osteopathic Medicine and Health Scis. 182
Univ. of Ottawa 558
Univ. of Pennsylvania 436
Univ. of Phoenix 25
Univ. of Pittsburgh 436, 664
Univ. of Portland 411
Univ. of Puerto Rico 448, 665
Univ. of Puerto Rico Central Office 665
Univ. of Puerto Rico Regional Colls. Administration 665
Univ. of Puget Sound 538
Univ. of Redlands 74

Univ. of Rhode Island 451, 667
Univ. of Richmond 529
Univ. of Rio Grande 396
Univ. of Rochester 358
Univ. of St. Mary of the Lake, Mundelein Sem. 163
Univ. of St. Michael's Coll. 558
Univ. of St. Thomas 273 (MN); 508 (TX)
Univ. of San Diego 74
Univ. of San Francisco 74
Univ. of Sarasota 122
Univ. of Saskatchewan 558
Univ. of Sci. and Arts of Oklahoma 405
Univ. of Scranton 437
Univ. of South Alabama 14, 576
Univ. of South Carolina Central Office 668
Univ. of South Carolina—Aiken 458, 668
Univ. of South Carolina—Beaufort 458, 668
Univ. of South Carolina—Coastal Carolina 458, 668
Univ. of South Carolina—Columbia 458, 668
Univ. of South Carolina—Lancaster 458, 668
Univ. of South Carolina—Salkehatchie 458, 668
Univ. of South Carolina—Spartanburg 459, 668
Univ. of South Carolina—Sumter 459, 668
Univ. of South Carolina—Union 459, 669
Univ. of South Dakota 462, 670
Univ. of South Florida 122, 600
Univ. of Southern California 74
Univ. of Southern Colorado 86, 593
Univ. of Southern Indiana 174, 609
Univ. of Southern Maine 223, 625
Univ. of Southern Mississippi 279, 635
Univ. of Southwestern Louisiana 220, 623
Univ. of Tampa 122
Univ. of Tennessee at Chattanooga 476, 672
Univ. of Tennessee at Martin 476, 672
Univ. of Tennessee System 672
Univ. of Tennessee, Knoxville 476, 672
Univ. of Tennessee, Memphis 476, 672
Univ. of Texas at Arlington 509, 678
Univ. of Texas at Austin 509, 678

Univ. of Texas at Brownsville 509, 678
Univ. of Texas at Dallas 509, 678
Univ. of Texas at El Paso 509, 678
Univ. of Texas at San Antonio 509, 678
Univ. of Texas at Tyler 509, 678
Univ. of Texas Health Sci. Ctr. at Houston 508, 677
Univ. of Texas Health Sci. Ctr. at San Antonio 508, 678
Univ. of Texas Medical Branch at Galveston 508, 678
Univ. of Texas of the Permian Basin 509, 678
Univ. of Texas Southwestern Medical Ctr. at Dallas 508, 678
Univ. of Texas System 677
Univ. of Texas—Pan American 510, 678
Univ. of the Arts 437
Univ. of the Dist. of Columbia 100
Univ. of the Ozarks 30
Univ. of the Pacific 74
Univ. of the Sacred Heart 448
Univ. of the South 476
Univ. of the State of New York Regents Coll. Degrees 358
Univ. of the Virgin Islands 518
Univ. of Toledo 396, 658
Univ. of Toronto 558
Univ. of Tulsa 405
Univ. of Utah 513, 680
Univ. of Vermont 516, 681
Univ. of Virginia 520, 529, 682
Univ. of Virginia Central Ofc. 682
Univ. of Washington 538, 685
Univ. of Waterloo 558
Univ. of West Florida 122, 600
Univ. of West Los Angeles 74
Univ. of West Virginia Coll. of Grad. Studies 542, 687
Univ. of West Virginia System 687
Univ. of Western Ontario 558
Univ. of Windsor 558
Univ. of Wisconsin Ctrs. 549, 688
Univ. of Wisconsin Ctr.—Baraboo-Sauk Co. 549
Univ. of Wisconsin Ctr.—Barron Co. 549
Univ. of Wisconsin Ctr.—Fond du Lac Co. 549
Univ. of Wisconsin Ctr.—Fox Valley 549
Univ. of Wisconsin Ctr.—Manitowoc Co. 549
Univ. of Wisconsin Ctr.—Marathon Co. 549
Univ. of Wisconsin Ctr.—Marinette Co. 550

Institutional Index

Univ. of Wisconsin Ctr.—Marshfield-Wood Co. 550
Univ. of Wisconsin Ctr.—Richland Co. 550
Univ. of Wisconsin Ctr.—Rock Co. 550
Univ. of Wisconsin Ctr.—Sheboygan Co. 550
Univ. of Wisconsin Ctr.—Washington Co. 550
Univ. of Wisconsin Ctr.—Waukesha Co. 550
Univ. of Wisconsin System 688
Univ. of Wisconsin—Eau Claire 550, 688
Univ. of Wisconsin—Green Bay 550, 688
Univ. of Wisconsin—La Crosse 550, 688
Univ. of Wisconsin—Madison 550, 688
Univ. of Wisconsin—Milwaukee 551, 688
Univ. of Wisconsin—Oshkosh 551, 688
Univ. of Wisconsin—Parkside 551, 688
Univ. of Wisconsin—Platteville 551, 688
Univ. of Wisconsin—River Falls 551, 688
Univ. of Wisconsin—Stevens Point 551, 688
Univ. of Wisconsin—Stout 551, 688
Univ. of Wisconsin—Superior 551, 688
Univ. of Wisconsin—Whitewater 551, 688
Univ. of Wyoming 553
Univ. System of New Hampshire 643
Upper Iowa Univ. 182
Upsala Coll. 318
Upson Tech. Inst. 138
Urbana Univ. 397
Ursinus Coll. 437
Ursuline Coll. 397
Utah State Univ. 513, 680
Utah System of Higher Ed. 680
Utah Valley Comm. Coll. 514, 680
Utica Coll. of Syracuse Univ. 355
Utica Inst. of Tech. (see: State Univ. of New York Inst. of Tech. at Utica/Rome)
Utica Sch. of Commerce 358

V

Valdosta State Coll. 138, 602
Valdosta Tech. Inst. 138
Vale Tech. Inst. (see: National Ed. Ctr.—Vale Tech. Inst. Campus)
Valencia Comm. Coll. 122, 599
Valley City State Univ. 377, 656
Valley Commercial Coll. 75
Valley Forge Christian Coll. 437
Valley Forge Military Jr. Coll. 437
Valparaiso Univ. 174
Van Nuys Coll. of Bus. 75
Vance-Granville Comm. Coll. 372, 654
Vancouver Sch. of Theol. 558
Vanderbilt Univ. 476
VanderCook Coll. of Music 163
Vanderschmidt Sch. 291
Vanguard Inst. of Tech. 510
Vassar Coll. 358
Vatterott Educational Ctrs. 291
Vatterott Educational Coll. 291
Vegas Dealing Sch. 303
Vennard Coll. 182
Ventura Coll. 75, 590
Ventura Co. Comm. Coll. Dist. 590
Vermilion Comm. Coll. 273, 633
Vermont Coll. 516
Vermont Comm. Coll. (see: Comm. Coll. of Vermont)
Vermont Law Sch. 516
Vermont State Colls. 681
Vermont Tech. Coll. 516, 681
Vernon Regional Jr. Coll. 510, 678
Victor Valley Coll. 75, 590
Victor Valley Comm. Coll. Dist. 590
Victoria Coll. 510, 678
Villa Julie Coll. 232
Villa Maria Coll. of Buffalo 358
Villanova Univ. 437
Ville Platte Tech. Inst. 220
Vincennes Univ. 175, 609
Virginia Coll. 520, 529, 682
Virginia Commonwealth Univ. 529, 682
Virginia Comm. Coll. System 682
Virginia Hair Acad. 529
Virginia Highlands Comm. Coll. 529, 684
Virginia Inst. of Tech. 529
Virginia Intermont Coll. 530
Virginia Marti Sch. of Fashion and Art 397
Virginia Military Inst. 530, 682
Virginia Polytechnic Inst. and State Univ. 530, 682
Virginia Sch. of Cosmetology 530
Virginia State Univ. 530, 682
Virginia Union Univ. 530
Virginia Wesleyan Coll. 530
Virginia Western Comm. Coll. 530, 684
Vista Coll. 75, 587
Visual Arts Sch. (see: Sch. of Visual Arts)
Viterbo Coll. 552
Voc. Ed. Region 1 (Purchase) 616
Voc. Ed. Region 2 (Pennyrile) 616
Voc. Ed. Region 3 (Green River) 617
Voc. Ed. Region 4 (Barren River) 617
Voc. Ed. Region 5 (Elizabethtown) 618
Voc. Ed. Regions 6 and 8 (Jefferson) 618
Voc. Ed. Region 7 (Northern Kentucky) 619
Voc. Ed. Region 9 (Buffalo Trace) 619
Voc. Ed. Region 10 (Fivco) 619
Voc. Ed. Region 11 (Big Sandy) 620
Voc. Ed. Region 12 (Kentucky River) 620
Voc. Ed. Region 13 (Cumberland Valley) 620
Voc. Ed. Region 14 (Lake Cumberland) 621
Voc. Ed. Region 15 (Bluegrass) 621
Voc. Inst. 122
Vogue Coll. of Hair Design 207
Volunteer State Comm. Coll. 476, 672
Voorhees Coll. 459

W

WKG-TV Video Electronic Coll. 220
Wabash Coll. 175
Wabash Valley Coll. 163, 606
Wabash Valley Tech. Inst. (see: Indiana Vo-Tech Coll.—Wabash Valley Tech. Inst.)
Wade's Fashion Merchandising Coll. (see: Miss Wade's Fashion Merchandising Coll.)
Wadhams Hall Sem./Coll. 358
Wagner Coll. 358
Wake Forest Univ. 373
Wake Tech. Comm. Coll. 373, 654
Walden Univ. 273
Waldorf Coll. 182
Walker Coll. 14
Walker State Tech. Coll. 14
Walker Tech. Inst. 138

Institutional Index

Walker Vo-Tech Ctr. (see: James L. Walker Vo-Tech Ctr.)
Walla Walla Coll. 538
Walla Walla Comm. Coll. 538, 686
Wallace State Comm. Coll. (see: George C. Wallace State Comm. Coll.)
Wallace State Comm. Coll. (see: George Corley Wallace State Comm. Coll.)
Wallace State Comm. Coll. 14, 575
Wallace State Jr. Coll. (see: Lurleen B. Wallace State Jr. Coll.)
Walsh Coll. 397
Walsh Coll. of Accountancy and Bus. Administration 262
Walters Coll. (see: Raymond Walters Coll.)
Walters State Comm. Coll. 477, 672
Ward Stone Coll. 123
Warner Pacific Coll. 411
Warner Southern Coll. 123
Warren Co. Comm. Coll. Commission 568
Warren Wilson Coll. 373
Wartburg Coll. 182
Wartburg Theol. Sem. 182
Washburn Univ. of Topeka 189
Washington and Jefferson Coll. 437
Washington and Lee Univ. 531
Washington Bible Coll. 232
Washington Bus. Inst. 163
Washington Bus. Sch. of Northern Virginia 530
Washington Coll. (see: Harold Washington Coll.)
Washington Coll. (see: Mary Washington Coll.)
Washington Coll. 232
Washington Co. Adult Skill Ctr. 530
Washington Co. Vo-Tech Inst. 223
Washington Higher Ed. Coordinating Board 685
Washington Holmes Area Vo-Tech Ctr. 123
Washington Inst. of Tech. 437
Washington State Board for Comm. Coll. Ed. 685
Washington State Comm. Coll. 397, 658
Washington State Comm. Coll. 6th Dist. 686
Washington State Comm. Coll. 17th Dist. 686
Washington State Univ. 538, 685
Washington Theol. Union 232
Washington Univ. (see: George Washington Univ.)
Washington Univ. 291

Washtenaw Comm. Coll. 262, 632
Waterbury State Tech. Coll. 95, 596
Waterloo Lutheran Sem. 559
Waters Coll. (see: Edward Waters Coll.)
Watterson Career Ctr. 207
Watterson Coll. 75 (CA); 207 (KY); 291 (MO)
Watterson Coll. Pacific 75
Watterson Sch. of Bus. and Tech. 437
Waubonsee Comm. Coll. 163, 608
Waukesha Co. Tech. Coll. 552
Waycross Coll. 138, 602
Wayland Baptist Univ. 510
Wayne Coll. 396
Wayne Comm. Coll. 373, 654
Wayne Co. Area Voc. Ed. Ctr. (see: Kentucky Tech—Wayne Co. Area Voc. Ed. Ctr.)
Wayne Co. Comm. Coll. 262, 632
Wayne State Coll. 300, 641
Wayne State Univ. 262, 632
Wayne's Sch. of Unisex Hair Design (see: Mr. Wayne's Sch. of Unisex Hair Design)
Waynesburg Coll. 437
Weatherford Coll. 510, 678
Webb Inst. of Naval Architecture 358
Webber Coll. 123
Weber State Univ. 514, 680
Webster Career Coll. 75
Webster Coll. (see: Daniel Webster Coll.)
Webster Coll. 542
Webster Co. Area Voc. Ed. Ctr. (see: Kentucky Tech—Webster Co. Area Voc. Ed. Ctr.)
Webster Univ. 291
Weeks Welding Laboratory Testing and Sch. (see: M. Weeks Welding Laboratory Testing and Sch.)
Welbes Coll. of Massage Therapy (see: Dr. Welbes Coll. of Massage Therapy)
Welder Training and Testing Inst. 437-438
Weldor Training Ctr. 263
WeldTech Welding Ed. Ctr. 262
Wellesley Coll. 246
Wells Coll. 358
Wenatchee Valley Coll. 538, 686
Wentworth Inst. of Tech. 246
Wentworth Military Acad. and Jr. Coll. 291
Wentworth Tech. Sch. 247
Wesley Biblical Sem. 279

Wesley Coll. (see: John Wesley Coll.)
Wesley Coll. 97 (DE); 279 (MS)
Wesley Theol. Sem. 100
Wesleyan Coll. 138
Wesleyan Univ. 95
West Central Alabama Skills Ctr. 14
West Chester Univ. of Pennsylvania 438, 664
West Coast Christian Jr. Coll. 75
West Coast Training 411
West Coast Univ. 76
West Georgia Coll. 138, 602
West Georgia Tech. Inst. 138
West Hills Comm. Coll. 76, 590
West Hills Comm. Coll. Dist. 590
West Jefferson Tech. Inst. 220
West Kentucky State Vo-Tech Sch. (see: Kentucky Tech—West Kentucky State Vo-Tech Sch.)
West Kern Comm. Coll. Dist. 590
West Liberty State Coll. 542, 687
West Los Angeles Coll. 76, 585
West Shore Comm. Coll. 263, 632
West Side Inst. of Tech. 397
West Suburban Coll. of Nursing 164
West Tech. Ed. Ctr. 123
West Tennessee Bus. Coll. 477
West Texas State Univ. 510, 676
West Valley Coll. 76, 590
West Valley-Mission Comm. Coll. Dist. 590
West Virginia Bus. Coll. 542
West Virginia Career Coll. 542
West Virginia Coll. (see: Coll. of West Virginia)
West Virginia Inst. of Tech. 542, 687
West Virginia Northern Comm. Coll. 543, 687
West Virginia Sch. of Osteopathic Medicine 543, 687
West Virginia State Coll. 543, 687
West Virginia Univ. 543, 687
West Virginia Univ. at Parkersburg 543, 687
West Virginia Wesleyan Coll. 543
Westark Comm. Coll. 30
Westbrook Coll. 223
Westchester Bus. Inst. 358
Westchester Comm. Coll. 358, 651
Westchester Conservatory of Music 359
Westech Coll. 76
Western Baptist Coll. 411
Western Bus. Coll. 411
Western Career Coll. 76
Western Career Inst. 76
Western Carolina Univ. 373, 655

Institutional Index

Western Connecticut State Univ. 95, 596
Western Conservative Baptist Sem. 411
Western Culinary Inst. 411
Western Dakota Vo-Tech Inst. 462
Western Evangelical Sem. 411
Western Illinois Univ. 164, 605
Western International Univ. 25
Western Iowa Tech Comm. Coll. 182, 612
Western Kentucky Univ. 207, 615
Western Maryland Coll. 232
Western Medical Coll. of Allied Health Careers 412
Western Michigan Univ. 263, 632
Western Montana Coll. 295, 639
Western Nebraska Comm. Coll. 300, 641
Western Nevada Comm. Coll. 303, 642
Western New England Coll. 247
Western New Mexico Univ. 323, 646
Western Oklahoma State Coll. 405
Western Oregon State Coll. 412, 662
Western Pentecostal Bible Coll. 559
Western Piedmont Comm. Coll. 373, 654
Western Sch. of Health and Bus. Careers 438
Western State Coll. of Colorado 86, 594
Western State Univ. Coll. of Law of Orange Co. 76
Western State Univ. Coll. of Law of San Diego 76
Western States Chiropractic Coll. 412
Western Tech. Coll. 76
Western Tech. Inst. 510
Western Texas Coll. 510, 678
Western Theol. Sem. 263
Western Truck Sch. 76 (CA); 412 (OR)
Western Washington Univ. 539, 685
Western Wisconsin Tech. Coll. 552
Western Wyoming Coll. 553, 689
Westfield State Coll. 247, 629
Westland Coll. 77
Westlawn Sch. of Marine Tech. 95
Westminster Choir Coll. 319
Westminster Coll. 292 (MO); 438 (PA)
Westminster Coll. of Salt Lake City 514
Westminster Theol. Sem. 438
Westminster Theol. Sem. in California 77

Westmont Coll. 77
Westmoreland Co. Comm. Coll. 438, 664
Weston Sch. of Theol. 247
Westside Tech. Inst. 220
Westside Vo-Tech Ctr. 123
Westwood Educational 263
Wharton Co. Jr. Coll. 510, 678
Whatcom Comm. Coll. 539, 686
Wheaton Coll. 164 (IL); 247 (MA)
Wheeling Barber Coll. 543
Wheeling Jesuit Coll. 543
Wheelock Coll. 247
White Pines Coll. 306
Whitewater Tech. Inst. (see: Indiana Vo-Tech Coll.—Whitewater Tech. Inst.)
Whitman Coll. 539
Whitney Regional Vo-Tech Sch. (see: Eli Whitney Regional Vo-Tech Sch.)
Whittier Coll. 77
Whitworth Coll. 539
Wichita Area Vo-Tech Sch. 189
Wichita Bus. Coll. 189
Wichita State Univ. 189, 613
Wichita Tech. Inst. 189
Widener Univ. 438
Widener Univ. Sch. of Law 97
Wilberforce Univ. 397
Wilbur Wright Coll. 164, 606
Wiley Coll. 511
Wiley's Hairstyling Acad. (see: Lynn Wiley's Hairstyling Acad.)
Wilkes Comm. Coll. 373, 654
Wilkes Univ. 438
Willamette Univ. 412
William and Mary Coll. (see: Coll. of William and Mary)
William Carey Coll. 279
William Jennings Bryan Coll. 477
William Jewell Coll. 292
William Marsh Rice Univ. 511
William Mitchell Coll. of Law 273
William Paterson Coll. of New Jersey 319, 645
William Penn Coll. 182
William R. Moore Sch. of Tech. 477
William Rainey Harper Coll. 164, 608
William T. McFatter Vo-Tech Ctr. 123
William Tyndale Coll. 263
William Woods Coll. 292
Williams Baptist Coll. 30
Williams Coll. (see: Roger Williams Coll.)
Williams Coll. 247
Williamsburg Tech. Coll. 459, 669

Williamson Free Sch. of Mechanical Trades 438
Williamsport Sch. of Commerce 438
Willmar Comm. Coll. 273, 634
Willmar Tech. Coll. 273
Wilma Boyd Career Schs. 438
Wilmington Coll. 97 (DE); 397 (OH)
Wilshire Computer Coll. 77
Wilson Coll. (see: Lindsey Wilson Coll.)
Wilson Coll. (see: Warren Wilson Coll.)
Wilson Coll. 439
Wilson Rehabilitation Ctr. (see: Woodrow Wilson Rehabilitation Ctr.)
Wilson Tech. Comm. Coll. 373, 654
Windham Regional Vo-Tech Sch. 95
Windward Comm. Coll. 142, 603
Winebrenner Theol. Sem. 397
Wingate Coll. 373
Winnipeg Bible Coll. 559
Winona State Univ. 273, 634
Winston Co. Area Voc. Ctr. 14
Winston-Salem Barber Sch. 374
Winston-Salem State Univ. 374, 655
Winter Park Adult Voc. Ctr. 123
Winthrop Coll. 459, 669
Wisconsin Conservatory of Music 552
Wisconsin Indianhead Tech. Coll. 552
Wisconsin Lutheran Coll. 552
Wisconsin Sch. of Electronics 552
Wisconsin Sch. of Prof. Psychology 552
Withlacoochee Voc. and Adult Educational Ctr. 123
Without Walls Coll. (see: Coll. Without Walls)
Wittenberg Univ. 397
Wofford Coll. 459
Wood Comm. Coll. (see: John Wood Comm. Coll.)
Wood Co. Voc. Sch. 544
Wood Jr. Coll. 279
Wood Sch. 359
Woodbridge Bus. Inst. 232
Woodbury Coll. 517
Woodbury Univ. 77
Woodrow Wilson Rehabilitation Ctr. 531
Woods Coll. (see: William Woods Coll.)

Institutional Index

Woodsbend Boys' Camp (see: Kentucky Tech—Woodsbend Boys' Camp)
Wooster Bus. Coll. 398
Wooster Coll. (see: Coll. of Wooster)
Wor-Wic Tech Comm. Coll. 233, 627
Worcester Polytechnic Inst. 247
Worcester State Coll. 247, 629
Worcester Tech. Inst. 247
World Coll. West 77
World Evangelism Bible Coll. and Sem. 567
World Supreme Tech. and Beauty Coll. 448
Worldspan Travel Acad. 292
Worsham Coll. of Mortuary Sci. 164
Worthington Comm. Coll. 273, 634
Wright Bus. Sch. 189 (KS); 405 (OK)
Wright Coll. (see: Wilbur Wright Coll.)
Wright Inst. 78
Wright Sch. of Architecture (see: Frank Lloyd Wright Sch. of Architecture)
Wright State Univ. 398, 658
Wycliffe Coll. 559
Wyoming Comm. Coll. Commission 689
Wyoming Tech. Inst. 554
Wytheville Comm. Coll. 531, 684

X

Xavier Univ. 398
Xavier Univ. of Louisiana 220
Yakima Valley Comm. Coll. 539, 686

Y

Yale Univ. 95
Yavapai Coll. 25, 579
Yeshiva and Kolel Bais Medrash Elyon 568
Yeshiva and Kollel Harbotzas Torah 569
Yeshiva and Mesivta Kol Torah 569
Yeshiva Beth Moshe 439
Yeshiva Beth Yehuda-Yeshiva Gedolah of Greater Detroit 263
Yeshiva Derech Chaim 359
Yeshiva Gedolah Bais Yisroel 568
Yeshiva Gedolah Imrei Yosef D'Spinka 568
Yeshiva Karlin Stolin Beth Aaron V'Israel Rabbinical Inst. 359
Yeshiva Mikdash Melech 359
Yeshiva of Nitra—Rabbinical Coll.
Yeshiva Farm Settlement 359
Yeshiva Ohr Elchonon-Chabad/ West Coast Talmudic Sem. 78
Yeshiva Shaar HaTorah Talmudic Research Inst. 359
Yeshiva Toras Chaim Talmudic Sem. 87
Yeshiva Univ. 359
Yeshivah and Mesivta Torah Temimah Talmudical Sem. 359
Yeshivath Viznitz 359
Yesivath Zichron Moshe 359
York Coll. 300 (NE); 359 (NY); 449 (PR)
York Coll. of Pennsylvania 439
York Inst. 359
York Tech. Coll. 459, 669
York Tech. Inst. 439
Yorktowne Bus. Inst. 233 (MD); 439 (PA)
Yosemite Comm. Coll. Dist. 590
Young Harris Coll. 138
Young Memorial Tech. Inst. 220
Youngstown State Univ. 398, 658
Yuba Coll. 78, 591
Yuba Comm. Coll. Dist. 591